The U.S. Financial System:
MONEY, MARKETS, AND INSTITUTIONS

"Of course, it's hard to make it singing and dancing, so I'm going to take a lot of economics in case I have to fall back on banking."

The U.S. Financial System

MONEY, MARKETS, AND INSTITUTIONS

Sixth Edition

George G. Kaufman

The John F. Smith Professor of Finance and Economics
Loyola University of Chicago

PRENTICE HALL, *Englewood Cliffs, New Jersey* 07632

Library of Congress Cataloging-in-Publication Data

Kaufman, George G.
    The U.S. financial system : money, markets, and institutions /
George G. Kaufman.—6th ed.
        p.   cm.
    Includes bibliographical references and index.
    ISBN 0-13-122912-5
      1. Finance—United States.   I. Title.   II. Title: US financial system.
    HG181.K34   1995
    332'.0973—dc20
                                                                        94-9691
                                                                        CIP

Acquisition Editor: Leah Jewell
Editorial Assistant: Eileen Deguzman
Production Editor: Judy Winthrop
In-house Project Liaison: Alana Zdinak
Copy Editor: Margo Quinto
Interior Design: Dorothy Bungert
Cover Design: Maureen Eide
Manufacturing Buyer: Patrice Fraccio
Assistant Editor: Teresa Cohen

*Cartoon on p. ii courtesy of "Keeping Up" by William Hamilton.
Copyright 1979, Universal Press Syndicate. Reprinted with permission.
All rights reserved.*

© 1995, 1992 by Prentice-Hall, Inc.
A Simon and Schuster Company
Englewood Cliffs, New Jersey 07632

Printed in the United States of America
10   9   8   7   6   5   4   3   2   1

ISBN   0-13-122912-5

Prentice-Hall International (UK) Limited, *London*
Prentice-Hall of Australia Pty. Limited, *Sydney*
Prentice-Hall Canada Inc., *Toronto*
Prentice-Hall Hispanoamericana, S.A., *Mexico*
Prentice-Hall of India Private Limited, *New Delhi*
Prentice-Hall of Japan, Inc., *Tokyo*
Simon & Schuster Asia Pte. Ltd., *Singapore*
Editora Prentice-Hall do Brasil, Ltda., *Rio de Janeiro*

Contents

Preface xvii

PART I MONEY AND FINANCE

1 Introduction and Overview 1

Importance of the Financial Sector 5

Financial Intermediation 10

Economic and Financial Theory 13

Questions 14
References 15

2 Money and Prices 16

Money Defined 16
What Money Is Not 16
What Money Is 16
Functions of Money 18

History of Money 18
Inconvenience of Coins and Currency 19

Measures of Money 20

The Value of Money 21
Real Values 26

Prices 27
Past Prices 27
Future Prices 30
Hyperinflation 30

Money Management 34

Summary 34
Questions 35
References 35
EXHIBIT 2-1 COPING WITH HYPERINFLATION IN BRAZIL 32

PART II FINANCIAL MARKETS AND INTEREST RATES

3 Financial Markets 37

Private Financial Market 38

Intermediation Financial Market 40

The Intermediation Process 43

Classification of Financial Markets 49

Financial Centers 53

Summary 55
Questions 56

References   57

EXHIBIT 3–1 GLOBEX: A WORLDWIDE 24-HOUR ELECTRONIC SECURITIES TRADING NETWORK   54

4   Financial Instruments   58

Money-Market Instruments   61

Capital-Market Instruments   68

Summary   76
Questions   76
References   77

5   Interest Rates and Bond Prices   78

What Interest Rates Are   78

Mathematics of Interest Rates and Bond Prices   79
  Present Value   80
  Yield to Maturity   81
  Current Yield   90
  Realized Yield   91

Summary   92
Questions   93
References   94

Appendix 5A   95
  Duration   95
  References   100

Appendix 5B   101
  Closed-Form Macaulay Duration Equations   101

6   The Level of Interest Rates   102

Inflation Premium   102

Determinants of the Interest Rate Level   110
  Loanable Funds   110
  Liquidity Preference   112

Interest Rates over the Business Cycle   114

Summary   115
Questions   116
References   117

7   The Structure of Interest Rates I   118

Term to Maturity   118
  Expectations Theory   120
  Market-Segmentation Theory   126
  Yield Curve over the Business Cycle   127

Risk of Default   129

Summary   136
Questions   137
References   138

EXHIBIT 7–1 METHODOLOGY USED BY STANDARD & POOR'S TO RATE INDUSTRIAL FIRMS   133

8 The Structure of Interest Rates II   139

Tax Treatment   139

Marketability   140

Special Features—Options and Covenants   141

Interrelationships among Rates   144

Winning with Bonds   145

Realized Returns   149

Summary   150
Questions   150
References   151

PART III   FINANCIAL INSTITUTIONS

9 Financial Intermediaries: An Overview   153

Institutions on the Private Financial Market   153
   Investment Banks   153
   Mortgage Banks   157

Institutions on the Intermediation Financial Market: Overview   158

Summary   168
Questions   168
References   169

10 Commercial Banks: History and Management   170

History of Banking   170
   Fractional Reserve Banking   171
   Bank Failure   173
   Capital and Liquidity   174
   Deposit Banking   178

Bank Balance Sheet   180

Bank Management   185
   Bank Performance   186

Summary   187
Questions   188
References   189

EXHIBIT 10–1 LIFE AT A BANK'S MONEY DESK   176

11 Commercial Banks: Safety and Structure   190

Bank Failure   190
   Bank Runs   191
   History of Bank Failures   195
   Reasons for the Increase in Failures   196
   Reform of Deposit Insurance   199

Bank Structure and Organization   200
   Charter   201
   Branching   202
   Holding Companies   203
   Bank Size   206
   Structure and Performance   208

International Banking   210

U. S. Overseas Offices   210
Foreign Offices in the United States   211

Summary   214
Questions   215
References   215

EXHIBIT 11-1 CHRONOLOGY OF A BANK FAILURE: WHAT GOES ON BEHIND CLOSED DOORS AT THE FDIC BEFORE AN INSURED BANK'S DOORS ARE CLOSED   192

EXHIBIT 11-2 DOES WORLD SIZE MATTER IN BANKING?   208

12   **Thrift and Insurance Intermediaries**   **217**

Thrift Institutions   217
Savings and Loan Associations   217
Savings Banks   226
Credit Unions   227

Insurance Intermediaries   228
Life Insurance Companies   230
Casualty Insurance Companies   233

Summary   235
Questions   236
References   237

EXHIBIT 12-1 LIFE INSURANCE COMPANIES: AN SLA COPYCAT DISASTER?   232

13   **Other Nonbank Financial Intermediaries**   **238**

Investment Companies   238
Mutual and Closed-End Funds   238
Money-Market Funds   241

Other Financial Intermediaries   243
Pension Funds   243
Finance Companies   247

Nonfinancial Firms   251

Summary   252
Questions   252
References   253

EXHIBIT 13-1 PAWNSHOPS: THE CONSUMER'S LENDER OF LAST RESORT   248

14   **The Payments System**   **255**

Paper Transfer Systems   255
Currency   256
Checks   258
Credit Cards   265

Electronic Funds Transfer Systems   266
Wire Transfers   266
Automated Clearinghouse   267
Automated Teller Machines   268
Point-of-Sale Transfers   269

Summary   271
Questions   272
References   272

15 Depository Institutions and the Supply of Money   275

Currency   275
  A Digression: The Case of the "Excess" Currency   276

Transaction Deposits   278
  An Individual Bank   278
  The Banking System   280
  The Deposit Multiplier   282

Money Supply   284

Summary   286
Questions   286
References   287

Appendix 15A   288
  Deposit Expansion Process   288
  Reference   290

16 Regulation of the Financial System   292

Reasons for Government Regulation   293

Types of Regulation   295
  Safety   295
  Structure   301
  Monetary Control   303

Evaluation of Regulation   304

Regulatory Agencies   306
  Comptroller of the Currency   306
  Federal Reserve System   308
  Federal Deposit Insurance Corporation   308
  Office of Thrift Supervision   310
  National Credit Union Administration   310

Bank Examination   311

Summary   314
Questions   315
References   315

PART IV CURRENT ISSUES IN FINANCIAL MARKETS AND INSTITUTIONS

17 Managing Interest Rate Risk   317

A Hypothetical Bank Balance Sheet   318

Duration Analysis   321

Managing Interest Rate Risk   325

Practical Problems with Applying Duration Gap Analysis   331
  Advantages of Duration Gap Analysis   333

Summary   336
Questions   336
References   337

18 Deposit Insurance   339

Determination of Premiums   341

Total versus Insured Deposits   342
Flat versus Risk-Related Premiums   343

Percent of Deposits Insured   346

Who Should Pay the Premiums?   348
Who Pays Now?   348

Who Should Provide Insurance?   349
Narrow Banks   352

How Should Failed Banks Be Treated?   352
Early Intervention and Closure   354

The FDIC As Insurer and Regulator   355

Recent Developments in Deposit Insurance   356

Summary   360
Questions   361
References   361

19 *Deregulation and Regulatory Reform*   364

Reform of Regulations   365
Product Powers   366
Geographic Powers   373
Interstate Banking   375
Deregulation and Bank Safety   377

Reform of Regulatory Agencies   378
The Case against Multiple Agencies   381
The Case for Multiple Agencies   383
Prospects for Reform   384

Summary   386
Questions   387
References   388

EXHIBIT 19-1 BOOTLEGGERS AND BAPTISTS—THE EDUCATION OF A REGULATORY ECONOMIST   367

EXHIBIT 19-2 MIXING COMMERCE AND BANKING: THE GERMAN CASE   371

20 *Separation of Commercial and Investment Banking*   390

History   390

The Banking Act of 1933   391
Reasons for the Banking Act   392

Permissible Bank Securities Activities   394
Underwriting and Trading Securities   394
Brokerage Activities   396
Private Placements   397
Customer Money Management Services   398

Nonpermissible Bank Securities Activities   399
Sponsoring Mutual Funds   399

Should Banks Be Permitted to Engage in Full Securities Activities?   400
Competition and Concentration   400
Economies of Scale and Scope   402
Bank Stability and Risk   402
Conflict of Interest and Other Abuses   403

Summary 405
Questions 405
References 406

21 The Mortgage Market 408

Effect of Regulation Q 410

The Mathematics of Mortgages 411
Fixed-Rate Mortgage (FRM) 411

Alternative Mortgage Plans 416
Graduated-Payment Mortgage (GPM) 417
Variable-Rate Mortgage (VRM) 418
Price-Level-Adjusted Mortgage (PLAM) 419

Interest Rate Risk and Financial Intermediation 420

The Secondary Market 423

Summary 425
Questions 426
References 427

22 Financial Derivatives: Futures and Options 428

Financial Futures and Forwards 428
Hedging 433
Hedging Fixed-Rate Loans 436
Speculating 438
Forward and Futures Interest Rates 439

Financial Options 439

Summary 444
Questions 444
References 445

23 Financial Innovation 447

New Institutions 448

New Instruments 452

New Technology 467

Summary 468
Questions 469
References 469

EXHIBIT 23-1 EXAMPLE OF INTEREST RATE SWAP 460

PART V INTERNATIONAL FINANCE

24 Foreign Exchange Rates and the Balance of Payments 472

Exchange Rates 473
Fixed versus Flexible Exchange Rates 477

Balance of Payments 483
Relation to Exchange Rates 485
Balance of Payments History 486

Summary 487
Questions 487
References 488

25 *International Financial Institutions and Markets* 490

International Monetary Fund (IMF) 490
  Borrowing Facilities 491
  Special Drawing Rights (SDRs) 493

World Bank 494
  International Development Association 495

Eurodollars 495

International Financial Markets 499
  Short- and Intermediate-Term Financing 500
  International Bond Financing 500

Summary 503
Questions 504
References 504

EXHIBIT 25-1 ECU, WHO? 502

PART VI MONETARY THEORY AND POLICY

26 *Economic Goals* 506

The Goals of the Economy 506
  Full Employment 506
  Economic Growth 509
  Price Stability 510
  Stability in the International Balance of Payments and Foreign Exchange Rates 511
  Equitable Distribution of Income and Wealth 512
  Efficiency 514

Responsibility for Goals 515

Economic Policy 516

Economics and Politics 517

Summary 520
Questions 520
References 521

27 *The Federal Reserve System: Purposes and Organization* 523

Structure of the Federal Reserve 524
  Board of Governors 524
  Federal Open Market Committee (FOMC) 525
  Regional Banks 526

Independence of the Federal Reserve 527

Federal Reserve Balance Sheet and Reserves 529
  Assets 530
  Liabilities 531
  Control of Reserves 532
  Interpreting the Balance Sheet 533

Summary 535
Questions 535
References 536

28 The Federal Reserve System:
Tools and Instruments   538

Quantitative Tools   538
  Changing the Multiplier (*k*)   539
  Changing the Amount of Reserves (*R*)   540
  Target Rates of Monetary Expansion   545

Qualitative Tools   547
  Regulation Q   548
  Margin Requirements   548
  Moral Suasion   549
  Minimum Down Payment   549
  The Credit Control Program of 1980   549
  Evaluation of Qualitative Tools   550

Summary   551
Questions   552
References   552

29 Monetary Theories   554

The Role of Theory   554

Quantity Theory   556

Keynesian Theory   560
  Speculative Demand for Money   560
  Total Demand for Money   562

The Supply of Money   564

Interest Rates   566

Summary   567
Questions   568
References   569

30 Money and Economic Activity   570

The Financial Sector   571

The Real Sector   573
  Consumption   573
  Investment   576
  Government   577
  Total Spending   578

Full-Employment Income   579

Summary   581
Questions   582
References   582

31 Monetary Policy   584

Strength of Monetary Policy   585
  Slope of the LM Function   585
  Slope of the IS Function   586

The Transmission Mechanism   588
  Policy Lags   593

Summary   597
Questions   597
References   598

EXHIBIT 31-1 THE LIQUIDITY TRAP 587

EXHIBIT 31-2 DIGRESSION ON FISCAL POLICY, DEFICITS, CROWDING IN, AND CROWDING OUT 590

32 Monetary Policy in the Post-World War II Period 600

Overview 600

1947–1960: Years of Economic Innocence 604

1960–1970: Years of Economic Experimentation and Promise 606

1970–1980: Years of Economic Pain, Frustration, and Disillusionment 608

1980–1990: Return to Stability 610

1990– Into the Great Unknown—Again 612

Summary 614
Questions 615
References 615

PART VII CURRENT ISSUES IN MONETARY POLICY

33 Interest Rates, Indicators, and Targets 617

Complete Money-Interest Rate Relationship 617
　Price-Expectations Effect 619
　Empirical Evidence 621

Indicators of Monetary Policy 623
　Interest Rates 624
　Money Supply 625

Intermediate Targets for Monetary Policy 625
　Interest Rates or Money Supply? 626
　Uncertainty in the Financial Sector 628
　Uncertainty in the Real Sector 628
　Federal Reserve Targets 630
　How Good Has Federal Reserve Control Been? 634

Fed Watching 635

Summary 637
Questions 637
References 638

EXHIBIT 33-1 BEAT INFLATION OR LOSE YOUR JOB 635

34 Inflation, The Phillips Curve, and Central Bank Independence 640

Costs of Inflation 642
　Aggregate Income Loss 643
　Bank Failures 644
　Income and Wealth Redistribution 645

The Phillips Curve 651
　Stability of the Phillips Curve 653
　Rational Expectations 658

Central Bank Independence 659

Summary 661

Questions   662
References   662

35 Keynesianism, Monetarism, and Other Isms   664

Keynesians versus Monetarists   664
   Differences in Transmission   665
   Differences in Assumptions   672
   Differences in Policy Recommendations   673

Other Monetary Theories   675
   Availability Theory   675
   Bankers Theory   677

Summary   679
Questions   680
References   680

Index   683

Preface

The sixth edition of *The U.S. Financial System: Money, Markets, and Institutions* has been revised and thoroughly updated to incorporate both the many dramatic structural, legislative, regulatory, and operational changes that have occurred at almost breathtaking speed in recent years and the comments and suggestions of users of the earlier editions. In particular:

- ▼ The discussions of the SLA and bank crises of the 1980s have been expanded and put into historical perspective.
- ▼ The deposit insurance reforms focusing on structured early intervention and resolution that were adopted as a consequence of the banking crises in both FIRREA (1989) and FDICIA (1991) are discussed throughout the book and in detail in Chapters 16 (Regulation of the Financial System) and 18 (Deposit Insurance).
- ▼ The scheduled coming of interstate branching in 1997 and its implications are introduced and discussed.
- ▼ Additional emphasis on the increasing importance of the globalization of banking, financial institutions, and financial markets is provided throughout the book.
- ▼ The discussion of financial instruments in Chapter 4 has been expanded.
- ▼ The discussions of bank management in Chapter 10 (Commercial Banks: History and Management) and of ongoing changes in banking structure in Chapter 11 (Commercial Banks: Safety and Structure) have been expanded.
- ▼ The Clinton administration's proposal for consolidating the bank regulatory agencies is discussed in Chapter 19 (Deregulation and Regulatory Reform).
- ▼ The discussions of financial derivatives (futures and options) in Chapter 22 and innovation in Chapter 23 have been revised and expanded.
- ▼ A discussion of the desirability of and empirical evidence on the independence of central banks has been added to Chapter 34, which has been retitled "Inflation, the Phillips Curve, and Central Bank Independence."
- ▼ A discussion of the recently developed credit channel of the transmission of monetary policy has been introduced in Chapter 35 (Keynesianism, Monetarism, and Other Isms).
- ▼ New current boxed exhibits have been added to increase emphasis on the practical applicability of important concepts, e.g., the near life insurance crisis in Chapter 12.
- ▼ The number of end-of-chapter questions has been significantly increased.

▼ A new study guide for students has been prepared by Donald Yarzebinski (Western Michigan University). Cynthia Latta (DRI Inc.) has updated and expanded the instructor's manual and the test bank.

The sixth edition retains its emphasis on constructing a consistent general framework at a basic level in the first chapters of each section, within which students can analyze and understand financial markets and institutions and Federal Reserve monetary policy. In the chapters that follow, the theory that was developed is applied to analyze specific important real-world issues, such as bank safety, deposit insurance reform, separation of commercial and investment banking, and inflation. One-third of the chapters are devoted to such issues. These chapters are at a somewhat higher level than the earlier chapters and are based on the concepts developed there.

The book remains an introductory undergraduate and MBA text for courses both in financial institutions and markets in business schools and in money and banking in economics departments that emphasize "commercial" rather than "central" banking. However, it may be used for a second course by emphasizing the current-issues chapters, particularly in quarter-term programs. The chapters remain brief in length but large in number so that the instructor can pick and choose among topics to tailor the course to his or her own needs and to the issues particularly important at the time.

Acknowledgments

Many people and institutions have assisted me in this revision as well as in the earlier editions. I am particularly indebted to:

Peter Alonzi (*Chicago Board of Trade*)
Harvey Anderson (*Federal Reserve Bank of Chicago*)
Herbert Baer (*World Bank*)
G. O. Bierwag (*Florida International University*)
Joseph Bisignano (*Bank of International Settlements*)
Paul Burik (*Ennis, Knupp and Associates*)
Michael Butler (*University of Northern Alabama*)
James A. Cacy (*Federal Home Loan Bank of Atlanta*)
Henry Cassidy (*Federal Home Loan Mortgage Corporation*)
Hanson Cheng (*Federal Reserve Bank of San Francisco*)
Kurt Dew (*Consultant*)
J. Kimball Dietrich (*University of Southern California*)
Gunter Dufey (*University of Michigan*)
Robert Eisenbeis (*University of North Carolina*)
Elinda Fishman (*Resolution Trust Corporation*)
James Gatti (*University of Vermont*)
Maureen Dunne (*Framingham State College*)
William Gibson (*Consultant*)
Ian Giddy (*New York University*)
Henry Goldstein (*University of Oregon*)
Charles E. Hegji (*Auburn University at Montgomery*)
Austin Jaffe (*Pennsylvania State University*)
Christopher James (*University of Florida*)
Scott Johnson (*Federal Reserve Bank of Chicago*)

Charles Klensch (*Citicorp*)
Gary Koppenhaver (*Iowa State University*)
Joseph Kvasnicka (*Federal Reserve Bank of Chicago*)
Steven Langford (*Federal Reserve Bank of Chicago*)
Leonard Lardaro (*University of Rhode Island*)
Cynthia Latta (*DRI Inc.*)
Paul Leonard (*State University of New York at Albany*)
Jo Malins (*Citicorp*)
Inayat Mangla (*Western Michigan University*)
Thomas Mayer (*University of California, Davis*)
Robert McLeod (*University of Alabama*)
David Melnicoff (*Temple University*)
Thomas Mondschean (*DePaul University*)
George Morgan (*Virginia Polytechnic Institute*)
James Moser (*Federal Reserve Bank of Chicago*)
Larry Mote (*Federal Reserve Bank of Chicago*)
Anne Marie Muelyndike (*Federal Reserve Bank of New York*)
Gerard Olson (*La Salle University*)
Douglas Pearce (*North Carolina State University*)
William Quinn (*Michigan State University*)
Martin Regalia (*U.S. Chamber of Commerce*)
Robert Rogowski (*Bank of America*)
Harvey Rosenblum (*Federal Reserve Bank of Dallas*)
Paul M. Taube (*University of Texas-Pan American*)
Michael Salemi (*University of North Carolina*)
Jeffrey Schaefer (*Securities Industry Association*)
David Schutte (*Texas A&M University*)
Robert Schweitzer (*University of Delaware*)
Sherman Shapiro (*Consultant*)
Joan Silverman (*Citicorp*)
Jean Sinquefield (*Chicago Board of Trade*)
Frank Steindl (*Oklahoma State University*)
Steven Strongin (*Goldman Sachs*)
John Tucillo (*National Association of Realtors*)
David Walker (*Georgetown University*)
Stanton Warren (*State University of New York at Albany*)
Frances Wrocklage (*Federal Home Loan Mortgage Corporation*)
Jeffrey A. Zimmerman (*Clarkson University*)

In addition, I was aided greatly by the staffs of the research department, public information department (Nancy Goodman), and library (Betty Maynard and Dorothy Phillips) of the Federal Reserve Bank of Chicago.

The many drafts of the manuscripts for this edition were typed by Mary Kukla, Mary Lellouche, and Linda Stack at Loyola University. John Duszynki, Kristine Gustitus, Wieslawa Shank, and Alice Djung (Loyola University) provided research assistance. At Prentice Hall, the production editor was Judy Winthrop, the designer was Dorothy Bungert and the editor was Leah Jewell. David Hildebrand was the original acquisitions editor. I was also aided by the responses of my students and other readers who were more than generous with their suggestions for improvements.

The U.S. Financial System:
MONEY, MARKETS, AND INSTITUTIONS

Introduction and Overview

Webster's Dictionary defines finance as "the science of managing money."[1] Because we all manage money, at least our own, a day rarely passes for most of us without some contact with finance. We get paid in money. We spend money to buy goods and services. We save the money we do not wish to spend immediately on goods and services for later use by lending it to someone or some institution that either spends it or, in turn, relends it to a third party. In return for the temporary use of our money, the borrower gives us an IOU in the form of a financial security—for example, a deposit, note, or bond—which generally promises to pay us interest until the money is returned. We borrow money against income we have not yet earned by creating our own IOU. The IOU commits us to repay the money in the future and in the meantime pay interest to the lender. Borrowing permits us to spend before we have earned the necessary income. Because of our everyday use of money, money has been a subject of fascination throughout history.

Financial terms such as **money, checking accounts, banks, savings and loan associations, interest rates, foreign exchange rates, stocks, bonds, mortgages, credit cards, money-market funds,** and **monetary policy** are part of our everyday language. Financial events are in the news daily—bank failures, savings and loan crises, junk bond crises, changes in the rate of inflation, changes in interest rates, changes in stock prices (including stock market crashes and meltdowns), new types of securities, and pronouncements by the chairman of the Board of Governors of the Federal Reserve System.

Although important, and the focus of much study, money still remains a mystery to many of us. Money has been accused of being the root, alternately, of all happiness and of all evil, the source of power, and the cause of corruption. Critics have suggested that it be abolished, and societies have at times tried to operate without it. Yet it exists in all modern economies. As the famous economist John Stuart Mill wrote almost 200 years ago:

> Confusion . . . envelopes the whole matter; partly from a lingering remnant of . . . misleading associations, and partly from the mass of vapoury and baseless speculation with which this, more than any other topic of political economy, has in later times become surrounded.[2]

It is hoped that this book will take some of the mystery out of the topic and replace speculation with fact.

---

[1] A tongue-in-cheek definition of finance is "the science of reconciling *principal* with *principle*."

[2] John Stuart Mill, *Principles of Political Economy*, 4th ed. (London: John Parker and Sons, 1857), vol. 2, p. 16.

Managing money and finance is important at the personal, business, international, and government levels. At these levels, it is referred to as ***personal finance, business finance, international finance,*** and ***public finance,*** respectively. The better we understand finance and how to manage money, the better off we will be as individuals, organizations, and societies. Good financial management is important at all levels. If we mismanage our personal finances, primarily we harm ourselves. If we mismanage the finances of a firm, we harm not only the owners but also the employees, suppliers, and customers. If we mismanage the finances of a governmental unit, including the federal government, we harm all its citizens. This book does not tell you how to manage money. Rather, it examines primarily the financial environment in which you manage your own money or that of others, and in which others manage your money, and how the government manages money in order to affect levels of economic performance. The book will provide you with the tools and understanding both for designing and for evaluating financial strategies.

The object of financial management at all four levels is both (1) to meet payments in full when due—that is, to avoid default and bankruptcy; and (2) to manage money efficiently until the time it is needed to meet future payments. If the funds are available before the scheduled payment date, the money may be invested in financial securities or real assets in such a way that the expected rate of return for a given level of risk of loss, or failure to receive payment in full, will be maximized (or the risk for an expected rate of return will be minimized). If one does not have the necessary funds to meet a current payment, one may borrow the funds until the expected future revenues are received by issuing securities in such a way as to minimize the interest cost for the risk the lender assumes that you may not make the required payments on the securities in full and on time.

Finance has two important dimensions—return and risk of loss. The two are closely related, and one is difficult to interpret without the other. Indeed, the strategy of finance is to determine the combination of return and risk that is most appropriate for achieving one's objectives. Return is measured by the increase or decrease in wealth, generally on an annual basis. But, because we live in a world of uncertainty, expectations are not always realized. The returns we expect to make on an investment before it is made may not be the return we realize after the investment period is finished. The risk investors assume is the risk that at any time the realized (ex-post) return may be less than the expected (ex-ante) return. It stands to reason that the greater risk of a loss, the higher the return an investor would demand as compensation for assuming the risk. Table 1–1 shows the average annual rates of return on selected investments in the United States between 1960 and 1992 and the associated risks as measured by the annual variability in the rate of returns. (Some of these investments are plotted in Figure 1–1 for a somewhat shorter time period.) Because it is difficult to measure risk directly, variability is frequently used as a proxy variable.

The more variable the return on an investment, the greater the likelihood of selling the security at a lower than expected price and realizing a return below the expected return. For example, a recent study found that from 1960 through 1990 the annual return on stocks averaged more than 50 percent higher than that on three-month Treasury bills. Yet if stocks were held for shorter periods, they did not do nearly as well. If stocks had been

TABLE

1-1   RETURN AND RISK FOR SELECTED INVESTMENTS, 1960–1992

	Return[a]	Risk[b]
	(annual percent)	
Common stock (S&P 500)	10.3	15.7
Long-term corporate bonds	7.3	11.0
Long-term Treasury bonds	6.8	10.8
Short-term Treasury bonds	6.3	2.8
Residential real estate	13.3	8.6
Farm real estate	10.6	9.6
Business real estate	8.6	7.8
Gold[c]	10.2	38.2
Silver[c]	3.7	81.7
Inflation	4.9	3.3

SOURCE: © *Stocks, Bonds, Bills, and Inflation* 1993 *Yearbook*™, Ibbotson Associates, Chicago (annually updates work by Roger G. Ibbotson and Rex A. Sinquefield). Used with permission. All rights reserved.

© *EnCorr Software*™, Ibbotson Associates, Chicago. Used with permission. All rights reserved.

[a]Geometric mean of annual observations.
[b]Standard deviation of annual observations.
[c]For 1971–1992 only.

sold after only one year, they would have outperformed the bills only 60 percent of the time. If stocks had been sold after five-year periods, they would have outperformed the bills 70 percent of the time. Only when the stocks were sold after 20-year periods, would they have outperformed the bills every time.

The data in Table 1–1 indicate that residential real estate had the highest average return of major types of investment from 1960 through 1992, followed by farm real estate, common stocks, and gold. Their risks varied greatly, however. The risk or variability in annual returns for residential real estate was lower than that for the other three, particularly gold, which had more than four times as much risk. Silver displayed both the lowest return and the greatest risk. Thus, all investments were not equally efficient in terms of achieving comparable returns for comparable risks, and investors were not always successful in obtaining a higher return for riskier investments. But averages hide many individual gains, and not all investors trade securities on an annual basis, so that annual variability may not be the appropriate risk measure. Nevertheless, it is unlikely that investors always met the goals they had in mind when they purchased the investments. Although all investments outpaced the rate of inflation in this period, this is not always the case. At times, the return on an investment, even if positive, may be less than the increase in the general price level, so that the investor suffers a loss in purchasing power.

To understand how to practice finance and have the best chance of achieving our objective of maximizing return and minimizing risk, we must understand (1) the financial instruments (securities) we can create to borrow money or those created by others in which we can invest our tem-

FIGURE

1—1

Wealth indices of six alternative investments, 1971–1992

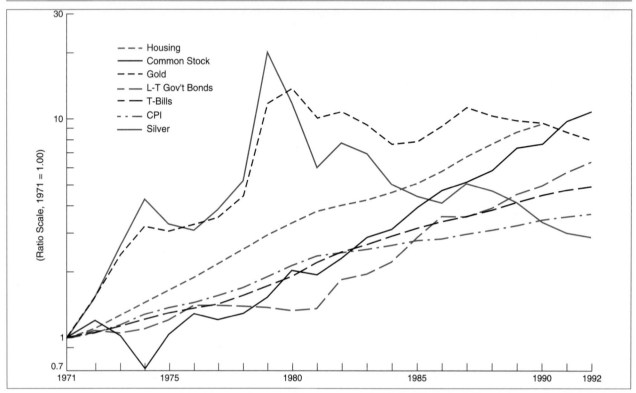

porarily surplus money; (2) the financial markets on which these instruments are traded; and (3) the financial institutions that both create and trade financial instruments. The complex of financial markets and institutions is referred to as the **financial sector** of the economy. The **financial system** encompasses the instruments, institutions, markets, and rules governing the conduct of trade that expedite the routing of funds from buyers to sellers and from savers to lenders. (That part of the financial system that encompasses only the institutions, including the central bank, that are involved in the creation and distribution of money only is referred to as the **monetary system.**) A financial system is an integral part of a modern, developed economy; it makes possible the highly complex, specialized, and efficient methods of production that create much of the wealth of the economy. Without finance, trade would be sharply reduced and individuals would be severely restricted in what, how, and when they can produce and consume. The more developed the financial system, the more freedom people have making these decisions, and the higher is their material well-being.

Importance of the Financial Sector

The importance of financial management increases as an economy develops. Thus, finance becomes more important and the financial sector becomes larger as the economy becomes wealthier and more complex. The financial sector produces services that increase the efficiency of trade, facilitate saving and accumulation of wealth, and minimize risk. It is among the most dynamic and innovative sectors in the economy. As the economy becomes wealthier and more complex, the need for new and different kinds of financial services increases. Many of today's common financial services were not available a few years ago. Special low- or no-minimum-balance checking accounts began in the mid-1950s; credit cards were not used widely until the 1960s; money-market funds and automatic 24-hour, remote bank teller machines (ATMs) became available only in the 1970s; check-writing privileges on interest-bearing accounts (such as negotiable order of withdrawal—NOW—accounts and money-market deposit—MMD—accounts) and zero-coupon securities came into widespread use only in the early 1980s; and debit cards in the early 1990s. For business firms, such popular short-term investment instruments as Eurodollars (dollar deposits at banks in foreign countries) and CDs (large, negotiable bank certificates of deposit) were unavailable before 1960; simple mortgage-backed securities were not introduced until the 1970s; newly issued junk bonds and more complex mortgage-backed securities, such as CMOs (collateralized mortgage obligations), until the 1980s; and splitting bonds into separate principal only (PO) and interest only (IO) securities until the early 1990s.

Likewise, securities that are created not to finance nonfinancial transactions either directly or indirectly, as are bonds and stocks (which thus derive their value from these activities), but to lock in the future prices of bonds and stocks, such as futures, option, and swap contracts (and thus derive their value from the associated underlying bond or stock), did not trade actively until the late 1970s. Can you visualize a world without MMD accounts, Eurodollars, CDs, CMOs, futures, swaps, and options? Your parents and, possibly, older siblings certainly can. Indeed, an entire new industry of financial engineering has developed to design financial instruments to satisfy the rapidly expanding needs of participants in today's financial markets.

Similarly, the institutions of the financial sector are continuously changing. A listing of the major types of financial institutions by size shows a considerably different rank ordering in 1950 and 1992 (see Table 9–5). The older types of institutions have lost ground to newer types. Private pension funds, which provide financial security after retirement, have expanded rapidly in size, climbing from the seventh to the second largest type of financial institution. In the process, they have passed savings banks, finance companies, casualty insurance companies, savings and loan associations, and even life insurance companies, which were 10 times as large in 1950. Money-market mutual funds are even more recent; these permitted households and small business firms to realize market interest rates on their savings at times when deposits were subject to below-market rate ceilings without incurring large transaction costs. They did not exist in 1970. In 1977, they were the smallest of the 11 major types of financial institutions. By year-end 1981, money-market funds had surpassed in size their older sibling, equity and bond mutual funds, long-established savings banks, and the previously fastest-growing credit unions and had almost caught up to finance companies and casualty insurance companies. Their growth slowed for a while after 1982, when commercial banks and thrift institutions were permitted to pay competitive interest rates on their deposits, such as MMD accounts, but money-market funds did not disappear and they remain a major financial institution.

Most financial institutions in the United States tend to specialize, being restricted by law or tradition in the types of activities in which they may engage and in the geographic markets in which they may have offices. This state of affairs has begun to unravel in recent years, however, for three primary reasons.

One, dramatic advances in computer and telecommunications technology have sharply reduced the cost and increased the speed of transferring funds and information across distances, including national boundaries. Thus, financial institutions are able to attract funds from beyond their traditional market areas and design financial products that closely resemble those of their competitors in other subsectors of the financial services industry. Two, equally dramatic increases in the level and volatility of interest rates in the early 1980s not only encouraged both institutions and customers to circumvent legal ceilings on interest rates that could be paid on certain types of financial products at the time, but also reduced the profitability of the chief products of some financial institutions, such as fixed-rate residential mortgages for thrift institutions, and encouraged them to develop more profitable products. Three, there was a reversal in economic and political philosophy toward reduced government intervention in the economic marketplace. As a result, many regulations on financial institutions that restricted the types of products offered and the locations at which products may be offered have been liberalized or removed altogether. This process is referred to as **deregulation** and has paved the way for the potential establishment of nationwide institutions offering many if not all financial product lines. Financial institutions are freer to choose their own products, market areas, and prices. The importance of this change is evident by noting that, until a few years ago, commercial banking, thrift institutions, insurance companies, and stock brokerages were viewed as separate industries. Now they are popularly combined under the new classification of **financial services industry.** The structure of financial institutions in the twenty-first century promises to be greatly different from that throughout most of our history.

Like financial institutions, financial markets also evolve. Markets on which financial securities, such as Treasury bills and mortgage contracts, may be traded for future delivery started only after 1970, those for options on these securities and for junk bonds only after 1980, and those for swap contracts only after 1990. The advances in computer and telecommunications technology have also permitted the quick and cheap transfer of funds not only within a country but also across national boundaries and among countries. Indeed, just as local financial markets gave way to national markets some years ago, national financial markets are now giving way to international markets. Today, financial markets are truly global, and funds flow easily from country to country in search of the highest lending rate or lowest borrowing rate.

In addition, new instruments and institutions are being developed almost daily. You might have read about or even participated in experiments in which funds can be transferred from your checking account to someone else's via your touch-tone telephone or a store's cash register. Many of you may have your employer automatically credit your salary to your bank account directly via computer. These are examples of financial services that are becoming increasingly available through the continued development of the ***electronic funds transfer system*** **(EFTS).**

Where do the efficiency and productivity of the financial sector come from? Unlike the case in many other efficient sectors in our economy, they do not arise primarily from large stocks of physical capital. Until recently, the only major physical capital most financial institutions owned was their office buildings. Even the acquisition of sophisticated electronic computers in recent years represented only a relatively small investment. The primary source of the productivity is human capital, or brain power. As we will demonstrate in later chapters, much of the value produced by financial institutions comes from human ingenuity and creativity in developing new financial instruments, institutions, and markets that can better serve the needs of both borrowers and lenders. The payoff for success is very high. Top salaries, commissions, and bonuses in finance are among the very highest in any profession. This course may change your life plans!

On the other hand, the penalty for financial failure is also great, ranging from personal bankruptcy, to corporate bankruptcy, to national bankruptcy in the form of high levels of inflation and unemployment. In addition, because money is used to conduct trade in all sectors of the economy, financial mismanagement by the federal government that produces either too little or too much money affects all sectors and produces more harm than the mismanagement of any other single good or service.

Although the financial sector is large and important, it is not as well understood as are most other sectors of the economy. This lack of understanding of the financial sector may, to a large extent, be attributed to the fact that it deals in intangibles. Money and financial instruments often appear to be created out of thin air; they are at most only pieces of paper and sometimes only entries on memory cores of computers.

In contrast, most of us are more familiar with tangible goods and the methods by which they are produced. For example, all of us understand in some basic way how an automobile works, even if it is only that it requires gasoline to run or that the wheels are connected to the engine. We would not feel completely lost in an automobile assembly plant, and most of us could probably follow the automobile as it proceeds along the assembly line. We would probably laugh if we were told that the wheels go inside the body of the car or that the gasoline tank is placed on the roof. But we would probably not know enough to laugh at equally absurd statements about commercial banks, savings and loan associations, or life insurance companies. Their production processes appear mysterious.

Because of the widespread lack of confidence in their understanding of how the financial production process works, many members of the public tend to stand in awe of the financial process and withdraw from making judgments about the process. They defer on questions of private or public policy to those in charge of the process—bankers or regulators. After all, like medical doctors and members of the clergy, they may be assumed to know the process with which they deal and therefore can be entrusted to do what is best. Such action confers substantial importance and power on bankers and regulators. An annual survey of business and government leaders conducted by *U.S. News & World Report* through the mid-1980s found that in more than half of the years surveyed, the chairman of the Board of Governors of the Federal Reserve System was ranked either second or third in national importance, closely behind the president of the United States. Banks were ranked as the fifth most important institution affecting the welfare of the nation, behind the White House, television, and the Supreme Court, but ahead of the U.S. Senate, U.S. House, the president's cabinet, and Wall Street.[3] The novelist Morris West captured the essence of the source of power of the financial community in his description of a hypothetical bankers' club:

> The Bankers' Club in Milan is only a whit less venerable than the Chess Club in Rome. It is, however, much more impressive because the focus of its power is clearer and all members are fluent in a single international language—money. It is a religious language reserved to priests and acolytes, like Church Latin or the time symbols of the Incas. It is precise, flexible, subtle and quite unintelligible to the profane populace.[4]

In large part because of the widespread failure to understand financial institutions, underlying problems in commercial banks and, particularly, savings and loan associations (SLAs) were permitted to go uncorrected during the 1970s and 1980s. By 1992, these institutions, as a whole, had lost more than $250 billion, and many could not pay their depositors in full and on time. Because most of the deposits were fully insured by federal government deposit insurance agencies, for banks, the loss was borne primarily by the remaining solvent institutions. For SLAs, the losses exceeded the resources of the insurance agency and were borne primarily by the taxpayers. This restitution represented payments from taxpayers who did not have insured deposits at insolvent institutions to those who did and would have suffered losses. Few of the paying taxpayers appreciated this transfer!

In reality, firms that produce intangible financial products are no more complex or more mysterious than firms that produce tangible products. This book will demonstrate the truth in this statement. Upon completing the book, you should feel as familiar with financial institutions as you do with nonfinancial institutions. The mystery should have disappeared.

The study of the financial system is fascinating and important in its own right. But equally important is the unique relationship of the financial sector to the rest of the economy. It is this relationship that makes the study of the financial system particularly important to students of business and the economy as well as to the average citizen who simply wants to

---

[3] "12th Annual Survey: Who Runs America," *U.S. News & World Report*, May 20, 1985, pp. 54–64.

[4] Morris West, *The Salamander* (New York: Morrow, 1973), p. 216.

understand how our economy as a whole works. As we will see in the next section, because they are used to finance real assets, the amount and changes in financial assets correspond closely with the amount and changes in real assets. As a result, the behavior of the financial and real sectors is closely interwoven. What happens in one sector will affect the other. Smooth operation of the financial system will improve the performance of the real sector, and smooth operation of the real sector will improve the performance of the financial sector. Conversely, difficulties in either sector will be transmitted to the other and may impede its performance.

As a result, the government has a strong and continuing interest in the financial sector. This interest is reflected in two ways. First, the government tries to promote conditions conducive to the safe and efficient operation of the financial sector through **regulatory policy.** Second, it effects changes in the financial sector intended to affect conditions in the real sector and to help the economy attain its economic goals through **monetary policy.** These two policies are types of **government**, or **public policies.** In this book, we discuss first the operation of the financial sector and then proceed to examine how the financial sector both affects and is affected by the real sector. A clear understanding of the operation of either the financial or the real sector and of public policies in these areas requires a clear knowledge of the fundamental structure of each.

Financial sectors have not always operated smoothly. Breakdowns in this sector in terms of increases in the number of failed institutions or excessive volatility in financial prices or interest rates have at times intensified or possibly even led to breakdowns in the real sector. For example, the severe worldwide depression of the early 1930s, which resulted in record levels of unemployment (approaching 25 percent in the United States) and which helped to bring leaders such as Adolf Hitler to power, was intensified by the collapse of the commercial banking system. Some also blame Hitler's rise to power on an earlier period of hyperinflation in Germany (discussed in Chapter 2) that was fueled by very rapid rates of money growth generated by the government and that wiped out, politically as well as financially, a large part of the German middle class.

On the other hand, fears of breakdowns in the financial sector (that are based on experiences such as the Great Depression) spilling over into the real sector and causing severe damage to the macroeconomy worldwide have at times led to the adoption of regulatory and monetary policies that reduced the efficiency of both sectors. Some of these policies shift losses from private units to the general public (taxpayer), restrict price and interest rate movements, or create excessive macroliquidity. For example, fear of contagion from the failure of individual banks to the banking system as a whole and eventually to the real economy has lead to temporary government support of a number of large banks in recent years, most noticeably the Continental Illinois National Bank (Chicago) in 1984 and most large Texas banks between 1986 and 1989. In the process, losses were shifted from uninsured depositors at these banks to the Federal Deposit Insurance Corporation (FDIC).

Unexpected volatility in interest rates and prices of financial assets is often viewed as symptomatic of a malfunctioning financial system. Thus, the sharp 500-point (nearly 25 percent) drop in stock prices on "Black

Monday," October 19, 1987, led to concern about possible further share price declines and consequent reductions in real spending that might trigger a downturn in the economy. Some analysts recommended that public policy stabilize prices by imposing limits on the magnitude of daily price changes. If these limits are hit, trading is halted for the day. The increased price stability, however, is achieved at the expense of reduced market liquidity for those wishing to buy or sell securities when trading has been halted. (As the economist Milton Friedman is fond of reminding us, there are no free lunches.)

Whether these financial "breakdowns" damage the real sector more than any immediate or delayed damage from the proposed cures is difficult to judge. Neither theory nor empirical evidence to date is sufficiently strong to convince everyone one way or the other. But as long as the perception that the damage from problems in the financial sector may be severe is widespread, public policy, for good or for bad, will weigh safety above efficiency.

In the absence of evidence to the contrary, perceptions, if held long enough, often become accepted "truths" that are difficult to dispel. As you work your way through this book, it is likely that you will encounter statements that run counter to your perceptions. When this occurs, you might wish to reexamine the issues in light of the information presented. Doing so may not be as easy as it sounds. Most of us do not confess to our errors either quickly or easily. Although Allan Bloom was discussing philosophy and not finance or economics, the origins of unsubstantiated perceptions or myths and the dangers of exorcising them are well described in his book, *The Closing of the American Mind*:

> Myths are made by poets. . . . The aim of philosophy is to substitute truth for myths. . . . Socrates['] . . . death at the hands of his countrymen for not believing in their myths epitomizes the risks of philosophy.[5]

The aim of finance and economics (financial economics) may be viewed similarly.

Financial Intermediation

Because finance is a study of managing money, it is useful to begin our study by discussing money and what can be done with it. Money is an asset that is a direct claim against all other assets, both financial and real. Financial assets are ownership claims against real assets, either directly or indirectly through other financial claims. Real assets are the tangible goods and services that we produce and require for our material well-being. If you hold money, you can collect on your claim at almost any time at face value. If you hold other financial claims, you are often restricted in the time when you can exercise the claim, and the future value of the claim may not be known with certainty. Many people do not wish to consume their income immediately upon receipt. They prefer to defer their spending to a later date. In the meantime, they save part of their income and add to their wealth. They can hold their wealth in either financial or real assets. Some

---

[5] Allan Bloom, *The Closing of the American Mind* (New York: Simon and Schuster, 1987), p. 207.

prefer to save in the form of financial assets for a number of reasons, including greater divisibility, greater ability to diversify among different assets, lower transactions costs in buying and selling, ease of storage and protection, ability to avoid direct participation in the operation and maintenance of the real assets, and a wider range of risks and returns from which to choose. The savers know that they can convert their financial claim into real assets whenever it is convenient to them, although not necessarily at face value.

Others prefer to hold their savings in real assets because they believe they can manage these assets more efficiently. These people may be able to increase their holdings of real assets by creating financial claims against the additional assets and selling the claims to those who prefer to save in financial form. As we shall see later in the book, this exchange makes it easier both for investors in real assets to raise funds for their projects and share some of the risk with others and for savers to find profitable outlets for their temporarily excess funds with varying degrees of risk. This exchange not only permits individual preferences to be satisfied but encourages capital accumulation. Capital, in the form of plant and equipment, increases the ability of the economy to generate increased output for a given level of input and for aggregate material well-being to increase. The composition of household assets is shown in Table 1–2. Financial assets account for only 28 percent.

The financial sector facilitates the creation of financial securities and their transfer from issuers to investors or borrowers. This process is referred to as *financial intermediation.* Financial securities are IOUs or receipts issued by those spending units (households, business firms, governments) that spend more than their current income on consumption and investment. These units are called borrowers, or more technically, *deficit spending units,* or **DSUs.** DSUs can issue two types of securities on themselves. Securities that promise the holder periodic payments of interest and/or principal financed from a first claim on the issuer's earnings are called *bonds;* those that promise the holder a share of the ownership of the issuer and of any profit generated are called *equities* or *stocks.* Because profits are uncertain, the return on stocks tends to be less certain than on bonds, and,

TABLE 1–2	COMPOSITION OF HOUSEHOLD ASSETS, 1989	
		Percent
Financial		28
Nonfinancial		72
Automobile	4	
Residence	32	
Other Real Estate	15	
Other Business Investment	18	
Other	3	___
Total		100

SOURCE: Arthur Kennickell and Janice Shack-Marquez, "Changes in Family Finances from 1983 to 1989," *Federal Reserve Bulletin,* January 1992, p. 3.

as can be seen from Table 1–1, stocks are riskier to investors. To satisfy their needs for funds, DSUs have three options. They can

1. Reduce their money balances,
2. Dissave by selling financial securities issued by others that they had purchased earlier when they were savers, or *surplus spending units (SSUs),* or
3. Borrow by selling new financial securities issued on themselves.

DSUs can, of course, engage simultaneously in any or all of the three alternatives.

Financial securities are purchased by units that spend less than their current income on consumption and investment. These units are savers, or SSUs. Their alternatives are the opposite of those of the DSUs. They can

1. Build up their money balances,
2. Reduce their debt by buying back securities they issued earlier when they were DSUs, or
3. Lend by buying securities issued by others.

SSUs can also engage simultaneously in any combination of the three alternatives. If there were no financial markets in which SSUs could transfer their temporarily surplus funds to DSUs in exchange for securities, SSUs would only be able to build up their money balances and DSUs to draw down money balances that they had previously accumulated when they were SSUs. Potential buyers of large ticket items, such as houses, automobiles, or factories, would need to save first and buy later rather than to buy first and save later. This would reduce the incentives to be either an SSU or a DSU and reduce the accumulation and flow of loanable funds. Thus, gains from being able to trade financial securities clearly exist.

It follows that, in a large economy with a large number and variety of DSUs and SSUs, there would be a large number of different financial securities outstanding. Indeed, recent advances in telecommunications technology have made it easier for SSUs and DSUs to search each other out not only in their own country but nearly across the world. The internationalization of financial markets has increased the number and variety of securities even further.

The more efficient the financial system, (1) the more smoothly are the "correct" financial securities created and transferred from the "right" DSUs to the "right" SSUs at the "correct" prices; and (2) the greater is the overall flow of funds from savers to borrowers to finance investment. The first dimension is referred to as *allocative efficiency* and the second as *operational efficiency.*

Financial intermediation involves the transfer of securities from DSUs to SSUs and the reverse flow of funds from SSUs to DSUs. As we will see later, this exchange can occur directly, although generally with the assistance of security brokers or dealers to locate the counterparty SSU or DSU. But more likely it occurs indirectly through a process in which a financial intermediary institution transforms the security issued by the DSU into one more to the liking of SSUs. This channel generally improves the efficiency of the intermediation process.

We shall find that there are disagreements about how the financial sector and the rest of the economy work. These disagreements arise because analytical tools are not yet good enough to explain all happenings to everyone's satisfaction. Having an understanding of the relationships in the economy means that we do not need to wait until an event has already occurred to be able to respond to it, and, in the case of economic policy, to correct or offset it if necessary. Such knowledge would permit us to predict the event. An explanation of how and why a particular event occurs is called a **theory.** It follows that the value of a particular theory is only as good as its ability to predict the appropriate event. Theory enhances understanding.

Theories that attempt to explain financial or economic events are called *financial theories* or *economic theories.* Unfortunately, just as with tomorrow's weather, many financial and economic events are not predicted very well by current theories. As a result, alternative theories often exist to explain the same phenomena. The large number of theories and their relatively poor predictive powers confuse many people, who therefore tend to downgrade the role and usefulness of theory. But what would replace theory? Facts describe only the past. Theory attempts to describe (predict) the future, as well as to explain the past, by fitting the individual facts into a logical and consistent framework. That tomorrow will (or will not) look like yesterday is only a theory until tomorrow has come and gone. Then, if it happens, it becomes fact. The importance of economic theory and ideas has been emphasized by Lord John Maynard Keynes in an often-quoted statement:

> The ideas of economists and philosophers, both when they are right and when they are wrong, are more powerful than is commonly understood. Indeed the world is ruled by little else. Practical men, who believe themselves to be quite exempt from any intellectual influences, are usually the slaves of some defunct economist. Madmen in authority, who hear voices in the air, are distilling their frenzy from some academic scribbler of a few years back. I am sure that the power of vested interests is vastly exaggerated compared with the gradual encroachment of ideas.[6]

Keynes should know whereof he speaks. Along with those of his economist predecessors, Adam Smith (1723–1790) and Karl Marx (1818–1883), Keynes's (1883–1946) ideas have had as much effect on world history as those of almost anyone else in the last thousand years.[7]

Financial and economic theories can be extremely useful. Without them we would have little or no idea of the consequences for you, your family, or the economy as a whole of changes in the money supply, interest rates, tax rates, regulation, or any other financial action by the private or government sector. In discussing the operation of the financial sector and

---

[6] John Maynard Keynes, *The General Theory of Employment, Interest, and Money* (New York: Harcourt Brace, Jovanovich, 1964), p. 383.

[7] It may be of interest to collectors of trivia that Keynes was born in the year that Marx died and on the same day 160 years later as Adam Smith.

the economy as a whole, we shall pick those theories that appear to be the most useful. When more than one theory appears to be equally useful or is accepted widely, we shall examine each of them and their supporting evidence.

QUESTIONS

1. What reasons can you think of that may account for the relative efficiency of the financial sector? Do you think that labor or capital is more important in the financial sector relative to other sectors of the economy? Why? Differentiate between *allocative* and *operational* efficiency. Can you think of an example of each type of inefficiency in today's financial system?

2. Discuss some new services and products introduced by commercial banks and other financial institutions in your geographic area in recent years. Why do you think they were introduced at this time?

3. How does the ability to sell a wide variety of different financial instruments permit owners of real (nonfinancial) assets either to increase or decrease the degree of risk they wish to incur?

4. How does the availability of a wide variety of financial instruments affect your willingness and ability to save? How might you save in the absence of these instruments?

5. "A theory that is not fine in practice is not fine in theory either." Discuss this statement. Support your argument with real-world examples. Do you think that this statement is more controversial in some disciplines than in others? If so, why?

6. Currently are you a SSU or a DSU? Why? When were you last the opposite? Why? What do you expect to be 10, 25, and 40 years from now? Why? Why might it be easier for you to be a SSU or a DSU now than it was for your great-grandparents when they were your age?

7. As can be seen from Table 1–1, stocks have generated a significantly higher rate of return, on average, than bonds. Why then do some SSUs continue to invest in bonds? Even though a particular investment, for example stocks, has generated a specific volatility of returns, why may its risk be perceived differently by different investors?

American Banker (a daily, authoritative newspaper covering financial news).

Congressional Research Service, Library of Congress, A *Reference Guide to Banking and Finance*. U.S. Congress, Committee on Banking, Finance and Urban Affairs, 97th Cong., 1st sess., May 1981.

Dobson, Steven W., "Development of Capital Markets in the United States," *Business Review*, Federal Reserve Bank of Dallas, April 1976.

Downes, John, and Jordan E. Goodman, *Barron's Finance and Investment Handbook*. Woodbury, N.Y.: Barron's Educational, 1990.

Friedman, Benjamin M., et al., *Postwar Changes in the American Financial Markets*. New York: National Bureau of Economic Research, Reprint 150, 1980.

Friedman, Milton, and Anna J. Schwartz, A *Monetary History of the United States, 1867–1960*. Princeton, N.J.: Princeton University Press, 1963.

Greenwald, Carol S., *Banks Are Dangerous to Your Wealth*. Englewood Cliffs, N.J.: Prentice Hall, 1980.

Kane, Edward J., *The S & L Insurance Mess: How Did It Happen?* Washington, D.C.: Urban Institute Press, 1989.

Kennickell, Arthur, and Janice Shack-Marquez, "Changes in Family Finances from 1983 to 1989," *Federal Reserve Bulletin*, January 1992, pp. 1–18.

Mayer, Martin, *The Bankers*. New York: Weybright and Talley, 1974.

Mumm, Glenn G., *Encyclopedia of Banking and Finance*, 8th ed. Boston: Bankers Publishing, 1983.

Smith, George David, and Richard Sylla, "The Transformation of Financial Capitalism: An Essay on the History of American Capital Markets," *Financial Markets, Institutions & Instruments*, May 1993.

Stigum, Marcia. *The Money Market*, 3rd ed. Homewood, Ill.: Dow Jones-Irwin, 1990.

Wall Street Journal (a daily, authoritative newspaper covering business and financial news).

Zweig, Phillip L., *Belly Up: The Collapse of the Penn Square Bank*. New York: Crown, 1985.

Money and Prices

Because this book is about money, it is important that we define it. William Shakespeare wrote, "That which we call a rose by any other name would smell as sweet." It is likely that this saying would apply equally well to money. Indeed, it may be more applicable to money because, unlike that of a rose, the definition of money is ambiguous and has changed considerably over time. Perhaps the best way to discuss why this is so and what money is and what it is not is to review its development.

Money Defined

What Money Is Not

Money means different things to different people. We have all heard or used expressions such as, "How much money do you want for this?" "How much money do you make?" "They have a lot of money." It is obvious that *money* does not mean the same thing in each of these expressions. In the first expression, *money* refers to a price; in the second, to income; and in the third, to wealth. The confusion arises because money is the standard in terms of which we value all material goods and services. To avoid confusion, we shall use **money** only to mean a financial asset with certain properties, which are discussed in the next section.

For most of us, both income and wealth are considerably greater than our holdings of money. **Income** is the compensation we receive for the sale of our services or of the products of our services. Although income is generally paid in the form of money, we hold it as such only until we spend it on goods and services or invest it in other financial assets. Over a period of time—say, one year—our income tends to be much larger than the amount of money we hold. **Wealth** is the accumulation of past savings of income. Most of us hold only a small part of our wealth in the form of money. The larger part is in our homes, automobiles, investments in life insurance, pension funds, stocks and bonds, and, equally important, in our own productive capabilities.

What Money Is

Money is an invention used to simplify trade. Because the earliest people were effectively self-sufficient and engaged in little trade, they had no need for money. Money did not exist. In time, however, people discovered that they were not all equally good at satisfying their own needs for food, shelter, protection, clothing, recreation, and so on. They learned that people would be better off materially if they specialized in what they could do best

16

and traded for the goods and services others could produce more efficiently. This led to the swapping or **barter** of goods and services they produced for goods and services produced by others.

It can easily be seen that, although such a system of trade might work reasonably well for small groups, it is not very efficient for larger groups. Neither would it work well for those who wished either to delay or to accelerate their purchases relative to the need to provide the goods they used in trade; that is, those who wished to save or to borrow, respectively. Frequent trading of a large number of items would involve an inordinate amount of time that could be used more efficiently in other ways. For example, the price of any item in a barter system would need to be quoted in terms of all the other goods that are traded. This results in a troublesomely large number of prices and complicates the trading process.

Assume a simple economy producing only four goods: bananas, skateboards, Frisbees, and radios. There would be three prices for bananas, one each in terms of skateboards, Frisbees, and radios. Likewise, each of the other three goods would be priced in terms of the remaining three. This results in a total of 4×3, or 12 prices. But, because the banana–Frisbee price is the reciprocal of the Frisbee–banana price, each price is in effect stated twice, and the number of different prices would be only half of 12, or 6. The general formula for the number of different prices in a barter economy is

$$N = \frac{n(n-1)}{2}$$

where: N = total number of prices

n = number of different goods and services

In a world of 1,000 different items, a relatively small number if you think about it, there would be 499,500 different prices, a relatively large number. You would need to compare all possible cross-prices to determine whether you were buying an item at the lowest possible price or selling an item at the highest possible price. This large number of prices would make trade both costly and inefficient.

To reduce the number of prices and simplify trade, one item, either one already traded or a new one, could be chosen to serve as the common standard value, or **numeraire,** in terms of which all other items would be valued or priced. This would reduce the number of different prices to either n (if a new item were chosen as the numeraire) or $n - 1$ (if an existing item were selected).

If we selected Frisbees to serve as the numeraire in the example of a four-good economy, there would be three prices rather than six. The price of each of the other three goods would be stated in terms of Frisbees. Likewise, if we used one of the 1,000 items to serve as the numeraire in the second example, the number of prices would decline sharply from 499,500 to 999. However, although all goods would now be valued on a common basis, trade might still be difficult if the good selected as the numeraire (1) were not sufficiently divisible to permit exchange in all and any quantities; (2) fluctuated widely in purchasing-power value; and (3) were not easily transferable, so that payment continued to be made in other goods. It follows that trade costs could be further reduced by selecting a numeraire that is readily divisible, stable in value, and relatively costless to store and transfer. Such a numeraire would be money.

The introduction of money into a barter economy increases aggregate economic welfare in two ways. One, by sharply reducing the number of prices, it reduces the amount of time and information required to carry on trade efficiently. Two, by permitting persons to specialize in what they can do best, it does not require them to be self-sufficient and thereby produce inefficiently.

Functions of Money

To serve successfully as money, a good must perform three basic functions. It must be a

1. Medium of exchange,
2. Standard of value, and
3. Store of value.

The first and second functions are discussed in the preceding section; the third is new.

Money as a store of value permits it to be used to separate the act of spending from the receipt of income. This greatly increases the usefulness of money. If income could be held in a form that maintains its value in terms of purchasing power, spending units that do not wish to purchase goods and services immediately upon the receipt of their income—that is, wish to save—would be willing to defer their expenditures. At a price, they would be willing to lend the money to other spending units that wish to spend before the receipt of the necessary income. Each unit would then be able to spend its income when it was most convenient. To permit this, money must be durable both physically and in terms of what can be bought with it. A good whose physical nature deteriorates, such as fish, or whose purchasing power deteriorates as a result of rapid increases in supply, such as rabbits, would serve poorly as money and would soon be replaced by a more durable good that is a better store of value.

Stability in purchasing power is not easy to achieve, and the failure to achieve it has plagued almost all forms of money throughout history. In the example in the preceding section, the value or price of Frisbees as money is easy to fix in nominal terms—1, 2, 3, and so on—but not in purchasing power or real terms. That depends on how many bananas, skateboards, or radios can be exchanged for each Frisbee at any time. How stability in the real value of what serves as money may be achieved so that it may serve as a satisfactory store of value is a major topic of the remainder of this book.

History of Money

Items that have served as money have varied greatly through time. The earliest forms of money were common items with which all participants were familiar and that they could accept as a standard of value. Such items included cattle (the word *pecuniary* is derived from the Latin word for cattle), skins, shells (wampum, which was used as money by some American Indian tribes, was made from shells), and corn. However, these tended to be both poor media of exchange and, because their supply was subject to abrupt changes, poor stores of value, so they were soon replaced by metals, such as gold, silver, and copper. Metals were both physically durable and available in relatively fixed quantities, so that they served as good stores of value. In addition, metals were relatively easy to store and were divisible into almost any amount so that they served as good media of exchange. To increase their usefulness even further, governments molded the metals into coins of standard size whose nominal values were fixed.

These coins were full valued, or **specie.** However, they quickly displayed a serious weakness: they had two values. One was their **monetary** or **exchange value,** fixed by the government. The government accepted all coins at this value in payment of taxes and stood ready to buy all of the particular metal offered at that value less a service charge. The other was their **intrinsic value,** determined by the demand for and supply of the metals for their own use. Because the government stood ready to buy all of the particular metal offered to it at the monetary value, the metal's intrinsic value effectively could not decline below its monetary value but it could rise above the designated monetary value. Through time, there was no reason for these two values to remain the same or to change together.

When the two values changed relative to each other, the amounts of the metal used as money changed. If the demand for, say, gold for use as jewelry increased, the intrinsic price of gold would rise above its monetary value. Holders of gold coins would melt down their coins and sell the gold for its own sake. This would reduce the supply of money.[1] If the demand for gold for its own sake declined and reduced its intrinsic price below its monetary value, holders of gold would sell the gold to the government for use as coins. This would increase the supply of money.

But changes in the amount of money are more important for the economy than changes in the amount of other commodities. As was discussed in Chapter 1, the amount of money in circulation directly affects the volume of trade. Thus, changes in the amount of money change the volume of trade and thereby also the economic well-being of the economy. It follows that by changing the amount of money, changes in the intrinsic price of a metal serving as money would have important implications for the performance of the economy and are a matter of concern for public policy. Countries using specie coins as money are said to be on a **metallic money standard.**

Inconvenience of Coins and Currency

In addition, coins became a less convenient medium of exchange as the volume of trade expanded. As the commercial and industrial revolution spread and as more and more people migrated from farms to the cities, a new form of money was invented—**paper notes.** These notes were initially

[1] As recently as the mid-1960s, a rapid increase in the price of silver threatened the disappearance of silver-based coins in the United States until the silver content was reduced. Similarly, in 1973, a temporary rise in the price of copper encouraged people to withhold pennies from circulation in hopes of selling the copper content for more than one cent. However, the price of copper declined again to the point where its intrinsic value in a penny was below the exchange value.

issued by commercial banks and were collateralized by the coins they replaced. Thus, like coins, they were subject to variations in supply as the monetary and intrinsic values of the coins changed relative to each other. In time, partly to avoid these difficulties and to provide a more stable money supply, the power to issue notes (or **currency,** as they became known) was transferred to the government, and the link with metal was cut. The definition of money expanded to include both coins and currency. Since after the separation of currency from metal, the nominal value of the currency was far greater than the intrinsic value of the paper on which it was printed, currency had only a monetary value, and its supply was determined entirely by the government. Such money is referred to as **fiat** money, and countries using it are said to be on a **paper money standard.**

As trade continued to expand, currency also became increasingly inconvenient for larger transactions. Commercial banks began to accept deposits, which could be exchanged with currency at par (face value) and could be transferred by the owner to a third party on demand upon a written order, called a **check,** in any amount less than the size of the owner's balance. (The history of banking and checking accounts is described in Chapter 10.) **Demand deposits,** or checking accounts, were a convenient medium of exchange, free of storage problems and safe from theft. Their major disadvantage was the possibility that the issuing bank would fail and would not be able to exchange the deposit for currency at par at all times. At such times, the exchange value of demand deposits declined, and checks became an inferior form of money to coin and currency. As the use of checks became widespread, the definition of money was expanded to include demand deposits as well as coin and currency. Starting in the 1970s, checks could be written on some interest-bearing accounts, such as NOW and MMD accounts, and the definition of money was expanded to cover some or all checkable, or transaction, deposits at all depository institutions. It is estimated that more than 90 percent of the dollar volume of all retail transactions in the United States is ultimately paid for by check.

But the development of money has not stopped. Advances in technology have decreased the need to transfer funds by check. Funds can now be transferred by telegraphic wire, telephone, or computer terminal. It is evident that the definition of money is not fixed. Money is a "living" definition that changes with changes in needs, technology, and the economic environment. Thus the definition of money will vary both over time and from person to person at any moment of time. Nevertheless, it is clear that any definition of money at any time consists of a grouping or subset of available financial assets.

Measures of Money

The Federal Reserve System, the central bank of the United States and the primary collector of financial statistics, regularly publishes data on four alternative definitions of money supply:

▼ M1—Coins, currency, demand deposits at commercial banks, and other unlimited checkable deposits at banks and thrift institutions (NOW and share draft accounts)

▼ M2—M1 plus limited checking deposits (MMDAs), noncheckable savings and small time-deposit accounts at depository institutions, and shares at retail money-market funds

▼ M3—M2 plus large time deposits at depository institutions, shares at institutional money-market funds, and large repurchase agreements

▼ L—M3 plus liquid assets, such as savings bonds, short-term Treasury securities, and commercial paper

More precise definitions and values for these definitions of money at year-end 1993 are shown in Table 2–1. Although all these definitions have different values and change by different amounts, they generally tend to change in the same direction, as can be seen for M1 and M2 on Figure 2–1, except for short periods, when new deposit accounts are developed or interest ceilings make some types of deposits less desirable.

Which definition of money one chooses is largely a matter of personal preference and the uses to which it is to be put. As was noted in the first chapter (and will be developed more completely in later chapters), money directly affects national income and price levels in later periods. But it is unlikely that all definitions of money affect income and prices equally. Thus, business managers would be interested in finding a definition that predicts future income, costs, price levels, and interest rates more accurately. Similarly, Federal Reserve policymakers would want to operate on a definition of money supply that affects income and prices more predictably. Unfortunately, the evidence in favor of any one definition of money over the others is not overwhelming.

Where does that leave one in terms of defining money? It is difficult to say. Most analysts emphasize the medium-of-exchange characteristic and prefer M1. But others do not view the distinction between transaction accounts and savings accounts or MMDAs, particularly since MMDAs have limited transaction properties, as important in affecting economic behavior, and prefer M2—or even M3—which includes larger time deposits, such as certificates of deposit in minimum denominations of $100,000, trading as money-market instruments similar to Treasury bills. Still others prefer to include all liquid assets. But where should one stop? How about stocks and long-term bonds, which are excluded even from the Fed's broadest L definition?

At least for the sake of semantics, it is preferable to have a common definition of money. In the remainder of this book, **money** will be defined as M1 (coin, currency, and transaction deposits), its most common definition. The term **monetary aggregates** is frequently used to refer to any of the definitions of money supply.

The Value of Money

What is the value or price of money? This may appear to be a silly question. After all, money has a price stamped right on it—10 cents, $1, $100, and so on. But this price is of limited use. It means only that you can exchange $1 for 10 dimes and $100 for 100 $1 bills. Because money is ultimately a claim against real goods and services, a more meaningful value is the amount of goods and services it can claim and for which it can be exchanged. That is,

TABLE
2–1
DEFINITIONS OF ALTERNATIVE MEASURES OF MONEY SUPPLY

Item	M1	M2	M3	L
Currency in circulation	X	X	X	X
Travelers' checks of nonbank issuers	X	X	X	X
At commercial banks				
Demand deposits (except those due to domestic banks, U.S. government, foreign banks, and official institutions)	X	X	X	X
NOW (negotiable order of withdrawal) accounts	X	X	X	X
At thrift institutions				
Demand deposits	X	X	X	X
NOW accounts	X	X	X	X
Credit union share draft balances	X	X	X	X
At commercial banks				
Overnight RPs (repurchase agreements)		X	X	X
Small time deposits (less than $100,000)		X	X	X
Savings deposits		X	X	X
MMD (money-market deposit) accounts		X	X	X
At thrift institutions				
Savings deposits		X	X	X
Small time deposits (less than $100,000)		X	X	X
MMD accounts		X	X	X
Other				
Overnight Eurodollar deposits of U.S. residents		X	X	X
Retail money-market mutual fund shares		X	X	X
At commercial banks				
Large time deposits ($100,000 or more), including large negotiable certificates of deposit			X	X
Term RPs			X	X
At thrift institutions				
Large time deposits ($100,000 or more)			X	X
Term RPs at savings and loan associates			X	X
Other				
Institutional money-market fund shares			X	X
Term Eurodollars held by U.S. residents				X
Bankers' acceptances				X
Commercial paper				X
U.S. Treasury bills and other liquid Treasury securities				X
U.S. savings bonds				X
Amount outstanding December 1993 (Billions of dollars, seasonally adjusted) (Currency = 321)	1,128	3,571	4,228	5,134

SOURCES: Adapted from Dale K. Osborne, "What Is Money Today?" *Economic Review*, Federal Reserve Bank of Dallas, January 1985, p. 4; and Federal Reserve System, *Statistical Release H.6*, February 10, 1994.

FIGURE

2–1   M1 and M2 tend to move in the same direction.

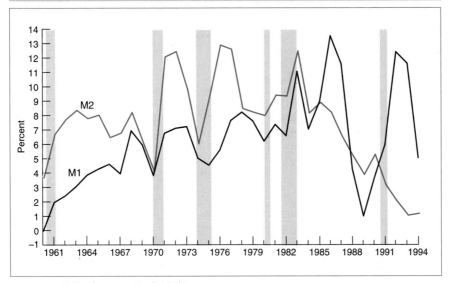

SOURCE: Federal Reserve Bank of Chicago.
NOTE: Shaded areas represent periods of economic recession.

the price of money is the exchange rate between money and other goods. The more you can buy with a given unit of money, the more it is worth.

In a market economy, the prices of all goods and services are denominated in terms of money. In the United States, the standard unit of money is the dollar, and everything is valued in dollars. Your teacher's salary might be $50,000 per academic year; the price of one of your textbooks, $50; and the price of a loan to finance your tuition, $10 per year per $100 of the outstanding balance. The value of goods and services and the value of the dollar are inversely related, so that one is the reciprocal of the other. Thus, the value of $1 is $1/$50,000, or 0.00002 of your teacher's salary; or $1/$50, or 0.02 of the textbook. That is, your teacher sells 0.00002 of his or her working time for $1, and you can sell 2 percent of the pages of your textbook for $1. As the price of an item increases, the purchasing power of money in terms of that item decreases. If the price of the textbook increased to $65, the value or price of the dollar would drop to 0.015 in terms of textbooks. You would now be willing to sell only $1\frac{1}{2}$ percent of the book for $1. (In periods of price inflation, it might pay you to hold onto your textbook to gain a higher price later. However, the author may write a newer edition that would render your decision almost worthless. Your willingness to bear this risk will affect your decision to store your wealth in the form of textbooks.)

Because we all use money to buy many goods and services, it is more useful to measure both prices and the value of the dollar in terms of a collection or "market basket" of goods and services rather than of individual items. If we let $q_{s,n}$ represent the quantity of good s purchased in period n and $p_{s,n}$ the price of good s in period n, then a market basket can be represented by the sum (Σ) of all goods purchased at these prices, or $\Sigma p_{s,n} q_{s,n}$. This may be abbreviated as $P_n Q_n$, where $P_n = \Sigma p_{s,n}$ and $Q_n = \Sigma q_{s,n}$.

How many dollars would it take to buy a standard market basket? Because we all tend to buy different types and quantities of items, we would all value the dollar somewhat differently. Nevertheless, representative market baskets can be put together that have reasonably accurate relevance for each of us. The U.S. Department of Labor collects monthly prices on a representative constant collection of items purchased by households living in urban areas, according to a survey conducted most recently in 1982 to 1984. The average price of this market basket is known as the **Consumer Price Index (CPI).** The major categories of items included and their relative weights in 1992 are shown in Table 2–2. The CPI is the most representative measure of prices paid by the "average" American. As a result, it is sometimes referred to as the cost-of-living index. Thus, the CPI provides a measure of the price level of the economy.

The CPI is known as a **constant market basket price index.** This means that the same market basket is priced every time. To simplify the interpretation of changes in prices, the market value of the market basket in any period is divided by the market value of the same market basket in an arbitrary but constant base period. This converts the dollar value into a relative, or *index*, number. The value of the index in the base period is set at 100. If prices in some other period are greater than in the base period, the value of the index number would be greater than 100. If prices are less than in the base period, the index number for that period would be less than 100. In equation form, a constant market basket index is defined in the first line of Table 2–3. Period 1 is shown as the base period, but any period could be chosen as the base without affecting the interpretation of price changes. On the other hand, since tastes change through time, the period in which the market basket (Σq) is determined does matter and could affect the results.

You must be careful about how you use the CPI. The index does not apply equally well to everyone and, in fact, applies very poorly to some of

TABLE
2–2

RELATIVE IMPORTANCE OF ITEMS INCLUDED IN CONSUMER
PRICE INDEX, 1992

	Percent
Food and beverages	17.4
Housing	41.0
Apparel	6.0
Transportation	17.0
Medical care	6.9
Entertainment	4.4
Education	4.0
Other	3.3
Total	100.0

SOURCE: U.S. Department of Labor, Bureau of Labor Statistics.

TABLE 2–3

DEFINITIONS OF CONSTANT MARKET BASKET AND
CURRENT MARKET BASKET PRICE INDEXES

Index Type	Period		
	1	2	3
Constant market basket	$\dfrac{P_1Q_1}{P_1Q_1}$	$\dfrac{P_2Q_1}{P_1Q_1}$	$\dfrac{P_nQ_1}{P_1Q_1}$
Current market basket	$\dfrac{P_1Q_1}{P_1Q_1}$	$\dfrac{P_2Q_2}{P_1Q_2}$	$\dfrac{P_nQ_n}{P_1Q_n}$

where: Q_n = total quantity of goods and services in market basket in period n
P_n = prices of goods and services in market basket in period n
n = period

us. Remember that the "average" American family has 3.2 persons and that you can drown in a river whose average depth is only 1 inch. There may not be any American who buys precisely the items included in the CPI market basket, and if there is, it certainly is unlikely to be you. Students are not likely to make nearly half their total expenditures on housing and only 4 percent on education. Moreover, college football and basketball tickets are not specifically included. Likewise, if you prefer opera, take frequent long ski trips, meditate on mountaintops, hang glide, live on a farm, or are a vegetarian, the CPI would not measure very accurately the prices you pay.

Nor does the CPI take into account price increases as the result of buying higher-quality items because your income has increased. The fact that the price of the new sports car that you plan to buy upon graduation is higher than that of the stripped-down sedan you bought when you entered college, or that the rent on the apartment into which you will move is much higher than that on the dormitory room in which you are currently living, does not mean prices have gone up. But your cost of living has gone up. The CPI prices only the same goods and services month in and month out. Finally, because the CPI prices a constant market basket, changes in relative prices that cause changes in the relative quantities of the goods and services used are not reflected. For example, if sharp increases in gasoline prices cause sharp reductions in gasoline usage, the CPI will overstate the increase in prices actually paid. This happened in the late 1970s, early 1980s, and again briefly in the early 1990s.

The Department of Labor also prices other collections of goods and/or services representative of other sectors, such as the **Producer Price Index (PPI),** formerly called the Wholesale Price Index. The PPI measures prices received by producers of commodities in all stages of processing in primary or wholesale markets. It is reported separately for finished goods, intermediate goods, and crude materials. Because it prices some items before they are sold to consumers, some analysts believe that changes in the PPI lead to changes in the CPI. Similar to the CPI, the PPI is a fixed market basket index. The current (1994) PPI is based on a 1982 survey and includes 75,000 monthly quotes on 3,100 commodities.

To maintain the current relevance of fixed market basket indexes, the market basket is periodically updated. Otherwise, the index would still be pricing horse-drawn carriages and silent movies.

Some indexes price current market baskets in each period. An example of such an index is the implicit **GDP *deflator,*** which prices all final goods and services produced in the economy in the particular period, rather than in a constant period. Such a ***current market basket price index*** is defined in the bottom row of Table 2–3. Note that the index prices a different market basket in each period.

In periods when substantial changes in relative prices result in significant changes in the composition of goods actually bought in favor of those that experience a slower price increase—such as when energy prices rise rapidly and buyers conserve energy—the current market basket GDP deflator will generally show slower rates of inflation than constant market basket indexes, such as the CPI. Although they price the current collection of items bought, by comparing somewhat different baskets of goods and services in each period, these indexes affect the interpretation of price comparisons over time. No price index is perfect or "for all seasons." Generally, all broadly based price indexes move in the same directions and emit the same signals. However, because some or all of the income of many people is tied to a price index, for example, social security payments and some wage contracts, even relatively small differences in movements in indexes may matter. Employees whose wage contracts are tied to an index would favor indexes that show faster price increases, whereas their employers would favor indexes that show slower increases. Thus, one should care to which index one's income or expense contract may be tied.

The value of the dollar may be gauged in terms of any of these indexes. Most frequently, however, the ***purchasing power of the dollar*** (PPD) is computed in relation to the CPI. The PPD measures the number of market baskets that can be bought with $1.00. It is computed as the reciprocal of the CPI. As an index number, the PPD = 10,000/CPI. In 1993, when the CPI was 145 relative to a base of 100 in 1982–1984, the PPD was 10,000/145 = 69. Thus in 1993, $1.00 could buy only 69 percent of the market basket it could buy in 1982–84. The values of the CPI and PPD between 1929 and 1993 are shown in Table 2–4. It can be seen that $1.00 could buy 11 times as many market baskets in 1933 as in 1993. This assumes, of course, that one had a dollar in 1933, the worst year of the Great Depression!

Real Values

The economic welfare of members of a society is not as much determined by the nominal or dollar amount of their income and expenses as by the purchasing power equivalent of these amounts. Thus, a wage earner may be worse off in a year in which he or she received $30,000 than in a previous year when he or she received only $20,000 but when the price level was only half as high. This may be seen by converting the nominal or ***current*** amounts into purchasing power—***real*** or ***constant-dollar*** amounts—by dividing the dollar amounts by the appropriate price index for the same period:

$$\text{Real value of } X = \frac{\text{Current value of } X}{\text{Price index}}$$

TABLE 2–4	CONSUMER PRICE INDEX AND PURCHASING POWER OF THE DOLLAR 1929–1993	
	Consumer Price Index	Purchasing Power of the Dollar
	(1982–1984 = 100)	
1929	20	513
1933	13	769
1940	14	714
1950	24	415
1960	30	338
1970	39	258
1980	82	121
1982–1984	100	100
1990	131	77
1993	145	69

SOURCE: Council of Economic Advisers, *Annual Report*, 1994, p. 335.

In this example, the wage earner would have $20,000 real income in the first year, but only $15,000 in the second year when the price index is 200 percent. He or she would be obviously worse off in the second year, although the dollars received are more. Likewise, you would view a 10 percent increase in your annual salary much more favorably if prices were expected to increase by only 2 percent over the year, rather than by 10 or 20 percent. In the latter cases, the salary increase would be an increase in name only. Individuals who evaluate decisions only in dollar and not real terms are said to be operating under **money illusion** and are not likely to make optimal choices.

Similarly, performance measures for the economy as a whole may be misleading unless they are first converted into real terms. For example, GDP can be measured in either current or constant dollars. In 1993, GDP was $6,375 billion. This was 530 percent greater than in 1970, when it was $1,011 billion. But when measured in 1987 dollars, GDP in 1993 was only $5,133 billion, only 80 percent greater than in 1970 when it was $2,874 billion in 1987 dollars. The GDP price deflator increased from 35 in 1970 to 100 in 1987 and to 124 in 1993. (Check the computation of the real GDP yourself.)

Prices

Past Prices

Data on prices are some of the oldest economic data collected. In the United States, data on wholesale prices are available as far back as 1720 and on consumer prices as far back as 1800. Wholesale prices since 1790 are plotted in Figure 2–2. Three points are readily discernible. First, throughout the entire period, prices have increased, on average. **Inflation** may be defined as a prolonged increase in broadly based price indexes. Thus, on average, the United States has experienced inflation throughout

FIGURE

2–2

HISTORY OF U.S. WHOLESALE PRICES SINCE 1790

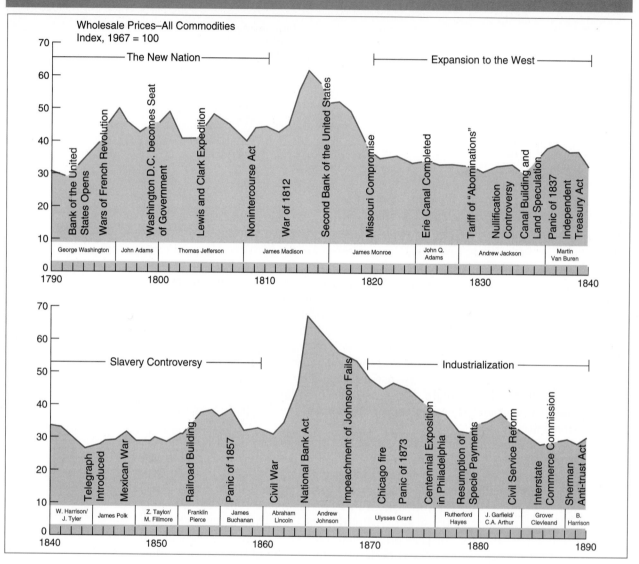

its history. The value (price) of the dollar has declined. At the end of 1993, prices were nearly 12 times their levels in 1790; that is, the dollar was worth only 9 percent of what it was worth in 1790. But the rate of inflation has not been even in all periods, and prices have declined (***deflation***) in some. Second, prices almost always rose most steeply at the outbreak of wars—1812, 1861, 1898, 1916, 1942, 1950, and 1966. Third, until the post–World War II period, prices declined sharply after the wars. One study has shown that if the war periods were omitted, consumer prices would have been no higher in the early 1960s than they were in 1800. Prices increased both during periods of armed conflicts and during some periods of peace, although

FIGURE

2-2

(CONTINUED)

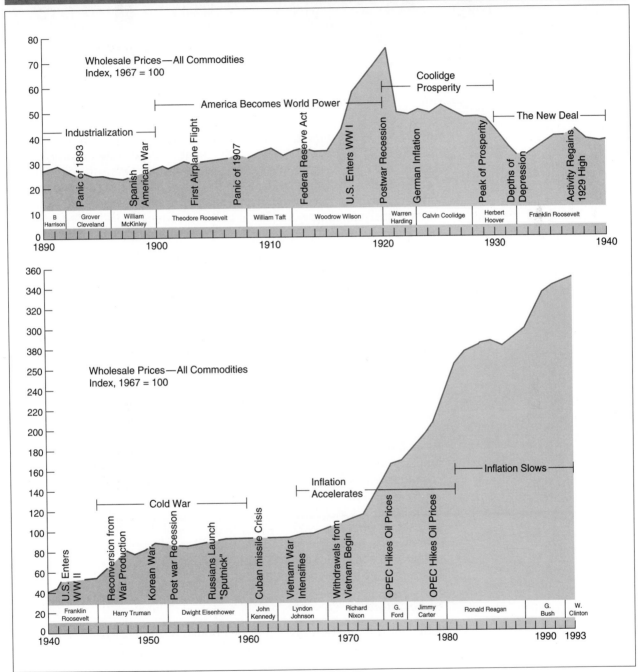

SOURCE: THE WIZARD OF ID by permission of Johnny Hart and Field Enterprises, Inc.

they tended to rise more slowly in the latter periods, with two exceptions. In 1973–1975 and again in 1978–1981, inflation accelerated sharply to the fastest rate in U.S. peacetime history. These spurts can be attributed largely to special factors discussed later in the book. The underlying rate of inflation in the post-World War II period, however, is largely the result of overexpansive monetary and fiscal policies designed to achieve and maintain high levels of employment. These policies are also examined later.

Future Prices

Since 1900, prices in the United States have increased at an average annual rate of about $2\frac{1}{2}$ percent. Since 1970, however, the rate has been about $5\frac{1}{2}$ percent annually. What would prices look like if the rate of inflation were 5, 10, or 15 percent, say, for the 50 years from 1994 to 2044? At 10 percent, an hourly wage of $6 in 1994 would increase to $704, and the equivalent annual income from $12,480 to $1,465,038. But remember, if all prices were to go up equally, your costs would also increase and you would not be better off. Some representative prices you would be paying in 2044 if prices increased by 10 percent per year are shown in Table 2–5. A $176 Sunday newspaper, a $3,500 pair of jeans, and a $3,000 plus ticket to a Chicago Bears football game! The table also shows 2044 prices if the annual rate of inflation slowed to 5 percent or accelerated to 15 percent. Will any of these scenarios actually happen? Who knows? But you will probably be able to give a better answer when you reach the chapters in this book that discuss both the causes and implications of inflation and possible cures. The Table also shows prices in 1980 to give you an idea of the actual effects of inflation over the 14 year period to 1994. We will see that inflation almost always redistributes income within an economy so that there are both winners and losers and, at times, reduces total income.

Hyperinflation

Although the inflation rates just mentioned are rapid by U.S. standards, many countries experience considerably faster rates of inflation. It is not unusual for some South American countries to experience annual rates in excess of 50 percent. One of the fastest inflations occurred in Germany after World War I. In 1921, prices were 35 times their 1913 level. By 1922, they had increased to 1,500 times as much; and by year-end 1923, to 1 *trillion* times as much. (For 1923, this represents an increase of 1 billion percent, or 5.84 percent per day if compounded daily—the power of compound interest.) Prices increased by the hour, and wages increased commensurately. Restaurant prices occasionally increased while a meal was being eaten.

TABLE

2–5

31

▼

MONEY AND
PRICES

INFLUENCE OF VARYING PERCENTAGE RATES OF INFLATION ON SELECTED PRICES, 1994–2044					
			50 Years after 1994 (1/1/2044)		
	12/31/80[a]	1/1/94	5%	10%	15%
Recreation					
Newspaper, Sunday edition	$ 0.75	$ 1.50	$ 17.20	$ 176.09	$ 1,625.49
Movie admission	4.00	7.50	86.01	880.43	8,127.43
Professional football game ticket (Chicago Bears)	11.50	27.00	309.62	3,169.55	29,258.75
Drugs and toiletries					
Soap bar	0.35	.75	8.60	88.04	812.74
Clothing					
Levi's jeans	16.99	29.99	343.91	3,520.55	32,498.89
Groceries					
Sugar (2 pounds)	1.51	1.27	14.56	149.09	1,376.24
Eggs (dozen)	0.98	.99	11.35	116.22	1,027.82
Miscellaneous					
Regular gasoline (1 gallon)	1.23	1.18	13.53	138.52	1,278.72
Big Mac hamburger	1.33	1.99	22.82	233.61	2,156.48
Stamp, first-class postage	0.15	.29	3.33	34.04	314.26
Cup of coffee	0.40	1.00	11.47	117.39	1,083.66

[a] December 31, 1980 prices from survey of Chicago prices reported in Jack Star, "Oh, My Aching Buck." Reprinted by permission from *Chicago Magazine*; © 1980 by WFMT, Inc.

Trade was seriously hampered. Professor Hans Bethe, who spent his childhood in Germany during this period before coming to the United States and winning the Nobel Prize for Physics in 1967, vividly recalls the trials and tribulations of the times:

> My father, who headed the Physiology Department at the University of Frankfurt, got his salary twice a week to keep pace with the continuing devaluation. I was the only person in the family who could at least deal with the numbers and grasp the fact that a million of today's marks were worth only five hundred thousand of yesterday's. So it was my job to collect my father's salary and spend it as quickly as I could. The money was generally paid by the university cashier at ten o'clock in the morning. By one o'clock, the money had to be spent, because the stores closed between one and two. The new dollar value of the mark would be published during this hour, and in the afternoon everything would be twice as expensive as it had been in the morning—or, sometimes, only one and a half times. Fortunately, I didn't have school in the morning—only in the afternoon—so I would go twice a week on my bicycle to get the money and spend it immediately. I had a list of the food items I was to buy, and after I returned home with the food the family had something to eat for the next few days.[2]

Another consequence of hyperinflation is described by a character in a novel based on the German experience:

[2] Jeremy Bernstein, "Master of the Trade," *New Yorker Magazine*, December 17, 1979, p. 48.

EXHIBIT

2–1

Coping with Hyperinflation in Brazil

It was a balmy evening in Rio, the sort of weather that invites one to relax at an outdoor cafe in Copacabana or Ipanema and take in the beachfront action.

But on this particular recent evening the hottest spot in town wasn't one of the cafes, bars, or restaurants that line the city's coast. The place to be was the gas station.

"The price of gas is going up 60% at midnight, so I want to fill up my tank before that happens," explained a taxi driver as he pulled into the line at the Petrobras gas station on Copacabana's Avenida Atlantica. It was close to 11:30 P.M. and there were a good 30 cars ahead of him. "I hope I reach the pump before midnight," he said. "Otherwise, my money will buy only 20 liters instead of 34."

So it goes these days in Brazil as prices continuously test the limits of Brazilians' resiliency—and patience. The question of how to break out of the inflationary spiral will be the biggest challenge facing president-elect Fernando Collor de Mello when he takes office on March 15. His advisers are busy drawing up shock measures to implement in his first days in office.

INFLATION OF 19,000%

In 1987, inflation was 365%. In 1988, it was 934% and pundits started to say that the country was on the verge of collapse. But in 1989, inflation reached 1,765% and the country has held together. Some wonder how long this can go on. For the month of January, inflation is expected to reach about 55%—an annual rate of about 19,000%.

By some measures that puts Brazil in the unenviable club of countries suffering from hyperinflation. Some economists say hyperinflation is when the monthly rate exceeds 50 percent. Other economists say hyperinflation can't be defined by a number, but occurs when the economy is in a state of total disorganization, which isn't yet the case. Brazilian economist Carlos Langoni has a more vivid definition: "Hyperinflation," he says, "is when you discover that it's a better deal to pay for lunch before the first course than after dessert."

INVESTING IN GROCERIES

Every day, the newspapers are full of articles announcing new price rises. Newspapers also offer advice on such matters as whether it's better to stock up on food and consumer products to anticipate price increases or invest one's money. (The answer: Go shopping. Since mid-November, supermarket prices have risen an average of 218 percent, while the stock market and gold rose by 175 percent, the dollar by 163 percent, and the overnight—a one-day savings account that most Brazilians place their money in as a hedge against inflation—by 137 percent.)

Prices vary. Going to supermarkets to compare prices has become a favorite recreational activity. Noemia Souza Pauferro, a 45-year-old book distributor in San Paulo, says inflation has forced her to cut back on traveling. And what does she do instead? "We go to the supermarket to see the prices," she says.

Brazilians are also constantly trying to devise the best way of paying for goods. Daniel Cherman, a 24-year-old employee in a real estate promotion company, has four different credit cards that fall due at different dates. He always tries to use the one payable at the latest date so that by the time his

"Herr Kroll," I say, "allow us to give you another short analysis of the times. The principles by which you were raised are noble, but today they lead to bankruptcy. Anybody can earn money now; almost no one knows how to maintain its purchasing power. The important thing is not to sell but to buy and to be paid as quickly as possible. We live in an age of commodities. Money is an illusion; everyone knows that, but many still do not believe it. As long as this is so the inflation will go on till absolute zero is reached. Man lives seventy-five per cent by his imagination and only twenty-five per cent by fact—that is his strength and his weakness, and that is why in this witch's dance of numbers

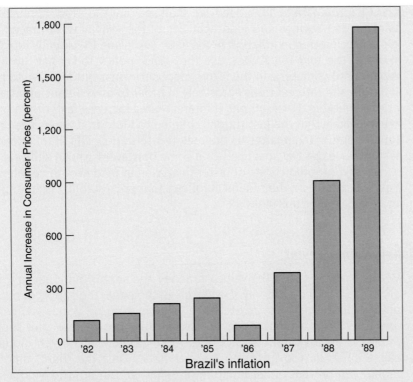

SOURCE: International Monetary Fund.

account is debited, the cost of the purchase has been cut in half.

Businesses are wising up, however. Most restaurants no longer accept credit cards. And most stores now have price tags with two different prices: one if you pay cash, and one, much higher, if you pay with a credit card. At the Mesbla department store in Sao Paulo,

for instance, a pair of Levi's jeans sells for 859 cruzados novos in cash and 1,561 cruzados novos with a credit card.

Businesses are also frustrated by the near-impossibility of making any long-term plans and keeping accounts current. The Pao de Acucar supermarket group keeps its accounts in its own invented currency unit,

SOURCE: Abstracted from Thomas Kamm, "Daily Inflation Struggle Obsesses Brazil," *The Wall Street Journal*, January 29, 1990, p. A14. Reprinted by permission of *The Wall Street Journal* © 1990, Dow Jones & Company, Inc. All Right Reserved Worldwide.

▲

there are still winners and losers. We know that we cannot be absolute winners; but at the same time we don't want to be complete losers. If the three-quarters of a million marks you settled for today is not paid for in two months, it will be worth what fifty thousand is worth now. Therefore . . . "[3]

The inflation ended in a sharp but short depression when the money supply was reduced and the currency revalued.

The economic and financial mischief done by inflation, including the harm to financial institutions, is discussed in greater detail in Exhibit 2–1

[3] Erich M. Remarque, *The Black Obelisk* (New York: Harcourt Brace Jovanovich, Inc., 1957), p. 15. Reportedly, muggers in this period were seen keeping the wallets they stole and throwing away the money!

and Chapters 12 and 34. Indeed, we shall see that the cause of much of the banking and savings and loan debacles of the 1980s can be traced to the rapid acceleration in inflation in the early 1980s and the equally rapid slow-down in the mid-1980s. Because they lend money today and do not get repaid until sometime in the future, depository institutions have to predict inflation and interest rates accurately in order to make financial intermediation profitable. For example, if interest rates increase faster than predicted, it is likely that the institutions charged too low an interest rate on their longer-term loans relative to their shorter-term deposits. If inflation slows faster than expected, it is likely that some borrowers, whose ability to repay was based on predictions of faster increases in income and collateral values, will default on their loans. It follows that price stability is an important prerequisite for bank stability.

Money Management

Because prices reflect the value of money, the supply of money is a strategic variable in the economy. *Ceteris paribus*, the larger the supply of money at any moment, the lower its exchange value in terms of goods and services, and the higher average prices. It follows that control over the supply of money is an important aspect of economic policy. Too much money can cause inflation; too little can hamper trade. Only the "right" amount of money can prevent either inflation or deflation. But how do we obtain the "right" amount of money? Writing more than a hundred years ago, the keen British financial observer Walter Bagehot noticed that money does not manage itself. Either society manages money or it will manage society. And if we choose to manage money, we must do so wisely or bear the consequences. In the United States, the responsibility for managing the supply of money in the public interest is delegated to the Federal Reserve System. How and why the Fed manages money is the primary topic of the second half of this book. The first part of the book discusses the characteristics and operation of the markets for money and financial instruments and how they affect money management at the private level.

SUMMARY

Money is defined as something that serves as a good medium of exchange, store of value, and standard of value. Because different financial assets possess these characteristics to varying degrees, there may not be a unique definition of money, and what serves as money has changed through time. The Federal Reserve publishes four definitions of money for the United States. Money is a necessity in any modern market economy: It reduces the number of exchange prices to a manageable size and thereby minimizes transactions costs. Money is worth what one can buy with it. The less one can buy, the lower the value of money. Prices indexes are used to value money by seeing how much is required to buy a designated basket of goods and services through time. The most common price index is the Consumer Price Index (CPI). Inflation is a sustained increase in the price level and deterioration in the value of money. Prices have increased throughout much of U.S. history, particularly in war periods and since 1960. To avoid inflation or deflation, it is necessary to manage money properly. In the United States, this is the function of the Federal Reserve System.

QUESTIONS

1. How does the introduction of money into a barter economy increase aggregate economic welfare? What gives contemporary money value? How does it increase aggregate economic welfare?

2. What is the major weakness of metallic coins or metallic-backed currencies? What economic harm can such monies cause? How was this problem remedied?

3. Compare the growth rates of the four alternative definitions of money supply during the last two years. (This information may be obtained from the *Federal Reserve Bulletin*.) Why do you think these rates differed by the amounts they did?

4. Obtain the latest monthly value of the Consumer Price Index. Using the CPI, compute the rate of inflation over the past 5 and 10 years. What happened to the price of the U.S. dollar in this period?

5. Discuss the differences in the computation between the CPI and the price deflator for GDP. Which do you consider more useful for your personal purposes? How would your personal CPI differ from the published CPI? Do you think your personal CPI would have risen faster or slower than the published CPI? Why?

6. How significant is the fact that the Producer (Wholesale) Price Index in 1993 was 12 times its value in 1790? Why do you think prices have failed to decline after most recent wars as they did after wars before World War II?

7. Why might a very rapid rate of inflation, say more than 50 percent per year, reduce aggregate output in the economy? How might your everyday work life differ from the way it is today? How would it affect your bank balance? Why?

REFERENCES

Bordo, Michael David. "The Classical Gold Standard: Some Lessons for Today," *Review*, Federal Reserve Bank of St. Louis, May 1981, pp. 2–17.

Brauer, David, and Lucille Wu, "An Overall View of Inflation Management," *Quarterly Review*, Federal Reserve Bank of New York, Summer 1991, pp. 25–29.

Brunner, Karl, and Allan H. Meltzer, "The Uses of Money: Money in the Theory of an Exchange Economy," *American Economic Review*, December 1971, pp. 784–805.

Davis, Richard G., "Inflation: Measurement and Policy Issues," *Quarterly Review*, Federal Reserve Bank of New York, Summer 1991, pp. 13–24.

Federal Reserve Bank of New York, *Coins and Currency*. New York, 1977.

Galbraith, John K., *Money: Whence It Came, Whence It Went*. Boston: Houghton Mifflin, 1975.

Gordon, Robert J., "The Consumer Price Index: Measuring Inflation and Causing It," *Public Interest*, Spring 1981, pp. 112–34.

Hessler, Gene, *The Comprehensive Catalog of U.S. Paper Money*. Chicago: Henry Regnery, 1974.

Humphrey, Thomas M., *Essays in Inflation*, 4th ed. Federal Reserve Bank of Richmond, 1983.

Nussbaum, Arthur, A *History of the Dollar*. New York: Columbia University Press, 1957.

Osborne, Dale K., "Ten Approaches to the Definition of Money," *Economic Review*, Federal Reserve Bank of Dallas, March 1984, pp. 1–23.

Shapiro, Max, *The Penniless Billionaires*. New York: Times Books, 1980.

Tauman, Ellis W., "Inflation: How Long Has This Been Going On?" *Economic Review*, Federal Reserve Bank of Atlanta, November/December 1993, pp. 1–12.

Throop, Adrian W., "Decline and Fall of the Gold Standard," *Business Review*, Federal Reserve Bank of Dallas, January 1976.

Veazey, Edward E., "Evolution of Money and Banking in the United States," *Business Review*, Federal Reserve Bank of Dallas, December 1975.

Wallace, William H., and William E. Cullison, *Measuring Price Changes*, 4th ed. Federal Reserve Bank of Richmond, 1981.

Walter, John R., "Monetary Aggregates: A User's Guide," *Economic Review*, Federal Reserve Bank of Richmond, January/February 1989, pp. 20–28.

Financial Markets

Financial markets channel funds from savers (or SSUs) to borrowers (or DSUs) by expediting the creation and trading of financial instruments (securities). This permits funds to be directed to those DSUs that can use them most efficiently as evidenced by a promise to pay the highest risk-adjusted returns for them. In addition, financial markets provide liquidity; so that both SSUs and DSUs may make changes in their portfolios quickly and at low cost even before a security matures. The development of new and more efficient means of achieving these transfers underlies the high value added that is produced by the financial sector.

In financial markets, actual and potential SSUs search for compatible actual and potential DSUs, and DSUs search for SSUs. Without financial markets, spending units would have less incentive to save and less ability to borrow. Spending on large-ticket, durable goods items (such as automobiles, homes, and business plant and equipment), whose costs are large relative to the buyer's income and that generate services for a number of years, would be particularly hampered. Potential buyers could not borrow to purchase these items. They would have to save the total amount of the expenditure first and make the purchase later. The burden of saving would precede the benefits generated by the asset rather than be concurrent with them. This would discourage the purchase of such goods. Individual preferences could not be accommodated as fully. For example, homeownership would be less likely for many people, and business firms would be hampered in their ability to acquire large-scale plant and equipment.

Because in the absence of well-developed financial markets SSUs are less likely to receive the maximum interest on savings by leasing their purchasing power to others, their incentive to save is less. There would be both fewer SSUs and less saving by the remaining SSUs. To the extent that many of the goods financed through borrowing are capital goods needed for the efficient production of other goods, the inability to transfer funds from SSUs to DSUs reduces aggregate investment in the economy. The reduced ability to satisfy wants and the lower rate of investment spending both act to reduce the aggregate level of economic well-being. It follows that financial markets increase economic well-being, and the more efficient these markets are, the higher is the level of well-being.

Spending units are neither permanent SSUs nor permanent DSUs. They are likely to be both through time, switching back and forth as their incomes change, their tastes change, and interest rates change. Most people follow a fairly predictable pattern over their lives. They are born DSUs, financed by their parents until or after college age. Upon permanent employment, they become SSUs. After marriage, they purchase their first home and become DSUs again. Thereafter, they slowly regain SSU status until their children enter college, at which time they again revert to being

DSUs. This is likely to be their last large expenditure, and after the graduation of the last child, they become SSUs until retirement. They finish their years as they started them—as DSUs—although this time they consume their own savings. Any savings remaining upon their death are transferred to their heirs. This pattern may change with unforeseen events and changes in interest rates. The higher the interest rate in any period, the more likely these units are to be SSUs at the time and the less likely to be DSUs.

Efficiency in financial markets may be measured in two dimensions. **Allocative efficiency** considers whether funds are channeled to the sectors promising the highest interest returns after adjustment for differences in risk and other unique features of the securities. That is, are the funds getting to the "right" users? If they are not, the funds could be put to better economic use and output increased. Allocative efficiency requires that all information available to the market is reflected fully in the prices of all securities, so that no "false" signals are transmitted to market participants. **Operational efficiency** considers whether the channeling is conducted at the lowest possible cost consistent with the survival of the market. The lower the costs, the more efficient the market and the greater output per unit of input. Maximization of aggregate welfare requires that financial markets are both allocatively and operationally efficient. In this way, funds are transferred quickly and at the lowest cost, from SSUs who offer the lowest interest rates to DSUs who bid the highest interest rates. The history of financial markets is the history of the development of more efficient techniques of moving funds from SSUs to DSUs.

In the absence of developed financial markets, SSUs and DSUs would have to search each other out. This could be very costly. A DSU would not only have to knock on a number of doors to find an SSU, but would have to find an SSU who wishes to lend exactly the amount of funds the DSU wishes to borrow, for just the same period of time, and assume exactly the same risk of default as is associated with the project being financed by the DSU. A DSU might expect to have to knock on a great many doors before finding such a compatible SSU and vice versa. This may help a DSUs' social life, but it does little to enhance his or her economic life.

Private Financial Market

Despite the difficulties, funds do flow directly between lenders and borrowers without the assistance of third-party intermediaries. The most common type of this flow is trade credit, in which you can charge a purchase directly to the seller without using a third party (such as a bank credit card), or, more frequently, a retail or manufacturing firm can borrow directly from a supplier. In these transactions, however, the two parties had already located each other before the financial exchange. But this is not the usual case.

To expedite the transfer of funds from SSUs to DSUs, third-party middlepersons developed. The first middlepersons were **brokers,** such as stockbrokers. Much as marriage brokers match compatible men and women, financial brokers match DSUs and SSUs on the basis of compatibility in maturity, denomination, default risk, and the like. By being in continuous contact with DSUs and SSUs, brokers reduce search costs. Also, like mar-

" Mr. SSU, meet Mr. DSU!"

riage brokers, financial brokers do not take possession of the item traded. They buy and sell securities for their customers and generate income by charging a commission.

Dealers developed after brokers. Dealers purchase the security from the DSU to resell it to the SSU. Thus, unlike brokers, securities dealers have "goods on the shelves" when customers come in. This permits the flow of funds between SSUs and DSUs who may not wish to conduct business at precisely the same time as would be required through the use of brokers. Dealers increased the efficiency of the financial markets further. Their profits are derived from being able to sell the securities at a higher price than that at which they were purchased. If interest rates change unfavorably while the securities are in inventory, the prices of the securities will decline, and dealers will experience smaller profits than expected, or even losses. The possibility of such profits or losses makes the risks of a dealer somewhat higher than those of a broker.

Today, many middlepersons are both brokers and dealers, depending on the security traded. Brokers and dealers are also known as *security dealers* or *investment bankers.* One such firm is Merrill Lynch, Pierce, Fenner & Smith, which is the largest investment banking organization in the United States—in fact, in the world.

Funds transmitted from SSUs to DSUs either directly or indirectly through the aid of a broker or dealer are said to be transmitted on the *private, or direct, financial market.* In this market, the security traded is created by an ultimate DSU—that is, a DSU who is an enduser of the funds and who uses them to purchase nonfinancial goods and services. Such a secu-

FIGURE

3–1 CHANNELS FOR TRANSFER OF FUNDS FROM SSUs TO DSUs

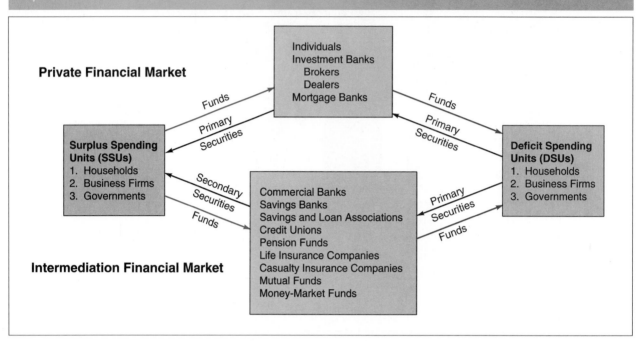

rity is called a **primary,** or ***direct, security.*** In transactions on the private financial market, the SSU purchases the primary security. The flow of funds in the private financial market from SSUs to DSUs and the reverse flow of primary claims from DSUs to SSUs either directly or with the assistance of investment banks are shown diagrammatically in the top of Figure 3–1. The transactions can be summarized by the use of **T accounts,** which are abbreviated balance sheets. Assets are shown on the left side, liabilities on the right. A plus sign indicates an increase in an account; a minus sign, a decrease. After a sale of a primary security to an SSU, T accounts of both sides of the trade show the following entries:

where: PS = primary security
M = money

The primary security is an asset to the SSU and a liability to the DSU.

Intermediation Financial Market

The entry of brokers and dealers into the financial market lowered trade costs significantly and increased efficiency. Many new participants were attracted, and the volume of funds transferred increased. However, through no fault of their own, brokers and dealers could not reduce costs as much as was possible. The difficulty lay with the primary securities. Because of the nature of the ultimate DSUs, many primary securities issued by them did not appeal to a large number of SSUs or potential SSUs. The securities had large and limited denominations (generally in multiples of $5,000 or larger) and limited maturities. The large minimum denominations priced many smaller SSUs out of the market and restricted the ability of many others to reduce their risk through diversification among different securities as much as they might wish. It is a well-known truism that risk can be reduced by not putting all one's eggs in one basket.

Many primary securities have default risk and require costly credit evaluation. Information about the financial condition of most DSUs and the characteristics of the primary securities they issue is difficult both to obtain and to evaluate. Investors must also monitor their portfolios frequently over the life of the securities to determine both changes in the issuers' financial situation and compliance with the provisions of the security contract so that the promised payments are received on schedule. For many SSUs, particularly smaller ones, the costs involved may exceed the expected returns.

Necessity is said to be the mother of invention. Because of the remaining inefficiencies in the financial markets, there was money to be made by finding a better way of encouraging saving and lending the funds to DSUs. Bankers found the better way. Banks could transform primary securities, many of which lack the characteristics that many SSUs want, into new securities that would have those characteristics. The new securities are issued on themselves. Because these securities are liabilities of the bank and not of the ultimate DSUs, they are called **secondary,** or **indirect, securities.** With the funds they borrow through the sale of the secondary securities, the banks can purchase primary securities and lend to the ultimate DSUs. They pass the funds through from SSUs to DSUs. As long as the interest return on the primary securities they purchase is greater than the interest rate they pay on the secondary securities they sell plus their costs of operations, this type of intermediation is profitable to the banks.

Banks have a comparative advantage over many individual SSUs in obtaining financial information about DSUs, evaluating their credit quality, and, after the loan is made, monitoring the performance of the borrower frequently to increase the probability of full and timely repayment. Bankers specialize in credit analysis. They gather much of this information cheaply as a by-product of providing DSU customers with other services, such as checking accounts and financial advice. Such *private information* may not be as easily available to SSUs directly and may not become *public information*. In effect, banks are the beneficiaries of *asymmetric information* about the borrower. As a result, many SSUs delegate the functions of credit evaluation, screening, and monitoring to the bank as their agent. Indeed, some analysts view modern banking as primarily information processing and intermediation.

In equilibrium, any individual intermediary institution will sell secondary securities up to the point where the sum of interest paid, other costs of sale, and its target profit equal the interest it earns on the primary securities (loans) it purchases with the proceeds from the sale of the secondary securities less transactions and servicing costs. But because it needs to redeem its secondary securities in full at maturity, the intermediary will not invest all the proceeds in primary securities. It will generally hold some in cash in order to pay maturing secondary securities on time and in full. How much cash depends on the type of secondary security sold and varies from intermediary to intermediary. The larger the amount of cash held per dollar of proceeds from the sale of secondary securities, the less profitable is the intermediation. It follows that changes in the interest and other costs of secondary securities and in the interest earnings on primary securities will change the amount of intermediation in which an intermediary institution engages and thus the dollar amount of secondary securities outstanding.

Bank is only a generic term for a financial intermediary that issues securities on itself for the purpose of purchasing primary securities issued by others, rather than purchasing nonfinancial goods and services. More specifically, these institutions are commercial banks, savings banks, savings and loan associations, life insurance companies, casualty insurance companies, mutual funds, and many more. All differ slightly in the characteristics of the primary securities they purchase and the secondary securities they sell. The secondary securities issued by banks are generally called *deposits*; those issued by life insurance companies, *policies*; those issued by mutual funds, *shares*; and so on. The intermediaries attract business from the private financial market by providing a better product for some DSUs and SSUs. They do this by tailoring their secondary securities in terms of time to maturity, size of issue (denomination), risk of default, and so on, to the particular needs of different SSUs and their primary securities to the particular needs of different DSUs. Financial intermediary institutions are primarily in the financial tailoring business, but "banker" sounds classier than "tailor"! The characteristics of the different types of secondary securities created are examined in Chapter 4, and the characteristics of the financial intermediaries in Chapter 9 through 13.

Funds that are transferred from SSUs to DSUs through financial intermediaries are said to be transferred on the **intermediation,** or **indirect, financial market.** In contrast to transfers on the private financial market, transfers on the intermediation market involve two separate, although almost simultaneous, transactions: The intermediary sells secondary securities to the SSU, and the intermediary buys primary securities from the ultimate DSU. These transactions may be summarized in T accounts as follows:

SSU		Financial Intermediary		DSU	
+SS		+PS	+SS	+M	+PS
−M		+M			
		−M			

where: SS = secondary security

Note that, unlike the case on the private financial market, the SSU who uses the intermediation market holds a secondary, not a primary, security. One can therefore always tell which market an SSU used to put his or her savings to work. If the SSU used the private financial market to invest surplus funds, he or she would hold a primary claim issued by an ultimate DSU, such as the U.S. Treasury or General Motors; if the SSU used the intermediation market, he or she would hold a secondary claim issued by an intermediary institution, such as a commercial bank, thrift institution, or insurance company, operating in this market. The path of the flow of funds through the intermediation market is shown in the bottom part of Figure 3–1.

The Intermediation Process

The development of the intermediation financial market reduced trade costs and further increased the efficiency of the financial markets. By opening these markets to spending units that were previously excluded from participation, the intermediation market has increased the flow of funds from SSUs to DSUs. It has done so by increasing the incentives of SSUs to save and of DSUs to borrow. Financial institutions operating on the intermediation market stimulate saving in at least six ways:

1. *Denomination (size) intermediation.* Secondary securities can be created in a wide range of denominations, from one dollar up to many millions of dollars. Commercial banks, for example, accept deposits in any amount. Some intermediaries specialize in small-denomination secondary securities and others in larger-denomination securities. Banks that specialize in selling secondary securities in small denominations generally *pool* the funds so collected to buy primary securities (make loans) in larger denominations.

2. *Maturity intermediation.* Secondary securities can be created in a wide range of maturities, from one to more than one hundred years. Equity securities have no maturity and are *perpetuals*. Commercial banks accept demand deposits for as short a period as a single day, whereas life insurance companies sell policies that mature only upon the SSU's death or retirement.

3. *Credit-risk intermediation.* Secondary securities can be created in a wide range of risks of default, from very low to very high. Because of their moderate wealth, many SSUs prefer minimal risk. Credit risk intermediation has two dimensions: (1) diversification and (2) credit screening. Diversification may be achieved by pooling the funds obtained through the sale of secondary securities and purchasing a wide variety of different primary securities. As a result, each secondary security is effectively collateralized by a small share of each primary security. Because at any one point, only some of the primary securities may default or decline in price while others may increase in price, the risk of loss through default or price change is reduced by diversification among different securities. Because of its easier access to credit information and economies of scale in evaluating large numbers of credit requests, the intermediary may reasonably be expected to screen out poor credit risks and monitor performance after the loan is made better than individual SSUs can. Thus, the institution can offer secondary securities with less credit risk than is contained in many primary securities. In the process, the institution assumes *credit risk*.

4. *Interest rate sensitivity intermediation.* Secondary securities can be created with different sensitivities in their prices to changes in interest rates. As will be seen in Chapter 5, for a given coupon interest rate, bond prices and interest rates vary inversely. Increases in market interest rates reduce the market value of fixed-coupon securities. Holders of such securities assume **interest rate risk.**

Secondary securities can be created with coupons that change in value at any period up to their final maturity. Securities with coupons that remain unchanged in value over the life of the security are referred to as **fixed-coupon (rate) securities;** those with coupons that may change in value before maturity are referred to as **variable-** or **floating-coupon (rate) securities.** The coupons on the latter generally change or are **reset** at specified **coupon change intervals (CCIs)** in line with comparable market rates according to a predetermined schedule. At these times, the securities are said to be **repriced.** The longer the term to maturity on a fixed-rate security or to the next repricing period for a variable-rate security, the greater is the interest rate risk assumed. Many SSUs, however, are risk-averse and do not wish to incur much, if any, interest rate risk. Intermediaries can issue secondary securities of a given maturity with a wide range of interest sensitivities to SSUs who wish to assume different degrees of interest rate risk. The risk is shifted from the SSU to the intermediary.

Differences between the CCIs on the secondary securities sold by the institution and the primary securities purchased cause the interest rate sensitivity of the two sides of its balance sheet to differ and represent the net interest rate risk assumed by the intermediary. Thus, interest rate intermediation is evidenced by mismatched CCIs on the securities on the two sides of an institution's balance sheet. Because financial intermediaries specialize in finance, they are generally better prepared to assume and manage interest rate risk than are most individual SSUs.

5. *Foreign currency intermediation.* Intermediaries can create secondary securities not only in the domestic currency of the country in which the intermediary is located (dollars in the United States, pounds in the United Kingdom, marks in Germany, and so forth), but also in the currency of any country the SSUs may wish. SSUs may want securities in foreign currencies, either because they will have bills to pay in those currencies or because they are betting on an increase in the value of one or more foreign currencies. Of course, at maturity the intermediary has to redeem the security in the currency specified or in its equivalent domestic value. Because, as we will see in Chapter 25, the market values of foreign currencies in terms of a domestic currency change through time, the intermediary assumes **foreign currency risk** if the secondary securities it sells are not denominated in the same currency as the primary securities it buys. Securities denominated in currencies other than the domestic currency of the country in which the institution is located have been widely offered at intermediaries outside the United States for many years. Such securities are said to be denominated in **Eurocurrencies,** and when in U.S. dollars, as **Eurodollars.** More recently, banks in the United States have begun to offer domestic customers deposits at their banks denominated in

major foreign currencies, such as British pounds or Japanese yen. Such deposits may be referred to as **Amercurrencies,** for example, **Amerpounds** or **Ameryen.** Foreign currency intermediation increased in importance as financial markets became increasingly globalized. (A fuller discussion of Eurodollars appears in Chapters 4 and 25 and of Amercurrencies in Chapter 23.)

6. *Reduce search costs.* SSUs can purchase many secondary securities with lower search and transactions costs than those for primary securities. The availability of many types of secondary securities is widely publicized through advertisement by the issuing intermediary, the credit quality of the securities is relatively easily obtainable, and purchase is possible at convenient offices. Search and transactions costs must be deducted from the gross interest rate on a security to obtain the net rate to the saver. To the extent that these costs are lower on secondary than on primary securities, the net interest rate on securities with equal gross rates is higher. Secondary securities often yield higher net interest returns than primary securities yielding higher gross returns. Search and some transactions costs vary from person to person. Thus, net interest rates for the same gross interest rate also vary among individuals and are not readily measurable. Interest rates observed in the market are gross rates.

Financial institutions on the intermediation market also stimulate borrowing in six ways:

1. *Denomination (size) intermediation.* Because they acquire a pool of funds through the sale of secondary securities, intermediaries can purchase primary claims in a wide range of denominations so that they can be precisely equal to the amounts particular DSUs wish to borrow. You could borrow exactly $4,233 from a bank or finance company to finance the purchase of a used car. Borrowing this amount on the private financial market directly from an SSU would be difficult. The size preferences of the SSU and DSU need no longer match.

2. *Maturity intermediation.* Because secondary securities can be created in any maturity and new securities sold as outstanding ones mature, intermediaries can, in turn, purchase primary securities of almost any maturity consistent with the price risk the intermediary is willing to incur. Among the different types of intermediaries, the maturity preferences of almost all ultimate DSUs could be accommodated.

3. *Interest rate sensitivity intermediation.* Like SSUs, many DSUs are averse to the risk of interest rate increases. DSUs can protect themselves against increases in interest rates by issuing long CCI variable-rate or fixed-rate securities. But many SSUs may not prefer investing in such securities, which put the interest rate risk on them. Both because they sell secondary securities to a variety of SSUs with different CCI preferences, from, say, every 6 months to every 30 years, and because they are better able to assume and manage interest rate risk, the intermediaries can buy primary securities with a sufficiently wide variety of coupon change periods for every maturity to accommodate most DSUs, even if these preferences do not match those of SSUs.

4. *Foreign currency intermediation.* Some DSUs require funds to finance purchases from foreign countries payable in the currency of that country.

Because they may create secondary securities denominated in foreign currencies—such as Eurocurrencies—intermediaries can buy primary securities in the same foreign currencies. Moreover, even if it does not sell secondary securities in a particular currency, an intermediary can still buy a primary security in that currency if it is willing to assume the exchange rate risk between the time the security is purchased and the time it matures.

5. *Reduce search costs.* Because the nature of their business is widely known, offices are conveniently located, denomination and maturity can be tailored to need, and credit evaluation is quick and efficient, DSUs' search and transactions costs in marketing primary securities to financial intermediaries are low. This can raise the DSUs' net interest cost on securities sold to intermediaries by less than on primary securities marketed directly to SSUs, for which search and transactions costs are frequently higher.

6. *Information and assistance services.* Because primary securities are generally not tailored to the SSU, and the DSU and SSU usually do not know each other, transactions on the private financial market generally involve only the transfer of funds. In contrast, because they tailor the loan closely to the DSU's needs, intermediaries frequently know the DSU well and are in a position to provide information, expert assistance, and other services that DSUs need in addition to the financing. For example, business DSUs who market products in distant markets or foreign countries can obtain information from the intermediary on the legal, tax, and financial environment in those areas. Individual DSUs who purchase homes can get information on tax rates and insurance needs.

It can now be seen that financial institutions on the intermediation market are in the financial custom-tailoring business. They design financial instruments to fit the particular characteristics of their SSU and DSU customers so that the two are well suited. Of course, the intermediaries do not engage in this tailoring or security transformation process for their health or out of altruism. They do it for expected profits from charging prices that they hope more than cover their costs. Part of the expected profit comes from the value added in the production of the new securities and part from the risks they assume in providing these services. In the process, the intermediaries assume risks of loss from credit defaults (credit risk), unfavorable interest rate changes that reduce the value of their assets more than their liabilities (interest rate risk), bad management and excessive operating costs (operating risk), fraud risk, and so forth. The greater the risks assumed intentionally, the higher is the price charged for the particular service. In the United States, financial institutions on the intermediation market have traditionally specialized in particular primary securities and particular secondary securities. These institutions are described in detail in Chapters 9 through 13.

SSUs and DSUs use the private financial market or the intermediation market, depending on which best serves their particular needs. On the whole, smaller spending units use the intermediation market more frequently than larger units do. Many units use both markets, switching back and forth according to interest rate changes. For example, many large business firms borrow both directly from individuals and other nonfinancial business firms through the sale of commercial paper on the private financial market and indirectly through business loans from commercial banks and life insurance companies on the intermediation market.

Disintermediation. The historical trend in most countries has been toward faster growth in the intermediation market than in the private financial market, particularly as financial markets are opened to smaller units that had not previously participated and as new types of intermediaries are organized that tailor securities to new demands. In the United States, some 85 percent of total funds are normally channeled through the intermediation financial market.

At times, however, funds shift back to the private financial market. This primarily reflects imperfections in the market, sometimes deliberately imposed by government action. In the United States, the government has, in the past, restricted the interest rates some financial intermediaries (such as commercial banks and savings and loan associations) may pay on certain types of deposits. This was intended primarily to exert downward pressure on the interest rates those intermediaries charge on primary securities, particularly on residential mortgages. Although well intentioned, these restrictions often have unintended, undesirable effects. As market rates of interest on primary securities rose above the rates that some intermediaries could legally pay on comparable secondary securities, an increasing number of SSUs, who preferred higher to lower interest returns, transferred funds from commercial banks and thrift institutions to Treasury securities and commercial paper on the private market or to institutions on the intermediation market whose secondary securities were not subject to interest rate ceilings, such as money-market funds. Other SSUs did not prefer or were not able to make this shift. They received a lower return on their savings than other SSUs, and may have saved less. At times of forced or involuntary transfers to less-preferred markets, market efficiency and the total flow of funds were reduced. Funds may even be reduced to the very sectors that the interest rate ceilings were intended to assist.

The shift of funds from the intermediation financial market to the private financial market is known as **disintermediation.** Disintermediation occurred periodically in the post–World War II years when market rates of interest rose above ceiling rates set on secondary securities at major depository-type institutions. These ceilings, which were in effect through 1986, were popularly referred to as Regulation Q, after the letter of the regulation that applied to commercial banks that were members of the Federal Reserve System. The term *disintermediation* is also used widely but less accurately to describe the outflow of funds from one type of institution on the intermediation financial market subject to deposit rate ceilings, for instance, savings and loan associations, to another type of institution not subject to deposit ceilings, such as money-market funds. This churning from one institution on the intermediation market to another may be referred to as *gross disintermediation*, and shifts of funds from the intermediation market to the private market as *net disintermediation*.

The percentage of total funds channeled through the private financial market from 1963 to 1987 is plotted in Figure 3–2. The remaining funds are channeled through the intermediation financial market. Periods of net dis-

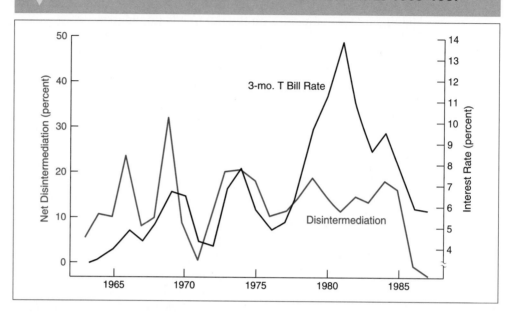

FIGURE

3–2   NET DISINTERMEDIATION AND INTEREST RATES 1963–1987

intermediation are seen to have occurred in 1966, 1969, 1973, and 1979. In those periods, market interest rates increased well above the deposit rates commercial banks and thrift institutions were permitted to pay on their smaller deposit accounts. Thus, SSUs were maximizing their interest income by shifting funds to the private financial market. Until the late 1970s, interest rates and net disintermediation were closely correlated.

After 1978, this relationship changed. Interest rates increased sharply through 1981, but net disintermediation stabilized. This reflects the introduction of money-market funds, which are in the intermediation market but were not subject to deposit rate ceilings. The ability to obtain higher rates at other institutions in the intermediation market reduced the need to shift funds from banks and thrift institutions to the private financial market and thereby also net disintermediation. Both net and gross disintermediation declined sharply only after banks and thrift institutions were permitted in 1983 to offer deposit accounts that were not subject to any deposit rate ceilings and allowed them to compete on an equal basis with money-market funds. Because of the removal of all rate ceilings on time deposits in 1986, disintermediation of any kind may be expected to be far less severe in the future than in the past, and, if it does occur, it will reflect voluntary choice by individual SSUs or institutions.

Securitization.   In order to increase their market share, firms on the private financial market recently have attempted to compete with institutions on the intermediation market by designing new primary-like securities that possess many of the desirable characteristics of secondary securities, but trade on the private financial market. Thus, they hope to get SSUs to voluntarily disintermediate back to the private financial market. The new securities are created not to finance new activities directly but to transform existing primary securities that were issued in small and odd denominations and with unique features so that they were not highly marketable. Examples include the transformation of residential mortgages or consumer loans into large, standard-denomination securities of the same overall dollar amount with minimum unique features. The new securities are collateralized by the pool of the old securities. This transformation, referred to as **securitization,** has been aided greatly by advances in computer technology, which permits credit information to be quickly and cheaply available to SSUs directly and reduces the advantage banks had in this area. Securitization is discussed at greater length in Chapter 23.

Liquidity.   It is desirable to have financial markets operate as efficiently as possible so that DSUs and SSUs can trade securities quickly and cheaply at prices that reflect accurately the underlying forces of supply and demand. This requires a large number of continuous market participants and sufficient middlepersons—dealers, brokers, and other institutions—to process the volume and provide competition. A necessary prerequisite for an efficient market is liquidity.

Market liquidity (sometimes referred to as **microliquidity**) refers to the ability to trade securities in the particular market quickly, cheaply, and at prices that do not improve (increase for sellers or decrease for buyers) solely as a result of having additional time to solicit additional bids or offers. That is, the more liquid a market, the less likely are fire-sale prices. (In contrast, **macroliquidity** refers to sufficient money supply in the aggregate economy to permit it to operate efficiently.) All securities and markets are not equally liquid. For example, if you want to sell a Treasury bill in the Treasury securities market you will receive numerous bids immediately at or very near the price you would get if you held out longer, *ceteris paribus*. On the other hand, if you were selling equity shares in a small local firm or IOUs from your professor in the corresponding markets, you would receive few immediate bids, and these bids would likely be significantly below those you would solicit by waiting for the number of bids to increase. The Treasury bill market is said to be highly liquid and the professor IOU market relatively illiquid.

This difference is shown in Figure 3–3, which plots the length of time necessary to search out the highest potential bidder in two markets, A and B. The shorter the time the more liquid the market. The Treasury bill market is shown by A and the professor IOU market by B. The immediate or fire-sale loss on professor IOUs is likely to be greater than that on a Treasury bill of equal ultimate value and rises to the ultimate value more slowly. (The factors that determine the marketability of individual securities are discussed in Chapter 8.) Liquid markets are often also referred to as **broad** or **deep markets.** All markets tend to become less deep and fire-sale losses greater when everyone or nearly everyone tries to sell particular securities at the same time, i.e. at market crashes such as in 1929 and 1987.

Classification of Financial Markets

Financial markets may be classified according to a number of other characteristics, such as the type of securities traded, the trading procedures used, and the location of the market, in addition to the division between private financial market and intermediation market.

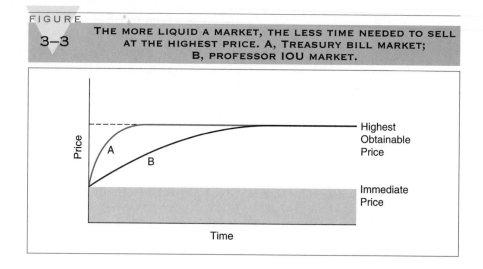

FIGURE

3–3

THE MORE LIQUID A MARKET, THE LESS TIME NEEDED TO SELL AT THE HIGHEST PRICE. A, TREASURY BILL MARKET; B, PROFESSOR IOU MARKET.

Primary Market.   The market on which newly issued primary and secondary securities are traded for the first time. The market for "new" securities.

Secondary Market.   The market, sometimes referred to as the **aftermarket,** on which already outstanding or "used" financial securities are traded. The secondary market provides liquidity for investors who wish to change their portfolios before their maturity dates.

Money Market.   The market for shorter-term securities, generally those with one year or less remaining to maturity, such as six-month Treasury bills or 30-year bonds with six months left to maturity.

Capital Market.   The market for longer-term securities, generally those with more than one year to maturity.

Bond Market.   The market for debt instruments of any kind.

Stock Market.   The market for common and preferred stock (at times, referred to as *equity* to indicate an ownership claim) of private corporations. In contrast to a bond, which promises scheduled coupon payments and repayment of principal at maturity, and payment of which has a first claim on the earnings of the issuer, a common stock promises no scheduled return and has only a residual claim on the earnings of the issuer. However, if a firm's earnings increase beyond the amount required to satisfy prior claims, the earnings accrue to the stockholders and the value of the stock rises. Because of this characteristic, the prices of stocks tend to be more volatile than those of bonds. Because stocks have no maturity date and are claims in perpetuity, the stock market is a subset of the capital market.

Auction Market.   A market on which trading is conducted by an independent third party according to a matching of prices on orders received to buy and to sell a particular security. The trader is an agent of the market. The bids and offers stipulate both price and volume. Bids are ranked from the

TABLE 3–1	HYPOTHETICAL BID AND ASKED PRICES ON AN AUCTION MARKET, IN DOLLARS	
Bid		**Asked**
		48.50
		48.40
		48.30
		48.20
48.10		48.10
48.00		48.00
47.90		47.90
47.80		
47.70		
47.60		
47.50		

highest price down; offers, from the lowest price up. Trades are consummated for those prices at which there are both bids and offers, until all the securities offered for sale are either sold or fail to get matching bids. Hypothetical bid and asked prices received by a trader on an auction market are shown in Table 3–1. Note that the bid (buying) prices tend to be below the asked (selling) prices. Where the two prices match, shown in the shaded area in the table, trades are achieved. Where they do not match, trades are not achieved and the orders are left outstanding until the price is matched or the offer is withdrawn. There are no direct negotiations between buyers and sellers to reach a compatible price.

To improve the matching, the trader can aggregate or subdivide individual bids and offers. Because bids and offers are received regularly and those not filled remain on the trader's books until canceled, trading tends to be continuous. Buyers and sellers do not trade with each other and generally do not know the identity of the other party. The market is impersonal. The New York Stock Exchange is an example of an auction market.

Negotiation Market. A market in which buyers and sellers negotiate with each other with respect to both price and volume, either directly or through a broker or dealer. If trade is through a dealer or broker, the identity of either party may or may not be known to the other. This market is useful for infrequently traded securities and for very large trades that may cause large short-run fluctuations in an auction market until sufficient orders are developed on the other side. Negotiation permits time for buyers and sellers both to find each other and to revise either price or volume in order to clear the market.

Organized Market. A market with fixed trading rules, established at a central physical location in which trading is generally conducted by auction. Organized markets are frequently referred to as exchanges, such as the New York Stock Exchange (NYSE). Standardized securities, such as equity securities, are generally sold on organized exchanges.

Over-the-Counter Market.   A market located at the offices of individual brokers or dealers and of the issuers of secondary securities, such as commercial banks and life insurance companies. Because trading occurs in many locations, it is primarily a telephone, telex, or computer market. Debt securities are generally sold over the counter. Over-the-counter markets are also primarily negotiated markets. Because they are negotiated markets, non-standardized and customized securities are traded here, if at all.

Spot Market.   The market on which securities are traded for immediate delivery and payment. *Immediate* is defined by the respective market and generally ranges from the same day to a week later, depending on the type of security. It is sometimes referred to as the *cash market.*

Futures Market.   The market on which securities are traded for future delivery and payment. *Future* is generally defined as one week and longer. The instrument traded is called a **futures contract.** The securities stipulated in the futures contract may be already outstanding securities or may be securities that will be issued before the maturity date of the futures contract. If a futures contract is traded over the counter by negotiation, it is referred to as a **forward contract** and the market as a **forward market.** The futures market is discussed in greater detail in Chapter 22.

Options Market.   The market on which securities are traded for conditional future delivery. The instrument traded is an **options contract.** The contract is executed at the option of the owner. The two most common types of option contracts are **call options** and **put options.** A call option permits the owner to purchase a particular security from the seller or writer of the option at a particular price before a particular maturity date. A put option permits the owner to sell a particular security to the writer of the option at a particular price before a particular date. Option contracts need not be executed and may be permitted to lapse at maturity. The options market is discussed in Chapter 22.

Foreign Exchange Market (FOREX).   The market on which foreign currencies—say, the British pound, German mark, or French franc—are traded either against domestic currency, (in the U.S., the dollar) or against each other. Trading may be for either spot or future delivery, and on organized markets, such as the International Monetary Market of the Chicago Mercantile Exchange or the Chicago Board of Trade, or over the counter at large commercial banks or foreign currency dealers. The foreign exchange market is by far the largest of all financial markets. It is discussed in greater detail in Chapter 25.

The categories just described are not mutually exclusive. In the course of its life, a particular long-term debt security may, for example, be sold first, even before issue, on the futures market; upon issue, on the over-the-counter, primary, capital market; later, on an organized, secondary market; and finally, after the passage of sufficient time, on a secondary money market. Thus, 30-year Treasury securities trade on both the capital and the money market, although those that trade on the latter have only a short term remaining before they mature. It should also be noted that these markets are separate primarily by classification only, not by physical location.

Many financial markets in the same physical location trade securities in more than one classification without distinction; for example, the over-the-counter Treasury securities market includes trading of short-term (money market) and long-term (capital market) as well as new (primary market) and outstanding (secondary market) securities.

Financial Centers

Markets exist for some financial securities in almost every community (for instance, the market for bank deposits). However, the majority of financial transactions occur in a limited number of communities. This is particularly true for larger transactions and for those that are conducted on organized exchanges. The major financial center in the United States is New York City. As you will see from the tables in Chapter 9, five of the seven largest commercial banks are located in New York City, as are five of the six largest savings banks, four of the five largest life insurance companies (Newark is right across the Hudson River from New York City), the ten largest investment bankers, and the largest two organized securities markets (the New York and American Stock Exchanges). In addition, many of the financial firms not headquartered in New York maintain offices there. In 1985, one-third of all persons employed in the securities industry in the U.S. were located in New York City.

New York City is both the largest national and the largest international financial market. International markets trade the securities of both domestic and foreign DSUs. Smaller, more regional financial markets in the United States are located in Chicago (home of the two largest financial futures exchanges), San Francisco, Los Angeles, Philadelphia, and Boston. Regional organized stock exchanges are located in those cities. Major international markets overseas include those in London, Zurich, Frankfurt, Tokyo, and Hong Kong. (Table 3–2 lists stock markets by size in selected

TABLE

3–2   STOCK MARKETS IN MAJOR COUNTRIES BY SIZE, 1981 AND 1991

| Country | Market value | | | |
| | 1981 | | 1991 | |
	$ Billions	Percent	$ Billions	Percent
United States	1,333	53.3	4,180	38.8
Japan	431	17.2	3,131	29.1
United Kingdom	181	7.2	1,003	9.3
Germany	63	2.5	394	3.7
France	38	1.5	374	3.5
Canada	106	4.3	267	2.5
Italy	24	1.0	154	1.4
Other	326	13.0	1,257	11.7
Total	2,502	100.0	10,760	100.0

SOURCE: John Mullin, "Emerging Equity Markets in the Global Economy," *Quarterly Review*, Federal Reserve Bank of New York, Summer 1993, p. 71.

EXHIBIT

3-1

GLOBEX: A Worldwide 24-Hour Electronic Securities Trading Network

In mid-1992, Reuters, the British electronic news and information service, began operating a worldwide electronic trading network connecting major futures and options exchanges in different countries. This system was named GLOBEX. The Chicago Board of Trade and the Chicago Mercantile Exchanges are charter members and partners in this venture. In 1994, the Board of Trade withdrew as a member. By permitting trading when the exchanges are not open for floor trading, GLOBEX provides nearly 24-hour trading in major contracts. Users around the world may trade in listed contracts on any member exchange. By mid-1993, GLOBEX could be used by traders at terminals in the United States, the United Kingdom, France, Germany, Japan, Switzerland, the Netherlands, Belgium, and Hong Kong to trade futures and options contracts, including foreign currency contracts, on the two U.S. exchanges and the largest French exchange (MATIF). The regular and GLOBEX business day trading hours for contracts on the two major Chicago exchanges in mid-1993 are shown below:

	BOARD OF TRADE	MERCANTILE EXCHANGE
Regular trading hours (Central Time)	7:20 A.M.–2:20 P.M. 6:20 P.M.–9:05 P.M.	7:20 A.M.–2:00 P.M.
GLOBEX (Central Time)	10:30 P.M.–6:00 A.M.	2:30 P.M.–4:00 P.M. 6:00 P.M.–6:00 A.M.

major countries.) Most financial markets are in continuous contact with one another by telephone, telegraph, computer, and telex, so that participants can both trade securities not sold on their own market and arbitrage securities common to more than one market to keep prices on the different markets in line. It is now possible to trade some securities around the clock on markets in different countries whose operating hours follow the sun. In 1992, the Chicago Mercantile Exchange in cooperation with Reuters began worldwide electronic trading from the close of their regular trading hours to the opening of floor trading the next day through a joint system called GLOBEX (described in greater detail in Exhibit 3–1).

The importance of financial markets differs in different countries. One measure of relative importance is the volume of securities outstanding in each country. Data are available on securities by currency of denomination. Although, as is discussed in Chapter 25, not all securities of a particular currency need to have been issued in that currency's home country, most are. Those that are not reflect the importance of that currency as an international currency and the importance of that country as an international financial center. Not surprisingly, the largest volume of financial securities is denominated in U.S. dollars. As is shown in Table 3–3, the combined volume of bonds and stocks in U.S. dollars in 1992 represented nearly 50 per-

TABLE
3–3

OUTSTANDING PUBLICLY ISSUED BONDS AND STOCK YEAR-END
MARKET VALUES BY MAJOR CURRENCY, 1975–1992

	Outstanding (U.S. $ Billions)				Percent of Total			
	1975		1992		1975		1992	
	Bonds	Stocks	Bonds	Stocks	Bonds	Stocks	Bonds	Stocks
U.S. dollar	786	704	6,876	3,871	48	61	47	43
Japanese yen	130	142	2,603	2,359	8	12	18	26
German deutschemark	212	51	1,407	302	13	4	10	3
Italian lira	106	11	764	99	6	1	5	1
French franc	51	35	684	302	3	3	5	3
Canadian dollar	57	51	356	192	3	4	2	2
U.K. sterling	85	86	338	850	5	7	2	10
Belgian franc	46	9	315	56	3	1	2	1
Swedish krona	38	2	229	63	2	—	2	1
Dutch guilder	41	18	217	131	3	2	2	1
Danish krona	32	4	215	26	2	—	2	—
Swiss franc	25	17	188	172	2	2	1	2
European currency unit	—	—	160				1	
Other	27	20	420	545	2	2	3	7
Total	1,636	1,150	14,772	8,912	100	100	100	100

SOURCE: Salomon Brothers, various publications, by permission.

cent of the world's total. Thus, the United States has the world's largest
financial securities market, and the U.S. dollar is the world's most important currency. The second largest volume of securities is denominated in
Japanese yen. German deutschemarks and British pounds trail far behind as
currencies of choice for securities.

Although only one-half as large as those denominated in U.S. dollars,
Japanese yen securities, particularly stocks, are growing rapidly. As a result,
the U.S. stock market may be losing its long-held global dominance.

SUMMARY

Financial markets are markets where SSUs and DSUs buy and sell financial
securities. These markets channel funds from SSUs to DSUs. The more efficient financial markets are, the higher will be aggregate economic welfare.
Financial markets consist of numerous smaller financial submarkets that
specialize in different types of securities, different types of customers, and
different minimum amounts of transactions. The most important breakdown by type of market is by whether the funds are channeled from SSUs
to DSUs directly or indirectly. Direct channeling, in which the SSU purchases the primary security issued by the DSU, occurs on the private financial
market with the possible assistance of brokers or dealers. Indirect channel-

ing, in which a financial intermediary purchases the primary security and effectively transforms it into a secondary security with characteristics more desirable to SSUs, occurs on the intermediation financial market. Through time, a progressively larger proportion of funds has been channeled through the intermediation markets. At times, however, primarily owing to government-prescribed ceilings on rates that depository-type financial intermediaries may pay for their funds, increasing amounts of funds will be redirected through the private financial market. This rerouting is termed *net disintermediation*. *Gross disintermediation* occurs when funds are rerouted from some institutions on the intermediation market to other institutions on this market.

Financial markets are also classified by whether they trade in new (primary) or used (secondary) securities, in short-term (money-market) or long-term (capital-market) securities, in debt (bond) or equity (stock) securities, in small (retail) or large (wholesale) dollar amounts, and in current (spot) or future (futures) securities. Financial markets are organized in a few central trading locations (organized exchanges) or in many decentralized, over-the-counter locations at the individual offices of all traders. Securities may be traded by competitive auction or by negotiation. The major financial market in the United States by far is New York City, followed by Chicago, San Francisco, Los Angeles, Boston, and Philadelphia. London is the major foreign financial center.

QUESTIONS

1. Discuss the importance of efficiency in financial markets. How do institutions on the private financial market differ from institutions on the intermediation market? Name one new institution on each market. Why did each develop?

2. How could intermediation simultaneously increase the net interest rate to savers and decrease the net interest rate to borrowers? What are some new types of intermediaries? Why did they develop?

3. "Disintermediation due to regulation reduces the efficiency of financial markets." Discuss your agreement or disagreement with this statement. Distinguish between gross and net disintermediation. How can disintermediation alter the allocation of credit?

4. In what types of markets do the following institutions operate? (List more than one if appropriate.)

   a. New York Stock Exchange
   b. Commercial banks
   c. Security brokers
   d. Security dealers
   e. Pension funds

5. Why do financial markets tend to exist more frequently in the largest cities? How do you think improvements in communications and transportation have affected the location of financial markets?

6. In a world of only fixed-rate bonds, why would maturity and interest rate intermediation be one and the same thing? Why were variable-rate bonds developed? Under what economic conditions might this have been most likely to occur? How do variable-rate bonds separate maturity and interest rate intermediation?

7. Why may *securitization* be called "the revenge of the private market"? How does securitization improve market efficiency? Why might institutions on

the intermediation market, for example, banks, invest in securitized instruments?

8. "Primary securities trade only on primary markets and secondary securities only on secondary markets." Do you agree or disagree with this statement? Why? How can you tell whether an SSU purchased a security on the private (direct) or the intermediation (indirect) market? How can the same security trade on the primary and secondary markets? On the capital and money markets?

REFERENCES

Altman, Edward I., *Handbook of Financial Markets and Institutions*, 6th ed. New York: John Wiley, 1987.

Brick, John R., H. Kent Baker, and John A. Haslem, *Financial Markets: Instruments and Concepts*, 2nd ed. Reston, Va.: Reston Publishing, 1986.

Cook, Timothy Q., and Robert K. LaRoche, eds., *Instruments of the Money Market*, 7th ed. Federal Reserve Bank of Richmond, 1993.

Corrigan, Gerald E., "A Perspective on the Globalization of Financial Markets and Institutions," *Quarterly Review*, Federal Reserve Bank of New York, Spring 1987, pp. 1–9.

Department of the Treasury, et al., *Joint Report on the Government Securities Market*, Washington, D.C.: Government Printing Office, January 1992.

Dobson, Steven W., "Development of Capital Markets in the United States," *Business Review*, Federal Reserve Bank of Dallas, April 1976.

Dougall, Herbert E., and Jack E. Guamnitz, *Capital Markets and Institutions*, 5th ed. Englewood Cliffs, N.J.: Prentice Hall, 1986.

Fabozzi, Frank J., and Franco Modigliani, *Capital Markets: Institutions and Instruments*. Englewood Cliffs, N.J.: Prentice Hall, 1992.

Fabozzi, Frank J., and Frank G. Zarb, *Handbook of Financial Markets: Securities, Options, Futures*, 2nd ed. Homewood, Ill.: Dow Jones-Irwin, 1986.

First Boston Corporation, *Handbook of Securities of the United States Government and Federal Agencies and Related Money Market Instruments*. Chicago, Ill: Probus Publishing, biannual.

Fraser, Donald R., and Peter S. Rose, eds., *Financial Institutions and Markets in a Changing World*, 3rd ed. Dallas: Business Publications, 1987.

Havrilesky, Thomas M., and Robert Schweitzer, eds., *Contemporary Developments in Financial Institutions and Markets*, 2nd ed. Arlington Heights, Ill.: Harlan Davidson, 1987.

Kolb, Robert W., *The Financial Institutions and Markets Reader*, 2nd ed. Miami, Fla.: Kolb Publishing, 1993.

Madden, Carl H., *The Money Side of "The" Street*. New York: Federal Reserve Bank of New York, 1959.

Schwartz, Robert A., *Equity Markets*. New York: Harper & Row, 1988.

Stigum, Marcia, *The Money Market*, 3rd ed. Homewood, Ill.: Dow Jones-Irwin, 1990.

Van Horne, James C., *Financial Market Rates and Flows*, 3rd ed. Englewood Cliffs, N.J.: Prentice Hall, 1990.

"Why the Big Apple Shines in the World's Markets," *Business Week*, July 23, 1984, pp. 100–08.

Financial Instruments

Financial instruments (securities or claims) are IOUs created by ultimate or intermediate DSUs when they borrow. Like modern money, financial securities have no intrinsic value. They have only exchange value for future intrinsic value.

Securities are legal contracts or indentures specifying the amount of the transaction and the terms and conditions for repayment. To the extent that the securities are created in the same legal and institutional environment, the contracts will tend to be similar in language, format, and legal provisions. They will differ, however, in a number of ways that reflect the particular needs of the issuing DSU or of the SSUs to which the instruments are tailored. Each security was developed to fill a particular financing need that was not being satisfactorily filled by the already existing securities. Some securities are not expected to trade and change ownership before their maturity. These are nonmarketable, and the differences among them are generally greater than among marketable securities, which must satisfy a broader range of investors in order for sellers to find buyers readily. This section will examine the types and distinguishing characteristics of major marketable securities—those of larger and better-known DSUs.

Financial securities differ among themselves with respect to

1. *Denomination (size).*
2. *Maturity.*
3. *Claim against issuer.* Securities may be either ownership claims (equities) or debt claims (bonds). Holders of equities participate in the management of solvent issuers, generally indirectly through voting for members of the board of directors. Equity owners participate on a pro rata basis in the earnings of the issuer after all prior claims have been satisfied. Payments are called **dividends.** Dividends are not paid automatically, but must be voted each time by the issuing firm. Dividends need not be paid, and there are no penalties if they are omitted. There are two types of equity: preferred and common. Preferred stock stipulates a maximum amount of dividends that may be received. Common stock dividends have no maximums, but may be paid only after preferred stock dividends have been paid in full. Equity has no maturity or repayment date.

Debt securities are scheduled, priority claims on the earnings of the issuer. Failure to pay the promised interest on schedule forces the issuer to declare bankruptcy and lose all or some ownership control. Debt-security holders participate in the management of only bankrupt issuers. Most debt securities promise periodic coupon payments and repayment of principal at maturity.

4. *Collateral.* The type of collateral determines the credit quality of the security. The primary collateral of all securities is the revenue generated by the issuing DSU, either overall or from the particular project being financed. Debt securities have prior claim on the earnings and assets of the issuing firm over equity securities. The smaller or more volatile the issuer's revenues relative to the promised payments on outstanding debt securities and to other claims that must be satisfied to avoid bankruptcy, such as wages and accounts payable, the lower the credit quality of the DSU and the greater the risk of default. In case of default, the principal and unpaid coupons on debt securities and any return on equity securities may need to be paid by liquidating the issuer's assets. Some debt securities are secured by specifically identified assets or by prior claim on all assets. The claims of the holders of these must be satisfied in full from the funds obtained from the assets before the claims of holders of other, subordinated securities are paid. Bonds not collateralized by specific assets are referred to as **debentures.** Thus, default risk on a particular security is also dependent upon the type of assets specified as collateral and the order of the claim on the assets. The less valuable the assets being liquidated and the lower the order, the higher is the potential loss on default. Equity securities have a residual, but unlimited, claim on the issuer's earnings after all other claims have been satisfied.

5. *Term to repricing.* The dollar amount of each scheduled coupon payment on a bond may change at predetermined times up to the final maturity date according to predetermined rules. Bonds whose coupon rates are fixed throughout their maturities are referred to as **fixed-coupon (rate) bonds;** those whose coupon rates may change before maturity are referred to as **variable-** or **floating-coupon (rate) bonds.** The intervals at which the coupon rates can change or be reset and the securities be *repriced* are referred to as **term to repricing (TTR)** or **coupon change intervals (CCIs).** Generally, changes in coupon rates are tied to changes in rates on predetermined comparable securities, such as the three-month Treasury bill rate or long-term Treasury bond rate. Fixed-coupon bonds are in effect a special case of variable-coupon bonds whose coupon change intervals are equal to their terms to maturity. Variable-rate bonds are designed to fluctuate less in price as a result of interest rate changes than fixed-rate bonds.

6. *Marketability.* The marketability of a security is related to the costs of trading it on the secondary market before maturity. The lower these costs, the higher the marketability. The following factors can lower the cost of trading a security and increase its marketability: (1) when the issuer of a security is well known, information costs are lower; (2) when the outstanding dollar amount is large, search and transaction costs are lower; (3) when the security has few unique characteristics, analysis and monitoring costs are lower. Securities that are highly marketable are also said to be *liquid.*

7. *Form of interest payment.* Interest on debt securities can be paid either by coupons or by appreciation in the principal of the securities purchased at a discount from par value. Coupons are paid in cash, whereas capital appreciation is realized only when the security is sold or matures.

However, good accounting practice requires that the discount be amortized annually over the remaining life of the security and added to the principal value to obtain the *amortized value*.

8. *Tax treatment*. The tax treatment of coupon-interest income to investors depends not only on the identity of the investor but also on the identity of the issuer. By tradition, most government units do not tax interest income paid on bonds issued by other government units. Thus, the federal government does not tax coupon income received from most bonds issued by state and local governments (*municipal bonds*), and state and local governments that levy income taxes do not tax coupon income received by their taxpayers from federal government securities. Because the federal income tax is substantially higher than state or local income taxes, municipal bonds are frequently referred to as **tax-exempt bonds.**

In addition, income derived from the amortization of bond discounts is taxed differently depending on whether the bond was originally issued at a discount (*original issue discount*) or if it declined to a discount from an increase in market rates of interest after it was issued (*market discount*). Income from original issue discounts is taxed as ordinary income; income from market discounts as capital gains income.

9. *Interest computation*. Traditionally, interest rates at which different debt securities trade have not been computed similarly. Rates on some securities, primarily short-term, are computed on a 360-day year, and on others, primarily long-term, on a 365-day year. Interest on most government and corporate bonds is paid and compounded semiannually; interest on residential mortgages is paid and compounded monthly. Rates on short-term securities with zero coupons that are sold at an initial discount, such as Treasury bills, are sometimes computed on the basis of par value of the security, rather than on current market value, the basis on which the rates on most other securities are computed. (See Chapter 5.) This computation is referred to as the **discount basis.**

10. *Options*. Options permit either the issuer (DSU) or the investor (SSU) to modify the security contract. Options that are included in the security contract are referred to as *embedded options*. The most popular embedded options are *call options* (permit the issuer to redeem the security before maturity), *put options* (permit the investor to sell the security back to the issuer before maturity), and *convertibility options* (permit the investor to convert from one security to another, for example, a bond to a stock).

11. *Currency*. Most securities are denominated in the domestic currency of the country in which the issuing DSU is located. But, at times, a security may be issued in a foreign currency. Although U.S. securities are almost always denominated in U.S. dollars, securities issued in foreign countries are frequently denominated in U.S. dollars or other major foreign currencies. These are referred to as **Eurobonds.** (Foreign currency bonds are discussed in Chapter 25.)

The types of major securities, the amounts outstanding, and their trading volume are shown in Table 4–1. With rare exception, these securi-

TABLE 4-1 — MAJOR FINANCIAL INSTRUMENTS

	Outstanding Dec. 31, 1992[a] ($ Billions)	Trading on Secondary Market[b]
Treasury securities:		
Bills	658	H
Notes	1,609	M-H
Bonds	473	M
U.S. government agencies:		
Federal Home Loan Banks	115	M
Federal Home Loan Mortgage Corporation	30	M
Federal National Mortgage Association	116	M
Farm Credit Banks	52	M
Student Loan Marketing Association	40	—
Resolution Funding Corporation	30	—
Tennessee Valley Authority	24	—
Commercial paper	549	L
Bankers' acceptances	38	M
CDs	409	L-M
Corporate bonds	1,740	L
Foreign bonds	143	L
Municipal bonds	1,155	L
Mortgages	4,193	L-M
Stock	5,128	L-M

SOURCE: Federal Reserve System.

[a] Stock valued at market price, other securities valued at par.

[b] Trading estimated by daily dollar trading volume as a percent of dollar amount outstanding: H = heavy trading, M = moderate trading, L = light trading.

ties are traded over the counter on a negotiated basis. Securities on the capital market are larger in dollar volume than those on the money market but trade less frequently. Note that although the market value of stocks is greater than the par value amount of mortgages outstanding, the largest single type of debt security, it is small compared with the par value of all debt securities outstanding. Mortgages are followed in importance by U.S. Treasury securities and corporate bonds.

Money-Market Instruments

Treasury Bills. These securities, often referred to as **T-bills,** are the major trading instrument in the money market and have the broadest primary and secondary markets. Daily trading volume averages 15 to 20 times that on the NYSE. The Treasury sells the bills at a discount price without coupons. Thus, Treasury bills are **zero-coupon securities.** The maximum maturity is one year. Interest is created by the amortization of the discount but is realized only upon sale or maturity. The price on the primary market is determined by competitive auctions conducted by the Treasury. Most new bills are issued on a regular schedule. Because of their short maturities, T-bills are sold frequently on the primary market. Bills with maturities of 91 (three months) and 182 (six months) days are sold by the Treasury weekly; those with maturities of 364 days monthly, and those with other maturities as the Treasury needs the funds. After issue, bills trade on the secondary market. Bills are traded on the basis of yields, not prices. The interest yield is typically computed on a 360-day discount basis. These yields understate the yield to maturity, the yield at which most other securities trade.

Because the T-bill market is so deep, dealer spreads average only one-sixth to one-quarter as wide as those on stocks traded on the NYSE. End-of-day bid and asked yields and the corresponding discount yields on the secondary markets are reported the next day in most major newspapers in the country. **Bid yields** are those at which dealers are willing to buy bills, and **asked yields** are those at which they are willing to sell bills. Because yields and prices are inversely related, bid yields are higher than asked yields so that the associated bid price is lower than the asked price. That is, the dealers attempt to buy bills at a higher yield or lower price than that at which they expect to sell them. The difference, or **spread,** between the dealers' bid and asked prices represents their markup. A listing of bid and asked yields for bills traded on November 17, 1993, is shown in Figure 4–4 (see page 70). Individual bill issues are identified by their maturity date. Also generally shown are the yields to maturities associated with the asked discount yields. This simplifies comparisons with yields on longer-term securities that are quoted on a yield-to-maturity basis. There are some 40 dealers who make continuous secondary markets for Treasury bills. About 10 of these are dealer affiliates of large commercial banks; the others are investment bankers.

To reduce transactions, security, and storage costs, all bills (as well as all new Treasury securities) are sold by the Treasury in **book-entry form** on computers at the Bureau of Public Debt at the Treasury Department or at the Federal Reserve Banks. Purchasers receive nonnegotiable receipts as evidence of ownership rather than engraved certificates. Ownership changes are recorded on the computer. Daily trading in Treasury bills far exceeds that in stocks on the New York Stock Exchange. (For all Treasury securities, daily dollar volume exceeds that on the New York Stock Exchange by a factor of 10.)

Three and six-month Treasury bills are auctioned every Monday by the Treasury for delivery on the following Thursday. Other bills are auctioned less frequently. All auctions are conducted by the Federal Reserve Banks as the fiscal agent for the Treasury Department. The auctions are competitive, although smaller investors can submit noncompetitive bids up to a total of $1 million. Competitive bidders, generally securities dealers and large institutional investors, may submit as many bids as they wish at different interest rates, obviously demanding a larger amount of bills at higher rates. The Federal Reserve sums all the bids submitted from the lowest interest rate up. The rate at which the aggregate quantity equals the amount the

Treasury wishes to sell that week, the **stopout rate,** is the highest rate accepted. All bids at interest rates below this rate are accepted at their respective bid rates. Thus, bids are accepted at different interest rates. (Noncompetitive bids are awarded at the average rate on accepted competitive bids.) Bidders bidding a low rate increase their chances of winning the bills but at the cost of receiving a below-market interest rate. Moreover, for the three-month bill, an existing issue sold as a six-month bill three months earlier is available in the secondary market. These factors help restrict the primary market for T-bills to more sophisticated investors relative to the secondary market.

Federal funds. Federal funds, or **Fed funds** as they are frequently called, are reserve balances that depository institutions, primarily commercial banks, have on deposit at their Federal Reserve Bank. Most institutions use these balances to satisfy their legal reserve requirements. The institutions can lend out reserves in excess of the required amount. Moreover, the required reserves need not be maintained daily but only as a biweekly average. Thus, on some days the institutions can lend out reserves that would put them below their requirements, as long as they hold more reserves than required on other days during the week to compensate.

The reserves can be lent to institutions that are deficient in their reserve requirements. These interinstitution loans are called **Fed-funds loans.** Fed-funds loans are generally overnight loans effective the same day as contracted and repayable the morning of the next day. In the Fed-funds market, lending is referred to as *sales* and borrowing as *purchases*. Trading and notification of the Federal Reserve Banks to transfer the appropriate balances are done by telephone. The minimum trading unit is generally $1 million, and therefore trading is primarily among larger institutions. The credit quality of these institutions is well known to all other institutions, permitting the transactions to be consummated quickly and cheaply on an unsecured basis. The interest rate of Fed funds is determined by the reputation of the borrowing institution. Because most Fed funds are one-day loans and are not traded on the secondary market, they are not technically a marketable money-market instrument. But because their brief maturity and rapid turnover give them characteristics very similar to those of securities traded on the secondary market, they are generally classified as such. Fed funds were developed to provide institutions with a low-cost, quickly available source of very-short-term liquidity.

Commercial Paper. These are primarily unsecured promissory notes of large, nationally known corporate firms, with initial maturities of less than 270 days and in minimum denominations of $25,000. Commercial paper was developed by the issuing firms as a substitute for short-term bank loans. The credit quality of the paper is a reflection of the financial strength of the issuing firm. Similar to corporate bonds, larger issues have credit ratings assigned to them by the credit-rating agencies. If the maturity is less than 270 days, the issuer is not required to register the security with the Securities and Exchange Commission.

Firms sell commercial paper either directly to investors or indirectly through dealers. In recent years, dealer-placed paper has grown more rapidly than directly-placed paper. This growth reflects the broader marketing and distribution facilities of dealers, an increasing percentage of which are commercial banks. By selling commercial paper, firms avoid compensating deposit balance requirements that many banks tie to their loan agreements, and so they pay lower effective interest rates. However, commercial paper is frequently "collateralized" by a line of credit at one or more large commercial banks. This is particularly true for commercial paper sold by finance companies. In addition, banks are purchasers of commercial paper.

Although originally developed as unsecured notes, some commercial paper has recently been collateralized by credit card and other short-term trade receivables. Such **asset-backed commercial paper** is issued by special-purpose vehicles (SPVs), which purchase the receivables from participating firms with funds raised by selling commercial paper collateralized by a pool of the receivables.

The credit quality and risk of default of commercial paper are rated by the major rating agencies. The best known of these rating agencies are Moody's and Standard & Poor's. The role of private rating agencies is discussed in greater detail in Chapter 7. The rating symbols and their definitions are shown in Table 4–2. Industrial firms are the primary issuers of commercial paper, followed by nonbank financial firms—such as finance companies—public utility companies, and bank holding companies. Money-market mutual funds are the primary investors in commercial paper, followed by pension funds, households, nonfinancial business firms, and life insurance companies.

The dollar volume of paper has expanded rapidly in recent years as progressively more large, high-quality business firms have found such financing cheaper than bank loans. Commercial paper is the second largest money-market instrument, exceeded only by Treasury bills. However, unlike that for Treasury bills, the secondary market for commercial paper is quite narrow. Commercial paper is generally sold on a discount, 360-day-year basis. The minimum round-lot trading unit is $100,000.

TABLE

4–2

SHORT-TERM RATINGS OF COMMERCIAL PAPER
BY THE MAJOR CREDIT-RATING AGENCIES

Category	Duff & Phelps Credit Rating Co.	Fitch Investors Service	Moody's Investors Service	Standard & Poor's Corporation
Investment grade	Duff 1+	F-1+		A-1+
	Duff 1	F-1	P-1	A-1
	Duff 1−			
	Duff 2	F-2	P-2	A-2
	Duff 3	F-3	P-3	A-3
Noninvestment grade	Duff 4	F-S	NP (Not Prime)	B
				C
In default	Duff 5	D		D

SOURCE: Mitchell Post, "The Evolution of the U.S. Commercial Paper Market Since 1980," *Federal Reserve Bulletin*, December 1992, p. 882.

Bankers' Acceptances.   Bankers' acceptances are one of the oldest types of financial securities, dating back to the earliest days of banking. They are used primarily to finance international trade. Buyers and sellers are generally less well known to each other in international trade than in domestic trade, and credit arrangements need to be worked out more carefully. A banker's acceptance is a draft on a commercial bank, generally payable to the exporter, based on funds that will be deposited at the bank by the importer by the maturity date. The draft is secured by the goods traded. The bank on which the draft is written can "accept" the obligation for the funds, guaranteeing the funds at maturity and thereby adding its name to that of the borrower. This raises the credit quality of the instrument and transforms the draft into a bankers' acceptance. The bank charges an acceptance fee. Thus, a banker's acceptance is two-name paper; a direct liability of the importer and a contingent liability of the accepting bank, which must pay the exporter if the importer defaults. A banker's acceptance is shown in Figure 4–1.

The exporter can either hold the acceptance to maturity or sell it. Acceptances trade on an old and well-established secondary market on the reputation of the accepting bank, which is better known than that of the borrower. Because the acceptance finances a particular transaction and is collateralized by the goods, its denomination is frequently in an odd amount. Maturity periods are generally less than 180 days.

Once a major money-market instrument, bankers acceptances have declined sharply in use in recent years. In the early 1930s, bankers acceptances financed nearly one-half of U.S. exports and imports. Since then the proportion has declined to near 15 percent. As can be seen in Figure 4–2, after increasing sharply in the late 1970s and early 1980s, primarily to finance foreign (third-country) shipments and storage, the volume of bankers acceptances declined slowly and by year-end 1992 was only one-half as great as 10 years earlier in 1982. At year-end 1991, acceptances arising from exports from the United States and imports into the United States accounted for more than 50 percent of the total volume of acceptances out-

FIGURE

4–1   A BANKER'S ACCEPTANCE

SOURCE: Courtesy of Continental Illinois National Bank and Trust Company of Chicago.

FIGURE

4–2   BANKERS ACCEPTANCES OUTSTANDING BY TRANSACTION TYPE

SOURCE: Robert L. LaRoche, "Bankers Acceptances," *Economic Quarterly*, Federal Reserve Bank of Richmond, Winter 1993, p. 77.

standing, and those arising from shipments of goods among foreign countries or the temporary storage of goods there accounted for another 40 percent. Trading of bankers acceptances on the secondary market is limited. Because the denomination of bankers acceptances is large, the secondary market is basically an institutional market.

Certificates of Deposit **(CDs).**   CDs are large time deposits at large depository institutions, generally commercial banks, with a specific maturity date and a specified interest rate, and evidenced by a certificate issued to the depositor. The certificate is negotiable and can be traded on a secondary market. The minimum denomination is generally $1 million. This differentiates CDs from consumer certificates, which are considerably smaller in denomination and generally not negotiable. The credit quality of the certificate is that of the issuing institution. CDs of larger, better-known institutions generally require lower interest rates than those of smaller, regional institutions. A CD is shown in Figure 4–3.

CDs are a relatively new money-market instrument. They were developed in 1961 to provide commercial banks with a means of competing with other DSUs for the temporary excess money balances of larger corporations and government units. These SSUs were reluctant to buy regular nonnegotiable or nonmarketable time deposits because they did not want to tie up their funds unconditionally until maturity. By simultaneously encouraging a secondary market for CDs to other depositors, the banks were able to provide investors with the opportunity to sell their investments before maturity without losing the deposits themselves. CDs have become a major means by which larger banks provide their intermediate liquidity needs. Small rate increases by an individual large institution will quickly attract large deposit inflows. The volume of CDs is volatile and reflects the need

SOURCE: Courtesy of Continental Illinois National Bank and Trust Company of Chicago.

for funds by larger depository institutions. Most CDs have a maturity of less than one year. Those with a maturity of more than one year are referred to as *term* CDs. CDs in U.S. dollars are also issued by foreign banks and overseas branches of U.S. banks. These are referred to as *Eurodollar* CDs. Eurodollars are discussed later in this chapter.

CDs have expanded rapidly and are the third largest money-market instrument in terms of dollar volume outstanding. Most CDs are coupon instruments that are issued at par value and trade on a 360-day basis. A reasonable secondary market exists for CDs of large prime banks.

Repurchase Agreements. Repurchase agreements, or RPs or *repos* as they are frequently called, are short-term collateralized loans in which the borrower sells securities to the lender (investor) with a provision to repurchase them on a specified future date at a specified price. The difference between the selling and repurchase prices represents the interest on the transaction. Borrowers are said to enter into a repurchase agreement and lenders into a *reverse repurchase agreement* (*reverse repo*) or *matched sale-purchase agreement*. Most repurchase agreements are for very brief periods of time, overnight to a few days. The use of securities to ensure performance by the borrower decreases the risk of the transaction relative to unsecured loans and reduces the interest rate on the agreement. Thus, interest rates on RPs are below the Fed-funds rate on comparable maturities.

Repurchase agreements are frequently used by security dealers and trading departments of commercial banks to finance their securities inventory. Most frequently, the collateral security is transferred not to the investor, but to an independent third party acting as a trustee custodian. The securities are returned at the maturity of the transaction. The market value of the collateral securities generally exceeds the dollar amount of the agreement to provide protection against a decline in market value during the agreement period. In recent years, a few repurchase agreement lenders suffered losses because they failed either to verify that the securities were transferred to a third party or that the value of the securities was greater than that of the loan. Thus, when the borrower defaulted, the lender ended up with only a partially collateralized or uncollateralized loan.

Eurodollars.[1]   Eurodollars are deposits at foreign offices of U.S. or foreign banks denominated in dollars rather than in the local currency of the country in which the issuing bank is located. The deposits are generally time deposits that mature in a period from a few days to more than a year. As noted in Chapter 3, large banks are willing to provide deposits in currencies other than the local currency if the interest cost of such deposits is less than the interest return on primary securities denominated in the same currency or in different currencies after adjustment for currency exchange costs and risks.

The demand for Eurodollars developed in the post–World War II era because the U.S. dollar had become the major currency used to finance international trade. As a result, many traders preferred to use a uniform currency that did not require continuous conversion into other currencies, with all the associated costs and risks. Eurodollars also permit investors to search out the most profitable investment opportunities worldwide without concern about additional exchange rate movements during the investment period. By reducing the costs of transferring funds internationally, Eurodollars have increased the efficiency of capital markets in all countries. There is now a worldwide capital market for many types of securities of larger private and government issuers. Markets have also developed for deposits denominated in other nonlocal currencies, such as the German mark, Swiss franc, and Japanese yen. These are called **Eurocurrencies.**

The market of Eurocurrencies is basically a wholesale market to finance large transactions. The minimum denomination is generally $1 million. Eurocurrency CDs trade in secondary markets. The default risk and marketability are dependent on the issuing bank. Thus, the market is limited to only the largest banks that have international reputations. The market distinguishes even among these banks, so that interest rates vary from bank to bank. Banks can use Eurocurrencies as a liquidity-adjustment instrument. The major market for Eurocurrencies is in London; other markets exist in the financial centers of most countries that are important in international finance.

 ## Capital-Market Instruments

Treasury Notes and Bonds.   These are long-term coupon securities of the U.S. Treasury. **T-Notes** have initial maturities of between one and ten years, and **T-bonds** of more than ten years. These securities are default-free and enjoy the broadest market of any capital-market instrument. Denominations are in multiples of $1,000. At the end of 1993, there were some 200 different note and bond issues outstanding. Notes and bonds are sold by the Treasury to refinance maturing issues or to raise new funds. The Treasury sells these securities at periodic auctions. New notes are generally auctioned with maturities of 2, 3, 5, and 10 years and new bonds with 30

---

[1]Eurodollars are analyzed in detail in Chapter 25. This discussion simply introduces Eurodollars as a money-market instrument.

years. Like the competitive multiple-price auction for T-bills, the auction for most Treasury coupon issues awards the securities to the participants bidding the lowest yields (highest prices) at these yields. In recent years, the Treasury has experimented with a *Dutch auction* technique in which all the securities are awarded to the winning bidders at the same interest rate rather than at the rate that they bid. By eliminating the risk that some buyers could be accepting a yield lower than that of others, the single price Dutch auction is hypothesized to increase the demand for the securities by increasing the number of bidders and thereby lower the interest cost to the Treasury.

Similar to T-bills, notes and bonds are sold on a book-entry basis rather than in tangible form. The identity of the owner of the security is recorded, and coupon payments are made automatically. The days of investors storing securities and clipping coupons have disappeared in the computer age. More recently, the Treasury, on request, will separate the coupon and principal components on their notes and bonds to effectively create zero-coupon instruments. These securities are referred to as STRIPS.

The secondary market for these securities is broad, and prices change with changes in market rates of interest. Unlike Treasury bills, Treasury notes and bonds are traded on a price basis. End-of-day prices are reported daily in most major newspapers. Parts of such a price list are shown in Figure 4–4 for securities traded on November 17, 1993. These listings identify each security by its coupon rate and maturity date. The bid and asked prices are shown, as are the changes in the asked price from the previous day and the yield to maturity computed on the basis of the closing asked price. Fractional prices are stated in 1/32nds, which are equivalent to 3.125 basis points. Plus and minus signs after the prices represent additional 1/64ths. Thus, 100.8+ is equivalent to 100 plus 17/64 or 100.266. Interest yields are computed on the basis of a 365-day year.

Government Agency Securities. These are securities issued by agencies established by the federal government primarily to implement the various government lending programs. The agencies either are owned by the federal government or were previously owned and converted to quasi-independent or "sponsored" status under private ownership, now referred to as **government-sponsored enterprises (GSEs).** The agencies sell securities to finance their lending operations. The largest proportion of government agency securities are issued by the sponsored agencies. These include agencies involved in residential housing finance and in agricultural finance, such as:

1. *Federal Home Loan Banks* (FHLB). These banks make loans to savings and loan associations, savings banks, and, since 1989, mortgage-oriented commercial banks. Commercial banks now account for more than one-half of FHLB's member institutions.
2. *Federal Home Loan Mortgage Corporation* (*Freddie Mac*). This agency is charged with supporting the secondary market in conventional and insured residential mortgages. Since 1990, Freddie Mac has been privately owned; before that, it was a subsidiary of the old Federal Home Loan Bank Board, which was the primary regulatory agency of savings and loan associations.
3. *Federal National Mortgage Association* (FNMA, *or Fannie Mae*). The associa-

FIGURE

4–4 **TREASURY SECURITIES ON THE SECONDARY MARKET, NOVEMBER 17, 1993**

Treasury Bonds, Notes & Bills

Representative Over-the-Counter quotations based on transactions of $1 million or more

Govt. Bonds & Notes

Rate	Mo/	Yr	Bid	Asked	Chg.	Ask Yld
$5\frac{1}{2}$	Nov	93n	100:02	100:04	....	1.31
5	Dec	93n	100:07	100:09	....	2.48
$7\frac{5}{8}$	Dec	93n	100:16	100:18	− 1	2.61
7	Jan	94n	100:18	100:20	....	2.88
$4\frac{7}{8}$	Jan	94n	100:11	100:13	....	2.77
$6\frac{7}{8}$	Feb	94n	100:27	100:29	− 1	3.00
$8\frac{7}{8}$	Feb	94n	101:11	101:13	....	2.89
9	Feb	94	101:12	101:14	....	2.88
$5\frac{3}{8}$	Feb	94n	100:19	100:21	....	2.97
$5\frac{3}{4}$	Mar	94N	100:28	100:30	− 1	3.11
$8\frac{1}{2}$	Mar	94n	101:28	101:30	− 1	3.06
7	Apr	94n	101:15	101:17	....	3.14
$5\frac{3}{8}$	Apr	94n	100:29	100:31	....	3.17
7	May	94n	101:24	101:26	....	3.23
$9\frac{1}{2}$	May	94n	102:31	103:01	+ 1	3.20
$13\frac{1}{8}$	May	94n	104:25	104:27	− 2	3.07
$5\frac{1}{8}$	May	94n	100:29	100:31	− 1	3.27
5	Jun	94n	100:31	101:01	....	3.29
$8\frac{1}{2}$	Jun	94n	103:03	103:05	....	3.27
8	Jul	94n	102:30	103:00	....	3.34
$4\frac{1}{4}$	Jul	94n	100:17	100:19	....	3.38
$6\frac{7}{8}$	Aug	94n	102:15	102:17	....	3.38
$8\frac{5}{8}$	Aug	94n	103:23	103:25	....	3.41
$8\frac{3}{4}$	Aug	94	103:26	103:28	....	3.40
$12\frac{5}{8}$	Aug	94n	106:20	106:22	− 1	3.40
$4\frac{1}{4}$	Aug	94n	100:18	100:20	....	3.43
4	Sep	94n	100:13	100:15	....	3.44
$8\frac{1}{2}$	Sep	94n	104:06	104:08	− 1	3.46
$9\frac{1}{2}$	Oct	94n	105:07	105:09	....	3.52
$4\frac{1}{4}$	Oct	94n	100:20	100:22	....	3.51
6	Nov	94n	102:10	102:12	....	3.54
$8\frac{1}{4}$	Nov	94n	104:15	104:17	− 1	3.55
$10\frac{1}{8}$	Nov	94	106:10	106:12	− 1	3.51
$11\frac{5}{8}$	Nov	94n	107:27	107:29	− 1	3.43
$4\frac{5}{8}$	Nov	94n	101:01	101:03	....	3.53
$4\frac{5}{8}$	Dec	94n	101:02	101:04	....	3.59
$7\frac{5}{8}$	Dec	94n	104:10	104:12	+ 1	3.59
$8\frac{5}{8}$	Jan	95n	105:16	105:18	− 1	3.67
$4\frac{1}{4}$	Jan	95n	100:20	100:22	− 1	3.66
3	Feb	95	100:16	101:16	+ 1	1.77
$5\frac{1}{2}$	Feb	95n	102:03	102:05	....	3.71
$7\frac{3}{4}$	Feb	95n	104:26	104:28	....	3.69
$10\frac{1}{2}$	Feb	95	108:04	108:06	....	3.69
$11\frac{1}{4}$	Feb	95n	109:01	109:03	− 1	3.68
$3\frac{7}{8}$	Feb	95n	100:05	100:07	....	3.70
$3\frac{7}{8}$	Mar	95n	100:03	100:05	....	3.76
$8\frac{3}{8}$	Apr	95n	106:04	106:06	− 1	3.81
$3\frac{7}{8}$	Apr	95n	100:01	100:03	....	3.81
$5\frac{7}{8}$	May	95n	102:28	102:30	....	3.83
$8\frac{1}{2}$	May	95n	106:21	106:23	....	3.82
$10\frac{3}{8}$	May	95	109:11	109:13	− 1	3.82
$11\frac{1}{4}$	May	95n	110:20	110:22	− 1	3.80
$12\frac{5}{8}$	May	95	112:21	112:25	− 1	3.72
$4\frac{1}{8}$	May	95n	100:11	100:13	....	3.85
$4\frac{1}{8}$	Jun	95n	100:10	100:12	....	3.88
$8\frac{7}{8}$	Jul	95n	107:26	107:28	− 1	3.92
$4\frac{1}{4}$	Jul	95n	100:14	100:16	....	3.94
$4\frac{5}{8}$	Aug	95n	101:00	101:02	− 1	3.99
$8\frac{1}{2}$	Aug	95n	107:17	107:19	....	3.94
$10\frac{1}{2}$	Aug	95n	110:29	110:31	− 1	3.92
$3\frac{7}{8}$	Aug	95n	99:24	99:26	− 1	3.99
$3\frac{7}{8}$	Sep	95n	99:22	99:24	....	4.02
$8\frac{5}{8}$	Oct	95n	108:10	108:12	....	4.01
$3\frac{7}{8}$	Pct	95n	99:20	99:22	....	4.04
$5\frac{1}{8}$	Nov	95n	102:00	102:02	....	4.04
$8\frac{1}{8}$	Nov	95n	108:12	108:14	....	4.04
$9\frac{1}{2}$	Nov	95n	110:10	110:12	− 1	4.02
$11\frac{1}{2}$	Nov	95	114:02	114:06	− 1	4.01
$9\frac{1}{4}$	Jan	96n	110:13	110:15	− 1	4.13
$7\frac{1}{2}$	Jan	96n	106:30	107:00	....	4.14

Rate	Mo/	Yr	Bid	Asked	Chg.	Ask Yld.
$10\frac{3}{8}$	Nov	07-12	139:22	139:26	− 2	6.10
12	Aug	08-13	156:14	156:18	+ 5	6.12
$13\frac{1}{4}$	May	09-14	171:19	171:23	+ 3	6.05
$12\frac{1}{2}$	Aug	09-14	164:03	164:07	− 2	6.10
$11\frac{3}{4}$	Nov	09-14	156:22	156:26	− 2	6.13
$11\frac{1}{4}$	Feb	15	156:13	156:15	− 2	6.36
$10\frac{5}{8}$	Aug	15	149:14	149:16	− 2	6.38
$9\frac{7}{8}$	Nov	15	140:21	140:23	− 3	6.40
$9\frac{1}{4}$	Feb	16	133:11	133:13	− 3	6.41
$7\frac{1}{4}$	May	16	109:21	109:23	− 4	6.43
$7\frac{1}{2}$	Nov	16	112:18	112:20	− 2	6.44
$8\frac{3}{4}$	May	17	127:25	127:27	− 2	6.44
$8\frac{7}{8}$	Aug	17	129:11	129:13	− 4	6.44
$9\frac{1}{8}$	May	18	132:26	132:28	− 2	6.44
9	Nov	19	131:15	131:17	− 2	6.44
$8\frac{7}{8}$	Feb	19	129:30	130:00	− 1	6.45
$8\frac{1}{8}$	Aug	19	120:21	120:23	− 2	6.46
$8\frac{1}{2}$	Feb	20	125:19	125:21	− 1	6.46
$8\frac{3}{4}$	May	20	128:30	129:00	− 1	6.45
$8\frac{3}{4}$	Aug	20	129:05	129:07	+ 4	6.44
$7\frac{7}{8}$	Feb	21	118:05	118:07	+ 3	6.45
$8\frac{1}{8}$	May	21	121:09	121:11	− 2	6.46
$8\frac{1}{8}$	Aug	21	121:11	121:13	− 1	6.46
8	Nov	21	119:31	120:01	− 2	6.45
$7\frac{1}{4}$	Aug	22	110:16	110:18	− 2	6.44
$7\frac{5}{8}$	Nov	22	115:23	115:25	+ 5	6.42
$7\frac{1}{8}$	Feb	23	109:21	109:23	+ 2	6.39
$6\frac{1}{4}$	Aug	23	100:28	100:30	− 8	6.18

Treasury Bills

Maturity		Days to Mat.	Bid	Asked	Chg.	Ask Yld.
Nov 26	'93	7	2.72	2.62	−0.04	2.66
Dec 02	'93	13	2.90	2.80	−0.02	2.84
Dec 09	'93	20	2.90	2.80	−0.01	2.84
Dec 16	'93	27	2.97	2.87	....	2.92
Dec 23	'93	34	2.95	2.91	....	2.96
Dec 30	'93	41	2.84	2.80	−0.02	2.85
Jan 06	'94	48	2.97	2.93	+0.01	2.98
Jan 13	'94	55	3.02	2.98	−0.02	3.04
Jan 20	'94	62	3.09	3.07	....	3.13
Jan 27	'94	69	3.06	3.04	....	3.10
Feb 03	'94	76	3.07	3.05	....	3.11
Feb 10	'94	83	3.09	3.07	....	3.13
Feb 17	'94	90	3.09	3.07	....	3.14
Feb 24	'94	97	3.10	3.08	....	3.15
Mar 03	'94	104	3.09	3.07	−0.01	3.14
Mar 10	'94	111	3.11	3.09	....	3.16
Mar 17	'94	118	3.10	3.08	−0.01	3.15
Mar 24	'94	125	3.07	3.05	−0.01	3.13
Mar 31	'94	132	3.08	3.06	....	3.14
Apr 07	'94	139	3.16	3.14	−0.01	3.22
Apr 14	'94	146	3.17	3.15	....	3.24
Apr 21	'94	153	3.18	3.16	....	3.25
Apr 28	'94	160	3.19	3.17	−0.01	3.26
May 05	'94	167	3.21	3.19	−0.01	3.28
May 12	'94	174	3.22	3.20	−0.01	3.30
May 19	'94	181	3.23	3.21	−0.01	3.31
Jun 02	'94	195	3.22	3.20	−0.02	3.30
Jun 30	'94	223	3.24	3.22	....	3.32
Jul 28	'94	251	3.30	3.28	−0.01	3.39
Aug 25	'94	279	3.32	3.30	....	3.41
Sep 22	'94	307	3.33	3.31	....	3.43
Oct 20	'94	335	3.37	3.35	....	3.48
Nov 17	'94	363	3.41	3.39	−0.02	3.53

tion was created to stabilize the residential mortgage market by buying and selling mortgages. Its stock is privately owned.

4. *Farm Credit System*. This agency was established in 1971 to supervise the other three farm credit agencies. Since 1979, Farm Credit Banks have issued bonds to replace the financing activities of the three major farm agencies: the Federal Land Banks (which extend credit to farmers for long-term needs collateralized by real estate); the Federal Intermediate Credit Banks (which extend secured credit to farmers to finance current production); and the Bank for Cooperatives (which extends credit to agricultural cooperatives that engage in production, purchasing, or marketing of farm products). In 1987, Congress authorized the *Farm Credit System Financial Assistance Corporation* to assist farm credit system institutions experiencing financial difficulty and the *Federal Agricultural Mortgage Corporation* (*FAMC or Fannie Mac*) to provide a secondary market for agricultural loans.

5. *Student Loan Marketing Association* (*Sallie Mae*). This agency encourages the flow of credit to students in higher education by buying student loans originated by private lending institutions, most of which are guaranteed by the federal government under the Guaranteed Student Loan Program and Health Education Assistance Loans.

6. *Resolution Funding Corporation* (REFCO). This agency was established in 1989 to help finance the savings and loan bailout and to keep the debt off the federal budget and, thus, is not subject to debt-ceiling restrictions.

Government-owned agencies that issue securities include the Government National Mortgage Association (GNMA or Ginnie Mae) and the Federal Housing Authority (FHA) in residential housing, and the Export-Import Bank (X-M Bank) in international trade. Securities of many of the government-owned agencies are no longer sold directly to the public but are instead sold to the Federal Financing Bank, a government agency housed in the Treasury Department that has the authority to borrow from the Treasury. In this way, the borrowing of the different agencies is coordinated and consolidated, and marketing and interest costs to the government are reduced.

The default risk of government agency securities is dependent on the relationship of the issuing agency to the Treasury Department. Almost all the securities issued by the government-owned agencies are fully guaranteed or insured by the Treasury. The independent agencies have the legal ability to borrow some funds from the Treasury. As a result, the market views these securities as only slightly riskier than Treasury bonds and assigns them an interest rate higher than on comparable Treasury securities but lower than on comparable private securities. The secondary market is only somewhat less active than that for Treasury securities.

Corporate Bonds. Corporate bonds are issued by large business firms. Corporations borrow directly from SSUs in the form of publicly issued bonds as an alternative to borrowing long-term from intermediaries in the form of either long-term bonds or privately placed nonmarketable bonds. Corporate bonds are also bought by some intermediaries. Many corporations have a number of different bond issues outstanding. For example, in 1991, General Motors Acceptance Corporation (GMAC) had some 75 different bond issues outstanding, ranging in size from $50 million to $750 million, in maturity from 1991 to 2015, and in coupon rate from 5 percent to 15 percent. In addition, the collateral for all the issues was not the same so that they carry different risks of loss in case of default. However, a default on one bond issue automatically causes a default in all others. Commonwealth Edison in Chicago had about 65 different bond issues outstanding and American Telephone and Telegraph had more than 20 issues outstanding, even after its breakup. (A sample AT&T bond is shown in Figure 4–5). In total, there are more than 4,000 corporate bond issues outstanding, including about 1,500 issues of 600 issuers that are traded on the New York Stock Exchange.

Almost each one differs from the rest in coupon rate, maturity, special features such as call or convertible option, and, most important, in terms of the priority of the claim on the issuer and the type and amount of collateral. Corporate bond indentures are typically long and complex legal documents. As a result, credit evaluation of the bonds can be a complex

FIGURE

4–5

**BOND ISSUED BY AMERICAN TELEPHONE
AND TELEGRAPH COMPANY**

SOURCE: Courtesy of American Telephone and Telegraph Company.

and costly process. To help investors, particularly smaller investors, to evaluate the risk of loss on a bond in case of default by the issuer, independent agencies, such as Moody's and Standard & Poor's, will undertake their own evaluation and provide the results to the public.

In recent years, an increasing number of low-credit-quality bonds have been issued, particularly in connection with the sale of the issuing firm. Unlike that of most other bonds, a primary source of repayment for these bonds is scheduled to come from the sale of some of the firm's assets as a result of a restructuring of the firm by the new owners to increase profits. These bonds are often referred to as **junk bonds** or **high-yield** and are rated below "investment grade" by the rating agencies. Junk bonds trade at higher yields to compensate investors for the greater likelihood of loss from default and for higher premiums that need to be paid to sell them on the secondary market than on higher-credit-quality bonds. As a result, the realized return on these bonds is more variable. In some years, junk bonds accounted for more than 20 percent of the dollar volume of total new corporate bond issues and accounted for nearly 15 percent of all corporate bonds outstanding.

Corporate bonds are initially sold on the primary market either in a *public issue* through dealers or directly to investors in a *private placement*. Public issues have to be registered with the Securities and Exchange Commission and require disclosure of material financial, economic, and managerial information about the issuer. Private placements need not be registered with the SEC and information is provided at the request of the investor. As a result, private placements are by law restricted to large, sophisticated investors and cannot trade freely on the secondary market without registration. Issuers using private placement can benefit from tailoring the issue to the specific needs of the investor but may experience reduced competition for the issue as few investors, often only a single investor, will be involved. Commercial banks may underwrite public issues to a limited extent in separately capitalized affiliates and assist issuers in locating investors for private placements. Banks may buy corporate bonds for their investment portfolio. Trading on the secondary market occurs both on organized exchanges, for example, the New York Stock Exchange, and on the over-the-counter market.

Corporate bonds may be denominated in foreign currencies as well as in U.S. dollars. These are referred to as **foreign bonds**. Bonds issued by foreign borrowers in U.S. dollars and sold in the United States are referred to as **Yankee bonds.** Those issued in U.S. dollars but sold outside the United States are referred to as **Eurodollar bonds.** U.S. borrowers can issue bonds abroad denominated in foreign currencies, such as German marks or Swiss francs, or in Eurodollars. These bonds are discussed in greater detail in Chapter 25.

Municipal Bonds.   These are bonds issued by state and local governments. The most distinguishing feature of municipal bonds is that the coupon income is exempt from income taxes levied by the federal and many state and local governments. The number of different municipal bond issues outstanding is very large, totaling about 1.5 million. This large number reflects both the 90,000 political subdivisions that may issue bonds and the serial form in which new bonds are typically sold by the issuer to underwriters. Serial bonds are packages containing individual bonds with different terms to maturity and, generally, different coupon rates. The underwriter buys the package as a whole and resells the bonds to investors one at a time.

State and local governments sell new bonds to underwriters by either competitive bid or negotiation. More complex issues and issues from newer issuers are generally sold by negotiation to permit the underwriter to become familiar with the issue and to help tailor it to the liking of ultimate investors. Regular and more straightforward issues are generally sold by competitive bid to attempt to attract the lowest interest rate by maximizing the number of bidders.

Municipal securities are collateralized either by the full taxing power (full faith and credit) of the issuing government unit or by the revenues from user charges applied to the particular project financed by the bonds. The former are referred to as *general obligation* **(GO)** *bonds* and the latter as *revenue bonds.* As already noted, interest income on most municipal bonds is exempt from federal income taxes and in some states also from the home state's income taxes. Because investors value after-tax income, they are willing to accept a lower interest rate on these municipal bonds than on private bonds of comparable maturity and risk. As a result, the market for municipal bonds is restricted to investors in higher income brackets, for whom this feature is relatively more valuable. These include casualty insurance companies and wealthy individuals.[2] Because it is so restricted, the market for municipal bonds is more volatile than that for other bonds. In recent years, some municipalities issued bonds that were not tax-exempt because they did not use the proceeds from the bond issue for an eligible "public" use.

Mortgages.   Mortgage loans are the largest single type of debt instrument, even larger than all U.S. Treasury securities combined. Mortgages are used to finance purchases of both residential and commercial buildings. Because home mortgages are in relatively small and odd denominations, are secured by costly-to-evaluate collateral in various parts of the country, have complex repayment provisions, and are costly to service (collect relatively small monthly payments), they are not very marketable on the secondary market. Unlike most other securities, which repay principal at maturity and make smaller coupon payments until then, mortgages generally stipulate equal monthly installment payments that include both interest and repayment of the principal. Thus, the monthly payments are larger than on bonds and the average life of a mortgage is considerably shorter than its maturity. In addition, interest is paid and compounded monthly rather than semiannually as on most other debt securities. Mortgages typically permit prepayment (the borrower can call the mortgage before maturity) with a small or no prepayment fee, so that the average life is also uncertain.

[2]The Tax Act of 1986 reduced the importance of commercial banks as buyers of municipal bonds by not permitting them to deduct as an expense their interest costs on an equivalent dollar amount of deposits for newly purchased municipal bonds. Banks can also expense for tax purposes only 80 percent of the interest costs on deposits equivalent to the amount of municipal bonds held before 1987.

Most residential mortgages outstanding have constant-level monthly payments. In recent years, a wider variety of residential mortgages have been developed tailored to the particular needs of the lender or borrower. Among these are **graduated payment mortgages,** on which the monthly payments increase through time on a prearranged schedule, and **variable-** or **adjustable-rate mortgages,** on which the contract interest rate and monthly payments vary in line with market rates of interest.

Most mortgage loans have been made by thrift institutions and, more recently, commercial banks. Thrift institutions specialize in residential mortgages, while commercial banks invest in residential and commercial mortgages in nearly equal proportions.

In recent years, an increasing number of mortgages have been made more marketable by pooling individual mortgages and issuing new securities, collateralized by the original mortgages but with more standardized and thus more marketable characteristics. The issuer assumes the servicing of the mortgages, so that the new securities involve only financing. These securities are referred to as **mortgage-backed securities (MBSs)** and are mostly in the form of **pass-through certificates,** which are a composite of the underlying mortgages whose payments are "passed through" to the certificate holders on a pro rata basis. The securities are created by private mortgage lenders as well as by government agencies, such as Ginnie Mae, and by GSEs, such as Fannie Mae. Some are guaranteed by the government either directly or indirectly by limiting the collateral mortgages to insured Veterans' Administration (VA) and FHA mortgages.

More recently, many MBSs have been repackaged to separate the payments into new securities that contain only the first few interest and principal payments in a short-term security, the next few payments in an intermediate-term security, and so on, which are then sold separately. These second-generation mortgage-backed securities are referred to as **collateralized mortgage obligations (CMOs)** and **real estate mortgage investment conduits (REMICs).** A third-generation bit of financial engineering has further separated the interest and principal on these securities payments into new securities called **interest only (IO)** and **principal only (PO) securities.** Mortgages and the mortgage market are discussed in greater detail in Chapter 21.

Stock. Stocks, or equities, have no maturity value or date and do not promise fixed payments. Stock is a residual claim on the earnings and assets of the issuer after all prior claims, including those of bondholders, have been satisfied. Common stock is subordinated to preferred stock, which is a hybrid between perpetual debt and common stock. Stockholders share in the earnings of the issuing firm after all prior claims, including interest has been paid, and vote on the management of solvent firms. The price of a stock is determined by the earnings prospects of the issuer and fluctuates as those prospects fluctuate. Because the earnings prospects of firms are closely tied to the state of the economy, stock prices generally vary with economic prospects.

At the end of 1992, more than $5 trillion in market value was outstanding. This makes stocks the largest single type of security outstanding, except when stock prices are low, but they are less than half as large as the total of all debt instruments. The stocks of most major corporations are traded on one or more organized exchanges, such as the New York Stock Exchange. The remainder are traded on smaller, regional exchanges or over the counter at dealers throughout the country who make markets in the particular stocks. In contrast to bonds, which are issued in large denominations, most stocks are priced at less than $50. Although the stock markets receive the most publicity and stock prices are a popular topic of conversation, trading on the secondary market is considerably smaller than for many debt instruments both in dollar volume and in turnover. Nevertheless, because stocks are perpetual securities and have no maturity date, few new equity securities are issued, and trading on the secondary market dominates trading on the primary market. This is the reverse of the ratio for debt securities, for which volume on the primary market is many times greater than that on the secondary market.

Because stocks have no maturity value, they are secured only by a firm's future earnings. Because future earnings are in the realm of speculation, investors are likely to disagree more about the value of individual stocks than about that of bonds. Nevertheless, stocks are simpler security instruments than bonds for the average investor to understand. This fact, along with their smaller denominations and the hope of making a "killing," probably accounts for their popularity, their more widespread individual ownership, and great public interest in their day-to-day price movements.

SUMMARY

Financial instruments are securities created by ultimate DSUs when they borrow. Each instrument stipulates the amount borrowed, the terms and conditions under which repayment is to be made, the amount and timing of any interest payments, the source from which payments are to be made, and the collateral. Thus, the securities reflect the characteristics of the DSU, the particular needs for which the funds are borrowed, and the market on which the securities are traded. Securities differ in credit quality, denomination, maturity, coupon change period, currency of denomination, marketability, interest computation, priority in default, and involvement in the management of the DSUs (debt versus equity). More important short-term securities are Fed funds, Treasury bills, commercial paper, bankers' acceptances, CDs, and Eurodollars. More important longer-term securities include Treasury bonds and notes, corporate bonds, municipal bonds issued by state and local governments, mortgages, and equities. Longer-term securities, including equities, tend to be larger in dollar amount outstanding but smaller in dollar amount traded than shorter-term securities.

QUESTIONS

1. Many private firms sell both debt and equity securities. Why might the equity securities have a broader market? Why would the legal documentation for the debt security be lengthier and more complex than for equities?

2. How are Treasury bills, commercial paper, bankers' acceptances, and negotiable CDs alike? How are they different?

3. Why might you wish to hold a deposit at a U.S. bank denominated in a for-

eign currency? What risks would you take relative to having a dollar deposit? How would the risks differ from those of a Eurodollar deposit?

4. Select a bond issued by a major U.S. corporation. Use Moody's or Standard & Poor's *Bond Manuals* (in your library) to describe the important characteristics of this bond. What determines its degree of default risk?

5. Select a general obligation bond issued by a municipality. Again use Moody's or Standard & Poor's to describe its characteristics. How do its risks of default and collateral differ from those of a corporate bond? How might the type of investors in municipal bonds differ from investors in corporate bonds?

6. What factors might affect your decision to purchase a Treasury bond rather than a corporate bond, a municipal bond, or a mortgage? Would this decision be affected either by the length of time you expected to hold the security or by your income level? If so, how?

7. In the financial pages of newspapers and when you discuss finance with your friends, stocks are likely to get more attention than bonds, although the dollar volume of bonds outstanding is considerably greater than the dollar volume of stocks outstanding. Why might this be? Why do some security analysts consider junk bonds more like stocks than like higher-quality bonds?

REFERENCES

Brick, John R., H. Kent Baker, and John A. Haslem, *Financial Markets: Instruments and Concepts*, 2nd ed. Reston, Va.: Reston Publishing, 1986.

Cook, Timothy Q., and Robert K. LaRoche, eds., *Instruments of the Money Market*, 7th ed. Federal Reserve Bank of Richmond, 1993.

Crabbe, Leland E., "Anatomy of the Medium-Term Note Market," *Federal Reserve Bulletin*, August 1993, pp. 751–71.

Crabbe, Leland E., Margaret H. Pickering, and Stephen D. Prowse, "Recent Developments in Corporate Finance," *Federal Reserve Bulletin*, August 1990, pp. 593–603.

Fabozzi, Frank J., and Irving M. Pollack, eds., *The Handbook of Fixed Income Securities*, 3rd ed. Homewood, Ill.: Business One, 1991.

First Boston Corporation, *Handbook of Securities of the United States Government and Federal Agencies*. Chicago, Ill: Probus Publishing, biannual.

Hahn, Thomas K., "Commercial Paper," *Economic Quarterly*, Federal Reserve Bank of Richmond, Spring 1993, pp. 45–67.

LaRoche, Robert K., "Bankers Acceptances," *Economic Quarterly*, Federal Reserve Bank of Richmond, Winter 1993, pp. 75–85.

McAndrews, James J., "Where Has All the Paper Gone? Book-Entry Delivery-Against-Payment System," *Business Review*, Federal Reserve Bank of Philadelphia, November/December 1992, pp. 19–30.

Moran, Michael, "The Federally Sponsored Credit Agencies: An Overview," *Federal Reserve Bulletin*, June 1985, pp. 373–88.

Oliva, William C., et al., *Structure and Operation of Selected United States Federal Agencies and Multilateral Development Institutions*. New York: Salomon Brothers, July 1987.

Stigum, Marcia, *The Money Market*, 3rd ed. Homewood, Ill.: Dow Jones-Irwin, 1990.

Stigum, Marcia, and Frank J. Fabozzi, *The Dow Jones-Irwin Guide to Bond and Money Market Instruments*. Homewood, Ill.: Dow Jones-Irwin, 1987.

Tucker, James F., *Buying Treasury Securities at Federal Reserve Banks*. Federal Reserve Bank of Richmond, 1989.

Interest Rates and Bond Prices

As you may have noticed by now, it is almost impossible to discuss money or the financial system without mentioning interest rates. This and the following three chapters discuss what interest rates are, how they are related to bond prices, how they are determined, and why they differ at different times and on different securities.

Any asset is demanded primarily for the services it generates. For example, residential houses are demanded for shelter, automobiles for transportation, and textbooks for education. To enjoy these services, one must either purchase or rent the associated assets. One can obtain shelter either by buying one's own home or by renting someone else's, transportation by buying one's own automobile or by renting one or space in one (taxicab), and education by buying the textbook or by renting it from the library. As a result, every asset has two prices: an ownership price and a rental price. The two prices are related.

What Interest Rates Are

The owner of an asset who does not need it at the moment can sell it and surrender possession permanently or rent it and regain possession at the maturity of the rental period. In the absence of a psychological preference for owning an asset, per se, the owner (or buyer of the services) would be indifferent between selling (buying) or renting the asset if the sum of the expected rental fees over its expected life, discounted to the present by the market rate of interest (the **present value**), were equal to the price of the asset. If the price exceeded the sum of the discounted expected rental values, the owner would prefer to sell the asset and the buyer would prefer to rent it. The price and rental fees would adjust until they were in equilibrium again.

Of course, many of us get a psychological kick out of owning an asset rather than renting one. Owning our own home, automobile, or even book gives us a sense of pride and success that cannot be obtained from renting their counterparts. This value of ownership can be converted into monetary terms and added to the ownership price. Ownership pride is less important to business firms, which are motivated more by monetary values.

The annual rental fee may be viewed as the owner's return on the asset. Assume that you required transportation services for the next year that could be accommodated only by an automobile. You have the option of buying an automobile and selling it after one year or of leasing the automobile for the year. If you rented, the market rental fee would be the sum of two component fees—the pure rental price and depreciation. During the duration of the rental contract, the rental agency would not be able to use the services of the automobile. As a result, you would have to compensate the agency for the value of the services it could not use. This fee may be viewed as the pure rental price. As you use the automobile, you consume transportation services and use up part of the automobile's ability to generate additional services, which reduces its market value. This reduction represents depreciation of the automobile, for which the lender must also be compensated. The greater the cost of either component, the greater the overall rental fee is.

Money is an asset and may be analyzed in a similar way. The service money generates is purchasing power. In Chapter 2 we discussed the ownership price of money; it is what can be bought with it, or the reciprocal of the price level. Temporary control over purchasing power may be obtained by renting money. As with the automobile rental, money owners must be compensated both for not using the purchasing-power services themselves during the rental period and for any depreciation in the purchasing-power value of the money. If $1 could purchase 10 market-basket units at the beginning of a loan and only 9 a year later, the depreciation is one unit, or 10 percent. If the price level were perfectly stable between the beginning and the maturity of a loan, there would be no depreciation, and the total rental fee would be equal to the pure rental fee. Thus, the pure rental fee of money is the constant purchasing-power fee and is referred to as the real rental fee. The faster the rate of inflation, the greater the depreciation, and the higher would be the overall or market rental fee for money above the real rental fee. Thus, the above 10 percent annual depreciation would be added to the real rental fee to obtain the market rental fee. If prices declined, the market rental fee would be less than the real rental fee. For money, the rental fee is called **interest** and is frequently expressed as a percentage based on an annual payment per $100 loan. This is the **interest rate.**

The interest rate is the rental price of money. In the words of Keynes, "The rate of interest is the reward for parting with liquidity for a specified period."[1] The rental of money is also referred to as credit, so that the interest rate is also the price of credit. When money is lent, the borrower creates an IOU stipulating the repayment date, the amount and timing of any periodic cash interest (coupon) payments, and the other terms of the agreement. If there is a firm commitment to pay the lender specific amounts at specific intervals, the IOU is a debt instrument and is called a bond. The market value, or price, of a bond is related to the interest rate promised by the borrower, generally referred to as the **coupon** or **contract rate,** and the interest rate prevailing in the market for that type of bond. The mathematics of this relationship is examined in the next section.

Mathematics of Interest Rates and Bond Prices

Bonds are legal debt contracts written by the borrower setting forth the conditions for repayment. Most bonds promise lenders (investors) a stream of scheduled periodic, coupon payments until the maturity of the bond and

[1] John Maynard Keynes, *The General Theory of Employment, Interest and Money* (New York: Harcourt Brace Jovanovich, 1964), p. 167.

repayment of the principal amount at maturity. What price would one pay for such a promise? The price will obviously depend on

1. The dollar maturity value of the bond
2. The size and frequency of coupon payments
3. The term to the final or maturity payment
4. The frequency and magnitude by which the coupon amount can change prior to maturity (the length of the coupon change interval)
5. The risk that some or all of the promises will not be kept (risk of default)
6. The time value the investors put on money
7. Any options or conditions that affect the timing or size of any of the payments

More broadly, the price one pays for a particular bond at any moment in time reflects

1. The characteristics of the issuer
2. The characteristics of the issue (security)
3. The prevailing condition of the market

Risks that can occur when one buys a bond include the risk that the borrower may not keep his or her promise to make all coupon and principal payments on time and in full (*default risk*) and that market interest rates may change through time (*interest rate risk*).

Present Value

Money to be paid in the future has two values: a nominal value and a present value. If you were promised $1 twenty years from now even with full certainty, this dollar would be less valuable to you than $1 promised to you 10 years from now. This dollar, in turn, is less valuable to you than a dollar that you currently have in hand. The present value of any dollar paid in the future is less than $1. The time value put on money is the interest rate required to compensate someone for not being able to use the purchasing power of the money until a later date. Thus, the price you would pay for a bond with a given set of promised future payments is the present value of these payments computed by discounting them by the interest rate that reflects your time value of money. The more you value a dollar now rather than in the future, the higher is the interest rate you will use. In addition, if either the amount or the timing of the payments were not certain, future payments would be valued even less and the interest made would be higher. The relationship between the present value or price of a simple bond making only a single future payment at maturity in period m and the interest rate may be written in equation form as

$$PB = \frac{A}{(1 + i)^m} \qquad (5-1)$$

where: PB = price of the bond
  A = amount of the payment in year m
  i = interest rate for m periods
  m = number of years until the payment date

If your personal time value of money or annual interest rate is 10 percent, the present value or price of a bond to you that makes a single $1,000 payment one year from now is $909. If the payment were not made until 2, 5, 10, or 30 years from now, the price of this bond would decline to $826, $621, $386, and $57, respectively. Part A in Table 5–1 shows the present values at different interest rates of $1 paid at the end of various future years at various interest rates.

If we multiply both sides of equation 5–1 by $(1 + i)^m$, we get

$$PB (1 + i)^m = A$$

Written in this form, it's easy to see that the present value or bond price is equivalent to the amount that, invested at interest rate i for m years, will accumulate to the amount of the future payment, or the **future value.** Part B of Table 5–1 shows future values at the end of various periods for $1 paid today. It can be seen from that table that, if invested at a 10 percent annual rate, $100 paid today will accumulate to $121, $161, $259, and $1,745 2, 5, 10, and 30 years from now. Likewise, $57, $386, $621, $826, and $909 will accumulate to $1,000 in 30, 10, 5, 2, and 1 year, respectively.

Yield to Maturity

It stands to reason that not everyone has the same time value of money and, thereby, not the same interest rate. The average of all individual interest rates is the **market rate.** Thus, the market price of a regular, option free bond is the present value of the stream of all future coupon and maturity payments promised by the bond discounted by the current market rate of interest for that type of bond. Similarly, the market rate of interest on this bond is the rate that will discount the promised future payments to its current market price. Because regular bonds pay interest in more than one period, the equation for bond prices is somewhat more complex than the simple present-value equation 5–1, but it is of the same general form.

Fixed-Rate Bonds. The price of a regular fixed-coupon rate bond making equal coupon payments at the end of each year and a final payment of the principal amount at maturity is[2]

$$PB = \frac{C}{(1 + i)} + \frac{C}{(1 + i)^2} \cdots + \frac{C}{(1 + i)^m} + \frac{A}{(1 + i)^m} \qquad \text{(5–2A)}$$

This reduces to

$$PB = \sum_{n=1}^{m} \frac{C}{(1 + i)^n} = \frac{A}{(1 + i)^m} \qquad \text{(5–2B)}$$

---

[2] This pricing equation holds only for dates on which coupon payments are scheduled. Because coupons are paid at the end of each coupon period, the prices of bonds traded between coupon dates must be adjusted for payment by the buyer to the seller of a proportionate amount of the coupon accrued up to the date of the sale but not paid.

Interest Rate

A. Present Values
($1.00 Paid at End of Period)

Number of Periods	1%	2%	3%	4%	5%	6%	7%	8%	9%	10%	12%	14%	15%
1	0.990	0.980	0.971	0.962	0.952	0.943	0.935	0.926	0.917	0.909	0.893	0.877	0.870
2	0.980	0.961	0.943	0.925	0.907	0.890	0.873	0.857	0.842	0.826	0.797	0.769	0.756
3	0.971	0.942	0.915	0.889	0.864	0.840	0.816	0.794	0.772	0.751	0.712	0.675	0.658
4	0.961	0.924	0.889	0.855	0.823	0.792	0.763	0.735	0.708	0.683	0.636	0.592	0.572
5	0.951	0.906	0.863	0.822	0.784	0.747	0.713	0.681	0.650	0.621	0.567	0.519	0.497
6	0.942	0.888	0.838	0.790	0.746	0.705	0.666	0.630	0.596	0.564	0.507	0.456	0.432
7	0.933	0.871	0.813	0.760	0.711	0.665	0.623	0.583	0.547	0.513	0.452	0.400	0.376
8	0.923	0.853	0.789	0.731	0.677	0.627	0.582	0.540	0.502	0.467	0.404	0.351	0.327
9	0.914	0.837	0.766	0.703	0.645	0.592	0.544	0.500	0.460	0.424	0.361	0.308	0.284
10	0.905	0.820	0.744	0.676	0.614	0.558	0.508	0.463	0.422	0.386	0.322	0.270	0.247
11	0.896	0.804	0.722	0.650	0.585	0.527	0.475	0.429	0.388	0.350	0.287	0.237	0.215
12	0.887	0.788	0.701	0.625	0.557	0.497	0.444	0.397	0.356	0.319	0.257	0.208	0.187
13	0.879	0.773	0.681	0.601	0.530	0.469	0.415	0.368	0.326	0.290	0.229	0.182	0.163
14	0.870	0.758	0.661	0.577	0.505	0.442	0.388	0.340	0.299	0.263	0.205	0.160	0.141
15	0.861	0.743	0.642	0.555	0.481	0.417	0.362	0.315	0.275	0.239	0.183	0.140	0.123
16	0.853	0.728	0.623	0.534	0.458	0.394	0.339	0.292	0.252	0.218	0.163	0.123	0.107
17	0.844	0.714	0.605	0.513	0.436	0.371	0.317	0.270	0.231	0.198	0.146	0.108	0.093
18	0.836	0.700	0.587	0.494	0.416	0.350	0.296	0.250	0.212	0.180	0.130	0.095	0.081
19	0.828	0.686	0.570	0.475	0.396	0.331	0.276	0.232	0.194	0.164	0.116	0.083	0.070
20	0.820	0.673	0.554	0.456	0.377	0.312	0.258	0.215	0.178	0.149	0.104	0.073	0.061
25	0.780	0.610	0.478	0.375	0.295	0.233	0.184	0.146	0.116	0.092	0.059	0.038	0.030
30	0.742	0.552	0.412	0.308	0.231	0.174	0.131	0.099	0.075	0.057	0.033	0.020	0.015

B. Future Values
($1.00 Paid at Beginning of Period)

Number of Periods	1%	2%	3%	4%	5%	6%	7%	8%	9%	10%	12%	14%	15%
1	1.010	1.020	1.030	1.040	1.050	1.060	1.070	1.080	1.090	1.100	1.120	1.140	1.150
2	1.020	1.040	1.061	1.082	1.103	1.124	1.145	1.166	1.188	1.210	1.254	1.300	1.323
3	1.030	1.061	1.093	1.125	1.158	1.191	1.225	1.260	1.295	1.331	1.405	1.482	1.521
4	1.041	1.082	1.126	1.170	1.216	1.262	1.311	1.360	1.412	1.464	1.574	1.689	1.749
5	1.051	1.104	1.159	1.217	1.276	1.338	1.403	1.469	1.539	1.611	1.762	1.925	2.011
6	1.062	1.126	1.194	1.265	1.340	1.419	1.501	1.587	1.677	1.772	1.974	2.195	2.313
7	1.072	1.149	1.230	1.316	1.407	1.504	1.606	1.714	1.828	1.949	2.211	2.502	2.660
8	1.083	1.172	1.267	1.369	1.477	1.594	1.718	1.851	1.993	2.144	2.476	2.853	3.059
9	1.094	1.195	1.305	1.423	1.551	1.689	1.838	1.999	2.172	2.358	2.773	3.252	3.518
10	1.105	1.219	1.344	1.480	1.629	1.791	1.967	2.159	2.367	2.594	3.106	3.707	4.046
11	1.116	1.243	1.384	1.539	1.710	1.898	2.105	2.332	2.580	2.853	3.479	4.226	4.652
12	1.127	1.268	1.426	1.601	1.796	2.012	2.252	2.518	2.813	3.138	3.896	4.818	5.350
13	1.138	1.294	1.469	1.665	1.886	2.133	2.409	2.720	3.066	3.452	4.363	5.492	6.153
14	1.149	1.319	1.513	1.732	1.980	2.261	2.579	2.937	3.342	3.798	4.887	6.261	7.076
15	1.161	1.346	1.558	1.801	2.079	2.397	2.759	3.172	3.643	4.177	5.474	7.180	8.137
16	1.173	1.373	1.605	1.873	2.183	2.540	2.952	3.426	3.970	4.595	6.130	8.137	9.358
17	1.184	1.400	1.653	1.948	2.292	2.693	3.159	3.700	4.328	5.054	6.866	9.276	10.761
18	1.196	1.428	1.702	2.026	2.407	2.854	3.380	3.996	4.717	5.560	7.690	10.575	12.375
19	1.208	1.457	1.754	2.107	2.527	3.026	3.617	4.316	5.142	6.116	8.613	12.056	14.232
20	1.220	1.486	1.806	2.191	2.653	3.207	3.870	4.661	5.604	6.728	9.646	13.743	16.367
25	1.282	1.641	2.094	2.666	3.386	4.292	5.427	6.848	8.623	10.835	17.000	26.462	32.919
30	1.348	1.811	2.427	3.243	4.322	5.743	7.612	10.063	13.268	17.449	29.960	50.950	66.212

where:
PB = price of the bond or present value of the payments
C = promised coupon payments
A = par or maturity value at m
i = interest rate for m periods
m = term to maturity
n = number of periods to each scheduled payment
Σ = algebraic sum

The interest rate calculated in this fashion is called the **yield to maturity** or, more technically, the **internal rate of return.** It is the yield promised when you buy a bond on the assumption that all payments will be made in full and on time and that interest rates will not change before you sell the bond. Prices of all bonds on the market are determined on this basis. As in equation 5–1, we can multiply both sides of this equation by a common term $(1 + i)^m$. This yields

$$PB(1 + i)^m = C(1 + i)^{m-1} + C(1 + i)^{m-2} \ldots + C + A$$

Both sides of the equation now express the future value of the bond, or the value to which the bond accumulates at maturity. This equation shows that all coupon payments are assumed to be reinvested at the same interest rate for the remaining term to maturity. As a result, interest is earned on interest. This defines **compound interest** and is an important assumption of the yield to maturity. (In the computation of **simple interest,** the coupon income is not reinvested and interest is earned only on the principal or maturity amount of the bond.)

It can be readily seen that the price of a bond varies directly with the size of C and A. The larger C or A is, the higher is the bond price. It can also be seen that PB varies inversely with i. The higher i is, the lower is the present value of the future payments, and the lower is PB. The inverse relationship between interest rates and bond prices, or, for that matter, the price of any asset, is one of the most important relationships in finance. This relationship can be demonstrated numerically.

Most coupon bonds are initially issued at their **par value.** This requires that the **coupon rate (c),** which is defined as C/A, equal the relevant market interest rate at the time. Assume a three-year fixed-rate bond with a par value of $1,000 that promises constant coupon payments of $100 at the end of each year. The coupon rate on this bond is $100/$1,000 or 10 percent. Assume that the market rate of interest for three-year bonds is also 10 percent. Although the bond promises an investor total payments of $1,300, its current market price is only $1,000. This price may be obtained by using equation 5–2A:

$$PB = \frac{\$100}{(1.10)} + \frac{100}{(1.10)^2} + \frac{100}{(1.10)^3} + \frac{1,000}{(1.10)^3}$$
$$= \$90.91 + 82.64 + 75.13 + 751.31$$
$$= \$1,000$$

After issue, the bond may trade in the financial marketplace. The market rate of interest on the bond is likely to change as the demand for and supply of the bond changes. Thus, the market yield to maturity at any moment may differ from the coupon rate. Because the coupons and par value of the bond are fixed, the change in interest rates will change the bond price. If the interest rate were to immediately rise to 12 percent, the price of the $1,000 bond would decline to $952 as the present value of each scheduled payment declines:

$$PB = \frac{\$100}{(1.12)} + \frac{100}{(1.12)^2} + \frac{100}{(1.12)^3} + \frac{1,000}{(1.12)^3}$$
$$= \$89.29 + 79.72 + 71.18 + 711.80$$
$$= \$951.99$$

If the interest rate fell immediately to 8 percent, the bond price would rise to $1,052. Conversely, if the bond price declined to $952, the interest rate would rise from 10 to 12 percent, and if the bond price rose from $1,000 to $1,052, the interest rate would decline to 8 percent.

It follows that an increase in market interest rates lowers bond prices and a decrease raises bond prices. This inverse relationship is shown in Figure 5–1 for our three-year, 10 percent coupon bond. Note that a two-percentage point increase in interest rates will lower the bond price by less ($49) than the same two-percentage point decrease in rates will increase the price ($52). Thus, the relationship between bond prices and interest rates is curvilinear (convex) rather than a straight line. One can also see

FIGURE

5–1   INTEREST RATES AND BOND PRICES VARY INVERSELY

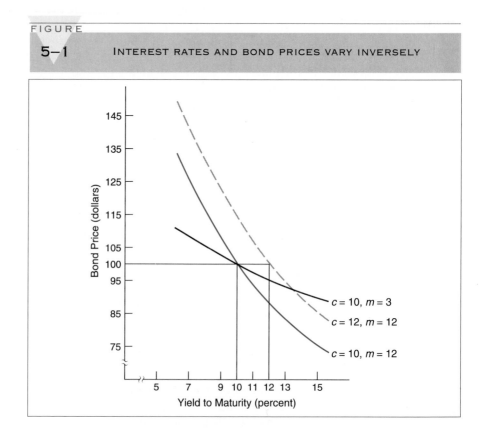

from the figure that the lower the interest rate, the greater is the change in the price of a bond for a given change in interest rate. Last, as noted earlier, the higher the coupon rate, the higher is the price of the bond as it pays more dollars. In Figure 5–1, the higher is the coupon rate, say, 12 percent instead of 10 percent, the higher is the bond price–interest rate curve.

Bonds that sell above their par value (A) are said to sell at a **premium;** those that sell below their par value, at a **discount.** Whether a bond trades at its par value, at a premium, or at a discount is determined by the relationship of its coupon rate (c) to the current market rate (i) for that bond.

$$
\begin{aligned}
\text{If} \quad & i = c, \quad \text{then} \quad && PB = A \text{ (par bond)} \\
& i < c, \quad && PB > A \text{ (premium bond)} \\
& i > c, \quad && PB < A \text{ (discount bond)}
\end{aligned}
$$

(Note that a discount bond is not necessarily a bond sold at a clearance sale like a discount suit or dress that represents a good buy.) Bonds may trade at discounts for two reasons: (1) because they were initially issued with a coupon rate below the market rate of interest at the time—this is referred to as an **original issue discount** (OID)—or (2) because the market rate of interest increased after issue to above the coupon rate—**market discount.** The discount on any particular bond may be due to either one or a combination of the two reasons. As the market rate changes through time, the same bond is likely to trade at par, at a premium, and at a discount at different times through its life. This can be seen from Figure 5–1 for our three-year, 10 percent coupon bond. When the market rate of interest is 10 percent, it sells at par value. For market rates below 10 percent, its market price rises to a premium; for rates above 10 percent, its market price drops to a discount.

For bonds that sell at par, all the annual interest return is in the form of cash coupon payments. For premium and discount bonds, the annual interest return consists only partially of cash; the remainder consists of the annual adjustment or **amortization** of the difference between the buying price and the maturity value. For premium bonds, the annual amortization is negative and must be subtracted from the corresponding coupon payments to obtain the interest return. For discount bonds, the amortization is positive and must be added to the coupon payments.

The time path followed by the price of a premium and a discount bond as each approaches par value at maturity is plotted in Figure 5–2 for the case in which interest rates do not change. Prices on this path are referred to as **amortized values.** Thus, the prices of premium and discount bonds change just from the passage of time. In addition, if interest rates change in the future, the prices of premium and discount bonds will rise above or fall below their amortized values, depending on whether interest rates declined or increased, respectively. In contrast to the cash coupon payment, the amortization component is accrued and realized only at the sale of the bond or at its maturity. The price change for premium and discount bonds from period t to the next period $t + 1$ may be divided into two parts:

$$
PB_{t+1} - PB_t = (PB_{t+1} - \overline{PB}_{t+1}) + (\overline{PB}_{t+1} - PB_t)
$$

where $\overline{PB}_{t+1}$ is the amortized value at $t + 1$. The first term on the right-hand

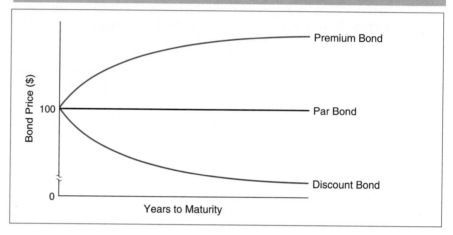

FIGURE

5–2 BOND PRICES APPROACH $100 AS BONDS APPROACH MATURITY

side is a function of interest rates and the second term is a function of time, or

$$(PB_{t+i} - \overline{PB}_{t+1}) = f(\overline{i})$$

$$(\overline{PB}_{t+1} - PB_t) = f(\overset{+}{\overline{t}})$$

The sign above the variable on the right side of the equations shows the direction of the relationship with the left side, or the change in price. For discount bonds, the price change is directly related to time so that, *ceteris paribus*, prices increase with the passage of time, and for premium bonds, inversely to time so that prices decrease with the passage of time.

As can be seen from equation 5–2, the computation of either the bond price or the yield to maturity is not easy without an electronic calculator or a computer. Fortunately, bond books have been prepared that permit one to obtain either the yield to maturity or the price of a bond given the other, the coupon rate, the par value, and the term to maturity. A page from such a book for bonds with 10 percent coupons and between 10½ and 14 years to maturity for market interest rates of between 6 and 14 percent is shown in Figure 5–3. You can see that the price of a bond with a par value of $1,000, coupon rate of 10 percent, and 12 years remaining to maturity is 100.00, or $1,000 par value, when the market rate of interest is also 10 percent. If the interest rate were 9 percent, the price of the bond would be $1,072.50. If the market rate were 12 percent, the bond price would be only $874.50. (In the real world, most bonds pay coupon interest semiannually and the interest rate is compounded semiannually. These assumptions are built into the bond tables.)

The bond book also shows that a given change in interest rates will have different effects on the prices of bonds with different terms to maturity. You can see from the table in Figure 5–3 that if interest rates declined by one percentage point from 10 to 9 percent, the 12-year, 10 percent coupon

FIGURE 5–3   BOND PRICE TABLE

Coupon Rate = 10%

Years and Months

Yield	10–6	11–0	11–6	12–0	12–6	13–0	13–6	14–0
6.00	130.83	131.87	132.89	133.87	134.83	135.75	136.65	137.53
6.20	129.01	129.98	130.92	131.83	132.72	133.58	134.41	135.22
6.40	127.22	128.12	128.99	129.84	130.66	131.45	132.22	132.96
6.60	125.46	126.30	127.10	127.88	128.64	129.37	130.08	130.76
6.80	123.74	124.51	125.25	125.97	126.66	127.33	127.98	128.61
7.00	122.05	122.75	123.43	124.09	124.72	125.34	125.93	125.50
7.20	120.38	121.03	121.65	122.25	122.83	123.38	123.92	124.44
7.40	118.75	119.34	119.90	120.44	120.97	121.47	121.96	122.43
7.60	117.15	117.68	118.19	118.68	119.15	119.60	120.04	120.46
7.80	115.58	116.05	116.51	116.94	117.37	117.77	118.17	118.54
8.00	114.03	114.45	114.86	115.25	115.62	115.98	116.33	116.66
8.10	113.27	113.66	114.04	114.41	114.76	115.10	115.43	115.74
8.20	112.51	113.88	113.24	113.58	113.91	114.23	114.53	114.83
8.30	111.76	112.11	112.44	112.76	113.07	113.37	113.65	113.92
8.40	111.02	111.34	111.65	111.95	112.24	112.51	112.78	113.03
8.50	110.28	110.58	110.87	111.15	111.41	111.67	111.91	112.14
8.60	109.55	109.83	110.10	110.35	110.60	110.83	111.06	111.27
8.70	108.83	109.09	109.33	109.56	109.79	110.00	110.21	110.41
8.80	108.12	108.35	108.57	108.78	108.99	109.19	109.37	109.55
8.90	107.41	107.62	107.82	108.01	108.20	108.37	108.54	108.71
9.00	106.70	106.89	107.07	107.25	107.41	107.57	107.73	107.87
9.10	106.01	106.17	106.34	106.49	106.64	106.78	106.92	107.04
9.20	105.31	105.46	105.60	105.74	105.87	105.99	106.11	106.23
9.30	104.63	104.76	104.88	105.00	105.11	105.22	105.32	105.42
9.40	103.95	104.06	104.16	104.26	104.36	104.45	104.54	104.62
9.50	103.28	103.37	103.45	103.54	103.61	103.69	103.76	103.83
9.60	102.61	102.68	102.75	102.81	102.88	102.94	102.99	103.05
9.70	101.95	102.00	102.05	102.10	102.15	102.19	102.23	102.27
9.80	101.29	101.33	101.36	101.39	101.42	101.45	101.48	101.51
9.90	100.64	100.66	100.68	100.69	100.71	100.72	100.74	100.75
10.00	100.00	100.00	100.00	100.00	100.00	100.00	100.00	100.00
10.10	99.36	99.34	99.33	99.31	99.30	99.28	99.27	99.26
10.20	98.73	98.70	98.66	98.63	98.60	98.58	98.55	98.53
10.30	98.10	98.05	98.01	97.96	97.92	97.88	97.84	97.80
10.40	97.48	97.41	97.35	97.29	97.24	97.18	97.13	97.08
10.50	96.86	96.78	96.71	96.63	96.56	96.50	96.43	96.37
10.60	96.25	96.16	96.07	95.98	95.90	95.82	95.74	95.67
10.70	95.65	95.54	95.43	95.33	95.24	95.15	95.06	94.98
10.80	95.05	94.92	94.80	94.69	94.58	94.48	94.38	94.29
10.90	94.45	94.31	94.18	94.05	93.93	93.82	93.71	93.61
11.00	93.86	93.71	93.56	93.42	93.29	93.17	93.05	92.94
11.10	93.28	93.11	92.95	92.80	92.66	92.52	92.40	92.27
11.20	92.70	92.52	92.35	92.18	92.03	91.88	91.75	91.62
11.30	92.12	91.93	91.75	91.57	91.41	91.25	91.10	90.96
11.40	91.55	91.35	91.15	90.97	90.79	90.63	90.47	90.32
11.50	90.99	90.77	90.56	90.37	90.18	90.01	89.84	89.63
11.60	90.43	90.20	89.98	89.77	89.58	89.39	89.22	89.05
11.70	89.87	89.63	89.40	89.18	88.98	88.78	88.60	88.43
11.80	89.32	89.07	88.83	88.60	88.38	88.18	87.99	87.81
11.90	88.78	88.51	88.26	88.02	87.80	87.59	87.39	87.20
12.00	88.24	87.96	87.70	87.45	87.22	87.00	86.79	86.59
12.20	87.17	86.87	86.59	86.32	86.07	85.84	85.61	85.40
12.40	86.12	85.80	85.50	85.21	84.95	84.70	84.46	84.24
12.60	85.09	84.75	84.43	84.13	83.85	83.58	83.33	83.09
12.80	84.07	83.71	83.38	83.06	82.76	82.48	82.22	81.98
13.00	83.07	82.70	82.34	82.01	81.70	81.41	81.14	80.88
13.20	82.09	81.70	81.33	80.99	80.66	80.36	80.07	79.81
13.40	81.13	80.72	80.34	79.98	79.64	79.33	79.03	78.76
13.60	80.18	79.76	79.36	78.99	78.64	78.31	78.01	77.72
13.80	79.25	78.81	78.40	78.02	77.66	77.32	77.01	76.72
14.00	78.33	77.88	77.46	77.06	76.69	76.35	76.03	75.73

SOURCE: Reprinted from *Expanded Bond Values Tables*, Pub. No. 83, p. 1166, copyright © 1970, Financial Publishing Company, Boston, Mass.

bond would increase in price from $1,000 to $1,072.30, but a 14-year bond would increase to $1,078.70. This occurs because a longer stream and therefore a larger amount of coupon payments are discounted by the lower interest rate. At the same time, if interest rates rise by one percentage point from 10 to 11 percent, longer-term bonds would decline more in price than shorter-term bonds. (Prove this for yourself from the bond book table.)

Although most debt securities in the United States promise both periodic fixed-coupon payments and repayment of the principal at maturity, some debt securities have different cash-flow characteristics. Four special types of securities should be noted.

Zero-Coupon Bonds. These securities make no coupon payments. They promise only a single payment at maturity. Zero-coupon bonds sell at a discount, and all the interest return is obtained from the appreciation in the value of the bond to its maturity value. Zero coupon bonds are original issue discount bonds. The longer the maturity of the bond or the higher the market rate of interest, the more is the price of the bond below the par value and the greater is the discount. If market rates of interest increase after issue, the price of the bond declines to a market discount below the original issue discount or the amortized price. The most common examples of zero-coupon securities are Treasury bills and U.S. savings bonds. Corporate zero-coupon bonds have been issued since 1981. The price of a zero-coupon *m* year maturity bond is given by equation 5–1:

$$PB = \frac{A}{(1 + i)^m}$$

(If zero-coupon bonds traded at par value, they would yield no interest. If they traded at a premium above par, they would yield negative interest as the investor would receive less in total payments than paid for the bond. Thus, zero-coupon bonds always trade at a discount.)

The price of a zero-coupon bond that pays $1,000 three years from now if current market rates of interest are 10 percent is $751.31. Through time, the market price of this bond will increase along a path similar to the one for the discount bond in Figure 5–2 and equal $1,000 at maturity. Of course, if market rates of interest change during this period, so will the price of the bond to above or below the amortized price. But it will never rise above $1,000. Note that this bond is equivalent to the principal payment of the regular bond analyzed earlier on page 83. It follows that the price of that bond is the sum of the present value of the scheduled flow of coupon payments and the price of a zero-coupon bond that pays the principal amount at maturity.

Interest rates on many zero-coupon money-market securities, such as Treasury bills and commercial paper, are quoted on a 360-day *bank discount basis* rather than on a yield-to-maturity basis. In this method, the dollar difference (discount) between the market price and par value is divided by the par value rather than the market price as follows:

$$d = \frac{360(100 - P)}{m} \qquad\qquad (5–3A)$$

where P is the dollar price per \$100 of the zero-coupon security and m is the number of days to maturity. Thus, a 90-day Treasury bill trading at \$98 has a discount yield of:

$$d = \frac{360\,(100 - 98)}{m} = \frac{720}{90} = 8.0\%$$

As can be seen in Figure 4–4, this yield understates the yield to maturity. A first approximation relationship between the discount basis (d) and the 365-day yield to maturity (i) is given by

$$i = \frac{d}{1 - dm/36{,}500} \qquad (5\text{–}3\text{B})$$

Thus, the yield to maturity of our 90-day Treasury bill trading at a discount rate of 8 percent is:

$$i = \frac{8}{1 - 8 \times 90/36{,}500} = \frac{8}{0.98} = 8.16\%$$

Consol Bonds. Consols promise only coupon payments. They have no maturity date and never repay their principal. They are perpetual bonds. The price of a fixed-rate coupon consol is the present value of all the future coupon payments, or

$$PB = \sum_{n=1}^{\infty} \frac{C}{(1 + i)^n} \qquad (5\text{–}4)$$

where ∞ is infinity. This equation reduces to the very easy formula:

$$PB = \frac{C}{i} \qquad (5\text{–}5)$$

Thus, the mathematics required for pricing consol bonds is very simple. Unfortunately, consols are rare in the United States. They are more common in other countries.[3]

The price of a 10 percent coupon consol bond when market rates of interest are 10 percent is \$100. The price will increase to \$111 if interest rates decline to 9 percent and decrease to \$91 if interest rates increase to 11 percent.

Variable-Rate Bonds. These securities have coupon or contract rates that may change periodically before maturity according to prearranged terms. When the coupon rate is changed or reset, the bond is said to be **repriced.** For example, a 20-year bond may have coupons whose value may be reset, say, every two years to maintain a given constant relationship with a pre-

---

[3] There is one consol currently traded on the New York Stock Exchange. It is a 4 percent bond issued by the Canadian Pacific Railroad in the 1920s. During 1973–1993, its price ranged between \$190 and \$550. The U.S. Treasury issued its one and only consol bond in 1900 at 2 percent. It was redeemed in 1935.

designated *reference* or *index* market rate of interest, say, the rate on two-year Treasury securities.

The purpose of variable (floating)-rate securities is to keep their market prices at or close to their par values and avoid large price losses when interest rates rise sharply. If there are no constraints on the amounts by which the coupons may change to maintain their relationship to the reference rate, and if the length of the coupon change interval or term to repricing is equal to the remaining maturity of the reference bond, the price of the variable-rate bond should be $100 at each repricing date. Between repricing periods, the price of the bond may vary and behaves like that of a fixed-rate bond with a term to maturity equal to the remaining term to repricing rather than to its final maturity. Thus, a long-term variable-rate bond generally behaves like a short-term fixed-rate bond. However, because the variable-rate bond is long term, it saves both issuers and investors transaction costs of rolling over a series of short-term bonds summing to the same maturity. As noted in Chapter 23, variable bonds have become very popular in recent years in the United States in response to the increased volatility of interest rates that has increased the downside price risk of long-term fixed-rate bonds.

Amortized Loans.   Rather than repaying the principal of the loan in one lump sum at maturity, these securities repay the loan principal through time in scheduled periodic installment payments that include both interest and principal. Many amortized loans are designed so that installments are of equal dollar amounts. Most mortgage loans used to finance the purchase of residential property are amortized loans (see Chapter 21). If an amortized loan had no maturity date it would be a consol bond. An amortized loan can be either fixed or variable rate. Amortized securities are frequently called **annuities.**

Relationship among Bonds.   The bond types just mentioned are not as different as they may appear at first. They are all based on a limited number of common elements—principal amount, coupon amount, term to maturity, and coupon change interval (term to first repricing). The similarities and differences in each of these elements for the bonds are shown in Table 5–2. Consol and zero-coupon bonds are the simplest. They have no common elements. The other bonds are effectively combinations of the two bond types and therefore they have common elements and are more complex. Fixed-rate bonds, for example, are a combination of a zero-coupon bond for the principal repayment at maturity and an amortized loan or annuity until maturity for the stream of coupon payments. The price of the bond is the sum of the prices of the two components.

Current Yield

The yield to maturity is not the only interest rate used in the market. Some people prefer to focus only on the cash coupon return currently received and compute the **current yield,** which is defined as C/PB. This yield, of course, omits the amortization of any discount or premium and thus reflects only part of the total interest return on the bond. It effectively assumes that the bond will not change in price. For zero-coupon bonds, the

TABLE
5-2

BASIC CHARACTERISTICS OF
DIFFERENT TYPES OF BONDS

| Type of Bond | Bond Characteristic | | | |
	A	C	m	CCI
Consol	0	>0	∞	∞
Zero-coupon	>0	0	<∞	m
Fixed-rate	>0	>0	<∞	m
Variable-rate	>0	>0	<∞	<m
Amortized (annuity)	0	>0[a]	<∞	$\underset{<}{=}m$[b]

[a]A cash amount containing both the interest payments and amortization of the principal.
[b]Can be either fixed-rate (CCI = m) or variable-rate (CCI < m).

A	= principal amount	>	= greater than
C	= coupon amount	<	= less than
CCI	= coupon change interval	∞	= infinity
m	= term to maturity	0	= zero

current yield is zero. This is obviously not the yield that the buyer expects to earn. Indeed, the current yield is equal to the yield to maturity only for par bonds and for consols. It overstates the yield to maturity for premium bonds, as it fails to recognize the scheduled loss from buying the bond above its value at maturity, and it understates the yield to maturity for discount bonds, as it does not include the scheduled gain from buying the bond at below its maturity value. Thus, although simple to calculate, the current yield is not very meaningful for most bonds.

Realized Yield

The yield to maturity is the return promised to the investor at the time the bond is purchased. However, it may not be realized if interest rates change between the purchase and sale or maturity of the bond or if the issuer defaults and the coupons and/or principal payments are not made in full or on time. The interest return that one realizes on a bond upon sale or maturity is called the **realized** or **holding-period yield.** The annualized realized rate is computed by summing the price of the bond at sale or maturity, all the coupon payments received, and the interest earned on the reinvestment of the coupons, dividing by the purchase price, taking the nth root for the number of years held, and subtracting one. This is shown algebraically in equation 5–6:

$$h = \left[\frac{PB_s + \Sigma C + RI}{PB_p} \right]^{1/n} - 1 \qquad (5\text{–}6)$$

where:

h = annualized total rate of return on a bond
PB_s = sale price of the bond
PB_p = purchase price of the bond
ΣC = dollar amount of coupons received
RI = income from reinvesting the coupons
n = number of periods held

The realized yield can be greater than, smaller than, or equal to the yield to maturity promised at the time of purchase so that

$$h \underset{<}{\overset{>}{=}} i$$

If interest rates change after a bond is purchased, the return realized will not be equal to yield to maturity, even if all the coupon payments are made in full and on time. But the direction of the error is not always clear. For example, if interest rates rise, the selling price of the bond will be lower than if rates did not rise, but the interest income from reinvestment of the coupons will be higher.

Interest Rate Risk.   The effect of changes in interest rates on changing the realized return on a bond from its promised return is referred to as **interest rate risk.** The effect on only the price of the bond is referred to as **price risk** and on coupon reinvestment income as **reinvestment risk.** Price changes vary inversely with interest rates (if interest rates rise, bond prices fall) and reinvestment income changes vary directly (if interest rates rise, income from reinvestment also rises). For price risk, the following three rules of thumb are frequently used:

For a given change in interest rates, the percent change in the price of a bond will be greater, the

   1. lower the coupon rate,
   2. lower the market rate of interest, and
   3. longer the term to maturity.

As is shown in Appendix 5A, the third rule of thumb does not hold for long-term deep discount bonds. For other bonds, the greater price change for longer-term bonds can be seen in Figure 5–1 by comparing the change in bond price for a 1 percent change in yield to maturity for the 3-year (black line) and 12-year (green line) 10 percent coupon bonds. The curve for the 12-year bond is steeper.

Whether, for a given change in interest rates, price risk or reinvestment risk is the stronger depends on the length of time the bond is held. The shorter the period, the more price risk will dominate reinvestment risk. Conversely, the longer the investment period, the more reinvestment risk will dominate. Thus, an increase in interest rates will lower returns below the promised yields for short investment periods but raise returns above the promised yields for long investment periods. Managing interest rate risk is discussed in greater detail in Chapter 17.

SUMMARY

The interest rate is the price of renting money in order to use its purchasing-power services. The rate is paid by the borrower to the lender, who cannot use the funds until the loan is repaid. A bond is an IOU issued by the borrower, generally promising to repay the face value of the loan at maturity and to make periodic coupon interest payments in the meantime. The market value of the bond is the present value of all promised future payments discounted by the appropriate market rate of interest. Thus, bond prices and interest rates vary inversely. When one goes up, the other goes down. Generally, the longer the term to maturity of a bond, the greater will be the change in its price for a given change in interest rates.

Bonds may trade at par value, at a discount, or at a premium, depending on whether their coupon rates are, respectively, equal to, lower than, or greater than the market rate of interest on that type of bond at the time. The interest yield on a bond consists of two components; coupon payments and amortization of any discount or premium. Par bonds pay only coupons; discount bonds yield both coupon payments and amortization of the discount; and premium bonds yield coupons less the annual amortization of the premium. Zero-coupon bonds make no coupon payments; they make only a single principal payment at maturity. Consol or perpetual bonds make no principal repayments; they make only coupon payments to infinity. Amortized loans repay principal through time rather than only at maturity. Variable- or floating-rate bonds make coupon payments that change in magnitude with changes in market rates of interest to keep the price of the bond at or close to par value.

Yields to maturity are the interest yields promised investors when they repurchase the bonds. However, these may not be realized if interest rates change or the issuer defaults. Realized yields maybe greater than, equal to, or smaller than the yield to maturity.

QUESTIONS

1. How may depreciation on an automobile be compared to the effect of inflation on money in computing the market and real rental rates?

2. A U.S. Treasury bond with 20 years to maturity, a coupon rate of 8 percent, and par value of $1,000 promises to pay $80 per year and $1,000 at maturity, for a total of $2,600. How much would you pay for this bond today? (Look in the *Wall Street Journal* for the current interest rate on the nearest such bond.) How much more or less would you have paid a year ago for this bond? What accounts for the difference?

3. What can you say about the price of a bond whose coupon rate is less than the current market rate? How could the yield on this bond be equal to the market rate? If interest rates do not change, what will happen to the price of this bond through time? Why? For such a bond, would the current

yield or yield to maturity be greater? Why?

4. Assume two fixed-rate bonds with equal par values and terms to maturity but different coupon rates. At a given market rate of interest, would you pay a higher price for the bond with the lower coupon rate or the one with the higher coupon rate? Why? Would this still be true if market rates of interest changed? Why or why not? Under what conditions would you pay a premium for a zero-coupon bond? Why?

5. Assume a 20-year fixed-rate bond with a coupon rate of 6 percent that is trading at a market rate of interest of 4 percent. What could you say about the market price of this bond? If this were a consol bond, what would be its price? Would this be higher or lower than the price on the 20-year bond? Why? At what interest rate would both these bonds trade at 100? How does a

bond paying a 6 percent coupon yield only 4 percent?

6. Could the market price of a bond change if market interest rates do not? If it could, for what kind of bonds? Why? For what kind of bonds could this *not* happen? Could a bond be both an original issue and market discount bond at the same time? Why or why not?

7. Assume that a 20-year, 6 percent fixed-coupon rate bond trades at 80:07. What is its market rate of interest? Assume that you could also buy a 6 percent coupon, 10-year bond at the same price. Would you? Why or why not? At what price would you be indifferent between buying the 10-year bond and the 20-year bond at 80:07? Why? At what coupon rate would a 10-year bond trade at the same price as the 20-year bond when market rates of interest were 8 percent?

8. Assume that both 90- and 180-day Treasury bills are trading at discount rates of 5 percent. What are their respective prices? What would be the equivalent yields to maturity? If the discount rate doubled to 10 percent, what would happen to the difference between it and the associated yields to maturity? Why?

9. Assume two fixed-rate bonds with equal coupon rates and par values but different terms to maturity. If the market rate of interest exceeded the coupon rates, would you pay more for the shorter- or longer-term bond? Why? What if market interest rates fell to the coupon rates? Below the coupon rates? If the two bonds were variable-rate bonds with equal coupon change intervals, would the term to maturity affect their price? Why or why not?

10. Why might you not realize the return promised you at the time you bought a bond even if the bond did not default? Differentiate between price risk and reinvestment risk. If you planned to hold a long-term bond for only one month, which risk would be the more important? Why?

REFERENCES

Cissell, Robert, Helen Cissell, and David C. Flashpholer, *Mathematics of Finance*, 8th ed. Boston: Houghton Mifflin, 1990.

Fabozzi, Frank J., *Fixed Income Mathematics*. Chicago: Probus Publishing, 1988.

Fabozzi, Frank J., *Bond Markets, Analysis and Strategies*, 2nd ed. Englewood Cliffs, N.J.: Prentice Hall, 1993.

First Boston Corporation, *Handbook of Securities of the United States Government and Federal Agencies and Related Money Market Instruments*. Chicago, Ill.: Probus Publishing, biannual.

Homer, Sidney, and Martin L. Leibowitz, *Inside the Yield Book: Tools for Bond Market Strategy*. Englewood Cliffs, N.J.: Prentice Hall, 1972.

Livingston, Miles, *Money and Capital Markets*. Englewood Cliffs, N.J.: Prentice Hall, 1990.

Sharpe, William F., and Gordon J. Alexander, *Investments*, 4th ed. Englewood Cliffs, N.J.: Prentice Hall, 1990.

Spence, Bruce M., Jacob Y. Graudenz, and John J. Lynch, Jr., *Standard Securities Calculation Methods: Current Formulas for Price and Yield Computations*. New York: Securities Industry Association, 1973.

Trainer, Richard D.C., *The Arithmetic of Interest Rates*. Federal Reserve Bank of New York, 1983.

Appendix 5A

Duration

As discussed in this chapter and shown in Figure 5–1, the relationship between bond prices and interest rates is curvilinear rather than linear. The lower the interest rate, the greater will be the change in the price of a bond for an equal change in interest rates. As a result, it is difficult to predict what will be the change in the price of a bond for a given change in interest rates without knowing both the direction of the change in interest rates and the initial level of interest rates. The relationship between bond prices and interest rates may be simplified through the use of the concept of **duration.**

Duration describes the major timing characteristic of a stream of payments, such as a bond or mortgage, better than does maturity. Term to maturity describes only the length of time to the date of the final payment of the stream. However, as noted in the body of the Chapter, all but zero-coupon streams make payments before maturity, and these payments help determine both the price (present value) of the stream and the sensitivity of the price to changes in interest rates. Duration takes into account the length of time to the final payment as well as all earlier payments. Thus, it may be viewed as a measure of the "average life" of a bond or mortgage. Much like your average test score for a number of examinations in this class, there are a number of ways of computing duration depending on the weights that are assigned to the observations, in this case the lengths of time to each payment.

The simplest measure of duration is the Macaulay measure, named after Frederick Macaulay, one of the earlier students of interest rate behavior, who introduced the concept in 1938. It weights the length of time to the date that each payment is scheduled to be made by the present value of that payment computed using the yield to maturity as the discount rate. It may be computed as follows:

$$D = \frac{\sum_{n=1}^{m} \frac{nC}{(1+i)^n} + \frac{mA}{(1+i)^m}}{\sum_{n=1}^{m} \frac{C}{(1+i)^n} + \frac{A}{(1+i)^m}} \tag{5A–1}$$

where D is duration and the other terms are defined as in the text. Like term to maturity, duration is scaled in units of time, for example, years. (Alternative computational procedures are shown in Appendix 5B.)

While simple, the Macaulay duration assumes that interest rates are the same for all maturities—that is, the yield curve of interest rates is flat—and that, if interest rates change, they will change by the same amount for all terms to maturity so that the yield curve remains flat. These are the same assumptions that underlie the yield-to-maturity calculation that is discussed in the body of this chapter. As will be seen in Chapter 7, these assumptions are not very realistic. More realistic but complex assumptions about the yield curve will change the weights and may even require more than a one-term, or *factor*, measure of duration. Nevertheless, for many purposes, the single-factor Macaulay duration, as defined in equation 5A–1, has been found to serve as a good approximation of the true duration.

The relationship between the duration of a bond and its term to maturity for a given market rate of interest is shown in Figure 5A–1. Duration is plotted on the vertical axis and term to maturity on the horizontal axis. As can be seen from equation 5A–1, duration is equal to maturity for single-payment, zero-coupon bonds.

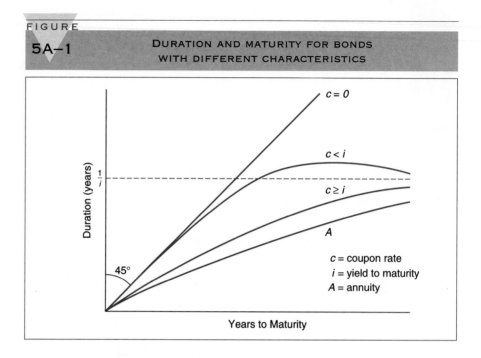

FIGURE

5A-1

DURATION AND MATURITY FOR BONDS
WITH DIFFERENT CHARACTERISTICS

This is plotted as a 45-degree line from the origin, on which all points are equidistant from both axes. For all other bonds, the coupon payments make duration shorter than the term to maturity; and the larger the coupon payments, the shorter the duration. For consol or perpetual bonds without a maturity payment, duration approximates $1/i$. Thus, these bonds are not as long as they appear to be. The higher the market rates of interest are, the smaller the present value of the more distant payments and the shorter the duration. The duration of a consol bond is shown by the dotted line.

Regular coupon bonds may be viewed as a combination of a zero-coupon maturity payment and a stream or annuity of coupon payments until maturity. The duration of an annuity is plotted on Figure 5A-1 by line A. The duration increases with maturity but at a decreasing rate, slowly reaching the duration of the consol shown by the dashed line. The duration of a regular bond is a complex average of the two components and will lie somewhere between the two. For par or premium

bonds, duration is greater than for an annuity of equal maturity and increases with maturity. As the present value of the relatively large but progressively later final payment becomes smaller, the bond's duration slowly approaches the duration of a consol. For coupon discount bonds, duration increases somewhat faster (as the final payment is relatively more important) and temporarily rises above that of a consol for some maturities, but falls back to this value as the maturity becomes longer. Thus, for coupon discount bonds, duration may decrease as maturity increases. It can be seen from the figure that discount bonds of different maturities can have the same duration.

Because the calculation of duration can be time-consuming without a computer, tables have been published showing duration for bonds. A sheet from such a table is shown in Figure 5A-2 for default- and option-free bonds with coupon rates of 8 percent and terms to maturity of from 19 to 25 years when market rates of interest vary from 4 to 15 percent. Note that when the interest rate is 15 percent, so that the

DURATION TABLE

Coupon Rate 5 8%

Years and Months

Yield	19–0	19–6	20–0	20–6	21–0	21–6	22–0	22–6	23–0	23–6	24–0	24–6
4.00	11.78	11.98	12.18	12.37	12.56	12.75	12.93	13.12	13.29	13.47	13.64	13.81
4.20	11.70	11.89	12.09	12.27	12.46	12.64	12.82	13.00	13.17	13.34	13.51	13.67
4.40	11.61	11.80	11.99	12.18	12.36	12.53	12.71	12.88	13.04	13.21	13.37	13.53
4.60	11.53	11.71	11.90	12.08	12.25	12.42	12.59	12.76	12.92	13.08	13.24	13.39
4.80	11.44	11.62	11.80	11.98	12.15	12.31	12.48	12.64	12.80	12.95	13.10	13.25
5.00	11.36	11.53	11.71	11.88	12.04	12.20	12.36	12.52	12.67	12.82	12.97	13.11
5.20	11.27	11.44	11.61	11.78	11.94	12.10	12.25	12.40	12.55	12.69	12.84	12.97
5.40	11.19	11.35	11.52	11.68	11.83	11.99	12.14	12.28	12.43	12.57	12.70	12.84
5.60	11.10	11.26	11.42	11.58	11.73	11.88	12.02	12.16	12.30	12.44	12.57	12.70
5.80	11.01	11.17	11.33	11.48	11.63	11.77	11.91	12.05	12.18	12.31	12.44	12.56
6.00	10.93	11.08	11.23	11.38	11.52	11.66	11.80	11.93	12.06	12.18	12.30	12.42
6.20	10.84	10.99	11.14	11.28	11.42	11.55	11.68	11.81	11.93	12.06	12.17	12.29
6.40	10.76	10.90	11.04	11.18	11.31	11.44	11.57	11.69	11.81	11.93	12.04	12.15
6.60	10.67	10.81	10.95	11.08	11.21	11.34	11.46	11.58	11.69	11.80	11.91	12.02
6.80	10.58	10.72	10.85	10.98	11.11	11.23	11.35	11.46	11.57	11.68	11.78	11.88
7.00	10.50	10.63	10.76	10.88	11.00	11.12	11.24	11.34	11.45	11.55	11.65	11.75
7.20	10.41	10.54	10.67	10.79	10.90	11.02	11.12	11.23	11.33	11.43	11.53	11.62
7.40	10.33	10.45	10.57	10.69	10.80	10.91	11.01	11.11	11.21	11.31	11.40	11.49
7.60	10.24	10.36	10.48	10.59	10.70	10.80	10.90	11.00	11.09	11.18	11.27	11.36
7.80	10.16	10.27	10.39	10.49	10.60	10.70	10.79	10.89	10.98	11.06	11.15	11.23
8.00	10.07	10.18	10.29	10.40	10.50	10.59	10.69	10.77	10.86	10.94	11.02	11.10
8.20	9.99	10.10	10.20	10.30	10.40	10.49	10.58	10.66	10.74	10.82	10.90	10.97
8.40	9.90	10.01	10.11	10.20	10.30	10.38	10.47	10.55	10.63	10.70	10.77	10.84
8.60	9.82	9.92	10.02	10.11	10.20	10.28	10.36	10.44	10.51	10.59	10.65	10.72
8.80	9.73	9.83	9.92	10.01	10.10	10.18	10.26	10.33	10.40	10.47	10.53	10.59
12.00	8.44	8.49	8.53	8.57	8.61	8.64	8.67	8.69	8.72	8.74	8.76	8.78
12.20	8.37	8.41	8.45	8.49	8.52	8.55	8.57	8.60	8.62	8.64	8.66	8.68
12.40	8.29	8.33	8.37	8.40	8.43	8.46	8.48	8.51	8.53	8.54	8.56	8.57
12.60	8.22	8.25	8.29	8.32	8.35	8.37	8.39	8.41	8.43	8.45	8.46	8.48
12.80	8.14	8.18	8.21	8.24	8.26	8.29	8.31	8.32	8.34	8.35	8.37	8.38
13.00	8.07	8.10	8.13	8.16	8.18	8.20	8.22	8.23	8.25	8.26	8.27	8.28
13.20	7.99	8.02	8.05	8.08	8.10	8.12	8.13	8.15	8.16	8.17	8.18	8.19
13.40	7.92	7.95	7.97	8.00	8.02	8.03	8.05	8.06	8.07	8.08	8.09	8.09
13.60	7.85	7.87	7.90	7.92	7.93	7.95	7.96	7.97	7.98	7.99	8.00	8.00
13.80	7.78	7.80	7.82	7.84	7.85	7.87	7.88	7.89	7.90	7.90	7.91	7.91
14.00	7.71	7.73	7.75	7.76	7.78	7.79	7.80	7.80	7.81	7.81	7.82	7.82
14.20	7.64	7.66	7.67	7.69	7.70	7.71	7.71	7.72	7.73	7.73	7.73	7.73
14.40	7.57	7.58	7.60	7.61	7.62	7.63	7.63	7.64	7.64	7.64	7.64	7.64
14.60	7.50	7.51	7.53	7.54	7.54	7.55	7.56	7.56	7.56	7.56	7.56	7.56
14.80	7.43	7.44	7.45	7.46	7.47	7.47	7.48	7.48	7.48	7.48	7.48	7.48
15.00	7.36	7.37	7.38	7.39	7.39	7.40	7.40	7.40	7.40	7.40	7.40	7.39

bond is at a deep discount, the duration of the bond falls from 7.40 to 7.39 years as maturity increases from 24 to 24½ years.

Duration is useful because it simplifies the bond price–interest rate relationship. Duration represents the slope of a straight line that is tangent to the curvilinear bond price–interest rate relationship at the intersection of the current bond price and interest rate. This is shown in Figure 5A:–3 for price P_0 and interest rate i_0 for a bond with a given maturity and coupon. (Technically, the axes should be scaled in logarithms and interest rates as $(1 + i)$ to reflect compound interest.) At the point of tangency, the slopes of the curve and the straight line (D_0) are the same. Small changes in interest rates, say, i_0 to i_1, can be read off the straight line rather than off the actual curve.

Price Risk. The relationship between the change in interest rates and the percentage change in bond prices may be approximated by the following equation:[1]

$$\frac{\Delta P}{P} = -D\frac{\Delta i}{(1 + i)} \cong -D\Delta i \qquad (5A–2)$$

Recall from your college algebra that $(\Delta P/P)/(\Delta i/[1 + i])$ is the equation for the slope of a straight line. Thus, if the duration of a security is known, the effect of a given change in interest rates on bond prices can be estimated easily without a bond book or calculator, and without having to know the initial level of interest rates. The longer the duration, the more sensitive is a security to interest rate changes and the greater its interest rate risk. Moreover, unlike with maturity, the interest rate–bond price relationship is linear. Thus, if the duration of one bond is twice as long as that of another, regardless of the differences in their terms to maturity, a given change in interest rates will change the price of the first bond twice as much as that of the second bond.

The steeper the line in Figure 5A–3, say, D_1, the larger is duration and the greater

[1] The term $D/(1 = i)$ is frequently referred to as *modified duration*

will be the change in the price of a bond for a given change in interest rates. Because the location of the actual curvilinear relationship between bond price and interest rates shifts with changes in a bond's maturity and/or coupon, it is possible for the curves of a large number of different bonds to be tangent to straight lines with the same slope or duration. (Note, these need not all be the same line, but could be any line parallel to the initial straight line.) Thus all bonds, regardless of maturity or coupon rate, that have the same duration have the same price sensitivity to equal changes in interest. Because bonds of different terms to maturity may have equal durations, and those of the same maturity may have different durations, duration is a more useful measure of a bond's price sensitivity to interest rate changes, and therefore the bond's price risk, than is its term to maturity.

It may be seen from Figure 5A–3 that for progressively larger changes in interest rates from i_0 the distance between the true curvilinear bond price–interest rate relationship and the straight line becomes greater. Thus, duration becomes an increasingly poorer approximation of the bond's price sensitivity. This difference between the straight and curvilinear lines, or the error, is referred to as *convexity.* Convexity can be reduced by using more complex multiple-term measures of duration rather than simple one-term measures, but these are more costly to use.

Return Risk. Duration is also useful in explaining differences between promised and realized yields. The relationship between the duration of a bond and the investor's intended holding or planning period reflects the degree of interest rate return risk assumed by bondholders. Investors may hedge or lock in the interest rate for a particular maturity promised to them at the time of purchase by selecting default-free bonds with durations equal to the length of that period. This strategy is referred to as *immunization* through *duration matching.* When a coupon bond is duration matched, its maturity is longer

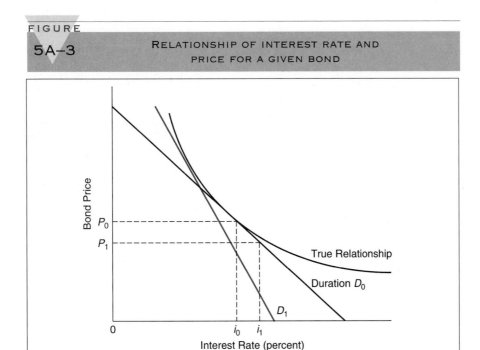

FIGURE
5A–3

RELATIONSHIP OF INTEREST RATE AND
PRICE FOR A GIVEN BOND

than the investor's planning period. But any change in interest rates will cause the change in the price of the bond (price risk) when the bond is sold at the end of the planning period to be exactly equal in magnitude but opposite in sign to the change in income from reinvesting the coupons (reinvestment risk) until the end of the planning period. The bond effectively behaves like a default-free zero-coupon bond with a maturity, and thus also a duration, equal to the planning period. Because such a zero-coupon bond makes its only payment with certainty, its return is certain by definition. Duration may also be defined as the length of time over which an investor is guaranteed to realize the promised return on a default-free bond.

When the duration of a selected bond is either longer or shorter than the investor's planning period, the bond will experience interest rate risk so that its realized return may be greater or smaller than the yield to maturity at time of purchase depending on the direction of the interest rate change. The price risk is now either greater or less than the reinvest-

ment risk. The greater the mismatch between the duration of a bond and the investor's planning period, the greater is the interest rate risk assumed by the investor. At first approximation, the relationship between the interest return an investor may expect and the promised yield is given by

$$E(i_j) = i_0 + \left(\frac{PL - D_j}{PL} \right)(\hat{\imath}_1 - i_0) \quad (5A\text{–}3)$$

where: $E(i_j)$ = expected interest return on bond with duration j

i_0 = initial yield to maturity

$\hat{\imath}_1$ = interest rate predicted immediately after purchase

PL = investor's planning period

Note that duration matching eliminates interest rate risk by setting to zero the first part of the second term in equation 5A–3 so that the expected return will be equal to the initial yield to maturity regardless of changes in interest rates. Note also that to win when using an **active** interest rate strategy in which duration is not matched to the investor's planning period, the investor must predict correctly at least the direction of any interest rate changes. Thus, duration permits investors to manage the degree of interest rate risk expo- sure they wish to assume. If interest rates are expected to change some time after purchase, equation 5A–3 is of the same form but slightly more complex.

REFERENCES

Bierwag, G.O., *Duration Analysis: Managing Interest Rate Risk*. Boston: Ballinger, 1987.

Bierwag, G.O., George G. Kaufman, and Cynthia M. Latta, "Duration Models: A Taxonomy," *Journal of Portfolio Managment*, Summer 1988.

Bierwag, G.O., George G. Kaufman, and Alden Toevs, "Duration: Its Development and Use in Bond Portfolio Management," *Financial Analysts Journal*, July/August 1983.

Hawawini, Gabriel A., ed., *Bond Duration and Immunization*. New York: Garland, 1982.

Appendix 5B

Closed-Form Macaulay Duration Equations

Annuity

$$D = \frac{1 + i/n}{i/n} - \frac{m(n)}{(1 + i/n)^{m(n)} - 1}$$

If $n = 1$:

$$D = \frac{1 + i}{i} - \frac{m}{(1 + i)^m - 1}$$

Regular Coupon Bond

$$D = \frac{1 + i/n}{i/n} - \frac{m(n)c/n + 1 - [m(n) - 1]\,(i/n)}{\left(\dfrac{i - c}{n}\right) + (1 + i/n^{m(n)}(c/n)}$$

If $n = 1, c = i$:

$$D = \frac{1 + i}{i} - \frac{1 + i}{i(1 + i)^m}$$

where:
$i =$ yield to maturity
$n =$ number of coupon payments per year
$c =$ coupon interest rate
$m =$ years to maturity

The Level of Interest Rates

The discussion in Chapter 5 showed that the price of a bond depends on its coupon rate, par value, term to maturity, and market rate of interest. This chapter examines the factors that determine the level of the market rate of interest for default-free bonds and changes in this level. As shown in Chapter 5, the interest rate may be viewed as the nominal rental fee on money in percentage terms, and as such has two components: (1) a **real rate,** equivalent to the pure rental rate discussed earlier for other assets, to compensate the owner in fixed purchasing power or real terms for not using the purchasing-power services of the money and to pay for letting borrowers accelerate their spending before the receipt of the necessary income; and (2) an **inflation premium,** to compensate the owner for any depreciation in the purchasing power of the dollar over the life of the loan.

Just as the rental fee for an automobile depends on its year, make, and, in the absence of insurance, risk of accident by the driver, the interest rate on money depends on the bond's length to maturity, risk of default by the borrower, and so on. It is, however, possible in the case of both automobiles and credit to talk about a basic, stripped-down model that contains only features common to all other models. Such a credit instrument would be a short-term default-free, fully taxable, highly marketable bond. An example would be a 91-day bill issued by the U.S. Treasury. Because the federal government has the ability to print money, it is always in a position to redeem its debt at full nominal value. The interest rate of these Treasury bills may be considered the basic or representative market interest rate. Changes in this rate will affect interest rates on all other securities to varying degrees. The reasons for different interest rates on different types of bonds are examined in Chapters 7 and 8.

Because the inflation premium component is an important determinant of the basic interest rate, it is useful to analyze this component in greater detail. The inflation premium is commonly referred to as the Fisher effect, after Irving Fisher, one of the first well-known American economists, who analyzed it in about 1900.

Inflation Premium

Is either a lender or borrower better or worse off when the market interest rate is, say, 12 percent than when it is 6 percent? One cannot answer this question accurately without having information about the rates of inflation in both periods. Just as the welfare of wage earners is gauged by their real wages and not their nominal dollar wages, the welfare of lenders and borrowers must be gauged in real or constant purchasing-power interest rates, not in nominal interest rates. Thus, the inflation premium must be identified and separated out. This may be done as follows.

Assume that the real (constant purchasing-power) interest rate for one-year, default-free, nontaxable bonds is 3 percent and that this rate remains unchanged through time. That is, the real rate is independent of the expected rate of inflation. Assume further that in the first year, prices are not expected to change. The inflation premium will be zero, so that the market rate of interest will also be 3 percent. At the end of the year, the lender receives back the principal of the loan—say $100—and $3 interest in compensation for the surrender of the purchasing power for the year. At the beginning of the second year, however, both lenders and borrowers expect prices to rise by 2 percent during the year. To maintain the purchasing-power value of their one-year loans and keep the real rate constant, lenders will now demand an inflation premium to compensate them for the expected 2 percent depreciation, from $100 to $98, in the purchasing power of the money lent. The premium that will do so is obviously 2 percent, which is equal to the expected rate of inflation. If the real rate were unchanged, the equilibrium market rate would increase from 3 percent to 5 percent.[1]

At the end of the year, the lender will receive $105. However, he or she will expect to be no better off then in the previous year, because the expected purchasing power of the $105 will be only $103 [$105 − (0.02)($100)]. Likewise, although the borrower pays $2 more than in the previous year, the $2 is just equal to the expected increase in prices, so that the expected cost of the loan in real terms is no higher than before. That is, although the market rate of interest increased, neither the lender nor the borrower would expect to be any better or worse off at the time the loan is contracted. If at the end of the year the expected 2 percent rate of inflation were realized, neither lender nor borrower would be any better or worse off than in year 1 when in market interest rate was only 3 percent. The real rate would be 3 percent in both years.

Of course, because our expectations are not always realized, the actual rate of inflation realized at the end of the year may differ from that expected at the beginning of the year. If the actual inflation rate at the end of the year differed from the 2 percent expected at the beginning, there would be a redistribution of income between lender and borrower. If, for example, the actual inflation rate turned out to be 4 percent, the borrower benefits from paying only 5 percent instead of a higher rate and the lender is harmed as he or she now receives back only $101 [105 − (0.04)($100)] in purchasing power. Of course, neither party expected this rate at the beginning of the year when the loan was made or he or she would have negotiated at a different rate.

Now assume that at the beginning of the third year, the rate of inflation was expected to accelerate to 5 percent. The market rate of interest on one-year loans would climb to 8 percent. This series of events is summarized in Table 6–1. In the fourth year, inflation is expected to slow to 3 percent. The market rate now declines to 6 percent—3 percent real rate and 3 percent inflation premium. Note that the interest rate has declined even

---

[1] Technically, the market rate will increase somewhat more to also offset the decline in the purchasing power of the coupon payment.

TABLE
6–1

EFFECT OF EXPECTED INFLATION RATES ON INTEREST RATES FOR ONE-YEAR BONDS (PERCENT)

Year (1)	Real Rate (2)	Expected Inflation Rate (3)	Market Rate (4) = (2) + (3)
1	3	0	3
2	3	2	5
3	3	5	8
4	3	3	6
5	3	−1	2
6	3	−5	0

though prices are still rising. This is because the market rate of interest is related to the rate of inflation, so changes in the market rates are related to changes in the rate of inflation.

In the fifth year, prices are expected to fall by 1 percent; that is purchasing power is expected to appreciate in value rather than depreciate. The dollar is expected to be worth more at the end of the year than at the beginning. As a result, the depreciation factor is negative, and the market rate will be 2 percent, or less than the 3 percent real rate. However, although the borrower now pays only $2 in interest rather than the $3 at which he or she values the ability to accelerate spending ahead of the receipt of income, the $1 gained is equal to the $1 expected to be lost at the end of the year by the need to repay the nominal $100 principal that has a purchasing-power value of $101.

In the next period, prices are expected to decline by 5 percent. This makes it difficult to determine an equilibrium rate of interest. At first it would appear that the market rate should decline to −2 percent. At this rate, the purchasing power of the $98 payment at the end of the year is equal to $103 during periods of stable prices. But although borrowers are no worse off, lenders have a better alternative. They could hold the money and not lend it. Then their purchasing power at the end of the year would be $105 rather than $103. Lenders are better off to hold money, even at a zero rate of interest, than to lend at negative rates of interest.

The problem is now obvious. The lender will not lend at −2 percent and the borrower will not borrow at 0 percent. The market does not clear and there will be no business. Funds will not be transferred from savers to borrowers. Investment will be hampered, and business activity will decline. Fortunately, this problem need not concern us greatly today. It is unlikely that prices will decline sharply in the near future. It is, however, a serious problem during periods of severe business depressions such as the 1930s.

In equation form, the Fisher effect for a loan of a given maturity may be written as

$$i = r + IP \tag{6–1}$$

where: i = nominal market rate of interest
r = real rate of interest
IP = inflation premium

As was shown, the inflation premium is determined by the rate of inflation expected at the time the loan is made over the life of the loan. Thus, equation 6–1 may be rewritten in an approximate form:[2]

$$i = r + b\dot{P}_E \qquad (6\text{–}2)$$

where: $\dot{P}_E$ = expected rate of change in the price level (P) over the life of

the loan from time period t to $t + n = \dfrac{P_{Et+n} - P_t}{P_t} = \dfrac{\Delta P_E}{P_t}$, where t = time

and b = sensitivity of market rate of interest to price expectations

The inflation premium is equal to $b\dot{P}_E$. The nominal market rate of interest is equal to the real rate only when $\dot{P}_E = 0$, or prices are not expected to change in the period. Because this rarely happens and even when it does the expectations may be not realized, contrary to its name, the real interest rate is not visible and cannot be observed directly. It can be estimated only indirectly by first estimating price expectations and subtracting the inflation premium from the observed market rate.

$$r = i - b\dot{P}_E \qquad (6\text{–}3)$$

The failure to differentiate between nominal and real interest rates is referred to as **interest rate illusion**. Because, unless they operate under interest rate illusion, savers and investors will change the amount of their saving and investing if the real rate rather than the nominal rate changes, it is important to try to isolate the inflation premium. Otherwise, investors and savers will be unable to make optimum decisions. Investors need to know the real interest rate in order to decide whether to invest in financial securities or real assets, whose returns are largely protected from price changes. Likewise, the failure of investment spending to decline in a period of accelerating inflation and rising market rates of interest or to pick up in a period of slowing inflation and declining market interest rates would be difficult to explain without distinguishing between market and real rates of interest.

Four problems arise in trying to divide the market rate into its two components in practice. First, the real rate of interest may not be constant through time as the rate of inflation changes, as was assumed in our simple example. As will be seen later in this chapter, real rates are affected by changes in both money supply and national income. In addition, the real rate may not be independent of inflation or inflationary expectations. Second, the price expectations of market participants are difficult to measure, and SSUs and DSUs may neither have the same expectations nor, if they do, adjust their behavior at equal speeds. Third, even if they could be measured accurately, the expectations may not be realized. Thus, the real rate expected at the beginning of the loan period may not be the same as the real rate realized at the end of the loan period. Fourth, so far we have abstracted from taxes. In a world of zero taxes, changes in interest rates and changes in expected inflation should vary on a one-to-one basis and the value of b in equation 6–2 should be equal to 1. But income from most

[2] The precise form is

$$i = r + b\dot{P}_E + brP_E$$

	Market Interest Rate on 1-Year Treasury Securities	Change in CPI in Next Year	Realized Real Interest Rate	
Year			Tax Rate = 0	Tax Rate = 30%[a]
(1)	(2)	(3)	(4)	(5)
1965	4.14	2.9	1.2	0.0
1970	6.90	4.3	2.6	0.5
1974	8.18	9.1	−0.9	−3.4
1975	6.76	5.8	1.0	−1.1
1979	10.67	13.5	−2.8	−6.0
1982	12.27	3.2	9.1	5.4
1985	8.43	1.9	6.5	4.0
1989	8.53	5.4	3.1	0.6
1990	7.89	4.2	3.7	1.3
1992	3.89	3.0	0.9	−1.0

TABLE 6–2 MARKET AND REALIZED REAL RATES OF INTEREST FROM 1965 TO 1992 (PERCENT)

[a] Computed by applying a 30 percent tax rate to the interest shown in column 2.

bonds is taxable. If we incorporate taxes, the value of the inflation premium to the investor is reduced through taxation and the theoretical value of b in equation 6–2 should be greater than 1 in order to maintain constant the after-tax purchasing-power value, or real rate, on the bond.[3]

The actual relationship between market rates of interest and realized rates is approximated in Table 6–2 for selected years from 1965 to 1992. The average interest rate on one-year Treasury securities for selected recent years is shown in column 2. The actual change in the CPI in the following year is shown in column 3. This may be assumed to have been the rate of inflation expected in the year when the Treasury bill was traded. The realized real rate of interest, computed by solving for r in equation 6–3 by subtracting the rate of price change in column 3 from the interest rate in column 2, is shown in column 4. This computation assumes that the tax rate is zero and that all the interest is available to help offset the depreciation in purchasing power. Thus, $b = 1$. What if the tax rate were not zero but, say, 30 percent? Then only 70 percent of the interest payment received by the investor would be available to help offset the depreciation in the real capital value of the bond. The realized real rate under this assumption is computed by subtracting the rate of price change from 70 percent of the market rate in column 2. This rate is shown in column 5.

It is readily apparent from Table 6–2 that, as expected, the real rates of interest actually realized on one-year bonds were lower than the market

[3] If the income tax rate (q) is greater than zero, the Fisher equation becomes

$$i = r + \left(\frac{b}{1 - q} \right) \dot{P}_E$$

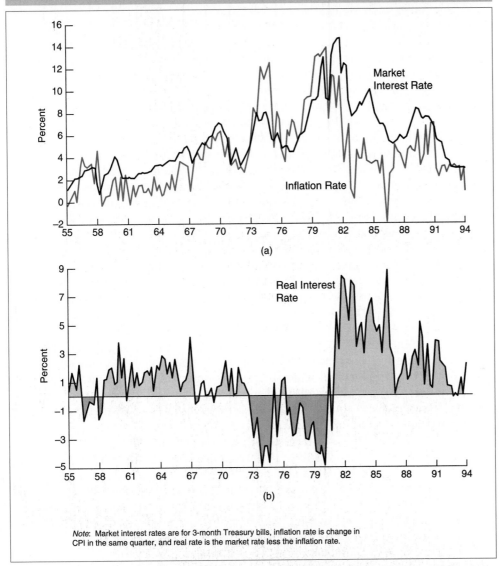

FIGURE
6–1

CHANGES IN MARKET INTEREST RATES MIRROR CHANGES
IN INFLATION RATE, SO REAL RATE FLUCTUATES LESS.

Note: Market interest rates are for 3-month Treasury bills, inflation rate is change in
CPI in the same quarter, and real rate is the market rate less the inflation rate.

SOURCES: Federal Reserve Bank of Chicago.

rates under either tax assumption. However, the real rates were not constant and varied greatly from year to year. The real rates appear to have
been affected by the rate of inflation rather than being independent of it, as
was hypothesized by Fisher. In the 1970s, when inflation was generally
accelerating, the realized real rates were small and frequently negative,
even at a zero tax rate. (See also panel b of Figure 6–1). The value of *b* was
likely to have been less than 1. Nominal market rates increased more slow-

ly than the rate of inflation. For a 30 percent tax rate, the realized after-tax real rate was almost always negative.[4] Thus, although the one-year market rate in 1979 was more than twice that of 1965, the realized real rate was far smaller, indeed negative.

Although at the beginning of each year both lenders and borrowers expected to be equally well off, this did not happen and income was unintentionally redistributed during these years. Lenders performed poorly and borrowers paid little or nothing for their loans when interest is calibrated in constant purchasing-power terms. Interest paid by them is mostly tax deductible. Interest rates were not as high as they appeared!

In the early 1980s, when inflation was generally slowing, the situation reversed. Nominal one-year market rates declined less than the decline in the rate of inflation, and real rates realized rose sharply to positive levels, even after taxes. The value of b was likely to have exceeded 1. Lenders benefited and borrowers paid high. Interest rates were not as low as they appeared! In the mid-1980s, inflation stopped slowing and began to accelerate again, but at a lower rate. At least through 1992, market rates of interest changed at about the same rate. Thus, in this period, one-year realized real rates remained relatively constant at near 3 percent and b was near the hypothesized value of 1. It is of interest to note that in 1974, 1985, and 1989, one-year market interest rates were near 8.5 percent. Yet, the realized rates differed greatly. As the rates of inflation were 9 percent, 2 percent, and 5 percent in 1974, 1985, and 1989, respectively, the corresponding one-year real rates were −0.9 percent, 6.5 percent, and 3.1 percent.

One must note, however, that because of the assumptions required in arithmetically backing-out the real rate by equation 6–3, it may well be that the after-the-fact real interest rates computed above were not the real rates expected by savers and investors at the beginning of the year. This could explain why SSUs lent at all when real rates were negative in the 1970s, while DSUs did not borrow more.

Indeed, there is evidence that people form their price expectations with a lag and thus tend to underestimate the rate of inflation when inflation accelerates and overestimate the rate when inflation slows. This can be clearly seen in Figure 6–2, which plots the actual rate of inflation from 1970 to 1990 and the difference or error between this rate and the rate people expected one year earlier, based on surveys of consumers. The two lines trace an almost mirror image of each other. When actual inflation accelerated sharply in the mid- and late 1970s, people underestimated the rate, and when inflation slowed in the mid-1970s and mid-1980s, people overestimated the rate. Apparently, people were fooled at these times. This suggests that the expected real rate of interest may have been more stable than the computed ex-post real rates. Expectations were just not always realized.

Although not as close as suggested by theory, the Fisher effect is clearly noticeable. The high correlation between past price changes and, in particular, short-term interest rates is evident from panel a in Figure 6–1, which plots quarterly the three-month nominal rate of interest and the

---

[4] Indeed, because the highest marginal tax rate until 1987 and again since 1993 was closer to 50 percent, realized after-tax real rates were even more negative than shown in the table.

FIGURE

6–2

ERROR IN PREDICTING INFLATION VARIES INVERSELY
WITH THE INFLATION RATE, 1970–1990

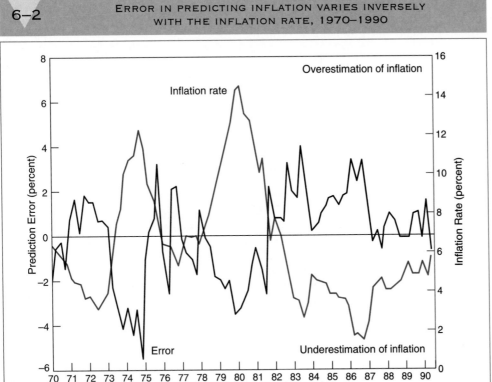

SOURCE: Federal Reserve Bank of Cleveland and Federal Reserve Bank of Chicago.

actual changes in the rate of inflation for the same period from 1955 through 1993. In addition,changes in the inflation premium appear to have accounted for the larger part of the changes in interest rates in many recent years. Thus, the changes in the rate and volatility of inflation in many recent years appear to be the principal cause of the changes in the level and volatility of market interest rates in this period. Nor does the Fisher relationship appear to be restricted to the United States. As can be seen from Figure 6–3, market rates of interest have been highest in countries that have experienced the most rapid inflation (e.g., Italy and the United Kingdom) and lowest in countries that have experienced the slowest inflation (e.g., Japan). In all these countries, the market rate of interest was greater than the rate of inflation as hypothesized by the Fisher effect.

The data in Table 6–2 show that the real after-tax cost of borrowing and the real after-tax reward for lending depend on the borrower's and lender's respective tax rates. The higher the tax rate, the lower both the cost and the reward. Lower-income households and less-profitable firms face higher real after-tax interest costs for a given nominal interest rate than do higher-income households and more-profitable firms. On the other hand, the former households and firms would receive higher after-tax income for the same nominal interest rate than would higher-income households and more-profitable firms. Changes in the expected rate of inflation thus affect differently the borrowing and lending decisions of different market participants, depending on their tax brackets.

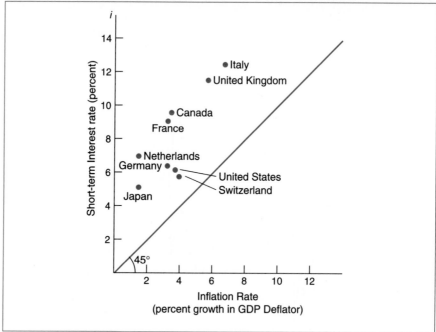

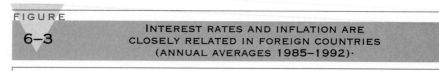

FIGURE **6–3**

INTEREST RATES AND INFLATION ARE CLOSELY RELATED IN FOREIGN COUNTRIES (ANNUAL AVERAGES 1985–1992)·

SOURCES: Federal Reserve Bank of Chicago, and the Federal Reserve Bank of St. Louis, *International Economic Conditions,* July 1993.

Determinants of the Interest Rate Level

Two theories attempt to explain both the level and changes in the level of the market rate of interest: the loanable-funds theory and the liquidity-preference theory.[5]

Loanable Funds

The **loanable-funds theory** uses the framework developed in Chapter 3 and focuses on the demand for and supply of loanable funds for a given period of time, generally one quarter or one year. As was shown in Figure 3–1, loanable funds travel from SSUs (surplus spending units) to DSUs (deficit spending units) on either the private or intermediation financial market, and the DSUs send receipts or securities back to the SSUs on the same market.

The supply of loanable funds originates from household (*HH*) and business (*B*) SSUs, who prefer to spend less than their current income, from government (*G*) units, who run budget surpluses, and from the Federal

---

[5] As was noted in Chapter 1, the purpose of a theory is to predict events. Thus, the value of a theory lies in its predictive ability. When two or more theories explaining a particularly phenomenon are held widely, it suggests that the evidence in favor of any one is not sufficiently strong to convince everyone of its superiority. Theories are discussed in greater detail in Chapter 28.

Reserve (*FR*), which can increase the money supply. The higher the interest rate, the more SSUs are willing to save and loan their funds and the more units are induced to be SSUs. Labelling savings provided by each sector by *S* and letting *SF* be the total supply of loanable funds, this relationship may be written as

$$HHS + BS + GS + FR = SF = f(\overset{+}{i})\qquad(6\text{--}4)$$

The positive relationship between the total supply of loanable funds and interest rates is shown in Figure 6–4 as schedule *SL*. When SSUs lend, they receive primary or secondary securities as evidence of their claims on DSUs. Thus, the supply of loanable funds is the other side of, and equivalent to, the demand for securities.

The demand for loanable funds originates from household, business, and government DSUs who prefer to spend more than their current income. To do so, they must borrow, and in the process issue primary securities. The lower the rate of interest is, the more these units are willing to borrow and the more units are induced to be deficit spending units. The demand for loanable funds is thus inversely related to interest rates and may be written as

$$HHD + BD + GD = DF = f(\overset{-}{i})\qquad(6\text{--}5)$$

where D is the demand for funds by each sector and *DF* is the total demand for loanable funds. This relationship is drawn to Figure 6–4 as schedule *DL*. The demand for loanable funds is equivalent to the supply of securities. The equilibrium interest rate occurs where *SL* = *DL*. In equation form

$$i = f(\overset{+}{DL},\ \overset{-}{SL})\qquad(6\text{--}6)$$

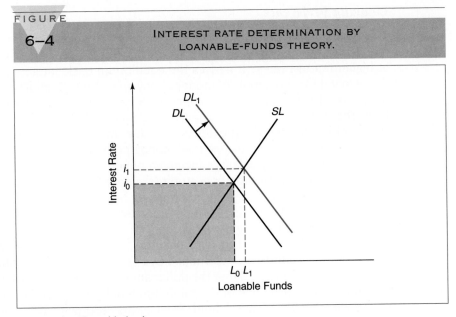

SL = supply of loanable funds;
DL = demand for loanable funds.

In Figure 6–4, this is shown as rate i_0. The corresponding equilibrium amount of loanable funds (or securities) is L_0. *Ceteris paribus*, increases in the demand for loanable funds, shift the demand schedule from DL to DL_1 and increase interest rates, say, from i_0 to i_1. Increases in the supply decrease interest rates. Expectations of an acceleration in the rate of inflation will raise interest rates by increasing the demand for loanable funds at every interest rate and decreasing the supply. The Federal Reserve can lower interest rates by increasing the money supply through techniques discussed in Chapters 27 and 28, thereby shifting the supply of loanable funds to the right. It can also raise interest rates by decreasing the money supply and shifting the supply of loanable funds to the left.

The loanable-funds theory is frequently used to predict interest rates in different economic sectors (e.g., households, business firms, and governments) and different financial sectors (e.g., mortgage loans and corporate loans), as well as the basic interest rate. The ability to predict interest rates by sector makes the loanable-funds theory particularly important to many practitioners in the financial markets who limit their activities to only a few sectors, such as short-term money-market instruments, mortgages, or municipal securities. Until recently, tables projecting the supply and demand in important sectors by quarter or year were prepared regularly by major financial institutions to assist analysts in predicting interest rates. These tables are referred to as **sources and uses of funds** or **flow of funds** tables. Using such a table, analysts could identify "pressure points" where the supply of funds appeared inadequate (overabundant) relative to rates in other sectors. However, the trend toward deregulation, technology that permits cheaper and faster transfer of funds among institutions, and lessened enforced specialization have reduced the types of credit associated with particular types of financial institutions and thereby also the usefulness of these tables.

Liquidity Preference

The **liquidity-preference theory** asks the question, Why do people hold money balances rather than either spend the funds or lend them to others at higher interest rates? It derives the equilibrium basic interest rate from the demand for and supply of money at any given time. Spending units are postulated to demand money balances to be held for liquidity to spend later. The demand for money balances is directly related to the income or wealth of the holder; the greater the income, the greater the demand for money. However, to the extent that money promises no or little interest return, holding money balances incurs an opportunity cost. The higher the interest rate, the higher the opportunity cost and the smaller the demand for money balances. Thus, the quantity of money demanded is related inversely to the interest rate. The determinants of the demand for money are analyzed more thoroughly in Chapter 29.

As will be discussed in later chapters, the supply of money in the United States is effectively determined by the Federal Reserve System. The Fed does so by changing either the dollar amount of cash reserves financial institutions have available or the minimum required ratio of cash reserves to deposits that they have to hold. Thus, at first approximation, the quantity of money at any moment may be assumed to be determined by the Fed.

The equations for the demand for and the supply of money may be specified in functional form as follows:

$$DM = f(\overset{+}{Y}, \overset{-}{i})$$

$$SM = M \tag{6-7}$$

where: DM = demand for money balances
SM = supply of money balances
Y = gross national product
M = money supply
i = market rate of interest

The sign above a variable indicates the direction of its relation with the dependent variable on the left side of the equation. A plus sign indicates that the relation is direct; a minus that it is inverse. In equilibrium, the demand for money is equal to the supply of money:

$$DM = SM$$

Substituting from above

$$f(\overset{+}{Y}, \overset{-}{i}) = M$$

and solving for i

$$i = f(\overset{-}{M}, \overset{+}{Y}) \tag{6-8}$$

But, as discussed earlier in this chapter, the interest rate that exists in a world without price changes is the real rate. Thus, equation 6–8 determines the real rate. To determine the nominal or market rate of interest, people's expectations of future price changes need to be included. Thus, the complete liquidity-preference theory may be written as

$$i = f(\overset{-}{M}, \overset{+}{Y}, \overset{+}{\dot{P}_E}) \tag{6-9}$$

where $\dot{P}_E$ is the rate of change in the price level expected at the beginning of the loan period for the same period as the term to maturity of the loan. The equation indicates that the level of nominal market interest rates varies directly with income and price expectations and inversely with money supply. That is, increases in income and/or expectations about the future rate of inflation exert upward pressure on interest rates, while increases in money supply exert downward pressure.

Also, as discussed earlier in this chapter, if prices are not expected to change, the nominal interest rate is equal to the real interest rate. Thus, equation 6–8 explains real, not nominal, interest rates and underlies the assumption in the Fisher effect that the real rate remains constant when expectations of inflation do not change. The real rate is assumed to be affected only by changes in aggregate income and in aggregate money supply by the Federal Reserve System. The relative strengths of each of the three determinants in equation 6–9 on market interest rates are discussed in greater detail in Chapter 33.

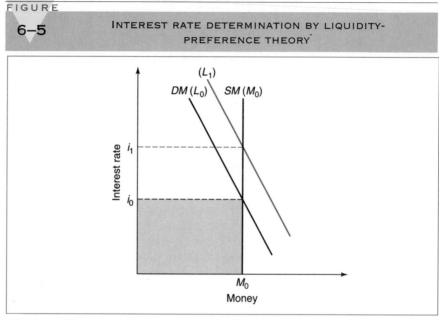

FIGURE **6–5**

INTEREST RATE DETERMINATION BY LIQUIDITY-
PREFERENCE THEORY

DM = demand for money balances at given levels of income and price expectations;
SM = supply of money balances.

The determination of the equilibrium interest rate under the liquidity-preference theory is shown graphically in Figure 6–5. The demand for money balances for given levels of income and price expectations is shown as schedule L_0. As shown in equation 6–7, the demand varies inversely with market interest rates, so that the schedule slopes downward to the right. Because, at first approximation, the supply of money may be assumed to be determined completely by the Fed without regard to the level of interest rates, the supply schedule is shown as completely vertical at M_0. (The role of the Federal Reserve in controlling the supply of money is discussed more thoroughly in Chapters 27 through 31.) The equilibrium interest rate is given by the intersection of the L_0 and M_0 schedules at i_0. If income and/or price expectations increase, the demand for money increases and the L schedule shifts out to the right, say, to L_1. Interest rates rise to i_1. If the Federal Reserve increases the money stock, the M schedule shifts to the right and interest rates decline. (However, as will be discussed later in Chapter 33, the initial change in interest rates brought about by a change in the money supply is likely to be only temporary.)

 Interest Rates over the Business Cycle

As shown in Figure 6–6 interest rates have tended to rise throughout most of the post–World War II period, particularly in the late 1970s when the rate of inflation accelerated. However, a distinct cyclical pattern can be observed superimposed on the trend. Interest rates tend to move directly with the business cycle. On average, rates are relatively high when the economy is close to full employment just before a peak in business activity and relatively low when the economy experiences recessions and higher levels of unemployment (shaded areas). This pattern of changes in the level of inter-

FIGURE

6–6

INTEREST RATES TEND TO RISE IN BOOMS
AND DECLINE IN RECESSIONS. (SHADED AREAS)

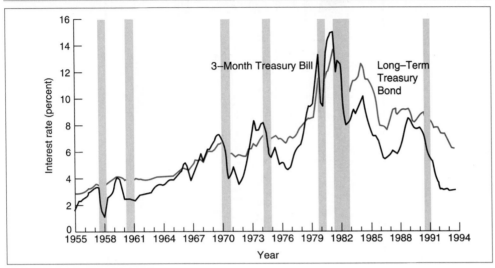

SOURCE: Federal Reserve Bank of Chicago.

est rates is easily explained by both the loanable-funds and liquidity-preference theories. In periods of economic expansion, the demand for loanable funds to finance additional investment and consumption expenditures increases, and the supply of loanable funds for these purposes shrinks. In terms of the liquidity-preference equation 6–9, when the economy is strong, income is high and rising and the rate of inflation is widely expected to accelerate. Both effects exert upward pressure on interest rates. At these times also the Fed can reasonably be expected to slow the rate of monetary expansion. Because money supply is inversely related to interest rates, this also exerts upward pressure on rates. Conversely, during recessions, income declines, the rate of inflation is expected to slow, and the Fed will accelerate the growth in the money supply. All three forces will cause interest rates to decline. The major exception to this pattern is the 1983–1987 and 1991–1993 periods when interest rates declined, although the economy was not in a recession. This may be attributed to an unusually dramatic slowing of inflation during periods of economic expansion. Bond prices, of course, will change in the opposite direction, declining during booms and accelerations in inflation and increasing during recessions and slowdowns in inflation.

SUMMARY

The market interest rate is made up of two components—the cost of borrowing if prices are steady (*real interest rate*) and an *inflation premium*. The real rate compensates the lender for the use of the purchasing power during the life of the loan. The inflation premium, also termed the *Fisher effect*, compensates the lender for any expected deterioration in the purchasing value

SOURCE: From *The Wall Street Journal*; permission, Cartoon Features Syndicate. Copyright © 1978.

of the dollar in this period. The faster the expected rate of inflation, the greater is the inflation premium and the higher is the interest rate. The evidence from recent years indicates that real interest rates have been below nominal rates, although not always by the realized rates of inflation hypothesized by the Fisher theory. In the 1970s, nominal rates increased more slowly than inflation, and real rates were low and even negative, particularly after adjusting for taxes. In the 1980s, nominal rates declined more slowly than inflation and real rates were high. Nevertheless, market interest rates and inflation were highly correlated in the United States as well as in other industrial countries.

Two competing theories explain the level of interest rates. The *loanable-funds* theory focuses on the supply and demand for funds in any one period. The *liquidity-preference* theory focuses on the supply and demand for money at any point of time. The two theories give the same results. Interest rates vary directly with the business cycle: They are high when income and inflation are high, and low when income and inflation are low. Although the two theories will provide the same answers, the liquidity-preference theory contains fewer variables and is easier to use to predict the overall level of rates.

QUESTIONS

1. Why do market rates of interest tend to be high in periods of rapid inflation and low in periods of slow inflation? How is it that borrowers frequently step up their borrowings in inflationary periods despite a sharp rise in market interest rates?

2. Why is it difficult to measure the real

rate of interest? Why is it important to do so? How would you do so? Why can realized real rate be negative?

3. If inflation increases from 5 percent in year 1 to 8 percent in year 2 would SSUs (lenders) or DSUs (borrowers) be better off? Why? Under what conditions would borrowers be worse off? Lenders? Neither?

4. Assume that the market rate of interest on one year bonds is 8 percent. If, in a world of zero income taxes, the expected real rate of interest was 5 percent, what is the consensus expected rate of inflation for the next year? If the tax rate was 50 percent and the pre-tax expected real rate remained at 5 percent, what would be the expected rate of inflation? If, on the other hand, the expected rate of inflation stayed at its earlier expected level, what would have been the expected pre-tax real rate? If the actual rate of inflation for the year was 4 percent, what would have been the realized pre- and after-tax rates if income taxes were zero and if they were 50 percent?

5. What is the empirical evidence with respect to the existence of the Fisher effect in the United States? How did the experiences of the 1970s, 1980s, and the early 1990s differ? How do you explain this difference?

6. Assume that the rate of inflation is expected to accelerate from 4 to 6 percent two years from now. If nothing else changes, what would happen today to the interest rate on one-year bonds and on five-year bonds? Why? What happens to their market prices?

7. Would the loanable-funds and liquidity-preference theories predict, on average, the same level of interest rates? Why or why not? Why might different analysts prefer to use one or the other theory? How is inflation incorporated in each theory?

8. How can the liquidity-preference theory describe the observed cyclical pattern in interest rates? Why might you prefer this theory if you were a policymaker, but the loanable-funds theory if you were a commercial banker?

9. What happened to the long-term Treasury rate over the past year? In terms of the liquidity preference theory, how could you explain this? What forces do you believe were the strongest? Why?

REFERENCES

Board of Governors of the Federal Reserve System, *Flow of Funds Accounts.* Washington, D.C., quarterly.

Gibson, William E., "Interest Rates and Inflationary Expectations," *American Economic Review*, December 1972, pp. 854–65.

Humphrey, Thomas M., "The Early History of the Real/Nominal Interest Rate Relationship," *Economic Review*, Federal Reserve Bank of Richmond, May/June 1983, pp. 2–10.

Humphrey, Thomas M., "Can the Central Bank Peg Real Interest Rates? A Survey of Classical and Neoclassical Opinion," *Economic Review*, Federal Reserve Bank of Richmond, September/October 1983, pp. 12–21.

Kopcke, Richard W., "Inflation, Taxes, and Interest Rates," *New England Economic Review*, Federal Reserve Bank of Boston, July/August 1988, pp. 3–14.

Mullineaux, Donald J., and Aris Protopapadakis, "Revealing Real Interest Rates: Let the Market Do It" *Business Review*, Federal Reserve Bank of Philadelphia, March/April 1984, pp. 3–8.

Santoni, G.J., and Courtenay C. Stone, "The Fed and the Real Rate of Interest," *Review*, Federal Reserve Bank of St. Louis, December 1982, pp. 8–18.

Van Horne, James C., *Financial Market Rates and Flows*, 4th ed. Englewood Cliffs, N.J.: Prentice Hall, 1994.

The Structure of Interest Rates I

As already noted, there is more than one interest rate in the real world. If you look at the financial pages of your newspaper, you find many bonds listed. Almost every one will have a different market interest rate. Frequently, for the sake of expediency, bonds with similar characteristics are grouped together and an average interest rate is reported. Table 7–1 shows the average rate in January 1993 on a number of important bond sectors. It is evident that interest rates on different bonds differ. Which bonds should you buy or sell? Which bonds are overpriced or underpriced? These are the questions we shall try to answer in this chapter. Knowing why and how interest rates differ on different bonds would assist you both in pricing the bonds correctly and in selecting the best bonds to buy as investments or to sell in order to raise funds; that is, in your portfolio strategy—to choose bonds with shorter or longer maturities, lesser or greater risk of default, lower or higher taxes, and so on.

It seems reasonable that the differences in interest rates are related to the differences in the characteristics of the underlying securities. Each characteristic is priced by the market according to its desirability or undesirability to investors and bond issuers. This will change the price of the security and, thus, its interest rate. Bond market analysts have identified five major sources of rate differences:

1. Term to maturity (or term to repricing for variable-rate bonds)
2. Risk of default
3. Tax treatment
4. Marketability
5. Special features

We shall examine how each of these factors affects interest rates one by one, holding each of the other factors constant. In this chapter we consider the first two—term to maturity and risk of default. In Chapter 8, we will consider the remaining factors.

Term to Maturity

Figure 7–1 shows the relationship between the term to maturity and the interest rate for fixed-coupon U.S. Treasury securities on eight dates—June 1980, 1981, 1982, 1985, 1986, 1988, 1991, and December 1993. At first approximation, these securities differ only in term to maturity. (Unconstrained variable-coupon-rate securities with equal coupon change intervals will have equal interest rates regardless of their terms to maturity.) They may be assumed to have the same risks of default (in this case, zero), tax treatment, marketability, and types of special features. The remaining years to maturity of each Treasury security outstanding at a given

TABLE 7–1	INTEREST RATES, JANUARY 1993	
		Percent
Treasury bills (3 months)[a]		3.00
Prime bankers' acceptances (3 months)[a]		3.14
Certificate of deposit (3 months)		3.19
Prime commercial paper (3 months)[a]		3.25
Treasury securities (1 year)		3.50
Treasury bonds (long term)		7.17
Corporate bonds, Aaa (long term)		7.91
Corporate bonds, Baa (long term)		8.67
Municipal bonds, Aaa (long term)		5.91
Municipal bonds, Baa (long term)		6.28

SOURCE: Federal Reserve Bulletin.
[a]Discount basis.

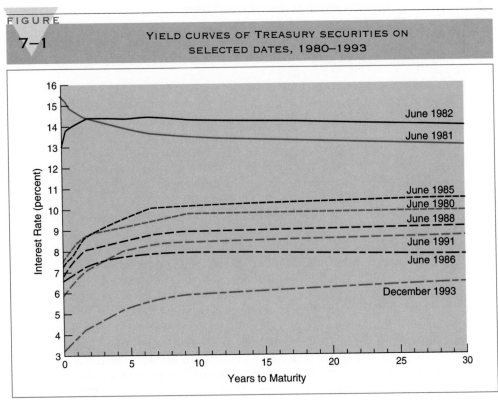

FIGURE 7–1

YIELD CURVES OF TREASURY SECURITIES ON SELECTED DATES, 1980–1993

SOURCE: Federal Reserve Bank of Chicago.

point in time are measured along the horizontal axis, and the corresponding market yield to maturity obtained from newspapers at each date is plotted along the vertical axis. A line drawn to connect these observations is called the **yield curve** or **term structure.** A yield curve shows the relationship of yields on short- and long-term bonds. Interest rates for any maturity can be read off this curve. For example, in December 1993, one-year securities yielded about 3½ percent, two-year securities about 4 percent, and so on. Daily yield curves are widely published in the financial press, such as the **Wall Street Journal.**

You can see from Figure 7–1 that yield curves shift and twist through time. In June 1980, the yield curve for Treasury securities was upward-sloping to the right with short-term rates below long-term rates. One year later, in June 1981, the overall level of interest rates had risen sharply, but short-term rates had risen much more than long-term rates so that the yield curve sloped downward. This is sometimes referred to as an *inverse yield curve.* By June 1985, interest rates had declined again, but short-term rates had declined sharply and long-term rates less, so that the yield curve sloped upward again. In December 1993, the yield curve was also upward sloping but at a much lower level. The reasons for the vertical up-and-down shifts in the yield curves reflect changes in the general level of interest rates that were discussed in Chapter 6. In this chapter, we consider the reasons for changes in the shape of the yield curve. The shape of the curve and changes in the shape of the curve are explained by two competing theories:

1. **The expectations theory**
   a. **unbiased-expectations**
   b. **liquidity-premium (biased-expectations)**
2. **The market-segmentation theory**

Expectations Theory

The **expectations theory** postulates that the yield curve is determined by lenders' and borrowers' expectations of future interest rates, and changes in the shape of the curve by changes in these expectations. The argument underlying this theory may be explained best through a numerical example. Assume that today's interest rate on a one-year default-free Treasury bond on the spot or cash market is 3 percent and on a two-year fixed-coupon Treasury bond is 4 percent. These rates lie on the observed yield curve. Assume further that you want to invest for two years, at which time you need the funds to pay for an automobile you plan to purchase. Which bond would you buy?

If you said you don't have sufficient information to make an intelligent decision, you were right. You know the average annual return for the two years that you would expect on the two-year bond, but not on the one-year bond. To make a decision, you need to know what you will do with the funds for another year at the end of the first year. If you buy the one-year bond and do not reinvest the proceeds, your average return for the two years will be only 1½ percent [(3 + 0)/2], and you would be better off to buy the two-year bond. But if you expected to be able to reinvest the funds in the second year at 9 percent, the average annual return you would receive is 6 percent [(3 + 9)/2]. This is higher than the 4 percent you could expect from the fixed-coupon two-year bond. You would buy the one-year bond and reinvest the proceeds in another one-year bond at the end of the first year.

Assume that you could enter into a contract today for a one-year bond to be delivered and paid for one year from today, at the beginning of the second year. The interest rate on this bond would be determined today. Such a bond is called a **forward bond** and the interest rate the **forward rate.** You would be indifferent between the two alternative bond strategies if the current observed rate on a two-year bond were equal to the average of the current observed rate on a one-year bond in the spot market and the forward rate on a one-year forward bond starting in year 2 in the forward market. This equilibrium expression may be written as follows:[1]

$$i_2 = \frac{i_1 + {_2f_1}}{2} \tag{7-1}$$

where: i_1 = observed rate of interest on one-year bond
i_2 = observed rate of interest on two-year bond
${_2f_1}$ = forward rate of interest on one-year forward bond bought for delivery one year from now (year 2)

This equation can be solved for the forward rate that would satisfy the equality condition:

$${_2f_1} = 2i_2 - i_1$$

In the example above, in which the one-year rate is 3 percent and the two-year rate is 4 percent, the equilibrium forward rate on a one-year bond for delivery one year from now would be 5 percent:

$${_2f_1} = 2(4) - 3 = 8 - 3 = 5$$

You would receive 4 percent per year whether you invested in the two-year bond or in the one-year bond and in a one-year forward bond.

Note that, even if a forward security did not exist, as long as we assume investors will never knowingly choose a lower-return alternative, an implied equilibrium forward rate may be computed from the two observed market interest rates. A similar analysis permits us to compute unobserved equilibrium forward interest rates from observed market rates for all years up to the maturity of the longest bond outstanding. For example, for three-year securities

$$i_3 = \frac{i_1 + {_2f_1} + {_3f_1}}{3} \tag{7-2}$$

and

$${_3f_1} = 3i_3 - i_1 - {_2f_1}$$

[1] This is a slight simplification of the precise equation that requires compound interest and is in terms of geometric rather than arithmetic means:

$$(1 + i_2) = [(1 + i_1)(1 + {_2f_1})]^{1/2}$$

Although this equation has two unknowns—$_2f_1$ and $_3f_1$—it can be solved for $_3f_1$ as the value for $_2f_1$ may be obtained from equation 7–1. Thus, implied forward rates may be computed from observed yield curves.

The expectations theory assigns a meaning to these computed equilibrium forward rates. There are two slightly different versions of the expectations theory: the unbiased-expectations theory and the liquidity-premium (or biased-expectations) theory.

Unbiased-Expectations Theory. The unbiased-expectations theory postulates that the implied forward rates computed according to the equation above from today's observed interest rates are the market's best or unbiased estimates of the interest rates actually expected on these bonds in the future. That is

$$_{t+n}f_1 = {}_{t+n}\rho_1 \tag{7–3}$$

where: $_{t+n}\rho_1$ = the expected one-period interest rate in period $t+n$
n = number of periods in the future

(Of course, expected rates may not be realized.) Unobserved expected future rates may thus be estimated from observed current rates and computed forward rates. In the above example, when the market rate on one-year bonds is 3 percent and on two-year bonds is 4 percent, the computed forward rate is 5 percent and is hypothesized to be the rate that the market expects one year from now.

Since long-term bonds may be viewed as composites of a sequential series of shorter-term bonds, the unbiased-expectations theory predicts that the observed long-term rates are averages of the current short-term rate and all future short-term rates expected during the life of a particular bond. It follows that, because the yield curve traces interest rates on bonds with increasing terms to maturity, if future interest rates are expected to

1. Increase, today's yield curve will slope upward.
2. Decrease, today's yield curve will slope downward.
3. Stay the same, today's yield curve will be flat.

Conversely, today's yield curve, based on today's observed interest rates, contains information about the market's expectations of tomorrow's short-term interest rates. If the yield curve

1. Slopes upward, the market expects short-term rates to be higher in the future than they are now.
2. Slopes downward, the market expects short-term rates to decline.
3. Is flat, the market expects short-term rates to remain unchanged.

Changes in the shape of the yield curve reflect changes in expectations about future interest rates. Assume that you and everyone else suddenly expected the one-year rate next year to be 7 percent rather than 5 percent, as in the previous example. You would now expect to be better off for a two-year investment by buying the one-year bond yielding 3 percent and reinvesting the proceeds next year at 7 percent than by buying the two-year bond at 4 percent. That way, you would expect to obtain an annual rate of 5 percent [(3 + 7)/2] for the two-year period rather than 4 percent. As a result, investors are assumed to arbitrage this difference by restructuring their portfolios by selling two-year bonds and reinvesting in the one-year bond. In the process, the price of the two-year bonds would decline (interest rates rise) and that of the one-year bond would rise (interest rates decline). The prices would change until the interest rate on the two-year bond rose sufficiently—say, to 4¾ percent—and that on the one-year bond fell sufficiently—say, to 2½ percent—so that the annual return on the two-year bond would be the same as on the two successive one-year bonds [(2.5 + 7)/2 = 4.75]. As a result, the yield curve would twist and slope upward more steeply. This is shown in Figure 7–2. More generally, the interest rate on a security of any maturity is strongly affected by the rate on securities of nearby maturities, or

$$i_j = f(i_{j \pm n})$$

where: j = term to maturity
   n = number of periods

It is evident that changes in expectations about interest rates in any maturity sector will set forces in motion that change interest rates in all other sectors. All maturity sectors are closely interrelated, and SSUs and DSUs both view securities of different terms to maturity as perfect substitutes for each other. Market participants are sensitive only to the expected returns on their portfolio and are indifferent to maturities of the individual securities—maturities do not matter. No maturity sector is an island unto itself.

The same reasoning suggests that if future interest rates were expected to be lower than before, market participants would restructure the maturities in their portfolios and the yield curve would twist down at the right. Thus, upward twists in the yield curve reflect upward revisions in future short-term interest rates; downward twists, downward revisions.

FIGURE

7–2   CHANGES IN RATE EXPECTATIONS SHIFT THE YIELD CURVE.

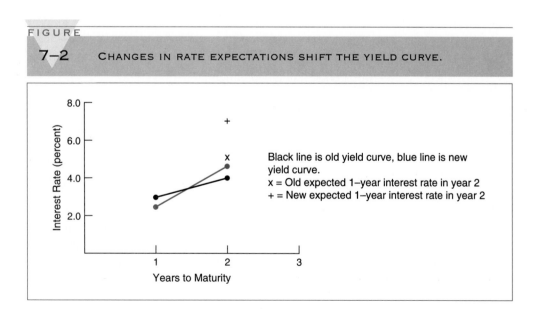

Black line is old yield curve, blue line is new yield curve.
x = Old expected 1–year interest rate in year 2
+ = New expected 1–year interest rate in year 2

Liquidity-Premium Theory. The liquidity-premium theory focuses on the fear that, in a world of uncertainty, the interest rates expected in the future may not be realized. If actual interest rates turn out to be higher than investors predicted, investors who purchased long-term fixed-coupon-rate bonds rather than short-term bonds would suffer losses. To protect themselves against such losses, risk-averse investors are postulated to charge a premium for long-term commitments over short-term commitments. This premium is termed the **liquidity** or **term premium.** The more distant the future period being predicted, the greater the probability of error, and so the longer term the bond, the greater the liquidity premium charged.

For example, if current one-year rates were 3 percent and the one-year rate expected next year were 5 percent as above, the expected average annual return on two successive one-year bonds would be 4 percent. But if interest rates increased, the rate on the one-year bond in year two will be higher than 5 percent and the return on this strategy would be higher than on the purchase of a two-year bond at 4 percent. Thus, investors will demand a higher return on longer-term bonds to compensate themselves for this risk. If investors demanded a liquidity premium of ¼ percent on the two-year bond, the two-year rate would be 4¼ percent rather than 4 percent. However, although the rate is higher, investors expect to be no better off holding the two-year bonds than the two successive one-year bonds because the higher rate will just compensate them for the actuarially fair value of the expected loss.

From equation 7–1, the implied forward rate for year 2 under this scenario would be

$$_2f_1 = 2i_2 - i_1 = 2(4\tfrac{1}{4}) - 3 = 5\tfrac{1}{2}$$

Thus, unlike under the unbiased-expectations theory, forward rates computed from the observed long-term rates are postulated to provide a biased estimate of expected future interest rates. They overestimate the expected future rate by the liquidity premium in our example by ½ percent. That is, the liquidity-premium theory postulates that the forward rate is equal to the expected rate for the particular future period plus a liquidity premium, or

$$_{t+n}f_1 = {}_{t+n}P_1 + {}_{t+n}L_1 \qquad (7\text{–}4)$$

where: $_{t+n}L_1$ = one-period liquidity premium in period $t + n$

Solving for the expected rare yields

$$_{t+n}P_1 = {}_{t+n}f_1 - {}_{t+n}L_1$$

The expected rate is lower than the forward rate. It follows that observed long-term rates are higher than the average of the current and expected future short-term rates over the loan period by an amount equal to the average liquidity premium.

Borrowers are assumed to be willing to pay the liquidity premium and the resulting higher interest rates on longer-term fixed coupon rate bonds because they prefer to lock in a known interest cost for their borrowing period rather than take a chance that interest rates may rise during this period.

As a result, the shape of the yield curve is a product of both expected interest rates and liquidity premiums and slopes more steeply upward (or less steeply downward) for a given set of expected future rates than it would under the unbiased-expectations theory. However, the shape primarily reflects expected future short-term rates so that expected higher future rates will result in an upward-sloping yield curve and expected lower future rates in a downward-sloping yield curve. But both yield curves will be higher than those predicted by the unbiased-expectations hypothesis by an amount equal to the liquidity premium. If tomorrow's interest rates are expected to be the same as today's, the liquidity-premium theory will predict an upward-sloping yield curve rather than a flat yield curve.

The differences between the yield curves predicted by the unbiased- and biased-expectations theories for expected increasing, decreasing, and constant future interest rates are shown in Figure 7–3. Conversely, for a given yield curve of any shape, from which forward rates are computed, the liquidity-premium theory will predict lower future rates than the unbiased-expectations theory by the amount of the liquidity premium. This is shown in Figure 7–4 for an upward-sloping yield curve.

Changes in interest rates in any maturity sector will cause investors to reshuffle their portfolios in order to obtain the highest expected returns. But in the liquidity-premium theory, unlike for the unbiased-expectations

FIGURE 7–3

YIELD CURVES PREDICTED BY THE UNBIASED-EXPECTATIONS AND LIQUIDITY-PREMIUM THEORIES FOR RISING (A), CONSTANT (B), AND FALLING (C) EXPECTED FUTURE INTEREST RATES

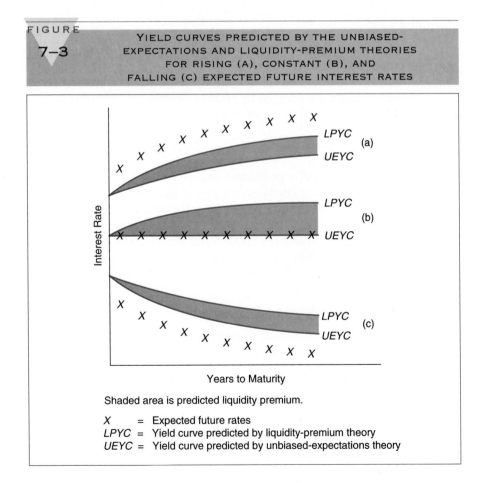

Shaded area is predicted liquidity premium.

X   = Expected future rates
LPYC = Yield curve predicted by liquidity-premium theory
UEYC = Yield curve predicted by unbiased-expectations theory

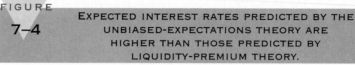

EXPECTED INTEREST RATES PREDICTED BY THE
UNBIASED-EXPECTATIONS THEORY ARE
HIGHER THAN THOSE PREDICTED BY
LIQUIDITY-PREMIUM THEORY.

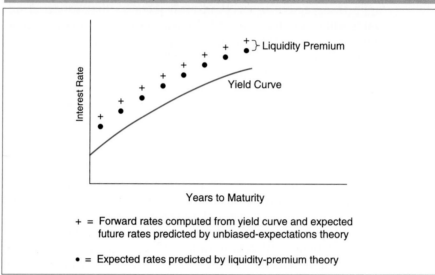

+ = Forward rates computed from yield curve and expected
future rates predicted by unbiased-expectations theory

• = Expected rates predicted by liquidity-premium theory

theory, all maturities are not viewed as perfect substitutes. Longer-term bonds are considered riskier by investors and require higher gross returns. To the investor, maturities matter but are not everything. Interest rates in any maturity are affected by rates in neighboring maturities and the liquidity premium for that premium:

$$i_j = f(i_{j \pm n}, L_j)$$

Unless the liquidity premiums change in value, changes in the yield curve would still reflect changes in investor expectations of future interest rates as market participants restructure the maturities in their portfolios to obtain the highest expected returns. What happens in one maturity sector affects all other maturity sectors, but less so than in the unbiased-expectations theory. Empirical evidence appears to support the existence of liquidity premiums, albeit small.

Market-Segmentation Theory

The ***market-segmentation theory*** postulates that the shape of and changes in the yield curve are determined not by borrower and lender expectations of future interest rates, but by current demand and supply behavior in each maturity sector. That is

$$i_j = f(D/S)_j$$

where: j = maturity sector
  D = demand for funds of maturity j
  S = supply of funds of maturity j

The computed value of the implicit forward rate has no meaning other than that whoever made the calculations is showing off his or her mathematical skills! If the demand for short-term funds were greater relative to the supply of these funds than the demand for long-term funds were to their supply, short-term interest rates would be higher than long-term rates and the yield curve would slope downward. If the demand for short-term funds fell sharply while the demand for longer-term funds and the supply of all funds remained unchanged, short-term rates would decline and the yield curve would slope upward. In functional form, the shape of the yield curve predicted by the market segmentation theory may be written as

$$(D/S)_{s\text{-}t}:(D/S)_{l\text{-}t}$$

where $s\text{-}t$ is short-term funds and $l\text{-}t$ is long-term funds.

The market-segmentation theory assumes that most borrowers and lenders have preferred maturity sectors determined by their borrowing and lending needs and will match the maturities (durations) of the securities they buy or sell to their needs. Borrowers who need funds to finance inventories will borrow only short term; those who need funds to finance new plants will borrow long term. Likewise, lenders who do not need their funds for some years will lend long term; those who have scheduled money outflows in the near future only will lend short term. In contrast to the expectations theories, in which all maturity sectors of the market are highly interrelated, the market-segmentation theory postulates that there is little if any connection among the different sectors. To both SSUs and DSUs, maturities are about all that matter. What happens in one sector will have only minor if any influence on the others. Market participants will only rarely leave their preferred sectors and therefore

$$i_j \neq f(i_{j \pm n})$$

Changes in the shape of the yield curve arise not from changes in expected future interest rates but from current changes in demand and supply of funds of different maturities. Thus, the market-segmentation theory requires a knowledge of who the players are in every maturity sector and what they are doing.

It is readily apparent that the market-segmentation theory of the term structure of interest rates is related to the loanable-funds theory of the level of interest rates discussed in Chapter 6. The demand for and supply of funds in major maturity sectors is important in both theories. However, similar to the loanable-funds theory, market-segmentation theory becomes progressively less useful as deregulation permits financial institutions to participate in broader ranges of activities. The basic components of the three theories of the yield curve are summarized in Table 7–2.

Yield Curve over the Business Cycle

As noted in Chapter 6, interest rates vary directly with the business cycle, rising in periods of economic expansion and declining in periods of economic contraction. Figure 6–6 showed that short-term rates tend to fluctuate more over the cycle than long-term rates. Short-term rates rise above

TABLE

7–2   SUMMARY OF THREE THEORIES OF YIELD CURVE

| | Expectations Theories | | Market-Segmentation Theory |
	Unbiased	Liquidity-Premium	
Shape of yield curve Relationship of securities	$_{t+n}f_1 = _{t+n}\rho_1$ All maturities are perfect substitutes for each other; maturity does not matter $i_j = f(i_{j\pm n})$	$_{t+n}f_1 = _{t+n}\rho_1 + _{t+n}L_1$ All maturities are imperfect substitutes; longer-term securities have greater interest rate risk $i_j = f(i_{j\pm n},\ L_j)$	$(S/D)_j\text{: }(S/D)_{j\pm n}$ Securities of different maturities are not interchangeable $i_j \neq f(i_{j\pm n})$
Change in shape of yield curve	$\Delta_{t+n}f_1 = \Delta_{t+n}\rho_1$	$\Delta_{t+n}f_1 = \Delta_{t+n}\rho_1 + \Delta_{t+n}L_t$	$\Delta(S/D)_j\text{: }\Delta(S/D)_{j\pm n}$

t = moment in time
n = number of periods
j = maturity

long-term rates at expansion peaks and drop below at recession troughs. The yield curve may be viewed as a cross-sectional slice of the time path of interest rates on bonds of different terms to maturity at a given moment in time. Thus, near expansion peaks, when short-term rates are above long-term rates, the yield curve is downward-sloping; near recession troughs, when short-term rates are below long-term rates, upward-sloping; and near mid-expansions and mid-contractions, flat. These patterns are shown in Figure 7–5. The solid line in the top panel traces the short-term rate and the dashed line the long-term rate.

Unfortunately, at least for being able to differentiate between the two theories easily, both the expectations and the market-segmentation theories can explain the cyclical movements observed in the yield curve. The expectations theory argues that, near expansion peaks, both borrowers and lenders expect interest rates to decline in the future as rates of income growth and inflation are expected to slow. Thus, current long-term rates, which are averages of the current and expected future short-term rates, will be lower than current short-term rates and the yield curve will slope downward. Near recession troughs, interest rates are widely expected to rise and current long-term rates will be above current short-term rates.

Alternatively, the market-segmentation theory argues that in periods of expansion, business firms wish to increase their inventories as sales increase and the demand for inventory financing, which is short-term, rises sharply. At the same time, many short-term lenders find internal uses for their funds and the Fed cuts back on new money through the banks. As a result, short-term rates rise sharply relative to rates for longer funds, the demand and supply for which are based on longer-term considerations and are less cyclically volatile. The yield curve slopes downward. In recessions, inventory demands are low, short-term funds for external use are plentiful, and the Fed steps up the provision of new money. Short-term rates fall sharply relative to longer-term rates and the yield curve turns upward.

FIGURE

7–5

129

▼

THE STRUCTURE OF
INTEREST RATES I

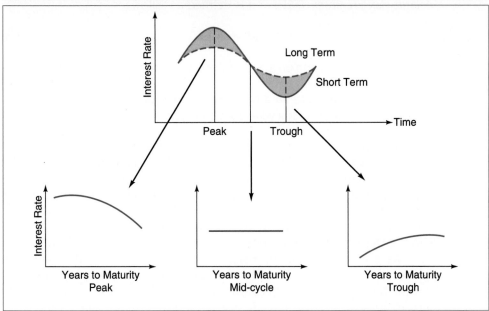

INTEREST RATE AND YIELD CURVE PATTERNS
OVER THE BUSINESS CYCLE

To the extent that one accepts either of the two versions of the expectations theory, the yield curve contains useful information about market expectations of future interest rates and therefore also of future business conditions. If the yield curve slopes downward, the market expects lower interest rates in the future. Recall that the liquidity-preference theory, developed in Chapter 6, relates the level of interest rates to income and price expectations directly. Thus, the lower future rates would most likely reflect expectations of deteriorating business conditions, slower inflation, or both. If the yield curve slopes upward, the market expects higher future rates. This probably reflects expectations of improving business conditions, accelerating prices, or both. Many business analysts make the yield curve a central part of their prediction-making tool kit.

Risk of Default

As we have seen, a bond is a promise by the borrower to pay the lender the full coupon amounts at the scheduled future time periods and to repay the principal amount (par value) at maturity. If the promise is not kept and the borrower cannot meet these payments in the amount and at the dates promised, the bond is in default. The investor receives less than promised. To compensate for potential losses from default, the investor will increase the interest rate charged. The greater the investor perceives the risk of default to be, the greater the increase in the rate demanded. The issuer is willing to pay the higher rate in order to attract investors. After all, investors can always buy bonds with lower risks of default, such as Treasury securities.

The difference between the interest rate on a bond subject to default risk and that on a bond equal in all respects but free of this risk—say, a bond issued or guaranteed by the U.S. Treasury—represents the market *default-risk premium* **(DRP)** and is defined as follows:

$$DRP = i_n^R - i_n \qquad (7-5)$$

where: $i_n^R =$ interest rate on a bond subject to default risk with n years to maturity

$i_n =$ interest rate on a bond free of the rate of default (U.S. Treasury security) with n years to maturity

Measured in this way, default-risk premiums reflect the market's consensus estimate of the expected losses on a default. It is the premium that would leave the marginal investor indifferent between otherwise comparable default-risk and default-free bonds, or the premium to entice investors away from default-free bonds to bonds subject to default risk. Of course, investors can be wrong, and realized losses from default can exceed or fall short of the expected losses impounded in the default-risk premium.

We can compute default-risk premiums established by the market for the securities shown in Table 7–1. Let us choose three-month prime commercial paper and long-term corporate Aaa bonds. Both securities are subject to losses from default. To use equation 7–5, we need to identify default-free securities that are comparable to these two in other characteristics. The best we can do is the three-month Treasury bill for the short-term security and the long-term Treasury bond for the long-term security. Both lie on the default-free yield curve. Substituting the relevant interest rates for January 1993 in the equation for DRP yields:

▼ Prime commercial paper: $3.25 - 3.00 = 0.25$
▼ Corporate Aaa bond: $7.91 - 7.17 = 0.74^2$

Thus in January 1993, the market perceived the corporate bonds to be riskier than shorter-term commercial paper. Note that one could not necessarily tell this from the yields on the two securities alone. For example, two years earlier, in January 1991, the yield on the corporate bond was higher than on the commercial paper, yet its default risk premium, computed as above, was smaller. Thus, it was viewed by the market as less credit risky. The relative levels of the interest rates on commercial paper and corporate bonds reflect the shape of the yield curve at the time, not the market's evaluation of possible losses from default. If the yield curve is upward-sloping, long-term bonds will always yield more than short-term bonds but will not necessarily have greater default risk. If the yield curve is downward-sloping, long-term bonds will always yield less than short-term bonds but may or may not have greater default risk.

Bonds with different maturities cannot be compared directly without first adjusting for yield differences attributable to the shape of the yield

---

[2] In actuality, some of the differences between the three-month commercial paper and Treasury bill yields reflect the fact that interest on Treasury bills is exempt from state and local income taxes and that bills are far more marketable in the secondary market. These factors are discussed in Chapter 8.

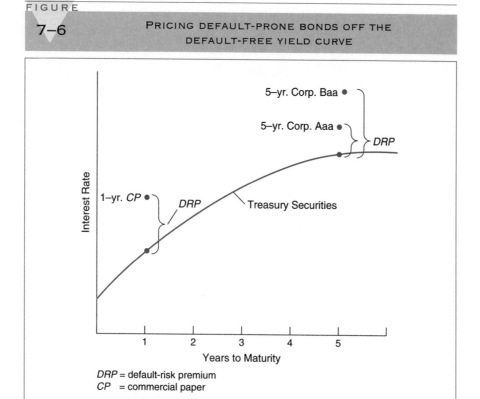

FIGURE
7–6

PRICING DEFAULT-PRONE BONDS OFF THE
DEFAULT-FREE YIELD CURVE

curve. This is shown in Figure 7–6. Default-risk premiums measure a bond's distance from the yield curve for default-free, say, Treasury securities, at the same maturity. Bonds with default risks are said to be priced "off the yield curve." The more the interest rate on a risky bond is above the yield curve for a comparable-maturity Treasury bond, the more does the market estimate its potential loss from default. Table 7–1 also shows that the municipal bonds have lower yields than the Treasury bond. However, this does not indicate that they are less risky. As we shall see in the next chapter, tax treatment of the two bonds is significantly different. These factors must be held constant.

To evaluate the size of a default-risk premium for a particular bond, investors must analyze the financial conditions and prospects of the borrower and the terms of the bond contract. The first set of factors is issuer-specific and reflects the probability of default; the second set is issue-specific and reflects the potential loss to the investor in case of default. All bonds are not treated equally when an issuer declares bankruptcy. Bonds that are specifically collateralized by particular assets of the issuer have priority in case of default over uncollateralized bonds or **debentures** of the same issuer and thus may incur smaller losses. Similarly, some bonds may be designated at issue as **senior** in case of default to other **junior** bonds.

For most smaller investors, the credit evaluation can be costly relative to the return on the investment. To broaden the market to such investors, a number of private firms evaluate the credit quality of bonds at the

Moody's	Standard & Poor's	Explanation
Aaa	AAA	Best quality
Aa	AA	High quality
A	A	Upper medium quality
Baa	BBB	Medium quality
Ba	BB	Speculative elements
B	B	Lack desirable characteristics
Caa[a]	CCC	Poor
Ca[a]	CC	Highly speculative
C[a]		Extremely poor
	D	In default

[a]May be in default.

Note: In addition, Moody's assigns numbers 1, 2, and 3, and S&P assigns plus (+) and minus (-) to each rating to indicate relative position within the rating.

SOURCE: Moody's Investors Service, Standard & Poor's Corporation. Reprinted by permission.

expense of the issuer and release their evaluations publicly in the form of ratings. The issuer expects to more than recoup the expense of the ratings by attracting additional investors and thereby lowering the interest cost. The two major bond-rating firms are Moody's and Standard & Poor's (S&P). The two firms' rating classifications are shown in Table 7–3. The ratings for commercial paper were shown in Table 4–2. Aaa is the highest Moody rating, and indicates the lowest probability of default and smallest resulting loss. Fewer and/or later letters of the alphabet indicate progressively lower credit quality and increasing risk. A listing of some of the factors analyzed by S&P in determining the credit quality of bonds issued by industrial firms is shown in Exhibit 7–1.

A bond's credit quality as reflected in its rating affects the interest rate required by investors. The lower the credit quality (rating), the higher the yield. As can be seen from Table 7–1, corporate Baa bonds yielded 76 basis points more than corporate bonds rated Aaa by Moody's, which in turn yielded 74 basis points more than default-free Treasury bonds. (A basis point is 1/100th of a percentage point so that 100 points are equivalent to 1 percentage point.) However, as the rating agencies live or die by their credibility in the marketplace, it is the underlying credit quality of a bond rather than the rating per se that determines the interest yield on the bond. Rating agencies effectively sell credibility. A rating agency that frequently misclassifies bonds is unlikely to be given much credibility by investors and is thus unlikely to continue to sell its services to issuers successfully.

Many issuers have more than one bond issue outstanding. Because of differences in their collateralization, different bond issues from the same DSU may represent different credit qualities and have different ratings. Issues rated Ba or lower are not considered to be investment grade and are frequently referred to as **high-yield** or **junk bonds.** Bonds are rated at their initial issue date and periodically through their life. Thus, bonds may change in rating through time. In 1992, for example, Standard & Poor's upgraded 260 corporate bond issues and downgraded 488. Many low-rated bonds were initially higher rated and reflect subsequent financial problems

EXHIBIT

133

▼

THE STRUCTURE OF
INTEREST RATES I

7–1

Methodology Used by Standard & Poor's to Rate Industrial Firms

I. Industry Risk:
    Defined as the strength of the industry within the economy and relative to economic trends. This also includes the ease or difficulty of entering this industry, the importance of any diversity of the earnings base and the role of regulation and legislation.
    A. Importance in the economic cycle.
    B. Business cyclicality: earnings volatility, lead-lag and duration, diversity of earnings base, predictability and stability of revenues and earnings.
    C. Economic forces impacts: high inflation, energy costs and availability, international competitive position, social-political forces.
    D. Demand factors: real growth projections relative to GNP and basis for projections, maturity of markets.
    E. Basic financial characteristics of the business: fixed or working capital intensive, importance of credit as a sales tool.
    F. Supply factors: raw materials, labor, over/underutilized plant capacity.
    G. Federal, state, foreign regulation.
    H. Potential legislation.
    I. Fragmented or concentrated business.
    J. Barriers to entry/ease of entry.

II. Issuer's Industry Position—Market Position:
    The company's sales position in its major fields and its historical protection of its position and projected ability for the future.
    A. Ability to generate sales.
    B. Dominant and stable market shares.
    C. Marketing/distributing requirements of business—strengths, weaknesses, national, international, regional.
    D. R&D—degree of importance—degree of obsolescence—short or long product life.
    E. Support/service organization.
    F. Dependence on major customers/diversity of major customers.
    G. Long-term sales contracts/visibility of revenues/backlogs/prepayments (e.g., subscriptions).
    H. Product diversity.

III. Issuer's Industry Position—Operating Efficiency:

This covers the issuer's historical operating margins and assesses its ability to maintain or improve them based upon pricing or cost advantages.
A. Ability to maintain or improve margins.
B. Pricing leadership.
C. Integration of manufacturing operations.
D. Plant and equipment: modern and efficient or old and obsolete. Low or high cost producer.
E. Supply of raw material.
F. Level of capital and employee productivity.
G. Labor: availability, cost, union relations.
H. Pollution control requirements and impact on operating costs.
I. Energy costs.

IV. Management Evaluation:
    A. The record of achievement in operations and financial results.
    B. Planning—extent, integration and relationship to accomplishments. Both strategic and financial. Plan for growth—both internal and external.
    C. Controls—management, financial, and internal auditing.
    D. Financing policies and practices.
    E. Commitment, consistency and credibility.
    F. Overall quality of management; line of succession—strength of middle management.
    G. Merger and acquisition considerations.
    H. Performance vs. peers.

V. Accounting Quality:
    Overall accounting evaluation of the methods employed and the extent to which they overstate or understate financial performance and position.
    A. Auditor's qualifications.
    B. LIFO vs. FIFO inventory method.
    C. Goodwill and intangible assets.
    D. Recording of revenues.
    E. Depreciation policies.
    F. Nonconsolidated subsidiaries.
    G. Method of accounting and funding for pension liabilities. Basic posture of the pension plan assumptions.
    H. Undervalued assets such as LIFO reserve.

VI. Earnings Protection:
    Key measurements indicating the basic

long-term earnings power of the company including:
A. Returns on capital.
B. Pretax coverage ratios.
C. Profit margins.
D. Earnings on asset/business segments.
E. Sources of future earnings growth.
F. Pension service coverage.
G. Ability to finance growth internally.
H. Inflation-adjusted earning capacity.

VII. Financial Leverage and Asset Protection:
Relative usage of debt, with due allowance for differences in debt usage appropriate to different types of businesses.
A. Long-term debt and total debt to capital.
B. Total liabilities to net tangible stockholders' equity.
C. Preferred stock/capitalization.
D. Leverage implicit in off-balance-sheet financing arrangements, production payments, operating rentals of property, plant and equipment, nonconsolidated subsidiaries, unfunded pension liabilities, etc.
E. Nature of assets.
F. Working capital management—accounts receivable, inventory, and accounts payable turnover.
G. Level, nature and value of intangible assets.
H. Off-balance-sheet assets such as undervalued natural resources or LIFO reserve.

VIII. Cash Flow Adequacy:
Relationship of cash flow to leverage and ability to internally meet all business cash needs.
A. Evaluation of size and scope of total capital requirements and capital spending flexibility.
B. Evaluation of variability of future cash flow.
C. Cash flow to fixed and working capital requirements.
D. Cash flow to debt.

E. Free cash flow to short-term debt and total debt.

IX. Financial Flexibility:
Evaluation of the company's financing needs, plans, and alternatives and its flexibility to accomplish its financing program under stress without damaging credit-worthiness.
A. Relative financing needs.
B. Projected financing plan.
C. Financing alternatives under stress—ability to attract capital.
D. Capital spending flexibility.
E. Asset redeployment potentials—nature of assets and undervalued liabilities.
F. Nature and level of off-balance-sheet assets or liabilities. This would include unfunded vested pension benefits and LIFO reserves.
G. High level of short-term debt/high level of floating rate debt.
H. Heavy or unwieldy debt service schedule (bullet maturities in future)—either of debt or sinking fund preferred stock.
I. Heavy percentage of preferred stock as a percentage of total capital.
J. Overall assessment of near-term sources of funds as compared to requirements for funds/internal financial self-sufficient/need for external financing.
K. Ownership/affiliation.

SOURCE: Standard & Poor's, *Credit Overview: Corporate and International Ratings* (New York, 1982), pp. 90–91. Reprinted by permission.

of their issuers. In the 1980s, however, original-issue junk bonds became popular and expanded rapidly in volume.

Not all bond issues are rated. Some smaller issuers do not consider the potential interest-cost savings large enough to justify the expense, and some issues are privately sold only to large institutional investors, who do their own independent credit analysis. Most investment and commercial bank underwriters also do independent credit evaluations both for customer reference and to compare with Moody's and S&P.

Individual investors can compare their own default-risk premiums on particular bonds with those existing in the market. If their own premiums are smaller than the market's, the bond should be a good buy, as part of the market's premium will become income rather than compensation—if the investors are right in retrospect. If the investors' own premiums are larger than the market's, the bonds should not be a good investment.

Default-risk premiums are not constant through time. Thus, investors do not always consider commercial paper and corporate bonds equally risky, as they did in our earlier example. In some periods, investors consider commercial paper relatively less risky than corporate Aaa bonds, and in other periods more risky. Overall, default-risk premiums tend to vary contracyclically, widening during recessions when business failures are high and expectations turn rosier. Figure 7–7 shows this behavior for corporate bonds. Periods of economic recession are shaded.

Bonds default when they miss a scheduled coupon or principal payment. If the probability of a default change during the life of a bond, both its risk premium and its price will change, but in opposite directions. Thus, if the likelihood of a default increases, the market price of a bond will decline and is likely to decline further if a default actually occurs. The prices of bonds that defaulted between 1971 and 1991 are shown in Table 7–4 by the original rating of the bonds. The average traded at $37.54 per $100 immediately after default. That is, it suffered a loss of more than 60 percent from its principal value. Bonds that were originally rated higher by rating

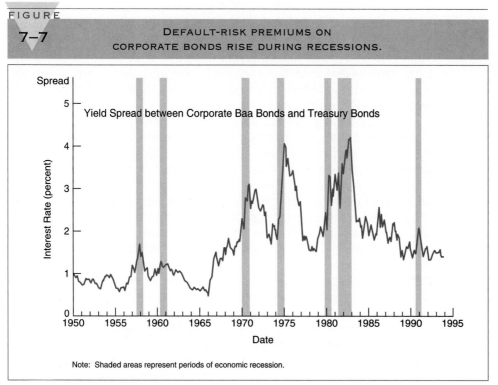

FIGURE

7–7

DEFAULT-RISK PREMIUMS ON
CORPORATE BONDS RISE DURING RECESSIONS.

Note: Shaded areas represent periods of economic recession.

SOURCE: Federal Reserve Bank of Chicago.

TABLE 7–4	AVERAGE MARKET PRICE OF BONDS THAT DEFAULTED BETWEEN 1971 AND 1991 BY ORIGINAL BOND RATING

Original Rating	Average Price After Default (per $100)
AAA	78.68
AA	69.24
A	47.24
BBB	38.54
BB	30.32
B	35.68
CCC	30.23
C	13.13
Average	37.54

SOURCE: Edward I. Altman, "Defaults and Returns on High Yield Bonds," *Extra Credit* (Merrill Lynch), July/August 1991, p. 26. Reprinted by permission.

agencies traded at higher average prices after default than on initially lower quality bonds, suggesting that investors expected to recover more on these bonds from the sale or merger of the company, liquidation of the firm's assets, or the issuance of new securities in a restructuring. Many higher rated bonds are collateralized by specific assets. Bonds in default still trade on markets until they are redeemed or declared worthless.

SUMMARY

Interest rates differ on different types of securities, according to the underlying characteristics of the securities. The most important differences among securities are term to maturity, risk of default, tax treatment, marketability, and special features such as options.

Two competing theories attempt to explain differences in rates attributable to differences in maturity. The expectations theory postulates that the relationship between rates and term to maturity, or the yield curve, is determined by decision units' expectations of future interest rates. Observed long-term rates are averages of observed short-term rates and unobserved expected short-term rates in the future. If interest rates are expected to increase, long-term rates will be higher than short-term rates, and the yield curve will slope upward. The market-segmentation theory postulates that the shape of the yield curve is determined by supply and demand conditions for funds in each of the differing maturity categories. Both theories explain why yield curves are upward-sloping in early periods of economic expansion and downward-sloping in the late periods of an expansion.

Securities that have a higher risk that the issuing DSU may default on the coupon or maturity payments require a higher interest rate to compensate the investing SSU for the potential loss. Default-risk, premiums reflect the average loss investors expect to suffer on the associated securities relative to otherwise comparable default-free securities.

1. Look through issues of *The Wall Street Journal*. How does the yield curve look today? How did it look exactly one year ago? Why do you think it changed as it did? What does today's yield curve suggest about what short-term rates will be like one year from now?

2. Why would the expectations theories of the yield curve be more useful to you than the market-segmentation theory if you were an economic forecaster? How would either theory help to explain the observed cyclical pattern in the yield curve?

3. Assume the interest-rate structure in years 1 and 2 shown in the table. Compute the one-year forward rate for Treasury bonds one year from now. How would (a) the unbiased-expectations theory; (b) the liquidity-premium theory; and (c) the market-segmentation theory each interpret this number?

4. Using the information in question 3, state what each of the three theories of the term structure says about the state of economic conditions in year 2 relative to year 1. Why do they say this? What is likely to happen to the term structure of rates in year 3 if the country enters a recession in that year?

5. Use the information in the table to discuss your agreement or disagreement with the following statements:
   a. The market views commercial paper as having greater default risk in year 2 than in year 1.

	Year 1	Year 2
	(percent)	
3-month Treasury bill	7.0	10.0
3-month commercial paper	8.0	10.5
1-year Treasury bond	7.5	9.5
2-year Treasury bond	8.0	9.0
5-year Treasury bond	8.1	8.8
20-year Treasury bond	8.3	8.6
20-year corporate bond		
Aaa	8.5	9.0
Baa	9.5	9.5
20-year municipal bond		
Aaa	6.0	6.5
Baa	7.0	8.5

   b. Long-term Treasury bonds had greater default risk in year 2 than in year 1 but less than Treasury bills in year 2.

6. What is a *junk bond*? Why do junk bonds usually have higher interest rates than other bonds? Why may some investors prefer not to buy these bonds? Would it matter if a junk bond were a senior, collateralized, or debenture bond? Why?

7. Why do Moody's, S&P, and other agencies rate bonds? Why risks do they evaluate and which do they not? Who is most likely to rely on these ratings? Why? How much influence do you think rating agencies have over interest rates on particular bonds? Why do some borrowers pay to have their bonds rated and others prefer not to get a rating?

Abken, Peter A., "Innovations in Modeling the Term Structure of Interest Rates," *Economic Review*, Federal Reserve Bank of Atlanta, July/August 1990, pp. 2–27.

Altman, Edward I., and Scott Nammacher, *Investing in Junk Bonds*. New York: John Wiley, 1987.

Cook, Timothy, and Thomas Hahn, "Interest Rate Expectations and the Slope of the Money Market Yield Curve," *Economic Review*, Federal Reserve Bank of Atlanta, September/October 1990, pp. 3–26.

Defaults and Distressed Securities: Evaluating Risks and Opportunities. New York: Merrill Lynch, January 1990.

Ederington, Louis E., Jess B. Yawitz, and Brian Roberts, "The Information Content of Bond Ratings," *Journal of Financial Research*, Fall 1987, pp. 211–26.

Fabozzi, Frank J., T. Dessa Fabozzi, and Irving M. Pollack, eds., *The Handbook of Fixed Income Securities*, 3rd ed. Homewood, Ill.: Business One Irwin, 1991.

Fisher, Lawrence, "Determinants of Risk Premiums on Corporate Bonds," *Journal of Political Economy*, June 1959, pp. 217–37.

Hickman, W. Braddock, *Corporate Bond Quality and Investor Experience*. New York: National Bureau of Economic Research, 1958.

Malkiel, Burton G., *The Term Structure of Interest Rates*. Princeton, N.J.: Princeton University Press, 1966.

Merrill Lynch & Co., *Extra Credit*, bimonthly.

Rosengren, Eric S., "The Case for Junk Bonds," *New England Economic Review*, Federal Reserve Bank of Boston, May/June 1990, pp. 40–49.

Sharpe, William F. and Gordon J. Alexander, *Investments*, 4th ed. Englewood Cliffs, N.J.: Prentice Hall, 1990.

Standard & Poor's, *Credit Overview: Corporate and International Ratings*, New York, 1982.

Standard & Poor's, *Corporate Finance Criteria*, New York, 1991.

Van Horne, James C., *Financial Market Rates and Flows*, 4th ed. Englewood Cliffs, N.J.: Prentice Hall, 1994.

The Structure of Interest Rates II

In this chapter, we consider the impact of differences in tax treatment, marketability, and inclusion of special features, such as options, on the interest rates and prices at which bonds trade. We then test to see how well these theoretical factors explain actual differences in interest rates on bonds and how this information may be used in constructing bond portfolio strategies to permit you to try to outperform other investors. Last, the chapter examines how well bond investors have performed in recent years.

Tax Treatment

Market participants are interested in after-tax income. Thus, they must adjust pretax interest rates to an after-tax basis. The greater the tax disadvantage, the greater is the pretax interest rate investors will demand. Not all interest income on a bond is taxed equally. The income tax rate applied to bonds depends on three factors:

1. The investor's taxable income,
2. The form of the income from the bond, and
3. The issuer of the bond.

An investor's taxable income is determined both by his or her legal status and by his or her income status. Some investors, such as pension funds, including individual IRA and Keough funds, are legally exempt from taxes. Taxes are paid by the recipient upon payout. Taxes paid by nontax-exempt investors depend on their tax bracket; generally the higher their income, the higher the applicable federal tax rate.

As discussed in Chapter 5, interest earned on bonds can be in two forms: (1) cash coupon payments and (2) amortization of any discount or premium between the purchase price and the sale or maturity value. The two components not only have different liquidity implications, but are frequently taxed at different rates. For tax purposes, discounts on bonds are of two types. **Original issue discounts (OID)** occur when issuers initially sell the bonds on the primary market at below their principal or par value. Annual gains from the amortization of OIDs, although not realized in cash, are taxed as ordinary income, similar to coupon income. **Market discounts** arise on the secondary markets when interest rates increase above the rate at time of issue and drive the price of a bond below its par or, if an OID bond, below its amortized value. Gains from the amortization of market discounts are taxed as capital gains.

In the United States, income from capital gains is generally taxed at a lower rate than is ordinary income for higher-income investors. Thus, on bonds issued by private issuers, many investors will value a pretax dollar of capital gains more highly than a pretax dollar of ordinary income (coupon or OID) and will accept a lower pretax return to achieve the same after-tax return. In addition, as noted earlier, income from the amortization of OID is taxed in the year it accrues, regardless of whether a cash payment is received, while income from the appreciation of market discounts is taxed only at the time of sale or maturity. However, this is not true for bonds issued by public issuers. Many taxing units in the United States do not tax investors' income from coupon payments or amortization of original issue discounts on bonds issued by other government units. Thus, the federal government does not tax coupon payments or annual amortization of OIDs on state and local (municipal) bonds, and state and local governments do not tax coupon payments or amortization of OIDs on federal government bonds. (Some municipal bonds issued for private purposes are taxed by the federal government. These are referred to as **taxable municipal bonds.**) In addition, many state and local governments do not tax coupon or OID income from bonds issued by themselves or their political subdivisions. However, all governments tax the amortization of market discounts. Thus on tax-exempt municipal bonds, markets discounts carry a tax disadvantage.

The value of these tax factors to the investor depends on the investor's marginal income tax rate. The higher the marginal tax rate, the more beneficial are bonds whose returns are subject to lower or zero tax rates. For example, an 8 percent tax-free coupon rate on, say, a municipal bond is equivalent to (1) a 9¼ percent fully taxable coupon on a par bond for a person in the 14 percent marginal tax rate; (2) an 11⅛ percent taxable coupon on a par bond for someone in the 28 percent marginal tax rate; and (3) a 13⅓ percent taxable coupon at the 40 percent marginal rate. Thus, bonds that are issued by state and local governments yield lower pretax market interest rates than comparable bonds issued by the U.S. Treasury or private firms. This explains why the long-term municipal Aaa bonds traded at a lower taxable interest rate than the corporate Aaa bonds in Table 7–1. The investor should expect similar after-tax yields on both these bonds. It also explains why the municipal bond with default risk traded at a lower interest rate than the default-free Treasury bond. But, as with all general rules, beware of occasional exceptions. In general, pretax yields are not very good guides to after-tax yields.

Marketability

Investors may wish to sell bonds they own before their maturity dates. This involves searching for the highest bidder on the secondary market. But not all bonds can be sold to the highest potential bidder with equal ease, speed, or cost. As noted in Chapter 4, the ability to sell a particular bond depends on the reputation of the issuer, the dollar amount of the particular issue outstanding, the trading volume of the issue on the secondary market, and any unique or complex features of the issue. The higher the reputation of the issuer, the larger the dollar volume of the issue outstanding, the larger its trading volume, and the fewer its unique features, the lower are transactions costs and the more liquid are the bonds. (See Figure 3–3).

Active markets exist for only a small number of bonds, generally those issued by large, well-known borrowers in standard denominations, standard contract form, and large overall amounts. Thus, bonds issued by the U.S. Treasury are more marketable than those issued by General Motors, which, in turn, are more marketable than those issued by a smaller, regional corporation, and so on. Probably the least marketable bonds are those issued by you and, certainly, me. The more marketable a bond, the more liquid it is. Because all of us at some time might have to sell any bonds we hold before maturity, we value marketability, and the more difficult, time-consuming, and costly a bond is to market, the higher the yield we demand in compensation. The difference between the rate on a less marketable bond and a bond similar in all respects but more marketable is referred to as the **marketability yield premium (MYP)** and may be defined as follows:

$$MYP = i_n^{lm} - i_n^{mm} \tag{8–1}$$

where: i_n^{lm} = interest rate on a less marketable bond
i_n^{mm} = interest rate on a more marketable bond

The most liquid and marketable securities in U.S. financial markets are Treasury bills followed by other short-term high-credit-quality private securities, longer-term Treasury bonds, equities, corporate bonds, and so on down to junk bonds. The last carry large marketability yield premiums in addition to large default-risk premiums, as many investors painfully discovered in the late 1980s, when many holders of junk bonds wanted to sell at the same time. Similar to the other bond premiums, the marketability premium changes over time.

Special Features—Options and Covenants

The most common special features added to plain vanilla bond contracts are options that permit the lender or borrower to change the nature of the bonds in specified ways at specified times before maturity. Each embedded option will be priced by investors and issuers and thereby will affect the interest rate on the bond to which they are attached, according to the advantage or disadvantage it produces for them. Frequently used options embedded in bonds are call, put, and convertible options. (Options that are traded separately are discussed in Chapter 22.)

A **call option** permits the issuer to call (buy back or prepay) the bond before maturity at no more than a predetermined price, referred to as the **call price.** (Remember that a borrower can always buy back the bonds at the going market price.) Thus, its maturity is uncertain. The issuer is likely to exercise a call option when interest rates have decline significantly below the coupon rates on the bonds so that they could be refinanced at lower interest costs, or when the receipt of revenues is greater than expected so that the bonds can be retired early. Thus, as interest rates decline, the price of an immediately callable bond will not rise above the call exercise price, which is generally at or above the bond's par value. The approximate relationship between the price of a callable bond and interest rates is shown by the blue line in panel b of Figure 8–1. The call price is designated as *CP*.

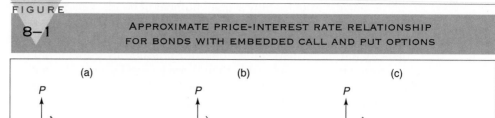

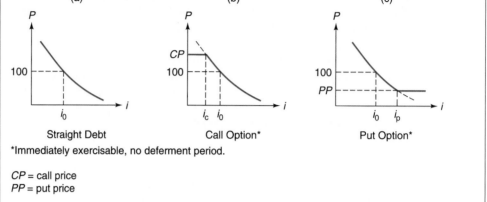

Straight Debt   Call Option*   Put Option*

*Immediately exercisable, no deferment period.

CP = call price
PP = put price

Without the call option, the price of the bond would have followed the dotted line when interest rates declined below i_c, the rate consistent with the call price—similar to the price behavior of the straight debt issue plotted in panel a. Some callable bonds have initial *deferment periods* during which the bonds may not be called. During the deferment period, the price of a callable bond can rise above its call price.

The investor, of course, will receive a lower interest rate on reinvestment in other bonds if the bonds are called away when rates are low and will charge a higher rate on callable bonds as self-protection. The call is an advantage to the issuer of the bond, and the issuer would be willing to pay the higher interest on a bond with a call provision than on a bond that does not give this option. The difference in interest rates between callable and comparable noncallable bonds is known as the **call yield premium.** It reflects the expected loss to investors (gain to borrowers) if the bonds are called. The yield on a callable bond after the call yield premium is deducted is referred to as the **option-adjusted yield.** Similar to any option, a call option need not be exercised. The sharp increases in the dollar volume of bonds that were called and refunded at lower interest rates both in 1985–1986 and again in 1992–93 when interest rates fell sharply and declined below the levels at which these bonds were issued in earlier years in higher interest rate environments are shown in Figure 8–2. Obviously, few bonds will be called when interest rates are high. If a callable bond is not called—the option is not exercised by the issuer—the investor keeps the call yield premium.

A **put option** permits the investor to sell the bond back (put the bond) to the issuer before maturity at a predetermined price, called the **put price.** Investors are likely to use this option when interest rates rise and the market price of the bond declines. A put places a floor on the price of a bond at the put exercise price, which is generally at or below par value. The approximate relationship between the price of a putable bond and interest rates is shown by the blue line in panel c of Figure 8–1. The put price is designated as *PP*.

FIGURE

8–2

VOLUME OF CORPORATE BONDS CALLED
INCREASES SHARPLY WHEN INTEREST RATES DECLINE

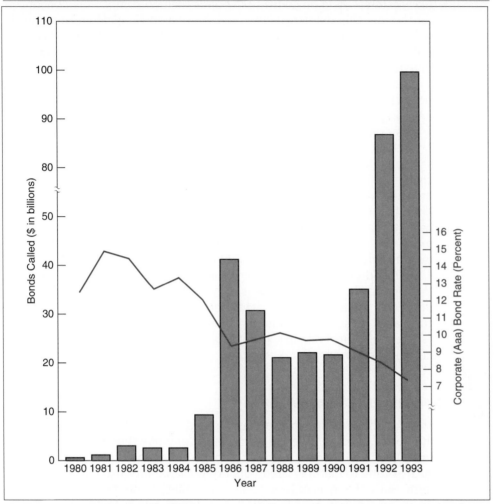

SOURCES: Henry Kaufman and Jeffrey Hanna, *Prospects for Financial Markets in 1987* (New York: Salomon Brothers, 1986), p. 8, updated by Salomon Brothers; *Economic Report of the President*, 1994, p. 352.

Because the put option is advantageous to the investor, the investor will require a lower yield on bonds with put privileges than on comparable bonds without such privileges. This difference is referred to as the **put yield premium** (really a discount). Callable bonds sell at higher yields and putable bonds at lower yields than comparable bonds without these options.

A **convertible option** permits the investor to convert the bond into another security at a predetermined price, such as a variable-coupon bond into a fixed-coupon bond or, more commonly, a bond of a private issuer into the issuer's stock. As a result, until conversion, the investor has a more valuable instrument. In the case of stock convertibility, if the issuer's earnings increase, the investor can share in them by converting the bond into stock. If the issuer's earnings decline, the investor is protected because the coupon payments are more likely to be continued than dividend payments. Thus, the price of the bond is unlikely to fall as much as that of the associated stock. The investor pays a price for these advantages in the form of a lower interest yield on convertible bonds than on comparable nonconvertible bonds. This difference is termed the **convertible yield premium** (again, really a discount). The price movements of stock-convertible bonds tend to follow those of the issuer's stock when earnings are rising sharply and those of regular bonds when earnings are in the doldrums.

Options are added to the basic bond contract to reduce the risk of potential losses to either the investor or the issuer. Options generally gain favor in periods of increased interest rate and economic uncertainty, such as has existed in the United States since the early 1970s. The proliferation of options in this period has transformed the old, straightforward, plain vanilla bonds into new, multiflavored, high-tech bonds. Because the analysis and pricing of options are highly complex, the relatively simple arithmetic required to analyze vanilla bonds is no longer sufficient. Analysis of the high-tech bonds requires commensurate space-age mathematics, such as a stochastic calculus, that is the province of Ph.D.s. Although this has made the job of bond analysts more difficult, it has also given them professional status equivalent to that of scientists, and even higher incomes.

In addition to options, bonds may include agreements, or **covenants,** that restrict the freedom of the issuer, particularly in the ability to increase dividends, issue additional debt, and make risky investments. Because covenants reduce the likelihood of default, they favor bond investors and reduce the interest rate investors require relative to comparable bonds with no or looser covenants.

 ## Interrelationships among Rates

This and the previous chapter have argued that the differences we observe in interest rates on different securities at any one time may be attributed primarily to differences in the characteristics of the underlying securities, such as term to maturity, credit quality, marketability, tax treatment, and so forth. But a theory is only as good as its ability to predict. What is the evidence? If the argument is correct, we should expect to see more similar interest rate changes on securities with similar characteristics than on securities with different characteristics. This may be tested empirically by correlating monthly interest rate changes on any one security, say, three-month Treasury bills, with interest rate changes on other securities for the same month. The results are shown in Table 8–1 for the period 1955 to 1992. Perfect correlation or lock-step behavior between interest rates is indicated by 1; no correlation is indicated by 0; and perfect inverse correlation by -1.

It is evident from Table 8–1 that the degree of correlation of changes in three-month Treasury bill rates with changes in rates of other securities varies greatly, but is greater for securities with shorter maturities, higher credit qualities, and no special tax treatment than for securities with longer maturities and lower credit qualities. For example, the coefficient of correlation between changes in interest rates on three-month Treasury bills and changes in rates on 12-month Treasury bills is 0.91, falls off to 0.61 as the maturity of the Treasury security is lengthened to long term, further to 0.56 as the credit quality of the security is reduced from default-free to corpo-

TABLE 8–1	SIMPLE CORRELATION COEFFICIENTS OF MONTHLY CHANGES IN MARKET YIELDS ON THREE-MONTH TREASURY BILLS COMPARED WITH OTHER SECURITIES, 1955–1992		
	Correlation Coefficient with Change in Yield on Other Security[a]		
Other Security	Same Month	One Month Later	Two Months Later
Commercial paper, 3 months	0.90	0.27	−0.13
Treasury bills, 6 months	0.96	0.35	−0.10
Treasury bills, 12 months	0.91	0.37	−0.09
Treasury bonds, 5 years	0.73	0.37	−0.08
Treasury bonds, long term	0.61	0.34	−0.08
Corporate bonds, Aaa	0.63	0.30	−0.12
Corporate bonds, Baa	0.56	0.18	−0.14
Municipal bonds, Aaa	0.50	0.15	−0.12
Municipal bonds, Baa	0.53	0.16	−0.20
Common stock, dividend yield	0.18	−0.13	−0.26

[a]Perfect correlation between interest rates would be represented by 1.00. A zero would indicate no correlation.

rate Baa bonds, and still further to 0.50 for municipal bonds, whose tax status differs. That is, as expected, the closer the similarities or *linkages* among the bonds, the more do the interest rates on these bonds move together. This suggests that all securities are to some extent substitutes for each other and that SSUs and DSUs will swap among them as interest rate differentials become large enough to compensate for the differential costs of the different characteristics. No bond or interest rate sector appears to be an island unto itself. Knowledge of the characteristics of a security is helpful in understanding the movements in its interest rate relative to rates on other securities, and thus in evaluating the price that should be paid for the particular security.

Moreover, to the extent that changes in Treasury bill rates affect other interest rates, they do so quickly. This may be seen from comparing the coefficients of correlation between changes in interest rates in the same month (the first column of Table 8–1) with the correlations between changes in the Treasury bill rates and changes in the other rates one month later (the second column) and two months later (the third column). The latter correlations are substantially lower, indicating that, to the extent interest rate shocks in one sector effect rates in other sectors, most of the transmission occurs in the same month.

Winning with Bonds

Until the 1970s, the bond market was viewed as unexciting. Indeed, because prices did not change greatly, so that most of the return on bonds came from fixed-rate coupons, bonds were frequently called **fixed-income securities,** and they appealed primarily to orphans, little old people in tennis shoes, and professors. But no more. The increase in interest rate volatility has caused violent swings in bond prices and has transformed the quiet bond market into a risky, noisy market not greatly different from the stock

FIGURE

8–3

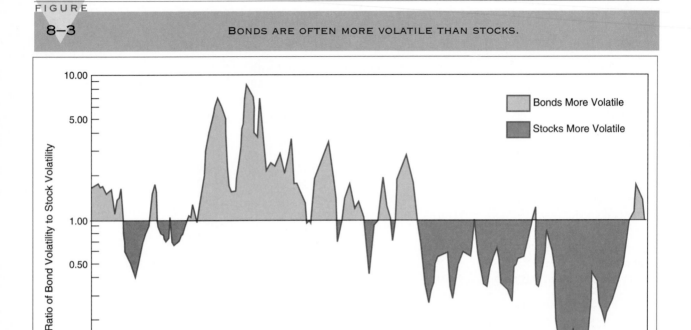

BONDS ARE OFTEN MORE VOLATILE THAN STOCKS.

Note: Bond volatility index based on deviations from a moving average of yields of new issue AAA–equivalent, corporate bonds, and stock volatility index based on deviations from a moving average of daily changes in rate of return (the change in dividend yield and expected earnings per share) of the S&P 500–stock index.

SOURCE: Allen Sinai, Lehman Brothers, Inc. Reprinted by permission.

market. It has become "macho." Indeed, as can be seen from Figure 8–3, expected returns on bonds have been more volatile than on stocks in many years. Moreover, realized returns frequently differ from promised yields to maturity at the time the bonds were purchased. In no way do bonds still yield fixed income, and in many years they do not even yield income! (Realized returns on the bond market are shown in Table 8–2 and analyzed in the next section.) One can now get very rich or very poor on the bond market. To attempt to get rich, the better of the two alternatives, requires the application of some investment strategy. A number of bond strategies have been developed. These are shown in the form of a decision tree diagram in Figure 8–4.

The first strategy decision is whether (1) to choose bonds randomly and hope to be lucky; or (2) to use the information about the basic relationships among bonds developed in this chapter in a systematic strategy. If you choose the latter, you have two further strategy decisions. You can choose (1) to achieve, on average, today's promised yield (yield to maturity) adjusted for yield premiums on bonds with the default risk, marketability, tax, and other characteristics that you wish; or (2) to try to outperform

TABLE

8–2

AVERAGE ANNUAL RETURNS REALIZED ON DIFFERENT
SECURITIES FROM 1946 TO 1992 (PERCENT)

| | 1946–92 | | | 1946–69 | 1970–79 | 1980–89 | 1990–92 |
	Highest	Lowest	Average	Average	Average	Average	Average
Treasury bills	14.7	.4	4.8	2.5	6.3	8.9	5.6
Long-term Treasury bonds	40.4	−9.2	4.9	0.9	5.5	12.6	11.0
Long-term corporate bonds	43.8	−8.1	5.5	1.4	6.2	13.0	11.9
Common stock	52.6	−26.5	11.7	12.0	5.9	17.5	10.8
Consumer prices	13.3	−1.8	4.5	3.1	7.4	5.1	4.0

SOURCES: © *Stocks, Bonds, Bills, and Inflation 1993 Yearbook*™, Ibbotson Associates, Chicago (annually updates work by Roger G. Ibbotson and Rex A. Sinquefield).
© *EnCorr Software*™ Ibbotson Associates, Chicago. Used with permission. All rights reserved.

the market to realize a higher return. The first strategy is referred to as a
passive strategy and the second as an ***active strategy.***

Passive strategies basically involve purchasing bonds with maturities
(or, more accurately, average lives or ***durations***) equal to your planned
investment period. On the average, you should come close to realizing a
return equal to that promised to you at the time you purchased the bonds,

FIGURE

8–4

BOND INVESTMENT STRATEGY DECISIONS

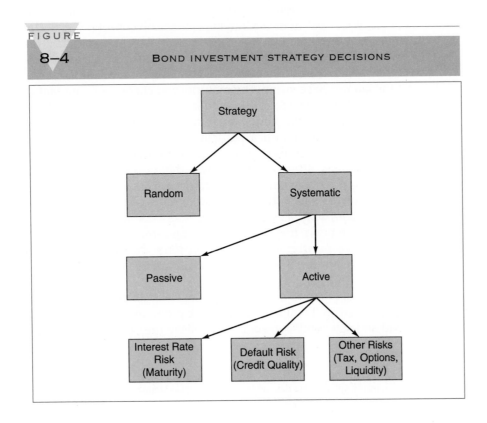

less any default risk and other premiums built into this yield.[1] (Recall that the yield to maturity on any bond at any time incorporates the market's consensus on the value of any default risk, tax feature, marketability, and embedded options. These may be viewed as the best "guestimates" of the actual values.) This strategy implicitly implies that your default-risk premium is equal to the market's, your marketability premium is equal to the market's, and so forth.

Active strategies involve betting against the *ceteris paribus* spreads that currently exist in the market between bonds of different maturities, or different risks of default, or different marketability, and so on. Investors are willing to assume interest rate risk, credit risk, or other risks in pursuit of higher returns. Investors will *swap* among bonds, selling bonds they believe to be overpriced (yielding too little) and buying bonds they believe to be underpriced (yielding too much). You may believe the current market spreads among bonds are incorrect because of differences in

1. Interest rate forecasts,
2. Risk of default evaluations, or
3. Marketability, tax, or option feature evaluations.

For example, if you predict that interest rates are going to rise more (or fall less) than is implied by the expectations theory's interpretation of the current yield curve (which incorporates the market's best guess), the maturity of the bond you buy matters importantly. You would purchase short-term bonds. If you are right, you would avoid large capital losses (the longer the maturity or duration of the bond, the greater its price change for a given change in interest rates) and would be able to reinvest the proceeds of the maturing short-term bonds in other bonds at higher yields. Of course, if interest rates decline more than the consensus expectation, you will do poorly and realize less than the initial yield to maturity. Conversely, if you expected rates to be lower than the market does, as reflected in the current yield curve, you would purchase long-term bonds to take advantage of the greater price swing. The maturity you choose, or your **maturity strategy,** reflects the degree of interest rate risk that you are willing to assume.

But "short term" and "long term" are relative. The degree of interest rate risk associated with a particular security is dependent on both the duration of the security and the time horizon of the investor. If the two are equal, there is little risk; if the two differ, interest rate risk exists and increases with the length of the difference. Thus, a security with a duration of, say, five years has little interest rate risk for an investor with a five-year time horizon, but has risk for other investors. It behaves like a five-year zero-coupon bond. It is viewed as a "long-term" bond for an investor with a shorter time horizon and as a "short-term" bond for an investor with a longer time horizon. (Duration strategies are discussed at greater length in Appendix 5A.)

If you evaluate a bond as having less default risk than the market assigns to it in its current default-risk premium, you would purchase this bond and sell bonds for which you believe the default risk is underestimat-

---

[1] As discussed in Appendix 5A, for default- and option-free bonds, investors immunize against interest rate risk and lock in the promised return by matching the duration of a security to the investor's planning period.

ed, and so on for other bond features. In all these cases, if you are right, you will do better than the market. If you are wrong—better luck next time! These strategies involve expectations of higher returns than can be obtained from passive policies, but also entail higher risk of failure. Note that in the bond market, you always know the views that are held by the average investor. Then you can bet with the market or against it. But beware! Many students of finance believe that financial markets are efficient in the sense that all the information publicly available is quickly impounded in current market prices and interest rates. Thus, to do better, you must either have access to private information that has not hit the market yet or disagree with the market's evaluations for some other reason. Thus, it may not be easy to "beat the market." Indeed, between 1982 and 1992, only 25 percent of all active bond managers were able to outperform the bond market as a whole.[2] In the same 10-year period, less than half of all bond funds beat the bond market as a whole in more than one-half the years.[3]

Realized Returns

We have seen that in the bond market, as elsewhere, promises are not always kept. So how do returns realized compare with those promised?

Table 8–2 shows annual realized rates of return for short-term Treasury bills, long-term Treasury bonds, and long-term high-grade corporate bonds in the post–World War II period. The table also reports the annual realized returns for the common stocks included in the S&P 500 average.

It is evident from examining the table that the returns vary from period to period. For the period overall, common stocks had by far the highest realized annual returns, but their margin over bonds has varied through time and has even been negative in some subperiods. Until the mid-1980s, long-term bonds had performed poorly through much of the period, as interest rates increased more than was generally expected. But the higher interest rates increased the returns realized on short-term bonds.

The table also shows the highest and lowest annual returns realized for each security. This range is sometimes used as an estimate of the risk of not realizing the promised or expected return when you sell the security. The range is generally greatest for common stock and narrowest for Treasury bills. The range has increased greatly for long-term bonds in recent years to almost the same magnitude as common stocks, but the average return has remained lower than on stocks.

Last, the table shows the average annual rates of change in the consumer price index. As discussed in Chapter 6, if the rate of change in prices is subtracted from the market return for the same period, the real rate of return may be approximated. The numbers in Table 8–2 suggest that, until the 1980s, the average before-taxes real rates of return realized on all debt securities were close to zero and were even negative in some years, particularly in the 1970s. Indeed, in the 1970s, even stocks recorded negative real

---

[2] Barbara D. Granito, "Bond Managers Beat the Pack by Finding Market Inefficiencies," *Wall Street Journal*, July 20, 1993, pp. C1, C9.

[3] 1992 *Consistency Study*, SEI Corporation (Chicago, Ill.: 1993.)

rates of return. This suggests that none of these investments were very good inflation hedges in all periods. As is discussed in Chapter 34 and shown in Figure 34–3, financial assets as a whole do better in outperforming the CPI in periods of low inflation, while nonfinancial assets do better in periods of high inflation.

These results are only suggestive and must be used with caution. Investors are assumed to want to hold the securities for the length of the periods shown. As we know, however, bonds promise that the principal will be repaid at maturity regardless of interest-rate changes. At any other time, the sales price is affected by a change in interest rates. Thus, the returns realized for periods shorter than the term to maturity, such as annually as in Table 8–2, may not reflect the return that would have been realized if longer-term bonds had been held to maturity. Moreover, the appropriate interest rate to associate with risk is the unobserved expected return, not the observed realized return. After all, expectations are not always realized!

SUMMARY

This chapter examined factors that explain differences in interest rates on different bonds, in addition to term to maturity and risk of default that were discussed in Chapter 7. The pretax interest rates on bonds subject to taxes are higher than the rates on comparable securities subject to lower or no tax rates, in order to yield an investor the same after-tax yield. Thus, tax-exempt municipal bonds trade at lower pretax yields than comparable-risk corporate bonds. Their after-tax yields will be the same, however, for the marginal investor. The more marketable a security is on the secondary market, the lower will be its interest rate.

Many bonds contain special features, such as *call options* that permit DSUs to buy back their bonds before maturity at no more than a fixed maximum price; *put options* that permit SSUs to sell their bonds before maturity at no less than a fixed minimum price; and *convertibility options* that permit SSUs to convert their bonds into another type of security, generally the stock of the corporate issuer. These options either raise or lower the interest rate on the associated bonds depending on whether they benefit the issuer or the investor.

Knowledge of these interrelationships among bond rates permits more knowledgeable investment and borrowing strategies. However, the promises contained in yields at the times bonds are purchased may not always be kept, so that realized returns frequently differ from expected returns. Investors may formulate strategies to try to outperform the market if they value these factors differently than the market does at the time they purchase their bonds. But the evidence suggests that few investors "beat the market" consistently.

QUESTIONS

1. Refer to the interest rate structure shown in Chapter 7, question 3. Discuss your agreement or disagreement with the following statements:

   a. The market viewed corporate Baa bonds as having equal default characteristics in both years.

   b. Municipal Aaa bonds had the least

risk of default of any security in both years.

2. If the tax exemption on municipal bond coupon interest were removed, what would be likely to happen to municipal bond yields relative to other yields? What changes might occur in the types of investors in municipal bonds? Why? Does the tax treatment of original issue discount and market discount matter greatly for municipal bonds?

3. Why do corporate bonds that trade at market discounts generally have lower market yields than comparable par and premium bonds? When would you and when would you not buy such discount bonds? Would it matter to you whether the discount on the bond was an original discount or a market discount? Why?

4. Assume that a par corporate Aaa bond yielded 8 percent and a par municipal Aaa bond 6 percent. Under what personal conditions would you purchase the corporate bond, purchase the municipal bond, or be indifferent between the two bonds? How may it be that the loss of revenue to the Treasury Department from not taxing the above municipal bond could be greater than the benefit to the municipality from the tax exemption?

5. Differentiate among a call, put, and convertibility option. For which options would the associated bond trade at lower interest rates? Why? When would these option yield premiums represent additional income to investors? Why would issuers be willing to pay them?

6. Empirical evidence suggests that Treasury bill rates do not change in lock-step fashion with rates on other securities. What are the characteristics of the securities whose rates move most like Treasury bill rates? What are the characteristics of the securities whose rates move least like Treasury bill rates? Do you think that the evidence supports or refutes the hypothesis that differences in interest rates among securities reflect systematic differences in their characteristics? Why? What is the evidence with respect to the transmission of interest rate changes across securities? What does this suggest?

7. Differentiate between active and passive bond portfolio strategies. Under what conditions would you choose one over the other? If you were reasonably certain that interest rates were going to decline, what kind of bond would you purchase? Would it matter to you if the market believed that rates were going to fall by more or by less?

REFERENCES

Brennan, Michael, "The Case for Convertibles," in *Issues in Corporate Finance*. New York: Stern Stewart Putnam & Macklis, 1983.

Chatfield, Robert E., and R. Charles Moyer, "Putting Away Bond Risk," *Financial Management*, Summer 1986, pp. 26–33.

Fabozzi, Frank J., T. Dessa Fabozzi, and Irving M. Pollack, eds., *The Handbook of Fixed Income Securities*, 3rd ed. Homewood, Ill.: Business One Irwin, 1991.

Fong, Gifford, "Portfolio Construction: Fixed Income," in John L. Maginn and Donald L. Tuttle, eds., *Managing Investment Portfolios*. Boston: Warren, Gorham and Lamont, 1983.

Fong, Gifford, and Frank J. Fabozzi, *Fixed Income Portfolio Management*. Homewood, Ill.: Dow Jones-Irwin, 1984.

Malitz, Ileen, "On Financial Contracting: The Determinants of Bond Covenants," *Financial Management*, Summer 1986, pp. 18–25.

Reiter, Sara Ann, "The Use of Bond Market Data in Accounting Research," *Journal of Accounting Literature*, Vol. 9, 1990, pp. 183–228.

Sharpe, William F. and Gordon J. Alexander, *Investments*, 4th ed. Englewood Cliffs, N.J.: Prentice Hall, 1990.

Siegel, Jeremy J., "The Equity Premium: Stock and Bond Returns Since 1802," *Financial Analysts Journal*, January/February 1992, pp. 28–38, 46.

Van Horne, James C., *Financial Market Rates and Flows*, 4th ed. Englewood Cliffs, N.J.: Prentice Hall, 1994.

Financial Intermediaries: An Overview

Financial institutions produce financial services by creating and/or trading financial securities on financial markets. As discussed in Chapter 3, the financial market may be divided into two submarkets: (1) the private (direct) financial market, on which ultimate SSUs purchase the primary (directly issued) securities of ultimate DSUs; and (2) the intermediation financial market, on which SSUs purchase secondary (indirect) securities issued by financial intermediaries, who, in turn, use the funds to purchase primary securities.

Financial institutions may be divided similarly, into (1) those that operate on the private financial market and help ultimate SSUs locate compatible ultimate DSUs, or conversely, help DSUs locate compatible SSUs; and (2) those that operate on the intermediation market, buying primary securities from DSUs (for example, making loans) and selling secondary securities to SSUs (for example, accepting deposits).

In the United States, these two functions have generally been performed by different financial institutions. However, an increasing number of institutions are beginning to operate on both the private and intermediation financial markets.

This chapter is the first of five that examine the underlying similarities and differences among major private financial institutions and describe the basic operation of each. Together, these institutions constitute the *financial services industry*. We shall consider first institutions operating primarily on the private financial market.

Institutions on the Private Financial Market

Investment Banks

Investment banks derive their name from their major traditional function: to locate and collect funds for clients so they can finance new investment projects. Investment banks generally do not finance the projects themselves. Unlike commercial banks, investment banks are not portfolio investors. Rather, they operate primarily on the private financial market as brokers and dealers and are sometimes referred to as **securities dealers** or **broker/dealers.** Some firms specialize in one or the other of these activities, but most engage in both. Investment banks serve as brokers for securities traded on organized exchanges, such as the New York Stock Exchange, and as dealers for securities traded over the counter. In over-the-counter trading, the firms themselves "make" the market by standing ready to buy or sell particular securities. They participate in almost all financial markets, including equity and debt markets, spot and futures markets, and primary and secondary markets.

On the primary market, an investment bank's major function is to **underwrite** new debt and equity securities issued by private or government DSUs who require funding for new capital expenditures. Investment banking firms generally purchase all the new securities issued by a DSU, either in a competitive (public) sale or through direct negotiation. Then they resell or **distribute** these securities in smaller units to individual and institutional investors in a **public offering.** Thus, they assume the risk of unfavorable price changes between the time they agree to buy the securities at a given price and the time they resell them. Alternatively, investment bankers may arrange for one or more large institutional investors to buy all the securities of an issuer in a **private placement.** For this service, their compensation is in the form of a commission.

The sale of new securities to raise new funds for a firm is termed a **primary offering.** At times, the amount of securities a DSU issues is too large for a single underwriting firm to handle by itself. When this occurs, the single firm will form a temporary partnership with other investment-banking firms. Such a temporary association is called a **syndicate.** For new issues of smaller, less well-known DSUs, underwriters frequently agree to purchase only as many new securities as they can successfully resell on a **best-effort basis,** or serve only as brokers and assist in the search for compatible SSUs. In the process of assisting their clients in raising new capital, investment bankers design the appropriate types of financial claims. In recent years, this has resulted in a virtual explosion of new and different financial instruments. These are discussed in Chapter 23.

Unlike institutions on the intermediation market, investment banks tend to raise funds for one specific DSU or one specific project per bond or stock sale. At times, larger investment banks may temporarily loan their own funds in a financing until more-permanent funding is found. Such operations are referred to as **merchant banking** and the short-term loans as **bridge loans.** To finance their short-term lending, merchant banks raise funds through the sale of commercial paper.

Although in their early years investment bankers operated principally on the primary market as underwriters, they expanded their activities on the secondary market as the financial markets developed. Today, most of their revenues are derived from trading on the secondary market as broker/dealers. As dealers, investment banks stand ready to create continuous markets for outstanding securities in which they specialize. As brokers, they provide continuous contact with the organized securities exchanges throughout the country for securities traded on these exchanges. Investment banks also assist in negotiating the trade of large blocks of outstanding securities among institutional investors and in redistributing such blocks more widely through a **secondary offering.** The largest volume of all security trading on the secondary market is on the over-the-counter market by dealers on a negotiated basis.

The relative importance of these different activities to investment banks may be seen from a breakdown of their revenues by source. This is done in Table 9–1. As can be seen from the table, the relative importance of the revenue sources has changed dramatically since 1973. In that year commissions from brokerage activities were by far the largest source of rev-

TABLE
9–1

REVENUE SOURCES OF INVESTMENT BANKS

	Percent of Total Revenues	
Activity	1973	1992
Commissions	56	18
Trading and investing	8	27
Underwriting	9	12
Margin lending	13	4
Commodities	4	2
Other	10	37
Total	100	100

SOURCE: Securities Industry Association, *Trends*, June 29, 1979, p. 3; and Securities Industry Association. Reprinted by permission.

enues, accounting for 56 percent of total revenues. In 1992, this source had declined to only 18 percent. This sharp falloff reflects the abandonment in 1975 of the "fixed-rate commission" system, under which all trades, regardless of dollar size, were charged the same percentage commission even though the larger the transaction, the relatively cheaper the costs of the trade. Because this both discriminated unfairly against some customers and dampened competition among firms, the Securities and Exchange Commission, the regulatory agency for investment banks, halted this practice. The combination of artificially high brokerage fees before 1975 and competition between security firms forced the firms to offer customers other services free. The reduction in fees led to a reduction in free services so that the reduction in brokerage revenues did not necessarily lead to a like reduction in net earnings from brokerage services. After the demise of fixed commissions, **discount brokers,** who offer low prices for trades but provide few additional services or advice, developed and grew rapidly.

In 1992, the largest single source of revenue was from dealer activities in the form of spreads between buying and selling prices and from gains in the market price of securities held in inventory as short-term investments. These accounted for 27 percent, more than three times the percentage in 1973, underwriting activities generated 12 percent, and revenues from margin loans to customers to finance their securities purchases accounted for 4 percent. The largest increase in revenues came from activities that were either new or relatively unimportant in the 1970s. These include fees for assistance in mergers and acquisitions (M&A), private placement of securities, investment advice, sales and management of mutual funds, and sales of real estate and other partnership arrangements. These activities now account for more than one-third of total revenues.

For the most part, investment bankers are not permanent investors. They need to finance only a small percentage of the securities they purchase, which are held in temporary inventory. Their profits are highly volatile, fluctuating with the volume of trade, the prices at which the securities are traded, and interest rates, which affect the market value of the securities they hold in inventory. All of these vary greatly from year to year. In 1992, all investment banks earned a pre-tax return of 23 percent on their equity capital. This compares with a record 49 percent in 1980, and a loss of 3 percent in 1973.

Investment banks come in all sizes and shapes. As of year-end 1992, more than 5,000 firms were members of the National Association of Securities Dealers (NASD), an association that promotes and self-regulates the securities business, and another 3,000 firms were smaller nonmembers. The very largest firms tend to operate in all securities sectors. Most firms, however, specialize in a limited number of sectors according to issuer (corporate, federal government, or municipal government), maturity (money or capital market), size of transactions (retail with individuals or wholesale with institutions), or geographic location of the issuer (state, local region, domestic, or foreign).

Wholesale firms generally not only direct their trading at institutional investors, such as banks, mutual funds, and pension funds, but tend to participate heavily in underwriting new securities and in advising large private and public entities. They tend to have few offices, located in major financial centers. Retail firms tend to focus on brokerage business and have many sales offices in their market areas. Smaller, specialized firms are referred to as *boutiques.*

Because of the diversity of their activities, it is difficult to rank investment banks categorically. Ranking by total revenues, for example, would favor retail-oriented firms over wholesale firms that emphasize, say, underwriting. Table 9–2 ranks the largest firms by the size of their capital at year-end 1992. Also shown are the number of their offices and employees and the dollar volume of securities underwritten. It is evident that there are wide differences in the importance of each firm in each category. The largest

TABLE

9–2   SELECTED CHARACTERISTICS OF LARGEST INVESTMENT BANKS, 1992

	Capital		Offices		Employees		Total Underwriting	
	$ Billions	Rank	Number	Rank	Number	Rank	$ Billions	Rank
Merrill Lynch	15.4	1	510	3	40,100	1	141	1
Goldman Sachs	9.0	2	28	41	7,389	9	104	2
Morgan Stanley	7.4	3	23	49	7,400	2	65	7
Shearson Lehman[a]	5.9	4	413	5	32,000	2	100	3
Salomon Brothers	4.9	5	18	53	6,823	10	75	6
Bear Stearns	2.6	6	13	65	6,037	11	53	8
Paine Webber	2.2	7	271	8	13,600	5	19	11
First Boston	1.4	8	9	70	3,725	16	81	4
Dean Witter Reynolds	1.3	9	339	6	15,500	4	b	b
Prudential Securities	1.3	10	297	7	16,339	3	29	9
Smith Barney[a]	1.2	11	106	11	7,487	7	8	15
E. D. Jones	0.2	38	2,185	1	5,800	12	b	b

SOURCES: Securities Industry Association, *Securities Industry Yearbook,* 1993–94; *Investment Dealer's Digest,* January 11, 1993. Reprinted by permission.
[a] Retail operations merged in 1993.
[b] Not ranked among top 15.

investment banking firm in 1992 was Merrill Lynch. It is a department-store-type full-service firm, engaging in a wide range of both wholesale and retail activities. Merrill Lynch ranked first in the dollar amount of capital, number of employees, and volume of security underwriting; and third in number of offices. Goldman Sachs was the largest wholesale house. It ranked second in capital and security underwriting, but only forty-first in number of offices, with 28. Almost all larger investment banking houses also have offices in major foreign countries.

On the other end of the spectrum are firms that primarily serve retail customers. By far the largest number of branch offices are operated by E. D. Jones (St. Louis), which has more than 2,000. This is four times the number operated by Merrill Lynch. Although the number is large, the size of its offices is small. With only 2,262 registered representatives, who are licensed to deal with the general public, for its 2,185 offices, the average number of salespersons per office is only one. E. D. Jones ranks twelfth in number of employees and only thirty-eighth in amount of capital. It participates in few underwritings.

An increasing number of investment banking firms have merged with other types of financial and nonfinancial firms in recent years. Prudential, the largest life insurance company in the country, merged with Bache Halsey Stuart Shields; American Express, which operates the American Express card and sells traveler's checks, merged first with Shearson Loeb Rhoades and then with Lehman Kuhn Loeb, a major wholesale firm and itself the result of a recent merger, and E. F. Hutton, before divesting itself of its brokerage business; Phibro, a large commodity dealer, purchased Salomon Brothers; Sears Roebuck, the nation's largest retailer, with a network of stores throughout the country, purchased Dean Witter Reynolds, which it later sold; General Electric purchased Kidder Peabody; and Primerica, a finance company, bought Smith Barney before buying the brokerage business of Shearson Lehman Brothers from American Express to form Smith Barney Shearson in 1993, the second largest retail-oriented firm.

Until recently, investment banking in the United States, in terms of both underwriting and market making was, in large part, legally restricted to firms that are not also commercial banks. This separation primarily began in 1933, when commercial banks were forced to discontinue or spin off their investment-banking activities for perceived reasons of safety as part of the Glass-Steagall Act of that year. Exemptions were granted to permit commercial banks to underwrite and trade in Treasury, federal agency, and municipal general obligation (GO) securities. In recent years, the Federal Reserve and the courts have reinterpreted the act and permitted larger commercial banks to expand their underwriting and securities activities. What securities activities may engage in, what they are doing, and the pros and cons of this issue are examined in Chapter 20.

Mortgage Banks

Mortgage bankers underwrite residential and commercial mortgages. They buy (*originate*) new mortgages from DSUs and sell (*distribute*) them to SSUs, primarily institutional investors such as thrift institutions and life insurance companies. Some mortgage bankers serve as mortgage origination agents or correspondents for large institutional investors. They provide these investors with a retail network. The mortgage banker may serve either as a broker and charge the SSU a commission, or as a dealer and hold the mortgages in inventory (*warehouse* them) for a brief period of time before selling them to an investor. Generally, the mortgage banker will continue to *service* the mortgage in terms of collecting the monthly payments and other administrative monitoring. By stripping the servicing from the financing, the mortgage becomes a more marketable instrument.

To further increase the marketability of the residential mortgages, mortgage bankers will at times pool individual odd-denomination mortgages into larger, standard-denomination pass-through securities or sell the mortgages to an agency, such as Fannie Mae or Freddie Mac, that will pool them. Although the pass-through security is a newly created instrument, it is not a liability of the mortgage banker but remains collateralized directly by the underlying individual mortgages. All monthly payments, prepayments of principal, and defaults are passed through to the investor. Thus, these securities are in effect primary securities.

Mortgage banks generate income from three major sources: (1) origination fees and commissions, (2) spreads from selling mortgages at higher prices than those at which they were originated, and (3) servicing the mortgages they originated. Because they do not own the mortgages that they originate for any significant length of time, mortgage banks, like investment banks, may be ranked by size according to the volume of their major activity—servicing mortgages.

In 1993, there were about 3,000 mortgage-banking firms. Many have offices in more than one state. Mortgage-banking activities are also conducted by many financial institutions, such as savings and loan associations and commercial banks, and many mortgage-banking firms are subsidiaries of commercial banks and other financial institutions.

Institutions on the Intermediation Financial Market: Overview

All institutions on the intermediation financial market are both similar and different. They are similar in that they all sell secondary securities to SSUs and use the proceeds to buy primary securities from DSUs. Thus, they are all primarily portfolio investors. They are different in the characteristics of the secondary securities they sell and the primary securities they buy.

The secondary securities may be divided into debt and equity. Debt securities may be further divided into unconditional and conditional contracts. **Unconditional debt** is paid in full according to the characteristics of the security, such as on maturity and coupon dates, for example, deposits. **Conditional debt** is paid according to the characteristics of the security and the nature of the future event triggering the payment, such as death, retirement, or being the victim of an accident, for example, insurance policies. Both types of debt may also be divided by risk and by whether the market value of the security is fixed or variable.

Likewise, primary securities may be divided according to debt or equity, term to maturity, and degree of risk. For any particular type of intermediary, the two sides of its balance sheet are related. Because the intermediary must honor its secondary securities as contracted, usually invests in primary securities that provide it with the best chances of doing so. Likewise, if it wishes to purchase particular types of primary securities, the institution generally sells secondary securities that are compatible with the risk characteristics of the particular primary securities.

Most intermediaries will engage in some but not all the types of intermediation discussed in Chapter 3. As a result, the secondary securities they offer will differ from each other. Because of externally imposed legal and regulatory constraints or self-imposed philosophical constraints, financial institutions in the United States have tended to specialize in particular segments of the market. In recent years, however, innovations in the marketplace and changes in laws aimed at deregulation have permitted institutions to invade each other's "turf" more easily, and the differences among institutions are becoming less significant. More and more financial services previously the domain of one of a limited number of institutions— for instance, checkable deposits and mortgage loans—are being offered by other types of institutions. As a result, the institutions are becoming less specialized and more alike. This has intensified competition both among the different types of institutions on the intermediation financial market— commercial banks versus savings and loan associations, insurance companies, and money-market funds—and between institutions on the intermediation market and those on the private financial market.

The major types of private financial institutions are shown in Table 9–3, along with the principal characteristics of their primary and secondary securities. These institutions will be examined individually in the next chapters. Here, we will present only an overview to place them in perspective. As can be readily observed from the table, most of the intermediaries deal in debt securities on both sides of their balance sheets, although most mutual funds deal in equity securities on both sides. Money-market mutual funds deal with debt on the asset side (primary securities) and equity (shares) on the liability side. On the whole, the secondary securities issued are tailored to have smaller denominations, shorter maturity periods, and less risk than the primary securities purchased. Financial intermediaries issuing debt secondary securities tend to be heavily leveraged, so that equity ownership represents only a small source of funds, generally less than 10 percent. (**Leverage** is defined as the ratio of borrowed, or another person's funds, to equity, or one's own funds). Most of the intermediaries' earnings from DSUs are "passed through" to SSUs.

The composition of the earning assets of major intermediaries is shown in Table 9–4. The degree of their specialization is now seen in more complete perspective. Table 9–5 shows the ranking, dollar size, growth rate, and market share of the institutions from 1950 through 1992. From Table 9–5, we see that they vary significantly in importance and rate of growth. Commercial banks, which are the least specialized, are by far the largest intermediary. However, their growth rate in this period has been somewhat below the average annual growth rate for all financial intermediaries. As a result, their market share dropped sharply from more than 50 percent of all assets of financial intermediary institutions in 1950 to less than 30 percent in 1992.

In contrast, private pension funds and mutual funds, other than money-market funds, have grown very rapidly and have enlarged their market shares from 2 to 18 percent and from 1 to 8 percent, respectively.

TABLE

9–3

CHARACTERISTICS OF MAJOR PRIVATE FINANCIAL INTERMEDIARIES

Intermediary	Assets (Primary Securities)		Liabilities (Secondary Securities)		
	Debt or Equity[a]	Major Security	Debt or Equity[a]	Variable Value	Major Security
Commercial bank	Debt	Business loan	Debt	Fixed	Transaction and time deposits
Savings and loan association	Debt	Residential mortgage loan	Debt	Fixed	Time deposit
Savings bank	Debt	Residential mortgage loan	Debt	Fixed	Time deposit
Credit Union	Debt	Consumer loan	Debt	Fixed	Time deposit
Life insurance company	Debt	Corporate bond	Debt	Both	Insurance policy
Casualty insurance company	Debt	Municipal bond	Debt	Fixed	Insurance policy
Private pension fund	Equity	Corporate stock	Debt	Both	Pension Plan
State and local government pension fund	Debt	Corporate stock	Debt	Both	Pension plan
Mutual funds	Equity	Corporate stock	Equity	Variable	Fund share
Money-market funds	Debt	Short-term liquid securities	Equity	Fixed	Fund share
Consumer finance company	Debt	Consumer loan	Debt	Variable	Bank loan
Business finance company	Debt	Business loan	Debt	Variable	Bond

[a]Characteristics shown are for majority of securities.

Money-market funds, which did not even exist in 1970, have also grown rapidly. Indeed, before slowing somewhat, at year-end 1982, after banks and thrifts were given the ability to compete for funds without Regulation Q deposit rate ceilings, money-market funds had become larger than long-established savings banks and casualty insurance companies. At year-end 1992, they were still larger than savings banks, whose market share has plummeted from 8 to only 2 percent. Savings and loan associations expanded very rapidly through the mid-1980s from 6 to 16 percent, only to drop back sharply to 6 percent as a result of the S&L crisis of the 1980s, which saw the number of institutions decline by over half. Life insurance

TABLE

9–4

COMPOSITION OF EARNINGS ASSETS OF MAJOR FINANCIAL INSTITUTIONS ON THE INTERMEDIARY FINANCIAL MARKET, 1992 (BILLIONS U.S.$)

	Total Financial Assets	U.S. Government Securities[a]	Municipal Securities	Foreign & Corporate Bonds	Business Loans[b]	Mortgages[c]	Consumer Loans[d]	Corporate Equity
Commercial banks	3,629	670	98	91	789	903	330	—
Private pension funds	2,347	305	4	227	93	30	—	1,052
Life insurance companies	1,625	293	12	648	32	250	71	125
Mutual funds	1,057	244	173	135	22	—	—	466
State and local government pension funds	988	275	1	183	31	20	—	464
Savings and loan associations	832	131	1	43	8	515	29	—
Finance companies	808	—	—	—	297	238	122	—
Casualty insurance companies	629	148	139	102	50	7	—	130
Money-market funds	548	134	95	—	176	—	—	—
Credit unions	266	45	—	—	—	53	93	—
Savings banks	245	45	1	11	7	138	5	—
Total intermediaries	12,974	2,290	524	1,440	1,505	2,154	650	2,237
Total outstanding	[e]	4,817	1,155	1,883	[e]	2,899	870	5,128

SOURCE: Board of Governors of the Federal Reserve, *Flows of Funds Accounts, Financial Assets, and Liabilities Quarterly Levels*, Fourth Quarter 1992, March 1993.

[a] Includes government-sponsored mortgage pools ($1,294).

[b] Includes open-market paper.

[c] Commercial and residential, excludes mortgage pools ($1,294).

[d] Includes policy loans, excludes asset-backed securitized loans except in total ($119).

[e] Unknown

companies have also lost market share from 22 to 13 percent, although their share appears to have stabilized since the 1980s as they introduced a number of new products to remain competitive.

These changes in market share reflect changes in the financial needs of the public, on the one hand, and differing abilities of intermediaries to provide for those needs, on the other. As noted earlier, all institutions are not permitted to offer all types of financial services. However, these figures do not take into account some activities in which institutions manage but do not own the assets so that they are not recorded on their balance sheets, such as commercial bank managed mutual funds and securities held in

TABLE

9–5

Intermediary	1992 Asset Rank	1992 ($Billions)	Annual Percent Growth (1950–1992)	Market Share (Percent of total assets, year-end)				
				1950	1960	1970	1980	1992
Commercial banks	1	3,629	7.7	52	38	38	36	28
Private pension funds	2	2,347	14.4	2	6	9	11	18
Life insurance companies	3	1,625	7.8	22	20	15	12	13
Mutual funds	4	1,057	14.4	1	3	4	2	8
State and local govern-ment pension funds	5	988	13.1	2	3	5	5	8
Savings and loan associations	6	832	9.5	6	12	14	16	6
Finance companies	7	808	10.9	3	5	5	5	6
Casualty insurance companies	8	629	9.7	4	5	4	5	5
Money-market funds	9	548	—	—	—	—	2	4
Credit unions	10	266	13.9	—	1	1	2	2
Savings banks	11	245	5.7	8	7	6	4	2
Total		12,974	9.3	100	100	100	100	100

SOURCES: Board of Governors of the Federal Reserve System, *Flow of Funds Accounts, Flows and Outstanding*, Fourth Quarter 1992, March 10, 1993; and Board of Governors of the Federal Reserve System, *Flow of Funds Accounts 1949–1978*, December 1979.

trust accounts. The relative growth rates of the institutions are also affect-ed by the interest rates that they pay on the secondary securities they issue and that they charge on the primary securities they purchase. SSUs will channel their funds to the institutions that pay the highest interest rate on the same security, and DSUs will borrow from institutions that charge the lowest rate for the type of security the DSU wishes to issue. Table 9–6 lists the 10 largest firms in each category of institution on the intermediation market.

TABLE

9–6

TEN LARGEST FIRMS IN EACH FINANCIAL INDUSTRY DECEMBER 31, 1992 (BILLIONS OF DOLLARS)

Commercial Bank Holding Companies (and Largest Owned Bank)

Commercial Bank Holding Companies (and Largest Owned Bank)		. Assets
1. Citicorp (New York)		214
Citibank (New York)	164	
2. BankAmerica Corp. (San Francisco)		181
Bank of America (San Francisco)	133	
3. Chemical Banking Corp. (New York)		140
Chemical Bank (New York)	109	
4. NationsBank Corp. (Charlotte, N.C.)		118
Nations Bank of Texas (Dallas)	35	
5. J. P. Morgan & Co. (New York)		103
Morgan Guaranty Trust (New York)	77	
6. Chase Manhattan Corp. (New York)		97
Chase Manhattan Bank (New York)	74	
7. Bankers Trust New York Corp. (New York)		72
Bankers Trust (New York)	56	
8. Banc One Corp. (Columbus, Oh.)		61
Bank One (Dallas)	16	
9. Wells Fargo & Co. (San Francisco)		53
Wells Fargo Bank (San Francisco)	51	
10. PNC Bank Corp. (Pittsburgh, PA)		51
Pittsburgh National Bank (Pittsburgh, PA)	22	

SOURCES: Veribanc, Inc. and *American Banker*, April 15, 1993, p. 6. Reprinted by permission.

Commercial Bank Trust Departments

		Assets	
	Discretionary	Nondiscretionary	Total
1. State Street (Boston)	113	1,165	1,278
2. Morgan Guaranty (New York)	38	694	733
3. Bank of New York	30	685	715
4. Citibank (New York)	23	399	422
5. Northern Trust (Chicago)	37	341	378
6. Mellon Bank (Pittsburgh)	37	324	361
7. Bankers Trust (New York)	129	222	351
8. Chase Manhattan (New York)	17	339	356
9. Boston Safe Deposit	19	217	236
10. Bank of America (San Francisco)	112	107	219

SOURCE: Federal Financial Institutions Examination Council, *Trust Assets of Financial Institutions–1992*, pp. 66–67.

Table 9–6 *cont.*

Savings and Loan Associations	Assets
1. Home Savings of America (Irwindale, Calif.)	48
2. Great Western Savings (Chatsworth, Calif.)	37
3. World Savings and Loan (Oakland, Calif.)	26
4. First Nationwide Bank (San Francisco)	19
5. Glendale Federal (Glendale, Calif.)	18
6. American Savings Bank (Irvine, Calif.)	17
7. California Federal Bank (Los Angeles)	17
8. Citibank (San Francisco)	11
9. Household Bank (Newport Beach, Calif.)	10
10. Standard Federal Bank (Troy, Mich.)	10

SOURCE: Veribanc, Inc. (reprinted by permission).

Savings Banks	Assets
1. Washington Mutual (Seattle)	9
2. Dime Savings Bank (New York)	9
3. Emigrant Savings Bank (New York)	7
4. CrossLand Federal (Brooklyn)	6
5. Green Point (Brooklyn)	6
6. Manhattan Savings Bank (New York)	6
7. Long Island Savings Bank (Melville, N.Y.)	6
8. Peoples Bank (Bridgeport, Conn.)	6
9. Hudson City Savings Bank (Paramus, N.J.)	4
10. Apple Bank for Savings (New York)	4

SOURCE: *American Banker*, May 14, 1993, p. 8 (reprinted by permission).

Credit Unions	Assets
1. Navy Federal (Merrifield, Va.)	7
2. State Employees (Raleigh, N.C.)	3
3. United Airlines (Chicago)	2
4. Boeing (Seattle)	2
5. Pentagon Federal (Alexandria, Va.)	2
6. American Airlines (Dallas)	1
7. Hughes Aircraft (Manhattan Beach, Calif.)	1
8. The Goldon 1 (Sacramento, Calif.)	1
9. Alaska Federal (Anchorage)	1
10. Orange County Teachers (Santa Ana, Calif.)	1

SOURCE: Veribanc, Inc. (reprinted by permission).

Table 9–6 *cont.*

Life and Health Insurance Companies	Assets
1. Prudential Insurance Company of America (Newark)	154.8
2. Metropolitan Life Insurance Company (New York)	118.2
3. Aetna Life Insurance Company (Hartford, Conn.)	50.9
4. New York Life Insurance Company (New York)	46.9
5. Equitable Life Assurance Society (New York)	46.6
6. Connecticut General Life Insurance (Hartford)	44.1
7. Northwestern Mutual Life Insurance (Milwaukee)	39.7
8. John Hancock Mutual Life (Boston)	39.1
9. Principal Mutual Life (Des Moines, Iowa)	35.1
10. Travelers Insurance Company (Hartford, CT)	34.2

SOURCE: A. M. Best Company (reprinted by permission).

Property and Casualty Insurance Groups	Assets
1. State Farm Group (Bloomington, Ill.)	53.4
2. American International Group (New York)	24.7
3. Allstate Insurance Group (Northbrook, Ill.)	24.7
4. CNA Insurance Companies (Chicago)	22.2
5. ITT Hartford Insurance Group (Hartford, CT)	22.0
6. Aetna Life & Casualty Group (Hartford, CT)	20.2
7. Liberty Mutual Group (Boston)	20.1
8. Travelers Insurance Group (Hartford, CT)	17.7
9. Nationwide Group (Columbus, Oh.)	16.5
10. CIGNA Group (Philadelphia)	14.1

SOURCE: A. M. Best Company (reprinted by permission).

Private Pension Funds	Assets
1. Teachers Insurance and Annuity Association/College Retirement Equities Fund	108
2. AT&T	53
3. General Motors	40
4. General Electric	36
5. IBM	30
6. Ford Motor	26
7. E. I. duPont	21
8. NYNEX	17
9. GTE	17
10. Bell South	15

SOURCE: *Pensions and Investments*, January 25, 1993, p. 20 (reprinted by permission).

Table 9–6 *cont.*

Public Pension Funds	Assets
1. California Public Employees	69
2. New York State and Local	53
3. New York City	53
4. California State Teachers	42
5. New York State Teachers	36
6. State of New Jersey	34
7. Texas Teachers	32
8. Florida State Board	30
9. Ohio Public Employees	27
10. State of North Carolina	25

SOURCE: *Pensions and Investments*, January 25, 1993, p. 20 (reprinted by permission).

Mutual (Open-End) Fund Investment Management Companies[a]	Assets
1. Fidelity Investments (Boston)	104.5
2. The Vanguard Group (Valley Forge, PA)	77.7
3. Capital Research & Management (Los Angeles)	69.8
4. Franklin Group of Funds (San Mateo, CA)	66.7
5. Putnam Funds (Boston)	39.7
6. Merrill Lynch Asset Management (New York)	38.2
7. Dean Witter (New York)	33.3
8. IDS Mutual Fund Group (Minneapolis)	32.8
9. Kemper (Chicago)	29.0
10. The Dreyfus Corporation[b] (New York)	27.3

SOURCE: Investment Company Institute, Washington, D.C. (reprinted by permission).
[a]Other than Money Market Funds
[b]To be acquired by Mellon Bank (Pittsburgh) in 1994.

Table 9–6 *cont.*

Money-Market Mutual (Open-End) Fund Management Companies	Assets
1. Fidelity Investments (Boston)	67.0
2. Merrill Lynch Asset Management (New York)	64.6
3. The Dreyfus Corporation[a] (New York)	47.6
4. Shearson Lehman Bros.(New York)	43.9
5. Federated Investors (Pittsburgh)	40.8
6. The Vanguard Group (Valley Forge, PA)	22.5
7. Goldman Sachs & Co. (New York)	16.8
8. Dean Witter (New York)	16.4
9. Kemper (Chicago)	15.1
10. SEI Financial Services (Philadelphia)	14.5

SOURCE: Investment Company Institute, Washington, D.C. (reprinted by permission).
[a]To be acquired by Mellon Bank (Pittsburgh) in 1994.

Finance Companies	Assets
1. General Motors Acceptance Corp. (Detroit, MI)	93.7
2. General Electric Capital Corp. (Stamford, CT)	92.6
3. Ford Motor Credit Co., (Dearborn, MI)	55.0
4. Associates Corp. of North America (Dallas, TX)	24.0
5. Household Finance Corp. (Prospect Heights, IL)	18.1
6. Chrysler Financial Corp. (Southfield, MI)	17.5
7. American Express Credit Corp. (Wilmington, DE)	13.6
8. ITT Financial Corp. (St. Louis, MO)	13.6
9. CIT Group Holdings, Inc. (New York)	13.0
10. Sears Roebuck Acceptance Corp. (Wilmington, DE)	12.4

SOURCE: *American Banker,* "Top 50 Finance Companies in Assets," December 29, 1993 (reprinted by permission).

SUMMARY

Financial institutions on the private financial market bring together SSUs and DSUs so that the SSUs can purchase primary securities issued by DSUs. They do not invest in the securities themselves. Investment banks, known more popularly as brokers and dealers, make both (1) a primary market for new securities issued to raise funds for new investment through underwriting and distributing the securities and (2) a secondary market for outstanding securities to provide liquidity for SSUs who wish to change their securities or to become DSUs through selling securities they own to others. Mortgage bankers originate mortgage loans that they sell to investors either as is or in a package collateralizing a new security. In either case, they generally continue to service the loan.

Financial institutions on the intermediation financial market buy primary securities issued by others with funds obtained by selling newly created secondary securities issued on themselves. In the United States, most of these intermediaries specialize in the types of primary securities they purchase and secondary securities they sell. Commercial banks are the largest and least specialized financial intermediary. They operate in most segments of the debt market and as fiduciaries for their customers in the stock market through their trust operations. Thrift institutions sell primarily shorter-term savings-type deposits and purchase primarily longer-term fixed and variable-rate residential mortgages. Mutual funds buy either bonds or equities and sell pro rata shares in these securities. Credit unions, money-market funds, other mutual funds, and pension funds are the fastest-growing intermediaries. After growing very rapidly through the mid-1980s, and doubling their market share, savings and loan associations declined sharply and, by 1992, had lost all of their gain in market share since 1950.

QUESTIONS

1. How do investment banks differ from commercial banks? If you were a businessperson, what important services could you get from which institution? If you managed a household, which services could you get from which institution?

2. Why and how would the management of an investment bank and commercial bank differ? How would the risks the two types of institutions incur differ? Do you think that management personnel in the two types of institutions are basically interchangeable?

3. What functions do *mortgage banks* perform? What makes them institutions on the private financial market rather than on the intermediation market? By what measures may mortgage

banks be simultaneously both larger and smaller than mortgage lenders on the intermediation market? Would it matter to you whether you receive a mortgage from a mortgage banker or from an institution on the intermediation market? Why or why not? What would make it matter?

4. Why and how would the asset and liability sides of the balance sheets of financial institutions on the intermediary financial market be related in terms of type, risk, maturity, and so on? How are all institutions on the intermediation market both similar and different?

5. Why do different types of financial intermediary institutions expand at different rates? Can you explain the

very rapid growth rate of money-market funds in recent years and the very slow growth rate of life insurance companies?

6. From information available in your library, list the three largest
   a. Commercial banks
   b. Savings and loan associations or savings banks

c. Credit unions headquartered in the state in which your university is located. How do these institutions compare in size with the largest similar institutions in the United States?

REFERENCES

Altman, Edward I., *Handbook of Financial Markets and Institutions*, 6th ed. New York: John Wiley, 1987.

Bloch, Ernest, *Inside Investment Banking*. Homewood, Ill.: Dow Jones-Irwin, 1986.

Dougall, Herbert E., and Jack E. Gaumnitz, *Capital Markets and Institutions*, 5th ed. Englewood Cliffs, N.J.: Prentice Hall, 1986.

Eccles, Robert G., and Dwight B. Crane, *Doing Deals*: *Investment Banks at Work*. Boston: Harvard University Press, 1988.

Friend, Irwin, et al., *Investment Banking and the New Issues Market*. Cleveland, Ohio: World, 1967.

Hayes, Samuel L., "Evolving Competition in Investment Banking," *Harvard Business Review*, January 1979.

Kaufman, George G. and Larry R. Mote, "Is Banking a Declining Industry? A Historical Perspective," *Economic Perspectives*, Federal Reserve Bank of Chicago, May/June 1994, pp. 1–21.

Keenan, Michael, *Profile of the New York Based Security Industry*. New York Center for the Study of Financial Institutions, New York University, 1977.

Kouwenhoven, John A., *Partners in Banking*: *An Historical Portrait of a Great Private Bank, Brown Brothers Harriman & Co. 1818–1968*. New York: Doubleday, 1968.

Kroos, Herman E., and Martin R. Blyn, *A History of Financial Intermediaries*. New York: Random House, 1971.

Redlich, Fritz, *The Molding of American Banking*: *Men and Ideas*. New York: Hafner, 1951.

Rosenblum, Harvey, and Christine Pavel, "Banking Services in Transition: The Effects of Nonbank Competitors," in Richard C. Aspinwall and Robert A. Eisenbeis, eds., *Handbook for Banking Strategy*. New York: John Wiley, 1985.

Securities Industry Association, *The U.S. Securities Markets: How They Work, Their Role in the National Economy*. New York: Securities Industry Association, 1980.

West, Richard, and Seha Tinic, *The Economics of the Stock Market*. New York: Praeger, 1971.

Willis, H. Parker, and J.I. Bogen, *Investment Banking*. New York: Harper, 1929.

Commercial Banks:
History and Management

Commercial banks are the oldest, largest, and least specialized of all financial intermediaries. They are 50 percent larger in asset size than private pension funds, the next largest financial intermediary, more than twice as large as life insurance companies, and hold almost 30 percent of the combined assets of all 11 major types of financial intermediaries listed in Table 9–6.

Commercial banks are frequently referred to as "department stores of finance." Several of their major types of secondary securities—for instance, demand deposits and NOW accounts—serve as the principal media of exchange in the United States, accounting for some two-thirds of the money supply.

By examining commercial banks in detail, we can gain considerable knowledge about the operation of all types of financial intermediaries. In the process, we shall develop a framework that will make it easier to understand the function of the other intermediaries. A thorough knowledge of commercial banking will also provide us with a base that we can use later to analyze the national payments system and monetary policy.

History of Banking

Although modern commercial banking is quite complex, the underlying principles are relatively simple. They may be demonstrated most directly by a stylized history of the development of banking. Assume that an economy has only recently moved from a barter to a money system. As noted in Chapter 2, such an economy relies on coins for money. But, as was pointed out, coins were clumsy to transport and difficult to store securely. Theft was easy and frequent. Robin Hoods and other highwaymen required few of the skills that were later refined by the Jesse Jameses and Butch Cassidys. Their targets were lingering highway travelers or unguarded homes. The size of a traveler's purse, generally carried in a visible location, was a good gauge of the rewards for the taking.

Some tradesmen who dealt in valuable merchandise had vaults on their premises. Among these were goldsmiths, who designed and fabricated articles of the precious metals in which they traded. The goldsmiths saw an opportunity to supplement their incomes by storing coins for their customers at a fee. The "depositors" of the coins were given receipts that were returned when coins of the same value, not necessarily exactly the same coins as deposited, were withdrawn. If fewer than all the coins in storage were withdrawn, a new receipt was issued for the amount that remained in the vault. If the customer used the coins to buy goods and services, it was likely that the seller would redeposit all or most of the coins with a goldsmith, possibly even the same one. A new receipt in the name of the new owner (seller) was created. The balance sheet of a hypothetical goldsmith engaging in this activity would effectively show the coins in storage as an asset and the receipts as a liability. If we assume that the goldsmith accepted coins valued at 10,000 units of the local currency, whatever it might have been, and issued an equivalent amount of receipts, the balance sheet would read:

Coins	10,000	10,000	Receipts

Of course, the goldsmith could abscond with the coins. The customer's receipts would then be worthless. To reduce the chances of such loss, receipt holders would demand periodic independent audits of the goldsmith's vaults and would conduct their business only with goldsmiths whose spotless reputations were certified by the auditors.

After a number of years, the son of one of the goldsmiths, who was working as an apprentice in the shop, observed that a great deal of time and expense was involved in rewriting receipts each time coins were withdrawn. Why not, he mused, prepare receipts in common denominations, such as 1, 5, and 10? Moreover, because the coins were generally deposited after use and a new receipt written to the new owner, why not also make the receipts payable to bearer rather than to the owner? In this way, not only could the same receipts be used over again, which would reduce preparation costs, but because the receipts were less clumsy to carry about and easier to secure, they could be used to finance the transaction in place of coins. The buyer would effectively transfer ownership of the specified number and type of coins stored at the goldsmith to the seller.

As long as the seller believed that the goldsmith issuing the receipt had not absconded with the coins, he or she was willing and happy to accept the receipts in payment. The receipt was transformed into money. The two forms of money traded at the same value. The receipts, or **notes** as they became known, supplemented coins as money but did not increase the money supply. The offsetting amounts of coins were in the goldsmiths' vaults.

However, there was an important difference between the two forms of money. Coins were only an asset and no one's liability. Notes were an asset to the holder but a liability to the issuing goldsmith. Thus, if there were doubts about the ability of the goldsmith to convert the notes into coins at par, notes would fall in value relative to coins and their value as money was diminished.

Fractional Reserve Banking

The idea of issuing bearer receipts in standard denominations caught on. The originating goldsmith prospered and was able to send his daughter to the local college, where she took a course in statistics and probability. During the summers when she had worked at her father's goldsmith shop, she had observed that not all the receipts were redeemed for coins at any one time. Indeed, most of the coins remained in the vaults. For her term project in the course, she computed the probabilities that different amounts of receipts would be exchanged for coins on any one day. This would indicate the shop's need for coins on hand to satisfy receipt holders and remain solvent. If the goldsmith could not exchange the receipts for the full amount of the coins immediately, he would have to declare bankruptcy and be forced to close.

The coins not needed to accommodate possible withdrawals were idle. Why not, our enterprising student mused, lend the coins out? After all, as long as depositors received the full value of their coins upon presentation of their receipts, why should they care about what the coins were doing in the meantime? Moreover, who would know the financial condition of potential borrowers and their ability to repay better than the goldsmith who stored their money? By lending the coins, the goldsmith would be able to supplement the income he received from storage fees with income from the interest charged on the loans. On the basis of this analysis, the daughter successfully persuaded her father to engage in lending activities on a small scale as a pilot project.

The first loans indicated that the borrower would accept notes in the amount of the loan as readily as coins. Thereafter, the goldsmith extended loans in the form of additional notes until the ratio of coins to notes was at the lowest level he considered necessary to meet all notes brought in for redemption. If the ratio were 50 percent, the balance sheet of our hypothetical goldsmith would now read:

Coins	10,000	20,000	Notes
Loans	10,000		
Total	20,000	20,000	Total

The loans are evidenced by IOUs of the borrowers. Note that now the lending has increased the supply of money. The new notes are not offset by an equal shift of coins from circulation to the vaults. Vault coins serve as reserves to accommodate note redemptions. A system in which cash reserves are smaller than the related liabilities is referred to as **fractional reserve banking.** This contrasts with **100 percent reserve banking,** in which the amount of reserves is exactly equal to the amount of liabilities, as in our earlier case.

Before long, income from lending greatly exceeded the other sources of income for many goldsmiths. To reflect this new activity, goldsmiths changed their name to *commercial banks.* The new title indicated the fact that most of the borrowers were business firms and that the loans financed commerce. The first loans were short-term, generally to finance inventory. They were repaid as the inventory was sold. Thus, they were effectively self-liquidating and involved minimum risk of default.

Not only had the bank now "created" money, but the amount it created depended on the percentage of reserves it held. For a given amount of coins, the smaller the necessary reserve percentage, the larger the amount of notes the bank could create. Because the bank earned interest income on loans and not on coins, it was encouraged to increase its loans and thereby its note issue to the amount consistent with continued solvent operation. The bank was solvent as long as all the bank's noteholders were able to convert their notes for an equal amount of coin upon demand. And exactly the same holds true today. (The details of bank credit expansion are examined in Chapter 15.)

Bank Failure

What would happen if the banker underestimated the demand to exchange notes into coins and was unable to pay in full? (Recall that the first objective of financial management at all levels, including commercial banking, is to meet all scheduled payments in full and on time. Only if this objective is satisfied, will a banker be able to satisfy the second objective of investing the funds until needed at the highest risk-adjusted return.) First, the banker would try to stall the noteholder by offering him or her coffee and small talk while an employee was sent out the back door to sell some loans for an equal value of coins or to borrow the coins from other banks. If this failed, the banker would change places with the employee and run out the back door as fast and as far as he or she could. The noteholders would probably not be able to obtain par value for their notes. Any remaining cash reserves would be divided among all noteholders. In time, the noteholders would also receive funds from the liquidation of the loans, but this would probably yield less than the full amount of the notes.

At first the banker wanted to keep the fractional reserve nature of the business secret from customers to avoid upsetting them. As the concept expanded, the secret became more difficult to keep. Noteholders became aware of it. However, as long as things went smoothly, the noteholders did not care. Coins and notes traded at the same value and were interchangeable. But the likelihood that the bank would experience difficulties and not

SOURCE: Drawing by Tom Wilson. © 1981 Universal Press Syndicate. Reprinted with permission. All rights reserved.

be able to pay noteholders in full was greater under fractional reserve banking than under 100 percent reserve banking. After all, borrowers could default on their loans and reduce the loans' market value. This made holding notes riskier than before.

If noteholders believed rightly or wrongly that the issuing bank would be unable to redeem their notes at par, the noteholders would try to convert from notes to coins. Because only the first noteholders would be able to convert into coins successfully, noteholders were very sensitive to any report or rumor of the bank's inability to exchange at par. It can be readily seen that if sufficient noteholders wanted to convert, the bank may not be able to accommodate them immediately and in full no matter how good the bank's loans were or how little the reserves were short of 100 percent. It takes some time to sell loans, and "fire sales" are likely to draw lower maximum prices. Moreover, the less liquid the loan, the lower the sales value is likely to be relative to the loan's face value. A simultaneous attempt by a large number of noteholders to exchange their notes for coins (or possibly notes of other banks) is called a **run** on a bank. A run was often characterized by lines of noteholders outside the bank waiting their turn to redeem their notes. By forcing the bank to sell loans hastily to obtain cash and thereby suffer possible *fire-sale* or *liquidity* losses, runs could cause some banks to fail.

Moreover, if there was a run on one bank, noteholders of other banks might begin to worry. Better to be safe than sorry! These noteholders also began to exchange their notes for coins. Again, none but the first ones are likely to do so successfully. The more banks that were affected by a run, the more loans had to be sold, the fewer buyers would there be, the harder it became for the banks to raise the necessary coins quickly by selling their loans to other banks, and the more likely they were to default. If the coins withdrawn from one bank were redeposited at other banks that were perceived to be safer and exchanged for their notes so that total notes in circulation remain unchanged, the run would not have serious spillover effects on other banks or the economy. But if the coins were not redeposited bank runs could be self-feeding and devour sound, well-managed banks as well as poorly managed banks. They could start an economic crisis or intensify a crisis started elsewhere in the economy.

Bank runs were often ignited by rumors of a bank's inability to exchange notes for coins at par. What would start a rumor? It could have been theft of coins, defaults due to fraudulent loans or good loans that turned bad, or bad economic conditions that adversely affected many loans. The fear of a run exerted influence on banks to maintain the quality and liquidity of their assets.

Capital and Liquidity

We can now introduce two refinements on the banks' balance sheets. First of all, some funds are raised from the owners of the bank by the sale of equity capital (stock). Equity has no maturity and does not need to be redeemed. Any payments on equity are subordinated to payments on notes, which technically are debt. Thus, a bank can charge any losses it incurs on loan defaults or on the hurried sales of good loans to its capital accounts up to the amount of capital. Because the losses are not charged against notes, the losses do not reduce the value of the notes. Capital protects the noteholder by being a buffer against losses. The greater the capital relative to notes, the safer are the noteholders. But to the bank, equity capital is costly both in terms of the high return required to compensate the owner for the greater risk that is assumed and in terms of sharing management with others. Bankers prefer to hold the minimum capital consistent with solvency and any regulations that may be imposed by chartering and regulatory agencies. Similar to funds raised by the sale of notes, funds raised by the sale of equity capital can be used to buy loans.

Second, not all loans are equally marketable at near their par value. More liquid loans—say, those that mature shortly or that the bank can sell the same day at near par value with low transaction costs—typically carry a lower interest rate than less liquid loans. Although lower, the rate is higher than on coins that do not bear interest. Thus, to some extent, liquid loans could be used to replace coins as reserves without loss in overall reserve liquidity. Loans that can be used for this purpose are called **secondary reserves** to differentiate them from the cash or **primary reserves.** Because secondary reserves are less liquid than primary reserves, it is likely that banks will use a greater amount of these assets to replace a given amount of primary reserves. If we assume that our banker sold 2,000 units of capital and replaced 4,000 units of non-interest-yielding coins with 5,000 units of interest-yielding liquid assets, the balance sheet would now read:

Primary reserves (coins)	6,000	20,000	Notes
Secondary reserves	5,000	2,000	Capital
Loans	11,000		
Total	22,000	22,000	Total

The bank now has proportionately more income generating assets than before the introduction of capital.

The composition of a bank's assets depends on its estimate of note redemptions and on the amount of capital. The smaller the likelihood of note redemptions or the greater the amount of its capital, the smaller is the proportion of liquid, but low-earning primary and secondary reserves the bank needs for a given amount of notes outstanding. The bank's choice of assets involves a trade-off between the liquidity of its assets and their expected returns. Note that the bank's management of its asset liquidity **(liquidity management)** and its capital **(capital management)** are related. The more capital a bank has, *ceteris paribus*, the less liquid its assets need be. The less capital, the more asset liquidity it needs.

It follows that the objective of bank liquidity management is to provide both sufficient liquidity and sufficient earnings to maintain solvency and earn a competitive return. Total liquidity, say only coins, would guarantee solvency but would not generate sufficient earnings to adequately compensate equity investors and encourage them not to remove their funds and close the bank. Asset liquidity management thus involves, given the characteristics of the bank's liabilities, choosing the mix of (1) zero-return 100 percent liquid primary reserves (coins), (2) low-yielding highly liquid secondary reserves (investments), and (3) high-yielding relatively illiquid loans that would maximize net income consistent with a given high probability of solvency. (How a modern large bank manages its cash balances is described in Exhibit 10–1.) Likewise, the objective of capital man-

EXHIBIT

10–1

Life at a Bank's Money Desk

A bank has to maintain enough liquidity to handle outgoing payments—that is, to cover any net deposit withdrawals, loan extensions, and securities purchases. It also has to leave enough on deposit at the Federal Reserve to meet its reserve requirements. However, a bank doesn't want to keep more funds at the Fed than are needed to meet those requirements, since that would entail a loss of potential interest income.

The challenge is particularly great at money-center and regional banks. Many customers of those banks—including large corporations, domestic and foreign correspondent banks, and securities firms—manage large money positions themselves and have a heavy volume of financial transactions. They receive and pay out far more each day than they keep in their accounts overnight. These transactions can have a major impact on their banks' reserve positions. Coping with such money flows is the task of a bank's "money-position" managers. Their main aim is to acquire funds to meet their bank's reserve requirements at the lowest possible cost.

A bank's reserve account at the Fed is constantly buffeted by the payments and receipts of its customers as well as by its own (as when it buys or sells securities). When the bank is presented through the clearing process with a check drawn on a customer's demand deposit account, for instance, the check is effectively paid through a transfer of funds to another institution from the bank's reserve account at the Fed. Similarly, when checks are deposited at the bank by its customers and then are collected, that raises the bank's balance in its Fed account.

Most of the activity through a money-center bank's reserve account results not from checks but from large-value electronic payments and receipts on behalf of customers. To make a payment, one of these customers sends an instruction to its bank by cable, computer link-up, or even over the telephone for the bank to pay funds to a specific party with an account at another bank. A clerk then instructs the bank's "money transfer"

computer to send out an electronic payment message.

The largest volume of such electronic payments is made over a Federal Reserve transfer network known as Fedwire. The sending bank's computer tells another computer at the Fed to transfer funds from the sender's to the receiver's reserve account and to inform the receiving bank of the transfer. The payment is made instantly—in the form of entries on the books of the Federal Reserve.

Most other electronic payments are handled by the New York Clearing House system known as CHIPS. To make a CHIPS payment, a bank transmits the relevant data electronically to the CHIPS computer, which will immediately advise the receiving bank—again, electronically—of all the details. However, unlike transactions via Fedwire, the actual transfer of funds will not occur until later that day. At 4:30 P.M. eastern time, CHIPS stops accepting payment instructions from its members and totes up the day's activity. Offsetting payments between CHIPS members are netted out, and each participating bank is informed of how much it owes other CHIPS participants or is owed by them. Then by 6:00 P.M. all banks owing money to other banks "settle" their CHIPS positions by making payments out of their reserve accounts over the Fedwire.

The ebb and flow of money through a bank's Fed account, much of which results from CHIPS and Fedwire transactions occurring late in the business day, can require a bank's money-position managers to scramble to acquire or dispose of federal funds late in the day. They want neither to leave more funds at the Fed than are required nor to let their bank's Fed account become overdrawn.

WATCHING THE NUMBERS

In meeting its reserve requirements, what counts for a bank is each day's balance in its Fed account as of 6:30 P.M. eastern time, when the Fedwire shuts down for the night and the Fed strikes a closing balance in each bank's reserve account. A bank does not have to hold the same amount of reserves each day, but rather must maintain an average closing balance in its Fed account over each Thursday-to-Wednesday weekly period which equals or exceeds that week's reserve requirements. Its only latitude is that it can end the week up to 2 percent short of its requirements.* In that event, it has to make up any deficiency in the following week, and it also cannot "under-reserve" in that period.

A bank's money-position managers start each day with a target for the bank's account balance at the Fed that evening. Critical to that objective are the customer inflows and outflows which the bank is likely to have, as well as the amount of funds that the bank's own activities may require. That permits a tentative decision concerning what amount to "buy" or to "sell"—i.e., to borrow or lend—on an overnight basis in the federal funds market. However, that decision is never final until Fedwire closes for the day, for unexpected inflows and outflows can net to a very large amount—sometimes approaching or even exceeding the bank's reserve requirement.

Typically, as the day goes on, a bank can't readily tell whether its estimate of net inflows or outflows is going to be correct. All day long, its balance at the Fed will be changing—up hundreds of millions of dollars one minute, and down just moments later. The bank might need to raise or lower the amount of money it borrows that day in the federal funds market. But to make the right decision, the money managers need to be able to tell, for instance, whether a 3:00 P.M. shortfall of funds means that they underestimated the day's funding requirements or simply that the shortfall will be made up by customer inflows between then and the close of Fedwire at 6:30 P.M.

If the day is a Wednesday—settlement day—falling below that day's reserve-account target could mean that the bank would not have maintained sufficient funds to meet its weekly-average reserve requirement and would have to borrow from the

Fed's discount window to close the gap. Since that can easily wear out a bank's welcome at the window, it will ordinarily try to obtain the needed amount in the funds market. But it is not uncommon for a bank to go ahead in such circumstances and buy additional Fed funds, and then find out later on that more money has arrived over the wire. And when that happens, it leaves a bank with an excess of funds to try to sell off within the final moments of the reserve week, a time when most of the banking system is often already sitting with enough funds to meet its reserve requirements and has no interest in borrowing any more money overnight. If the bank could sell the funds, the rate on such a transaction might well be lower than that at which the funds were previously bought.

For illustrative purposes, consider a money-center bank having a $500-million weekly-average reserve requirement. The day is Friday, and the bank starts out in the morning knowing that Thursday's closing balance was $500 million. The bank plans on holding another $500 million in its Fed account Friday night. However, by 6:00, the bank has a reserve balance of $900 million rather than the intended $500 million.

Unless the bank can sell its excess funds to another institution in the next few moments, the bank will accumulate a substantial reserve excess for three days of its reserve week, relative to its $500 million requirement. Such a reserve excess would sharply reduce the bank's flexibility in managing its Fed account in the remaining days of the reserve-settlement week. After keeping $500 million for one day and $900 million for three days at the Fed (Friday, Saturday, and Sunday), all that the bank would have to keep on the following Monday through Wednesday—for its weekly holdings to average $500 million—would be $100 million per night. Thus, virtually no matter what might happen to the federal funds rate in the next three days, the bank's latitude to alter its own federal funds activity would be almost nil.

SOURCE: Abstracted from "Life at a Bank's Money Desk," *Morgan Guaranty Survey* (Morgan Guaranty Trust Company), November 1981, pp. 11–15. Reprinted by permission.
* In 1984, the reserve period was lengthened to two weeks.

agement is to provide sufficient capital to absorb all but the most unusual and unexpected losses from the sale of assets or other risks, but not too much capital to reduce the bank's ability to pay shareholders a competitive return. Liquidity and capital are sufficient when a bank is able to accommodate all but the most unusual runs. It follows that, on the whole, bank failure is a problem of poor asset quality relative to a bank's capital rather than a problem of runs.

Deposit Banking

Through time, trade developed further, and payment by note, like coin before it, became increasingly cumbersome. The daughter of our goldsmith-turned-banker, who had innovated fractional reserve banking and had taken over the bank upon her father's retirement, turned to her son, who had recently been awarded an MBA at the leading university in the country, and asked him to put his training to practical use and develop alternatives to notes. After surveying a scientifically selected sample of noteholders, the son concluded that the major disadvantages of notes were their limited denominations and their physical form, which made them clumsy to store and difficult to secure. Why not let the bank customers create their own money when they needed it, in just the right amounts? This could be done by having customers deposit coins and notes in their banks as before but receive as evidence of the deposit only an account in the form of a record on the banks' books. The depositor could use the funds in the account by ordering the bank (in writing) to pay a specified amount to a third party named on the order. The amount, of course, had to be less than the depositor's balance at the bank. The orders would be called *checks,* and the accounts on which they could be written, *checking accounts* or *demand deposits* (deposits to be paid on demand). Because it did not exist physically until it was created by writing the check, the check money presented neither storage nor security problems to the holder, other than bank robbery or fraud.

The bank adopted the son's suggestion and offered its customers checking accounts. They proved popular, and the concept was introduced by other banks. Demand deposits soon replaced notes as the banks' major form of liability, and banks expanded more rapidly than before. Because checks were generally deposited immediately, while notes were used in hand-to-hand transactions for some time before returning to the issuing bank for redemption, banks required more liquidity against checking accounts than against notes.

As the importance of notes diminished, the government took over the task of note issue. The notes changed from liabilities of banks, whose value was affected by the ability of the issuing bank to exchange them into the same nominal amount of coins, to liabilities of the government. To keep changes in the intrinsic value of the metal into which the note could be converted from affecting the value of the notes and therefore their amount, governments soon separated the value of the note from the value of the metal by not guaranteeing free conversion from one to an other. Paper notes became inconvertible except into coins. They were "backed" no longer by the value of metal but only by the strength of the government in protecting their purchasing power in terms of goods and services.

This was an important change, since it permitted governments to change the amount of money freely without being constrained by their holdings of the particular metal. This change introduced the modern age of active government monetary management. Moreover, as coins became less important, governments were able to weaken the link between their monetary value and the intrinsic value of the composite metal. They stopped buying all metal offered at the nominal coin value. As a result, the intrinsic market value of the metal was permitted to decline below its monetary exchange value. Moreover, by reducing the metallic content of coins when the intrinsic value of the metal increased, the government could now always exchange its notes into an equal nominal amount of coins. Notes became known as **currency.** Banks could hold currency as well as coin as reserves to meet deposit outflows. Depositors now had to be concerned with the ability of the banks to exchange deposits—bank money—into currency—government money—at par value.

The development of the financial sector spurred economic growth and increased the demands for credit. Commercial banks found it increasingly difficult to meet this need and again took innovative steps to increase their ability to raise funds. They developed *time-deposit* accounts, on which checks generally could not be written. Except for savings deposits, which may be redeemed at any time, time deposits were, until recently, repayable only at a specific date. Because they were less likely to be withdrawn unpredictably, the banks could invest the proceeds in less liquid assets and thus were able to pay a higher interest rate than on demand and other transactions accounts. Recently, time deposits surpassed demand deposits as the major source of bank funds. Banks also developed secondary securities that technically were not considered deposits and became referred to as borrowings. In economic terms, borrowings are indistinguishable from deposits. Both are debt.

In time, larger banks learned that they could directly and quickly influence the amount of funds they desired by making small changes in the interest rates they offered on interest-sensitive secondary securities, such as CDs, Fed funds, and Eurodollars. These funds are called **purchased** or **managed funds.** The higher the rate a bank was willing to pay, the more purchased funds it could attract. Not only could a bank raise additional funds if it had profitable investment opportunities, but it could offset a deposit loss. This would obviate the need to sell assets and reduce reserves. Liquidity could be obtained on the liability side through **liability liquidity management.** For larger banks, liability management reduced but did not eliminate the need for **asset liquidity management.** When the quality of its assets deteriorate so that the likelihood of failure increases, liability management becomes difficult for a bank because SSUs became increasingly reluctant to purchase the bank's secondary securities. At these times, a bank has to rely on traditional asset management for its liquidity. Thus, liability liquidity management is primarily reserved for larger and financially strong institutions.

The increasing importance of banking and its growing relationship to the rest of the economy made the government more concerned with the safety, efficient operation, and economic influence of banks and banking. Central banks were established to regulate both the operation of commercial banks and the aggregate amount of bank deposits. The central banks prescribed legal minimum reserve requirements, at first to enhance bank safety through minimum liquidity standards, but later to control the money supply. The central banks also established deposit facilities for the commercial banks to hold their reserves and provisions for extending short-term credit to them. The balance sheet of a modern commercial bank might be as follows:

Cash reserves:			
Currency	300	10,000	Demand deposits
Deposits at		19,000	Time deposits
central bank	3,700	1,000	Borrowings
Secondary reserves	7,000	3,000	Capital
Loans	22,000		
Total	33,000	33,000	Total

Bank Balance Sheet

We can now turn from the stylized account of commercial banking to the banking of the real world.

The oldest operating bank in the world is the Monte dei Paschi di Siena Bank in Italy. It dates back to 1472. The three next-oldest banks are also Italian, followed by two British banks. The first commercial bank in the United States was established in 1782 in Philadelphia as the Bank of North America. It still operates today as the First Pennsylvania Bank. Two years later, the Bank of New York and the Massachusetts Bank (now known as the Bank of Boston) opened, and banking was off and running. The 10 oldest U.S. banks still in operation are listed in Table 10–1.

Table 10–2 shows the balance sheet of all commercial banks in the United States at year-end 1992. Banks provide funds to (make loans to or buy primary securities from) a wide variety of borrowers, not only businesses but also farmers, consumers, and governments. Loans involve three functions: (1) origination, (2) financing, and (3) servicing (monitoring financial condition and collecting interest and principal payments on a timely basis). And they are often specially tailored or customized to the needs of the DSUs. They frequently involve an ongoing bank–loan customer relationship. Loans that are issued to large, well-known DSUs and are evidenced by standard IOUs or securities in standard denominations are referred to as **investments.** Investments are impersonal; they do not involve a bank–customer relationship. Loans are less marketable and liquid than investment securities, many of which serve as secondary reserves. Cash, which accounts for only 8 percent of total assets, is held as balances at Federal Reserve Banks or other, *correspondent banks,* or in the banks' own vaults.

Between 1950 and 1992, banks increased sharply the importance of loans in their portfolios at the expense of investments. This is shown in Figure 10–1. Through time, the relative importance of traditional commercial loans has declined and that of real estate loans has increased. Indeed, by 1992, real estate loans were by far the largest type of loan at both large and small banks. Banks also lengthened the maturities of their loans. They make intermediate-term loans, called **term loans,** to business firms and

TABLE

10–1   THE TEN OLDEST BANKS IN THE UNITED STATES

Current Name of Bank	Original Name of Bank	Year Chartered
1. First Pennsylvania (Philadelphia)	Bank of North America	1782
2. Bank of New York	Bank of New York	1784
First National (Boston)	The Massachusetts Bank	1784
4. Fleet National (Providence, R.I.)	Providence Bank	1791
5. Connecticut National (Hartford, Conn.)	Hartford Bank	1792
6. Chase Manhattan (New York)	Bank of the Manhattan Co.	1799
7. Bank of New England— Old Colony (Newport, R.I.)[a]	Newport National	1803
Norstar Bank (Albany, N.Y.)	State Bank of Albany	1803
Philadelphia National	Philadelphia Bank	1803
10. New Jersey National (Trenton, NJ)	Trenton Banking Co.	1804

SOURCE: *American Banker: 150th Anniversary*, 1986, p. 138. Reprinted with permission from American Banker. Updated by author.

[a] The assets of the bank were acquired by the Citizens Savings Bank and Trust Company (Providence, R.I.) in 1991 when the Bank of New England and its affiliates failed.

long-term mortgage loans to both businesses and households. The longer-term loans were made possible by the reduced fears of bank runs and sudden large deposit losses after the introduction of the Federal Deposit Insurance Corporation (FDIC), the increased liquidity of secondary reserves as a result of improvements in the money markets, and the greater ability of the banks to attract funds quickly through liability management to offset deposit losses. Commercial banks are the largest single suppliers of credit to business firms, consumers, real estate buyers, the federal government, and state and local governments.

As may be seen from Figure 10–1, transaction deposits have become a less important source of funds for commercial banks. At year-end 1992, they accounted for about 30 percent of total deposits, down sharply from 75 percent in 1950. This decline may be attributed both to the rise in interest rates, which made holding non-interest-bearing demand deposits more costly to depositors, and to the development of checkable time deposits. In addition, the Depository Institutions Deregulation and Monetary Control Act of 1980 removed the traditional legal monopoly commercial banks had over checkable deposits by permitting thrift institutions to offer them also. Time deposits that have specific maturity dates are referred to as certificates of deposit, or **CDs,** and those in denominations of $100,000 or more as ***negotiable certificates of deposit.*** Time deposits that may generally be withdrawn without penalty at any time include savings accounts and money-market deposit accounts (MMDAs). These pay a lower interest rate. Consumer certificates of deposit may be redeemed before maturity only at a reduction in interest rate. Large CDs may not be redeemed before matu-

	All Banks		Large Banks[a]		Small Banks[b]	
	$Billions	Percent	$Billions	Percent	$Billions	Percent
Assets						
Cash reserves	298	8	236	10	22	6
Loans	2,032	58	1,466	59	178	51
Real estate	868	25	550	22	98	28
Agriculture	35	1	8	—	18	5
Commercial	536	15	433	17	30	9
Consumer	385	11	280	11	30	9
Banks	38	1	36	1	—	—
Other	170	5	159	6	2	1
Investment securities	733	22	460	19	116	34
U.S. Government	608	17	359	14	94	27
Other	125	4	101	4	22	6
Other Assets	403	12	318	13	30	9
Total	3,506	100	2,480	100	346	100
Liabilities and Capital						
Domestic transaction deposits	811	23	540	22	92	27
Demand Deposits	511	15	370	15	44	13
Other (incl. NOW accts.)	300	9	170	7	48	14
Domestic nontransaction deposits	1,601	46	982	40	215	62
Savings	298	8	182	7	38	11
MMDAs	455	13	324	13	38	11
Large time (> $100,000)	227	6	148	6	27	8
Small time deposits and other	621	18	329	13	112	32
Foreign deposits	287	8	283	11	0	0
Borrowings	404	12	371	15	4	1
Other liabilities	105	3	96	4	2	0
Capital	298	8	208	8	33	10
Total	3,506	100	2,480	100	346	100
Number of banks	11,461		380		8,290	

SOURCE: Federal Deposit Insurance Corporation, *Statistics on Banking*, 1992, pp. C-2–C-9.
[a] Banks with assets of more than $1 billion.
[b] Banks with assets of less than $100 million.

rity, but may be sold to other investors. Thus, bank deposits are basically fixed-value securities. The Federal Deposit Insurance Corporation insures deposits up to $100,000 per account.

The balance sheets of individual banks will vary from those for all other banks or the average bank. The operation of individual banks reflects the characteristics both of management and of the surrounding market area. As can be seen from Table 10–2, smaller banks hold proportionally smaller cash reserves and loans than larger banks, but more securities. By type of loan, they hold proportionately more mortgage (real estate) and agriculture loans and fewer business loans than larger banks. Similar dif-

FIGURE

10–1

LOANS INCREASE AND TRANSACTION DEPOSITS DECREASE IN
IMPORTANCE AT COMMERCIAL BANKS, 1950–1992.

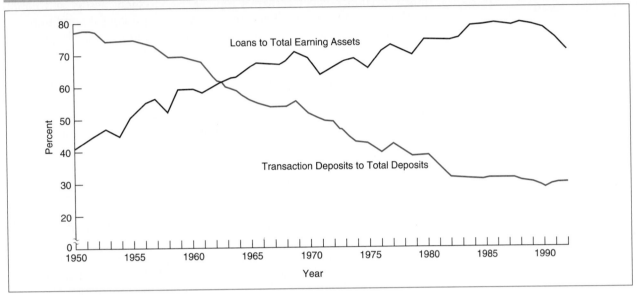

SOURCE: Federal Reserve System.

ferences may be observed on the liability side. Smaller banks rely more heavily on small time deposits and larger banks on managed or borrowed funds, such as Fed funds, Eurodollars, and on deposits at overseas branches. Note that all banks are highly leveraged, with capital equal to less than 10 percent of assets. Capital generally consists of common stock, preferred stock, subordinated debt, and retained earnings. Capital serves both as a source of funds like deposits and as an absorber of losses unlike deposits.

Off-Balance-Sheet Accounts.   Besides the items listed on the balance sheet, which include the full value of transactions that involve a concurrent transfer of funds, many banks also have **off-balance-sheet** activities, which include current commitments that do not involve the transfer of funds until some time in the future. These contingencies include the following:

▼ *Loan commitments*—an agreement in which a bank agrees, for a fee, to provide up to a maximum amount of future funding at the option of a borrower, generally at a prearranged interest rate;

▼ *Commercial letters of credit*—an agreement in which a bank, for a fee, will provide future funding for financing a particular transaction upon its completion;

▼ *Standby letters of credit*—an agreement in which a bank, for a fee, will provide future funding if a specified third party fails to perform on a contract; and

▼ *Futures and forward contracts*—An agreement in which a bank buys or sells securities and foreign exchange for future delivery and payment at a specified price.

The banks charge for many types of off-balance-sheet services and collect *fee income,* which is a rapidly growing source of income for many banks.

When the transfer of funds occurs, the activity goes *on-balance-sheet.* Thus, off-balance-sheet activities represent contingent assets and liabilities that need to be considered in evaluating the financial condition of a bank as a whole. When the funds are ultimately committed, the bank is likely to incur credit or interest rate risk similar to that incurred in on-balance-sheet activities. These activities are off-balance-sheet only for accounting purposes, not for financial purposes. Off-balance-sheet transactions in the form of guarantees are among the oldest type of bank activity. Valuable financial guarantees could be provided only by wealthy and credible members of the community, such as goldsmiths. For some large banks, off-balance-sheet accounts exceed on-balance-sheet accounts in dollar size.

Other Activities.   Although commercial banks may not own equity securities for their own account (except when obtained as collateral on a defaulted loan), they may hold these as well as other securities in a fiduciary capacity for their customers through their trust operations. Trust departments service and, at times, manage investments for a variety of clients, ranging from individuals to corporations to universities to pension funds to closed-end investment funds. Ownership of the assets is held by the customers. To avoid conflicts of interest between the trust and other activities of a bank, regulations were imposed to restrict the investment of trust funds in the equities of bank loan customers and to prevent firms whose stocks are heavily owned by trust accounts from receiving preferential loan treatment. These regulations require a *Chinese Wall* to separate a bank's commercial and trust operations. Information obtained by one cannot be transmitted to the other. Nevertheless, trust operations increase the economic importance and influence of commercial banks.

Only about one-third of all commercial banks operate trust departments. At year-end 1992, assets of bank trust departments totaled more than $9 trillion. This is more than twice as large as the total on-balance-sheet assets of the banking system as a whole. Trust funds may be either *discretionary trust funds* managed by the bank or *nondiscretionary trust funds* that are managed by nonbank managers but serviced by the bank in terms of record keeping, security transfers, and safekeeping. Although discretionary funds are by far the most profitable, as the bank also collects a management fee, they account for the smaller part of all trust funds.

The importance of trust funds operations varies considerably among banks; trust operations are more important for large than for small banks. Five of the ten largest trust departments in 1992 belonged to bank holding companies that ranked among the ten largest in the country. Two of the other banks were among the ten largest banks, although not bank holding companies, and two of the remaining three banks, including the one with largest trust assets were basically trust companies with relatively small deposit business. The largest trust department by a full-service bank is operated by Morgan Guaranty Bank in New York. Its trust assets were nearly ten times its on-balance sheet assets. (See Table 9–6).

In addition to trust operations, commercial banks engage in a large number of activities either directly or through their parent holding companies, that are not evident from the balance sheet. These activities include credit cards, traveler's checks, safe-deposit facilities, underwriting and trading Treasury, municipal, and other permitted debt securities, buying and selling securities for customers as brokers, credit advice, payroll accounting, investment advice, trading in foreign exchange, and many more.

The market area served by a bank varies directly with the bank's size. Large banks in major cities conduct business with large firms throughout the country and even internationally. Small banks rely more heavily on local customers. Likewise, larger firms with larger credit needs have access to banks outside their own cities and possibly even overseas. Households and smaller business firms are generally restricted to banks in their own city or even neighborhood. Advances in technology that have permitted funds to be transferred quickly across large distances have weakened somewhat the reliance of banks on their local markets, particularly for time deposits.

Bank Management

The objective of bank management is to maximize profits subject to the constraint of remaining solvent and not going out of business. This implies earning more on the bank's assets than paying on its deposit liabilities, so that it has a positive *interest rate spread* and, thus, also a positive *return on assets* (ROA) and *return on equity* (ROE). But return must be evaluated in conjunction with the risks assumed. The higher the return, generally the higher too are the risks of insolvency. Otherwise, banks, like any other investor, would make only the highest-yielding loans. Solvency requires the skillful use of both (1) *liquidity management* to ensure that deposit outflows will be paid on time and in full and (2) *capital management* to ensure that any losses incurred, such as on the sale of assets, higher interest costs on deposits, losses from loan defaults, or unfavorable interest rate changes, will be charged against capital and not against deposits. These, in turn, involve managing the various types of intermediation risks discussed earlier.

The chief risks banks incur are default (credit) risk, interest rate risk, foreign currency (foreign country exposure) risk, liquidity risk, fraud risk, and operations (poor management) risk. Although individual banks can choose not to assume some of these risks, most of their profits come from assuming risk, so they cannot eliminate all risk taking and remain in business. Rather, they must price and manage the risks successfully. The determination of how much of each kind of the above risk as well as how much overall risk to assume, or **risk management,** is generally referred to as **asset and liability management** and is generally made by a bank's *asset and liability management committee,* or ALCO, which is made up of the bank's most senior officers.

Default risk has been the traditional source of bank risk. Profitable bank lending consists of three functions: (1) loan origination, (2) loan monitoring, and (3) loan collection. As some bankers have discovered to their sorrow, the first is generally much easier than the third. In recent years, banks have experienced large losses from loans to energy, real estate, and less developed country (LDC) borrowers, and many have failed as a result. Appropriate loan origination involves careful evaluation of the financial and personal characteristics of borrowers to estimate the probabilities of default and potential losses. After origination, to maximize the probability of full and timely repayment, the bank must carefully and frequently monitor the performance of its loan customers with respect to compliance with the conditions of their loan agreement.

In recent years, interest rate risk has become of more concern to bank management as rates have become substantially more volatile and have increased the risk of loss from unfavorable rate changes. As discussed in Chapter 3, interest rate risk arises when the sensitivity of the securities on the two sides of the balance sheet to interest rate changes is not the same because of differences in the times when coupon rates may change and the securities may be repriced. This makes the values of the two sides respond differently to interest rate changes and affects the value of the bank's capital and earnings. The greater the imbalance or *gap* between the rate sensitivity of the assets and that of the liabilities, the greater the risk; the smaller the imbalance, the smaller risk.

The management of the interest rate sensitivity of both sides of the balance sheet to alter the degree of interest rate risk exposure is generally referred to as **gap management;** it is an important part of liquidity management in today's environment. In periods when interest rates did not fluctuate greatly, interest rate risk was not great, and banks engaged actively in interest rate intermediation by making, say, intermediate-term loans at non-rate-sensitive fixed-coupon rates and by raising funds by short-term, effectively variable or rate-sensitive deposits. But as interest rate volatility increased, banks began to realize losses from this activity, and many banks lost their enthusiasm for interest rate intermediation. To reduce their risk exposure, they synchronized the rate sensitivity of the two sides of their balance sheets more closely, primarily by making variable coupon loans, thereby reducing the size of their gap. In the process, they shifted a greater share of the risk to their loan and deposit customers. For example, in mid-1993, loans with floating coupons accounted for 76 percent of long-term business loans. This was double the 37 percent of such loans in mid-1977. Bank gap management is discussed in greater detail in Chapter 17.

The senior managers of a bank have to determine how much and what types of risks their bank should assume. For example, the bank may wish to assume both credit and interest rate, only credit risk, or only interest rate risk. When a bank wishes to assume only one type of risk, it will attempt to hedge the other risks. This strategy is referred to as *risk-controlled arbitrage*. A bank can eliminate credit risk by investing in only U.S. Treasury securities and eliminate interest rate risk by matching the maturities (durations) of their assets and liabilities. (The last strategy is referred to as *matched-book* or *immunization* and is discussed in Chapter 17.) How well banks do at managing their risks may be gauged by examining their performance both relative to their competitors and through time.

Bank Performance

Through time, as competition for deposits has intensified and more non-bank firms have entered into lending activities, the spread between the interest banks earn on their loans and investments and interest they pay on deposits has tended to narrow. As a result, banks have relied more on providing financial services for which they charge a fee up front, but do not necessarily provide long-term financing, such as loan origination and ser-

TABLE 10–2 BANK NONINTEREST FEE INCOME AS A PERCENTAGE OF TOTAL INCOME: SELECTED COUNTRIES, 1980–82 AND 1990		
	1980–1982	1990
Canada	21.6	31.0
France	14.6	24.9
Germany	30.6	34.9
Italy	26.0	26.8
Japan	20.4	35.9
Switzerland	46.6	49.1
United Kingdom	28.5	41.1
United States	30.0	38.0

SOURCE: Bank for International Settlements, *Annual Report, 1992,* p. 196.

vicing but not financing by holding the loans in their portfolios, financial advising, and mutual fund management and brokering. These are basically off-balance sheet activities. In 1992, *noninterest* or *fee income* accounted for 21 percent of total bank income, up from only 11 percent in 1985. Only about 20 percent of this amount was derived from service charges on deposits. When measured as a percent of total assets, noninterest income amounted to 1.95 percent in 1992, compared with 7.47 percent for more traditional interest income. Noninterest income is more important at larger banks than at smaller banks. In 1992, noninterest income averaged 2.59 percent of assets at the 10 largest banks in the country, but only 1.14 percent at banks with less than $300 million in assets. Yet interest income as a percent of assets was the same at both groups of banks. Although noninterest fee income is often described as a U.S. phenomenon, Table 10–3 shows that off-balance sheet activities are large and growing for banks in many major countries. (Note that the definition of noninterest income used in Table 10–3 differs somewhat from that given above.)

Interest expense averaged 3.57 percent of assets for all banks in 1992. When this is subtracted from interest income of 7.47 percent, the banks earned a **net income margin** of 3.90 percent. After adding in noninterest income and deducting operating and other expenses, the banks earned a pre-tax return on assets of 1.33 percent and an after-tax return of 0.92 percent. This represented a 12.8 percent return on equity; 1992 was a very good year for banks. The return on assets was the highest on record and 10 times the low return recorded five years earlier in 1987, when banks suffered unusually large loan defaults. The return on equity was also high, but was not a record level.

SUMMARY

Modern commercial banks developed from goldsmiths who stored gold and other coins for their customers and issued receipts. In time, the receipts circulated as money, first directly in the form of notes and then indirectly in the form of checks written on demand-deposit accounts. The bank held cash reserves equal to some fraction of its deposit liabilities (fractional reserve banking) in order to satisfy the claims of depositors in full and on time. If it could not do so, it failed. In their operations, banks assume default (credit) risk, interest rate risk, foreign currency risk, liquidity (fire sale) risk, and fraud risk in addition to the usual operations risk. To reduce the probability of failure, banks maintain capital, which is subordinated in its claims on assets to deposits, and liquid assets, which can be sold quickly at almost face value. In recent years, larger banks could also obtain liquidity by selling liabilities that were sensitive to interest rates and could be used to raise funds quickly when other deposits declined.

Modern commercial banks make a large variety of different loans and investments and issue an almost equally large variety of demand and time deposits. Although constrained to investing in debt securities for their own accounts, banks may invest in equity securities as fiduciaries for their trust department customers. Banks are the largest and broadest financial intermediary. However, the Depository Institutions Deregulation and Monetary Control Act of 1980 removed their legal monopoly on checkable deposits and reduced the importance of demand deposits. To achieve their objective of maximizing profits without going insolvent, banks engage in liquidity and capital management.

QUESTIONS

1. Define 100 percent reserve banking. What arguments can you make for or against it? How would commercial banks earn their income under such a system? Is 100 percent reserve banking more or less risky than fractional reserve banking? Why?

2. Obtain the balance sheet of the largest and smallest commercial banks in the city in which your school is located. (These may be obtained from Rand McNally's or Polk's Bank Directories.) How do the compositions of their balance sheets differ from each other and from the balance sheet for all banks shown in Table 10–2? Why?

3. In early days, bank noteholders attempted to convert their notes into gold upon rumors of bank difficulties. More recently, depositors have attempted to convert deposits into currency. What is the basic reason for this behavior? Why the increased faith in currency? What can be done to reduce the likelihood of such behavior?

4. Why should bank management be concerned with both return and risk? Discuss the difference between risk management and risk minimization.

What are the major risks that banks need to manage? Do all banks assume all of these risks? If not, what determines which risks they assume?

5. Liquidity management may be practiced on either the asset or the liability side of a bank's balance sheet. How are asset and liability liquidity management similar, and how do they differ? Why is liability management easier for larger and more solvent banks than for smaller banks?

6. What is the basic function of capital in a bank? On which side of the balance sheet is capital recorded? In what forms may it be? How is capital similar to deposits and how is it different? Why should depositors be concerned with the level of their bank's capital?

7. How and why are liquidity and capital management for a commercial bank related? How is each affected by an abrupt large deposit loss? How is each affected by interest rate risk or gap management?

8. Why are some bank activities classified as *on-balance-sheet* and others as *off-balance-sheet*? Give two examples of each type of activity. Some activities change through time from one classification to the other. Give an example

of one off-balance-sheet activity that does change and one that does not. How does income derived from on- and off-balance-sheet activities differ in form? For large banks, which is growing more rapidly? Why?

REFERENCES

Auerback, Ronald Paul, *Historical Overview of Financial Institutions.* Washington, D.C.: Federal Deposit Insurance Corporation, n.d.

"Bank Scoreboard," *Business Week.* An annual feature.

Brunner, Allan D., and William B. English, "Profits and Balance Sheet Developments of U.S. Commercial Banks in 1992," *Federal Reserve Bulletin,* July 1993, pp. 649–73 (annual article).

Cagan, Phillip, "The First Fifty Years of the National Banking System," in Deane Carson, ed., *Banking and Monetary Studies.* Homewood, Ill.: Irwin, 1963.

Cleveland, Harold van B., and Thomas F. Huertas, *Citibank: 1812–1970,* Cambridge, Mass.: Harvard University Press, 1985.

Davis, Steven I., *Excellence in Banking.* New York: St. Martin's Press, 1985.

Gardner, Mona J., and Dixie L. Mills, *Managing Financial Institutions,* 2nd ed. Chicago: Dryden Press, 1991.

Green, Timothy, "From a Pawnshop to Patron of the Arts in Five Centuries: Il Monte dei Paschi di Sienna," *Smithsonian Magazine,* July 1991, pp. 59–69.

Groseclose, Elgin, *Money and Man: A Survey of Monetary Experience,* 4th ed. Norman, Okla.: University of Oklahoma Press, 1976.

Hammond, Bray, "Banking before the Civil War," in Dean Carson, ed., *Banking and Monetary Studies.* Homewood, Ill.: Irwin, 1963.

Hammond, Bray, *Banks and Politics in America.* Princeton, N.J.: Princeton University Press, 1957.

Havrilesky, Thomas M., and John T. Boorman, *Current Perspectives in Banking: Operations, Management, and Regulation,* 2nd ed. Arlington Heights, Ill.: AHM, 1980.

Hempel, George H., Alan B. Coleman, and Donald G. Simonson, *Bank Management,* 3rd ed. New York: John Wiley, 1990.

Kaufman, George G. and Larry R. More, "Is Banking a Declining Industry? A Historical Perspective," *Economic Perspectives,* Federal Reserve Bank of Chicago, May/June 1994, pp. 1–21.

Klebaner, Benjamin, *Commercial Banking in the United States: A History.* Hinsdale, Ill.: Dryden Press, 1974.

Koch, Timothy W., *Bank Management,* 2nd ed. Chicago: Dryden Press, 1992.

Kolb, Robert W., ed., *The Commercial Bank Management Reader,* Miami, Fla.: Kolb Publishing, 1992.

Krooss, Herman E., and Martin R. Blyn, *A History of Financial Intermediaries.* New York: Random House, 1971.

MacLeob, Henry, "The Theory and Mechanism of Banking," in *A History of Banking in Great Britain,* in William G. Sumner et al., *A History of Banking in Leading Nations,* Vols. 1–4. New York: Journal of Commerce and Commercial Bulletin, 1896.

Mayer, Martin, *The Bankers.* New York: Weybright and Talley, 1974.

Robertson, Ross M., *The Comptroller and Bank Supervision: A Historical Appraisal.* Washington, D.C.: Office of the Comptroller of the Currency, 1968.

Rose, Peter S., *Commercial Bank Management.* 2nd ed. Homewood, Ill.: Irwin, 1993.

Selgin, George A., and Lawrence H. White, "The Evolution of a Free Banking System," *Economic Inquiry,* July 1987, pp. 439–57.

Sinkey, Joseph F., Jr, *Commercial Bank Financial Management,* 4th ed. New York: Macmillan, 1992.

Veasey, Edward E., "Evolution of Money and Banking in the United States," *Business Review,* Federal Reserve Bank of Dallas, December 1975.

Commercial Banks: Safety and Structure

Bank Failure

As discussed in Chapter 10, banking is a risky business. It always has been and always will be. Because it is risky, banks can fail. Commercial banks fail when they are unable immediately to convert their maturing deposits (including demand deposits withdrawn on demand) into currency or deposits at other banks at full face value. This may occur because of losses incurred in their intermediation activities from:

▼ Credit risk
▼ Liquidity (fire-sale) risk
▼ Interest rate risk
▼ Foreign exchange risk
▼ Fraud risk
▼ Operations risk

Banks maintain cash and secondary reserves to accommodate expected deposit outflows. Losses experienced when secondary reserves or other noncash assets are sold may be charged against capital. If these losses do not exceed the amount of the bank's capital, they do not reduce the value of the deposits. But, as may be seen from the bank balance sheet shown in Table 10–2, the ratios of primary plus secondary reserves of capital to deposits are reasonably small. Unexpected deposit losses that require the hurried sale of less-liquid loans and investments at below-market fire-sale prices may be expected to create larger losses. Larger losses may also be realized when an unexpectedly large number of borrowers default on their loans, or interest rates rise more than expected. If losses exceed the amount of capital, they must be charged against deposits. At that point, the market value of a bank's assets is less than that of its deposit liabilities, and the bank fails in economic terms. (Legally, a bank fails when its chartering agency or the FDIC determines that the book value of its assets is less than that of its deposits or fails to meet minimum capital requirements established by law.)

Like the failure of any business firm, the failure of a bank is a serious event, causing losses to its owners (shareholders), creditors (for banks, the FDIC and uninsured depositors), employees, suppliers, and, for banks, some loan customers. But bank failures may have more serious repercussions on a community than the failure of other firms. Because bank services are used by almost everyone in a community and bank deposits finance almost every sizable trade, the failure of a bank affects a large number of persons either directly or indirectly.

Bank Runs

Before a bank fails, some depositors, who are aware of the bank's problem, will attempt to withdraw their funds. This may start a run on the bank. Because banks operate on a fractional reserve basis, they may not have sufficient cash to meet all withdrawals and have to sell earning assets, possibly at a fire-sale loss, to raise the necessary cash. Thus, they are likely to incur liquidity problems. When they run, depositors may pursue one or more of three strategies. One, if they believe that the bank's problems are unique to that bank or a small group of banks and are not representative of the state of the entire banking system, they will redeposit their funds at other banks that they perceive to be safe. This is referred to as a **direct redeposit.** In this scenario, deposits are lost to the deposit-losing bank, but not to the banking system as a whole. Indeed, if the banks receiving the deposits believed that the bank suffering the run was solvent, they may recycle the funds through loans to the bank or purchasing assets from the bank. This would reduce the need for the bank to suffer fire-sale losses and prevent a liquidity problem from becoming a solvency problem.

Two, if depositors did not consider other banks safe, they could flee to perceived safe nonbank securities, say, U.S. Treasury securities. If the seller of the securities redeposited the proceeds in a bank, as is likely, or he or she would not have sold the securities, the reserves and deposits again do not leave the banking system. They just move among banks, and fire-sale losses are unlikely. This scenario represents a **flight to quality** and an **indirect redeposit.** Because banking services are largely interchangeable, much of the slack at the failed bank is taken up by the others. The failure is contained to the bank and its market area.

Moreover, failed banks are rarely liquidated and thus do not disappear as physical entities. Generally, a failed bank is sold or merged and remains in existence but under different management and possibly not as an independent entity. (The process of resolving a bank failure is described in Exhibit 11–1.) Most bank customers also have more than one banking connection and can shift to another bank or similar institution for their deposit and loan needs without great difficulties. Particularly in more recent years, many traditional banking services are being increasingly offered by other financial institutions and even basically nonfinancial firms, such as Sears and General Electric. Thus, the failure of individual banks should not inconvenience either their customers or communities proportionately more than the failure of any other business of comparable size.

Three, but what if both depositors and the sellers of safe securities fear that the problems are general? Then they may lose faith in all banks and become hesitant to redeposit the funds they have withdrawn. Rather, they may prefer to hold the funds as currency outside the banks. This is referred to as a **flight to currency.** The run on individual banks is now transformed into a run on the banking system. A loss of currency to the banking system is equivalent to a loss of reserves. Because banks operate on a fractional reserve basis so that (as is discussed in Chapter 15) deposits are a multiple of a bank's reserves, the currency loss will start a multiple con-

██████████████ EXHIBIT ██████████████

11–1

▼

Chronology of a Bank Failure:
What Goes on behind Closed Doors at the FDIC
before an Insured Bank's Doors are Closed

Every failing bank situation is different. It varies by the bank's size, its location, the cause of the problems, the state of its books, the attitude of the management, and the complexity of solution. But with the recent surge in failures the last few years, the FDIC has its system of handling failures pretty much down to a routine.

Here is what typically goes on behind closed doors at the FDIC before a bank's doors are closed for good, based on interviews with FDIC insiders.

TWO WEEKS BEFORE THE CLOSING

After months of speculation on the part of the bank's chartering authority about the bank being in danger of failing, the regulator by now will have a date in mind to shut down the bank. The ball game, in effect, is over.

The state regulator or the Comptroller of the Currency, whichever is the bank's chief regulator, will know that a closing is imminent from a recent or a current examination. Or maybe it's the recognition that the bank can't make a deadline for raising new capital.

Also at this time, the FDIC's regional division of bank supervision begins working with other regulatory agencies on a list of banks, holding companies, and other potential investors who might be willing and able to bid for the failing bank's deposits and certain assets. The FDIC prefers deposit assumptions to payoffs of insured deposits—it's usually less expensive for the insurance fund and much less traumatic for the local community.

A WEEK BEFORE CLOSING

Those who might be in a position to buy the bank are quietly contacted to come to a "bidder's conference" the next week regarding an undisclosed failing bank. FDIC regional staffers also are busy preparing financial data and other background on the bank to hand out at that meeting.

In addition, the agency's regional liquidation division begins establishing the team that will be working at the bank closing. This will include phone calls to field offices to find out how many liquidation specialists they can spare. In rare cases of large bank closings, phone calls may go out to other regions

asking for reinforcements.

MONDAY, TUESDAY, WEDNESDAY

On-site examinations by the chartering authority and the FDIC could continue on these days and might even go through the end of the week. FDIC staffers in Washington remain in contact with the regional office and synchronize their regulatory watches for the upcoming closing.

The regional liquidation office also begins making clandestine arrangements for a visit to the town later in the week. Its staff will make reservations at a local motel, usually for a group disguised as representatives of a fictitious computer firm so as not to start rumors. "We may have a whole bunch of mini-computers shipped in, so the name has to tie in," explains an FDIC official.

THURSDAY

The bidders conference takes place. This often can be an all-day affair, usually in a drape-drawn hotel room away from public view. It could be in the same city as the failing bank or as much as 100 miles away, to accommodate potential bidders.

The number of prospective bidders can vary. "A few weeks ago, we invited about 100 people for a relatively small bank and about seven showed up," says an FDIC spokesman. "Sometimes we invite 10 and they all show up." At the meeting, the secret identity of the bank is given out, as well as the background material about the bank and a rundown of FDIC bidding procedures and other considerations, such as regulatory requirements for capitalizing an acquisition.

There are stiff warnings that the identity of the failing bank is to remain a secret to the outside world. "They're told that if the information is revealed and we can determine who revealed it, that party won't be invited back in the future," says an FDIC spokesman.

By this day, the first of the FDIC's bank closing team arrives in town. The "computer specialists" will roam around in their car, checking out the bank to be closed. They'll scope out the size and location of its bank's offices. They'll talk secretly with the FDIC examiner in charge of the bank about what it looks like on the inside.

FRIDAY

D-Day has arrived. Bank closings typically occur on a Friday, giving the government the entire weekend to go through the books, calm down the depositors and the employees, and maybe have a new owner ready for the next business day. There has, though, been a movement recently to close banks on Thursdays, especially if the procedure appears likely to be routine.

By late morning, the entire FDIC closing team, usually 40 or 50 staffers, has arrived in the area.

Then, about 15 minutes before the bank is scheduled to end its business day, several FDIC officials who will be leading the closing team quietly enter the bank. There they'll seek out representatives of the chartering authority, who already have been inside the bank and are likely to be in closed session with the bank's board members, giving them the bad news.

When the lobby doors are closed at the end of the business day, the representatives of the chartering authority will add the real finishing touch—a notice on the door that the bank is closed. An official then will read aloud an order terminating the charter and appointing the FDIC receiver. Immediately, FDIC liquidation specialists put seals on bank records and other property to avoid any tampering.

Also, FDIC officials on the scene begin explaining the situation to bank employees, who are wondering if they have a job on Monday.

"One characteristic that all closing managers must have is compassion," an FDIC official said. "You have to remind yourself that you are dealing with people's lives."

Part of the briefing involves warning them that 40 or so more FDIC staffers will be swarming in within minutes. The FDIC doesn't send in the rest of their massive closing until the employees have been "forewarned and prepared" for that sight, says an FDIC spokesman.

It isn't until the bank is closed that the FDIC's regional officials will begin opening any bids for the bank. They then have a conference call with agency officials in the Washington headquarters, and soon the FDIC board will call a meeting to choose a winning bidder. If no bids come in that are acceptable to the FDIC, the agency may decide to pay off insured depositors.

Back in Washington, FDIC staffers are putting in "courtesy calls" to the congressmen and senators telling them of the closing. Also in Washington, the agency's corporate communications office begins making conference calls to members of the local and national media, informing them of the situation.

The FDIC's closing team likely will work late into the night and will always come back the next day, balancing and closing out the bank's books, plus making an inventory of the bank's assets.

THE NEXT WEEK

If a buyer has been found for the bank, on Monday morning the bank will reopen under a new name and new ownership. If there is to be a deposit payoff, a local announcement will be made that the bank's doors will be open, and customers are invited to receive their checks. FDIC attorneys and liquidators will continue working on the aftermath of the failed bank's problems—a matter that could take years to complete. And somewhere else in the United States, a mysterious group of computer salespeople will be checking into a motel, asking where they might be able to rent a few tables and chairs.

SOURCE: Abstracted from Jay Rosenstein, *American Banker*, September 2, 1986, p. 11. Reprinted by permission.

▲

traction in deposits (money) and credit. If a large number of banks were simultaneously required to liquidate assets to meet deposit withdrawals, fire-sale losses would be expected even on the best and most liquid assets. There would be few buyers for these assets, and their prices would fall sharply. Healthy, well-managed banks would be affected as well as weaker, sick banks. In this scenario, liquidity problems turn into solvency problems, and bank failures, unlike the failures of most other firms, are contagious, rippling out from the first banks to fail and knocking down other banks nationwide in domino fashion. Instability at individual banks leads to instability in the entire financial system. Under such circumstances, bank failures are more serious than the failure of comparable nonbank firms for a number of reasons:

1. Bank deposits constitute a large proportion of the total money supply. Reductions in the money supply from bank failures would seriously disrupt business activity nationwide and either start or intensify a downturn.
2. Not only is the amount of bank debt (including deposits) high relative to capital, but the number of creditors is large and the composition diverse. Many depositors, particularly smaller ones, do not view themselves as creditors. Rather, they consider commercial banks as safe depositories where they can store that part of their wealth they can least afford to lose. Bank failures reduce the core savings of many households, which reduces their spending and exerts further downward pressure on business activity.
3. Bank failures break ongoing loan relationships. Households and business-firm customers that have relied on bank financing must curtail activity until they find other sources of funds.

Although receiving widespread publicity when they do occur, for most of U.S. history, commercial bank failures have been less prevalent than failures of nonbank firms. Because loan defaults increase during economic downturns, bank failures similar to the failure of other firms, is more frequent in such periods. Thus, increases in the rate of bank failures tend to occur in periods of major national economic crisis, such as in 1819, 1837, 1857, 1877, 1884, 1893, 1907, and particularly in the Great Depression of 1929–1933. Between 1929 and 1933, more than 10,000 banks failed, reducing the number of banks from more than 25,000 to fewer than 15,000. These failures probably intensified the severity of the economic downturn. Not all bank failures, however, occur during national recessions or lead to such crises. During the 1920s, an average of 600 banks failed annually. Almost all of these were small banks in rural areas and reflected the sharp decline in farm product and land prices, which caused an equally sharp increase in farm loan defaults. Although large in number, these failures remained contained and did not spill over to other parts of the country. Indeed, nationwide contagious bank failures appear likely to have occurred only twice in U.S. history—in 1893 and 1929–1933.

Nevertheless, because of the substantial potential damage of bank failures and the widespread fear they invoke, attempts have been made throughout American history both to reduce the likelihood of individual bank failures and to contain them before they spread. The earliest attempts focused on restricting the note issue of banks by having the government periodically force the immediate conversion of bank notes into coin. This caused banks to hold greater cash reserves and less-risky assets. But this strategy was unpopular with the public as well as the banks, because it conflicted with the growing needs of the rapidly expanding economy for bank money and credit. A later attempt, after the Civil War, to increase the collateral that banks were required to maintain in the form of treasury securities (National Bank Acts of 1864 and 1865) against their note issue was effectively subverted by the rapid expansion of deposit banking.

In 1913, the Federal Reserve System was established to promote a healthy economic climate that would deter the spread of individual bank failure to other banks, to supervise banks more effectively, and to assist banks experiencing liquidity difficulties by providing credit assistance as the **lender of last resort.** But the failure of the Federal Reserve to prevent the depression of 1929 by not injecting sufficient reserves into the banking system to offset the currency withdrawn from banks by depositors led to the worst wave of bank failures in American history. In 1933, federal deposit insurance was established to deal with the basic cause of contagious bank failures—widespread attempts to convert deposits into currency. If depositors knew that their deposits were safe, they would be less likely to demand conversion. Individual bank failures would also be viewed more as isolated events and less likely to ignite a chain reaction of other failures nationwide. Insurance was initially provided for deposits up to $2,500 per account, and over the years, the amount was increased to $100,000. The Federal Deposit Insurance Corporation (FDIC) was established to administer the program. The FDIC charges banks premiums for the insurance and can borrow funds from the U.S. Treasury when necessary to finance payouts. (At the same time, the Federal Savings and Loan Insurance Corporation—FSLIC—, now the Savings Association Insurance Fund—SAIF— of the FDIC, was established to provide similar insurance for savings and loan associations.)

History of Bank Failures

Since the introduction of the FDIC, the average number of bank failures declined from more than 500 per year in the 1920s, and 2,000 per year in the early 1930s, to fewer than 100 per year in the mid- and late 1930s, and to fewer than 10 per year through the 1970s. However, the number of failures sharply increased in the 1980s, before declining again in the 1990s. (See Figure 11–1.) From World War II until 1973, bank failures almost disappeared from public attention. In that year, the United States National Bank of San Diego, with deposits of $1 billion, failed. This was the first large bank to fail since the establishment of the FDIC. The next year, the Franklin National Bank in New York failed. Before its failure, it had more than $3 billion in deposits and was the twentieth largest bank in the country.

By the end of the 1980s, the number of bank failures reached 200 per year and would have been even greater if the definition of failure was based on economic rather than accounting values. As is discussed later, with federal deposit insurance, economically insolvent institutions can continue to attract insured deposits and remain open. The resulting losses are borne mostly by the other banks through higher insurance premiums and, if these are insufficient, by the government instead of the banks' depositors. The number of S&L failures increased even faster. The losses borne by the FSLIC increased well beyond its ability to pay, and only the fallback guarantee on the federal government prevented a run from developing on the banking system as a whole. Finally, in 1989, Congress enacted the Financial Institutions Reform, Recovery and Enforcement Act (FIRREA) that abolished FSLIC, raised additional funds to reorganize and recapitalize the most insolvent savings and loan associations, shifted deposit insurance to the FDIC, and made it somewhat harder for SLAs to get into the same mess again. By that time, close to 1,000, or one-third of all S&Ls, with half of the $1.2 trillion total assets in the industry, were economically insolvent or close to it.

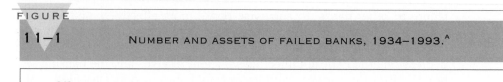

FIGURE

11–1   NUMBER AND ASSETS OF FAILED BANKS, 1934–1993.[A]

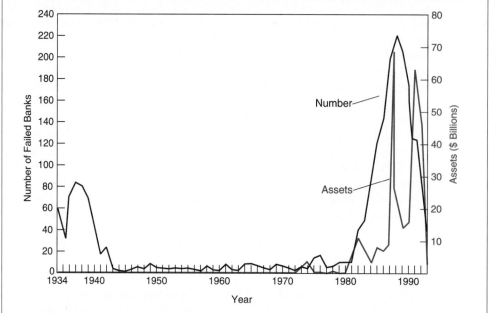

SOURCE: FDIC *Annual Reports* (various years).
[a] Failed banks include savings banks insured by the Bank Insurance Fund (BIF) and provided financial assistance by the FDIC.

Although failures of commercial banks were smaller, a number of very large banks failed, including in 1984 the Continental Illinois National Bank (Chicago), the seventh largest bank in the country at the time, nine of the ten largest banks in Texas between 1987 and 1989, and the Bank of New England in 1991. The FDIC incurred losses of more than $3 billion each in the failure of the First Republic and MCorp Banks in Texas, and more than $1 billion each in the failure of the Bank of New England Corp., the First City Bank (Texas), which failed twice, the Texas American Bank, and the Continental Illinois Bank. These losses were enlarged because the FDIC chose to protect all depositors fully in large bank failures rather than protect only the first $100,000 per account as required by law, as it did in the failure of many smaller banks. The largest commercial bank failures are shown in Table 11–1.

Reasons for the Increase in Failures

Between 1982 and 1992, some 1,500 banks failed. This represented three-quarters of all bank failures since the introduction of the FDIC in 1934. The losses incurred in the failures strained the resources of the FDIC almost to the breaking point, but the recovery in banking in the early 1990s prevented it from going the way of FSLIC. In 1993, the number of bank failures declined to 42, less than one-fifth the 221 banks that failed in 1988 and the lowest number since 1982. The reasons for the large increase in failures in

TABLE

11–1

197

COMMERCIAL
BANKS: SAFETY
AND STRUCTURE

LARGEST COMMERCIAL BANK FAILURES

Institution	Location	Date	Assets ($Billions)	Estimated Loss ($Billions)
First Republic Corp.	Dallas	July 29, 1988	33.4	3.7
Continental Illinois Bank	Chicago	Sept. 26, 1984	33.0	1.0
Bank of New England	Boston	Jan. 6, 1991	21.8	1.4
MCorp	Dallas	March 29, 1989	15.7	3.0
First City Bankcorp	Houston	April 20, 1988	11.2	1.1
Southeast Bank	Miami	Sept. 19, 1991	10.9	—
First City Bancorp	Houston	Oct. 30, 1992	8.8	0.1
Texas American	Fort Worth	July 20, 1989	4.8	1.1

SOURCE: FDIC.

the 1980s varied greatly, but in large measure reflected both high interest rates that sharply increased the interest cost of deposits to thrift institutions relative to their revenues from generally fixed-rate mortgage loans and a sharp reversal in the fast runup of real estate, agriculture, and petroleum prices that caused severe economic recessions in geographic regions specializing in these activities and sharp increases in defaults on loans. Economic stability and, to the extent that inflation affects interest rates, price level stability may be seen as important prerequisites for bank stability.

A substantial number of failures also reflected fraud and self-dealing by bank officers or directors. Such behavior had more serious results after the deregulation of deposit rates and the increase in deposit insurance coverage from $40,000 to $100,000 per account in 1980. As a result, these institutions could quickly attract large amounts of funds from outside their normal market areas through nationwide advertising and the use of money brokers (*brokered accounts*). The institutions promised high-interest returns on insured deposits, which depositors considered safe from loss regardless of the riskiness of the institution. Indeed, for many depositors, the riskier the bank under these circumstances, the better. Runs developed not from bad banks to good banks, as they did before deposit insurance, but from good banks to bad banks.

Many large commercial banks also were weakened by losses on commercial real estate loans and on loans to less developed countries (LDCs), particularly Latin American countries, which were unable to meet their scheduled debt service payments. Nevertheless, these failures and near-failures did not spread to other banks or cause financial panics. No national economic downturn was started by bank failures, and multiple bank failures were not set off by any economic recession. Funds withdrawn from troubled banks were redeposited at other banks perceived to be safe. While lost to the individual banks, the funds were not lost to the banking system as a whole. There was no net currency drain from the system and, thus, no multiple contraction in bank deposits or money. By removing the need to withdraw insured deposits to avoid losses, federal deposit insurance has

FIGURE

11–2   COMMERCIAL BANKING INDUSTRY CAPITAL: ASSETS RATIO, 1993.

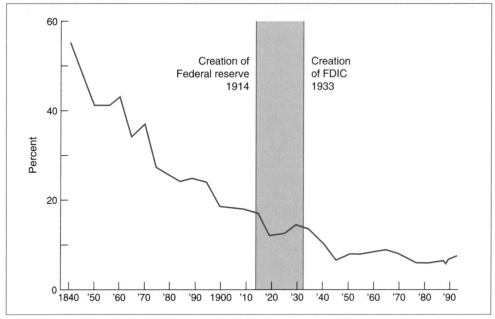

SOURCE: U.S. Treasury Department, *Modernizing the Financial System*, updated by author..

successfully cured the potential contagiousness of bank failures; instability at individual banks is contained to those banks and does not affect the national economy.[1] But, as will be argued in Chapter 18, the cost of this macrostability has been high; deposit insurance has reduced public concern over bank risk taking and unintentionally encouraged banks to become riskier.

By reducing the concern of depositors over the safety of their banks, the introduction of federal deposit insurance reduced the capital levels at which banks felt safe to operate without a withdrawal of deposits. As can be seen from Figure 11–2, the ratio of bank capital to on-balance-sheet assets has declined steadily from near 50 percent in 1840 to 20 percent in 1900 and 15 percent in the 1920s. But these figures understate the effective amount of capital available to absorb losses, as shareholders in all national banks and some state banks were liable for additional amounts up to the par value of their shareholdings in case of insolvency. Since 1940, capital ratios have declined to near 6 percent and even lower for SLAs; and the system of *double liability* has been abolished. As has become evident by the large num-

---

[1] In 1985, the failure of state-chartered savings and loan associations in Ohio and Maryland and in 1991 of credit unions in Rhode Island, which were insured by state-sponsored rather than federal insurance agencies, wiped out the resources of their insurance funds. Because, unlike the federal government, a state does not own the printing presses for money, Ohio, Maryland, and Rhode Island had no nontax resources to protect depositors at other similarly insured institutions, and depositors started a run on those institutions. The runs were finally contained when the state institutions were closed or required to obtain federal deposit insurance.

FIGURE

11-3

PROFITABILITY AMONG BANKS HAS VARIED MORE SINCE DEREGULATION IN THE EARLY 1980s.

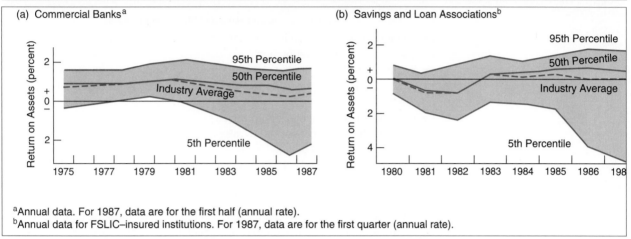

(a) Commercial Banks[a]

(b) Savings and Loan Associations[b]

[a]Annual data. For 1987, data are for the first half (annual rate).
[b]Annual data for FSLIC–insured institutions. For 1987, data are for the first quarter (annual rate).

SOURCE: Thomas D. Simpson, "Developments in the U. S. Financial System Since the Mid-1970s," *Federal Reserve Bulletin*, January 1988, p. 5

ber of bank failures, such low capital ratios are insufficient in a volatile economic environment. At the same time, financial institutions that are not covered by the federal safety net carry much higher capital ratios. For example, securities firms, casualty insurance companies, and finance companies all have capital ratios of 15 percent or more.

Since the beginning of broad deregulation in the early 1980s, the profitability of individual commercial banks has diverged significantly. Before this period, almost all banks moved in lock-step fashion within a narrow profit band around the mean. Since then, as can be seen from panel a in Figure 11–3, the band has widened greatly. A substantial number of banks have increased their profitability sharply, while an almost equal number have become problem banks or failed. (The same change has occurred in the savings and loan association industry as can be seen from panel b.) This pattern reflects both the greater freedom of the banks to make their own decisions (including the freedom to make their own mistakes) and intensified competition. A similar pattern has been observed in the airline industry after their deregulation in the late 1970s. Airline failures also increased sharply in the 1980s.

Reform of Deposit Insurance

The sharp increase in the number, size, and cost of bank failures in the late 1980s threatened to bankrupt the FDIC and shift the burden of the losses onto the taxpayer, much as the bankruptcy of the FSLIC from S&L losses had done earlier. Both to prevent additional losses and to reduce the incentives for risk taking inherent in the structure of deposit insurance, Congress enacted the Federal Deposit Insurance Corporation Improvement Act (FDICIA) at year-end 1991. This act dramatically changed the ground rules by which banks and thrift institutions operate. When the performance of an institution begins to deteriorate, the regulators are required to intervene

TABLE

11–2   THE FDIC IMPROVEMENT ACT OF 1991: HIGHLIGHTS

Deposit Insurance Reform and Prudential Regulation

▼ Requires early structured intervention by regulators tied to bank's capital ratio to discourage capital deterioration.

▼ Requires timely recapitalization or liquidation of a bank when its capital asset ratio declines below 2 percent to avoid losses to the Bank Insurance Fund (BIF) of the FDIC.

▼ Introduces risk-based deposit insurance premiums.

▼ Restricts the ability of the FDIC to raise deposit insurance coverage above $100,000 per account in failed banks.

▼ Reduces the incentive of the Fed to provide discount window loans to failing banks.

Product Powers

▼ Little. Permits well-capitalized banks to continue raising brokered deposits and selling insurance, where permitted, and generally restricts state banks to same powers as national banks.

Geographical Powers

▼ None

Regulatory Powers

▼ None

Other

▼ Liberalizes lending powers of thrift institutions.

Note: The provisions were phased in through time and became effective at various dates through 1995.

and impose sanctions similar to those the market would impose on troubled firms in nonfederally insured industries to try to turn the institution around. If the institution continues to deteriorate, the sanctions become harsher and more mandatory. If all else fails and the institution runs down its capital to low levels, the regulators are required to resolve the institution through sale, merger, or liquidation before its capital turns negative. Thus, at least in theory, losses are confined to shareholders who expect to take risk and not spread to depositors or the FDIC. Only few institutions may be expected to sink through all these sanctions and fail. The major prudential and deposit insurance reform provisions of FDICIA are summarized in Table 11–2 and are discussed in greater detail in Chapters 16, 18, and 19.

Bank Structure and Organization

At the end of 1993, there were fewer than 11,000 commercial banks in the United States. As can be seen from Figure 11–4, until recently this number has remained relatively unchanged at near 15,000 since 1933 but is less than half as many as the record 31,000 banks in 1921. For reasons peculiar to this country (discussed later), the number of banks in the United States is far greater than those in other industrialized countries, even after adjustment for differences in population and income. With the exception of the

FIGURE

11—4   NUMBER OF COMMERCIAL BANKS AND BRANCHES, 1915–93

201

COMMERCIAL
BANKS: SAFETY
AND STRUCTURE

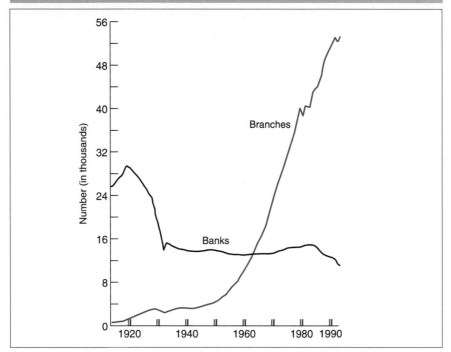

SOURCE: Board of Governors of the Federal Reserve System. *1989, Historical Chart Book,* p. 82, updated by author.

Bank of North Dakota, which is owned by the state of North Dakota, all commercial banks are privately owned. Commercial banks differ among themselves according to the source of their charter, number of offices, type of ownership, and size. These characteristics are referred to as **bank struc-ture.**

Charter

With the exception of a few small, long-standing, nonincorporated banks, all commercial banks have special charters. Banks may obtain charters from either the federal or a state government. The existence of both a national and a state chartering agency is known as the **dual banking system.** For the most part, there is not much difference between a national and a state charter. Federally chartered banks must include "national" (or "national association"—"N.A.") in their title and must be members of both the Federal Reserve System and the Federal Deposit Insurance Corporation. State banks cannot use the title "national" and are not required to join either the Fed or the FDIC but may apply for membership. In effect, all banks have federal deposit insurance.[2] Since 1980, state nonmember banks are subject to the same Federal Reserve System reserve requirements as Fed member banks. (The bank regulatory agencies are discussed in Chapter 16.)

[2] Deposits at the Bank of North Dakota are guaranteed by the State of North Dakota.

The powers of commercial banks are spelled out in their charters. National banks, for example, may exercise

> all such incidental powers as shall be necessary to carry on the business of banking; by discounting and negotiating promissory notes, drafts, bills of exchange, and other evidence of debt; by receiving deposits; by buying and selling exchange, coin and bullion; [and] by loaning money on personal security. . . .[3]

National banks also must conform to many of the regulations applicable to state-chartered banks, including restrictions on branch offices. Small differences exist in some operating powers of national and state banks, and they are regulated and examined by different agencies. (The product powers are discussed in greater detail in Chapter 16.)

Although of relatively minor importance today, dual banking has a long tradition in the United States and is zealously guarded by bankers. At year-end 1993, only one-third of the total number of commercial banks had national charters. However, these tended to be the larger banks and account for more than half of all banking assets.

The most important remaining major nonchartered private commercial bank is Brown Brothers Harriman. Private banks are partnerships and are not eligible to belong to the Fed or FDIC. They are not examined by government bank examiners. At year-end 1993, there were only four private banks in the country.

Branching

Unlike most other business firms, commercial banks are restricted in the number and location of offices they may operate. The ability to operate branch offices is determined by state law. Except for a few, primarily "grandfathered" banks, banks may not currently operate full-service branch offices in more than one state, although Congress in 1994 enacted legislation that will permit them to do so generally after June 1997. That helps to explain the large number of banks in the United States. Nationwide branching is permissible in most other countries. Indeed, until recently, there were even some **unit-banking** states, in which banks may have only one full-service office. In 1991, Colorado, the last remaining unit-banking state in the country, began to permit branching on a limited basis. While there are no unit-banking states left in the U.S., there are unit banks by their own choice. In about 10 percent of the states, banks are permitted to operate branch offices only within a limited geographic distance of their main office. These are **limited branch** states. In the remaining 90 percent of the states, banks may operate branch offices throughout the state. These are **statewide-branch** states. In recent years, there has been a trend toward more liberal branch laws, and more states have adopted less restrictive limited- or statewide-branch banking. In the 1960s, approximately one-third of the states permitted only unit banking and only one-third permitted statewide branching. As would be expected, the more restrictive the branching legislation in a state, the greater the number of banks per person. However, the

---

[3] *Federal Reserve Act and Other Statutory Provisions Affecting the Federal Reserve System* (Washington, D.C.: Board of Governors of the Federal Reserve System, 1983), pp. 89–90.

total number of banking offices per person is spread more evenly among the states. The liberalization of intrastate branching restrictions helps to explain the recent decline in the number of banks.

Geographically, the unit-banking states were located predominantly in the Midwest, the limited-branch states in the East, and the statewide-branch states in the West. The unit banking in the Midwest reflected the legacy of farmer distrust of banks and creditors in the early days of this country. Then, and ever earlier, when their forebears were in Europe, many farmers had been in debt to banks for many years. In years of bad harvest, they were frequently unable to repay their loans, and some were forced to sell their farms. Banks were only permitted reluctantly to organize in these states, which tried to curtail their power by prohibiting them from expanding through branch offices.

The number of full-service offices has expanded sharply in recent years. At year-end 1993, there were some 55,000 such branch offices, seven times the 1950 number and nearly four times the number of commercial banks. Bank affiliates of the BankAmerica Corp. alone have more than 2,000 branches in 11 states. In 1920, there were fewer than 1,500 branches of all banks. The increase reflects the shift of population from cities to suburbs, liberalized branching laws, more restrictive requirements for chartering new banks than for establishing additional offices, improved computer and telecommunications technology for managing large and geographically diverse banking systems, and the need to compete for customers by offering greater location convenience during the years that deposit rate ceilings (Regulation Q) prohibited competition on the basis of interest rates.

Holding Companies

Commercial banks may be either independent or owned by a holding company. A holding company is an organization that owns other firms. Holding companies are generally used in banking to (1) increase flexibility (such as operating banks in more than one state when interstate branching is prohibited and engaging in activities not permitted commercial banks themselves), (2) increase accessibility to capital (particularly for smaller banks in unit-banking states), and (3) decrease risk through diversification. At the end of 1993, about three-quarters of all banks were owned by some 5,500 bank holding companies. These banks accounted for more than 90 percent of total bank assets. As a result of multiple ownership of banks by holding companies, the number of independent banking organizations in the United States is only about 8,000.

Since 1933, bank holding companies have been regulated by the federal government. In 1956, the Bank Holding Company Act restricted holding companies that owned two or more banks (multibank holding companies, or **MBHCs**) from (1) engaging in nonfinancial activities and limited financial activities basically to those permitted banks themselves and (2) expanding through the acquisition of banks in states that did not explicitly permit acquisition by out-of-state holding companies (the Douglas Amendment to the act).

During the 1960s, there was a significant expansion in the formation of holding companies that owned only one bank (one-bank holding companies, or **OBHCs**), in order for banks to enter into activities that neither

WORLDWIDE ACTIVITIES OF CITICORP AS OF SEPTEMBER 30, 1993

A. IN THE UNITED STATES (MORE THAN 1,500 OFFICES IN 43 STATES AND THE DISTRICT OF COLUMBIA)

Subsidiary	Function	Scope
Citibank, N.A.	Full-service bank (see overseas operations below)	275 branches concentrated in New York City metropolitan area
Citibank Delaware	Wholesale banking; credit-related insurance	New Castle, Del.
Citibank (Florida), N.A.	Full-service bank	11 Florida branches; 1 Cayman Is. branch
Citibank (Maine), N.A.	Full-service bank	7 branches throughout Maine
Citibank (Nevada), N.A.	Consumer bank; bankcard activities	5 branches throughout Nevada
Citibank (New York State)	Full-service bank	29 branches in upstate New York
Citibank (South Dakota), N.A.	Primarily bankcard activities	Sioux Falls, S.D.
DeAnza Bank	Full-service bank	2 branches in northern California
Citibank, Federal Savings Bank	Primary vehicle for home mortgages	225 branches and 40 loan offices/service centers in 18 states and D.C.
Citibank International[a]	Edge Act international banking corporation	6 branches and 2 representative offices in 4 states
Citicorp Banking Corporation	Domestic holding company for U.S. and foreign operations (see below)	26 direct U.S. subsidiaries with offices in 20 states and D.C.
Citicorp Credit Services, Inc.	Customer service and collections for credit card business	22 offices in 13 states
Citicorp Diners Club Inc.	Travel and entertainment cards	16 offices in 11 states
Citicorp Investment Services[a]	Broker/dealer	550 offices in 11 states and D.C.
Citicorp Mortgage, Inc.	Mortgage securities; consumer loans	3 offices in 2 states
Citicorp North America, Inc.	Commercial lending and leasing	29 offices in 16 states and D.C.
Citicorp Real Estate, Inc.[a]	Project finance; commercial mortgages	10 offices in 6 states and D.C.
Citicorp Securities, Inc.	Securities underwriting, trading and distributing; credit card marketing	4 offices in 3 states
Citicorp Services, Inc.	Citicorp travelers checks; payment instruments; remittance services	7 offices in 6 states
Quotron Systems, Inc.	Financial information services	14 offices in 8 states and D.C.
The Student Loan Corporation	Student loans and all related services; 20% publicly held and NYSE listed	Headquartered in Pittsford, N.Y.
Transaction Technology, Inc.	Financial Communications and delivery systems for Citicorp	Head office in Santa Monica, Calif.

B. Overseas (about 2,000 offices in 91 countries and territories)

Subsidiary	Function	Scope
Citibank, N.A.	Commercial and consumer banking	312 branches and 13 representative offices in 69 countries
Citibank Overseas Investment Corporation[a]	Edge Act investment corporation and financial services holding company	535 subsidiaries and 29 affiliates with offices in 60 countries
Citicorp Banking Corporation	Overseas commercial banking; subsidiaries engage in investment and merchant banking; insurance; venture capital (see U.S. also)	4 branches in 4 countries; 3 intermediary holding companies and 23 other direct subsidiaries with presence in 29 countries
Citicorp Deutschland AG[b]	German holding company for diversified financial services	Separate bank subsidiaries for consumer (305 branches) and corporate banking (8 branches) in Germany
Citibank Canada[b]	Commercial banking; leasing; venture capital; securities brokering/dealing	9 branches; 6 subsidiary offices (5 in Canada and 1 in Texas)
Citibank Espana S.A.[b]	Commercial banking; insurance, mutual funds	101 bank branches and 10 subsidiary offices in Spain
Citibank Investments Limited[b]	U.K. holding company: merchant banking, foreign exchange, insurance	40 direct U.K. subsidiaries with holdings in 9 additional countries
Citibank Limited[b]	Australian commercial bank with diversified financial subsidiaries	17 bank branches; 17 savings bank branches; 12 consumer finance offices

SOURCE: Citicorp.
[a]Direct subsidiary of Citibank, N.A.
[b]Subsidiary of Citibank Overseas Investment Corporation.

individual banks nor MBHCs could engage in. By 1970, OBHCs engaged in approximately 100 different nonbanking activities, including agriculture, mining, manufacturing, transportation, and retail trade. In that year, Congress brought OBHCs under all the provisions of the Bank Holding Company Act and restricted the activities in which nonbank affiliates of any bank holding company could engage to those "so closely related to banking or managing or controlling banks as to be a proper incident thereto." Determination of this criterion was delegated to the Board of Governors of the Federal Reserve System. OBHCs engaging in other types of activities had to divest themselves of these.

Relatively few bank holding companies hold substantial nonbank assets. In 1992, nonbank assets totaled only 7 percent of the total assets of some 250 bank holding companies that had significant nonbank operations. The largest dollar amount of assets in permissible nonbank activities was in thrift institutions followed by securities brokerage, finance companies, and mortgage banking. Although they could not operate full-service offices across state lines until the 1980s, bank holding companies were able to operate their nonfull-service banking offices across state lines. By the late 1970s, many bank holding companies operated nonfull-service offices in major cities in a number of states and some had such offices in every large city in the country.

In the 1980s, the limitation on full-service bank expansion across state lines through the holding company format started to ease. The Garn-St. Germain Act of 1982 permitted bank holding companies to purchase large failed banks and any size failed savings and loan associations in other states, and some states permitted these associations then to be converted into banks. More important, states began to adopt legislation that satisfied the provisions of the Douglas Amendment and explicitly permitted out-of-state ownership of banks, although primarily on a reciprocal basis. By 1994, every state had enacted legislation that permitted acquisitions by out-of-state bank holding companies, although sometimes only from neighboring or regional states, and generally only by acquiring existing banks rather than being able to start banks new or *de novo*. This transformation to full-service interstate banking is discussed more fully in Chapter 19.

Larger bank holding companies also operate in foreign countries. The worldwide activities conducted by Citicorp (New York), which is the parent holding company of Citibank, the largest bank in the country, are shown in Table 11–3. Citicorp is the largest bank holding company in the United States and, through its acquisition of four savings and loan associations, also the largest SLA holding company. It is also by far the largest bank issuer of credit cards. In 1992, over half of its deposits and one-half of its business loans were outside the United States. In some years, half of its net income was also derived from outside the United States. This makes Citicorp truly an international bank.

Bank Size

Commercial banks vary greatly in size. At year-end 1992, assets at Citibank, the largest bank in the United States, totaled about $165 billion, an amount about 10,000 times as large as at the smallest banks and more than 500 times as large as at the average bank. At year-end 1991, the average insured bank asset size was slightly less than $300 million. However, as can be seen from Table 11–4, most banks were relatively small—over 90 percent smaller than average. About 50 percent of all banks had assets of less than $50 million and held only 4 percent of all bank assets. On the other end, 179 banks had assets of more than $3 billion. Although they accounted for only 1 percent of all banks, they held 60 percent of all assets.

Moreover, the relative importance of large banking organizations would be even greater if one considered bank holding companies, which may own more than one bank, rather than only banks. For example, Citibank alone accounted for 4.7 percent of total bank assets, but its parent holding company, Citicorp, accounted for 6.1 percent. If only domestic assets were considered, BankAmerica Corp., the parent holding company of the Bank of America, would be the largest single banking organization, accounting for 5.2 percent of total domestic deposits. In contrast, Citicorp holds only 2 percent and ranks only fourth. This reflects the greater importance of Citicorp as an international bank.

Do big banks have an advantage over small banks? The answer depends on what is meant by *advantage*. The fact that banks of such different sizes coexist suggests that no one size is inherently more profitable than any other. And indeed, this is borne out by the data. Any advantage large size has for a given type of bank service appears to be offset by the cost of additional branch offices and of other, new types of activities that tend to accompany increases in bank size. Much the way supermarkets and small convenience grocery stores coexist by catering to customers who make different-sized purchases, large and small banks cater to large and small loan and deposit customers, respectively. As banks get larger, they add additional services for larger regional, national, and eventually international business and government customers. Thus, large banks bear no more similarity to small banks than supermarkets do to convenience stores. While large banks have been getting larger in recent years, often through

TABLE

11–4 SIZE DISTRIBUTION OF INSURED COMMERCIAL BANKS, 1991

Asset Size ($Millions)	Banks		Total Assets	
	Number	Percent	$Billions	Percent
Less than 25	2,844	24	44	1
25–50	3,164	27	113	3
50–100	2,773	23	197	6
100–300	2,119	18	342	10
300–500	389	3	149	4
500–1,000	263	2	183	5
1,000–3,000	189	2	336	10
3,000–10,000	130	1	714	21
10,000 and over	49	[a]	1,352	40
Total	11,920	100	3,430	100

SOURCE: Federal Deposit Insurance Corporation, *Statistics on Banking 1991*, p. 28.
[a]Less than 0.5 percent.

EXHIBIT

11–2

▼

Does World Size Matter in Banking?

Some observers argue that a visible indicator of weakness in the U.S. banking system relative to banks in other countries is the decline in the number of U.S. banks among the largest 25, 50, or 100 in the world. In the mid-1970s, the Bank of America was the largest bank in the world, and five U.S. banks were among the largest 25. Some 15 years later in 1991, no U.S. banks were among the top 25, and only five were among the top 100. (U.S. organizations would rank higher if holding companies rather than banks were used.) Japanese banks were the seven largest, and eight Japanese banks were among the top ten. Is this a sign of weakness that requires urgent public policy attention?

Those that argue it does focus on the prestige that world size per se brings, as well as the additional profitability of being able to service the world's largest corporations and governments. Moreover, to them, size is a sign of strength, and only the strongest banks can grow to be world-class size.

Others, however, argue that size per se, either in the U.S. or worldwide, is not important. What really matters in terms of both contribution and prestige is the bottom line—profitability. And, as is discussed in this chapter, there is no convincing evidence of economies of size that make the largest banks automatically more efficient and profitable than other banks, except the very smallest. Indeed, during the U.S. banking problems in the 1980s, larger regional banks were far more profitable on average than the largest money-center banks located in New York and California that operated both nationally and internationally.. Moreover, if some banks are viewed by regulators as "too big to fail" now, would encouraging even larger banks be wise public policy? Smaller banks can and do serve large clients by joining forces and participating in consortium or syndicate loans. Few major corporations limit their banking relationship to a single bank. To support their argument, the proponents point out that ranking of the world's most profitable banks in 1991 found that 4 of the 10 most profitable banks among the world's 300 largest banks and 19 of the 50 most profitable banks were U.S. institutions. In contrast, the most profitable large Japanese bank ranked only 109th.

mergers, many new, small banks have entered the industry. Whether bank size matters globally as well as domestically is discussed in Exhibit 11–2.

Structure and Performance

We are interested in the structure of banking not only for its own sake but also because economic theory suggests that, by affecting the intensity of competition, the structure of an industry is an important determinant of its performance in terms of prices charged or paid, profitability, and the quality and innovativeness of services offered. But structure (S) is not the only variable to affect a bank's performance. It is also influenced by regulation (R), legislation (L), economic conditions in the bank's market area (E), the quality of bank management (*M*), and other factors (*X*). This relationship may be written in function form as:

$$P = f(S, R, L, E, M, X)$$

where *P* is a measure of performance.

Because at least some of the structure variables, such as chartering new banks and permitting mergers among existing banks, are under the control of bank regulators, it may be possible to change the performance of banks in a community if we are disappointed with their performance by easing or tightening the chartering of new banks, easing or tightening the approval of mergers, permitting greater branch banking, and so on. The evidence suggests that bank performance is slightly, but statistically significantly, affected by the number of banks in a market area—the larger the number, the lower loan rate charged and the higher deposit rates paid. But the relevant market area is likely to differ for different-sized banks; for different bank services (for example, small and large business loans) and different bank customers (for example, households and farmers). Some banks and bank customers operate in a national market, others in a regional market, and still others in a local market. The concentration ratios—the percent of deposits held by the largest *X* banking organizations—differ for different market areas. In 1992, the largest three bank holding companies in each market area held 12 percent of domestic deposits nationally, 68 percent in metropolitan areas, and 89 percent in nonmetropolitan areas. Thus, concentration is not very great at the national level but increases substantially at local levels. Not surprisingly, the smaller the market, the fewer the banks and the greater the concentration.

Nationwide, as can be seen from Table 11–5, the percent of domestic deposits held by the top 10, 25, 50, and 100 banking organizations has been increasing, particularly in recent years, primarily as a result of an increase in the acquisitions of banks by holding companies as expansion across state lines was liberalized. In addition to the number of banks, the availability of bank substitutes, such as SLAs and finance companies, will also affect the intensity of competition.

TABLE

11–5   NATIONWIDE BANK CONCENTRATION RATIOS, 1960–1992[a]

Year	Percent of Domestic Deposits Held by			
	Top 10	Top 25	Top 50	Top 100
1960	21	32	40	50
1970	20	31	39	48
1980	19	29	37	47
1990	20	35	49	61
1992	24	39	52	63

SOURCE: Board of Governors of the Federal Reserve System.
[a]For bank holding companies.

International Banking

Firms that engage in international trade frequently prefer to do business with their own banks rather than with foreign banks. Domestic banks may be expected to be familiar with the firm's history and particular financing needs, talk its own language, and practice the same customs. Also, it is more comfortable to conduct business with domestic banks. As international trade and finance have increased, so has the movement of commercial banks across national boundaries—both to pursue their domestic customers and to search for new business. International banking, however, is conducted primarily by the largest banks. In 1990, fully 50 percent of all assets at overseas offices of U.S. banks were owned by only four large bank holding companies and 80 percent by only 10 such companies. About half of the deposits of the largest U.S. money-market-center banks were at overseas offices.

In recent years, foreign operations became less glamorous to many U.S. banks. A number of Latin American and East European countries that had borrowed heavily from large U.S. banks began to experience severe financial strains and were unable to meet their debt service payments in full. As a result, the earnings of these banks were significantly reduced and these banks have become more hesitant to make additional major loans to foreign countries. Foreign country risk exposure became a major concern of bank management.

U.S. Overseas Offices

U.S. banks operate overseas banking offices in three major forms: branches, subsidiaries, and Edge Act offices. At year-end 1992, 120 U.S. banks operated some 775 subsidiaries and branch offices with more than $500 billion assets. As is shown in Table 11–3, Citibank alone operated more than 300 branch offices in some 70 countries. As already noted, over half of its total deposits are at overseas offices.

After growing rapidly, the overseas activity of U.S. banks has decreased slightly in recent years. In 1960, only eight U.S. banks operated 131 branch offices with less than $4 billion in assets. In 1985, 163 banks operated nearly 1,000 branches. The largest number of U.S. branches are in Argentina, the United Kingdom, Hong Kong, and the Bahama and Cayman Islands. The branches in these islands are primarily "shell" operations to avoid U.S. taxes and restrictions.

Edge Act corporations are special subsidiaries of U.S. and foreign firms in the United States that engage primarily in international banking and financial operations. They may have domestic and foreign offices. They have wider powers than U.S. banks to participate in operations permitted foreign banks in their own countries, but are prohibited U.S. banks in the United States by U.S. laws. In 1992, there were 94 Edge Act corporations operating some 44 branches in the U.S. and abroad. Seventy-seven of the Edge Act corporations are owned by U.S. banks. U.S. banks also own majority interests in a wide variety of types of foreign financial institutions, such as finance companies, investment banks, lending companies, and so on, including those they cannot own in the United States. For example, in the mid-1980s U.S. banks owned 12 investment banking firms in the United Kingdom, 6 in Hong Kong, 5 in Australia, and 4 each in Singapore and Switzerland.

In 1981, domestic and foreign banks in the United States were given permission to establish *international banking facilities* (IBFs) in this country, which could accept time deposits from foreign customers without being subject to either reserve requirements or deposit-rate ceilings and could extend credit to foreign borrowers. Except for being located in the United States, IBFs function like overseas branches. Their primary purpose was to increase the competitiveness of U.S. banks in attracting international banking activities that were being conducted by foreign banks and branches. In particular, the absence of reserve requirements was intended to permit U.S. banks to offer terms to foreign depositors comparable to those on Eurodollars and thus attract these funds to domestic offices.

But after an initial rash of new charters, IBFs have not turned out to be as popular as expected, primarily because of deregulation of domestic offices. By yearend 1993, there were 524 IBFs in operation. This was down slightly from their peak. At last count, nearly half of these, holding more than three-quarters of the assets, were located in New York State. Most of the remainder were in California and Florida. Less than half of the IBFs were owned by U.S. banks. Although IBFs have attracted business that were formerly conducted offshore, they do not appear to have increased the overall volume of international business conducted by U.S. banks or foreign banks in the United States. Business was primarily shifted to the IBFs from offshore U.S. banks and from U.S. offices of foreign banks.

Foreign Offices in the United States

At year-end 1992, there were some 700 commercial banking affiliates of 300 foreign banks in the United States. Although the rate of increase has slowed in recent years, this was more than five times the number in 1973. Sixty-five percent of the affiliates and 85 percent of the assets were in New York and California. By far, the largest number were operated by Japanese banks. Total assets at the domestic affiliates of foreign banks were nearly $1.2 trillion and accounted for 30 percent of total banking assets in the United States and fully 45 percent of business lending.

U.S. affiliates of foreign banks are principally in the form of agencies, branches, and subsidiary banks. Branch offices are the largest and the most rapidly expanding type of foreign office. They are generally full-service offices. The number of U.S. offices increased from 32 to 378 between 1973 and 1992, and assets jumped from $10 billion to nearly $600 billion. Since the International Banking Act of 1978 and until 1997, foreign banks may establish full-time service branches only in their designated home state. However, they may operate agencies and limited-service branches in other states and may continue to operate any full-service branches that they had in these states at the time the act was enacted. Thus, many foreign banks operate in more than one state. Two-thirds of all foreign branches are in New York State, followed by Illinois and California, with nearly 15 percent each.

Agencies may lend and transfer funds but cannot accept regular deposits from domestic residents. They are established when the foreign bank wishes to avoid some aspect of state law that would apply to full-service offices, such as mandatory FDIC insurance or reciprocity in establishing offices of U.S. banks in the foreign country. In 1992, there were about 250 agency offices with $95 billion in assets operating mostly in New York and California.

Subsidiary banks are chartered as U.S. banks and operate under the same regulations. They may be owned by foreign bank or nonbank interests. At year-end 1992, controlling ownership in 90 U.S. banks was held by foreign banks and that of others was held by nonbank foreigners. Subsidiary banks operate primarily in New York, California, and Illinois. Some have many offices and engage in domestic retail as well as international activities. A few concentrate on the needs of particular ethnic groups associated with the home country of the parent bank. For example, the Sumitomo Bank in California has branch offices statewide serving the Japanese community. Others have not emphasized their foreign affiliation, except in their names. The European-owned European-American Bank and Trust Company purchased the assets and offices of the failed Franklin National Bank of New York in the mid-1970s and aimed to serve the same clientele. Still others show even less of their foreign ownership. For example, the Marine Midland Bank in New York, the thirtieth largest bank in the country, is owned by the Hong Kong and Shanghai Bank, but shows little outward sign of its foreign ownership.

Eleven of the foreign-owned subsidiary banks rank among the 100 largest banks in the United States; these are identified in Table 11–6. This number is down slightly from 14 in the mid-1980s. The asset share of for-

TABLE

▼

11–6

**LARGEST FOREIGN-OWNED BANKS IN THE
UNITED STATES, DECEMBER 1992**

U.S. Bank	Major Foreign Owner (country)	Assets $Billions	Rank
Union Bank (California)	Japan	16.9	27
National Westminster (New York)	United Kingdom	16.3	29
Marine Midland (New York)	Hong Kong	16.3	30
Harris Trust (Illinois)	Canada	9.7	54
Bank of Tokyo (New York)	Japan	8.5	66
Bank of California	Japan	8.1	70
Sanwa Bank (California)	Japan	7.3	77
LaSalle Bank (Illinois)	Netherlands	7.1	78
First National (Maryland)	Ireland	6.8	81
National Westminster (New Jersey)	United Kingdom	6.7	84
European American (New York)	Netherlands	5.6	99

SOURCE: Board of Governors of the Federal Reserve System and *American Banker.* Reprinted with permission from *American Banker.*

TABLE 11–7	ASSETS OF FOREIGN BANKS HAVE GROWN RAPIDLY IN MOST MAJOR COUNTRIES (PERCENT OF TOTAL ASSETS OF ALL BANKS IN SELECTED COUNTRIES)			
Host Country	1960	1970	1980	1985
Belgium	8.2	22.5	41.5	51.0
France	7.2	12.3	15.0	18.2
Germany	0.5	1.4	1.9	2.4
Italy	a	a	0.9	2.4
Japan	a	1.3	3.4	3.6
Luxembourg	8.0	57.8	85.4	85.4
Netherlands	a	a	17.4	23.6
Switzerland	a	10.3	11.1	12.2
United Kingdom	6.7	37.5	55.6	62.6
United States	a	5.8	8.7	12.0

SOURCE: Bank for International Settlements, *Recent Innovations in International Banking*, April 1986.
Note: For some countries, data are closest reporting date to year shown.
a =No figures available.

eign-owned banks and bank offices has grown rapidly from near zero percent of total bank assets in the United States in the early 1970s to 15 percent in the early 1980s and to 25 percent in 1992. Most of the increase in recent years has been from Japanese-owned banks. These institutions have more than doubled their market share from 5 to 12 percent between 1982 and 1992 and now account for nearly one-half of the assets of all foreign banks in the United States.

The trend to international banking is not restricted to either the United States or U.S. banks. The importance and rapid growth in the percentage of banking assets held by foreign banks in major countries are shown clearly in Table 11–7. In 1985, assets at foreign bank institutions accounted for 85 percent of all bank assets in Luxembourg, for 63 percent in the United Kingdom, and 57 percent in Belgium. In 1960, none of these percentages were greater than 10 percent. In the United States, assets at foreign banks accounted for 12 percent of total bank assets, nearly 50 percent more than in 1980 and double that in 1970. The integration of the economies of the 12 major European countries that are members of the European Community (EC) promises to increase even more the percentage of bank assets held by foreign banks in the other countries in the EC.

The rapid growth in international banking has reduced the importance of U.S. banks in this area. As can be seen in Table 11–8, in 1984, U.S. banks held the largest share of total international bank assets or bank claims on nondomestic customers—26 percent. By 1992, although international assets at U.S. banks increased by 10 percent, their relative importance had declined to 11 percent. This was well behind the 28 percent held by Japanese banks and the same percentage as those in France and Germany.

| TABLE 11–8 | INTERNATIONAL BANK ASSETS BY COUNTRY, 1984–1992 |

Parent Country of Bank	December 1984		December 1992		Percent Increase 1984–1992
	$Billions	Percent Share	$Billions	Percent Share	
France	201	9	656	11	226
Germany	143	6	684	11	378
Italy	91	4	407	7	347
Japan	518	23	1,678	28	324
Switzerland	83	4	397	6	378
United Kingdom	169	8	294	5	73
United States	595	26	656	11	10
Other	451	20	1,272	21	182
Total	2,251	100	6,044	100	169

SOURCE: *Federal Reserve Bulletin*, February 1990, p. 40, and Bank for International Settlements.

SUMMARY

Commercial bank failures are frequently considered more serious than the failure of most other types of business firms. The consequences could spread far beyond the stockholders and employees of the failed institution. Money supply and liquid wealth in the service area may be reduced, and credit arrangements that finance ongoing operations disrupted. In addition, if depositors lose faith in all banks and hold their funds as currency outside of banks, bank failures are contagious, spreading to other, financially health institutions and disrupting economic activity nationwide. To reduce both the probability of individual bank failure and the impact on other banks, government deposit insurance was introduced in the United States in 1933, after 40 percent of the banks in the country failed during the Great Depression. After having declined sharply to less than 10 per year, the lowest rate in U.S. history, bank failures have increased sharply in recent years. Nevertheless, primarily because of federal deposit insurance, the individual failures have not destabilized the banking system as a whole.

There are nearly 11,000 commercial banks in the United States. Banks may obtain charters from either the federal government (national banks) or the state government (state banks) and may operate branch offices if state law permits. Through mid-1977, banks could not branch across state lines. Individual banks may be independent or owned by a holding company that may also own other banks and affiliates that offer permitted nonbank activities. Most of these nonbank activities and, since 1980, an increasing amount of full-service banking itself may be conducted across state lines. By 1994, every state permitted interstate acquisitions of banks by bank holding companies, some on a regional basis and others on a national basis. Banks vary greatly in size, from less than $10 million in deposits to more than $100 billion. Most banks are relatively small. A few very large banks hold a large proportion of the dollar amounts of all deposits.

In recent years, U.S. banks have expanded their overseas operations sharply, and foreign banks have increased the number of their offices in the United States. This reflects the continued internationalization of finance and the growing transnational structure of banking.

QUESTIONS

1. Discuss the reasons why a bank failure may be considered more important than the failure of most other business firms. On the other hand, why may it not?

2. The worst wave of bank failures in U.S. history occurred after the establishment of the Federal Reserve System in 1913. Why did these failures occur? What could the Fed have done to prevent them? What was finally done to put an end to these failures? How successful has this been?

3. "If the Fed had done its job in the early 1930s, the FDIC would not have been established." Discuss your agreement or disagreement with this statement.

4. What is a *bank run*? Why does it usually occur in a fractional banking system? What starts a run on a particular bank? What does a bank experiencing a run need to do to avoid insolvency? What problems may it encounter in doing so?

5. How may federal deposit insurance have contributed to the sharp increase in bank and SLA failures in the 1980s? Why was the failure rate so much higher in this period than in the previous 30 years? Why were some runs in this period from good to bad banks rather than from bad to good banks as in earlier periods?

6. List the commercial banks in your market area. Are any of these owned by out-of-state holding companies? If so, when were they purchased? Are any of the banks owned by holding companies chartered in your state that have acquired banks in some other states? Why do you think bank holding companies in your area have been more (or less) aggressive in acquiring out-of-state banks? (A good starting point for a listing of the ownership of banks is Rand McNally's or Polk's bank directories in your library.)

7. Differentiate between interstate banking on a branching and on a holding company basis. Why did national holding company banking occur first? Why are the activities of bank holding companies limited?

8. "Large banks are inherently more profitable than small banks and will drive small banks out of business." Evaluate the theory and evidence for this statement. If it is true, what remedies may there be?

9. What three choices do depositors have if they consider their bank unsafe? What are the implications of each for other banks, the local community, and the national economy?

10. Are there any offices of foreign banks in your state? If so, are they branches, agencies, or subsidiary banks? Do any of the domestic banks have offices abroad? If so, where?

REFERENCES

"Appendices to the Statement by Paul A. Volcker," *Hearings*, Subcommittee on Commerce, Consumer and Monetary Affairs of Committee on Government Operations, U.S. House of Representatives, 99th Cong., 2nd. sess., Washington, D.C., June 1986.

Aspinwall, Richard C., and Robert A.

Eisenbeis, eds., *Handbook for Banking Strategy*. New York: Wiley-Interscience, 1985.

Barth, James R., R. Dan Brumbaugh, Jr., and Robert E. Litan, *The Future of American Banking*, Armonk, N.Y.: M.E. Sharpe, 1992.

Benston, George J., "Interest on Deposits and the Survival of Chartered Depository Institutions," *Economic Review*, Federal Reserve Bank of Atlanta, October 1984, pp. 42–56.

Benston, George, et al., *Perspectives on Safe and Sound Banking*. Cambridge, Mass.: MIT Press, 1986.

Benston, George J., and George G. Kaufman, *Risk and Solvency Regulation of Depository Institutions* (Monograph 88–1). New York: Graduate School of Business Administration, New York University, 1988.

Chrystal, Alec K., "International Banking Facilities," *Review*, Federal Reserve Bank of St. Louis, April 1984, pp. 5–11.

Dewald, William G., et al., "Bank Market Studies: Review and Evaluation," *Journal of Money, Credit, and Banking*, November 1984, pt. 2, special issue.

Elliehausen, Gregory, and John D. Wolken, "Banking Markets and the Use of Financial Services by Households," *Federal Reserve Bulletin*, March 1992, pp. 169–81.

England, Catherine, and Thomas Huertas, eds., *The Financial Services Revolution*. Boston: Kluwer Academic, 1988.

Golembe, Carter H., and David S. Holland, *Federal Regulation of Banking, 1986–87*. Washington, D.C.: Golembe, 1986.

Haraf, William S., and Rose Marie Kushmeider, eds., *Restructuring Banking and Financial Services in America*. Washington, D.C.: American Enterprise Institute, 1988.

Havrilesky, Thomas M., Robert Schweitzer, and John T. Boorman, *Dynamics of Banking*. Arlington Heights, Ill.: Harlan Davidson, 1985.

Houpt, James V., *International Trends for U.S.*

Banks and Banking Markets. Staff Study 156. Washington, D.C.: Board of Governors of the Federal Reserve System, May 1988.

Hultman, Charles W., *The Environment of International Banking*. Englewood Cliffs, N.J.: Prentice Hall, 1990.

Humphrey, David B., "Cost Dispersion and the Measurement of Economies in Banking," *Economic Review*, Federal Reserve Bank of Richmond, May/June 1987, pp. 24–38.

Kaufman, George G., ed., *Banking Structures in Major Countries*, Boston, Mass.: Kluwer, 1991.

Kaufman, George G., and Roger C. Kormendi, eds., *Deregulating Financial Services: Public Policy in Flux*. Cambridge, Mass.: Ballinger, 1986.

Kaufman, George G., "Bank Contagion: A Review of the Theory and Evidence," *Journal of Financial Services Research*, April 1994, pp. 123–50.

Mester, Loretta, "Owners versus Managers: Who Controls Banks," *Business Review*, Federal Reserve Bank of Philadelphia, May/June 1989, pp. 13–22.

Rose, Peter S., *The Changing Structure of American Banking*. New York: Columbia University Press, 1987.

Savage, Donald T., "Interstate Banking: A Status Report," *Federal Reserve Bulletin*, December 1993, pp. 1075–1089.

Sprague, Irvine H., *Bailout: An Insiders' Account of Bank Failures and Rescues*. New York: Basic Books, 1986.

Terrell, Henry S., et al., "The Activities of Japanese Banks in the U.K. and U.S., 1980–88," *Federal Reserve Bulletin*, February 1990, pp. 39–50.

U.S. Congress, House Committee on Banking, Finance, and Urban Affairs, *Formation and Powers of National Banking Associations—A Legal Primer*, 98th Cong., 1st sess. Washington, D.C., May 1985.

Zweig, Phillip L., *Belly Up: The Collapse of the Penn Square Bank*. New York: Crown, 1985.

Thrift and Insurance Intermediaries

Most nonbank financial intermediaries engage in some of the same activities as commercial banks do. Thus, the insights that we gained about commercial bank operations in the preceding two chapters will make it easier to understand how the intermediaries described in this chapter function.

Nonbank financial institutions operating on the intermediation market may be classified into four general types:

1. Thrift
2. Insurance
3. Investment
4. Other

This chapter examines thrift depository and insurance intermediaries.

Thrift Institutions

Thrift institutions are depository intermediaries that sell secondary securities primarily in the form of time and savings deposits and invest principally in residential mortgage and consumer loans. They compete with commercial banks in both their deposit and lending activities. The thrift industry encompasses three types of institutions: savings and loan associations, savings banks, and credit unions.

Savings and Loan Associations

Savings and loan associations (SLAs or S&Ls), are primarily specialized mortgage-lending consumer thrift institutions. They raise funds almost completely through fixed-value time deposits. SLAs were initially organized in the mid-1800s by groups of people who wished to buy their own homes but did not have enough savings to finance the purchase. At the time, neither commercial banks nor life insurance companies, the major financial intermediaries of the day, lent money for residential mortgages. The members of the groups pooled their savings and lent them back to a few members to finance their home purchases. As the loans were repaid, funds could be lent to the other members of the group. The first savings and loan association in the United States was established in 1831 in Pennsylvania as the Oxford-Provident Building Association.

The associations were originally organized on a mutual basis: every member had voting power proportionate to the size of his or her deposit. Because these institutions emphasized lending, they were originally named *building and loan associations*. Through time, as the demand for home building increased faster than member savings, the associations had to expand beyond their own group to search for funds as well as to appeal to a broader range of SSUs. To publicize this change, the associations added *savings* to their titles. As the affiliation with particular groups of borrowers diminished, many new associations were organized as private stock associations, and older ones converted to stock ownership to make it easier to raise additional capital. In recent years, primarily to reduce the stigma of being labeled an SLA, many changed their names to Federal Savings Bank (FSB) but maintained their savings and loan charter.

At year-end 1992, there were some 1,900 privately owned savings and loan associations in the United States. In addition, nearly 100 institutions were operated by the RTC (Resolution Trust Corporation) while in the process of being resolved.) This number is down more than 70 percent from the nearly 6,500 associations operating 30 years earlier in 1960 and fully 85 percent from the record 12,400 in 1924. Despite the sharp decline in numbers, total assets of the industry grew rapidly through the mid-1980s, so that SLAs briefly became the second largest intermediary after commercial banks before declining sharply. By yearend 1992, SLAs were only the sixth largest type of financial institution. The number of SLA branches increased sharply from 3,000 in 1965 to more than 20,000 in 1989 before declining to 14,000 in 1992. Like commercial banks, SLAs can be chartered by either the federal government (these have *federal* in the title) or the home-state government. On average, federally chartered associations tend to be somewhat larger. They account for 75 percent of the number of all associations, but nearly 90 percent of total association assets. For all practical purposes, it makes little difference to the depositor whether the association is federally or state chartered.

Since 1989, savings and loan associations have been regulated by the Office of Thrift Supervision (OTS), which, like the Comptroller of the Currency, is housed in the U.S. Treasury Department. Before 1989, SLAs were regulated at the federal level by the Federal Home Loan Bank Board (FHLBB), which was disbanded by the Financial Institutions Reform, Recovery, and Enforcement ACT (FIRREA) of 1989. Deposits may be insured up to $100,000 per account by the Savings Association Insurance Fund (SAIF), operated by the FDIC. Before 1989, SLAs were insured by the Federal Savings and Loan Insurance Corporation (FSLIC), operated by the FHLBB.

Federal associations are required to be members of SAIF; state associations may apply for this insurance. In 1993, all associations were so insured. Until the mid-1980s, deposits at state-chartered SLAs in a few states were insured by state-sponsored insurance agencies. But well-publicized difficulties in Ohio and Maryland as a result of the insolvencies of a few large state-insured institutions led to runs on these and all other state-insured institutions and to large losses to the states and also losses to some depositors. As a result, effectively all states required federal deposit insurance for all their associations. Branching laws are more liberal than for commercial banks at both the federal and state levels, and limited interstate branching is permitted. A number of commercial banks have purchased SLAs and some have converted them to bank branches.

The asset size of the average federally insured SLA at year-end 1992 was about $425 million, which is almost 50 percent larger than that of the average commercial bank. However, the largest SLAs are considerably smaller than the largest commercial banks. Home Savings of America in California, the largest SLA in the country, had nearly $50 billion of assets,

TABLE 12-1	SAVINGS AND LOAN ASSOCIATION BALANCE SHEET AT YEAR-END 1992[a]	
	$Billions	Percent
Assets		
Cash and bank deposits	29	4
Real estate loans	496	60
Mortgage-backed securities	156	19
U.S. government securities	19	2
Corporate bonds and loans	22	3
Consumer loans	30	4
Other assets	68	8
Total	820	100
Liabilities and Net Worth		
Checkable deposits	66	8
Savings deposits and MMDAs	185	22
Time deposits	401	49
Borrowings	105	13
Other liabilities	6	1
Net worth	57	7
Total	820	100

SOURCE: FDIC, *Statistics on Banking*, 1992.
[a]SAIF-insured institutions.

which is only about 30 percent of the $160 billion asset size of Citibank (New York). Some 25 percent of SLA assets are held by the largest eight associations, each with assets in excess of $10 billion. As can be seen from Table 12–1, mortgage lending still dominates SLA lending. At year-end 1992, real estate loans and mortgage-backed securities accounted for nearly 80 percent of SLA assets. Time and savings deposits accounted for 70 percent of their funds.

The S&L Mess.   After enjoying many years of rapid growth and profitability in the post–World War II period, during which their market share of financial institutions jumped from 6 to 16 percent (Table 9–5) and they became the largest single provider of residential mortgage loans, SLAs have suffered rocky times in more recent years.

In the late 1970s, the SLAs began to experience severe financial strains from their interest rate intermediation activities. As we saw in Chapter 7, long-term rates are averages of current short-term rates and the short-term rates expected in the future. Thus, SLAs must price long-term fixed-rate mortgages (FRMs), which were basically the only type of mortgage they were permitted to make, so that the mortgage rate charged, less the costs of operations, is no lower than the average of the current and future short-term deposit rates they expect to pay over the life of the mortgage. If rates rise unexpectedly, the SLA will have priced their long-term fixed-rate mortgage too low and will realize lower profits than it had expected, or even losses. Like almost everyone else, SLAs underestimated the sharp acceleration in the rate of inflation during the 1970s and early 1980s and, therefore also the sharp rise in interest rates. As a result, many mortgages extended in this period had interest rates that were too low in retrospect, were unprofitable, and produced financial strains on the associations. This problem is examined in greater detail in Chapter 21.

The interest rate risk exposure of SLAs could be reduced by shortening the duration of their assets and lengthening the duration of their deposits. In the early 1980s, Congress and the regulators permitted SLAs to offer variable- or adjustable-rate mortgages (VRMs), to invest in consumer and commercial loans, which are typically shorter-term, and, by removing deposit rate ceilings (Regulation Q), to pay competitive rates on longer-term deposits. By the mid-1980s, SLAs as a whole had dramatically increased their lending in the form of VRMs and moderately increased their investments in consumer and commercial loans. Some institutions used these new powers more aggressively than others.

In the period before either the lengthening of deposits or the shortening of assets could be implemented, the government imposed ceilings on the interest rates SLAs could pay on their deposits, similar to those previously placed on commercial banks. These held down SLA costs in periods of rising interest rates. But whenever market rates of interest on comparable securities rose above the rates the SLAs could pay on their deposits, disintermediation occurred and funds flowed out of the institutions. More and more depositors redirected their funds from SLAs to the private financial market or to institutions not subject to the rates restrictions, such as money-market funds. This reduced the availability of funds to the thrift industry and accelerated the drive to deregulation of deposit rates in order to prevent the industry from withering away.

Deregulation came too late, however, to prevent many SLAs from experiencing severe financial problems from interest rate risk exposure. By 1982, about two-thirds of all associations were estimated to be economically insolvent, so that the market value of their assets was less than that of their deposits, and 85 percent were suffering losses. The net worth of the industry as a whole was negative by about $100 billion, an amount equivalent to almost 20 percent of their assets. Because **generally accepted accounting principles (GAAP)** require associations to recognize losses from adverse interest rate movements only when the assets are actually sold, the official number of insolvent institutions was far less. Nevertheless, by 1982, the number of insolvent associations had become too large for the FSLIC to deal with efficiently and the losses too large for FSLIC to pay without endangering its own reserves. As a result, the Federal Home Loan Bank Board searched for ways to delay official recognition of failed associations.

Both the Depository Institutions Deregulation and Monetary Control Act of 1980 and the Garn-St. Germain Act of 1982 permitted the Board to lower capital requirements. In addition, the Garn-St. Germain Act permitted the Board to provide some economically and even GAAP insolvent associations with paper capital, termed **net worth certificates,** in order to permit them to continue to operate legally and defer the need for FSLIC to make out-of-pocket payments. Indeed, it was hoped that by buying additional time for the associations to operate, particularly if interest rates declined, they would be able to regain their profitability and remove the need for any FSLIC payments altogether. This represents a form of **capital forbearance.** In addition, the board temporarily permitted associations to

FIGURE

12–1

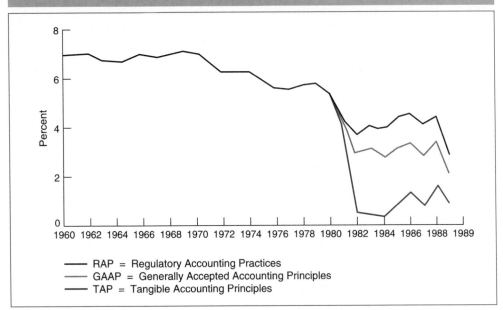

ALTERNATIVE MEASURES OF THE DECLINE IN
CAPITAL TO ASSET RATIOS AT SLAS: 1960–1989

SOURCE: Adapted from James R. Barth, et al., "The Need to Reform the Federal Deposit Insurance System," *Contemporary Policy Issues*, January 1991, p. 26. Reprinted by permission.

use accounting techniques, termed ***regulatory accounting principles* (RAP),** that permitted a more favorable reporting of their net worth position.

The results of both lowering capital requirements and encouraging accounting practices that permitted an association's capital to be reported at substantially above its market or economic value can be seen in Figure 12–1. Between 1980 and 1982, capital in the S&L industry as a whole declined from about 6 percent of assets to near 4 percent on an RAP basis, to near 3 percent on a GAAP basis, and to only 1 percent on a more conservative ***tangible accounting principles* (TAP)** basis. But even TAP overstated the actual economic value of capital at that time, as it does not make a full adjustment for losses from interest rate risk on assets that are not sold.

Depositors were willing to continue to place funds in insolvent but operating associations in amounts up to $100,000, as long as they continued to be fully insured by FSLIC. Indeed, because their revenues were insufficient, some insolvent institutions used the newly attracted deposits to pay the interest on their existing deposits and even operating expenses. That is, they borrowed from Peter to pay Paul in what is commonly referred to as a *Ponzi scheme.*[1] Note that, in the absence of federal guarantees, Ponzi

[1] The use of newly attracted funds to pay interest on old funds is frequently referred to as a **Ponzi scheme.** Charles Ponzi was a "con man" in Boston in the early 1920s who had perfected the "borrow-from-Paul-to-pay-Peter-principle." At first he promised to double and then, after initial success beyond his fondest dreams, promised to triple investors' funds. This worked well as long as new funds kept rolling in. However, because his investors were not protected by federal deposit insurance, they stopped sending him their funds when the method of his operation was exposed by a local newspaper. At the close of the operation, the earliest investors had done well, while the later ones were left holding the bag. If only Ponzi had thought of federal deposit insurance!

schemes collapse when the source of the "profits" becomes public knowledge and the supply of new Peters dries up.

Interest rates declined sharply from 1982 through 1984 as inflation slowed. Losses from interest rate intermediation were reversed, and the industry almost regained economic solvency. But new losses arose to offset these gains. The new losses stemmed from a number of reasons, including

- ▼ Sharp regional economic recessions, first in the mid-1980s in the energy and agricultural states of Texas, Oklahoma, Arkansas, and Louisiana and then in the late 1980s in New England and the mid-Atlantic states, that led to sharp increases in defaults on mortgage loans.
- ▼ Risky investments, particularly by economically insolvent or near-insolvent institutions, that had little of their own funds to lose but much to gain if the gambles paid off. In effect, they may be said to have "gambled for resurrection." Most lost! The resulting losses were enlarged by advances in telecommunications that, combined with an increase in deposit insurance coverage from $40,000 to $100,000 in 1980 and the lifting of deposit rate ceilings, permitted risk-seeking institutions to attract funds from throughout the country rather than from only their immediate market area.
- ▼ Outright fraud, which was abetted by the heavy caseload of the FHLBB from the crisis that impeded its ability to adequately monitor and police the institutions.
- ▼ Delays by Congress and the administration in introducing corrective actions because of their failure to understand the nature and magnitude of the problem, unwillingness to appropriate funds and increase the reported federal government budget deficit, and successful lobbying by the SLA industry to prevent solutions costly to their membership. Thus, for example, of the near 200 failed SLAs resolved by the regulators in 1988, over half had been insolvent by generally accepted accounting principles for three years or longer and fully two-thirds had been insolvent that long on a market-value basis. In the years the insolvent associations were permitted to continue to operate, most gambled for resurrection in an attempt to regain profitability before they were closed and succeeded only in substantially increasing their losses and the costs to the taxpayers.
- ▼ Changes in federal tax laws that first in 1981 encouraged investments in commercial real estate and then in 1986 abruptly discouraged new investments and penalized old investments. As a result, many projects suddenly turned from profitable on an after-tax basis to unprofitable, real estate values fell sharply, and many loans made on the basis of future income from such projects and/or collateralization by such real estate went into default.

Because the new losses were primarily from credit risk rather than from interest rate risk as earlier and less likely to reverse on their own accord, they caused greater concern. By 1987, GAAP capital had declined to only 3 percent of assets, TAP capital to only 1 percent, and the market value of assets at insolvent SLAs was some $40 billion less than the par value of deposits, almost all of which were insured by FSLIC. This amount was many times greater than FSLIC's reserves. Despite the more lenient accounting, some 670 SLAs—nearly one-quarter of all associations—were insolvent on

"And to my children and grandchildren I leave the rescue of the savings and loan industry."

SOURCE: *Federal Home Loan Bank Board Journal,* June 1989. Cartoon by Peter Steiner. Reprinted with permission.

a TAP basis, 520 on a GAAP basis, and even 350 on a RAP basis. Only the widespread belief that the federal government would support FSLIC's guarantee prevented a run by depositors on all SLAs.

In response, in the Competitive Equality Banking Act of 1987, Congress appropriated about $11 billion to recapitalize FSLIC. This amount would be paid by the industry, primarily from deposit insurance premiums. However, Congress also made it more difficult for regulators to close insolvent institutions. Both because the amount provided was greatly inadequate and because the act did not correct the underlying causes of the problem, the losses continued to increase rapidly.

Finally, in 1989, the number of failing SLAs and the dollar magnitude of their losses became so great that continued denial of the problem by policymakers and continued forbearance and postponement of remedial actions were no longer possible. By this time, the FSLIC deficit was estimated to be in excess of $100 billion. In response, newly elected President George Bush proposed and Congress enacted the Financial Institutions Reform, Recovery, and Enforcement Act. This Act provided another $100 billion to recapitalize insolvent associations and significantly reorganized the SLA regulatory structure. Because the $100 billion plus deficit was far too large to be paid by the SLA industry, most of it was billed to the taxpayer, although deposit insurance premiums were raised on both SLAs and commercial banks. (It should be noted that the funds raised were used to prevent losses to SLA depositors at insolvent associations, not to SLA shareholders.)

Among other things, FIRREA "punished" the Federal Home Loan Bank Board and the Federal Savings and Loan Insurance Corporation by abolishing it (see Table 12–2). It transferred the chartering, examination, supervisory, and regulatory duties to a new Office of Thrift Supervision within the

TABLE 12–2   MAJOR PROVISIONS OF FIRREA (1989) AFFECTING SAVINGS AND LOANS

SLA *Operations*

▼ Increases required capital.

▼ Increases deposit insurance premiums.

▼ Increases percent of assets required to be in residential mortgage loans.

▼ Increases restrictions on nonresidential mortgage lending.

▼ Restricts lending powers of state-chartered associations to approximately same as federally chartered.

▼ Restricts loans to single borrower.

▼ Permits purchase by commercial bank holding company.

Regulatory Structure

▼ Abolishes FHLBB and FSLIC.

▼ Transfers regulation, supervision, and examination authority to new Office of Thrift Supervision (OTS) in Treasury Department.

▼ Transfers deposit insurance to new Savings Association Insurance Fund (SAIF) in FDIC and makes it a full-faith and credit guarantee of the U.S. government.

▼ Transfers FHL Banks to New Federal Housing Finance Board.

Resolution of Insolvent SLAs

▼ Establishes Resolution Trust Corporation (RTC) to supervise and manage sale or liquidation of insolvent associations.

▼ Raised about $100 billion in new government funds to make whole insured depositors at insolvent associations.

Treasury Department, the insurance function to a new Savings Association Insurance Fund within the FDIC, and the provision of financing and services to SLAs provided by the 12 regional Federal Home Loan (FHL) Banks to a new Federal Housing Finance Board. In addition, the act established a new Resolution Trust Corporation (RTC) to manage and liquidate the insolvent institutions and their assets, required positive but still low capital standards for SLAs, made it easier for the FDIC to remove insurance from insolvent associations, reversed some SLA powers to make nonmortgage loans, and permitted SLAs to be acquired by bank holding companies.

But FIRREA underestimated the dollar size of the problem and the difficulty of recapitalizing and reprivatizing the insolvent institutions. By mid-1990, almost 500 SLAs, about one-sixth of the industry, with $200 billion of assets, had been taken over by the RTC. In total, some 1,200 institutions with $500 billion in assets were estimated to be insolvent on a market-value basis. The cost of resolving the problem had increased to near $200 billion and greatly angered taxpayers.

In 1991, SLAs, similar to commercial banks, became subject to the capital levels, prompt corrective action, and least cost resolution provisions of the FDIC Improvement Act. These provisions were discussed briefly in Chapter 11 and are discussed at greater length in Chapters 16 and 18. As a result, SLAs intensified their efforts to raise additional capital, and weakly capitalized associations were more likely to be closed. In 1995, responsi-

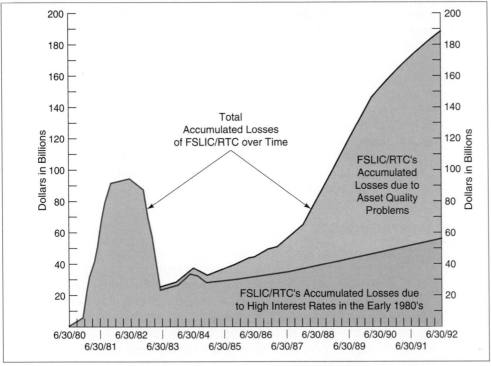

FIGURE
12–2

FSLIC/RTC'S ACCUMULATION OF LOSSES DURING
THE 1980S AND EARLY 1990S

SOURCE: Bert Ely, "Savings and Loan Crisis" in David R. Henderson, ed., *The Fortune Encyclopedia of Economics*, New York: Warner Books, 1993, p. 372. Reprinted by permission.

bility for new failures is scheduled to be shifted from the RTC to the FDIC. Through that period, despite a sharp fall in interest rates and a more favorable real estate market that resurrected many previously insolvent SLAs, the RTC had taken over nearly 750 associations with assets of $400 billion.

The estimated losses to the government and taxpayer of the SLA debacle from 1980 through 1992 are plotted in Figure 12–2. The total accumulated loss at mid-1992 was near $200 billion for some 1,200 failed institutions. The losses are divided between those caused by the sharp rise in interest rates in the late 1970s and early 1980s and those caused by primarily real estate losses in the late 1980s. As was described in this chapter, the real estate losses did not occur until the sharp decline in interest rates in 1982–1983 had almost rescued the industry. The losses were charged first to the FSLIC until it was abolished in 1989 and thereafter to the RTC.

As a direct outgrowth of the crisis, the market share of SLAs fell abruptly from 16 percent in the mid-1980s to only 6 percent in 1992, their lowest market share since 1950. SLAs also declined abruptly from the second largest financial institution in the mid-1980s to only the sixth largest and were exceeded by commercial banks as the largest provider of mortgage loans. In addition to the impact of failures, this reduction reflected the cost of higher deposit insurance premiums, the end of above-market interest rates paid for deposits by insolvent and near-insolvent institutions who wanted to "grow" out of the problems, and the purchase of the deposit bases of closed associations by commercial banks. The decline in interest rates in 1992 and 1993, accompanied by a widening of the spread between short- and long-term rates, and a bottoming out of real estate market permitted many surviving SLAs to record substantial profits and to improve their capitalization. By year-end 1992, 95 percent of solvent SLAs had equity capital-asset ratios of 4 percent or higher. Nevertheless, the future for SLAs is not nearly as bright as 20 years earlier. It is apparent that they will not regain their prominence as a financial intermediary and are likely to evolve either into full-service consumer-oriented banks or into niche players as specialized residential mortgage lenders. Indeed, an increasing number of SLAs are being acquired by commercial bank holding companies and losing their independent identity.

Savings Banks

Savings banks (SBs) are institutions very similar to savings and loan associations.[2] Their principal source of funds is time deposits, and their principal use of funds is to make mortgage loans. SBs have had somewhat broader lending powers than SLAs. As a result, they invest a slightly smaller percentage of their assets in mortgages. (The balance sheet of all SBs is shown in Table 12–3.) Unlike SLAs, however, savings banks have grown slowly during the postwar period and have declined from being the third largest private intermediary in 1950, larger than SLAs, to the smallest of the 11 major intermediaries. Until recently, all savings banks were mutually organized (MSBs). But in recent years, an increasing number have converted to stock ownership to increase their capital base.

The declining popularity of SBs in large measure reflects their limited location. SBs are located principally in the north and central east coast states, the population of which has experienced below-average growth in the post–World War II period. In 1992, nearly half of the 414 SBs were located in Massachusetts. In all, SBs operate in only sixteen states, only three of which are west of the Mississippi River. In part, the limited geographic expansion reflects the unavailability of federal charters until 1978.

Although SBs are smaller in the aggregate, their average size is considerably greater than that of either commercial banks or SLAs. At year-end 1992, the average SB had assets of near $525 million. Savings banks are among the older intermediaries in the country. The first was opened in 1816 in Philadelphia "to promote economy and the practice of saving amongst the poor and laboring classes of the community." It is still in existence today, operating as the Meritor Savings Bank, and is one of the largest savings banks in the country. SBs were organized by wealthy people who wanted to encourage saving among poorer working groups by providing

---

[2] Since 1982, savings and loan associations have been able to convert to federal savings banks, but this represents primarily a change in title only and these institutions are not included as savings banks in this section.

TABLE
12–3 · SAVINGS BANK, BALANCE SHEET AT YEAR-END 1992[a]

	$Billions	Percent
Assets		
Cash and bank deposits	6	3
Real estate loans	124	58
Mortgage-backed securities	28	13
U.S. government securities	13	6
Corporate bonds and loans	15	7
Consumer loans	7	3
Other assets	22	10
Total	215	100
Liabilities and Net Worth		
Checkable deposits	19	8
Savings deposits and MMDAs	81	38
Time deposits	82	38
Other liabilities	18	8
Net worth	17	8
Total	215	100

SOURCE: FDIC, *Statistics on Banking*, 1992.
[a]BIF-insured institutions.

accessible and safe savings facilities. In contrast to SLAs, the emphasis was on saving, not on lending. Many SBs catered to particular segments of the population, a fact that remains embedded in their names. Thus, New York City has an Emigrant Savings Bank and a Dime Savings Bank; Boston has a Five Cents Savings Banks.

Because their balance sheet resembles that of SLAs, SBs have experienced many of the same interest rate and credit risk problems in recent years. Indeed, because they are located in slower-growth areas, SBs had a larger proportion of low interest rate, fixed-rate mortgages in their portfolios and were hurt more severely, on average, by the unexpected rise in interest rates in the late 1970s. A number of large institutions, particularly in New York City, were temporarily saved from failure only by financial assistance from the FDIC similar to that provided to SLAs by the FSLIC. Many of the reforms granted SLAs by the Depository Institutions Deregulation and Monetary Control Act (DIDMCA) and the Garn-St. Germain Act and by government regulatory agencies were also granted SBs. Deposits in SBs are insured up to $100,000 by the Bank Insurance Fund (BIF). Because of the similarity to SLAs, the future of savings banks, as that of SLAs, is uncertain.

Credit Unions

Credit unions (CUs) are small but among the fastest-growing depository institutions. Credit unions originated in Europe in the mid-1800s and arrived in the United States in the early 1900s. They were principally consumer-oriented savings institutions, organized as cooperative associations among people who have common employment or geographic locations. Credit unions exist at business and government offices to serve the employees, at neighborhood centers, and among professional and union groups. Most credit unions are based on common employment. About 40 percent serve employees of private firms, 20 percent serve employees of government agencies, and 16 percent serve employees of educational institutions. Most of the remaining are operated by social, fraternal, or labor organizations. Often, the facilities and some of the time of the personnel are donated by the employer or sponsor. Less than one-half of the employees are full-time, the remainder are part-time and volunteers. Credit unions are the only private intermediaries that are completely exempt from federal income taxes.

Although their aggregate dollar size is small, there are many credit unions. At year-end 1992, there were about 13,500 credit unions. This number was 20 percent greater than the number of commercial banks, nearly 7 times the number of savings and loan associations, and 35 times the number of savings banks. The average credit union has only $20 million in assets, one-fifteenth as much as the average commercial bank, one-twentieth as much as the average SLA, and one-twenty-fifth as much as the average savings bank. Only 4 percent of all credit unions have assets in excess of $100 million. Like both commercial banks and SLAs, credit unions can be chartered by either the state or federal government.

As in the other thrift institutions, the principal secondary securities of credit unions are time deposits, called **shares.** The deposits may be insured up to $100,000 by the National Credit Union Share Insurance Fund (NCUSIF), and about 97 percent of the CUs holding about the same percentage of the assets of the industry are so insured; almost all of the rest are insured by state agencies. Credit unions invest primarily in small consumer loans to their shareholders, but in recent years their investment in residential mortgage loans has increased rapidly. The balance sheet of all credit unions is shown in Table 12–4.

Credit unions are the third largest provider of consumer and personal credit, behind commercial banks and finance companies. As they have expanded, credit unions have acquired permission to offer additional services, including mortgage and credit-card loans, IRAs, and interest-bearing checking accounts, called **share drafts.** Credit unions are evolving into complete household financial centers. Because of their small average size and the volunteer nature of their management, credit unions tend to fail far more frequently than other financial institutions.

Insurance Intermediaries

Insurance intermediaries sell secondary securities in the form of insurance policies. Insurance policies may be classified as conditional or contingent debt; they are paid at the time certain stipulated conditions occur. Policyholders or their beneficiaries receive payment when a stated event occurs that results in financial loss to the insured party—such as an accident, theft, fire, injury, retirement, or death. Policies may be purchased for different time periods, ranging from one day to a lifetime. Policyholders pay premiums to the insurance intermediary for this protection. The insurance

TABLE

12–4

TABLE 12–4 CREDIT UNIONS, BALANCE SHEET AT YEAR-END 1992		
	$Billions	Percent
Assets		
Cash and bank deposits	49	18
U.S. government securities	45	17
Mortgage loans	53	20
Consumer loans	93	35
Miscellaneous assets	26	10
Total	266	100
Liabilities and Net Worth		
Checkable shares (deposits)	32	12
Savings shares (deposits)	214	81
Miscellaneous liabilities	3	1
Net worth	17	6
Total	266	100

SOURCE: Board of Governors of the Federal Reserve System, *Flow of Funds Accounts*, Fourth Quarter 1992.

company uses the proceeds from the premiums to invest in primary securities with maturities and risks that will permit them to pay the amounts of the policies when required. (Note that insurance companies insure only against financial losses occurring from particular events, not against the occurrence of the event itself. Thus, life insurance does not insure you against death, nor accident insurance against accidents.)

Losses from insured events tend to be large relative to the financial resources of the person purchasing the insurance but small relative to the resources of the company. This is so because the insurance company pools the risks by selling many policies on similar but independent events, and by the law of large numbers, the probability that a large loss will occur at any given time is small. The insurance company reduces its exposure to risk by diversifying and not "putting all its cars on the same highway at the same time."

Policyholders purchase insurance in order to share with others the risk of loss in any one period and avoid the experience of a large sudden loss that would produce severe financial strains. The cost of the loss is spread over a long period and is thereby less painful. At times, the insured event may occur early in the policy period when premiums paid in are small relative to the loss, and the policyholder ends up gaining. At times, the insured event may occur late in the policy period after most of the premiums have been paid. Then the cost of insurance is high relative to the loss. In many cases, there may never be a loss. Then, in retrospect, the policyholder would have been better off without insurance. In addition, the insurance company may reduce risk further by prescribing conditions for insurance that reduce either the probability that an event will occur or the dollar amount of the resulting loss; for example, burglar and fire alarms, or safety equipment.

The insurance company charges a premium for assuming the risk. The size of the premium is computed by first multiplying the probability that the particular event will occur in a specified period by the financial value of the loss, then subtracting the expected income the company derives from investing the premiums received until payment is required, and finally adding the costs of operations and a target profit amount. The greater the expected loss, the higher the premium. The greater the expected earnings, the lower the premium. If the premium is correctly estimated, the sale of insurance is profitable. If it is underestimated, losses will be realized. However, insurance companies may not sell policies for all risks. Events for which probabilities cannot be computed with confidence, or for which the financial loss is too large for any one or group of private insurance sellers, are termed **uninsurable risks.**

Like depository intermediaries, insurance intermediaries tend to specialize in particular segments of the market. Life insurance companies specialize in assuming risks of income losses due to death, illness, or retirement; casualty insurance companies assume risks primarily attributed to personal injury or property damage. The probabilities that different types of events will occur differ and cannot be estimated with equal confidence. For example, the probabilities that any person in the United States will die at any particular age are well defined on the basis of a large number of historical observations and only slow changes in the causes of death. On the other hand, the probabilities of losses from automobile accidents are more difficult to compute and depend on more rapidly changing factors, such as speed limits, the price of gasoline, the cost of repairs, and the design of automobiles. As a result, insurance companies selling different types of secondary securities and assuming different kinds of risks will purchase different types of primary securities in order both to be able to pay the insurance claim when required and to maximize their return.

Life Insurance Companies

Life insurance companies are the oldest type of intermediary in the United States. The first life insurance company was organized in 1759 in Philadelphia, almost 20 years before the independence of the United States from Great Britain and 23 years before the first commercial bank. The firm was established as the Corporation for Relief of Poor and Distressed Presbyterian Ministers and of the Poor and Distressed Widows and Children of the Presbyterian Church. Now called the Presbyterian Ministers' Fund, this is the oldest continuous life insurance company in the world.

About 70 percent of all adults in the United States carry some life insurance. Most people purchase life insurance for their remaining life or working years. Thus, the maturities of the policies are long-term. Frequently, policy buyers will purchase both insurance that pays if and when an event occurs and a flow of additional payments—*annuities*—that will be made under any circumstances. Payment for the second service represents savings by the policyholder. Life insurance companies invest the funds they obtain through the sale of policies primarily in longer-term, taxable, not highly marketable primary securities, such as corporate bonds and commercial mortgages. (The balance sheet of all life insurance companies at year-end 1992 is shown in Table 12–5.) The federal tax code permits

TABLE

12–5

231

▼

THRIFT AND
INSURANCE
INTERMEDIARIES

LIFE INSURANCE COMPANIES BALANCE SHEET AT YEAR-END 1992		
	$Billions	Percent
Assets		
U.S. governmental securities	282	18
Corporate and foreign bonds	654	41
Corporate stock	192	12
Mortgages	247	15
Policy loans	72	4
Miscellaneous assets	167	10
Total	1,614	100
Liabilities and Net Worth		
Policy reserves	1,353	84
Other liabilities	165	10
Surplus and net worth	96	6
Total	1,614	100

SOURCE: Board of Governors of the Federal Reserve System, *Flow of Funds Accounts, Quarterly Levels*, Third Quarter 1993, December 8, 1993.

life insurance companies to exempt from taxable income that income that will in time be paid to the policyholders. It is viewed as a return on the policyholders' investment. Thus, life insurance companies are in relatively low tax brackets and do not find tax-exempt municipal securities a good investment.

In recent years, these companies have increased their investment in equity securities, in order to satisfy the demands of insurance buyers who wish to index their future benefit payments to the future market value of equities rather than receive predetermined nominal amounts. Such policies are called **variable-rate annuities.** These funds are managed in *separate accounts* so as not to affect the other common account.

Partially because of a relatively low return paid on the savings part of insurance policies and partially because of the newer forms of savings for retirement, such as pension programs, life insurance companies have been among the slowest-expanding major private financial intermediaries in asset size. In the postwar period, their market share has declined from 22 percent to 13 percent. To increase their growth rate, they have entered a number of new areas, such as health insurance. They have also stepped up their activities to attract and manage pension funds. Pension funds that are managed and guaranteed by insurance companies are referred to as **insured pension funds.**

Life insurance companies provide payment to the beneficiaries of the insured upon death and to the insured upon illness or retirement. The companies pay a majority of their benefit payments to the policyholder. In 1991, they paid out more than $90 billion in benefits on life insurance policies— $68 billion directly to the policyholder and $25 billion in death payments to beneficiaries.

Similar to SLAs, the earliest life insurance companies were mutual associations in which the policyholders were the owners. Newer companies

EXHIBIT

12–1

Life Insurance Companies: An SLA Copycat Disaster?

In the early 1990s, a record number of life insurance companies, including some large ones, were declared insolvent and closed by their respective home state supervisory agencies. Coming on the heels of the costly SLA debacle in the mid-1980s and the barely averted banking crisis in the late-1980s, widespread fears arose that life insurance companies would be the next trouble spot.

As discussed in this chapter, life insurance companies invest in long-term securities, such as corporate bonds and commercial real estate mortgages. However, unlike SLAs and banks, their liabilities also tend to be longer-term. Thus, their balance sheets are relatively maturity matched and they were not hurt badly by the sharp rise in interest rates in the late 1970s and early 1980s. But they were hurt by the sharp fall in commercial real estate prices in the late-1980s, and some companies had invested heavily in junk bonds, whose prices also declined sharply in those years. Starting in 1989, the number of financially impaired life insurance companies jumped sharply. The number peaked in 1991, when 58 companies, or $2\frac{1}{2}$ percent of all companies, accounting for over 3 percent of industry assets, failed.

Among the failures in 1991 were four large companies: First Executive Corporation with assets of $18 billion (California and New York); First Capital with assets of $10 billion (California); Mutual Benefit Life with assets of $14 billion (New Jersey); and Monarch with assets of $5 billion (Massachusetts). The first two companies suffered large losses in junk bonds and the last two in commercial real estate. These companies all sold policies nationwide.

Although life insurance policies tend to be long-term, a number of companies, including many of the failed institutions, developed a new type of secondary security in the late-1970s that permitted large policyholders to lock in the high interest rates of the period. Many of these *guaranteed interest contracts* (GICs) also permitted the holders, mostly pension funds, to cancel their contracts without any or only very short advance notice. As a result, when rumors circulated about financial difficulties at some companies, these policyholders ran on these institutions, much as depositors run on banks and SLAs. This intensified the companies' problems as they were forced to liquidate their assets quickly at fire-sale prices to accommodate the policy outflows. As with the banks and SLAs, the runs precipitated the closure actions by the regulators. In most cases, however, closure occurred only after an institution's net worth was negative, and losses accrued to policyholders.

Unlike banks and SLAs, insurance companies are regulated and supervised only by state agencies. The state agencies exchange information through the National Association of Insurance Commissioners (NAIC). Policyholders are also insured by state guaranty associations, which now exist in almost all states and protect policyholders in their states, generally up to $100,000. The guaranty funds will, however, restrict withdrawals and reduce the interest rates paid. The guaranty funds are financed by assessments on the surviving companies. Because of the widespread difficulties and large losses, some observers argued for federal regulation, supervision, and insurance, as for banks and SLAs.

The number and size of failures declined in 1992 and 1993, although real estate problems remained serious. As did the banking agencies, the insurance regulators improved and intensified their supervision after the problems surfaced. At the time of publication of this book, it appeared that the worst of the life insurance company problems were behind us and that an SLA-type debacle had been averted.

have tended to be private stock companies. In contrast to most other types of financial intermediaries, the number of life insurance companies has been increasing. In 1991, there were about 2,100 life insurance companies, some 400 more than 10 years earlier, but down 250 from their peak in 1986. Only 5 percent were mutual. However, these tended to be the older and larger firms and accounted for nearly 45 percent of total assets.

In the early 1990s, like banks and S&Ls, some life insurance companies encountered financial difficulties from losses on commercial real estate loans and investments in junk bonds. Unlike depositors, however, policyholders are not protected by federal insurance. However, most states have state sponsored insurance funds but their resources are far smaller and some policyholders at failed institutions suffered losses from not having their claims paid in full or on time. For a while, there was fear that the industry might go the way of the SLAs. Fortunately, this did not happen. This near miss is discussed further in Exhibit 12–1.

Casualty Insurance Companies

The investment policies of property-casualty insurance companies are determined by the unique characteristics of their business. These differ in three significant ways from those of life insurance companies. First, unlike life insurance policies, which are generally for long periods of time, casualty insurance policies are for much shorter periods, such as only a single event—say, goods in transit until they reach their destination or an entertainment performance—or for a year, as with fire, theft, and automobile insurance. Second, the probabilities that the losses will occur are more difficult to compute and less reliable than those for death. And third, all the income of casualty companies is taxable. As a result, casualty companies invest the revenues from premiums in marketable securities that can be liquidated quickly. The largest share of assets is in Treasury securities, followed by tax-exempt municipal securities, corporate stocks, and corporate bonds. The balance sheet of all casualty insurance companies at year-end 1992 is shown in Table 12–6. They had 5 percent of all assets of financial institutions, almost the same market share they have had since 1950.

At the end of 1992, there were some 3,900 casualty insurance companies. Many companies prefer to specialize in a limited number of activities, such as household, business, fire, automobile, personal liability, or shipping. At times when the event insured is too large for a single firm, the risk will be divided among a number of different firms. The best-known example of such risk sharing by insurance companies is the operation of Lloyds of London, which is an association of individual insurance firms each of which may accept a desired portion of a given contract. Casualty insurance companies are organized either as private stock or mutual firms. The form of organization does not affect their operation.

In the mid-1980s, many casualty insurance firms experienced financial difficulties because they had underestimated the sharp decline in interest rates and therefore the interest returns that they earned on their investments. As a result, they had charged lower premiums for their insurance coverage than, in retrospect, were required to be profitable. These losses were worsened by unexpected, large loss claims, particularly on personal

TABLE

12–6

PROPERTY-CASUALTY INSURANCE COMPANIES BALANCE SHEET AT YEAR-END 1993

	$Billions	Percent
Assets		
U.S. government securities	151	25
Municipal bonds	134	23
Corporate and foreign bonds	98	16
Corporate stock	97	16
Miscellaneous	117	20
Total	597	100
Liabilities and Net Worth		
Policy contracts	439	74
Surplus and net worth	168	26
Total	597	100

SOURCE: Board of Governors of the Federal Reserve System, *Flow of Funds Accounts, Quarterly Levels*, Third Quarter 1993, December 8, 1993.

liability policies. In the later 1980s, the combination of higher returns on investments and higher premiums restored most firms to profitability. Nevertheless, the firms continued to experience unexpected large losses, particularly in 1992. That year's catastrophes included Hurricane Andrew in Florida, the most costly natural catastrophe in recent U.S. history, Hurricane Iniki in Hawaii, and riots in Los Angeles. Table 12–7 lists the ten costliest insured catastrophes and the estimated insured losses both in

TABLE

12–7

THE TEN COSTLIEST INSURED CATASTROPHES IN U.S. HISTORY AS OF 1994

Event	Date	Estimated Insured Loss ($millions) Current Dollars	1992[a] Dollars
Hurricane Andrew (Florida)	October 1992	16,500	16,500
Hurricane Hugo (Carolinas)	September 1989	4,200	4,680
Los Angeles earthquake	January 1994	2,500	2,438
Blizzard (East Coast)	March 1993	1,750	1,706
Hurricane Iniki (Hawaii)	September 1992	1,600	1,600
Oakland, Calif. fire	October 1991	1,200	1,232
San Francisco earthquake	October 1989	960	1,070
Countrywide cold snap	December 1983	880	1,221
Los Angeles riots	April 1992	775	775
Hurricane Frederic (Southeast)	September 1979	753	1,390

SOURCE: Insurance Information Institute and author.
[a]Computed using Gross Domestic Product (GDP) deflator.

current dollars and in 1992 dollars. For many types of insurance, such as automobile insurance, premiums and policy terms are regulated by the state in which the policy is purchased. This often slows the adjustment in premiums to rapidly changing conditions.

SUMMARY

Thrift institutions accept primarily savings and time deposits and extend primarily residential mortgage loans. The major types of thrift institutions are savings and loan associations, savings banks, and credit unions. The SLAs are the largest and the credit unions the fastest-growing. In recent years, the performance of thrift institutions has been highly volatile. Primarily as a result of a sharp increase in the rate of inflation in the 1970s, interest rates on shorter-term deposits increased faster than expected and were not incorporated in the rates on the longer-term mortgage loans made previously. This exerted downward pressures on profits. In response, SLAs and SBs, at first, encouraged the imposition of ceilings on deposit rates by the government. However, this resulted in disintermediation in periods when market rates of interest increased above the ceiling rates, and the ceilings were eventually phased out. At the same time, many SLAs and SBs reduced their exposure to interest rate risk by shortening the effective maturities of their assets through making variable-rate mortgages (VRMs).

Because of the new powers granted them by the Depository Institutions Deregulation and Monetary Control Act of 1980 and the Garn-St. Germain Act of 1982, which includes the authority to offer checkable deposits and make limited consumer and commercial loans, thrift institutions are becoming less specialized and more like commercial banks. Nevertheless, many SLAs and SBs became insolvent from losses from higher interest rates and required assistance from the FSLIC and FDIC. Time did not heal the problem. Indeed, some institutions suffered further deterioration from default losses as their market areas experienced economic downturns, some "gambled for resurrection" and lost, and some engaged in outright fraud. As a result, by the mid-1980s the FSLIC was itself economically insolvent and required both explicit funding assistance from Congress and an implicit congressional guarantee that additional funding would be appropriated to reassure depositors of the viability of the insurance program.

By 1989, the cost of recapitalizing insolvent institutions had increased to near $100 billion and Congress enacted the Financial Institutions Reform, Recovery, and Enforcement Act (FIRREA), which provided funds to do so to be paid for by the taxpayer. In addition, Congress abolished FSLIC and its parent Federal Home Loan Bank Board and reconstituted deposit insurance for SLAs in the Savings Association Insurance Fund (SAIF) operated by FDIC and regulation of the industry in the Office of Thrift Supervision in the Treasury Department. But these actions were both too late and too little to resolve the crisis, and it was still ongoing in the early 1990s. By then, the cost estimate had increased to near $200 billion and some 1,200 had failed. Thereafter, the higher capital requirements required by FDICIA and a sharp decline in interest rates combined to improve the condition of the surviving thrift institutions and reduced the ultimate cost of resolving the insolvencies. Both SLAs and SBs survive as much smaller industries.

Insurance-type intermediaries raise funds by selling policies that make prearranged payments when a particular event occurs. Life insurance companies sell policies that make payments to beneficiaries of the insured upon death or to the insured upon illness or retirement. Because the probabilities that these events will occur may be computed accurately and the policies are generally long-term, life insurance companies generally tend to invest in long-term debt securities. Casualty insurance companies provide financial compensation to the insured for loss of property from, say, fire or theft, or for loss of income from injury. Because the odds of these events occurring are more uncertain, casualty insurance companies invest in marketable debt and equity securities.

QUESTIONS

1. Differentiate among the development and history of savings and loan associations, mutual savings banks, and credit unions.
2. Traditionally, savings and loan associations and savings banks have lent long term at fixed interest rates and borrowed short term. What difficulties may arise from such practices? What has actually occurred? What remedies would you suggest?
3. Why did the old Federal Savings and Loan Insurance Corporation (FSLIC) become insolvent in the 1980s? What was "the great S&L bailout"? Who was bailed out? Why? How could economically insolvent institutions continue to operate? Why did the regulators permit this?
4. How were provisions enacted in the Financial Institutions Reform, Recovery, and Enforcement Act (FIRREA) in 1989 and the FDIC Improvement Act (FDICIA) in 1991 intended to correct the underlying causes of the SLA crisis? What was the function of the Resolution Trust Corporation (RTC)? Who now insures deposits at SLAs?
5. In 1989, Congress punished the Federal Home Loan Bank Board for not preventing the SLA debacle by abolishing it. Describe the current regulatory structure for SLAs. Discuss whether you believe that this restructuring will prevent or reduce greatly the likelihood of a future recurrence of the large number of costly SLA failures.
6. What do you think is the future for SLAs and SBs? Do you feel the same way about credit unions?
7. Why do most people prefer to purchase automobile and fire insurance from an insurance company rather than to be self-insured? Why then do most people not buy bicycle insurance from an insurance company? What reasons might there be for buying trip life insurance at airports?
8. How do the investment strategies of life insurance and casualty insurance companies differ? What similarities do these companies have?
9. Life insurance companies have experienced slow asset growth among the major financial intermediary institutions since World War II. What changes has the industry introduced to accelerate its growth rate?

American Council of Life Insurance, *Life Insurance Fact Book.* Washington, D.C.: annual.

Auerback, Ronald P., *Historical Overview of Financial Institutions in the United States.* Washington, D.C.: Federal Deposit Insurance Corporation.

Barth, James R., *The Great Savings and Loan Debacle.* Washington, D.C.: AEI Press, 1991.

Benston, George J., and George G. Kaufman, "Understanding the S&L Debacle," *The Public Interest,* Spring 1990, pp. 79–95.

Brewer, III, Elijah, Thomas H. Mondschean and Philip E. Strahan, "Why the Life Insurance Industry Did Not Face an S&L Type Crisis," *Economic Perspectives,* Federal Reserve Bank of Chicago, September/October 1993, pp. 12–23.

Brumbaugh, R. Dan, Jr., *Thrifts under Siege.* Cambridge, Mass.: Ballinger Press, 1988.

Credit Union National Association, CUNA *Yearbook,* Madison, Wis., annual.

Curry, Timothy, and Mark Warshawsky, "Life Insurance Companies in a Changing Environment," *Federal Reserve Bulletin,* July 1986, pp. 449–62.

Day, Kathleen, S&L *Hell,* New York: W.W. Norton, 1993.

Federal Home Loan Bank of San Francisco, *The Future of the Thrift Industry.* San Francisco, 1988.

Insurance Information Institute, *Insurance Facts.* New York, annual.

Kane, Edward J., *The S&L Insurance Mess.* Washington, D.C.: Urban Institute Press, 1989.

Kopcke, Richard W., "The Capitalization and Portfolio Risk of Insurance Companies," *New England Economic Review,* Federal Reserve Bank of Boston, July/August 1992, pp. 43–57.

Kopcke, Richard W., and Richard E. Randall, eds., *The Financial Condition and Regulation of Insurance Companies,* Boston, Mass.: Federal Reserve Bank of Boston, 1991.

Lowy, Martin, *High Rollers: Inside the Savings and Loan Debacle.* New York: Praeger, 1991.

Mayer, Martin, *The Greatest-Ever Bank Robbery: The Collapse of the Savings and Loan Industry,* New York: Charles Scribner's, 1990.

Moysich, Alane K., "An Overview of the U.S. Credit Union Industry," *FDIC Banking Review,* Fall 1990, 12–19 pp. 12–26.

National Commission on Financial Institution Reform, Recovery and Enforcement, *Origins and Causes of the S&L Debacle: A Blueprint for Reform,* Washington, D.C., July 1993.

Pearce, Douglas K., "Recent Developments in the Credit Union Industry," *Economic Review,* Federal Reserve Bank of Kansas City, June 1984, pp. 3–19.

Pizzo, Stephen, Mary Fricker, and Paul Muolo, *Inside Job: The Looting of America's Savings and Loans.* New York: McGraw-Hill, 1989.

Polakoff, Murray E., Thomas Durkin, et al., *Financial Institutions and Markets,* 2nd ed. Boston: Houghton Mifflin, 1981.

White, Lawrence J., *The S&L Debacle.* New York: Oxford University Press, 1991.

Other Nonbank Financial Intermediaries

The remaining nonbank financial intermediaries, which specialize in a wide variety of financial activities, are relatively newer institutions. These tailor their primary or secondary securities (or both) to DSUs and SSUs who were either not serviced or were poorly serviced by the intermediaries that existed. The need for some of these institutions arose because of changes in economic and social development. For example, the need for financial security after retirement increased both because more people lived longer and because many shifted to highly specialized jobs in urban areas from self-sufficient types of employment. The need for other institutions may be attributed to artificial restriction or legal barriers on the activities of existing intermediaries. For example, the need for secondary securities that offered SSUs market rates of interest arose in periods in which Regulation Q ceilings prevented depository institutions from offering competitive rates on their deposits. This chapter discusses the most important remaining nonbank financial intermediaries.

Investment Companies

Mutual and Closed-End Funds

Investment companies organize and sponsor **investment funds** to invest funds of SSUs in securities. The funds engage almost totally in denomination and credit-risk (diversification) intermediation. Monies are raised through the sale of secondary securities, called *shares*, generally in small denominations, and are pooled to purchase a wide variety of primarily primary securities in larger denominations. The shares represent ownership or equity claims in the fund. Technically, the shareholders vote annually to approve the investment company and its operation of the fund.

Because the shares have a claim against the entire asset portfolio (each share is effectively collateralized by a small slice of every primary security), they are less risky than if the same dollar amount were invested in only one or a small number of securities. Except for the differences in denomination, investment company shares closely resemble the primary securities held in the portfolio. Unlike the secondary securities of depository intermediaries, all investment fund shares are not fixed in value. The fluctuation of the market value of their secondary securities corresponds to the fluctuation of the market value of their portfolios of primary securities. Thus, unlike most other financial institutions whose liabilities are fixed-value debt (bank deposits, for example), investment companies cannot default on their secondary securities or become insolvent.

Most investment funds specialize in particular sectors of the financial market. Some trade only in equity securities, some only in debt securities, and some in both. Within equities, a fund may concentrate on only a few industries, such as energy or electronics, on risky growth or less risky income stocks, on foreign stocks, or so on. Within debt securities, funds may specialize in corporate, federal government, or tax-exempt municipal issues or in short-term **(money-market fund)** or long-term **(bond fund)** instruments. In its particular sector, an investment fund will diversify its portfolios to reduce risk. The first investment funds were equity funds; in recent years, the number of debt funds has expanded rapidly.

Investment funds are organized either as mutual stock or as regular stock firms. Unlike other intermediaries, the form of organization affects the characteristics of the secondary securities. **Mutual funds** are technically **open-end companies** that offer shares at the current pro rata net asset value of their portfolios and redeem outstanding shares upon presentation at the same price, or in the case of many money-market funds, at a fixed price. These shares do not trade in secondary markets.

Shares of some mutual funds are sold by salespeople who earn a commission. Because these commissions are paid at the time of purchase, the funds are called **load funds.** Funds that are sold directly to the public without a salesperson and do not impose a sales fee are called **no-load funds.** Both types of funds charge periodic service fees. Although mutual funds were traditionally load funds, no-load funds have increased in popularity in recent years, particularly as a result of the rapid growth of money-market funds. The number of outstanding shares in mutual funds is not fixed, but is changed to accommodate demand at the offer price. This is similar to the way most other intermediaries offer secondary securities.

In contrast, regular stock investment funds are **closed-end funds.** These are authorized to issue a given number of shares at a time. Like new stock issues by other private firms, the shares are sold at an initial offering. After that, they trade on the over-the-counter, secondary market at prices determined by supply and demand. The market price of the shares is generally close to the current pro rata market value of the portfolio; but the price maybe below or above that value, depending on several factors, such as quality of management and marketability. The fund does not redeem its own shares.

In large measure because of their greater liquidity, mutual funds are larger and have expanded faster than closed-end funds. In 1994, there were more than 5,000 different mutual funds. This far outnumbered the 3,000 individual stocks listed on the New York Stock Exchange. The assets of more than 3,000 larger stock and bond mutual funds, other than money market funds, totaled more than $1 trillion at year-end 1992, compared to less than $100 million at 315 closed-end funds. The size distribution and composition of major mutual funds at year-end 1992 are shown in Table 13–1. (See also Table 9–4).

Unlike those of many other financial intermediaries, the assets of investment funds are generally valued at market price rather than at cost. Thus, the growth of these funds is affected by changes in the market value of their assets as well as by the sale of new shares. Because stock prices have increased sharply on average in the post–World War II period but have

Type of Fund	No. of Funds	Combined Assets ($ thousands)	Percent of Total	Size of Fund	No. of Funds	Combined Assets ($ thousands)	Percent of Total
Common Stock				Over $1 billion	227	602,825	60.1
Maximum capital gain	97	$ 57,780	4.1	$500 million–$1 billion	216	152,896	15.2
Growth	207	135,809	9.6	$300 million–$500 million	208	81,157	8.1
Growth and income	363	127,305	9.0	$100 million–$300 million	644	115,339	11.5
Specialized				$50 million–$100 million	409	29,354	2.9
Government mortgage-				$10 million–$50 million	744	20,931	2.1
backed	74	51,255	3.6	$1 million–$10 million	289	1,441	0.1
Government securities	202	104,781	7.4	Under $1 million	42	18	0.0
International equity	165	41,431	2.9	Total	2,779	1,003,961	100.0
Small company growth	65	22,907	1.6				
Utilities	27	16,110	1.1				
Other	100	16,352	1.2				
Balanced Funds							
Balanced	61	24,067	1.7				
Equity income	64	22,333	1.6				
Bond Funds							
Corporate bonds	195	61,087	4.3				
Corporate high-yield	76	32,394	2.3				
International bond	70	25,274	1.8				
Municipal Bond Funds							
Municipal bond	405	111,074	7.9				
Municipal single state	185	84,214	6.0				
Money-Market Funds							
Taxable money market	365	362,500	25.7				
Tax-free money market	178	76,600	5.4				
Other							
Asset allocation and							
other	59	9,675	0.7				
Flexible income	54	30,391	2.2				
Total	2,996	1,410,362	100.0				

SOURCE: Reprinted by permission from the Wiesenberger Investment Companies Service, *Investment Companies Yearbook 1993*, Warren, Gorham, and Lamont, Inc., Boston, Mass, p. 18, and CDA/Wiesenberger.

been highly volatile and many mutual funds invest totally in equity, the market share of all mutual funds has also both increased sharply and been highly volatile. Mutual funds accounted for only 1 percent of total financial assets in 1950, 4 percent in 1970, 2 percent in 1980, and 8 percent in 1992. During this period, they climbed from the ninth largest institution to the fourth largest.

Investment companies hire investment advisers, frequently the sponsoring organization, to manage the funds. Management fees vary but are generally between 0.5 and 1 percent of the assets of the fund per year. In return, shareholders receive professional management of their investment portfolios. Much recent evidence suggests that, on average, management companies are not able to outperform the market when the returns are adjusted for differences in risk. This evidence has caused some investors to question the value they have received from having their portfolios actively managed, particularly in the case of equity funds. As a result, many funds have reduced the amount of trading they do in order to reduce costs. In addition, a small number of equity funds have tied or indexed the composition of their portfolios to a broad market average in order to realize the average market return. These funds, called **index funds,** downgrade the role of active management and emphasize the benefits of diversification. The investment company also arranges to sell the fund shares to the public either directly, generally through the mail or telephone, or indirectly through an independent sales force, including brokers working for security dealers, banks, and insurance companies.

Many investment companies offer a number of different funds, or a **family of funds,** including equity growth, equity income, bond, and other funds. The individual funds may be managed by the same or different advisers. At year-end 1992, Fidelity Investments sponsored funds with more than $100 billion of assets. This made Fidelity almost as large as both the third largest commercial bank in the country (Chemical Bank in New York) and the largest private pension fund and much larger than any other private or public pension fund. Indeed, if its money market mutual funds were included, Fidelity would effectively be tied with BankAmerica Corp. as the second largest financial institution in the U.S. after Citicorp (Table 9–6).

Most U.S. households that invest in stocks and bonds now do so through mutual funds. In 1992, some 27 percent of all households owned mutual funds. Among those households, ownership of mutual funds accounted for nearly 40 percent of their total financial assets. Bank deposits accounted for 36 percent, and individual stocks and bonds only 20 percent. Household investors accounted for nearly two-thirds of total mutual fund assets. The other one-third was owned by institutional investors. Mutual funds are much more important in the United States than in other countries, accounting for more than one-half of total fund assets worldwide. But, these funds are growing rapidly in other countries too. In 1992, after the United States, mutual funds were most important in France, followed by Japan.

Money-Market Funds

During the 1970s and early 1980s, Regulation Q ceilings on time deposits at commercial banks and thrift institutions encouraged smaller savers to shift their funds away from these institutions as market rates rose above the ceiling rates. The shift was either to the private financial market or to institutions in the intermediary market that were not constrained by these ceilings. At first, depositors shifted their funds to the private financial market. But the large minimum denominations on this market restricted this escape route primarily to larger depositors. Through time, new institutions developed on the intermediation market that purchased the most liquid of the securities on the private market (Treasury bills and commercial paper) as well as on the intermediation market (large bank CDs) and sold secondary securities in small denominations that effectively represented shares in the pool of these securities. These money-market funds were organized as mutual (open-end) funds. Because their secondary securities were not subject to deposit-rate ceilings, they permitted smaller depositors to escape the ceiling constraints and earn market rates of return. Although the market value of the funds' assets changes with interest rates, the short-term nature of the assets reduces the effect of these changes on their prices. Because of the small fluctuations, the Securities and Exchange Commission (SEC) permits money-market funds to redeem their shares at a fixed value, for example, always at $1.00, if the average maturity of their assets is less than 90 days. Likewise, although the shares are not insured by the FDIC or other government agency, the high quality of the investments and the diversification among many different issuers reduce the default risk. To reduce risk even further, some money-market funds invest only in U.S. Treasury securities. In addition, most money-market funds permit investors to withdraw their funds by writing checks above some minimum amount, usually $250, on the fund's account at a commercial bank. These checks serve, in effect, as orders to sell the same dollar amount of shares and transfer the proceeds to the bank. Thus, shares at money-market funds closely resemble deposits at depository institutions.

For these reasons, money-market funds grew phenomenally in the late 1970s and early 1980s. At year-end 1977, the 50 money-market funds had only $4 billion and represented only 5 percent of the total assets of all mutual funds. By November 1982, just before banks and thrift institutions were authorized to offer unregulated MMD accounts, money-market funds had grown to $232 billion offered by 280 funds. This accounted for almost 80 percent of all mutual fund assets—or four times as large as all other funds—and 30 percent of the total number of funds. This was the fastest rate of growth of any financial institution and made them the sixth largest financial institution in less than 10 years of existence; larger than credit unions, casualty insurance companies, and savings banks. After November 1982, money-market funds temporarily declined in size, as customers redeposited their funds with commercial banks and thrift institutions at competitive rates. However, they had recovered their losses by year-end 1984 and have continued to expand, although at a slower rate. Because of the rapid increase in stock prices, assets at money-market funds declined to about 30 percent of total mutual fund assets. At year-end 1992, there were nearly 600 taxable money-market funds with assets of $450 billion. Another $95 billion of assets was held in 280 short-term tax-exempt (municipal bond) funds. Because of their similarity to bank deposits, the Federal Reserve classifies consumer money-market fund holdings as part of M2 and institutional money-market holdings as part of M3.

The largest money-market funds are operated by Fidelity Investments, which also operated the largest family of nonmoney-market mutual funds. At year-end 1992, Fidelity funds totaled $67 billion and were roughly equivalent in size to the sixth largest commercial bank and larger than any thrift institution. It is interesting to speculate whether money-market funds would have been developed in a world without Regulation Q. They do not exist in countries such as Canada that do not have deposit rate ceilings. The balance sheet for money-market funds at year-end 1992 is shown in Table 13–2.

	$Billions	Percent
TABLE 13–2 MONEY-MARKET FUNDS, BALANCE SHEET AT YEAR-END 1992[a]		
Assets		
Cash and bank deposits	49	9
U.S. government securities	134	24
Municipal bonds	95	17
Commercial paper	176	32
Repurchase agreements	69	13
Miscellaneous	25	5
Total	548	100
Liabilities		
Shares	548	100
Total	548	100

SOURCE: Board of Governors of the Federal Reserve System, *Flow of Funds Accounts, Flows and Outstandings, Fourth Quarter 1992*, March 10, *1993*.

[a]Includes short-term tax-exempt funds.

Other Financial Intermediaries

Pension Funds

Pension funds sell employees and self-employed people secondary securities in the form of contractual agreements that provide for benefit payments upon the participant's retirement. Employers, unions, and other related groups frequently establish pension funds. The first employer pension plan in the United States was established by the American Express Company in 1875. Since then, pension funds have grown rapidly. Combined, private (second largest) and public (fifth largest) pension funds have 26 percent of all financial assets, up from only 4 percent in 1950 and are exceeded in asset size only by commercial banks.

The magnitude of the deferred payments in a pension plan may either be stipulated in the contract **(defined benefit)** or be related to the magnitude of the contributions and the earnings on them **(defined contribution).** In defined-benefit plans, the magnitude and timing of the contributions are related to the amount of the defined benefits, the expected earnings on the contributions, and the time period from when contributions are made until benefit payments begin. The magnitude of the benefits is generally related to the participants' final years' earnings and the number of years of participation in the pension plan. Given the size and timing of the benefits, which are liabilities of the fund that must be met to avoid default, and the estimated rate of return, the amount and timing of the contributions can be computed. A defined-benefit plan is said to be **fully funded** if the present value of the contributions and earnings thereon are expected to be enough to pay the benefits in full at the contracted time. If the contributions and expected earnings are insufficient, the plan is **underfunded.**

In pension funds established by an employer, the contributions are frequently shared between the employer and employees. In general, the employees' required contributions are not tax deductible. However, many employees may make additional tax-deductible contributions. In addition, employees do not get taxed on the employer's contributions until payout.

The earnings of the fund depend on the type of primary securities purchased. Because for each participant the benefits are promised in the future, the secondary securities are effectively long-term and the primary securities may also be long-term. In an attempt to increase earnings as much as possible and thereby reduce the necessary contributions for a given level of benefits, private pension funds have invested heavily in corporate stocks. The next largest investment is in corporate bonds. Defined-contribution plans often leave the risk-return composition of their investment strategy to the contributor by offering a choice among different plans, much as investment companies do. Table 13–3 shows the balance sheet for all private pension funds not managed by an insurance company.

Pension funds may manage themselves or be managed either by a trustee—say, a commercial bank or investment advisor—appointed by the sponsoring organization (firm, union, government unit, or the like) or by a life insurance or investment company. As noted earlier, if an insurance company manages the fund, it assumes the liability. But this is not so for other managers. Through the years, a number of problems have developed that have reduced the ability of some pension plans, particularly defined-benefit plans that are trustee-administered, to satisfy their obligations in full and on schedule. These problems involve under-funding, improper investment, abrupt termination, incomplete coverage by too-restrictive eligibility requirements **(vesting)**—such as requiring 20 years or more of service for eligibility for benefits—and inability to transfer pension rights to other employers or even other offices of the same employer **(portability).** These

TABLE 13–3	PRIVATE, NONINSURED PENSION FUNDS, BALANCE SHEET AT YEAR-END 1992	
	$Billions	Percent
Assets		
Cash and bank deposits	154	6
U.S. government securities	305	13
Corporate and foreign bonds	227	10
Corporate stock	1,130	48
Other assets	531	23
Total	2,347	100
Liabilities		
Pension plans	2,347	100
Total	2,347	100

SOURCE: Board of Governors of the Federal Reserve System, *Flow of Funds Accounts, Flows and Outstandings, Fourth Quarter 1992,* March 10, 1993.

problems reduce the value of some employers' contributions to the employees.

In recent years, self-employed persons and others have been permitted to initiate their own pension plans on a tax-deferred basis. Taxes on the contributions are deferred until payout, when the recipient is presumably in a lower income tax bracket. The self-employed may contribute 20 percent of their net income up to $30,000 annually in Keogh plans (named after Congressman Eugene Keogh, who sponsored the enabling legislation). In addition, from 1982 through 1986, all employees whether or not covered by other pension funds could contribute up to $2,000 of their wages and salaries annually ($2,250 if the spouse was unemployed) in a qualified **Individual Retirement Account (IRA).** In 1987, this provision was restricted to lower-income households and those not covered by other pension plans.

Private Pension Funds. Private pension plans cover more than 75 million employees. Plans managed by life insurance companies are referred to as **insured plans;** those managed by private trustees are called **noninsured plans.** Private noninsured pension funds are the third largest financial intermediary and are twice as large as insured plans. The largest private pension plan is Teachers Insurance and Annuity Association/College Retirement Equities Fund (see Table 9–6).

To improve the operation of private pension funds and reduce the risk to participants, Congress enacted in 1974 the **Employee Retirement Income Security Act (ERISA).** This act strengthens the fiduciary responsibilities of the trustee of the funds, establishes reporting and disclosure requirements, imposes minimum vesting requirements, and provides for insurance of the benefit payments in case of default or termination of defined benefit plans. The act applies only to private pension funds; funds operated by federal, state, or local government are exempt. In 1993, defined-benefit pension plans that were not guaranteed by insurance companies were insured by the **Pension Benefit Guaranty Corporation (PBGC)** up to some $2,500 per month per participant. The PBGC is a government agency housed in the Department of Labor and governed by a board of directors that consists of the Secretaries of the Treasury (chairperson), Labor, and Commerce. The corporation charges pension plans premiums for the insurance. It may also borrow up to $100 million from the U.S. Treasury.

As a result of the bankruptcy of such large corporations as LTV, Western Union, Pan Am, and Eastern Airlines, which left large underfunded pension plans (defined as plans the present value of whose assets fall short of the present value of their liabilities to plan participants), the PBGC found itself underfunded and asked Congress to permit it to levy large increases in premiums. Congress acquiesced on some but not all the premium increases and, for the first time, partially scaled the premiums to the riskiness of the pension fund as measured by the degree of its underfunding. Nevertheless, the incentive for troubled companies to increase the risk to the PBGC both by not funding their pension plans and by awarding employees with future benefits rather than with current compensation was not greatly reduced. As a result, the pension insurance program remains a ticking time bomb that has the potential for exploding into a smaller version of the S&L debacle. At year-end 1992, the PBGC actuarial deficit was estimated to be as large as $30 billion and growing.

TABLE 13–4	STATE AND LOCAL GOVERNMENT RETIREMENT FUNDS, BALANCE SHEET 1992	

	$Billions	Percent
Assets		
Cash and bank deposits	14	1
U.S. government securities	275	28
Corporate and other bonds	183	19
Corporate stock	464	47
Other assets	52	5
Total	988	100
Liabilities		
Pension plans	988	100
Total	988	100

SOURCE: Board of Governors of the Federal Reserve System, *Flow of Funds Accounts, Flows and Outstandings, Fourth Quarter 1992,* March 10, *1993.*

Public Pension Funds. There are two types of public pension plans. One type covers specific employees such as federal, state, or municipal employees, and is similar in general design to private plans. The other is Social Security (technically, **Old Age and Survivors Insurance Fund),** operated by the federal government for almost all employees in the United States. State and local government employee retirement funds cover some 17 million employees and are the fifth largest financial intermediary. Like the case with private funds, the largest portion of state and local funds is invested in corporate stock. (The balance sheet is shown in Table 13–4.) These are mostly defined-benefit plans. Contributions are generally made by both the participant and the employing government unit.

In recent years, some state and local governments have increased deferred pension benefits sharply, partially as a substitute for larger increases in current wages and salaries. At the same time, the government delayed making the necessary contributions, to avoid raising tax rates. Underfunding of this kind will require higher taxes in the future. This has contributed to the concern that municipal bond investors have about the ability of these governments to meet their debt obligations, and has exerted upward pressure on interest rates on municipal bonds. It is feared that households and business firms may vote against tax-rate increases or abandon the jurisdiction if tax rates are raised. The largest state or local pension fund is operated by the state of California (see Table 9–6).

The federal government operates large employee pension funds for its civil service and military employees and separate, smaller funds for employees of the foreign service, federal judiciary, Tennessee Valley Authority, and Board of Governors of the Federal Reserve System.

The largest pension fund is Social Security. It covers almost the entire nonfederal labor force. In 1992, more than 175 million people had some earnings credit in Social Security, and more than 165 million were fully insured. Forty million were receiving some benefits. Social Security is intended to provide minimum retirement income security to all retirees. Its financing differs significantly from that of other pension plan: participants do not contribute directly to their own benefits. Social Security is primarily financed on a "pay-as-you-go" basis; current contributions are used to pay current benefits to others. Contributions have been financed by payroll taxes on both employer and employee.

As the growth in population slows and the percentage of retirees increases relative to the labor force, payroll taxes have been increased almost annually and may be expected to continue to be increased in the future to maintain current benefits. As a result, Congress has considered alternative ways to finance Social Security in the future, such as through income taxes. Because contributions are channeled directly from contributors to recipients who use their benefit payments primarily for consumption expenditures, Social Security, unlike most other pension funds, does not foster aggregate saving and investment in the economy. Moreover, it may reduce the incentive of some participants to save as much as they would otherwise during their working years. If so, this would contribute to a slower rate of economic growth.

Finance Companies

Finance companies lend to a wide variety of borrowers for an equally wide variety of purposes. In contrast to most financial intermediaries, which emphasize tailoring secondary securities to the particular needs of the SSU, finance companies specialize in tailoring credit to the particular needs of the borrower. Thus, their credit service is highly personalized. For purposes of analysis, finance companies may be divided into three groups, although some larger *diversified* firms engage in two or even all three types of activities.

Consumer finance companies, often called *small-loan companies* (and in some states, *industrial* or *Morris Plan banks*), make small to medium-sized installment loans to households, either to purchase particular items, such as television sets and vacation trips, or to refinance various types of maturing, small debt obligations. Much of the credit extended by consumer finance companies is to households that are unable to obtain credit elsewhere. These loans generally have high origination costs and high risks of default and, as a result, carry high interest rates. Because a large proportion of the clientele are low-income and less-educated households, consumer finance companies are regulated by the states with respect to the maximum size loans they may extend, the maximum interest rates they may charge, and the terms and conditions of collection. The maximum permissible rates are often higher than the rates commercial banks may charge.

Although no firm figures are available, it is estimated that there are some 1,750 consumer finance companies that operate more than 10,000 offices throughout the country. These offices range from small, one-office firms on upper floors of older commercial buildings to large, national firms that advertise widely, such as Household Finance, with some 500 offices in the United States and Canada. In recent years, commercial banks have increased their consumer lending by establishing finance companies through their parent holding companies. Unlike the bank itself, these affiliates may branch across state lines. A colorful competitor for small loans to low-income households are pawnshops. These are described in Exhibit 13–1.

EXHIBIT

13-1

Pawnshops: The Consumer's Lender of Last Resort

Pawnshops play a specialized role in consumer finance. They cater to those consumers whose credit needs are not accommodated by mainstream financial institutions. Broadly speaking, pawnshop customers have two characteristics. First, these customers have high credit risk and so cannot borrow on an unsecured basis. Second, pawnshop customers typically require very small denomination loans that traditional lenders are unable or unwilling to provide on a secured basis.

While there are no estimates of the percentage of the population whose risk characteristics exclude them from mainstream consumer credit sources, available evidence suggests that the number is large. Moreover, the poor and poorly educated are disproportionately represented. Not only are many low-income consumers excluded because of their income, but they are also much more likely than the middle class to have unstable incomes, and employment patterns. In addition, many consumers, especially those with low incomes and little education, do not maintain bank accounts, almost ensuring they would not pass the typical screening requirements of a bank or finance company. For example, the Federal Reserve Board's 1983 Survey of Consumer Finances found that 12 percent of all families did not have a checking or savings account. Of these families, 57 percent fell into the lowest quintile for family income, and 59 percent were headed by individuals without a high school education.

Financial historians trace the birth of institutionalized pawnbroking in the Western world to the later Middle Ages. Starting in fifteenth-century Italy, charitable groups or governments in Continental Europe and Latin America opened nonprofit pawnshops as a public service for the poor, a tradition persisting to this day. In England and the United States, on the other hand, pawnshops were almost exclusively privately owned and operated for profit.

In examining the pawnbroking industry [in the United States] over time, three observations stand out. First, the number of pawn-shops and pawnshops per capita is now larger than it was at the beginning of the century. Second, over time the industry has shifted from a concentration in older major urban areas, primarily in the Northeast, to Southern and Central Mountain states. Third, in the 1980s, the pawnbroking industry grew in almost all states for which there are data; and in some states the growth was extremely strong.

Pawnshop loans have three features: the loans are for very small amounts and short maturities, they are fully collateralized by personal property, and interest and other charges are extremely high relative to other types of lending.

Most pawnshop loans are for relatively small amounts. For example, in Indiana, Oklahoma, and Oregon, average loan sizes range from $40 to $60 (see the table). In most states, pawnbrokers make loans with one-month or two-month maturities. However, it is not uncommon for customers to renew these loans by paying the interest on the loan at the end of the month.

To prevent a loss in case of default, a broker lends a customer a percentage of the value the broker believes the collateral would bring in a sale. The loan-to-collateral ratio varies over time and across pawnshops, but typically the amount loaned is 50 to 60 percent of the resale value of the collateral. Though brokers almost always make a one-time profit from a default, almost all say they prefer customers repay the loan. Such customers are likely to return to the same pawnshop for future credit needs. Indeed, brokers report about 70 to 80 percent of their customers are repeat customers. Moreover, credit customers often purchase goods the shop sells and, if they blame the broker for the loss of their collateral, they are less likely to patronize the shop.

Another feature of pawnshop credit is its high cost. Each of the states listed in the table imposes a ceiling on pawnshop interest rates. The ceiling interest rates in these states for an average size loan range from 0.5 percent per month in Pennsylvania to 20 percent per month in Oklahoma. In addition, several of the states allow storage and insurance fees, which raise the effective price of the loan. For each state, the dollar outlay for a two-month, $51 loan plus applicable fees is shown in the table. For comparison with other types of consumer credit, annual percentage interest rates (APR) inclusive of fees are also illustrated. Thus, for borrowers from pawnshops in these states, effective interest rates range from 36 percent APR in New Jersey and Pennsylvania to 240 percent APR in Oklahoma. Such high rates are not uncommon. In more than half of the states, pawnshops levy effective interest rates of 120 percent APR or more on average-size loans.

CHARACTERISTICS OF PAWNSHOP LOANS, SELECTED STATES

	Indiana	New Jersey	Oklahoma	Oregon	Pennsylvania
Average loan size	$43.11	n.a.	$41.00	$61.31	n.a.
Default rate, number of loans	20.6%	n.a.	22.2%	13.9%	n.a.
Default rate, value of loans	13.8%	n.a.	19.6%	9.3%	n.a.
Legal interest rate ceiling (monthly)	3.0%	3.0%	20%	3.9%	0.5%
Interest charge on two-month $51 loan	$3.06	$3.06	$20.40	$3.06	$0.51
Permissible storage and insurance fees (for item left on pledge two months)	$3.00	none	none	$5.00	$2.55
Implicit APR interest rate on two-month $51 loan (includes storage and other fees)	71.3%	36.0%	240.0%	94.8%	36.0%

SOURCE: Abstracted from John P. Caskey and Brian J. Zikmund, "Pawnshops: The Consumer's Lender of Last Resort," *Economic Review*, Federal Reserve Bank of Kansas City, March/April 1990, pp. 5–18.

Sales finance companies finance both consumer purchases of large durable goods, such as automobiles, pleasure boats, refrigerators, and television sets, and retailer inventories of these goods. Many of the larger sales finance companies are "captive" firms, owned by either the manufacturer of the goods financed or the retailer from whom the goods were purchased. General Motors owns General Motors Acceptance Corporation (GMAC), which finances both consumer purchases of GM products and dealer inventories of GM products and is the largest finance company in the nation; and Sears Roebuck owns Sears Roebuck Acceptance Corporation, which finances consumer purchases of all goods and services at Sears retail outlets. Note from Table 9–6 that at year-end 1992, GMAC's assets exceeded $90 billion, which made it larger than all but three commercial banks.

Sales finance companies compete directly with commercial banks, which make similar loans to both consumers and retailers; with credit unions, which make consumer loans; and, for smaller purchases, with bank credit cards. For many borrowers, loans from sales finance companies may be obtained faster and at lower transactions costs particularly at the place of purchase, such as the automobile dealer, than from commercial banks or credit unions. In recent years, a number of large local retailers have supplemented or replaced their own consumer credit operations with national credit cards.

Business finance companies finance inventory and equipment of almost all types and sizes of business firms. Their competitive advantage is specialization and careful tailoring of the entire financing package. Some finance companies have developed expertise in the textile industry and provide credit to firms by purchasing or *factoring* their accounts receivable. The finance company advances credit to the firm at the time of sale and receives payment directly from the firm's customers. Other finance companies specialize in various types of equipment used by small and medium-sized business firms and provide credit for the purchase of such equipment on mortgage terms. Larger business finance companies also engage in leasing. Upon agreement with a customer, the finance company purchases the equipment and leases it to the customer at a prearranged rental fee for a prearranged number of years. Such arrangements are particularly popular in the railroad industry for financing rolling stock and in the airline industry for financing jetliners.

Finance companies obtain their funds primarily through the sale of debt securities in large denominations to larger SSUs. At the end of 1992, the major source of funding for finance companies was commercial paper. These sources are supplemented by credit lines at commercial banks, which can be activated when the funds on the private capital markets become too costly, and loans from parent companies. The particular type of secondary securities sold varies greatly among different finance companies. Captive sales finance subsidiaries, whose names and credit quality are well known, rely more heavily on commercial paper, business finance companies rely on longer-term bonds, and locally owned small-loan companies rely on nonmarketable long-term debt and equity. The balance sheet of finance companies is shown in Table 13–5.

TABLE 13–5	FINANCE COMPANIES, BALANCE SHEET AT YEAR-END 1992	
	$Billions	Percent
Assets		
Cash and bank deposits	11	1
Consumer loans	122	15
Business loans	297	37
Mortgage loans	238	30
Miscellaneous assets	140	17
Total	808	100
Liabilities and Net Worth		
Bank loans	44	6
Commercial paper	338	42
Bonds	181	22
Miscellaneous liabilities	178	22
Net worth	67	8
Total	808	100

SOURCE: Board of Governors of the Federal Reserve System, *Flow of Funds Accounts, Flows and Outstandings, Fourth Quarter 1992*, March 10, 1993.

Nonfinancial Firms

In recent years, a number of basically nonfinancial firms have entered into various types of financial activities. Most have confined these activities to services connected with their nonfinancial activities, such as financing their customers through affiliated finance companies. Some, however, have expanded far afield in search of greater earnings, such as investment banking, insurance, and real estate finance.

Perhaps the best known firm to attempt to become a "nonfinancial" financial firm was Sears Roebuck. For many years, Sears operated a large finance company; Allstate Insurance Company, the third largest casualty-property insurance firm in the country, as well as a smaller life-health insurer; a consumer-oriented Sears Savings Bank in California; Sears Mortgage Corporation, a mortgage banker; and Homart Development Company, a developer and operator of shopping centers and office buildings. In the early 1980s, it purchased Dean Witter, one of the largest investment banking firms, and Coldwell Banker, at one time the nation's largest real estate broker. The retail services offered by many of these firms were provided under one roof at financial services centers located in Sears stores throughout the country. In 1985, Sears introduced a general consumer credit card—the Discover Card—through a small bank that it owned in Delaware. According to its president in the early 1980s, Sears' goal was "to become the largest consumer-oriented financial service entity."[1]

However, by 1989, it became apparent that this strategy was not working. Many people did not want "to buy their stocks where they bought their socks." Sears sold part of Coldwell Banker and much of its savings and loan business and cut back on the number of Dean Witter offices in its stores. In the early 1990s, it sold most of its remaining financial services affiliates, including a segment of Allstate Insurance (which Sears had owned since it was organized in 1931) and Dean Witter (along with its Discover credit card), to raise funds to support its basic retail merchandising activities, which had not been benefiting from the strategy.

Likewise, American Express, perhaps the largest and most aggressive financial supermarket, with worldwide operations in commercial banking, investment banking, insurance, mutual funds, finance companies, travel services, and cable television, as well as credit cards, also found such diversity not as profitable as it had expected and started to sell off some of its newer activities, including its Shearson securities firm, to concentrate on its original banking, travel, and credit-card operations.

Nevertheless, many nonfinancial firms continue to view financial services as a promising addition to their product lines. For example, General Electric, which owns GE Capital, the second largest finance company, and Kidder Peabody, a large investment bank, has stated that it is aggressively searching to acquire additional financial firms. The ability of such firms to enter banking would be made easier if nonfinancial firms were permitted to own bank holding companies as is sometimes recommended. The pros and cons of combining banking and commerce are examined in Chapter 19.

---

[1] "Sears to Offer Money Market Trust Service, Maps Major Real-Estate Brokerage Role," Wall Street Journal, September 2, 1981, p. 2.

SUMMARY

Investment funds operated by investment companies engage primarily in denomination and risk intermediation. They purchase large-denomination and/or high-risk primary securities and sell pro rata shares to SSUs in small denominations. Risk is reduced by diversifying securities of many different issuers. Investment funds tend to specialize in the types of securities they buy. These can range from risky equities to income-type equities, to municipal bonds, to short-term money-market debt. Investment companies are organized as either mutual open-end funds or closed-end funds. Mutual funds are the more common. These funds continuously issue shares at the net market value of their asset portfolio and redeem outstanding shares at the same price. Initially, money-market mutual funds expanded rapidly by investing in short-term, low-risk securities and offering savers a low-risk, highly liquid deposit-like instrument at yields higher than Regulation Q permitted on deposits until it was phased out. Closed-end funds have a limited number of shares outstanding that after initial issue trade on stock markets just like any other type of share.

Pension funds provide income to member retirees. They raise funds through regular payments by members and their employers during their working years. Pension funds invest in longer-term securities. The largest single pension fund is the national Social Security System which covers almost all employees everywhere in the United States. Most other pension funds cover only their own employees.

Finance companies lend to DSUs ranging from large corporations to lower-income households. They tailor their loans more closely to the individual DSU than do most other financial intermediaries. Finance companies raise funds by selling both short- and long-term debt to larger SSUs. Some basically nonfinancial firms also offer a variety of financial services, particularly loan services.

QUESTIONS

1. "Investment funds are the most basic type of financial intermediary institution." Evaluate this statement. Differentiate among investment funds according to organization, objective, and type of securities traded.

2. Wiesenberger and some other investment services' reports, which are generally available in your library, track the performance of individual investment funds by measuring their rates of return. Pick three investment funds that specialize in different securities. How has their performance compared over the past 1, 5, and 20 years? What accounts for these differences?

3. At year-end 1992, the largest family of mutual funds, the largest finance company, and the largest pension fund all were as large as all but the largest two commercial banks. This represents a change from earlier years in which the largest banks were relatively much larger. Discuss the reasons you believe for the more rapid growth by the nonbank financial intermediaries. What might be some of the implications for the banks and public policy?

4. Trace the growth in money-market funds from 1974 to the present. Why do you think these funds did not dis-

appear when Regulation Q ceilings were removed from bank and thrift institution deposits? What is the most comparable account at a bank? How does the current return of money markets funds compare with that at banks? Why is there a difference?

5. Differentiate between defined-benefit and defined-contribution pension plans. How might the investment strategies of the two types of plans differ? Which type is more likely to encounter financial difficulties? Why?

6. "Mutual funds cannot fail." Discuss the truth of this statement. What happens to investor claims when the market value of a fund's assets decline? How can risk-averse investors protect themselves against excessive risk in mutual funds?

7. Although money-market funds are not insured by the federal government, surveys have shown that many households have greater confidence in them than in banks. Why might this be? How could the funds quickly lose this confidence?

8. How does Social Security differ from private and most other public pension funds? In recent years, Social Security taxes have been raised significantly. Why was that necessary? What arguments are there for and against financing Social Security out of income taxes?

9. How can the different types of finance companies compete against commercial banks? What is the maximum interest rate that consumer loan companies can charge in your state? What is the maximum size loan they may make? For what kind of loan might you personally use a consumer loan company? When?

REFERENCES

Abken, Peter A., "Corporate Pensions and Government Insurance; Déjá Vu All Over Again?," *Economic Review*, Federal Reserve of Atlanta, March/April 1992, pp. 1–16.

American Council of Life Insurance, *Life Insurance Factbook*, Washington, D.C., annual.

Congressional Budget Office, *Controlling Losses of the Pension Benefit Guaranty Corporation*, Washington, D.C.: Government Printing Office, January 1993.

Dougall, Herbert E., and Jack Gaumnitz, *Capital Markets and Institutions*, 5th ed. Englewood Cliffs, N.J.: Prentice Hall, 1986.

Elliehausen, Gregory E., and John D. Wolken, "Banking Markets and Use of Financial Services by Households," *Federal Reserve Bulletin*, March 1992, pp. 169–81.

General Accounting Office, *Pension Plans: Hidden Liabilities Increase Claims against Government Insurance Program*, Washington, D.C., December 1992.

Investment Company Institute, *Mutual Funds Fact Book*. Washington, D.C., annual.

Laderman, Jeffrey M., and Geoffrey Smith, "The Power of Mutual Funds," *Business Week*, January 18, 1993, pp. 62–68.

Munnel, Alicia H., "ERISA—The First Decade," *New England Economic Review*, Federal Reserve Bank of Boston, November/December 1984, pp. 44–63.

Paré, Terrence P., "Tough Birds That Quack Like Ducks," *Fortune*, March 11, 1991, pp. 79–84.

Pavel, Christine, and Harvey Rosenblum, "Banks and Nonbanks: The Horse Race Continues," *Economic Perspectives*, Federal Reserve Bank of Chicago, May/June 1985, pp. 3–17.

Polakoff, Murray E., Thomas A. Durkin, et al., *Financial Institutions and Markets*, 2nd ed. Boston: Houghton Mifflin, 1981.

Remolona, Eli M., and Kurt C. Wulfekuhler, "Finance Companies, Bank Competition and Niche Markets," *Quarterly Review*, Federal Reserve Bank of New York, Summer 1992, pp. 25–38.

Rose, Peter S., and Donald R. Fraser, *Financial Institutions*, 4th ed. Plano, Tex.: Business Publications, 1993.

Rosenblum, Harvey, and Christine Pavel, "Financial Services in Transition: The Effects of Nonbank Competitors," in Richard C. Aspinwall and Robert A. Eisenbeis, eds., *Handbook for Banking Strategy*, New York: John Wiley, 1985.

Utgoff, Kathleen, "The PBGC: A Costly Lesson in the Economics of Federal Insurance," in Mark S. Sniderman, ed., *Government Risk Bearing*, Boston: Kluwer, 1993, pp. 145–60.

Wiesenberger Investment Companies Service, *Investment Companies*. New York: Warren, Gorham and Lamont, annual.

The Payments System

An efficient national payments system is a prerequisite for efficient trade and maximum economic well-being. Money that is not widely accepted, or is accepted only at different prices in different locations, is not very useful. If you were unable to use your currency or checks at full face value to finance purchases when you were away from home, you would purchase far less. Payments are made by

▼ Coin and currency,
▼ Checks, and
▼ Electronic transfer.

In the United States, a truly national payments system in which both currency and checks were acceptable throughout the country at par value did not exist until after 1914, when the Federal Reserve System was established. Commercial banks are the most important private financial institution in the payments system. Commercial banks in the United States not only issue almost all transaction deposits, which account for 70 percent of the money supply (M1) and finance an estimated 90 percent of the dollar volume of all noninterbank transactions, they also operate much of the interbank funds-transfer mechanism, which is the heart of the national payments system.[1] Since 1981, when they were given the authority to offer checkable deposits nationwide, savings and loan associations, savings banks, and credit unions have played an increasingly important, but still small, role in the payments system. Some 80 percent of all families in the United States have one or more checking accounts. Thus, a study of the payments system requires a knowledge of how depository institutions and, in particular, commercial banks operate. The use of each major form of payment in 1987 is shown in Table 14–1.

Paper Transfer Systems

In early days, the acceptance of coins was dependent on the value of the underlying metal. There was an inverse relationship between the value of the metal and the acceptance of the coin at face value. The greater the face value stamped on the coin relative to the intrinsic value, the less widely the coin was accepted at its face value. To standardize their value, governments began accepting coins with specified metallic content at face value in pay-

---

[1] In 1986, households financed 56 percent of their expenditures by check; 36 percent by coin, currency, and money orders; and 8 percent by credit card. Business firms, of course, rely much more heavily on payment by check or by electronic transfer. It is not necessary for the issuance of money and the operation of the payments system to be vested in the same institutions. In many countries, money is issued by the banks, but the payments system is operated by the government.

TABLE

14–1

VOLUME AND VALUE OF TRANSACTIONS BY
PAYMENT METHOD, 1987

Type of Payment	Number of Transactions		Volume of Transactions		Average Transaction ($)
	Billion	Percent	$Trillion	Percent	
Nonelectronic					
Cash	278.6	83.4	$ 1.4	0.4	$ 5
Check	47.0	14.1	55.8	16.3	1,187
Other	7.3	2.2	0.4	0.1	57
Subtotal	332.9	99.7	57.6	16.8	173
Electronic					
Wire transfer	0.1	a	281.0	82.1	3,345,238
Automated clearinghouse (ACH)	1.0	0.3	3.6	1.1	3,530
Subtotal	1.1	0.3	284.6	83.2	258,727
Total	334.0	100.0	342.2	100.0	1,024

SOURCE: David VanHoose and Gordon Sellon, Jr., "Daylight Overdrafts, Payments System Risk, and Public Policy," *Economic Review*, Federal Reserve Bank of Kansas City, September/October 1989, p. 11.

[a]Less than 0.1.

ment of taxes and fees. People frequently attempted to obtain extra value from their coins by "clipping" or "sweating" part of the metal off without reducing their exchange value. By reducing their homogeneity, this practice reduced the usefulness of coins in trade and sped the changeover from a metallic to a paper transfer system.

Currency

Before collateral on national bank notes was standardized in 1863, the acceptance of bank notes (currency) in the United States depended on the credit worthiness of the issuing bank. The less faith the potential recipient had in the ability of the bank to redeem the note in coin at full value, the less likely was the note to be accepted at face value. Because of the predominance of unit banking in this period, there were a large and expanding number of banks, and banks failed frequently. But, because news traveled only slowly and the cost of information was high, the notes issued by failed banks remained in circulation for some time afterward. It followed that the larger the number of banks or the more distant the issuing bank, the less knowledgeable the note recipient was likely to be about the bank and the less likely that the note would be accepted at face value. Notes of equal denomination but issued by different banks circulated at different values.

Once a note left the vicinity of the issuing bank, redemption became both less certain and more difficult. For payment in coin, the note had to be returned to the issuing bank. Possibilities for gain presented by this requirement were not lost on some less-than-honest entrepreneurs. They established banks in frontier areas of the country that were reportedly more hospitable to wildcats than to humans. This made the process of redeeming the notes even more difficult, and gave rise to the term **wildcat banking.** Wildcat banks printed many more notes than they had reserves to redeem in the normal course of business. The notes were put into circulation as far away from the bank as possible, frequently at a discount. Although enough notes eventually found their way back to the issuing bank to bankrupt it, they generally did not do so until after the owners had made their profits and left town. In addition, even less scrupulous people simply counterfeited notes from more obscure banks.

To help people evaluate the notes in circulation and identify counterfeit issues, directories listing all banks were published. These showed the important financial particulars for each bank with notes in circulation and the characteristic markings of each note. Because there were many banks, and each bank had notes in a number of different denominations, these publications tended to be rather thick and cumbersome. Clearly, this system was hardly conducive to efficient trade.

Periodic attempts were made by the federal and state governments, some larger banks, and others to standardize the value of the notes of different banks. These attempts generally centered on one of three approaches. In the first, notes issued by selected banks were collected and presented to the banks unannounced in large batches for redemption. The knowledge that such redemptions were a possibility caused banks to pursue more conservative policies and to maintain larger reserves. This strategy was employed by the First (1791–1811) and Second (1816–36) Banks of the United States. These banks were early, unsuccessful attempts to establish a central bank in the United States. In part because their actions caused a slower rate of monetary expansion than many felt was desirable, Congress terminated the charters of these banks.

In the second approach, groups of cooperating banks agreed to maintain deposits with each other to be used to redeem each other's notes at par value. This approach was tried most notably by a group of New England banks in 1825. The plan was referred to as the **Suffolk System** after the Suffolk Bank, which played the key role. The third method was to impose fees on cooperating banks. The fees were to be used to compensate noteholders and other creditors of insolvent banks. New York State used this approach in 1829; it may be viewed as a forerunner of government deposit insurance.

Each of these plans was successful for only a brief period. They eventually failed because the coordinating institution was terminated, as in the case of the First and Second Bank of the United States, or because the coverage was insufficient in terms of both banks and amounts.

The value of notes was finally standardized by the National Bank Act of 1863. This act provided for national charters for commercial banks and authorized these banks to issue uniformly sized currency collateralized by Treasury bonds. (Notes previously came in almost as many sizes and colors as there were banks.) To discourage state banks from issuing competing notes not similarly collateralized, the act taxed these notes. The tax effectively prevented state banks from issuing notes and left only national bank notes in circulation.

Although supplemented by a limited amount of Treasury notes, national bank notes were the major form of currency in the United States until after World War I. In 1913, Congress granted the new Federal Reserve Banks power to issue Federal Reserve notes and these gradually became the primary form of currency. (The issuing district Federal Reserve Bank is identified on each note by its number and corresponding letter of the alphabet; for example, Boston is 1 and A, New York is 2 and B; and so on.) In 1935, the last of the national bank notes were withdrawn from circulation. Today, almost all currency is Federal Reserve notes. Although, as can be seen from Table 14–1, currency is used to finance more than 80 percent of the number of all transactions, it finances less than 1 percent of the dollar volume.

Checks

The national payments system created by circulating currency of equal value did not last long. The expansion of deposit banking created the same problems that had previously plagued note banking—fear of nonconvertibility into specie or currency. Checks written on deposits at unknown and distant banks were accepted by sellers only at discount, if at all. (This discount was independent of the faith that the check recipient had that the check writer had sufficient funds in his or her account to cover the check.) Because, unlike notes, checks do not circulate hand to hand, collecting funds from the bank on which the check was written—the paying bank—increased in importance.

Particularly in the United States with its restrictions on branching and the resulting large number of banks, most checks are not deposited at the same banks on which they are written. By itself, receiving a check does not do a bank much good. It needs to collect the funds. For payment, checks had to be presented physically at the bank on which they were drawn. Until the funds were collected, the receiving bank could not invest the proceeds. Moreover, if it had paid the check depositor, either in currency or by permitting the amount credited to the deposit account to be drawn down, the bank had, in effect, extended an interest-free loan.

The process by which the check is sent from the receiving bank to the paying bank and payment is transmitted the other way is termed **check clearing** and is shown below:

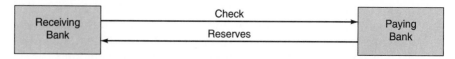

In the early days, check clearing did not function efficiently. Even under the best of circumstances, the state of transportation and communications in the middle and late 1800s did not favor rapid clearings. To travel from one region to another and return took many days, and round trips between coasts often took weeks. Moreover, although it was in the receiving bank's interest to send the check to the paying bank as directly as possible, it was in the paying bank's interest to transmit payment as indirectly and slowly as possible.

Banks in different parts of the country collected checks and transmitted payment through other banks with which they had working agreements. These banks are called *correspondent banks.* Banks maintained deposit balances at correspondent banks to which proceeds from check collection could be credited and payments debited. Upon receipt of a check on a distant bank, the receiving bank would send the check to a correspondent closer to the paying bank for collection. This bank might, in turn, send the check to its correspondent bank, and so on. Given a large number of banks, the state of transportation, and the conflicting objectives of the receiving and paying banks, it is not difficult to visualize the inefficiency inherent in this process.

To improve the efficiency of interbank check clearing in a given market area, banks joined together to establish clearinghouses. The operation of a clearinghouse may be seen best by tracing the path a check takes from the time it is written to the time payment is completed.[2]

Example of a Local Clearinghouse. Assume that Mr. Smith purchases some general merchandise from the Atlanticville Store in his hometown of Atlanticville and pays for the purchase by writing a check on the Atlanticville Bank. At the end of the day, the Atlanticville Store deposits the check in its demand-deposit account at its bank, the First State Bank. This is shown as entry (a) in Table 14–2. The First State Bank credits the store's deposit account and prepares to send the check to the Atlanticville Bank for collection. It records the check on its books as an asset entitled *cash item in the process of collection,* or **CIPC,** shown as entry (b). This is similar to accounts receivable on the books of other business firms. It reflects funds owed but not yet paid. (CIPC on the books of commercial banks is also referred to as *bank float.*)

TABLE

14–2 CHECK CLEARING

Mr. Smith			Atlanticville Bank		
(a) Merchandise +					
Bank balance −					
(b)					
(c)			Cash reserves −	−	Mr. Smith

First State Bank			Atlanticville Store		
(a)			Merchandise −		
			Bank balance +		
(b) CIPC	+	+ Atlanticville Store			
(c) CIPC	−				
Cash reserves +					

[2] Clearinghouses also exist for the transfer of securities, including bonds, stocks, futures, and options. All serve to expedite the transfer of funds and to reduce the risk of default in delivery of the securities.

During the night, the First State Bank sorts the checks drawn on other banks that it has received during the day. The next day, messengers are sent with these checks to the appropriate banks (or their correspondents) for payment. At the same time, the other banks in Atlanticville follow a similar procedure and send their messengers. If they are careful not to crash into each other, each messenger reaches his or her destination. Upon receipt of the checks drawn on it, the Atlanticville Bank discovers that Mr. Smith has written his check, verifies the account for sufficient funds, debits the account for the amount, and sends payment to the First State Bank by the same messenger, thereby reducing its reserves. (If Mr. Smith has insufficient funds in his deposit account to cover the amount of the check, the Atlanticville Bank rejects the check and returns it to the First State Bank which reserves the credit to the Atlanticville Store's account.) When the messenger returns with payment, the First State Bank offsets the CIPC entry and records the increase in cash reserves, entry (c). The transfer is complete.

At the same time as this transaction, the First State Bank may be sending payment to the Atlanticville Bank by another messenger. It is not surprising to some of us, of course, that the size of Mr. Smith's account may not always be the same on his records and on the bank's records. Mr. Smith reduces his balance on his records at the time the check is written, but the Atlanticville Bank does not reduce his balance on its records until it receives the check some time later. Thus, the amount of deposits on the books of a bank generally overstates the amount on the records of its customers. Aware of this, Mr. Smith, as a few of us are sometimes tempted to do, may write a check knowing that he has insufficient funds in his account at that time but that he will make a deposit before the check clears and is presented for payment. This is called living off bank float, or **check kiting.** Legally, it is quite naughty and may be said to be an example of "checks without balances."

After a few midtrip collisions among messengers, it quickly became obvious to the banks in Atlanticville that the clearing process could be greatly expedited if everyone brought their checks to a central location. They agreed to cooperatively establish a clearinghouse to which all checks would be brought at specified times, generally once or twice a day. The clearinghouse actually consists of only a room in which tables are placed in a circle. Each bank has a designated table. Representatives of each bank walk along the outside of the tables and place the checks drawn on each bank (or their correspondents) on the appropriate table. These are verified and the amount totaled. The checks are delivered to the bank. The tallies are brought to a representative of the clearinghouse, who compares the amount owed each bank with the amount which that bank owes the others. These amounts are offset or **netted** against each other, so that only net payments are transferred.

The time and effort saved by a clearinghouse through netting are demonstrated in Table 14–3 for a hypothetical three-bank system. Assume that at the end of a business day, bank A has received $1,000,000 in checks drawn on bank B and $1,200,000 drawn on bank C. Bank B has received checks of $700,000 drawn on bank A and $300,000 on bank C. Bank C, in turn, has $800,000 in checks on bank A and $500,000 on bank B. Each bank could send messengers the next morning to deliver the checks to the

TABLE
14–3

HYPOTHETICAL EXAMPLE OF CHECK CLEARING
THROUGH CLEARINGHOUSE

Checks Drawn on Bank	Checks Deposited at Bank			Total Owed
	A	B	C	
A		$ 700,000	$ 800,000	$1,500,000
B	$1,000,000		500,000	1,500,000
C	1,200,000	300,000		1,500,000
Total received	2,200,000	1,000,000	1,300,000	4,500,000
Total owed	1,500,000	1,500,000	1,500,000	4,500,000
Net	+700,000	−500,000	−200,000	0

appropriate bank and collect payment. Thus, bank A would send messengers to banks B and C to collect $1,000,000 and $1,200,000, respectively, from each. There is a good chance that they might collide with the messengers sent by banks B and C to collect payment on the checks they received from bank A. Moreover, upon their return, they are likely to pass each other carrying cash to each other's banks, the messenger from bank A carrying cash from bank B while the messenger from bank B carries cash from bank A. In total, the messengers carry $4,500,000 from bank to bank.

More efficiently, all three banks could send messengers to a central clearinghouse. The clearinghouse would sum all the checks by bank. It would find that each bank had $1,500,000 in checks drawn on it and deposited at the other two banks (Table 14–3). This payment would be deducted from the amount each bank would collect from the others. Thus, bank A collects $2,200,000, but owes $1,500,000; bank B collects $1,000,000, but owes $1,500,000; and bank C collects $1,300,000, but owes $1,500,000. Only the net amounts would change hands. Bank B pays the clearinghouse $500,000, and bank C pays $200,000. The clearinghouse, in turn, pays bank A $700,000. The messengers can return to their own banks without any further stops, and carrying only $700,000 rather than $4,500,000. Local clearinghouses are found in almost any city or area with three or more banks.

Intercity Clearing.   Check clearing among banks in different regions of the country is more difficult. Suppose Mr. Smith had made his purchase while on vacation in Pacificville, at the opposite end of the country from his home in Atlanticville. The store deposited the check with the Pacificville Bank. The Pacificville Bank forwarded the check to its San Francisco correspondent, which, in turn, forwarded it to a correspondent closer to Atlanticville. After passing through a number of banks, the check eventually reached the Atlanticville Bank, Mr. Smith's account was debited, and the payment was started on its long trip west. Because of the long time delays in collecting payment, many banks were reluctant to accept checks drawn on distant banks, accepted checks did not permit the depositor to use the funds until after collection, or charged the depositor a discount from the par value of the check. The last practice was referred to as **nonpar banking** and particularly restricted using checks in distant places. Stores did not know for what value to accept checks on distant banks. Thus, buyers from outside the region were discouraged from purchasing larger-ticket items typically paid for by check, and trade was reduced.

The Federal Reserve System was enacted in 1913 to, among other things, reduce the cost of interarea check clearings. It effectively established a national clearinghouse. Banks, and more recently any depository institutions, could present their checks on other banks anywhere in the country to their district Fed bank or branch for collection. The receiving Fed bank would send the check to the Fed bank or branch of the paying bank, which, in turn, would send it to that bank. At the same time, the Fed committed itself to pay the bank according to a predetermined time schedule based on the distance between the two banks. The injection of the Federal Reserve in the clearing process is shown below:

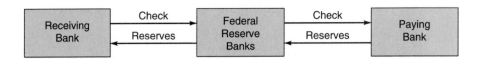

Through time, as transportation and communications have improved, the Fed's schedule has been shortened. At present, the maximum delay in the United States is two days, and many checks are cleared overnight. To the extent that the actual collection time is longer than the scheduled time, part of the float is transferred from the depository institutions to the Federal Reserve. Most intercity checks are cleared through the Federal Reserve at 48 Regional Check Processing Centers (RCPs). The Depository Institutions Deregulation and Monetary Control Act of 1980 required the Federal Reserve to make its check-clearing facilities available to all depository institutions but to charge for the service. As a result, a number of large commercial banks and other firms have begun to offer competitive intercity check-clearing services, and the volume of clearings through the Fed has declined.

The intercity collection process through the Federal Reserve is traced through T accounts in Table 14–4 and schematically in Figure 14–1. Assume that, after crediting the account of the Pacificville Store and debiting CIPC, the Pacificville Bank sends the check on the Atlanticville Bank to, say, the Federal Reserve Bank of San Francisco (FRBSF). This is shown as entry (a) in Table 14–4. The FRBSF promises to pay the Pacificville Bank in two days. This promise is recorded on the FRBSF's books as a liability, entitled *deferred availability cash item,* or **DACI.** (DACI is similar to accounts payable on the books of other firms.) Similar to the commercial bank, the FRBSF debits CIPC in an equal amount, entry (b). The FRBSF then sends the check by air to the Federal Reserve Bank of New York (FRBNY) for presentation to the Atlanticville Bank. (For the sake of simplicity, we will consolidate the two Reserve Banks' accounts into one.) Upon receipt, the FRBNY sends the check to the Atlanticville Bank.

Two days later, the FRBSF pays the Pacificville Bank by crediting its reserve balance and debiting DACI, entry (c). The Pacificville Bank records payment and credits CIPC. If payment is made by the Fed to the Pacificville Bank before payment is received from the Atlanticville Bank, the CIPC entry remains on the Fed's books. The net differences between CIPC (funds to be

FIGURE

14–1

TYPICAL DEPOSIT TRANSFERS

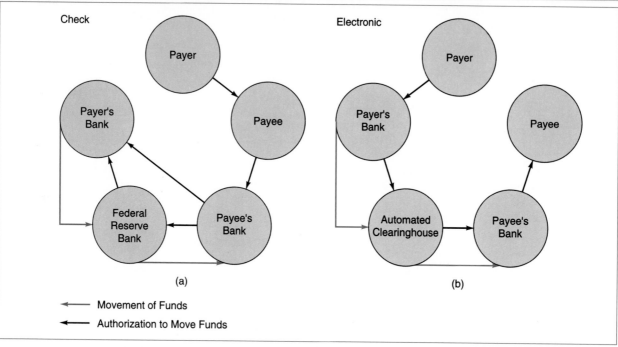

SOURCE: George W. Mitchell and Raymond Hodgdon, "Federal Reserve and the Payments System," *Federal Reserve Bulletin*, February 1981, p. 112.

collected) and DACI (funds owed) on the Fed's books is referred to as **Fed float.** (For example, if a bank sends the Fed a $1,000 check, and it takes the Fed three days to collect payment from the bank on which it is written but the Fed pays the first bank after only two days, Fed float is zero for the first two days and increases to $1,000 for the third day.) Unlike bank float, Fed float provides reserves to support deposits at both the receiving and paying banks. When the Atlanticville Bank pays the FRBNY, its reserve account is debited and CIPC is credited, entry (d). (If Mr. Smith does not have enough funds in his account to cover the amount of the check, or if the check is forged, the Atlanticville Bank can refuse payment and return the check.) In 1987, the average check took one and a half days to complete its trip from the receiving to the paying bank on which it was drawn.[3]

As restrictions in branching are eased and the number of banks decreases, progressively more checks will be deposited at branches of the same banks on which they are written. More clearing will occur within each bank, and interbank clearing will decrease in importance.

[3] Your bank may take longer than this in permitting you to withdraw funds after you have deposited checks. This reflects the bank's concern that the writer of the check may not have sufficient funds in his or her account at the paying bank so that the check will "bounce" after you have received the proceeds but your bank will not receive payment. Bounced checks are termed **not sufficient funds** or **NSF** checks. On average, it takes five days for a bounced check to be returned by the paying bank to the receiving bank. However, some banks froze deposited funds received by check for substantially longer than this. Congress enacted legislation in 1987 that shortens these delays.

TABLE 14–4	CHECK CLEARING THOUGH FEDEAL RESERVE

Pacificville Bank			Federal Reserve Bank		
(a) CIPC	+	+ Pacificville Store			
(b)			CIPC	+	+ DACI
					− DACI
(c) CIPC	−				+ Deposit Pacificville Bank
Reserve deposit at Fed	+				
(d)			CIPC	−	− Deposit Atlanticville Bank

Atlanticville Bank		
(a)		
(b)		
(c)		
(d) Reserve deposit at Fed	−	− Mr. Smith

Check Volume. Checks are used to pay for 10 percent of the number of non-interbank transactions but nearly 95 percent of the dollar volume. In 1992, some 58 billion checks, or about 160 million a day, were written. Of these, about one-third were cleared through the Fed. After increasing rapidly in the post–World War II period, the use of checks has begun to slow in recent years. The cost of check clearing and servicing is not small. The average cost to the receiving and payer banks is estimated to be more than 50 cents per check. This includes the explicit charge imposed by the Fed, or its competitors, since 1981 for clearing. (The clearing fee schedule charged by the Federal Reserve Bank of Chicago is shown in Table 14–5.) As a result, there is considerable impetus to reduce the costs of funds transfers. In the 1960s, banks began to imprint the user's bank and account identities and the amount of the check on the bottom of the check in magnetic ink. This process is called **magnetic-ink character recognition,** or **MICR.** MICR greatly accelerated the speed at which the checks could be sorted through computers.

A number of European and Asian countries, in which the use of personal checking is not as widespread as in the United States and that have far fewer commercial banks, have developed *giro* payments systems. Although they differ in details, these systems frequently combine the billing and check-writing functions, so that the payer receives and verifies a statement from the seller in the form of a transfer authorization to the sell-

TABLE

14–5

SELECTED PRICES FOR CHECK PROCESSING AT THE FEDERAL RESERVE BANK OF CHICAGO, 1993

265

THE PAYMENTS
SYSTEM

Checks Sorted by Area of Paying Bank	Deposit Deadline	Cents per Check	
		Collection	Return
Chicago, Detroit, Indianapolis, Des Moines, or Milwaukee[a]			
Regular	6:30 A.M.	2.2	30.0
Premium	7:30 A.M.	2.7	30.5
Other areas in Chicago district[a]			
Regular	12:01 A.M.	3.5	35.5
Premium	1:00 A.M.	4.2	39.0
Other Federal Reserve districts[b]			
	[c]	6.1	59.9

SOURCE: Federal Reserve Bank of Chicago.
[a]Plus $1.50 per bundle.
[b]Plus $2.00 per bundle.
[c]Various times.

er's bank. After verification, the payer sends the statement to his or her bank rather than to the seller. If more than one bank is involved, the funds are transferred by wire. The paper order is kept by the receiving bank and is not transferred or returned to the originator. (Checks legally have to be presented physically to the paying bank in order to be honored, although some banks are now experiencing with truncating the flow at the receiving bank and sending forward only summary records. The paying bank would periodically send depositors summary computer printouts, much like monthly bank credit-card statements.) In some countries, all giro entries are handled centrally by a national bank or the post office. Giro systems are particularly efficient for preauthorized transfers of repetitive payments such as utility, rent, interest, and the like. Giro systems reduce but do not eliminate the need for paper transfers.

Credit Cards

In the United States, the use of credit cards has expanded rapidly since the mid-1960s. These cards are issued by commercial banks, thrift institutions, retail stores, gasoline companies, and other firms. Most banking institutions issue cards of one or both of the two major international bank-oriented card systems—MasterCard and Visa. A few banks issue their own cards. The three major nonbank cards, referred to as *travel and entertainment* (T&E) *cards*, are American Express, Diners Club, and Carte Blanche. Large retail stores issue credit cards good only at the particular store or chain. In 1985, Sears Roebuck issued a general-use bank credit card named Discover, which it sold in 1993. In 1990, AT&T introduced a MasterCard through a small bank in Georgia.

Credit cards may be divided between those that may be used solely or primarily to finance purchases from the issuing vendor—two-party store-specific cards—and those that may be used at a large number of vendors—

three-party general-purpose or *universal* cards. All three-party credit cards work basically alike. The card issuer (the bank, in the case of bank cards) makes arrangements with merchants to accept the card in payment of purchases. Upon presentation of the receipts, the issuer will provide immediate payment to the merchant for these purchases. The issuer charges a fee in the form of a discount from the amount of the purchase, determined by negotiation with the merchant. Depending on volume, the discount is generally between 2 and 6 percent. When the card issuer pays the merchant, it is extending credit to its credit-card users. Generally, interest is not charged the purchaser who pays in full within a specified number of days after the monthly billing. The customer who does not do so is charged interest, generally at an annual rate of between 10 and 24 percent on the unpaid balance. In 1992, credit extended on bank cards totaled $136 billion. This accounted for almost one-third of all consumer credit extended by banks, but only 5 percent of total bank credit extended.

Credit cards are widely held. It is estimated that some 80 percent of all households in the United States hold at least one credit card and almost all of these hold a bank credit card. In 1992, some 80 million households held nearly 300 million bank credit cards. In 1990, credit cards financed some $450 billion of purchases, or 13 percent of all consumer expenditures. Because the card user pays the issuer with only one check per month for all transactions, the number of checks written is reduced, so also are the transactions balances of credit-card users. But neither the paperwork nor the cost is reduced. Credit-card slips replace checks and, like checks, must be cleared to the appropriate bank for payment. Moreover, because these slips are not of uniform size, generally are made of flimsy and difficult-to-sort paper, and are not imprinted in magnetic ink, their clearing costs are higher than those for checks.

In more recent years, some credit-card issuers have also introduced debit cards. These are used like credit cards, but customers make immediate payment from their bank balances rather than receiving credit. In this way, debit cards work much like checks or giro systems. Because payment is made immediately, debit cards have not yet achieved the popularity of credit cards. The development of credit and debit cards has resulted less in a checkless economy than in a less-check economy! (Credit cards as a financial "innovation" are discussed in Chapter 23.)

Electronic Funds Transfer Systems

Rather than attempting to reduce costs by perfecting the paper transfer system, the electronic funds transfer system (EFTS) attempts to reduce payment costs by replacing the paper currency and check system with an electronic system. EFTSs are of several types that are currently in a variety of states of implementation and experimentation. EFTSs reflect the dramatic advances in computer and transmission technology in recent years that permit rapid, low-cost transfers of information and funds.

Wire Transfers

The earliest form of electronic transfer of funds was by telegraphic wire, first among Federal Reserve Banks and, later, larger commercial banks. The

Fedwire was completed in 1918 and permitted rapid transfers of reserve balances. It is owned and operated by the Federal Reserve System. It is used by some 7,500 depository institutions. Fed-funds transactions involving more than one Federal Reserve Bank are conducted by this wire. Treasury and federal agency securities may also be transferred by this wire. In 1990, Fedwire was used daily for some 250,000 transactions totaling nearly $800 billion. In addition, some 45,000 Treasury securities, with an average value of $400 billion, were transferred among banks daily on Fedwire. Another electronic wire system was established by the New York Clearing House Association, termed **CHIPS (Clearing House Interbank Payments Systems),** to serve major New York City banks. It largely handles international transfers. CHIPS handles about 90 percent of all dollar payments moving between countries in the world. In 1990, the number of transfers using CHIPS averaged 115,000 daily and totaled nearly $900 billion. Thus, although used somewhat less than Fedwire, CHIPS transactions were of larger average size. It is now possible for customers of any bank to transfer funds to another bank for same-day delivery. As can be seen from Table 14–1, by far the largest dollar volume of funds are transferred by wire. However, as can be seen from the large average size of these transactions, this process is used almost entirely to transfer funds among banks and not to finance purchases. The number and dollar amount of large payment transfers have increased very rapidly in recent years. As can be seen from Table 14–1, by 1987, wire transfers accounted for 82 percent of the dollar volume of all transactions, although they accounted for less than one-tenth of 1 percent of the number.

Automated Clearinghouse

Automated clearinghouse (ACHs) permit payments to be made by magnetic computer tape rather than by paper. Payments to other accounts are imprinted by the payer—say, a large employer—on tape or disk showing the amount of the transfer, the account and bank from which the transfer is to be made, and the date of the transfer. The tape is then sent, either directly or through the payer's bank, to the ACH, where the information is transferred to the tapes of the appropriate banks that make and receive the payments. These tapes are, in turn, returned to the banks, where the information is transferred to the individual accounts. Payment is made on the scheduled date. This path is traced in Figure 14–1b.

ACHs have a number of advantages over paper transfers. The imprints may be put on the tapes at the payer's convenience anytime before the payment date, the tapes may be cleared at the convenience of the ACH, and the information may be transferred to the individual receivers' accounts at the convenience of the receiving bank, again at any time before payment. The transfers can be completed quickly and cheaply. They are more secure against theft, although not necessarily against fraud. Computer safeguards are a major problem with all types of EFTSs. Unscrupulous computer experts are the modern-day Jesse Jameses, and a number of banks already have suffered losses at the hands of some of them.

The initial costs of establishing an ACH are very high. Because of the high degree of automation, variable costs are small. As a result, average costs per transaction decline sharply as the volume of transactions increases. In 1982, the average cost of each item processed in the smallest ACHs was 6.4 cents, compared with only 4.1 cents in the largest. Overall, the average cost per item was 4.8 cents. In contrast, the Fed's cost of clearing paper checks averaged only 1.4 cents per check. By 1993, as volume and technology both improved, the average cost declined sharply to near 1.7 cents by item. In contrast, the cost of paper checks increased slightly to 1.5 cents. Moreover, the cost differences are far less when they are compared with the average dollar amount of the transaction, which is considerably greater for the items cleared through ACHs. In addition, the processing costs at the paying and receiving banks are substantially smaller.

ACH transfers are particularly economical for large numbers of simultaneous or "batch" transactions, such as payroll payments, dividend or interest payments, and Social Security payments. The federal government is the largest user of ACHs. About 85 percent of all Social Security payments are made through ACHs as automatic transfers to the recipient's account at a commercial bank or thrift institution. One-third of all households are estimated to receive at least some direct deposits. Although growing very rapidly, the overall usage of ACHs is still small, however. The number of ACH transfers in 1992 was equivalent to only 4 percent of the total number of checks written in the year and only 12 percent of the dollar volume. In 1991, the number of payments made by the U.S. Government through ACHs for the first time exceeded those made by check.

The first ACH was established in California by 100 participating banks in 1968. There are currently four operators of ACHs. The Federal Reserve operates 13, one at each district reserve bank and another one in Los Angeles. The other three are operated privately by clearinghouse associations in New York and Arizona and by Visa in San Francisco. A national ACH system linking the individual regional systems was completed in 1978. Currently, nearly all banks and SLAs participate in the ACH system.

Automated Teller Machines

Automated teller machines (ATMs), or remote service units, are self-contained units located either on or off the premises of the bank or thrift institution that owns them. ATMs can provide a variety of services, depending on the preferences of the owning institution and the restrictions imposed by state laws.

ATMs are mechanically able to accept deposits, make deposit withdrawals, transfer funds between accounts, collect bills, and extend small loans. When using an ATM, customers identify themselves by their personal identification number (PIN) and a plastic identification card issued by the financial institution. After positive identification, the customer tells the unit what service to perform. The unit is connected to a computer that contains the customer's records. If the service requested by the customer can be performed within the restrictions of the customer's account and the machine's authorization, the unit will perform the service. Many depository institutions have banded together to create shared regional or national networks of ATMs that can be used by customers of any of the participating institutions. Many of these networks cross state lines. However, commercial bank customers cannot make deposits to out-of-state banks, although SLA customers may.

The major advantage of ATMs is convenience. Unlike offices with people, ATMs operate 24 hours a day, seven days a week. ATMs are a particularly convenient way for households or small business firms to conduct routine individual transactions otherwise completed in the office of the financial institutions.

By 1993, about 95,000 ATMs had been installed by more than 5,000 depository institutions and had been used by almost half of all households. To date, ATMs have not been used as much as they were expected to be and have not been profitable for many institutions, because the units are costly to purchase and install. About 75 percent of the transactions are cash withdrawals. Because of high installation costs, the key to profitability is high transactions volume. Almost all ATMs are shared with at least one other institution in regional or nationwide sharing systems.

Point-of-Sale Transfers

The heart of EFTs for individual transactions is the **point-of-sale transfer system (POS).** POS systems are on-line computer networks linking customers and merchants with financial institutions that permit instant transfers of funds without paper. POS requires substantial underlying communications networks among the principals. The greater the number of participants, the more complex the network; the smaller the number of participants, the less useful the system. Participating institutions may be either commercial banks or thrift institutions.

Computer transfer terminals may be connected to ATMs, home computers, telephones, cash registers, or other convenient equipment. POS systems offer flexibility to perform a large variety of transactions. They may be used to pay for purchases, make deposits and withdrawals, transfer funds among participating financial institutions, verify checks and credit cards, obtain loans, make loan repayments, and so on. As visualized most frequently, POS is used by merchants to receive payment for goods sold. Transfer terminals are attached to one or more cash registers at checkout counters. The terminals are connected either to individual financial institutions in the area or to a central clearing system for all participating institutions. (The sequence of events for a POS system including more than one bank is traced in Figure 14–2.)

Participating customers have plastic identification debit cards with the customer's personal identification number and the institution at which the account is maintained imprinted on them. Customers without accounts or with accounts at nonparticipating institutions would not be able to pay by this method. At the checkout counter, the plastic card is inserted into the terminal. Upon completion of the sale, the amount of the payment is automatically transferred from the customer's demand or time account to the store's account. The transfer can be programmed to be immediate or after a delay of one or two days to "simulate" bank float. This would make the payment similar to payment by check. The customer may also have overdraft or other credit arrangements with the participating financial institution. Both the customer and the merchant receive written verification of the transactions from the institutions.

POS systems have increased sharply in recent years. In 1993, there were more than 150,000 terminals in operation—a threefold increase over

FIGURE

14–2   ELECTRONIC POINT-OF-SALE SYSTEM

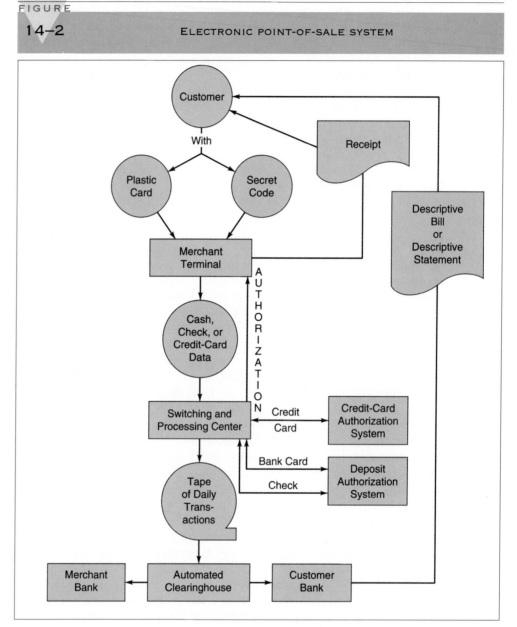

SOURCE: Mary G. Grandstaff and Charles J. Smaistrla, "A Primer on Electronic Funds Transfer," *Business Review,* Federal Reserve Bank of Dallas, September 1976, p. 12.

only three years earlier in 1990. Nearly one-half of the terminals were in supermarkets, one-third at gas stations, and the remainder scattered among different types of retailers. (Supermarkets are also the largest cashers of checks.) Accompanying the sharp increase in POS terminals has been a sharp increase in the number of debit cards.

In the most comprehensive scenarios, POS systems include terminals not only at retail establishments but also in residential dwellings—in-house banking. If you were a participant, you would be able to transfer funds at any time to the account of any other participant and make any type of purchase by keying the information on a terminal connected to your touch-tone telephone, television set, or home computer. In addition, you would be able to request all your bank records to be displayed in the form of **videotex** on your screen through a cable connection, along with information on prices at various shops, interest rates on different types of investment, and even investment advice. You could then execute any financial transactions you wished. Thus, nearly all banking services would be delivered into your home, almost obviating the need for you to ever step inside a bank building. You would require a personal identification number, known only to yourself and your financial institution; the identification numbers of your institution and of the account and institution to which the funds are to be transferred; the amount to be transferred; and the date of the transfer. You would receive written verification of the transfer either within a few days or in regular periodic statements.

As discussed earlier, EFTSs have been developed to reduce the costs of our increasingly more complex payments system that threatens to overload the paper transfer system. But, as checks were at the beginnings of the paper system, EFTS is being accepted only slowly. Many household customers distrust computers and are reluctant to engage in impersonal, automatic transactions without receiving simultaneous physical documentation. They prefer to deal with live tellers and loan officers. In addition, most households do not appear to be greatly dissatisfied with paper transfers and, unless the costs of such transfers increase sharply, have little motivation to change. EFTSs have been more widely accepted by business firms and government units for batch transactions. However, as the number of participating institutions and merchants is increased, and customers become more familiar with the systems, POS systems should become even more popular.

Although EFTSs protect against physical theft, computer security is a serious problem. Foolproof safeguards have not been developed. Computer fraud, through access to the computer program, has increased sharply as the use of computerized systems has increased. Such fraud is generally not uncovered until long after it has occurred.

SUMMARY

The *payments system* describes the process by which funds are transferred from buyer to seller. The system has gone through much change over time. The earliest payment systems were metallic. As trade increased and notes and bank deposits became accepted as money, a paper transfer system was developed. This system involved collecting funds in the form of coins, currency, or reserves for the money received by the seller from the institution for which the buyer's money was a liability. This was not easy, and until the establishment of the Federal Reserve System in 1914, most payment systems did not operate efficiently much beyond the immediate geographic area where the payment occurred. There was no national payments system, and trade was hampered.

The Fed introduced a national clearing system for checks that made collection from any part of the country operate smoothly. But the progressive increase in the volume of transactions has decreased the relative efficiency of tangible paper transfers, despite the increased use of credit cards.

Electronic funds transfer systems (EFTSs) have been developed in which funds are recorded on and transferred by computers. Funds are in the form of intangible electronic imprints. Automated clearinghouses (ACHs) process computer tapes rather than checks. Automated teller machines (ATMs) conduct many types of retail banking services around the clock without personal contact. Point-of-sale (POS) systems automatically initiate funds transfers arising from purchases and, combined with home computers, will in time permit full in-house banking. Home computers also promise to bring a wide array of banking and payments services, into the home. EFTS is growing rapidly and may reasonably be expected to become the dominant payments system of the future, particularly for larger and repetitive types of financial transfers.

QUESTIONS

1. Why is an efficient national payments system important? Why was the national payments system not very efficient until after the establishment of the Federal Reserve System?

2. What is a *clearinghouse*? Why are clearinghouses less important in countries that have nationwide branch banking? What might this tell you about the future of clearinghouses in the United States? Why?

3. Suppose your bank account has insufficient funds but you expect a sufficiently large deposit momentarily. Why might you be more likely to write a check on this account when you are traveling than when you are at home? As technology permits checks to be cleared faster, what does it do to students' abilities to "play-the-float"? How can banks play the float game with you?

4. Differentiate between *bank float* and *Fed float*. Why is it that Fed float increases the aggregate money supply in the country, but that bank float does not? Why do banks try to minimize the amount of float on their balance sheet?

5. In what ways have credit cards improved the efficiency of the payments system? In what ways may credit cards have reduced that efficiency? Differentiate between credit and debit cards. Do you think debit cards will be as successful as credit cards?

6. How does the electronic funds payments system differ from the paper-funds payments system? Why is EFTS expanding rapidly? In the next few years, in which areas do you expect to see EFTS develop fastest, and in which areas slowest?

7. Describe four different types of electronic funds transfer facilities. Which have you used? What are your reaction to them and your prediction about their success?

8. Speculate on how continued development of EFTS will change banking from how we know it today. Include a discussion on the importance and function of branch banks. When do you think the country will be ready for in-house banking? What are some of the barriers that will have to be overcome?

REFERENCES

American Bankers Association, *Statistical Information on the Financial Services Industry*, 5th ed. Washington, D.C., 1989.

Avery, Robert B., et al., "The Use of Cash and Transaction Accounts by American Families," *Federal Reserve Bulletin*, February 1986, pp. 87–108.

Baer, Herbert, et al., "Payments System

Issues," in George G. Kaufman, ed., *Research in Financial Services*, vol. 3. Greenwich, Conn.: JAI Press, 1991.

Bank for International Settlements, *Payments Systems in the Group of Ten Countries*, Basle, Switzerland, December 1993.

Belton, Terence M., et al., "Daylight Overdrafts and Payments System Risk," *Federal Reserve Bulletin*, November 1987, pp. 839–52.

Board of Governors of the Federal Reserve System, *Credit Cards in the U.S. Economy: Their Impact on Costs, Prices, and Retail Sales*. Washington, D.C., July 17, 1983.

Calem, Paul S., "The Strange Behavior of the Credit Card Market," *Business Review*, Federal Reserve Bank of Philadelphia, January/February 1992, pp. 3–14.

Federal Reserve Bank of Atlanta, "The ACH in a New Light," *Economic Review*, March 1986.

Federal Reserve Bank of Atlanta, "The Automated Clearinghouse Alternative: How Do We Get There from Here," *Economic Review*, April 1986.

Felgran, Steven D., "From ATM to POS Networks: Branching, Access, and Pricing," *New England Economic Review*, Federal Reserve Bank of Boston, May/June 1985, pp. 44–61.

Felgran, Steven D., and R. Edward Ferguson, "The Evolution of Retail EFT Networks," *New England Economic Review*, Federal Reserve Bank of Boston, July/August 1986, pp. 42–56.

Gorton, Gary, "Private Clearinghouses and the Origins of Central Banking," *Business Review*, Federal Reserve Bank of Philadelphia, January/February 1984, pp. 3–12.

Grandstaff, Mary G., and Charles J. Smaistrla, "A Primer on Electronic Funds Transfer," *Business Review*, Federal Reserve Bank of Dallas, September 1976, pp. 7–14.

Horvitz, Paul M., "Payments System Developments and Public Policy," in George J. Benston, ed., *Financial Services*. Englewood Cliffs, N.J.: Prentice Hall, 1983.

Humphrey, David B., *The U.S. Payments System: Costs, Pricing, Competition and Risk*. New York: Salomon Brothers Center for the Study of Financial Institutions, New York University, 1984.

International Banking and Payment Services, *Journal of Bank Research*, 1986 (special issue).

Junker, George, et al., "A Primer on the Settlement of Payments in the United States," *Federal Reserve Bulletin*, November 1991, pp. 847–58.

Kaufman, George G., *Research in Financial Services* vol. 3, Greenwich, Conn.: JAI Press, 1991.

Knudson, Scott E., Jack K. Walton II, and Florence M. Young, "Business-to-Business Payments and the Role of Financial Electronic Data Interchanges," *Federal Reserve Bulletin*, April 1994, pp. 269–78.

Long, Donald G., "The Business Case for Electronic Banking," *Journal of Retail Banking*, June 1982, pp. 14–22.

McAndrews, James J., "The Evolution of Shared ATM Networks," *Business Review*, Federal Reserve Bank of Philadelphia, May/June 1991, pp. 3–16.

McAndrews, James J., "Where Has All the Paper Gone? Book-Entry Delivery-Against-Payment System," *Business Review*, Federal Reserve Bank of Philadelphia, November/December 1992, pp. 19–30.

McAndrews, James, "The Automated Clearinghouse System: Moving Toward Electronic Payment," *Business Review*, Federal Reserve Bank of Philadelphia, July/August 1994, pp. 15–23.

Mandell, Lewis, *The Credit Card Industry: A History*. Boston: Twayne Publishers, 1990.

Mengle, David, "Behind the Money Market: Clearing and Settling Money Market Instruments," *Economic Review*, Federal Reserve Bank of Richmond, September/October 1992, p. 3–11.

Mitchell, George W., and Raymond Hodgdon, "Federal Reserve and the Payments System," *Federal Reserve*

Bulletin, February 1981, pp. 109–16.

Parkinson, Patrick, et al., "Clearance and Settlement in U.S. Securities Markets," *Staff Study (163)*, Board of Governors of the Federal Reserve System, March 1992.

Summers, Bruce J., "Clearing and Payments Systems: The Role of the Central Bank," *Federal Reserve Bulletin*, February 1991, pp. 81–91.

VanHoose, David, and Gordon H. Sellon, Jr., "Daylight Overdrafts, Payments System Risk, and Public Policy," *Economic Review*, Federal Reserve Bank of Kansas City, September/October 1989, pp. 9–29.

Whiteside, Thomas, *Computer Capers: Tales of Electronic Thievery*. New York: Crowell, 1978.

Depository Institutions and the Supply of Money

CHAPTER

15

Because money significantly affects our daily lives, it is important to understand what determines its amount and how changes occur in its amount outstanding. We noted in Chapter 2 that the definition of money is ambiguous. It is a matter of personal preference. Different analysts include different types of financial assets in their definitions. Moreover, the particular definition favored by an analyst may change through time as changes occur in the needs of the economy, in financial instruments and financial institutions, and in the regulations governing the types of financial instruments in which financial institutions may trade and the interest rates they may pay. For the sake of expediency, we shall define money narrowly to include only currency and transaction deposits (demand deposits, NOW accounts, and share drafts) at commercial banks and other depository institutions (M1), the principal medium of exchange. At the end of 1992, the amount of money outstanding in the United States was $1,046 billion. Of this, $295 billion, or about 28 percent, was in the form of coin and currency (from now on referred to only as *currency* because coin accounts for only 10 percent of the total) and $751 billion, or more than 70 percent, in the form of transaction deposits at depository institutions. Thus, similar to the exploration of the payments mechanism, an exploration of how money changes requires a study of how depository institutions operate. This chapter discusses the determinants of currency first and then those of transaction deposits.

Currency

In contrast to the situation in the early United States, or to the present situation in less developed countries, currency is a relatively small part of the contemporary U.S. money supply. Moreover, even the stock of currency overstates its importance for economic control. Although a large proportion of transactions are financed by currency, it is estimated that only 1 percent of the dollar amount of all transactions are so financed and even less than 3 percent of all nonelectronic payments.

Indeed, currency is so unimportant in the United States today for purposes of monetary control that the Federal Reserve, which issues almost all the currency in circulation, will provide as much currency as people wish to hold. (In technical terms, the supply function of currency is perfectly elastic at the face value of the currency.) The Fed cares what the overall money supply is, but not how much is held in currency and how much is held in transaction deposits. The Fed can follow such a policy because increases in currency are generally paid for by reductions in transaction deposits and, contrary to what you might think, people will not hold as currency all that they can get their hands on. After all, there are better ways to hold one's

275

money, such as in checkable deposits. As we well know, currency is clumsy to use, unsafe to store, and bears no interest.

Most people will carry only the minimum amount of currency necessary to pay for their small daily transactions. Similarly, business firms will hold in their cash registers only the minimum amount of currency necessary to make change and accommodate their customers. Excess currency will be taken to the banks and exchanged for deposits. Of course, there are always a few people who prefer to carry large bankrolls. Nevertheless, the Federal Reserve finds it easier to control the money supply by controlling deposits and letting currency go. (In many less developed countries where currency is the major form of money, the central bank controls the money supply by controlling the amount of currency.)

But having recognized this, we might ask why it is that there is still so much currency in circulation. A quick calculation indicates that the $295 billion outstanding at year-end 1992 was equivalent to about $1,150 per person, or $4,600 per family of four. Do you know anyone who carries or possesses this much currency? Certainly, not very many faculty members do. Moreover, since 1960, currency generally has been increasing faster than transaction deposits.

The increase in currency is particularly surprising in the light of all the changes in recent years that should have made currency less attractive. Interest-bearing checking accounts have increased in popularity. Bank and other credit cards have reduced the need to carry currency for day-to-day purchases as well as on business and vacation trips. Traveler's checks and money orders have been advertised widely as safer than currency and not much costlier. Nevertheless, currency appears to be in increasing demand. We will take a few pages to see whether we can account for this phenomenon.

A Digression: The Case of the "Excess" Currency

A large number of wonderful, imaginative, and colorful theories have been woven to explain the large and growing amounts of currency outstanding. These include increased criminal activity (organized or unorganized), increased smuggling, increased drug dealing, increased tax evasion and avoidance, increased use of vending machines, increased use of U.S. currency abroad, increased importance of a "subterranean" or "underground" economy of artisans and sidewalk vendors, increased illegal payments by U.S. business firms to foreign nationals in exchange for goodwill, and increased activity by U.S. intelligence agencies in protecting "friendly" and changing "unfriendly" governments. Unfortunately, by themselves each of these theories appears to be able to explain only a small part of the currency increase. However, taken together, they probably come close to explaining most of it.

Until the 1980s, average federal income tax rates had not changed much. However, the sharp acceleration in the rate of inflation in the 1970s "promoted" many taxpayers into much higher marginal brackets in the very progressive federal income tax structure through 1986 and again since 1993. This could have increased the incentive of these people to try to get a greater proportion of their incomes in currency in order to evade income taxes. In addition, increases in Social Security taxes may have encouraged an increasing number of employees and employers to avoid these taxes on both parties by paying salaries in currency and not maintaining records. Recent studies estimate that the underground economy in the United States may be equivalent to somewhere between 10 and 25 percent of GNP and growing. Currency undoubtedly is a more important medium of exchange in this economy than in the visible, aboveboard economy.

Crime appears to have increased rapidly. However for currency to increase significantly as a result of the increase in crime, it must remain in the form of currency and not be converted into deposits. Although this is likely to have occurred for unorganized crime—in particular, smaller-scale dope trafficking—it is less likely to have occurred for organized crime. After all, even the largest crime organization may find it difficult to purchase business firms, hotels, gambling casinos, or even Rolls-Royces with currency.

At some point, the currency is converted into transaction deposits. The Watergate, Irangate, and Bank of Credit and Commerce (BCCI) adventures have indicated that considerable progress has been made in "laundering" deposits so that the original sources cannot be identified. Laundering is achieved by transferring the deposits among a large number of domestic and foreign banks under an equally large number of account names.

Until recently, it was unlikely that a substantial proportion of the increase in U.S. currency is held overseas. In most years, the value of the U.S. dollar frequently had been falling with respect to most of the countries generally mentioned as increased users of the dollar. Thus, in contrast to the early post–World War II period, when the dollar was the strong currency in the world, it would not have been profitable for citizens of most foreign countries to traffic in U.S. currency relative to that of other countries or of their own. However, the collapse of the USSR in the early 1990s and the introduction of new currencies of uncertain value in the resulting newly independent and other former communist countries may have temporarily increased the demand for U.S. dollars abroad as a day-to-day medium of exchange. However, to the extent that U.S. currency is transferred overseas for safekeeping, it is likely to be put into a foreign (very likely Swiss) bank deposit account. (After all, currency could be held in U.S. vaults.) The bank receiving the currency would have little use for it and would ship it back to the United States in exchange for a deposit at a U.S. bank.

Vending machines also have not absorbed a significant amount of the increased currency. Most vending machines use coins, and coins represent only 10 percent of the sum of coin and currency. This is up only slightly in recent years.

Although the number of artisans selling wares at fairs and on streets has increased rapidly in recent years, this also is unlikely to account for much of the increase in currency. A significant percentage of their sales is likely to be drawn from other small merchants, rather than to represent net additions. And these merchants, as well as many street vendors, probably deposit their receipts in a bank daily. In addition, casual observation suggests that many accept personal checks and credit cards.

But currency hoards do exist. Periodically, there are reports of discoveries of large currency caches. One of the largest such finds was uncovered in 1971 when Paul Powell, who was the long-time secretary of state of

Illinois, died. Powell turned out to have been a most prodigious "saver" in his lifetime! About $1 million in currency of various denominations was found in shoe boxes scattered throughout his hotel room, which had served as his principal residence in the state capital. As far as was known, Mr. Powell had no reported major source of income in addition to his state salary. Both in his previous political positions and as secretary of state, Powell had influence over matters such as the assignment of horse-racing dates at tracks and the weight and other specifications for trucks using the state's highways. Some went so far as to question whether the source of the savings may not have been connected with some of these activities. It would appear that the hotel maids either never cleaned Powell's room or helped themselves to generous tips. If they had, then the amount of Powell's "savings" would very likely have exceeded the cache discovered.

Reports frequently circulate of well-known entertainers, Texas oil producers, Arab potentates, and suspected drug dealers who are seen flashing large rolls of currency in public. But it takes a very large number of very large bank rolls to account for an average of more than $1,000 in currency for every man, woman, and child in the United States.

A survey by the Federal Reserve System found that in 1986 the average individual held only about $111 in currency. This accounted for only 15 percent of the total currency per capita then outstanding. Even in including estimated illegal transactions, the amount of currency that can be accounted for would increase to less than 20 percent of the total amount actually outstanding. Another Federal Reserve study concluded that, while high, aggregate currency holdings actually declined somewhat as a proportion of either GDP or personal consumption expenditures since 1960 and per capita holdings had remained constant in real terms. Moreover, currency holdings in the U. S. are not high relative to those in other industrial countries either per capita or as a percent of GDP. Fortunately, a solution to the mystery of the excess currency is not really necessary for an understanding of how the money supply in the United States is determined or changes. So we will leave this mystery unsolved and focus on the determinants of the amount of transaction deposits.

Transaction Deposits

The Federal Reserve controls the money supply by controlling the amount of transaction deposits. If it wishes to increase the amount of money, it increases deposits; if it wishes to decrease the amount of money, it decreases deposits. Transaction deposits are secondary claims issued by depository institutions, primarily commercial banks. Thus, the Federal Reserve can control the money supply by affecting the behavior of these institutions. In this section, we will examine how the Fed does this; why and when the Fed does so is examined in later chapters.

An Individual Bank

The dollar amount of deposits a bank has is related to the dollar amount of reserves it has. (For the sake of simplicity, we will refer to all depository institutions generally as *banks*.) Changes in the amount of deposits are related to changes in the amount of reserves and to changes in the ratio of reserves to deposits. In Chapter 10 we observed that even before there were any central banks or special bank regulations, banks voluntarily held cash reserves against their deposits in order to accommodate deposit withdrawals and to avoid insolvency. Let us assume that, on the basis of experience, the management of a particular bank feels that it needs to hold cash reserves equal to 10 percent of its checkable-deposit liabilities, the only liabilities it has. If its deposits were $1,000,000, it would hold cash reserves of $100,000 and earning assets of $900,000. The relationship between reserves and transaction deposits for bank A may be written as follows:

$$TR_A = r_{DA}D_A$$

where: TR_A = total cash reserves held by bank A
r_{DA} = reserve ratio desired by bank A
D_A = transaction deposits at bank A

Note that TR and D are in dollar terms and r_{DA} is in percentage terms. We will assume that all banks hold their reserves either in currency or on deposit at the Federal Reserve. The bank's balance sheet reads:

Assets		Liabilities	
Reserves	$ 100,000	$1,000,000	Transaction deposits
Loans	900,000		
Total	1,000,000	1,000,000	Total

If for some reason, such as a sudden fear of increased deposit losses, the bank felt it needed to hold cash reserves equal to 20 percent of its transaction deposits, it would either (1) have to sell $100,000 of its loans to depositors at other banks to increase its cash reserves to $200,000 or (2) have to sell $500,000 of loans to its own depositors in order to reduce its deposits to $500,000. (The depositors would need to use $500,000 to pay for the loans.) In either case, after the transactions, reserves will be equal to 20 percent of the bank's deposits. But in the first case, as we have seen in Chapter 14, some other bank would experience an equal outflow of deposits and reserves as its depositors paid the selling bank for the loans, and it would need to acquire additional reserves in order to maintain its desired reserve-deposit ratio. Thus, the need to contract deposits is passed on to other banks until deposits at all banks are reduced sufficiently. Although the cases differ for individual banks, for the banking system as a whole, the end result will be a reduction in deposits of $500,000.

This process may also be analyzed in terms of the model of financial intermediation we developed in Chapter 3. Recall that any financial intermediary will sell secondary claims on itself as long as the interest and other costs it incurs are less than the interest it earns on the primary claims it purchases with the proceeds. Not all the proceeds from the sale of the secondary claim are invested in primary claims, however. Some part is held as nonearning cash reserves to redeem the claim. The larger the proportion of the proceeds derived from the secondary claim held as reserves, the less profitable the secondary claim. If now the bank believes it necessary to increase the amount of its cash reserves, it will sell loans of an equal amount. This will reduce its earnings. It may be unable to find sufficient primary claims that yield high enough income at the same level of risk to offset the earnings loss. Thus, it will reduce its intermediation by offering below-market rates on its deposits and letting them run off. The bank will also contract its deposits if interest rates on its deposits increase relative to its loan rate. In either case, it will decrease its operations up to the point where intermediation is profitable again.

Conversely, if the bank suddenly believed that it could meet all its expected deposit withdrawals with reserves equal to only 5 percent of transaction deposits rather than 10 percent, it could purchase $50,000 of loans and securities from other banks. This would reduce its own reserves from $100,000 to $50,000. Alternatively, if a bank were confident that sellers would maintain all their proceeds with it, it could purchase $1 million of loans and securities from the public and, in the process of paying for them, increase its deposits by $1 million to $2 million. In either case, reserves would be equal to 5 percent of the bank's deposits. But in the first case, some other bank would probably have more cash reserves than it wants to hold. The deposit-expanding effects of the lower reserve ratio are passed on to other banks. Reductions in deposit rates relative to loan rates will also encourage banks to expand their deposits by bidding reserves away from other banks.

The Banking System

The relationship between cash reserves and transaction deposits holds for all banks in the banking system as well as for individual banks. For all banks, we can write the relationship as

$$TR = r_D D$$

If all banks voluntarily held $1 million in cash reserves and wanted these reserves to be equal, on the average, to 10 percent of their deposits, deposits would total $10 million. However, if suddenly all banks wanted to hold cash reserves equal to 20 percent of deposits, the analysis would differ from that for the individual bank. Although any one individual bank can sell loans (securities) to other banks to increase its own reserves, all banks together cannot increase their aggregate reserves this way. The banks buying the loans (securities) lose reserves, offsetting the reserve gains of the banks selling loans. All banks together can increase their reserves only by selling loans (1) to the public for currency, which is unlikely, or (2) to the central bank. The second alternative will increase the banks' reserve balances at the Fed. No bank loses reserves. But this alternative is possible only at the discretion of the central bank and begins to suggest the potential role and power of the Fed in determining the amount of deposits.

Except for currency and, as we will see later, bank borrowing from the Fed, the dollar amount of reserves in the banking system as a whole is set by the Fed through the amount of deposits it is willing to sell to the banks. But neither currency nor bank borrowing from the Fed is completely under the control of the banks. Currency is determined primarily by the public, and the Fed can affect the amount it lends to banks at the discount window. Thus, although any individual bank can bid reserves away from other banks by paying a higher deposit rate, all banks cannot increase their dollar amount of reserves in this way. Only the Federal Reserve can effectively change the overall amount of reserves in the banking system. How the Fed does this is examined in Chapters 27 and 28.

Thus, in the absence of the sale of loans to the public for currency or to the central bank, which increases aggregate reserves, if the banking system as a whole wanted to increase its ratio of reserves to deposits, it could do so only by contracting its deposits. In our example of a desired increase in the ratio from 10 to 20 percent when reserves are $1 million, deposits must decline from $10 million to $5 million.

Likewise, if all banks wished to hold reserves equal to only 5 percent of their deposits rather than 10 percent, they could do so by buying loans from (making loans to) the public, paying for them either in currency or, more likely, with deposits. In the process of doing this, banks would expand their deposits. Alternatively, they could buy loans from the central bank. This would decrease their reserve balances at the Fed. Loans bought from other banks would only start a game of musical chairs. At some point, some bank will use the reserves to buy loans from the public and create new deposits. But even though reserves may move from bank to bank, they do not leave the banking system. Deposits will expand until the $1 million of reserves supports $20 million of deposits rather than $10 million.

Now let us assume that the central bank imposes legal minimum-reserve-requirement ratios against transaction deposits that all banks have to maintain. The dollar reserves the banks hold to satisfy this requirement are called **required reserves (RR).** We will also assume that banks hold exactly the amount of reserves required, so that total reserves are equal to required reserves. That is, $TR = RR$. The aggregate deposit–total-reserve ratio relationship can be written as

$$TR = rr_D D$$

where: $TR =$ dollar amount of aggregate total reserves
               $rr_D =$ legal reserve-requirement ratio on transaction deposits

It can easily be seen that if the central bank wished to increase transaction deposits for a given dollar amount of reserves, it would lower reserve requirements, and if it wished to reduce transaction deposits, it would raise reserve requirements. In our simple example with $1 million of required reserves, an increase in reserve requirements from 10 to 20 percent would reduce transaction deposits from $10 million to $5 million; a decrease from 10 to 5 percent would increase deposits from $10 million to $20 million.

It should be noted than when reserves stopped being held voluntarily and became required by law, they lost some of their liquidity. Required reserves are now available to meet deposit outflows only to the extent that they are equal to the percent reserve requirement times the dollar outflow. The remaining required reserves are needed by the bank to meet the requirements against its remaining deposits. The additional reserves needed to meet the deposit drain must come from any excess reserves the bank may hold or from the sale of assets. Thus, the primary role of bank reserves has changed from providing liquidity to providing monetary control by the Federal Reserve. However, to the extent that the Fed does not require banks to meet their reserve requirements hourly but only over a two-week period, reserves do provide limited liquidity.

The Deposit Multiplier

The previous examples show that aggregate bank deposits are a multiple of the dollar amount of aggregate reserves. If we let k be the value of the multiple, or the **deposit multiplier,** we can write

$$D = kTR$$

We can also solve the earlier equation for D:

$$D = \frac{1}{rr_D} \ (TR)$$

It can be readily seen that

$$k = \frac{1}{rr_D}$$

The deposit multiplier and reserve requirements vary inversely. If reserve requirements were 10 percent, the value of the multiplier would be 10. If the requirements were raised to 20 percent, the multiplier would fall to 5; and if the requirements were lowered to 5 percent, the multiplier would increase to 20.

Similarly, for a given multiplier, a change in the aggregate dollar amount of reserves will produce a change in aggregate deposits in the same direction by an amount equal to the value of the multiplier times the change in the reserves

$$\Delta D = k\Delta TR$$

where Δ means change. If for some reason—say, an inflow of currency or a purchase of loans by the Fed—aggregate reserves increased by $10,000 when the transaction deposit multiplier was 5, transaction deposits in the banking system would increase 5 × $10,000, or $50,000. If aggregate reserves decreased by $10,000 when the multiplier was 10 because of a currency outflow or a sale of loans by the Fed, deposits would decrease by 10 × $10,000 or $100,000. These changes are unlikely to occur immediately. Rather, the change in reserves is felt first by one bank, then is transmitted to other banks through time as the affected banks adjust. The step-by-step process by which such an expansion occurs is traced in the appendix to this chapter.

In reality, the deposit multiplier is more complex than the one we just derived, because the bank balance sheet is more complex and includes more than just required reserves, loans, and transaction deposits. It is worthwhile to develop some but not all of the complications.

Excess Reserves. When the central bank imposes legal reserve-requirement ratios, these may be greater or smaller than the ratios that the banks themselves would maintain voluntarily. If the required-reserve ratios were greater than the voluntary ratios, the banks would hold more reserves than they wished. If the required ratios were less than the voluntary ratios, the banks would hold more reserves than were legally required. The difference between the total amount of reserves that the banks hold and the required legal amount is referred to as **excess reserves,** and is defined as

$$ER = TR - RR$$

where: ER = excess reserves
         TR = total reserves

Excess reserves are excess or surplus only in the legal sense; the banks are not required to hold them. But they are not excess in the economic sense; the banks want to hold them. Some banks might want to hold excess reserves because they expect larger deposit outflows than they believe can be accommodated by the amount of legally required reserves, or because they do not want to take the chance of not meeting their legal reserve requirements and be subject to penalties by the Fed. Others might want to hold excess reserves because they do not feel that the income they could earn from investing the last dollar of excess reserves is worth the cost and trouble involved. Each bank determines the amount of excess reserves, if any, it wishes to hold.

If banks hold cash beyond the amount legally required, so that total reserves are greater than required reserves, they are making fewer loans than they could otherwise. The deposit-total reserve multiplier is smaller than if excess reserves were zero and total reserves were equal to required reserves. If we assume that the average bank wishes to hold excess reserves equal to e percent of its transaction deposits ($ER = eD$), the deposit multiplier is

$$k' = \frac{1}{rr_D + e}$$

Thus, if rr_D = 10% and e = 2.5%, then

$$k' = \frac{1}{0.10 + 0.025} = \frac{1}{0.125} = 8$$

One million dollars of total reserves will now support only $8 million of deposits, rather than $10 million of deposits if there were no excess reserves. e is sometimes referred to as a **leakage.**

Currency.   The public determines how much of its money supply it wishes to hold in the form of transaction deposits and how much in the form of currency. Currency may be bought from the Federal Reserve, which issues it. (Technically, currency is printed by the Bureau of Engraving and Printing of the U.S. Treasury Department, but it is sold to the Federal Reserve before issue.) It is much easier for most people, however, to obtain currency from their bank in exchange for a deposit. (If you obtain currency from a store, it, in turn, has to obtain it from a bank.) The bank buys the currency from the Fed. When a bank exchanges currency for a deposit, it is equivalent to a deposit outflow. The bank loses an equivalent dollar amount of reserves.

If the public as a whole wishes to hold more of its money stock in currency, a given amount of reserves provided by the Federal Reserve will support a smaller amount of deposits. If we assume that the public wishes to hold currency (C) in an amount equal to c percent of its transaction deposits ($C = cD$), the deposit multiplier is

$$k'' = \frac{1}{rr_D + e + c}$$

If, as before, $rr_D = 10\%$ and $e = 2.5\%$, and $c = 7.5\%$, then

$$k'' = \frac{1}{0.10 + 0.025 + 0.075} = \frac{1}{0.20} = 5$$

Because $\Delta D = k''\Delta TR$, the $1 million of reserves in the banking system will now support only $5 million of deposits. The banking system will be drained of $375,000 of reserves in the form of currency (0.075 × $5,000,000), leaving only $625,000 of reserves with the banks. Note that $625,000 × 8, the multiplier for reserves left in the banking system, is $5,000,000. Note also that the value of the deposit decreases as additional leakages are included. The previous examples are summarized in Table 15–1.

We can continue to make the multiplier more complex by recognizing that all banks are not subject to the same reserve requirements. Larger banks are subjected to higher requirements. We can also derive multipliers for total bank deposits and bank loans. Moreover, reserve requirements do not have to be satisfied every day but only on a two-week average basis. On any one day, a bank may be over or under its reserve requirement with a smaller or larger deposit multiplier as long as its dollar reserves for the period average out to no less than its average reserve requirements for that period. Nevertheless, the basic principle and general form of the equation would be unchanged. Depository institutions have deposits that are a multiple of their reserves.

If the Federal Reserve wished to change the amount of transaction deposits, it could do so by changing reserve requirements (rr), thereby changing the value of the deposit multiplier (k), or by changing the dollar amount of total reserves (TR). How the Fed does either of these is discussed in Chapter 28. Banks respond to a change in reserves by changing deposits in the same direction by a multiple of the change in reserves. The multiple is, of course, given by the value of the multiplier. Thus, if we assume only transaction deposits and that the multiplier is 5, banks will increase deposits by $5,000 for every $1,000 increase in their total reserves and decrease deposits by $5,000 for every $1,000 decrease in total reserves. If the multiplier were 10, the $1,000 increase in reserves would expand deposits by $10,000.

Money Supply

Now that we have seen how transaction deposits are related to total reserves, it is a simple step to see how the amount of money is related to reserves. Remember that we define *money* as

TABLE 15–1	SUMMARY OF BANK DEPOSIT EXPANSION	

Assumptions	Multiplier	Transaction Deposits per $1,000 Change in Reserves
$rr_D = 0.10;\ e,\ c = 0$	$\dfrac{1}{0.10} = 10$	$10,000
$rr_D = 0.10;\ e = 0.025;$ $c = 0$	$\dfrac{1}{0.10 + 0.025} = 8$	$8,000
$rr_D = 0.10;\ e = 0.025;$ $c = 0.075$	$\dfrac{1}{0.10 + 0.025 + 0.075} = 5$	$5,000

$$\Delta M = \Delta C + \Delta D$$

From the earlier sections, we can write

$$C = cD$$
$$D = kTR$$

where k is any measure of the multiplier we wish to assume. Substitution of these expressions one at a time in the definition of money yields

$$\Delta M = \Delta C + \Delta D = c\Delta D + \Delta D = \Delta D(1 + c)$$
$$\Delta M = k(1 + c)\Delta TR$$

Thus, just as the Fed can change the amount of transaction deposits, it can change the supply of money by changing either the dollar amount of total reserves (TR) or the value of the multiplier (k), which is done by changing the reserve-requirement component. How the Fed does this is discussed in Chapter 28.

Although the Fed can change the money supply, this does not necessarily mean that it can determine the amount of money precisely to the last dollar. This imprecision occurs because, although reserve requirements are under the control of the Federal Reserve, they are only one component of the deposit multiplier. As we have seen, neither excess reserves nor currency (nor, for that matter, the other components that we did not derive) are under the control of the Fed. Excess reserves are determined by the banks, and currency by the public. To determine what the implications of a change in total reserves or reserve requirements will be on the money supply, the Fed must predict what will happen to e and c. The more accurately the Fed can predict those values, the more precisely it can determine the value of the multiplier and hence also of the money supply. How well the Fed can predict those components not under its control, and for what time period— daily, weekly, monthly, or annually—is one of the hotter current controversies in monetary policy. It is also one of the major bones of contention between the neo-Keynesian and monetarist schools of economic thought that we will explore later in the book.

SUMMARY

Although most of us have greater daily personal contact with currency, most of the money supply is in the form of transaction deposits at depository institutions (banks). Banks are constrained in issuing transaction deposits by the explicit or implicit interest rate they must pay on the deposits, the interest rate they can earn on the primary securities they buy with the funds raised, the percentage of deposits required to be held in nonearning assets (cash reserves), and the dollar amount of cash reserves made available by the Federal Reserve. The banks must expect to earn more on assets than they pay on deposits. Deposits are equal to a multiple of bank reserves. The percentage of reserves banks are legally required to hold affects the size of the bank deposit-reserve multiplier. The higher the legal reserve ratio, the smaller the value of the multiplier. For all banks, changes in reserves cause multiple changes in deposits: $\Delta D = k\Delta TR$ and, more generally, $\Delta M = k\Delta(1 + c)TR$. Because the Fed can set both the legal reserve-requirement percentage and the dollar amount of cash reserves for the banking system as a whole, it can affect the money supply.

But the value of the multiplier is also affected by variables not under Federal Reserve control, such as the banks' demands for excess reserves and the public's demand for currency. The greater these leakages are, the smaller the multiplier is. The Fed can change the amount of transaction deposits for a given dollar amount of reserves by changing the legal reserve ratio in the opposite direction. Multipliers may be derived for any set of bank deposits. From these, it is easy to derive similar multipliers for any definition of money supply.

QUESTIONS

1. In what ways is currency both important and unimportant in the United States today? How is the supply of currency determined in the United States? How can you explain the current high level of per capita currency holdings?

2. Why can the banking system as a whole expand deposits more for a given increase in reserves than an individual bank can? Do you think that a bank in a small or a large city can expand deposits more for a given reserve inflow? Why?

3. Why would a bank hold excess reserves? How would the amount of excess reserves held vary with bank size? How do excess reserves affect the deposit multiplier?

4. How is the money multiplier related to the transaction-deposit multiplier?

How would a bank loan multiplier be related to the deposit multiplier? Is the deposit multiplier unique to commercial banks? Why or why not?

5. At any one time, a given dollar amount of total bank reserves in the banking system may be consistent with many different levels of money supply. Discuss the reasons for this. How do you think this affects the ability of the Federal Reserve to control the money supply?

6. Assume that reserve requirements against transaction accounts are 20 percent, banks' demand for excess reserves is 5 percent, and the public's demand for currency is 10 percent. Compute the transaction deposit multiplier. How many deposits can be supported by every $1,000 of bank reserves? What would happen to

deposits if alternatively (a) banks increased their demand for excess reserves to 7 percent, (b) the public decreased its demand for currency to 7 percent, or (c) the Fed doubled reserve requirements to 40 percent? What would be the value of the multiplier if all three changes occurred at once?

7. Why is it important for the Federal Reserve to be able to predict the banks' demand for excess reserves and the public's demand for currency if it is to control the money supply? What happens if it cannot do so reasonably accurately? What might happen to the banks' demand for excess reserves if the Fed were to double reserve requirements? Why?

REFERENCES

Avery, Robert B., et al., "The Use of Cash and Transaction Accounts by American Families," *Federal Reserve Bulletin,* February 1986, pp. 87–108.

Bureau of Engraving and Printing, *Paper Money.* Washington, D.C.: U.S. Treasury Department, 1962.

Burger. Albert E., *The Money Supply Process.* Belmont, Calif.: Wadsworth, 1974.

Carson, Carol S., "The Underground Economy: An Introduction," *Survey of Current Business,* May 1984, pp. 21–37; July 1984, pp. 106–17.

Federal Reserve Bank of Atlanta, *Fundamental Facts about United States Money.* Atlanta, 1989.

Federal Reserve Bank of Richmond, *Bank Deposits and the Money Supply: Concepts, Measurement, and Interpretation.* Rich-mond, 1980.

Gonczy, Anne Marie, *Modern Money Mechanics.* Federal Reserve Bank of Chicago, 1992.

Houston, Joel F., "The Underground Economy: A Troubling Issue for Policymakers," *Business Review,* Federal Reserve Bank of Philadelphia, Sep-tember/October 1987, pp. 3–12.

Jordan, Jerry L., "Elements of Money Stock Determination," *Review,* Federal Reserve Bank of St. Louis, October 1969, pp. 10–19.

Kaufman, George G., *Money, the Financial System and the Economy,* 3rd ed. Boston: Houghton Mifflin, 1981.

Porter, Richard D., and Amanada S. Bayer, "A Monetary Perspective on Underground Economic Activity in the U.S.," *Federal Reserve Bulletin,* March 1984, pp. 177–90.

Russell, Steven, "The U.S. Currency System: A Historical Perspective," *Review,* Federal Reserve Bank of St. Louis, September/October 1991, pp. 34–61.

"The Underground Economy's Hidden Force," *Business Week,* April 5, 1982, pp. 64–70.

Whitehead, David D., "Explaining the Cash Explosion," *Economic Review,* Federal Reserve Bank of Atlanta, March 1982, pp. 14–18.

Appendix 15A

Deposit Expansion Process

This appendix traces, step by step, the effects of a change in total reserves on the amount of transaction deposits in the banking system. For the sake of simplicity, we will assume the following:

1. Banks have only transaction deposits as liabilities and cash reserves and loans as assets.
2. All banks wish to hold cash reserves equal to 10 percent of their transaction deposits. This is also the legal required-reserve ratio, so that desired excess reserves are zero. Reserves are required to be held in the same period as the associated deposits.
3. The public wishes to hold no additional currency.

Mr. Bigpockets finds that his pockets are not quite big enough to hold all his currency, and he exchanges $10,000 of currency for a transaction deposit at bank A. Because currency serves as reserves, bank A now has an additional $10,000 of reserves. But it legally needs to hold only $1,000 (0.10 × $10,000) of required reserves against the additional $10,000 of deposits. The remaining $9,000 is excess reserves. This is shown in the first column of T accounts in Table 15A–1. Because excess reserves are nonearning assets, the bank will want to convert them into more profitable earning assets. It will make a $9,000 loan to Ms. Buynow, whose credit application was next in line. Ms. Buynow accepts the loan in the form of a deposit at bank A. After the loan extension, bank A has $19,000 in new deposits ($10,000 + $9,000), $10,000 in reserves, and $9,000 in loans. It is in equilibrium.

Ms. Buynow uses the $9,000 to make a down payment on a house sold to her by the owner, Ms. Moveon. Ms. Moveon takes the check for $9,000 written on bank A and deposits it in her bank, bank B. Bank B gives her a transaction deposit of $9,000 and sends the check to bank A for payment. In the meantime, it lists the check as a cash item in the collection process. Bank A receives the check and reduces Ms. Buynow's account by $9,000. At the same time, it sends $9,000 in reserves to bank B. Bank A's deposit liabilities decline to $10,000; its reserves to $1,000; and its loans to $9,000. The balance sheet now balances ($10,000 on both sides), and the bank's reserves are equal to 10 percent of its deposits. The bank remains in equilibrium. Upon receipt of the payment, bank B has $9,000 in new deposits and $9,000 of new reserves (column 2, Table 15A–1). But it is not in equilibrium. It needs to hold only $900 in required reserves; it can lend out $8,100. And so it does, making a loan of this amount to Mr. Spendaway.

Mr. Spendaway uses the $8,100 for a down payment on a Mercedes Benz from Richperson's Auto Sales. Mr. Richperson, the owner, deposits the check in his bank, bank C. Bank C increases Richperson's deposit account by $8,100 and sends the check for collection to bank B. Bank B reduces Mr. Spendaway's deposit by the $8,100 and pays bank C. Bank B now has $9,000 in deposits, $900 in reserves, and $8,100 in loans. Its balance sheet balances, and its reserves are 10 percent of deposits. Bank B is in equilibrium. Bank C has $8,100 in new deposits and the same amount in reserves. Thus, it is not in equilibrium. Bank C has excess reserves and will lend out $7,290 to increase its earnings.

Note that total deposits in the banking system are becoming larger with each round. Bank A has an additional $10,000 of deposits; bank B, $9,000; and bank C, $8,100. This sums up to $27,100. But the

Bank A		Bank B		Bank C	
Reserves $10,000	$10,000 Deposit Mr. Bigpockets	Reserves +$9,000	+$9,000 Deposit Ms. Moveon	Reserves +$8,100	+$8,100 Deposit Mr. Richperson
Required 1,000 Excess 9,000		Required 900 Excess 8,100		Required 810 Excess 7,290	
Reserves $10,000	$10,000 Deposit Mr. Bigpockets	Reserves 9,000	$9,000 Deposit Ms. Moveon		
Required 1,900 Excess 8,100	+9,000 Deposit Ms. Buynow	Required 1,710 Excess 7,290	+8,100 Deposit Mr. Spendaway		
Loans +9,000		Loans 8,100			
Reserves −9,000	−9,000 Deposit Ms. Buynow	Reserves −8,100	−8,100 Deposit Mr. Spendaway		
Reserves 1,000	$10,000 Deposit Mr. Bigpockets	Reserves 900	$9,000 Deposit Ms. Moveon		
Required 1,000 Excess 0		Required 900 Excess 0			
Loans 9,000		Loans 8,100			
Total $10,000	$10,000 Total	Total $9,000	$9,000 Total	Total $8,100	$8,100 Total

process will not stop here, because bank C has excess reserves. The expansion will continue until there are no more excess reserves. At that point, the entire $10,000 of new reserves injected into the banking system by the initial inflow of currency from Mr. Bigpockets serves as required reserves. This sequence is summarized step by step in a T account for the entire commercial banking system in Table 15A–2. Of course, the deposits need not always go to another bank. In equilibrium, when the expansion process is complete, total reserves are higher by $10,000, required reserves by $10,000, excess reserves by $0, loans by $90,000, and total transaction deposits by $100,000. This is

shown on the bottom line of Table 15A–2 and is traced in Figure 15A–1. Because no deposits have left the banking system, no reserves have left either. The final amount of reserves is equal to the initial amount plus the $10,000 currency inflow. The deposits in the banking system have expanded by a multiple of the initial inflow in reserves. After the initial inflow, the dollar amount of reserves has not changed. The amount of the deposit expansion for the entire banking system is given by the product of the multiplier (10)—which is the reciprocal of the required reserve ratio (1/0.10)—and the initial increase in reserves ($10,000).

It can be seen from Table 15A–1 that for

TABLE			STEP-BY-STEP AGGREGATE BANK		
15A–2			DEPOSIT EXPANSION PROCESS		

	Aggregate Bank Balance Sheet				
	Assets				Liabilities
	Reserves			Loans	Transaction Deposits
Banks[a]	Total	Required	Excess		
A	$10,000	$ 1,000	$9,000	0	$ 10,000
A + B	10,000	1,900	8,100	$ 9,000	19,000
A + B + C	10,000	2,710	7,290	17,100	27,100
•					
•					
•					
•					
All − 1	10,000	9,999	1	89,999	99,999
All	$10,000	$10,000	0	$90,000	$100,000

[a]Before the extension of loans by the last bank.

any individual bank, the deposit expansion is only equal to its initial inflow of reserves. This is so because any one bank is subject to deposit outflows to other banks. But in the absence of a currency drain, the deposits stay in the banking system as a whole. To the extent that any individual bank does not believe it will experience a deposit outflow, it too can expand deposits by a multiple of its initial reserve gain. But it is taking a chance. If it is wrong, it will need to sell earning assets quickly to accommodate the deposit loss. This is risky!

A reduction in reserves attributed to, say, a currency outflow to accommodate a deposit customer will result in a multiple contraction in deposits through a similar domino effect in reverse. The initial bank will have insufficient reserves to meet its reserve requirements. It sells loans to obtain reserves. The purchaser is likely to have a deposit at another bank. Reserves are transferred from the second to the first bank, and the purchaser's deposits are reduced. The first bank regains equilibrium, but this transaction leaves the second bank deficient in reserves and out of equilibrium. The adjustment process goes on until aggregate deposits are contracted to the point where the smaller amount of reserves in the banking system satisfies the reserve-requirement ratio once more.

REFERENCE

Humphrey, Thomas M., "The Theory of Multiple Expansion of Deposits," *Economic Review*, Federal Reserve Bank of Richmond, March/April 1987, pp. 3–11.

CUMULATIVE EXPANSION IN DEPOSITS ON BASIS OF $10,000 OF NEW RESERVES AND RESERVE
REQUIREMENTS OF 10 PERCENT

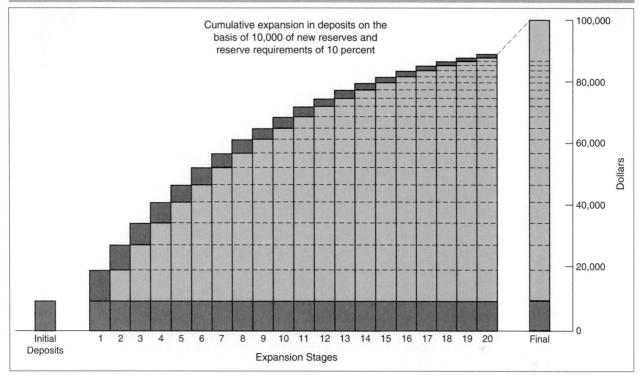

Cumulative expansion in deposits on the
basis of 10,000 of new reserves and
reserve requirements of 10 percent

SOURCE: Anne Marie Gonczy, *Modern Money Mechanics*, Federal Reserve Bank of Chicago, 1992, p. 11.

Regulation of the Financial System

The financial system in the United States, as in most countries, is highly regulated by the government. This reflects the great importance of the sector not only in itself but also to the well-being and efficient operation of the economy as a whole and the potential for severe economic harm if the financial system were to seriously malfunction. Regulation and legislation in the public interest that are intended to maximize banking's contribution to society are referred to as **public policy.** This chapter discusses public policy toward banking; the previous chapters emphasized private policies to maximize the firms' own objectives.

Firms are regulated primarily by the marketplace or by the government. These two forms of regulation compete with each other. If one is perceived to be inducing suboptimal performance by firms in an industry, it tends to be replaced by the other. Historically, in a free enterprise, free market economy, firms traditionally tend to be regulated by the government rather than by the marketplace only if competition is believed to be inadequate to provide efficient production at low prices. The leading candidates for regulation for this purpose are firms in an industry widely believed to be a **natural monopoly.** Natural monopolies are industries whose costs per unit of output decline continuously as output is increased. As a result, their optimal scale of operation is as large as the market permits. It is efficient for firms in such industries to merge with other firms in the industry to achieve the benefits of the economies of scale until only one firm remains. At that point, the firm and the industry are the same. Industries that are generally believed to be natural monopolies include communication, transportation, and power.

(It is important to recognize that not all activities of firms in these industries may be natural monopolies. For example, although telephone transmission lines may be natural monopolies, terminal telephone equipment is not. Similarly with railroads, it is the tracks and not the rolling stock that constitute a natural monopoly. Unlike most railroads, trucking firms do not own highway rights of way and are not as frequently viewed as natural monopolies.)

If a natural monopoly is permitted to operate without constraints, there is no guarantee that the resulting single firm will price its output at the lowest cost warranted by the economies of scale. Governments impose regulations to attempt to achieve the advantages of both large-scale, low-cost production and competitive pricing. The intent of the regulation is to simulate competition and force the firms to pass on to consumers the benefits of lower production costs. This is achieved by establishing performance norms in terms of prices and rates and return on capital consistent with those that would exist under a competitive structure.

To be effective, regulation needs to be accompanied by verification through monitoring and examination to determine compliance. This process is referred to as **supervision.**

Reasons for Government Regulation

As we discussed in Chapter 11, there is little evidence that size is advantageous in banking or that banks may be classified as natural monopolies. Although, until recently, there were significant restrictions on the entry of new banks, the fact that a large number of different-sized banks coexisted even in branch-banking states provides strong evidence that any economies of scale that may exist are not overwhelming. There is similar evidence indicating that other major types of financial institutions are not natural monopolies. Why, then, are they regulated by the government?

The courts have ruled that any industry may be regulated by the government if it is "clothed in the public interest." And commercial banks and other financial institutions most certainly are. The public interest aspects of banking include safety, payments system, structure—economic concentration, efficiency, conflict of interest (fairness)—consumer protection, and monetary policy.

Safety. As we saw earlier, the failure of depository financial institutions is widely perceived to have more serious implications for the community than the failure of many other types of business firms. Almost every household, business firm, and government unit is a creditor of these institutions, and many are also debtors. They may experience significant losses and disruptions if their bank fails. Moreover, the failure of large individual banks, unlike that of most other firms, could ignite panic, which can spread to customers of other banks and cause a domino effect of bank failures that could reduce the aggregate money supply and dampen national income. Last, the high debt leverage made possible by deposit insurance might tempt bank owners to become less risk-averse. They are likely to take chances that they would not take if more of their own money were invested in the firm. If they win, they win big; if they lose, they lose only other people's money! Government regulation is believed necessary to prevent runs on and failures of individual banks from spilling over to other, financially healthy banks. Many recent prudential regulations reflect the government's need, as the ultimate guarantor of the par value of deposits and in response to the high cost of the SLA failures of the 1980s, to protect the deposit insurance fund and taxpayers.

Payments System. Depository institutions both provide the major form of payment in the United States and operate the major part of the funds-transfer system. It is in the public interest to have the payments mechanism operate as efficiently as possible on a national scale. Regulation is intended to broaden the availability of the payments system, increase its operational efficiency, standardize the days of operation, and maintain operation at all times. For example, banks are permitted to be closed only on days designated by the state.

Structure.   Industry structure deals with questions of efficiency, concentration, and fairness. Because money and credit are used pervasively in all sectors and activities in the economy, control over them is more powerful than control over any other sector or activity. Monopoly power in money and credit may lead both to inefficient operation and to monopoly powers in other sectors. A monopoly creditor may influence the behavior of borrowers. For example, borrowers may be required to do business only with parties that are also customers of the creditor. Lenders that offer many financial services may encounter conflicts of interest that are resolved to the disadvantage of the customer. For example, lenders, who are also stockholders may be confronted with serious conflicts of interest when firms they own and to whom they may also have extended credit become poor credit risks and cannot obtain credit elsewhere. The lenders may be tempted to lend to them against their better business judgment. Lenders, who are also investment bankers, may exert pressure to sell to their loan customers or place in their own portfolios new security issues that they cannot market profitably through normal channels. (The pros and cons of separating commercial and investment banking are discussed in Chapter 20.) Because of the strength of monopoly power in finance, it may spill over into excessive social and political power. Fear of "big banking" has been particularly strong in the United States. This fear helps to explain the long-standing restrictions against interstate branching and the separation of banking and commerce. Indeed, some states actually prohibited commercial banks in the early days of U.S. history; and, even by 1850, banks were prohibited in California, Texas, Florida, and Iowa. Regulation is intended to prevent such excessive power and restrict abuses.

Consumer Protection.   This is the most recent type of regulation, dating back only to the Truth in Lending Act in 1968. The objectives of this regulation are to (1) prevent abuse in the extension and collection of consumer credit; (2) provide for full disclosure of credit costs and terms; and (3) protect against discrimination in the provision of credit for reasons other than economic.

Consumers are viewed as being in need of protection because they are small relative to the depository institution and thus may be taken unfair advantage of and because the costs and terms of most financial transactions are difficult to analyze accurately, even by experts. Thus, the Truth in Lending Act and the Truth in Savings Act, which was part of FDICIA in 1991, require depository institutions to clearly and uniformly state their loan and deposit rates and fees. The Expedited Funds Availability Act (1987) imposes restrictions on the number of days that a bank may delay payment on checks deposited with it. Although new, more specific legislation has been enacted in this area in recent years than in the other areas combined. Some of the more important federal acts are listed in Table 16–1.

Although not strictly consumer protection, the Community Reinvestment Act (CRA) enacted in 1977 is generally grouped in this category. The act uses banks to help achieve social objectives. It encourages banks to make loans in their local communities, including low-income and minority neighborhoods, and requires the bank regulatory agencies to assess how well the banks are doing. The performance evaluations may be used by the regulators to grant or deny an application by a bank for permission to

TABLE 16–1	MAJOR CONSUMER PROTECTION ACTS, 1968–92	

	Year Enacted
Consumer Credit Protection Act (Truth in Lending Act)	1968
Fair Housing Act	1968
Fair Credit Reporting Act	1970
Equal Credit Opportunity Act	1974
Real Estate Settlement Act	1974
Home Mortgage Disclosure Act	1975
Consumer Leasing Act	1976
Community Reinvestment Act	1977
Electronic Fund Transfer Act	1978
Expedited Funds Availability Act	1987
Truth in Savings Act	1991

engage in a new activity, such as a merger with another bank, the opening of a branch office, or offering a new product service. Similarly, the Home Mortgage Disclosure Act (HMDA) of 1975 and its later amendments require banks to publish residential mortgage loan data by type of loan and racial characteristics of the borrowers to help assess whether a bank is providing mortgage loans on a nondiscriminatory basis.

Monetary Policy.   Changing the money supply is one of the major ways the federal government can affect levels of economic activity. Deposits at commercial banks and other depository institutions account for the larger share of any definition of money supply. Thus, the deposit size of the banking system is controlled by the Federal Reserve System. In addition, the Fed at times attempts to influence economic activity in individual sectors by affecting the flow of credit to these sectors. This involves them in regulating the composition of earning assets and deposits as well as the overall amount.

Types of Regulation

Banking regulations may be classified according to what they restrict: (1) prices (interest rates) paid or charged, (2) products offered, and (3) number of firms and geographic location, as well as by their principal objectives. In this section, we shall examine government regulations that are imposed by purposes of safety, structure, and monetary control. Some regulations may have more than one objective.

Safety

Most of our banking regulations were initially imposed to increase the safety of the banking and payments systems. *Prudential regulations* are generally introduced after periods in which the systems broke down and widespread injury resulted from bank failures, such as during the Great Depression of the early 1930s, when the number of banks declined sharply by 40 percent from 25,000 to 14,000, and during the 1980s.

Entry.   People wishing to establish commercial banks or other types of depository financial institutions must obtain charters from the federal or state government before they can commence business. (In addition, it is now almost impossible for a bank to be granted a charter unless it first qualifies for deposit insurance from the appropriate federal insurance agency.) Charters are not issued freely. Among the requirements for a charter, applicants frequently have been asked to demonstrate that there is a need for their services and that they will not endanger the solvency of other, similar institutions. To further ensure the safety of both new and existing institutions, the regulators, in evaluating applications for a new charter, also

1. Stipulate minimum capital requirements,
2. Evaluate projected earning prospects, and
3. Consider the banking experience and reputation of the applicant.

As a result of these restrictions, the number of institutions may be expected to be smaller. Without charter requirements, firms may be expected to enter an industry if they consider the profit potentials favorable— either because the market is growing or because they could capture a share of the existing market from other firms. By restricting entry, these regulations restrict the intensity of competition and reduce the likelihood of failures; inefficient firms do not die as quickly. Restricted entry results in restricted exit and in the support of inefficient firms. In recent years, charting restrictions have been eased substantially. In addition, primarily because of advances in telecommunications technology, nonbanking firms, such as Sears and Merrill Lynch, have been able to offer many banking-type services without chartering themselves as commercial banks.

Amount and Type of Earning Assets.   The safety of financial institutions is enhanced by restricting the types of loans and investments they may make to those of high quality and by limiting the amount of any one type of loan or investment so as to reduce the severity of any losses through diversification. For example, federal regulations restrict national commercial bank investment in corporate and municipal bonds primarily to "investment quality," which is interpreted to mean the four highest ratings assigned by the national credit-rating agencies. For Moody's, this implies Baa or higher and some nonrated issues. In addition, the Glass-Steagall Act (1933) prohibits commercial banks from underwriting and dealing in many private securities.

With respect to loan size, national commercial banks are not permitted to lend an amount in excess of 15 percent of the bank's capital to any single borrower. Neither are these banks permitted to make real estate loans in the aggregate in excess of their capital or 70 percent of their time and savings deposits, whichever is the greater.

Capital Adequacy.   The bulwark against bank failure is bank capital, consisting primarily of common stock, preferred stock, and retained earnings.

As long as losses can be charged against the bank's capital account no losses accrue to depositors or the FDIC and the bank remains solvent. Thus, the capital account is the focus of bank safety regulations. As noted previously, a new bank must satisfy minimum capital requirements in order to be granted a charter and deposit insurance, and after chartering, the amount of capital is monitored closely. For example, the three federal bank regulatory agencies require that all commercial banks maintain minimum equity capital-to-asset or **leverage** ratios of at least 3 percent. But, most banks are required to maintain higher minimum ratios. However, the amount of capital required by any institution cannot be evaluated in isolation; the size and operational characteristics of the institution must be considered. The lower the quality of its assets and the less stable the quantity of its deposit liabilities, the more capital is required to ensure any given degree of safety. In recent years, the U.S. bank regulatory agencies have worked with their counterparts in other major financial countries to develop uniform risk-based capital standards that could be applied to banks worldwide.

The FDIC Improvement Act of 1991 increased the importance of capital even further. The act requires that each depository institution be assigned to one of five capital zones according to the ratios of its tier 1 (equity) and total capital to total and risk-based assets. The capital zones, their numerical definitions and the respective major sanctions are shown in Table 16–2. The lower the assigned capital zone, the progressively harsher and more mandatory are the regulatory sanctions applied to the institution in an attempt to dissuade it from continuing down the path toward failure and to persuade it to reverse its direction before it is too late. The sanctions serve as speedbumps and are designed to resemble those that the market would impose on a non-FDIC insured firm. If, however, these *prompt corrective action* (PCA) measures fail to work, the regulators are required to attempt to resolve the institution through sale, merger, or liquidation before its capital is fully depleted and losses accrue to depositors. This *least cost resolution* (LCR) or "closure" rule goes into effect when the institution's equity capital declines to 2 percent of its assets and it becomes **critically undercapitalized.**

Because all bank activities are not equally risky, the market is unlikely to impose the same capital standards on all. Higher standards would likely be imposed on riskier activities and lower standards on safer activities. In an attempt to reflect these differences, the regulators developed risk-based capital standards in which each on- and off-balance sheet activity is weighed by a risk factor. The greater the perceived riskiness of the activity, the greater the risk weight, and the greater the risk-adjusted asset base against which capital must be held. The risk weights assigned to major on-balance sheet asset categories are shown in Table 16–3. These standards were developed at meetings held at the Bank for International Settlements (BIS), a multinational agency organized after World War I, in Basle, Switzerland. As a result, they are often referred to as the **BIS** or **Basle standards.**

Ongoing information on a bank's capital position is obtained from regular reports submitted by the institution and from periodic examinations conducted by the regulatory agencies on the institution's premises. (Examinations are discussed later in this chapter.)

TABLE

16–2

FEDERAL DEPOSIT INSURANCE CORPORATION IMPROVEMENT ACT:
PROMPT CORRECTIVE ACTION CAPITAL ZONES AND SANCTIONS

	Capital Ratios[a]		
	Risk-Based Assets		Total Assets
	Total	*Tier 1* *(percent)*	*Tier 1*
Well Capitalized	>10	>6	>5
Definition: Significantly exceeds required capital standards.			
Sanctions: None			
Adequately Capitalized	>8	>4	>4
Definition: Meets minimum required standards.			
Sanctions: Few, but cannot underwrite insurance where permitted by state law, and FDIC approval required to accept brokered funds.			
Undercapitalized	<8	<4	<4
Definition: Fails to meet minimum required standards.			
Sanctions: Above, plus close agency monitoring, capital restoration plan required; limits on asset growth; approval required for acquisition, branches, and new activities.			
Significantly Undercapitalized	<6	<3	<3
Definition: Is significantly below required minimum standards.			
Sanctions: Above, plus required recapitalization by sale of new stock; activities, transactions with affiliates, and interest rates paid on deposits restricted; management compensation restricted; divestiture of troubled affiliates required.			
Critically Undercapitalized			<2
Definition: Less than 2 percent eligible capital-to-asset ratio.			
Sanctions: Above, plus interest payment on subordinated debt prohibited and institution generally placed in receivership or conservatorship within 90 days.			

[a]Tier 1 basically includes equity capital and excludes subordinated debt. Numerical values assigned by bank regulatory agencies, except for 2 percent ratio for critically undercapitalized.

TABLE 16–3	WEIGHTS FOR MAJOR ASSET CATEGORIES IN RISK-BASED CAPITAL REQUIREMENTS

Category 1—Zero Percent Weight

Cash

Balances due from Federal Reserve Banks and claims on central banks in other (OECD) countries

U.S. Treasury and government agency securities and claims on or unconditionally guaranteed by OECD central governments

Federal Reserve stock

Category 2—20 Percent Weight

Cash items in the process of collection

All claims on or guaranteed by U.S. depository institutions and banks in OECD countries

General obligation bonds of state and local governments

Loans and other claims secured by bank deposits or U.S. government securities

Loans or other claims conditionally guaranteed by the U.S. government, its agencies, or other OECD central governments

Securities and other claims on U.S. government–sponsored agencies

Category 3—50 Percent Weight

Loans secured by first liens on 1–4 family residential property

Certain privately issued mortgage-backed securities

Revenue bonds of state and local governments

Category 4—100 Percent Weight

All loans and other claims on private obligors not placed in a lower risk category

Bank premises, fixed assets, and other real estate owned

Industrial development revenue bonds

Intangible assets and investment in unconsolidated subsidiaries, provided they are not deducted from capital

SOURCE: Kenneth Spong, *Bank Regulation*, Federal Reserve Bank of Kansas City, 1990, p. 68.

Deposit Rate Ceilings. *Ceteris paribus*, the higher the interest rate paid on deposits, the lower are bank profits. In earlier years, it was widely believed that overaggressive deposit behavior characterized by paying high interest rates forced banks to pursue overaggressive lending policies to acquire earning assets that paid sufficiently high interest. These tended to be riskier loans and investments, and caused the institution to be riskier than otherwise. If the loans turned bad, the banks experienced financial difficulties.

Many analysts initially placed a large amount of the blame for the widespread bank failures during the depression years of 1929 to 1933 on such aggressive behavior. However, later, more thorough analysis indicated that the banks that failed were not necessarily those that paid relatively high deposit rates. Nonetheless, as an ad hoc response to the banking crisis, a prohibition was placed on the payment of any interest on demand deposits in 1933, and ceilings were placed on the maximum interest rates commercial banks could pay on time and savings deposits. Congress delegated the determination of the ceiling to the appropriate bank regulatory agency. These ceilings were commonly referred to as **Regulation Q,** after the regulation applicable to banks that are members of the Federal Reserve.

In 1966, deposit rate ceilings were extended to thrift institutions to reduce the cost pressures on them from sharply higher short-term interest rates. As discussed in Chapter 8, only interest rate changes expected at the time a fixed-rate mortgage loan is made are included in the long-term mortgage rate when the loan is made. The deposit rate ceilings were intended to give the thrift institutions time to roll over their mortgages at the new, higher rates without experiencing financial strains. The ceiling rates were set somewhat higher than on commercial banks. This action was intended to encourage the flow of savings into thrift institutions that primarily make mortgage loans.

In time, these restrictions caused more difficulties than they solved. They prevented the affected financial institutions from offering competitive rates on deposits as interest rates on comparable primary securities climbed above the ceiling rate. Thus, Regulation Q encouraged larger depositors to shift their funds from intermediaries to the private financial market or to intermediaries not covered at the time, such as the newly organized money-market funds. The resulting disintermediation reduced the amount of funds available to the mortgage market. To the extent that Regulation Q was effective in periods of high interest rates in reducing cost pressures, it impinged principally on smaller depositors. The cost of shifting to primary securities for these depositors was too high in relation to the size of their deposits, and most endured receiving below-market rates of interest on their savings. However, transfer costs were relatively minor for large deposits, and the deposit ceilings caused the outflow of these deposits to higher-yielding primary securities on the private financial market. Because they were ineffective, in the early 1970s the ceilings were gradually removed from deposits in excess of $100,000.

Finally in 1980, Congress concluded that

> (1) limitations on the interest rates which are payable on deposits and accounts discourage persons from saving money, create inequities for depositors, impede the ability of depository institutions to compete for funds, and have not achieved their purpose of providing an even flow of funds for home mortgage lending; and
> (2) all depositors, and particularly those with modest savings, are entitled to receive a market rate of return on their savings as soon as it is economically feasible for depository institutions to pay such rate.[1]

The Depository Institutions Deregulation and Monetary Control Act (DIDMCA) of 1980 provided for the phase-out of all deposit rate ceilings on time deposits by 1986. The process was considerably speeded up by the introduction of nonregulated money-market deposit accounts by the Garn-St Germain Act of 1982. The prohibition on cash interest payments on demand deposits remains in effect, but it has been weakened considerably by the use of NOW accounts by households and of automatic **sweep** overnight repurchase agreements by business firms.

---

[1] U.S. Congress, *Depository Institutions Deregulation and Monetary Control Act of* 1980, p. 12.

Structure

Regulations that affect the structure of financial institutions are intended to restrict concentration and to encourage competition. At times, this objective conflicts with the objective of safety. Like most other firms, financial institutions are subject to the provisions of federal antitrust statutes, such as the Sherman and Clayton Acts. But, in addition, financial institutions are subject to special restrictions on the number of firms and offices, geographic location, horizontal consolidations, the activities in which they may engage, and the products they may offer.

Number of Firms and Offices.   The more firms there are, the lower the concentration of deposits and the more intense competition is likely to be. Although numbers do not guarantee competition, lack of numbers virtually guarantees a lack of competition. The number of competitors is meaningful only within the context of market area. Bank concentration on a national basis is far less in the United States than elsewhere. However, few, if any, bank customers have access to all 11,000 commercial banks, 1,900 SLAs, 400 SBs, and 13,500 CUs in the United States. Thus, this large number does not necessarily indicate intense competition. The market area for banks is difficult to delineate and may be expected to differ for each major type of service offered. The fact that a major metropolitan area has, say, 50 banks will be viewed differently by large- and medium-sized borrowers who have access to all these banks than by small household borrowers who may have access to only the one of two banks in their own neighborhoods. Moreover, any analysis of the number of depository institutions must consider not only the number of the same type of institution but also the number of other financial institutions, including nondepository institutions such as finance and insurance companies, that compete in one or more activities. Thus, while the number of commercial banks may be the most relevant to an analysis of the market for business loans, at minimum, the number of savings and loan associations and savings banks must also be included when the market for savings deposits or residential mortgage loans is analyzed.

Geographic Powers.   The number of firms in a market area is affected by both chartering and branching (office) restrictions. The more restricted branching is geographically, the larger will be the number of banking firms in the entire jurisdiction, but not necessarily in subsectors of the jurisdiction. A state that permits statewide-branch banking may have fewer different banking firms than a unit-banking state. But such a state could also have the same or more banking firms in local communities. In an extreme example, a unit-branch state with 100 communities might have 100 different banking firms, with one in each town. In contrast, a statewide-branching state might have only five banks in the entire state, but each bank might have a branch in each community. Thus, each community would have five banks. In this instance, households might have the same number of banking alternatives as larger business firms.

Restrictions on full-service interstate commercial bank branching protect against sharp reductions in the number of commercial banks in the country as a whole and the creation of very large national banks, but may also reduce the potential number of different banks in some states. Although the restrictions against interstate holding company acquisitions did not protect against a decline in the total number of banks, they did protect against a decline in the number of independent banks. Since the liberalization of interstate acquisitions of banks by bank holding companies in the early 1980s, the number of independent banking organizations has declined from 12,400 in 1981 to about 8,000 in 1993, and may be expected to decline more rapidly as interstate banking increases.

Horizontal Consolidation. Financial institutions may acquire other institutions of the same type **(horizontal consolidation)** either by merger or by acquisition through a holding company. Financial institutions are subject to the general provisions of the Sherman and Clayton Antitrust Acts. However, the applicability of these acts to financial intermediaries was not completely resolved until the early 1960s. Both to supplement these statutes and to spell out the responsibilities of the regulatory agencies in bank consolidations, Congress enacted additional legislation. Commercial bank mergers are subject to the Bank Merger Acts of 1960 and 1966. These acts stipulate that a merger may not be approved unless the responsible regulatory agency finds that it will not result in a monopoly and that:

> the anticompetitive effects of the proposed transaction are clearly outweighed in the public interest by the probably effect of the transaction in meeting the convenience and needs of the community.[2]

In its determination, the responsible agency receives advisory reports on the competitive effects of the proposed merger from the other two federal regulatory agencies and from the U.S. Department of Justice. If the Department of Justice disagrees with the ultimate decision of the agency, it can delay the merger and challenge it in court.

Consolidations among commercial banks by holding company acquisitions are restricted by the Bank Holding Company Act of 1956. Responsibility for evaluating all applications by holding companies to acquire additional financial institutions is delegated to the Board of Governors of the Federal Reserve System. As with mergers, the Board may not approve any acquisition" whose effect in any section of the country may be substantially to lessen competition, or to tend to create a monopoly." Mergers and holding-company acquisitions for savings and loan associations, savings banks, and credit unions must be approved by the respective regulatory agency. Until the late 1980s, mergers between commercial banks and thrift institutions were restricted.

Concern about the anticompetitive implications of the structure of banks has been reduced in recent years as the barriers to the entry of new firms were lowered. As a result, fewer bank mergers and holding acquisitions have been denied.

Permissible Products. The products and services that banks may offer, either directly or through holding company affiliation, are restricted. The restric-

---

[2] Board of Governors of the Federal Reserve System. *Federal Reserve Act*, 1976, p. 101. In 1989, FIRREA extended the Bank Merger Act to SLAs and made the Office of Thrift Supervision the responsible federal agency.

tions are intended to limit aggregate economic concentration, the potential for conflict of interest, and bank risk. In the United States, banks are not permitted to offer nonfinancial products—the separation of finance and commerce. The primary statutes restricting the type of activities in which commercial banks may engage are the national and state banking codes, the 1970 amendments to the Bank Holding Company Act of 1956, and the Glass-Steagall Act of 1933. As noted in Chapter 11, the 1970 amendments prohibit bank holding companies from acquiring firms that are not "so closely related to banking . . . as to be a proper incident thereto." In determining whether an activity satisfies this criterion, the act requires that the Board of Governors of the Federal Reserve System

> . . . consider whether its performance by an affiliate of a holding company can reasonably be expected to produce benefits to the public, such as greater convenience, increased competition, or gains in efficiency, that outweigh possible adverse effects, such as undue concentration of resources, decreased or unfair competition, conflicts of interest, or unsound banking practices.[3]

As noted in Chapter 11, activities undertaken most frequently by bank holding company subsidiaries include operating finance companies, credit insurance agencies, and mortgage banking. With some exception, banks may not sell insurance other than credit life extended in conjunction with the extension of loans. While multiple SLA holding companies are subject to similar regulations, unitary SLA holding company regulations are less restrictive.

The Glass-Steagall Act prohibits commercial banks from engaging directly in many types of securities activities, such as underwriting and trading of corporate securities and mutual funds. In recent years, however, banks have been permitted by regulation to engage in a progressively wider range of securities activities but largely in holding company affiliates. Current securities activities of commercial banks are discussed in greater detail in Chapter 20.

Monetary Control

Most important, the Federal Reserve System regulates the overall deposit size of depository institutions to affect the rate of inflation and levels of economic activity in the real sector of the economy. As will be discussed in greater detail in Chapter 28, the Fed does so primarily by controlling the dollar amount of reserves and deposits in the banking system, changing required reserve ratios, and changing the discount rate it charges on direct bank borrowing of reserves. On occasion, the Fed has also influenced the composition of bank liabilities, to affect either levels of aggregate activity or activity in particular sectors, through deposit rate ceilings and reserve requirements on different types of deposits. In past periods of emergency, the Fed was authorized to affect the mix of bank assets by establishing minimum down payments and maximum maturity schedules on different types of credit and by imposing differential reserve requirements on different

---

[3] Ibid., p. 116.

types of bank earning assets in addition to their liabilities. This would affect the relative profitability of different earning assets and the incentives of banks to extend different types of loans. The higher the reserve requirements on any particular type of earning asset, the lower the return on that asset, and the less likely banks are to allocate funds to it.

 ## Evaluation of Regulation

Although regulations are imposed in the public interest to improve the efficiency of the financial system and prevent breakdowns, it does not necessarily follow that the more regulation, the better. Regulation can have undesirable and counterproductive side effects. Attempts to provide for safety and "orderly" competition by restricting entry and aggressiveness may result in less efficient economic performance. Interest rates charged on loans may be higher than otherwise and those paid on deposits lower. The quality of services may deteriorate. Responsiveness to changes in consumer demands and methods of production may be reduced. Innovations may be adopted more slowly. As a result, regulation may protect competitors rather than competition. In the 1960s, when banking was highly regulated and bank failures rare, a senior congressman knowledgeable about banking startled his colleagues by arguing that what this country needed was more bank failures. He felt that regulation had taken the zest out of banking and had shortchanged consumers. Excessive regulation may also reduce efficiency by imposing excessive reporting burdens. These may cause managerial resources to be shifted from more-productive operating activities to less-productive compliance activities. Regulation has implications for the welfare of both the industry as a whole and the individual firms.

The evidence from other regulated industries is unclear with respect to who benefits from regulation. At times it appears to be the consumers, at times the industry, at times the labor force, and at times only the regulators. Those who argue that regulation favors the industry—***regulatory capture***—point to the close relationship between the regulators and the industry. Because the technical aspects of regulation necessitate a knowledge of the industry, regulators are often selected from the industry itself and/or maintain close contact with the industry and become over sympathetic to its problems. Moreover, even if regulation was initially established through consumer pressures, many consumers quickly lose interest in the industry; the industry, however, has a strong incentive to remain involved. On the other hand, those who argue that regulation favors the consumer point to the increasing spirit of consumerism and the growth of "Naderism."

It is most likely that the benefits of regulation vary over time and, in particular, over the business cycle. It is not uncommon for an industry to press for regulation when demand is weak and prices are declining from excess supply. (For individual firms, regulation involves a trade-off between greater security in maintaining stable profits and market share and greater uncertainty with a possibility of increasing profits and market share at the cost of possible reductions in both.) Nor is it uncommon for consumers to press for regulation when demand is strong and prices are rising sharply.

The contradictory nature of the evidence alone should promote caution in supporting regulation to achieve purposes other than control over natural monopolies. And even in this area, the case for government intervention is not clear. The President's Council on Wage and Price Stability concluded that, on the basis of its experiences from 1974 and 1980, "there appear to be very few areas today in which economic regulation can be justified on the basis of natural monopoly arguments. Even where elements of natural monopoly exist, the theoretical case for intervention may be outweighed by the failure of government to improve efficiency when it has intervened."[4]

Primarily because of the inconclusive evidence, public sentiment in favor of regulation is highly variable. If the market does not appear to function well, regulation is viewed as desirable; if regulation does not appear to function well, a freer market is viewed as desirable. After four decades of increased regulation, dissatisfaction with the performance of many regulated industries caused public sentiment to swing toward deregulation in the late 1970s. Dramatic changes in the economy since the existing regulations were introduced, on the whole, to correct the problems of an earlier day, had made the system unresponsive to present needs. The first sectors "deregulated" were transportation, such as airlines; energy, such as natural gas; and communications, such as the telephone company. But, once introduced, regulation becomes difficult to remove. Many regulatees benefit and become accustomed to operating within the regulatory ground rules. They do not favor a change—often abrupt—to a freer, more competitive market and new ground rules, and lobby vigorously to maintain the status quo.

But in banking, deregulation could not be stalled totally. Market forces operated to make many of the regulations, particularly those adopted for purposes of safety during the Great Depression, ineffective. High and volatile interest rates caused by high and volatile inflation rates provided the incentive to bypass deposit rate ceilings and product restrictions; and technical advances in telecommunications and computers, which permitted quick and cheap transfer, storage, and manipulation of information and funds, provided the means to bypass these regulations. As discussed above, Congress progressively validated the de facto product changes de jure in DIDMCA of 1980 and the Garn-St. Germain Act of 1982 and, more recently, de facto interstate banking in the Banking Modernization Act of 1994. But like regulation, deregulation has distributional as well as aggregate impacts. The more deregulation permits the extension of one player's turf onto that of others, the more opposition to further change is likely to strengthen. Moreover, as competition and risk taking increased, the number of bank and thrift institution failures also increased and concern for safety again increased in priority. The experience of the 1980s led to an increase in prudential regulations mandated by FDICIA of 1991.

Compliance with the continuing increases in regulation for prudential, consumer protection, and social objective purposes have imposed a high regulatory cost burden on the banks. A study by the bank regulatory agencies reported that regulatory costs to the banking industry in 1991 ranged between $7.5 and $17 billion, or between 6 and 14 percent of the

[4] Thomas D. Hopkins, et al., A *Review of the Regulatory Interventions of the Council on Wage and Price Stability: 1974–1980* (Washington, D.C.: Council on Wage and Price Stability, January 1981), p. vii.

banks' total noninterest expenses. The costs have reduced bank profits and put the banks at a competitive disadvantage with their non- or less-regulated competitors. As a result, increased attention has been directed in recent years at ways of reducing this burden without reducing prudential standards.

Regulatory Agencies

Regulation of financial intermediaries is shared by federal and state agencies. At the federal level, three agencies have principal responsibilities for commercial banks, another for savings and loan associations, and another for credit unions. In addition, all or some of the activities of these institutions come under the purview of other federal agencies, such as the Department of Justice, the Securities and Exchange Commission, the Federal Trade Commission, and the Department of Housing and Urban Development. State-chartered institutions are also subject to regulation by one or more agencies in their home states and in any other state in which they operate branch offices (Table 16–4). We will discuss only the major federal agencies.

Comptroller of the Currency

The Office of the Comptroller of the Currency is the oldest federal regulatory agency. The office was established by the National Bank Act of 1863. It is housed in the Treasury Department. The comptroller is appointed for a five-year term by the president of the United States, subject to confirmation by the U.S. Senate.

Contrary to the name, the comptroller does not control currency. The name is a legacy of U.S. history. When the office was established in 1863, currency was the major form of money, and the National Bank Act made national bank notes the major form of currency. Thus, the comptroller was able to affect the amount of currency outstanding. But as we have seen, deposit banking developed rapidly shortly thereafter, and demand deposits replaced currency as the major form of money. Moreover, after the establishment of the Federal Reserve, Federal Reserve notes replaced national bank notes as the major form of currency.

Today, the comptroller has primary responsibility for chartering national banks, passing on applications for branch offices of national banks where permitted by state law, evaluating applications for bank mergers where the surviving bank is a national bank, providing advisory opinions to the responsible agency on other bank mergers and holding company acquisitions, declaring national banks insolvent, establishing and enforcing operating regulations for national banks, and examining national banks. The office is sometimes referred to as the Administrator of National Banks. It is financed by assessments on those banks. At year-end 1993, there were about 3,300 national banks. Although they account for only 30 percent of all commercial banks, they tend to be larger and hold 57 percent of total bank deposits.

FINANCIAL INSTITUTIONS AND THEIR FEDERAL REGULATORS

	Office of the Comptroller of the Currency	Federal Reserve System	Federal Deposit Insurance Corporation	National Credit Union Administration	Office of Thrift Supervision
Origin	1863 Currency Act	1913 Federal Reserve Act	1933 Banking Act	1934 Federal Credit Union Act	1989 Financial Institutions Reform, Recovery and Enforcement Act
Affiliation	Bureau of the Department of the Treasury	Independent agency within government, central bank of United States	Independent agency within government, insurer of bank and thrift deposits	Independent agency within government, regulator and insurer of credit unions	Bureau of the Department of the Treasury
Organization	Chief executive—Comptroller of the Currency; 6 district offices throughout country	Seven-member Board of Governors, appointed by the president; 12 autonomous Federal Reserve Banks overseen by Board	Five-member Board of Directors, including the Comptroller of the Currency, the director of the Office of Thrift Supervision, and three other presidential appointees; 12 regional offices	Three-member Board of Directors appointed by president; 6 regional offices	Chief executive—director; headquarters In Washington, D.C.; district offices.; throughout country
Funding	Congressional appropriations	Income from interest on government securities, loans to financial institutions, fees for services to financial institutions; profits to Department of Treasury (about 90% of revenues)	Assessments on insured banks and thrifts, earnings on investments	Assessments on insured credit unions, earnings on investments	Congressional appropriations
Examination Responsibilities	Federally chartered (national) banks	State-chartered banks members of Federal Reserve System, bank holding companies	Insured state-chartered banks not members of Federal Reserve System, insured state-chartered thrifts, insured state-licensed branches of foreign banks	Federally chartered credit unions, federally insured state-chartered credit unions	Federally chartered savings associations
Chartering Responsibilities	National banks	None	None	Federal credit unions	Federal savings associations

SOURCE: Federal Reserve Bank of Chicago, *On Reserve*, December 1989, pp. 2–3.

Federal Reserve System

The Federal Reserve System was established by the Federal Reserve Act of 1913 to, among other purposes, "establish a more effective supervision of banking in the United States." Its other major function is the formulation and execution of monetary policy. The prescription of this function, as well as of the organization and structure of the Fed, is postponed until Chapter 27. With respect to bank regulation, the Fed has primary responsibility for establishing and enforcing operating regulations for commercial banks that are members of the system.

All national banks are required to be members, and state banks may apply for membership. Because Fed reserve requirements were higher than those imposed by most states, few state banks joined the Fed, and an increasing number withdrew from membership after World War II. To prevent further membership erosion and improve Federal Reserve control of the money supply, DIDMCA (1980) extended Fed reserve requirements to nonmember banks and checkable deposits at thrift institutions. In return, all depository institutions were granted equal access to most Fed services, such as the discount window and check-clearing services. As a result, Federal Reserve membership lost much of its meaning. At year-end 1993, about 1,000 state-chartered banks and all 3,300 odd national banks were members of the Fed.

The Fed's regulatory responsibilities are similar to those of the comptroller, except that the Fed does not have the authority to charter new banks. To reduce the degree of overlapping with the comptroller, the Fed has primary supervisory responsibilities of state-chartered member banks. The Fed also has sole responsibility for approving bank holding company acquisitions and for determining which nonbank activities are close enough to banking to be permissible to holding company affiliates. Operating funds are obtained primarily from interest earned on its very large portfolio of Treasury securities.

Federal Deposit Insurance Corporation

The FDIC was established in 1934 to provide deposit insurance to commercial and savings banks primarily to prevent individual bank failures from spreading to other banks. In 1989, its powers were expanded to assume the operations of the Federal Savings and Loan Association (FSLIC) and provide deposit insurance for savings and loan associations through a new Savings Associations Insurance Fund (SAIF). FSLIC had previously been housed in the Federal Home Loan Bank Board. Deposit insurance for commercial and savings banks was reorganized as the Bank Insurance Fund (BIF) of the FDIC. For the first time, the Financial Institutions Reform, Recovery, and Enforcement Act (FIRREA) explicitly placed the full faith and credit of the federal government behind both funds up to the legal maximum account coverage, which had been raised through time from $2,500 to $100,000 per qualified account.

All national and Fed member commercial banks are required to have FDIC-BIF insurance. Nonmember state commercial banks as well as state savings banks may apply for insurance. At year-end 1992, effectively all domestic commercial and savings banks were so insured. However,

FIGURE

16–1

309

▼

REGULATION OF
THE FINANCIAL
SYSTEM

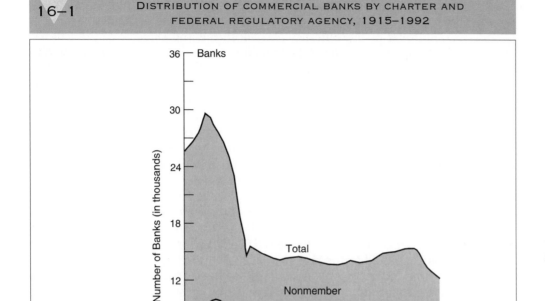

DISTRIBUTION OF COMMERCIAL BANKS BY CHARTER AND
FEDERAL REGULATORY AGENCY, 1915–1992

SOURCE: Board of Governors of the Federal Reserve System, 1987 *Historical Chart Book*. Updated from annual reports.

because the accounts that are not fully insured tend to be very large, only about 78 percent of the dollar amount of all bank deposits are federally insured. Likewise, effectively all savings and loan associations are insured by FDIC-SAIF. Because SLAs have few deposit accounts in excess of $100,000, almost all SLA deposits are fully insured. As noted, both banks and SLAs pay premiums for the insurance coverage, which are computed as a percentage of their total domestic deposits and are related to their risk exposure.

The FDIC's regulatory and supervisory responsibilities pertain to insured banks. To avoid duplication with the comptroller and the Fed, its primary concern is with state-chartered insured banks that are not members of the Federal Reserve System. (The distribution of commercial banks among the three bank regulatory agencies is shown in Figure 16–1.) The FDIC also has the responsibility for liquidating insolvent banks or disposing of their insured liabilities by some other means, such as sale to a solvent bank. Although it does not charter banks directly, the FDIC does affect chartering indirectly by considering the potential bank's application for deposit insurance. Because all federally chartered banks are required to be insured, many states require insurance before they will grant a state charter. Thus FDIC approval is effectively required to open a new bank.

The FDIC is an independent federal agency, managed by a five-person board of directors appointed by the president of the United States for six-year terms and subject to Senate confirmation. One of the members is the Comptroller of the Currency and another is the Director of the Office of Thrift Supervision. One of the remaining three members is appointed chairperson by the president for a five-year term.

Office of Thrift Supervision

The Office of Thrift Supervision (OTS) was established by the Financial Institutions Reform, Recovery, and Enforcement Act (FIRREA) in 1989 to replace the discredited Federal Home Loan Bank Board as the chief regulator/supervisor of savings and loan associations. It also charters federal associations, examines them, and declares then insolvent. The chief administrative officer is the Director of the OTS. The OTS is modeled after the Office of the Comptroller of the Currency. Thus, similar to the Comptroller, it is housed in the U.S. Department of the Treasury. The director is appointed by the president and confirmed by the Senate.

The Federal Home Loan Bank Board also operated 12 regional Federal Home Loan Banks, which were owned by the member savings and loan associations. Among other things, the regional banks raised funds through the sale of bonds and relent the proceeds to SLAs in the form of **advances.** Because the regional banks had emergency access to the U.S. Treasury, their bonds frequently sold at lower interest rates than those at which the associations could raise deposit funds, and the cost savings were passed through to the associations. The banks also provided check clearing and other services to member associations. FIRREA reorganized the regional banks under a new Federal Housing Finance Board directed by the five-person board appointed by the president for staggered seven-year terms, and permitted commercial banks to become members. The secretary of Housing and Urban Development is a permanent member of the board.

National Credit Union Administration

The National Credit Union Administration (NCUA) was established in 1970. Before then, responsibility for federally chartered credit unions was vested in the Farm Credit Administration in 1934, shifted to the FDIC, then transferred to the Department of Health, Education and Welfare. The National Credit Union Administration is governed by a three-person board appointed by the president and subject to Senate confirmation. The administration charters, regulates, and supervises federally chartered credit unions. Slightly less than half of all credit unions have federal charters.

In 1970, Congress established the National Credit Union Insurance Fund (NCUSIF) to provide deposit insurance to credit unions similar to that provided commercial banks and SLAs. All federally chartered credit unions must be insured. In 1992, about 97 percent of all credit unions, accounting for about 82 percent of total credit union assets, were insured by the fund. Almost all of the remainder are insured by state insurance agencies.

In 1978, Congress established the Central Liquidity Facility, housed in the NCUA, to provide liquidity to credit unions by making loans to them or by purchasing assets from them. The facility finances its activities by selling debt and also has a $500 million line of credit with the Treasury Department to meet emergency situations.

Bank Examination

All chartered financial intermediaries are subject to periodic, surprise, on-site examination by, at minimum, the chartering agency. We will discuss only commercial bank examinations. Examinations of other financial intermediaries are similar.

Bank examinations to evaluate safety and soundness are required by FDICIA to be at least annual for all but some small banks. Prudential examinations are primarily a management appraisal rather than a financial audit. The examination is intended to appraise the quality of bank management and directors, check regulatory compliance, evaluate financial condition, and identify potential problems while they are still minor and can be corrected quickly and at low cost. The examination verifies the quantity and evaluates the quality of a bank's assets and liabilities. Cash on hand and securities are audited to see whether all are accounted for. Spot checks are made of other asset documents, and the quality of the assets is appraised. Loans are classified in declining order as "good," "substandard," "doubtful," and "loss." Troublesome assets are flagged for special attention. The sufficiency of loan loss reserves is evaluated, particularly for loans classified as less than good. Bank operations are checked to verify that they are in compliance with bank statutes and regulations, including consumer protection and nondiscrimination provisions. The quality of internal record keeping and management controls is evaluated, as well as the adequacy of external audits. The net credit quality of the institution is determined. The adequacy of the bank's capital in relation to its riskiness and thereby its soundness is then evaluated. The evaluation of capital adequacy is the heart of the bank examination process.

A summary examination report is submitted to the bank. If the examination finds violations of law, poor operating procedures, insufficient loss reserves relative to the quality of loans, an insufficient amount of capital in relation to the bank's size or degree of risk, or other problems of serious concern, management is notified. Representatives of the examining agency meet with senior bank personnel and the bank's board of directors to discuss their concerns and offer recommendations. The progress of the bank in correcting the difficulties is carefully monitored, and additional examinations are scheduled. Most banks take corrective actions voluntarily. They prefer not to "get in bad" with the agency. Sooner or later, bank management knows it will want to get a favorable opinion from the agency on an application for a branch, merger, new activity, or so on. Regulators, like elephants, have long memories! For serious problems, the regulatory agencies require a written "memorandum of understanding" **(MOU)** or, if this is insufficient, they can serve "cease and desist" **(C and D)** orders on the bank. C and D orders require speedy compliance under penalty of law.

Although the three commercial bank regulatory agencies examine the banks under their jurisdictions somewhat differently, they have recently adopted a uniform supervisory rating system. The examiners focus on five

THE WALL STREET JOURNAL

SOURCE: From *The Wall Street Journal*; permission, Cartoon Features Syndicates..

performance dimensions: capital adequacy, asset quality, management, earnings, and liquidity. (This system is referred to as **CAMEL,** after the initial letters of the dimensions. The equivalent acronym for thrift institutions examined by the OTS is **MACRO,** which stands for management, asset quality, capital adequacy, risk management, and operational results.) Each dimension is rated on a scale from 1 to 5, where 1 is the highest rating and 5 indicates unsatisfactory performance. A composite rating is then determined for the bank overall. The interpretation of the composite rating is shown in Table 16–5.

In 1979, standardization was improved further by the establishment of the Federal Financial Institutions Examination Council (FFIEC), comprising representatives of the three commercial bank regulatory agencies as well as of the Office of Thrift Supervision and the National Credit Union Administration, to prescribe uniform principles, standards, and report forms for federal examination of all financial institutions. Since 1982, the council has prepared and published a quarterly Uniform Bank Performance Report (UBPR) for each insured commercial bank, which is designed to be an analytical tool for bank supervisory, examination, and management purposes. This report shows important balance sheet and income statement information for each commercial bank and compares it with the same information both for all banks and for a group of "peer" banks having similar characteristics in terms of size, branches and location.

All agencies monitor the operations of the institutions under their primary jurisdiction. The lower is an institution's rating, the more closely and frequently is it monitored. Institutions that are viewed as having inadequate capital or other problems are placed on a problem-bank list for clos-

TABLE	
16–5	UNIFORM COMPOSITE BANK EXAMINATION RATINGS

313

▼

REGULATION OF
THE FINANCIAL
SYSTEM

Composite 1

Banks in this group are sound institutions in almost every respect; any critical findings are basically of a minor nature and can be handled in a routine manner. Such banks are resistant to external economic and financial disturbances and capable of withstanding the vagaries of the business cycle more ably than banks with lower composite ratings.

Composite 2

Banks in this group are also fundamentally sound institutions but may reflect modest weaknesses correctable in the normal course of business. Such banks are stable and also able to withstand business fluctuations well; however, areas of weakness could develop into conditions of greater concern. To the extent that the minor adjustments are handled in the normal course of business, the supervisory response is limited.

Composite 3

Banks in this group exhibit a combination of weaknesses ranging from moderately severe to unsatisfactory. Such banks are only nominally resistant to the onset of adverse business conditions and could easily deteriorate if concerted action is not effective in correcting the areas of weakness. Consequently, such banks are vulnerable and require more than normal supervision. Overall strength and financial capacity, however, are still such as to make failure only a remote possibility.

Composite 4

Banks in this group have an immoderate volume of asset weaknesses, or a combination of other conditions that are less than satisfactory. Unless prompt action is taken to correct these conditions, they could reasonably develop into a situation that could impair future viability. A potential for failure is present but is not pronounced. Banks in this category require close supervisory attention and monitoring of financial condition.

Composite 5

This category is reserved for banks whose conditions are worse than those defined under Composite 4. The intensity and nature of weaknesses are such as to require urgent aid from the shareholders or other sources. Such banks require immediate corrective action and constant supervisory attention. The probability of failure is high for these banks.

SOURCE: George R. Juncker, "A New Supervisory System for Rating Banks," *Quarterly Review*, Federal Reserve Bank of New York, Summer 1978, p. 49.

er surveillance. At year-end 1992, 863 insured banks were listed by the FDIC as problem banks, falling into rating 4 or 5 of the uniform rating system. This was down from a record 1,575 at year-end 1987, when such banks accounted for more than 10 percent of all insured banks. Problem banks are divided into different categories, depending on the probability that financial assistance will be required. Experience indicates that about one-third of the banks classified as having serious problems fail. The banks on the list are not always the same. In 1992, 421 of that year's 863 problem banks were added to the list, while 648 banks on the 1991 list were removed, 114 by failure. Six banks that failed were not on the 1991 problem bank list.

In addition to the examinations, the bank regulatory agencies receive information about the banks from quarterly income statements and balance sheet reports, plus a number of special reports providing ongoing and current status data. The reports are monitored carefully to detect any dramatic changes in the financial position of a bank or deviations from average performance for comparable banks.

Regulators also examine depository institutions for compliance with consumer protection requirements specified in CRA, HMDA, and other acts. These compliance examinations are generally every 18 months, but can be more frequent for poor compliers and less frequent for good compliers.

SUMMARY

The financial system in the United States is highly regulated by the government for several reasons: (1) to provide safety in banks; (2) to protect against excessive economic concentration and unfair practices; (3) to conduct monetary policy and promote an efficient payments system. Regulation takes the form of restricting, among other things, the entry of new institutions, the types and amounts of earning assets the institutions may hold, the types of liabilities they may offer, interest rates that may be paid on deposits, the types of business activities in which bank holding companies may engage, consolidations among institutions, the number of branch offices they may have, and the minimum amount of reserves, liquidity, and capital with which they may operate.

Although regulation is imposed in the public interest, its effects may not always be in the public interest. To the extent that regulation reduces competition in the name of safety, it is likely also to reduce economic efficiency and protect the institutions more than the depositors. After years of increasing regulation, changes in the economic environment and technology in the late 1970s and early 1980s decreased the effectiveness of the regulations by encouraging endruns around them and provided the inducement for deregulation. The Depository Institutions Deregulation and Monetary Control Act (DIDMCA) of 1980 and the Garn-St Germain Act of 1982 represented the first major federal legislative steps in a reversal toward less government regulation and more by the private marketplace. In response to the costly bank and SLA failures of the 1980s, the Federal Deposit Insurance Corporation Improvement Act of 1991 increased prudential regulations to protect the insurance fund and the taxpayer.

The major commercial bank regulatory and supervisory agencies are the Office of the Comptroller of the Currency for national banks; the Federal Reserve System for monetary policy and state-chartered member banks; the Federal Deposit Insurance Agency for all insured banks and, in particular, insured state-chartered banks that are not members of the Fed; and the individual state banking agencies. The Office of Thrift Supervision regulates savings and loan associations, and the National Credit Union Administration regulates credit unions. All regulatory agencies periodically examine the operations of the institutions under their jurisdiction to evaluate their performance, safety, and compliance with laws and regulations.

Institutions that appear to be deficient in any of these areas are put on a list for closer surveillance and corrective actions as required by FDICIA.

QUESTIONS

1. Evaluate the arguments and evidence on whether commercial banks are "natural monopolies." Contrast the arguments relating to banks with the arguments for two other industries often considered natural monopolies.
2. Other than as a natural monopoly, why do we regulate commercial banks? "In the absence of government regulation, banks are not subject to any regulation whatsoever." Discuss this statement.
3. Identify two specific current regulations that are justified by each of the reasons listed in your answer to question 2. Discuss their benefits and their costs. Why do many banks claim that they are overregulated?
4. What is meant by "bank structure"? Discuss the importance of bank structure in affecting bank performance. How can public policy affect bank structure?
5. "Bank regulation is in the public interest. Thus, the more regulation, the better the public interest is served." "Deregulation has made bank failures more likely." Explain why you agree or disagree with each of these two statements.
6. What is the purpose of bank examinations by the regulatory agencies? How might this function have changed in the past 50 years? How can bank examinations prevent bank failures? How does a prudential examination differ from a compliance examination?
7. Identify the major regulators of commercial banks and thrift institutions. Which regulator is the primary regulator for which institutions? Why do we have multiple bank regulators in the United States? Why is there substantial overlapping of authority? Give two examples of such overlapping.
8. Discuss three restrictions on depository institution operations that have been liberalized or removed in recent years by federal legislation. Why were they removed? Do you agree with the changes? Why? What do you think is the most important remaining restriction that should be removed? Why?
9. FDICIA imposes new capital criteria on banks and thrifts. Why did it establish five capital zones rather than implicitly only three—adequately capitalized, undercapitalized, and solvent—as previously. What happens as a bank sinks through these zones? Why are such actions mandated? What happens if these actions do not work? How does the lowest capital zone differ in FDICIA from the lowest rating used before FDICIA?

REFERENCES

Benston, George, *Bank Examination*. New York: Institute of Finance, New York University, May 1973.

Benston, George, et al., *Perspectives on Safe and Sound Banking*. Cambridge, Mass.: MIT Press, 1986.

Comptroller General of the United States, *Federal Supervision of State and National Banks*, Washington, D.C., 1977.

Federal Financial Institutions Examination Council, *Annual Report*. Washington, D.C., annual.

Federal Reserve Bank of Atlanta, "Warning Lights for Bank Soundness: Commercial Bank Surveillance," *Economic Review*, November 1983.

Federal Reserve Bank of Chicago, *Leveling the Playing Field: Review of the DIDMCA of*

1980 and the Garn-St Germain Act of 1982. Chicago, 1983.

Federal Reserve Board Staff, *Appendices to Statement by Paul A. Volcker before Subcommittee on Commerce, Consumer and Monetary Affairs of Committee on Government Operations*, U.S. House of Representatives. Washington, D.C., June 1986.

Gilbert, R. Alton, "Requiem for Regulation Q: What It Did and Why It Passed Away," *Review*, Federal Reserve Bank of St. Louis, February 1986, pp. 22–37.

Golembe, Carter H., and David S. Holland, *Federal Regulation of Banking, 1986–87*. Washington, D.C.: Golembe Associates, 1986.

Havrilesky, Thomas M., Robert Schweitzer, and John T. Boorman, *Dynamics of Banking*. Arlington Heights, Ill.: Harlan Davidson, 1985.

Holder, Christopher L., "Competitive Considerations in Bank Mergers and Acquisitions," *Economic Review*, Federal Reserve Bank of Atlanta, January/February 1993, pp. 23–36.

Junker, George R., "A New Supervisory System for Rating Banks," *Quarterly Review*, Federal Reserve Bank of New York, Summer 1978, pp. 47–50.

Kaufman, George G., ed., *Reforming Financial Institutions and Markets in the United States*. Boston: Kluwer, 1994.

Lash, Nicholas A., *Banking Laws and Regulations*. Englewood Cliffs, N.J.: Prentice Hall, 1987.

Mahoney, Patrick I., et al., "Responses to Deregulation," *Staff Study No. 151*. Washington, D.C.: Board of Governors of the Federal Reserve System, January 1987.

McCarthy, F. Ward, Jr., "The Evolution of the Bank Regulatory Structure: A Reappraisal," *Economic Review*, Federal Reserve Bank of Richmond, March/April 1984, pp. 3–21.

Robertson, Ross M., *The Comptroller and Bank Supervision*. Washington, D.C.: Office of the Comptroller of the Currency, 1968.

Saunders, Anthony, and Lawrence J. White, eds., *Technology and the Regulation of Financial Markets*. Lexington, Mass.: Lexington Books, 1986.

Savage, Donald T., "Interstate Banking Developments," *Federal Reserve Bulletin*, February 1987, pp. 79–92.

Scott, Kenneth E., "The Patchwork Quilt: State and Federal Roles in Bank Regulation," *Stanford Law Review*, April 1980, pp. 687–742.

Spong, Kenneth, *Banking Regulation: Its Purposes, Implementation, and Effects*, 3rd ed. Kansas City: Federal Reserve Bank of Kansas City, 1990.

U.S. Congress, Senate Committee on Banking, Housing, and Urban Affairs, *Compendium of Major Issues in Bank Regulation* (Committee Print), 94th Cong., 1st sess., May 1975.

U.S. Congress, Senate Subcommittee on Financial Institutions of the Committee on Banking, Housing, and Urban Affairs, *Compendium of Issues Relating to Branching by Financial Institutions* (Committee Print), 94th Cong., 2nd sess., October 1976.

Wells, F. Jean, and Pauline H. Smale, *Commercial Banks, Thrifts, and Credit Unions: The Federal Regulatory Structure*, Washington, D.C.: Congressional Research Service, Library of Congress, August 1993.

Winningham, Scott, and Donald G. Hagan, "Regulation Q: An Historical Perspective," *Economic Review*, Federal Reserve Bank of Kansas City, April 1980, pp. 3–17.

Managing Interest Rate Risk

As discussed in Chapter 3, depository institutions assume a number of risks in performing their intermediation function between SSUs and DSUs. Among the most important of these is interest rate risk. This risk arises when the interest rate sensitivity (coupon change intervals or the times to the earliest date of repricing) on the secondary claims that an institution sells to depositors differs from that of the primary claims it purchases from loan customers. Thus, the two sides of its balance sheet are not equally sensitive to interest rate changes and unexpected change in interest rates will change the institution's income and capital. Starting in the mid-1990s, interest rate risk will supplement credit risk as a component of the risk-based capital standards that banks and thrift institutions are required to maintain. But the measurement of interest rate risk is complex. This chapter discusses a relatively new technique, called **duration gap analysis**, for assessing a depository institution's exposure to interest rate risk.

An institution may engage in interest rate intermediation to meet the needs of its loan and deposit customers. When it does, unexpected changes in interest rates will affect the two sides of its balance sheet differently. (As discussed in Chapter 7, information about expected changes in interest rates is already included in the yield curve and should not change market values.) For example, if the coupon change interval of the institution's asset side is longer than that of the liability side, unexpected increases in market rates of interest will both (1) increase the revenues from its assets more slowly than they increase the expenses on its deposits, so that the institution's income is reduced, and (2) decrease the market value of the assets more than that of the deposits so that its net worth (the difference between assets and liabilities) decreases. Conversely, unexpected decreases in interest rates will increase both the income and net worth of an institution with such a balance sheet structure. If the institution changed the composition of its assets and deposits so that the coupon change interval of its assets were shorter than that of its liabilities, increases in interest rates would increase both its income, as revenues would increase faster than its interest rate expenses, and its net worth, as the value of its assets would decline less than the value of its deposits. The more volatile are interest rates, the greater is the risk in interest rate intermediation.

A depository institution does, of course, charge its loan and deposit customers for providing interest rate intermediation services and assuming the associated interest rate risk. This fee is included in the difference between the loan rate charged and the deposit rate paid. If priced correctly, the income from interest rate intermediation should compensate the institution for any losses it may realize from unfavorable interest rate changes. Of course, the charges are imposed before the changes in interest rates occur and the losses are known only after the changes in interest rates occur. Thus, an institution may, in retrospect, charge too much, too little, or just enough.

Because interest rate intermediation is an important service that depository institutions provide, the management of interest rate risk is one of the more important functions of bank management. The institution can change the degree of risk exposure it assumes by changing the composition and thereby the interest rate mismatch of its balance sheet. In the 1970s and early 1980s, many depository institutions, in particular thrift institutions that made long-term fixed-rate mortgages financed by short-term deposits, badly underestimated the increase in interest rates and suffered severe losses by charging too little for the degree of risk they assumed. Some even failed.

Although the problems of interest rate risk are well known, accurate measurement of an institution's risk exposure is not easy. And, without such measurements, reliable management of this risk is not possible. After developing duration as a measure of interest rate risk, this chapter discusses alternative strategies for managing or controlling interest rate risk and the pros and cons of duration analysis relative to more commonly used procedures.

A Hypothetical Bank Balance Sheet

The implications of interest rate changes for a depository institution may be analyzed most easily with a simplified bank balance sheet.[1] The same principles apply to more complex and realistic situations. Here, we describe an institution that has only three types of assets:

1. Cash reserves (C),
2. 2¹/₂-year business loans, amortized monthly (BL), and
3. 30-year mortgage loans, amortized monthly (ML).

It also has only two types of deposits (P):

1. 1-year single-payment certificates of deposit (CD1), and
2. 5-year single-payment certificates of deposit (CD5).

These deposits make no coupon payments and may not be redeemed before maturity. The remaining item on the right side of the balance sheet is net worth or capital (K). The balance sheet shown in Table 17–1 describes an institution with total footings of $1,000. All accounts are valued at market. Cash is $100; business loans are $400; mortgage loans are $500; 1-year CDs are $600; and 5-year CDs are $300. To balance the balance sheet, the bank's capital is valued at $100, and its capital-to-asset ratio is 10 percent.

For the sake of simplicity, interest rates are assumed to be the same for all terms to maturity for all securities and deposits of a given default risk class. That is, the yield curve is assumed to be flat. All interest rates are compounded monthly. All payments are to be made on schedule; there are no assumed defaults, prepayments, or early deposit withdrawals. The inter-

---

[1] The examples in this chapter and other simulations of interest rate risk management can be demonstrated more thoroughly on a PC with a computer program developed by and available from the author directly (see Bierwag and Kaufman 1988 in references).

TABLE

17–1

INITIAL CONDITIONS

BALANCE SHEET

Assets (A)	Dollars[a]	D (yrs.)[b]	Liabilities	Dollars[a]	D(yrs.)
Cash	100	0	CD (1 yr.)	600	1.0
BL (2½ yr.)	400	1.25	CD (5 yr.)	300	5.0
ML (30 yr.)	500	7.0	Net worth (K)	100	
Total	1,000	4.0	Total	1,000	

DEPOSIT DURATION

$$D_P = \frac{600(1) \times 300(5)}{900} = 2.33 \text{ years}$$

PROJECTED ANNUAL INCOME STATEMENT FOR YEAR

	Interest Yield (percent)	Market Value ÷ Total Assets	Interest ÷ Total Assets (percent)
Revenues			
Cash	0	0.10	0
Loans	13	0.90	11.7 11.7
Expenses			
Deposits	11	0.90	9.9 9.9
Net income (*NI*)			1.8

SUMMARY ACCOUNTS

$$K = \$100$$
$$K/A = 10\%$$
$$NI/A = 1.8\%$$

[a]All accounts are valued at market (present value).
[b]Duration values are approximated for ease of use.

est rate on all business loans is initially assumed to be 13 percent and on all deposits, 11 percent. Cash reserves are assumed not to bear interest initially. The projected net income of the bank for the year may be computed by multiplying the market value of each account by the appropriate interest yield. This is shown in the summary income statement in Table 17–1. The bank's initial net income (*NI*) projected for the year is 1.8 percent on assets (*A*), which are $1,000, or $18. This income will be realized if interest rates do not change during the year.

If interest rates change, they are assumed to change by equal percentage points (basis points) for all securities. After a change in interest rates, all bank accounts are marked to their new market (present) values—the price for which the accounts could be sold, if necessary. The balance sheet is designed so that the accounts are not equally sensitive to interest rate changes.

Now let interest rates increase 200 basis points across the board. This reduces the market value of all accounts. The new balance sheet and

TABLE
17-2

ASSUME INTEREST RATE INCREASE OF 200 BASIS POINTS

BALANCE SHEET

	Dollars[a]			Dollars[a]	
Assets	Actual	Estimated[b]	Liabilities	Actual	Estimated[b]
Cash	100	100	CD (1 yr.)	588	588
BL (2½ yr.)	390	390	CD (5 yr.)	272	270
ML (30 yr.)	437	430	Net worth (K)	67	62
Total	927	920	Total	927	920

PROJECTED ANNUAL INCOME STATEMENT FOR YEAR

	Interest Yield (percent)	Market Value 4 Total Assets	Interest 4 Total Assets (percent)	
Revenues				
Cash	2	0.11	0.2	
Loans	15	0.89	13.4	13.6
Expenses				
Deposits	13	0.93	12.1	12.1
Net Income				1.5

SUMMARY ACCOUNTS

$$K = \$67$$
$$K/A = 7.1\%$$
$$NI/A = 1.5\%$$

[a]All accounts are valued at market (present value).
[b]By equation 17-2 or 17-4.

income statements are shown in Table 17–2. It is obvious that the accounts do not change by equal amounts. Longer-term accounts decline more in value than shorter-term accounts. For example, the market value of the business loan declines from $400 to about $390, while that of the longer-term mortgage loan declines from $500 to $437. Total assets decline to $927. Likewise, the market value of the 1-year CD declines from $600 to $588, the 5-year CD from $300 to $272, and total deposits from $900 to $860. The value of capital, which is the difference between the value of total assets and deposits, declines 33 percent, from $100 to only $67. Capital as a ratio of total assets declines from 10 percent to 7.1 percent. The increase in interest rates also decreases the projected annual net income by increasing the aggregate dollar interest cost of deposits more than the revenues from assets, even though cash is now assumed to yield a small interest return. This occurs because deposits now account for proportionately more of total footings than before, so that interest expense has increased in relative importance. The projected net income at the new interest rate level declines to 1.5 percent of total assets from 1.8 percent. It is evident that the increase in interest rates has harmed the institution.

An equal decrease in interest rates of 200 basis points would have opposite effects. As can be seen from Table 17–3, the values of all bank

TABLE
17–3 ASSUME INTEREST RATE DECREASE OF 200 BASIS POINTS

BALANCE SHEET					
	Dollars[a]			Dollars[a]	
Assets	Actual	Estimated[b]	Liabilities	Actual	Estimated[b]
Cash	100	100	CD (1 yr.)	612	612
BL (2½ yr.)	410	410	CD (5 yr.)	331	330
ML (30 yr.)	580	570	Net worth (K)	147	138
Total	1,090	1,080	Total	1,090	1,080

PROJECTED ANNUAL INCOME STATEMENT FOR YEAR			
	Interest Yield (percent)	Market Value 4 Total Assets	Interest 4 Total Assets (percent)
Revenues			
Cash	−2	0.09	−0.2
Loans	11	0.91	10.0 9.8
Expenses			
Deposits	9	0.87	7.8 7.8
Net Income			2.0

SUMMARY ACCOUNTS
K = $147
K/A = 13.5%
NI/A = 2.0%

[a]All accounts are valued at market (present value).
[b]By equation 17–2 or 17–4.

accounts except cash increase. Capital increases to $147, the capital-to-asset ratio to 13.5 percent, and net projected income to 2.0 percent of total assets. The institution is better off than it was before.

Duration Analysis

Changes in a bank's financial position due to interest rate changes can be analyzed with the help of *duration analysis*. As discussed in Appendix 5A, duration is a measure of the average life of a security. It has a number of interesting and important mathematical properties, particularly for measuring interest rate risk. In its simplest form, duration is computed by (1) multiplying the length of time to each scheduled payment of a default- and option-free security by the present value of that payment; (2) summing over all payments; and (3) dividing by the total present value (or price) of the security. In equation for

$$D = \frac{\sum_{t=1}^{m} t \cdot PVF_t}{\sum_{t=1}^{m} PVF_t} \qquad (17\text{–}1)$$

where: D = duration

t = length of time (number of months, years, etc.) to the date of payment

PVF_t = present value of the payment (F) made at (t), or $F_t/(1 + i)^t$

$\sum\limits_{t=1}^{m}$ = summation from the first to the last payment (m)

(Although notationally simple, equation 17–1 is difficult to use in practice. A more complex-looking but easier-to-use equation is presented in Appendix 5B.)

This measure of duration is referred to as Macaulay's duration, and is named after Frederick Macaulay, who first computed it in 1938 in his seminal study of the history of interest rates in the United States. Duration is a single number that is measured in units of time, for example, months or years. For securities that make only one payment at maturity, duration is equal to term to maturity; for all other securities, it is shorter than term to maturity. Duration effectively converts a coupon security into its zero-coupon (single-payment) equivalent. (Other properties of duration are discussed in Appendix 5A.) Most important for our purposes, at first approximation, duration relates changes in interest rates and percentage changes in bond prices linearly as follows:

$$\frac{\Delta S}{S} = - D \frac{\Delta i}{(1 + i)} \approx - D\Delta i \qquad (17\text{–}2)$$

where: S = price of a security

i = yield to maturity

Δ = change from previous value

Equation 17–2 is more accurate, the smaller are the interest rate changes.

Now we can readily see how the value of each account changed when interest rates increased. All we need do is compute the duration for each account by equation 17–1 and multiply by the 200 basis point increase in interest rates. The duration of each account computed by equation 17–1 is shown in Table 17–1. (For ease of following the analysis, the durations shown are approximate.) As was noted earlier, the duration of securities that generate periodic flows before maturity is less than their term to maturity. Thus, the initial duration of the 30-year monthly amortized mortgage yielding 13 percent is only seven years (7.14 years precisely). The durations of the single-payment CDs are equal to their maturities. The longer are the durations, the proportionately greater will be the price change predicted by equation 17–2 for a given change in interest rates.

The change in the market value of each account predicted by equation 17–2 is shown in Table 17–4. For example, if interest rates increased by 200 basis points, the market value of the one-year zero-coupon CD, whose duration also is one year, declines by 1 × 0.02, or 2 percent. At the same time, the duration of the 30-year maturity, seven-year-duration mortgage loan declines by 7 × 0.02, or 14 percent, which is seven times as much. Changes in interest rates of 200 basis points are large relative to the capabilities of equation 17–2. As a result, the predictions are only rough approximations and will be less accurate with longer durations. In actuality, changes of 200 basis points are unlikely to occur all at one time. In addition, the predic-

| TABLE 17–4 | USING DURATIONS TO MEASURE RISK EXPOSURE FOR INDIVIDUAL ACCOUNTS | | | | |

$$\Delta S \simeq - DS\Delta i$$

| | | | | ΔS | |
Account	D	S	Δi	Estimated	Actual
BL	1.25 yrs.	$ 400	0.02	$-10	$-10
ML	7.00	500	0.02	-70	-63
1-yr. CD	1.00	600	0.02	-12	-12
5-yr. CD	5.00	300	0.02	-30	-28
TA	4.00	1,000	0.02	-80	-73

tions are distorted because rounded rather than precise values of duration are used. The estimated changes in values will approach the actual changes in value as the assumed interest rate changes decrease in size and the precise values of duration are used.

Nevertheless, for all the balance sheet accounts, except capital, the computed dollar changes are reasonably close to the actual changes between Tables 17–1 and 17–2. For example, the actual decline in the market value of the 5-year CD is $28 (from $300 to $272) and the estimated decline is $30 (from $300 to $270). To the extent that changes in prices reflect the degree of interest rate risk assumed, duration represents a good first-approximation measure of risk because it is proportional to the price change. For example, the percentage price of the five-year CD will change five times as much for a given change in interest rates as the price of the one-year CD. This makes it five times as risky, which is reflected in a duration five times as great.

With a small adjustment, durations can also be used to measure the interest rate mismatch on the two sides of the balance sheet and therefore the interest rate exposure of the institution as a whole. As is evident from analyzing the changes in the balance sheet and income statement above, the increase in interest rates did not affect every account equally. It is thus necessary to specify precisely what account is most important to the institution. The selection of such a *target* account whose value is to be controlled and of a particular degree of risk exposure in that account is the function of the bank's senior management. For example, management may wish to control the bank's capital (net worth) account, capital-to-asset ratio, net income, or interest rate spread between loans and deposits. Because maximizing shareholders' wealth is generally considered to be the ultimate objective of business firms, in this chapter we will assume that bank management focuses only on the bank's capital account.

While the interest rate sensitivity or risk of individual accounts is related to the duration of the account, the interest rate risk of a target account for a bank is related to the difference, or *gap*, between the average duration of the assets of the institution and the average duration of the deposits. The **duration gap (DGAP)** measure for capital is

$$DGAP_K = (D_A - wD_P) \qquad (17\text{–}3)$$

where: A = total assets
P = total deposits
D_A = average duration of assets
D_P = average duration of deposits
w = a weight defined as $P/(P + K) = P/A$

The durations for total assets and total deposits are computed by weighting the durations for the individual securities by their relative market values.[2] For target accounts other than capital, the *DGAP* equation would differ somewhat from 17–3 but be of the same general format.

The value of the *DGAP* for capital for our hypothetical bank may be computed from the information provided in Table 17–1 as follows:

$$DGAP_K = (D_A - wD_P) = 4.0 - 0.9(2.3) = 1.9 \text{ years}$$

The equation for *DGAP* and therefore also its value will be different for other target accounts. The impact of interest rate changes on the bank's capital account may be estimated by substituting *DGAP* for *D* in equation 17–2. Thus

$$\frac{\Delta K}{A} \approx - DGAP_K\Delta i \qquad (17\text{–}4)$$

or

$$\Delta K \approx -DGAP_K A \Delta i$$

For our bank

$$\Delta K \approx -1.9(\$1,000)\Delta i = -\$1,900 \; \Delta i$$

If interest rates increased by 200 basis points, or 0.02, the bank's capital would be estimated to decline by $38, from $100 to $62. This is close to the actual decline of $33 shown in Table 17–2. As with *D*, the smaller change in interest rates, the more accurate is equation 17–4.

An institution can change its degree of interest rate exposure to any extent it wishes by changing the composition of its balance sheet in such a way as to obtain the desired duration gap for its target account. The greater the duration gap, the greater is the institution's risk exposure for a particular target account, and conversely, the smaller the gap, the smaller its exposure. Moreover, the relationship is linear. For example, if in the previous example the duration gap for capital were twice as large, say, 3.8 years, then the value of capital would decline twice as much, or $76, for a 200-basis-point increase in interest rates.

An institution can also reduce its risk exposure to zero by setting its target account duration gap to zero. As can be seen from equation 17–4, for capital this implies setting $D_A = wD_P$. The bank is then said to be **immunized**, and unexpected interest rate changes will not change the market value of the target account. The decision on how much interest rate risk

---

[2] If the securities do not all trade at the same interest rate, the appropriate weights are the prices at which the securities would trade at the duration date of the portfolio if interest rate did not change.

exposure to assume and the strategy of how to achieve this are referred to as interest rate risk management and are discussed in the next section. Interest rate risk management is the responsibility of the bank's **asset and liability management committee (ALCO)**.

Before introducing risk management, it is useful to emphasize a number of points:

1. If the institution does not specify a target account, it cannot measure its interest rate risk exposure accurately.
2. Interest rate exposure is directly related to the absolute size of the duration gap for the target account; the greater the gap, the greater the risk exposure.
3. Interest rate exposure can be removed or immunized in a target account by setting the appropriate duration gap to zero.
4. Although the bank balance sheet used in our examples includes only securities traded on the cash market, duration analysis applies equally well to off-balance-sheet accounts such as securities traded on the futures and options markets. (These are discussed in Chapter 22.) The durations of these securities can be computed and included in the appropriate duration gap measure to measure the overall interest rate exposure of the bank.

Managing Interest Rate Risk

Like any private business firm, a depository institution attempts to maximize its profits. However, profit maximization presumes a desired level of risk exposure. Required return and risk are directly related. The greater the risk of loss assumed, the greater must be the return required to compensate for the higher likelihood of loss; and, conversely, the smaller the risk exposure assumed, the smaller the return can be. The desired risk-return trade-off for an institution is determined by its senior management and may be expected to differ from bank to bank. Interest rate risk is only one type of risk a bank assumes. It generally also assumes credit quality risk, liquidity risk, foreign exchange rate risk, and so on. Thus, managing interest rate risk is part of overall risk management.

To manage any risk accurately, a bank must predict the probability of possible outcomes of undertaking the risky activity. To manage interest rate risk, it is necessary to predict, at minimum, the direction of interest rate changes. The effect of an interest rate change will differ depending on whether the bank has a positive duration gap (the duration of assets is greater than the duration of the appropriately weighted deposits) or a negative gap in the relevant target account. As may be seen in equation 17–4, a decline in interest rates will increase the value of a bank's capital account if its capital duration gap is positive and decrease the value if its gap is negative. An increase in interest rates will have the opposite effect, decreasing the value of the capital account if the duration gap is positive and increasing it if it is negative. The greater the gap, the greater will be the gain or loss. Thus, the bank must determine both the direction and the size of its gap on the basis of its predicted interest rates. Correct predictions will increase capital and incorrect predictions will decrease capital. A bank may pursue two interest rate risk strategies: an immunization strategy or an active strategy.

Immunization. For whatever reasons, a depository institution may wish to maintain a constant value of its target account regardless of changes in interest rates and immunize its interest rate risk exposure. This is a complete interest rate hedging strategy. It should be noted that banks generate profits if they assume interest rate risk and manage it correctly, and that this income may be reduced or lost altogether when it decides to immunize. The bank must then rely on income from managing other risks, such as credit risk or foreign exchange risk. On the other hand, immunizing the bank also decreases its chances of suffering losses if interest rate risk is mismanaged. As discussed earlier, to immunize fully the bank needs to set the appropriate duration gap to zero. Because the strategy matches the interest rate sensitivity of the two sides of the balance sheet, it is referred to as **duration matching**.

Assume that the bank chooses capital as its target account and wishes to immunize its current market value. In our example in Table 17–1, the initial value of capital is $100. To immunize capital, the bank needs to restructure its balance sheet so that its $DGAP_K = 0$. From equation 17–3

$$D_A - wD_P = 0 \qquad (17\text{--}5)$$

Initially $D_A = 4$ years, $D_P = 2.3$ years, and $P/A = 0.9$. This yields a duration gap of $4 - 0.9(2.3) = 1.9$ years. The bank is not immunized. It can reduce the gap to zero either by shortening the duration of its assets by 1.9 years from 4 years to 2.1 years to match the weighted duration of its deposits or by lengthening the duration of its deposits to 4.5 years, so that $0.9(4.5) = 4$ years and matches the duration of its assets. We will assume that the bank prefers to lengthen its deposits on the cash market. It can do so by reducing the dollar volume of its one-year CDs from $600 to about $110 and increasing the volume of its five-year CDs from $300 to $790. As is shown in Table 17–5, this increases the duration of the deposits from 2.3 to 4.5 years and satisfies equation 17–5.

Now let interest rates increase 200 basis points as before. (For the sake of ease in tracing the mechanics, the examples are created using the approximate duration values rather than the precise duration values. Thus, the bank will not be perfectly immunized in actuality.) Except for capital, which remains at $100, the market value of each account declines. Because the composition of assets was not changed, the decline in their market value is the same as in Table 17–2. The composition of the deposits was changed, however, by increasing the proportion of longer-term deposits. As a result, the decline in the value of total deposits is greater than before. Capital remains unchanged because the decline in the market value of the deposits is now exactly equal to the decline in the market value of the assets. But income is not immunized and increases to 2 percent.

Because, as can be seen from equation 17–1, the change in interest rates changes the duration of all securities, equation 17–5 is no longer satisfied after the change in rates and the bank is no longer immunized. $DGAP_K$ declines from 0 to -0.5. Thus, the bank must restructure its balance sheet so that it is immunized against the next interest rate change. Moreover, as may also be seen from equation 17–1, the durations of securities decline, even if there is no interest rate change, just from the passage of time. To remain immunized, the bank must continually restructure its

TABLE 17–5	IMMUNIZE K AND SET $DGAP = 0$ YEARS WHEN $D_A = 4$ AND $D_P = 2.3$

Strategy: Set $D_A - (P/A)D_P = 0$
Currently: $D_A = 4$, $(P/A)D_P = 2.1$ years
$$DGAP_K = 4 - 2.1 = 1.9 \text{ years}$$

Can satisfy by:

1. Shortening TA to $D_A = 2.1$ years
2. Lengthening P to $D_P = 4.5$ years $[(P/A)D_P = 9(4.5) = 4.0]$

Can act on:

1. Spot market
2. Futures market

Assume *lengthening P* on *cash* market by changing mix:

Assets	Dollars[a]	D (yrs.)[b]	Liabilities	Dollars[a]	D (yrs.)[b]
Cash	100	0	CD (1 yr.)	110	1
BL ($2^1/_2$ yr.)	400	1.25	CD (5 yr.)	790	5
ML (30 yr.)	500	7.0	Net worth	100	
Total	1,000	4.0	Total	1,000	

DURATIONS

$$D_P = \frac{110\,(1) \times 790\,(5)}{900} = 4.5 \text{ years}$$

$$DGAP_K = 4 = 0.9(4.5) = 4 - 4 = 0 \text{ years}$$

IF INTEREST RATES INCREASE BY 200 BASIS POINTS:

	Dollars[a]			Dollars[a]	
Assets	Actual	Estimated[c]	Liabilities	Actual	Estimated[c]
Cash	100	100	CD (1 yr.)	108	108
BL ($2^1/_2$ yr.)	388	390	CD (5 yr.)	715	712
ML (30 yr.)	435	430	Net worth	100	100
Total	923	920	Total	923	920

Projected Annual Income Statement

	Interest Yield (percent)	Market Value ÷ Total Assets	Interest ÷ Total Assets (percent)	
Revenues				
Cash	2	0.11	0.2	
Loans	15	0.89	13.4	13.6
Expenses				
Deposits	13	0.89	11.6	11.6
Net income				2.0

[a]All accounts are valued at market (present value).
[b]Approximate
[c]By equation 17–2 or 17–4.

balance sheet to offset this *duration drift*. For larger institutions that buy or sell Fed funds daily in the normal course of their business, this is not a problem. It is more of a problem for smaller institutions.

It is important to note that even though an immunized institution as a whole does not assume interest rate risk, the durations of the individual securities on the bank's balance sheets need not be matched, and the institution may still engage in interest rate intermediation in individual accounts. In our example, the bank has 30-year mortgages financed in part by one-year deposits. The reduction in overall risk exposure is achieved through diversification across individual securities with different durations. A portfolio of a given average duration can be structured from an almost infinite number of individual securities with different durations.

Active Management. Many banks do not wish to eliminate interest rate risk altogether, but prefer to manage it. They can do so by deliberately mismatching the durations of the two sides of their balance sheets. Such a strategy is referred to as an **active** interest rate strategy.

Because accepting risk exposure assumes that the bank will suffer losses if interest rates change in the wrong direction, the decision to accept such exposure presupposes that the bank is willing to predict interest rates and believes it can do so successfully. (If it is not, it is better off to immunize and to assume no risk for the same expected return.) Indeed, to determine the desired direction and magnitude of the duration gap, it is necessary, at minimum, for the bank to forecast the direction in which interest rates will change. If rates are predicted to increase, the DGAP should be negative, so that the average duration of the assets is shorter than that of the weighted deposits. This would make the bank behave as if it were a net liability, whose value declines as interest rates rise. The bank will benefit from an interest rate rise. On the other hand, if rates are predicted to decline, the institution would be better off if the DGAP were positive. Then the bank behaves like a net asset, whose value increases as interest rates decline.

Assume that the bank predicts that interest rates will decline. It will structure its portfolio to obtain a positive duration gap. The precise value of the gap it chooses depends on its risk-return preferences. The larger the gap, the higher the potential return but the higher also the risk of loss. The decision as to the precise risk-return matrix to assume and thus the value of the gap to achieve is generally made by the bank's top management in consultation with the asset and liability management committee. Assume that the bank is willing to accept risk in the value of its capital consistent with a positive duration gap of one year so that

$$D_A - wD_P = 1 \tag{17-6}$$

As can be seen from Table 17–6, it can achieve this value in our example either by shortening the duration of its assets from 4 to 3.1 years or by lengthening the duration of its deposits from 2.3 to 3.4 years. (We again use the approximate durations.) From equation 17–4, for every 100-basis-points decline in interest rates, the bank's capital value will rise by $10 (100 basis points × 1 year $DGAP$ = 1% of total assets). However, because the bank is

TABLE	
17–6	SET *DGAP* FOR $K = 1$ YEAR WHEN $D_A = 4$ AND $D_P = 2.3$

Strategy: Set $D_A - (P/A)D_P = 1$ year

Currently: $D_A = 4$, $(P/A)D_P = 2.1$ years

$DGAP_K = 1.9$ years

Can satisfy by:

1. Shortening *TA* to $D_A = 3.1$ years
2. Lengthening *P* to $D_P = 3.4$ years $[(P/A)D_P = 3.4$ and $0.9 D_P = 3]$

Can act on:

1. Spot market
2. Futures market

Assume *lengthening P* on *cash* market by changing mix:

Assets	Dollars[a]	D (yrs.)[b]	Liabilities	Dollars[a]	D (yrs.)b
Cash	100	0	CD (1 yr.)	360	1
BL (2½ yr.)	400	1.25	CD (5 yr.)	540	5
ML (30 yr.)	500	7.0	Net worth	100	
Total	1,000	4.0	Total	1,000	

DURATIONS

$$D_P = \frac{360\,(1) \times 540\,(5)}{900} = 3.4 \text{ years}$$

$$DGAP_K = 4 - 0.9(3.4) = 4 - 3 = 1 \text{ year}$$

IF INTEREST RATES INCREASE BY **200** BASIS POINTS:

	Dollars[a]			Dollars[a]	
Assets	Actual	Estimated[c]	Liabilities	Actual	Estimated[c]
Cash	100	100	CD (1 yr.)	353	353
BL (2½ yr.)	390	390	CD (5 yr.)	489	486
ML (30 yr.)	437	430	Net worth	85	80
Total	927	920	Total	927	920

Projected Annual Income Statement

	Interest Yield (percent)	Market Value ÷ Total Assets	Interest ÷ Total Assets (percent)	
Revenues				
Cash	2	0.11	0.2	
Loans	15	0.89	13.4	13.6
Expenses				
Deposits	13	0.91	11.6	11.6
Net income				1.8

[a]All accounts are valued at market (present value).

[b]Approximate

[c]By equation 17–2 or 17–4.

TABLE

17–7

CHANGES IN ACCOUNTS FOR ALTERNATIVE DURATION GAPS TARGETING CAPITAL ACCOUNT WHEN INTEREST RATES INCREASE BY 200 BASIS POINTS

$DGAP_K$ (years)	Estimated Changes[a]		
	K	K/A	NI/A
1.9	$-38	-3.1%	-0.2%
1.0	-20	-1.2	0.0
0.5	-10	0.2	+0.1
0	0	+0.8	+0.2

[a]Using equation 17–4 for K, and similar equations for K/A and NI/A.

highly leveraged with a capital-to-asset ratio of 10 percent, this implies an increase in net worth of 10 times as much, or 10 percent.[3]

In Table 17–6, the bank lengthens the duration of its deposits on the cash market to 3.4 years by reducing the dollar amount of one-year CDs from $500 to about $360 and increasing the dollar amount of five-year CDs from $300 to $540. Now, contrary to the bank's expectations, let interest rates increase by 200 basis points rather than decrease. The bank is worse off. Assets again decline to $927 as before, but the market value of capital declines by $15 to $85, or 15 percent. The bank has lost its bet on interest rates and has paid the price. As was noted earlier, to win with an active policy, the bank must both predict interest rates and be right. Also as before, the interest rate increase changes the durations of the accounts and thus the value of the duration gap. To maintain a gap of one year, or any other target amount, the bank must restructure its balance sheet accordingly.

As discussed earlier, different banks may prefer different target accounts. The *DGAP* equations for different target accounts differ. Thus, a particular value of *DGAP* for one target account, say, 0 for capital, will not be the same as that for other target accounts, say, the capital-to-asset ratio or net income. This is demonstrated in Table 17–7 in which changes in the values of these accounts are shown for alternative values of $DGAP_K$ in response to a 200-basis-point increase in interest rates. Note that when $DGAP_K = 0$, the change in interest rates will not change the value of the bank's capital account, but will change the values of both its capital-to-asset ratio and net income. Note also that these changes may not always be in the same direction. Thus, it is important for the bank to select its target account carefully.

---

[3] When $\Delta K/K$ rather than $\Delta K/A$ is the target account, the interest rate sensitivity equation becomes:

$$\frac{\Delta K}{K} = -DGAP_K \left(\frac{A}{K} \right)(\Delta i)$$

The term $DGAP_K(A/K)$ is sometimes referred to as the duration of capital. Because A/K tends to be large, the duration of capital could be large even for small duration gaps.

Practical Problems with Applying Duration Gap Analysis

Although theoretically appealing, duration gap analysis has some practical problems that have limited its use to date. Duration gap analysis imposes strenuous data demands. It requires complete data on the expected cash flow of each account (security) or, at minimum, each homogeneous group of accounts on the bank's balance sheet, including not only information on contract (coupon) interest rate and maturity but also on when a variable-rate account (security) can be repriced (its contract rate changed) before maturity and any constraints on the amount by which it can be repriced. In addition, it requires data on prepayment and other call provisions; due-on-sale, early deposit withdrawal, and other put provisions; and any other options that are included and the conditions for when and how they may be exercised.[4] This information requires full access to the bank's account origination files. The less information on individual accounts that is available, the less reliable will be the computed duration gaps.

Variable-rate contracts and contracts that contain option provisions have effective maturities that are shorter than their nominal maturities. For example, if a 10-year variable-rate bond can be repriced at $100 at the beginning of every year, its price behavior resembles that of a one-year bond rather than a 10-year bond. Likewise, a 10-year bond with a call option permitting the borrower to buy back (prepay) the bond at no more than a maximum price will behave like a shorter-term bond when interest rates decrease, so that the probabilities of a call are sufficiently high. The computation of durations for cash flows that involve either repricing or the exercise of option provisions requires forecasts of interest rates to determine when the cash flow pattern will be changed and by how much. As was demonstrated in Chapter 7, the best forecasts to use for this purpose are the rate forecasts that are implicit in the term structure of interest rates at the time.

A number of types of bank deposit accounts, such as demand deposits, savings, NOWs, and MMDAs, do not have specific maturity dates. Depositors may redeem these accounts at any time at par value. The accounts effectively have a put option exercisable by the holder on the bank at any time. What are the durations of such deposit accounts?

On the one hand, it may be argued that these are one-day accounts. If market rates of interest increase and the bank does not raise its deposit rates accordingly, either in cash or in services, the depositor may withdraw the funds. This is particularly likely in a world of deregulation in which institutions across the street are able and likely to compete by offering market rates. The deposits may be effectively viewed as variable-rate accounts that are repriced at par every day. Unlike our earlier examples, their market value will never decline below par value as interest rates rise. Their durations would be one day.

---

[4] Because the expected stream of cash payments is also determined by delayed or missed payments due to default, assumptions about the timing of default should also be included in the computation of duration.

On the other hand, in the old world of regulation and deposit rate ceilings and to some extent even today, all deposits are not equally interest sensitive. If a bank's deposit rates lag behind increases in market rates, all deposits will not leave the bank immediately. "Core" deposits will remain for some time and flow out only slowly. It may be possible to assign accurate probabilities to the timing of the net outflows, depending on the difference between the market and deposit rates. From this it is possible to compute the effective decline in the market value of the remaining deposit accounts by assuming them to be equivalent to certificates of deposit with maturity dates equal to the predicted outflow dates. Their durations would also be equivalent and thus would be longer than one day. If interest rates increase, it is then possible to value these deposits at less than their par value.

However, the correct duration to assign these deposits cannot be determined arbitrarily by the desirability of the assumptions. Rather, the actual price behavior of the accounts when interest rates change must be used. Otherwise, the interest rate sensitivity of the bank is misgauged. The correct duration awaits additional research. (To the extent that deposit rate deregulation has increased the availability of deposit accounts without specific maturity dates, such as MMDAs, it may have made it more difficult for banks to structure small positive or negative duration gaps and to decrease their interest rate exposure.)

As noted earlier, because the value of a security's duration is determined by the interest rate, changes in interest rates change its duration and may force a restructuring of the portfolio in order to maintain the desired duration gap. Moreover, even if interest rates do not change, periodic restructuring is necessary in a dynamic framework because the durations of coupon securities do not decline (or age) at the same rate as does time. They generally decline more slowly, although at times duration can increase as time passes. Thus, the durations of the two sides of the balance sheet are unlikely to change equally over time, and continual updating or restructuring of the balance sheet is required. In effect, every day is a new day for managing the gap. Restructuring, of course, is costly. But most depository institutions operate, at least in the Feds-funds market, daily, so that restructuring at the margin should not be much of a burden.

We have made a number of simplifying assumptions in the analysis. One of these was to assume that the yield curve is flat and that when interest rates change, they all change by the same amount. This is highly unlikely. But the duration measure define in equation 17–1 is dependent on it. Different and more complex assumptions about the shape of the yield curve and changes in interest rates yield different and more complex measures of duration. If the actual process that governs interest rate changes, referred to as the *stochastic process*, were known, the correct duration formula could be used. But this process is not known with certainty. The theory, however, assumes that the correct duration measure is used. Moreover, securities of different default-risk classes may be subject to different stochastic processes. Thus, the bank is likely to use an incorrect measure of duration, and this introduces a source of error.

In addition, the duration measures developed to date apply strictly only to securities that are free of the risk of default. Yet, many bank accounts, particularly on the asset side, have default risk. This introduces additional inaccuracies into the computation of the correct duration measure. Lastly, the analysis abstracts from transactions costs and taxes. Introduction of these complicates the analysis further.

Advantages of Duration Gap Analysis

Despite these disadvantages, duration gap analysis has substantial advantages over alternative techniques for measuring interest rate risk exposure accurately. The most widely used alternative measure technique involves classifying all asset and liability accounts by their terms to maturity or to first permissible repricing, whichever comes first. The accounts are grouped in a number of maturity-period "buckets": for example, 1 day, 1 to 3 months, 3 to 12 months, 1 to 5 years, and so on. Net balances, or **maturity gaps** in dollars, are computed for each bucket. The larger are the net balances in the shorter maturity buckets, the more income sensitive and less price sensitive the institution.

Duration analysis considers the timing of coupon and other intermediate cash flows as well as the timing of the final payment at maturity. This is particularly important for mortgages and other amortized loans for which the intermediate flows are significantly larger than the final payment. Yet the maturity bucket approach classifies such accounts only by the date of the final payment or of the first permissible repricing.

For practical purposes, the number of maturity categories must be limited. What should be the maturity cutoffs for each bucket? Should the shortest-term bucket include accounts maturing or eligible for repricing in 1–30 days, 1–60 days, or 1–90 days? The same question applies to the other bucket categories. Changing the limits of the buckets can give a different picture of a bank's interest rate sensitivity. Table 17–8, which groups the accounts in the balance sheets shown in Tables 17–1 and 17–5 in a number of alternative ways, illustrates this problem.

The more limited the number, the wider the category. But the wider the category, the less accurate is the informational content of each category. For example, a category of 6 to 12 months is frequently used on the Federal Reserve call report. This category would encompass 182-day securities as well as 364-day securities. If these were zero-coupon single-payment instruments so that the terms to their maturities were equal to their durations, equation 17–2 indicates that the price sensitivity of the 364-day security to a given interest rate change is exactly twice that of the shorter security. Thus, if the 182-day security were the only security on the asset side of the balance sheet and the 364-day security the only security on the liability side, the maturity bucket would indicate no gap and no interest sensitivity. Yet the bank's liability side would in fact be twice as price sensitive as the asset side. In reality, there will be larger numbers of securities with different maturities in all the buckets so that the average maturity in each is unlikely to be at one extreme of the maturity range. Nevertheless, accuracy is sacrificed.

As noted, the maturity gap analysis yields a number of gap values equal to the number of maturity categories used. These individual gaps cannot be simply summed. The overall degree of risk exposure is thus dif-

TABLE 17–8

ALTERNATIVE MATURITY GAP MEASURES (DOLLARS)

A. Balance sheet from Table 17–1

Maturity Bucket	Assets	Liabilities	Gap	Assets	Liabilities	Gap	Assets	Liabilities	Gap	Assets	Liabilities	Gap
0–3 mos.	100	0	+100									
3–6 mos.	0	0	0	100	600	−500	100	600	−500			
6–12 mos.	0	600	−600							500	600	−100
1–2½ yrs.	400	0	+400	400	0	+400						
2½–5 yrs.	0	300	−300	0	300	−300	400	300	+100			
5–10 yrs.	0	0	0	0	0	0				500	400	+100
> 10 yrs	500	100	+400	500	100	+400	500	100	+400			
Total	1,000	1,000	0	1,000	1,000	0	1,000	1,000	0	1,000	1,000	0

B. Balance sheet from Table 17–5

Maturity Bucket	Assets	Liabilities	Gap	Assets	Liabilities	Gap	Assets	Liabilities	Gap	Assets	Liabilities	Gap
0–3 mos.	100	0	+100									
3–6 mos.	0	0	0	100	110	−10	100	110	−10			
6–12 mos.	0	110	−110							500	110	+390
1–2½ yrs.	400	0	+400	400	0	+400						
2½–5 yrs.	0	790	−790	0	790	−790	400	790	−390			
5–10 yrs.	0	0	0	0	0	0				500	890	−390
> 10 yrs	500	100	+400	500	100	+400	500	100	+400			
Total	1,000	1,000	0	1,000	1,000	0	1,000	1,000	0	1,000	1,000	0

ficult to summarize. It is not readily observable, for example, from any of the alternative maturity gap groupings in Table 17–8, part B, that the balance sheet is one that immunizes the dollar value of capital. The gap in any one bucket, even the shortest one, is unlikely to be representative of the overall interest rate sensitivity of the institution. The impact of the value of the gap in the shortest-term bucket can be more than offset by the value of the gap in the next shortest bucket, so that the longest gaps can be in the same direction as the shortest gaps. More important, measured this way, the risk exposure is difficult to manage. A different strategy is required for each bucket. This involves considerable management and transactions costs. It is reasonable to assume that some of the bucket gaps are internally offsetting and that the use of external transactions to achieve the same objective is inefficient. In contrast, duration analysis yields a single number and only a single gap to manage. Any internal cancelling is already accounted for.

Maturity bucket gaps must generally be managed with securities in the same maturity category; for example, a gap in the 6–12 month bucket can be changed most easily by buying or selling other securities in this maturity range. This constrains management. The larger the number of buckets used to gain greater accuracy, the more constrained is management. On the other hand, duration gaps can be managed with a very wide range of maturities. For example, as was seen earlier, the duration of a 30-year amortized fixed-rate mortgage when interest rates are 13 percent is nearly equivalent to that of a seven-year zero-coupon bond. Moreover, even durations on individual securities on the two sides of the balance sheet need not be equal or different by the size of the gap as long as the average durations of all securities are. The desired target gap value may be achieved by diversifying amount individual securities of different but offsetting durations. Thus, bank management has an almost unlimited choice of maturities and can continue to provide a range of interest rate intermediation services to its customers within a given degree of net interest rate risk exposure to the institution. Even if the bank wishes to immunize itself, it may still engage in a wide range of interest rate intermediation for individual securities; it does not have to match cash flows in each maturity bucket. That is, a bank can simultaneously engage in macro immunization and micro interest rate intermediation and continue to accommodate its customers, who have a range of maturity preferences, with an equally wide range of products.

Maturity gap analysis provides the user with information on the changes in a bank's income if interest rates change on its assets and liabilities with terms to maturity shorter than the particular maturity gap considered. This period is referred to as the **gapping period** and is frequently chosen to be one year. But changes in interest rates change the market value of all bank's asset and liability items regardless of their terms to maturity. The changes in the values of items with maturities longer than the gapping period represent capital gains or losses. To be accurate, these gains and losses should be included in the bank's income. Thus, maturity gap analysis shows only part of the effect of a change in interest rates on a bank's income, and may be misleading.

Last and perhaps most important, the strenuous data demands made by duration analysis are not any more severe than those that alternative systems, including maturity gap analysis, would impose if they were to be equally accurate. All measuring techniques must forecast interest rates to know when repricing will occur and options will be exercised. The relative simplicity claimed for some alternative systems cannot be obtained by sweeping such problems under the rug. Only a complete and thorough cost-benefit analysis can differentiate among the alternative techniques. Simplicity and reduced cost are likely to be achieved only at the cost of reduced accuracy.

In sum, although duration-based models require further refinement, they appear the most promising tool for accurate asset and liability management for depository institutions. As bank accounts become more computerized, the use of duration analysis to manage interest rate risk exposure may be expected to increase rapidly.

SUMMARY

Interest rate intermediation may cause problems for depository institutions when interest rates are volatile. If the interest sensitivities of the two sides of an institution's balance sheet are not equal, it is exposed to interest rate risk. Changes in interest rates will affect the two sides differently and change the institution's income and net worth. If the institution is not careful and rates change the wrong way, the institution will experience losses and may even fail. Thus, banks need to manage their interest rate risk exposure. This is referred to as asset and liability management.

In order to manage interest rate risk correctly, it is first necessary to measure it accurately. The recently developed technique of duration analysis can be readily applied to this problem. Duration gap is both a relatively accurate measure of an institution's interest rate risk exposure and, because it is a single number, a simple concept to manage. But its application is complex, and the data required are costly. However, most of these complexities and costs also apply to alternative measures of interest rate risk, if they are to be equally accurate.

QUESTIONS

1. Compute the duration of a 10-year, 10 percent coupon bond when its market rate of interest is 6 percent. (For the sake of simplicity, assume, if you wish, that coupon payments are made annually and interest is compounded annually. You may also wish to review Appendices 5A and 5B.) What happens to its duration as the interest rate first increases to 10 percent and then declines to 4 percent? What would be the duration of a 10-year zero-coupon bond under each of these scenarios?

2. In what two major ways do unexpected changes in interest rates impinge on depository institutions? What are the

differences between the effects of expected and unexpected interest rate changes?

3. Why is duration gap a better measure than maturity gap of both the income- and price-interest sensitivity of asset and liability accounts? Define duration both mathematically and intuitively. Why is duration shorter than the maturity for all securities but zero-coupon bonds?

4. Why must a bank manager specify a target account before determining the institution's duration gap? What target account would you choose? Why?

5. What is meant by an *immunization* and

by an *active* strategy? When would an institution pick one over the other? What two conditions are necessary for an institution to be willing to pursue an active strategy? What could go wrong? What are the consequences?

6. "In light of the experiences of recent years, depository institutions should immunize." Do you agree or disagree? Support your answer.

7. How has the introduction of more complex securities containing call, put, and convertibility options made it more difficult for institutions to measure and manage interest rate risk? "The increasing use of these options makes it easier to use maturity gaps than duration gaps." Do you agree or disagree? Why?

8. Assume the following bank balance sheet:

Assets	$	Maturity
Cash	100	0 yr.
Loans	500	3
Securities	400	10
Total	1,000	

Liabilities	$	Maturity
CDs (zero-coupon)	300	1 yr.
CDs (zero-coupon)	600	4
Net worth	100	
Total	1,000	

Interest on the loans and securities is paid and compounded either annually or semiannually. Assume also that loan and security rates are 10 percent and deposit rates are 8 percent.

Compute the DGAP for net worth and the duration of net worth. Is the bank subject to interest rate risk? If market interest rates increase by 200 basis points, what happens to the institution's net worth? What happens if they decrease by 200 basis points? How would this institution do if inflation suddenly accelerated? How would you change the institution's deposit structure if you wanted to immunize net worth? Why would you want to?

REFERENCES

Bierwag, G.O., *Duration Analysis: Managing Interest Rate Risk.* Cambridge, Mass.: Ballinger Press, 1987.

Bierwag, G.O., Charles J. Corrado, and George G. Kaufman, "Computing Durations for Portfolios," *Journal of Portfolio Management*, Fall 1990, pp. 51–55.

Bierwag, G.O., and George Kaufman, *Bank Interest Rate Risk Management Tutorial—D Game 2.0.* (A tutorial computer program for IBM PCs.) Chicago: Center for Financial Studies, Loyola University of Chicago, 1988. (Available to faculty members from author.)

Bierwag, G.O., and George Kaufman, "Duration Gaps for Financial Institutions," *Financial Analysts Journal*, March/April 1985.

Bierwag, G.O., George Kaufman, and Alden Toevs, "Duration: Its Development and Use in Bond Portfolio Management," *Financial Analysts Journal*, July/August 1983.

Hawawini, Gabriel A., ed., *Bond Duration and Immunization.* New York: Garland, 1982.

Houpt, James V., and James A. Embersit, "A Method for Evaluating Interest Rate Risk at U.S. Commercial Banks,"

Federal Reserve Bulletin, August 1991, pp. 625–37.

Kaufman, George G., "Integrating Asset/ Liability Management to Finance Mortgage Portfolios," *Solving the Mortgage Menu Problem: Conference Proceedings*. Federal Home Loan Bank of San Francisco, December 1984.

Kaufman, George G., "Measuring and Managing Interest Rate Risk: A Primer," *Economic Perspectives*, Federal Reserve Bank of Chicago, January/ February 1984, pp. 16–29.

Kaufman, George G., G.O. Bierwag, and Alden Toevs, eds., *Innovations in Bond Portfolio Management: Duration Analysis and Immunization*. Greenwich, Conn.: JAI Press, 1983.

Williams, Bill, *Asset/Liability Measurement Techniques*. Rolling Meadows, Ill.: Bank Administration Institute, 1987.

Deposit Insurance

Until the early 1980s, federal deposit insurance had been widely credited with ending the history of periodic cumulative bank failures and financial crises in this country.[1] By guaranteeing most depositors that they will receive the full amount of their insured deposits whether or not a depository institution fails, government deposit insurance provides a safety net that effectively insulates or quarantines healthy banks from failing banks. Insured depositors no longer feel it necessary to run to their bank to withdraw their funds at the first indication that their bank or some other bank may be experiencing financial difficulties. Moreover, as was discussed in Chapter 11, even if they do, they will run to other, perceived safe banks rather than to currency that will be held outside the banking system as a whole. This effectively prevents both a loss of reserves from the banking system with its resulting multiple contraction in deposits and money (discussed in Chapter 15) and a potential spillover of the trouble at the one bank to other banks.

Although federal deposit insurance has been successful in eliminating a currency run on the banking system as a whole (good effects), it has its undesirable side (bad effects). The insurance increased the incentives both for excessive risk taking by individual depository institutions and for delay by regulators in reorganizing institutions as soon as they become economically insolvent. The first effect represents a *moral hazard problem*, discussed later in this chapter, in which insured parties who do not bear the full cost of any potential losses assume greater risk than otherwise. The second effect represents a *principal-agent* (or *agency*) *problem*, in which the bank regulatory agencies, who in effect serve as the delegated agents for the principals of the FDIC—the other banks and taxpaying public as the backstop—, are not operating in the principals' best interests to minimize their losses. By guaranteeing many depositors the par value of their deposits regardless of the financial condition of their institutions, deposit insurance has reduced the discipline to remain healthy that depositors exert on uninsured institutions to protect their funds. Because bankers know that depositors are not looking over their shoulders as much as they were before deposit insurance, they consciously or unconsciously have increased their risk exposure in two ways.

One, when deposit insurance was implemented in 1933, banks reduced their capital-to-asset ratio substantially to record low levels. This can be seen from Figure 11–2. In recent years, the banks' and thrifts' capital ratios have also been substantially below those of their noninsured competitors, such as finance and insurance companies. The capital-asset

---

[1] The United States was the second country to adopt federal government bank deposit insurance, after Czechoslovakia in 1924.

TABLE 18–1	CAPITAL-ASSET RATIOS FOR VARIOUS FINANCIAL INDUSTRIES, 1989[a]	
		Percent
50 largest commercial banks		5.0
Large national bank holding companies		6.3
Large savings and loan associations		5.1
Diversified insurance companies		10.9
Life insurance companies		12.4
Short-term business credit companies		13.3
Personal credit companies		13.8
Securities dealers		19.7
Property/casualty insurance companies		22.3

SOURCE: George G. Kaufman, "Capital in Banking: Past, Present, and Future," *Journal of Financial Services Research*, April 1992, pp. 385–402. Reprinted with permission.

[a]Book Values

ratios of banks, thrifts, and other financial firms in 1989 are shown in Table 18–1. In effect, the insured institutions have substituted the capital of the FDIC (and because the FDIC is supported by the full faith and credit of the federal government, also that of the taxpayer) for the capital of private shareholders. Thus, they are in poorer shape to absorb losses through their own resources. Indeed, to protect insured depositors against loss, the taxpayers did have to supply some $200 billion of additional capital to absorb the large losses that were generated in savings and loan associations in the 1980s.

Two, insured institutions increased their portfolio risk. They extended loans to less-creditworthy borrowers and entered new and riskier areas, such as commercial real estate. They also extended the maturities of their assets—for example, longer-term fixed-rate mortgages—but did not correspondingly extend the maturities of their liabilities; thus they assumed greater interest rate risk. Before deposit insurance, many depositors would not have deposited their funds, or would have withdrawn funds they already had deposited, at a bank with a low capital ratio or high portfolio risk profile (or would have demanded correspondingly high interest rates). As a result, the bank likely would have been hesitant to pursue a high-risk strategy.

By guaranteeing the par value of deposits regardless of the financial condition of a bank, deposit insurance also permits regulators to keep insolvent and near-insolvent institutions open and operating. Without insurance, depositors would run and withdraw their funds from such institutions, forcing their closure. As is discussed later in this chapter, regulators may practice such capital forbearance for a number of reasons, including fear of contagion to other banks, temporary reductions in credit availability to the local community, interruptions in the payments system, and adverse publicity from announcing a bank failure for an agency charged with promoting bank safety. Evidence suggests that keeping these banks in operation encourages them to "gamble for resurrection" as they have little of their own capital funds to lose and much to gain, such as keeping ownership of the bank. At least one-half of these bets are likely to be lost with big losses, increasing the losses borne by the FDIC and potentially the tax-payers.

From its inception in 1933 through the late 1970s, the good (conta-gion-deterrent) effects of deposit insurance outweighed the bad (high risk) effects. But the increase in the volatility and magnitude of prices, interest rates, and macroeconomic shocks over the next years increased the strength and visibility of the bad aspects by driving large numbers of insured depository institutions, particularly SLAs, into insolvency. As a result, reforming deposit insurance received serious public policy attention for the first time since its adoption in the Banking Act of 1933. Indeed, because these failings of deposit insurance were generally known at the time of its adoption, deposit insurance was enacted only after a long and hard political battle. Deposit insurance had been tried unsuccessfully on numerous occasions at the state level, and some 150 proposals for federal insurance had been introduced in Congress since the end of the Civil War before its eventual enactment.

Finally in 1991, Congress enacted major reforms in deposit insurance in the FDIC Improvement Act (FDICIA) that reduced the incentives both for banks to take excessive risk (reduce moral hazard) and for regulators to delay taking corrective actions (increase their agency responsibilities). The act maintains deposit insurance but attempts to make it effectively redun-dant by requiring regulators to act promptly to discourage institutions from performing poorly and reorganizing those who do not respond before their capital is fully depleted. If the regulators are successful, losses will accrue primarily to shareholders and only minimally, if at all, to uninsured depos-itors and the FDIC. This chapter examines the major problems with deposit insurance before FDICIA, some proposed solutions, and the solutions incorporated in FDICIA.[2] The major deposit insurance reform provisions were shown in Table 11–2.

Determination of Premiums

Insurance companies generally assess a premium for their insurance con-tracts to cover potential losses when payouts are required. The dollar pre-miums charged are the product of two components: the premium base and the premium rate. For deposit insurance, the definition of both compo-nents has been controversial. The current premium base is an insured insti-tution's total domestic deposits. Until FDICIA, the premium rate was a flat percentage. FDICIA changed the rate structure to one that is scaled to the riskiness of the institution. This section discusses the arguments for and against different definitions of the appropriate premium base and premium rate structure.

Insurance premiums have been increased sharply in recent years. In 1992, the premium rate was 23 basis points, or 23 cents per 100 dollars. Before the SLA crisis, insurance premiums for all institutions were only 8.33 basis points, and rebates were frequently made. The premiums were raised first on SLAs to help replenish FSLIC's reserves in the mid-1980s, then on

[2] Problems with government insurance programs are not limited to banks and thrifts, but extend to other activities, such as pension funds and mortgage loans. See articles by Peter Abken and George Kaufman (1987) listed in references.

SLAs again and banks for the first time in 1989 to help defray the large costs of SLA failures, and on the banks again in mid-1991 to replenish the Federal Deposit Insurance Corporation's reserves.

Premiums collected are held as reserves by the FDIC and are invested in Treasury securities. Together with the investment earnings, they represent the first line of protection against losses from the failure of insured institutions. Despite the premium increases, they were not nearly sufficient to cover the combined losses of failed banks and SLAs, and taxpayers' funds were required. In 1989, FIRREA formalized in law the full-faith and credit guarantee of the federal government behind deposit insurance. Although such a guarantee was previously widely believed by the public to exist, it had never been enacted by Congress.

In evaluating the size of the insurance fund, it is important to note that potential losses to the fund (1) are equal only to the difference between the amount of insured deposits and the market (sale) value of the failed bank's assets, not to the amount of the insured deposits, and (2) are generally smaller the more quickly the failed bank is declared insolvent after its net worth reaches zero so that no further losses occur that are charged against the insurance fund rather than against the bank's own capital. That is, the FDIC's losses depend on its *closure rule*.

Total versus Insured Deposits

Although premiums are currently charged on a bank's total domestic deposits, the legal (de jure) insurance applies only to the first $100,000 of each account. (In practice, a private depositor at an insured bank is eligible for insurance up to a maximum of $100,000 on accounts in his or her own name and a maximum of $100,000 on each of all accounts in joint names with other parties.) Larger banks tend to have larger-deposit accounts, with balances that exceed the insured maximums. Thus, larger banks tend to have a smaller proportion of insured deposits to total deposits than smaller banks do. If insurance premiums are based on total domestic deposits but less than the total amount of deposits is insured, large banks will pay a disproportionate share of the costs of the insurance. If large banks are not proportionately riskier than small banks, they in effect subsidize the insurance coverage of small banks.

On the other hand, premiums are not charged on deposits at overseas branches, which are more important for larger banks than for smaller banks. About half of the total deposits of some large money-center banks are at their overseas offices. In contrast, such deposits are insignificant at almost all small and medium-sized banks. While not legally insured, the FDIC had in practice (de facto) guaranteed these deposits as well as all other larger deposits at large banks as part of a policy referred to as *too-large-to-fail*, or TLTF. For example, this occurred in the insolvency of the Continental Illinois National Bank in 1984 and continued through the insolvency of the major Texas banks in the late 1980s, the Bank of New England in 1991, and many relatively smaller banks. To the extent that the FDIC continues this practice, the largest banks may be paying proportionately lower premiums than the other banks. On net, then, it is difficult to evaluate the equity of basing insurance premiums solely on a bank's total domestic deposits.

Flat versus Risk-Related Premiums

Private insurance companies typically scale their premiums to the probability or risk of the occurrence that gives rise to the financial loss. The higher the probability or risk, the higher is the premium for a given loss value. The premiums represent the actuarial fair value of the expected loss. Banks face default (credit quality) risk, interest rate risk, foreign currency risk, operations risk, and fraud risk. Most likely, not all commercial banks are equally risky. As we discussed in Chapters 10 and 11, the higher the ratio of its earning assets to total assets, demand deposits to total deposits, and total deposits to capital, the riskier a bank tends to be. Within these categories, loans are riskier, on average, than investments; and Treasury demand deposits, which are highly volatile and more likely to be withdrawn, are riskier than household savings deposits. Riskiness may be measured even more finely. Consumer loans tend to be riskier than residential mortgage loans; municipal Baa bonds riskier than municipal Aaa bonds or Treasury securities. Banks also differ in their exposure to interest rate risk. In terms of interest rate risk, the greater the gap between the durations (price sensitivities) of the bank's assets and deposits, the riskier the bank.

It is quite common for decision units to modify their behavior when the consequences of their actions are insured against loss so that they do not bear the full cost of any loss. This is referred to as **moral hazard.** Thus, we may be less careful about installing fire alarms or extinguishing cigarettes after we buy fire insurance, or about locking our cars or installing burglar alarms after buying theft insurance.[3] Likewise, banks may become riskier when they obtain insurance on their losses as depositors reduce their interest in the financial condition of their banks. Higher premiums on riskier ventures may serve to curb a bank's appetite for risk taking. Under a flat proportional fee structure, risk taking must be curbed by regulation and supervision in order to control the deposit insurance agencies' losses. Moreover, when premiums are based only on deposit size, riskier banks pay no more for a given amount of insurance than less-risky banks do. If all banks are not equally risky, less risky banks in effect subsidize riskier banks. This violates the law of equity.

Equally important, some banks may also be tempted to become riskier than otherwise in order to get full value for their premium dollar. To the extent that deposits are fully insured or, in the case of deposits in excess of $100,000, perceived to be fully insured because of FDIC policy of paying off all deposits in large bank failures, banks can raise funds at interest rates that are not fully related to the riskiness of the bank. Yet, the riskier their asset portfolios, the greater the expected revenue. If neither their costs of funds nor their deposit insurance premiums increase, the banks can pocket all of the higher revenue from taking greater risks and earn a higher return.

Proponents of premiums based on risk conclude that such a system would make for a more equitable and less-risky banking system than one based on proportional deposit premiums and strict regulation. In addition,

---

[3] Another example of moral hazard that may be more familiar to you generally exists when you go out to lunch or dinner with a group and decide ahead of time that the bill will be divided evenly among you. It is likely that some in the crowd, and possibly even you, will order more than they would otherwise or if they had to bear the full cost of their purchase.

the proponents argue that controlling bank risk through regulation is incompatible with the goal of improving efficiency through increasing the role of market forces. (An extreme proposal for restructuring risk through regulation rather than through price is the narrow bank proposal, which is discussed later in this chapter.)

Proponents of a flat premium structure argue that although risk-scaled premiums sound fine in theory, in practice they are difficult to implement. Evaluating the riskiness of banks is more difficult than evaluating that of, say, automobile drivers. For many assets, loss experiences are limited to particular periods and are subject to change as general economic conditions change. The proponents point out that municipal bonds experienced almost no defaults in the post–World War II period until 1975 and were widely viewed as almost completely riskless. The New York City crisis, however, increased their risk almost overnight. Would banks, which had purchased municipal bonds in earlier years, suddenly be assessed much higher premiums? Likewise, how would one have evaluated loans to less developed countries, energy firms, and agriculture in the mid-1970s, when many were made and viewed as "sure bets"? Only hindsight indicates the true risk that those loans incurred. How does one quantify the riskiness of each of the many individual loans and investments a bank holds? How much riskier are demand deposits than an equal dollar amount of time or savings deposits? Can these differences be sufficiently quantified to provide a basis for meaningful premium differences?

But equally important, modern finance theory suggests that it is not the risk of individual accounts or securities that affects the risk of an institution, but the risk of all the institution's accounts and securities taken together. Two individual accounts can both be very risky but, if their projected cash flows are not perfectly correlated, their combined risk is smaller than for either account alone. In the extreme, two risky accounts whose cash flows are perfectly negatively correlated so that changes in one exactly offset changes in the other would be completely riskless if combined. Thus, the appropriate risk measure is the bank's portfolio as a whole, not individual accounts. Likewise, interest rate risk applies to the two sides of the balance sheet as a whole, not to individual accounts on one side only (see Chapter 17). Moreover, if the risk classifications are not determined objectively on the basis of market values, they are susceptible to manipulation by the regulators to allocate credit toward socially or politically favored borrowers. Last, how large need the premium differentials be to affect bank behavior significantly? If they were too large, banks might not be willing to assume any risk whatsoever.

Although an evaluation of bank riskiness is made periodically by bank examiners during the course of their examinations, the regulatory agencies believe that these evaluations are too qualitative to be the sole criterion for setting premiums. Moreover, if they were used, the release of this information alone would call the attention of the public to the differential quality of the banks and encourage interbank deposit shifts. On the other hand, knowledge that this information would be made public might cause bank management to be more cautious to avoid the possibility of runs and also exert discipline on the examiners to do a good job.

It may also be argued that the insurance fund's losses are not really related to the riskiness of a bank, but to the speed with which the insurance agency reorganizes the bank after its capital is wiped out. As discussed earlier, if the bank is closed precisely at the point its capital is exhausted and sold or merged, there will be no loss to the fund. Thus, insurance losses are tied to the fund's ability to monitor a bank's financial condition accurately and to reorganize it speedily. The premiums should be scaled to the complexity and cost of operating such a monitoring system for each bank. This cost may or may not be related to the bank's risk exposure.

FDICIA required the FDIC to change to a system of risk-based insurance premiums no later than January 1, 1994. The FDIC imposed such premiums January 1, 1993. The premiums are based on both the capital position of the bank and the degree of the FDIC's supervisory concern. A bank's capital position is classified as well-capitalized, adequately capitalized, or undercapitalized (including significantly undercapitalized and critically undercapitalized) as defined in FDICIA (see Table 16–2). Supervisory concern is also classified into three groupings: healthy, generally consistent with CAMEL ratings of 1 or 2; supervisory concern, generally consistent with a CAMEL rating of 3; and substantial supervisory concern, generally consistent with a CAMEL rating of 4 or 5. (CAMEL stands for the five performance dimensions examined: capital adequacy, asset quality, management, earnings, and liquidity. CAMEL ratings are defined in Chapter 16.) Thus, each bank is placed into one of nine cells, and a different premium is assigned to each. The premium structure in effect in January 1994 is shown in Table 18–2.

In total, there are five different rates. However, the spread between the premiums on the safest and riskiest banks ranged from a low of 23 to a high of 31, or only 8 basis points. Some critics argue that this difference is insufficient to seriously dissuade risk-prone banks from taking risky actions as it is significantly smaller than the spread the market imposes on CD rates issued by the two types of banks. Some also argue that the premium rate charged the soundest banks is much higher than the benefit they receive from the insurance and that this discourages them from raising funds in the form of deposits as opposed to borrowings, which are not subject to premiums. As a result, the FDIC will collect smaller premiums and will not

TABLE

18–2 FDIC INSURANCE PREMIUM STRUCTURE, JANUARY 1994

Capital Position[a]	Supervisory Group		
	Healthy	Supervisory Concern (basic points)	Substantial Supervisory Concern
Well capitalized	23	26	29
Adequately capitalized	26	29	30
Undercapitalized	29	30	31
	Average premiums		
For banks	23.8		
For thrifts	24.7		

[a] As established by FDICIA for purposes of prompt corrective action.

replenish its fund as quickly and the public will be inconvenienced by having deposits less available. In 1994, 85 percent of all banks and 75 percent of all thrifts qualified for the lowest 23 basis point premium.

Percent of Deposits Insured

Would deposit insurance be more efficient if all deposits were insured, regardless of account size? Such a system is commonly referred to as **100 percent deposit insurance.** Full coverage would reduce the incentive of all depositors, not only of small depositors, to withdraw their funds from financially troubled banks and possibly permit a bank to weather a storm more successfully. Large, basically uninsured deposits are frequently withdrawn when large banks are perceived to be encountering financial difficulties. For example, deposits declined from $3.7 billion at the large Franklin National Bank at year-end 1973, four months before the first public announcement of the bank's troubles, to $3.2 billion on the date of the announcement, to $2.1 billion six weeks later, and to only $1.4 billion on October 8, 1974, when the bank was declared insolvent and sold. Similarly, runs by uninsured depositors on the large Continental Illinois National Bank in Chicago in 1984 and the Bank of New England in Boston in 1991 led to the takeover of the banks by the FDIC.

In addition, 100 percent deposit insurance would reduce the need for any depositor to search out information about the financial condition of commercial banks. The costs of such a search may be greater than for many other types of firms, in part because much information about banks, such as examination reports, is confidential and not available to depositors.

Those who oppose full deposit insurance argue that uninsured large depositors serve to keep bank management honest. They will make efforts to obtain information about their banks and monitor them more carefully as they do now for bonds. In recent years, a number of firms have begun to analyze and rate depository institutions, similar to Moody's and Standard & Poor's ratings of bonds. The threat of deposit outflows reduces the risk management is willing to undertake and encourages it to operate a sounder bank. Private market discipline reinforces the pressure of the bank regulatory agencies. Uninsured depositors are a protection against greater government and bureaucratic involvement in the day-to-day operation of individual banks that might be necessary in the absence of this discipline.

In addition, until the practice was stopped by FDICIA, by paying higher rates for insured deposits, troubled banks could attract nearly as many funds as they wished without either a cost penalty or having the depositor looking over the bank's shoulder when it made its loans. After all, why should fully federally insured depositors care if the bank folds? Thus, they will make deposits up to the fully insured ceiling in banks that they might otherwise avoid as being too risky. A bank's ability to attract insured deposits was made easier and faster by the introduction of "brokered" accounts, 800 telephone numbers, and other systems that permitted depositors to search out the highest deposit rate throughout the country and transfer their funds in insured amounts anywhere quickly and cheaply. In the old days, a bank could attract deposits readily only from its immediate market area. Indeed, in some brokered account transactions, the fully insured depositor did not even find out the name of the receiving institution until after the deposit was made and did not care. By reducing the proportion of uninsured deposits to total deposits, any market discipline exerted on bank management by uninsured depositors, who may be hurt by a big enough hit, is reduced. Runs will occur not from bad banks to good banks, as in the preinsurance days, but from good banks to bad banks that pay higher interest rates on fully insured and government-guaranteed deposits!

In the mid-1980s, a number of savings and loan associations, particularly in California, Florida, and Texas, were purchased by unscrupulous owners who, by offering very high interest rates on insured deposits, expanded the institutions' deposits by as much as a hundredfold in a few months and then systematically looted the institution through massive high risk and fraudulent operations. In effect, the owners operated the associations as their own personal piggy banks. When they were finally caught, the remaining value of their institutions' assets was only a small fraction of the insured deposits. The losses were borne by FSLIC. The depositors, however, were not only fully insured against the losses but benefited from the high deposit rates they received. Indeed, a large percentage of the banks and thrifts that failed in this period had experienced very rapid deposit growth.

A compromise proposal between insuring all deposits and only those up to $100,000 or less per account involves insuring transaction and other deposits without specific maturity dates in full, but time deposits with maturity dates not at all or only up to $100,000. This would prevent the immediate unexpected deposit withdrawals that cause forced asset sales, without eliminating private market discipline altogether. The timing and possible magnitude of deposit losses would then be known to the bank, which could prepare to deal with them in advance. In effect, the bank would be like any debtor with debt due on specific dates that it wishes to renew. But this is likely to drive out short-term time deposits, which would become inferior types of deposits and require higher deposit rates in compensation. A bank would then fund itself more fully with transaction deposits.

There is also debate about the maximum amount of insurance coverage per deposit account and the number of accounts belonging to one individual that may be covered. Account coverage has increased by a factor of 40 since the introduction of federal deposit insurance in 1933: from $2,500 to $5,000 in mid-year 1934; to $10,000 in 1950; to $15,000 in 1966; to $20,000 in 1969; to $40,000 in 1974; and to $100,000 in 1980. In contrast, over the same period prices had increased only by a factor of 6½ through 1980 and 10 by 1992. Indeed, some analysts attribute much of the ability of institutions to grow quickly to the 1980 increase in coverage from $40,000 to $100,000. It is much easier to divide large amounts into $100,000 chunks than into $40,000 chunks! On the one hand, reducing the maximum amount from $100,000 would increase the number of depositors at risk and, therefore, be more likely to exert market discipline on their banks. On the other hand, if the maximum amount was reduced too much, it might encourage depositors to hold funds withdrawn from banks perceived to be in trouble as currency outside the banking system rather than to redeposit them in perceived safer banks. Such action might ignite a multiple contraction of money and credit that could endanger the entire banking system.

Currently, all accounts up to $100,000 that any one individual has in different insured institutions, as well as in accounts in joint names in any one institution, are fully covered. Thus, wealthy individuals and other parties can fully insure some or all of their large deposits by dividing them among institutions. Some reformers recommend that the number of multiple accounts qualifying for insurance be limited to a small number, say, two or three, or that a lifetime limit of $100,000 be imposed on all depositors regardless of the number or size of their accounts. In addition, as discussed earlier, the FDIC has frequently in practice not imposed losses on deposits in excess of $100,000 at failed banks with negative net worths, particularly large banks, in a policy of too-large-to-fail. Although initially such banks were not permitted to fail legally, more recently the policy referred only to not imposing losses on uninsured depositors at these banks when they failed with losses to the FDIC. How FDICIA dealt with this problem is discussed later in the chapter.

Who Should Pay the Premiums?

Insurance premiums are generally paid by the party who wishes to be protected from a financial loss or liability that may accompany the occurrence of a particular event. Moreover, the purchase of insurance is at the discretion of the purchaser unless universal insurance is in the public interest. Thus, people can choose whether or not to purchase life insurance and how much to purchase, but they are required in most states to purchase minimum automobile liability insurance.

Who is protected by deposit insurance? Depositors are protected against loss from the failure of their bank. Banks are protected from failure and the loss of their owners' equity investment to the extent that insurance prevents depositor runs. The public is protected from a decline in the money supply, disruption or normal credit relationships, and the economic hardships that accompany widespread bank failures. Although all three groups benefit, the current FDIC premium structure assesses only banks for the full amount of the insurance. But a commercial bank, like any corporation, is an artificial entity that does not bear the ultimate incidence of costs. It is only a collector, acting for those who bear the final burden of the payments. Thus, we need to examine who really pays the insurance premiums.

By definition, risky ventures entail the possibility of loss. The loss is borne by the participants in the venture. Insurance reduces the burden of the possible loss to the participants by spreading it both over a longer period of time and over a larger number of participants. Insurance can be purchased from a separate entity (such as an insurance company), which in effect buys the risk, or from the participants in the venture themselves, through amortizing the cost of the expected loss over time. The latter alternative is **self-insurance.** Which alternative one chooses depends on which is cheaper. If explicit premium payments to an insurance company for a given loss value are considered cheaper than implicit premium payments to oneself to be self-insured, outside insurance is preferable. Conversely, if explicit premiums are considered to be higher than the implicit premiums, self-insurance is preferred.

Who Pays Now?

Under FDIC insurance, the premiums are paid by the insured bank. But this does not imply that all or any of the burden of the premium payments is borne by the bank. The insurance is only on the deposits. To the extent that deposits are less risky after the insurance, depositors are willing to accept a commensurately lower interest rate. This would be true not only for depositors whose entire deposit balances are insured, but also to a lesser extent for larger depositors, who know that by reducing the probability of bank runs FDIC insurance increases the safety of the noninsured portion of their deposit balances. Thus, some of the burden of the premiums is shifted to depositors in the form of lower deposit rates. But the premium paid by the bank may exceed the reduction in deposit rates. Because the bank is less likely to fail, the shareholders also assume less risk. Thus, the shareholders will require a commensurately lower return and assume part of the payment burden.

If the premium still exceeds the sum of these two reductions, the remainder must be shifted elsewhere. If deposit rates or shareholder returns are reduced more than is consistent with the respective risk reductions, the deposits or capital funds would be transferred to another bank, or even another industry, where the risk-adjusted return is higher. Some of the burden may be passed to bank borrowers in the form of higher loan rates in recognition of the more continuous availability of credit, or some may be passed to bank employees in the form of lower wages and salaries in recognition of their more stable employment. Note that, to the extent that all these parties assume commensurately less risk, the lower return or higher cost does not leave them any worse off. Conversely, if the premium is smaller than the reduction in deposit rates, benefits accrue to shareholders in the form of higher returns and to borrowers in the form of lower loan rates.

It is conceivable that some private depositors may not want $100,000 of deposit insurance. Certainly, depositors with accounts greatly in excess of $100,000 benefit less from this insurance. Some with accounts of less than $100,000 may also be willing to be totally or partially self-insured and place their funds with banks that they believe are more financially secure. They may wish to buy, say, only $5,000 or $10,000 of FDIC insurance. By requiring everyone to have a designated amount of insurance, the current system interferes with consumer freedom and economic efficiency.

An alternative policy would permit depositors to decide how much, if any, insurance they wish to purchase and to pay premiums only on that amount. Insurance counters or vending machines, much like those at airports, could be placed in bank lobbies to permit depositors to purchase their insurance up to any amount they wish. The premium may or may not be based on the risk classification of the bank assigned by the insuring agency. However, because comprehensive deposit insurance affects public behavior, increasing individual choice and permitting each depositor to choose the amount of insurance desired may reduce aggregate social welfare by increasing the probability of contagious bank failure if insufficient depositors buy the insurance.

Who Should Provide Insurance?

Most insurance policies on potential losses other than on bank deposits are provided by nongovernment-sponsored private stock or mutual insurance companies. To be able to stay in business, these firms must compute accurately the probability or risk that the insured event will occur in a particular period of time and the magnitude of the resulting loss. Premiums charged will be scaled to this risk. Some events are easier to predict than others. Deaths from natural causes are easier to predict than automobile accidents, which in turn are easier to predict than hurricanes or floods. The more difficult it is to compute the probabilities, the more uncertain is the expected value of the loss, and the higher is the premium that must be charged. If the probabilities are very difficult to compute, private insurance companies may be reluctant to assume the risk. These companies may also be unable to assume the risk if the value of the expected loss is very large. If private insurance firms cannot or will not provide insurance and the protection is deemed to be in the public interest, a case can be made for government insurance.

In his analysis of deposit insurance, William Gibson divided bank failures into two kinds: normal failure and depression or crisis failure. Normal failures include the failures of individual banks during basically healthy economic times. These are attributed to mismanagement, fraud, or just bad luck. Normal bank failures remain isolated independent events; they do not spread to other banks. From the late 1930s through the early 1980s, fewer than 20 of 15,000-odd banks in the United States failed in any on year. The probabilities of normal bank failures may be computed reasonably accurately and a large part of the risk to any one party diversified away.

Crisis or **systemic** failures include those that occur when national economic conditions are poor and a large number of bank borrowers are unable to repay their debts on schedule or interest rate changes depress the market value of the assets below that of the liabilities. As a result, many banks are likely to experience difficulties at these times. Individual bank failures are no longer independent but are positively correlated. The risk cannot be diversified away. The problems that any one bank has may spread to other banks. As noted earlier, such cumulative failures have not occurred very often in U.S. history, primarily only in the massive financial crisis of the 1930s. Nevertheless, contagious bank failures are widely perceived as a credible threat. Crisis failures are more difficult to predict, and for the associated losses are larger, than for normal failures.

Private insurance companies can be expected to assume the risks for normal bank failure but not for crisis failures. Federal government insurance may be appropriate for crisis failures. The large losses that could result from widespread bank failures would be too large for almost any group of private firms. Depositors would most likely be aware of this and not feel fully protected. This also helps to explain why there were runs on troubled state-insured savings and loan associations and credit unions in Ohio and Maryland in 1985 and in Rhode Island in 1991, but not on troubled federally insured institutions in these same states or elsewhere. Unlike the federal government, state governments have access neither to the money printing press nor to very large sources of tax revenues. If the viability of the private insurers is threatened in a banking crisis, the federal government may be expected to come to their rescue to support the banks indirectly. Thus, private insurance may only shift government insurance from the banks to the insurance companies. The case for government insurance is strengthened to the extent that crisis failures occur because of faulty government economic policies. The federal government would be directly to blame for the losses from these failures and could reasonably be expected to shoulder the cost.

Does it follow that, if private firms cannot insure all bank failures, provision of insurance should be left entirely to the government? Not necessarily. It may be efficient to have private companies insure normal failures. They can do this by including an "escape" clause in their insurance policies. Such a clause may be worded to say that if the number of bank failures in any one year or so exceeds a particular number or percentage of all banks, the policy would be void. At that point, government insurance would take over. Escape clauses are common in private insurance contracts. Life insurance policies do not cover deaths in combat zones, and most property insurance policies do not pay for flood and hurricane damage. Supplementary government insurance is available in many of these instances. Alternatively, private firms could be used to insure amounts above a specified minimum per account, say $1,000 or $10,000, or the current $100,000, that is believed to be necessary to discourage depositor runs into currency rather than to other banks.

Dividing the risks between private and government insurance companies may be in the public interest. Competing, private insurance firms would maintain economic efficiency during normal times, relating benefits to costs. Government intervention would be minimal. In crisis periods, the government could provide the necessary reserves to maintain the money supply and the banking system. On the other hand, it is possible to argue that such a division, or ***coinsurance,*** would be difficult to implement in practice. Because government insurance is necessary in any case, why not assign the government total responsibility? Too many insurers will only spoil the policy! Lastly, private insurers may not be either permitted or able to resolve economically insolvent banks as quickly as a government agency and thus not be able to limit losses to the same extent. As discussed earlier, losses from insolvencies occur because the institution is not resolved as soon as its net worth becomes zero.

As an alternative to insurance from private insurance companies, some have suggested that banks could cross-guarantee each other. Because losses from failures would then be borne directly by the surviving banks, the banks would monitor each other carefully and act early to exert sanctions to turn troubled banks around or to resolve failures at minimum cost. After all, who knows banks best and who is more suitable for monitoring them than other banks? Others argue, however, that such a scheme would be impractical both because there is insufficient capital in the banking system to pay for expected losses and because it is unlikely that the government would permit banks to impose sanctions, including closure, on their competitors.

It has also been suggested that depositors would care more about the fate of their funds and exert greater discipline on their institutions if they shared in any potential deposit loss through, say a deductible provision—for example, the depositor absorbs the first $1,000 of any loss per account—or a percent sharing provision—for example, the depositor shares any loss on a 25–75 basis with the government insurer. Most private casualty and property insurance contracts have such coinsurance provisions. But to the extent that risk sharing affects small depositors, it may not protect against the possibility of a run into currently and thus of a run on an individual bank from expanding into a contagious run on the banking system as a whole.

Narrow Banks

An alternative to deposit insurance are banks that are structured in such a way that they cannot fail. The most obvious such structure would be one in which the banks could hold only cash, as the early goldsmiths did (see Chapter 10). This would represent 100 percent banking and would not permit fractional reserve banks as are today's banks. Of course, even such banks could fail from theft and fraud. Because these banks would earn no income on their assets, they would need to charge rather than pay depositors. Some argue that the same degree of safety can be obtained by restricting banks to assets that have only a very small probability of falling in value. Such "safe" assets might include short-term securities issued by the Treasury or very-high-quality private issuers. This system would permit fractional reserve banking. Depositors would be willing to hold funds in safe banks without government insurance, as they do now in uninsured money market funds. Nevertheless, some versions of this proposal would provide insurance to protect against theft and fraud.

Critics have several problems with this restricted or ***narrow bank*** solution. Some argue that efficiency is reduced by not permitting these banks to make broader loans and make use of the unique information they have on the loan customer from their deposit relationship. To them, providing both lending and deposit services promotes valuable synergies that reduce costs to customers. Other critics argue that even if these "narrow" banks were permitted to make investments they would not earn enough on safe securities to pay competitive deposit rates. Thus, depositors would go elsewhere, and what would happen if those other, supposedly uninsured institutions experienced problems? Would not the government be under pressure to insure their depositors? If so, narrow banking primarily would shift deposit insurance to "broad" banks rather than eliminate it. Last, without a firm "closure" rule by which insolvent safe banks are resolved, depositors could still incur relatively large losses, particularly if the troubled bank attempted to gamble for resurrection.

How Should Failed Banks Be Treated?

The FDIC uses four alternative basic methods for resolving failed or failing insured banks and protecting depositors, depending on the cost to itself and the community. First, it can close and liquidate the bank. Depositors are paid the full value of their insured deposits up to the maximum amount in force at the time, and the remaining pro rata liquidation (sale) value of the bank's assets for any deposits in excess of this amount. (This is referred to as a ***deposit payoff.***)

Second, the FDIC can assist in the absorption of the bank by another, existing or new, insured bank. The FDIC auctions off the assets of the failed bank to the highest bidder. The winning bank purchases some or all of the assets and assumes the insured or more deposit liabilities of the failed bank and the FDIC pays the difference, if any. (Technically, this method is referred to as ***purchase and assumption,*** or **P&A.**) If the sale is to an existing bank, the failed bank is generally operated as a branch so that its services are not lost to the community. The depositors are protected up to the insured amount or more, depending on the FDIC's intentions, and the provision of banking services to the community is not disrupted. Uninsured depositors may be paid in full or in part, according to the estimated market value of the bank's assets and the FDIC's evaluation of the impact of the failure on the community. If uninsured depositors are paid less than the face value of their deposits, the FDIC usually pays a certain percentage of the uninsured amount, say, 60 percent, immediately, based on the estimated liquidation value of the assets, and the remainder upon actual liquidation. (This is referred to as a *modified P&A.*) If the proceeds from liquidation fall short of the initial percentage paid, the FDIC absorbs the shortfall.

Third, if the good assets of the failed bank are perceived to be small relative to its deposits or if the uncertainty about the bank's potential value is great, the FDIC may transfer the insured deposits to another nearby bank. It may provide the receiving bank with an equivalent amount of cash and liquidate (sell) all the assets of the failed bank or transfer the good assets to the bank. The uninsured deposits are paid from the proceeds on a pro rata basis. (This procedure is termed a *deposit transfer.*) Fourth, the FDIC can provide direct assistance to a bank in danger of closing if the bank's services are essential to the community or organize a temporary *bridge bank.* It may make loans to the bank, purchase shares in the bank, and even provide temporary management. (This procedure is termed *open bank assistance* or **OBA.**) Similar techniques are used to deal with failed savings and loan associations.

Between 1934 and 1992, about 30 percent of the nearly 2,000 failed commercial banks have been liquidated. The other 70 percent were merged with other banks or were assisted financially in some way. In general, it was the smaller banks that were liquidated and the larger ones that were merged. Through 1990, the average deposit size of liquidated commercial banks was $23 million and of absorbed and assisted banks $131 million. Only 20 of the 151 failed commercial banks with deposits of more than $100 million were liquidated and closed, as compared with one-third of those with deposits of less than $100 million. Particularly in recent years, the FDIC has also assisted, through direct infusions of capital, a limited number of primarily large banks that were in danger of closing. Each of the 10 largest bank failures in the 1980s involved financial assistance by the FDIC in the form of either merger assistance or open bank assistance.

The Federal Reserve has tended to support FDIC actions to keep larger banks open. For example, it has lent funds through the discount window to large banks that have failed in recent years, including the Franklin National Bank (1974), the Continental Illinois National Bank (1984), the major Texas banks in 1987–1989 and the Bank of New England in 1991, and has encouraged a change in state law to permit the trouble Seattle–First to be purchased by the out-of-state BankAmerica Corporation.

Before FDICIA, the method chosen in individual cases was determined by the estimated cost to the FDIC, the FDIC's cash position, and the needs of the community. The larger the bank, the more costly the deposit payoff is perceived to be by the FDIC. This accounts in part for the greater proportion of P&As than liquidations among larger banks. Another reason is that the closing of larger banks may cause greater inconvenience and economic harm, including the possibility of spilling over onto other, "healthy" banks.

For whatever reason, the fact that larger banks tend to be resolved by merger rather than liquidated has important implications for uninsured bank depositors. In liquidations, depositors with account sizes larger than the insured maximum are likely to experience losses. In contrast, in most P&As, all depositors were protected fully regardless of the size of their accounts. Uninsured depositors are better off, on average, in P&As than in liquidations. For example, only 225 of 1,086 bank failures between 1980 and 1989 involved losses to depositors. Of these, 210, or 93 percent of the banks, had deposits of under $100 million. Thus, large depositors were likely to be protected better if they held their deposits in larger banks. This reduced their incentive to hold uninsured amounts in smaller banks, and made for unequal treatment of banks differing only in deposit size. This practice was also likely to reduce the intensity with which large depositors monitored large banks. The distribution of deposits among banks and geographic areas is likely to be different than if all bank failures were treated equally regardless of bank size and no bank was considered too-large-to-fail and impose pro rata losses on uninsured depositors.

As noted earlier in this chapter, losses from bank failures are primarily a function of the time at which the bank is closed and reorganized. Banks fail economically when the market value of their assets declines below that of their liabilities, so that they cannot reasonably expect to meet all their deposit claims in full and on time, and the bank's capital turns negative. Recall that market values are present values that take into account the market's current expectations of future scenarios. If the bank is reorganized by the regulators just at the point at which its net worth touches zero, losses will accrue only to shareholders, but not to depositors or the deposit insurance agency. But, before FDICIA, banks were often not declared legally insolvent at the time they became economically insolvent for two reasons.

One, bank regulators view failures as a black mark on their record and frequently delayed recognition of this state in the hopes that the banks may regain solvency or, if not, fail during the terms of office of their successors. Instead, they provided *forbearance* to some capital-short banks. Two, banks and bank regulators use book value accounting systems rather than market value accounting systems. In these systems, losses are not recognized and assets are typically not marked down until there is a missed cash payment or sale. These are likely to happen some time after the loss actually occurs.

When an economically insolvent bank is kept open, it is operating fully on depositors' funds, which remain at the bank because of deposit insurance protection. Because, as discussed earlier, shareholders of such institutions have nothing more to lose, but will be credited with any profits, the bank is likely to engage in risky ventures in hopes of regaining solvency. Heads it wins, tails the FDIC loses! Similar to last-second "Hail-Mary" passes in football, few of these ventures are successful and the FDIC is likely to absorb larger losses on average than if it had reorganized the bank sooner.

Early Intervention and Closure

Because losses to the FDIC occur only if a bank is permitted to continue to operate after its economic net worth becomes negative, some analysts proposed that the regulators intervene earlier with troubled banks and require recapitalization by current shareholders before the bank's capital is totally depleted, for example, when capital falls to 3 percent of the bank's assets. If the shareholders prefer not to raise the additional capital, the bank would be sold to those who would raise it or be liquidated. If this is done in time, no loss is incurred by any party, including uninsured depositors, other than the shareholders. Losses would occur only in cases of inadequate monitoring by the regulators, failure by the regulators to require additional capital on time, and fraud. Deposit insurance would effectively be redundant and insurance premiums would be greatly reduced. This proposal was referred to as **structured early intervention and resolution,** or **SEIR.**

Such a scheme also envisioned higher capital requirements. It is argued that banks have been able to operate with their current low capital-to-asset ratios of 6 percent and less only because of federal deposit insurance. Other firms, including other types of financial institutions not covered by the safety net, such as insurance companies and finance companies, operate with capital ratios between 10 and 25 percent, and nonfinancial firms, with ratios in excess of 40 percent. Moreover, before the introduction of federal deposit insurance in 1933, banks tended to hold capital ratios of nearly 20 percent, and many shareholders were subject to double liability—they were liable not only for the amount of their investment, but also, in the case of failure, for an additional amount up to the par value of their shares.

To reduce the likelihood of a bank's capital being depleted, SEIR establishes a series of progressively stronger and more mandatory sanctions that would be imposed on the banks as their performance deteriorates. Thus, as a bank's capital-asset ratio declines, regulatory monitoring and supervision increases; restrictions are imposed on its powers, deposit growth, and dividend and interest payments; and an acceptable business plan must be prepared that spells out its program for recovery and raising additional capital. At the same time, healthy well-capitalized institutions would be awarded with broader permissible powers and less day-to-day supervision. Proponents argue that only the most stubborn of banks that really wants to fail would be able to work its way down through these safeguards to deplete its capital to the point where mandatory recapitalization or closure is triggered.

The FDIC As Insurer and Regulator

The FDIC's responsibilities as an insurance agency and as a bank regulatory agency may at times conflict. An insurance agency has the responsibility to limit the risks of the insured to those stipulated in the policy and to reduce both the probabilities of loss and the magnitude of losses by encouraging the insured to introduce self-protection measures. Thus, automobile insurance companies restrict insured drivers' coverage to that agreed upon in the policy—for example, recreational, business, or racing—and encourage them to reduce risk by adopting safety measures, such as seat belts and air bags. The FDIC has a similar obligation to protect its reserves by discouraging insured banks from entering new, riskier activities and to encourage less risk in their existing activities.

The FDIC can encourage safety through its examination, regulatory, and supervisory powers by questioning risky activities and by recommending additional bank capital. It can reduce the probability of individual bank failure directly by restricting the entry of new, competing banks and by reducing existing competition through the merger or competing institutions. The objective of safety, however, may conflict with the FDIC's objective as a regulator in promoting an efficient banking system. This objective requires encouraging bank competition and permitting some bank failures, although not necessarily losses.

Some analysts have concluded that these conflicting objectives have reduced the ability of the FDIC to perform efficiently either its insurance or its regulatory responsibilities. They recommend that the FDIC surrender one or the other of its duties. Because there are two other bank regulatory agencies, these analysts generally recommend that the FDIC's regulatory responsibilities be transferred to the other agencies or to a newly established agency. The FDIC would be reconstituted solely as an insurance agency. Opponents of such a reorganization argue that the FDIC's responsibilities as a bank regulatory agency are necessary for it to carry out its insurance functions if it is to do more than merely take note of any increased riskiness in the banking system. This is particularly true if the FDIC is to protect depositors at all banks adequately and maintain the provision of banking services in a community. If a conflict between safety and efficiency exists, proponents of this view would argue that the importance of maintaining a viable banking system should be reconciled in favor of safety. On the other hand, combining regulation and insurance in the same agency did not prevent the old Federal Home Loan Bank Board, which controlled the old FSLIC, from bankrupting itself and disappearing from the regulatory scene in 1989.

Recent Developments in Deposit Insurance

The SLA debacle of the 1980s, which led to the insolvency of FSLIC, and the accompanying large number of commercial bank failures, which reduced the reserves of the FDIC to near insolvency levels, forced a dramatic reevaluation of federal deposit insurance. The increases in the number and dollar size of the failures put substantial pressure on the FDIC and, in particular, the late FSLIC. To preserve the reported amount of their reserve funds, the agencies resorted both to "funny" accounting similar to that used by the institutions they insured to give the appearance of solvency and to delay the formal declaration of failures. They recorded only the actual cash outlays incurred in liquidating, selling, or merging failed and failing institutions and not the actuarial value of the assistance that they guaranteed to the acquirers to cover future losses on the assets transferred. But even so, the FSLIC ran down its reserves to the point that it could not close and reorganize large associations that were insolvent even on a book-value basis, no less on a more accurate market-value basis. In part, as a result, some of these insolvent institutions increased their risk taking in hopes of regaining solvency before FSLIC could close them, and others continued to loot the remaining good assets. To make matters worse, many of these "zombie" institutions deliberately continued to grow as rapidly as possible by offering rates well above market deposit rates to attract funds nationwide. In many instances, the inflows were used to finance not only new assets but also interest payments on existing deposits and operating expenses. This compounded the losses of both FSLIC and their healthier competitors.

By mid-year 1987, FSLIC's economic losses—measured as the difference between the market value of assets at all insured savings and loan associations and the par value of the deposits, almost all of which were in chunks of $100,000 or under and thereby fully insured—were estimated at more than $40 billion, although FSLIC's official estimates were much smaller. As the magnitude of the problem began to be realized more fully and as the extent of the fraud at some SLAs began to surface, Congress became more concerned. In 1987, the Competitive Equality Banking Act (CEBA) provided $11 billion to FSLIC by permitting it to borrow against future premium income. But this amount was much too little, too late. In addition, the act made it more difficult for the regulatory agencies to reorganize insolvent institutions, even if they had been prepared to do so. This reflected the strong political pressures brought to bear by groups that would be directly harmed by closure, such as owners, managers, large depositors, and even large borrowers, who would be forced to repay their loans on a more timely basis. Some of these groups sent large amounts of funds, frequently obtained from the institutions themselves, to lobby Congress and the regulators to weaken, delay, or prevent altogether corrective actions. Improper responses by those lobbied led to the resignations of both the speaker of the House of Representatives and Democratic House whip in 1989 and to the reprimand in 1991 of a number of senators (known as the "Keating Five" after Charles Keating, a failed SLA executive who lobbied these senators to avoid being closed down).

The progressively increasing number of failures and dollar losses also led the deposit insurance agencies to modify some of their policies, in particular, TLTF (too-large-to-fail). In the 1984 rescue of the Continental Illinois Bank, the FDIC had not failed the bank legally and had protected the par value of all depositors of the bank and of all creditors of the parent holding company. Starting in 1986, the FDIC began to impose pro rata losses on creditors of insolvent bank holding companies; in 1988, it forced the legal failure of insolvent large banks; and in 1989, it imposed pro rata losses on interbank balances held by solvent banks at insolvent bank affiliates of the same holding company. None of these changes were accompanied by runs on other large banks, as many regulators had feared. By late 1990, "too-large-to-fail" had been narrowed to "too large to impose losses on most uninsured depositors," but had also been broadened to include many not-so-large institutions. At the same time, FSLIC greatly accelerated the resolution of large insolvent SLAs, primarily in Texas. Because it had no funds, FSLIC used promissory notes and provisions in the federal tax code that permitted lower taxes to eliminate the negative capital at these institutions and to entice buyers. Many of these negotiations were done in haste, behind closed doors, and permitted the new owners to operate with minimum capital. As a result, the transactions increased the unfavorable public image of FSLIC.

Finally, in mid-1989, as estimates of the deficit in FSLIC approached $100 billion and criticisms of its operations mounted, Congress, at the request of newly elected President George Bush, enacted FIRREA. Unfortunately, both the additional $100 billion raised to finance FSLIC's deficit and resolve the SLA insolvencies and many of the provisions included were again too little, too late, and too often misdirected to either end the crisis or put federal deposit insurance on a sounder basis. Soon afterward, the first of a series of requests for additional funding began. In early 1991, the Treasury released its study of deposit insurance mandated by FIRREA. The Treasury recommended greater emphasis on early intervention and sanctions by the regulators to resolve institutions before their capital is fully depleted, reducing de facto insurance coverage to $100,000 per account per bank, eliminating the coverage for brokered deposits, and scaling insurance premiums to a bank's capital position.

The increase in bank failures, accompanied by a fear that the FDIC might also become insolvent as the FSLIC had and require taxpayer support, spurred Congress to legislate basic deposit insurance reform. It accepted the idea of SEIR over the alternative options and included it in somewhat weakened form in the form of prompt corrective action (PCA) and least cost resolution (LCR) as the centerpiece of FDICIA enacted at year-end 1991. Among other provisions, the act also mandated risk-based insurance premiums and restrictions on too-large-to-fail. Because it fundamentally changed the way depository institutions are prudentially regulated, FDICIA is the most important banking legislation since the Banking Act of 1933, which introduced federal deposit insurance.

For purposes of prompt corrective action by the regulators, insured institutions are divided into the five categories or zones discussed earlier and shown in Table 16–2. Each institutions's rating depends on its capital position, both total and risk-adjusted, and the restrictions on bank activity become progressively harsher and more mandatory the lower the capital zone. This approach should reduce the moral hazard problem and encourage banks to operate in the top, well-capitalized, zone or at least in the next, adequately capitalized, zone. The reduction in regulator discretion in the lower zones occurs only if the banks have not responded favorably to the discretionary actions in the higher zones and is intended to prevent the regulators from bowing to political and other pressures to delay taking the necessary corrective actions. This should help make the regulators better agents of the taxpaying public. If, despite these regulatory actions, an institution drops into the bottom, critically undercapitalized zone and has less than 2 percent total capital, FDICIA requires a recapitalization either by the current owners or by new owners through a sale or merger arranged by the FDIC or, if there are no buyers, liquidation. The least cost provision of the act requires the FDIC to use the resolution option that will minimize the cost to the fund. This will increase the number of times that losses or **haircuts** will be imposed on uninsured depositors.

The act also restricts the FDIC's ability to protect uninsured depositors at banks it considers too-large-to-fail. To do so, two-thirds of the Board of Directors of the FDIC and of the Board of Governors of the Federal Reserve and the secretary of the Treasury in consultation with the president (who might be expected to have more pressing items on his agenda) must agree in writing that not protecting the uninsured depositors at a failed bank "would have serious adverse effects on economic conditions or financial stability." In addition, any loss the FDIC incurs in such an action must be financed on a "pay-as-you-go" basis by a special assessment on the total deposits of all banks. This provision imposes the greatest cost on the largest banks, some of whom might be reluctant to pay to keep one of their competitors alive. In addition, the act for the first time restricts the ability of the Federal Reserve to lend to undercapitalized institutions through the discount window. Such lending effectively reinforced deposit insurance in providing a federal safety net under banks. A study had shown that some 90 percent of all banks that received extended, long-term discount window assistance from the Fed in the 1980s failed.

FDICIA basically maintains $100,000 insurance coverage per eligible account, but, as discussed earlier, requires that the premium rate be scaled to the riskiness of the bank. The act also maintains total domestic deposits as the base to which the premiums are applied.

Enactment of parts of FDICIA was vigorously fought by the regulatory agencies. Many regulators perceived the reduction in their prudential discretion as reducing their authority, visibility, and job challenge and therefore their career advancement or postcareer opportunities. Many regulators return to the financial services industry after their regulatory tenure and feared that FDICIA could slow the "revolving door" between government and industry. For their own visibility, it might be said that "financial crises are to regulators what wars are to generals." Because FDICIA delegates to the regulators the interpretation of many of the provisions and the drafting and implementation of the supporting regulations, the regulators can either reinforce or weaken the intent of the act. Together with weaknesses in the act itself that make it unlikely that FDIC losses from bank failures will be held to zero, this provision makes it too early to be able to tell whether FDICIA introduces effective deposit insurance reform in practice as well as in law. However, the sharp decline in both the number of bank failures and the magnitude of losses after its enactment suggests that the intent of the act, in part assisted by lower interest rates, which significantly increased bank profits, was being achieved.

Insolvencies have been resolved earlier, with smaller losses to the FDIC, and more uninsured depositors have shared in the losses. In 1990 and 1991, only 37 of the nearly 300 resolutions involved any losses to uninsured depositors, and all of these were at very small institutions. In 1992, the first year after the enactment of FDICIA, uninsured depositors in about one-half of the 120 failure resolutions incurred losses. In 1993, such losses were incurred in almost 90 percent of the 41 bank failures, including at the largest bank to fail.

In 1993, Congress enacted a national ***depositor preference*** provision, which gives uninsured domestic depositors and the FDIC preference over both nondeposit creditors, such as debtholders and Fed-funds sellers, and depositors at overseas branches in receiving payment from the sale of assets in failed institutions. Previously the FDIC shared losses with all uninsured depositors and creditors. This measure is intended to increase FDIC income both by reducing its losses from bank failures and by increasing its premium income, as some nondeposit creditors of banks may switch to become depositors in order to move up in priority in case of bank failure. The long-term implications are less certain, however, as foreign depositors,

Fed-funds sellers, and other creditors may demand collateral against their funds. If they succeed, this could put uninsured domestic depositors and the FDIC at greater risk, as they would have to bear a larger portion or in the extreme all of the losses from the sale of the assets of failed banks.

SUMMARY

Federal government deposit insurance, introduced in 1933, on the one hand, has contained problems at individual banks from spilling over onto other banks and has thereby stabilized the banking system as a whole. On the other hand, FDIC insurance has introduced problems that became evident only when the economy became more volatile in the late 1970s. By reducing the need of depositors to be concerned about the safety of their banks and charging premiums that were not scaled to the riskiness of the bank, deposit insurance unintentionally increased the incentive for banks to take risk. Partially as a result, the number of bank and thrift institution failures increased sharply in recent years. By the early 1980s, the failures overwhelmed the deposit insurance agencies, who, in part because of insufficient funds and in part because of pressures from both the industry and Congress, delayed closing and reorganizing insolvent institutions. This permitted many zombie institutions to gamble for resurrection, lose, and increase the losses that were passed onto the agencies, and, for FSLIC, onto the taxpayer. Critics claim that the insurance can be provided more efficiently. Some of the more important issues are:

How should the premiums be determined? Until recently, premiums were charged the insured banks on the basis of their total domestic deposits. No adjustment was made for the relative riskiness of the bank's asset or liability portfolios; risk was controlled through supervision and regulation. FDICIA introduced risk-based premiums.

What percent of deposits should be insured? Insurance up to $100,000 covers 99 percent of all bank accounts and nearly 80 percent of all bank deposits. Thus, large depositors could still start bank runs that might result in bank failures. On the other hand, because of their concern, depositors with large uninsured accounts might operate in a way that would keep bank management "honest" and brake the bank's risk exposure.

Should the premiums be paid by the insured bank? Banks, like any corporation, do not bear the burden of the premiums. The burden is shifted to individuals, but precisely to whom is uncertain. The premiums are unlikely to be paid only by fully insured depositors. It might be more efficient to let depositors determine whether they want insurance, and if so, how much, and then to pay the premiums directly.

How should insolvent banks be handled? Should insolvent or near-insolvent banks be permitted to continue to operate and all depositors at insolvent banks considered too-large-to-fail be fully protected, or should regulators require higher capital, intervene early to discourage banks from performing poorly, and mandate recapitalization or liquidation of troubled banks before their capital is fully depleted?

Should all or some deposit insurance be provided by private insurance companies? Should insurance be restricted to only safe "narrow" banks? Does the FDIC encounter conflicts of interest between its insurance function and its other regulatory functions, such as promoting competition and efficiency? At year-end 1991, Congress enacted FDI-CIA, which reforms deposit insurance through early structured intervention and resolution. By increasing the barriers to failure and decreasing the probability of losses, FDICIA makes insurance substantially redundant. The act also introduced risk-based premiums and restrictions on too-large-to-fail.

QUESTIONS

1. What is the underlying reason for federal deposit insurance? What are its positive and negative features? How successful has it been?
2. Define *moral hazard*. Is it limited to deposit insurance only? If not, give some examples from everyday life. How do private insurance companies attempt to deal with moral hazard problems? How does the FDIC?
3. Evaluate the arguments for and against flat percentage of total deposits insurance premiums and risk-related premiums. How are insurance premiums determined in most other areas? Why?
4. What causes losses to the FDIC from bank failures? Why might risk-related deposit insurance premiums by themselves not necessarily prevent losses to the FDIC? How would the average size of insurance premiums be related to the type of "closure rule" imposed by the regulators?
5. "Less than 100 percent deposit insurance is necessary in order to keep bank management on its toes." Discuss your agreement or disagreement with this statement.
6. Why not have private deposit insurance similar to private life, fire, or property insurance rather than government-provided insurance? How

does deposit insurance differ from other types of insurance in terms of losses to the insurer? Can you make a case for some minimal amount of government insurance?
7. Why are *narrow banks* proposed as a solution to the deposit insurance problem? Would such banks require insurance? Why? What are the arguments against this proposal?
8. In what way did the recent FDIC policy of treating failing banks appear to favor depositors at larger banks? Why may this policy weaken depositor monitoring of banks? Has the FDIC changed its policy? Why or why not?
9. "There is an inherent conflict between the FDIC as an insurance agency and as a bank regulator." Discuss your agreement or disagreement with this statement.
10. In what ways may SEIR be considered deposit insurance reform? How successful has it been as implemented in FDICIA? Why did some regulators oppose FDICIA?
11. Choose a recent bank or S&L failure in your state or region. (This information can be obtained from the state's banking department.) What happened to the institution, and how were the uninsured depositors treated?

REFERENCES

Abken, Peter A., "Corporate Pensions and Government Insurance: Déjà Vu All Over Again?" *Economic Review*, Federal Reserve Bank of Atlanta, March/April 1992, pp. 1–16.

Barth, James R., *The Great Savings and Loan Debacle*. Washington, D.C.: AEI Press, 1991.

Barth, James R., and R. Dan Brumbaugh, Jr., eds. *The Reform of Deposit Insurance*. New York: Harper Business, 1992.

Barth, James R., R. Dan Brumbaugh, Jr.,

and Robert E. Litan, *The Future of American Banking*, Armonk, N.Y.,: M.E. Sharpe, 1992.

Benston, George J., and George G. Kaufman, "Risk and Solvency Regulation of Depository Institutions: Past Policies and Current Options," *Monograph Series in Finance and Economics, 88-1*. New York: New York University, 1988.

Benston, George J. and George G. Kaufman, "Understanding the Savings and Loan Debacle," *The Public Interest*, Spring 1990, pp.79–95.

Benston, George J. and George G. Kaufman, "The Intellectual History of FDICIA," in George G. Kaufman, ed., *Reforming Financial Institutions and Markets in the United States*. Boston: Klower, 1994, pp. 1–19.

Benston, George J., et al., *Blueprint for Restructuring America's Financial Institutions*. Washington, D.C.: Brookings Institution, 1989.

Benston, George J., et al., *Perspectives on Safe and Sound Banking*, Cambridge, Mass.: MIT Press, 1986.

Bovenzi, John F., and Maureen Muldoon, "Failure-Resolution Methods and Policy Considerations, " FDIC *Banking Review*, Fall 1990, pp. 1–11.

Brumbaugh, R. Dan, Jr., *Thrifts under Siege*, Cambridge, Mass.: Ballinger Press, 1988.

Calamiris, Charles W., "Deposit Insurance Lessons from the Record," *Economic Perspectives*, Federal Reserve Bank of Chicago, May/June 1989, pp. 10–30.

Duwe Richard, et al., "Problem Banks," *Banking Studies*, Federal Reserve Bank of Kansas City, Special Issue, 1988.

England, Catherine, and Thomas Huertas, eds., *The Financial Services Revolution*. Norwell, Mass.: Kluwer, 1988.

England, Catherine, et al., "Is Private Insurance a Viable Alternative to Federal Deposit Insurance?" in *Proceedings of a Conference on Bank Structure and Competition*. Federal Reserve Bank of Chicago, May 1985, pp. 316–68.

Federal Deposit Insurance Corporation, *Deposit Insurance in a Changing Environment*, Washington, D.C., 1983.

Federal Deposit Insurance Corporation, *The First Fifty Years: A History of the* FDIC, Washington, D.C., 1984.

Federal Deposit Insurance Corporation, "Predecessors of the Federal Deposit Insurance Law," *Annual Report*, 1950, Washington, D.C., 1951, pp. 63–101.

Federal Home Loan Bank Board, *Agenda for Reform: A Report on Deposit Insurance to Congress*, Washington, D.C., 1983.

Flannery, Mark J., "Deposit Insurance Creates a Need for Bank Regulation," *Business Review*, Federal Reserve Bank of Philadelphia, January/February 1982, pp. 17–27.

Flood, Mark D., "The Great Deposit Insurance Debate," *Review*, Federal Reserve Bank of St. Louis, July/August 1992, pp. 51–77.

Gibson, William E., "Deposit Insurance in the United States: Evaluation and Reform," *Journal of Financial and Quantitative Analysis*, March 1972, pp. 1575–94.

Horvitz, Paul M., "The Case against Risk-Related Deposit Insurance Premiums," *Housing Finance Review*, July 1983, pp. 253–64.

Horvitz, Paul M., "A Reconsideration of the Role of Bank Examination," *Journal of Money, Credit, and Banking*, pt. 1, November 1980, pp. 654–59.

Horvitz, Paul M., et al., "Research on Federal Deposit Insurance," *Proceedings of a Conference on Bank Structure and Competition, 1983*, Federal Reserve Bank of Chicago, 1983, pp. 196–298.

Kane, Edward J., "Confronting Incentive Problems in U.S. Deposit Insurance," in George G. Kaufman and Roger C., Kormendi, eds., *Deregulating Financial Services*. Cambridge, Mass.: Ballinger, 1986, pp. 97–120.

Kane, Edward J., *The Gathering Crisis in Federal Deposit Insurance*. Cambridge, Mass.: MIT Press, 1985.

Kane, Edward J., "No Room for Weak Links in the Chain of Deposit Insurance

Reform," *Journal of Financial Services Research*, September 1987, pp. 77–111.

Kane, Edward J., *The S&L Insurance Mess: How Did It Happen?* Washington, D.C.: Urban Institute Press, 1989.

Kaufman, George G., "The Federal Safety Net: Not for Banks Only," *Economic Perspectives*, Federal Reserve Bank of Chicago, November/December 1987, pp. 19–28.

Kaufman, George G., "Too Large to Fail: Myth and Reality," *Contemporary Policy Issues*, October 1990, pp. 1–14.

Kaufman, George G., ed., *Reforming Financial Institutions and Markets in the United States*. Boston: Kluwer, 1994.

Kaufman, George G., ed., *Restructuring the Financial System*. Boston: Kluwer, 1990.

Kaufman, George G., et al., "Public Policy Toward Failing Institutions: The Lessons from the Thrift Industry," in *Proceedings of a Conference on Bank Structure and Competition*. Chicago: Federal Reserve Bank of Chicago, May 1987, pp. 267–340.

McCarthy, Ian S., "Deposit Insurance: Theory and Practice," *International Monetary Fund Staff Papers*, September 1980, pp. 578–600.

National Commission on Financial Institution Reform, Recovery and Enforcement, *Origins and Causes of the S&L Debacle: A Blueprint for Reform*, Washington, D.C., July 1993.

Scott, Kenneth, and Thomas Mayer, "Risk and Regulation in Banking: Some Proposals for Federal Deposit Insurance Reform," *Stanford Law Review*, May 1971, *pp.* 857–902.

Sprague, Irvine A., *Bailout*. New York: Basic Books, 1986.

U.S. General Accounting Office, *Deposit Insurance*. Washington, D.C., 1986 (2 vols.).

U.S. General Accounting Office, *Deposit Insurance: A Strategy for Reform*. Washington, D.C., March 1991.

U.S. Treasury Department, *Modernizing the Financial System*. Washington, D.C.: Government Printing Office, 1991.

White, Lawrence J., *The S&L Debacle*. New York: Oxford University Press, 1991.

Zweig, Phillip L., *Belly Up: The Collapse of the Penn Square Bank*. New York: Crown, 1986.

Deregulation and Regulatory Reform

The dramatic changes that have occurred in the financial sector since World War II have frequently clashed with the regulatory structure that was put in place for an earlier and different period. As a result, the banking system did not always operate as efficiently as it could, to the detriment of both the industry and consumers. This generated widespread calls for changes (generally, but not necessarily accurately, referred to as "reforms") in the regulatory structure. Most of the current structure has been developed in bits and pieces on an ad hoc basis in immediate response to developments and crises as they occurred. Regulation generally reflects the most pressing problems of the day. Much of our banking regulation still reflects the major financial disorders of the early 1930s and emphasizes safety at the expense of competition and efficiency. Thus, the Banking (Glass-Steagall) Act of 1933, among other things, prohibited interest payments on demand deposits, limited interest payments on time deposits, increased barriers to the entry of new banks, separated full-service commercial and investment banking, and introduced deposit insurance by the federal government. Many of the changes that were made at that time and since were not part of a well-developed or well-considered overall blueprint. Like Topsy, the regulatory structure just grew.

By the late 1970s, the regulations were widely viewed as excessively restrictive on the ability of the institutions to respond to changes in the environment that saw (1) advances in telecommunications and information processing technology permit interest rate and product restrictions to be easily and cheaply bypassed; (2) increases in interest rates provide the incentive for bypassing affected institutions; and (3) increases in the volatility of both prices and interest rates (recall from Chapter 6 that market rates of interest are in part determined by changes in the rate of inflation) undermine the solvency of thrift institutions. (The forces hammering down the regulatory wall, mostly built in the 1930s, are depicted in Figure 19–1.) As a result, the profitability of depository institutions was reduced and "nonbank" competitors grew rapidly. Many changes by banks occurred de facto as the affected institutions searched out ways around the de jure restrictions. In response, in the 1970s, Congress began to reexamine the entire structure of bank regulation.

The first major steps in systematically redesigning the regulatory and financial structure at the federal level were the enactment of the Depository Institutions Deregulation and Monetary Control Act (DIDMCA) in 1980 and the Garn-St Germain Depository Institutions Act (DIA) in 1982. These acts reduced the governmental operating restrictions on depository institutions and were consistent in thrust with the deregulation that was occurring in other industries, such as airlines, telephone, and trucking. (It is important to note that deregulation does not imply no regulation. Rather, as is dis-

FIGURE

19–1   HAMMERING THE REGULATORY WALL IN THE 1980S

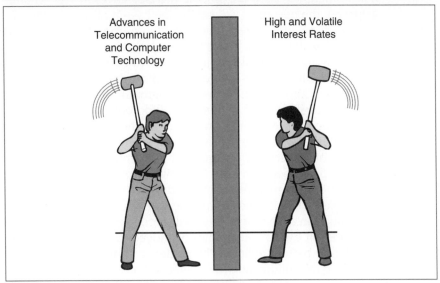

Advances in
Telecommunication
and Computer
Technology

High and Volatile
Interest Rates

cussed later in this chapter, deregulation refers to a shift in regulation from government agencies to market forces.) However, the reduced official emphasis on safety was widely questioned when bank and SLA failures, including some large institutions, increased sharply with large losses to the insurance agencies that required taxpayer funding. As a result, further de jure deregulation was pretty much put on the back burner until the new economic forces were sorted out. The Financial Institutions Recovery, Reform, and Enforcement Act in 1989 and the FDIC Improvement Act in 1991 were primarily responses to these debacles and focused on strengthening the capital base of insured institutions and forcing earlier regulatory intervention in the affairs of troubled institutions to attempt to prevent them from failing with large losses. Both acts focused primarily on prudential regulations and, on net, reregulated somewhat with respect to operational powers. But as the banks became financially healthier in the 1990s, their product and geographic powers were slowly expanded again. This chapter first discusses the reform of regulations and then of the regulatory agencies.

Reform of Regulations

Banking deregulation represents a change in the regulations or ground rules of the game of banking, similar to a change in the rules in any game, such as basketball (a 45-second time clock or prohibiting goal tending) or football (permitting bumping receivers past the line of scrimmage or downing a quarterback while still standing but in the grasp of a tackler). It follows that some teams and players will benefit from the new rules. Other teams and players that did well under the old rules, however, may do worse under the new rules. Why were the rule changes made? Because someone—the league, team owners, players, or public—thought that the game would be better for them because of the change—possibly more audience appeal, fewer injuries, more balanced teams, and so on. Sometimes they are right and sometimes they are not. If the objectives of the changes are not achieved, the new rules will be changed again or withdrawn.

With banking deregulation, some groups—bankers, regulators, consumers, legislators—believed that banking was not operating as effectively as they thought it should or that the old rules were not being observed and that their effectiveness could be improved by simultaneously changing some rules and "cleaning up" the rulebook. Under the new rules, some bankers, consumers, or regulators will do better and others will do worse. Competition among banks and other financial firms will intensify with all the ramifications that go with such as environment. Similar to the experiences in other recently deregulated industries, such as airlines and trucking, the spread between high- and low-performing banks has widened since the start of deregulation. Some of the more poorly performing banks that cannot keep up with the competition will exit the industry through merger or liquidation. But other banks will enter, either taking up any unfulfilled demands left by the failed banks or, indeed, causing the exit of these banks by offering better services. The evidence of recent years shows both the highest bank failure and the highest bank entry rates since the Great Depression. One author observed that "if we [want] the creativity and spontaneity of market forces, we [have] to accept the inequity—as well as the vulgarity—that [goes] with it."[1]

Today's regulations applicable to financial institutions primarily reflect responses to past structures and crises. Once adopted, regulations often develop a constituency of their own. Groups that benefit from them are reluctant to have any major changes occur (see Exhibit 19–1). As we have noted, the enactments of DIDMCA in 1980 and of DIA in 1982 were a belated recognition that the regulations were showing their age and that groups harmed by the regulations in the changed marketplace were getting the upper hand politically over the groups that benefited. Some of the major provisions of DIDMCA and DIA that are related to decontrol of financial institutions or modification of regulations are shown in Table 19–1. As was discussed in Chapter 18, to increase emphasis on safety in a world of greater product deregulation, Congress in 1991 reformed deposit insurance in FDICIA, but little else. In this chapter, we will examine two important regulations that are currently being reevaluated—product line and geographic market restrictions. The next chapter examines a third—the separation of commercial and investment banking. A fourth—deposit insurance—has already been examined in Chapter 18. (Another important regulation that is currently being reevaluated is the prohibition of interest payments on demand deposits. This has already been touched on in earlier chapters and in greater detail in Chapter 15 in the second edition of this book.)

Product Powers

As already discussed, financial institutions in the United States have tended to be specialized. Traditionally, commercial banks have had monopolies

---

[1] Aaron Wildavsky, "The 'Reverse Sequence' in Civil Liberties," *The Public Interest* (Winter 1985), p. 40.

E X H I B I T

19–1

367

▼

DEREGULATION
AND REGULATORY
REFORM

Bootleggers and Baptists—The Education of a Regulatory Economist

Economists from Adam Smith on (and including Karl Marx) have realized that government regulation is a sword that cuts in both directions, and all have called for reforms to improve the good regulations and prune the bad. But desiring reform and achieving it are obviously two different things. What we want to find out here is under what circumstances they can coincide. When can we achieve regulatory reform?

In my studies of the relationships between governments and business, my attention was first attracted to the unbelievably costly things that governments do when attempting to control businesses. It seemed, as Murphy might have said, that if there was a wrong way of doing something, the regulators would adopt it. I found countless cases where rules and regulations imposed tremendous costs while delivering little if any benefit.

▼ Freight rates for one class of shippers were subsidized by another class of shippers. As a result, factories were located on the basis of false signals, real costs were hidden, and goods were shipped great distances at lower fares to be processed in higher-cost plants.

▼ Catalytic converters were installed on automobiles for the purpose of reducing emissions. But, for the converters to operate properly, unleaded gas had to be used—and it is more expensive than regular. So cost-conscious drivers put leaded gas in their tanks, which turned the converters into so much junk and added more emissions to the environment than there would have been had engines been even slightly modified or some other plan introduced.

▼ Petrochemical plants were required to reduce emissions at each and every stack by the same percentage. If instead managers had been given plantwide targets and left free to attain them efficiently, the same degree of pollution control could have been achieved at much lower cost.

▼ Petroleum companies that found oil on Alaska's North Slope and sought to bring it to the lower 48 states by way of the West Coast were barred from doing so by complex environmental rules. Logic would then have dictated that the oil be shipped to Japanese refineries, which could have returned the refined product to the United States. But that was against the federal law too. Instead, the crude oil is being shipped from Alaska to Texas, where it is unloaded and refined, all at considerable extra cost.

The list could go on and on. Not only does government rarely accomplish its stated goals at lowest cost, but often its regulators seem dedicated to choosing the highest-cost approach they can find. Because of all this, I and others in academia became convinced years ago that a massive program in economic education was needed to save the world from regulation. If we economists could just teach the regulators a little supply and demand, countless billions of dollars would be saved.

My views began to change after I joined the Council on Wage and Price Stability in 1976. There my assignment was to review proposed regulations from the Enviromental Protection Agency (EPA), the Federal Trade Commission (FTC), the Department of Transportation (DOT), and parts of the Department of Health, Education, and Welfare (HEW). The field was white unto the harvest, and I was ready to educate the regulators. But then I began to talk with some of them, and I began to hear from people in the industries affected by the rules. To my surprise, many regulators knew quite a bit about economics. Even more surprising was that industry representatives were not always opposed to the costly rules and occasionally were even fearful that we would succeed in getting rid of some of them. It was in considerable confusion that I returned later to my university post, still unable to explain what I had observed and square it with the economics I thought I understood.

That marked the beginning of a new approach to my research on regulation. First, instead of assuming that regulators really intended to minimize costs but somehow proceeded to make crazy mistakes, I began to assume that they were not trying to minimize costs at all—at least not the costs I had been concerned with. They were trying to minimize *their* costs, just as most sensible people do. And what are some of those costs that keep regulators from choosing efficient ways of, say, reducing emissions of hydrocarbons?

▼ *The cost of making a mistake.* Simple rules applied across the board require fewer decisions where mistakes can be made.
▼ *The cost of enforcement.* Again, simple rules requiring uniform behavior are easier to monitor and enforce than complex ones, and they also have a false ring of fairness.
▼ *Political costs.* A legislator is likely to be unhappy with regulators who fail to behave in politically prudent ways—who fail, in the legislator's view, to remember the industries and the workers in his area.

Second, I asked myself, what do industry and labor want from the regulators? They want protection from competition, from technological change, and from losses that threaten profits and jobs. A carefully constructed regulation can accomplish all kinds of anticompetitive goals of this sort, while giving the citizenry the impression that the only goal is to serve the public interest.

Indeed, the pages of history are full of episodes best explained by a theory of regulation I call "bootleggers and Baptists." Bootleggers, you will remember, support Sunday closing laws that shut down all the local bars and liquor stores. Baptists support the same laws and lobby vigorously for them. Both parties gain, while the regulators are content because the law is easy to administer.

What all this implies is that the challenges of regulatory reform are institutional. Regulation is relief for some and a burden for others, so that reform is a burden for some and a relief for others. The fact that a regulation has come into being as a result of a costly political exchange means that reform can hardly be gained easily. This is not to suggest that all is for naught, that there are no opportunities for reducing net (overall) regulatory costs or removing the protective regulatory cocoons woven so tightly and carefully around this activity and that. But it is to say that we can scarcely expect full-scale deregulation to occur often. Not when the Baptists and the bootleggers vote together.

Putting all this together, we may say that there are strong possibilities for regulatory reform when the institutions involved are changing for other reasons anyway. One should not expect to see sudden and widespread transformation in regulation. Like all market processes, the market for regulation is relatively stable, the result of thousands of transactions and years of institutional development. Yet, also like other markets, the forces of supply and demand do change, and the agents for change can and do have marginal but significant impact on political demand and regulatory supply. Bootleggers and Baptists may have been agitating for a century or more, but the saloon is still with us—and usually on Sundays, too.

SOURCE: Abstracted from Bruce Yandle, "Bootleggers and Baptists—The Education of a Regulatory Economists," *Regulation*, May/June 1983, pp. 12–16. Reprinted by permission of The American Enterprise Institute. At the time this article was written, the author was executive director of the Federal Trade Commission, a major regulatory agency.

on checkable deposits, and thrift institutions have been restricted largely to short-term savings and long-term, fixed-interest-rate residential mortgages. SLAs must hold at least 60 percent of their assets in residential mortgage loans, government securities, or cash to qualify for favorable income tax status, and even higher percentages for other benefits. But the barriers that create these product specializations have been under attack on both the asset and liability sides of the balance sheet.

On the liability side, improvements in the electronic transfer of information and funds have tended to blur the distinctions between transaction and time deposits and even between deposits at depository institutions and funds at other financial institutions, such as money-market funds. Commercial banks have lost much of their traditional uniqueness as providers of transactions accounts. If funds can be transferred almost immediately from account to account or institution to institution, funds in time deposits or money-market funds can be transferred to demand deposits, to a third party, and back again to time deposits or money-mar-

TABLE 19–1	MAJOR DEREGULATION PROVISIONS OF THE DEPOSITORY INSTITUTIONS DEREGULATION AND MONETARY CONTROL ACT OF 1980 AND THE DEPOSITORY INSTITUTIONS (GARN-ST GERMAIN) ACT OF 1982

DEPOSIT RATE CEILINGS

▼ Required a phase-out of all deposit ceilings at all depository institutions over six-year period ending April 1, 1986.

▼ Removed ceiling-interest-rate differentials between commercial banks and thrift institutions.

LOAN RATE CEILINGS

▼ Preempted state usury ceilings on business and agricultural loans in excess of $25,000 for three years unless state reimposes ceiling.

▼ Eliminated state usury ceilings on residential mortgages unless state reimposes ceiling within three years.

FINANCIAL POWERS

▼ Permitted personal NOW accounts at all depository institutions (CBs, SLAs, SBs, CUs).

▼ Permitted federal thrift institutions to accept business demand deposits in connection with business loans.

▼ Permitted all federal credit unions to offer share drafts.

▼ Permitted federal SLAs to offer trust services.

▼ Permitted federal SLAs to offer credit cards.

▼ Permitted federal thrift institutions to invest in consumer loans (30 percent of assets), commercial loans (5 percent), commercial real estate loans (55 percent), leasing (10 percent), and corporate and municipal bonds.

▼ Permitted all depository institutions to offer money-market deposit accounts (MMDAs) without ceiling rate.

▼ Permitted all depository institutions to offer variable-interest-rate mortgages.

▼ Removed prohibition on due-on-sale provisions on mortgage loans made by all depository institutions.

GEOGRAPHIC RESTRICTIONS

▼ Permitted, with some size restrictions, interstate acquisitions of any type of failing depository institution by any other depository institution.

ket funds as fast and conveniently as from only demand to demand deposits. These transfers may be made by telephone, telegraph, teletype, or computer. Because interest-bearing deposits can be effectively used for third-party transfer, balances in non-interest-bearing demand deposits will be reduced. In response, all depository institutions were permitted to offer households interest-bearing checkable accounts, such as MMDs and NOW accounts. Thrift institutions were also permitted to accept business demand deposits on a limited scale. This has significantly reduced the differences among liabilities offered by the different depository institutions. Further reductions in differences await legal permission for all depository institutions to pay interest on demand deposits.

On the asset side, the high and volatile rates of price inflation in many recent years reduced the attractiveness of traditional fixed-rate residential mortgages to institutions that finance the mortgage loans with shorter-term deposits. As is discussed in Chapter 21, to be profitable, these institutions must predict accurately their future deposit rates and set the rate they charge on new fixed-rate mortgages equal to the average of the predicted deposit rates. If they underestimated future deposit rates, so that they increase more than expected or decline less than expected, the fixed-rate mortgages they originated earlier would be unprofitable. The increased volatility in the rate of inflation has added to the increase in the volatility in interest rates and made it more difficult to predict deposit rates with great accuracy. The rapid accelerations in the inflation rate (in the late 1970s and early 1980s) caught thrift institutions, which have been required by law to specialize in residential mortgage lending, and almost everyone else by surprise. As a result, the long-term mortgage interest rates set in earlier periods did not reflect the higher rates of inflation actually experienced, and short-term deposit rates went up more than expected. This exerted unfavorable pressures on the earnings of thrift institutions.

Because it is easier to predict interest rates when the time horizon is shorter and because rate predictions are not necessary at all when fixed-rate assets have the same durations as fixed-rate deposits, shorter-term loans would reduce the exposure of these institutions to unexpected interest rate changes. Starting in 1979, federally chartered and in 1982 all thrift institutions were permitted to make variable- or adjustable-rate mortgages on which the contract interest rate can be changed in line with changes in market rates or the cost of their funds. In addition, to reduce their credit-risk exposure through diversification, the institutions were granted powers to make both consumer, business, and commercial real estate loans. But many of these institutions may be expected to continue to specialize in a limited number of financial products, just as grocery stores voluntarily operate as supermarkets, convenience stores, gourmet shops, or old-fashioned "Ma and Pa" stores.

In contrast to its willingness to permit expanded powers for thrift institutions in the DIDMCA of 1980 and the Garn-St Germain Act of 1982, Congress has been more reluctant to expand the powers of commercial banks and bank holding companies. This reluctance may reflect a perception that the restrictions on commercial banks have not produced the financial havoc that occurred among thrift institutions, and therefore do not require urgent correction. Or Congress may consider the expansion of bank powers to be more a battle for turf among industries than a major public policy concern. Thus, despite the increased penetration of nonbanks into the banks' traditional turf and despite the increased use of new powers by banks in ways that circumvent the legal restrictions (such as joint ventures with and leasing of bank office space to legal providers), attempts to expand bank powers legally have languished in almost every recent session of Congress. At times, such bills have passed one or the other house of Congress, but not yet both at the same time.

Although the Federal Reserve has greatly expanded the authority of bank holding companies to trade and underwrite securities (the reasons for and against such underwriting are discussed in Chapter 20), banks are still prohibited from many financial activities, such as full-line insurance underwriting and brokerage, real estate brokerage, and most nonfinancial activities. But nonbank financial institutions generally are not similarly restricted and many insurance companies, investment banks, finance companies, and even some savings and loan associations are owned by nonfinancial firms. In some countries, commercial banks are permitted to engage in a wide range of financial and even nonfinancial activities. Such banks are referred to as **universal banks**. The (pros and cons of mixing banks and commerce are discussed in Exhibit 19–2).

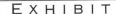

E X H I B I T

19–2

Mixing Commerce and Banking: The German Case

The appropriate relationship between banking and commerce is a central issue in the debate over banking reform. Reluctance to allow their commingling in the U.S. financial system has been marked by concerns over self-dealing and excessive risk taking that may destabilize the banking system and possible exploitation of the bank safety net.

The effects of mixing banking and commerce are discussed in light of the banking experience in West Germany. In West Germany, where "universal banking" is permitted, banks engage directly in investment banking, insurance, and real estate investment activities. They also own (or exercise proxy rights over) large blocks of shares in German industrial enterprises, and serve on the supervisory boards of German corporations. Approximately 80 percent of the 400 largest German corporations have bankers on their management committees, and about 15 percent of corporate equities are estimated to be held by banks. Over half of the shares of the top 100 or so German corporations are voted by banks.

In addition, there is no law prohibiting ownership of banks by commercial enterprises. One finds banks (and other depository institutions) owned by such diverse enterprises as bakeries, automobile manufacturers, retailers, and insurance companies. The German banking experience thus seems a natural laboratory for examining the effects of commingling banking and commerce.

IMPROVE EFFICIENCY?

A number of theoretical arguments can be made in favor of universal banking-type links to commercial firms. One is that the participation of the bank in managing a firm that is borrowing funds can facilitate efficient credit flow. Specifically, some economists have argued that bank lending is superior to open market financing for certain types of projects because banks can economically monitor those projects on an ongoing basis whereas credit markets cannot. It follows from this argument that if banks can improve their monitoring—by gaining entry to the internal decision making processes of a firm, for example, they can also identify and finance an otherwise unexploited set of projects.

Proponents of universal banking claim that the system has indeed improved the efficiency of Germany's economy. Alexander Gerschenkron and others, for example, believe that the empirical record implies that universal banking contributed to the rapid pace of German industrial development. (It is interesting to note in this regard that Japan, which presents another example of rapid economic development, also traditionally permitted affiliation of commerce and banking in the form of Zaibatsu groups.)

OTHER VIEWS

The view of universal banks as an efficiency-enhancing form of financial organization is not universally held. Within modern Germany, there is concern about the concentration of economic power that some feel results from the interlocking ownership of banking and commercial firms. They argue, for example, that these interlocks result in limited credit flows to smaller firms. The German Federal Monopolies Commission recently recommended that banks be allowed to own no more than 5 percent of the shares of a nonbank firm rather than the 25 percent limit enforced currently.

Another broad area of concern raised by the practice of universal banking is its effects on the stability of the banking system itself. In particular, can a bank that offers lending, investment banking, and securities trading services, and that has equity interests in nonbank firms (or vice versa) avoid conflicts of interest that may generate losses of confidence and destabilize the banking system?

Economists argue that competition is the bank customer's main protection against a bank trying to benefit itself or others at the customer's expense. A bank that is not careful to avoid conflicts of interest risks losing its customers (and reputation) to other banking firms. There is little evidence that German banking suffers from insufficient competition. At present there are approximately 4,800 banks able to provide universal banking services—250 commercial banks, 600 savings banks, and 4,000 cooperative banks. In addition, German banking is no more concentrated than U.S. or other European banking systems, and profits in the domestic German banking markets appear to be low.

EFFECTS OF DEPOSIT PROTECTION

A . . . thornier issue with universal banking is whether it is possible for government to provide some protection against systemic banking collapse without, ultimately, also shouldering what should be commercial risks. For example, if a bank can own corporate equities, and finance them with default-free debt (insured deposits), some risk effectively is transferred to the insuring entity. Similarly, if a commercial firm can own an insured bank, the possibility arises that the commercial firm will exploit the bank to finance risky investments.

Until 1976, Germany did not have explicit deposit insurance. Instead, it sought to reassure depositors through a stated general policy of protection the banking system against failure. The policy still exists and is imple-

mented through examination, capital regulation, lending limits, and laws against securities and other abuse. Evidence on whether this implicit deposit protection has extended into commerce is mixed. The fact that the traded equity and venture capital markets in Germany are very thin, for example, could suggest that banks enjoy artificially low costs of funds and out-compete other finance mechanisms.

In contrast, the prominence of German bank lending in corporate finance also would be expected if there were informational and control advantages to equity interlocks. That is, it need not signal an exploitation of governmental safety nets. This interpretation is reinforced by the fact that the ownership of banks by nonbanks, although permitted, is not widespread. Using asset measures, only about 5 percent of German banks have nonbank parents. This implies that any funding advantages present in those links are minor.

CONTINUE DEBATE

Universal banking has existed in a country that has enjoyed rapid postwar economic development and a relatively stable banking environment. To the extent that the Germans themselves have misgivings about their banking system, they do not appear to be our typical concerns about the stability of the banking sector or the desire for the banking system to be more supportive of business and industry. Rather, the misgivings seem to focus on universal banking's potential for concentrating economic power. This provides an interesting contrast to the content of debate about banking reform in the United States.

SOURCE: Abstracted from Randall Johnston Pozdena, "Commerce and Banking," *Weekly Letter*, Federal Reserve Bank of San Francisco, December 18, 1987.

Author's Note: West Germany, is now the major part of reunified Germany.

In early 1991, the U.S. Treasury Department recommended that healthy and well-capitalized banks be permitted to engage in a wide array of financial activities, including securities and insurance, generally through separate affiliates of the bank's parent holding company. The proposal also would permit nonbank financial and nonfinancial firms to own bank holding companies, which would be named *Financial Services Holding Companies* (FSHCs). This proposal would effectively repeal the Bank Holding Company Act restrictions. (The major recommendations of the Treasury study are shown in Table 19–2). The Treasury's recommendations were not included in the FDIC Improvement Act of 1991.

TABLE

19–2

373

DEREGULATION
AND REGULATORY
REFORM

RECOMMENDATIONS BY THE TREASURY DEPARTMENT FOR MODERNIZING THE FINANCIAL SYSTEM, 1991
PRODUCT POWERS
▼ Permit well-capitalized banks a wider range of financial and nonfinancial activities through holding company affiliates.
▼ Permit nonfinancial firms to own bank holding companies, renamed financial services holding companies.
GEOGRAPHIC POWERS
▼ Permit national banks to branch across state lines.
▼ Permit nationwide bank affiliates of holding companies.
DEPOSIT INSURANCE
▼ Generally restrict insurance coverage to $100,000 per account per bank.
▼ Scale insurance premiums to bank's capital adequacy.
▼ Early intervention by the regulators in problem institutions. Restrict their activities and operational discretion and force recapitalization to reduce probability of failure.
▼ Discretion by regulators to exempt depositors at some banks from suffering losses when their bank fails, if this is the lowest-cost resolution or if the bank is sufficiently large to spill the problem over to other banks.
REGULATORY AGENCIES
▼ National banks, national bank holding companies, and savings and loan associations would be regulated by a new Federal Banking Agency (Office of Depository Institutions Supervision) to be housed in the Treasury Department.
▼ State banks and state bank holding companies would be regulated by the Federal Reserve.
▼ The FDIC would monitor all insured banks and resolve failures, but not regulate or examine them directly.

SOURCE: U.S. Treasury Department, *Modernizing the Financial System: Recommendations for Safer, More Competitive Banks.* Washington, D.C.: Government Printing Office, 1991.

Geographic Powers

Unlike almost all other firms, depository institutions are restricted by federal and state law not only in their ability to enter the industry but also in their ability to operate and locate branch and holding company affiliated banking offices. Office expansion generally results in larger and more influential financial institutions, and the restrictions reflect the fear of undue concentration of power in banking and finance. Restrictions on branching have come under attack for four reasons:

1. The need for institutions to follow their customers to the suburbs and other newer areas into which they have moved in increasing numbers from central cities
2. The breakdown in specialization and calls for equal treatment of all institutions providing the same services
3. The ability to reduce credit risk through greater geographic diversification

4. The introduction of EFTS, which has reduced the need for costly brick-and-mortar offices and has increased the desirability of lower-cost remote service units (ATMs)

Most early commercial banks in the United States did not have branches. Branching was restricted by state statute. Early settlers had brought with them a distrust of banking that was reinforced, particularly in the agricultural states, by the traditional debtor-creditor conflict between farmer and bank. In periods of sharp price declines for agricultural products, farmers were often unable to meet their loan payments and were forced to default. The bank would auction off the farm. In some states, commercial banking was periodically prohibited altogether.

The National Bank Act of 1864, which authorized national charters for banks, was interpreted as restricting the national banks to a single office, except for those banks that converted to national charters from state charters. These were permitted to retain the branches they operated at the date of conversion but not to acquire additional ones. Branching was permitted for state-chartered banks in some states, but even there, branches were generally restricted to the same city as the main office either by statute or by the high costs of supervising distant offices. Effectively, no state permitted full-service branches at out-of-state banks. In 1900, fewer than 100 banks, or only 1 percent of all commercial banks, operated branch offices, and most of these had only one additional office. Even by 1920, fewer than 2 percent of all banks operated branches, and branches accounted for less than 5 percent of all banking offices.

Because of the increased use of the automobile and the improvement of highways, the dispersal of population away from the central city accelerated. Many banks lost their customers. At the same time, the same advances in transportation, along with advances in communication, made it easier for banks to supervise more distant branches offices. As a result, pressure intensified for more liberal branching regulations. However, the increase in the number of branch banks also rekindled the opposition to branching. In 1927, the McFadden Act permitted national banks to establish new branches for the first time, but only within their city limits and only in states that permitted state banks to branch. Although the act liberalized national bank branching regulations, it was more restrictive than some state statutes and subordinated federal branching statute to state statute. The act was viewed as a defeat for the proponents of branch banking. In the second half of the 1920s, 13 states acted to prohibit branch banking altogether. Most of these were states in which there were no or few branches. By 1930, branching was permitted in only 19 of the 48 states. In some states, banks were able to supplement or circumvent branching restrictions by organizing bank holding companies and acquiring or establishing other in- or out-of-state banks.

Public attitude toward branch banking changed dramatically after the beginning of the depression of the 1930s and the virtual collapse of the banking system. The failure of many of the banks, particularly smaller rural banks, was attributed to excessive concentration of deposits and loans in one sector. Branching was believed to reduce the risk of banking by permitting greater diversification. The Banking Act of 1933 broadened the ability of national banks to branch on an equal footing with state banks. Between 1930 and 1935, 12 states changed from prohibiting branches to permitting them, and three more states that already permitted branches further liber-alized their branching regulations. For the first time, serious consideration was also given to permitting banks to branch across state lines within "trade areas," but this was not enacted. Because of the weak financial posi-tion of banks in this period, most banks did not immediately rush into branching. By 1940, branch banks accounted for only 6 percent of all banks, but the number of branches had increased sharply to 20 percent of all bank-ing offices.

Then, a combination of factors—an acceleration in the rate of subur-banization after World War II, restrictive policies with respect to the char-tering of new banks, and ceilings on deposit rates that encouraged financial institutions to compete by building more branch offices closer to their cus-tomers and pressuring state legislatures to liberalize branching laws—caused the number of bank branches to jump from 3,700 in 1945 to some 52,000 in 1992. In that year, branches accounted for more than 80 percent of all bank offices. By 1992, no state prohibited intrastate branch banking. Finally in 1994, Congress authorized interstate branching effective for most banks in June 1997.

Interstate Banking

Interstate banking was restricted by the McFadden Act and state statutes, which prohibited out-of-state branches for national and state-chartered banks, respectively, and by the Douglas Amendment to the Bank Holding Company Act, which prohibited holding companies to acquire or establish banks in other states except if the laws of that state explicitly permitted such operations. Until the 1980s, few state statutes did.

The Commission on Money and Credit in 1961 and the President's Commission on Financial Structure and Regulation in 1971, both of which carefully studied the financial structure, recommended that commercial banks be permitted to branch throughout trade areas, such as metropolitan areas, regardless of state boundaries. Proponents argued that by removing local protections, interstate branching would intensify the degree of com-petition. The overall number of bank offices may also be expected to increase, which would increase the convenience of banking for consumers. It makes little sense not to have the same banks available to all households and business firms in the same area. Although interstate branching may encourage mergers and reduce the number of banks overall, proponents argue that it would increase the number of banks in many local market areas and lower costs through economies of scale. In addition, the restric-tion against interstate offices discriminates unfairly against commercial banks. These are increasingly competing in the same financial services with institutions, such as investment banks, which are not restricted at all in interstate offices, and savings and loan associations, which are less severe-ly restricted. Finally, interstate branching would permit banks to lessen their dependency on their local economies and to reduce their risk through diversification. Thus, fewer of the banks in Texas would have failed in the late 1980s and in New England in the early 1990s had they been permitted to operate in both areas (or better yet throughout the country), as New England was booming in the late 1980s and Texas was recovering in the early 1990s.

Opposition to interstate banking rested on the fear of increased concentration, reduced competition, and excessive economic and political power. State boundaries effectively limit the size of individual banks and prevent the formation of large, national banking systems. The experiences of other countries are interpreted to support the fears. In most developed countries, banks are permitted to branch nationwide. As a result, these countries generally have only a few very large banks, compared with 11,000 banks of various sizes in the United States. These banks are considered to have substantially greater domestic economic and political power than American banks. In addition, there is little evidence that significant economies of scale actually occur in banking, particularly through branching, so that price reductions are unlikely.

Moreover, through the early 1980s, opponents argued that commercial banks were already operating across state lines through loan production offices and the holding company form of organization in almost all permitted activities except full-scale retail banking. Citicorp, BankAmerica, and other larger bank holding companies operated offices, including nonbank banks, in almost all 50 states. Even in retail banking, the importance of brick-and-mortar offices was being reduced by automatic teller machines and the 800 telephone number. After all, money-market funds, which have been so successful in attracting deposits away from banks and thrift institutions, generally operate from only a single office with 800 numbers.

To the surprise of most analysts, the first changes in interstate banking laws occurred not on the national level, but on the state level. States entered into reciprocal banking arrangements in which out-of-state banks could establish offices through holding company affiliates if the state in which the bank was located would permit offices of the first state's banks. The only national action taken by 1993 was a provision in the Garn-St Germain Act that out-of-state banks could acquire failing banks and thrift institutions.

In 1975, Maine and New York were the first states to enact legislation that conformed with the Douglas Amendment and freely permitted bank holding companies in other states with similar legislation to acquire full-service banking offices in their states—*reciprocal interstate banking*. (Florida and Iowa had previously passed legislation permitting interstate operations only for very limited banks on a "grandfather" basis.) Starting in the early 1980s, an increasing number of states enacted similar legislation, but limited the eligible states to only those in the same region. Most of these states specifically omitted New York banks. In 1982, Alaska was the first state to permit free entry by any out-of-state bank. Many of the regional pacts contained *triggers* that automatically broadened the number of states or permitted national banking after a specified number of years. By 1994, every state had enacted some form of interstate banking. Few states, however, permitted out-of-state holding companies to start new (*de novo*) banks.

Although these arrangements breached the barriers to interstate banking, they were not viewed as either efficient or equitable by all parties. Some feared that the regional restrictions violated free and equal interstate commerce authorized by the Constitution. The legality of regional compacts that excluded some states were challenged by New York banks, but upheld by the Supreme Court in 1985. Others were concerned that many other financial institutions still had more advantageous full interstate branching powers and that interstate banking through holding company affiliates was less efficient than through branching.

What was evident to all was that for the first time in U.S. history, near nationwide full-service interstate banking was a reality. However, like so much else in banking regulation, it was evolving piecemeal and not necessarily rationally. As a result, some argued for a federal interstate policy that would provide for equal treatment of all banks and other depository institutions to avoid the regulatory confusion that plagued other areas of banking. On the other hand, others argued that it is only the existence of competition among regulatory agencies—federal versus federal, federal versus state, and state versus state—that led to the liberalization of interstate banking that had occurred. Indeed, they find it ironic that an issue that affects national banking practice and the national interest as much as interstate banking was significantly changed without any federal legislation whatsoever.

Although interstate banking now existed, it did so only on a bank holding company basis. Permitting interstate branching for national banks required modification of the McFadden Act at the federal level. This had been recommended by the Treasury Department, and legislation to this effect was introduced in Congress in 1991, but failed to be enacted. In early 1994, using a technicality in the National Bank Act, the Comptroller permitted a bank holding company with offices in Pennsylvania and New Jersey to combine them into a single branching system. Shortly thereafter, Congress authorized interstate branching as part of the Banking Modernization Act of 1994. The act formally repeals the Douglas Amendment effective mid-1995 and permits bank holding companies to consolidate affiliated banks across state lines into branching systems effective June 1997. Individual states may elect either to permit their banks to become branches of out-of-state banks sooner or to prohibit their banks from becoming such branches. The removal of state lines as barriers to branch banking should sharply reduce the overall number of banking organizations.

Deregulation and Bank Safety

Lack of government regulation of an industry does not necessarily imply that the industry is risky and that the failure rate is high. After all, most industries in the United States are not regulated by the government. But their performance is regulated. It is regulated by the private marketplace, which rewards successful firms with higher profits and punishes unsuccessful firms with failure. Because government regulation of banks was frequently intensified out of concern about bank safety, deregulation is sometimes believed to endanger bank safety.

Deregulation may increase bank failures in a number of ways. One, by permitting increased competition, the number of failures should increase by definition. Two, although deregulation grants banks new product and geographic powers to permit them to reduce their risk exposure through diversification, some of these powers may be risky by themselves and may be used by risk-seeking institutions to increase their risk exposure. Three, deregulation may be accompanied by reduced government monitoring and supervision of banks so that the FDIC may not have sufficient information or authority to identify poorly performing banks and to take corrective actions before they become insolvent. Four, because regulation was used to reduce risk exposure, deregulation must be accompanied by an offsetting increase in private market regulation to control risk. In particular, the regulators must permit failure, which is the strongest force of market discipline and provides the strongest incentive against excessive risk taking.

Unfortunately, policymakers did not permit the bank deregulation of the 1980s to be accompanied by a compensating increase in market regulation, in particular, by the threat of failure. Bank failures were viewed as undesirable because it was believed that they were contagious and could spill over to other banks, that banks were unique providers of money and credit to their communities, and that failures would be a black mark on the regulators' record. But the first two fears are unjustified, and the third fear, while true, reflects irresponsibility. As discussed in Chapter 11, with federal deposit insurance, runs on individual banks will not expand into currency runs on the banking system as a whole. As has been evident to all bankers for years, even if banks were sole providers of money and credit in the past, they certainly are not today. Many other types of financial institutions, such as finance companies and money-market funds, and even some nonfinancial firms offer traditional banking deposit and loan-like services. All of these institutions are noninsured and subject to greater market discipline. As a result, as was shown on Table 18–1, most operate with capital ratios at least twice as high as for commercial banks and thrift institutions.

The lessening of government regulation of risk without increasing monitoring by the regulators and market regulation resulted in an increase in risk taking by institutions. The delay in recognizing the seriousness of the problem in the late 1980s and the reluctance of the regulators to force insolvent institutions to be recapitalized, sold, merged, or liquidated permitted these institutions second, third, and even more chances to roll the dice. Because proportionately few big gambles pay off, the resulting losses were passed on to the federal deposit insurance agency and, in the case of the FSLIC, eventually to the taxpayer. By imposing stricter capital requirements, greater freedoms for well-capitalized institutions, earlier and more mandatory regulatory intervention in the affairs of troubled institutions, and closure of a troubled institution before its capital is fully depleted, FDICIA attempts to reconcile safety and deregulation.

Reform of Regulatory Agencies

Like that of regulations, the structure of the regulatory agencies reflects American history, in particular the division between federal and states' rights and the tendency to establish new agencies to deal with new concerns. As we saw in Chapter 16, responsibilities among the regulatory agencies substantially overlap, so that many functions are shared by two or more agencies, often at the same level of government. Some argue that there are too many cooks in the regulatory kitchen! A report issued by a congressional committee referred to this structure as a "crazy quilt" and lamented the fact that it evolved from historical accident rather than from a well-conceived master plan. Arthur Burns, a former chairman of the Board of Governors of the Federal Reserve System, called the existing structure "a jurisdictional tangle that boggles the mind." The degree of parallel and overlapping regulatory and supervisory relationships for commercial bank-

FIGURE

19–2   THE TANGLED WEB OF BANK REGULATION

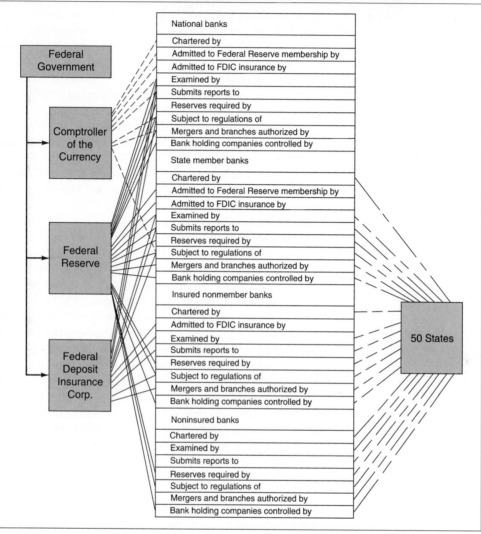

SOURCE: Raymond Natter, *Formation and Powers of National Banking Associations—A Legal Primer.* Washington, D.C.: Congressional Research Service, Library of Congress, 1983, pp. 1–10.

ing alone is evident from Figure 19–2. It is frequently claimed that the different agencies get in each other's way, squabble among themselves, administer the same regulations unevenly, issue conflicting edicts, engage in "competition in laxity," impose parochial views, and rule with a heavy hand. In addition, supervision of some institutions and activities may fall between the cracks. As a result, there have been almost continual calls for changes in the structure. Most of these recommend reducing the number of agencies and simplifying the relationships. In this chapter, we analyze the arguments for and against changes in the existing structure of financial regulations.

Proposals for reform date back many years. The Commission on Money and Credit recommended in 1961 that most federal regulatory functions be transferred to the Federal Reserve. Ten years later, the President's Commission recommended a more drastic overhaul. The Comptroller of the Currency would be renamed the Office of the National Bank Administrator, moved out of the Treasury Department, and given supervisory and regulatory responsibility for all federally chartered commercial banks, savings banks, and savings and loan associations whose checking accounts totaled more than 10 percent of their total deposits. A new agency, called the Office of the Administrator of State Banks, would be established to supervise and regulate all state-chartered, insured commercial banks, savings banks, and savings and loan associations whose checking accounts totaled more than 10 percent of their total deposits. Most of the supervisory duties of the Fed would be shifted to this agency. Another new agency, the Federal Deposit Guarantee Administration, would incorporate the deposit insurance functions of the FDIC, FSLIC, and NCUSIF. The former Federal Home Loan Bank System and the National Credit Union Administration would have retained most of their powers. The Fed would be freed to concentrate on monetary policy.

In 1982, a Task Group on Regulation of Financial Services was appointed by then President Reagan and chaired by Vice President Bush (Bush Commission). It issued its report in 1984, after a long series of public hearings and submissions and intense political lobbying by the regulatory agencies. Partially as a result, the recommendations were not as sweeping as those of some of the earlier commissions. The proposed changes focus on reducing duplication of supervision and regulation. The Office of the Comptroller of the Currency (OCC) would be reorganized as the Federal Banking Agency (FBA) and have primary authority over national banks and bank holding companies. Much of the supervision of state banks would be vested solely in state banking agencies. The Federal Reserve would share primary authority with the new FBA over the very largest "international class" bank holding companies and have temporary authority over all insured state banks until the state agencies are ready to take over. The Fed would then concentrate primarily on monetary policy. The FDIC would lose its supervisory responsibilities and serve solely as a deposit insurance agency. Thrift institution regulatory agencies would be left pretty much as they were.

In 1991, the Treasury Department recommended that the number of regulatory agencies be reduced to two, one of which, not surprisingly, would be itself. The other one would be the Federal Reserve. The FDIC would remain as the insurer of banks and thrifts, but would have no regulatory and supervisory responsibilities except for resolving failed institutions. A new Federal Banking Agency (later renamed the Office of Depository Institutions Supervision) housed in the Treasury would have regulatory and supervisory powers over all institutions but state-chartered commercial banks. These would be under the Fed, which would also have responsibility for bank holding companies that have a state-chartered bank subsidiary.

At year-end 1993, the Clinton administration proposed a new Federal Banking Commission (FBC), which would regulate, supervise, and examine all federally insured banks and savings associations. Thus, it would consolidate the current regulatory functions of the Comptroller, the Fed, the FDIC, and the Office of Thrift Supervision (OTS). Credit unions would not be included; they would continue to be under the supervision of the National Credit Union Administration. States would continue to have responsibility for state-chartered institutions. Although out of bank regulation, the Fed would retain its monetary policy, lender of last resort, and payments system functions. The FDIC would continue to provide deposit insurance and resolve failed institutions. The OCC and OTS would be abolished. The FBC would have five members. Three, including the chair, would be appointed by the president, the chair for a four-year term and the other two for staggered five-year terms. The remaining two members would be the secretary of the treasury and the chairman of the Federal Reserve Board.

Numerous other proposals have been offered for combining the three federal regulatory agencies into a smaller number or even into one agency, for example, the Brookings Study (1937), the Hoover Commission (1949), the Financial Institutions and the Nation's Economy (FINE) Study (1975). Although this idea has generated considerable support, differences exist as to which agency would absorb the others. Each of the existing agencies is willing to absorb the others, but none is willing to be absorbed or lose much of its "turf."

Despite all the studies, through 1993, the only major restructuring of the bank regulatory agencies in the post–World War II period was enacted by FIRREA in 1989 for the SLAs in the wake of the debacle in the industry. The Federal Home Loan Bank Board was widely perceived as having failed to prevent the crisis at a high dollar cost to the taxpayers and the credibility of Congress. As punishment, rather than as the result of any particular reorganization blueprint, the agency was abolished and its powers distributed among existing agencies. Its regulatory responsibilities were transferred to a new Office of Thrift Supervision (OTS) in the Treasury Department and its deposit insurance functions in the FSLIC were transferred to a new Savings Association Insurance Fund (SAIF) in the FDIC.

The Case against Multiple Agencies

The most obvious case against multiple agencies is the high cost of inefficiency produced by a duplication of activities, overcrowding, and lack of a central authority with which the regulated institutions can communicate and from which they can obtain an ultimate decision or agreement. Widespread economies could be achieved by reducing the number of agencies. Staff and training programs could be combined; travel time of examiners reduced, personnel specialization increased for complicated problems such as trust activities, international operations, computer data processing, and so on; uniform regulations promulgated; and uniform reports compiled.

Another, equally important cost of the present multiagency structure is the differing treatment of similar financial institutions by the different agencies and differing interpretations of the same regulations or legislation. To a large degree, nonuniform enforcement stems from competition among the agencies, their differing objectives reflecting their other responsibilities, and simply different personnel. Former Federal Reserve Board Chairman Burns noted that:

The present regulatory system fosters what has sometimes been called "competition in laxity." Even viewed in the most favorable light, the present system is conducive to subtle competition among regulatory authorities, sometimes to relax constraints, sometimes to delay constructive measures. I need not explain to bankers the well-understood fact that regulatory agencies are sometimes played off against one another.[2]

Applicants denied a charter for a new financial institution by the state may try the federal government, or vice versa. A bank denied a merger or a particular activity by one agency may change or threaten to change jurisdictional agency by changing its charter.

An example of the ability of banks to play one agency off against another is the reversal by the FDIC of a previous denial of a proposed merger between two small banks in Texas. In his dissent to the majority view, Frank Willie, chairman of the FDIC at the time, wrote:

> I suppose it is indelicate to suggest that the real reason for the Board's reversal has something to do with the explicitness of Mr. ____'s (the purchaser) reminder that he can recast the proposal so that the resulting bank would be a national bank, thus permitting the Comptroller of the Currency alone to approve the desired transaction under the Bank Merger Act.[3]

A single, strong regulatory agency might have been able to prevent the deterioration in bank capital levels during the 1970s that endangered the solvency of many banks.

Moreover, for reasons already discussed, the differences among all types of financial institutions are breaking down. The institutions are increasingly offering the same or similar products and services. Both logic and equity suggest that all competitors should be treated evenly and be subject to the same rules and regulations, and they weaken the case for maintaining different regulations and regulatory agencies for different types of institutions.

Regulatory agencies that also have nonregulatory responsibilities may reasonably be expected to take the objectives of these other duties into account in evaluating the activities of the institutions under their jurisdiction. Besides bank regulation and supervision, the Fed is concerned with monetary policy and, since 1981, the marketing of check clearing and other bank services, and the FDIC is concerned with the solvency of the deposit fund. Concern over the safety of one or more larger banks for reasons that are not closely associated with the current state of the economy and the need to provide the necessary liquidity as lender of last resort could induce the Fed to pursue a more expansive monetary policy than it would otherwise.

Because responsibilities over even the same bank are divided among different agencies, action at times of immediate crises may be slowed

---

[2] Arthur F. Burns, "Maintaining the Soundness of Our Banking System," speech to American Bankers Association Convention, Honolulu, Hawaii, October 21, 1974, pp. 18–19.

[3] Frank Willie, *Dissenting Statement, FDIC Approves Merger in Alice, Texas,* news release, FDIC, August 18, 1975.

because of the need for all the involved agencies to meet and to coordinate their actions. For example, while the FDIC has the responsibility to protect depositors at floundering institutions, until FDICIA, it could not payoff depositors until the bank has been legally declared insolvent by the chartering agency—either the comptroller or the respective state—and this could depend on how long, if at all, the Fed was willing to provide liquidity through the discount window to keep the bank afloat. For example, Stanley Silverberg, former director of research at the FDIC, noted that in the Continental Bank case:

> If the FDIC had wanted to pay off Continental in May [1984], I don't think we could have gotten there. I suspect the Fed would have continued to fund it and the Comptroller would not have closed it.[4]

Yet it is the FDIC's funds and not those of the chartering agencies that are at risk if delayed closure enlarges losses. It is thus ironic that, in its reform of the SLA regulatory structure, FIRREA separated the chartering and insurance powers, which had previously been united in the Federal Home Loan Bank Board (recall that FSLIC was housed with the FHLBB) between the Office of Thrift Supervision in the Treasury Department and the FDIC.

The Case for Multiple Agencies

Opponents of fewer bank regulatory agencies or a single agency, while admitting that competition among the agencies results in inefficiency and possible laxity, argue that such competition among government regulatory agencies is as desirable as is rivalry among private business firms. Although competition may force some firms to duplicate services offered by other firms and to fail, it also encourages greater efficiency, responsiveness, and willingness to experiment and innovate—advantages that are generally believed to outweigh the disadvantages. Similarly, although a single, all-powerful regulatory agency might be able to adopt more restrictive standards and to enforce them uniformly, it could do so only at the cost of reducing the responsiveness of the institutions and their willingness to experiment and innovate. Risk taking would be reduced, and safety and caution would be given increased priority. Also, the agency could be unduly rigid and arbitrary. There would be no system of "checks and balances" or availability of informed and influential critics such as exist in a multiauthority structure.

Although "shopping" among agencies does at times result in decisions that may be contrary to the public interest, such shopping may also result in decisions that are in the public interest, such as granting permission to offer new activities or forming a more competitive banking structure by permitting more liberal branching into the home areas of other banks. For instance, the increase in the number of commercial banks in the early 1960s after a long period of decline may be attributed to a more liberal chartering policy introduced by a newly appointed comptroller, James Saxon, at a time that most states were pursuing a more restrictive policy.

[4] Stanley Silverberg, "Resolving Large Bank Problems," paper delivered at Symposium on Issues and Options in Dealing with Large Bank Problems and Failures, Dartmouth College, New Hampshire, August 29–30, 1984, p. 2.

Likewise, until stopped by the Competitive Equality Banking Act of 1987, the decision of the comptroller in the early 1980s to grant bank charters to institutions that did not qualify as commercial banks under the Bank Holding Company Act's definition—an institution that provides both business loans and demand deposits—and that therefore did not come under the supervision of the Fed, and of the FDIC to insure these "nonbank banks" against the opposition of the Fed, permitted the establishment of a larger number and variety of competing depository institutions. Finally, the birth of interstate banking discussed earlier in this chapter resulted from competition among state regulatory agencies.

As evidence of the potentially restrictive nature of single regulatory agencies, critics point to the alleged inefficiency and unresponsiveness of industries regulated by a single agency, such as ground transportation (railroads, barge lines, and trucks) by the Interstate Commerce Commission and, until their deregulation, airlines by the Civil Aeronautics Board. Most of these industries are widely considered to have performed poorly compared with nonregulated industries. In contrast, at least until 1981, the financial sector is generally considered to have performed well in the post–World War II period. The institutions have grown rapidly despite dramatic events in the financial and economic environment, such as inflation, rapidly rising and volatile interest rates, currency devaluations, some big-bank failures, and rapid acceleration in the transmission of funds through EFTSs and in the automation of many banking functions. Commercial banks have been innovative in adjusting to the changed environment and in creating new instruments and techniques of intermediation. Financial markets have functioned efficiently and, if anything, have become more competitive. Until some larger banks encountered troubles in the 1980s, one would be hard pressed to find many major industries that have been as dynamic as commercial banking has been in recent years. The financial institutions that have experienced the greatest problems in recent years have been the savings and loan associations, despite being regulated at the time by only one federal agency—the Federal Home Loan Bank Board.

Thus, supporters of the existing regulatory structure see little reason for substantial changes. In general, they recommend minor changes in structure that focus primarily on increased cooperation among the agencies, such as the establishment of the Federal Financial Institutions Examination Council in 1979. Better to let well enough alone! To them, the solution to the problem of the optimal structure is similar to that given by President Lincoln when he was asked about the optimal length of a soldier's legs. "Long enough to reach the ground," he is reported to have replied.

Prospects for Reform

The lack of widespread agreement about the optimal type of regulatory structure explains both the wide range of recommendations for differing structures and the failure to adopt any substantial changes since the major crisis of the 1930s. Moreover, both because banking is viewed by most members of the public as highly complex and outside their own areas of expertise, and because the financial system has served the public reasonably well, there is little public groundswell for change until it breaks down and stops working.

It is important to recognize that significant benefits are derived by many institutions under the current hydra-headed organization that would be lost under alternative organizations. As a result, congressional hearings on reform are attended principally by bankers, officials of other financial institutions and regulators—all of whom have a great deal to lose or gain from any changes—and by academicians—who often view themselves as in the business of designing more logical structures. The hearings receive little coverage in the general press. Regulatory reform may be likened to tax reform; it is always good for the other guy! Regulators generally favor consolidation as long as their agency is the surviving agency.

It is not difficult to see why major reforms are adopted only when there is widespread dissatisfaction with the existing structure or when there are fears of an actual or perceived financial crisis. Only then are large losses likely to be inflicted on other important sectors of the economy. At other times, it is generally considered wise to let sleeping dogs lie and introduce patchwork improvements that will carry the structure over a current crisis. The concerned parties view proposals for consolidation as battles over turf, and protection of their own turf becomes their primary objective. For example, although most experts have long argued that the Fed's regulatory powers frequently conflict with its monetary policy powers and distract from its most important function, the Fed has been unwilling to surrender its regulatory functions. Thus, the Fed announced its opposition to the Clinton administration's proposed Federal Banking Commission, arguing that:

> It is the long-held conviction of the Board that a hands-on role in banking supervision is essential to carrying out the Federal Reserve's responsibilities for the stability in the financial system and is vital for the effective conduct of monetary policy. While the Board recognizes the overlaps in bank supervision that have emerged in recent years, it is essential that any proposal for change preserve the important benefits of the current system.[5]

Only FIRREA, which was enacted when the sleeping dogs awoke and barked loudly, made major changes in the regulatory structure, and it did so primarily to punish an agency, FHLBB, that the public believed had failed badly to perform its duties rather than to improve the efficiency of the regulatory structure. The FHLBB's functions were primarily distributed to two other agencies—the FDIC and the Treasury—that welcomed them with open arms. On the other hand, neither DIDMCA nor DIA, which made major changes in the regulations administered by the regulatory agencies, made real changes in the agencies themselves. How much, if any, of the Clinton administration's proposed sweeping restructuring will be enacted remains to be seen. But if history is a guide, the proposal will have a tough road ahead. In recognition of the strong opposition, the Clinton administration was forced to move its reform proposal to a rear burner in mid-1994.

---

[5] Board of Governors of the Federal Reserve System, "Press Release," Washington, D.C., November 23, 1993.

Kenneth Scott attributes the failure to move faster toward a more "rational" structure to the failure to have a "comprehensive and powerful theory of the political process and regulation. A large body of rather elegant theory and accumulated data can be brought to bear on the functioning of economic markets, but not on the working of political markets."[6]

Judge Richard Posner, a well-known student of regulation, describes a "life-cycle" theory of administrative regulation that appears to be particularly applicable to banking regulation. This theory postulates that an agency is created by the legislature when there is strong public and legislative interest in the area as a result of some crisis or important disclosure. As time passes, the problem tends to become less important relative to other, newer problems, and the public and legislature shift their attentions elsewhere. Less time is devoted to monitoring the performance of the industry and of the regulatory agency. The performance of both may deteriorate unnoticed and unopposed, even though, as the economy grows and becomes more complex, administrative efficiency becomes more important. Nevertheless, unless major problems arise, the regulatory structure continues unaltered except for periodic cosmetic changes.

SUMMARY

Calls to reform bank regulations have appeared for as long as banks have been regulated. But the calls have become more frequent and widespread as the economic, financial, and technical environments in which banks operate have changed greatly. In contrast, most regulations and regulatory structures reflect the depression conditions of the 1930s and emphasize safety at the expense of competition and efficiency. The Depository Institutions Deregulation Act (1980) and Garn-St Germain Act (1982) validated many of the de facto changes that had been brought about by market forces; most important, removing interest rate ceilings and reducing the restrictions on the products that primarily thrifts can offer. Depository institutions can now offer a wide range of deposit services, including some transaction deposits, at any interest rate they wish. To permit them to reduce their risk exposure through diversification, thrift institutions were permitted to offer variable-rate mortgage loans and shorter-term commercial and consumer loans. Despite no new national legislation until 1994, full-service interstate banking has become widespread in recent years on a holding company basis. National legislation enacted in 1994 will also permit it on a branching basis effective June 1997 for most banks. As long as market forces continue to change, de facto as well as catch-up de jure, changes in bank regulations may be expected to continue. However, when failures increase and induce concerns about safety, some reregulation, as was contained in FIRREA (1989) and summarized in Table 12–2, may be expected. Partially as a result, no significant changes in product or geographic powers were included in the FDIC Improvement Act of 1991. But

---

[6] Kenneth E. Scott, "The Patchwork Quilt: State and Federal Roles in Bank Regulation," *Stanford Law Review*, April 1980, p. 742.

when the health of the banking industry improves, as it has in the early 1990s, additional powers are more likely to be granted.

The most important change proposed in the regulatory structure is to reduce the number of bank regulatory agencies. Proponents argue that this would increase efficiency and uniformity, and avoid "competition in laxity" among the agencies. Opponents argue that the faults of regulation are in the nature of the beast and cannot be corrected by changing only the number of beasts. They note that other single-agency regulators have been no more successful in achieving the original goals of regulation, and some have been far worse. Moreover, competition among regulators, like competition among banks, is favorable on net. But because regulatory agency restructuring frequently boils down to a battle over turf, little has occurred. The same fate appears likely for the recent Clinton Administration proposal for regulatory agency consolidation.

QUESTIONS

1. What is meant by "reform" of financial regulatory agencies? Why has support for reform increased in recent years?

2. In 1993, the Clinton administration proposed a major reorganization and consolidation of the bank regulatory agencies. Trace what has happened to this proposal since. What were some of the arguments made for and against this proposal?

3. If there were only one agency to regulate all major financial intermediary institutions, which existing or newly created agency would you favor? Why?

4. Why were banks and bank holding companies limited in the products and services that they could offer? Why are similar restrictions not imposed on other firms? Do you think that these restrictions are productive today? Why or why not?

5. It appears that because of recent regulatory changes and technological advances, distinctions among major depository institutions are disappearing. Do you foresee any future for specialized intermediaries? Discuss your argument?

6. Weigh the case for and against interstate branch banking. Would you include remote automatic teller machines as branch offices? Why, or why not?

7. How was it possible that interstate holding company banking was possible without permissive federal legislation? Why and how did it come about? Could the same thing happen for interstate branching? How? As nationwide banking through the holding company format basically exists today, is interstate branching as necessary? Discuss.

8. Most other countries permit their banks broader geographic and product powers than does the United States. Why might that be? From casual observation, can you reach any preliminary conclusions as to how well permitting banks broader powers has worked and why?

9. How far have each of the proposals recommended by the Treasury Department in 1991 and summarized in Table 19–2 progressed to date? Why have some progressed further than others?

REFERENCES

Benston, George J., ed., *Financial Services: The Changing Institutions and Government Policy*. Englewood Cliffs, N.J.: Prentice Hall, 1983.

Benston, George J., et. al., *Perspectives on Safe and Sound Banking*. Cambridge, Mass.: MIT Press, 1986.

Bentson, George J., and George G. Kaufman, *Risk and Solvency Regulation of Depository Institutions: Past Policies and Current Options*. New York: Salomon Brothers Center, New York University, 1988.

Blueprint for Reform: Report of the Task Group on Regulation of Financial Services. Washington, D.C.: U.S. Government Printing Office, July 1984.

Boyd, John H., and Stanley, L. Graham, "Investigating the Banking Consolidation Trend," *Quarterly Review*, Federal Reserve Bank of Minneapolis, Spring 1991, pp. 3–15.

Cargill, Thomas F., and Gillian G. Garcia, *Financial Policy Reform in the 1980's*. Stanford, Calif.: Hoover Institution Press, 1985.

Commission on Money and Credit, *Report: Money and Credit*. Englewood Cliffs, N.J.: Prentice Hall, 1961.

Council of Economic Advisers, "Rethinking Regulation," *Economic Report of the President*. Washington, D.C.: Government Printing Office, January 1989, pp. 187–222.

Edwards, Franklin R., ed., *Issues in Financial Regulation*. New York: McGraw-Hill, 1979.

England, Catherine, and Thomas Huertas, eds. *The Financial Services Revolution*. Boston: Kluwer, 1988.

Evanoff, Douglas D., et al, "Financial Industry Deregulation in the 1980s," *Economic Perspectives*, Federal Reserve Bank of Chicago, September/October, 1985.

Federal Reserve Bank of Atlanta, "Interstate Banking Laws," *Economic Review*, March 1985.

Horvitz, Paul M., "Reorganization of the Financial Regulatory Agencies," *Journal of Bank Research*, Winter 1983, pp. 245–63.

Kane, Eward J., "Accelerating Inflation, Technological Innovation and the Decreasing Effectiveness of Banking Regulation," *Journal of Finance*, May 1981, pp. 355–67.

Kaufman, George G., "The Current State of Banking Reform," in Dimitri Papadimitriov, ed., *The Stability of the Financial System*. New York: Macmillan, forthcoming.

Kaufman, George G., *Reforming Financial Institutions and Markets in the United States*. Boston: Kluwer, 1994.

Kaufman, George G., and Roger C. Kormendi, eds., *Deregulating Financial Services: Public Policy in Flux*. Cambridge, Mass.: Ballinger, 1986.

Kaufman, George G., Larry Mote, and Harvey Rosenblum, "Consequences of Deregulation for Commercial Banks," *Journal of Finance*, July 1984, pp. 789–803.

Noll, Roger G., and Bruce M. Owen, *The Political Economy of Deregulation*. Washington, D.C.: American Enterprise Institute, 1983.

Posner, Richard A., "Theories of Economic Regulation," *Bell Journal of Economics and Management Science*, Autumn 1974, pp. 335–58.

Pozdena, Randall J., and Kristin L. Hotti, "Developments in British Banking: Lessons for Regulation and Supervision," *Economic Review*, Federal Reserve Bank of San Francisco, Fall 1985, pp. 14–25.

President's Commission on Financial Structure and Regulation, *Report*. Washington, D.C.: U.S. Government Printing Office, 1971.

Shull, Bernard, "How Should Bank Regulatory Agencies Be Organized?" *Contemporary Policy Issues*, January 1993, pp. 99–107.

Spong, Kenneth, *Banking Regulation*, 3rd ed. Kansas City, Federal Reserve Bank of Kansas City, 1990.

Sprague, Irvine H., *Bailout: An Insiders Account of Bank Failures and Rescues*. New York: Basic Books, 1986.

U.S. Congress, House Committee on Banking, Currency and Housing. *Financial Institutions and the Nation's Economy (FINE): A Compendium of Papers Prepared for the* FINE *Study*, Vol. 1, 94th Cong., 1st sess., Novenber 1975.

U.S. Congress, Senate Committee on Banking, Housing and Urban Affairs, *Compendium of Major Issues in Bank Regulation*, 94th Cong., 1st sess., August 1975.

U.S. Treasury Department, *Modernizing the Financial System*. Washington, D.C.: Government Printing Office, 1991.

Weidenbaum, Murray, L., *Business Government, and the Public*, 4th ed. Englewood Cliffs, N.J.: Prentice Hall, 1990.

Weiss, Leonard, et al., *Regulatory Reform: What Actually Happened*. Boston: Little, Brown, 1986.

White, Laurence, J., *The S&L Debacle*. New York: Oxford University Press, 1991.

Separation of Commercial and Investment Banking

For much of recent U.S. history, commercial banking (accepting deposits and making loans) has been legally separate from full-service investment banking (underwriting and trading in securities). (Investment banks were described in Chapter 9.) In addition, U.S. commercial banks have not been permitted to invest in corporate equities for their own accounts. In these ways, U.S. banks differ significantly from their counterparts in many other countries, where commercial banks are permitted to underwrite a wide range of securities as well as invest in equity securities for their own accounts.

History

Unlike commercial banks, investment banks need not obtain special charters. Until recently, most investment banks were not even incorporated. Even today, some investment banking houses are still organized as partnerships. Because they were not incorporated and therefore were not subject to the regulations that apply to corporations, the early investment banks could engage in almost any activity they wished, other than issuing bank notes, and have offices in any location. Owing to the nature of their business, investment banking houses developed almost exclusively in major financial centers. Many offered deposit banking as well as underwriting services, although their investment banking activities of raising long-term funds for business firms and governments tended to dominate their commercial banking activities. The early investment banks were generally organized by people who had made private fortunes in other lines of business and found that they could put these funds to profitable use by underwriting, distributing, and trading securities, as well as investing their own funds in these enterprises.

The golden era of private banking was the period immediately after the Civil War, when the great banking houses of J. P. Morgan, Lehman Brothers, Kuhn Loeb, and Goldman Sachs were established. These houses helped raise the capital, both in the United States and abroad, that financed the rapid industrialization of the country in the period between the Civil War and World War I.

The earliest commercial banks in the United States were chartered exclusively to issue notes (and later to accept deposits) and make primarily short-term business loans. Through the years, however, some states began to permit their state-chartered banks to enter into various aspects of investment banking, although they were not permitted to own equity for their own accounts. At the same time, trust companies were organized in many states under general incorporation laws that gave them broader powers than commercial banks. These companies managed funds for individuals and others in a fiduciary capacity. In the process, they became involved in the trading of existing securities for their customers and then in underwriting new securities. In time, many trust companies requested and were granted deposit powers. By the turn of the twentieth century, many trust companies were indistinguishable in their banking operations from state-chartered commercial banks.

In the meantime, the National Bank Act of 1864 granted the newly created national-chartered banks "incidental powers as shall be necessary to carry on the business of banking." This was initially interpreted by both the Comptroller of the Currency and the courts as prohibiting most aspects of investment banking other than investing in government securities. However, competitive pressures from state banks soon forced increasingly broader interpretations. At first, national banks were permitted to underwrite and trade securities in which they were permitted to invest, which were primarily those of the federal government and municipalities. In time, this authority was extended to corporate bonds to keep the national banks on an equal footing with state-chartered banks.

In 1927, the McFadden Act was enacted to explicitly equalize competitive conditions between national and state banks. National banks were permitted to branch in the states in which they were headquartered on approximately the same basis as state-chartered banks and to de jure underwrite and trade all types of securities, except equities. By 1930, commercial and investment banking were almost fully integrated. Commercial banks played an increasingly important role in the securities markets. In 1930, commercial banks, trust companies, and their affiliates underwrote an estimated 60 percent of all new bond issues, the major type of security at the time, up from 37 percent only three years earlier.

The Banking Act of 1933

For reasons to be discussed later, the Banking Act of 1933 (widely referred to as the Glass-Steagall Act, after its major sponsor, Senator Carter Glass, who was also a principal draftsman of the Federal Reserve Act of 1913), effectively separated commercial and investment banking.[1] The act

1. Prohibited, with certain exceptions, commercial banks that are members of the Federal Reserve System from underwriting, distributing, and dealing as principals in stocks, bonds, or other securities (other than those issued by the bank itself). The exceptions were federal government bonds, municipal bonds collateralized by the full faith and credit—i.e., taxing power—of the issuer (general obligation or GO bonds), and deposit-type securities, such as CDs.
2. Limited purchases of securities for a commercial bank's own account to debt securities approved by the bank regulatory agencies.
3. Prohibited commercial banks that are members of the Federal Reserve System from affiliating with firms *engaged principally* in investment banking.

[1] The Banking Act of 1933 also introduced federal deposit insurance, prohibition of interest payments on demand deposits, ceilings on time deposit rates, and margin requirements. The act combined Rep. Steagall's House bill establishing federal deposit insurance with Sen. Glass's bill separating commercial and investment banking.

4. Prohibited firms and individuals engaged in investment banking from simultaneously engaging in commercial banking.

Banks were given the choice of being one or the other but not both. Almost all primarily commercial banks chose to remain commercial banks, and almost all primarily investment banks chose to remain investment banks. They divested themselves of the prohibited activities. Thus, the National City Bank (the predecessor of today's Citibank), the Chase National Bank (the predecessor of the Chase Manhattan Bank), and the Harris Trust and Savings Bank of Chicago dissolved their securities affiliates. The First National Bank of Boston spun off as a separate entity its affiliate, the First Boston Corporation, which has remained a major investment banking firm (see Table 9–2).

Lehman Brothers and Kuhn Loeb, both now part of American Express, were examples of the majority of investment banks that discontinued their deposit business. J. P. Morgan and Company and Brown Brothers Harriman and Company were among the few investment banks that chose to retain their deposit business and discontinue their securities activities. J. P. Morgan reorganized as the Morgan Bank, first as a private deposit bank and then incorporated as a state-chartered bank. Today it is the Morgan Guaranty Trust Company. Brown Brothers Harriman remained a private deposit bank and is today the only such large institution in the country. Some senior officers of both firms left their organizations to remain in the securities business and established the firms of Morgan Stanley and Brown Harriman (which became part of the late firm of Drexel Burnham Lambert of junk bond fame), respectively.

Reasons for the Banking Act

The Glass-Steagall Act was a product of its times—the Great Depression, widespread bank failures, severe loss of public confidence in the stability of the economic and political system, and the search for quick solutions to prevent similar disasters in the future. Its purpose was threefold:

1. *To restore confidence in the commercial banking system by separating commercial from investment banking.* Many investment banks experienced severe financial difficulties at the onset of the depression. The attempts by some banks to come to the aid of their troubled securities affiliates were viewed as weakening their already precarious capital positions. There was a widespread belief that the securities activities of the banks increased their susceptibility to financial strains and had contributed significantly to their financial troubles. (You should recall that this occurred before the introduction of FDIC insurance, and depositors probably had good cause to be anxious about the ability of their banks to meet deposit demands at full par value.)

2. *To prevent a channeling of funds from "legitimate" commercial uses to "speculative" uses.* Such channeling was considered easier if commercial banks could engage in securities activities and were able to advise their deposit customers to purchase securities. Increased credit flows into the securities markets were believed to increase the instability of the financial system and to have contributed greatly to the cumulative nature, and

thus the severity, of the 1929 stock market crash. Customers had bought stock on credit, and when the market price of the shares declined below the value of the associated loan, the banks were forced to sell the stocks. These forced sales exerted further downward pressure on stock prices.

3. *To eliminate the conflicts of interest and self-dealing that were perceived to exist in the marriage of commercial and investment banking.* A number of such alleged abuses had received national publicity in congressional hearings and, coming at a time of massive bank failures, had created a public outcry for strong and immediate remedial action. (The alleged abuses are described later in this chapter.)

In the years since the separation of commercial and investment banking in 1933, the financial system has changed greatly. Wide-scale, domino-type bank failures are no longer a major concern. The creation of the Securities and Exchange Commission and the enactment of statutes on security disclosure and registration have reduced the threat of self-dealing and conflict of interest. The development of new financial instruments and services has led commercial banks to enter or request to enter areas not envisioned in 1933, such as financial futures, mutual funds, mortgage-related securities, swaps, and tax-deferred retirement programs. In addition, some securities, such as municipal revenue bonds and mutual funds, which were relatively unimportant in the 1930s when the act was passed and which the commercial banks were not permitted to underwrite or trade, have become more important today. At the same time, investment banks have expanded successfully into activities traditionally served by commercial banks, such as assisting business firms in cash management (collecting revenues, minimizing deposit balances, and investing surplus funds), providing liquid and even checkable "deposits" through money-market funds, and extending loans through credit cards. This expansion was accompanied by several well-publicized mergers between large investment banks and other large financial institutions: Bache Halsey Stuart with Prudential Life Insurance Company; Shearson Loeb Rhoades, Lehman Brothers Kuhn Loeb, and E. F. Hutton with American Express and then partly sold to Primerica; and Salomon Brothers with Phibro, a large commodities trading firm; and between large investment banks and large nonfinancial firms: Dean Witter Reynolds with Sears and Kidder Peabody with General Electric.

The commercial banks feared that these and other, similar mergers would create large institutions that would have the strength and ability to penetrate further into traditional commercial banking activities. The old walls separating commercial and investment banking have been breached in a number of places and threaten to collapse entirely with or without legal sanction. As a result, there has been wide support for a reexamination of the prohibition of commercial bank participation in investment banking and of investment banking participation in commercial banking. Legislation to extend bank powers in the securities market and to liberalize or repeal the Glass-Steagall Act altogether has been introduced in most recent sessions of Congress and was recommended in the 1991 Treasury Department study, but has not been enacted to date.

Permissible Bank Securities Activities

In recent years, commercial banks have increased their securities activities significantly as some of the more traditional bank lending activities have grown more slowly at the same time that perceived profits in full-service investment banking have increased rapidly and advances in computer information-processing technology have promised increased efficiency in providing a broader range of financial services. As a result, many banks have become more aggressive in seeking out securities activities that either were not denied them by the Glass-Steagall Act or would not force a head-on confrontation with the prohibitions. In this, they have been increasingly abetted by the bank regulatory agencies, which have interpreted the language of Glass-Steagall more liberally. In particular, the agencies have broadened their interpretation of the provision in the Glass-Steagall Act that prohibits commercial banks from affiliating with entities, including affiliates of the same holding company, that are "engaged principally" in full-service investment banking.

A list of the major securities activities that are permitted and those not permitted commercial banks that are members of the Federal Reserve System is shown in Table 20–1. By 1990, banks, particularly the largest banks, were able to participate in almost all the securities activities they were able to engage in before the enactment of Glass-Steagall in 1933.

Underwriting and Trading Securities

Commercial banks are explicitly permitted by law to underwrite, distribute, and trade as principals for their own account securities of the federal government and federal government agencies and those of state and local (municipal) governments that are secured either by the full faith and credit of the issuer (general obligation bonds) or, since 1968, by revenues derived from housing, dormitory, or university activities (some revenue bonds). Larger money-market banks are major dealers in most of these securities directly or through bank holding company affiliates. They accounted for about one-quarter of the approximately 40 Treasury security dealers that made sufficiently broad and continuous markets in 1993 to be required to report to the Federal Reserve Bank of New York. Bank-related dealers account for about one-fifth of all recorded transactions in Treasury and federal agency securities, which are by far the most actively traded securities in the secondary markets. In addition, commercial banks underwrite a substantial percentage of the dollar volume of municipal general obligation bonds.

In 1987, member banks were permitted by the Federal Reserve to underwrite, distribute, and trade through holding company affiliates all municipal revenue bonds, commercial paper, and securities backed (collateralized) by the bank's mortgage and consumer loans. In 1989, this authority was extended to corporate bonds and, in 1990, to corporate equity. To engage in these activities, the securities affiliates had to be separately and adequately capitalized. In addition, the volume of business in the newly permitted securities had to be limited to a maximum percentage both of the affiliate's volume, so that they were not "engaged principally" in that

TABLE 20–1	SECURITIES ACTIVITIES OF DOMESTIC COMMERCIAL BANK HOLDING COMPANIES (JANUARY 1994)

Permissible	Year Started[a]
Underwriting, distributing, and dealing	Always
U.S. Treasury securities	Always
U.S. federal agency securities	Various years
Commercial paper	1987
Mortgage and other asset-backed securities	
Collateral originated by other banks	1987
Collateral originated by issuing bank	1989
Municipal securities	
General obligation	Nearly always
Some revenue bonds	1968
All revenue bonds	1987
Corporate bonds	1989
Corporate equity	1990
Financial and precious metal futures brokerage and dealing	1983[b]
Private placement (agency capacity)	Always
Sponsor closed-end funds	1974
Underwrite deposits with returns tied partially to stock market performance	1987
Offshore dealing in Eurodollar securities	Always
Mergers and acquisitions	Always
Trust investments	
Individual accounts	Nearly always
IRA commingled accounts	1982
Automatic investment service	1974
Dividend investment service	Always
Financial advising and managing	
Closed-end funds	1974
Mutual funds	1974
Restricted	Always
Brokerage	
Limited customer	Always
Public retail	1982
Securities swapping	Always
Research advice to investors	
Separate from brokerage	1983
Combined with brokerage	
Institutional	1986
Retail	1987
Nonpermissible	
Mutual funds sponsorship and underwriting	

[a]After the Civil War. Different dates may apply to national and state banks and among state banks. With some exceptions, the earliest date is shown. Regulatory rulings frequently concluded that a specific activity was permissible before the date of ruling. If the activity was halted by enactment of the Glass-Steagall Act, the date of renewed activity is given.

[b]Restricted to futures contracts for which banks may hold the underlying security or that are settled only in cash.

activity, and of the total market in that particular security. Otherwise, they would violate Section 20 of the Glass-Steagall Act. To satisfy these conditions, bank holding companies transferred to their securities affiliates the trading and underwriting of the securities that a bank could do itself under Glass-Steagall. Because, such securities activities are relatively more important for larger banks, the restrictions favored those banks. Moreover, the requirement to establish special subsidiaries reduced the efficiency of these transactions. The securities affiliates became known as *Section 20 subsidiaries*, after the section of the Glass-Steagal Act that was satisfied by this reorganization. Banks may also trade in futures contracts for securities which they are permitted to trade on the cash or spot markets. In 1993, both J. P. Morgan and Citicorp ranked among the largest 15 underwriters in the country.

Brokerage Activities

Commercial banks' brokerage services are expanding rapidly. Until the enactment of the Glass-Steagall Act, security trading as an agent (broker) and a principal (dealer) were generally treated alike. But Glass-Steagall distinguished between the two. Section 16 of the act states that for national banks:

> The business of dealing in securities and stock by the association shall be limited to purchasing and selling such securities and stock without recourse, solely upon the order and for the account of customers, and in no case for its own account, and the association shall not underwrite any issue of securities and stock.

There are a number of provisions permitting dealing in bonds backed by the full faith and credit of federal, state, and local governments and in some municipal revenue bonds.

Unlike dealers, brokers do not buy and sell securities for their own account, but receive commissions from trades between buyers and sellers arranged through their assistance. Brokerage is a pure agency relationship. Until the 1980s, banks did not publicize their brokerage activities or actively solicit such business. Most banks regarded it as a convenience and accommodation service provided to good customers. Indeed, a ruling by the Comptroller of the Currency in 1936 stated that these services had to be provided at cost without profit and that the customer must already have had a nonsecurities activity relationship with the bank. In 1948, the Comptroller liberalized the restriction against profits and removed it altogether in 1957.

In the early 1980s, commercial banks began to expand their security brokerage services and to solicit business from the public. In 1981, BankAmerica Corporation acquired the Charles Schwab Corporation, then the largest *discount broker* in the United States. Schwab traded securities at low commissions, extended margin credit, and provided custodial services but did not offer investment advice. Through nationwide branch offices and the use of a free 800 telephone number, Schwab solicited customers nationwide. (When the Bank of America encountered financial difficulties in the mid-1980s, Schwab was sold at a profit for cash.)

At almost the same time, the Security Pacific National Bank (Los Angeles), which later merged with the Bank of America, announced a cooperative venture with the Fidelity Group, a large sponsor of mutual funds and a registered broker-dealer firm, in which Fidelity would execute and clear security trades and maintain accounts for Security's customers on a contract basis. Shortly thereafter, Security Pacific received permission from the Comptroller of the Currency first to establish a *de novo* subsidiary of the bank itself to provide brokerage services, then to purchase an established discount broker and operate it as an affiliate of the bank, and finally to form a subsidiary to provide "back office" brokerage support to other banks.

Many banks moved quickly into the active brokerage business in all four basic forms—through the bank itself, through an affiliate of the bank, through an affiliate of the bank holding company, or jointly with an established broker-dealer firm. The first bank brokers served the retail market. Almost all charged commission fees that were below those charged by full-service brokers for comparable transactions and were similar to those of nonbank discount brokers. In 1983, the Comptroller permitted a bank to establish a subsidiary to provide investment advice to its retail customers, including buy-and-sell advice on individual securities and an investment advisory letter. The bank already had a discount brokerage subsidiary. In a series of rulings from 1986 to 1988, the Fed expanded bank brokerage authority to include services to institutional investors as well as to retail customers and to provide investment advice. Thus, banks were effectively permitted to be full-service brokers.

In penetrating this market the banks have made use of two advantages they have over many investment banks. First, many banks have overseas broker and dealer operations and are familiar with foreign securities and securities markets. With the increasing interest of U.S. investors in foreign securities, these banks are able to offer established worldwide brokerage services. Second, the banks can use the continuing buy-and-sell orders of the funds managed by their trust departments to provide a wide range of immediate transactions for their customers. Nevertheless, securities brokerage has not been as profitable as many banks thought it would be, and a number have curtailed or terminated their activities.

Private Placements

Private placements represent the sale of a new securities issue directly by the issuer to one large investor or a small group of them. This process is often cheaper than public underwriting, since it bypasses some or all of the middlemen, does not require SEC registration, and can be completed quickly. Registration is waived because large investors are presumed to be sufficiently knowledgeable and informed about the issue, from their own investigations as well as their negotiations with the issuer, and to be aware of the risks involved. Security issuers often use the services of an intermediary to help design the security, locate promising investors, and negotiate financing terms. The Federal Reserve Board, the Comptroller of the Currency, and the U.S. Supreme Court have all ruled this activity permissible within Glass-Steagall as long as the banks do not purchase the securities for their own accounts. The major type of security placed privately by banks is commercial paper issued by their customers.

Customer Money Management Services

Commercial banks have traditionally managed funds for individuals and institutions in a fiduciary capacity in their trust departments or subsidiaries. Trust customers encompass a wide range including individuals and estates; pension and other benefit programs of business firms, non-profit organizations, and labor unions; endowment funds, such as of universities and hospitals; and so on. At year-end 1991, some 3,200 commercial banks operated trust departments and managed assets totaling some $8.5 trillion.

As a fiduciary, the bank may purchase and sell any type of security at the request of the customer or, with the prior approval of the customer, at its own discretion. At first, banks managed each trust account separately. But over time, it became evident that significant cost savings were possible, particularly for smaller trusts, if the accounts were pooled for investment purposes and managed as larger common funds with the same investment objectives. Commingling of trust accounts for such purposes has been permitted as long as the commingling is not used to solicit accounts for primarily investment purposes rather than for the fiduciary services generally associated with a trust account. That is, banks may pool trust accounts as long as the service is sold to customers primarily as a fiduciary trust service and not as an investment service. The latter activity was defined to constitute the sale of securities in mutual funds, which is prohibited by the Glass-Steagall Act. Banks can, however, manage mutual funds as long as they do not buy or sell the shares to the public directly from the fund's own account. An exception applies to Individual Retirement Accounts (IRAs), for which banks legally serve as trustees and therefore can purchase all types of investments, including commingled accounts managed by their own trust departments.

Banks offer a variety of investment plans on an agency basis. In Automatic Investment Services (AIS), a prearranged amount approved by the customer is deducted regularly (e.g., monthly) from a participating customer's account. The bank prepares a list of a limited number of large, well-known firms in which the bank is willing to make share purchases, but individual recommendations are not made. The customer selects the individual shares and amounts, and becomes the sole owner of the securities. The customer benefits from any lower brokerage fee the bank pays from purchasing the stocks in larger quantities. The bank profits from higher brokerage activity or shares in the brokerage commissions directed at other brokers.

Banks also offer dividend reinvestment plans. Basically, these plans provide for the automatic reinvestment of all or part of the dividends received by customers in additional shares of the paying firms, which have arranged with a bank for such a program. The attraction of these plans is that customers may share in any commission cost savings the bank may experience through pooling funds and purchasing in larger quantities. In addition, some firms offer to sell shares purchased through dividend programs at discounts from current market value.

Lastly, banks may sponsor, sell, and manage closed-end investment funds in which the number of shares is fixed and the bank does not repurchase the shares. Because of the one-time issuance of securities, the courts have ruled that, unlike open-end (mutual) funds, closed-end funds are not principally engaged in the public sale of securities, which is prohibited by the Glass-Steagall Act.

Nonpermissible Bank Securities Activities

Sponsoring Mutual Funds

Commercial banks or bank holding companies may not sponsor mutual funds and underwrite or distribute ownership shares sold directly to customers, where the bank stands ready to repurchase the shares at the current price for the fund's own account. This would be similar to dealing as principals in any security. That is, banks may not be investment companies. Banks may, however, broker mutual funds as third parties, as well as manage and advise mutual funds. Moreover, most of the profits from mutual funds come from managing and selling the funds, not from sponsoring them per se, which primarily involves recordkeeping. A bank may broker funds managed by others that are also marketed by others or that are marketed exclusively by the bank. The latter funds are referred to as ***private-label funds***. Since 1992, banks may even broker mutual funds managed by the banks' own affiliate but sponsored by a separate investment company. Funds managed in-house by a bank affiliate and brokered to investors solely by the bank are referred to as ***proprietary funds.*** Funds sold by banks but managed by others are referred to as ***nonproprietary funds***. Banks are required to inform customers that unlike deposits, mutual fund shares are not obligations of the bank and their par value is not insured by the FDIC.

Banks have increased their sales of mutual funds in recent years, particularly as declining interest rates have encouraged many of their customers to search for higher yields than are available on bank deposits. In 1992, more than 90 percent of all banks offered mutual funds, double the percent only seven years earlier in 1985. In the first half of 1992, banks accounted for more than one-third of all mutual fund sales. Nearly all of the sales were for money-market funds. Only 5 percent represented sales of longer-term bond and stock funds. These accounted for only some 15 percent of total industry sales. About 40 percent of bank sales of both money-market and longer-term funds represented proprietary funds. At end-year 1993, some 11 percent of all mutual fund assets outstanding were being managed by banks (23 percent of money-market funds and 6 percent of other funds). In 1994, the Mellon Bank (Pittsburgh), the twelfth largest bank in the country announced its intentions to buy the Dreyfus Funds, the third largest sponsor of money-market funds and tenth largest sponsor of stock and bond mutual funds.

In addition, in the 1980s, the banks developed deposit accounts whose returns are partially tied to changes in stock prices. These ***market index deposits* (MIDs)** resemble equity mutual funds closely. (MIDs are discussed in greater detail in Chapter 23.)

While waiting for nonpermissible activities to be approved, some banks have been offering them indirectly through joint agreements with other firms for whom the service is permissible. The bank provides its customer list, space in its offices if necessary, and performs the permitted part of the service, while the partner provides the prohibited part. The bank receives a fixed amount per sale or a percentage of the partner's revenues. Thus, some banks lease lobby office space to full-service stock brokers and mutual funds (as well as insurance and real estate brokers, also prohibited to the banks). Indeed, through arrangements such as joint agreements, aggressive commercial banks can, in practice, participate in almost any type of securities activities that they wish, although often on a second best and less profitable basis.

Should Banks Be Permitted to Engage in Full Securities Activities?

Both because the regulatory agencies and the courts have been interpreting the Glass-Steagall prohibitions increasingly less stringently and have expanded the type of securities in which banks may deal, and because banks have been successful in developing ways of bypassing many of the remaining restrictions, Congress has begun to reconsider removing the Glass-Steagall restrictions entirely. The arguments for and against commercial bank activities in the securities markets can be grouped under four headings: competition and concentration, economies of scale and scope, bank stability and risk, and conflict of interest and other abuses.

Competition and Concentration

Banks have argued that their failure to provide customers with full-service investment banking puts them at a competitive disadvantage relative to nonbank security dealers. Those who favor increased commercial bank participation in securities activities argue that because investment banks have expanded into some traditional commercial bank areas, it is only fair to permit commercial banks to protect themselves and invade some traditional investment bank areas. They assert also that bank entry would increase the number of firms, thereby enhancing competition and improving the quality of the service to seller (borrower) and buyer (investor) alike. This would be particularly true for the underwriting of corporate securities issued by smaller, regional firms. Commercial banks are located in almost every community of any size and take a close interest in the financial welfare of the community. Many smaller cities do not have offices of investment banking houses. And when they do, there are few offices, and those are retail branches of firms headquartered elsewhere, frequently in other states. The banks would provide alternative, local bidders.

Proponents of greater bank participation cite studies that provide favorable evidence on bank involvement in the market for new security issues. As noted earlier, commercial banks could until recently bid on new municipal GO bonds but not on many new municipal revenue bonds. These studies show that during this period, on average, new GO bonds received more bids and sold at lower interest rates than revenue bonds with the same credit rating. They conclude that permitting banks to bid on new revenue issues would increase the number of bids and thereby lower interest yields and provide significant cost savings to state and local governments.

By implication, similar savings would accrue to private corporations on the underwriting of their new securities and to individuals and institutions in their purchase and sale of both newly issued securities on the primary market and outstanding securities on the secondary market.

Opponents of greater bank participation in the securities markets argue that commercial banks have an unfair advantage over investment banks. They have more intimate knowledge of the financial conditions of many firms and government units acquired in the process of providing lending and federally insured deposit services to these customers; have easier access to funds through their deposit activities and the Fed discount window; and have a ready, "captive" market for the securities they underwrite in their own portfolios, in those of their correspondent banks, and in those of their trust accounts. As a result, according to the opponents, although bank entry may intensify competition in the short run, in the longer run it would lead to the failure and exit of many investment banks and result in a lower number of firms and reduced competition. As evidence of the importance of these advantages, the opponents point to the very rapid increase in the percentage of new securities underwritten by the commercial banks in the late 1920s, after national banks had been given approval to engage in these activities, and to their eventual domination of this market shortly before the Glass-Steagall Act.

Those opposing greater securities powers for commercial banks are not impressed by the studies claiming that interest rates would be lowered on municipal revenue bonds if commercial banks could bid on them. They assert that the researchers did not hold enough other things constant. GO bonds of a particular credit rating are not equivalent in default risk to revenue bonds of the same credit rating. The ratings are relative for each class of bonds. Generally, an Aa-rated revenue bond has a greater risk of default than an Aa-rated GO bond. Permitting banks to underwrite revenue bonds would not transform them magically into GO bonds of the same rating. As a result, the number of overall bids and interest rates would remain unchanged; commercial banks might simply take a share of the market from investment banks.

Because of the all-pervasive nature of money, the opponents also argue that concentration in the financial markets is even more undesirable than concentration in other markets. They claim that the commercial banking market is already highly concentrated. Only 1 percent of the total number of banks hold some 60 percent of all bank deposits, and 3 percent of all banks hold about three-quarters of the dollar amount of assets held in bank trust accounts. If commercial banks drive investment banks out of business, concentration in all financial services would be greatly increased. The evidence from countries in which commercial and investment banking are fully integrated suggests much higher degrees of concentration. In addition, in some countries, banks have acquired significantly greater political power as well as economic power.

Moreover, the opponents say that bank entry may not even increase competition in the short run. Instead of entering the new lines of activity as separate entities (*de novo*), commercial banks may merge in ownership or in bidding (in the form of a temporary **syndicate**) with investment banks. Commercial banks frequently appear to combine with investment banks in a syndicate in submitting bids on GO bonds. On the other hand, it may be argued that if commercial banks were permanently permitted to bid on all types of securities they would be more willing to incur the heavy start-up costs required to have their own marketing and distribution system and be more apt to increase the number of bidding syndicates.

Finally, the opponents argue that commercial banks have other unfair advantages over investment banks. Deposits provide them with an artificially low cost of funds because they are insured by a federal government agency, and borrowings at the Fed discount window are often priced below market. In contrast, investment banks must obtain many of their funds through bank loans on which banks charge a markup over their own cost of funds.

Economies of Scale and Scope

Advocates of expanded commercial bank powers argue that corporate securities underwriting, brokerage, and complete money-management services are not significantly different from many of the financial services currently offered by commercial banks. Commercial banks already possess trained and qualified personnel, much of the capital equipment necessary for these activities, and substantial financial information about their customers. Adding the new services would result in lower average costs to consumers through economies of scale (size) and scope (complementarities of different services). Moreover, the greater convenience that would be provided consumers by offering these services at the 60,000-odd commercial bank offices throughout the country would reduce their effective cost and increase the demand for these services further. Consumers could satisfy all their financial needs at one place, and commercial banks could truly offer full-service banking.

Opponents argue that significant economies and lower costs are unlikely to be realized. Personnel trained in lending activities or in underwriting government securities cannot be readily transferred to analyzing equities or underwriting corporate securities without considerable retraining. Investment banks are geared up to handle the total volume of underwriting, money-management, and brokerage services currently prohibited for commercial banks. Transfer of some of this business to commercial banks would leave investment banks with excess capacity. Any cost saving at commercial banks would be offset by higher costs at investment banks. To the extent that this makes investment banks less effective competitors, commercial banks would not be forced to pass through to their customers any economies they might realize.

Bank Stability and Risk

Proponents of wider commercial bank securities powers argue that it would contribute to reducing bank risk and failure. They point to studies that have reported investment banking to be less risky than commercial banking. Far fewer investment banks failed in the 1980s than commercial banks. Moreover, to the extent that variability in investment banking earnings from trading and underwriting is not perfectly correlated with variability in commercial bank earnings from nonsecurity activities, diversification into full-service investment banking should help stabilize bank earnings and reduce overall risk to the bank as a whole.

Not so, argue the opponents. Although the number of failures may be smaller, investment banking is riskier than commercial banking; that is why investment banking firms maintain higher capital ratios than do commercial banks. Commercial banks would need to increase their capital ratios substantially in order to be able to assume these risks without endangering themselves or the FDIC. Moreover, even if they use securities activities to reduce their risks, many depositors are likely to perceive these activities as risky and to withdraw some of their funds, FDIC insurance notwithstanding. This outcome would reduce the efficiency of the financial system. But commercial banks need not use their new securities powers to reduce their portfolio risk through diversification. Instead, as many savings and loan associations did in the 1980s with the new powers granted them, commercial banks could misuse these activities to increase their risk exposure.

Last, if a securities affiliate were to get into financial difficulties, it is argued that the commercial bank would be likely to come to its rescue by providing resources in order to maintain the bank's reputation. Proponents of this line of reasoning point to this experience in the early 1930s and more recently in the mid-1970s, when many banks came to the rescue of affiliated, and even nonaffiliated but similarly named, real estate investment trusts (REITs). This produced a significant drain on the banks' capital, increasing their riskiness. However, opponents note that there are specific regulations that limit the ability of banks to use funds to help floundering affiliates that have been put in place since then.

Conflict of Interest and Other Abuses

Opponents of permitting commercial banks increased powers to participate in securities markets point to the alleged abuses that occurred when the banks were permitted these activities before the Glass-Steagall Act. Congressional hearings at the time disclosed numerous instances of alleged serious conflicts of interest and self-dealing. Many commercial banks were accused of having forced securities they had underwritten on their customers, their own trust departments, or their correspondent banks without regard to risk or the interests of the buyers.[2] Many of these buyers suffered subsequent losses. The opponents claim that, at times, the bank itself purchased the securities to prevent one of its own underwritings from being unsuccessful, thereby reducing the credit quality of the bank's own investments portfolio.

Some commercial banks were found to have paid large additional salaries and bonuses to their officers who were also officers of the banks' securities affiliates. These payments were viewed as reducing the capital base of these banks and increasing their vulnerability to the financial crisis that occurred a short time later.

Congress also focused on other potential conflicts inherent in conducting commercial and investment banking under the same roof. It was

[2] Similar well-publicized perceived conflicts between underwriting and investing led many states to separate investment banking and life insurance in the early 1900s.

feared that many of the banks' transactions might not be independent or at "arm's length," that is, determined solely by their economic merits. Firms that agreed to use a bank's underwriting facilities might be provided credit on more liberal terms than otherwise, and firms that used other underwriters might be denied credit. Customers might be provided more liberal credit on securities underwritten by the bank, particularly on those the banks had difficulty selling. Good loan customers of the banks might be given preferential treatment in the underwriting and marketing of their securities. The sale of new equity securities might be recommended to capital-deficient loan customers, primarily to protect the quality of the bank's loans.

Moreover, in the conduct of their business, commercial banks are apt to acquire information not available to others about a customer that is important in evaluating the customer's financial prospects. Thus, for example, a bank may obtain information on a loan customer that would affect its decision to underwrite or invest in the customer's securities, or on a customer whose securities it had underwritten that would affect the bank's decision to extend credit to the firm. Such "inside" information may lead to both conflicts of interest between the different departments within the bank and a comparative advantage over firms that engage in only one of these activities.

Proponents of broader commercial bank securities powers admit that abuses may have occurred, but no more than for other underwriters. Indeed, recent evidence suggests that commercial bank underwritten securities in the 1920s had lower default rates than those underwritten by investment banks. Moreover, legislation enacted since the 1930s has greatly reduced the possibilities of a recurrence. Among the legislation on the books, they cite the establishment of the Securities and Exchange Commission, the numerous disclosure requirements and investor-protection provisions enacted by the Securities Act of 1933 and the Securities Exchange Act of 1934, the introduction of margin requirements on stock purchases, and the increased regulation of commercial banking affiliates by the Federal Reserve under the Bank Holding Company Act. In addition, bank regulatory agencies have been provided with additional powers to ferret out, halt, and penalize abusers; and bank examination practices have been upgraded. Lastly, easier entry into banking has increased the number of alternatives for bank customers, who may believe that they are victims of unfair treatment. Competition and the availability of alternative suppliers, they argue, are the best protection against conflict of interest abuses.

Moreover, the often cited conflicts of interest abuses are not limited to commercial banks. The potential for such abuses are present any time underwriting and trading operations and managing investment funds for others are conducted under a single roof, as occurs at almost all investment banks. This was evident in the 1980s. Recent mergers between investment banks and insurance companies have increased the scope for activities. Thus, it makes little sense to restrict the activities of only commercial banks and not those of similarly situated firms. These proponents recognize that not all potentials for abuse can be eliminated from commercial banking any more than from any other industry. They argue that with proper protection, however, the public can obtain the benefits of greater bank participation in securities activities without exposure to the problems and abuses of the earlier era.

SUMMARY

405
▼
SEPARATION OF
COMMERCIAL AND
INVESTMENT
BANKING

The "appropriate" powers of commercial banks have been a subject of controversy since the beginning of banking. Early state-chartered banks in the United States had a wide range of powers and by the late 1800s could engage in most types of financial activities, with the primary exception of owning equities for their own accounts. National banks were generally more restricted, although their powers were broadened considerably in the 1920s to compete with the state banks. In some activities, such as the underwriting and trading of securities, commercial banks competed with investment banks. The Banking (Glass-Steagall) Act of 1933 separated commercial and investment banking in most activities. Commercial banks were restricted to underwriting and trading only securities of the U.S. government or its agencies and of state and local governments collateralized by general taxes (general obligation municipal bonds). Investment banks were prohibited from engaging in deposit banking. The separation was intended to reduce both the riskiness of commercial banking and any potential conflicts of interest between banks' underwriting and investing in their own or their customers' portfolios.

Because of the dramatic changes in the financial environment in recent years and the development of needs and technologies not envisioned in 1933, commercial banks asked for more liberal security powers, including underwriting and trading of all types of securities and mutual funds and full-line stock brokerage services. The banks argue that these powers are fair compensation for the invasion by investment banks of their traditional deposit and cash-management turf that has put them at a competitive disadvantage. Opponents argue that, if banks were granted these powers, the alleged abuses that led to the separation would reappear. In addition, because commercial banks have an inherent advantage in raising low-cost federally insured deposit funds, they could drive investment banks out of business, thereby reducing competition in the long term.

In recent years, banks have increased their securities activities greatly, although not always in the most efficient way, in part as a result of more liberal regulatory and judicial interpretations of the Glass-Steagall restrictions and in part as a result of greater aggressiveness on the part of the banks themselves. In addition, banks can engage in almost any type of securities activity that they wish through joint agreements with institutions that can offer them legally. As a result, at least large commercial banks have regained almost all the securities powers they had before enactment of Glass-Steagall without congressional repeal of the prohibitions in Glass-Steagall.

QUESTIONS

1. Differentiate between the basic functions of commercial banking and of investment banking.
2. Discuss the reasons for the separation of commercial and investment banking in 1933.
3. Identify ways in which commercial banks have increased their activities in the securities market in recent years and ways investment banks have increased their "commercial banking" activities.

4. Why have commercial banks increased their securities activities substantially in recent years? Why have their attempts been challenged by investment banks?

5. Discuss the arguments for and against permitting commercial banks to engage in full-service investment banking in today's environment. How has the environment changed from the 1920s, if at all?

6. What are "Section 20 subsidiaries"? How did they come about? What banks do they favor? Why? Do you think that it is still necessary to repeal Glass-Steagall now? Discuss.

7. How might securities activities increase the risk exposure of commercial banks? Which activities are likely to induce the greatest risks, per se, and which the least, per se? How do these risks compare with those of activities currently permitted banks?

8. Call your bank. Do they offer mutual funds? If so, which ones? Who serves as adviser to these funds? Are they sold directly by the bank itself? If not, who sells them? Did they tell you that these funds are not insured by the FDIC? Does the fact that they are not insured disturb you? Why or why not?

REFERENCES

Ang, J.S. and T. Richardson, "The Underwriting Experience of Commercial Bank Affiliates Prior to the Glass-Steagall Act," *Journal of Banking and Finance*, March 1994, pp. 351–96.

Benston, George J., *The Separation of Commercial and Investment Banking*. New York: Oxford University Press, 1990.

Bierwag, G.O., et al., "Interest Rate Effects of Commercial Bank Underwriting of Municipal Revenue Bonds: Additional Evidence," *Journal of Banking and Finance*, March 1984, pp. 35–50.

Carosso, Vincent, *Investment Banking in America: A History*. Cambridge, Mass.: Harvard University Press, 1970.

Carosso, Vincent, "Washington and Wall Street: The New Deal and Investment Bankers, 1933–1940," *Business History Review*, Winter 1970, pp. 425–45.

Felgran, Steven D. "Bank Entry into Securities Brokerage: Competitive and Legal Aspects," *New England Economic Review*, Federal Reserve Bank of Boston, November/December 1984, pp. 12–33.

Fischer, Thomas G., William H. Gram, George G. Kaufman, and Larry R. Mote, "The Securities Activities of Commercial Banks: A Legal and Economic Analysis," *Tennessee Law Review*, Spring 1984, pp. 467–518.

Kaufman, George G., "The Securities Activities of Commercial Banks: Recent Changes in the Economic and Legal Environments," *Journal of Financial Services Research*, January 1988, pp. 183–96.

Kaufman, George G., and Larry Mote, "Glass-Steagall: Repeal by Regulatory and Judicial Reinterpretation," *Banking Law Journal*, September/October 1990, pp. 388–421.

Krooss, Herman, and Martin Blyn, A *History of Financial Intermediaries*. New York: Random House, 1971.

Kroszner, Randall and Raghuram Rajan, "Is the Glass-Steagall Act justified? A Study of the U.S. Experience with Universal Banking before 1933," *American Economic Review*, .forthcoming.

Mote, Larry R., "Banks and the Securities Market: The Controversy," *Economic Perspectives*, Federal Reserve Bank of Chicago, March/April 1979, pp. 14–20.

Peach, W. Nelson, "The Security Affiliates of National Banks," *Johns Hopkins University Studies in Historical and Political Science*, Series 58, No. 3, 1941.

Perkins, Edwin J., "The Divorce of Commercial and Investment Banking: A History," *Banking Law Journal*, June 1971, pp. 483–528.

Sametz, Arnold W., ed., *Securities Activities of*

Commercial Banks, Lexington, Mass.: Lexington Books, 1981.

Sametz, Arnold W., et al., "The Securities Activities of Commercial Banks: An Evaluation of Current Developments and Regulatory Issues," *Journal of Comparative Corporate and Securities Law*, November 1979, pp. 155–93.

Saunders, Anthony, and Ingo Walter, *Universal Banking in the United States*. New York: Oxford University Press, 1994.

Securities Industry Association, "Bank Securities Activities: Memorandum for Study and Discussion," *San Diego Law Review*, November 1977, pp. 751–822.

Shugart, William F., II. "A Public Choice Perspective of the Banking Act of 1933," in C. England and T. Huertas, eds., *The Financial Services Revolution*, Boston: Kluwer, 1987.

Walter, Ingo, ed., *Deregulating Wall Street*. New York: John Wiley, 1985.

Willis, H. Parker and J. I. Bogen, *Investment Banking*. New York: Harper, 1929.

Willis, H. Parker, and John M. Chapman, *The Banking Situation*. New York: Columbia University Press, 1934.

The Mortgage Market

The largest single type of private debt outstanding is mortgage debt, or loans collateralized by land and buildings. At year-end 1992, about $4 trillion of mortgage debt was outstanding. This was about one-third greater than U.S. Treasury securities and accounted for one-third of all debt securities. However, the total was less than the market value of all corporate equities outstanding. About three-fourths of the mortgage debt was created to finance purchases of residential homes; smaller amounts were created to purchase multifamily, commercial, and agricultural structures.

Mortgages are important not only because of their large overall volume, but because they finance the single largest expenditure most households make in their lifetimes and the largest part of most households' wealth. The United States is a country of homeowners. Almost two-thirds of all households own at least one home. After increasing rapidly throughout the post–World War II period, home ownership stabilized in the 1980s·at near 65 percent. In contrast, in 1970, 63 percent of all households were homeowners; in 1950, 55 percent; and in 1940, only 44 percent. Before then, the percentage varied between 40 and 50. An efficient mortgage market is a prerequisite for satisfying the country's housing needs, supporting a strong construction industry, and providing reasonable liquidity for wealth invested in housing.

Mortgage lending may be divided into three parts: (1) origination (making the loan initially, including credit evaluation and documentation), (2) financing (holding the mortgage as an investment), and (3) servicing (collecting and recording the monthly payments). All three parts need not necessarily be done by the same party. Moreover, the financing and/or servicing may be transferred from one party to another over the life of the mortgage. Mortgage loans are originated either by institutions that generally expect to hold and/or service the loan, such as savings and loan associations, or by institutions that generally expect to sell off either or both the financing and/or servicing, such as mortgage bankers (discussed in Chapter 9) that specialize in origination and servicing but do not finance the loan.

The breakdown of residential mortgages by ultimate lender or investor at year-end 1950, 1960, 1970, 1980, and 1992 is shown in Table 21–1. The ownership composition of mortgages has changed rather dramatically in the post–World War II period, reflecting both the rise and fall of savings and loan associations and the development of mortgage pools or mortgage-backed securities (MBSs), which are discussed later in this chapter. Savings and loan associations grew rapidly in this period through the mid-1980s to become by far the largest providers of mortgage loans. As is shown in Table 21–1, by 1980, they provided more than 35 percent of all mortgage funds and held twice as many mortgages as commercial banks, the next largest mortgage lenders. This was twice their market share in 1950. However, by

TABLE

21–1 TOTAL MORTGAGES BY LENDER, SELECTED YEARS, 1950–1992

Lender	1950	1960	1970	1980	1992
Total ($ billion)	73	209	470	1,460	4,006
Percent distribution					
Commercial banks[a]	19	14	16	19	29
Savings and loans[a]	19	29	31	37	16
Life insurance	22	20	16	9	6
Government	3	4	3	5	5
Government-sponsored enterprises	1	3	5	7	5
Savings banks[a]	11	13	12	8	4
Households	24	16	11	8	4
Finance companies	1	1	2	3	2
Mortgage-backed securities[b]	—	—	1	3	25
Other	—	—	3	1	4
Total	100	100	100	100	100

SOURCE: Board of Governors of the Federal Reserve System, *Flow of Funds Accounts* (various years).
[a]Includes allocation of mortgage-backed securities.
[b]Unallocated to specific institutions.

1992, reflecting their major financial problems, savings and loan associations had shrunk to the extent that their market share was less than it had been in 1950. On the other hand, commercial banks increased their mortgage lending sharply in this period and replaced SLAs as the major provider of such funds. Households and life insurance companies declined from being the largest lenders in 1950 to only relatively minor lenders in 1992, although particularly life insurance companies may hold sizeable amounts of MBSs. Mortgage-backed securities accounted for only 1 percent of all mortgages in 1970, for 10 percent of all mortgages in 1980, and for more than 35 percent in 1992. Similar to other mortgages, MBSs are held by lenders. However, the available data do not permit the holders of the MBSs to be completely identified. Even after adjustment to allocate ownership as much as possible, MBSs still account for some 25 percent of outstanding mortgages in 1992. Thus, the identity of 25 percent of all mortgage investors is unknown.

The creation of new mortgage debt tends to vary contracyclically. Because the large outlay required to purchase a home typically necessitates that it be financed through long-term borrowing, in which interest costs are a substantial expense, the demand for housing is very sensitive to interest rates, which, as we have seen, fluctuate procyclically. Most potential homebuyers are currently housed and are able to postpone purchasing another home if they believe interest rates are high and are going to fall. Thus, housing demand tends to be low in periods of relatively high business activity and high in periods of relatively low business activity and in early periods of the following expansion.

The cyclical inflow of savings into thrift institutions was examined earlier in the book when we discussed disintermediation. When interest rates increase more than expected, these institutions may not be able to afford to pay a competitive deposit rate if their income is derived from fixed-contract-rate mortgages (FRMs), as typically was the case until recent years. To reduce the cost pressures on the institutions in periods of rising interest rates, as well as to reduce the intensity of competition among institutions and the interest rate on mortgages, ceilings were placed on the interest rates the institutions could pay on deposits (Regulation Q) in 1966. However, when market interest rates climbed above the ceiling rates, SSUs tended to redirect their funds to new institutions not subject to Q (for instance, money-market funds) and to the private financial market (such as Treasury bills). As disintermediation intensified and thrift institutions were forced to cut back on their mortgage lending, the ceilings were gradually phased out and eliminated altogether in 1986. This should reduce the cyclical nature of both deposit inflows into thrift institutions and mortgage lending by these institutions.

Effect of Regulation Q

Because ceilings on deposit rates are frequently justified on the basis that they reduce mortgage rates, it is of interest to analyze their effects on the volume and cost of mortgage credit. This is done in Figure 21–1. In the absence of deposit ceilings, the supply of savings (demand for deposits) increases with interest rates along schedule S. The institutions' demand for funds (supply of deposits), derived from the demand for mortgage funds, decreases with interest rates along schedule D. The equilibrium interest rate is i_0 at deposit amount A. If, for the sake of simplicity, we assume that the mortgage rate charged is a fixed markup over the deposit rate, the mortgage rate would be i_m, which is not shown. (As is shown later in this chapter, this assumption is more useful for variable-rate mortgage loans than for fixed-rate mortgages, which have a different term to maturity than that of the deposits.) Now introduce a ceiling on deposit rates of i_c, below i_0. At

FIGURE

21–1   REGULATION Q REDUCES SAVINGS FLOW AND MAY OR MAY
NOT REDUCE MORTGAGE RATE.

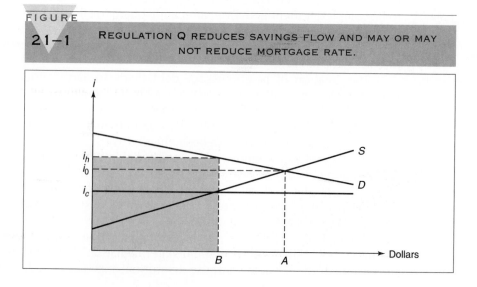

this rate, the amount of deposits supplied is only B. If SLAs continued to follow a markup strategy in pricing their mortgages, the new mortgage rate would be below the old, nonceiling rate. But the SLAs could also charge a higher mortgage rate, above i_h, based on their demand for funds, which reflects the demand for mortgage loans. In either instance, if effective, fewer mortgage loans are made.

What happens to the unsatisfied loan customers? It is likely that they will attempt to obtain funds from other institutions or private parties. In the process, they will bid up the interest rate to the point where new loan funds will flow into the market, in part financed by the savings that were diverted from the thrift institutions because of the ceilings. In the short run, reductions in mortgage credit may occur. However, in time, the final total amount of mortgage loans will probably not differ greatly from that before the ceilings, but at a somewhat higher cost to compensate for the less efficient intermediation process. Note that, if SLAs priced on a constant-markup basis, some mortgage borrowers would have received their mortgage loans at lower rates with a ceiling than without. At this rate, the quantity of mortgage loans demanded is greater than the quantity supplied, and the institutions have to ration their loans in some way. They would probably prefer to accommodate better credit risk borrowers. Thus, higher-income groups, which tend to be better credit risks, may be receiving mortgage loans at lower interest costs than lower-income groups. Moreover, as argued in Chapter 16, any lower mortgage rates are financed by forcing below-the-market returns on the savings of primarily lower-income households. Because of the distortions in both the price and the quantity of savings and mortgage loans caused by these deposit ceilings, Congress finally mandated the orderly dismantling of deposit rate ceilings by March 1986 in the Depository Institutions Deregulation and Monetary Control Act of 1980 and accelerated the process in 1982 by authorizing ceiling-free MMD accounts in the Garn-St Germain Act to permit banks and thrifts to compete with money-market funds. In terms of Figure 21–1, interest rate deregulation is more likely to even out the mortgage rate at i_0 to all borrowers than to raise mortgage rates across the board and to stabilize the supply of loans.

The Mathematics of Mortgages

Fixed-Rate Mortgage (FRM)

Primarily because of their large size and long terms, almost all mortgage loans call for the repayment of the principal amount to be spread or **amortized** over the life of the loan rather than being repaid in a lump sum at maturity. Thus, mortgage loans differ significantly from most other debt instruments. Their periodic, generally monthly, payments combine (1) a contract interest amount and (2) a repayment of the remaining or unpaid principal of the loan. From the 1930s through the 1970s, the standard mortgage instrument in the United States was the fixed-rate, constant-payment mortgage (FRCPM). In this mortgage plan, the periodic payments are of equal size. The mathematical formula for this mortgage plan differs somewhat from that of a bond, as developed in Chapter 5. Because there is no large final payment at maturity, the price of a mortgage is just the present value of the equal-sized payments, similar to the coupon payments on a fixed-coupon-rate bond, or of an annuity promising a periodic stream of equal payments through a maturity date. If

P = amount of the mortgage (unpaid loan principal)
Q = amount of the periodic payments
i = contract interest rate (yield to maturity)
m = number of periods to maturity

then

$$P = \frac{Q}{(1+i)} + \frac{Q}{(1+i)^2} + \cdots \frac{Q}{(1+i)^m} \qquad (21\text{--}1)$$

This reduces to

$$P = \frac{Q}{i}\left[1 - \frac{1}{(1+i)^m}\right] \qquad (21\text{--}2)$$

The periodic payment (Q) consists of an interest payment (I) and the amortization or repayment of the outstanding principal (R), or

$$Q = I + R \qquad (21\text{--}3)$$

If the contract interest rate (i) and loan amount (P) are known, I is computed by multiplying the unpaid principal at the beginning of the period (n) by the interest rate:

$$I_n = iP_n \qquad (21\text{--}4)$$

For a loan of a given dollar size and maturity, the higher the interest rate, the higher is I and thus also Q. The amount of the interest component changes through time as the amount of the unpaid principal changes. From equation 21–3, the difference between the amount of the total monthly payment and the amount of the interest payment is the amount of the amortization of the principal:

$$R_n = Q - I_n \qquad (21\text{--}5)$$

As I changes through time, so also does R. In contrast to bonds, the periodic payments for mortgages are typically made monthly, and interest is compounded monthly.

Assume a $100,000 fixed-rate constant-payment 30-year mortgage with an annual contract rate of 10 percent. The amount of the monthly payment may be obtained by solving equation 21–2 for Q. In our example, the number of monthly periods is 360 (30 years × 12 months). If the annual interest rate is 10 percent, the monthly rate will be 0.833 percent. Substituting these values into the equation yields monthly payments of $878. The monthly interest payment component is computed from equation 21–4 by multiplying the unpaid principal for the first month (the total $100,000 amount of the mortgage) by the monthly interest rate 0.833 percent. This yields $833. The amount of principal repayment is given by equation 21–5 as the difference between the total $878 payment and the $833 interest payment, or $45. This reduces the unpaid principal of the loan to

FIGURE

21–2

413

▼

THE MORTGAGE
MARKET

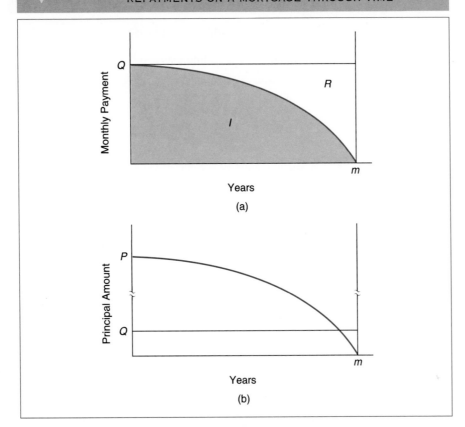

CHANGES IN PRINCIPAL AMOUNTS, INTEREST PAYMENTS, AND
REPAYMENTS ON A MORTGAGE THROUGH TIME

$99,955 after the first month, and the next and following month's interest and principal repayment amounts are computed on this amount. Thus, through time, as the mortgage loan is repaid, the unpaid principal and the interest component (I) of the monthly payment both decline and the amortization component (R) increases. This is plotted in Figure 21–2.

The amounts of the monthly interest payment, the principal repayment components, and the unpaid principal for a number of dates before maturity are shown at the top of Table 21–2 and are plotted at the top of Figure 21–3 for a 14 percent mortgage. To avoid having to make these computations each time, mortgage tables have been published. Like the bond tables discussed in Chapter 5, these tables show the monthly payments and the interest and principal components for different contract interest rates and terms to maturities. If market rates of interest decline, new mortgages of a given maturity and dollar amount will have lower periodic payments (Q) and repay the principal (R) more quickly. Conversely, if interest rates increase new mortgages will have higher monthly payments and the principal will be repaid more slowly.

Since 1980, a number of other mortgage plans, to be described later in the chapter, have become popular. In these newer plans, the contract

TABLE

21-2   MONTHLY PAYMENTS ON A 30-YEAR, $100,000 MORTGAGE

Years Remaining to Maturity	Monthly Payment ($)			Unpaid Principal[a] ($)
	Total	Interest	Principal	
A. Fixed-Rate, Constant Payment: 10 Percent				
30	878	833	45	99,955
20	878	757	121	90,729
10	878	548	327	65,753
1	878	76	802	8,300
B. Variable-Rate: 12 Percent[b]				
20	1,001	909	92	90,758
C. Variable-Rate: 8 Percent[b]				
20	760	606	154	90,696

SOURCE: *Monthly Payment Direct Reduction Loan Schedules*, 13th ed. (Boston: Financial Publishing Company, 1980).
[a]After one monthly payment is made.
[b]Rate changes for first time from 10 percent.

interest rate may change during the life of the loan, the monthly payments may change, the maturity may change, or any combination of two or all three of these factors may change. Although these plans are more complex than the FRCPM, the mathematics is of the same basic form as shown in the previous equations and demonstrated in the example above.

Similar to other securities, mortgages may trade on the secondary market after origination. Their market value at any time will depend on the term remaining to maturity and the relation between the contract and market interest rates at the time. As market rates of interest rise, the market price of FRMs declines. The market value of variable-rate mortgages (VRMs) will depend on how their contract rates change. If the rate changes are perfectly correlated with market rates on securities with equal coupon change intervals in both timing and magnitude, the market price will always be at par value at the date of repricing. If, according to the provisions of the mortgage contract, the contract rate changes are not perfectly correlated with changes in such market interest rates, the market value may be above or below par value at the repricing date.

Like other bonds, mortgages often include option features that affect both their contract and market interest rates. Call options are referred to as **prepayment provisions**, and put options as **due-on-sale clauses**. Many mortgage contracts contain both options. Prepayment provisions permit the borrower to repay part or all of the mortgage before the scheduled due dates either because the house is sold or because the house can be refinanced at a lower interest rate. Due-on-sale provisions permit the lender to put the loan to the borrower at any time the borrower sells the collateral property. This cancels the loan and requires the new purchaser to obtain new financing. Mortgages with due-on-sale clauses are referred to as **nonassumable**. Call and put options take on particular significance for mortgages

FIGURE

21–3

COMPARISON OF NOMINAL AND REAL MONTHLY PAYMENTS AND
OUTSTANDING BALANCES ON A 14 PERCENT, $100,000, 30-YEAR
FIXED-RATE CONSTANT-PAYMENT MORTGAGE (FRCPM) AND A
PRICE-LEVEL-ADJUSTED MORTGAGE (PLAM), ASSUMING A 10 PERCENT
STEADY RATE OF INFLATION AND A 4 PERCENT REAL INTEREST RATE

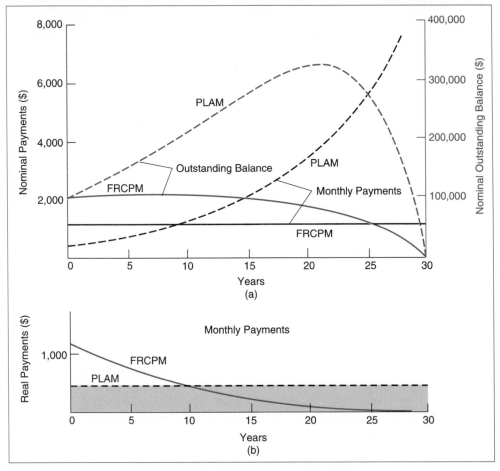

SOURCE: Adapted from Henry J. Cassidy, "Price-Level Adjusted Mortgages Versus Other Mortgage
Instruments," *Federal Home Loan Bank Board Journal*, January 1981, p. 5.

because the collateral is frequently sold before the maturity of the loan. It
is estimated that the average American moves once every five years, so that
prepayment and/or due-on-sale provisions are frequently activated regardless of market interest rates at the time. As a result, the average 30-year
fixed-rate assumable mortgage is repaid in about 12 years and even sooner in periods of sharply falling interest rates; nonassumable mortgage loans
have shorter lives.

A 1989 survey reported that 20 percent of all home mortgage holders
had prepaid and refinanced their outstanding mortgages to take advantage
of lower interest rates compared with only 8 percent up to 1977, when interest rates were lower and less volatile. The refinancing varied greatly among
regions of the country, ranging from 13 percent in the South to more than

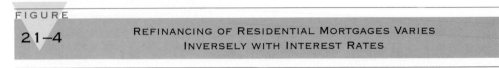

FIGURE

21–4

REFINANCING OF RESIDENTIAL MORTGAGES VARIES
INVERSELY WITH INTEREST RATES

SOURCE: Mortgage Bankers Association and *Economic Report of the President.*

25 percent in the Northeast and West. Refinancing also varied greatly from year to year. The sharp drop in interest rates in the early 1990s encouraged existing mortgage borrowers to refinance their old mortgages at lower interest rates in record numbers. In 1993, nearly three-quarters of all new residential mortgage originations were refinancings. Indeed, some borrowers refinanced two and even three times as interest rates continued to decline. In periods of high interest rates, refinancings drop off. The inverse relationship between refinancings and interest rates can be seen from Figure 21–4.

Alternative Mortgage Plans

Similar to all financial instruments, mortgages are tailored to the needs of borrowers and lenders. The rapid and volatile inflation in the late 1970s and early 1980s was particularly hard on the mortgage market in two ways. On the one hand, the combined effects of higher interest rates and higher home prices increased monthly mortgage payments faster than household income and increased the burden of mortgage debt for many new borrowers. On the other hand, the higher interest rates were for the most part unexpected and produced losses that made traditional mortgage lenders, such as savings and loan associations, reluctant to make new fixed-rate mortgages. (The reasons for this reluctance are analyzed in the next section.) This resulted in the development of new types of mortgage plans, tailored more specifically to the changing needs of particular mortgage borrowers and lenders.

On the whole, home mortgage borrowers prefer fixed-rate mortgages, so that they need not assume the risk of unexpected interest rate increases during the life of their loans. Under noninflationary conditions, most home buyers would also prefer constant monthly payments, so that they can plan their budgets more precisely. But for many, particularly first-time home buyers, constant monthly payments develop drawbacks as the rate of inflation accelerates. The early payments become too large for their incomes. For example, in 1971, monthly payments on an average 7¾ percent, fixed-rate, constant-payment 30-year 90 percent mortgage on an average $24,800 home were $160. In 1980, the average rate on this same mortgage plan had increased to 12.5 percent and the monthly payments to $238. But the price of the average house had also increased, to $62,200. Thus, the monthly payments for a new buyer would have risen to $597. As a percentage of average family income, the mortgage payments increased from 19 percent in 1971 to 34 percent in 1980.[1] This increase surely discouraged some first-time buyers who, for the large part, represent younger households with below-average current income. The higher relative initial payments also make it more difficult for these households to meet lender standards to qualify for mortgage loans, which are generally stated in terms of no more than a maximum percent, say, 25 percent, of annual household income. These households may find either a graduated payment mortgage or a price-level-adjusted mortgage better suited to their needs.

Financial institutions may be expected to make any type of mortgage loan that they expect to be profitable. As is discussed in the next section, mortgage-lending institutions have traditionally engaged heavily in interest rate intermediation, transforming basically short-term deposits into long-term fixed-rate mortgage loans. Thus they incurred interest rate risk and charged a premium for this service based on their expectations of realizing a loss. In the 1970s, many of these institutions underestimated the degree of risk they assumed and, consequently, the losses they experienced and, in retrospect, charged too small a premium for their "interest rate insurance." As a result of being badly burned, many have preferred to pull out of the interest rate intermediation business partially or altogether and to concentrate on variable-rate mortgages.

Graduated-Payment Mortgage (GPM)

Graduated-payment mortgages (GPMs) are tailored to the needs of younger, first-time home buyers whose current income is low but expected to increase faster than average as they enter their more productive years. Monthly payments on GPMs start low, lower than on a comparable constant-payment mortgage, and increase at a predetermined rate, presumably in line with the borrower's income. Later monthly payments will be sufficiently high to offset the low early payments and will be higher than on a comparable constant-payment mortgage. Early payments may be totally

---

[1] It is of interest to note that, for households that had purchased their homes in 1971, when interest rates were low, and whose incomes increased at the average rate, mortgage payments in 1980, when interest rates were high, represented less than 10 percent of their income. For similar households that also bought in 1971 but moved in 1980, the burden of their new monthly payments relative to income increased sharply, but because their wealth also increased substantially from the sale of the previous home, the burden of the new mortgage was less severe than for first-time buyers. Nevertheless, the higher rates reduced household mobility.

interest and may even be insufficient to cover the entire interest amount due. Any shortfall is added on to the unpaid principal in the form of **negative amortization**. Of course, at some later time, the monthly payments must increase sufficiently to permit full repayment of the loan. GPMs may be either fixed or variable rate. Fixed-rate GPMs were first introduced in the mid-1970s. The lower early payments increase the likelihood that households, which have low current income that is expected to increase, can qualify for mortgage loans.

Variable-Rate Mortgage (VRM)

Variable-rate mortgages (VRMs) are mortgage loans for which the contract interest rate may change in line with market rates of interest. The loan contract specifies the market *index* or *reference* interest rate to which the variable mortgage rate is tied, the frequency at which the mortgage rate may be changed (for example, monthly, quarterly, semiannually, annually, and so on), the maximum magnitude of any individual or cumulative interest rate changes, how interest rate changes are translated into changes in monthly payments, the maximum amount of negative amortization permissible, and so on.

The workings of a VRM may be demonstrated for the mortgage described in Table 21–2. Let market interest rates change for the first time at the beginning of year 10, when the loan has 20 years remaining to maturity and an unpaid principal of $90,850. If rates increased and the formula included in the VRM contract called for the VRM rate to rise from 10 to 12 percent, the monthly payment would increase from $878 to $1,001. However, the interest component would increase by a greater proportion, so that the reduction in the unpaid principal would still be less than under the FRM—only to $90,758 after one month rather than $90,729. If the contract also called for monthly payments to remain unchanged for a period after the rate increase, such as three or five years, the $31 difference between the $909 in interest payments required for full amortization and the $878 payments permitted would be negative amortization and added to the unpaid principal. If market interest declined so that the VRM rate fell to 8 percent, the monthly payment would be smaller but repayment of principal would be greater so that the unpaid principal at month end would be smaller, $90,696 rather than $90,729. If VRMs are tied to short-term rates and short-term rates are below long-term rates, then VRMs may increase the number of households that can qualify for mortgage loans. Lenders, however, must be cautious that borrowers can continue to meet their mortgage payments as short-term rates rise and mortgage payments increase accordingly.

VRMs were first introduced on a wide scale in California in 1975. In 1979, the Federal Home Loan Bank Board permitted federal SLAs nationwide to offer VRMs, subject to substantial limitations with respect to individual and overall rate changes. In 1981, primarily in response to the sharp increase in volatility in interest rates, both the FHLBB and the Comptroller of the Currency authorized unrestricted VRMs, with the provisions to be determined by the individual borrower and lender. In the mid-1980s, most new mortgages were VRMs. As both the level and volatility of interest rates declined, FRMs reemerged as the dominant mortgage form in the later 1980s. VRMs go under many names, such as **renegotiable-rate mortgages (RRMs)**, **roll-over mortgages**, or **adjustable-rate mortgages (ARMs)**. In 1987, when mortgage rates began to increase, some institutions offered new **convertible** **VRMs** that permitted borrowers to convert to FRMs at the going market rate at the time and protect themselves against further rate increases.

The popularity of VRMs varies with the level and expected direction of changes in interest rates. When interest rates are high, lenders prefer to offer VRMs to protect themselves against further increases, while borrowers prefer VRMs to avoid locking themselves into high rates. When interest rates are low, borrowers prefer fixed-rate contacts to protect against rate increases. Thus, in the high-interest-rate periods in the early 1980s, VRMs accounted for nearly 60 percent of all new residential mortgages. In the early 1990s, when interest rates were lower, VRMs accounted for only some 20 percent of total new mortgages.

Price-Level-Adjusted Mortgage (PLAM)

A disadvantage of standard FRCPMs or VRMs is that the early monthly payments on new mortgages can be very large relative to borrowers' incomes in periods of high and accelerating inflation. This occurs because, as seen in Chapter 6, increases in inflationary expectations are immediately incorporated into interest rates and thus factored into the monthly payments on new mortgages in one lump sum; yet the borrower's income increases through time at only an average rate close to the rate of inflation. Thus, the early mortgage payments are large in relation to income, and the burden of the mortgage increases. The faster the rate of inflation, the greater the initial burden. Of course, in time, income will increase and the burden of the mortgage debt will be reduced. This may be seen from Figure 21–3, which shows the pattern of real or constant purchasing power of monthly payments on a $100,000, 30-year, 14 percent FRCPM when the annual inflation rate is 10 percent. The real value of the monthly payments starts high and declines through time.

PLAMs would be offered at a mortgage rate that assumes no increase in prices, that is, at the real interest rate (recall $r = i - bP_E$ from Chapter 6). In Figure 21–3, this would be 4 percent. Thus, the rate is low and the first monthly payment is small. Subsequent monthly payments will increase (or decrease) with changes in an appropriate price-level index to which the payments are tied. At the same time, the unpaid principal of the mortgage loan will also increase (or decrease) with the price level. This may be seen in Figure 21–3. Note that both the monthly payments and the unpaid principal rise to amounts far above those for the FRCPM. At first, this may appear scary. However, if the borrower's income increases in line with the general price level, the ratio of monthly payments to income will remain constant over the life of the loan. The real monthly payments will also remain constant. This is shown in Figure 21–3b.

PLAMs have been introduced in the United States only on a very limited scale, but they are in wider use in a number of countries that have had longer experience with rapid inflation, such as Brazil and Israel.

Interest Rate Risk and Financial Intermediation

An important consideration in the evaluation of alternative mortgage plans is who bears the risk of unfavorable interest rate changes. For FRMs, the risk is borne entirely by the lender, either the intermediary institution or the ultimate SSU. The implications of FRMs for financial intermediaries may be seen from the following diagrammatic multiperiod analysis.

Assume a financial institution operating on the intermediation financial market, such as a savings and loan association, that engages in interest rate intermediation by issuing short-term, one-period deposits and investing in long-term, fixed-rate mortgage loans. The interest rate on the deposits may change every period. Thus, through time, the deposits are equivalent to long-term, variable-rate deposits, and the coupon change intervals on the two sides of the institution's balance sheet are mismatched. (Recall the analysis in Chapter 17.) For the sake of simplicity, assume also that the mortgage loan is a nonamortized loan, so that it resembles a regular coupon bond. If the institution makes an M-period fixed-rate loan, what interest rate should it charge?

Recall that the expectations theory of the term structure of interest rates discussed in Chapter 7 postulates that in equilibrium, the long-term (M-period) rate is the average of the current short-term (one-period) rate and the short-term (one-period) rates expected over the remainder of the M-period loan. Thus, if we include operating costs, any liquidity premium, and a competitive profit rate in the deposit rate, the rate of an M-period fixed-rate loan should be the average of the current one-period deposit rate and the institution's best predictions of the one-period deposit rate to M periods from now. If the current one-period deposit rate were A percent and future one-period deposit rates were expected to increase through period M along straight line AC in panel a of Figure 21–5 (the current yield curve is upward-sloping), the appropriate M-period rate would be B percent. At this rate, the institution expects to break even on the loan. At current period 0, the institution would make a gain of BA above its competitive profit. But if deposit rates increase as expected, the "excess" profit becomes smaller and smaller and eventually turns into a loss from period P through M. However, as long as deposit rates change only as expected, the present value of the loss, represented by the area in the triangle CDE, would be exactly equal to the area in the earlier present value "gain" triangle ABE.

Two things can be noted at this point: First, the excess profits at the beginning of the loan period are not really profits but "reserves." They are required to offset expected losses later and should not be used to finance higher deposit rates. At times when deposit rates are expected to decline—say, along line RS in panel b (the current yield curve is downward-sloping), the loss period precedes the gain period. (Note that in this case, it is profitable for an institution to borrow at a higher rate than it lends at as long as the short-term borrowing rate declines below the long-term lending rate as expected.) Although the institution again expects to break even, it may experience a *liquidity* problem in which it will have insufficient cash inflows from its loans to pay the necessary deposit rate. This problem is temporary and self-correcting, however, and is not much different from liquidity problems experienced by any firm, such as an airplane or heavy-machinery man-

FIGURE

21–5

DETERMINATION OF INTEREST RATE ON FIXED-RATE MORTGAGES
DEPENDS ON PROJECTION OF FUTURE DEPOSIT RATES..

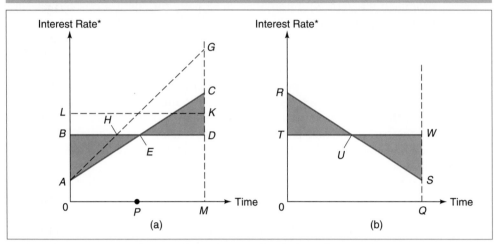

*Technically, interest rate on the vertical axis is measured in the form of $\ln(1 + i)$.

ufacturer, that incurs production costs before it receives cash inflows from the sale of products that require long development and construction times. The solution is basically to borrow additional funds to tide over the loss period until the expected profits begin. Note that the more steeply upward-sloping the yield curve the greater the immediate profits from long-term fixed-rate lending, but the greater also are the best current estimates of locked-in future losses. Upward-sloping yield curves are temptations that often entrap thrift institution managers, whose eyes are on short-term profits—*the trap of the upward-sloping yield curve.*

Second, the analysis is all fine and dandy if the institution's deposit rate expectations are realized, but what if they are not? If actual deposit rates increase less than expected in panel a, the deposit line will rotate down to the right, and the gain triangle will become larger and exceed the loss triangle. The institution will experience permanent excess profits. But little shouting and screaming is likely to develop; the institution's officers are only apt to spend more time on the golf course! If actual deposit rates increase more than expected, the picture is different. The deposit line will rotate up to the left—say, to *AG*—and the gain triangle (*ABH*) will become smaller and fall short of the loss triangle (*GDH*). Permanent losses will occur, and the institution will experience a more serious *solvency* problem. Because this may lead to the failure of the institution and a potential diminution in mortgage lending, loud shouts for corrective measures will arise. In retrospect, the institution should have charged a higher rate—say, *LK* in panel a. As was discussed in Chapter 17, the greater is the mismatch between the coupon change intervals on the two sides of the balance sheet, the greater is the interest rate risk assumed by the institution.

It is likely that, just like almost everyone else, most mortgage-lending institutions in the 1970s underestimated the rate of price inflation, and thus also the market rate of interest, and charged rates on their FRMs that turned out to be too low. Losses occurred. One solution attempted was to impose ceilings on deposit rates to keep costs down. But, as noted earlier, these ceilings did not deal with the cause of the problem and primarily resulted in disintermediation and at least temporary loss of funds from the mortgage markets. An alternative is to have the institutions reduce their interest rate intermediation and thus their exposure to interest rate risk. This may be achieved by having the institutions make M-period variable-rate loans on which the coupon rate can change every period to match their M-period variable-rate deposits. Any change in deposit rates, whether or not expected, would be passed through to mortgage rates. The institutions' profits would not be affected; they would be immunized.[2] In terms of Figure 21–5, the mortgage rate line would coincide with the deposit rate line. All the interest rate risk is passed through to the borrower. Variable-rate mortgages have been adopted by most SLAs in recent years to reduce their interest risk or to shed it altogether.

But most home buyers are not anxious to assume all the interest rate risk on their mortgage loans. With VRMs, they would be uncertain of the dollar amount of their monthly payments and might fear that sharp increases in payments in periods of increased interest rates might outrun the increases in their incomes and hamper their ability to make the debt payments. Although interest rates may have an equal probability of rising and falling, so that borrowers have an equal probability of gaining or losing on a VRM, most borrowers are risk-averse and weigh a loss more heavily than an equal dollar gain. As a result, VRM plans frequently entail some degree of interest rate risk sharing between lender and borrower. This is achieved by limiting the magnitude and frequency of individual rate changes and/or the magnitude of the overall permissible change over the life of the loan. The smaller and less frequent the rate changes, the smaller is the risk assumed by the borrower. For example, some VRMs limit the overall change in the mortgage rate over each year of the mortgage to no more than some percentage points, say 2, on either side of the initial rate and over the life of the mortgage to a larger amount, say, 5 percentage points. The risk of interest rate changes smaller than this amount is borne by the borrower; the risk of changes larger than this is borne by the lending institution.

Of course, the less risk a lender assumes, the lower the expected return required. Thus, the more risk a mortgage plan places on the borrower, *ceteris paribus*, the lower its rate. The wider the risk band included in a risk-sharing VRM, the lower the interest rate. The band serves the same purpose as a deductibility clause in an accident or theft insurance policy. The analogy is appropriate when one recalls that a lender that offers FRMs is including interest rate insurance with the financing. It can also be seen now that the profitability and thus the availability of FRMs depend on an institution's ability to predict interest rates and charge the appropriate risk premium. For most years of their lives, mortgage-lending institutions were either able to do so or, in retrospect, overestimated increases in interest rates and FRMs were profitable. The inflation of the late 1970s and early 1980s made interest intermediation more risky and less profitable and reduced the supply of FRMs. As is now clear from the analysis, FRMs flourish in low and stable interest rate and inflation environments.

---

[2] The institutions would also be immunized from interest rate risk if they offset their long-term fixed-rate mortgages with deposits of equal duration, as was discussed in Chapter 17, or used the futures market, as will be discussed in Chapter 22.

The Secondary Market

An individual residential mortgage is difficult and costly to trade after origination for a number of reasons. It is issued in an odd amount, related to the price of the home; the loan amount is relatively small, so that a credit evaluation of either the collateral property or the borrower's income is relatively expensive; the monthly payment schedule entails frequent servicing costs; the new types of variable-rate or graduated-payment mortgages are complex and require high processing costs; and the legal provisions differ from mortgage contract to mortgage contract. In other words, residential mortgages are small, unique, and expensive-to-service securities. The limited marketability has restricted the ownership of whole mortgages pretty much to originating lenders, thereby both reducing the supply and increasing the variability of funds. To increase the marketability of mortgages, it is necessary to consider each of the factors that limit their marketability.

The unique features of a mortgage loan may be reduced by using a standard mortgage contract. Model contracts have been prepared by the Federal National Mortgage Corporation and the Federal Home Loan Mortgage Corporation, which are major buyers of residential mortgages, and the Federal Housing Administration for government-insured mortgages. But many borrowers and lenders prefer finer tailoring than is permitted in these contracts. Moreover, state laws frequently specify particular provisions of mortgage contracts. Thus, maximum allowable fees for prepayment differ in different states, and some states prohibit negative amortization if it involves interest on interest. In addition, many provisions of the new types of mortgage plans were deliberately left open-ended by the regulators so that the plans could be finely tailored to the changing needs of the particular borrowers and institutions involved.

The financing and servicing aspects of a mortgage may be separated. This would make mortgages more attractive to investors who do not wish to perform both functions. As noted earlier in the book, mortgage bankers have traditionally separated the two aspects. They originate regular mortgages, keep the servicing function, and spin off and sell the financing to investors who do not wish to be burdened with servicing the loan. The mortgage bankers charge a fee for the servicing, which they deduct from the monthly payments they collect. The remainder is paid to the investors, who are willing to accept the lower gross return to avoid the servicing costs.

The small and odd size of the individual mortgages may be corrected by pooling a large number of mortgages into a larger, standard-denomination package. The new security is collateralized by the pool of individual, whole mortgages. Such **securitization** is particularly useful for mortgages that have few if any unique features and for which the servicing has been spun off. Such mortgage packages would resemble other marketable securities more closely and expand the market by appealing to investors who were not interested in individual mortgage instruments. In addition, it is possible to divide the cash flows from the monthly payments into segments according to maturity, say, three or four, and construct a different package for each to attract investors with different maturity preferences. Since their development in the 1970s, **mortgage-backed securities** have become very popular and have grown rapidly. By year-end 1992, more than $1.2 trillion of such securities were outstanding, accounting for more than 40 percent of the dollar volume of residential mortgages outstanding.

The most common type of MBS are *mortgage pass-through* or *participation securities*. These securities are collateralized by a given number and amount of individual whole residential mortgages. As payments are made on the individual mortgages, the proceeds (interest plus principal), less a servicing charge, are "passed through" to the investor. Thus, the income pattern and lives of the pool of underlying mortgages and of the security are the same. Unlike mortgage bondholders, the holders of these securities receive large and not necessarily constant monthly payments. The securities are issued in standard denominations and contracts.

The first widely used pass-through security was developed by Government National Mortgage Association (GNMA), which was discussed in Chapter 4, in 1970 to expedite its operations in the secondary mortgage markets. Mortgage pools in this program are created and securities issued by private mortgage lenders. The pools include only FHA- and VA-insured mortgages. The securities are guaranteed against default by GNMA. This makes them more marketable. In 1971, the Federal Home Loan Mortgage Corporation (FHLMC) began to issue pass-through securities based on pools of conventional, nongovernment-insured mortgages that they had purchased. The corporation guarantees the interest and principal payments. The maturity of fixed-rate pass-through securities is generally 30 years, but prepayments reduce the maturity to about 12 years. In 1984, reflecting their increased use in the primary market, VRMs began to be used to collateralize some MBSs.

In 1977, the Bank of America sold the first privately issued pass-through mortgage securities without a government guarantee. Since then, they have been issued by an increasing number of commercial banks, thrift institutions, and more recently, private "conduit" firms that purchase regular mortgages from different smaller lending institutions. Generally, at least part of the interest and principal payments are guaranteed by private mortgage-insurance companies. Thus, financial intermediaries are on both the selling and buying sides.

In 1983, the FHLMC developed a new security tailored to the needs of investors with different maturity preferences by effectively dividing the cash flows on MBSs into groups and issuing new securities, termed **collateralized mortgage obligations (CMOs)**, against each group. Thus, both lenders who preferred only short-term loans and those who preferred only long-term loans could satisfy their preferences with mortgages. Initially, the MBSs were divided into three classes or tranches: short-term, intermediate-term, and long-term. More recently, many have been tailored more precisely to the needs of investors and may have more than 30 classes. Because they modify a previous innovation, CMOs may be viewed as a second-generation product. Like the underlying MBSs, CMOs proved popular and were also issued by other issuers and also securitized by whole mortgages. In 1987, the tax law permitted a more flexible type of CMO called **real estate mortgage investment conduit (REMIC)**.

More recently, the coupon interest streams on both MBSs and CMOs have been *stripped* from the principal of the security and sold separately. This provides investors with securities having greatly different interest rate sensitivities both from each other and from the MBS and may be viewed as a third-generation transformation. Primarily because prepayments on mortgages vary inversely with interest rates, increasing when interest rates decline and decreasing when rates rise, the price of the *principal-only strip* (PO), which acts like a series of zero-coupon bonds and sells at a discount, tends to vary inversely with interest rates. For the same reason, the price of the *interest-only strip* (IO), which acts like a series of premium bonds, tends to vary directly with interest rates. Because of the complexities of newly created third and beyond generation securities, such as IOs and POs, they are often referred to as **exotic securities**.

The new mortgage securities appear to be successful in attracting new investors into the mortgage markets, in expediting the flow of funds from mortgage-lending institutions in capital-surplus areas to institutions in capital-short areas, and in permitting traditional mortgage lenders, who no longer wanted to hold long-term loans, to hold only shorter-term mortgages. Commercial banks and life insurance companies are the biggest buyers of CMOs and REMICs. Banks concentrate their purchases on the shorter-term classes, and insurance companies on the longer-term classes. The ability of these institutions to purchase only the maturities they want rather than the entire mortgage security has helped to both enlarge and stabilize the flow of mortgage funds. In the process, MBSs have become major trading instruments and have created a viable secondary market for mortgages. In terms of turnover—trading volume relative to dollar amount outstanding—MBSs are, despite their brief existence, just as active as federal agency securities, which is a veteran trading vehicle.

As a result of the new securities, the mortgage market is no longer segmented from other parts of the capital market. In the 1980s, changes in rates on Treasury securities were reflected in changes in mortgage rates more than five times as rapidly as in the 1970s. This, of course, also makes mortgage rates more volatile.

SUMMARY

Mortgage credit is the largest single type of private debt outstanding. Commercial banks have replaced savings and loan associations as the largest holders of mortgages, accounting for about one-third of all mortgages. The amount of residential mortgages fluctuates contracyclically, reflecting the pattern in both the construction of new homes and the inflow of savings funds to traditional mortgage lenders. Because housing is a long-lived, large-expense item, it is generally financed by long-term debt for which interest rates are a large factor. Thus, the demand for housing is highly interest-sensitive.

Mortgage loans have traditionally been fixed-rate, constant-payment plans. However, the increased rate and volatility of inflation in recent years produced higher and more volatile interest rates and spawned the birth of new types of mortgage plans. Many first-time home buyers could not afford the high early monthly payments required by FRCPMs in an inflationary environment and preferred a graduated-payment mortgage on which the payments start low and increase through time. Many thrift institutions suffered losses on FRMs as deposit rates increased more than they had expected at the time they set the mortgage rate. In periods of volatile interest rates, they prefer to make primarily variable-rate mortgages on which the contract rate changes in step with their deposit costs. Thus, they reduce the degree of interest rate intermediation in which they engage and the degree of interest rate risk which they incur.

To expand and stabilize the supply of residential mortgage funds, individual mortgage contracts are being made more marketable by standardizing the contract, separating the servicing from the financing, and pooling them into packages that can be used to secure new large-denomination mortgage pass-through securities with the same or different terms to maturity and other characteristics. These go under the names of mortgage-backed securities (MBSs) and collateralized mortgage obligations (CMOs).

QUESTIONS

1. How does a mortgage loan differ from a regular bond? Why is it so designed? Why does the interest component of the monthly payments on an FRCPM decline through time?

2. Assume a 14 percent, $100,000, 25-year FRCP mortgage. What will the monthly payments be? How much will the interest component be in the first month and in the thirteenth month? Assume that this was a variable-rate mortgage and the mortgage rate rose to 15 percent after one year. What would the new monthly payments be and the interest and principal components? How could negative amortization arise on this mortgage?

3. What is the interest rate on a new 30-year, $100,000, fixed-rate mortgage that makes monthly payments of $733.76? (Use either mortgage tables or a calculator.) At the end of the first year, how much of the payment is interest, how much is repayment of principal, and what is the remaining balance? At the end of 10 years? of 20 years? If interest rose to 15 percent what would be the monthly payments on a similar mortgage? What would be the remaining balance after 20 years? By how much does this balance differ from that of an 8 percent mortgage?

4. Discuss the reasons underlying the development of the variable- (adjustable) rate and graduated-payment mortgages. What advantages do you see for different households for each type of mortgage? Any disadvantages? How about for a mortgage-lending thrift institution?

5. If you purchased a new house today, would you finance it with a fixed- or variable-rate mortgage? What would be some of the factors that you would consider? What would be the importance to you of annual and lifetime upper bounds on interest rates on VRMs? Would expectations of how long you expected to own the house be important? If so, how?

6. How does the price-level-adjusted mortgage differ from other mortgage plans? How does this plan affect a thrift institution's interest rate intermediation activities? How might a PLAM affect default risk?

7. Why were mortgage-backed securities developed? What are some major forms of MBSs? How do both differ from individual whole mortgages? Who might purchase them? To whom does the mortgage borrower send the monthly payment check? What if there is a default?

8. Why may mortgage prepayment provisions be seen as a call option? Why are prepayments generally accepted at par value rather than at a higher call price premium as for regular bonds discussed in Chapter 8? How might this difference affect mortgage rates? Why would it so affect them?

REFERENCES

Barth, James R. and R. Dan Brumbaugh, Jr., "Turmoil among Depository Institutions: Implications for the U.S. Real Estate Market," *Housing Policy Debate*, Vol. 3, No. 4, 1992, pp. 907–26.

Belton, Terrence M., "Option Adjusted Spreads," *Secondary Mortgage Markets*, Winter 1988–89, pp. 6–11.

Brick, John R., "A Primer on Mortgage-Backed Securities," *Bankers Magazine*, January/February 1984, pp. 44–52.

Brown, Peter G., et al., *Introduction to Mortgage and Mortgage-Backed Securities*. New York: Salomon Brothers, September 1987.

Canner, Glenn B., and Charles Luckett, "Mortgage Refinancing," *Federal Reserve Bulletin*, August 1990, pp. 604–14.

Fabozzi, Frank J., ed., *The Handbook of Mortgage-Backed Securities*, 3rd ed. Chicago: Probus Publishing, 1992.

Fabozzi, Frank J., and Franco Modigliani, *Mortgage and Mortgage-Backed Securities Markets*. Boston: Harvard Business School Press, 1992.

Federal Home Loan Bank Board, *Alternative Mortgage Instruments Research Study*, Vols. 1–3. Washington, D.C.: U.S. Government Printing Office, 1977.

Federal Home Loan Mortgage Corporation, *Secondary Mortgage Markets* (quarterly).

Federal Home Loan Mortgage Corporation, *The Secondary Market in Residential Mortgages*. Washington, D.C., 1983.

Gilbert, Alton R., "Will the Removal of Regulation Q Raise Mortgage Rates?" *Review*, Federal Reserve Bank of St. Louis, December 1981, pp. 3–12.

Guttentag, Jack, et al., "Conference on Housing Finance," *Housing Finance Review*, July 1984.

Kaufman, George G., and Eleanor Erdevig, "Improving Housing Finance in an Inflationary Environment: Alternative Residential Mortgage Instruments," *Economic Perspectives*, Federal Reserve Bank of Chicago, July/August 1981.

McKenzie, Joseph A. "Mortgage-Related Instruments," in John R. Brick, H. Kent Baker, and John A. Haslem, eds., *Financial Markets, Instruments, and Concepts*. Reston, Va.: Reston Publishing, 1986.

Peek, Joe, and James A. Wilcox, "A Real, Affordable Mortgage," *New England Economic Review*, Federal Reserve Bank of Boston, January/February 1991, pp. 51–66.

Rosen, Kenneth T., "Securitization and the Thrift Industry," in *Thrift Financial Performance and Capital Adequacy*. Federal Home Loan Bank of San Francisco, 1986.

Roth, Howard L., "Volatile Mortgage Rates—A New Fact of Life," *Economic Review*. Federal Reserve Bank of Kansas City, March 1988, pp. 16–28.

Ryding, John, "Housing Finance and the Transmission of Monetary Policy," *Quarterly Review*, Federal Reserve Bank of New York, Summer 1990, pp. 42–55.

Sellon, Gordon, "Securitization of Housing Finance," *Economic Review*, Federal Reserve Bank of Kansas City, July/August 1988, pp. 3–20.

Senft, Dexter, "Mortgages," in Frank J. Fabozzi and Irving M. Pollack, eds., *The Handbook of Fixed Income Securities*, 3rd ed. Homewood, Ill.: Dow Jones-Irwin, 1990.

Tuccillo, John A., *Housing Finance: A Changing System in the Reagan Era*. Washington, D.C.: Urban Institute Press, 1983.

U.S. Congress, House Committee on Banking, Finance and Urban Affairs, *Housing—A Reader* (Committee Print), 98th Cong., 1st sess., July 1983.

Weicher, John C., "The Future Structure of the Housing Finance System," in W. Haraf and R. Kushmeider, eds., *Restructuring Banking and Financial Services in America*. Washington, D.C.: American Enterprise Institute, 1988.

Financial Derivatives: Futures and Options

22

Futures and options markets for financial instruments were developed in recent years to increase investor and borrower certainty in a world of uncertainty. In contrast to spot or cash markets, in which payment for and delivery of the traded financial instrument are completed at or close to the time the trade is arranged, in futures and option markets payment and delivery are postponed to some specified or optional date after the trade is arranged but at the arranged price. Thus, these markets permit you to do now what you would like to do in the future. In this way, you can shift the risk until the time of delivery to someone else who is prepared and willing to assume it. Because futures and options contracts are contracts to eventually buy or sell the underlying securities, their values are derived from these securities, and the contracts are sometimes referred to as **derivative securities** and their markets as **derivative markets.** (Derivatives also include CMOs which were discussed in Chapter 21 and swap agreements which are discussed in Chapter 23.)

Although developed only recently, financial derivatives are the fastest growing financial instruments. Almost all derivatives are based on underlying debt instruments, commonly referred to as interest rate instruments or on foreign currencies. In 1992, derivative contracts outstanding totalled more than $17 trillion, fully 50 percent greater than in 1989. Of these, 62 percent were based on interest rate securities and 37 percent on foreign currencies. By type, 18 percent were futures contracts, 42 percent were forward contracts (futures contracts traded over-the-counter), 13 percent were option contracts, and 27 percent were swap contracts.

Financial Futures and Forwards

A futures contract is an agreement that you will accept (or make) delivery of a particular asset (either real or financial) on some date in the future at a price determined today. Thus, if you wish to buy an asset in the future, you could do so today by buying a futures contract. In this way, you would know with certainty the price you will pay and will avoid the possibility of a price rise. If you wish to sell an asset in the future, you could sell it at a known price through a futures contract and avoid the consequences of the price decreasing between now and the planned selling date.

Assume that you wished to buy, say, an automobile six months from now as a graduation present to yourself. You would have three alternatives: You could (1) wait until then to buy a car, (2) purchase the car now and either not use it until then or lease it to someone else until then, or (3) buy a contract to have the car delivered to you six months from today at an agreed-upon price. The third alternative is termed a **forward contract.** Selection among the alternatives would depend on a number of factors, including the availability and cost of financing, storage costs, and, very important, the current price relative to the price that you expect six months from now. If you like today's price (the **spot price**) and are afraid the price might rise in the next six months (so that the expected future spot price will be higher than the current spot price or the current price of a forward contract), you could either buy the auto today or purchase a forward contract. If you purchase the forward contract, you need make no payment, except possibly for a small "good-faith" check, until delivery. You have protected yourself, or **hedged,** against a higher spot price than the price specified in your forward contract (the **forward price**).

Whether you actually benefit or not from the futures transaction, of course, depends on what happens to spot prices during the six months. If they increase to more than the forward price, you experience a gain. Because you do not actually realize income on this transaction but only avoid a loss, the gain may be viewed as an opportunity gain. If spot prices increase to less than the forward price, you experience an opportunity loss. You could have purchased the automobile at a lower price by waiting. Nevertheless, you gained greater certainty by buying the forward contract. The risk of an unfavorable spot-price increase was eliminated. In addition, you have avoided any borrowing and storage costs that you may have incurred had you purchased the automobile immediately. The use of forward contracts is similar to buying insurance or hedging and may be viewed as part of your **risk management.**

The forward contract "locks in" the price. The price of the contract cannot be higher than the current spot price plus the cost of borrowing, storage, and depreciation, if any, for the period until delivery. Otherwise everyone would purchase the item now rather than later.

Of course, broad, organized markets do not exist for forward contracts on automobiles. These contracts and forward contracts on other items, including financial securities, which are generally tailored to the specific needs of the participants, trade over-the-counter (OTC). But organized markets do exist for a large number of items, including grains and feeds (wheat, corn, soybeans); livestock (cattle, hogs, porkbellies); metals (copper, silver, gold); lumber; and financial assets (foreign currencies, stocks, and debt instruments). These markets are known as **futures markets,** the instruments traded as **futures contracts,** and the prices as **futures prices.** The daily prices of futures contracts for these items are published on the financial pages of major daily newspapers.

Any asset can be traded for future delivery between two parties on whatever terms are agreeable to them through a forward contract. When the forward contract is for a standardized amount of a carefully defined asset for delivery on a specific date and subject to the terms and conditions established by the organized market on which it is traded, it becomes a futures contract. The futures contract locks in the price at which the security underlying the contract will be traded at the delivery date. However, most futures markets prescribe daily marking of the futures contract to its current market price (**mark to market**) and settlement of any gains or losses to reduce the risk of default at its maturity. Thus, if the price of the futures contract declines before either the sale or the maturity date, the buyer is required to pay the dollar amount of the daily decline to the seller to reduce the likelihood that he or she will not accept delivery and buy the asset elsewhere at the lower price. Conversely, if the price of the futures contract increases, the seller must pay the gain to the buyer daily to increase the likelihood that he or she will deliver at the agreed-upon price. By being marked to market daily and settling any changes in value daily, the futures contract in effect maintains the same value at the start of every trading day as it had on the day it was initially created. The daily as well as the final payments are generally made through a central clearinghouse.

Note that, in the futures market, default refers to a failure to meet all terms of the contract on time and not to the failure to make payments on the underlying security. Thus, there can be default on a Treasury security futures contract, even though there is no default on the underlying Treasury security. The clearinghouse of the futures market guarantees timely completion of the contract between trading firms. To protect themselves against losses from default on either the daily or final payment, the futures exchanges and the clearinghouses require small margin payments (equal to a percentage of the daily dollar value of contract) to be maintained throughout the life of the contract by the member dealers. These *margin requirements* may generally be satisfied by cash or short-term Treasury securities. The trading firms, in turn, require margin accounts from their customers of at least the same size.

The existence of organized futures markets also provides a secondary market for the trading of contracts before maturity and therefore liquidity. This increases the usefulness of futures contracts to many decision units. Almost all financial futures contracts are reversed, or *offset*, before their maturity or delivery dates by buying or selling, as the case may be, an equal number of contracts. Indeed, for some contracts, such as on stock market indexes, there is no physical asset to deliver, only a market value at expiration.

There exist a number of organized futures markets or *exchanges* that specialize in contracts for particular items. The Chicago Board of Trade (CBOT) trades futures contracts in grains and feeds (such as wheat, corn, soybeans, and oats), plywood, gold, silver, and a number of financial assets: Treasury bonds, Treasury notes, municipal bonds, and stock market indexes. The Chicago Mercantile Exchange (Merc) trades futures contracts in livestock and meat, lumber, foreign currencies, Eurodollar time deposits, three-month Treasury bills, and the Standard & Poor's 500 stock market index. The New York Mercantile Exchange trades in oil, potatoes, silver coins, and platinum. Other organized futures markets include the Kansas City Board of Trade; the Minneapolis Grain Exchange; the New York Coffee, Sugar and Cocoa Exchange; the New York Commodity Exchange; the New York Futures Exchange; the London International Financial Futures Exchange; The French MATIF, and the Tokyo Stock Exchange.

Although organized futures markets for commodities have existed for many years, and for foreign currencies since 1972, organized futures markets for financial instruments were established more recently. The first such market—for GNMA mortgage certificates—was established in 1975. Contracts for financial instruments are generally traded for up to two years in the future, mostly spaced three months apart to mature in March, June,

TABLE

22–1

PRICES FOR TREASURY BOND FUTURES ON CHICAGO BOARD
OF TRADE, NOVEMBER 17, 1993

Delivery Date	Open	High	Low	Settle-ment[a]	Change[b]	Yield Settle-ment	Change
	(Percent per $100,000; points are 32nds of 100%)					(%)	
Dec.	117-09	117-31	116-22	116-30	−8	6.477	+0.020
Mar94	116-00	116-24	115-14	115-21	−9	6.581	+0.023
June	115-01	115-21	114-15	114-19	−9	6.668	+0.023
Sept.	114-15	114-15	113-17	113-19	−9	6.751	+0.023
Dec.	113-18	113-31	113-04	113-04	−9	6.791	+0.024
Mar95	113-05	113-05	112-15	112-14	−9	6.849	+0.024

SOURCE: *The Wall Street Journal*, November 18, 1993, p. C16. Reprinted by permission of *The Wall Street Journal*, © 1993 Dow Jones & Company, Inc. All Rights Reserved Worldwide.

[a]Settlement is the equilibrium closing price.
[b]Point change from previous day's close

September, and December. Prices for futures contracts on Treasury bonds on the Chicago Board of Trade on November 17, 1993 are shown in Table 22–1.

To simplify trade, the contracts are generally for specially created homogeneous instruments rather than for actual existing instruments. This permits trading in a wider variety of actual instruments. For example, the basic contract trading unit for the Treasury bond is an 8 percent coupon 20-year bond. If the bond is delivered, the seller may fulfill the contract with a number of different bond issues according to a prescribed conversion formula. Specifications for three major financial futures contracts are shown in Table 22–2. At year-end 1992, more than $3 trillion futures contracts were outstanding. In contrast, forward contracts totalled $7.5 trillion, or more than twice the amount. But some three-quarters of these were short-term foreign currency contracts of 7 days or less.

Trading in the futures market for financial instruments has expanded rapidly since it was established and now dominates futures trading in older contracts. In 1992, futures contracts on Treasury bonds had become by far the most actively traded futures contract of all the 100-odd futures contracts of any kind traded on all U.S. commodity exchanges. The volume far exceeded that in the spot market, but it should be remembered that far less cash changes hands in futures trading than in spot trading. Contracts on short-term Eurodollars were the second-most actively traded contracts and on the S&P 500 stock index the fourth. Crude oil futures contracts were a distant third and corn contracts, the most actively traded agricultural contract, were sixth. Futures contracts on debt instruments are sometimes referred to as *interest rate futures.* Trading in interest rate futures accounted for nearly 50 percent of all contracts traded on U.S. commodity exchanges in 1992, and trading in all financial futures contracts, including foreign currencies, accounted for about 65 percent of total trading volume, up from only 1 percent in the early 1970s. At any one time, only three or so interest rate futures contracts trade actively, despite the development of

	91-Day Treasury Bill	Three-Month Eurodollar Time Deposit	Long-Term U.S. Treasury Bond
Trading unit	$1,000,000 par value	$1,000,000 par value	$100,000 par value
Delivery months	March, June, September, and December	March, June, September, and December	March, June, September, and December
Price quotation	IMM Index = 100 − discount yield on a 3-month U.S. Treasury bill	IMM Index = 100 − yield on 3-month Eurodollar time deposit	In points ($1,000) and $1/_{32}$ of a point; for example, 80-16 equals $80^{16}/_{32}$.
Tick size and minimum fluctuation	1 basis point (0.01) = $25 per contract	1 basis point (0.01) = $25 per contract	$1/_{32}$ point = $31.25 per contract
Daily price movement limits	No limits	No limits	3 points ($3,000) above or below the previous day's settlement price
Year of introduction	1978	1981	1977
Exchange	Chicago Mercantile Exchange	Chicago Mercantile Exchange	Chicago Board of Trade

SOURCE: Chicago Board of Trade, *Community Trading Manual*, 1989, pp. 296, 306.

contracts on a large number of different debt securities. For reasons discussed in Chapter 23, most of the new contracts innovated by financial engineers through time have failed to pass the market test for survival.

The increase in trading volume in financial futures contracts can also be explained by the considerably lower transactions costs on futures markets than on the markets for the underlying securities. Because the prices of futures contracts and the underlying securities move together, on average, some transactions have been transferred to the futures markets from the stock and bond markets. This is particularly true for **program trading,** in which trading is conducted in packages of many different securities at a time according either to the needs of portfolio managers or to rules incorporated in computer programs and activated by opportunities identified by the computer from continuous online monitoring of all securities markets. Most frequently, program trading is used to arbitrage mispricing in different markets, particularly between the cash and futures markets, and to hedge risky positions. Program trading is generally conducted by larger institutional investors and therefore involves large dollar amounts. Because of both the rapid speed of the transactions and the large volumes involved, program trading is sometimes accused of increasing volatility in stock prices. In particular, some have accused program trading of aggravating the freefall in stock prices on "Black Monday," October 19, 1987, and at other times and have suggested limitations on its use.

Similar to prices on the spot markets, prices on the futures market change inversely with interest rates. When interest rates rise, futures contract prices decline. Also as on the spot market, changes in futures prices affect buyers and sellers symmetrically in opposite directions. Increases in contract prices benefit buyers and harm sellers. (This is shown in the top

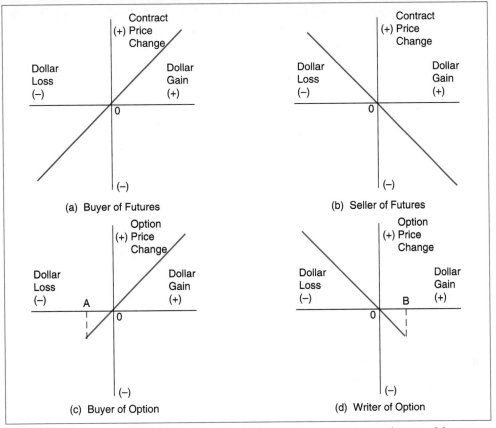

The upper-right quadrant of chart a shows that the buyer of a futures contract gains as the price of the contract rises, which occurs when the interest rate on the underlying asset falls. In the lower-left quadrant of chart a, he loses as the price of the contract falls (interest rates rise). In chart b, the seller of a futures contract gains as prices fall and loses as prices rise.

Movements in financial option prices are determined by changes in interest rates on the underlying asset. In chart c, the buyer of an options contract gains as the price of the option rises. This occurs for a call option when interest rates fall or for a put option when interest rates rise. As the option price falls, however, the buyer's maximum loss is limited to the premium paid, represented by OA in chart c. In chart d, the writer of an options contract loses as the price of the option rises, but if the option price falls, his maximum gain is limted to the initial premium received, OB.

SOURCE: Bluford H. Putnam, "Financial Options: Passing the Risky Buck," *Economic Observer* (The Chase Manhattan Bank), September/October 1981, p. 5.

panels of Figure 22–1.) Conversely, decreases in contract prices benefit sellers and harm buyers.

Trading on futures markets is regulated by the Commodity Futures Trading Commission, an agency of the federal government.

Hedging

Participants in the futures market, either buyers or sellers, may be classified as **hedgers** or **speculators.** Hedgers are risk-averse; they wish to reduce their uncertainty. They trade in futures contracts not to make a profit, but only to avoid a loss. Hedgers buy or sell futures contracts to counterbalance an existing spot position or commitment that is associated with their normal business activities, and to avoid the risk of unfavorable price changes in that asset until the close or unwinding of the position. Thus, food processors may hedge by contracting for crops and livestock at a fixed price before they wish to accept delivery, and farmers may hedge by selling futures contracts to deliver crops and livestock at a fixed price before they are ready to be delivered. Likewise, individual and institutional investors that will have funds to invest, say, six months from now, as a result of a scheduled receipt at that time, can purchase futures contracts for the desired security to obtain a known yield, and potential borrowers can sell futures securities to lock in a known interest cost.

As will be shown later in this chapter, financial-intermediary institutions may also use futures contracts to hedge some or all of their interest rate intermediation. For example, a bank or thrift institution that extends long-term, fixed-rate loans financed by shorter-term deposits may reduce its risk exposure by selling a series of short-term CD futures contracts with progressively later delivery dates. Thus, the lender would know its cost of funds for the loan period at the time the loan is made.

A unit that owns an asset is said to have a ***long position*** in the asset. If it wishes to sell the asset at a future date, the unit can offset or hedge the long spot position against price declines during the period up to the future sales date by establishing a ***short position*** in the futures market through selling a futures contract. The position is referred to as *short* because, when it sells a futures contract, the unit must make delivery at a later date on an asset that it may not currently own. A unit that plans to purchase assets in the future but does not own them now is said to have a short position in the spot market. If such a unit wishes to acquire the assets at a known price, it can hedge its short spot position with a long futures position by buying a futures contract.

Although prices on the spot and futures markets for the same or similar assets change by approximately the same amount, they need not move precisely alike. The difference between spot and futures prices is called the ***basis.*** A complete or ***perfect hedge*** requires that the basis be the same at the time when the investor takes his or her money out as it was when the investor initiated the hedge; then the spot and futures prices will have changed by exactly the same amounts. If the basis changes, the effectiveness of the hedge is reduced. The more similar the assets traded on the spot and futures markets, the more likely spot and futures prices are to move together and the basis to remain the same. Because futures-contract markets exist in only a limited number of assets, it is not always possible in practice to trade in the same assets on both markets. Thus, the ability to hedge completely depends on the availability of a futures market in the same asset as the one whose price the unit wishes to lock in, or in a similar asset.

For the purpose of illustration, we shall assume that a hedger trades an asset for which there is both a spot- and a futures-contract market and for which the basis remains constant. For this asset, the change between the current buying price of a futures contract and the future selling (or current selling and future buying) price of the contract is exactly equal in amount but opposite in sign to the change between the current and future spot prices. If holders of short spot positions buy futures contracts now to protect against a potential price increase before they are ready to accept delivery, the opportunity loss from buying the item later at a spot price higher than the current one is exactly offset by the gain realized at that time from the sale of the futures contract. The hedge is successful. This can be illustrated by a simple example.

Assume that on March 1 an institutional investor expects an inflow of $1 million in three months (on June 1) and wishes to invest this amount in 20-year Treasury bonds. The current yield on such bonds is 8.42 percent, and the investor fears that the yield will decline (price will increase) in the next three months. To hedge, he can purchase now $1 million of the 20-year Treasury bonds for future delivery—say, in September, or six months from now in the form of ten $100,000 contracts. These bond futures contracts yield 8.57 percent. Because the investor effectively invests funds that he does not yet have, he can be said to have a short spot position. He offsets the short spot position with a long position in the futures market. (This sequence of transactions is traced in Table 22–3.) Suppose yields decline. Three months later, on June 1, when the investor receives the $1 million, he or she buys the 20-year Treasury securities at 8 percent, or at a price $40,000 higher than their spot price on March 1. This represents an opportunity loss of $40,000 relative to the March 1 price of the securities. But at the same time, the September bond futures contracts have also increased in price and are sold at 8.09 percent, for an offsetting gain of $40,000. The investor has successfully locked in the 8.42 percent yield by doing now what he wished to do in the future.

Likewise, if the investor were long on the spot market and wished to lock in the current 8.07 percent yield when he needs to sell the bonds in two weeks on March 15, he could go short on the futures market by selling a comparable amount of, say, September futures bond contracts. Assume that these yield 8.18 percent. On March 15, the spot yield has increased

| TABLE 22–3 | "PERFECT" LONG HEDGE |

Cash Market	Futures Market
March 1 Decides to lock in yield of 8.42% on $1 million of 20-year, 8% U.S. Treasury bonds at 96-00.	March 1 Buys 10 September bond futures contracts at 95-08 (yield 8.57%).
June 1 Buys $1 million of 20-year 8% U.S. Treasury bonds at 100-00 (yield 8.00%). OPPORTUNITY LOSS: $40,000	June 1 Sells 10 September bond futures contracts at 99-08 (yield 8.09%). GAIN: $40,000

SOURCE: Chicago Board of Trade, *Hedging Interest Rate Risks* (Chicago, 1977), p. 8. Reprinted by permission.

Note: Commissions and exchange service fees are not included. Fractional bond prices are in thirty-seconds.

TABLE 22–4	"PERFECT" SHORT HEDGE

Cash Market	Futures Market
March 1	March 1
Owns $1 million of 25-year 8% U.S. Treasury bonds at 99-08 to yield 8.07%.	Sells 10 bond futures contracts at 98-16 (yield 8.18%).
March 15	March 15
Sells $1 million of 25-year 8% U.S. Treasury bonds at 94-08 to yield 8.56%.	Buys 10 bond futures contracts at 93-16 (yield 8.79%).
LOSS: $50,000	GAIN: $50,000

SOURCE: Chicago Board of Trade, *Hedging Interest Rate Risks* (Chicago, 1977), p. 8. Reprinted by permission.

Note: Commissions and exchange service fees are not included. Fractional bond prices are in thirty-seconds.

sharply to 8.56 percent and the prices have declined. The investor effectively lost $50,000 for each $1 million he did not sell spot on March 1. But the price of the futures contract also dropped, and so the investor is able to buy back the futures contracts at 8.79 percent. This represents a $50,000 gain, offsetting the $50,000 loss. The steps in this "perfect" short hedge are traced in Table 22–4.

These two examples describe perfect hedges, in which the current yield is protected exactly. But it is more likely that the price of the futures contract will not change in perfect synchronization with the spot price. The basis is likely to change. Thus, the gain on one market will not be exactly the same amount as the loss in the other, the current price will not be fully protected, and the hedge will be only partial. (It is, of course, possible for the spot and futures prices to change in such a way that the hedger is better off in terms of profits. But this is not the intent of the hedger and may be attributed to luck.) Also, it may not always be possible to find a futures contract in precisely the same asset as is positioned on the spot market. A different but related instrument must be selected—say, long-term mortgages or Treasury bonds for long-term corporate bonds, or Treasury bills for bankers' acceptances. Under such conditions, the hedge is likely to be imperfect. A hedge involving two different assets is referred to as a **cross-hedge** and incurs *basis risk*.

Hedging Fixed-Rate Loans

As we have seen, the combined effects of the sharp rise in the level and increases in the volatility of interest rates in the 1970s and early 1980s produced losses at many financial institutions that engaged in interest rate intermediation and financed their long-term, fixed-rate loans with short-term deposits. The interest costs of the deposits increased more than was expected or incorporated in the fixed rates charged on the loans. This experience made many of these institutions reluctant to continue to make long-

TABLE					
22–5		FINANCING FIXED-RATE LOANS			

		Cost of 1-Year CDs Sold On			
	24-Year Fixed Loan Rate	Spot Market (percent)			Futures Market in Year 1 (percent)
Year	(percent)	A	B	C	
1	10	9	9	9	9[a]
2	10	$9^1/_4$	$9^1/_2$	$9^1/_2$	$9^1/_4$
3	10	$9^1/_2$	$11^1/_2$	9	$9^1/_2$
4	10	$10^1/_4$	14	$8^1/_2$	$10^1/_4$
Average	10	$9^1/_2$	11	9	$9^1/_4$

[a]First-year CD sold on spot market.

term fixed-rate loans that were not financed by equally long-term deposits. As these deposits were more difficult to market, they preferred to make variable-rate loans, on which the rates change more or less alike with rates on short-term deposits. But, as noted in Chapter 21, variable-rate loans shift the interest rate risk onto the borrowers, some of whom may be reluctant to accept it and may reduce their demand for loans.

An alternative strategy is for the institution to continue to make fixed-rate loans but to hedge them on the futures market by selling deposits in the form of large CDs for delivery at regular intervals in the future. Thus, at the time the fixed-rate loan is originated, the interest costs of the deposits over the term of the loan and profitability of the loan are known with certainty. The interest rate risk is shifted to other users of the futures market, who are more eager to assume it.

The mechanics of a fixed-rate loan hedge are traced in Table 22–5. Assume that a bank wished to make a four-year loan financed by one-year CDs. It has three options: (1) it can make a variable-rate loan with the interest rate tied at a fixed markup, say, ½ percent over the one-year CD rate; (2) it can make a fixed-rate loan and assume the interest rate risk itself by selling equal amounts of one-year CDs on the spot market in the future; or (3) it can make a fixed-rate loan and simultaneously sell equal dollar amounts of one-year CDs in the futures market for delivery at the beginning of years 2, 3, and 4.[1] In both option 1 and option 3, the bank avoids interest rate risk and locks in the interest rate risk spread. In option 2, however, this spread will not be known until the last year of the loan.

Let the fixed four-year rate for the particular type of loan be 10 percent, the current one-year CD rate by 9 percent, and the target interest rate gross profit or spread be ½ percent. As discussed earlier in this book, the expectations theory of the yield curve argues that the long-term rate is an average of the current short-term rate and the expected future short-term rates over the life of the loan. Assume that the expected one-year CD rates in years 2, 3, and 4 are 9¼, 9½, and 10¼, percent, respectively, or an average of 9½ percent. The bank's expected spread on the fixed-rate loan would

[1] Although three-month CD futures contracts traded actively in the mid-1980s, the market for these contracts is currently inactive.

then be ½ percent, and it would make the loan. If, through time, these expected rates are realized, so that the bank can sell its CDs at the beginning of each year at them, it will realize its target spread (scenario A in Table 22–5). Note that there is a profit even though the deposit rate in year 4 exceeds the loan rate.

But what if the expected CD rates are not realized? Then the expected spread is not realized. In scenario B, CD rates rise faster than expected, reaching 14 percent in year 4. The actual annual cost of deposits averages 11 percent, and the bank will realize a loss of 1 percent annually. In scenario C, actual rates are lower than expected. They average only 9 percent, and the bank will realize a gain of 1 percent.

The bank can eliminate or hedge this interest rate risk, if it so wishes, by using the futures market. Assume, as is discussed later in this chapter, that the bank can sell futures contracts on its CDs at the current expected one-year interest rates, that is at 9¼, percent for year 2, 9½ percent for year 3, and 10¼, percent for year 4. (This is shown in the last column in Table 22–5.) In this scenario, the bank's cost of funds for the entire four-year period is locked in today at an average annual rate of 9½ percent. In effect, the bank has created a **synthetic** four-year fixed-rate deposit, paying 9½ percent. This locks in the ½ percent target spread. Note, however, that hedging is a two-sided sword. Although one avoids losses, one also gives up the opportunity of making greater profits if interest rates unexpectedly change in a favorable direction as in scenario C.[2]

Speculating

Speculators do not use the futures market to reduce uncertainty by offsetting a spot position. Rather, they generally are risk seekers. They trade in futures contracts to make a profit, believing that the current futures price of an asset will not be equal to the spot price of that asset in the future. The asset is selected because of profit potential in its anticipated price movements and not because the speculator has a use for it or the services it generates in the normal course of his or her business. For example, if the current futures price of an asset is below its expected future spot price, speculators will buy the futures contract and hope to sell the contract in the future at a profit as its price increases to conform to the spot price at the time. If the current futures price is above the speculator's expected future spot price, the speculator will sell futures contracts on the expectation of being able to repurchase them later at a lower price. If the speculator's expected future spot price is realized, the speculator wins' if it is not, he or

---

[2] To be successful, hedging on the futures market requires a thorough knowledge of the market. This point was brought home to many bankers in dramatic fashion by an article in the *American Banker*. The article described the experiences of an unwary savings and loan association that hedged the cost of its deposits in July 1982 against a rise in future interest rates by selling futures contracts. Instead of rising, however, interest rates declined sharply, and the value of the futures contracts rose. Changes in the value of futures contracts are settled daily, so that the SLA had to come up with large cash payments to the buyer before it could realize the benefit from the use of the futures contracts at the end of the six-month hedge period. The cash payments caused substantial financial distress. To make the situation even worse, the SLA found itself making the cash payments to lock in a significantly higher deposit rate than was then available on the market. (John Morris, "New Jersey S&L Hit by Futures 'Bloodbath': Thrift Is Out $1.5 Million on Interest Rate Hedge That Did Its Job," *American Banker*, November 22, 1982, pp. 1, 15.)

she loses. Because, expect for a small good-faith deposit as a maintenance margin and settlement of daily losses, payment of the futures price is not made until delivery, speculators find the futures market more attractive than the spot market. Speculators and hedgers need not be different persons. The same market participant may be a speculator one time and a hedger the next, depending on market conditions and preferences at each time. Because speculating in futures and forward contracts is so easy and cheap, substantial concern has been raised in recent years about the safety of the participants, particularly banks, who use these and other derivative contracts.

Forward and Futures Interest Rates

In Chapter 7, we discussed three competing theories of the term structure of interest rates, or how interest rates are related on securities differing only in term to maturity. Two of these theories—the unbiased-expectations theory and the liquidity-premium theory—argue that the one-period forward rates that are implied in the term structure and that can be computed from observed interest rates through some simple computations contain information about the market's expectations of future interest rates. The third theory—the market-segmentation theory—puts no significance whatsoever on the computed forward rates. The empirical validity of these theories has not been established clearly. But the development of futures markets has permitted additional evidence to be generated. The computer forward rates can be compared with the observed future rates. Prices for progressively future three-month Treasury bill futures contracts on November 17, 1993 (Table 22–1) declined. This indicates that, in the absence of large liquidity premiums, short-term interest rates in the future were expected to be somewhat higher than those on the trade date. On the same date, the yield curve for Treasury securities was upward-sloping over the same time horizon. More rigorous but still preliminary analysis also supported the expectations theories. The computed forward rates approximated the comparable futures rates reasonably closely. Some differences between observed futures and implicit forward rates are to be expected, because actual futures contracts and implicit forward contracts involve transactions costs, and, as noted, not all payments are made only at delivery; intervening losses and gains are settled daily in dollars whose present values exceed those at the delivery date.

Financial Options

Another financial derivative instrument that is designed to reduce uncertainty is the **financial option contract.** Similar to a futures contract, an options contract is for the future purchase or sale of a security. An option is a right to buy (or sell) a given number of units of a particular security on the cash or futures market at a particular price before a particular expiration date. However, unlike a futures contract, an options contract is a conditional contract. The right may or may not be exercised by the holder, depending on the profitability of doing so before the expiration date. An options contract is written by a second party. The buyer of the option pays the writer or seller of the option a **premium** for the right. Thus, unlike a futures contract, an options contract has immediate value. However, like a futures contract, payment for the purchase or sale of the underlying security at the prespecified price is not made or received until the option is exercised.

An option for the right to buy a security is termed a **call option.** An option to sell a security at a particular price is termed a **put option.** Generally, options are written by parties other than the issuer of the associated security. At times, however, they may be written by the issuer and be sold in a combined package. Thus, in Chapter 8, we discussed bonds that include call and put options, and in Chapter 21 we noted that prepayment options on mortgages are, in effect, embedded call options, and due-on-sale clauses are embedded put options exercisable when the mortgaged home is sold. (For bonds that come with call options, the call is effectively written by the investor, not the issuer.)

Similar to futures contracts, options contracts may be used both to hedge and to speculate. Buyers of call options profit when prices increase above the call price in a security they wish to buy, and buyers of put options when prices decrease in a security they hold below the put price. Writers of call options bet that the price of the security will not rise much above the **exercise,** or **strike price,** and writers of put options that the price of the security will not decline much below the exercise price. Buyers of call and put options may lose the **premium** that they pay for the option if they do not find it profitable to exercise the right by the expiration date. Writers of call and put options lose, respectively, the increase in the price of the security above the exercise price or the decrease below the exercise price less the premium for which they sold the options contract. Thus, the gains and losses on options trading are not symmetrical as on futures trading. This asymmetry is shown in the bottom panels of Figure 22–1.

When a call option is exercised, the writer must immediately deliver the contracted securities at the exercise price. If the writer owns the securities at the time the call option is initially sold, he or she is said to sell a **covered call.** If the writer does not own the securities at the time, he or she is said to sell an **uncovered,** or **naked, call.** Obviously, sales of naked calls are riskier than covered calls, as the writer has to purchase the securities to be delivered at current market prices, which may be expected to be above the call price when the option is exercised.

The price of an option is importantly related to four factors:

1. *The difference between the strike price and the current market price of the underlying security.* The greater the immediate benefit of the difference to the holder (the greater the market price is above the strike price for call options, so that the holder can buy the security below market price, and the greater the market price is below the strike price for put options, so that the holder can sell the security at above market price), the greater is the value of the option to the holder. If the strike price of an option is equal to the current market price of the underlying security, the option is said to be *at-the-money*; if the strike price is favorable to the holder, it is *in-the-money*; if it is unfavorable, it is *out-of-money*. These relationships are summarized in Table 22–6. Obviously, in-the-money options are priced higher than at-the-money options, which in turn are priced higher than out-of-the-money options.

TABLE 22–6	TAXONOMY OF OPTION CONTRACTS	
	Call Option	*Put Option*
In-the-money	Strike price < market price	Strike price > market price
At-the-money	Strike price = market price	Strike price = market price
Out-of-the-money	Strike price > market price	Strike price < market pric

2. *The volatility of the underlying security.* Options are traded to be exercised in the future, and the future market price of the security is not known. Nevertheless, the future price is more likely to be favorable to the holder of the option and more likely to be exercised, the greater is the volatility in the market price of the security. Thus, the greater the volatility, the greater the value of the option.

3. *The time to expiration of the option (the time during which it can be exercised).* The longer the holder of an option has to exercise the option, the greater is its value.

4. *Market rate of interest.* The strike price is the price to be paid at some future date when the option is exercised. Because the funds can be invested until that time, the price of interest to the holder of an option is its present value. Because present value and interest rates vary inversely, the higher the market rate of interest, the lower is the present value of the strike price. A lower present-value strike price is to the advantage of holders of call options and to the disadvantage of holders of put options.

The major determinants of the market price of an option can be summarized in functional form as:

$$
\begin{array}{cccc}
+ & - + + + & \text{Call option} \\
- & + + + - & \text{Put option}
\end{array}
$$

$$PO = f(MP,\ SP,\ V,\ T,\ i) \tag{22-1}$$

where

PO = market price of the option
MP = market price of the underlying security
SP = strike (exercise) price of the option
V = volatility in the market price of the underlying security
T = time to expiration
i = market rate of interest

Note that the direction of the relationship between the price of the option and both the market price of the underlying security and the strike price differs for call and put options.[3]

---

[3] Very precise formulating using these and less important factors have been developed to compute the value of options. The best-known of these was constructed by Fischer Black and Myron Scholes and is referred to as the Black-Scholes model. These option-pricing models are described in John C. Cox and Mark Rubenstein, *Options Markets* (Englewood Cliffs, N.J.: Prentice Hall, 1985).

TABLE

22–7

POTENTIAL GAIN AND LOSS FROM HOLDING $100,000 BOND AND BUYING AN IN-THE-MONEY PUT OPTION (STRIKE PRICE = $70, PREMIUM = $2,000) OR AN OUT-OF-THE-MONEY PUT OPTION (STRIKE PRICE $68, PREMIUM = $1,000) WHEN BOND PRICE IS $70

If Bond Price Is	Gain or Loss on Bond	Gain or Loss on At-the-Money Put[a]	Net Gain or Loss[a]	Gain or Loss on Out-of-the Money Put[a]	Net Gain or Loss[a]
75	+5,000	−2,000	+3,000	−1,000	+4,000
74	+4,000	−2,000	+2,000	−1,000	+3,000
73	+3,000	−2,000	+1,000	−1,000	+2,000
72	+2,000	−2,000	Breakeven	−1,000	+1,000
71	+1,000	−2,000	−1,000	−1,000	Breakeven
70	Breakeven	−2,000	−2,000	−1,000	−1,000
69	1,000	−1,000	−2,000	−1,000	−2,000
68	−2,000	Breakeven	−2,000	−1,000	−3,000
67	−3,000	+1,000	−2,000	Breakeven	−3,000
66	−4,000	+2,000	−2,000	+1,000	−3,000
65	−5,000	+3,000	−2,000	+2,000	−3,000

[a]Includes premium paid.

The potential gain from the use of put options can be seen from Table 22–7. Assume that an investor owns a $100,000 face value bond that has a market price of $70 and wishes to protect against a decline in value caused by a rise in interest rates. The investor can hold the bond and purchase a put option, say, one with a strike price at $70 or one with a strike price at $68. The first at-the-money option sells at a premium of $2,000. The second out-of-the-money option is less valuable and sells at a premium of only $1,000. If the investor's fears were realized and the price of the bond declined to $65, she would record a $5,000 loss on the bond. But, at the same time, she could exercise (or sell) the put option. With the initial at-the-money put, the bond would be sold at $70, and the investor would recover the loss. But, because she paid a $2,000 premium for the right to do so, her net recovery would be only $3,000. Thus, she would suffer a net loss of $2,000. With the initial out-of-the-money put, the bond would be sold at $68. This time, the investor would recover only $3,000 of the $5,000 loss. After accounting for the $1,000 premium, the recovery is only $2,000 and the investor will experience a net loss of $3,000. Indeed, for each alternative, these losses are the maximum losses the investor will suffer regardless how low the bond price drops. On the other hand, if the bond price increases above $70, the investor will not exercise the option. She will gain from the rise but less than otherwise, as the cost of the premium on the unused put must be subtracted. The net gains and losses for each bond price are shown in Table 22–7 and are plotted for the in-the-money put in Figure 22–2. Note that the investor has in effect bought insurance to guarantee that the value of the bond will not fall below the strike price and that the net loss will never be more than the amount of the premium below the

FIGURE

22–2

PAYOFF SCHEDULES FOR BOND, PUT OPTION WITH STRIKE
PRICE = $70 AND PREMIUM = $2,000, AND
SIMULTANEOUS PURCHASE OF BOND AND PUT OPTION

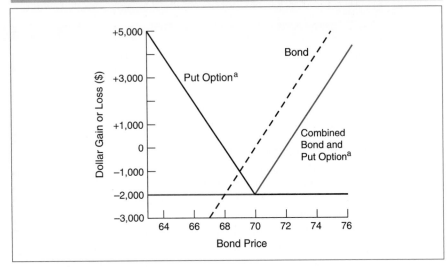

[a]Includes $2,000 premium.

strike price. The insurance costs more for the at-the-money option, as the potential losses from any given bond price are smaller.

The same results could also have been achieved if the investor had sold the bond and simultaneously purchased a call option to repurchase the bond at $70 or $68, respectively. This suggests that different combinations of options (and futures) can be used to achieve the same objectives. Designing alternative combinations of options and futures is referred to as **financial engineering.** Keeping the prices of the different security combinations (*synthetic securities*) in line, so that all that produce similar results and sell at the same price, has increased the opportunities for arbitrage, or eliminating unjustified price differences.

Trading in call and put options has existed informally over the counter for almost as long as assets have been traded. In 1973, options contracts on stocks were introduced on the Chicago Board of Options Exchange (CBOE). Since then, options contracts have been developed on a wide range of financial instruments, including Treasury securities, foreign currencies, stock market indexes, and even swap contracts **(swaptions)**, on both the cash and futures markets on a large number of organized exchanges both in the United States and abroad.

In 1992, there were more than $2 trillion of financial option contracts outstanding. The most actively traded options contract was for U.S. Treasury bond futures on the CBOT, followed by Eurodollar futures on the

Merc. Options trading on debt securities and futures contracts accounted for more than half of all options trading and on all financial instruments, including foreign currencies, for more than 70 percent.

SUMMARY

Financial futures instruments are contracts for future delivery of financial instruments. The price of the financial instrument at future delivery is established at the date of trade, although payment of this price is delayed until the scheduled delivery date. (Changes in the market value of the contracts are settled daily.) Futures instruments permit decision units to lock in a current price on a future purchase or expenditure. The risk of price (interest rate) changes in the period between the trade and the delivery is shifted to units who are prepared and willing to assume it. Futures instruments are traded on futures markets. Traders on futures markets are either hedgers or speculators. Hedgers are risk-averse units who wish to offset an existing spot or future position with a transaction in the opposite direction. Thus, they eliminate the risk of unexpected price changes. Speculators are generally greater risk seekers who wish to profit by betting on future outcomes. Because effectively no payment is made until delivery, futures contracts provide a low-cost trading vehicle to speculators.

Organized futures markets for financial instruments have expanded rapidly since their introduction in the mid-1970s. Active markets currently exist for contracts on Treasury bills, Treasury bonds, Eurodollar time deposits, foreign currency, and stock market indexes.

Financial options contracts permit the holder to purchase or sell a security at a particular price at his or her discretion at any time up to the expiration date and thus be protected against price changes in an undesirable direction. Options contracts sell at prices determined by the interaction of the strike price and the level and variability of the price of the associated security. Financial options contracts are traded on organized exchanges for a large number of different equity and debt instruments on both the cash and futures markets.

QUESTIONS

1. Why are futures contracts referred to as *derivative securities*? Discuss how the use of futures contracts in financial instruments may reduce risk. What is the underlying reason?

2. What types of financial intermediary institutions are most likely to make use of the current futures contracts in financial instruments? What kinds of contracts would they use?

3. Why are futures contracts in financial instruments attractive to speculators as well as hedgers? What precautions do most organized futures markets take to prevent defaults?

4. Distinguish between a *perfect hedge* and a *cross-hedge*. Which is riskier? Why is the riskier hedge used? Give examples of its use.

5. Check the quotes on Treasury bill futures contracts in last Tuesday's *Wall Street Journal*. What are the implications for future interest rates? What would a yield curve based on these

futures rates look like? Compare this yield curve with the actual curve over the same range.

6. When would you use a call option or a put option? How does an options contract differ from a futures contract? Is it possible to have options on futures contracts? Why?

7. Why do the volatility of the underlying security and the time remaining to expiration affect the price of both put and call options in the same direc-

tion? Why do the market price and the strike (exercise) price affect the price of put and call options in opposite directions?

8. Why does the current market rate of interest affect the prices of put and call options? Why is the effect in opposite directions for put and call options? Why are in-the-money options more expensive than out-of-the-money options? Why do you think anyone buys the latter?

REFERENCES

Burger, Albert E., Richard W. Lang, and Robert H. Rasche, "The Treasury Bill Futures Market and Market Expectations of Interest Rates," *Review*, Federal Reserve Bank of St. Louis, June 1977, pp. 2–9.

Campbell, Tim S., and William Kracaw, *Financial Risk Management.* New York: Harper Collins, 1993.

Carlton, Dennis W., "Futures Markets: Their Purpose, Their History, Their Growth, Their Success and Failures," *Journal of Futures Markets*, Fall 1984, pp. 237–71.

Change, Don M., *An Introduction to Options and Futures.* Chicago: Dryden Press, 1989.

Chicago Board of Trade, *Financial Instruments Guide Future.* Chicago, 1989.

Chicago Board of Trade, *Strategies for Buying and Writing Options on Treasury Bond Futures.* Chicago, 1983.

Chicago Board of Trade, *Treasury Futures for Institutional Investors.* Chicago, 1990.

Edwards, Franklin R., and Cindy W. Ma, *Futures and Options.* New York: McGraw Hill, 1992.

Figlewski, Stephen, *Hedging with Financial Futures for Institutional Investors.* Cambridge, Mass.: Ballinger, 1986.

Kolb, Robert W., *Financial Derivatives.* Miami: Kolb, 1993.

Kolb, Robert W., *Options: An Introduction.* Miami, Kolb, 1991.

Kolb, Robert W., *Understanding Futures Markets*, 3rd ed. Miami: Kolb, 1991.

Koppenhaver, G.D., "Futures and Options and Their Uses by Financial Institutions," *Economic Perspectives*, Federal Reserve Bank of Chicago, January/February 1986, pp. 18–31.

Koppenhaver, G.D., "Futures Market Regulation," *Economic Perspectives*, Federal Reserve Bank of Chicago, January/February 1987, pp. 3–15.

Kuprianov, Anatoli, "Money Market Futures," *Economic Review*, Federal Reserve Bank of Richmond, November/December 1992, pp. 19–37.

Kwast, Myron, ed., *Financial Futures and Options in the U.S. Economy.* Washington, D.C.: Board of Governors of the Federal Reserve System, 1986.

Moriarty, Eugene, Susan Phillips, and Paula Tosini, "A Comparison of Options and Futures in the Management of Portfolio Risk," *Financial Analysts Journal*, January 1981, pp. 61–67.

Peck, A.E., *Selected Writings on Futures Markets: Explorations in Financial Futures.* Chicago: Chicago Board of Trade, 1985.

Powers, Mark, and David Vogel, *Inside the Financial Futures Market*, 3rd ed. New York: John Wiley, 1991.

Remolona, Eli M., "The Recent Growth of Financial Derivative Markets," *Quarterly Review*, Federal Reserve Bank of

New York, Winter 1992–93, pp.28–43.

Siegel, Daniel R., and Diane R. Siegel, *Futures Markets*. Chicago: Dryden Press, 1990.

Smithson, Charles W., "A LEGO Approach to Financial Engineering: An Introduction to Forwards, Futures, Swaps, and Options," *Midland Corporate Finance Journal*, Winter 1987, pp. 16–28.

U.S. General Accounting Office, *Financial Derivatives: Actions Needed to Protect the Financial System*, Washington, D.C.: May 1994.

Financial Innovation

The dramatic changes in the twentieth century in our economy—higher incomes, longer life expectancies, greater specialization of labor and capital, larger-scale operations, higher and more volatile rates of price inflation or interest and exchange rates, higher levels of education, more active economic intervention by governments, and technological improvements in transportation, communications, and information processing—have stimulated equally dramatic changes in the financial sector. Large numbers of new DSUs and SSUs have entered the financial sector for the first time, and the financial needs of established units have changed greatly. As the nature of their markets changed, established financial institutions were forced to innovate to maintain or expand their profits and shares of the market. Consequently, new institutions and instruments developed.

As discussed in earlier chapters, financial intermediaries are like tailors. They take financial instruments that do not fit perfectly the current characteristics of investors or borrowers and reshape them, in terms of denomination, maturity, repricing periods (coupon change intervals), credit quality, cash flow characteristics, and so on, so that they do. Of course, "banker" sounds much classier than "tailor." Because the number of investors and borrowers is large and diverse, the number of securities custom-tailored to supplement the standard securities available on the rack is large. In addition, the needs of market participants change as both the economic and financial environment and regulations and legislation change. In response to the rapid changes in these factors in recent years, financial tailors have been very busy designing new and redesigning old instruments to reduce or enlarge risk exposure, circumvent regulations, and make use of the latest technology.

Like those of clothing designers, however, the imaginations of financial designers at times outrun the permanent or mass demand, and more new instruments are designed than eventually survive. Again, like clothing designers, financial designers appear to have little trouble finding customers who are willing to be the first to try a new design before all the advantages and disadvantages of the material, cut, color, and so on are fully known. There appears to be a certain prestige in being the first on the block, in the country, or in the world to be seen using a new financial security, just as there is in being the first to be seen wearing a new outfit. However, the price of the first-of-a-kind security, like that of a first-of-a-kind outfit, is high. If successful, the new security or process stops being custom-tailored and starts being mass produced for off-the-rack purchases. But many of the financial designs, like clothing designs, do not last long enough to move into mass production, even at much lower prices. Moreover, many of the new securities and processes developed are highly complex and require substantial financial sophistication on the part of users both to understand their workings and to price them correctly, so that the value they perform will be worth their cost. Some of the more recently innovated securities are so complex that they are frequently referred to as **exotic securities.** As the value of financial tailoring increased, the activity came to be called **financial engineering,** a term that sounds more high-tech than "banker".

Innovations are designed to improve efficiency in financial markets by both reducing costs and easing the flow of funds around distortions that prevent them from going to those DSUs who are willing to pay the highest for them. Such distortions include regulations, taxes, and transactions costs that do not bear equally on all market participants. In the process, the innovations permit risk to be shifted to those who believe that they can bear it best and thus charge the least for it. As a result, the value added to the economy by financial markets will increase.

Innovations may be classified as either *product* or *process* innovations. Product innovation is the development of a new product, such as credit cards, zero-coupon bonds, or mortgage-backed securities. Process innovation is the development of a new process for producing the same, or nearly the same, product, such as new channels of financial intermediation between DSUs and SSUs by existing or new institutions, for example, money-market funds. Either type of innovation in the financial sector is stimulated by a number of forces, including:

1. Changes in the needs of DSUs and SSUs,
2. Changes in the needs of financial intermediaries,
3. Changes in technology,
4. Changes in legislation or regulation.

It is evident that innovation is the lifeline of the financial services industry. Indeed, the more and the faster the economic and financial environment changes, the more important financial innovation becomes. This helps to explain why the financial sector relies so heavily on human capital. As noted in Chapter 1, brain power is its major resource! Successful new ideas bring big payoffs. The promise of such payoffs and the excitement of developing new products have lured many finance academics to Wall Street in recent years. Such "in-house" academics are now a common sight in almost every major investment-banking house.

The United States appears to be the world leader in financial innovation and engineering. In part, this distinction reflects the large size and high sophistication of the financial market in the United States. But, in part, it may also reflect a conducive legal environment for innovation. In contrast to the legal systems of many countries, which prohibit all activities except those specifically permitted by law, the legal system in the United States permits all activities except those specifically prohibited by law. Generally, new products can be introduced without first having to change the law through regulatory "loophole mining." In many other countries, the law must be changed before new instruments can be adopted. This constraint can be expected to dampen the incentive to innovate.

New Institutions

If existing institutions cannot satisfy the needs of potential users of financial services, new institutions will be established. As we have already seen, goldsmiths developed into full-blown commercial banks when, in the wake of the commercial and industrial revolutions, trade increased sharply and produced a need for more efficient financing. Casualty insurance companies were established in response to the expansion in the number and importance of distant countries in the increased volume of trade that required the shipment of more goods and materials across longer distances. The need of shippers to be protected from losses during transit gave rise to a demand for financial institutions that could insure shipments against loss.

The commercial and industrial revolutions created a more industrial and urban economy, in which fewer and fewer people were self-sufficient. Because they were not in a position to satisfy all their own needs, these workers and their dependents required greater financial security in case of the disability or death of the breadwinner. Life insurance companies were developed to fill this need. Pension funds were established to improve the means by which workers could provide for their own financial security after retirement as their life expectancies increased. The acceleration in the growth and, in particular, the mobility of the population, combined with longer life expectancies and the desire of young adults to own their own homes, increased people's need to purchase homes before they could save the necessary financing rather than after, as had been the practice earlier. Why wait until one is too old to enjoy it before purchasing one's own home? Savings and loan associations were established especially to accommodate this demand through residential mortgage loans. Such mortgages also provided an ideal investment for other savings-oriented intermediaries, such as savings banks. The desire of consumers to obtain more credit for small-ticket items than existing institutions were willing to extend stimulated groups of workers to band together to collect their own pool of loanable funds. Credit unions, which stressed consumer lending, were the outcome.

After World War II, rising personal incomes brought more and more people to the point where they were willing and financially able to seek somewhat riskier outlets for their savings, but they were still unable to assume the risks of ownership of shares in only one or two business ventures. Investment companies (mutual funds) were established to provide the advantages of higher returns with only moderately higher risk, reflecting the ability to diversify among many different investments. The poor performance of the stock market in the 1970s and the increasing volatility in interest rates encouraged the development and growth of investment companies that specialize in debt instruments rather than equities. At the same time, increases in market rates of interest to far above the maximum rates commercial banks and thrift institutions were permitted to pay on time and savings deposits encouraged the development of investment companies that offered SSUs shares in short-term, money-market securities, tailored to the requirements of the owners of the affected deposits. These money-market funds invest in short-term Treasury securities, CDs, commercial paper, and other short-term, highly liquid debt securities. Like deposits, the shares provide almost instant liquidity and little price risk and serve as good substitutes. A change in the tax law in 1976, permitting investment companies to pass through the tax exemption on municipal bond coupons to investors, stimulated the development of municipal bond mutual funds, and a similar change in 1986, permitting the pass-through of mortgage interest to investors without taxation of the middleman stimulated the development of mortgage mutual funds called **real estate mortgage invest-ment conduits,** or **REMICs,** which could issue CMOs more efficiently.

Some of the new institutions were successful and grew rapidly. Until Regulation Q was removed from time deposits at commercial banks and thrift institutions, money-market funds had replaced credit unions as the fastest-growing major financial institution since World War II. They expanded almost eightyfold in just five years, from $3 billion at year-end 1977 to a peak of $230 billion near year-end 1982, before the lifting of rate ceilings on bank deposits and the introduction of MMDAs and NOWs. By year-end 1983, assets of money-market funds had declined to $163 billion. However, while reduced in size, money-market funds did not disappear and began to expand again in 1984. By year-end 1986, their volume had returned to their 1982 levels. In contrast, the volume of MMDAs, which did not exist in 1982, was $570 billion, or more than twice as large as money-market funds.

A few new intermediaries have faltered because their services were unsuccessful or the need for them subsided. Real estate investment trusts (REITs) expanded rapidly in the late 1960s as commercial real estate development proved to be a profitable investment, but declined equally rapidly as prospects in this sector diminished in the mid-1970s. New financial institutions are listed in Table 23–1. Part of the growth of the new institu-

| TABLE 23–1 | | INNOVATIONS IN FINANCIAL MARKETS | |

Innovation	Year Introduced[a]	Primary Reason for Introduction	Introduced by
Instrument			
Term loan (fixed rate)	1950	Tailor	Banks
Term loan (variable rate)	1970s	Reduce risk	Banks
Federal funds	1920s, 1960s	Tailor	Banks
Special checking account	1935, 1950s	Tailor	Banks
Eurodollars	1950s	Tailor	Bank depositors
Amercurrencies	1990	Tailor	Banks
CD (fixed rate)	1961	Tailor	Banks
CD (variable rate)	1977	Tailor Reduce risk	Banks
CD (zero coupon)	1981	Tailor	Banks
Credit card	1920s, 1960s	Tailor	Banks
Mortgage-related securities	1970	Liquidity	Government
Collateralized mortgage obligations (CMOs)	1983	Tailor	Government
Real estate mortgage investment conduits (REMICs)	1987	Tax law	Investment banks
Leasing	1960s	Tax law	Banks
Financial futures contract	1975	Tailor	Market maker
Variable-rate residential mortgage	1920s, 1975	Reduce risk	Savings and loan association
Graduated-payment residential mortgage	1976	Broaden Market	Government
Municipal bond mutual shares	1976	Tax law	Mutual funds

TABLE
23–1   (CONTINUED)

Innovation	Year Introduced[a]	Primary Reason for Introduction	Introduced by
Money-market shares	1974	Regulation	Mutual funds
Original-issue discount bonds (OIDs), including zero coupon	1981	Tailor	Investment banks
Repurchase agreement (business)	1960s	Regulation	Banks
Repurchase agreement (consumer)	1980	Regulation	Depository institutions
Financial options	1920s, 1980s	Reduce risk	Market maker
Options on financial futures contracts	1982	Reduce risk	Market maker
Money-market deposit accounts (MMDA)	1982	Regulation	Depository institutions
NOW accounts	1972	Regulation	Savings bank
Market index deposit account (MID)	1987	Regulation	Banks
Variable-rate preferred stock	1982	Tailor	Investment banks
Stock market index futures contract	1982	Tailor	Market maker
Share draft	1974	Regulation	Credit unions
Zero-coupon Treasury collateralized (animal) bonds	1982	Tailor	Investment banks
Zero-coupon Treasury bonds (STRIPS)	1985	Tailor	U.S. Treasury
Foreign currency swaps	1981	Tailor	World Bank
Interest rate swap	1982	Reduce risk	Investment banks
Certificates of automobile receivables (CARs)	1985	Tailor	Investment banks
Certificates of amortized revolving debts (CARDs)	1986	Tailor	Investment banks
Junk (high-yield) bonds	1970s	Tailor	Investment banks
Service			
Automatic teller machines	1974	Technological change	Banks
Point of sale	1974	Technological change	Savings and loan associations
Telephone deposit transfers	1975	Regulation	Savings and loan associations
Preauthorized deposit transfers	1970	Tailor	Savings and loan associations
Mortgage insurance	1968	Reduce risk	Insurance companies
Municipal bond insurance	1971	Reduce risk	Insurance companies
Shelf registration (SEC Rule 415)	1982	Tailor	Investment banks
Institution			
REITs	1920s, 1960s	Tax law	
Money-market mutual funds	1974	Regulation	
Municipal bond mutual funds	1976	Tax law	
Municipal bond unit trust	1961	Tailor	
Federal agency mutual funds	1978	Tailor Regulation	

[a] Second year cited represents year major modification introduced.

NOTE For additional innovations, see Table 21–1 in the second edition of this book.

tions was at the expense of older institutions. Commercial banks, life insurance companies, and savings banks, the three largest intermediaries at the end of World War II, have grown much more slowly and lost some of their market share (see Table 9–5). SLAs, which grew rapidly and nearly tripled their market share between 1945 and 1985, declined sharply in relative market share during the resolution of the thrift crisis to their lowest levels since the early 1950s.

New Instruments

As the economy changes through time, so do the financial needs of existing DSUs and SSUs, and new units enter the market. It is likely that the new needs require modified or new instruments. It is also likely that some of the existing needs can be accommodated more satisfactorily than is possible with the existing instruments. In addition, new instruments were developed by financial institutions to get out from under restrictive regulations or taxes, to exploit new markets, or to change the amount of interest rate risk they would have to assume.

Although, as we have seen, there are some legal restrictions, most financial institutions operating on the intermediation financial market can generally offer a variety of different financial instruments. As a result, the number of new instruments developed has been far greater than the number of new institutions. Moreover, at times DSUs themselves will design new instruments better suited to their needs. Some of the more important instruments developed since the Great Depression are identified in Table 23–1. Also shown in the table are the year each new instrument was introduced, by whom it was initially introduced, and the primary reason for its introduction. Some of these new securities have already been discussed in previous chapters. Here, we shall examine the development of a few of these instruments to get a better picture of the innovation process.

Special Checking Accounts. Before World War II, commercial banks catered primarily to business firms, government units, and wealthier individuals on both the deposit and lending sides. A large segment of the population was too poor to maintain the minimum demand-deposit balances necessary for the account to be profitable. Minimum balances were frequently as high as $1,000 (in 1930 dollars, which would be equivalent to nearly $10,00 today!). Most people paid for their purchases in currency. Transfers of large amounts of money or transfers over distances by these household units were made by money orders, which were sold by commercial banks, other financial institutions, and the U.S. Post Office.

Personal incomes increased rapidly in the post–World War II years. In the process of shaking off the ultraconservative and defensive attitudes they had assumed during the preceding period of widespread bank failures, banks increasingly viewed the consumer market as one of potentially high profits. Payment by currency and money order was clumsy, and many low- and middle-income households covered the ease of payment by check enjoyed by the higher-income groups. Most of them still could not afford the high minimum balances required for profitable operations, but they could afford to pay for the services directly. Special no-minimum-balance demand-deposit accounts, with charges per check written, were first introduced by some banks on a wide scale in the mid-1950s. They were accepted enthusiastically. Ten years later, hardly a commercial bank in the country, large or small, did not offer special checking accounts. The convenience of payment by check was extended to almost every household that wanted it.

Negotiable Certificates of Deposit (CDs).   In the first 15 years after World War II, commercial banks grew considerably more slowly than most other financial intermediaries. Between 1946 and 1960, these banks saw their market share of funds at all private financial institutions erode from 57 to 39 percent, and their share of the depository institution market from 82 to 66 percent. One major factor in this decline was the primary emphasis of most banks on demand deposits. These deposits had been built up to very high levels during the war years, because (1) items to purchase were scarce; (2) many business firms were uncertain about the strength of the economy after the war and preferred to build liquidity; and (3) interest rates were low, so that the opportunity cost of holding "idle" balances was also low. After the war, these conditions changed, and demand deposits increased only slowly.

Banks stepped up their search for ways to halt the decline in their market share of financial services. Most banks had always accepted interest-bearing time certificate deposits from business firms but did not seek these funds aggressively. After all, demand deposits did not require cash interest payments. On the other side, business firms did not actively seek out such deposits. They preferred to hold their temporary money balances in short-term securities that could be quickly sold on short notice. Bank certificates of deposit had to be held to maturity. This made them less desirable to investors than Treasury bills and commercial paper.

In 1961, Citibank (formerly the First National City Bank of New York) developed a large-denomination certificate (generally in denominations of $1 million) that was legally negotiable. But trade requires not only negotiability but also marketability. So the bank arranged for the First Boston Corporation, a large investment banking firm, to start a secondary market for the certificates. (A bank cannot make a market in its own CDs, because that would be equivalent to redeeming a time deposit before its scheduled maturity date.) This made CDs not only negotiable, but also marketable. The CD satisfied both large depositors' needs for quick liquidity and the banks' needs for funds with a specified maturity. Business and government customers could hold the certificates for as short a period as they wished. The bank, of course, would retain the funds until the certificate matured. Only the owner would change. Thus the negotiable CD was born, and other major banks quickly marketed their own CDs.

CDs caught on. They offered a slightly higher interest rate than did Treasury bills, and many investors found this to be a profitable swap. By year-end 1963, less than two years after their introduction, CDs had grown to $10 billion, 30 percent greater than the dollar volume of commercial paper and eightfold the amount of bankers' acceptances. At year-end 1992, the amount of commercial bank CDs was $409 billion. This made it the third largest money-market instrument.

Credit Cards.   The most publicized bank innovation of the post–World War II period is the bank credit card. Like the special checking account, the credit card represented an attempt by the banks to increase their participation in the consumer credit market. Credit cards had been used by large department stores and gasoline companies since the early 1900s. Use of these credit cards was restricted largely to purchases at the issuing merchant. These were ***two-party credit cards.*** Immediately after World War II, Diners Club was established to market ***three-party credit cards*** for use in restaurants. Its use was later extended to transportation and entertainment, and the cards became known as T&E charge cards. Similar cards were soon marketed by American Express and Carte Blanche. Because of the type of purchases that could be financed, these cards appealed principally to businesses and wealthy individuals.

Some commercial banks saw an opportunity to develop a card that had broader appeal by making it acceptable at many different merchants in the banks' service areas. (See Chapter 14.) Income would be derived both from charging participating merchants a discount for immediate payment on sales paid by charge card and from charging cardholders interest on the amounts charged and an annual service fee. The first general-purpose or ***universal*** bank credit-card plan was established in the early 1950s. Most of the banks offering charge cards were smaller banks. Although broader than the individual merchant and T&E cards, the use of these cards was still limited, because the bank generally failed to enroll both larger merchants and merchants outside the bank's immediate service area. The cards also involved high start-up costs. As a result, most of these plans did not prosper. The few larger banks that marketed their own cards experienced similar difficulties. For example, Chase Manhattan Bank terminated its card plan in 1962, only three years after it was introduced.

In the late 1960s, however, after more careful planning, a number of larger banks introduced new credit cards. Substantial efforts were made to enroll as many merchants as possible, and to do this, the banks had to show a large number of card customers. Some banks engaged in massive, unsolicited mailings of cards to people on various and sundry mailing lists. Theft and fraud became almost commonplace until this practice was finally phased out. But sufficient cardholders had been enrolled.

The banks also broadened the coverage of the cards, so that they could be used at merchants outside the banks' areas as well as within. To achieve this, the banks joined together first in regional and then in national groups. Banks that were members of a group would honor charges at their merchants made by credit-card customers of other banks in the same group. The credit-card sales slip would then be sent to the customer's bank for reimbursement. By 1970, there were two major competing groups—BankAmericard (originally organized by the Bank of America, but now independent and called Visa) and MasterCard—and a small number of regional groups. Bank credit cards became a success. A number of banks did attempt to continue or start their own cards independently of the two major groups, but these generally were not successful. In 1985, Sears Roebuck introduced a general three-party credit card, named the Discover Card, issued through a bank affiliate in Delaware, to compete with the two major groups. (It sold the card in 1993.) In 1990, American Telephone and Telegraph introduced its Universal Card issued as a MasterCard through a small bank in Georgia, and within two years became the second largest issuer of credit cards in the United States after Citicorp. Other major retailers and even manufacturers, such as General Electric and General Motors, followed suit shortly thereafter.

Bank credit cards are now the most widely used credit cards, surpassing retail store credit cards. In 1992, 80 million households held nearly 300 million bank credit cards. About one-half of all cardholders use their cards for transactions purposes only and pay off their balances in full within the interest-free grace period, generally 20 days or so. The other half borrow for longer periods of time and pay interest. In 1992, Visa had 150 million credit cards outstanding in the United States on which $190 billion was charged during the year and 304 million cardholders worldwide who charged $458 billion; MasterCard had 100 million cardholders and $113 billion charged domestically and 188 million cardholders worldwide who charged $259 billion; and Discover had 39 million cardholders and $28 billion charged. The cards are accepted by many merchants that also operate their own card system or accept other, nonbank cards and by merchants in many foreign countries.

NOW Accounts. NOW accounts were developed by thrift institutions to circumvent their prohibition against offering demand deposits and to break the commercial banks' monopoly on such deposits. To the extent that regulation limits profit potentials, it encourages the search for and development of ways to circumvent the barriers. Edward Kane refers to this process as the "regulatory dialectic."[1] The regulatory agency and those being regulated, be they financial institutions or users of financial services, are viewed as opposing forces locked in a continuing struggle between political and economic power, respectively. When political actions by regulators reduce the economic power of the institutions and/or users of financial services, the latter go "loophole mining" until they strike a "loophole lode." The regulators' political power is thereby reduced. To regain their lost political authority, the regulators expand their regulations to close the loophole. And so the process continues in a series of actions and reactions. Alternatively, this process may be viewed as a battle between the "heavy hand" of regulation and the "invisible hand" of the marketplace.

In the United States, commercial banks historically had a monopoly on the issuance of deposits subject to transfer check to third parties. Thrift institutions long viewed checking accounts as a service that would both profitably supplement their own deposit and lending services to households and attract additional customers through the convenience of "one-stop, full-service" banking. They considered the commercial banks' monopoly as unfair. After all, they argued, if the commercials could offer interest-paying time and savings accounts in competition with the thrifts, why couldn't the thrifts offer checking accounts?

In May 1972, after two years of litigation in the courts, a state-chartered savings bank in Massachusetts was allowed to permit its household depositors to write drafts (which are very similar to checks) payable to third parties on their interest-paying accounts. The drafts were in the form of

[1] Edward J. Kane, "Good Intentions and Unintended Evil: The Case against Selective Credit Allocation," *Journal of Money, Credit and Banking*, February 1977, pp. 55–69.

negotiable orders of withdrawal, and the accounts on which such drafts could be written became known as **NOW** *accounts.* In June 1972, savings banks in Massachusetts began offering NOW accounts. Three months later, in September, savings banks in New Hampshire received court approval to offer them to household customers.

As might be expected, these events spurred charges of unfair competition both from commercial banks, which could offer check-writing services only on non-interest-bearing deposits, and from savings and loan associations, which could not offer any check-writing deposits. In August 1973, the U.S. Congress authorized all depository institutions (except credit unions) in Massachusetts and New Hampshire to issue NOW accounts. In 1975, NOW accounts became permissible for state-chartered thrift institutions in Maine and Connecticut. At the same time, Illinois permitted state-chartered SLAs to issue non-interest-bearing NOW accounts (NINOW *accounts*), and Oregon permitted savings banks to offer non-interest-bearing checking accounts. In February 1976, Congress extended the authority to issue NOW accounts to all depository institutions (except credit unions) in all six New England States (Maine, Vermont, New Hampshire, Massachusetts, Connecticut, and Rhode Island). Later in the year, New York State authorized noninterest demand deposits at state-chartered savings banks and SLAs, and in 1978, Congress permitted federally chartered SLAs in the state to offer NOW accounts. Not to be outdone, the National Credit Union Administration in August 1974 permitted federally chartered credit unions to offer *share draft accounts.* These accounts permitted depositors to write checks on their interest-paying deposits (called shares at credit unions) drawn on the credit union's account at its commercial bank. Finally, in 1980, the Depository Institutions Deregulation and Monetary Control Act extended NOW accounts to all depository institutions everywhere. (A chronology of these events appears in Table 15–1, pp. 262–65, in the second edition of this book.)

The actions since 1970 broke down some of the traditional barriers between commercial banks and other depository institutions and intensified the competition for deposits. Through the early 1990s, NOW accounts accounted for almost all of the growth in transaction deposits and exceeded demand deposits in dollar size.

MMD *and* **SNOW** *Accounts.* Most of the funds collected by money-market funds in their rapid growth from $3 billion in 1977 to $235 billion five years later in 1982 either came from or would otherwise have been put in depository institutions subject to Regulation Q ceilings. (Of course, since money-market funds invest partially in CDs, some of these funds were not totally lost to, at least, the larger institutions.) To permit depository institutions to compete on more equal footing, Congress in the Garn-St Germain Act authorized, effective year-end 1982, MMDAs that had a minimum balance but no rate ceiling and permitted limited transaction usage. Shortly thereafter, the regulatory agencies authorized minimum-balance consumer NOW accounts not subject to rate ceilings termed super-NOWs (SNOWs). Depository institutions marketed these accounts vigorously. Within one year, the dollar amount of MMDAs exceeded money-market funds, even at their peak, by 50 percent as well as demand deposits, savings accounts, and CDs, and were equal in dollar amount to all transactions balances, including NOW and SNOW accounts. MMDAs are now the largest single type of deposit at commercial banks after consumer certificates of deposits. Most banks merged SNOW accounts with NOW accounts after regulation Q was removed.

Zero-Coupon and Original-Issue Discount Bonds. As interest rates increased to record levels in early 1981, investors experienced substantial losses on their holdings of long-term, fixed-coupon-rate bonds. As a result, many shied away from buying additional bonds of this type and shifted their demands to either short-term or variable-coupon bonds. Some investors, however, believed that interest rates would begin to decline again and attempted to lock in the high rates. This could be done best with long-term, zero-coupon bonds **(ZCBs).** Since these bonds make only a single payment at maturity, they are sold by the issuer in the primary market at original-issue discounts from par value and continue to trade at a discount in the secondary market until their maturity date. ZCBs are frequently referred to as original-issue discount bonds, or **OIDs.** Because they make no coupon payments, zero-coupon bonds also eliminate the risk to investors of receiving lower interest returns on the reinvestment of the coupon payments. On the other hand, ZCBs have longer durations than coupon bonds of the same maturity and, therefore, carry more price risk.

Although zero-coupon Treasury bills were the dominant security in the money market for many years, few such securities existed in the capital market. One reason for the scarcity was that, for bonds issued by private firms, most investors had to declare the annual amortization of the discount as ordinary income for federal income tax purposes and had to pay the tax annually even though the cash income was not realized until the bond either was sold or matured. Nevertheless, in 1981, the first private ZCBs were issued by J. C. Penney and PepsiCo. The Penney bonds had an 8-year maturity and were sold at $332 per $1,000 maturity value. For the reason above, the buyers were tax-exempt investors, such as life insurance companies and pension funds. With the broadening of eligibility for tax-deferred IRAs (investment retirement accounts) to all taxpayers in 1982, a number of ZCBs were tailored especially for this market, featuring small denominations. In addition, mutual funds were established that invested only in such bonds. Because, similar to coupon payments, the amortization of original-issue discounts on municipal bonds is exempt from federal income taxes, municipal ZCBs (sometimes called *accrual bonds*) were developed for taxable investors.

To reduce the risk of default and broaden their appeal, Merrill Lynch issued small-denomination ZCBs that were fully collateralized by equal amounts of a U.S. Treasury bond issue that had been previously purchased by Merrill Lynch for this purpose and held by a trustee. These ZCBs, termed **Treasury investment growth receipts** or **TIGRs,** were issued in serial form (a package containing individual bonds with different maturities), in which each maturity date and amount was matched precisely to the coupon amount and date of the collateral Treasury bond, but sold to investors in separate maturities. The Treasury bond was effectively stripped of its coupons and each, as well as the principal amount, was sold as individual ZCBs. Because of the advantages of default-free ZCBs, Merrill Lynch sold the newly created TIGRs at a higher price than the price of the associated underlying collateral, so that the TIGRs traded at a lower yield than otherwise comparable Treasury securities. Merrill Lynch was able to create these synthetic Treasury securities because the U.S. Treasury Department chose not to market ZCBs. Other institutions quickly followed with similar instruments, the most popular of which were Salomon Brothers' **certificates of accrual on Treasury securities,** or **CATS.** (Because of the acronyms, these bonds are sometimes referred to as "animal" bonds.)

Finally, in 1985, the U.S. Treasury started selling its own long-term ZCBs indirectly in the form of coupons on its regular bonds. The coupons, which are effectively small ZCBs maturing on the payment date, and the principal amount at maturity are assigned separate registration numbers and can be traded separately from the associated bond. They are known as **STRIPS (separately traded registered interest and principal securities).** The bonds, including the coupons are sold by the Treasury. Bond dealers who purchase the bonds strip off the coupons and sell them separately. STRIPS have reduced the demand for animal bonds and no new issues have been created since STRIPS were introduced.

Variable-Rate Securities.   The increase in interest rate volatility in the 1970s made longer-term traditional fixed-rate securities riskier. This encouraged many investors to restrict their investments to short-term securities, whose prices fluctuated less with changes in market interest rates. However, these securities involved transactions costs when they were rolled over at maturity. SSUs had to locate other comparable securities, and DSUs had to obtain new financing. To reduce transactions costs and increase the certainty of the commitment to both parties, long-term contracts were designed with short terms to repricing or coupon-change intervals (CCIs). As the coupon rates on these instruments are likely to change over the maturity of the security, they were termed **variable-** or **floating-rate securities (VRSs).**

The coupon rates on VRSs are tied to the interest rate on an outstanding fixed-rate *index* or *reference* security with a term to maturity equal or close to the length of the CCI and are generally free to change by an amount necessary to equate it to the rate on the index security. Thus, the price of the security returns to par value at each repricing date. Some variable-rate securities, however, constrain the amount by which the coupon can change. For these securities, the price returns only partially to par value on repricing dates. The shorter the CCI, the closer the security trades to par value.

Since their introduction in the mid-1970s, variable-rate designs have been applied to all major forms of debt securities from corporate bonds, to mortgages, to bank loans and deposits, and so on. (Variable-rate residential mortgages were examined in Chapter 21.) The demand for variable-rate securities fluctuates with the volatility in inflation and interest rates. The more volatile the rates of inflation or interest, the greater is the demand by investors for variable-rate relative to fixed-rate securities. In some periods, the demand for variable-rate securities has almost completely dominated that for fixed-rate securities.

To reduce the interest rate uncertainty on unconstrained variable-rate securities, some financial institutions offer borrowers a maximum interest rate guarantee, referred to as **interest rate caps.** If interest rates rise above the cap rate, the institution will make the additional interest payments.

Contracts have also been designed to provide protection against both interest rate increases and decreases by specifying a ceiling and floor rate, or **interest rate collars.** Within the collar range, the borrower (investor) pays (receives) the interest. Outside the collar range, the seller of the collar contract pays (receives) the additional or reduced interest. Caps and collars trade in secondary markets separately from the associated variable-rate security.

Financial Futures and Options Contracts.   As discussed in detail in Chapter 22, futures and options contracts permit DSUs, SSUs, and intermediaries to reduce their uncertainty and protect themselves against adverse future price changes. Although futures contracts were long used in markets for agricultural and other raw-material commodities and options contracts for stocks, both have only recently been introduced in the market for financial instruments on organized exchanges. The development of futures contracts in financial instruments differs from that of the previously discussed innovations. The futures contracts were developed by institutions operating organized trading markets rather than by those marketing the financial instruments. The first financial futures contracts were in foreign currency. These were first traded in 1972 on the new International Monetary Market, a subsidiary of the Chicago Mercantile Exchange, which trades in nonfinancial futures contracts. The first futures contracts on financial securities were in GNMA mortgage-participation certificates on the Chicago Board of Trade in 1975, also a long-time major market for nonfinancial futures trading. The first options contracts on financial debt instruments were traded on the Chicago Board of Options Exchange (CBOE) in 1982. The board had previously started trading options on stocks in 1973.

Swaps.   Many financial institutions engage in interest rate intermediation. Thus, changes in interest rates will affect the market values of their assets and deposits differently. Their net income also will be affected when market rates of interest change as the interest revenues from their earning assets and the interest expenses on their deposits will change differently. The institutions can reduce their exposure to interest rate risk, if they wish, by reducing the mismatch in the interest rate sensitivities of the two sides of their balance sheets through duration matching on the cash market (discussed in Chapter 17) or on the futures market (discussed in Chapter 22).

    In recent years, institutions have developed a third way to reduce the mismatch by exchanging or *swapping* the flow of cash interest payments generated by some of their securities or deposits on one side of their balance sheet for the cash flows of securities or deposits held by other institutions that are better synchronized with the interest sensitivity of the cash flows on the other side of their balance sheet. For example, if one institution was financing long-term fixed-rate mortgages with short-term deposits and a second institution was financing variable-rate mortgages with long-term fixed-rate deposits, both institutions would have large interest rate mismatches and would be exposed to substantial interest rate risk. Both could reduce their risk exposure if they swapped the cash flows from the fixed-rate mortgages for those from the variable-rate mortgages. Such a swap is referred to as an **interest rate swap.** Unlike an ordinary transaction, the principal amounts are not exchanged. After the swap, the first institution would

EXHIBIT

23–1

Example of Interest Rate Swap

Assume a commercial bank and a thrift institution of equal credit quality and equal dollar size. The initial accounts for the two institutions are shown in part (a) of the table. The commercial bank has variable-rate loans yielding 12 percent, financed by long-term fixed-rate deposits paying 11 percent. The thrift institution has long-term fixed-rate loans (mortgages) of equal credit quality yielding 13 percent and variable-rate deposits paying 10 percent. Thus, each institution is assuming interest rate risk. This accounts for at least some of the differences in interest margins between the two institutions. Note that the variable-rate securities yield 1 percent less than the comparable fixed-rate securities, although this can change through time as market rates of interest change. If interest rates rise, the bank's interest margin increases and the thrift's decreases.

Both institutions can reduce their interest rate risk exposure by swapping the income stream on their assets. Thus, the bank would send its variable income stream, initially 12 percent, to the thrift institution, and the thrift would send its income stream, fixed at 13 percent, to the bank. Now the bank has only variable-rate inflows and the thrift only fixed-rate inflows. Because only the income streams and not the principal amounts of the securities are traded, the balance sheets do not change; only the income flows are affected. The after-swap accounts are shown in part (b) of the table. Note that the interest margins are now the same for both institutions at 2 percent and will remain so, as neither institution incurs interest rate risk, at least on its interest spread. Thus, this spread reflects equal differences in credit risk.

CASH FLOWS FOR COMMERCIAL BANK AND THRIFT INSTITUTIONS BEFORE AND AFTER INTEREST RATE SWAP

	Commercial Bank		Thrift Institution	
(a) Before Swap				
Loan ($100)	Variable-rate loan	12%	Fixed-rate loan	13%
Deposit ($100)	Fixed-rate deposit	11	Variable-rate deposit	10
(b) After Swap				
Loan ($100)	Variable-rate loan	12%	Fixed-rate loan	13%
Interest ⎤ Outflow	Variable-rate outflow	12	Fixed-rate outflow	13
Swap ⎦ Inflow	Fixed-rate inflow	13	Variable-rate inflow	12
Deposit ($100)	Fixed-rate deposit	11	Variable-rate deposit	10

effectively be financing variable-rate mortgages with short-term deposits and the second institution would effectively be financing long-term fixed-rate mortgages with long-term fixed-rate deposits. Their interest rate mismatches would be reduced. (An example of such a swap arrangement is shown in Exhibit 23–1.)

In swap transactions, ownership of the underlying securities that generate the cash flows remains with the original holders, who would continue to service the loans and, generally, retain the risks of default. Thus, the institutions continue to originate loans in their preferred maturity sectors and maintain their customer base. Swaps may also be used by SSUs and

DSUs among themselves. The two sides in a swap agreement are referred to as **counterparties** and, if one or both also were the ultimate users of the swap arrangement, as **endusers.** In 1991, nearly 60 percent of all endusers of swap arrangements were financial institutions and 30 percent were non-financial corporations. In most cases, interest rate swaps are arranged by a third party, generally a commercial or investment bank, acting either as a broker or, more frequently, as a dealer, who temporarily buys the offsetting position from the enduser. Because endusers could default on their payment obligations, swap contracts involve credit risk and some of the intermediaries also generate fees by enhancing the credit quality of a swap by guaranteeing timely payment on both ends. But, because the nondefaulting counterparty will not make its payment, the loss is restricted to the contracted interest rate that the nondefaulting counterparty could have earned.

Cash flow swaps may be used for purposes other than managing interest rate risk. At times, a firm's credit quality may be priced differently on the variable- and fixed-rate markets, in terms of interest rate spread above the yield on Treasury securities of like maturity, so that the firm can borrow relatively more cheaply on one than the other. It may, however, not prefer the security with the cheaper rate, such as the variable-rate loan because of, say, unwanted interest rate risk exposure. If it could find another firm whose borrowing costs on variable- and fixed-rate loans do not differ as much, it could swap its variable-rate cash flows for the other firm's fixed-rate cash flows, adjusted for differences in across-the-board credit quality between the two firms. Both firms would benefit from such a swap by sharing in the elimination of the higher interest rate spread between the variable- and fixed-rate obligations of the first firm. Such swaps are referred to as **credit quality swaps.** Swaps may also be used by institutions and firms that operate in different currencies on the two sides of the balance sheet and wish to reduce their exposure to changes in exchange rates or foreign currency risk. Such swaps are known as **foreign currency swaps.**

Cash flow swaps came into widespread use only in the early 1980s. By 1993, the dollar amount of securities (the principal or *notional* amount) swapped worldwide approached $5 trillion and exceeded the outstanding amount of interest rate futures and options. (Recall, however, only the periodic interest payments are swapped.) Interest rate swaps outstanding accounted for more than $3 billion of this amount, and currency swaps for about $1 billion. About one-half of the swap contracts were denominated in U.S. dollars and the rest in foreign currencies, primarily in Japanese yen. Many of these swaps are substitutes for other types of interest rate hedges, such as futures contracts. A survey of chief finance officers of major U.S. corporations found that they use swaps far more frequently to hedge than futures or options. The basic differences between swaps and futures contracts are shown in Table 23–2.

Unlike futures contracts, although similar to forward contracts, swap contracts may be tailored to the particular needs of endusers and become far more complex than the plain vanilla contracts described above. Swaps may be traded in the secondary market.

Market Index Deposits (MIDs). Although commercial banks may manage mutual funds and act as brokers in selling mutual funds managed by oth-

TABLE

23–2   PRINCIPAL DIFFERENCES BETWEEN SWAPS AND FUTURES

	Swaps	Futures
Maturities covered	One month to 20 years	Six to eight quarters
Liquidity in the markets	Out to 10 years	Next two quarters
Quotes	From commercial banks/ investment banks/ brokers	Traded market: Chicago Mercantile Exchange and Chicago Board of Trade
Credit risk control method	Credit-line	Mark-to-market mechanism
Costs	Bid/offer spreads and/or fees	Commissions/margin
Dealing amounts	Any amount over $10 million	Units of $1 million up to market liquidity
Dealing dates	Any dates	Fixed quarterly cycle
Reversing positions	Simple	Simple
Contract documentation	Simple	Simple
Management	Simple	Complex
Normal accounting	Loan deposit	Mark-to-market

SOURCE: *Intermarket*, October 1986, p. 16. Reprinted by permission.

ers, the Glass-Steagall Act prohibits them from selling and distributing mutual funds that they themselves sponsor. This would be equivalent to banks dealing in securities as principals, which is prohibited (see Chapter 20.) From the beginning of the bull stock market in 1982 through 1986, the number of equity and long-term bond mutual funds tripled, and their assets expanded sevenfold. The funds were highly profitable to both managers and distributors. In 1987, Chase Manhattan Bank developed a technique by which it could offer a product effectively equivalent to a mutual fund.

Chase offered investors a time-deposit account whose return is partially tied to increases in the Standard & Poor's 500 stock index. (Recall that since the demise of Regulation Q, banks can offer any rate on time deposits that they wish.) This account is referred to as a ***market index deposit*** or **MID.** The bank offers depositors a choice of a combination minimum-guaranteed return, say, 0 or 4 percent, and a proportional share in any increase in the S&P index, say, 70 or 50 percent, for a specified term to maturity. The higher participation in stock market increases is paired with lower guaranteed returns. The precise numbers offered are changed as market conditions change. As a deposit, of course, the account cannot decline below its principal or maturity value and is insured by the FDIC up to $100,000. This is an advantage that mutual funds cannot offer.

To earn a return that has characteristics similar to that it is offering on MIDs, Chase invested in futures contracts on the S&P 500 stock index. As discussed in Chapter 22, changes in futures prices move closely with changes in spot prices for the same item. Because at maturity the S&P 500 futures contract can be settled only in cash, it is not viewed as a security by the regulators. Thus, banks are not prohibited from dealing in these contracts for their own accounts.

Other banks introduced their own MIDs. Many differ somewhat in terms of the minimum-guaranteed rate–stock market gain participation combination offered depositors. A few banks have tied the returns to increases in other prices, such as gold prices, and some have even tied the increases in return to decreases in a stock index, effectively permitting depositors to sell the stock market index short. MIDs tied to gains in stock prices are referred to as *bull* **MIDs** and those tied to decreases as *bear* **MIDs.** MIDs have expanded the product mix commercial banks may offer SSUs and have made them more competitive with mutual funds.

Securitization. As discussed in Chapter 8, securities that are not highly marketable trade at a higher interest rate than otherwise comparable highly marketable securities to compensate the investor either for the additional time necessary to find the highest bidder, if the security is sold before maturity, or for the "fire-sale" loss incurred, if it is necessary to sell the security immediately. The marketability of a security is a function of a number of its characteristics, including its denomination, cash flow pattern, and credit quality. The smaller and odder the denomination, the more unique and unpredictable the cash flow, and the lower the credit quality and more costly the credit evaluation, the less marketable the security. Less-marketable securities include residential mortgages, consumer loans, automobile loans, and business loans. But recent advances in information-processing technology have permitted nonmarketable securities to be transformed into marketable securities and permit primary securities to compete more with secondary securities. This is achieved through a process termed *securitization.* The securities are referred to as *asset-backed securities* or **ABSs.**

In securitization, a financial entity, such as a commercial bank, investment bank, or similar institution, puts together a pool or package of less-marketable, small whole securities. These are generally transferred to a third party that serves as a trustee. New securities are created that are collateralized by the existing pooled securities, but are more highly marketable by designing large standard denomination, more-predictable cash flows, and higher credit quality. The payments on the old securities are passed through to the new securities. Credit quality is enhanced because pooling reduces risk through diversification. In addition, for some securities, insurance may be purchased by the issuer to guarantee the timely payments of coupons and principal. The issuer retains responsibility for servicing the original loans, so that the pure financing part of the loan is spun off and sold separately, but generally does not assume the risk of default. (Although securitized securities are new securities, their payment stream is tied directly to that of the specific underlying primary securities, so that they resemble these securities more than they do secondary securities of depository institutions.) These steps are traced in Figure 23–1.

The first type of securitized loans were residential mortgage loans that were transformed into pass-through certificates in the 1970s. These and other types of mortgage-backed securities were analyzed in Chapter 21. In more recent years, a wide range of other whole loans have been securitized,

FIGURE

23–1

PASS-THROUGH, ASSET-BACKED SECURITIES: STRUCTURE
AND CASH FLOWS

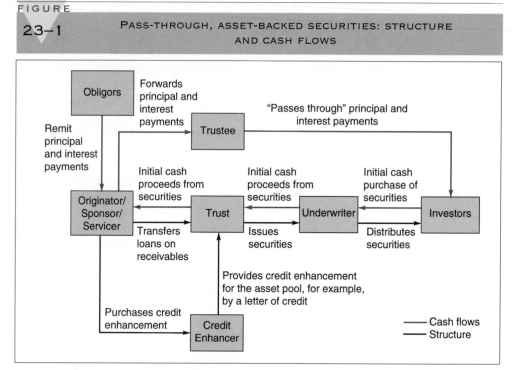

SOURCE: Thomas R. Boemio and Gerald A. Edwards, Jr., "Asset Securitization: A Supervisory Perspective," *Federal Reserve Bulletin*, October 1989, p. 661.

including consumer credit-card loans (termed ***certificates of amortizing revolving debts*** or **CARDs**), automobile loans (termed ***certificates of automobile receivables*** or **CARs**), and business loans. Many commercial banks and other financial institutions have used securitization to increase the liquidity and diversification of their asset portfolios.

By enabling banks and thrifts to sell their assets more easily, securitization has also permitted them to move some assets off their balance sheet and avoid holding the capital required by the regulators' risk-based capital standards. In addition, by creating more efficient primary securities, securitization has also permitted some DSUs to bypass institutions on the intermediation financial market and obtain funding on the private financial market.

Junk Bonds. As noted in Chapter 7, *junk,* or *high-yield, bonds* are bonds that have credit ratings below Baa. These ratings are frequently considered below investment grade. For many years before they became popular, below-investment-grade bonds on the market were generally bonds that were initially issued as investment grade (Baa or higher), but were later downgraded because of the financial misfortunes of their issuers. They were referred to as ***fallen angels.***

Starting in the late 1970s, some investment bankers believed that new below-investment-grade bonds could be sold to finance capital expenditures of smaller, riskier firms if the interest premium over investment grade bonds was sufficiently high. These bonds substituted for funds previously raised primarily from banks, venture capital firms, or not raised at all. After a slow start, the issuance of new junk bonds, or **original issue junk,** accelerated sharply in 1983, when it was discovered that these bonds were also useful in financing highly leveraged acquisitions or "buyouts" (LBOs) of large companies either by another company or by its management. LBOs became highly popular in the mid-1980s. The guiding spirit in the development of original-issue junk bonds was Michael Milken, who was in charge of bond activities at Drexel Burnham, the major investment banking firm in both the primary and secondary junk bond markets in their formative years.

Yields to maturity on junk bonds were, at times, some 300 to 400 basis points above those of Treasury bonds of the same maturity. Many investors considered these spreads greater than their perceived default risk premiums and increased their demand for these bonds. Junk bond mutual funds grew rapidly in size and importance. As a result, the volume of new issue junk bonds increased sharply from only $1 billion in 1982 to more than $33 billion in 1986. In 1987, these bonds accounted for nearly 25 percent of all new corporate bond issues. As is shown in Table 23–3, during much of this period, the return realized on junk bonds significantly exceeded that on higher-quality bonds.

However, in the late 1980s conditions changed dramatically. A number of highly publicized leveraged buyouts of earlier years financed by junk

TABLE

23–3

NEW ISSUES OF JUNK BONDS AND ANNUAL RETURNS, YIELDS, AND SPREADS ON
JUNK BONDS AND TEN-YEAR TREASURY SECURITIES, 1978–1993

Year	Return (percent)			Promised Yield (percent)			New Issues ($ billions)
	Junk	Treas.	Spread	Junk	Treas.	Spread	
1993	17.18	12.08	5.11	9.61	5.80	3.81	57.2
1992	18.16	6.50	11.66	11.28	6.69	4.59	39.8
1991	34.58	17.18	17.40	13.11	6.70	6.41	10.0
1990	−4.36	6.88	−11.24	17.58	8.83	8.75	1.4
1989	1.62	15.99	−14.37	15.41	7.93	7.48	28.8
1988	13.47	9.20	4.27	13.95	9.00	4.95	31.1
1987	4.67	−2.67	7.34	12.66	8.75	3.91	30.5
1986	16.09	24.08	−7.99	14.45	9.55	4.90	33.3
1985	22.51	31.54	−9.03	15.40	11.65	3.75	15.7
1984	8.50	14.82	−6.32	14.97	11.87	3.10	15.2
1983	21.80	2.23	19.57	15.74	10.70	5.04	7.8
1982	32.45	42.08	−9.63	17.84	13.86	3.98	2.7
1981	7.56	0.48	7.08	15.97	12.08	3.89	1.5
1980	−1.00	−2.96	1.96	13.46	10.23	3.23	1.4
1979	3.69	−0.86	4.55	12.07	9.13	2.94	1.4
1978	7.57	−1.11	8.68	10.92	8.11	2.81	1.6
Arithmetic Average							
1978–1993	12.78	10.97	1.81	14.03	9.43	4.60	

SOURCE: High Yield Securities Research Department of Merrill Lynch. Reprinted with permission.

bonds failed, and others came close to defaulting on their interest payments. In addition, significant abuses in the issuance and trading of junk bonds were reported. Combined, these events scared many investors away from junk bonds, and they dropped sharply in value. In 1989 and 1990, the return realized on junk bonds averaged some 13 percentage points below that on long-term Treasury bonds despite promising yields of 7 percentage points more. The number of newly issued junk bonds also dropped sharply from $25 billion in 1989 to fewer than 10 new issues totaling only $1 billion in 1990.

The collapse of the market both reflected and accounted for the failure of Drexel Burnham and the conviction of Michael Milken for fraudulent activities. The loss of Drexel Burnham as the major dealer caused severe disruption on the secondary market and a sharp spike in liquidity premiums until other dealers entered. But the market rebounded strongly in the early 1990s. In 1991 and 1992, realized returns were more than double the returns on long-term Treasury bonds. In 1992, new issues rose to a record $40 billion and accounted for 13 percent of all new corporate issues. New issue volume jumped sharply again in 1993 to $57 billion. Having survived this test, junk bonds appear to be a permanent major financing vehicle for risky corporate ventures.

Amercurrencies.   As discussed in Chapter 3, banks can engage in foreign currency intermediation. That is, they can accept deposits (sell secondary securities) denominated in one currency and make loans (buy primary securities) denominated in another. And neither has to be the domestic currency of the country in which the bank is located. Such deposits permit customers the flexibility to avoid exchange rate risks and transactions costs when temporarily storing funds received in a foreign currency or to speculate on favorable exchange rate movements. As discussed in Chapters 4 and 25, banks in foreign countries have been offering Eurocurrencies, or deposits in currencies other than their own, particularly in U.S. dollars, for many years.

In the mid-1970s, the Bank of America requested permission from the Federal Reserve to offer customers deposits at its U.S. offices denominated in major foreign currencies. The Fed denied the request both because such deposits might be too risky for smaller depositors and because it was difficult to determine appropriate interest rate ceilings for each currency as existed at the time for U.S. dollar deposits under Regulation Q. (Although they did not yet exist, this author introduced the term *Amercurrencies* for such deposits in the first edition of this book, published in 1980.) Finally, at year-end 1988, the Fed agreed to permit banks to offer such deposits effective 1990, and by midyear 1990, a small number of larger banks had.

Amercurrencies are issued in both money-market deposit and fixed-rate time deposit forms. Interest rates paid differ according to the market rate of interest in the currency's home country. For example, on March 1, 1990, Citibank (New York) offered the interest rates shown in Table 23–4 on three-month time deposits in five foreign currencies. Rates were more than twice as high on British pound deposits (14.41%) as on Japanese yen deposits (6.63%). At the time, rates on three-month U.S. dollars CDs were about 8¼ percent. However, the return realized on Amercurrencies is the sum of the interest yield and the gain or loss from any change in exchange rates relative to the dollar.

TABLE 23–4	YIELDS AND REALIZED RETURNS ON THREE-MONTH AMERCURRENCY DEPOSITS, MARCH–JUNE 1990		
Currency	Interest Yield (percent)	Exchange Rate Gain or Loss (percent, annual rate)	Total Return (percent)
British pound	14.41	6.29	20.7
Canadian dollar	12.38	5.12	17.5
German mark	7.69	9.01	16.7
Japanese yen	6.63	−4.73	1.9
Swiss franc	8.56	25.94	34.5

SOURCE: Reprinted by permission of *The Wall Street Journal*, July 11, 1990, pp. C1, C19, © 1990 Dow Jones & Company, Inc. All Right Reserved Worldwide.

NOTE: Rates offered by Citibank (New York).

At maturity on June 1, the dollar exchange rate had changed for all five of the above currencies. The Swiss franc had appreciated sharply and gained holders of Amerfrancs a total annualized return of 35 percent. On the other hand, the Japanese yen had depreciated relative to the dollar, and the return realized on Ameryen deposits in this three-month period was only 2 percent, considerably less than the 6.63 percent promised yield. Thus, Amercurrency deposits are riskier than dollar deposits, at least for participants who do not have scheduled payments in foreign currency.

New Technology

New markets are also opened by changes in technology. The development of the computer and electronic telecommunications has made possible an entirely new way of processing and transmitting financial data. Electronic entry on computer tapes and disks can replace paper entry on traditional records. This represents a process innovation. Some of the new services that have resulted from this change have already been discussed in Chapter 14. These include remote service units, point-of-sale systems, in-home banking, and automated clearinghouses. Videotex on the home computer screen, from which hard copy can be printed, can replace both the need to request current account records from bank personnel and periodic mailed statements.

The cost of electronic processing has declined astronomically in recent years, making it cheaper as well as more flexible than previous payment processes. Between 1960 and 1980, the rental cost of computer memory declined by a factor of 50, and processing costs by a factor of 10. In 1960, the newly developed, widely used IBM 650 computer required an air-conditioned 18-square-foot room. Its main "brain" unit alone was 5 feet high and 6 feet wide. It could do 33,000 additions per second. By 1982, personal computers could do 700,000, or 20 times as many, additions per second. In 1982 dollars, the 1960 IBM 650 cost about $600,000, not including operating costs. Today's far more powerful personal computer costs less than one-hundredth this amount. Data-processing costs have declined commensurately. What cost a dollar to record and process in 1964, costs less than a nickel today. Computers can be activated from a wide variety of distant terminals located anywhere in the world, and information entered into terminals is quickly and cheaply transmitted.

These innovations will continue to revolutionize institutions and markets further in coming years as the new technology permits most financial services to be provided more conveniently and more cheaply. In the process, new and different markets will be developed and further innovations encouraged. The use of 24-hour-a-day trading and globalized markets will accelerate.

The new technology not only increased the variety of financial services possible, but opened the provision of financial services to nonfinancial firms. For example, cash management services, which involve the monitoring of funds in one or more customer deposit accounts to see that they do not accumulate over a specified amount and ordering the transfer and/or investment of any funds that do, can be provided by nonfinancial firms. All that is necessary for such *sweep systems* is a computer and a communications network. By permitting the rapid transfer of funds, the technological advances have made particularly significant inroads in the traditional role of commercial banks as the sole providers of transactions balances and lessened their importance in the economy. With a large computer, almost anyone can technically offer services similar to bank transaction deposits.

Likewise, the availability of greater, cheaper, and more current information on the financial condition of the world's largest corporations has made it easier for many of these firms to borrow funds from DSUs directly on the private financial market through commercial paper than to borrow indirectly from banks. This has eroded the traditional commercial bank market for business loans.

SUMMARY

The financial environment in the United States has changed dramatically since World War II. In part, this reflects changes in the economy and in part technological advances in communications and transportation. Higher incomes have enlarged the number of participants in financial markets, and large-scale production has increased the need for larger financing and thus the collection of larger pools of savings. Also, more volatile rates of inflation, interest rates, and exchange rates have increased financial risk; speedier transportation and communications have increased the unification of previously partitioned regional markets into national markets, and national markets into international markets, and permit almost instantaneous record maintenance; and greater government regulation has stimulated the search for institutions and instruments not subject to the regulations. The financial sector has responded to these changes by creating new institutions and instruments that accommodate the new needs and conditions.

Credit unions, which have favorable tax treatment and regulation, have grown faster than other depository institutions. Pension funds, which provide for a growing need in a progressively more complex economy, have also expanded rapidly. Newly established money-market funds prospered when regulation diminished the attractiveness of depository institutions. New instruments created include special, no-minimum-balance checking accounts that are tailored to lower-income households; NOW accounts that permit interest rates to be paid on transaction deposits; futures instruments and variable-rate securities that reduce interest rate risk exposure; MMD accounts that were free of deposit rate ceilings and permit banks to compete on more level terms with money-market funds; MID accounts that permit banks to compete with mutual funds; zero-coupon bonds that lock in current interest rates; futures and options contracts on debt securities that permit interest rate risk to be managed more efficiently; assets backed securities that permit a pool of not very marketable primary securities that securitize the new securities to become more marketable; Eurocurrencies and Amercurrencies that permit depositors to hold bank deposits denominated in other than the local currency; and swaps of income streams between two market participants that permit both parties to better balance their interest rate or foreign currency positions or to arbitrage peculiar credit quality differences.

QUESTIONS

1. Discuss the reasons for innovation in the financial markets and the major types of innovation. Why has innovation appeared to accelerate in the years since 1970?

2. Identify two new major financial intermediary institutions that were established in recent years, and discuss the reasons underlying their developing and growth.

3. Identify three new financial instruments that financial institutions introduced in recent years in response to the needs of their customers. What purpose did each instrument serve?

4. Identify three new financial instruments that financial institutions introduced in recent years in response to their own needs. How did each instrument satisfy this need?

5. Why did commercial banks develop *market index deposits*? How do they basically work? What advantages and disadvantages relative to mutual funds might they have for investors?

6. Why were *junk bonds* an innovation? How did junk bonds before 1980 differ

from those after? What is their appeal to investors? To issuers? What has been the actual experience of investors? What was the importance of Drexel Burnham on both the primary and secondary markets?

7. Describe a *swap agreement*. What motivates such transactions? What gets swapped and what does not? Why is the reported volume of swaps so large relative to activity on other markets?

8. Discuss how the increase in the volatility of inflation in recent years has affected financial innovation. What do you think might happen to the new instruments and institutions if the volatility in inflation decreases significantly?

9. How do Amercurrencies differ from Eurocurrencies? How are they alike? Why may banks offer such deposits and why may depositors demand them? How can banks manage the additional risk exposure associated with these deposits?

REFERENCES

Altman, Edward I., "Setting the Record Straight on Junk Bonds: A Review of the Research on Default Rates and Returns," *Journal of Applied Corporate Finance*, Summer 1990, pp. 82–95.

Bank for International Settlement, *Recent Innovations in International Banking.* Basel, Switzerland, April 1986.

Bruck, Connie, *The Predators' Ball: The Inside Story of Drexel Burnham and the Rise of the*

Junk Bond Raiders. New York: Penguin Books, 1989.

Campbell, Tim S., and William A. Kracaw, *Financial Risk Management*. New York: Harper Collins, 1993.

Canner, Glenn B., and Charles Luckett, "Developments in the Pricing of Credit Card Services," *Federal Reserve Bulletin*, September 1992, pp. 652–66.

Center for Research in Government Policy and Business, *Government Credit Allocation*. San Francisco: Institute for Contemporary Studies, 1975.

Dufey, Gunter, and Ian Giddy, *The Evolution of Instruments and Techniques in International Financial Markets*. Tilburg, Netherlands: Société Universitaire Européenne de Recherches Financiers, 1981.

Effects of Information Technology on Financial Services Systems. Washington, D.C.: U.S. Congress, Office of Technology Assessment, OTA-CIT-202, September, 1984.

Felgran, Steven D., "Interest Rate Swaps: Use, Risk, and Prices," *New England Economic Review*, Federal Reserve Bank of Boston, November/December 1987, pp. 22–32.

Finnerty, John D., "Financial Engineering in Corporate Finance," *Financial Management*, Winter 1988, pp. 14–33.

Fridson, Martin S., and Jeffrey A. Bersh, "What Caused the 1977–78 Takeoff in High Yield Finance?" *Extra Credit* (Merrill Lynch), November/December 1993, pp. 4–25.

Goodfriend, Marvin, et al., "Recent Financial Innovations," *Economic Review*, Federal Reserve Bank of Richmond, March/April 1980, pp. 14–27.

Hargreaves, D.K., "Swaps: Versatility at Controlled Risk," *World Financial Markets*. New York: Morgan Guarantee Trust & Co., April 1991, pp. 1–22.

Holdcraft, James P., Jr., and Edward L. Neuberg, "The Wizards of Wall Street," *Secondary Mortgage Markets*, Winter 1988–89, pp. 16–20.

Kane, Edward J., "Accelerating Inflation, Technological Innovation, and the Decreasing Effectiveness of Banking Regulation," *Journal of Finance*, May 1981, pp. 355–68.

Kaufman, George G., "Financing the National Debt: Time for Innovation," *Backgrounder* (No. 202), Heritage Foundation, August 1982.

King, Stephen R., and Eli M. Remolona, "The Pricing and Hedging of Market Index Deposits," *Quarterly Review*, Federal Reserve Bank of New York, Summer 1987, pp. 9–20.

Loeys, Jan G., "Interest Rate Swaps," *Business Review*, Federal Reserve Bank of Philadelphia, May/June 1985, pp. 17–25.

Mandell, Lewis, *The Credit Card Industry: A History*. Boston: Twayne Publications, 1990.

Marshall, John F., and Kenneth R. Kapner, *The Swap Market*, 2nd ed. Miami: Kolb, 1993.

Marton, Andrew, "Brokers and Investors Are Being Inundated with New Futures Contracts That They Didn't Ask For and Don't Understand," *Institutional Investor*, August 1984, pp. 238–50.

Miller, Merton, "Financial Innovation: The Last Twenty Years and the Next," *Journal of Financial and Quantitative Analysis*, December 1986, pp. 459–71.

Miller, Merton, et al., "Financial Innovation," *Journal of Applied Corporate Finance*, Winter 1992, pp. 4–47.

Monroe, Ann, "New-Securities Ideas Are Often Hatched But Most Are Flops," *Wall Street Journal*, March 25, 1986, pp. 1, 22.

Pavel, Christene A., *Securitization*. Chicago: Probus, 1989.

Rawls, S. Waite, III, and Charles Smithson, "The Evolution of Risk Management Products," *Journal of Applied Corporate Finance*, Winter 1989, pp. 18–26.

Remolona, Eli M., "The Recent Growth of Financial Derivative Markets," *Quar-*

terly Review, Federal Reserve Bank of New York, Winter 1992–93, pp. 28–43.

Silber, William L., "The Process of Financial Innovation," *American Economic Review*, May 1983, pp. 89–95.

Smith, Clifford W., Jr., Charles W. Smithson, and Lee M. Wakeman, "The Evolving Market for Swaps," *Midland Corporate Finance Journal*, Winter 1986, pp. 20–32.

Van Horne, James C., "Of Financial Innovations and Excesses," *Journal of Finance*, July 1985, pp. 621–31.

Walmsley, Julien, *The New Financial Instruments: An Investor's Guide*. New York: John Wiley, 1988.

Foreign Exchange Rates and the Balance of Payments

As noted throughout this book, financial markets in major countries are no longer separate and distinct markets. In recent years, because of both increased international trade among countries and advances in computer and telecommunications technology that have reduced sharply the cost and transmittal time of international payments, national financial markets have progressively become integrated into a single international marketplace. What happens in any one country's marketplace will quickly affect the markets in all other countries. Thus, to understand the operation of the U.S. financial system, it is increasingly necessary to study not only that system but also the international or global financial system.

International finance differs from domestic finance in that more than one country is involved. Thus, it is likely that an international financial transaction will involve more than one

▼ Currency
▼ Language
▼ Institutional and legal environment
▼ Culture and custom
▼ Economic policy

These differences tend to increase the risk and cost of international finance relative to domestic finance. Indeed, one can say that international finance is interpersonal finance made more difficult. On the other hand, because their geographical scope is broadened beyond the boundaries of any individual country, market participants may have access to more DSUs or SSUs and to more individual markets. If this reduces costs by more than they are increased by the additional difficulties, international finance enhances the efficiency of the domestic financial system. In this chapter, we discuss the link between international trade and international finance. In the next chapter, we shall discuss the international financial system, including international financial institutions and markets.

International trade, or trade among different countries, occurs for the same reasons that interpersonal trade does. Individuals trade when they are not self-sufficient in the satisfaction of their needs and find it advantageous to exchange some of their production (or payment for their production) for the production of others. Such trade reflects the specialization of labor and results in higher aggregate incomes than would occur in the absence of trade and under complete self-sufficiency.

Some jacks-of-all-trades may be happier people than specialists, but they generally have lower material incomes. Like individuals, countries are not equally good at producing all items. By specializing in producing those goods in which they are relatively most efficient (in which they have a *comparative advantage*) and trading for those goods in which other countries are

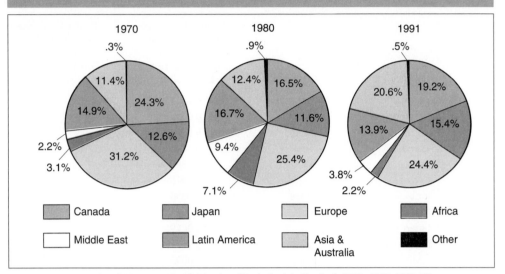

FIGURE
24–1   U.S. TRADE BY REGION AS A PERCENTAGE OF TOTAL U.S. TRADE

SOURCE: International Monetary Fund, *Direction of Trade Statistics Yearbook*, 1992, 1985, 1968–72.

relatively more efficient, countries acquire higher incomes, both individually and in the aggregate.

In large measure because it is so large and its economy so highly diversified, the United States does not rely as much on international trade as do most other countries. In the early 1990s, international trade (as measured by exports in the balance of payments) was equivalent to about 10 percent of GDP for the United States. In contrast, the proportion of international trade to GDP was near 25 percent for the United Kingdom, 35 percent for Germany, and 50 percent for the Netherlands. However, 10 percent in the United States is about twice the proportion of 20 years earlier and reflects the rapid internationalization of our economy. In addition, the pattern of U.S. trade has shifted in recent years. As can be seen in Figure 24–1, trade with Asian countries has increased substantially in the 21 years between 1970 and 1991 at the expense of Canada, Latin America and, since the oil embargo in the mid and late 1970s which pushed up oil prices sharply, oil-exporting countries such a those in the Middle East. Unfortunately, as will be seen later in this chapter, the new important trade partners include many with which the United States has large trade deficits.

Exchange Rates

Because most countries have different currencies, payments for goods, services, and securities purchased from other countries (***imports***) and receipts for goods, services, and securities sold to other countries (***exports***) involve traders who use currencies other than their own. Domestic currencies must be exchanged for foreign currencies, and foreign currencies for domestic currencies. Thus, international trade involves two prices rather than one:

TABLE

24–1   FOREIGN CURRENCY EXCHANGE RATES, 1992

Country	Currency	Foreign Exchange Rate (One Unit of Foreign Currency per U.S. Dollar)	Dollar Exchange Rate (One U.S. Dollar per Foreign Currency Unit)
Australia	dollar	0.7354	1.36
Belgium	franc	0.0311	32.14
Canada	dollar	0.8264	1.21
China (PR)	yuan	0.1811	5.52
France	franc	0.1890	5.29
Germany	mark	0.6410	1.56
India	rupee	0.0356	28.15
Italy	lira	0.0008	1231.20
Japan	yen	0.0079	126.79
Netherlands	guilder	0.3922	2.55
Spain	peseta	0.0098	102.33
Sweden	krona	0.1728	5.82
Switzerland	franc	0.7092	1.41
United Kingdom	pound	1.7673	0.57

SOURCE: *Federal Reserve Bulletin*, February 1993, p. A68.

(1) the price of the item in the currency of the country in which it is produced; and (2) the price of the currency of the producing country in terms of the currency of the buying country. The second price is called the **exchange rate.** The value of the exchange rate for dollars is important to you because it affects the price you will pay for imported goods.

The currencies of some countries and their exchange rates in 1992 are shown in Table 24–1. Currencies of most countries have different names and different values. For example, the currency unit is the United Kingdom is the pound sterling; in France, the franc; in Germany, the mark; and in Japan, the yen. The currencies of some countries have the same names as those in others but have different values. Thus, the Canadian dollar is not the same as the U.S. dollar, the Swiss franc is not the same as the French franc, and the Irish and Egyptian pounds are not the same as each other or as the British pound. The **foreign exchange rates** in the table are the prices of one unit of the foreign currency in terms of U.S. dollars. Thus, in 1992, one Canadian dollar cost 83 U.S. cents; one French franc, 19 U.S. cents; one Japanese yen, less than 1 U.S. cent; and one British pound, 177 U.S. cents.

It is also useful to value domestic currency in terms of foreign currencies. The price of one unit of domestic currency per foreign currency (or the number of foreign currency units per one unit of domestic currency) is referred to as the **domestic exchange rate** and for U.S. dollars, the **dollar exchange rate.** Thus, in 1992, one U.S. dollar cost 1.21 Canadian dollars, 5.3 French francs, 127 Japanese yen, and 0.57 British pounds. The foreign exchange rate is the reciprocal of the dollar exchange rate, or:

$$E_F = \frac{1}{E_D} \qquad (24\text{--}1)$$

where: E_F = foreign exchange rate (cost of one unit of foreign currency in U.S. dollars)

E_D = dollar exchange rate (cost of one U.S. dollar in foreign currency)

The dollar cost of foreign goods is given by the following relationship:

$$P_{US} = P_F \times E_F \qquad (24\text{--}2)$$

where: P_{US} = dollar price
P_F = price in foreign currency
E_F = foreign exchange rate (price of foreign currency in dollars)

A U.S. importer would effectively buy both the foreign goods and the foreign currency to pay the exporter in his or her local currency. Thus, if a particular product sold for 100 francs in France and the French exchange rate was, say, 20 cents, the dollar price would be $20. Likewise, the cost of U.S. products in foreign currencies is given by

$$P_F = P_{US} \times E_D \qquad (24\text{--}3)$$

where: E_D = dollar exchange rate (price of one U.S. dollar in foreign currency)

A foreign importer would effectively buy both the U.S. goods and the U.S. dollar to pay the U.S. exporter in dollars. A product that cost $10.00 in the United States would cost 50 French francs, if the dollar exchange rate were 5.

The higher the dollar exchange rate, that is, the more the dollar costs in foreign currencies, the cheaper are foreign goods in the United States and the more expensive are U.S. goods in the foreign countries. Conversely, the higher the cost of a particular foreign currency in terms of dollars, the lower the dollar exchange rate, and the more expensive are imports in the United States, and the cheaper are exports from the United States. If the exchange rate of a currency increases so it can buy more of another currency, the rate is said to be **appreciating.** If the exchange rate decreases, the rate is **depreciating.** Because two currencies are being exchanged for each other, it follows that if one of the currencies is appreciating, the other is depreciating. A depreciation of the dollar makes U.S. goods less expensive in foreign countries in terms of their own currencies, which are appreciating and can purchase more dollars, but foreign goods more expensive in the United States in terms of dollars.

Thus, if the foreign exchange rate for French francs in terms of U.S. dollars appreciated from 20 to, say, 25 cents, the dollar cost of our 100-franc product would increase from $20 to $25 as the value of the dollar depreciated from 5 francs to 4 francs. You might import less of it. At the same time, the franc cost of our $10 U.S. product would decline from 50 to 40 francs. The French might now buy more of this and other U.S. products. It can be readily seen that changes in exchange rates affect the volume of exports and imports.

The easiest way to understand changes in exchange rates is to treat foreign currencies (or **foreign exchange**) just like any other goods. An exchange rate is a price and, just like any other price, is determined by the demand for the particular currency and the supply of that currency. The domestic demand for a foreign currency arises out of the need either to pay bills for imports from that country or the desire to make financial investments in that country. The domestic supply of the foreign currency arises from receipts for exports to the country or from investments by the country in the United States. Hypothetical demand and supply schedules for a particular foreign currency—in this case, the French franc—in terms of U.S. dollars are drawn in Figure 24–2. The equilibrium exchange rate is 20 cents. (Note, the lower the dollar price of the franc, the higher the franc price and the exchange rate of the dollar.) If, as a result of an increase in the demand for U.S. exports to France, the supply of francs to the United States increases, the supply schedule shifts out from S_0 to S' and the franc exchange rate declines to 15 cents. (The dollar exchange rate climbs from 5 to 7 francs.) If the demand for U.S. exports decreases and the U.S. supply of francs declines (shown by a decline in the supply schedule to S''), the franc exchange rate increases to 25 cents. Changes in imports would shift the demand schedule and thereby change exchange rates in like fashion.

The exchange rate of a particular foreign currency changes as the underlying supply and demand conditions in that country or its trading partners change. Such shifts may occur because of changes in tastes, technological improvements, weather, political upheavals, wars, and so on. A poor harvest in one country will increase its demand for agricultural products from other countries and, unless offset by a reduction in import demand in some other product or an increase in its exports, will cause its exchange rate to decline in terms of the currencies of crop-exporting countries. Likewise, a technological improvement reducing the domestic cost of production of a good may increase the quantity of that good demanded by foreign as well as domestic markets. Unless exports of some other product

FIGURE

24–2   U.S. EXCHANGE RATE FOR FRENCH FRANCS

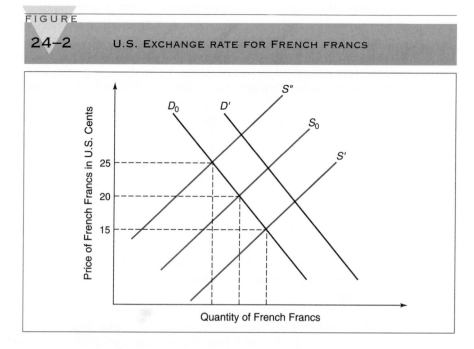

Quantity of French Francs

decline or imports climb by the same amount, the domestic exchange rage will increase in terms of foreign currencies.

Fixed versus Flexible Exchange Rates

Because exchange rates affect the value of all goods and services traded internationally, they affect employment and income both in a country's export industry and in its domestic industries that may compete with potential imports. In addition, changes in exchange rates redistribute income across national boundaries. Thus, they are widely considered to be more important than most other individual prices and of special government concern. Few governments can afford to ignore exchange rate movements.

For many years, governments attempted to hold their exchange rates constant for as long a time as possible. This policy is referred to as a **fixed exchange rate** policy. It was believed that by reducing the uncertainty of future exchange rates, fixed exchange rates would encourage international trade and investment, increase international specialization of labor and capital, and maximize economic efficiency and income in all countries. Fixed exchange rates were written into the international financial system created after World War II, which was supervised by the then newly created **International Monetary Fund (IMF).**

But wishing that exchange rates were fixed and achieving such stability are two different things. Time must almost be made to stand still. In the immediate post–World War II era, most major foreign countries were rebuilding after the war damage they had experienced. They had little to export and for their daily economic survival relied greatly on imports from the United States. This exerted downward pressure on their exchange rates. To maintain the rates, the United States provided these countries with substantial loans and grants-in-aid, such as the Marshall Plan.

By 1960, most industrial countries had reduced their dependence on the United States and had begun to compete vigorously with U.S. goods in both domestic and foreign markets. The tables began to turn. Dollars changed from being scarce to being in surplus, and the dollar exchange rate came under pressure. To maintain the dollar exchange rate and prevent it from depreciating, major foreign countries accelerated repayment of their debts and extended loans of their currencies to the United States. This increased the U.S. supply of foreign currency and postponed a devaluation. In addition, the United States sold some of its reserves of gold and foreign currency that it had built up during its surplus years. (This is not to say that no rate adjustments were made in this period. Small adjustments were made periodically by some major countries, and major adjustments were made more frequently by smaller countries.)

But in time, the forces of the marketplace set in motion by different economic conditions in different countries overcame the commitment of governments to fixed exchange rates. In 1971, exchange rates were realigned. The dollar was devalued relative to the currencies of most industrial countries for the first time since 1934. But the realignment was insufficient, and downward pressures on the dollar continued. In 1973, fixed exchange rates were abandoned by most major countries. **Flexible** or **floating exchange rates** were adopted, and currencies were permitted to change

PEGGED					
Single Currency				Currency Composite	
U.S. Dollar	French Franc	Russian Ruble	Other	SDR[a]	Other
Angola	Benin	Armenia	Bhutan	Libyan Arab	Algeria
Antigua and	Burkina Faso	Azerbaijan	(Indian	Jamahiriya	Austria
Barbuda	Cameroon	Belarus	rupee)	Myanmar	Bangladesh
Argentina	Central	Georgia	Estonia	Rwanda	Botswana
Bahamas, The	African Republic	Kazakhstan	(deutsche	Seychelles	Burundi
Barbados	Chad		mark)		
		Kyrgyzstan	Kiribati		Cape Verde
Belize	Comoros	Moldova	(Australian		Cyprus
Djibouti	Congo		dollar)		Fiji
Dominica	Côte d'Ivoire		Lesotho		Hungary
Ethiopia	Equatorial		(South		Iceland
Grenada	Guinea		African		
	Gabon		rand)		Jordan
Iraq			Namibia		Kenya
Liberia	Mali		(South		Kuwait
Marshall	Niger		African		Malawi
Islands	Senegal		rand)		Malaysia
Mongolia	Togo				
Nicaragua			Swaziland		Malta
			(South		Mauritania
Oman			African		Mauritius
Panama			rand)		Morocco
St. Kitts and Nevis					Papua
St. Lucia					New Guinea
St. Vincent and					
the Grenadines					Solomon Islands
					Tanzania
Suriname					Thailand
Syrian Arab					Tonga
Republic					Vanuatu
Yemen					
					Western Samoa
					Zimbabwe
NUMBER OF COUNTRIES					
23	14	7	6	4	27

relative to each other. Changes in supply and demand forces were permitted to be reflected in changes in exchange rates.

Although the major countries adopted flexible exchange rates, many countries continued to practice some form of fixed exchange rates. As can be seen from Table 24–2, in 1993, nearly one-half of all IMF member coun-

TABLE

24–2 (CONTINUED)

Flexibility Limited against a Single Currency or Group of Currencies		More Flexible			
Single Currency	Cooperative Arrangements	Adjusted According to a Set of Indicators	Other Managed Floating	Independently Floating	
Bahrain	Belgium	Chile	China	Afghanistan,	Nigeria
Qatar	Denmark	Colombia	Ecuador	Islamic State of	Norway
Saudi Arabia	France	Madagascar	Egypt	Albania	
United Arab	Germany		Greece	Australia	Paraguay
Emirates	Ireland		Guinea	Bolivia	Peru
				Brazil	Philippines
	Luxembourg		Guinea-Bissau		Romania
	Netherlands		Indonesia	Bulgaria	Russia
	Portugal		Israel	Canada	Sierra Leone
	Spain		Korea	Costa Rica	South
			Lao People's	Dominican Republic	Africa
			Democratic	El Salvador	Sudan
			Republic		
				Finland	Sweden
			Maldives	Gambia, The	Switzerland
			Mexico	Ghana	Trinidad and
			Pakistan	Guatemala	Tobago
			Poland	Guyana	Uganda
			Sao Tome and		Ukraine
			Principe	Haiti	
				Honduras	United
			Singapore	India	Kingdom
			Somalia	Iran, Islamic	United
			Sri Lanka	Republic of	States
			Tunisia	Italy	Venezuala[a]
			Turkey		Zaire
				Jamaica	Zambia
			Uruguay	Japan	
			Viet Nam	Latvia	
				Lebanon	
				Lithuania	
				Mozambique	
				New Zealand	
				Nepal	

NUMBER OF COUNTRIES

4	9	3	22	48

SOURCE: International Monetary Fund, Annual Report, 1993, p. 132–33.
[a] Special drawing rights.

tries pegged their currency to that of some other country or to an average of the currencies of a group of other countries. However, these countries tended to be small. Thirteen countries, including most European countries, tied their currencies to each other but floated against outside currencies. The currencies of the remaining countries, including the United States, Canada, United Kingdom, and Japan, floated independently. Even for these countries, however, the float is by no means "clean." The respective governments retained sufficient concern for the rate to periodically intervene in the market by buying and selling foreign currencies to offset abrupt changes and head off what they considered to be speculative raids. Thus, the current system is sometimes termed a *dirty* or *managed float.*

Until 1971, the U.S. dollar was fixed in terms of both gold and foreign currencies. Between 1934 and 1971, the dollar was officially priced at $35 per ounce of gold, and the United States stood ready to sell gold to foreign countries at that price. In 1971, it was depreciated to $38 per ounce, and to $42.22 per ounce in 1973. (The price of gold on the private markets is much higher and has fluctuated between $100 and $850 per ounce.) However, the United States stopped selling gold to foreign countries at any price in 1971. Thus, the United States officially abandoned the gold standard, and the "official" U.S. gold price had little meaning.

The exchange rates of major currencies in terms of the U.S. dollar from 1971 to 1993 are shown in Figure 24–3. Also shown is the average foreign exchange rate of all U.S. trading partners, termed the *trade-weighted dollar.* As can be seen, since 1971 the dollar first depreciated against most foreign

FIGURE

24–3   FOREIGN EXCHANGE RATES SINCE 1971 (THE COST OF ONE UNIT
OF FOREIGN CURRENCY IN U.S. DOLLARS)

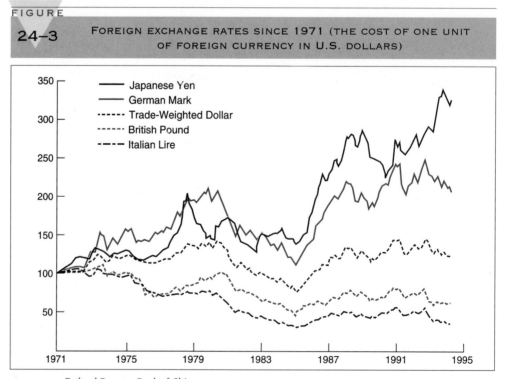

SOURCE: Federal Reserve Bank of Chicago.
NOTE: 1971 = 100

currencies (one unit of foreign currency became more expensive) except the British pound and the Italian lira, appreciated sharply from 1981 through 1985, depreciated again through year-end 1990 and has remained relatively stable through year end 1993. The major exception shown on the chart is the Italian lira. On average, the dollar depreciated so that foreign currencies cost some 50 percent more in dollar terms in 1990 than in 1971.

The Theory. Whether a fixed or a flexible exchange rate standard is superior for major countries has been debated for many years. Proponents of fixed exchange rates focus on greater short-run stability, reduced uncertainty, lower costs of trade, smaller speculative capital flows, increased international economic cooperation, and greater government commitment to anti-inflationary policies. Proponents of flexible exchange rates say that most of these advantages are illusory. Any increased stability in the short run is likely to result in greater instability in the longer run when the cumulative forces can no longer be held back. Better, they argue, to have small daily adjustments than large periodic changes. Short-run stability not only is expensive in terms of subsidizing inefficient activities and misallocating resources, it also does not fool long-term investors who look at the basic underlying economic forces. Moreover, although exchange rates are free to change under such a system, flexible exchange rates per se do not imply volatile exchange rates any more than noncontrolled automobile or chewing-gum prices imply volatility in those prices. Exchange rates will be volatile only if the underlying forces are volatile and proper stabilizing policies are not pursued.

Advocates of flexible exchange rates also point out that if one country does not pursue intelligent economic policies, fixed exchange rates will speed the transmission of disturbances from that country to others. Another country can protect itself only by introducing restrictive and harmful trade measures.

This process can be seen in the following example. Assume that country A inflates relative to its trading partner, country B, as a result of, say, overexpansive monetary or fiscal policy. Domestic prices increase. If the exchange rate does not change, imports become relatively cheaper in price in country A, and the quantity of imports demanded increases. At the same time, exports from A become relatively more expensive in B's currency (reflecting the higher price in A's currency and the unchanged exchange rate), and the quantity demanded in B declines.

Country B, on the other side of this exchange, experiences a pickup in exports to A and a decline in imports from A. Its supply of A's currency increases. To maintain the exchange rate, its government needs to purchase the excess supply of A's currency created by this imbalance. Unless offset by the central bank by means described in Chapter 28, the increase in B's official holdings of foreign currency increases the reserves of its commercial banks and, thereby, its money supply. The increased money supply will, in turn, reinforce the stimulative pressures already exerted by the increase in exports and strengthen inflationary pressures. This process is referred to as **imported inflation.**

In contrast, it is argued, under flexible exchange rates, the higher prices in A would also lead to a higher price for B's currency and a depreciation in A's exchange rate. The price of A's imports would rise in line with

that of A's domestic goods, and the foreign price of its exports would be unchanged. As a result, imports and exports would not be affected, B would not experience greater stimulus, and the inflation would be confined largely to A.

Nevertheless, flexible exchange rates may not be for everyone. It is generally agreed that they may be less desirable for smaller countries. International trade tends to be relatively more important for those countries, and, for many of them, the major exports or imports are highly concentrated in only one or two sectors. The more important international trade, the greater the effect of exchange rate changes on all domestic prices and the more difficult it is for the country to maintain stable prices. Moreover, the fewer the number of different goods that are involved in trade, the more will the domestic price level go the way of these goods. For these reasons, as we have seen, most smaller countries have retained some form of fixed exchange rate system. However, even these countries have to make periodic adjustments in their exchange rates if their domestic rates of price inflation differ widely from those of their major trading partners.

The Evidence.   The empirical evidence to date on the relative advantages of fixed and flexible exchange rates is mixed. Foreign trade and investment prospered under fixed exchange rates from 1945 to 1970. Trade and capital restrictions, such as tariffs, quotas, and currency controls, were reduced, and transactions across national boundaries increased manyfold. However, the effects of greatly different rates of economic development and different economic policies among the trading countries began to accumulate and moved the system increasingly away from equilibrium. Disturbances at first believed to be only short-term and self-reversing became longer-term and unidirectional. The costs of exchange rate maintenance to surplus countries increased dramatically in terms of both financial assistance to deficit countries and domestic misallocation of resources; by 1973 most major countries considered the game no longer worth the cost.

Indeed, exchange rates did not remain unchanged. Between 1948 and 1967, only 13 of the then 109 IMF member countries did not devalue their currencies at least once with respect to the U.S. dollar. The average overall devaluation by country was almost 50 percent. Moreover, it is generally agreed that fixed exchange rates could not have survived the abrupt quadrupling of petroleum prices in 1973, which transformed many surplus countries into deficit countries and vice versus almost overnight.

But exchange rates have been more volatile under flexible rates than many proponents expected, despite substantial intervention by governments. This has undoubtedly discouraged some international trade and investment by increasing risk, at least until individuals, institutions, and governments become more familiar with the system. Nor did flexible exchange rates prevent the spread of the sharp acceleration in the rate of inflation from country to country in 1974 and 1979. Inflation was worldwide. However, a significant portion of the inflation in these periods may be attributed to the delayed reactions to very sharp worldwide increases in the money supply in the final years of the fixed exchange rate standard, and to increases in the prices of important internationally traded commodities, such as grains and petroleum, that sell at an equivalent price in all countries. Changes in exchange rates will not offset these price increases. On the other hand, the prediction of a collapse of the international financial system made by some fixed-rate advocates were not realized. It appears that flexible exchange rates have functioned sufficiently well to disarm those who advocate a speedy return to fixed rates but not well enough to convince them of the lasting superiority of flexible rates. A recent IMF study concluded that even for developing countries, which generally have less-diversified economies than developed countries, the pros of floating exchange rates outweigh the cons if correct domestic economic policies, particularly monetary policy, are in place.[1]

Balance of Payments

The demand and supply forces affecting exchange rates are reflected in the balance of payments of the respective countries. A **balance of payments** is a double-entry bookkeeping record of every transaction between a country and its trading partners during a particular period of time—say, one year. It is not unlike a record that you would keep if you were interested in maintaining a file of all your expenditures and receipts.

All transactions in the balance of payments that result in an inflow of payments from abroad are recorded under *Receipts*. For the United States, these would include exports of merchandise; income on investments in other countries; foreign investments in the United States (exports of securities); travel by foreigners in the United States; gifts, aid, and remittances from other countries; and U.S. borrowings in other countries. *Payments* include those transactions that result in immediate or delayed cash outflows from the United States to other countries, such as imports of goods; payments on foreign investments in the United States; investment overseas (imports of securities); travel abroad; gifts, aid, and remittances abroad; and foreign borrowing in the United States.

Because of the nature of double-entry bookkeeping, the sum of all payments must equal the sum of all receipts. Technically, the balance of payments always balances! But although this is true by definition (every trade has two sides), it is not analytically useful. Subbalances can be calculated at different places that provide information about the strengths of the pressures on exchange rates and whether they are temporary or permanent in nature. A particular subbalance is said to be in *surplus* if receipts exceed payments and in *deficit* if payments exceed receipts. A number of the more widely used subbalances are shown for the United States in Table 24–3. The first balances reflect international exchange of nonfinancial products. The **balance of trade** indicates the net difference between merchandise exports and imports. Because trade patterns are unlikely to change dramatically in the short run, the trade balance is viewed by many analysts as a measure of the basic ability of a country to compete internationally and as a force exerting fundamental pressure on the exchange rate. The more the trade balance is in surplus, the stronger the exchange rate and the cheaper the imports. The United States experienced a large trade deficit in 1992.

[1] Peter J. Quirk and Herman Cortes-Douglas, "The Experience with Floating Exchange Rates," *Finance and Development*, June 1993, pp. 28–31.

TABLE

24–3 U.S. BALANCE OF PAYMENTS: SELECTED SUMMARY MEASURES
FROM 1946 TO 1992 (BILLIONS OF DOLLARS)

	Balance on			Change in Foreign Official Holdings of U.S. Assets	Change in U.S. Official Reserves[a]
	Trade	Goods and Services	Current Account		
1946	6.7	7.8	4.9	N.A.	0.6
1950	1.1	2.1	−1.8	N.A.	−1.8
1955	2.9	2.9	0.4	N.A.	−0.2
1960	4.9	5.1	2.8	1.3	−2.1
1965	5.0	8.3	5.4	0.0	−1.2
1970	2.6	5.6	2.3	6.9	−2.5
1975	8.9	22.7	18.1	7.0	0.8
1980	−25.5	9.0	1.9	15.5	8.2
1985	−122.1	−97.3	−110.0	−1.1	3.9
1990	−108.9	−57.5	−90.4	33.9	2.2
1992	−96.3	−31.1	−62.4	40.3	−3.9

SOURCE: Council of Economic Advisers, *Annual Report* 1993, *pp.* 462–63 *and* Federal Reserve Bulletin, June 1993, p. A3.

[a] Includes gold, special drawing rights, foreign currency, and reserve position in IMF.

N.A. = Not available.

Imports and exports of services, which include income on foreign investment and travel in foreign countries, are also not likely to be highly volatile from year to year and may be added to the trade balance for a broader measure of the more fundamental forces. This net balance is referred to as the **balance on goods and services.** Exports of services, particularly income from foreign investments, have historically tended to be very large for the United States. However, this margin has not been large enough in recent years to offset the trade deficit, so that the balance on goods and services was also in deficit in 1992. Private and government aid and remittances tend to be less stable than international transactions in goods and services. Yet these accounts are not as unstable as flows of financial capital, which respond to changes in volatile interest rates and profit opportunities. The net balance that includes aid and remittances is termed the **balance on current account.** The U.S. current account was also sharply in deficit in 1992.

The **capital account** indicates changes in the ownership of financial assets. Thus, it reflects financial flows. Because it includes all transactions not in the current account, except for any statistical discrepancies in measurement, it must balance the current account in order for the balance of payments to balance. If the current account is in surplus, the capital account must be in deficit to provide the means of payment for other countries. If the current account is in deficit, the capital account must be in surplus for the country to acquire the foreign currencies to pay for the imports. But the fact that the capital account must by definition offset the current account does not imply cause and effect. Indeed, in recent years, international financial transactions have far exceeded international trade transactions, at least for the United States.

The capital account is divided between short-term and long-term and between private and government (official) capital. Private capital flows are motivated by interest rate and profit differentials. Thus, these flows affect the exchange rate and thereby trade exports, imports, and the current account. On the other hand, official short-term capital flows are generally not motivated by interest rate differences and are considered *compensatory* and indicative of pressures on the country's exchange rate. In 1992, capital inflows into the United States were greater than capital outflows but by not quite enough to make the surplus in the capital account large enough to more than offset the deficit in the current account. As a result, the United States suffered a small decrease in foreign reserves. At the same time, foreign governments sharply increased their holdings of dollar reserves.

Relation to Exchange Rates

Under "clean" flexible exchange rates, government compensatory financial movements to affect the exchange rate do not occur, and the exchange rate absorbs any changes in demand or supply. Increases in import demand would drive the domestic exchange rate down, increasing import prices and reducing the quantity of imports demanded until equilibrium is restored. Changes in the balance of payments and its components would provide little additional information about a country's international economic position beyond that reflected in changes in the exchange rates.

Under fixed exchange rates, the story is different. Because exchange rates (prices) cannot move, the accounts (quantities) on the balance of payments must. If, for example, import demand increases, there will be no immediate offsetting increase in price, and the quantity of imports will increase. Unless offset by a decline in some other import sector or an increase in exports, the additional imports must be financed from past savings in the form of foreign assets or gold, current short-term borrowing abroad, or both. The sum of these two accounts would indicate the net deficit or surplus in the balance of payments and the pressure on the exchange rate to change its value. It follows that the "less clean" or "more dirty" the exchange rate float, the more meaningful are changes in the balance of payments.

Foreign Reserves. Government savings for international transactions purposes are referred to as **foreign** or **international reserves.** These reserves are held in the form of gold and special drawing rights, or SDRs (which, because they are not a liability of any country, serve as primary international currencies), the currencies of major foreign countries, and unconditional claims on the IMF, referred to as **reserve position in the IMF.** (SDRs are created by the International Monetary Fund and are discussed in Chapter 25.) Foreign reserves play the same role for countries as personal savings do for individuals—namely, tiding the country over temporary deficit periods when it is spending (importing) more than it is receiving (exporting) without a change in the exchange price of its currency. In 1992, foreign currencies accounted for 90 percent of world international reserves, gold and reserve positions each 4 percent, and SDRs 2 percent. For the United States the distribution was 56, 15, 17, and 12 percent, respectively.

Foreign reserves are used to affect exchange rates under managed flexible or fixed exchange rate regimes. It is unlikely that a country on a fixed exchange rate standard would have a zero balance in its official accounts year in and year out. If the deficits and surpluses are small and alternate more or less regularly, the exchange rate could be maintained unchanged. However, if the deficits or surpluses are large and consistently in the same direction, a change in the exchange rate would be inevitable. A country continually in deficit would in time exhaust its foreign reserves and borrowing powers. (Its currency is said to be *overvalued*.) At that time, it can no longer offset the downward pressures on its exchange rate, and the rate depreciates. The country must then cut back on its scale of living and generate surpluses to pay its cumulated debts plus accrued interest and to rebuild its reserves. Likewise, a country continually in surplus is like a miser who worships money for how it looks rather than for what it buys. (Its currency is said to be *undervalued*.) At some point, the country's populace would want to increase its consumption and scale of living. At that time, the country stops lending and building up reserves. Its exchange rate will increase, and imports will become cheaper.

Balance of Payments History

Major components of the U.S. balance of payments in recent years are shown in Table 24–3. Until the 1970s, the United States traditionally had surpluses on its balance of trade. However, the rapid recovery of other industrial countries and their ability to replace war-damaged plants and equipment with new, more efficient counterparts made many of their products attractive both in the United States and in foreign markets that had been importing U.S. goods. The fixed exchange rate permitted these goods to be sold at favorable prices relative to those of U.S. goods, and so these foreign goods often replaced U.S. goods. The size of U.S. trade surpluses shrank through the late 1960s and finally disappeared in 1971. Since 1976, the trade balance has remained negative reflecting, at different times, higher rates of domestic inflation and favorable domestic investment opportunities for foreigners that increased the dollar exchange rate and decreased exports.

The United States traditionally generated a large income from its overseas investments, which, until recently, more than offset the equally traditional deficit on foreign trade. Through 1981, the balance on goods and services was in surplus in every year but three. Since 1982, it has been in deficit every year. The current account performed somewhat more poorly as the United States traditionally transfers more funds abroad as gifts and pensions than it secures. Partially to finance the deficits and partially because of a favorable investment climate, foreigners have sharply increased their holdings of U.S. assets. The increase in foreign government holdings of U.S. assets reflects the deteriorating trade position of the United States.

SUMMARY

487

▼

FOREIGN EXCHANGE
RATES AND THE
BALANCE OF
PAYMENTS

Unless restricted by artificial barriers, funds flow as freely among countries as within countries. However, different countries use different currencies. Thus, funds must be exchanged from one currency into another. The price of one unit of foreign currency in terms of the domestic currency is termed the *exchange rate*. If the price of the foreign currency increases, the exchange rate of the domestic currency depreciates; if the price of the foreign currency decreases, the exchange rate appreciates. Changes in exchange rates affect the domestic price of imports and the foreign price of exports.

Like any other price, changes in exchange rates reflect changes in demand and supply. Exchange rates may either be permitted to fluctuate freely in response to those forces (flexible exchange rates) or be kept fixed by official intervention to offset the effects of the destabilizing forces. In the early 1970s, most major countries converted from fixed to flexible exchange rates as the efforts to offset the impact of changes in supply and demand and to stabilize rates become too costly.

The balance of payments is a double-entry bookkeeping record of all transactions between one country and its trading partners. Although the overall balance of payments is always in balance, subtotals need not be, and they reflect pressures on exchange rates. The most useful subtotals for gauging economic performance are the balance of trade and the balance on current account. The meaningfulness of these balances, however, has been reduced with the use of flexible exchange rates.

For a variety of reasons, the U.S. balance of payments has deteriorated in the past two decades. This has been accompanied by a decline in the dollar exchange rate in most of the period since the introduction of floating exchange rates in 1973, except for a sharp but brief recovery from 1981 through 1985. The period also saw considerable intervention by the U.S. government in the foreign exchange market to dampen both undesirable declines and undesirable increases. Such intervention by the United States and other governments has resulted in a "dirty" floating exchange rate standard for major countries.

QUESTIONS

1. Why do countries engage in international trade? How may trade affect aggregate and individual income in a country differently?

2. What determines the price you pay for an imported good? How does this differ from the determinants of domestically produced goods?

3. What was yesterday's foreign exchange rate for British pounds, German marks, Japanese yen, and French francs? What are the associated dollar exchange rates? What were the foreign exchange rates exactly one year ago? What have the changes over the year implied for the prices of imports to the United States and exports from the United States for each of these countries?

4. Differentiate between *fixed* and *flexible* exchange rates. Which may be expected to experience the greater volatility? How would the domestic price of an imported good be affected under each exchange rate system as the domestic rate of inflation accelerates?

5. Why are many countries reluctant to operate a free or unmanaged floating (flexible) exchange rate system? What is a *managed float*? What system do you think the United States has followed in the 1990s? What evidence to you have?

6. In the 1930s, many countries engaged in policies of competitive depreciation of their currencies. Why do you think that they might have done so? What is the cost to the domestic economy? Why do you think these strategies eventually broke down?

7. What is the *balance of payments*? If the balance of payments is always in balance, how can it reveal information about the international financial position of a country? Look up balance of payments data for the United States in recent years. How has the United States been doing in its international position? Support your answer.

8. How may the interpretation of the balance of payments differ under fixed and flexible exchange rates? How does the role of international reserves differ under the two exchange rate systems?

REFERENCES

Balbach, Anatol, "The Mechanics of Intervention in Exchange Markets," *Review*, Federal Reserve Bank of St. Louis, February 1978, pp. 2–7.

Bank for International Settlements, *Annual Report*. Basle, Switzerland, Annual.

Batten, Dallas S., and Mack Ott, "Five Common Myths about Floating Exchange Rates," *Review*, Federal Reserve Bank of St. Louis, November 1983, pp. 5–15.

Bordo, Michael D., and Barry Eichengreen, A *Retrospective on the Bretton Woods System*. Chicago: University of Chicago Press, 1993.

Chrystal, K., Alec. "A Guide to Foreign Exchange Markets," *Review*, Federal Reserve Bank of St. Louis, March 1984, pp. 5–18.

Crabbe, Leland, "The International Gold Standard and U.S. Monetary Policy from World War I to the New Deal," *Federal Reserve Bulletin*, June 1989, pp. 423–40.

De Vries, Margaret G., *The IMF in a Changing World, 1945–85*. Washington, D.C.: International Monetary Fund, 1986.

Dufey, Gunter, and Ian Giddy, *The International Money Market* 2nd ed. Englewood Cliffs, N.J.: Prentice Hall, 1994.

Fieleke, Norman, *The International Economy under Stress*. Cambridge, Mass.: Ballinger, 1988.

Fieleke, Norman. "International Payments Imbalance in the 1980s: An Overview," *New England Economic Review*, Federal Reserve Bank of Boston, March/April 1989, pp. 3–15.

Fieleke, Norman S., *What Is the Balance of Payments*? Boston: Federal Reserve Bank of Boston, 1985.

Gay, Gerald D., and Robert W. Kolb, eds., *International Finance: Concepts and Issues*. Englewood Cliffs, N.J.: Prentice Hall, 1983.

Grabbe, J. Orlin, *International Financial Markets*. New York: Elsevier, 1986.

Graboyes, Robert, "International Trade and Payments Data: An Introduction," *Economic Review*, Federal Reserve Bank of Richmond, September/October 1991, pp. 20–31.

Humphrey, Thomas M., "International Aspects of Inflation," in *Essays on Inflation*, 4th ed. Federal Reserve Bank of Richmond, 1983.

International Monetary Fund, IMF *Survey*. Washington, D.C., biweekly.

International Monetary Fund, *International Financial Statistics*. Washington, D.C., monthly.

Kenen, Peter, *Financing, Adjustment and the IMF.* Washington, D.C.: Brookings Institution, 1986.

Kolb, Robert W. *The International Finance Reader.* Miami: Kolb, 1991.

Kumar, Vikram, and Joseph A. Whitt, Jr., "Exchange Rate Variability and International Trade," *Economic Review,* Federal Reserve Bank of Atlanta, May/June 1992, pp. 17–32.

Kvasnicka, Joseph G., ed., *Readings in International Finance,* 3rd ed. Chicago: Federal Reserve Bank of Chicago, 1987.

Mayer, Martin, *The Fate of the Dollar.* New York: New York Times Books, 1980.

Meltzer, Alan, "U.S. Policy in the Bretton Woods Era," *Review,* Federal Reserve Bank of St. Louis, May/June 1991, pp. 54–83.

Pauls, B. Dianne, "U.S. Exchange Rate Policy: Bretton Woods to Present," *Federal Reserve Bulletin,* November 1990, pp. 891–908.

Quirk, Peter J., and Herman Cortes-Douglas, "The Experience with Floating Rates," *Finance and Development,* June 1993, pp. 28–31.

Rolfe, Sidney, and James L. Burtle, *The Great Wheel: The World Monetary System.* New York: McGraw-Hill, 1975.

Rolnick, Arthur J., and Warren E. Weber, "A Case for Fixing Exchange Rates," 1989 *Annual Report,* Federal Reserve Bank of Minneapolis, 1990.

International Financial Institutions and Markets

International Monetary Fund (IMF)

There are two major official international financial institutions promoting stable growth in international trade and finance. They are the **International Monetary Fund** and the **World Bank.** The IMF was established at the end of World War II as a cooperative venture among countries to create an international economic system that would "facilitate the expansion and balanced growth of international trade, and . . . contribute thereby to the promotion and maintenance of high levels of employment and real income and to the development of the productive resources of all members."[1] Membership in the IMF has expanded steadily, from 30 countries in 1945 to 177 in 1993. The former communist countries have joined only recently. The IMF engages in a number of activities, including

1. Monitoring economic developments in member countries
2. Establishing rules for international trade and finance
3. Assisting in the establishment and management of exchange rates
4. Reviewing restrictive trade and capital policies imposed by countries
5. Providing borrowing facilities for member countries experiencing balance of payment difficulties
6. Providing technical economic and financial assistance to member countries
7. Providing machinery for international monetary cooperation
8. Collecting and analyzing international trade and financial data and other economic intelligence for member countries
9. Issuing limited amounts of international money

Exchange rates and orderly conditions in exchange markets have been the key concerns of the IMF. Before 1973, the IMF established rules for maintaining fixed exchange rates and consulted with each country before its exchange rate was altered. Since 1973 and the adoption of flexible exchange rates by most industrial countries, the IMF has maintained an active surveillance over exchange rate policies of member countries, in order to

1. Prevent manipulation of exchange rates by any member to gain an unfair competitive advantage by deliberately undervaluing its currency to stimulate exports,

[1] International Monetary Fund, *Articles of Agreement*, p. 2.

2. Restrict official intervention by countries with flexible exchange rates to counter disorderly short-term conditions in exchange markets, and

3. Encourage only intervention that takes into account the interests of other member countries.

Member countries are assigned quotas based on their national income and importance in world trade. The quotas determine the amount each country pays into the fund, its voting power, and its right to draw on the facilities of the fund. Subscription payments represent the fund's basic source of operating funds. Normally, each country pays 25 percent of its quota to the IMF in gold or a reserve currency and 75 percent in its own currency.

Borrowing Facilities

To maintain orderly exchange rates and unrestricted international trade and financial transfers, it is necessary to provide facilities where member countries can borrow foreign currency "to correct maladjustments in their balance of payments without resorting to measures destructive to national or international prosperity."[2] The provision of adequate reserve borrowing facilities has been one of the IMF's major achievements. As additional countries joined the IMF, as international trade became more important, and as destabilizing shocks became larger and more pervasive, the need for borrowing by IMF member countries increased sharply.

Borrowing facilities are particularly important for countries on a fixed exchange rate standard that are experiencing what appear to be temporary reductions in their ability to acquire sufficient foreign currency. This may occur because of temporary deterioration in their export industry (such as a poor harvest for agricultural countries, a sharp decline in the price of their mineral exports owing to an economic recession in the importing country, or an increase in competition for their exports); a temporary rise in the demand for or the price of imports (such as foodstuffs following a bad harvest, or higher import prices for oil); or both. Any of these factors exert downward pressure on the country's exchange rate by shifting its supply of foreign currency in (say, from S_0 to S'' in Figure 24–2) or its demand for foreign currency out (say, from D_0 to D' in Figure 24–2). Borrowing facilities permit IMF member countries to offset these downward pressures by increasing their supply of foreign currencies (say, from S_0 to S' to offset the increase in demand to D', or from S'' to S_0 to offset the shortfall in exports). Of course, borrowing is not free. Interest must be paid until the foreign currency is repaid, and sufficient additional foreign currency must be earned to repay the loan at maturity.

There are two types of IMF borrowing facilities: (1) general and (2) specific. The general facilities permit borrowing against the country's quota. A country can borrow up to 25 percent of its quota (referred to as the **reserve tranche**) automatically for general balance of payments purposes at any time. It can also borrow up to 100 percent of its quota in four equal 25 per-

---

[2] International Monetary Fund, *Articles of Agreement*, p. 2.

cent steps (referred to as ***credit tranches***) for periods up to five years, to support domestic economic measures designed to overcome balance of payments difficulties. Application must be made for such borrowing, and the acceptance criteria become increasingly more restrictive with each higher tranche.

Although the quotas have been increased periodically and the magnitude and criteria for the credit tranches liberalized, the general tranches have not been able to keep up with the borrowing needs of less developed countries, particularly those that rely for foreign exchange on only one or two export commodities, generally raw materials, whose prices tend to be highly volatile. In response, the IMF established a number of specific borrowing facilities, in part funded by borrowing from surplus member countries. Specific facilities include

- ▼ *Extended facility*—medium-term financing for up to 10 years to overcome serious structural balance of payments maladjustments.
- ▼ *Enlarged access facility*—to finance larger, more persistent payment imbalances for periods up to seven years.
- ▼ *Compensatory and contingency financing facility* (CCFF)—established in 1963 and expanded in 1988 to compensate for temporary shortfalls in export earnings and/or increased cost of food imports due largely to circumstances beyond the country's control—financing up to five years.
- ▼ *Buffer stock financing facility*—to finance buildup of buffer stocks in designated internationally traded commodities to stabilize their prices subject to approved international commodity agreements—financing up to five years.
- ▼ *Structural adjustment facility* (SAF)—established in 1986 to provide medium-term assistance in conjunction with the World Bank and other international lenders to low-income countries that face protracted balance of payments problems while undertaking comprehensive corrective policies. The loans are for a maximum of 10 years at an annual interest rate of 0.5 percent.
- ▼ *Enhanced structural adjustment facility* (ESAF)—established in 1987 to provide additional funding to the poorest member countries that are burdened with high levels of debt repayment, to adopt strong policies for stimulating domestic growth and improving their balance of payments. The loan terms are the same as for SAF.
- ▼ *Systemic transformation facility* (STF)—the newest special assistance program established in 1993 to help countries facing severe disruptions from shifting from international trading at nonmarket, negotiated prices to market-determined prices. This facility, which is expected to be only temporary, is aimed primarily at countries that formerly were part of the Soviet Union or traded primarily with the Soviet Union. The loan rate is the same as for borrowings from the IMF's general funds.

Borrowings are made in the currencies of the countries required by the borrowing country by exchanging its own currency for the foreign currencies. Repayment is made by repurchasing the country's own currency with the same or other foreign currencies ruled eligible by the IMF.

Special Drawing Rights (SDRs)

What distinguishes a central bank (such as the Federal Reserve System in the United States or the Bank of England in the United Kingdom) from other government financial institutions (such as the Federal Home Loan Bank or the Federal Land Bank) is its ability to create money in a form that has a fixed nominal value and is not viewed as anyone's liability that needs to be repaid. In the United States, this form of money is currency or reserves at the Fed. Until 1969, the IMF was not a central bank; it was an international financial intermediary that borrowed from surplus countries and lent to deficit countries. In 1969, it obtained permission from its member countries to issue a new form of international money, named *special drawing rights,* more popularly **SDRs,** to supplement other forms of international reserves, which were believed to be insufficient to finance maximum international trade. SDRs have a fixed value and are not the liability of any member country. Since 1975, SDRs are also the standard of value in which all IMF accounts are valued. Between 1969 and 1993, 21.5 billion SDRs (equivalent to U.S. $29 billion) had been created.

SDRs can be used by countries to pay their debts to other countries. SDRs originally supplemented and then replaced gold, whose use and importance are being phased out by the IMF. (Variations in the price of gold now reflect changes in private demand and supply forces, stemming primarily from speculation on the values of major currencies as a store of value.) There are some restrictions on the use of SDRs. Member countries must agree to repurchase from other countries any SDRs they have spent that reduce their holdings to less than 30 percent of the amount they were initially allocated by the IMF. This prevents countries from using SDRs as a permanent source of capital.

The IMF pays interest to holders of SDRs. Countries, however, must pay the same interest on the total amount of SDRs they were allocated. If a country has not spent its allocation, its interest receipts will equal its interest payments. If a country has spent some of its SDRs, it effectively pays interest to the recipient countries. Thus, interest is paid from deficit to surplus countries. The interest rate changed is set by the IMF equal to a percentage of the weighted average of short-term market interest rates in five major countries—the United States, the United Kingdom, France, Germany, and Japan. Thus, the SDR rate fluctuates in line with market interest rates. Since 1981, the rate has been 100 percent of the average market rate.

Unlike borrowings from the IMF, SDRs increase the world money supply. As a result, the IMF is cautious about creating additional SDRs. Changes in the total stock of SDRs require an affirmative vote by members having 85 percent of the quotas. The value of SDRs is determined in terms of a "basket" of currencies of the five countries to whose interest rates the SDR rate is tied, with the weight for each currency based on that nation's share of world trade and its exchange rate. The U.S. dollar accounts for 40 percent of the total weight. The current makeup is shown in Table 25–1. As the dollar changes in value, the value of the SDR changes in the opposite direction. For example, the SDR was equal to $1 in 1970, to $1.32 in 1979, to $1.05 in 1984, and back up to $1.43 in 1993. SDRs accounted for less than 2 percent of the total reserve holdings of IMF countries.

TABLE 25–1	COMPOSITION OF SDR BY CURRENCY AS OF 1993 (PERCENT)
U.S. dollar	40
Deutsche mark	21
Japanese yen	17
French franc	11
Pound sterling	11

SOURCE: International Monetary Fund, *Annual Report, 1993*, p. 95.

World Bank

The World Bank, technically known as the International Bank for Reconstruction and Development, was established at the same time as the IMF at the end of World War II in 1945. The two organizations supplement each other. The IMF promotes orderly conditions in foreign exchange markets to encourage higher incomes through international trade; the World Bank facilitates the provision of private long-term credit from developed to developing countries for the construction of basic capital projects necessary for higher incomes through more rapid domestic development. Loans may be made to either governments or private firms. The bank raises most of its funds through the sale of its bonds in surplus, developed countries. The bank lends these funds to deficit, developing countries for important economic and social capital projects that require foreign currency and might not be financed otherwise. The loans are generally repayable within 20 years but have a five-year grace period. The bank and the bondholders are repaid out of proceeds generated by the projects. The bank does not give grants or aid; the projects must show promise of being self-financing. However, the bank may, at times, charge below-market rates of interest. All loans have the unconditional guarantee of the government of the country in which the project is located.

The membership of the World Bank more or less parallels that of the IMF. In 1993, there were 176 member countries, each of which is required to subscribe to the capital of the bank according to its economic and financial strength. In 1993, capital subscriptions totaled $184 billion, with the U.S. share about 18 percent. Only 10 percent is paid in gold, dollars, or other acceptable currency; the remaining 90 percent is subject to call by the bank. As can be seen in Table 25–2, paid-in capital subscriptions account for only a small proportion of the bank's loanable funds.

As of June 30, 1993, the bank had nearly $160 billion in loans outstanding or committed. The largest borrowers were Indonesia, Mexico, India, Brazil, China and Turkey. All had loans in excess of $5 billion outstanding. The largest sectors financed were agriculture, rural development, energy, and transportation.

TABLE 25–2	WORLD BANK AND IDA SOURCES OF FUNDS AS OF JUNE 30, 1993 (BILLIONS OF DOLLARS)		
World Bank			
Borrowings			96.3
Capital subscriptions			
Subscribed		184.1	
Uncalled		165.6	
Net Paid-in			18.5
Other			10.5
Total			125.3
International Development Association (IDA)			
Subscription and contributions			72.8
Other			8.1
Total			80.9

SOURCE: World Bank, *Annual Report*, 1993 and World Bank

International Development Association

The International Development Association (IDA) is an affiliate of the World Bank. It was established in 1960 to make long-term, low-interest loans to the poorest countries. The loans are for 50 years and bear no interest other than a 0.75 percent annual service charge. They are amortized so that no repayments are made in the first 10 years, 1 percent of the loan is repaid annually in years 10 through 19, and 3 percent annually over the remaining 30 years. Because of the poor creditworthiness of the recipient country and the large magnitude of the repayment burden, it is unlikely that these loans would have been extended otherwise.

Most members of the World Bank are also members of the IDA. Member countries are divided into two categories: (1) high-income developed countries and (2) low-income less developed countries. Funds are raised primarily from the developed countries through capital subscriptions and periodic special contributions termed **replenishments.** Smaller amounts are raised from the less developed countries and from transfers from the World Bank. At midyear 1993, the IDA had $52 billion in loans outstanding or committed. The major borrower by far was India, with $15 billion in loans, or nearly one-third of the total loans made by the IDA. The next largest borrowers were Bangladesh, China, and Pakistan. The major sectors that have been provided with financing have been agriculture and rural development.

Eurodollars

As international trade and finance expanded, the need for a uniform currency increased. Exchange of currencies for each other involves at least two costs: (1) the transactions costs of exchange and (2) the risk of changes in exchange rates between the beginning and the end of the transactions period. The first cost increases proportionately with the number of currency conversions made. The second cost can be reduced through the use of futures contracts that permit traders to contract at the beginning of the period for a foreign currency at some future time at a known price. (Futures contracts are discussed in Chapter 22.) Nevertheless, the cost of futures contracts is still greater than the cost of using only a single currency.

In the post–World War II period, the U.S. dollar replaced the British pound sterling as the major currency used to finance international trade. Despite its later depreciation in value and the sharp rise in the economic power of other countries, the dollar still accounts for 60 percent of all holdings of currencies used as international reserves and finances an even larger percentage of international trade. But except for paper currency, which is not used greatly in international payments, U.S. dollars were available only as deposits at banks in the United States. This restricted their use for some foreign traders who preferred to do business with their own banks in their own countries. Typically, banks accept deposits (sell secondary securities) in the local currency. Thus, banks in the United States denominate their deposits in dollars, banks in the United Kingdom in pounds, and so on.

But there is no economic reason that banks could not denominate deposits in any other currency, if they and the depositors so wished. Other than any possible legal constraints, the only economic constraint is that they must be able to redeem the deposit in that currency or its equivalent value. Thus, banks in the United States could offer deposits in pounds, marks, francs, and so on, and banks in foreign countries could offer deposits in dollars and other foreign currencies. The banks could hold reserves either in the same currencies as the deposits or in some other currencies, including the domestic currency, and convert the reserves into the currency being withdrawn, when necessary. The second strategy is, of course, riskier, because exchange rates may change unfavorably so the bank is exposed to foreign currency risk.

Eurodollars are dollar-denominated deposits at commercial banks outside the United States. The first commercial banks to offer these deposits were in Europe, hence the term *Eurodollars.* Since then, dollar-denominated deposits have been offered by major banks in almost all major international financial centers, and the menu of foreign denominations has expanded to include German marks (Euromarks), French and Swiss francs (Eurofrancs), Japanese yen (Euroyen), and British pounds (Europounds). All foreign currency–denominated deposits at banks outside the United States are referred to as **Eurocurrencies.** Starting in 1990, a few banks in the United States began to offer domestic customers deposits denominated in major foreign currencies, including British pounds, Canadian dollars, German marks, Japanese yen, and Swiss francs. These foreign-denominated deposits at banks in the United States may be referred to as **Amercurrencies.** (Amercurrencies are discussed in greater detail in Chapter 23.) In T-account terms, examples of Eurodollars at, say, U.K. bank A, and of Amerpounds at, say, U.S. bank B, are shown below as the deposits in the shaded areas:

U.K. Bank A		U.S. Bank B	
Reserves £	£ Deposits	Reserves $	$ Deposits
Loans £	$ Deposits	Loans $	£ Deposits

The history of Eurodollars is interesting. Eurodollars were in part invented by the Russians. At the height of the cold war in the early 1950s, Russia owned substantial dollar balances at U.S. banks. Because of the fear of expropriation after the outbreak of the Korean War in 1951, Russia did not wish to hold these balances at U.S. banks, yet did not want to risk converting them into foreign currencies that, in those days, carried a high risk of depreciation. After negotiation with some large London banks, the Russians agreed to accept deposits denominated in dollars at these banks. In the exchange, the London banks obtained dollar balances on U.S. banks that they otherwise might not have obtained. This permitted them to increase their participation in the financing of international trade.

The Eurodollar and Eurocurrency markets have grown rapidly. At midyear 1992, Eurocurrencies totaled $4.3 trillion. Of these, Eurodollars totaled $2.3 trillion. This was about the same as the total dollar deposits at all banks in the United States. Euromarks, the next largest Eurocurrency, totaled about $0.6 trillion. Eurodollars are generally in the form of interest-bearing time deposits with maturities of from a few days to one year. There is an active secondary market for Eurodollar CDs.

The mechanics of the Eurodollar market are very similar to those of the domestic deposit market, explained in Chapter 15, and are shown in T-account form in Table 25–3. Assume that Mr. E. Z. Sell in London exported

TABLE 25–3   EURODOLLAR DEPOSIT ACCOUNTING

	Chase Manhattan Bank			Barclays Bank	
(a)	100,000	deposit —Mr. Bituff			
(b)	−100,000	deposit —Mr. Bituff			
	+100,000	deposit —Mr. E. Z. Sell			
(c)	−100,000	deposit —Mr. E. Z. Sell	dollar deposit at Chase Manhattan Bank	+100,000	+100,000	dollar deposit —Mr. E. Z. Sell
:	+100,000	deposit —Barclays Bank			
(d)			dollar loan to Ms. Borrow	+ 90,000	+ 90,000	dollar deposit —Ms. Borrow

some merchandise to Mr. Bituff in New York. Because he plans to use U.S. dollars to pay for some imports later, Mr. Sell bills in dollars. On the payment date, Mr. Bituff sends Mr. Sell a check for $100,000 drawn on his bank—say, the Chase Manhattan (step b). But Mr. Sell prefers to hold the dollar deposit at his own bank—say, Barclays Bank. The Barclays Bank agrees to give Mr. Sell a dollar-denominated 10-day time deposit at a competitive interest rate in exchange for his $100,000 deposit at the Chase Manhattan Bank. Barclays Bank now has the $100,000 deposit at the Chase Manhattan Bank as an asset and a $100,000 Eurodollar deposit liability to Mr. Sell (step c). Note three things: First, only the ownership and not the total amount of deposits at the Chase Manhattan Bank has changed. Second, the dollars never physically left the United States; only the ownership of the deposit balance changed. And third, the Barclays Bank dollar deposit at the Chase Manhattan Bank (or any other bank in the United States) effectively serves as reserves for the Eurodollars.

Until the maturity of the Eurodollar deposit, Barclays can extend additional loans, either in dollars or in some other currency, by converting part of the dollars into that currency. (Part of the dollar balance is held as reserves.) A multiple expansion of deposits in foreign banks may occur based on the deposit at the Chase Manhattan. The first step is shown as (d) in Table 25–3. Ms. Borrow in London wants to borrow $90,000 in U.S. dollars to pay for imports. The Barclays Bank provides Ms. Borrow with a $90,000 Eurodollar deposit. If she transfers this deposit to another bank outside the United States, that bank will receive $90,000 of the $100,000 deposit Barclays has at the Chase Manhattan Bank, reducing its dollar deposit balance to $10,000. The new bank can now make another Eurodollar loan. Unlike domestic U.S. banks, whose reserves in total are determined by the Federal Reserve, foreign banks can pretty much determine their own dollar reserve base by purchasing dollar deposits at U.S. banks. Moreover, as noted earlier, they do not really even need dollar reserves if they are willing to assume exchange rate risk and redeem dollar-denominated deposits at maturity by buying dollars on the foreign exchange market at that time. This effectively separates the Eurodollar system from the domestic U.S. dollar system. Interest rates on the two markets are, however, closely interrelated.

Eurodollars have increased the efficiency of international finance and trade. Because the costs and risks of converting from one foreign currency to another have been eliminated, Eurodollars permit SSUs to search out the most profitable investment opportunities in all major financial markets, and DSUs the cheapest source of borrowings. National capital markets have been linked more closely together to form a global capital market for some types of securities. The major Eurocurrency market is in London, which is the oldest continuing financial center in the world. Until replaced by New York City after World War II, it had been the major financial center in the world almost from the beginning of the commercial revolution in the 1600s. Some of the largest banks in the world are headquartered in London, and almost all major banks in the world maintain offices there. Communications with governments, banks, and traders throughout the world have long been established. London is the world's largest foreign exchange trading center. Thus, the institutions and personnel were in place for the development of this new market. Other large Eurodollar centers are in Luxembourg, Paris, Zurich, Geneva, Amsterdam, Rome, Brussels, Hong Kong, and Singapore.

International Financial Markets

Every developed country has one or more financial markets for financing domestic trade and investment. For a number of reasons, not all these markets may be equally efficient or equally able to accommodate domestic needs. Institutions that collect savings and that trade in financial instruments are better developed in some markets than in others. Likewise, the needs of domestic DSUs outstrip the resources of domestic SSUs in some markets (particularly in developing countries), whereas in others, the savings generated by domestic SSUs exceed the credit requirements of domestic DSUs. The climates for trading in financial claims also differ among markets, as do rates of inflation and confidence in the political and economic future of the economy. The higher or more uncertain the expected rate of inflation and the less the confidence in the future of the country, the more reluctant are SSUs to lend in that country. Last, financial markets in different countries differ not only because of different stages of secular development but also because of different stages of cyclical development. A particular national market today need not have been equally efficient last year or be so again next year. For example, until their removal in 1986, deposit rate ceilings (Regulation Q) caused the U.S. financial market to become less efficient in periods of rising market rates of interest.

Because of these differences, some, mostly larger, DSUs and SSUs may look outside their national borders for borrowing and lending opportunities. The continued increase in international trade and investment has generated a simultaneous increase in the need for international finance. By reducing search, transactions, and processing costs, technical advances in telecommunications and funds transfer have permitted a broadening of financial horizons across national boundaries similar to the earlier broadening within domestic borders and the development of international financial markets.

Larger DSUs have the choice of whether to borrow in their own country or in some other and whether to borrow in their own currency or in some other. Larger SSUs have the same choice, whether to lend at home or abroad and whether to lend in the domestic currency or another. Their decision depends on the need for a particular currency, on the interest rates in the different countries, and on their expectations of the future values of the relevant currencies. The more the exchange rate of a particular currency is expected to depreciate, *ceteris paribus*, the more will DSUs prefer to borrow in that currency and the less will SSUs prefer to lend in that currency. Thus, what happens in any one major national financial market will affect all other major national markets.

International financial markets include the trading of foreign currencies for each other (foreign exchange or FOREX market) and the trading of domestic currency for securities denominated in foreign currencies (foreign securities market). Both markets have grown rapidly in recent years as barriers to the free flow of funds across national boundaries have diminished. Financial markets have effectively become globalized. Trading volume on the world's foreign exchange markets in 1992 was estimated to be $220 trillion a year or nearly $1 trillion per business day and growing rapidly. This is some 15 times the daily volume on the U.S. Treasury securities market and makes the foreign exchange market by far the most active market in the world. About 30 percent of the volume is traded in London. Another 20 percent is traded in New York, and 12 percent in Tokyo. The other major trading centers are Zurich, Frankfurt, Singapore, Hong Kong, and Paris. The U.S. dollar was by far the most actively traded currency in world markets, accounting for some 83 percent of all transactions in 1992. However, this is down from 90 percent in 1989. West German marks were the most actively traded foreign currency in the United States, followed by Japanese yen, British pounds, and Swiss francs.

Similar to domestic borrowing, foreign borrowing can be short-term, intermediate-term, and long-term. Many borrowing arrangements in international markets are floating- or variable-rate arrangements in which the interest rate is tied to the London interbank offered rate (LIBOR), which is the rate at which the largest international banks lend to each other on a sort of an international Fed-funds market.

Short- and Intermediate-Term Financing

Short- and intermediate-term financing in international markets occur both through bank loans and the sale of notes. Large international commercial banks extend loans to foreign as well as domestic borrowers. These loans may be made in either the bank's loan currency or in Eurocurrencies. Bank loans are generally shorter-term, typically with maturities of under three years. Many have maturities of under one year. Some bank loans are made by groups or syndicates of banks, with each bank being liable for a particular proportion of the total package. These arrangements are referred to as **syndicated loans.**

Prime quality international borrowers may also sell paper in the form of notes. Most notes are issued in Eurocurrencies and termed **Euronotes.** They are frequently unsecured. Frequently, borrowers arrange for a line of credit from a *note-issuing facility* (NIF) at a bank or syndicate of banks, and draw down the amount needed at any one time by issuing the notes. The notes may be purchased by the participating banks or sold by them to other investors. The facility commitment is generally for five to seven years, while the notes are generally issued on a revolving basis for three to six months in the form of commercial paper. Maturities of other securities extend to more than five years. Most Euronotes are denominated in U.S. dollars.

International Bond Financing

Long-term financing in foreign countries is primarily through the sale of bonds. Such financing has been expanding rapidly. In 1992, bond sales in countries other than that of the borrower or in currencies other than that of the borrower's country exceeded $300 billion, and the amount of such bonds outstanding totaled nearly $1.7 trillion. The borrowing countries and currencies of issue are shown in Table 25–4. The bonds may be divided into two types: (1) *foreign bonds* and (2) **Eurobonds.**

| TABLE 25–4 | INTERNATIONAL BOND ISSUES OUTSTANDING, 1992 |

By Currency	U.S. $ Billions	By Borrower	U.S. $ Billions
U.S. dollar	681	Japan	357
Swiss franc	156	United States	155
Japanese yen	208	Canada	127
Deutsche mark	169	United Kingdom	158
British pound	121	France	124
European currency unit (ECU)	101	Other developed countries	482
Other	253	International institutions	225
		Other	61
Total	1,689	Total	1,689

SOURCE: Bank for International Settlements, *Annual Report, 1993*, p. 117, and *Quarterly*, August 1993, Table 13A.

Foreign bonds are bonds denominated in the domestic currency of the foreign country in which they are sold. They are generally purchased by residents of that country. Foreign bonds are the oldest type of foreign long-term borrowing. Interest payment and repayment of the principal amount must be made in the currency in which the bond is denominated. Thus, the risk of change in the exchange rate is borne by the borrower. If the borrower's domestic currency depreciates relative to the currency in which the bond is denominated, the cost of service and repayment increases to the borrower. Foreign bonds denominated in dollars and sold in the United States are referred to as **Yankee bonds.**

Eurobonds are bonds denominated in one or more currencies other than that of the country in which they are sold. The currencies are generally those for which there are markets in more than one country, so that the bonds can be sold in more than one national market either initially or later on the secondary market. This gives them an advantage over foreign bonds, which for all practical purposes can be sold only in the country in whose currency they are denominated. Eurobonds may also be denominated in more than one Eurocurrency, or in a bundle of currencies called a **unit of account,** to protect against unfavorable exchange rate changes in any one currency against the others. The most frequently used composite currencies are the IMF's SDR and the *European Currency Unit* or ECU. (The basics of the ECU are examined in greater detail in Exhibit 25–1.) The borrower again assumes the risk of devaluation in the domestic currency in terms of the Eurocurrencies used. The DSU may be either a foreign or a domestic borrower. The Eurobond market was developed in the early 1960s for many of the same reasons as the shorter-term Eurocurrency market.

At year-end 1992, Japan was by far the largest individual borrower of funds on the international bond market (Table 25–4). Some 40 percent of the bonds were denominated in U.S. dollars; smaller percentages were denominated in Swiss francs, Japanese yen, and Deutsche marks. This does

EXHIBIT

25–1

▼

ECU, *Who?*

What's an ecu? It's not an Australian bird or a Greek coin. Rather, the ecu stands for European Currency Unit, a synthetic composite currency consisting of fixed amounts of ten European currencies. Since its introduction in March 1979, the ecu has been used by the governments of countries participating in the European Monetary System (EMS). It has also played a rapidly growing role in private financial markets in many countries, including interbank markets, short-term deposit markets, the Eurobond market, and most recently, the futures and options markets.

The ecu was originally designed as an official instrument for payments and debt settlements among the central banks of countries participating in the European Monetary System (EMS), whose purpose is to limit the movements of member currencies against one another. The ecu was also intended to serve as a unit of account for the countries in the European Economic Community (EEC). Of the 12 members of the EEC, eight participate in the EMS. They are West Germany, France, Italy, the Netherlands, Belgium, Denmark, Ireland, and Luxembourg. The currencies of the other four—the United Kingdom [now a participant], Greece, Portugal, and Spain, float independently of their EEC partners.

The ecu consists of a fixed quantity of each of the EMS currencies plus those of the United Kingdom and Greece (included in anticipation of their future participation in the EMS). The quantity of each currency in the ecu is related to its country's relative economic strength. Currently, one ecu consists of 0.719 German marks, 1.31 French francs, 0.256 Dutch guilders, 3.71 Belgian francs, 0.14 Luxembourg francs, 0.219 Danish kroner, 140 Italian liras, 0.00871 Irish pounds, 0.0878 British pounds, and 1.15 Greek drachmas.

USE IN PRIVATE MARKETS

The ecus used by the EMS monetary authorities in their foreign exchange market activities against one another's currencies are known as official ecus. However, no ecu bills or coins exist. Nowhere is the ecu legal tender, and no central bank issues it or stands ready to redeem it. The ecu therefore lacks some of the characteristics associated with a national currency.

Nevertheless, the ecu can easily be created from or converted into its component currencies. In fact, the so-called "private ecu" exists because commercial banks guarantee its officially determined value by their commitment to convert ecus into national currencies at official rates. Thus, in private financial and other markets, the ecu has found increasing use as a unit of account, a store of value, and a medium of exchange—the traditional functions of money.

An increasing number of banks accept ecu deposits and make ecu loans. The Bank of International Settlements (BIS) reported that the share of ecus in total nondollar Eurocurrency banking assets rose from less than two percent at the end of 1982 to over nine percent at the end of the first quarter of 1986. With reported holdings equivalent to $61 billion in March of this year [1986], the ecu was the fifth most widely used unit for international bank lending behind the U.S. dollar ($1,290 billion), German mark ($228 billion), Swiss franc ($138 billion), and yen ($84 billion); the English pound and French franc trailed behind.

In commercial transactions, private use of the ecu has been expanding quickly as well, as indicated by the increasing number of trade contracts, export credits, and other transactions denominated in ecus. Some companies have chosen to invoice their transactions with foreign affiliates in ecus. Even ecu traveler's checks have recently become available.

Even though individual firms or investors may not need the ten component currencies in exactly the same proportions as they appear in the ecu, they find other benefits in the ecu. For one, commercial banks dealing in ecus may face much lower transaction costs than if they were to tailor their own baskets of currencies. In addition, the markets for some individual European currencies are not very liquid, and certain European capital markets are difficult to tap directly for funds because of remaining capital controls. Using the ecu therefore lowers transactions costs, enables indirect access to currencies otherwise not obtainable, and allows wider market diversification.

Yet another reason for the ecu's appeal stems from its use as a hedge against the dollar. Because the ecu currency basket excludes the dollar completely, the value of the ecu in terms of any of its component currencies is generally unaffected by changes in the value of the dollar. In contrast, the SDR has been perceived as an ineffective hedge against the dollar because the dollar constitutes such a large part of its construction that it has fluctuated a great deal in terms of its other component currencies (the German mark, French franc, pound, and yen).

SOURCE: Abstracted from Reuven Glick, *Weekly Letter*, Federal Reserve Bank of San Francisco, January 9, 1987.

not indicate, however, that the bonds were sold in these countries on a proportionate basis. Eurobonds, which are sold in countries other than the country in whose currency the bonds are denominated, account for the large majority of the new international bond issues and have been increasing in volume much faster than foreign bonds.

SUMMARY

Two official international agencies operate in the international financial markets to promote growth in trade and finance. The International Monetary Fund (IMF) acts to "shorten the duration and lessen the degree of disequilibrium in the international balance of payments." It does so by monitoring economic and financial conditions in member countries, collecting economic and financial data, providing technical assistance, establishing rules for international trade and finance, providing a forum for international consultation, and most important, providing resources that permit lengthening the time necessary for individual member countries to correct balance of payments disequilibriums. The IMF has established an international currency, SDRs (special drawing rights), to supplement its borrowing facilities.

The International Bank for Reconstruction and Development (World Bank) finances economic growth and productivity in developing countries. The bank raises funds primarily by selling bonds in developed countries. The loans it makes must both promote economic development and promise repayment of principal. More risky loans are channeled through a subsidiary, the International Development Association (IDA).

Increases in world trade and finance have encouraged the integration or globalization of national financial markets. International financial markets trade in market instruments. Eurodollars are dollar-denominated deposits at foreign banks. Because they provide a single currency and obviate the need to engage in multiple exchange transactions, Eurodollars and other Eurocurrencies are favorite international currencies and have expanded rapidly. Large borrowers may tap the resources of any developed currency by borrowing from large banks in these countries or selling notes and bonds, either in the local currency of that country (foreign bonds) or in other major foreign currencies (Eurobonds). Both types of financing have increased rapidly in recent years as restrictive barriers have been removed and telecommunications have improved. No major national financial market is an island on to itself; it is affected by changes in the other major financial centers.

QUESTIONS

1. How is the International Monetary Fund both similar to and different from the Federal Reserve System?

2. How do the functions and objectives of the IMF and World Bank differ? What might be a domestic equivalent to the World Bank?

3. What is the function of the IMF's specific borrowing facilities? Why has the number of these facilities been periodically expanded? Might the growth in the number be related to the growth in the number of IMF members? Why?

4. What are SDRs? In what ways are they like domestic money and in what ways are they not? Who controls the amount of SDRs outstanding? Could you imagine a conflict among member countries in determining how many SDRs to supply? What would be the nature of such a conflict?

5. Define *Eurodollars*. How do they differ from "regular" dollars? Why is there a demand for Eurodollars? How do Eurodollars affect the domestic U.S. money supply?

6. Why may borrowers prefer to borrow in different countries from their own? Why may lenders prefer to lend to foreign borrowers in foreign currency? Why has volume on the international money and capital markets expanded very rapidly in recent years? Do you think this growth will continue?

7. Discuss the reasons gold has lost most of its official domestic and international importance since World War II. Why has the price of gold risen sharply and become more volatile on the private gold markets since the 1960s?

REFERENCES

Abdullah, Faud, *Financial Management for the Multinational Firm*. Englewood Cliffs, N.J.: Prentice Hall, 1987.

Aliber, Robert Z., *Handbook of International Financial Management*. Homewood, Ill.: Dow Jones Irwin, 1989.

Bank for International Settlements, *Annual Report*. Basel, Switzerland, annual.

Bank for International Settlements, *Recent Innovations in International Banking*. Basel, Switzerland, April 1986.

"Beyond the Bretton Woods Era: Changing Bank and Fund Operations," *Finance and Development*, December 1977.

Boyd, John, et al., "Primer on the IMF," *Quarterly Review*, Federal Reserve Bank of Minneapolis, Summer 1983, pp. 6–15.

Chrystal, K. Alec, "A Guide to Foreign Exchange Markets," *Review*, Federal Reserve Bank of St. Louis, March 1984, pp. 5–18.

Coombs, Charles A., *The Arena of International Finance*. New York: John Wiley, 1976.

DeVries, Maragaret G., *The IMF in a Changing World: 1945–1985*. Washington, D.C.: International Monetary Fund, 1986.

DeVries, Rimmer, "Global Capital Markets: Issues and Implications," *Marcus Wallenberg Papers on International Finance*, International Law Institute, vol. 1, no. 4, pp. 1–45.

Dufey, Gunter, and Ian Giddy, *The International Money Market*, 2nd ed., Englewood Cliffs, N.J.: Prentice Hall, 1994.

Goodfriend, Marvin, "Eurodollars," *Economic Review*, Federal Reserve Bank of Richmond, May/June 1981, pp. 12–18.

Grabbe, J. Orlin, *International Financial Markets*. New York: Elsevier, 1986.

Holmes, Alan R., and Francis H. Schott, *The New York Foreign Exchange Market*.

New York: Federal Reserve Bank of New York, 1965.

Hultman, Charles W., *The Environment of International Banking*. Englewood Cliffs, N.J.: Prentice Hall, 1990.

International Monetary Fund, *Annual Report*. Washington, D.C., annually.

International Monetary Fund, IMF *Survey*. Washington, D.C., monthly.

Keil, John A., "Bretton Woods Revisited," *Durell Journal of Money Banking*, Fall 1993, pp. 25–35.

Kubarych, Roger M., *Foreign Exchange Markets in the United States*, rev. ed. Federal Reserve Bank of New York, 1983.

Kvasnicka, Joseph G., ed. *Readings in International Finance*. Chicago: Federal Reserve Bank of Chicago, 1983.

Laney, Leroy O., "The Secondary Market in Developing Country Debt," *Economic Review*, Federal Reserve Bank of Dallas, July 1987, pp. 1–12.

Maxwell, Watson, et al., *International Capital Markets: Developments and Prospects*. Washington, D.C.: International Monetary Fund, December 1986.

Melnick, Arie, and Steven E. Plaut, *The Short-Term Eurocredit Market*. New York: New York University Salomon Center, 1991.

Mikesell, Raymond F., "The Bretton Woods Debates: A Memoir," *Essays in International Finance* (192), Princeton, Princeton University, March 1994.

Morgan Guaranty Trust Company, *World Financial Markets*. New York, monthly.

Organization for Economic Cooperation and Development, *Financial Market Trends*. Paris, three times yearly.

Revey, Patricia A., "Evolution and Growth of the United States Foreign Exchange Market," *Quarterly Review*, Federal Reserve Bank of New York, Autumn 1981, pp. 32–44.

Solomon, Robert, *The International Monetary System, 1945–1976: An Insider's View*. New York: Harper, 1977.

Sommers, Davidson, and Roger Chavfourniel, "Bretton Woods at Forty: The World Bank from Reconstruction to Development," *Finance and Development*, June 1984, pp. 30–35.

Stonehill, Arthur, and David K. Eiteman, *Finance: An International Perspective*. Homewood, Ill.: Irwin, 1987.

Throop, Adrian W., "Decline and Fall of the Gold Standard," *Business Review*, Federal Reserve Bank of Dallas, January 1976.

Economic Goals

Although the financial sector is important, the material welfare of all of us is determined in the real sector by the quantity and quality of goods and services we produce and consume. It is useful to discuss the performance of the economy in relation to the economic objectives of our society. This will provide us with a framework within which to evaluate both the operation of the financial system and alternative government economic policies.

The Goals of the Economy

If we thought about it for a few minutes, we could each prepare a long list of goals we think the economy should achieve. Of course, the list would differ somewhat from person to person, but some goals are likely to be included on everyone's list. These would probably include, among others.

1. Full employment
2. Economic growth
3. Price stability
4. Stability in the international balance of payments and foreign exchange rates
5. Equitable distribution of income and wealth
6. Efficiency

We shall discuss each of these separately.

Full Employment

Full employment implies that every person of working age who wishes to work is employed at an acceptable position. Although clear in concept, full employment is difficult to define in practice. How should "person of working age" be defined? Should it mean only males, heads of households, those with appropriate work qualifications, and so on? How should "acceptable" be defined? Should it be commensurate with a person's training, ambition, qualifications, peer level? How should voluntary quits be handled? Should acceptable employment be available the next day, the next week, or the next month?

It is unlikely that a zero rate of unemployment could be achieved even for the most restrictive definitions. In a dynamic economy, employers expand as the demand for their products increases and contract as demand decreases. Workers laid off by firms whose markets are declining need to be employed by the firms whose markets are growing. Such switchovers cannot be accomplished immediately. The workers laid off may not have knowledge of the new employment opportunities. The new jobs may not require the same skills. They may be in another part of the city, state, or even country. Information, search, travel, and change in permanent residence are costly and time-consuming. Other people may quit their jobs voluntarily, because they wish to upgrade their positions, change their residences, or try a change of pace, or because they encounter crises at home that require their attention full-time. Thus, some minimum rate of unemployment consistent with the structural, sociological, and demographic characteristics of the economy is generally accepted as full employment.

Moreover, it is likely that even such a minimum rate is not a constant, but changes over time. For example, in the 1950s and 1960s, many analysts considered an unemployment rate of about 4 percent to be consistent with full employment for the United States. However, this rate has not been achieved since 1969, even though the economy has undergone periods of very rapid expansion and record rates of price inflation.

In part, the higher rates of unemployment reflected changes in the composition of the labor force that were independent of the state of the economy. Teenagers and adult women traditionally have had higher rates of unemployment than adult males, because of greater inexperience, less training, more frequent voluntary entry into and departure from the labor force, or discrimination. And these groups have become relatively more numerous in the labor force. In 1960, adult women represented 30 percent of the labor force, and teenagers 7 percent. In 1992, the proportion of adult women had increased to 46 percent and that of teenagers had declined to 5 percent after rising to 10 percent. Unemployment among adult women had, at times, been 50 percent higher than for adult males, and for teenagers three to five times higher. It has been estimated that this change in the composition of the labor force has increased the unemployment rate in 1980 that is comparable to a given rate in the 1950s by more than 1 percentage point. Thus, if full employment was considered to be 4 percent unemployment in 1960, the comparable unemployment rate by 1980 was at least 5 percent. Nevertheless, a look at Table 26–1 shows that actual rates

TABLE 26–1

SELECTED INDICATORS OF U.S. ECONOMY, 1960–1993 (PERCENT)

	Civilian Unemployment	Growth in per Capita Real GDP	Inflation[a]	Discomfort Index[b]
1960	5.5	2.2	1.6	7.1
1965	4.5	5.8	1.7	6.2
1970	4.9	−0.3	5.9	10.8
1975	8.5	−1.3	9.1	17.6
1977	7.1	4.7	6.5	13.5
1980	7.1	−0.2	13.5	20.6
1990	5.5	0.0	5.4	10.9
1993	6.8	2.9	3.0	9.8

SOURCE: Council of Economic Advisors, *Annual Report 1994.*
[a] Consumer Price Index.
[b] Sum of unemployment and inflation rates.

of unemployment have frequently exceeded even this rate by substantial amounts. But as women gain additional experience in the labor market and the proportion of teenagers continues to decline, the unfavorable effect of the change in the composition of the labor force on unemployment will decrease and even reverse. Indeed, by 1982 the unemployment rate among adult females had declined below that of adult males for the first time and has remained slightly below or roughly comparable since.

Although difficult to measure precisely, full employment is an important goal to achieve for two reasons. First, the greater the employment, the greater is the economy's aggregate output. The loss in output attributable to unemployment is shown in Figure 26–1 as the difference between the real GDP that the U.S. economy could have achieved at full employment (potential GDP) and the GDP that was actually produced. Second, the greater the unemployment, the more must the employed share their income with the unemployed through mechanisms such as unemployment insurance and food stamps. Thus, achievement of full employment makes everyone better off, with the possible exception of some employers who have to search harder for employees—and perhaps some people who enjoy seeing others less fortunate. This makes full employment a unique goal. As we shall see, the other goals help some but harm others. Thus, their acceptance is less universal.

FIGURE

26–1   ACTUAL AND POTENTIAL REAL GROSS DOMESTIC PRODUCT, 1964–1993

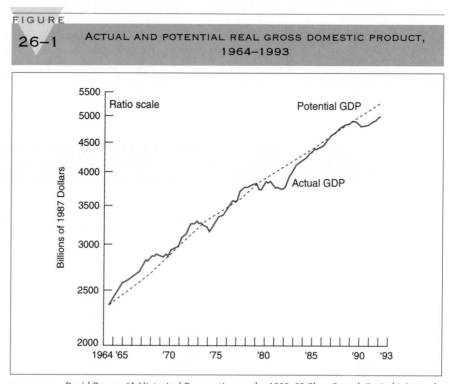

SOURCE: David Brauer, "A Historical Perspective on the 1989–92 Slow Growth Period," *Quarterly Review*, Federal Reserve Bank of New York, Summer 1993, p. 13.

Economic Growth

Economic growth is defined as a rising material standard of living measured by output per unit of input. Economic growth means that you will live better materially working 40 or fewer hours per week than your parents did working 40 hours and than their grandparents did working 50 to 60 hours a week. And your children may live even better working fewer hours!

Growth is made possible through increased productivity of labor and capital. Labor becomes more productive through increased education and training; capital, through technological improvements and more intensive use. Both processes require shifting resources away from current consumption to investment. Economic saving achieved by abstaining from consumption is a prerequisite for economic growth. The saving-investment process is helped by an efficient financial sector.

Unlike higher levels of employment, faster economic growth does not benefit everyone. Economic growth involves an exchange of a given amount of current consumption for a larger amount of future consumption. The faster the growth rate, the more current consumption must be postponed. Although you personally might benefit from a policy of faster growth from now on, it is unlikely that your parents would. They might not be alive in the future period when the gains are realized and would prefer to consume now. Thus, there are intergenerational differences. Through our personal decisions on how to divide our income between consumption and savings, we, in effect, determine our preferred growth rate. The closer this rate is to one that may be established by the government, the better off we are relative to those whose preferred growth rates differ more from that of the government.

Faster economic growth does, however, permit a less painful redistribution of income to lower-income households. The faster the rate of growth, the more can any income transfer to these households come from new income; the slower the rate of growth, the more will any income transfer come from other households' income. Faster economic growth may also slow inflation if more goods and services can be produced by the same labor force, increasing supply.

Economic growth may or may not result in greater personal happiness. Those who argue that it does not point to increased pollution and greater psychological strains and stresses from coping with a more urbanized environment. On the other hand, there are obvious advantages to urban living, such as greater access to other people and to a large variety of social and cultural activities. In addition, a closer look at history makes us consider whether today's major cities, such as New York, London, Paris, and Hong Kong, were any less polluted 100 years ago. Similarly, many waterways that pass through industrial areas are cleaner today than when the economy was more rural. Pollution is not so much a result of growth as it is of inappropriate measuring of economic growth and of inappropriate pricing of outputs that pollute.

A steel plant that pollutes the air should be charged for the "consumption" of the air it pollutes in the same way it is charged for the other inputs it consumes. This would increase the price of steel and motivate steel firms to discover ways to reduce costs to offset a decline in steel purchases. Likewise, the costs of pollution would be subtracted from economic growth rather than effectively added to it through the inclusion of the value of items produced to offset its damages, such as laundry and medical services. On the other hand, a number of beneficial outputs that are not priced by the market are omitted from GDP and thus economic growth. These include progress toward cleaner air and water and reduced noise pollution.

One study of the relationship between material well-being and happiness concluded:

> In all societies, more money for the individual typically means more happiness. However, raising the incomes of all does not increase the happiness of all. . . . Each person acts on the assumption that more money will bring happiness; and, indeed, if he does get more money, and others do not (or get less), his happiness increases. But when everyone acts on this assumption and incomes generally increase, no-one, on the average, feels better off. . . . What is true for the individual is not true for society as a whole.[1]

In a democratic society, the appropriate rate of growth is determined at the ballot box, through the election of parties that promise to implement policies that encourage savings to different degrees. Recent rates of economic growth in the United States as measured by GDP are shown in Figure 26–1 and as measured by GDP per capita are shown in Table 26–1.

Price Stability

Price stability refers to stability in the average price or price *level* of all goods and services we consume. It does not refer to *individual* or *relative* prices. In a market economy in which there is no central planner to dictate what, how much, and for whom goods are to be produced, individual prices signal suppliers what consumers want by reflecting changes in demand. If individual prices were not free to change, the signaling mechanism would break down and consumer preferences would not be accommodated at lowest cost.

Changing price levels are a different story. Within a country, one person's expenditures are another person's income. Thus, higher prices paid by buyers also represent higher revenues received by sellers. At first approximation, it may appear that, if we neglect the foreign sector, inflation would be a "zero-sum" game. If everyone were able to predict the rate of price change freely and correctly, he or she would adjust the prices for services accordingly, and inflation would do little more than increase the number of zeros after every price. No one would be any better or worse off. However, the evidence suggests that even if all predictions were right on the nose, neither the process of arriving at them nor the adjustments required by persons in their economic behavior would be costless and that not all members of an economy predict price changes or adjust their economic behavior equally well. Thus, rapid price changes increase the time and effort that must be expended by both sellers and buyers in conducting trade and cause resources to be shifted to this activity from more produc-

[1] Richard A. Easterlin, "Does Money Buy Happiness?" *The Public Interest*, 30 (Winter 1973), 4, 10.

tive activities. In this way, rapid inflation reduces aggregate income. In addition, everyone is not able to predict the future rates of inflation accurately. Depending on how well their predictions are realized, income is redistributed; some people gain and others lose. Those who predict and adjust best gain income at the expense of those who predict and adjust most poorly. Because this redistribution is not based on a person's economic contribution or economic need, it is arbitrary and likely to be inconsistent with the goal of an equitable distribution of income and wealth. Last, to the extent inflation was not expected and interest rates are higher than expected, financial intermediaries that financed long-term fixed-rate loans with short-term deposits (for example, savings and loan associations), experience financial difficulties. Price stability may be favored as a goal on the basis that it is the fairest and safest alternative.

Generally, until an inflation turns into a hyperinflation, the economic harm sown is not as evident as for, say, an increase in unemployment. This occurs primarily because the rise in unemployment affects a small proportion of people greatly and visibly, while inflation affects a large proportion of persons less severely and less visibly and creates winners as well as losers. Of course, as is described in Chapter 2, in periods of hyperinflation the economy grinds almost to a halt and the harm caused is clear to everyone. On the basis of experiencing both massive unemployment in the United States during the 1930s and hyperinflation in China during World War II, the political writer Theodore White wrote, "I learned to fear inflation as much as the cruelty of joblessness and depression in which I had grown up."[2]

Since the mid-1960s, the United States has experienced periods of fairly rapid and volatile price inflation. The economic implications of this inflation are examined in Chapter 34. It would be reasonable to argue that, if no one benefited from inflation, it is highly unlikely that government policy would have permitted the rate of inflation that was experienced or pursued policies that permitted continued inflation. Recent rates of inflation are shown in Table 26–1.

Stability in the International Balance of Payments and Foreign Exchange Rates

As we discussed in Chapter 24, the balance of payments is a record of all transactions between one country and all other countries. It records whether the country is buying more or less from other countries than they buy from it. Much like individuals, countries that continuously buy more from others than they sell to others are living beyond their means and either have to lower the price (exchange rate) at which they sell their products so they can sell more, sell assets they own, or go into debt. If they lower their exchange rate, the costs of imports increase. If they go into debt, they have to pay interest and, in time, pay off the loan. This can be done only by cutting down on the amount they purchase abroad and/or increasing the amount they sell abroad. Both these adjustments are painful and reduce domestic welfare. Because of the resulting changes in export and

---

[2] Theodore H. White, *In Search of History* (New York: Warner Books, 1981), p. 220.

import prices, some sectors gain and others lose, but painful dislocations occur. Countries that continuously sell more to others than they buy from them are not benefiting fully from their production efforts and are in effect financing other countries. Either their exchange rate will increase, which reduces the prices of imports and stimulates their purchase, or they will pile up debts on their trading partners. However, at some point they will refuse to extend further credit and demand payment. At this point, exports will decline and dislocations will occur.

Equitable Distribution of Income and Wealth

Almost all members of any economy would agree that income should be distributed in such a way that everyone benefits to some extent from the wealth of the economy and no one benefits excessively. However, what is meant by "some" and "excessively" is one of the oldest and most hotly debated subjects in world history. Probably more governments have fallen, either peacefully or violently, owing to disagreement on this issue than on any other. In this country, almost no political debate or election is complete without reference to this issue.

Is the distribution of income equitable when everyone is rewarded according to his or her contribution? If so, how is "contribution" to be measured? Is there a distinction between a person's economic and social contribution? Does a doctor or teacher contribute more than a used-car dealer or a stockbroker? What if people have greatly different skills and the resulting income distribution is very uneven? Is the distribution equitable when everyone is given the same income? If so, who is "everyone"—every person, every adult, every household? What if different people have different basic needs, so that one's medical needs greatly exceed another's? Who will judge "needs"? What are the effects of income distribution on economic incentives? To the extent that people work for income, will a transfer of income away from them cause them to cut back on their hours worked? If so, at what point? Would the decrease in aggregate income offset the gains to the recipients?

It is obvious that there is no "correct" distribution of income; only one imposed in some arbitrary ways. In this country, the distribution of income is determined primarily by consensus at the ballot box. The ultimate distribution is achieved basically in two steps. In the first step, income is rewarded by the marketplace according to supply and demand. In the second step, income is redistributed by the government expenditure and income tax systems according to the consensus of the electorate.

Analysis of the income distribution in the United States appears to indicate only moderate change in the post–World War II period between the income shares of the highest and lowest income groups. The proportion of before-tax money income received by families in the highest 20 percent of the distribution increased slightly to 45 percent, while that received by families in the lowest 20 percent declined slightly from 5 to 4.4 percent. The complete distribution is shown in Table 26–2. However, these data are subject to two limitations. First, the same families are not in the same group each year. Thus, a family is likely to move from a low-income group right after its formation to a higher group at its peak earnings periods, and to a lower group after retirement. A study of tax filers showed that more than

	Lowest Fifth		Second Fifth		Third Fifth		Fourth Fifth		Highest Fifth	
Year	Money[a]	Adjusted[b]	Money	Adjusted	Money	Adjusted	Money	Adjusted	Money	Adjusted
1952	4.9	7.8	12.2	14.8	17.1	18.8	23.5	23.3	42.2	35.3
1962	5.0	9.0	12.1	15.1	17.6	19.1	24.0	22.9	41.3	34.0
1972	5.5	12.6	11.9	16.1	17.5	18.4	23.9	20.9	41.4	31.9
1982	4.8	N.A.	11.2	N.A.	17.1	N.A.	24.2	N.A.	42.7	N.A.
1992	4.4	N.A.	10.5	N.A.	16.5	N.A.	24.0	N.A.	44.6	N.A.

SOURCE: U.S. Department of Commerce, Bureau of the Census, *Statistical Abstract of the United States, 1984*, p. 465; *Current Population Reports*, P60 1992, p. B-13; and Timothy Hannon, "Measuring Income Distribution in the United States," *Business Review*, Federal Reserve Bank of Philadelphia, March/April 1978, p. 7.

[a] Money income defined as sum of money wages and salaries, net income from self-employment, and income other than earnings.

[b] Adjusted income is money income adjusted to include government noncash income payments.

N.A. = not available.

one-half of the filers in each of the lowest 20 and next-to-lowest 20 percent in 1979 had climbed into the top 60 percent in 1988. Likewise, only two-thirds of the filers in the top 20 percent in 1979 remained there in 1988. Income mobility appears to be ongoing. Moreover, the composition of families does not remain constant through time. In recent years, families have become smaller, more likely to be headed by a single parent, particularly a female, and proportionately both older and younger. Other things equal, this should have widened the distribution of income.

If the U.S. population were adjusted for family size and age, so that perfect equality was defined as "equal incomes for all families at the same state of the life cycle," the lowest 20 percent of the families would be entitled to 13 percent of the total income in the 1970s.[3] The highest 20 percent would be entitled to 25 percent of total income. This shows income to be distributed more evenly, and the adjustment indicates that the distribution has become more equal since World War II, at least through the 1970s.

Second, the distribution of income is very sensitive to the definition of income used. The income measure used in Table 26–2 includes only money income. An increasing proportion of low-income-family expenditures are financed by food stamps, Medicare, Medicaid, government housing subsidies, and other noncash federal government benefits. If such noncash income is included in family income, the bottom 20 percent received 13 percent of total family income in 1972 rather than 5 percent and the top 20 percent, 32 percent rather than 41 percent.[4] As may be seen from Table 26–2, these estimates also indicate a reduction in inequality in the early postwar period. By changing the definition of income, the U.S. Department of Commerce reports that in 1989 the lowest quintal would have had between 1.5 and 5.1 percent of total income and the highest

[3] Morton Paglin, "Time Measurement and Trend of Inequality: A Basic Revision," *American Economic Review*, September 1975, pp. 598–610.

[4] Edgar K. Browning, "How Much More Equality Can We Afford?" *The Public Interest*, Spring 1976, pp. 90–110.

quital, between 44 and 51 percent. Likewise, although in 1991, 14 percent of all persons had before-tax and public-transfer-payments incomes below the federal poverty level of from $6,933 for one person to $13,924 for a family of four and $27,942 for a family of nine or more, only 10 percent had such income after the market value of all food, housing, and medical care non-cash transfers was included and taxes were deducted. If all transfer payments were omitted, the poverty rate would have been close to 22 percent.

There has also been a sharp change in the age composition of persons with incomes below the official poverty level. In 1970, 25 percent of persons 65 years or older, and 15 percent of persons 17 years or younger, were in this category. In 1991, the percentages had effectively reversed. Only 12 percent of senior citizens but more than 20 percent of teenagers lived in households that had incomes below the poverty level. For the country as a whole, the poverty rate increased slightly from 12.6 percent to 14.2 percent. For whites the poverty rate increased from 9.9 to 11.3 percent, while for blacks it declined slightly from 33.5 to 32.7 percent.

The apparent increase in the inequity of unadjusted income in the United States in recent years appears to also hold true in most other industrial countries, at least as far as it applies to the wage structure. However, it does not hold true in the more rapidly developing countries.[5]

It may be argued that wealth is a better measure of well-being than income. Estimates of the distribution of wealth are far less accurate or frequent than of the distribution of income. But, they suggest that wealth is far less equally distributed than income. In 1983, the wealthiest 1 percent of the population held 34 percent of total wealth, while the least wealthy 90 percent held only 32 percent. Likewise, in 1988, households in the top 20 percent of the income distribution held 45 percent of the total wealth. However, some people with low current income may have substantial wealth (retired people) or expect substantial wealth in the future (students). At the same time, some with high current incomes have little wealth. They would be disadvantaged by income redistribution but gain from wealth redistribution.

Efficiency

The more operatively and allocatively efficient (as is defined in Chapter 1) the economy, the greater is aggregate output and welfare. Because efficiency is objective and measurable, it is a favorite goal of economists and financial analysts. However, because it is impersonal and considers only aggregate measures and not individuals or sectors, it is generally not considered important by others. Thus, although the resources in a particular sector may be excessive as a result of market imperfections and total output in the economy could be increased by shifting the excessive resources elsewhere, members of the inefficient sector would be harmed by such a shift. They benefit from this inefficiency.

The basic justification for the marketplace as the distributor of goods and services is that it is the most efficient system in allocating them to where they maximize total output in the economy. Efficiency, however, has no "heart." It evaluates individuals and sectors only by their production, not

---

[5] Steven J. Davis, "Cross-Country Patterns of Change in Relative Wages," Working Paper 4085, Cambridge, Mass.: National Bureau of Economic Research, June 1992.

by their "needs" or "worthiness." Efficiency may not be "just." It may truthfully be said that the only constant supporters of the marketplace through thick and thin are economists, and sometimes even they waver.

It has been argued that by encouraging efficiency, the marketplace also safeguards individual choice and political freedom. This relationship was emphasized by Keynes in the concluding notes of his famous *General Theory*, which is best remembered for making the modern case for government intervention in the economy. Keynes wrote:

> Let us stop for a moment to remind ourselves what these advantages [of individualism] are. They are partly advantages of efficiency—the advantages of decentralisation and of the play of self-interest. The advantage to efficiency of the decentralisation of decisions and of individual responsibility is even greater, perhaps, than the nineteenth century supposed; and the reaction against the appeal to self-interest may have gone too far. But, above all, individualism, if it can be purged of its defects and its abuses, is the best safeguard of personal liberty in the sense that, compared with any other system, it greatly widens the field for the exercise of personal choice. It is also the best safeguard of the variety of life, which emerges precisely from this extended field of personal choice, and the loss of which is the greatest of all the losses of the homogeneous or totalitarian state. For this variety preserves the traditions which embody the most secure and successful choices of former generations; it colours the present with the diversification of its fancy; and, being the handmaid of experiment as well as of tradition and of fancy, it is the most powerful instrument to better the future.[6]

Responsibility for Goals

Although policymakers, legislators, and the public discuss these and similar goals as if their achievement were generally recognized to be the legal responsibility of the federal government, neither the goals nor the responsibilities of the government in achieving them, at least in the United States, are precisely defined in legislation. The first legislative statement of the goals appears in the Employment Act of 1946, which formally recognized the role of the government in this area. It reads:

> The Congress hereby declares that it is the continuing policy and responsibility of the Federal Government to use all practicable means consistent with its needs and obligations and other essential considerations of national policy, with the assistance and cooperation of industry, agriculture, labor, and state and local governments, to coordinate and utilize all its plans, functions, and resources for the purpose of creating and maintaining, in a manner calculated to foster and promote free competitive enterprise and the general welfare, conditions under which there will be afforded useful employment opportunities, including self-employment, for those able, willing, and seeking to work, and to promote maximum employment, production, and purchasing power.

[6] John Maynard Keynes, *General Theory of Employment, Interest, and Money* (New York: Harcourt Brace Jovanovich, 1964), p. 380.

The wording of this charge is obviously quite vague. What is meant by "all practical means," "able, willing, and seeking to work," "maximum employment," or "maximum purchasing power?" The vagueness reflects the political practicality of incorporating language that would satisfy a majority of legislators.

It is unlikely that an economy can achieve all or even most of its economic goals simultaneously at all times. Some may be mutually incompatible in the short run. For example, economic growth requires shifting resources from less to more efficient uses. But this may cause temporary unemployment among those employed in the less efficient sectors. Conversely, strict maintenance of full employment might prevent the shifts in resources necessary to generate continued growth. A more equal distribution of income may reduce incentives and productivity and interfere with the attainment of full employment and growth. To the extent that price pressures intensify as the economy approaches full employment, price stability may be difficult to realize at full employment. And so on. If such incompatibilities exist, priorities must be established and choices made.

Sometimes several goals are combined to construct a more inclusive index. One such is the ***discomfort index,*** constructed by summing the unemployment rate and the rate of price inflation. Values of this index are shown in the last column of Table 26–1. However, unless all of the individual goals included in such measures are assigned equal weight, this procedure does not escape the need to determine priorities and make policy choices. These may be included explicitly in a combined index by assigning a weight to each of the goals before summing: Perhaps unemployment would be weighted twice as heavily as inflation, or vice versa. But who will assign the weights?

Economic Policy

For a variety of reasons, the performance of economies frequently deviates from the levels of performance that are consistent with the economic goals they select. To assist their economies in operating close to their target levels, governments employ economic policies. The precise nature of these policies depends on the state of development of the economy, the form of economic organization, and the form of ownership of capital. An economy can be organized according to a central plan designed by the government or by the decisions of the individual spending units (households, business firms, and governments) in the marketplace. Ownership of capital may be public (socialist) or private (free enterprise). Most economies pursue hybrid forms of market organization and capital ownership.

The United States is principally a highly developed, market-oriented, free-enterprise economy. The government has available to it different types of economic policies for affecting levels of performance, including the following:

1. *Monetary policy.* Monetary policy is predicated on a predictable relationship between money and other variables in the financial sector of the economy and activity in the real sector. Increases in money stimulate private demand and exert upward pressure on employment, production, and prices. Conversely, decreases in money exert downward pressure on these variables.

2 *Fiscal policy.* Fiscal policy involves the spending and taxing powers of the federal government. When spending exceeds tax receipts at a given level of national income, additional income is injected into the economy and upward demand pressure is exerted on employment, production, and prices. Conversely, when tax receipts exceed spending at a given national income level, income is withdrawn and downward demand pressure is exerted on economic activity. Changes in tax rates may also be used to change work and investment incentives and thus alter supply.

3. *Incomes policy.* Incomes policy consists of controls over prices, wages, and profits, primarily to reduce inflationary pressures by restricting increases in these variables to predetermined magnitudes. Such controls are likely to change the share of aggregate income that accrues to any one sector or group of sectors at the expense of other sectors relative to what the distribution would have been in the absence of the controls. An incomes policy is generally a last-resort effort to slow inflationary pressures at times when imperfections are believed to hamper the efficient operation of the market mechanism and of monetary and fiscal policies.

In this book we focus primarily on monetary policy. We examine how the federal government manages money and uses the financial sector to attempt to stabilize the real sector. We also consider whether the federal government can use monetary policy or any other policy effectively to achieve its goals.

Economics and Politics

Economic policy is conducted by government personnel that have to satisfy the economic needs of the citizens in order to remain in office. While the economic marketplace allocates resources on the basis of prices, the political marketplace allocates them on the basis of votes. In democratic societies, members of the government must stand for reelection every few years. This frequency determines the time frame over which they are evaluated and must produce results. For many, their time horizon for policy actions and results cannot safely be longer than this time frame. Failure to satisfy a sufficiently large proportion to the public results in their defeat at the polls. Because many economic policies affect the economy only with long and varied time lags, elected officials may at times choose a less efficient but more visible and quicker-acting policy to one they know in their hearts to be superior. For example, economic policies tend to affect real income before prices. Thus, for short time horizons, the effects of expansive policies will be seen primarily in higher incomes—which is favorable—and not in prices—which is unfavorable. Through time, however, the effect on real income will decline and that on inflation will increase. The chairman of the Federal Reserve System warned Congress of this problem with respect to monetary policy:

> The lure of short-run gains from gunning the economy can loom large in the context of an election cycle, but the process of reaching for such gains can have costly consequences for the nation's economic performance and standards of living over the longer term. The temptation is

to step on the monetary accelerator, or at least to avoid the monetary brake, until after the next election. Giving in to such temptations is likely to impart an inflationary bias to the economy and could lead to instability, recession, and economic stagnation. Interest rates would be higher, and productivity and living standards lower, than if monetary policy were freer to approach the nation's economic goals with a longer-term perspective.[7]

Focusing decision making on outcomes in only a particular time period at the exclusion of outcomes in other periods is referred to as a *time inconsistency problem*. One study has blamed short-run projections for misleading Congress into adopting poor economic policies.[8] The differences between the partial short-term policy implications seen by Congress when it evaluates alternative policy proposals and the complete implications over a longer time frame are shown in Figure 26–2 for an expansive policy action. The unfavorable delayed effects of policy actions act like a time bomb waiting to go off after the policymakers take their bows for the favorable intermediate effects of their actions. We examine the time lags in monetary and fiscal policy in Chapter 31.

Even those policymakers appointed for longer terms of office are only partially insulated against this problem. Their appointments are recommended and approved by elected officials who have shorter time horizons and, after confirmation, they remain under varying degrees of pressure from these elected officials. Electoral mandates cannot be neglected. Like the Supreme Court, "independent" agencies tend to follow the ballot box.

In less democratic societies, the need of the governments to satisfy the economic needs of their citizens differs only in degree. Frequently, the time horizons are longer. But governments that do not achieve satisfactory economic results over some time period will be changed one way or another. Any government's life span is inversely related to the domestic rate of inflation, the rate of unemployment, and the dispersion in family incomes.

Thus, economics cannot be practiced in a vacuum. Solutions that are economically appealing may not be equally politically appealing. Conversely, solutions that are politically appealing may not be equally economically appealing. This is particularly true for restrictive economic policies to slow inflation, which by definition are intended to reduce someone's spending and income. Those affected are unlikely to sit by quietly. Alternative policies and solutions will be proposed that challenge the government. Until the cost of inflation becomes sufficiently visible and broad-based, restrictive economic policies that may be politically acceptable may well be those that are economically ineffective—all noise but little action.

Economics cannot easily be separated from politics. Indeed, until not very many years ago, economics as a discipline was referred to as **political economy**. However, economics and politics do at times conflict. Economists promise that there is no such thing as a "free lunch." Resources are scarce and choices must be made. But every choice or policy has its costs. Politicians, on the other hand, live by promises of "free lunches." As has been noted in *The Wall Street Journal*:

[7] Alan Greenspan, "Testimony," *Federal Reserve Bulletin*, December 1993, p. 1101.

[8] Preston J. Miller and Arthur J. Rolnick, "The CBO's Policy Analysis," *Journal of Monetary Economics*, April 1980, p. 181.

FIGURE

26–2

519

ECONOMIC GOALS

EFFECT OF TIME HORIZON ON EXPANSIVE POLICY IMPLICATIONS

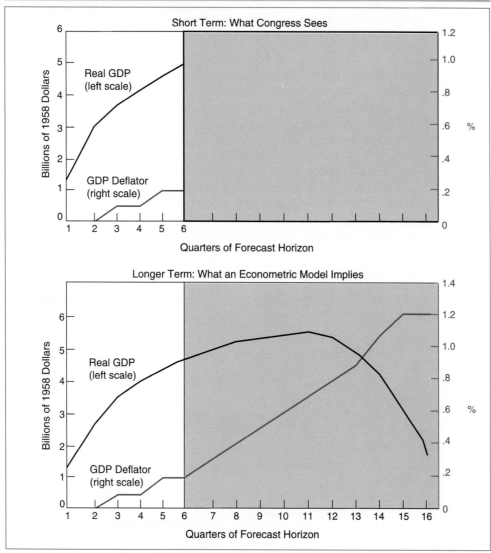

SOURCE: Preston J. Miller and Arthur J. Rolnick, "The CBO's Policy Analysis," *Journal of Monetary Economics*, April 1980, p. 181

The reason the economics profession is often held in disrepute isn't that economists don't have solutions to problems. The trouble is that the solutions they recommend may possibly be painful. . . . And, while economists propose, politicians dispose.[9]

The need for economists to recognize the political implications of their recommendations was stated clearly by Irving Kristol:

[9] Charles N. Stabler, "The Outlook," *Wall Street Journal*, April 1, 1985, p. 1.

A good economist has a mind like a razor, which is why he is so useful—and so dangerous. He is useful because he can make sense of a tangled and otherwise bewildering situation. He is dangerous because he can make only economic sense of it—and the world does not move by economic sense alone.[10]

Although economics and politics are intertwined, this should not affect the usefulness or validity of economic analysis. Economics may be defined as the art of efficient solutions, and politics as the art of possible solutions. Efficient solutions may not always be possible solutions. But they may shape what is and what is not possible and help to decide among alternative, "second-best" solutions. Economic analysis has important implications for the policies and economic performance of an economy, even those that are the most political.

The next chapters examine the Federal Reserve System as the nation's central bank, which is responsible for the formulation and execution of monetary policy; the structure of the economy—in particular, the relationship of the financial and real sectors; theories of monetary policy; and some current controversies in the use of monetary policy to achieve our economic goals.

SUMMARY

All economies have goals. Among the more important are full employment, economic growth, price stability, stability in the balance of international payments and exchange rates, equitable distribution of income, and economic efficiency. Although obvious in general terms, these goals are difficult to define precisely, and definitions differ from person to person. Regardless of their definitions, the goals may not always be attainable, particularly at the same time. Economic policies are used by governments to pressure the economy to operate closer to these target levels. Monetary policy involves changing variables in the financial sector, particularly money supply and interest rates, to affect levels of economic performance in the real sector.

Because economic policy significantly affects individual units and reflects the value judgments of policymakers, who are directly or indirectly responsible to the electorate, it is difficult to disentangle economics from politics in the short term. But economic solutions have important implications for political solutions in the longer term.

QUESTIONS

1. Why do you think an economy requires formal economic goals? How might these goals be interpreted differently in different economic systems? Would you introduce any goals in addition to those listed in the chapter?

2. Why is full employment the only goal that appears to benefit all economic units and harm none? Discuss the reasons the other goals do not do so. Why might the harm done by inflation not be as immediately visible as that done by unemployment?

[10] Irving Kristol, "The Corporation, A Last Word," *Wall Street Journal*, March 14, 1974, p. 16.

3. Evaluate the argument that the rate of unemployment consistent with a given degree of price pressure is higher now than in the 1950s. Would you consider it likely that this rate would continue to increase? Why, or why not?

4. How has the distribution of income changed in the United States in the post–World War II period? Why does there appear to be an unusual degree of confusion in formulating an answer to this question?

5. What is the basic purpose of economic policy in the United States? Why is there a need for more than one type of economic policy? Why do you think most of the policies have been designed to affect demand rather than supply?

6. "Economic and financial policy is in the end determined by politics." If this is so, why should we bother at all to study economic and financial analysis?

7. Do you think that the U.S. government cared about the state of the economy before the enactment of the Employment Act of 1946? Why or why not? If yes, why was the Employment Act passed? What difference may it have made? What are some of the problems in implementing it?

8. Look up the rate of inflation, the rate of GDP growth, and the unemployment rate for the last complete year. Do you think they indicate that the United States is achieving its economic goals? Why or why not? What has happened since? Is this an improvement or not? Why?

REFERENCES

Aaron, Henry J., ed. *Setting National Priorities: Policy for the Nineties*. Washington, D.C.: Brookings Institution, 1990.

Aaron, Henry J., et al., "Economists as Policy Advocates," *Journal of Economic Perspectives*, Summer 1992, pp. 59–77.

Blinder, Alan S., et al., "The Level and Distribution of Economic Well-Being," in Martin Feldstein, ed., *The American Economy in Transition*. Chicago: University of Chicago Press, 1980.

Bradbury, Katharine L., "The Changing Fortunes of American Families in the 1980s," *New England Economic Review*, Federal Reserve Bank of Boston, July/August 1990, pp. 25–40.

Browning, Edgar K., *Redistribution and the Welfare System*. Washington, D.C.: American Enterprise Institute, 1975.

Campbell, Colin D., ed., *Income Redistribution*. Washington, D.C.: American Enterprise Institute, 1975.

Commission on Money and Credit, *Money and Credit: Their Influence on Jobs, Prices, and Growth (Report)*. Englewood Cliffs, N.J.: Prentice Hall, 1961.

Council of Economic Advisers, "Government and the Level and Distribution of Income," *Economic Report of the President*. Washington, D.C.: Government Printing Office, 1992, pp. 115–54.

Eastburn, David, *Economic Man vs. Social Man*. Philadelphia: Federal Reserve Bank of Philadelphia, 1977.

Easterlin, Richard, "Does Money Buy Happiness?" *Public Interest*, Winter 1973.

Fischer, Stanley, and John Huizinga, "Inflation, Unemployment and Public Policy," *Journal of Money, Credit, and Banking*, February 1982, pp. 1–20.

Friedman, Milton, *Capitalism and Freedom*, Chicago: University of Chicago Press, 1962.

Hannan, Timothy, "Measuring Income Distribution in the United States," *Business Review*, Federal Reserve Bank of Philadelphia, March/April 1978, pp. 3–11.

Hargrove, Erwin, and Samuel A. Morley, *The President and the Council of Economic Advisers: Interviews with CEA Chairmen*. Boulder, Colo.: Westview Press, 1984.

Haslag, Joseph H., and Lori H. Taylor, "A Look at Long-Term Developments in the Distribution of Income," *Economic Review*, Federal Reserve Bank of Dallas, First Quarter 1993, pp. 19–30.

Kuperman, Martin, and Maurice D. Levi, *Slowth: The Changing Economy and How You Can Successfully Cope*. New York: John Wiley, 1980.

Lawrence, Robert Z., "Sector Shifts and the Size of the Middle Class," *Brookings Review*, Fall 1984, pp. 3–11.

Lekachman, Robert, and Michael Novak, "Is America Still the Land of Opportunity?" *Public Opinion*, June/July 1982, pp. 5–10, 52.

Levy, Frank, *Dollars and Dreams: The Changing American Income Distribution*. Philadelphia: Russell Sage, 1987.

Levy, Frank, and Richard Michel, "Work for Welfare: How Much Good Will it Do?" *American Economic Review*, May 1986, pp. 399–404.

Levy, Frank, and Richard J. Murmane, "U.S. Earnings Levels and Earnings Inequality," *Journal of Economic Literature*, September 1992, pp. 1333–81.

Murray, Charles, *Losing Ground: American Social Policy, 1950–1980*. New York: Basic Books, 1984.

Nasar, Sylvia, "Do We Live as Well as We Used To?" *Fortune*, September 14, 1987, pp. 32–46.

Nelson, Robert H., "The Economics Profession and the Making of Public Policy," *Journal of Economic Literature*, March 1987, pp. 49–91.

Okun, Arthur M., *Equity and Efficiency: The Big Tradeoff*. Washington, D.C.: Brookings Institution, 1975.

President's Commission on National Goals, *Goals for Americans*. Englewood Cliffs, N.J.: Prentice Hall, 1960.

Rector, Robert, and Kate W. O'Breirne, "Discompelling the Myth of Income Inequality," *Backgrounder*. Washington, D.C.: Heritage Foundation, June 6, 1989.

Sametz, A.W., "The Measurement of Economic Growth," in Eleanor Bernert, ed., *Indicators of Social Change: Concepts and Measurements*. New York: Russell Sage Foundation, 1968.

Santoni, G.J., "The Employment Act of 1946: Some Historical Notes," *Review*, Federal Reserve Bank of St. Louis, November 1986, pp. 5–16.

Schultz, George P., and Kenneth W. Dam, *Economic Policy beyond the Headlines*. New York: Norton, 1977.

Stein, Herbert, *Presidential Economics*. New York: Simon & Schuster, 1984.

Thurow, Lester, *The Zero-Sum Society, Distribution, and Possibilities for Economic Change*. New York: Basic Books, 1980.

U.S. Department of Commerce, Bureau of the Census, *Measuring the Effect of Benefits and Taxes on Income and Poverty: 1987–1988 (Supplementary Data)*. Washington, D.C., November 1990.

Weidenbaum, Murray L., *Business, Government, and the Public*, 4th ed. Englewood Cliffs, N.J.: Prentice Hall, 1990.

The Federal Reserve System: Purposes and Organization

The Federal Reserve System, or "Fed," is the central bank of the United States. It has primary responsibility for promoting conditions in the financial sector that are conducive to achieving the basic goals of full employment and balanced economic growth at stable prices. The Fed shares overall responsbility for national economic stabilization with the executive and legislative branches of the federal government, which have control over the other economic policies described in Chapter 26. In its stabilization activities, the Fed importantly affects both the money supply and interest rates. The Fed is also responsible for protecting the soundness and efficiency of the commercial banking system and the national payments system. Thus, understanding how the Fed operates is necessary for understanding how financial markets operate.

The Federal Reserve System was established by an act of Congress in 1913. The United States was late among developed countries in establishing a permanent central bank. The Bank of England was established in the 1600s and the Bank of France in 1800. Although the Fed is the first permanent central bank in American history, it was not the first central bank. Both the First (1791–1811) and Second (1816–1836) Banks of the United States performed this function, but their 20-year charters were not renewed by Congress upon expiration. It was believed by many that the operations of these banks resulted in excessive financial concentration, represented excessive federal government power, and that their policies slowed economic development and the settling of the frontier. The cost of dispensing with a central bank was periodic financial strain, characterized by bank failures and losses to depositors and investors. Whether or not a central bank would have been able to achieve the same rate of economic growth in these periods at a lower cost in financial disruption is a question for economic historians.

The combination of the closing of the frontier, rapid industrialization, equally rapid urbanization, and the growing importance of the financial sector in the economic well-being of the country finally increased the cost of financial breakdown in the early 1900s to the point where broad public support developed for a more orderly financial system. The Fed was the outcome of a thorough study of alternative financial systems sponsored by Congress in response to the financial crisis of 1907.

Like all major congressional legislation, the Federal Reserve Act represented a compromise among diverse and, at times, conflicting forces. The urban business community favored a highly centralized organization, independent of the federal government and dedicated to stabilizing the purchasing power of the dollar. Rural agricultural interests favored a decentralized, government-owned system oriented toward providing credit on liberal terms.

Decentralization was achieved by the establishment of 12 regional or district banks. These banks were "owned" by the member commercial banks, which also elected the majority of the directors. Centralization was achieved by creating a Board of Governors in Washington, D.C., whose members were appointed by the president and shared the responsibility for determining and executing policy with the regional banks. Independence from excessive government interference was achieved by providing the members of the board with very long terms and with an independent source of operating revenue.

Although the organization of the Fed has undergone considerable change since 1913, it still reflects its origins. The regional banks still exist, as does the Board of Governors. However, power has shifted from the regional banks to the board as the economy has become more centralized and the problems more national in scope.

The functions of the Federal Reserve have also changed over time. The Federal Reserve Act of 1913 stated that the purpose of the Fed was

> to furnish an elastic currency, to afford means of rediscounting commercial paper, to establish a more effective supervision of banking in the United States, and for other purposes.

An elastic currency did not mean "rubber checks." Because of its greater relative importance in those days, *currency* was the common term for money. *Elastic* referred to the ability of the money supply to support higher levels of economic activity. Before the Fed, the money supply was the responsibility of the Treasury Department, which did not have an easy way of changing the quantity of money.

In those days also the relatively primitive state of commuications and transportation was not conducive to an efficient national financial market. Rather, markets were segmented regionally and funds did not flow smoothly, quickly, or cheaply from surplus areas to deficit areas, including from urban to agricultural areas in the spring to finance planting and from agricultural to urban areas in the fall after harvests. This segmentation hampered trade. Regional money flows were lubricated by providing facilities for banks in deficit areas to borrow from the Federal Reserve at its discount window by rediscounting their loan notes, that is by using them as collateral. As rediscounting would be greater in deficit areas than in surplus areas, funds would flow in the same direction.

In addition, the Fed was charged with improving the check-clearing system to promote an efficient and nationwide payments system. (See Chapter 14.) Not until later did monetary policy become an important Federal Reserve function.

Structure of the Federal Reserve

Board of Governors

The Board of Governors is the heart of the Federal Reserve System. It consists of seven members appointed by the president subject to Senate confirmation. Terms of office are for 14 years. Members serving a complete term cannot be reappointed; those appointed to uncompleted terms may be reappointed to one complete term. The terms are staggered in such a way that, in the absence of resignations or deaths, one expires every two years. One member of the board is appointed chairman by the president for a four-year term. The chairman may be reappointed for additional terms within the constraints of the 14-year term as a member of the Board of Governors.

Alan Greenspan was appointed both a member of the Board of Governors and chairman in mid-1987. He was appointed by President Reagan and reappointed four years later by President Bush. Greenspan is the thirteenth chairman since the Fed was established in 1914 and only the seventh since it was reorganized in 1934. He followed Paul Volcker, who was appointed by President Carter in 1979 and reappointed by President Reagan in 1983. Greenspan is a business economist who had long experience both in private practice and in government. From 1974 to 1977 he served as chairman of the President's Council of Economic Advisers.

The Board of Governors has some responsibility for all tools of monetary policy. It has sole responsibility for changes in reserve requirements at all depository institutions and final responsibility for approving or denying changes in the discount rate recommended by the regional banks. The board shares responsibility for open-market operations with the regional banks. All seven board members are members of the 12-person Open Market Committee. The board has sole responsibility for all regulatory and supervisory duties assigned to the system by federal legislation. Some of these activities are, in turn, delegated to the regional banks.

The board publishes the monthly *Federal Reserve Bulletin*, which contains feature articles that analyze important current developments in the economy. The *Bulletin* also includes congressional testimony and selected statements of Federal Reserve officials, announcements of changes in Federal Reserve regulations and policies, and a wealth of economic and financial statistics. The board also publishes numerous statistical releases and an annual report that reviews and discusses Fed activities in the year. (Many releases and reports are available free of charge from the Board of Governors of the Federal Reserve System, Washington, D.C. 20551.)

Federal Open Market Committee (FOMC)

The Federal Open Market Committee (FOMC) consists of 12 members. All seven members of the Board of Governors are permanent members; the other five are presidents of regional reserve banks. The president of the New York Federal Reserve Bank is a permanent member; the presidents of the other reserve banks serve for one-year terms, with an established rotation so that four are members at any one time. The chairman of the Board of Governors always serves as chairman of the FOMC, and the president of the Federal Reserve Bank of New York as vice-chairman.

The FOMC is responsible for domestic open-market operations to affect money supply and interest rates and for transactions in foreign currencies to affect exchange rates. The FOMC meets about once every six weeks in Washington, D.C. Interim emergency meetings may be conducted by conference telephone.

Regional Banks

The 12 regional or district banks are located in Boston, New York, Philadelphia, Cleveland, Richmond, Atlanta, Chicago, St. Louis, Minneapolis, Kansas City, Dallas, and San Francisco. There are also 25 branches of the district banks. A map of the 12 districts is shown in Figure 27–1. The boundaries of the districts reflect the demographic and economic characteristics of the United States in 1913. There have been only minor adjustments in the boundaries since then.

The regional reserve banks are technically "owned" by the member commercial banks. Member banks subscribe to the stock of their district Fed in a fixed proportion of their capital, receive dividends, and elect some of the members of the regional board of directors. But the ownership does not carry the proprietary rights usually associated with private ownership. The shares are not transferable and must be sold back to the Fed when the bank leaves the system. Dividends are restricted to 6 percent of the par value of the stock. The member banks have little if any direct voice in monetary policy and, where they do have some, their actions are subject to review and denial by the Board of Governors.

Each regional bank has a nine-person board of directors. Three are bankers elected by the district member banks. Each member bank votes for one director from a bank of its own deposit-size group. Three directors are nonbankers, also elected by the member banks. The remaining three are appointed by the Board of Governors as "public" members. (In recent years, bills to broaden representation by increasing the number of public members have been introduced in Congress.) The board appoints one of the public members to be chairman and another to be deputy chairman. Each regional branch has a separate board of directors of five or seven people. The majority are appointed by the board of the home-district bank and the remainder by the Board of Governors.

The functions of the board of directors of each regional bank are to

1. Elect the president of the bank, subject to approval by the Board of Governors,
2. Review and change the discount rate, subject to final determination by the Board of Governors,
3. Approve and review loans to banks and other eligible financial institutions from the discount window,
4. Oversee the operations of the bank, and
5. Provide an ongoing two-way channel of communications between the Federal Reserve and the constituencies represented by each director.

The functions of the regional banks and branches include

1. Operating as clearing mechanism for paper checks and electronic funds,
2. Providing for rapid transfers of bank reserves by telegraphic wire,
3. Examining member banks,
4. Providing loans to depository institutions through the discount window,
5. Providing currency and other services for depository institutions,
6. Perform regulatory and supervisory duties delegated to them by the Board of Governors, including the preparation of analyses and advisory opinions on consolidations and holding company acquisitions,
7. Performing research activities for the bank president as a policymaker on the FOMC, and
8. Providing information to district member banks and the general public on monetary policy, the state of the economy, developments in the financial sector, and so on. All the banks publish periodic reviews, newsletters, and statistical releases. (Most of these may be obtained free of charge by writing to the reserve banks. Their addresses appear in the *Federal Reserve Bulletin*.)

Independence of the Federal Reserve

There is widespread agreement that government regulatory agencies should be insulated from short-run and partisan political pressures. Efficiency should be the overriding priority of the regulators. In this country, there is a long tradition of "independent" regulatory agencies. The role of Congress and the executive branch is to determine broad policy objectives, appoint the regulators, oversee and evaluate their operations, and consider necessary changes. But in its daily operations, the agency is to be free of partisan interference. Similarly, it is widely agreed that monetary policy should also be insulated from partisan short-run political pressure.

Independence is granted the Federal Reserve System by the long and staggered terms of the governors and a source of income that is not subject to congressional purse-string approval and thus to Congress's "golden rule"—he or she who has the gold, rules. In the absence of resignations, the president can appoint only two governors per four-year term, or a maximum of four over two four-year terms. The long terms tend to make appointees independent of their sponsors. The beginning date of the chairman's four-year term is not fixed but is dependent on the resignation of his or her predecessor. At present, the chairman's term expires in the middle of the third year of the president's term; but this is not fixed. On the whole, chairmen tend to serve lengthy periods. As noted earlier, there have been only seven chairmen between 1934 and 1994—Mariner Eccles (1934–1948), Thomas McCabe (1948–1951), William McChesney Martin (1951–1970), Arthur Burns (1970–1978), G. William Miller (1978–1979), Paul Volcker (1979–1987), and Alan Greenspan (1987—   ).

The Fed derives most of its revenues from interest income on its large portfolio of Treasury securities purchased in the course of open-market operations. In 1992, this source accounted for some 85 percent of the Fed's $20 billion total earnings. Revenues from charges on bank services, such as check clearing, accounted for 4 percent of revenues. Operating expenses totaled $1.4 billion, or only 7 percent. Less than 1 percent was paid in dividends to member banks. Almost all of the remainder was returned to the U.S. Treasury. Like Rockefeller, the Fed gains considerable independence from its income!

But, although insulated in the short term, the Fed is not insulated in the longer term. The limits of its independence are clearly delineated. The Fed was established by an act of Congress and, like any agency so created, can be changed or terminated altogether by Congress. What Congress creates it can destroy! As noted earlier, the lives of the First and Second Banks of the United States were terminated at the expiration of their charters. Although they did not terminate the Fed's charter, the Banking Acts of 1933 and 1935 drastically altered the structure of the system. Among other things, these acts shifted the power from the regional banks to the Board of Governors. Less major changes are made by Congress almost every session. By giving it control over reserve requirements on transaction deposits at some 30,000 depository instutitions rather than at only 5,000 member commercial banks, the Depository Institutions Deregulation and Monetary Control Act of 1980 greatly enhanced the Fed's power.

The Fed is subject to all the laws of the United States, including the Employment Act of 1946 and the Full Employment and Balanced Growth Act of 1978, which come closest to spelling out the economic responsibilities of the federal government discussed in Chapter 26. Board members and staff personnel testify in Congress almost weekly. The chairman or his representative generally meets weekly with counterparts at the Treasury, the Council of Economic Advisers, and the Office of Management and Budget, and occasionally attends cabinet meetings. Other board members and their staff meet regularly, with their counterparts in other areas of the government.

Moreover, although their terms are long in theory, most members of the Board of governors serve less than the full 14-year term. Many resign before the end of their terms, others are appointed to complete an unexpired term and are not reappointed, and a few have died in office. Only three of the 37 governors appointed since 1945, who were not in office on January 1, 1993, served 14 years or longer. (A member can serve more than 14 years if initially appointed to fill an unexpired term and then reappointed to his or her own term.) One-half served less than five years. The average term served was only seven years.[1] The length of service has been declining. Between 1945 and 1969, the average term served was nine years; between 1970 and 1992, it dropped to only five years. Both Presidents Nixon and Carter were able to appoint a majority of the seven board members, including the chairman, in their first term, and President Reagan appointed all seven board members in his two terms.

The Fed is sometimes referred to as "the Supreme Court of finance." And like the judicial court, board members have been known to "follow the ballot box." A study of Federal Reserve monetary policy in the post-World War II period found dramatic shifts in policy whenever the presidency changed, to bring it more in line with the policies of the new president regardless of the personal policies of the chairman or of the president who appointed him.[2] Former Chairman Martin liked to describe the Fed as "independent within the government, not of the government." How independent the Federal Reserve and other central banks actually are in practice is examined in Chapter 34.

Federal Reserve Balance Sheet and Reserves

Monetary policy is now the most important and visible function of the Federal Reserve. Monetary policy implies control of the money supply to help achieve the economic goals of the economy discussed in Chapter 26. As we saw in Chapter 15, the stock of money in circulation at any time is a multiple of the dollar amount of bank (depository institution) reserves. Where do bank reserves come from? For the most part, banks hold their cash reserves in the form of deposits at their regional reserve bank or at other larger banks that, in turn, hold reserves at the Fed. Banks also hold a small amount of cash in their vaults to satisfy customers who wish to cash checks or withdraw funds from their deposit accounts. Although the reserves are assets to the depository institutions, they are liabilities to the Fed. As such, they are created when the Fed sells secondary securities to the banks, much as bank deposits are created when banks sell their secondary securities to the public. The amount of secondary securities the Fed sells is affected by changes in the other accounts on the Fed's balance sheet. To understand why and how the dollar amount of bank reserves changes, it is necessary to identify the other accounts on the Fed's balance

[1] Excludes governors who died in office. Some of the resignations may have been encouraged by the relatively low salaries paid board members in comparison with similar positions in private industry. In 1993, the salaries of governors were $123,100. The chairman received an additional $10,500. Although low in comparison with private industry, those salaries compare favorably with those paid in academe. This may explain the longer term of service of the governors appointed from universities. The average term of office of those seven governors was nine years, compared with the overall average of seven years.

[2] Robert Weintraub, "Congressional Supervision of Monetary Policy," *Journal of Monetary Economics*, April 1978.

TABLE 27-1	CONSOLIDATED BALANCE SHEET OF FEDERAL RESERVE BANKS, SEPTEMBER 8, 1993 (BILLIONS OF DOLLARS, WEEKLY AVERAGES)		

| | Week Ending September 8, 1993 | Change from Week Ending | |
		September 1, 1993	September 9, 1992
Assets			
Gold and SDRS	18.1	—	−2.0
U.S. government securities	327.2	+1.3	+39.0
Float	32.0	+0.9	+0.4
Loans	0.6	+0.5	+0.6
Other assets	23.8	+0.4	+0.5
Total	401.7	+3.1	+38.5
Liabilities			
Currency	351.3	+2.9	+31.9
Treasury deposits	5.9	+0.4	—
Bank reserves at Fed	27.4	−0.6	+5.4
Other liabilities	17.1	+0.4	—
Total	401.7	+3.1	+38.5

SOURCE: Board of Governors of the Federal Reserve System, "Factors Affecting Reserve Balances at Depository Institutions," (H.4.1), September 9, 1993.

sheet and to examine why and how they change. The major accounts on the balance sheet are shown in Table 27–1 and are defined in the next sections.

Assets

Gold Certificates and SDRs (*G*). The Treasury Department sells gold to the Fed in exchange for money balances and buys gold from the Fed as a result of its transactions with foreign countries. In reality, the Treasury maintains the official gold stock of the country and issues certificates against it to the Fed. Changes in gold certificates or SDRs (special drawing rights), an international paper currency issued by the International Monetary Fund (see Chapter 25), reflect changes in the international financial position of the United States vis-à-vis foreign countries. Decreases in gold reflect official foreign government purchases. The gold is purchased with balances held by the foreign governments at U.S. commercial banks. Because the payment is, in effect, to the Fed, this transaction reduces bank deposits and bank reserves. Since 1971, gold has not been used as a major international currency, and changes in this account have been small. In this period, gold has been supplemented as the ultimate international reserve by SDRs. Causes of changes in SDRs are similar to those for gold, and the two may be combined for analyzing the causes of changes in bank reserves.

Loans (*L*). Like you and me, banks periodically need to borrow money. Banks may obtain loans for short periods of time at the Fed's discount window. (The discount window does not exist physically; it is only an expression.) Borrowers are charged an interest rate referred to as the **discount rate.** The discount window and the discount rate are discussed in greater detail in the next chapter.

Securities (S). These securities are the investment portfolio of the Fed. They consist mostly of Treasury securities, but the Fed is authorized to trade also in government agency issues. Changes in the securities account reflect transactions incurred in open-market operations, the major tool of monetary policy. These changes are discussed more fully in the next section and in the next chapter.

Fed Float (F). As discussed in Chapter 14, Fed float represents the difference between the asset account cash items in the process of collection (CIPC) and the liability account deferred availability of cash items (DACI). Float arises from the check-clearing process, when the Fed pays the amount of the check to the receiving bank (reducing DACI) before it has collected the proceeds from the paying bank (reducing CIPC). Increases in Fed float increase bank reserves; decreases decrease reserves.

Liabilities

Federal Reserve Notes (C). Federal Reserve notes constitute 90 percent of the coin and currency in circulation. The remainder is a perpetual liability of the Treasury.

Deposits (D). Three groups may hold deposits at reserve banks:

- ▼ U.S. *Treasury (TD).* The Treasury maintains its working balance at the Fed, from which it pays all its bills. (The next time you receive a check from the federal government for a tax refund or whatever, examine it. You will find that it is drawn on a regional Federal Reserve Bank.) This is a small account, however. The majority of Treasury funds are held at commercial banks, where they earn interest. When the Treasury wishes to replenish its working balance at the Fed, it transfers funds from the commercial banks, reducing bank reserves in the process. When recipients deposit their Treasury checks, bank reserves are rebuilt.
- ▼ *Foreign governments and official international institutions (FD).* These units hold some working balances at the Fed as an alternative to balances at commercial banks.
- ▼ *Banks (R).* These deposits are the reserves depository institutions are required to hold or want to hold in excess of the required amount, outside of the amount of coin and currency they hold in their own vaults (vault cash). Banks may also hold additional balances required for use of Fed check-clearing services. Balances held at the Fed do not earn interest. These reserves are assets of the commercial banks and liabilities of the Federal Reserve.

These accounts may be summarized in equation form by relying on one of the fundamental laws of finance: the balance sheet must balance, or total assets must equal total liabilities:

$$\text{Total assets} = \text{Total liabilities}$$
$$G + L + S + F = C + TD + FD + R$$

We can rearrange the terms in this equation to focus in on reserves:

$$R = G + L + S + F - C - TD - FD$$

It can be seen that changes in reserves vary directly on a one-to-one basis with changes in asset accounts and inversely with changes in liability accounts. Increases in assets increase reserves, and increases in liabilities decrease reserves. For example, when the Fed buys $1,000 of securities from the public, it pays for them with a check drawn on itself, S increases by $1,000. When the seller deposits the check at a bank, bank deposits increase by $1,000. The bank sends the check to the Fed for collection and receives a $1,000 increase in its reserve account, or R. The money supply can expand by a multiple of this amount.

If a bank customer withdraws $1,000 in currency, C increases. The bank will replenish its supply of currency from the Fed. In payment, the Fed will reduce the bank's reserve account by this amount. R declines by an equal amount. Note that an exchange of a deposit for an equal amount of currency leads to a reduction in the money supply. This occurs because the reduction in reserves from the currency outflow will decrease deposits by a multiple amount, so that deposits will decline by more than the increase in currency.

Control of Reserves

Can the Federal Reserve control the total amount of bank reserves? An analysis of the accounts on the Fed's balance sheet indicates that most of them are not under the control of the Fed. The Fed controls totally only the amount of securities in its portfolio. It controls loans to banks partially by setting the discount rate. Banks, of course, can choose to borrow or not at this price; many can raise funds quickly alternatively through Fed funds, CDs, or Eurodollars. The higher the discount rate, *ceteris paribus*, the less banks will want to borrow at the discount window. All other accounts on its balance sheet are outside Fed control.

The quantity of gold and SDRs is determined by the international position of the United States, Fed float by the public's check-writing patterns and by weather and other delays in check clearing, notes by the public's demand for currency (excess currency is returned to the banks for deposits), Treasury deposits by the Treasury, and foreign deposits by foreign governments. Thus, at first glance, it may appear that changes in bank reserves may or may not be attributed to Fed actions. But the Fed could, if it so wanted, act to offset reserve changes from accounts not under its control through open-market security transactions. (How they do so is described in the next chapter.) If an increase in currency threatened to reduce reserves by more than the Fed felt desirable, it could offset some or all of the decrease by purchasing Treasury securities.

This indeed happens. As Figure 27–2 shows, between 1950 and 1992, currency increased some $300 billion and gold decreased $10 billion. Yet, rather than decreasing by $310 billion, bank reserves increased about $30

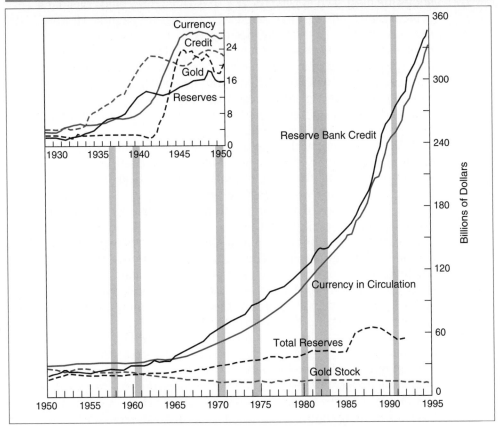

FIGURE

27–2   MAJOR CHANGES IN FED BALANCE SHEET, 1930–1992

SOURCE: Board of Governors of the Federal Reserve System, *1987 Historical Chart Book*, p. 2, updated by author.

billion. The major offsetting item was Fed credit (defined as security hold-ings, loans, and Fed float), which increased $320 billion. Thus, the Fed determines the total size of the reserve pie and the individual banks deter-mine how it is divided up among themselves.

Interpreting the Balance Sheet

Because of their relationship to both money supply and interest rates and because the Federal Reserve does not provide day-to-day information on its monetary policy operations, bank reserves are viewed as an important indicator of Federal Reserve policy. Changes in the Fed's balance sheet are carefully scrutinized by the financial community for clues to the Fed's intent. The Fed releases data on its balance sheet every Thursday afternoon for the week ending Wednesday. These data are published in many news-papers.

The balance sheet for the week ending September 8, 1993 is summa-rized in Table 27–1. The Fed's portfolio holdings of U.S. government securities increased $1.3 billion over the previous week. Because changes in this account are totally under Fed control and reflect open-market operations, many analysts assign particular attention to them. (Fed open market operations are discussed in Chapter 28.) These analysts would consider a weekly increase to indicate that the Fed is "easing up" slightly. However, bank reserves at the Fed actually decreased in this week.[3] This decrease in reserves gives a different interpretation of Fed policy—the Fed is "tightening up." The increase in Fed holdings of government securities appears to have been in response to a $2.9 billion increase in the public's holding of currency, probably for use over the long Labor Day weekend, which absorbed reserves. Without the Fed's increase in security holdings, bank reserves would have decreased by nearly $2 billion.

Thus, evaluating changes in securities in isolation from the other accounts may be misleading. Part or all of these changes may reflect Fed actions undertaken to offset changes in other balance-sheet accounts rather than to change reserves. Open-market operations conducted by the Fed for such purposes are referred to as **defensive** operations. The appropriate account to examine is the reserve account. But even the decline in reserves in the week just cited may not be indicative of increasing monetary restraint. Although the Fed conducts monetary policy to affect income, employment, and prices, in the short run it also operates to stabilize the money market to reduce sharp, self-reversing swings in interest rates. The Fed believes that such fluctuations discourage use of the financial markets and are detrimental to economic efficiency.

You may recall from Chapter 5 that, *ceteris paribus*, interest rates and reserves (or money) tend to be inversely related. Increases in reserves lower interest rates, and decreases raise rates. Thus, reserve changes in any one week could reflect the Fed's desire to offset pressures on interest rates from sources not originating on the Fed's balance sheet by injecting or absorbing reserves temporarily. For example, upward pressures on interest rates could originate from an increase in the demand for money, the issuance of a new, large bond issue, and so on. To be able to distinguish short-term defensive operations on the Fed's balance sheet from longer-term **dynamic** open-market operations conducted to affect income and prices; the analyst must trace changes in reserves for a longer period of time, maybe as long as three to six months. Changes in reserves that persist over such long periods may reliably be attributed to Fed actions to affect prices, employment, and production. Reserve changes over shorter periods are likely to reflect the Fed's attempts to smooth interest rate fluctuations.

This analysis indicates that the interpretation of the Fed's weekly balance sheet depends on the particular needs of the analyst. A daily participant in the money market, such as a securities dealer, would be interested in all Fed operations that affect interest rates, defensive as well as dynamic. Thus, he or she would analyze short-run changes in all the accounts. On the other hand, if you were a business manager, you might be interested primarily in predicting changes in prices, employment, and production. You would want to separate dynamic from defensive operations and look only at longer-term changes in reserves. Thus, to obtain useful information from

---

[3] This excludes balances banks hold to support their check-clearing activities and reserves held in the form of vault cash.

the Fed balance sheet requires considerable care and skill. A hasty reading may produce more misinformation than information.

SUMMARY

The Federal Reserve System is the central bank of the United States. It has the responsibility for conducting monetary policy to help achieve the goals of the economy. The primary policymaking groups in the Fed are the seven-person Board of Governors in Washington, D.C., and the 12-person Federal Open Market Committee, whose membership consists of the seven governors and five regional Federal Reserve Bank presidents. The chief Federal Reserve official is the chairman of the Board of Governors, who is appointed by the president.

Primarily because of its ability to create reserves and therefore money, and because of the long terms of the governors, the Fed is reasonably independent of short-run political pressures. But because it was created by Congress and can be changed by Congress, the Fed is not immune to long-term political pressures.

The Fed operates directly on bank reserves. These are a liability of the Fed and are affected by changes in all asset accounts and other liability accounts on the Federal Reserve balance sheet. Changes in the published weekly balance sheet are viewed as important clues to Fed monetary policy conduct. To interpret policy correctly, it is necessary to differentiate between the more frequent short-run defensive operations undertaken to stabilize the money market and the less frequent dynamic operations undertaken to affect levels of income, prices, and production.

QUESTIONS

1. Why may the Federal Reserve have succeeded where the First and Second Banks of the United States failed so that they were not rechartered by the federal government?
2. What were the major reasons for the establishment of the Federal Reserve in 1913? What was the importance of monetary policy at the time? How has technology played a part in changing the functions of the Fed over time?
3. Why do you think the power in the Federal Reserve System has shifted from the district reserve banks, when the system was organized in 1913, to the Board of Governors? Why might quasi-independent district reserve banks have been more suitable in 1913 than now?
4. Why is the Board of Governors the most important policymaking group in the Federal Reserve System? In your library, find the identities of the current members of the board. What are their professional backgrounds?
5. What is meant by the "independence" of the Federal Reserve System? What are the limitations to this independence?
6. Assume that Fed holdings of U.S. government securities increased $2 billion in a hypothetical particular week. Does this increase indicate that the Fed was pursuing an expansive monetary policy? Why or why not? If not, what more evidence would you want?
7. Why do many financial analysts and Fed watchers pay attention to weekly changes in the Federal Reserve balance sheet? Why might different analysts focus attention on different accounts and/or time periods? Is it possible for Fed holdings of Treasury securities and Fed reserves to change in opposite directions in a particular week? How could this happen?

REFERENCES

Board of Governors of the Federal Reserve System, *The Federal Reserve Discount Window*. Washington, D.C., October 1980.

Board of Governors of the Federal Reserve System, *The Federal Reserve System: Purposes and Functions*. Washington, D.C., 1984.

Broaddus, Alfred, *A Primer on the Fed*. Richmond, Va.: Federal Reserve Bank of Richmond, 1988.

Brockschmidt, Peggy, and Carl Gambs, "Federal Reserve Pricing—A New Era," *Economic Review*, Federal Reserve Bank of Kansas City, July/August 1981, pp. 3–15.

Dykes, Sayre F., "The Establishment and Evolution of the Federal Reserve Board: 1913–23," *Federal Reserve Bulletin*, April 1989, pp. 227–43.

"The Federal Reserve System—Its Purpose and Work," *Annals of the American Academy of Political and Social Science*, January 1922.

Gonczy, Anne Marie, *Modern Money Mechanics*. Chicago: Federal Reserve Bank of Chicago, 1992.

Greenspan, Alan, "Testimony," *Federal Reserve Bulletin*, December 1993, pp. 1101–1107. (The Chairman of the Fed explains the structure and operations of the system.)

Havrilesky, Thomas, *The Pressures on American Monetary Policy*, Boston: Kluwer Academic, 1992.

Johnson, Roger T. *Historical Beginnings . . . The Federal Reserve*. Boston: Federal Reserve Bank of Boston. 1977.

Kane, Edward J., "The Impact of a New Federal Reserve Chairman," *Contemporary Policy Issues*, January 1988, pp. 89–97.

Maisel, Sherman J., *Managing the Dollar*. New York: Norton, 1973.

Mayer, Thomas, "The Structure and Operation of the Federal Reserve System: Some Needed Reforms," in U.S. Congress, House Committee on Banking, Currency, and Housing, *FINE— Financial Institutions and the Nation's Economy: Compendium of Papers Prepared for the Fine Study*, Book II, 94th Cong., 2nd sess. (Committee Print), June 1976.

Melton, William C., *Inside the Fed: Making Monetary Policy*, Homewood, Ill.: Dow Jones-Irwin, 1985.

Meulendyke, Ann-Marie, *U.S. Monetary Policy and Financial Markets*, New York: Federal Reserve Bank of New York, 1989.

Meyer, Stephen A., "Non-Open-Market Monetary Policy Operations," *Business Review*, Federal Reserve Bank of Philadelphia, January/February 1988, pp. 3–15.

Murray, Alan, "Fed Banks' Presidents Hold Private Positions But More Public Role," *Wall Street Journal*, August 1, 1991, pp. A1, A7.

Parnow, C.J., *A Day at the Fed*. New York: Federal Reserve Bank of New York, 1980.

Parthemos, James, "The Federal Reserve Act of 1913 in the Stream of U.S. Monetary History," *Economic Review*, Federal Reserve Bank of Richmond, July/August 1988, pp. 19–28.

Partlan, John C., et al., "Reserves Forecasting for Open Market Operations," *Quarterly Review*, Federal Reserve Bank of New York, Spring 1986, pp. 19–33.

Reagan, Michael, "The Political Structure of the Federal Reserve System," *American Political Science Review*, March 1961, pp. 64–76.

Rowe, J.Z., *The Public-Private Character of United States Central Banking*. New Brunswick, N.J.: Rutgers University Press, 1965.

Samansky, Arthur W., *Statfacts: Understanding Federal Reserve Statistical Reports*. New York: Federal Reserve Bank of New York, 1981.

Stevens, E.J., "Comparing Central Banks," *Economic Review*, Federal Reserve Bank of Cleveland, Fall 1992, pp. 2–15.

U.S. Congress, Joint Economic Committee, *Monetary Reform and Economic Stability: Hearings*, 98th Cong., 2nd sess., May/June 1984.

U.S. Congress, Subcommittee on Domestic Finance, House Committee on Banking and Currency, *The Federal Reserve System after Fifty Years: Hearings*, Vols. 1, 2, 3, 1964.

Weintraub, Robert E., "Congressional Supervision of Monetary Policy," *Journal of Monetary Economics*, April 1978, pp. 325–88.

Wooley, John T., *Monetary Politics: The Federal Reserve and the Politics of Monetary Policy*. Cambridge: Cambridge University Press, 1984.

The Federal Reserve System: Tools and Instruments

The Federal Reserve uses two types of instruments or tools to influence financial and economic conditions in order to achieve the goals of the economy discussed in Chapter 26: (1) **quantitative tools** and (2) **qualitative** or **selective tools.** Quantitative tools affect the aggregate supply of money and credit. They are used to influence aggregate levels of income production, employment, and prices. Expansive policy actions that increase the supply of money are undertaken to stimulate aggregate spending, and restrictive actions that decrease (or slow the rate of growth of) the supply of money are undertaken to slow aggregate spending. Qualitative tools affect the ownership mix of money and credit. They are used primarily to change the distribution of spending and income among sectors of the economy. We can diagram the linkage between the Fed and the economy as

$$R \rightarrow M \rightarrow Y$$

The Fed operates directly on reserves (R) to affect the quantity and mix of money (M), which, in turn, affects levels and growth of economic activity (Y). In this chapter, we examine the link between R and M. In later chapters, we examine the link between M and Y. The complete transmission process, from the time the Fed takes a policy action that changes bank reserves and deposits (discussed in this chapter) to the time it affects the ultimate goals of policy, is described in Chapter 31.

Quantitative Tools

It was shown in Chapter 15 that the stock of money, however defined, is some multiple of the dollar amount of total bank reserves (R), where the value of the money multiplier (k) depends on the definition of money, on the reserve-requirement ratios established by the Federal Reserve, and on excess reserve and currency leakages:

$$M = kR$$

where

$$k = \frac{1 + c}{rr_D + e + c}$$

as defined in Chapter 15. Changes in the money supply may occur from changes in k or R. This may be written in approximate form as

$$\Delta M = k\Delta R + R\Delta k$$

Quantitative tools operate on either k or R. The Fed has one tool to affect k and two tools to affect R.

Changing the Multiplier (k)

Reserve Requirements.   Reserve requirements are the only variable in the money multiplier completely under the control of the Fed. By changing the required-reserve ratios, the Fed changes the value of the multiplier in the opposite direction. For example, if we assume only transaction deposits and no leakages, a *ceteris paribus* reduction in reserve requirements from 20 percent to 10 percent of deposits for all banks would increase the multiplier from 5(1/0.20) to 10(1/0.10) and the money supply from $500 to $1,000 for every $100 of reserves. This is shown in the following T account for the banking system as a whole:

Reduction in Reserve Requirements

A. $rr = 20\%$				B. $rr = 10\%$		
Reserves	10,000	50,000	Deposits	Reserves	10,000	100,000 Deposits
Loans	40,000			Loans	90,000	

An increase in reserve requirements from 20 percent to 25 percent would decrease this multiplier from 5 to 4 and the money supply from $500 to $400 for every $100 of reserves. Thus, when the Fed wishes to increase the money supply, it decreases reserve requirements, and when it wishes to decrease the money supply, it increases the requirements. The Depository Institutions Deregulation and Monetary Control Act of 1980 extended the Federal Reserve's reserve requirement powers from only member commerical banks to all commercial banks, savings and loan associations, savings banks, and credit unions offering transaction deposits.

In reality, statutory reserve requirements are more complex and vary according to both the type of deposit and the amount of the particular deposit held by the depository institution. Generally, reserve requirements are higher on transaction than on nontransaction deposits and increase the larger the amount of deposits at the institution. Since 1980, no reserve requirements have been levied on personal savings or time deposits, and since 1991 none has been levied on any savings or time deposits. Thus, reserve requirements are currently levied only on transaction deposits. Deposit flows among different types of deposits or different-sized depository institutions thus may affect the value of the actual multiplier. Reserve-requirement ratios for depository institutions in effect in January 1994 are shown in Table 28–1.

Reserve requirements may be changed by the Fed within limits established by Congress. Currently, reserves are required only against transaction balances and are computed against average deposits for a two-week reserve computation period, running from a Tuesday through the second Monday. The requirements may be satisfied on a daily-average basis. Thus, an individual institution may fall short of its dollar requirement on some days as long as it exceeds the requirement on other days, so that the average for the reserve period is no less than the required amount. The reserves must be held during a two-week reserve maintenance period, starting on

TABLE

28–1

RESERVE REQUIREMENTS FOR DEPOSITORY INSTITUTIONS (PERCENT), JANUARY 1994

| | Net Transaction Accounts[a] | | Time Deposits | |
			Savings and Personal Time Deposits	Non-personal Time Deposits[b]
	$0–52 Million	Over $52 Million		
In effect	3	10	0	0
Legal limits				
Minimum	3	8	0	0
Maximum	3	14[c]	0	9

SOURCE: Board of Governors of the Federal Reserve System.

NOTE: Required reserves must be held in the form of deposits with Federal Reserve Banks or vault cash. Non-Federal Reserve members may maintain reserves on a pass-through basis with certain approved institutions.

[a] Transaction accounts include all deposits on which the account holder is permitted to make withdrawals by negotiable or transferable instruments, payment orders of withdrawal, and telephone and preauthorized transfers in excess of three per month for the purpose of making payments to third persons or others. However, MMDAs and similar accounts that permit no more than six preauthorized, automatic, or other transfers per month, of which no more than three can be checks, are not transaction accounts (such accounts are savings deposits).

[b] Includes Eurocurrency liabilities.

[c] The Board of Governors may impose an additional 4 percent requirement in emergencies.

the Thursday after the start of the deposit computation period on Tuesday and ending on the second Wednesday. The dollar reserves may be held on deposit at the Fed or at a correspondent bank or in the bank's own vault.

The Fed does not change reserve requirements frequently. Since 1960, such changes have averaged fewer than two per year. In part, requirements have been changed sparingly because even a change of a small fraction—say, ¼ of one percentage point—will produce a large dollar change in deposits. Changes of less than ¼ of one percentage point are considered unnecessarily confusing to the banks. Changes in reserve requirements affect depository institutions quickly and generally are a strong indicator of Federal Reserve intent.

Changing the Amount of Reserves (R)

Discount Rate. The discount rate is the interest rate the Fed charges depository institutions for borrowing reserves at the discount window. The discount rate is the oldest tool of monetary policy and is referred to as the *bank rate* in some countries. Because, as the central bank, the Fed has the important responsibility of being the *lender of last resort* and providing liquidity to the economy, it is always ready to lend to banks in need. Banks may borrow at their Federal Reserve Banks under three programs:

▼ *Adjustment credit*—available on a short-term basis to assist in meeting temporary requirements for funds.

▼ *Seasonal credit*—available to smaller institutions for periods up to nine months to accommodate large recurring intrayear need for funds that is not met by corresponding deposit inflows.

▼ *Extended credit*—available to all institutions on a longer-term basis to meet serious liquidity strains or financial difficulties where failure to obtain credit would adversely affect the economy. The interest rate charged may be above the basic discount rate.

Since the enactment of the Depository Institutions Deregulation and Monetary Control Act in 1980, the Fed discount window is open to all depository institutions, not only to member commercial banks.

Although the discount window is never closed to needy institutions, the Fed can change the incentive for institutions to borrow by changing the discount rate relative to market interest rates on comparable sources of funds. The lower the discount rate, *ceteris paribus*, the more banks are encouraged to borrow at the Fed rather than elsewhere, particularly for adjustment or seasonal credit. Conversely, the higher the discount rate, *ceteris paribus*, the less banks are encourged to borrow from the Fed. As was discussed in Chapter 27 and is shown in the T account that follows, when a bank borrows at the Fed, the Fed credits its reserve account by the amount of the borrowing, and reserves increase for the banking system as a whole as well as at the indiviudal bank.

Reduction in Discount Rate Increases Borrowing from Federal Reserve
(*rr* = 20%)

A. Before Borrowing				B. After Borrowing			
Reserves	10,000	50,000	Deposits	Reserves	11,000	55,000	Deposits
Loans	40,000			Loans	45,000	1,000	Borrowing at at Fed

Deposits can expand by a multiple of the reserve injection. Thus, bank borrowing from the Fed differs from bank borrowing elsewhere, which primarily redistributes the existing amount of reserves among the banks but does not increase them or aggregate deposits in the banking system. Banks are not required to hold reserves against borrowings from the Fed, so that a dollar of borrowed reserves can expand bank loans more than a dollar of deposits or unborrowed reserves. This can be seen from the T account. A $1,000 increase in reserves obtained through open-market operations would increase loans by only $4,000, to $44,000 (see page 544), when reserve requirements are 20 percent, rather than by $5,000, to $45,000. Decreases in the discount rate are expansionary and increases are restrictive.

However, changes in the discount rate are difficult to interpret for several reasons. Because the incentive for bank borrowing is related to the discount rate relative to market rates that determine a bank's cost of borrowing elsewhere, the Fed may change the discount rate in response to changes in market rates just to maintain the same incentive. Some analysts give greater meaning to discount rate changes that alter its relationship with market interest rates than to those changes that maintain it.

In addition, although the discount rate is a bank's cost of borrowing from the Fed, it is not the only cost. The Fed does not view the discount window as a permanent source of funds to individual institutions and limits its nonemergency access to it by administrative surveillance. It considers discounting "a privilege, not a right." If it feels a bank is abusing its right to

FIGURE

28–1

FEDERAL RESERVE DISCOUNT RATE MOVES CLOSELY
WITH SHORT-TERM MARKET RATES

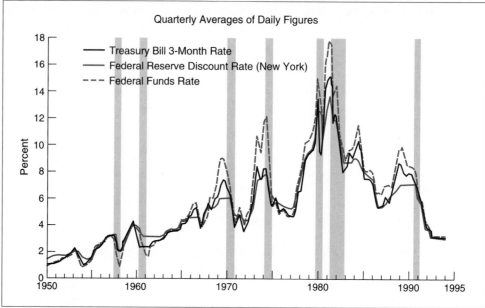

Quarterly Averages of Daily Figures

SOURCE: Federal Reserve Bank of Chicago.

NOTE: Shaded areas represent periods of economic recession.

tap the window, the Fed "reviews" the proper role of the facility with the bank's senior management. To avoid such administrative discipline, banks limit their use of the window for adjustment credit. Thus, the nominal discount rate may differ from the effective rate recognized by bankers and at times may explain poorly the amount of bank borrowing. This is the reason that the Fed funds rate is often above the discount rate in Figure 28–1. There is more to the discount rate than meets the eye of a nonbanker! (The Fed may charge above the discount rate for some extended borrowings and, since 1992, for seasonal borrowings.)

Because of the surveillance of the discount window to appropriate uses, the window is used most frequently by smaller banks, and borrowed reserves account for a larger percentage of total reserves and deposits at smaller banks, whose funding alternatives for adjusting their assets and liabilities are more limited than those of larger banks. This may be seen from Table 28–2. Except for very brief periods of time, borrowed reserves rarely account for more than 5 percent of total reserves.

The discount rate is changed much more frequently than are reserve requirements. In the 1980s, the discount rate was changed an average of about four times annually. Since 1960, the rate has fluctuated between a low of 3 percent and a high of 14 percent. Recent changes in the discount rate are shown in Figure 28–1. Not surprisingly, because the Fed generally tries to keep the discount rate in line with market interest rates, changes in the discount rate parallel changes in short-term market rates. The changes

Consecutive Reserve Weeks of Borrowing		Weeks of Borrowing within a 13-Week Period		Borrowings as a Percent of Domestic Deposits	
Size of Bank (domestic deposits)	Average	Size of Bank (domestic deposits)	Average	Size of Bank (domestic deposits)	Average
Less than $200 million	4–5	Less than $200 million	6–7	Less than $200 million	2%
$200 million–$1 billion	3–4	$200 million–$1 billion	5–6	$200 million–$1 billion	2%
$1 billion–$3 billion	2–3	$1 billion–$3 billion	4–5	$1 billion–$3 billion	1.5%
More than $3 billion	1–2	More than $3 billion	3–4	More than $3 billion	1%

SOURCE: Board of Governors of the Federal Reserve System, *The Discount Window* (Washington, D.C., October 1980) p. 8.

however, generally do not cause changes in market rates. The discount rate affects directly only the cost of borrowed reserves, which rarely total more than 10 percent of the total dollar amount of reserves. Thus, changes in the discount rate are a relatively weak tool of monetary policy. Nevertheless, because much of the public believes that changes in the discount rate do affect other rates indirectly, and because they are very visible and infrequent enough to be newsworthy, the strength of the discount rate is often overestimated.

Open-Market Operations.   Open-market operations are the most frequently used tool of monetary policy. **Open-market operations** refers to purchases from and sales to the public of Treasury securities and other authorized securities by the Federal Reserve. As discussed in Chapter 27, open-market operations change the dollar amount of federal government securities (S) on the Fed's balance sheet. The securities are purchased from sellers offering the lowest prices and sold to the highest bidders in a competitive, arm's-length process—hence the name, open-market operations. The transactions may be either permanent or temporary. Temporary purchases are called **repurchase agreements.** The seller agrees to repurchase the securities from the Fed within 15 days of the sale, at the original sales price plus an interest charge for the period. Temporary sales are called **matched sale-purchase** transactions. The security sale by the Fed is matched by a simultaneous purchase of the same security from the same purchaser for delivery a few days later. Other transactions are termed **outright** purchases or sales. Transactions are either *cash* transactions, for delivery and payment the same business day, or *regular* transactions, for delivery and payment the next business day.

     When the Fed purchases securities, it pays the seller for them by a check on itself. This increases reserves at depository institutions. The selling banks will use the new reserves to increase their earning assets by making loans and in the process expand deposits in the banking system as a whole by a multiple of the reserve injection. This effect is shown on the following T account:

Fed Open-Market Purchase of $1,000 of Securities ($rr = 20\%$)

A. Before Purchase			B. After Purchase		
Reserves	10,000	50,000 Deposits	Reserves	11,000	55,000 Deposits
Loans	40,000		Loans	44,000	

When the Fed sells securities, it pays the seller with a check on a bank. When the check is cleared, reserves in the banking system are reduced and deposits contract by a multiple of the reserve reduction, *ceteris paribus*.

All securities trading is conducted for the system as a whole at the open-market desk at the Federal Reserve Bank of New York by the manager of the Open Market Account for Domestic Operations and his or her staff. (There is, of course, no more a physical "open-market desk" than there is a "discount window.") The manager operates in accord with a directive adopted by the FOMC at its previous meeting. This directive stipulates the general targets the manager should achieve in terms of the ranges of growth rates in different definitions of money supply and interest rates until the next meeting of the committee. The directive is adopted at the end of each meeting of the FOMC. Meetings are held about one every six weeks in Washington, D.C. The committee is briefed on current economic and financial developments and on monetary policy options by the senior economics staff at the Board. The manager of the account reviews domestic open-market activity since the last meeting; then each of the 12 voting members (the seven governors and five voting Reserve Bank presidents) presents his or her own views in a "go-around." The seven nonvoting reserve bank presidents also attend and discuss their views. Traditionally, the chairman of the board speaks last, summarizing the previous discussion and suggesting one or more policy options for open-market operations until the next committee meeting. The committee then votes on a directive to be given as a guide to the manager.

The domestic policy paragraphs of the directive adopted by the FOMC at its meeting on May 18, 1993, read in part:

> The Federal Open Market Committee seeks monetary and financial conditions that will foster price stability and promote sustainable growth in output. In furtherance of these objectives, the Committee at its meeting in February established ranges for growth of M2 and M3 of 2 to 6 percent and ½ to 4½ percent respectively, measured from the fourth quarter of 1992 to the fourth quarter of 1993. The Committee expects that developments contributing to unusual velocity increases are likely to persist during the year. The monitoring range for growth of total domestic nonfinancial debt was set at 4½ to 8½ percent for the year. The behavior of the monetary aggregates will continue to be evaluated in the light of progress toward price level stability, movements in their velocities, and developments in the economy and financial markets.
>
> In the implementation of policy for the immediate future, the Committee seeks to maintain the existing degree of pressure on reserve positions. In the context of the Committee's long-run objectives for price stability and sustainable economic growth, and giving careful consideration to economic, financial, and monetary develop-

ments, slightly greater reserve restraint would or slightly lesser reserve restraint might be acceptable in the intermeeting period. The contemplated reserve conditions are expected to be consistent with appreciable growth in the broader monetary aggregates over the second quarter.[1]

Directives are not always adopted unanimously. The above was adopted by an 9–2 vote. One dissenter favored greater restraint and one, greater ease.

The directive discusses the *dynamic* operations undertaken to affect levels of aggregate economic activity. But these operations account for only a small percentage of the desk's overall volume of transactions, generally less than 10 percent of the dollar volume. The large majority of transactions are *defensive,* undertaken to offset the short-term effects on reserves of other accounts on the Fed's balance sheet and to stabilize short-term interest rates. The Fed's theory behind defensive operations is that greater stability in day-to-day interest rates would maximize the participation of both SSUs and DSUs in financial markets and increase aggregate income. Defensive operations are generally not included in the directive and are left up to the discretion of the manager. The manager does, however, check his daily security strategy in a conference telephone call each morning with a member of the Board of Governors and a voting Reserve Bank president.

In 1992, the desk bought $1,909 billion of securities outright or under a repurchase agreement (where the buyer must repurchase the securities at the same price within a specified period of time). In the same period, the desk sold $1,884 billion. Thus, the Fed's net holdings of securities over the year increased $25 billion. Total bank reserves, however, remained almost unchanged for the year. This represents the net sum of Fed dynamic operations. Because the purchase and sale of securities involve trading costs, some analysts have questioned the benefits of the large volume of defensive operations. They believe that the private market could stabilize short-run seasonal and random swings in interest rates as well as, if not better than, the desk and at a lower cost.

Open-market operations can be conducted every business day. They are flexible and can be undertaken in almost any dollar amount, from less than $1 million to more than $1 billion. They may be reversed quickly if conditions change unexpectedly. Purchases in the morning can be reversed by sales in the afternoon. Open-market transactions are generally not publicly announced at the time, although the net amount can be read from the weekly Federal Reserve balance sheet shortly afterward. A statistical separation of defensive from dynamic operations, however, is not possible until many months later.

Target Rates of Monetary Expansion

Since 1975, the Fed has specified, at least semiannually, the upper and lower ranges of the target rates of growth in M1, M2, and M3 it expects to achieve over the next 12 months through the use of all three tools. These are shown in Table 28–3. The target rates are good indicators of the intent of Fed dynamic policy. If the target growth rates are increased, monetary

---

[1] *Federal Reserve Bulletin*, September 1993, p. 865.

TABLE

28–3

SELECTED FEDERAL RESERVE TARGET AND ACTUAL GROWTH
RATES IN MONETARY AGGREGATES FROM 1978 TO 1994

Year 4Q to 4Q	M1 Target Low	High	Actual	M2 Target Low	High	Actual	M3 Target Low	High	Actual
				(percent, annual rate)					
1979	4.5	6.5	7.7	5.0	8.0	8.2	6.0	9.0	10.4
1980	4.0	6.5	7.4	6.0	9.0	8.9	6.5	9.5	9.5
1981	3.5	6.0	2.5	6.0	9.0	9.3	6.5	9.5	12.3
1982	2.5	5.5	8.8	6.0	9.0	9.1	6.5	9.5	9.9
1983	4.5[a]	8.5[a]	10.4	7.0	10.0	12.2	6.5	9.5	9.8
1984	4.0	8.0	5.4	6.0	9.0	8.0	6.0	9.0	10.7
1985	3.5[b]	7.5[b]	12.0	6.0	9.0	8.7	6.0	9.5	7.6
1986	3.0	8.0	15.5	6.0	9.0	9.2	6.0	9.0	9.0
1987	[c]	[c]	6.3	5.5	8.5	4.3	5.5	8.5	5.8
1988	[c]	[c]	4.2	4.0	8.0	5.2	4.0	8.0	6.3
1989	[c]	[c]	0.6	3.0	7.0	4.7	3.5	7.5	3.6
1990	[c]	[c]	4.3	3.0	7.0	4.0	1.0	5.0	1.8
1991	[c]	[c]	8.0	2.5	6.5	2.8	1.0	5.0	1.1
1992	[c]	[c]	14.3	2.5	6.5	1.9	1.0	5.0	0.5
1993	[c]	[c]	10.5	1.0[d]	5.0[d]	1.4	0.0[d]	4.0[d]	0.6
1994	[c]	[c]	—	1.0	5.0	—	0.0	4.0	—

SOURCE: Federal Reserve System.
[a] Range was changed from 4–6 to 5–9 percent during year.
[b] Range was changed from 4–7 to 3–8 percent during year.
[c] No target range specified.
[d] Range was changed from 2.0–6.0 and 0.5–4.5 percent during the year.

policy should become more expansionary. If they are decreased, policy should become more restrictive in the coming months. The table also shows the actual growth rates for the periods. As can be seen, the target rates have not always been achieved. The misses may reflect changes in target rates during the one-year period, difficulties in achieving target growth in more than one measure of money at a time, or periodic emphasis on interest rates rather than on money supply. The target and actual growth rates in M2 and M3 in 1992 are plotted in Figure 28–2. In this period, the growth rates in both M2 and M3 were slightly below the lower end of their target range.

As can be seen from the wording of the directive, the Fed specifies not only annual targets in a number of monetary aggregates but also shorter-run targets that may differ from the yearly target ranges. These are designed both to deal with temporary factors in the economy and to return the monetary aggregates to within the longer-term target ranges, if they have moved outside. Since 1986, M1 has not been used as a target.

It is evident that the multiple-monetary-aggregate targets specified in the directive may not all be mutually consistent and may make accurate control of any one target difficult. If all cannot be achieved simultaneously, explicit or implicit priorities must be set. The development of the directive,

FIGURE

28–2

547

▼

THE FEDERAL
RESERVE SYSTEM:
TOOLS AND
INSTRUMENTS

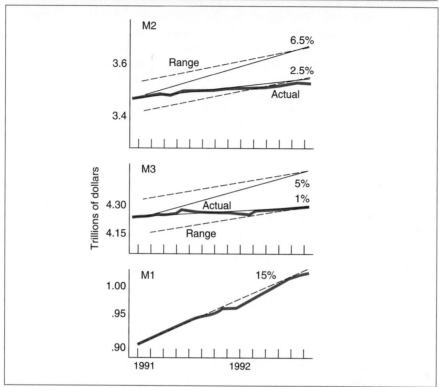

ACTUAL AND TARGET GROWTH RATES IN M2 AND M3 AND
ACTUAL M1 IN 1992

SOURCE: Board of Governors of the Federal Reserve System, *Annual Report, 1992*, Washington, D.C., 1993, pp. 30, 32.

the operating procedures currently used to achieve the target ranges, and the effectiveness of monetary control in practice are discussed in Chapter 33.

How the Fed uses each of the three quantitative tools to implement its policy is summarized below:

Tool	Policy Action	
	Expansive	Restrictive
Reserve requirements	Lower	Raise
Discount rate	Lower	Raise
Open-market operations	Purchase securities	Sell securities

Qualitative Tools

The use of qualitative (selective) tools indicates dissatisfaction with the ownership mix of money and credit determined by the market mechanism. This may reflect assumed imperfections in the market or different economic and social priorities for different individuals. Qualitative tools attempt to direct credit toward or away from specific sectors of the economy by legislative or regulatory edict on the assumption that the credit will be used in that sector to increase or decrease, respectively, spending in the sector and not elsewhere. Thus, the Fed might feel that insufficient credit is being channeled into, say, residential housing or agriculture to permit these sectors to operate at socially desirable levels. In general, qualitative tools modify the effective interest rate structure and thereby the incentive system of lenders and borrowers. Because the distribution or rationing of credit is not determined solely by prices set by market forces, qualitative tools are said to rely on **nonprice rationing.** In the United States, qualitative tools have been used most extensively during periods of emergencies, such as wars, but, because they are a visible sign of policy, they are also popular during periods when more "active" economic policy is favored. The major qualitative financial tools (selective credit controls) include Regulation Q, margin requirements, moral suasion, and minimum down payment.

Regulation Q

As has been discussed in Chapter 16, until it was repealed in 1986, Regulation Q restricted the maximum interest rate depository institutions could pay on their various types of time deposits. This was the most visible qualitative tool used over a long time period. The relationship between ceiling rates and market rates of interest on comparable securities affects the distribution of funds between (1) financial intermediaries and the private financial market; (2) commercial banks and thrift institutions; (3) large and small intermediaries of each type; and (4) sectors deriving credit primarily from the affected institutions. Regulation Q had been in effect for commercial banks since 1933 and for most thrift institutions since 1966. In the 1960s and 1970s, it was used primarily to encourage inflows into thrift institutions for relending in the mortgage market without their need to pay higher deposit rates. To achieve this, higher ceiling rates were permitted thrift institutions than commercial banks.

For reasons discussed earlier, ceilings on large deposits began to be phased out in 1970. The Depository Institutions Deregulation and Monetary Control Act of 1980 prescribed a phase-out of all ceilings on all time deposits at all institutions by 1986. The Garn-St Germain Act of 1982 authorized ceiling-free MMDAs. This served to accelerate the phase-out. As a result, market forces, rather than government edict, now allocate household and business firm savings.

Margin Requirements

Margin requirements, technically known as Federal Reserve Regulations U, T, and G, specify the minimum down payment that buyers may make on the purchase of stocks and convertible bonds on credit. The intent is to limit the flow of credit into the stock market and reduce speculation. Like Regulation Q, margin requirements were initially enacted in the 1930s. Excessive speculation on the stock market was widely viewed as an important contributing factor to the Great Depression and the accompanying financial chaos. In the intervening years, the stock market has frequently been seen as draining credit away from "more productive" sectors. The higher the margin requirement, the higher the minimum down payment required for the purchase of stocks, the fewer stocks will be purchased, and the less credit will be extended for such purposes. At the beginning of 1994, margin requirements were 50 percent. Thus, covered lenders could lend stock buyers only 50 percent of the market price of the stock used as collateral for the loan. This percentage has remained unchanged since 1974.

Moral Suasion

At times, the Federal Reserve and other government agencies request commercial banks and other lenders to voluntarily favor or disfavor certain sectors in their credit extensions. These requests are accompanied by appeal to the lender's patriotism or spirit of good citizenship. Not infrequently, the appeal for voluntary compliance is reinforced by a veiled threat of punitive action if compliance is not forthcoming. Moral suasion has been used by the Fed to limit bank lending overseas when the balance of payments was unfavorable, to slow the increase in bank lending rates to smaller business firms, and to encourage bank lending to small business and housing.

Minimum Down Payment

During wartime periods, such as World War II and the Korean War, the Federal Reserve has been authorized by Congress to impose minimum-down-payment requirements on the purchase of large-ticket items that consumers generally financed on credit. These included houses, automobiles, and other consumer durables. Changes in the down payment may be viewed as equivalent to a change in the effective interest cost of the loan. The higher the down payment, the higher the effective interest rate, and the smaller the demand for the affected good. The purpose of these requirements was both to reduce inflationary pressures by curbing demand and to shift credit from the private sector to the government sector without increasing nominal interest rates.

The Credit Control Program of 1980

In early 1980, the rate of price inflation jumped abruptly. In response, President Carter authorized the Board of Governors to implement provisions of the heretofore unused Credit Control Act of 1969, which permits the board "to regulate and control any or all extensions of credit." The Board imposed restrictions on consumer and large corporate borrowings. All financial consumer-lending institutions were required to hold reserves against further loan increases, including credit-card loans; higher reserve requirements were imposed on large deposits and other sources of funds at large banks; reserve requirements were imposed for the first time on increases in the assets of money-market funds; and a 3 percent surcharge was added to the discount rate for frequent borrowing by large banks. In addition, banks were required to limit voluntarily the growth in their loans to no more than 9 percent annual rate, which was the Fed's credit growth target at the time. Institutions were encouraged, however, to maintain their loans to small businesses, farmers, home buyers, and auto buyers.

These controls were imposed almost simultaneously with an unexpected sharp drop in GDP. Credit expansion slowed abruptly. Consumer installment credit declined for the first time in five years, applications for bank credit cards almost came to a complete halt, and business lending decreased significantly. All measures of monetary aggregates dropped sharply to below target levels. Partially in response to the severity of the decline, the restrictions were quickly relaxed and then removed altogether by summer.

Evaluation of Qualitative Tools

Qualitative tools have had mixed success. Because they attempt to divert credit from the directions determined in the marketplace by individual preferences and interfere with the self-interest dictum of "buy low, sell high," selective controls encourage subversion. Market participants search for ways to avoid or evade the controls. They invent new definitions, new financial instruments, new financial institutions, and new techniques that are not subject to the existing regulations. In the short run, the barriers set up by the controls may alter the flow of funds from the market solution and channel funds into the target sectors. In the longer run, however, the forces of self-interest, competition, and human inventiveness frequently reduce their effectiveness. In time, funds can be directed at almost any purpose their owners wish and are said to be *fungible* (interchangeable). This is particularly true since the substantial advances in telecommunications technology, which permit near-instantaneous and cheap transfers of funds and information from almost anywhere throughout the world.

Even if credit is directed toward selected sectors, it may not be used to finance expenditures in those sectors. For example, although qualitative controls may have increased the flow of funds into the mortgage market in the 1970s and increased mortgage debt as a ratio of both housing and total debt, the ratio of investment in residential housing to GDP has not increased. Mortgage credit replaced other forms of credit previously used, such as consumer and stock market credit. People financed vacations, automobiles, and even college tuitions through a second mortgage on their homes. At the same time, the ceiling rates on deposits at thrift institutions resulted in disintermediation in periods when market rates of interest exceeded these ceilings. As a result, less rather than more funds were channeled into the mortgage market at these times. This unintended side effect helped to feed the disillusionment with Regulation Q that eventually led to its removal.

Moreover, to the extent that selective controls have been effective in redirecting either financial or real resources, they are likely to have reduced efficiency. As one observer concluded:

> . . . where the market's "hidden hand" does not turn "private vices into public virtues," it may be hard to construct visible hands that effectively turn nonmarket vices into public virtues.[2]

[2] Charles Wolff, Jr., "A Theory of Nonmarket Failure: Framework for Implementation and Analysis," *Journal of Law and Economics*, April 1979, p. 113.

Thus, the net effect of selective controls on aggregate economic welfare is uncertain. What is more certain is that once introduced, they develop strong constituencies that benefit from them and make it difficult to remove them even after the original need for them has long since disappeared. Nevertheless, in time, most qualitative controls become ineffective in the face of market forces and are removed.

The brief experience with the credit control program of 1980 supports many of these observations. When banks were restricted in expanding consumer loans through credit cards, department stores advertised widely that their credit cards were not restricted. When banks located in the United States were urged to voluntarily curtail their lending to large corporations, overseas banks publicized their willingness to lend to these corporations. Questions about "special cases" quickly transformed the initial short and simple regulations and guidelines into long and detailed instructions. Nevertheless, it was probably only the early termination of the program in response both to the unexpected severity of the declines in income and to cries of "unfair" competition from unregulated suppliers of credit that prevented the development of constituencies with sufficient power to maintain the regulations in force.

Despite the evidence of their questionable long-run effectiveness, qualitative tools have strong popular appeal and may be expected to be used again when things are believed to be out of control. They appear to provide the Fed with a "rifle rather than a shotgun" so that they may aim their actions directly at the intended sectors. Above all, their use is a sign of action at times when the public is frustrated and impatient and urges policymakers, "Don't just stand there, do something."

SUMMARY

The Federal Reserve uses both quantitative and qualitative tools to execute its policies. Quantitative tools affect the aggregate supply of money and credit. The major quantitative policy tools are reserve requirements (which affect the value of the money multiplier) and the discount rate and open-market operations (which affect the dollar amounts of bank reserves). Open-market operations, which involve the buying or selling of U.S. government securities from or to the public, are the most frequently used and most important tool. They are conducted by the manager of the Open Market Account at the Federal Reserve Bank of New York in accord with a policy directive prepared every six weeks by the Open Market Committee. Increases in bank reserves increase money supply and stimulate economic activity. Decreases in bank reserves decrease money supply and restrain economic activity. Since 1975, the Federal Reserve has been required by Congress to make public its periodic growth-rate targets for monetary aggregates.

Qualitative or selective tools affect the ownership mix of money and credit. Their use primarily reflects dissatisfaction with the mix determined by the free market. The major qualitative tools have been Regulation Q ceilings on deposit rates, moral suasion, and minimum down payments on the purchase of securities (margin requirements) and periodically of other items. The long-run effectiveness and usefulness of qualitative tools is questionable, and most are eventually phased out when their undesirable and, generally, unintended side effects become sufficiently visible.

QUESTIONS

1. Differentiate between *quantitative* and *qualitative* tools of Federal Reserve policy. How do their objectives differ?
2. "The Federal Reserve controls interest rates through changing the discount rate." Discuss the validity of this statement.
3. What does the Fed mean when it says that "bank borrowing at the discount window is a privilege and not a right"? Why may the posted discount rate not always be the discount rate banks see? Why does a bank's borrowing from the Fed affect the aggregate money supply differently than if it had borrowed from another bank on the Fed fund's market?
4. Assume that reserve requirements on transaction balances are 10 percent and that the public's demand for currency and the banks' demand for excess reserves are both 5 percent of transactions balances. What is the transactions deposit multiplier? Assume that the Fed lowers reserve requirements by 50 percent to 5 percent. What would happen to deposits for every $1,000 of reserves in the banking system? Why might the Fed have taken such action? What would have happened to deposits if the Fed had increased reserve requirements

by 50 percent to 15 percent? Why are the changes not symmetrical?
5. Why are open-market operations the most frequently used tool of monetary policy? Differentiate between *dynamic* and *defensive* open-market operations.
6. Assume that the Fed buys Treasury securities from a nonbank securities dealer on the open market. Why might it want to buy the securities and why from a nonbank dealer? Trace the change in reserves on the balance sheet of the Fed, the securities dealer, and the banking system. What will happen to the money supply?
7. Why may it be difficult for the Fed to achieve all its money supply and interest rate targets simultaneously? Why do you think the Fed continues to have multiple targets?
8. Why is the use of qualitative tools by the Fed frequently viewed by the general public as more desirable than the use of quantitative tools? Why are most economists, however, opposed to their use? What do you think they know that the public doesn't?
9. Why do many analysts consider the use of qualitative tools to be more visible with immediate but less lasting impact than quantitative tools?

REFERENCES

Anderson, Clay J., A *Half-Century of Federal Reserve Policymaking, 1914–1964.* Philadelphia: Federal Reserve Bank of Philadelphia, 1965.

Board of Governors of the Federal Reserve System, *Annual Report.* Washington, D.C., annually.

Board of Governors of the Federal Reserve System, *The Federal Reserve Discount Window.* Washington, D.C., 1980.

Board of Governors of the Federal Reserve System, *The Federal Reserve System: Purposes and Functions.* Washington, D.C., 1984.

Board of Governors of the Federal Reserve System, *The Federal Reserve Reserve Requirements.* Washington, D.C., 1982.

Commission on Money and Credit, *Money and Credit: Report.* Englewood Cliffs, N.J.: Prentice Hall, 1962.

Federal Reserve Bank of St. Louis, "The FOMC in 19XX," *Review*, annually.

Feinman, Joshua N., "Reserve Requirements: History, Current Practice, and Potential Reform," *Federal Reserve Bulletin*, June 1993, pp. 569–89.

Goodfriend, Marvin, and Monica Hargraves, "A Historical Assessment of the Rationales and Functions of Reserve Requirements," *Economic Review*, Federal Reserve Bank of Richmond, March/April 1983, pp. 3–21.

Hetzel, Robert L., "Making Monetary Policy," *CATO Journal*, Spring/Summer 1992, pp. 255–77.

Institute for Contemporary Studies, *Government Credit Allocation*, San Francisco, 1975.

Kane, Edward J., "Accelerating Inflation, Technical Innovation and Decreasing Effectiveness of Banking Regulation," *Journal of Finance*, May 1981, pp. 355–67.

Kane, Edward J., "Good Intentions and Unintended Evil," *Journal of Money, Credit, and Banking*, February 1977, pp. 55–68.

McNees, Stephen K., "The Discount Rate: The Other Tool of Monetary Policy," *New England Economic Review*, Financial Reserve Bank of Boston, July/August 1993, pp. 3–22.

Meek, Paul, *Open Market Operations*. New York: Federal Reserve Bank of New York, 1985.

Mengle, David L., "The Discount Window," in Timothy Q. Cook and Timothy D. Rowe, eds., *Instruments of the Money Market*, 6th ed. Richmond, Va.: Federal Reserve Bank of Richmond, 1986.

Meulendyke, Ann-Marie, "Reserve Requirements and the Discount Window in Recent Decades," *Quarterly Review*, Federal Reserve Bank of New York, Autumn 1992, pp. 25–43.

Meulendyke, Ann-Marie, *U. S. Monetary Policy and Financial Markets*, New York: Federal Reserve Bank of New York, 1989.

Reich, Cary, "Inside the Fed," *Institutional Investor*, May 1984, pp. 137–62.

Roberds, William, "What Hath the Fed Wrought? Interest Rate Smoothing in Theory and Practice," *Economic Review*, Federal Reserve Bank of Atlanta, January/February 1992, pp. 12–24.

Roth, Howard L., "Federal Reserve Open Market Techniques," *Economic Review*, Federal Reserve Bank of Kansas City, March 1986, pp. 3–15.

Samansky, Arthur W., *Statfacts: Understanding Federal Reserve Statistical Reports*, New York: Federal Reserve Bank of New York, 1981.

Schreft, Stacey, "Credit Controls: 1980," *Economic Review*. Federal Reserve Bank of Richmond, November/December 1990, pp. 25–55.

Weiner, Stuart E., "The Changing Role of Reserve Requirements in Monetary Policy," *Economic Review*, Federal Reserve Bank of Kansas City, Fourth Quarter 1992, pp. 45–63.

Monetary Theories

Now that we know how the Fed affects the money supply, we shall examine how money, in turn, affects the behavior of aggregate economic variables, such as income, employment, and the price level. Then we can see how the Fed affects economic performance. To do so, we shall analyze a number of different theories that attempt to explain this relationship.

The Role of Theory

A theory is a general statement or story that describes the behavior of a particular event. It is based on important repetitious cause-and-effect relationships that we believe we know about the phenomenon from both thought and previous observation. For example, statements that cloudy skies produce rain and that winning football teams sell out sports stadiums are both theories. Theories can be either good or bad, useful or not useful, depending on how well and how simply they predict the actual event. Theories use assumptions to simplify or limit the "real-world" conditions under which they hold in order to focus as much as possible on the most important relationships. The two theories above generally include assumptions that the temperature is above 32° Fahrenheit and that the stadiums are located in the United States, respectively.

All theories are not equally useful. Evaluating a theory as to its usefulness is a two-step process. In the first step, the theory is examined for internal consistency. But no matter how aesthetically pleasing or internally consistent it may be, just as the proof of a pudding is in the eating, the proof of a theory is in the prediction. In the second step, therefore, the theory is tested empirically. It is quantified as much as possible and is fitted statistically to past data to see how well it has performed. Unless we know of some dramatic structural change in the meantime, the better a theory's performance in the past, the more likely it is to perform well in the future. When a theory is transformed into a format in which it can be tested, it is referred to as a **model.** The model is believed to be a representation of the actual phenomenon. In some areas, physical models can be constructed. This is obviously not very practical in economics or finance. In these areas, models are generally constructed in quantitative or equation forms, which capture the underlying relationships. Such models are termed **econometric models.** Models may be used both for prediction and to simulate the implications of particular policy actions or other changes. It is easier and less costly to conduct experiments on a model than on the economy itself.

Good theories are useful because they permit us to explain events and their consequences in advance rather than after they have occurred. Thus,

we can prepare for the event and, if possible and necessary, take appropriate action to forestall or offset the event or any undesirable effects. Monetary theory considers the causes of changes in financial variables, such as money supply and interest rates, and the effects of these changes on variables in the real sector, such as employment, production, and prices.

Monetary theories have been spun since the beginning of the use of money. Through time, they have been refined, modified, or rejected altogether as additional evidence became available with which to evaluate the quality of their predictions. Because these theories are constructed for a given structure of the economy, when the structure changes, many previously accepted theories become less useful and new theories are developed. We do not have the space here to review each of the numerous monetary theories that have been developed over the years. Many of these had only short lives and lie forgotten by almost everyone but students of the history of economic thought. We will confine our discussion in this and the following chapters to only a few theories that have been important in affecting economic policy in the past or that have relevance to today's economy. In the process, we will trace briefly the development of monetary theory from its beginnings.

At any one time, more than one theory of economic behavior may be widely accepted. This occurs because in most areas of economics and finance the empirical evidence in support of one of the competing theories is not sufficiently strong to convince everyone of its superiority over the others. In addition, empirical testing is costly, difficult, time-consuming, and often not completely convincing; and almost all of us have had some personal experience with many of the phenomena the theory is attempting to explain, albeit generally on a limited and superficial basis. For these reasons, many prefer to rely on intuition and "gut" feeling in choosing among alternative hypotheses.[1]

Quantity Theory

The earliest major theory attempting to explain the relationship between money and national income was the **quantity theory of money,** first developed in the late 1500s. The underpinnings of the quantity theory are quite simple. At the time, money was primarily a medium of exchange used to purchase goods and services. The more money in circulation, the more spending; and conversely, the less money, the less spending. At any moment in time, the amount of purchases required the use of an equal nominal amount of dollars (or whatever the unit of currency in the particular country). Through time, however, the amount of purchases could exceed the amount of dollars. The same dollar could be used over and over again to finance more than one purchase. The average number of times each dollar turns over in a particular period—say, one year—to finance the purchases in that period is termed the **velocity of money.**

The total value of goods and services purchased during a period may be divided into two components. One part is the physical quantity of the purchases, the other is the average price of the purchases. The earliest form of the quantity theory equated the flow of money in a particular period, generally one year—measured by the product of the amount of money (M) and the velocity of money (V)—with the total value of all goods and services sold in that period—measured by the product of the sum of the physical quantity of items purchased (Q) and their average price (P_T)—in an **equation of exchange:**

$$MV_T = P_TQ \tag{29–1}$$

P_TQ represents total transactions in the economy, and V_T is termed **transactions velocity.**

Most analysts, however, are interested in the state of the economy as reflected in employment and production. Aggregate employment and production are linked to the purchase of new physical goods and services in their final state (final output), rather than to the purchase of all items—old (used automobiles) as well as newly produced goods, intermediate (wheat and flour) as well as final (bread) goods, and financial (securities) as well as physical (automobile) goods. The equation of exchange may be rewrit-

---

[1] The difficulties of generating sufficiently strong empirical evidence in favor of one hypothesis over other competing ones, the tendency for the same problems to reappear, and the natural instinct for quick and costless solutions often permit economic and financial theories discarded as useless in one period to gain substantial support later. This characteristic appears to be much truer of theories in the social sciences than in the physical sciences. Milton Friedman in his *Essays in Positive Economics* noted that the problems in developing convincing tests render "the weeding-out of unsuccessful hypotheses slow and difficult. They are seldom downed for good and are always cropping up again."

ten to include only newly produced final goods and services included in real GNP (y) and their prices:[2]

$$MV_Y = P_Y y \qquad (29\text{-}2)$$

Note that the product of $P_Y y$ gives us Y, or GDP in current dollars. Note also that both the V and P in equation 29–2 will differ from those in equation 29–1. Because the equation now has income rather than total transaction on the right-hand side, V_Y is termed ***income velocity.*** M, of course, remains the same. Because Q is much greater than y, transaction V in equation 29–1 is much larger than income V in equation 29–2.

Equation 29–2 is true by definition. If any one variable were to change, one or more of the other variables would also need to change in order to maintain the equality. But so far, the equation does not specify which variable affects which other variables and by how much, so it is not a useful theory. For example, a change in M could lead to a change in V_Y, P_Y, or y, or in any combination of two or all three. This permits us to say little that is useful. To make the theory operational, it is necessary to introduce a number of assumptions. The assumptions transform equation 29–2 into the ***quantity theory of money.***

The early quantity theorists argued that, at first approximation and for moderately short periods of time, both velocity and the physical quantity of final output could be assumed to remain constant. This was not as outrageous an assumption in those days as it would be to us now. In the period before the mid-1880s, economies were basically agricultural. Most people were largely self-sufficient, and unemployment in the industrial sense of the word did not exist. As a result, physical output varied slowly with changes in population and labor force.

Financial sectors were not yet developed much beyond the goldsmith and early commercial bank stage. Savings were held in the form of their money or physical capital, such as land and houses, and people did not shift funds rapidly from one form to the other. Because there were few interest-bearing financial assets, interest rates did not affect the mix of savings greatly. The amount of money held was dependent principally upon the frequency with which people received payments. The longer between pay periods, the larger average balances units would have to hold in order to finance the same expenditures.

Just imagine that you are paid monthly and daily in alternate periods and spend your income more or less smoothly during each period. Certainly you would hold a larger average money balance when you were paid monthly than when you were paid daily. For example, assume that you were paid $300 a month and spent it more or less evenly through the month at the end of each day. If you were paid the entire amount at the beginning

---

[2] If the variables are measured in percent rates of change, equation 29–2 may be written in the following approximate form:

$$M + V = P + y$$

Thus, if $M = 5\%$, $P = 9\%$, and $y = 1\%$, V must equal 5%.

of the month, you would maintain an average daily balance of about ($300 + 0)/2 = $150. If you were paid $10 per day, your average daily balance would be $10. Because the time pattern of payments was unlikely to change greatly in the short run, the velocity of money was also unlikely to change greatly. Moreover, to the extent y or V did change, it was probably not the result of changes in money supply. These assumptions restricted the changes in the equation to only M and P. But which way did the relationship go, from M to P or from P to M?

During the development of the quantity theory, money was primarily in metallic form or was rigidly tied to metal. Thus, changes in the supply of money depended largely on new finds of the monetary metals or the exhaustion of old mines. These events were only slightly affected by the course of prices. (Of course, higher prices for the metal would have some effect on its supply. The higher prices would intensify the search and make some previously unprofitable mining operations profitable.) From this, the quantity theorists reasoned that changes in the money supply affect prices more than changes in prices affect the money supply so that the primary relationship went from M to P.

With these modifications, the equation of exchange assumes useful behavioral properties and becomes the quantity theory of money. Because V and y are assumed not to change as a result of changes in money, the quantity theory predicts that a change in the money supply results in an equal percentage change in the average price level in the same direction. Thus, if money increased by 10 percent during a period, prices would be expected to rise by 10 percent. This occurs because 10 percent more money would be chasing the same quantity of goods, so that prices would be bid up proportionately across the board. If money decreased by 10 percent, prices would decrease by the same 10 percent. Of course, money was not the only cause of changes in prices. Prices could change if either V or y changed independently, but the theory had little to say about this. It was concerned only with the effect of changes in money on the economy. Nor did the theory stipulate that money changes were followed immediately by equal proportional changes in the price level. The effects of changes in money supply took time to work their way through the economy. In the meantime, the change in money could temporarily affect the physical supply of goods and thus real income.

The quantity theory was simple and straightforward, and predicted reasonably well for many years. As a result, it attracted widespread use. People could predict the future consequences of changes in money supply. To the extent that money was under the control of the government, the quantity theory provided the government with a tool to achieve price stability.

However, as economies became more industrialized and the financial sector more developed, the quantity theory predicted more and more poorly. For example, in the 1980s, the money supply in the United States increased only slightly faster than in the 1970s. The quantity theory would have predicted that prices would have risen at about the same rate in the two decades. But, instead, prices increased more than twice as rapidly in the 1970s than they did in the 1980s. Obviously, V and y were not constant.

FIGURE

29–1

559

▼

MONETARY
THEORIES

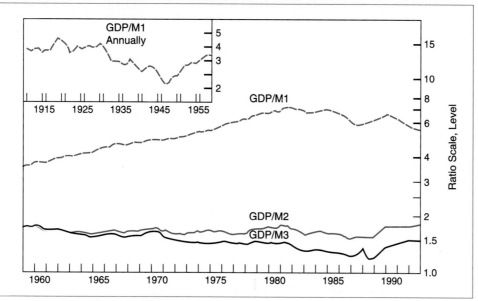

INCOME VELOCITY OF MONEY (GDP/M) 1910–1993

SOURCE: Board of Governors of the Federal Reserve System, 1987 *Historical Chart Book* (Washington, D.C.), p. 5; updated by the author.

V is strongly affected by interest rates and regulations that influence the mix of funds households and business firms hold in "idle" cash balances and in interest-bearing securities. The higher interest rates are, the more costly are idle balances, the smaller is the amount of money balances held, and the more intensively the smaller money balances are used, increasing V. Thus, V varies directly with interest rates and thereby also with income. In the 1980s, interest rates declined and, in part, as a result V, particularly for M1, also declined for the first time since World War II. Thus, increases in M1 had a smaller impact on prices. Moreover, the sharp slowdown in the growth of M1 velocity below its trend values in the 1980s and increases in its volatility have made its prediction more complicated.

The changes in income velocity for three definitions of money since 1910 are seen in Figure 29–1. Predictability of velocity is important for monetary policy. To determine the correct amount of money to provide to achieve a specified income target, the Federal Reserve must predict the value of velocity accurately. The greater difficulty in predicting M1 velocity in recent years helps to explain the Fed's decision to deemphasize M1 as a monetary target relative to M2 and M3.

Moreover, the rise in cyclical unemployment broke the fixed relationship between change in output and change in the labor force, so that y could not be assumed constant even in the short run. Theories useful for explaining modern economies must be able to explain the change in y as well as in P. Both variables are affected by M.

Keynesian Theory

Among the theories developed to correct the shortcomings of the quantity theory, the most widely accepted was proposed by John Maynard Keynes in the 1930s. Keynes argued that it was important to look not only at the supply of money, as the quantity theorists did, but also at the demand for money. He hypothesized that money is an asset that, like any other asset—such as automobiles or houses—is held both for the stream of services it generates and for the potential for appreciation in value. The service money renders is purchasing power, or perfect liquidity. Keynes's theory of the demand for money is often referred to as the **liquidity preference theory.** We have already discussed this theory with respect to the determination of the level of interest rates in Chapter 6. Money is typically not held for its own sake. Rather, it is held to finance immediate or deferred spending on goods and services. At any moment in time, money can be (1) spent; (2) lent; or (3) held. Except for coin and currency, money is held in the form of short-term, fixed-value loans to depository institutions—transaction deposits. Thus, the dividing line between holding and lending money is not very clear-cut.

Keynes hypothesized that both households and business firms hold money balances for two reasons: (1) to finance transactions and (2) to finance speculation. The demand for money balances for purchasing-power services to spend immediately on goods and services is referred to as the **transactions demand for money.** It is directly related to aggregate nominal income. The higher income, the more goods and services will be purchased and the more money will be required. But, as later analysts added, money balances not spent can be lent. Otherwise, the potential or *opportunity* interest income is foregone. Thus, the transactions demand for money is also related to the market interest rate, but inversely. The higher the interest rate, the smaller will be the quantity of money demanded. The transactions demand for money may be written:

$$DM_T = f(\overset{+}{Y}, \overset{-}{i})$$

where DM_T is the demand for money for transactions purposes, Y is GDP in current dollars, and i is the market rate of interest. (In actuality, this relationship is more accurately written in real- or constant-dollars terms in which both M and Y are deflated by the price level, i.e., $M/P = m$ and $Y/P = y$.) Similar to the quantity theory, the transactions demand for money views money only as a medium of exchange.

Speculative Demand for Money

The heart of Keynes' hypothesis, however, is the **speculative demand for money** balances, or the demand for money to hold as an asset rather than to spend immediately on goods and services or to lend longer term. Money typically yields no or low coupon income. Why then would anyone hold larger money balances in his or her asset portfolio than are required for transactions purposes? A person would reasonably hold on to money only if the value of money were expected to appreciate so that it would yield a return greater than that on other, comparable assets.[3] The return is proportional to the difference between its buying and selling prices. Like any other asset, money is held for expected profit.

Money appreciates in value if the physical quantity of goods and services that can be bought with it increases, and money depreciates in value if the amount that can be bought with it decreases. Keynes argued that people are most likely to "speculate" on the future value of money with respect to the prices of liquid investments, say, bonds. If the price of bonds were expected to decline in the future, people would either sell their bonds or postpone purchasing additional bonds. They would prefer to hold money, and their demand for speculative purposes would increase. If their expectations were realized and bond prices declined, they would experience a postive rate of return. Conversely, if the price of bonds were expected to increase, people would purchase bonds rather than hold money balances. The speculative demand for money declines because money is expected to yield a lower return. The speculative demand for money, thus, is an inverse function of expected bond prices. But expectations are generally not observable. Although one can specify hypotheses in terms of unobservable variables, doing so is not really "kosher," because there is no way of testing their empirical validity. Thus, they are not very useful. But with a little work, we can relate the unobserved expectations to observed interest rates.

You may recall that in Chapter 5 we demonstrated that bond prices vary inversely with market rates of interest. Bond prices fall as interest rates increase and rise as interest rates decrease. It follows that bond prices are expected to decline if interest rates are expected to increase, and vice versa. Thus, expectations of bond prices can be stated in terms of expectations of interest rates. Unfortunately, interest rate expectations are just as unobservable as bond price expectations.

However, most of us explicitly or implicitly have some "normal" or average level of interest rates in the back of our minds when we analyze current rates. Otherwise, we would not say that current rates are "high," or "low," or "just about right." They must be high, low, or just about right relative to this normal level. If interest rates are "too high," we expect them to drop back, and if rates are "too low," we expect them to rise. Thus, unobserved expected interest rates seem to be related inversely to the observed current level of interest rates. Because, from above, the demand for money for speculative purposes is related inversely to expected bond prices, it is

---

[3] Even some 60 years after Keynes provided the answer to this question, it was not obvious to all. Miss Piggy, a well-known financial guru to Muppets, noted that:

> . . . the fact of the matter is that just like almost everything else green (I specifically exclude emeralds . . .), money can get stale quite quickly. I know you wouldn't think of putting fresh asparagus in the back of a drawer and eating it months later, and yet otherwise sensible people do take sizeable amounts of money and let it rot.

[From Henry Beard, *Miss Piggy's Guide to Life* (New York: Knopf, 1981), p. 73.]

related directly to expected interest rates and, therefore, inversely to current observed interest rates. That is

$$DM_S = f(\overset{-}{i}) \tag{29–4}$$

where DM_S is the speculative demand for money. When interest rates are low, they are expected to rise, bond prices are expected to decline, and the demand for money balances for speculation increases. This relationship is plotted in Figure 29–2, *ceteris paribus*. The schedule is labeled Y_0 to indicate that income is held constant at level 0.

The slope of the schedule in Figure 29–2 is drawn so that it becomes flatter when the interest rate is lower. This reflects the increasing likelihood that interest rates will rise as their level drops lower, rather than fall farther, and that bond prices will decline. Buying bonds would not be very profitable on average. At some point, the likelihood of any further rate decreases is considered to be zero, and the slope of the money-demand function becomes perfectly flat with respect to interest rates. At this point no one would trade money for bonds; people would hold on to their money balances. On this part of the schedule, the costs of buying and then selling the bonds are also likely to be greater than the coupon income that will be earned on the bonds, particularly if the bonds are expected to be held for only a short period. The flat part of the schedule is referred to as the **liquidity trap.** The importance of the liquidity trap is discussed in Chapter 30.

Total Demand for Money

Although we may demand money balances for more than one purpose, it is unlikely that we compartmentalize our money holdings in different pockets—the money for transactions in one pocket and that for speculation in

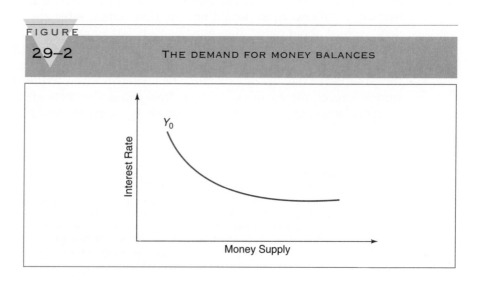

FIGURE

29–2   THE DEMAND FOR MONEY BALANCES

the other.[4] It makes sense to combine equations 29–3 and 29–4 and to write a single demand equation for total money balances:

$$DM = f(\overset{+}{Y}, \overset{-}{i}) \qquad (29\text{--}5)$$

Thus, the overall demand for money increases with increases in income and decreases with increases in interest rates.

This equation suggests that, if the supply of money increases, income has to increase and/or interest rates have to decrease in order for spending units to be induced to hold the additional money balances. But hold them someone must, since in equilibrium demand must equal supply! Because interest rates may change when money supply changes, the rigid proportional link between money and nominal income (or prices, if real income is assumed constant) postulated by the quantity theorists is broken. The more interest rates change as a result of a given change in money, the less will income change. A change in the money supply can now change real income, prices, velocity, or any combination thereof.

It also follows that, if the demand for money depends on interest rates, then velocity, which moves inversely with money if income is held constant, is also a function of interest rates. Since $MV = Y$, income is a function of interest rates. To the extent that interest rates are volatile, both velocity and income are volatile and, as was noted earlier, cannot be assumed to be constant for purposes of prediction. Interest rates become a key variable in the Keynesian transmission process. To Keynesians, any theory that attempts to explain the relationship between money and income must first explain velocity and interest rates. This requires a description of the factors determining the supply of money and will be provided in the next section.

The Keynesian specification of the demand for money has been refined over the years. At first, many analysts believed (1) that the demand function was not very stable, meaning that it would move about (or technically, that the values of the coefficients for income and interest rates in the function were not constant through time), so that predicting its location at any one time was difficult; and (2) that the interest rate coefficient was very large, so that small changes in interest rates would induce large changes in the quantity of money demanded and most of a change in the supply of money would be absorbed by a change in interest rates rather than a change in income. As we shall see in later chapters, both these conditions reduce the ability of monetary policy to stabilize income. Empirical evidence, however, does not support these assertions. Changes in money change not only interest rates but income as well, and, until the early 1980s, the demand function for money was reasonably stable and pre-

---

[4] Keynes also hypothesized a third, *precautionary* demand for money balances to be held for a "rainy day." However, the development of charge cards and very liquid interest-bearing securities has reduced much of the need for such balances in the United States. Or more simply, in Miss Piggy's words, "Many people think money is something to be set aside for a rainy day. But honestly, how much money do you really need for a dozen or so hours of inclement weather?" (Henry Beard, *Miss Piggy's Guide to Life*, p. 73.)

dictable for periods of, say, six months or longer. Moreover, as was suggested by Milton Friedman in an attempt to reconstruct the quantity theory, the stability of the money-demand function is increased if we broaden the concept of income to encompass income over some extended period of time, say a few years, and include expected as well as current income—a concept Friedman labeled *permanent income*—or use wealth. (Obviously, a person's consumption neither jumps nor drops abruptly if that person's income either jumps or drops for a brief period of time, such as a losing night at Las Vegas or expected unemployment for only the summer months.) With these changes, the basic Keynesian formulation of the demand for money described in equation 29–5 is useful today.

 ## The Supply of Money

In Chapter 15 we showed that the supply of money (defined as coin, currency, and transaction deposits) is a multiple of the dollar amount of bank reserves. Changes in money result from changes in the multiplier or in reserves. This relationship may be written approximately as

$$\Delta M = k\Delta R + R\Delta k \tag{29–6}$$

where

$$k = \frac{1 + c}{rr_D + e + c}$$

and rr_D = reserve requirement on transaction deposits
    c = ratio of currency to transaction deposits
    e = ratio of excess reserves to transaction deposits

In Chapter 28, we saw that the Fed has significant control over both the dollar amount of bank reserves and the ratio of required reserves to deposits. Thus, the Fed has significant control over the money supply. It can increase the money supply by (1) increasing the dollar amount of total reserves (R) through open-market purchases of securities or decreasing the discount rate to encourage bank borrowing at the discount window; or (2) increasing the multiplier (k) through reductions in reserve requirements. Conversely, it can reduce the money supply by open-market sales, increases in the discount rate, or increases in reserve requirements. It is at times useful to combine all three Federal Reserve quantitative tools into one composite variable. But two of the tools (open-market operations and the discount rate) change by a dollar amount and the third (reserve requirements) changes by a percentage. Thus, combining them is like adding apples and oranges. However, it is possible to transform a change in reserve requirements into an equivalent change in dollar reserves by multiplying the change in requirements times the dollar amount of deposits and reversing the sign. A reduction in reserve requirements, for example, is thereby transformed into an equivalent increase in dollar reserves and can be added to the aggregate dollar amount of reserves in the banking system. This composite variable is referred to as **effective reserves** and is designated R^E. R^E increases when the Fed buys securities on the open market, increases loans to banks through the discount window, and lowers reserve requirements; it decreases when the Fed sells securities on the open market, raises the discount rate, and raises reserve requirements.[5] The greater are effective reserves, the greater is the quantity of bank deposits and therefore of money that can be supported; and, conversely, the smaller are effective reserves, the smaller is the quantity of money that can be supported.

Of course, factors not under direct Fed control also affect the money supply. These include e and c in the deposit multiplier and other accounts on the Federal Reserve balance sheet, such as float and Treasury deposits. However, the Fed can pretty much offset these influences on the money supply if it so wishes, through the use of its monetary tools. Indeed, many analysts argue that technically the money supply is completely under the control of the Fed. It can make the money supply any amount it wishes. However, for reasons to be discussed later, it may not wish to do so. Other analysts argue that some importance should be given these independent factors in explaining changes in the money supply. Some of the factors are affected by interest rates. For example, the higher interest rates are, the lower are excess reserves held by banks. Because excess reserves are a leakage in the deposit-expansion multiplier, the lower they are, the larger is the value of the multiplier and the larger is the money supply that a given amount of bank reserves can support. The banks are using the reserves provided by the Fed more intensively. For the sake of simplicity, all factors not under Fed control may be assumed to be positive functions of the interest rate. We can now write the supply function for money as

$$SM = f(\overset{+}{R^E}, \overset{+}{i}) \tag{29-7}$$

where SM is the supply of money, R^E captures all the forces controlled by the Fed, and i all the forces outside of Fed control.

The greater the amount of effective reserves provided to the banks by the Fed or the higher the rate of interest, the greater is the amount of money supplied by the commercial banks. The relationship between the amount of money supplied by the banks and the interest rate is plotted in Figure 29–3 for a given amount of R^E. Increases in R^E shift the schedule outward to the right, and decreases inward to the left. The Fed may be assumed to supply reserves independently of interest rates. Thus, the more the slope of the schedule deviates from a perfectly vertical line for a given amount of effective reserves provided by the Fed, the greater is the importance of forces not under Fed control (either intentionally or unintentionally) in determining the supply of money. The Fed can, of course, if it so wishes, change R^E to offset any undesirable changes in money supply caused by changes in interest rates. It is the senior partner in determining the quantity of money outstanding at any time.

---

[5] In equation form at time t

$$R_t^E = R_{t-1}^E \pm \Delta R(OMO) \pm \Delta R(BR) \mp \Delta rr_D D_{t-1}$$

where: $OMO =$ open-market operations
$BR =$ borrowed reserves at the discount rate
$D =$ transaction deposits

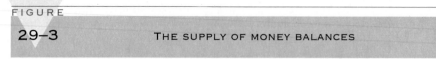

FIGURE

29-3   THE SUPPLY OF MONEY BALANCES

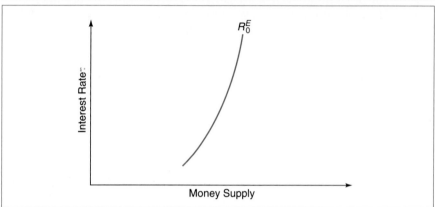

Interest Rates

The equilibrium level of interest rates is determined by the interaction of the demand schedule for money and the supply schedule of money. This point is obtained by equating equations 29–5 and 29–7:

$$DM = SM$$

$$\overset{+\,-}{f(Y,\,i)} = \overset{+\,+}{f(R^E,\,i)}$$

and solving for i:

$$i = \overset{-\quad+}{f(R^E,\,Y)} \tag{29–8}$$

This is two thirds of the formulation as developed in Chapter 6. The variable that is missing on the right-hand side of the equation is price expectations. This must be added to complete the specification. Thus

$$i = \overset{-\quad+\ +}{f(R^E,\,Y,\,\dot{P}_E)} \tag{29–9}$$

If we assume that the Fed has total control over the quantity of money, so that it is not a function of interest rates, this equation may be written:

$$i = \overset{-\ +\,+}{f(M,\,Y,\,\dot{P}_E)}, \tag{29–10}$$

which is the liquidity preference specification developed in Chapter 6.

Graphically, the equilibrium market rate of interest may be obtained by combining Figures 29–2 and 29–3. This is done in Figure 29–4. The

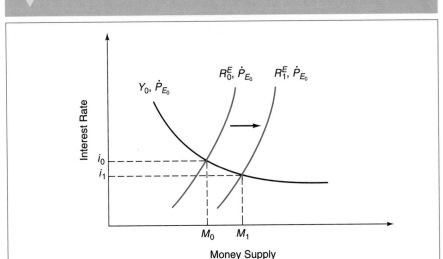

FIGURE

29–4   EQUILIBRIUM INTEREST RATE

demand for money is drawn for a given income, Y_0; the supply of money for a given effective reserve base provided by the Fed, R_0^E; and both schedules for a given rate of price expectations, $\dot{P}_{E_0}$. The higher the income or the lower the effective reserves, the higher the interest rate is. It follows that the Fed can affect the level of interest rates by changing effective reserves. An increase in effective reserves from R_0^E to R_1^E in Figure 29–4 increases the supply of money from M_0 to M_1 and lower interest rates from i_0 to i_1. A decrease in effective reserves (not shown) reduces the money supply and increases interest rates. But this is not the whole story, as we shall see later in Chapter 33. The initial change in interest rates brought about by the change in effective reserves by the Fed, referred to as the ***liquidity effect,*** in time affects income and price expectations in the opposite direction. These effects will feed back onto later interest rates through the process described in equation 29–9 and attenuate or even offset the initial change. Increases in money will initially lower interest rates but may in time cause them to increase as the lower rates increase income and expectations of future price increases. As a result, it is difficult to make precise statements on the basis of the analysis so far about the final direction of change and level of interest rates after a Fed policy action. Nevertheless, because changes in interest rates affect spending on goods and services, interest rates transmit Federal Reserve actions that change the money supply from the financial sector to the real sector.

In the next chapters, we shall put these theories to work to explain how monetary policy may be used to stabilize the economy.

SUMMARY

Monetary theories describe the relations between one or more financial variables, such as money supply and interest rates, and other variables in the financial sector as well as variables in the real sector. In particular, monetary theories attempt to identify the key variables on the linkage path along which a monetary policy action travels from the time the Fed initiates the action until it affects the intended goals of economic policy. The test of a theory is in its ability to predict. The earliest monetary theory is the quantity theory, which postulates a direct proportional relation between changes in the money supply and changes in prices. This relation was predicated on the assumption that neither money velocity nor real income varied greatly in the short run. When economies became more developed, the quantity theory predicted more poorly as both velocity and real income varied increasingly more.

Keynes switched the emphasis of monetary theory from the supply of money to the demand for money. He postulated that spending units demand to hold money balances for both transaction and speculative purposes and that both factors can be summarized by income and interest rates. The demand for money varies directly with aggregate income and inversely with interest rates. Changes in money no longer affect only income. The supply of money was described in earlier chapters as being determined jointly by the Fed and depository institutions. The Fed determines the amount of effective reserves, and the banks determine the intensity with which they will be used according to interest rates. When the demand for money is set equal to the supply of money, equilibrium interest rates are determined. Interest rates link the financial and real sectors. Fed actions that change the supply of money are transmitted to other sectors through changes in the interest rate.

QUESTIONS

1. "It may be good in theory, but it doesn't work in practice" is a commonly heard statement. Discuss your agreement or disagreement with the validity of this statement on the basis of your understanding of the role of theory.

2. How would you test the usefulness of a theory? Why? "Assume that the world is flat." When might this statement be absurd and when might it be useful in terms of getting from point A to point B?

3. Why and when are economic theories useful in explaining the behavior of the real world? How can one differentiate among alternative theories that attempt to explain the same occurrences?

4. Describe the quantity theory of money. Why was it used more frequently in the United States before the twentieth century than in the twentieth century? Go to recent *Federal Reserve Bulletins* in your library and compute income velocity annually for the last 10 years. How can you explain its behavior?

5. What major changes did Keynes introduce in monetary theory? How did these changes address the weaknesses of the quantity theory?

6. Why might there be a demand for money balances for purposes other than transactions? How does this demand vary with interest rates? Why?

7. Who is the primary determinant of the money supply? Why? What role do the other determinants play? Why is velocity an important variable for the Fed to predict? What happens if it misses?

Carlson, John B., "The Stability of Money Demand, Its Interest Sensitivity, and Some Implications for Money as a Policy Guide," *Economic Review*, Federal Reserve Bank of Cleveland, Third Quarter 1989, pp. 2–13.

Clower, R. W., ed., *Monetary Theory*. Middlesex, England: Penguin Books, 1969.

Dean, Edwin, ed., *The Controversy over the Quantity Theory of Money*. Lexington, Mass.: Heath, 1965.

Friedman, Milton, *Essays in Positive Economics*. Chicago: University of Chicago Press, 1953.

Friedman, Milton, and Anna J. Schwartz, *Monetary Trends in the United States and the United Kingdom*. Chicago: University of Chicago Press, 1982 (particularly Chapter 2).

Hein, Scott E., and Paul T. W. M. Veugelers, "Predicting Velocity Growth: A Time Series Perspective," *Review*, Federal Reserve Bank of St. Louis, October 1983, pp. 34–43.

Humphrey, Thomas M., "The Quantity Theory of Money: Its Historical Evolution and Role in Policy Debates," *Economic Review*, Federal Reserve Bank of Richmond, May/June 1974, pp. 2–19.

Humphrey, Thomas M., "Two Views of Monetary Policy: The Attwood-Mill Debate Revisited," *Economic Review*, Federal Reserve Bank of Richmond, September/October 1977, pp. 14–22.

Judd, John P., and John L. Scadding, "The Search for a Stable Money Demand Function," *Journal of Economic Literature*, September 1982, pp. 993–1023.

Laidler, David E. W., *The Demand for Money: Theories, Evidence, and Problems*, 3rd ed. New York: Harper-Collins, 1993.

Thorn, Richard S., ed. *Monetary Theory and Policy*. New York: Random House, 1966.

Wrightsman, Dwayne, *An Introduction to Monetary Theory and Policy*, 3rd ed. New York: Free Press, 1983.

Money and Economic Activity

The economy of the United States is highly complex. There are more than 250 million free spirits roaming about in the economy. Their tastes, preferences, and actions are difficult to chart and apt to vary greatly from person to person. These traits are not well defined, are subject to change without notice, and are buffeted by numerous and diverse forces. Because of the wide differences among individual traits, averages for large groups of households or business firms may not be very meaningful. Moreover, although we want to isolate only the economic behavior, it is difficult to separate this behavior completely from social, political, psychological, and other influences.

However, we can be relatively confident about some economic relationships. For example, *ceteris paribus*, the higher the price of any good or service, the less will be the quantity of it we demand. But even here, sometimes it is difficult to identify all the *ceteris paribuses*. Sales of automobiles are certainly higher now than 50 years ago, even though their price is much higher. But then personal incomes have risen, highways have improved, public transportation has faltered, and so on. Nevertheless, demand and supply relationships are among the most certain in economics and finance.

Most other relationships are less certain than demand and supply. They involve many variables that may interact with each other in complex and, at times, mysterious ways. A precise description of the economy is not easy to put together. But if we want to discuss happenings in the economy and their implications, we must have some framework in mind. Indeed, whenever we make a statement about economic behavior, we have some picture of the economy in mind, however hazy. Without any picture at all, one would not really know what to say, outside of purely random comments. The clearer the picture, the more precise, meaningful, and defensible the statement can be. In this chapter, we shall construct a simple, superficial, but useful model of the economy.

A model is a representation of the "real thing." Thus, we have model airplanes, model automobiles, model cities, and even "model" human beings. Models may be in either physical or mathematical form, such as a system of equations describing the underlying structure of the phenomenon being analyzed. A mathematical model is a theory stated in very precise language. For obvious reasons, models of the economy are cheaper and more useful in mathematical form than in physical form. It is also generally easier and cheaper to experiment on the model than on the real thing. But a model, regardless of how elaborate, is only as good as its description of the real thing. This, in turn, can be evaluated only by how well the model predicts actual observations.

The model developed in this and other chapters in this book provides us with a description of only the most basic relationships of the economy.

It does not furnish any details, refinements, or nuances. Moreover, it gives us only a partial description of the relationships it does consider. Nevertheless, it permits us some important insights into the operation of the economy and allows us to trace through the major consequences of economic policy actions.

The Financial Sector

With the strong caveats above, we will proceed to construct a one-diagram model of the domestic U.S. economy. The economy will be divided into two sectors, a financial sector and a real sector. The financial sector is described by the two demand and supply equations for money (29–5 and 29–7) developed in the preceding chapter. In equilibrium, the demand for money must equal the supply of money. If we temporarily neglect price expectations and set the two equations equal to each other, we obtain the equilibrium relationship between the interest rate and aggregate nominal income described in equation 29–8:

$$i = f(\overset{-}{R^E}, \overset{+}{Y}) \tag{30-1}$$

Unlike the interest rate–reserve or money relationship plotted in Figure 29–2, we now focus on the interest rate–income relationship. The *ceteris paribus* relationship between the interest rate and aggregate nominal income, holding constant the amount of effective reserves supplied by the Fed, is referred to as the **LM function.** (*L* refers to the demand for money or liquidity preference, and *M* for the supply of money.) An *LM* function is plotted in Figure 30–1 for a given R^E. Interest rate is measured on the vertical

FIGURE

30–1 THE *LM-IS* MODEL

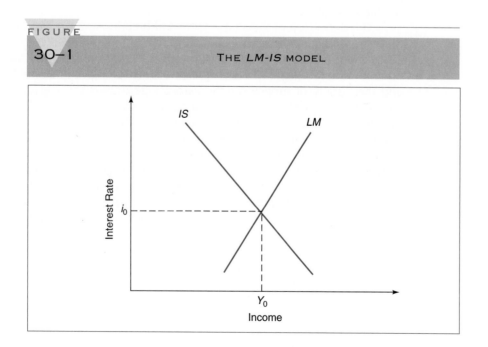

FIGURE

30–2

DERIVATION OF *LM* FUNCTION

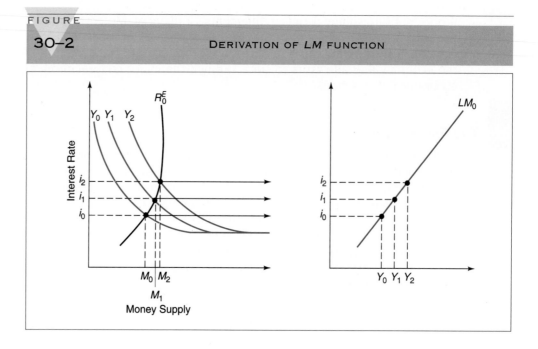

axis and income on the horizontal axis. All points on this line show values of i and Y that satisfy equation 30–1. As a result, the financial sector is in equilibrium at all points along the *LM* function. The function slopes upward to the right, so that interest rates increase as income increases. This occurs because as income increases, the public's demand for money balances increases and, holding the amount of reserves constant, exerts upward pressure on interest rates. The higher income is, *ceteris paribus*, the higher the interest rate.

The derivation of the shape of the *LM* function and the reason for the direct relationship between income and interest rates are shown in Figure 30–2. The panel on the left shows the demand for money function developed in Chapter 29 and plotted in Figure 29–2 for a given income level Y_0, and the supply of money function from Figure 29–3 for a given level of effective reserves R_0^E. Price expectations are held constant. The demand for money is equal to the supply of money where the two schedules intersect. This occurs at i_0, M_0. Now let aggregate income increase to Y_1, *ceteris paribus*. The demand for money function shifts up to the right, and the interest rate increases to i_1. If income increases again to Y_2, interest rates increase to i_2, and so on. The derived relation between income and interest rates may be transferred directly to the panel on the right, where income is measured on the horizontal axis and interest rate on the vertical axis. The points form the *LM* function. When income is Y_0, the interest rate is i_0. As income increases from Y_0 to Y_1 to Y_2 and monetary policy as depicted in changes in the R^E schedule remains unchanged, the interest rate increases from i_0 to i_1 to i_2.

Changes in effective reserves by the Fed shift the location of the *LM* function. Increases in R^E shift the *LM* function out to the right, and decreases in to the left.

The Real Sector

The real or commodity sector of the economy comprises three broad sectors: consumption (C), investment (I), and government (G). (For the sake of simplicity, the foreign sector, encompassing exports and imports, is omitted.) Spending on final goods and services in these sectors at current market prices sums to GDP (Y). This may be written:

$$Y = C + I + G \qquad\qquad (30\text{--}2)$$

We shall examine the principal determinants of spending in each of these sectors one at a time.

Consumption

Consumption goods are those that are totally used up immediately, or almost so. For purposes of definition, **consumption goods** are generally defined as goods consumed totally in one year or less, although, for the sake of expediency, the government considers all consumer durables, even automobiles, as consumption goods. (Reliable sources at the U.S. Department of Commerce, which puts out the GDP figures, assured me that this is not intended to be a commentary on the quality of the automobiles.) The aggregate demand for consumption goods in the economy is basically the sum of individual demands. What determines your personal demand for consumption goods? You would most likely include the following on your list:

1. Current income
2. Borrowing power or future income
3. Wealth or savings from past income
4. Current and expected prices
5. Current and expected interest rates
6. Tax rates
7. Family requirements
8. Individual tastes and preferences

These same variables are apt to determine other persons' consumption expenditures and thus aggregate consumption spending as well. The last two determinants may change for any individual from year to year but are likely to remain relatively stable for the economy as a whole. As one household starts upon family formation, another calls it quits.

One of the strongest relationships in economics is that between annual or longer-term income and spending on consumption. The higher income is, the higher consumption is. Although the other determinants of aggregate consumption expenditures just listed are also important, we shall ignore them for the moment and assume that aggregate consumption expenditures in current dollars are a function of only aggregate nominal income:

$$C = \overset{+}{f}(Y) \qquad\qquad (30\text{--}3)$$

This expression may be written in linear form as

$$C = a + bY \qquad\qquad (30\text{–}3\text{A})$$

where b is the change in consumption expenditures for every unit change in income, and a is a constant that reflects the net effect of all other forces on consumption.

The values of a and b are obtained through statistical techniques such as regression analysis that fit the equation to the actual observations of the variables. The term b is called the **marginal propensity to consume** out of income. Its value is less than 1 for all but exceptional periods. That is, aggregate expenditures on consumption goods and services will increase with increases in income, but less than proportionately. Equation 30–3A can be fitted statistically to annual observations of C and GDP in the United States since 1900. The resulting equation is

$$C = 2.7 + 0.63 \text{ GDP}$$

The R^2, or coefficient of determination, is 0.99. This indicates that 99 percent of the variance in annual consumption is statistically explained by the variance in annual GDP. The highest possible value of $R^2 = 1.0$, so this represents a pretty good fit. The estimated value of b is 0.63. This indicates that for every \$1 increase in GDP in this period, consumption expenditures increased on average by 63 cents. Actual changes in consumption expenditures in any one year may have been greater or less than 63 cents but, for the period as a whole, averaged to this amount. The aggregate marginal propensity to consume varies depending on the measure of income used. If only after-tax household income is used, the value increases to near 0.92 for the period since 1929, so that, on average, about 92 cents of every \$1 increase in disposable income is spent on consumption.

If we abstract for the moment from government spending, income that is not spent on consumption goods and services is saved. That is, $Y - C = S$, or $Y = C + S$. Thus, saving is also a function of income and may be written in linear form as:

$$S = d + sY \qquad\qquad (30\text{–}3\text{B})$$

where S is aggregate saving in current dollars, s is the **marginal propensity to save** and indicates the dollar amount of saving for every dollar change in income, and d is a constant. Dividing both sides of $S = Y - C$ by Y yields $s = 1 - b$. Thus, the higher the marginal propensity to save, the lower the marginal propensity to consume. If the marginal propensity to consume out of disposable income is 0.9, the marginal propensity to save is 0.1.

In addition to income, expenditures on consumption goods and services are affected by the interest rate both directly and indirectly. Directly, i affects C in two ways. One, some expenditures are financed by borrowing against future income. The lower the cost of borrowing, the more likely are consumers to finance expenditures in this way. Two, the interest rate helps consumers determine how to divide their income between consumption and saving. The lower the rate of interest, the lower the return on saving, the smaller will be saving, and the greater will be expenditures on consumption.

Indirectly, interest rates affect spending on consumption by affecting the market value of consumers' wealth (consisting of stocks, bonds, homes, and personal assets), which affects consumption directly. Recall from Chapter 5 that bond prices are inversely related to interest rates; the lower interest rates are, the higher bond prices are. Similarly, the present value or market price of any asset generating a stream of future services increases when the interest rate by which the value of the services is discounted declines. Thus, the lower are market rates of interest, the higher is the market value of wealth. This **wealth effect** may be written as

$$C = f(\overset{+}{W}) \qquad (30\text{–}4)$$

where

$$W = f(\overset{-}{i}) \qquad (30\text{–}4A)$$

The direct and indirect effects of interest rates on consumption expenditures may be observed in Figure 30–3. For any given market values of Y and W, say, Y_0 and W_0, interest rates vary inversely with expenditures on consumption. At interest rate i_0, consumption expenditures are C_0. Now let interest rates decline from i_0 to i_1. As a direct consequence, expenditures on consumption increase from C_0 to C'. But the decrease in interest rates also increases the market value of consumers' wealth to W_1. This is shown by an outward shift in the Y_0W schedule to Y_0W_1, indicating greater consumption expenditures at every level of interest rates. Thus, at i_1, consumption increases by an additional amount $C' - C_1$. The total increase in consump-

FIGURE

30–3

INTEREST RATES AFFECT CONSUMPTION DIRECTLY AND INDIRECTLY.

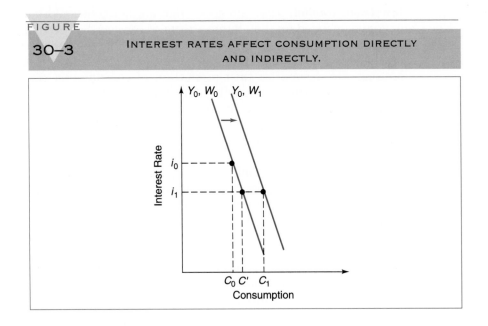

tion caused by the decline in interest rates is $C_0 - C_1$, equal to the sum of the direct effect $C_0 - C'$, and the indirect wealth effect, $C' - C_1$. Thus, the wealth effect reinforces the direct interest rate effect.

A more complete consumption function may now be written:

$$C = \overset{+ \ - \ +}{f(Y, i, W)} \tag{30–5}$$

and the corresponding savings function:

$$S = \overset{+ \ + \ +}{f(Y, i, W)} \tag{30–5A}$$

For the economy as a whole, aggregate income equals the value of aggregate output. Goods and services not consumed are, by definition, saved. For the economy as a whole, saving is undertaken in the form of durable or capital goods, or goods that are consumed slowly through time. (Recall that financial securities are claims on real goods, so that if someone saves in the form of financial securities, someone else either saves in the form of real goods or dissaves by selling securities.) Capital goods include business plant and equipment and residential housing. The consumption of capital goods through time is termed **depreciation.** The buildup of capital goods is termed **investment.**

If the marginal propensity to consume is greater than 1, the marginal propensity to save is negative and the economy will be consuming its capital stock. Investment will be negative. Aggregate dissaving is obviously not possible for long for any economy and is apt to occur only during deep depressions, such as that of the 1930s.

Investment

Investment (capital) goods are goods that are not consumed immediately but are demanded for their future stream of services. Business investment goods, such as plant and equipment, are desired for their ability to produce other goods and services. Household investment goods, such as residential housing, are desired for their production of consumption services. The demand for investment goods is a function of many factors, including the present value of the expected future stream of the services they provide less operating costs (expected profits for business firms), technological improvements, changes in the demand for the goods produced, prices, tax rates, and interest rates.

At any moment of time, investors are faced with a large number of alternative investment opportunities having different expected returns. The number of projects having a given expected rate of return may be expected to vary inversely with the level of returns, so that the higher the expected return the fewer the number of potential investment projects, and the lower the expected return the larger the number of projects available. Thus, the higher the interest rate, *ceteris paribus*, the fewer are the number of investment opportunities that promise to be profitable, and conversely. (In actuality, it is the real interest rate, defined as the nominal rate less some adjustment for expected price changes, not the nominal rate, that determines investment spending. Unless price expectations are incorporated in estimates of the future profitability of an investment, they must be sub-

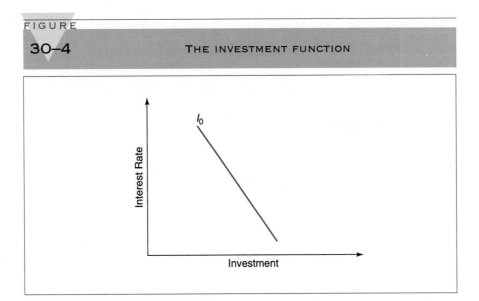

FIGURE

30–4   THE INVESTMENT FUNCTION

tracted from current market rates of interest to maintain comparability. But for the sake of simplicity, we shall use nominal rates.) The higher market interest rates and the cost of funds are, the lower is spending on investment goods. Interest rates are probably the most important single determinant of investment spending, so we can write a simple investment function as:

$$I = f(\overline{i}) \qquad\qquad (30\text{–}6)$$

The *ceteris paribus* investment–interest rate relationship is referred to as the **marginal efficiency of investment,** or *MEI*, schedule and is plotted in Figure 30–4.

Government

Most government spending is based on social and political criteria rather than on economic ones. Thus, governments provide funds for national defense, internal security, social welfare, health, education, and so on. It is reasonable to assume that these expenditures are independent of current interest rates, prices, and even national income beyond some minimum level. Most government spending in the United States is determined through the political process. Moreover, to the extent that government spending is motivated by economic factors, these are generally not the same factors as those that determine private spending. Economically motivated federal government spending is generally undertaken to offset changes in private spending and thereby to attempt to stabilize the economy. If private spending declines and is too low to provide full employment, government spending is increased. If private spending increases to the point that it creates inflationary pressures, government spending is reduced.

Federal government spending undertaken to stabilize the economy is termed **fiscal policy** and is discussed in greater detail in the next chapter. For purposes of our model, we shall assume that government spending is not determined by any of the other variables included in the model. Rather, it is determined solely by outside or **exogenous** forces and may be treated as given. Thus

$$G = G_0 \qquad\qquad (30\text{–}7)$$

Total Spending

We can now substitute the principal determinants of spending in each of the three sectors C, I, and G from equations 30–5, 30–6, and 30–7 in the equation for Y, equation 30–2. This gives[1]

$$Y = \overset{+\,-}{f(Y, i)} + \overset{-}{f(i)} + G_0$$

Collecting terms and solving for i:

$$i = \overset{-\,+}{f(Y, G_0)} \qquad\qquad (30\text{–}8)$$

The *ceteris paribus* equilibrium relationship between interest rates and aggregate nominal income for a given level of government spending is referred to as the **IS function.** (*I* refers to investment and *S* to saving, or $Y - C$.) An IS function is plotted in Figure 30–1 for a given level of government expenditures, G_0. Similar to the LM function, the interest rate is measured on the vertical axis and income on the horizontal axis. Thus, the IS and LM functions may be drawn on the same diagram. All points on the IS schedule are values of Y and i that satisfy equation 30–8. At all points along the IS function, the real sector is in equilibrium. Contrary to the LM function, the IS function slopes downward to the right. Higher incomes are associated with lower interest rates.

The reason for the negative slope may be seen from Figure 30–5. The investment–interest rate schedule shown in Figure 30–4 is plotted in the left panel. Also plotted is the saving relationship from equation 30–5A. The higher is the rate of interest, the greater will be the amount of income saved. But saving is also a function of income. As long as the marginal propensity to consume in equation 30–3A is less than 1, so that dollar expenditures on consumption increase less than increases in income, the marginal propensity to save, which is shown as s in equation 30–3B, is greater than 0 and saving increases as aggregate income increases. (Price expectations are again assumed to remain unchanged.) When aggregate income is Y_0, aggregate saving is S_0 and the equilibrium interest rate is i_0. Now let income increase. If income increases to Y_1, saving increases to S_1 and, as there is greater saving to finance investment, the interest rate declines to i_1; and if income increases further to Y_2, the interest rate declines further to i_2. The derived interest rate–income relationship can again be transferred from the left panel to the right panel, which shows only interest rate and income, to develop the IS function. When income is Y_0, the

---

[1] In actuality, C, I, and G are not independent of each other, and changes in one are likely to produce changes in the others.

FIGURE

30–5

579

MONEY AND
ECONOMIC ACTIVITY

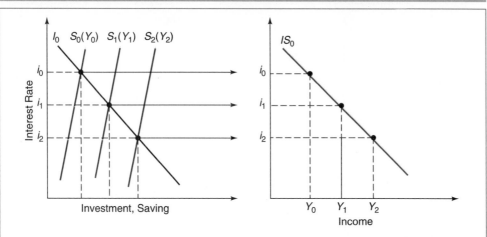

DERIVATION OF *IS* FUNCTION

interest rate is i_0. As income increases to Y_1 and Y_2, *ceteris paribus*, the interest rate decreases to i_1 and i_2.

Changes in government spending or fiscal policy (as well as in consumption spending for reasons other than a change in income and in investment for reasons other than a change in interest rates) shift the *IS* function. Increases in these exogenous expenditures shift the *IS* function out to the right, and decreases in to the left.

Equilibrium in both the financial and real sectors of the economy simultaneously and thus in the economy overall is achieved at the point of intersection of the *LM* and *IS* schedules. This is shown as Y_0, i_0 in Figure 30–1. Y_0 represents equilibrium aggregate nominal income. The entire economy in a nutshell, or at least in one diagram! But, as is true for almost all simplifications, the one-diagram *LM-IS* model does at times give incorrect and misleading answers.

Full-Employment Income

The *LM-IS* analysis developed above solves for equilibrium nominal income for given values of the exogenous variables (R^E and G) and under the restrictive assumptions discussed earlier. However, the equilibrium income solution may not be equivalent to the target income level—say, the level that is consistent with full employment at stable prices or any other one of combination of economic goals discussed in Chapter 26. If equilibrium income differs from target income, the federal government may use economic policy to attempt to equate the two. This is referred to as **contra-cyclical** or **stabilization policy.**

Figure 30–6a shows the case where equilibrium income derived from the *LM-IS* model happens to be equal to target income—say, full-employment–stable-price-level income (Y_F). In panel b, equilibrium income falls short of full-employment income. The distance on the horizontal axis between equilibrium income Y_D and full-employment income

FIGURE

30-6

EQUILIBRIUM INCOME AND INFLATIONARY
AND DEFLATIONARY GAPS

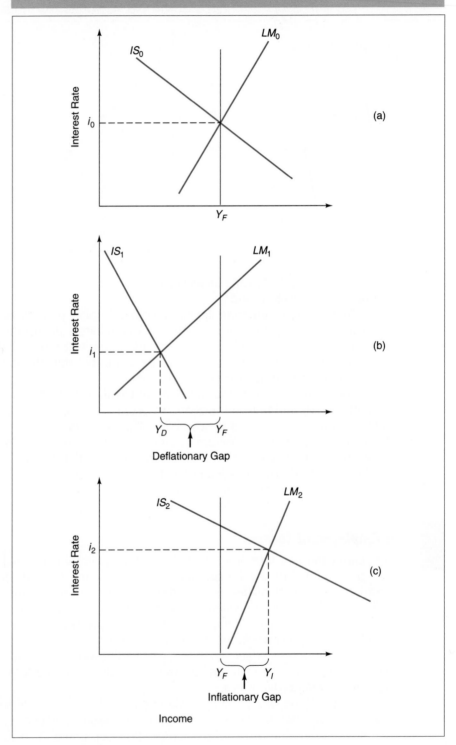

zontal axis between equilibrium income Y_D and full-employment income Y_F, or $Y_F - Y_D$, is referred to as a ***deflationary gap.*** Because some unemployment is generally accepted to be consistent with full-employment income, a deflationary gap indicates the presence of "excessive" unemployment. If equilibrium income exceeds full-employment income, an ***inflationary gap*** is said to exist. This is shown in Figure 30–6c. The inflationary gap is equal to $Y_I - Y_F$.

For the sake of simplicity, we shall assume that all of the deflationary gap represents excessive unemployment and all of the inflationary gap represents excessive rates of price inflation. In reality, unemployment is related to the difference between full employment and actual real income rather than nominal income. A real deflationary gap may exist whether or not a nominal deflationary gap exists. Inflation may disguise part or all of the real gap. In Chapter 34 we shall break nominal income into its real-income and price components and explore the implications of economic policy on each.

Shifts in either the *LM* or the *IS* function will shift equilibrium income up or down, toward or away from target income. The effects of deliberate shifts in the *LM* function by the Federal Reserve through changing R^E and in the *IS* function by the federal government through changing *G* or other variables under its control will be discussed in the next chapter. Changes in R^E represent Federal Reserve monetary policy, and changes in *G* represent fiscal policy.

Once again, keep firmly in mind that this model is a vast oversimplification of the actual economy and is useful only for limited purposes. The limited input into the model limits the output. Some of the results are only partial and can be misleading if interpreted out of context. We shall examine some of these problems in later chapters. But the model does permit us to trace some of the more important implications of monetary and fiscal policy changes for levels of economic activity. Much larger and more complete models of the U.S. economy are commonly used by business firms, the federal government, and others both to predict output and prices in total and in various sectors of the economy and to stimulate the implications of alternative policy strategies. Some of the larger models have more than 1,000 equations to predict the same number of sectors. In later chapters, we shall enlarge our model slightly to increase its relevance to the real world.

SUMMARY

This chapter constructs a simple one-diagram, two-sector model of the economy. The financial sector is summarized by the demand for and supply of money. When the two are in equilibrium, aggregate nominal income may be described as a function of the interest rate in the *LM* schedule. The *LM* schedule slopes up to the right. The real sector encompasses spending on consumption, investment, and government goods. In equilibrium, aggregate income is related to interest rates in the *IS* function. The *IS* function slopes down to the right. The economy is in equilibrium when the *LM* schedule intercepts the *IS* schedule.

But the equilibrium income determined by the intersection of the *LM* and *IS* schedules may not be the level consistent with the goals of economic policy. If the equilibrium income were greater than full-employment income were less, there would be a deflationary gap. Economic policy may be used to close these gaps. Shifts in the *LM* schedule caused by changes in R^E depict Federal Reserve monetary policy, and shifts in the *IS* schedule caused by changes in G depict federal government fiscal policy.

QUESTIONS

1. Derive the *LM* function shown in equation 30–1 from the demand and supply functions for money. Which way does the *LM* function slope on a graph with interest rate on the vertical axis and income on the horizontal axis? How can you explain this?

2. Derive the *IS* function shown in equation 30–8. Which way does it slope? What can cause this function to shift?

3. How is equilibrium income determined in the *LM-IS* model? What happens to equilibrium income if *M* increases? C increases? *I* decreases?

4. How are the following policy actions depicted in the *LM-IS* model?
   a. Reduction in reserve requirements
   b. Increase in the Fed discount rate
   c. Fed open-market purchases of Treasury securities
   d. Increase in government expenditures
   e. Increase in tax rates

5. Why may the equilibrium income determined by an *LM-IS* model not be the appropriate level of aggregate income that the economy wishes? If it is not, what can the government attempt to do? How?

6. Define *inflationary gap* and *deflationary gap* graphically and verbally. What economic stabilization policy actions would you recommend for each gap?

7. Assume:
$$C = 80$$
$$T = 30$$
$$I = 20$$
$$G = 10$$
$$W = 300$$

What is GDP (*Y*)? If we exclude the government sector, what is *S*? If we introduce the government sector, need *S* = *I* at all times? Why or why not? If now *T* = 15, what would *S* be? If interest rates increase, what happens to *C*, *I*, *W*, and *Y*? Why? For most countries, would you expect *Y* or *W* to be larger?

REFERENCE

Bennett, Paul, "The Influence of Financial Changes on Interest Rates and Monetary Policy," *Quarterly Review*, Federal Reserve Bank of New York, Summer 1990, pp. 8–30.

Boorman, John T., and Thomas M. Havrilesky, *Money Supply, Money Demand, and Macroeconomic Models*. Boston: Allyn & Bacon, 1972.

Carson, Carol, "National Income and Product Accounts in the U.S.: An Overview," *Survey of Current Business*, February 1981.

Dornbusch, Rudiger, and Stanley Fischer, *Macroeconomics*, 6th ed. New York: McGraw-Hill, 1993.

Gordon, Robert J., *Macroeconomics*, 6th ed. Glenview, Ill.: Scott Foresman, 1993.

Hirtle, Beverly, and Jeanette Kelleher, "Financial Market Evolution and the Interest Sensitivity of Output," *Quarterly Review*, Federal Reserve Bank of New York, Summer 1990, pp. 56–70.

Kaufman, George G., *Money, The Financial System and the Economy*, 3rd ed. Boston: Houghton Mifflin, 1981.

Laidler, David E.W., *The Demand for Money: Theories and Evidence*, 2nd ed. New York: Dun-Donnelley, 1977.

Poole, William, *Money and the Economy: A Monetarist View*. Reading, Mass.: Addison-Wesley, 1978.

Spencer, Roger, "Channels of Monetary Influence: A Survey," *Review*, Federal Reserve Bank of St. Louis, November 1974, pp. 8–26.

Tobin, James, "Monetary Policies and the Economy: The Transmission Mechanism," *Southern Economic Journal*, January 1978, pp. 421–31.

Monetary Policy

Monetary policy involves the manipulation of financial variables by the Federal Reserve in order to achieve the economy's ultimate goals of full employment and balanced economic growth at stable prices. A large body of empirical evidence collected over long periods of time in many developed countries indicates that changes in the money supply are a major cause of changes in aggregate income and prices. Indeed, if such evidence did not exist, there would not be much purpose in studying money or worrying about shifts in the *LM* function.

In addition to the ultimate goals, the Fed is also concerned with a number of sectoral goals, either because the achievement of them is considered a prerequisite for the achievement of the ultimate goals or because social and political priorities differ from the economic priorities determined by the marketplace. The first type of sectoral objective includes stability in the money and capital market; the second includes high levels of residential construction and "adequate" credit for small business and agriculture.

In Chapter 28 we discussed the Fed's tools of monetary policy—basically: open market operations, changes in reserve requirements, and changes in the discount rate—and in Chapter 30 we constructed a simple, one-diagram model of the economy. In this chapter, we trace the path by which the effects of Fed actions travel through the financial sector of the economy into the real sector and eventually impinge on the sectoral and ultimate goals of policy. We restrict our analysis to the Fed's use of quantitative tools—open-market operations, reserve requirements, and the discount rate—that affect aggregate effective reserves. In later chapters we shall examine a number of important problems that directly affect the effectiveness of monetary policy.

Monetary policy is depicted in the *LM-IS* model by parallel shifts in the *LM* function brought about by changes in effective reserves (R^E) by the Fed. These shifts change the amount of the money. (Shifts in the *LM* function may also occur for reasons other than Federal Reserve actions, such as a change in the public's demand for money balances.) The Fed may close deflationary gaps by increasing the money supply through purchasing securities on the open market, reducing reserve requirements, and/or reducing the discount rate. Through increasing effective bank reserves, these actions shift the *LM* schedule outward to the right by an amount necessary, it is hoped, to achieve the target income. (The transmission mechanism through which this occurs is discussed later in this chapter.) The Fed may close inflationary gaps by decreasing the money supply through selling securities on the open market, increasing reserve requirements, and/or increasing the discount rate. These actions shift the *LM* function inward to the left. (In reality, because the economy is growing, the Fed changes the rate of growth of the money supply rather than its absolute level, and income grows at a faster or slower pace rather than increasing or decreasing.) In the remainder of this chapter, we shall assume that shifts in the *LM* function reflect only deliberate changes the Fed makes in the money supply.

Strength of Monetary Policy

The strength of a monetary policy action may be measured by the resulting change in nominal income per dollar change in money supply, or $\Delta Y/\Delta M$. The change in income produced by a shift in the *LM* function depends on

1. The size of the shift.
2. The slope of the *LM* function, and
3. The slope of the *IS* function.

The first factor is self-evident. As can be inferred from Figure 31–1, the larger the shift in the *LM* function, the larger is the change in income, *ceteris paribus*.

Slope of the LM Function

The *slope* of a line is defined as the change in the variable that is measured on the vertical axis for each unit change in the variable that is measured on the vertical axis for each unit change in the variable that is measured on the horizontal axis. For the *LM* schedule in Figure 31–1, the slope is equal to $\Delta i/\Delta Y$. The slope of a function is also given by the value of the coefficient of the corresponding variable on the right-hand side in the equation describ-

FIGURE

31–1   THE STEEPER THE *LM* FUNCTION, THE MORE POTENT MONETARY POLICY IS.

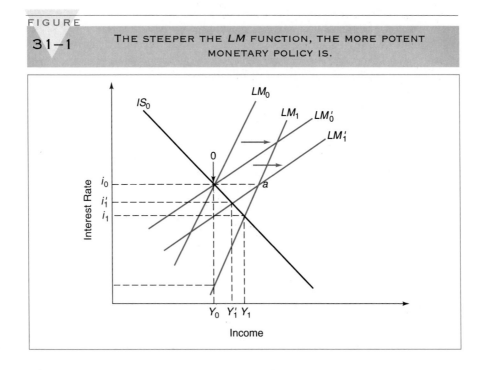

ing the function. For example, the value of b in equation 30–3A is the slope of the consumption-income schedule. The greater the slope, the steeper the line.

The slope of the LM function depends on the slopes of the underlying demand-for-money and supply-of-money schedules. The steeper the demand-for-money function or the supply-of-money function in Figure 30–2, that is, the less either the demand for or the supply of money depends on interest rates, the steeper the LM function.

The steeper the LM function, the greater will be the change in income per unit shift in the LM function. This is shown in Figure 31–1. Schedule LM_0 is steeper than schedule LM_0'. For both schedules, equilibrium income is Y_0 and equilibrium interest rate i_0. Let the Fed increase the money supply by a specified amount, from point 0 to point a. Both LM functions shift to pass through this point. But, with no change in the IS function, equilibrium income will increase to Y_1 as a result of the shift in LM_0 to LM_1 and only to Y_1' as a result of the shift in LM_0' to LM'_1. The larger increase in income with the steeper LM function occurs because of a greater decline in interest rates that stimulates greater investment spending. Interest rates decline to i_1 when the steeper schedule shifts and only to i_1' when the flatter schedule shifts.

In contrast, for an equal shift in the IS function, due to, say, a fiscal policy action, the steeper the LM function, the smaller will be the change in income. This occurs because interest rates will change more in the same direction as the IS function, the steeper the LM function, and help cushion the effect of the shift on income. Thus, the strength of fiscal policy depends on the shapes of the money demand and supply functions. If the LM schedule were perfectly vertical, all changes in income would be due to changes in money supply. Monetary policy would be all-powerful. Shifts in the IS schedule would affect only interest rates, not income. This is the classical quantity-theory case discussed earlier. The implications of a perfectly flat LM schedule are discussed in Exhibit 31–1.

Regardless of the slope of the LM function, expansive monetary policy appears to produce the best of all worlds—higher income and lower interest rates. But beware! As we shall discuss in Chapter 33, these interest rate changes may not be the final changes if the changes in monetary policy produce a change in investment (the IS function) or in price expectations.

Conversely, the steeper the LM function, the more will a unit decrease in money supply reduce aggregate income. Restrictive monetary policies are depicted by shifts in the LM function to the left, and reduce income and increase interest rates in this model.

Slope of the IS Function

Like the slope of the LM function, the slope of the IS function is determined by the slopes of its underlying saving (or consumption) and investment functions. The flatter the investment function in Figure 30–5, the more interest-sensitive it is and the flatter the IS schedule. As can be seen from Figure 31–2, the flatter the IS schedule, the greater is the change in Y for a given shift in the LM function, and the more potent monetary policy is. This occurs because the change in the interest rate caused by the change in

EXHIBIT

31–1

587

▼

MONETARY POLICY

The Liquidity Trap

Many early Keynesians hypothesized that near bottoms of deep recessions, when interest rates decline to very low levels, the demand schedule for money becomes perfectly flat, for reasons discussed in Chapter 29. As a result, the *LM* function also becomes perfectly flat or elastic and runs parallel to the horizontal income axis. The economy is said to be in a *liquidity trap*. Under such conditions, increases in the money supply from outward shifts in the *LM* function from, say, LM_0 to LM_1 would have no effect on income or interest rates, and monetary policy would be completely impotent. This is depicted in the figure below. Part of the *LM* function is shown as perfectly flat at interest rate i_0. (The *LM* function can also be perfectly flat if the Fed operates so as to peg interest rates at some stipulated level. Shifts in the *IS* function would be completely offset by shifts in

the same direction in the *LM* function. But this is not a structural fault in the economy.) Along the flat or liquidity-trap part of the *LM* schedule, income can be in equilibrium only at Y_0 for a given *IS* function regardless of the money supply.

If the economy is caught in a liquidity trap, monetary policy is impotent. Increased emphasis must be placed on fiscal policy actions that shift the *IS* function. This is the recommendation of those who believe the U.S. economy is periodically caught in a liquidity trap. However, the weight of the empirical evidence suggests that the *LM* function is not now and probably never was, even in the worst parts of the Great Depression of the 1930s, perfectly flat. Thus, monetary policy is a useful tool for economic stabilization at all income levels.

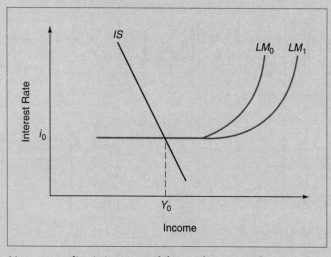

Monetary policy is impotent if the *LM* function is flat.

money supply will have a greater effect on investment spending. Increases in money supply indicated by the outward shift in the *LM* function from LM_0 to LM_1 increase income only from Y_0 to Y_1 if the *IS* schedule is steep (IS_0), and from Y_0 to Y_1' if the IS schedule is flatter (IS_0'). If the *IS* function is perfectly vertical, because interest rates have no effect on investment spending and saving whatsoever, monetary policy is totally impotent. In this

FIGURE

31–2

THE FLATTER THE *IS* FUNCTION, THE MORE
POTENT MONETARY POLICY IS.

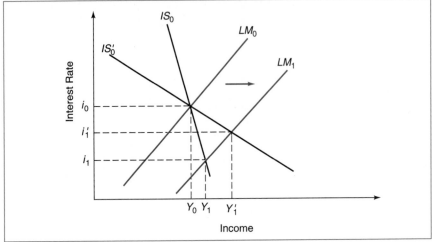

situation, shifts in the *LM* function would change only the interest rate but
not nominal income. Only fiscal policy would matter. (Perfectly vertical or
horizontal *LM* or *IS* functions are highly unlikely. Nevertheless, they are
useful to analyze in theory in order to identify the limiting cases and are
discussed further in Exhibit 31–2.)

The relationships of the *LM* and *IS* functions and the strength of monetary policy are summarized in the table below:

	Monetary Policy	
	Stronger	*Weaker*
Size of *LM* shift	Greater	Smaller
Slope of *LM* function	Steeper	Flatter
Slope of *IS* function	Flatter	Steeper

The Transmission Mechanism

The preceding section discussed the effect of changes in the money supply
on aggregate nominal income and the conditions under which monetary
policy is likely to be more or less potent. This section describes the path
along which the effect of monetary policy travels from the time the Fed acts
to the time income or some other final target of monetary policy is affected. This transmission mechanism or chain of variables cannot be traced in
detail in our single-diagram model. We can, however, trace the path more
completely with the help of the structural equations underlying the *LM-IS*
functions developed in Chapters 29 and 30.

Assume that the Fed increases effective reserves through open-market
purchases of securities, reductions in the discount rate, and/or reductions
in reserve requirements. This is indicated by an outward shift in the effec-

FIGURE

31–3

THE UNDERLYING TRANSMISSION SCHEDULES

589

MONETARY POLICY

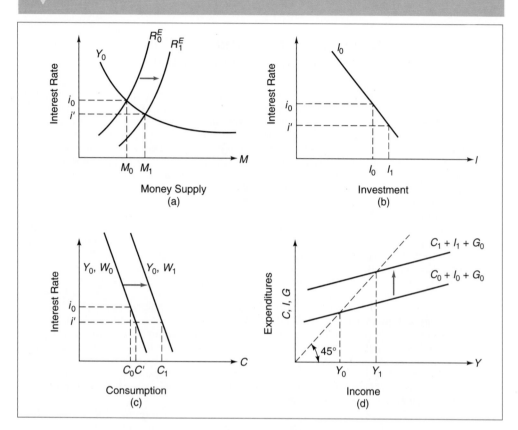

The underlying transmission schedules

tive reserves schedule in panel a of Figure 31–3 from R_0^E to R_1^E. Interest rates decline from i_0 to i' and money increases from M_0 to M_1. (In the corresponding *LM-IS* model depicted in Figure 31–4, this action is indicated by an outward shift in the *LM* schedule to LM_1.) Almost immediately, interest rates decline from i_0 to i_0. The lower interest rates stimulate investment spending in panel b of Figure 31–3 from I_0 to I_1.

The lower rates stimulate consumption expenditures in two ways. First, the lower interest rates reduce the cost of consumer credit and encourage additional spending. Consumption increases from C_0 to C' in panel c. Second, the lower rates increase the market value of wealth from W_0 to W_1 This shifts the consumption–interest rate function out to the right. The higher the market value of wealth, the greater consumption spending will be for any level of income. In Figure 31–3, consumption increases from C' to C_1. The total increase in consumption expenditures is C_0C_1, or the sum of the direct interest rate effect (C_0C') and the indirect wealth effect ($C'C_1$).

The increases in both investment and consumption spending, stimulated by the lower interest rates, cause the schedule that depicts total spending ($C + I + G$) as a function of income to shift upward, as shown in panel d. The increases in spending increase income from Y_0 to Y_1. By equa-

░░░░░░░░░░░░░░ EXHIBIT ░░░░░░░░░░░░░░

31–2

▼

Digression on Fiscal Policy, Deficits,
Crowding In, and Crowding Out

Fiscal policy supplements monetary policy as the major tool of economic stabilization in the United States. Fiscal policy involves changes by the federal government in its spending and taxing policies. Expansive fiscal policy is evidenced by *ceteris paribus* increases in government spending (*G*) or decreases in tax rates (*t*) that, in turn, increase private consumption and investment spending. (Changes in tax rates may affect supply as well as demand by affecting both work and saving incentives. These effects are termed *supply-side* economics.) In our model, expansive fiscal policy may be indicated by upward shifts directly in the *G* function and indirectly in the *C* and *I* functions and, hence, in the *IS* function. Restrictive fiscal policy involves spending cutbacks or tax-rate increases that reduce private spending. This shifts the *IS* function down. Similar to monetary policy, the strength of fiscal policy depends on (1) the magnitude of the fiscal policy action; (2) the slope of the *IS* function; and (3) the slope of the *LM* function. Fiscal policy is more potent (1) the greater the shift in the *IS* function; (2) the flatter the *LM* function; and (3) the steeper the *IS* function. The potency of fiscal policy may be measured by the change in income per unit change in government spending in the same direction ($\varnothing Y/\varnothing G$) or per unit change in tax revenues from a change in tax rates ($\varnothing Y$) in the opposite direction ($-\varnothing Y/\varnothing Y$).

If the *LM* function is perfectly vertical, so that income does not change as interest rates change, fiscal policy is impotent. Policy actions will affect only the equilibrium interest rate but not the equilibrium income. Equilibrium income is determined totally by the supply of money. This is the classical quantity case discussed in Chapter 29. Fiscal policy actions have an immediate effect on interest rates. Expansionary actions increase rates; restrictive actions decrease rates. The interest rate changes feed back onto private spending in a direction opposite to that of the fiscal action. Thus, expansive fiscal policies cut back private spending by the same amount as the increase in public spending or the decrease in tax revenues. Restrictive policies increase private spending by the

amount of the decrease in public spending or the increase in tax revenues. This feedback nullifies the intended effect of fiscal policy on income. Income remains unchanged. In the case of a perfectly vertical *LM* function, expansive fiscal policy is said to completely *crowd out* private spending and restrictive fiscal policies to completely *crowd in* private spending.

The less vertical the *LM* function, the smaller the crowding-out effects and the more potent is fiscal policy in terms of changing income for a given shift in the *IS* function. This may be seen from the figure on page 591 for *LM* functions LM_0 and LM'_0 and a shift in the *IS* function from IS_0 to IS_1. For steep function LM_0, income increases from Y_0 to Y_1; for flatter function LM_0, income increases farther to Y''_1. However, the flatter the *LM* function, the more may the fiscal stimulus be accompanied by an increase in the money supply from, say, a reduction in excess reserves by banks, and the less it represents a "pure" fiscal action.

For a given nonvertical *LM* function, the flatter the *IS* function, the less powerful is fiscal policy. For example, in the figure, income increases only from Y_0 to Y'_1 for flat function IS'_0 when an expansive fiscal action shifts it to IS'_1 but from Y_0 to Y_1 for a shift of equal size in steep function IS_0 to IS_1. This occurs, because the flatter the underlying investment interest rate schedule, the greater is the offsetting change in private investment spending to the change in government spending or tax rates for a given change in interest rates. If the *IS* function is perfectly horizontal, because the underlying investment function is perfectly horizontal, the effects of fiscal policy actions are completely offset by changes in private spending in the opposite direction. Fiscal policy totally crowds out private spending and is ineffective. Only monetary policy matters. This is equivalent to the liquidity-trap case for monetary policy.

The degree of crowding out of private spending is also dependent on how any budget deficit (surplus) is financed. Because the government pays for all the goods and services it buys, its expenditures must be financed either by taxes or by debt through the sale of bonds. Private units, in turn, will finance the taxes or bonds either out of savings or by cutting back on consumption expenditures. The more is financed from consumption, the greater will be crowding out and the transfer of resources from the private to the public sector. It is widely believed that a larger proportion of taxes than bonds is financed out of consumption. If so, tax finance results in proportionately more crowding out and is more restrictive than an equal amount of deficit financing through the sale of debt.

Because tax payments are involuntary, funds raised by taxes bypass the price system. However, funds raised by the sale of bonds can only be collected through the price system by outbidding other users through paying a higher interest rate on the new bonds. Thus, deficit finance may lead to higher interest rates, *ceteris paribus*, and impact particularly interest-sensitive sectors, such as housing and equipment. To partially or completely offset such an increase, the Fed may monetize part of the debt by providing additional reserves, shifting the *LM* schedule out to the right. Such action increases the expansiveness of the fiscal stimulus and reduces crowding out. However, the largest part of any crowding out is not dependent on how the increase in government expenditures is financed but rather is the direct result of the increase in spending itself. That increase shifts the resources from the private to the public sector. The choice of financing affects primarily the distribution within the private sector.

It can now be seen that the effectiveness of fiscal policy in changing aggregate income depends on the degree of crowding out that occurs from debt financing of a given amount of government spending relative to tax financing, which is assumed to crowd out private spending completely and make fiscal policy totally ineffective. The less debt financing crowds out, the more effective is fiscal policy. Thus, government spending financed by debt or the sale of bonds is more expansive than an equal dollar amount financed by taxes, but, unless there is no crowding out whatsoever, it is less expansive than an equal dollar injection of money. Conversely, the more debt finance crowds out, the less effective is fiscal policy. If debt and tax finance crowd out private spending equally, fiscal policy will not change aggregate income.

This discussion makes it appear that expansive fiscal policy is at a comparative disadvantage vis-å-vis expansive monetary policy. It increases income but also raises interest rates. Conversely, restrictive fiscal policy reduces income but, unlike monetary policy, also reduces interest rates. However, as we noted earlier, the model does not show the complete interest rate effects for monetary policy. These will lessen the final interest rate differences between the two policies.

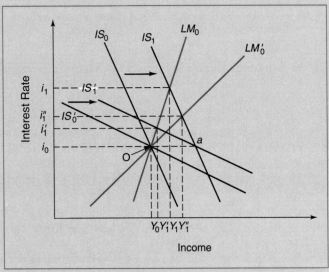

The steeper is *IS* function and the flatter the *LM* function, the more potent is fiscal policy.

"If you ask me, I'd say a tax cut is preferable to public works!"

SOURCE: GRIN and BEAR IT, by Lichty and Wagner. Copyright © 1978 King Features Syndicate. Reprinted with special permission of North American Syndicate.

tion 30–1, interest rates will increase. In Figure 31–4, this appears as downward movements along the IS schedule. At the same time, the increases in income from the additional spending exert upward pressure on interest rates along LM_1. The new equilibrium is achieved when the return on investment and consumption spending is equal to the market rate of interest. This occurs at the intersection of the IS and the LM_1 functions at Y_1, i_1. (As noted earlier, this analysis does not yet include the effects of changes in price expectations on interest rates and is therefore incomplete. Nor does the analysis encompass feedback from changes in income to the IS function, as is likely to happen in the real world, so that the IS function shifts in reaction to a shift in the LM function. Thus, the analysis and final equilibrium solutions are both oversimplifications of the actual process, but are useful for illustrative purposes. With some caution, a little learning need not be a dangerous thing!) To be meaningful, the change in nominal income needs to be divided between a change in real income and a change in prices. This will be done later in Chapter 34.

The major variables on the linkage scheme (or road map) along which monetary policy actions travel from the time they are taken by the Fed are

FIGURE

31–4

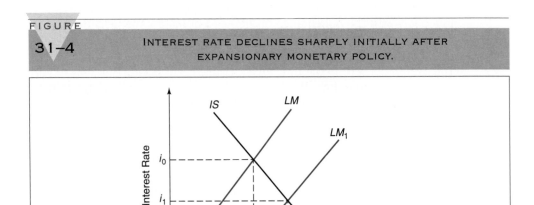

FIGURE 31–4 INTEREST RATE DECLINES SHARPLY INITIALLY AFTER EXPANSIONARY MONETARY POLICY.

SOURCE: Thomas R. Boemio and Gerald A. Edwards, Jr., "Asset Securitization: A Supervisory Perspective," *Federal Reserve Bulletin*, October 1989, p. 661.

shown in Figure 31–5. (As an exercise, trace through the direction of change in these variables when the Fed takes restrictive policy actions.)

Policy Lags

It stands to reason that the movement of Fed actions along the transmission mechanism depicted in Figure 31–5 is not instantaneous. An open-market purchase today by the Fed is unlikely to increase investment and consumption and therefore income today, or even tomorrow. It is also unlikely that the Fed either recognizes the need for a policy action instan-

FIGURE

31–5 TRANSMISSION MECHANISM FOR MONETARY POLICY

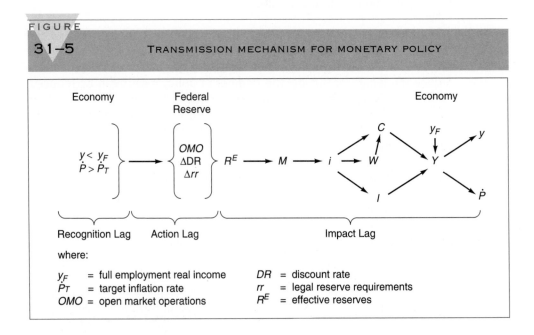

FIGURE 31–5 TRANSMISSION MECHANISM FOR MONETARY POLICY

where:

y_F = full employment real income
$\dot{P}_T$ = target inflation rate
OMO = open market operations

DR = discount rate
rr = legal reserve requirements
R^E = effective reserves

taneously with the appearance of the need or instantaneously determines the particular action to be taken.

Monetary as well as other economic policies operate with time lags. The overall delay from the time an economic event occurs that may require policy action to the time the effect of the action taken is felt on the ultimate targets may be divided into three discrete lags:

1. *The recognition lag*. The delay between the time an economic disturbance occurs and its recognition by the policy makers.
2. *The action lag*. The delay between the recognition that policy action should be taken and the taking of an action.
3. *The impact lag*. The delay between the taking of an action and the impact on the ultimate targets.

We will examine each of the lags individually.

The Recognition Lag.   The recognition lag occurs because we generally do not know what is happening in the economy at the time it is happening. It takes time to collect and analyze data. Although information on many financial variables is available for short periods, such as daily or weekly, soon after the end of the period, information on most real variables is available only for longer periods, such as monthly or quarterly, and then not until some time after the period has ended. Thus, information on most interest rates is available on the same day; on money supply, weekly after one week; on bank credit, weekly after a few weeks; on consumer prices, monthly after three weeks; and on GDP, quarterly three weeks after the last month of the quarter. In addition, many of the data series are revised at later dates.

Moreover, the appropriate time span over which to view some variables in order for them to be meaningful may be relatively long, such as one quarter, or even one year. Even if collected, GDP and employment figures vary too much from day to day to signal useful information about the economy. Analysts have to wait for sufficient time to pass to wash out the large random movements in these series.

The Action Lag.   The length of the action lag depends on institutional and organizational behavior. Generally, the more policymakers who are involved in the decision process, the longer it takes to reach a decision. To reduce the length of the lag, the number of policymakers can be reduced. However, this is not always feasible or desirable. The speed with which an action is taken should not be confused with the appropriateness of the action or its subsequent success. Quick actions need not necessarily be good actions!

The Impact Lag.   The impact lag is embedded in the structure of the economy—that is, in its institutions, customs, laws, and technology. The length of the lag depends on the characteristics of the transmission mechanism. Changes in the lag can be brought about only through structural changes in the economy, such as changes in the factors just mentioned. To the extend that structural changes are not easy to implement in the short run, the impact lag is a sticky one.

The length of the overall lag, the sum of the three individual lags, is important to the success of monetary or any other economic policy. To be

FIGURE

31–6

STABILIZING EFFECT OF ECONOMIC POLICY DEPENDS ON LENGTH OF LAG.

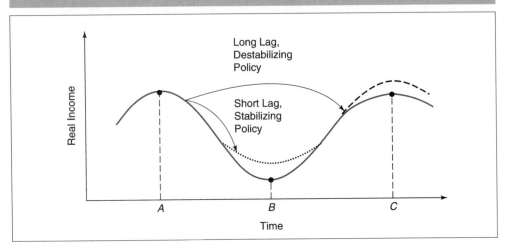

successful, the policy must have its intended effect during the time when the conditions requiring correction exist. If most of the intended effect comes at some other time, it can worsen rather than improve matters. Economic policy is one of a number of forces that affect income. In the absence of policy, income might be assumed to follow a cyclical pattern, such as that depicted by the solid line in Figure 31–6.

Assume that the Fed wished to offset the decline in real income during period A–B. It would take expansionary actions sometime near period A (the more it relied on forecasts, the earlier), intending to have its actions increase income before and shortly after period B. If the actions were successful, the recession might be moderated along the dotted line. If, however, the expansionary actions did not affect income until sometime near period C, they would exert upward pressures when they were not desired— say, along the dashed line—and might strengthen inflationary pressures. Similarly, restrictive policy actions designed to slow income growth before period C would be detrimental if they affected the economy after C and reinforced the downturn. A policy tool whose lags are longer than the length of the period of the condition it is intended to correct, or whose lags vary a lot and are difficult to predict, has little stabilization value.

If the lag appears to be too long to permit monetary policy to be used constructively, it may be possible to shorten it. The best bet is for a reduction in the recognition lag. The length of the recognition lag may be reduced by relying more on economic forecasting. Then policymakers would be able to spot undesirable events in advance and possibly prevent them from occurring or offset their effects shortly thereafter. (It is interesting to note that if a policy agency were totally accurate in predicting undesirable events and all-powerful in preventing them, the event would never occur, and the agency's batting average would be 0.000.) To be useful as a tool for economic stabilization, the lag associated with a particular policy must not only be sufficiently short to have its average effect in the appropriate phase of the business cycle, but the length of the lag must be stable enough to permit accurate predictions.

Empirical Estimates. Empirical measurements of each of the three lags for monetary policy are neither precise nor uniform. The recognition lag is generally accepted as being quite short, no more than three months. The action lag is also estimated to be short, one month at most. The Board of Governors or the Federal Open Market Committee can generally agree upon a course of action quickly after the recognition of the need. (Of course the action decided on is not necessarily the best or even correct.)

The impact lag is found to be longer and more variable. It is difficult to measure because it is not a bullet lag. Action taken today does not make income jump suddenly one way or another exactly *n* periods from now. Rather, it is apt to affect income over time, with some effects felt almost immediately and others not until a long time afterward. This type of lag is referred to as a *distributed lag*. Most econometric models of the economy estimate that the larger part of the effect of a monetary policy action is observed in real income from 3 to 12 months later, and on the price level from one to two years later, depending partly on the type and strength of the action. In sum, the total delay, from the time the event requiring correction occurs to the time most of the subsequent monetary policy action impinges on real income, appears to be between 3 and 15 months.

Since World War II, economic contractions in the United States have averaged 11 months, and economic expansions some 51 months. The lag in the use of restrictive monetary policy to slow the economy is generally of little concern, because it is short relative to the length of the expansion. But expansive monetary actions to stimulate the economy are likely to have at least some of their effects after the recession has already ended. These actions need to be carefully designed and monitored to restrict their effects to the desired period.

Fiscal policy also operates with a lag. The recognition lag is generally believed to be short, no longer than that for monetary policy. The impact lag is estimated to be considerably shorter than for monetary policy, particularly for changes in government spending. Most of the effect on income is estimated to occur within the first year. These models, however, fail to consider the lag between the time the funds are appropriated by Congress and the time programs are initiated. They generally assume that the two dates are the same. Because start-up costs may delay the start of the programs until many months after the funds are appropriated, many of these models may underestimate the length of the impact lag.

The action lag for fiscal policy is highly variable. It hinges on how fast Congress enacts spending or tax legislation. Congress generally operates reasonably quickly to initiate tax cuts and spending increases and more slowly to initiate tax increases and spending cuts. This is not entirely unexpected. Restrictive policies by their very nature are intended to be painful, at least at first, and hurt and impatient voters are not likely to reelect those responsible for the pain. Moreover, because economic policies tend to affect real variables before they affect prices, the undesirable aspects of restrictive policies—reduced output and higher unemployment than otherwise—are seen before the more desirable aspects—slower price inflation. Likewise, expansionary policies are more pleasant, at least at first. They are intended to expand income, and everyone loves Santa Claus! The less desirable impact of higher inflation is felt only later. Thus, fiscal policy may be more efficient in closing deflationary gaps than in closing inflationary gaps.

As was discussed in Chapter 26, the existence of policy lags makes it more difficult for either monetary or fiscal policymakers to employ stabilization policies effectively. The public is generally impatient and, if the actions do not have their intended effects quickly enough, will call for stronger or different policies and eventually for different policymakers. They care less about possible unfavorable effects later on and, when these do occur, tend to associate them with some events occurring at that time rather than with the earlier and quite removed policy action. Thus, stronger-than-optimal policies are frequently adopted that must be offset later when the undesirable side effects appear. Such a scenario decreases macro stability in the longer term.

SUMMARY

Monetary policy involves the manipulation of financial variables by the Federal Reserve in order to achieve the goals of economic policy. In our simple *LM-IS* model, monetary policy actions are reflected in shifts in the *LM* schedule. Shifts outward to the right represent expansive actions to close deflationary gaps; shifts inward to the left represent restrictive actions to close inflationary gaps. The greater the shift in the *LM* function, the steeper the slope of the *LM* function, and the flatter the slope of the *IS* function, the stronger monetary policy is. In the unlikely event that the *LM* function is perfectly vertical, only money determines income, and monetary policy is all powerful. In the equally unlikely event that the *LM* function is perfectly flat, the economy is in a liquidity trap, and monetary policy is completely ineffective. Changes in money have no effect on interest rates. The greater the shift in the IS function, the steeper the slope of the IS function, and the flatter the slope of the *LM* function, the stronger fiscal policy is. Fiscal policy is inoperative when the *LM* function is perfectly vertical.

When the Fed takes a policy action by changing reserve requirements or the discount rate or engages in open-market operations, it changes effective reserves. This shifts the *LM* function, and interest rates change. The change in interest rates in turn affects spending on goods and services. This causes income to change in the same direction and exerts pressures on interest rates in an opposite direction from the initial change along the *LM* schedule until a new equilibrium income is reached. This process takes time. The overall time delay may be divided into three sublags: (1) the recognition lag; (2) the action lag: and (3) the impact lag. For policy to be effective, the length of the combined lags must be shorter than the length of the economic condition that the policy action is intended to correct. Otherwise, some of the effect of the corrective action may take place when the economy is in the opposite phase of the cycle to that at which the action was initially directed. This would do more harm than good.

QUESTIONS

1. What determines the slopes of the *LM* and *IS* functions? If investment were more interest-elastic (sensitive) what would happen to the slope of the *IS* function? What would happen to the slope of the *LM* function? If *M* increased, what would happen to the slope of the *LM* function? Why?

2. Why is monetary policy stronger:
   a. The steeper the *LM* function

b. The larger the shift in the *LM* function

c. The flatter the *IS* function?

3. What is the "liquidity trap"? Why is it important for the effectiveness of monetary policy? Under what conditions might a liquidity trap exist? Is it likely to exist today?

4. Under what assumptions about the *LM* function would monetary policy be more appropriate than fiscal policy? Under what assumptions would fiscal policy be more appropriate? What is required for both monetary and fiscal policies to be effective?

5. What is meant by the "transmission mechanism" for monetary policy? Trace the transmission of an expansive monetary policy action through the economy from the time the action is taken to the new equilibrium income. How is this depicted on the *LM-IS* diagram?

6. Identify the subparts of the lag in the impact of monetary and fiscal policies. What determines the length of each? What are the implications for stabilization policy if the overall lag is much longer than the average length of the part of the business cycle at which the policy is aimed? What if the lag is highly volatile?

7. If you wished to speed up the effect of monetary policy, which lag would appear most amenable to being reduced? How would you reduce it? Why would the other two lags be more difficult to affect?

8. Why may well-intentioned policies to improve income or inflation have unpopular side effects? Politically, might it be easier to attempt to increase income or employment or to decrease inflation? Why?

REFERENCES

Belognia, Michael T., and James A. Chalfant, "Alternative Measures of Money as Indicators of Inflation: A Survey and Some New Evidence," *Review*, Federal Reserve Bank of St. Louis, November/December 1990, pp. 20–33.

Brayton, Flint, and Eileen Mauskoph, "Structure and Uses of the MPS Quarterly Econometric Model of the United States," *Federal Reserve Bulletin*, February 1987, pp. 93–109.

Chrystal, K. Alex, and Daniel L. Thornton, "The Macroeconomic Effects of Deficit Spending: A Review," *Review*, Federal Reserve Bank of St. Louis, November/December 1988, pp. 48–60.

Gibson, William E., and George G. Kaufman, *Monetary Economics: Readings on Current Issues*. New York: McGraw-Hill, 1971.

Havrilesky, Thomas M., and John T. Boorman, *Current Issues in Monetary Theory and Policy*, 2nd ed. Arlington Heights, Ill.: AHM Publishing, 1980.

Hetzel, Robert L., "The Rules versus Discretion Debate over Monetary Policy in the 1920s," *Economic Review*, Federal Reserve Bank of Richmond, November/December 1985, pp. 3–14.

Kaufman, George G., *Money, the Financial System, and the Economy*, 3rd ed. Boston: Houghton Mifflin, 1981.

Mayer, Thomas, *Monetary Policy in the United States*. New York: Random House, 1968.

McCulloch, J. Huston, *Money and Inflation*, 2nd ed. New York: Academic Press, 1982.

Meigs, A. James, *Money Matters*. New York: Harper, 1972.

Poole, William, *Money and the Economy: A Monetarist View*. Reading, Mass.: Addison-Wesley, 1978.

Romer, Christine, and David H. Romer, "New Evidence on the Monetary Transmission Mechanism," *Brookings Papers on Economic Activity*, 1, 1990, pp. 149–213.

Rosenbaum, Mary S., "Lags in the Effect of Monetary Policy," *Economic Review*, Federal Reserve Bank of Atlanta, November 1985, pp. 20–33.

Simpson, Thomas D., and Patrick M. Parkinson, "Some Implications of Financial Innovations in the United States," *Staff Studies*. Washington, D.C.: Board of Governors of the Federal Reserve System, September 1984.

Tobin, James, "Monetary Policies and the Economy: The Transmission Mechanism," *Southern Economic Journal*, January 1978, pp. 421–31.

Monetary Policy in the Post-World War II Period

The U.S. economy has changed dramatically since the end of World War II in 1945, and monetary policy has contributed to these changes for better or for worse.

Overview

On the whole, the post–World War II period was one of economic expansion. Real GDP expanded by a factor of four in the 45 years between 1947 and 1992 or, as can be seen from Table 32–1, at an average annual rate of 3.1 percent. This was more than twice as fast as the growth in population, so that real GDP per capita increased at a 1.9 percent average annual rate. These growth rates resemble those in earlier periods. Between 1900 and 1947, real GDP increased at an annual rate of about 3 percent and real GDP per capita at 1.8 percent.

Superimposed on this growth trend, however, were nine business cycles. (The turning points of the business cycles are identified in Table 32–2 and the changes in real income are plotted in Figure 32–1.) Through the beginning of the expansion that started in 1991, on average, the recessions were 11 months long and the expansions 51 months. This was shorter for recessions and longer for expansions than before World War II. Unemployment increased during the period, both secularly and cyclically. (See Figure 32–2.) In the immediate postwar period, full employment was considered to be equivalent to a 4 percent rate of unemployment. By the late 1960s, the rate had been increased to 4½ percent and was upped further to 5 percent by the 1970s and 6 percent by the early 1980s, before being lowered again to about 5 percent. As discussed in Chapter 26, the increase

TABLE

32–1   ANNUAL GROWTH RATES IN SELECTED MEASURES OF ECONOMIC PERFORMANCE, 1947–1992 (PERCENT)

Period	GDP Current Dollars	GDP Constant Dollars	Real GDP per Capita	Popu- lation	Civilian Labor Force	Con- sumer Prices	M1
1947–1960	5.7	3.3	1.6	1.6	1.1	2.0	1.6
1960–1970	6.3	3.6	2.4	1.2	1.6	2.5	3.9
1970–1980	9.3	2.8	1.8	1.0	2.4	7.1	6.1
1980–1990	6.5	2.4	1.5	0.9	1.0	4.3	6.6
1947–1992	7.5	3.1	1.9	1.3	1.4	4.2	5.0

SOURCE: *Economic Report of the President*, various years.

FIGURE

32-1

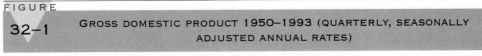

GROSS DOMESTIC PRODUCT 1950–1993 (QUARTERLY, SEASONALLY
ADJUSTED ANNUAL RATES)

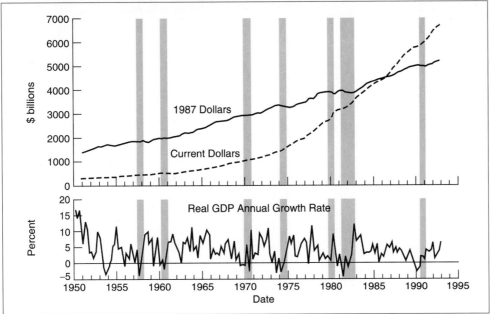

SOURCE: Federal Reserve Bank of Chicago.
NOTE: Shaded ares represent periods of economic recession.

in the unemployment rate that was considered to be consistent with equilibrium full employment was attributed primarily to the large increase in
the proportion of women and teenagers in the labor force in the 1970s.
Cyclical unemployment peaked at about 7 percent in 1949, 6 percent in
1954, 7½ percent in 1958, 7 percent in 1961, 6 percent in 1971, 9 percent in
1975, 7½ percent in 1980, 10½ percent in 1982, and 7½ percent in 1992.

FIGURE

32-2

PERCENT UNEMPLOYED, 1950–1993

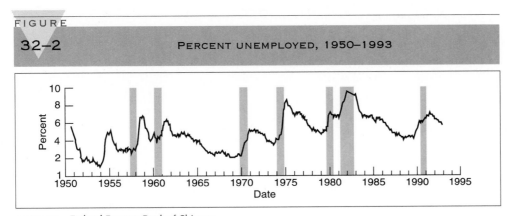

SOURCE: Federal Reserve Bank of Chicago.
NOTE: Shaded ares represent periods of economic recession.

TABLE

32–2

BUSINESS CYCLE EXPANSIONS AND CONTRACTIONS IN THE UNITED STATES, 1854–1994

| Business Cycle Reference Dates | | Duration in Months | | | |
| | | Contraction (trough from previous peak) | Expansion (trough to peak) | Cycle | |
Trough	Peak			Trough from Previous Trough	Peak from Previous Peak
December 1854	June 1857	—	30	—	—
December 1858	October 1860	18	22	48	40
June 1861	April 1865	8	46	30	54
December 1867	June 1869	32	18	78	50
December 1870	October 1873	18	34	36	52
March 1879	March 1882	65	36	99	101
May 1885	March 1887	38	22	74	60
April 1888	July 1890	13	27	35	40
May 1891	January 1893	10	20	37	30
June 1894	December 1895	17	18	37	35
June 1897	June 1899	18	24	36	42
December 1900	September 1902	18	21	42	39
August 1904	May 1907	23	33	44	56
June 1908	January 1910	13	19	46	32
January 1912	January 1913	24	12	43	36
December 1914	August 1918	23	44	35	67
March 1919	January 1920	-7	10	51	17
July 1921	May 1923	18	22	28	40
July 1924	October 1926	14	27	36	41
November 1927	August 1929	13	21	40	34
March 1933	May 1937	43	50	64	93
June 1938	February 1945	13	80	63	93
October 1945	November 1948	8	37	88	45
October 1949	July 1953	11	45	48	56
May 1954	August 1957	10	39	55	49
April 1958	April 1960	8	24	47	32
February 1961	December 1969	10	106	34	116
November 1970	November 1973	11	36	117	47
March 1975	January 1980	16	58	52	74
July 1980	July 1981	6	12	64	18
November 1982	July 1990	16	104	28	108
March 1991		8			
Average, all cycles:					
1854–1990 (31 cycles)		18	35	51	53
1854–1919 (16 cycles)		22	27	48	49
1919–1945 (6 cycles)		18	35	53	53
1945–1991 (9 cycles)		11	51	56	61
Average, peacetime cycles:					
1854–1990 (26 cycles)		19	30	46	48
1854–1919 (14 cycles)		22	24	46	47
1913–1945 (5 cycles)		20	26	46	45
1945–1991 (7 cycles)		11	44	46	53

SOURCE: *Business Conditions Digest*, January 1988, p. 104, updated by author.

NOTE: Underscored figures are the wartime expansions (Civil War, World Wars I and II, Korean War, and Vietnam War), the postwar contractions, and the full cycles that include the wartime expansions.

FIGURE

32–3

603

MONETARY POLICY
IN THE POST-WORLD
WAR II PERIOD

RATE OF INFLATION, 1950–1993

SOURCE: Federal Reserve Bank of Chicago.
NOTE: Shaded ares represent periods of economic recession.

Unemployment troughed at near 3½ percent in 1948, 2 percent in 1952–53, 4 percent in 1956–57, 5 percent in 1959, 3½ percent in 1969, 5 percent in 1972, 6 percent in 1978, 7 percent in 1981, and 5 percent in 1990.

Prices increased more than 500 percent in the 45 years between 1947 and 1992. This represents an average annual rate of inflation of 4.2 percent. As can be seen from Figure 32–3, inflation accelerated during the period, averaging about 2 percent in the early years and 7 percent in the 1970s, before slowing in the 1980s.

The balance of payments and foreign exchange value of the dollar both deteriorated throughout most of the period. At first, the deterioration reflected deliberate U.S. policy to assist in the economic recovery of countries severely damaged by World War II. Beginning in the 1960s, however, it reflected excessive domestic inflationary pressures and increasing non-competitiveness of U.S. goods in world markets. The switchover from fixed to flexible exchange rates in the early 1970s did not relieve the secular pressures on the dollar.

Monetary policy provided growth in the supply of money. Between 1947 and 1992, M1 increased at an average annual rate of 5 percent. This was somewhat faster than the rate of growth in consumer prices and 50 percent faster than the average annual growth rate in real GDP. Monetary expansion was not steady throughout the period, however; M1 expanded twice as rapidly in the 1960s as in the 1950s, and more than three times as rapidly in the 1970s and early 1980s before slowing again in the late 1980s. (The growth rates in M1, M2, and M3 are shown in Figure 32–4.) Interest rates increased sharply on average in the period, but traced a clear cyclical pattern. Until the 1980s, rates peaked at progressively higher levels during each period of business expansion. Three-month Treasury bill rates peaked at about 1 percent in 1949, 2 percent in 1953, 3 percent in 1957, 4 percent

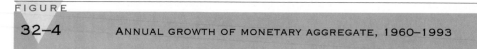

FIGURE

32–4   ANNUAL GROWTH OF MONETARY AGGREGATE, 1960–1993

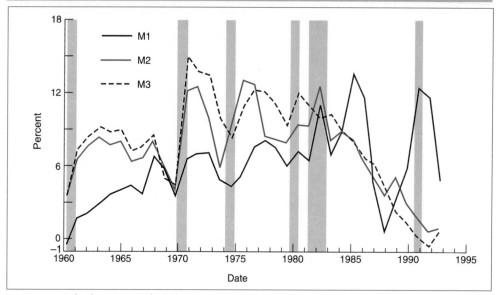

SOURCE: Federal Reserve Bank of Chicago.

NOTE: Shaded ares represent periods of economic recession.

in 1959, 7 percent in 1969, 8.5 percent in 1974, 17 percent in 1981, 10 percent in 1984, and 9 percent in 1989, before declining sharply to 3 percent in mid-1993. A similar pattern was traced by longer-term rates (Figure 32–5).

To examine the strategy of monetary policy and its effects more carefully, we shall divide the postwar period into five subperiods, 1947–1960, 1960–1970, 1970–1980, 1980–1990, and 1990—.

1947–1960: *Years of Economic Innocence*

The United States emerged from World War II as the major country undamaged by physical destruction. Despite widespread predictions that the nation would return to the economic depression and stagnation of the prewar years and that prices would decline, as had occurred in the aftermaths of previous wars, the economy boomed after a brief downturn resulting from the conversion from wartime to peacetime production. The expansion was fueled by a backlog of consumer demand that had not been satisfied during the war, when consumer goods were scarce, and ready financing from the large savings accumulated during the war years. The jump in consumer and business spending more than offset the sharp, almost overnight cutback in federal government spending. Government spending dropped from 42 percent of GDP in 1944 to 8 percent in 1946. Unemployment increased moderately from the unusually low wartime levels to 4 percent and remained substantially below the 20 percent rates experienced during much of the Great Depression of the 1930s until shortly before the war.

FIGURE

32–5

LONG-TERM BOND YIELDS, 1950–1993

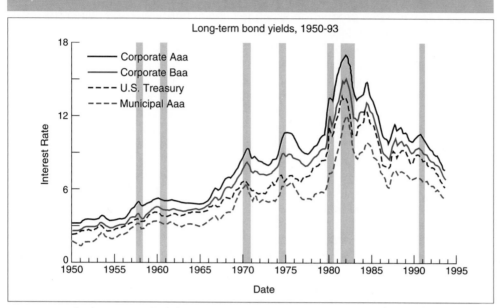

SOURCE: Federal Reserve Bank of Chicago.
NOTE: Shaded ares represent periods of economic recession.

Prices increased sharply as wartime price and credit controls were lifted. In part, the price increases reflected a shift from hidden to open inflation. Despite severe shortages, nominal prices increased only 10 percent during the war years, 1942 to 1945, but in the next three years they increased 33 percent. Economic activity peaked in late 1948, and the economy entered its first genuine postwar recession.

The recession lasted less than a year, and the economy began to improve again in late 1949. During the contraction, unemployment more than doubled, from almost 3 percent to 7 percent, and the rise in consumer prices slowed slightly.

Monetary policy contributed little to economic stabilization one way or the other. Policy was devoted primarily to preventing interest rates from rising sharply from the unusually low wartime levels. It was believed that rate increases would both cut back consumer spending, by decreasing the prices on the large volume of Treasury securities held, and increase significantly the interest burden of the debt. Because of the excessive liquidity, idle demand deposits built up during the war were run down, and M1 actually declined during much of this period. Short-term interest rates drifted up slowly, while longer-term rates remained constant.

The economic expansion that started in late 1949 accelerated sharply with the outbreak of the Korean War in mid-1950. Because of memories of shortages and price pressures in World War II, price and credit controls were quickly reimposed. Output spurted, and unemployment declined to almost 2 percent. Prices slowed after their initial surge, and the controls were lifted. The economy peaked in mid-1953 after almost four years of expansion. The subsequent recession in part reflected the adjustment from war to peacetime production. It was mild and lasted less than one year. Early in 1954, production expanded again, until mid-1957, when the economy declined into a brief but more severe recession. Unemployment jumped from 4 to 7½ percent. The economy troughed early in 1958 and turned up again, but only for two years. Unemployment declined only to 5 percent, but prices accelerated sharply by the standards of the period. However, particularly in view of the prewar experience, which was still fresh in many people's minds and shaped their expectations, and despite the volatility, most people believed that the economy was performing extraordinarily well in the period 1947 to 1960 as a whole.

Monetary policy became more active after the outbreak of the Korean War. The Fed was released of its obligation to peg interest rates at low levels by an "accord" with the Treasury Department in 1951. Interest rates drifted upward and traced a procyclical pattern. The Fed relied heavily on interest rates as an intermediate target for monetary policy in this period and followed a strategy referred to as "leaning against the wind." During periods of economic expansion and upward pressure on rates, this involved providing reserves but fewer than necessary to keep interest rates from rising altogether. During periods of economic slowdown and downward pressures on rates, it involved absorbing reserves but fewer than necessary to keep rates from falling. As a result, the money supply tended to move procyclically. But except for the spurt at the outbreak of the war, money supply increased only slowly.

Although more active than in the immediate postwar period, monetary policy could not be considered to have been used vigorously. It is unlikely that it contributed greatly to economic stability in this period, although the overall slow rate of monetary expansion provided little support for inflationary pressures. Fiscal policy was also used only moderately in this period. In large measure because of widespread satisfaction with the performance of the economy, policymakers did not test their powers greatly.

1960–1970: *Years of Economic Experimentation and Promise*

In the 1960s as a whole, aggregate real income increased somewhat faster than in the previous period, and per capita real income increased considerably faster as the rate of population increase slowed. Prices increased only slightly faster than before. But these summary figures are deceiving.

The 1960s was a decade of paradox. In the first half, everything was almost too good to be true. Nothing could go wrong. Economic growth was rapid, unemployment declined, and the inflation slowed to less than 2 percent annually. Even economic policy appeared foolproof; the policies implemented had their expected effects. Economists were in their glory, much in demand, and feeling their oats. Public expectations of economic performance were sharply upgraded. The new feelings of political self-confidence that swept the country after the election of President Kennedy spilled over into the economic arena.

In the second half of the decade, almost nothing went right. Economic growth slowed, the economy became less stable, and inflation accelerated sharply. Only unemployment performed well, declining to the lowest levels since the Korean War. Moreover, the seeds were sown for even worse economic performance in the 1970s. Few economic policies had the desired effects, although policy was used more frequently and more intensively in an attempt to make the economy perform up to the higher level of expectations. The more active policy was termed **fine tuning.**

Unlike the earlier period, the decade of the 1960s encompassed basically only one complete business cycle. After a brief eight-month recession ending in early 1961, the economy did not turn down again until almost nine years later, at year-end 1969. This was by far the longest uninterrupted expansion in U.S. history—106 months. The previous record had been 80 months, from 1938 through 1945, encompassing the World War II period.

Unemployment declined from 7 percent in 1961 to 3½ percent in 1969. In 1966, U.S. participation in the war in Vietnam expanded, abruptly setting off sharp increases in government spending on defense. At the same time, numerous social programs designed in the first half of the decade were brought online, increasing government spending further. By 1967, federal government spending on defense accounted for 11.4 percent of GDP, and total government spending 22.6 percent. Two years earlier, in 1965, the comparable percentages were only 9.8 and 20.1 respectively. The economy turned down as the decade ended.

Fiscal policy in this period was dominated by two major tax changes, one a tax cut and the other a tax increase. In 1964, federal income taxes were reduced sharply across the board. This was the first tax cut in U.S. history that was intended neither to reduce tax revenues from unusually high wartime levels nor to combat a recession. Instead, it was designed to speed up the ongoing economic expansion. This marked the beginning of the use of more active fiscal policy to stimulate the economy.

Monetary policy underwent dramatic changes during the decade. Like fiscal policy, it became progressively more active. In the first half, money supply increased at a slowly accelerating rate. Short-term interest rates increased moderately after declining sharply during the brief recession, and long-term rates remained stable. Reserve requirements were reduced in 1960 and effectively maintained until 1966. The discount rate was reduced in 1960 and then increased only three times through 1966.

In 1966, monetary policy turned more active. The rate of monetary expansion was slowed in 1966, accelerated sharply in 1967, and decelerated equally sharply in 1969. The average rate of growth M1 in the second half of the decade was almost twice as rapid as in the first half. Reserve requirements were increased in 1966, lowered in 1967, and increased again in both 1968 and 1969. The discount rate was changed more often as market rates of interest fluctuated more widely.

The quantitative tools of monetary policy were supplemented by qualitative tools. Margin requirements were expanded to cover all institutional lenders of credit for the purchase of securities, not only banks, brokers, and dealers, and to cover convertible bonds as well as stocks. Regulation Q was extended to thrift institutions in 1966 with somewhat higher ceilings than those on commercial banks to (1) encourage the flow of deposit funds into mortgage-lending thrift institutions to support housing and (2) discourage the flow of deposit funds into larger banks that financed loans to larger corporations. The Fed viewed spending by these firms to have been excessive in this period and to have contributed to inflation. When market rates of interest increased sharply and climbed above the ceiling rates on deposits in 1966 and 1969, disintermediation of deposit funds to the private financial market resulted. Restrictions were also imposed on bank lending overseas, in order to improve the balance of payments and alleviate the pressures on the dollar. The more vigorous use of qualitative tools was an integral part of the strategy of fine tuning.

 ## 1970–1980: *Years of Economic Pain, Frustration, and Disillusionment*

Economically, the years from 1970 to 1980 were the most frustrating years since the Great Depression of the 1930s. The bright promise of the final taming of economic forces through the intelligent use of economic policy and the achievement of unprecedented economic performance instilled in the first half of the 1960s and sustained through the disappointing performance in the second half evaporated in the 1970s. As the decade progressed, public trust in economists and policymakers crumbled, as did the confidence of these groups in their own abilities to achieve what they once thought they could.

The decade was highlighted by substantial cyclical instability and long periods of *stagflation*. (*Stagflation* is simultaneous rapid inflation and high unemployment.) Unemployment increased to the highest levels since the 1930s, averaging significantly higher than in the earlier periods even after adjustment for the changed composition of the labor force. Inflation skyrocketed to record peacetime rates. Pressures on the dollar led to devaluations in 1971 and 1973 and to continued declines in the exchange rate after the introduction of flexible rates. The economy was battered by higher food prices from poor harvests worldwide and higher energy prices from cutbacks in production and intensified monopoly pricing by OPEC. The latter actions gave rise to the energy crisis, which reshaped the social and political life of the country as well as its economic life. Finally, an incomes policy was introduced for the first time in peacetime. In contrast to the earlier period, economic expectations were downgraded sharply. Reflecting this more sober attitude, the stock market was no higher in 1980 than it was in 1970 after rising almost uninterruptedly since the end of World War II.

Overall, GDP in constant dollars increased at an average annual rate of 2.8 percent, well below the rate of the two earlier periods. Prices increased at an average annual rate of 7 percent, almost triple the rate of the earlier periods. At the end of the decade, inflation ran in double digits.

The recession that ended the record period of economic expansion in the 1960s lasted less than a year. But the following expansion appeared disappointing in the light of both the previous expansion and the expectations of even better performance in the future. Unemployment did not fall sharply, and the rate of inflation did not slow greatly. Reflecting these disappointments and the accompanying public dissatisfaction with the perceived ability of traditional monetary and fiscal policies in producing results quickly enough, President Nixon imposed price and wage controls in mid-1971. After initially slowing, inflation began to accelerate again as monetary and fiscal policies turned aggressively expansive.

The economy peaked at year-end 1973, after only three years, concurrent with the crop shortfalls and quadrupling of petroleum prices by OPEC. After declining slowly for one year, the economy dropped sharply in the last quarter of 1974 and first quarter of 1975. Real GDP declined at an annual rate of 8 percent in these two quarters, and unemployment jumped from 5½ to 9 percent. The decline was the steepest since the 1930s, and the recession was the longest, continuing 16 months before the upturn at the end of the first quarter of 1975. Despite the severity of the recession and the presence of price controls, inflation accelerated from 3.3 percent in 1972 to 11 percent in 1974 and 9 percent in 1975, spurred by the sharp jump in food and energy prices—the latter reflecting constraints on supply rather than increases in demand. Oil prices more than doubled. The incomes policy was terminated in mid-1974.

Like the preceding expansion, the one that started in 1975 was disappointing to many. Unemployment declined slowly from its peak to only 6 percent. Inflation declined sharply from 11 percent in 1974 to less than 6 percent in 1976 before accelerating sharply again thereafter to 14 percent in 1980, in part fueled by another round of OPEC price increases on the heels of the Iranian revolution in 1979. Adjusted for inflation, oil prices jumped to more than triple their 1972 prices. The exchange value of the dollar declined sharply, and the price of gold soared, from less than $150 per ounce in 1976 to more than $800 in 1980.

The economy slowed in 1979 and became highly erratic, emitting confusing signals about a downturn. Officially, the National Bureau for Economic Research (NBER), the nation's scorekeeper for business cycles, pronounced the first quarter of 1980 as the beginning of the seventh post–World War II recession. Although not too robust, the expansion had lasted five years. The following recession, on the other hand, was the shortest in U.S. history, lasting only six months.

Monetary policy continued to be active in this period—despite the announced greater emphasis on growth rates in monetary aggregates. The rate of growth of monetary aggregates accelerated sharply in 1971 and 1972 (despite the incomes policy), slowed in 1973 and again in 1974, accelerated sharply from 1975 through 1977, declined in early 1980, and accelerated at the fastest rate in the postwar period during the remainder of 1980. For the decade as a whole, money supply expanded at an unprecedented annual rate of over 6 percent. As in the 1960s, the activeness of monetary policy in the 1970s does not appear to have contributed greatly to economic stability.

Interest rates also were highly volatile around a sharp upward trend. Treasury bill rates declined from 7 to 4 percent on the heels of the 1969 recession, climbed to 8 percent in 1974, declined to 5 percent in 1976, spurted to 15 percent in early 1980, dropped abruptly to 8 percent by midyear, and returned to 16 percent by year-end 1980. Long-term rates showed a similar pattern. The increase in rate volatility is also seen from changes in the bank prime lending rate. This rate was changed about once a year in the 1960s, five times in 1970, 15 times in 1975, and 51 times in 1980 alone. The sharp increase in interest rate volatility reflected sharp increases in the volatility in the rate of inflation.

Also reflecting the increased volatility in market rates, the discount rate was changed much more frequently than in the past. Reserve requirements, however, were changed only rarely. Although the Fed announced greater emphasis on monetary aggregates and less on defensive open-market operations in 1970 and even more so in 1979, the volume of defensive operations increased sharply. In 1980, purchase of securities by the Open Market Desk exceeded $800 billion. This was up from only $75 billion in 1971.

Except for the brief period of credit controls in spring 1980, qualitative tools were used progressively less actively. Regulation Q ceilings were removed from short-term CDs in 1970, when the failure of the Penn Central Railroad and the potential failure of other large firms limited the market for commercial paper; and from all CDs in 1973, as interest rates increased and threatened large-scale disintermediation. Ceilings were maintained on deposits of less than $100,000, but were slowly liberalized when disintermediation occurred. Although this reduced the magnitude of disintermediation, it did not halt the flow to money-market funds in the late 1970s.

Ceilings on overseas lending by banks were dismantled. Changes in margin requirements were made annually in the early 1970s, and then not at all. Moral suasion was used during the periods when first price and wage controls and then credit controls were in effect, to exert downward pressure on bank loan rates, particularly to small business firms. But this served primarily to shift borrowing from the commercial paper market to the banks and was soon abandoned.

The credit control program in spring 1980 (1) imposed reserve requirements on consumer loan expansion at all financial institutions; (2) increased reserve requirements on purchased funds at large banks; (3) applied reserve requirements on additional assets at money-market funds; and (4) established a surcharge on the discount rate for frequent borrowings by large banks. In addition, the program urged depository institutions to voluntarily limit their overall credit expansion. Credit extension dropped abruptly thereafter, owing both to the program and to the sharp drop in real income in the second quarter.

Fiscal policy also moved increasingly away from fine tuning as the divergence between policy intent and policy results became more evident. Although less active, fiscal policy, like monetary policy, tended to be expansionary for most of the period.

1980–1990: *Return to Stability*

The economy entered the 1980s with double-digit inflation, relatively high unemployment, slow and volatile economic growth, record high interest rates, and considerable uncertainty. Disillusionment set in with the economic policy strategies that had held such great promise only a few years earlier. Doing more and more of the same was becoming less and less effective. The disappointing and frustrating performance of policy and the economy signaled a need for a return to the drawing boards.

In 1981, newly elected President Reagan introduced an economic program that represented the most dramatic break from past economic policies since President Roosevelt's program to combat the Great Depression some 50 years earlier. Emphasis was shifted from demand management to supply management. The program had three distinct parts: (1) sharp cuts in the growth in federal government spending to both lower inflationary expectations and reduce the role of the government in the economy, (2) sharp income tax reductions to stimulate longer-term output and investment by increasing incentives, and (3) slow growth in monetary aggregates.

But all things did not go according to plan. Economic activity declined in mid-1981, signaling the start of the eighth downturn since World War II. Coming only 12 months after the trough of the previous recession, the expansion was the shortest since 1920. Unemployment increased to nearly 11 percent, the highest since the Great Depression, after dipping to 7 percent during the expansion. Inflation, however, slowed significantly, dropping below double digits by year-end and to less than 4 percent by 1982. In measure, the slowdown reflected the absence and even reversal of forces that had contributed greatly to the earlier acceleration in the inflation rate, in particular, energy prices and mortgage rates. Because of the slowing in economic activity and inflation and the first round of tax cuts, federal tax revenues declined sharply and increased the budget deficit to over $100 billion for the first time. But then things improved.

The recession, the most severe since the Great Depression, ended in November 1982. The subsequent recovery was the longest in peacetime history, lasting through the summer of 1990 or nearly eight years. Unemployment declined slowly to near 5 percent in 1989, the lowest level since the 1970s. Inflation declined to only 1 percent in 1986, before increasing again to near 5 percent. The stockmarket almost tripled in value after having remained relatively stable during the 1970s. On October 19, 1987, the stock market declined nearly 25 percent and in a few weeks by about 40 percent, the sharpest decline in such a brief period in history. Although the break led to predictions of economic disaster, the macroeconomy was almost unaffected and the stock market staged a strong recovery. But all parts of the economy did not share equally throughout the improvement.

Energy, particularly oil, and agricultural prices fell as sharply in the 1980s as they had risen in the 1970s and produced severe and long-lasting recessions in the states in which these activities were heavily located, primarily Texas, Louisiana, and the plains states. This was followed in the late 1980s by real-estate-led recessions first in New England and then in the mid-Atlantic states. As a result, the United States witnessed a series of rolling regional recessions during the long expansion of the 1980s.

In mid-1990, at about the same time as Iraq's invasion of Kuwait and the beginning of the U.S. military involvement in the Persian Gulf area, the macroeconomy slipped into its ninth recession of the post–World War II period. A surge in energy prices following the outbreak of the war in August and an increase in uncertainty about the degree of both the damage and the U.S. involvement contributed to a simultaneous jump in the rate of inflation and a cutback in spending, particularly on construction.

Contrary to the Reagan blueprints, the federal government budget became mired in large deficits as spending increased sharply from near 20 percent of GDP in 1979 to 24 percent by the mid-1980s and remained near

23 percent, despite the strength of the economic recovery. At the same time government revenues did not recover fully from the sharp earlier income tax cuts and stabilized at near 20 percent of GDP. Last, imports of goods and services to the United States increased 50 percent faster than exports in the 1980s, and the balance on these items deteriorated from a surplus to record deficits. In part, this was attributed to a sharp 60 percent increase in the dollar exchange rate between 1980 and 1985. But the balance did not improve greatly as the dollar declined in international value to its earlier levels in the second half of the decade.

After slowing dramatically in the early 1980s, although increasing in volatility, the money supply increased rapidly and more smoothly during most of the early years of the economic expansion at well above the Fed's target levels. Yet inflation did not re-accelerate greatly. This reflected sharp and unprecedented declines in M1 and M2 velocities. In 1987, M1 velocity was 10 percent below its 1980 level and about equivalent to its 1976 level. In contrast, M1 velocity had trended upward at a relatively smooth 3 percent annual rate since the end of World War II. Because the strange behavior of velocity weakened the M1-GDP relationship, the Federal Reserve deemphasized controlling monetary aggregates after 1982, ending its brief three-year flirtation with monetarism, and focused additional attention on money-market conditions.

Interest rates declined sharply. By the end of 1982, three-month Treasury bill rates were only one-half of their 16 percent levels of mid-1981, and rates on longer-term Treasury securities were down to 11 percent from 14 percent one year earlier. Similar to money, the short-term volatility in rates also declined. Although down sharply, market rates of interest did not decline as sharply as the rate of inflation and ex-post real rates of interest climbed sharply to the highest levels since World War II. Market rates of interest continued to decline through 1986 and then fluctuated in a relatively narrow range (see Figure 32–5). Because the rate of inflation continued to slow through 1986 and then picked up only moderately, real rates of interest declined from their high levels of the early 1980s but, unlike the 1970s, remained positive.

In keeping with the national emphasis on deregulation, the Federal Reserve made little use of selective tools, and those in force, including Regulation Q, continued to be dismantled. Reserve requirements were not changed until 1990. The discount rate, however, was changed frequently to maintain contact with market interest rates. The Fed also increased its emphasis on smoothing short-term fluctuations in interest rates, and defensive open-market operations were used more often.

 ## 1990—Into the Great Unknown—Again

In early 1991, after building up its forces since August 1990, the United States invaded Kuwait and Iraq and won a decisive victory in a few days. The quick end of the conflict sharply increased economic confidence and certainty in the United States and appeared to signal an end to the decline in consumer and business spending that had existed since mid-1990. Real

GDP had declined by 1 percent. At the same time, the Federal Reserve had accelerated the growth in M1, reduced the discount rate from 7 to 5½ percent in three steps, and eliminated the remaining reserves requirements on time deposits. However, in part because of the large continuing deficit in the federal budget and in part because of the mildness of the recession, fiscal policy was not used to stimulate the economy. Interest rates, particularly short-term rates, declined. In mid-1991, three-month Treasury bills had declined from 8 to 5½ percent, and the bank prime lending rate from 11 to 8½ percent.

The recession lasted only eight months, from July 1990 to March 1991. But the subsequent expansion began so slow that many perceived the recession to have been significantly longer. Through mid-1993, GDP expanded at an average annual rate of less than 2 percent, too slow to absorb the increases in the labor force. As a result, unemployment continued to increase and did not peak until June 1992 at 7.7 percent. Inflation slowed from the runup at the time of the Persian Gulf War and averaged near 3 percent. Because of both the weak economy and slowdown in inflation, interest rates declined sharply to the lowest levels since the early 1970s. Treasury bill rates dipped to 3 percent and longer-term Treasury securities to near 6 percent. The slow growth of the economy also helped to keep federal government tax receipts low, which, combined with sharp increases in government spending, increased the budget deficit sharply. By early 1993, federal government spending represented 24 percent of the GDP, the highest level since 1983, receipts 19 percent, and the deficit near 5½ percent. In part to slow the growth in both government spending and the deficit, newly elected President Clinton introduced an economic program that reversed the Reagan tax cuts of 1981 and the tax simplification of 1986 by substantially increasing income taxes on higher-income households.

At the same time, bank lending as a percentage of total bank assets declined sharply from 1990 levels, particularly at financially weak banks that were constrained by their shortage of capital. As a result, many believed that the recovery was hampered by a "credit crunch" and exerted pressure on the bank regulators to ease up on the banking system in order to get bank lending flow more freely. In response, the regulators took a number of actions to encourage additional lending by banks.

By mid-1993, the rate of recovery accelerated. Unemployment declined more markedly and fears of renewed inflation became more widespread, although this was not yet reflected in either the CPI or PPI. Nevertheless, interest rates stopped their downward slide and began to creep upward. The prime lending rate, which had declined continuously from 11½ percent in 1989 to 6 percent in 1992, was increased in a number of steps in early 1994.

The Fed accommodated the decline in interest rates. The discount rate was lowered six times, from 6½ to 3 percent, between early 1991 and mid-1993. Growth rates in money differed greatly among the different definitions. M1 expanded at an annual rate of near 10 percent, while M2 and M3 expanded at less than 3 percent. As a result, the Fed intensified its search for consistent monetary targets. As the economy strengthened and interest rates increased again, the Fed raised its discount rate. But monetary expansion remained slow.

At the time of publication of this book, it was too early to tell whether the expansion would continue with or without a significant acceleration in the rate of inflation. That is, it was too early to tell whether policymakers have learned the lessons of the previous three decades or are unable to sacrifice temporary gains in the near term to achieve more-lasting gains over the longer term.

SUMMARY

The U.S. economy expanded rapidly on net in the post–World War II period. But superimposed on the expansion were nine business cycles and progressively worsening inflation, unemployment, and international balance of payments. The performance of the economy was viewed as satisfactory in the early postwar period, when it was generally compared with that of the depression era immediately preceding the war. The performance improved in the early 1960s and raised expectations of even further improvement. However, these expectations were not realized as the economy, buffeted in part by forces not of its own making, began to experience undesirably high inflation and unemployment through the 1970s and into the early 1980s. In the mid-1980s, the economy began to return to more satisfactory levels of performance. Inflation slowed substantially and unemployment declined steadily as the economy enjoyed the longest fully peacetime expansion in U.S.history. Even a sharp 25 percent freefall in stock prices on "Black Monday" October 19, 1987, had little lasting impact on either the stock market or aggregate economic activity. However, in mid-1990, the economy stalled after expanding for nearly eight years and slid into its ninth recession, concurrent with the outbreak of the Persian Gulf War. One year later in mid-1991, the economy entered the tenth expansion of the post–World War II period.

Monetary policy went through a number of phases. In the first years of the period, it was directed at preventing interest rates from rising. The inflationary pressures following the outbreak of the Korean War freed monetary policy to be used for broader stabilization purposes. The Federal Reserve moved cautiously to resist cyclical forces but did not attempt either to offset them in total or to direct the thrust of economic activity. In the 1960s, the Fed operated more actively, together with fiscal policy, to fine-tune the economy in an attempt to achieve levels of performance consistent with the higher expectations. However, the poor performance of the economy in the 1970s cast doubt on the ability of monetary policy to fine-tune successfully, and that policy was progressively deemphasized. The rapid growth in the money supply in both the early and late 1970s contributed significantly to the sharp acceleration in the rate of inflation in these periods. The slowing in monetary expansion in the 1980s and early 1990s contributed to the slowing in the inflation rate. The Federal Reserve appeared reluctant to permit monetary growth to accelerate back to the rapid rates of the 1970s, even during the recession of 1990–1991 and subsequent period of slow economic growth.

Through the period, the focus of Federal Reserve attention slowly shifted from the sole emphasis on interest rates to greater emphasis on monetary aggregates, particularly as concern about inflation increased. Nevertheless, concern about high interest rates never diminished completely, and the record rates of inflation in the 1970s were accompanied by record rates and volatility in the growth of money supply. After inflation slowed in the 1980s, the Fed pursued an operating strategy that mostly gave equal weight to interest rates and money supply, and reduced the volatility in both. In the 1990s, however, the Fed became increasingly dissatisfied with the performance of first M1 and then M2 and shifted its focus more towards short-term interest rates as policy targets.

QUESTIONS

1. How would you evaluate the performance of the U.S. economy in the post–World War II period relative to its economic goals?

2. Why could the years 1960 to 1970 be called "years of economic experimentation and promise"? What do you think motivated economic policy strategy in this period?

3. Why was the decade of the 1970s one of economic disillusionment and frustration? How did the 1980s differ? Why?

4. What is meant by economic "fine tuning"? What did fine tuning imply for the conduct of monetary policy?

5. How did monetary policy differ in each of the five subperiods of the post–World War II period? What accounted for these differences?

6. Trace the pattern of interest rates since 1960. Why are they relatively high in the 1970s and early 1980s and relatively low in the 1960s and since 1985? Do you think monetary policy has contributed to this pattern? If so, how and why?

7. What forces appear to have been important contributors to the poor economic and policy performance of the 1970s? Do you think this poor performance influenced policy in the 1980s and 1990s? Why? Does that make you more or less optimistic about good economic performance in the future?

8. Describe President Clinton's economic program. How have things worked out? How does it differ from the programs of former Presidents Reagan (1981) and Bush (1991)? What have the economy and monetary policy done since the publication of this book at year-end 1994?

9. Comparable data may be found for other major economies in your library. How does the performance of the U.S. economy compare with that of other countries since 1970 and since 1990? Speculate on the reasons for any major differences you observe.

REFERENCES

Blustein, Paul, et al., "Curbing of Inflation," *Wall Street Journal*, December 7, 10, and 11, 1984.

Board of Governors of the Federal Reserve System, *Annual Report*. Washington, D.C., annual.

Brauer, David, "A Historical Perspective on the 1989–92 Slow Growth Period," *Quarterly Review*, Federal Reserve Bank of New York, Summer 1993, pp. 1–14.

Burns, Arthur F., *Reflections of an Economic Policy Maker: 1969–1978*. Washington,

D.C.: American Enterprise Institute, 1978.

Carlson, Keith M., "Federal Fiscal Policy Since the Employment Act of 1946," *Review*, Federal Reserve Bank of St. Louis, December 1987, pp. 14–29.

Council of Economic Advisers, *Economic Report of the President*. Washington, D.C., annual.

Cullison, William E., "The Case of the Reluctant Recovery," *Economic Review*, Federal Reserve Bank of Richmond, July/August 1992, pp. 3–13.

Diabold, Francis X., and Glenn D. Rudebush, "Have the Patterns of U.S. Business Cycles Changed Since World War II?" *Business Review*, Federal Reserve Bank of Philadelphia, November/December 1991, pp. 13–20.

Federal Reserve Bank of St. Louis, "The Federal Open Market Committee," *Review*, annual.

Feldstein, Martin, *The U.S. Economy in Transition*. Chicago: University of Chicago Press, 1980.

Goodfriend, Marvin, "Interest Rate Policy and the Inflation Scare Problem," *Economic Quarterly*, Federal Reserve Bank of Richmond, Winter 1993, pp. 1–24.

Maisel, Sherman J., *Managing the Dollar*. New York: Norton, 1973.

Mayer, Martin, *The Fate of the Dollar*. New York: New York Times Books, 1980.

McNees, Stephen K., "The 1990–91 Recession in Historical Perspective," *New England Economic Review*, Federal Reserve Bank of Boston, January/February 1992, pp. 3–22.

Meltzer, Alan, "U.S. Policy in the Bretton Woods Era," *Review*, Federal Reserve Bank of St. Louis, May/June 1991, pp. 54–83.

Moore, John H., ed., *To Promote Prosperity: U.S. Domestic Policy in the Mid-1980s*. Stanford, Calif.: Hoover Institution Press, 1984.

Stein, Herbert, *Presidential Economics*. New York: Simon & Schuster, 1984.

Weibtraub, Robert E., "Political Economy of Inflation," in Karl Brunner, ed., *The Political Economy of Inflation: A Symposium*. Rochester, N.Y.: Center for Research in Government Policy and Business, University of Rochester, 1981.

Interest Rates, Indicators, and Targets

When we last looked at the relationship between money supply and interest rates, it appeared that expansive monetary policy actions depicted by outward shifts in the *LM* function would reduce market interest rates on net and that restrictive actions depicted by inward shifts would increase interest rates. But, this is only part of the story. As we discussed in Chapter 6, the liquidity preference theory specifies that interest rates are a function not only of reserves (or money supply) and income but also of price expectations in the same period t. In equation form

$$i_t = f(M, \overset{-}{Y}, \overset{++}{\dot{P}})_t \qquad (33\text{--}1)$$

If the rate of inflation is expected to accelerate, market rates of interest rise; if inflation is expected to slow, market rates decline.

Complete Money–Interest Rate Relationship

In addition to affecting aggregate income, monetary policy is apt to have some effect on the price level. Expansive policies tend, in time, to increase prices faster, although maybe not in the one-to-one relationship predicted by the early quantity theory of money, and restrictive policies tend to slow price increases. To the extent that expectations of future price changes are based on either current policy actions or current and past price changes, monetary policy actions affect price expectations.

The price-expectations effect can now be incorporated easily into our simple model of the economy. Changes in price expectations shift both the *LM* and *IS* schedules. If price increases are expected to accelerate, investors will want to purchase more investment goods at each nominal interest rate. (After all, by increasing earnings in dollar terms, inflation will increase the nominal return on the investments.) The *IS* schedule shifts out to the right to maintain the same level of real investment at the same real interest rate. At the same time, the demand for money balances will be greater at each nominal interest rate, since the faster inflation is expected to reduce the real value of the balances. More nominal money must be held to equal the same amount of real money balances as before the change in price expectations. Less money will be lent at each interest rate. With no increase in reserves, the *LM* function shifts in to the left.

If we assume that all households and business firms have the same price expectations and that they adjust interest rates by equal amounts in an equal time period, a change in price expectations will shift the *LM* and *IS* schedules in and out, respectively, by equal amounts. The new equilibri-

FIGURE

33–1   INTEREST RATES DECLINE, THEN INCREASE, AFTER
EXPANSIVE MONETARY POLICY.

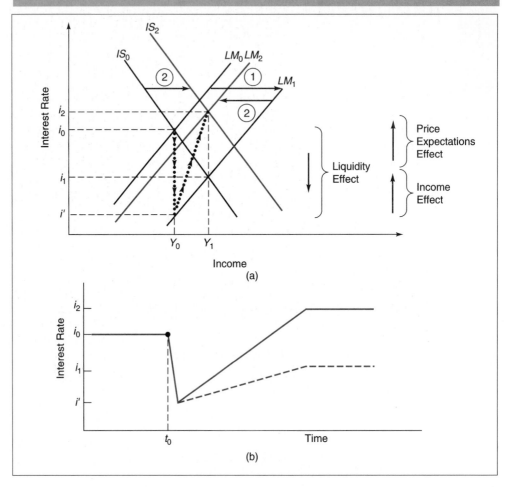

um solution will be at a different interest rate but the same income as before the change in price expectations. This is depicted in Figure 33–1 for an upward revision in price expectations following an expansive monetary policy action. As before, market rates of interest are measured on the vertical axis.

We can trace this process step by step. Before the action, equilibrium income was Y_0 and the equilibrium market interest rate i_0, determined by the intersection of schedules LM_0 and IS_0. Now assume that the Federal Reserve increases the money supply at time period t_0 by using one or more of its quantitative tools of monetary policy—buying Treasury securities on the open market, lowering reserve requirements, and/or lowering the discount rate. The banks use the increased reserves to increase their deposits and thereby the money supply. This is shown by a shift in LM schedule to LM_1 (shown as shift 1 in Figure 33–1a). In the absence of an immediate change in income and price expectations, this lowers the interest rate rather quickly to i'. This change in rates represents the **liquidity effect** and reflects that $i_t = f(\overline{M})_t$. But the reduction in interest rates in time stimulates additional spending and income, causing rates to rise along LM_1. Again, in the absence of a change in price expectations, the market rate will rise slowly through time from i' to i_1 as income expands to Y_1. This effect is termed the **income effect** and reflects that $i_{t+n} = f(\overset{+}{Y})_{t+n}$, where n is the number of periods in the future after t.

Price-Expectations Effect

But the expansive policy action itself, or any price increases that are generated by the resulting higher income, will eventually cause price expectations to be revised upward. To retain the same relationships between investment, lending, and interest rates in real terms, the IS schedule shifts out of IS_2 and the LM schedule in to LM_2 (shift 2 in Figure 33–1a). Investors will want to borrow more and money holders lend less than before at each nominal interest rate. After the shift, equilibrium income remains at Y_1 but the market rate of interest increases to i_2. The increase from i_1 to i_2 is the

price-expectations effect (Fisher Effect) and reflects that $i_{t+s} = f(\overset{+}{P})_{t+s}$, where s is the number of periods in the future after t.

Much of the income and price-expectations effects are likely to occur at the same time, so that the interest rate would climb from i to i_2 along the dotted line in Figure 33–1a. The time path along which these changes travel is shown in panel b. Note the quick and transitory liquidity-effect response and the slower but longer-lasting income and price-expectations effect responses. The vertical distance between i_2 and i_1, which represents the adjustment in interest rates to the change in price expectations, is equal to the value of the coefficient b in the Fisher-effect equation developed in Chapter 6. If there were taxes and full adjustment to the expectations of the faster rate of inflation, b would exceed 1 and i_2 would exceed i_1 by at least the amount of the increase in the expected annual rate of inflation.

In both panels of Figure 33–1, i_2 is drawn higher than i_0, the interest rate at the time the expansionary action was undertaken. This implies that the delayed combined income and price-expectations effects more than offset the initial liquidity effect. But this need not be. The final equilibrium interest rate may be above, equal to, or below the initial rate, depending on the slopes of the schedules and the magnitude of the adjustment to the revision in price expectations. It is reasonable that the closer the economy is to full employment at the time of the expansionary action, the greater will be the effect on prices and price expectations and the greater will be the increase in interest rates per dollar increases in the money supply.

Downward revisions in price expectations following a restrictive policy action will cause the LM and IS functions to shift down by equal amounts. Investors will borrow less and money holders lend more at each nominal interest rate. As a result, the final equilibrium will be at the same income level as would have occurred without the change in price expectations, but at a lower interest rate.

If all participants do not have equal price expectations or do not adjust by equal amounts in equal time periods, the IS and LM functions are not likely to shift by equal amounts. Market interest rates are apt to change in the same net direction as before, but by smaller amounts. Equilibrium

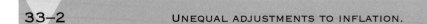

FIGURE

33–2   UNEQUAL ADJUSTMENTS TO INFLATION.

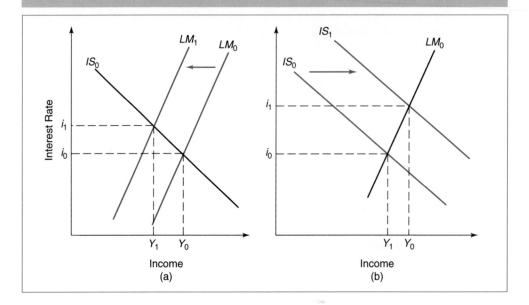

income will also differ from the solution above. For example, in panel a of Figure 33–2, lenders, depicted by the *LM* schedule, anticipate an acceleration in the rate of inflation, but investors, depicted by the *IS* schedule, do not. Thus, the *LM* schedule shifts up to LM_1. Interest rates climb to i_1, less than the rate that would occur if both functions shifted equally. Income declines to Y_1. In panel b, investors anticipate a faster rate of inflation, but lenders do not. The *IS* schedule shifts to IS_1. Interest rates rise to i_1, again lower than if both schedules shifted, and income rises to Y_1. In both instances, if inflation accelerates, there will be a redistribution of real income among borrowers and lenders, from those who adjust more completely to those who adjust less completely. If inflation does not accelerate, lenders lent too little in the first example and investors borrowed too much at high interest rates in the second example. In addition, there will be after-the-fact (*ex-post*) income redistributions regardless of the degree of adjustment if the realized rate of inflation either exceeds or falls short of the anticipated rate. The redistribution from unanticipated inflation is discussed in Chapter 34.

We can now trace the complete effect of monetary policy on interest rates. The policy action will have three effects on interest rates. The initial liquidity effect comes from the change in money supply and is opposite in direction to the money-supply change. If money supply increases, nominal interest rates decline, and conversely. Through time, the new interest rate is likely to change consumption and investment spending and also prices and price expectations. These two delayed effects operate in the opposite direction to the liquidity effect. Interest rates reverse. The final equilibrium rate can be higher, lower, or equal to the initial rate, depending on how sensitive aggregate income and price expectations are to the initial disturbance in the money supply. The more sensitive they are, the higher interest rates are likely to be ultimately.

The relationship between money and interest rates is thus more complex than the intuitive liquidity effect only. To the extent that changes in money supply affect both aggregate income and price expectations in later periods, the complete money–interest rate relationship may be written as:

$$i_t = f(\overset{-}{M_t}, \overset{+}{\Sigma M_{t-n}}) \qquad (34\text{–}2)$$

That is, interest rates are inversely related to money supply in more or less the same period, but positively related to changes in money in earlier periods $(t - n)$.

Thus, it is difficult to predict the final outcome of a monetary-policy action on nominal interest rates. Solutions generated only from the immediate liquidity effect, on which many analysts concentrate, or the combined liquidity and income effects, which are incorporated in the simple *LM-IS* model, may prove incorrect. As ironic as it may appear, expansionary actions may in time lead to higher interest rates than otherwise, and restrictive actions to lower rates. Likewise, this analysis shows why it is difficult and often self-defeating for policy to attempt to keep interest rates down for long through increases in the money supply. Like Alice in Wonderland, who had to run faster and faster to stay in the same place, the Fed will have to provide reserves faster and faster just to offset the effects of the previous increases in reserves and to keep interest rates in place!

Empirical Evidence

What has been the net relationship between changes in money supply and in interest rates in the past? This can be seen by plotting observations of market rates of interest and of the rate of change of money. The liquidity effect suggests an inverse relationship in which a line fitted to the points plotted would slope down from left to right, so that the greater the increase in money, the lower the interest rate. The income and price-expectations effects suggest a direct relationship in which this line would slope up from left to right, so that the greater the increase in money, the higher the interest rate.

Quarterly observations of the Treasury bill rate from 1960 through 1993 and of the corresponding growth rate of money in the United States are plotted in Figure 33–3. Interest rates are measured on the vertical axis and growth in money supply on the horizontal axis. If one were to draw a line through these points, it would slope positively up to the right. This suggests that on average the income and price-expectations effects dominate the liquidity effect and that interest rates change in the same direction as money supply. That is, increases in money tend to produce increases in interest rates quickly. But there is substantial dispersion around the average relationship. This suggests that the relationship is not very strong. A closer examination of the time period for each observation in Figure 33–3 suggests that the positive relationship is strongest in periods of more-rapid inflation, when inflationary expectations are high, and weakest in periods of more-modest inflation. In these periods the liquidity effect dominates.

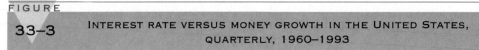

FIGURE

33–3

INTEREST RATE VERSUS MONEY GROWTH IN THE UNITED STATES,
QUARTERLY, 1960–1993

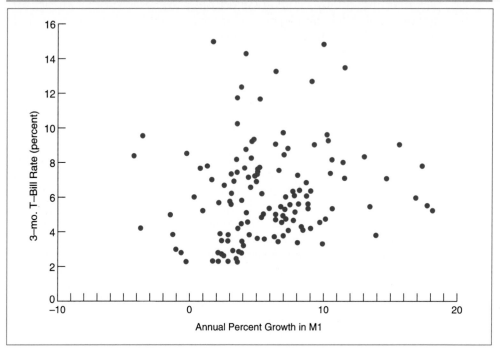

But maybe this relationship is unique to the United States and does not hold in other countries. Figure 33–4 shows plots of average short-term interest rates from 1979 to 1992 in 9 major industrial countries including the United States and the average annual rate of growth of money in the same period. Again, the relationship is clearly positive. Countries experiencing the fastest growth in money supply tended to experience the highest interest rates. Italy had the highest short-term interest rates (12½ percent) and the second fastest growth in money (11 percent). The United Kingdom had the next highest interest rates (11½ percent) and the fastest money growth (14 percent). Switzerland had the second lowest interest rates (6 percent) and by far the slowest money supply growth (1½ percent). However, breaking this down by subperiods shows that the positive relationship was stronger in the first half of the 1980s, when inflation was strongest, and weakest in the second half, when inflation weakened.

Thus, it is fair to conclude that in all countries the relationship between money and interest rates varies over time and depends greatly on the strength of price inflation and inflationary expectations at any time. In periods when inflation is strong, the relationship tends to be positive and increases in money are quickly reflected in increases in interest rates. The combined price expectations affects income and this, in turn, dominates the liquidity effect. In periods when inflation is mild, the relationship is harder to identify. At times, it is inverse, indicating that the liquidity effect dominates. Moreover, to the extent that central banks target nominal inter-

FIGURE

33-4

INTEREST RATE VERSUS MONEY GROWTH IN DIFFERENT
COUNTRIES, 1979-1992

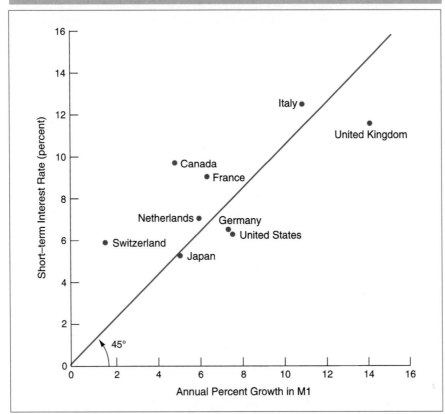

SOURCE: Board of Governors of the Federal Reserve System, *Federal Reserve Bulletin*, various issues, and Federal Reserve Bank of St. Louis, *International Economic Conditions*, annual edition, July 1993.

est rates rather than money supply directly in their policy operations, changes in money will not always be related to changes in observed interest rates. This is discussed later in the chapter.

Indicators of Monetary Policy

What is the Fed up to? This is important to know if you are trying to plan your future and want to predict income and inflation. But it may not be as easy for you or the general public to determine as it would appear. The tools of monetary policy may not always give a correct answer, because they may not all change in the same direction at the same time. As we have seen, some may be used to temporarily offset changes in others. Changes in the ultimate goals of monetary policy may not always give a correct answer, both because the goals are affected by many other forces in addition to monetary policy and because monetary policy affects the goals only after significant time lags. And asking the Fed may not always produce a correct answer, because in a world in which the transmission process is not known with certainty, the intent of policy may not be realized. Thus, "Fed watchers" must rely on other variables that they believe contain more reliable information about the current thrust of Federal Reserve monetary policy. These variables are termed **indicators of monetary policy.** The most popular indicators are nominal interest rates and money supply. Both are closer to the scene of Federal Reserve policy action than the ultimate targets, are important links in the transmission process, are quickly and reasonably accurately observable, and can signal information about policy sooner. But neither is perfect; both are also affected by non-Fed forces. Do high interest rates indicate restrictive or expansive monetary policy? How about rapid money growth? What if there were both high interest rates and rapid money growth?

Interest Rates

Interest rates are often used as an indicator of both monetary policy and financial conditions in general. Low and/or declining market interest rates are generally viewed as indicative of expansionary monetary policy, and high and/or rising market interest rates as indicative of restrictive policy. However, to the extent that money supply is indicative of monetary policy, the use of interest rates, as seen from the analysis just developed, has different, counterintuitive implications.

As we have discussed earlier in this chapter, nominal interest rates are frequently affected more by income and price expectations than by money supply. Thus, high and/or rising interest rates do not so much indicate restrictive monetary policy as they do rising income and price expectations, possibly as a result of expansive monetary policy in some earlier period. Low and/or falling interest rates do not so much indicate expansive monetary policy as they do declining income and price expectations, possibly as a result of earlier restrictive monetary policy. Thus, some analysts argue, high and rising interest rates indicate expansionary Fed monetary policy, be it sometime earlier, and low and/or falling interest rates indicate restrictive Fed monetary policy. It may not be correct to blame the Fed every time interest rates rise!

If even the direction of the relationship between interest rates and monetary policy is so uncertain, why then have interest rates been such a popular indicator of monetary policy, remaining so even today? It appears to be because we can "see, touch, and smell" interest rates. They are "real"! All of us have personal experiences with interest rates as savers, lenders, or borrowers. We know what they are, and we can understand them. They are a very visible price; on many securities, rates are known daily if not hourly. They are reported in the popular press and advertised widely. Changes in rates affect us in a very understandable way. *Ceteris paribus*, increases in rates encourage us to save more and borrow less, and decreases in rates to save less and borrow more. The non–*ceteris paribus* effect of inflation on rates takes time to decipher and sort out.

Moreover, we all know something about supply and demand. If money increases, there is more to lend, and interest rates should decline. If money decreases, interest rates should increase, reflecting the smaller supply of credit. Because the Fed controls the money supply, changes in interest rates should be the Fed's doing. Finally, market interest rates tend to follow a clear cyclical pattern, rising during periods of economic expansion and accelerating inflation, and declining during periods of economic contraction and slowing inflation. This pattern is consistent with our belief about the way monetary policy should be operating. Rates tend to be high when monetary policy should be restrictive and low when monetary policy should be expansive. This makes it easy to explain Fed stabilization policy as it should be.

Money Supply

Aggregate money supply, on the other hand, is a statistical artifact. It is not "real"! It bears little relation to our personal money supply, or to what many mistakenly call *money*. In contrast to interest rates, most people would be unable to define money supply and to differentiate among the numerous definitions, even if the definitions remained constant, which they do not. Also unlike nominal interest rates, which are observable and can be read accurately continuously throughout each working day, data on money supply are published weekly at best and only with a time delay of a few days and subject to periodic revisions. Nor do all measures of money supply always point in the same direction. The precise process by which money is created is not well understood, nor is the process by which money affects income. The money-income scenario has less intuitive appeal than the interest rate–income scenario and is often accused of resembling a "black box" in which money goes in one side and income comes out the other.

Nevertheless, while not perfect, the empirical evidence suggests that changes in monetary aggregates capture the future effect of Federal Reserve policy on the ultimate targets of income, employment, and prices more reliably than do interest rates. Increases in money growth foretell upward pressure on these variables and indicate more expansive monetary policy, and decreases indicate more restrictive policies. In contrast, increases in market rates of interest are more likely to indicate rising income and inflationary expectations than slowing monetary growth.

Intermediate Targets for Monetary Policy

Uncertainty about the relative importance of money supply and interest rates in the transmission process is the basis for another important controversy in monetary policy. Before long, almost any discussion of monetary policy reaches the sticky issue of whether the Federal Reserve should use money supply or market rates of interest as its **intermediate target.** Intermediate policy targets are generally considered necessary in a world of uncertainty when the time lag between policy action and its effect on the ultimate targets of policy (employment and inflation) is sufficiently long that the policymaker does not know the outcome of the action until it is too late to make corrections. As we have seen, such long lags exist for monetary policy. Intermediate targets are variables along the transmission process that are closer to the scene of the policy action than the ultimate objective and permit the policymaker to see the effects of policy actions sooner and to make midcourse corrections.

One occasions, the Fed uses a series of intermediate targets located progressively farther out on the transmission linkage in a way such that the

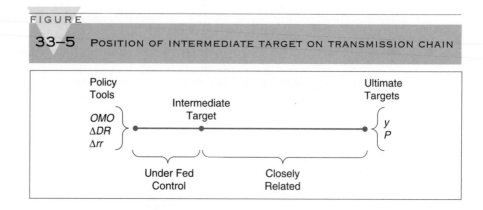

FIGURE

33–5 POSITION OF INTERMEDIATE TARGET ON TRANSMISSION CHAIN

nearest one to its operations affects the next nearest one, and so on. To differentiate among these targets, the nearest one is referred to as *operating targets*, the next nearest one as *instrumental targets*, and only the farthest out as *intermediate targets*. But, for the sake of analysis, we will assume only one such variable and target. (Intermediate policy targets may be likened to landmarks, located along a not very clearly marked path to an ultimate destination, that serve as near-term targets for a traveler and permit midcourse corrections to be made if he or she appears to stray from the initially charted course.) To be effective, variables that serve as intermediate targets must be under the control of the policymaker (although, unlike an indicator, not necessarily be set in value precisely by the Fed), important links in the transmission chain, close to the Fed on the transmission mechanism, quickly and accurately observable, and closely linked to the ultimate objective. The position of an intermediate target along the transmission linkage for monetary policy is shown in Figure 33–5. The Fed identifies the intermediate target it is using at the time in the final paragraph of its periodic open market directive.

Interest Rates or Money Supply?

In our world of uncertainty not all potential intermediate-target variables may be equally useful. For monetary policy, it is useful to use financial variables. They are the closest to the scene of the policy action and therefore the earliest to be observed. Interest rates and money supply are the most popular intermediate targets. However, as you may recall from your class in principles of economics, although producers can set either the price or the quantity supplied of a product, if they face an independent demand schedule, they cannot set *both* the price of the product and its supply. If producers set the quantity supplied, the price is determined by the demand; if the price is set, the quantity supplied is determined by the demand.

As is demonstrated in Figure 33–6, this principle also holds for the money market. If the Fed sets the supply of effective reserves and holds them constant at R_0^E, then the interest rate is determined by the demand for money. If the demand for money schedule increases from Y_0 to Y_1, in the absence of a change in price expectations, the interest rate increases from i_0 to i_1. In this operating regime, interest rates are volatile, but money supply is not. If the Fed does not want interest rates to change and pegs the

FIGURE

33–6

627

▼

INTEREST RATES,
INDICATORS, AND
TARGETS

THE FED CAN SET EITHER *M* OR *I* BUT NOT BOTH.

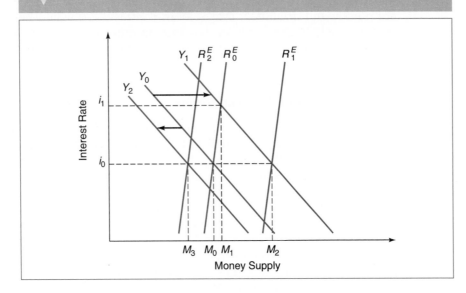

interest rate at i_0, it must supply the amount of effective reserves necessary to prevent shifts in demand from changing the rate. In this case, the Fed must increase reserves to R_1^E to keep the interest rate from rising to i_1. Money supply increases from M_0 to M_2. Conversely, if income declines from Y_0 to Y_2, the Fed must decrease the money supply to M_3 to keep interest rates unchanged. In effect, the supply schedule becomes flat at i_0. In this regime, money supply is volatile, but interest rates are not.

The choice of using interest rates or money supply as the intermediate target is related to your view of the transmission process. If you are a monetarist and believe that money is significantly linked to income in future periods, you would prefer to have the Fed operate on money supply. To increase income, the Fed would increase the money supply, and to decrease income, it would decrease the money supply. You would argue that by the setting of interest rate targets, changes in the demand for money would be accommodated to the detriment of the economy as a whole. Increases in the demand for money arising from higher incomes and inflation would call for increased money supply to prevent interest rates from rising. Conversely, decreases in money demand from lower incomes and inflation would call for lower money supply to prevent interest rates from declining. The resulting changes in the money supply would be pro-cyclical and would intensify rather than stabilize the business cycle. Moreover, to the extent that spending may be sensitive to interest rates, it is sensitive to the real rate of interest and not to the nominal market rate and to after-tax, not before-tax, rates. Thus, the Fed should affect the real rate. But even as powerful and knowledgeable a person as the chairman of the Board of Governors of the Federal Reserve System may be unable to estimate the real rate accurately.

On the other hand, if you were a Keynesian, you would prefer to have the Fed operate on interest rates. You would believe that these rates affect economic activity in known directions. A reduction in rates would stimulate spending, and an increase would discourage spending. Interest rates are directly affected by Federal Reserve operations, and data on interest rates are quickly and accurately available. In contrast, you would believe that money supply is unreliable in its effect on other variables, is difficult to measure and control, and has too many definitions to be useful as an intermediate-target variable.

Uncertainty in the Financial Sector

William Poole has developed a simple framework for analyzing the effectiveness of alternative intermediate targets based on the effects on aggregate income. Let the economy be summarized by the LM-*IS* model developed in Chapter 30. Assume that we know the position of the *IS* function with certainty but are uncertain about the position of the *LM* function because of uncertainty about the demand for money, *L*. The supply of money is controlled by the Fed and thus is known by it. However, assume that the bounds within which the *LM* function can shift due to volatility in demand are known and are shown by LM_1 and LM_2 in Figure 33–7. Let target full-employment income be Y_0 at interest rate i_0.

If the Fed set a money supply (or effective reserves) target, there would be no change in the quantity of money (or effective reserves) if the demand for money shifted. A shift in the *LM* function from LM_0 up to LM_1 caused by an increase in the demand for money from L_0 to L_1 would reduce income to Y_1 at higher interest rate i_1. A shift out to LM_2 caused by a decrease in the demand for money would increase income to Y_2 at lower interest rate i_2. Thus, a money supply target would have income fluctuate between Y_1 and Y_2 in response to the instability in the demand for money.

If the Fed set an interest rate target at, say, i_0, a shift in the *LM* schedule to LM_1 from an increase in the demand for money that threatens to raise interest rates would be offset by an equal increase in the money supply to return the function to LM_0 and keep the interest rate at i_0. That is, the increase in *L* would be exactly offset by an increase in *M*. Income would be stabilized at Y_0. Likewise, a shift to LM_2 from decreases in the demand for money that threaten to lower rates is offset by equal decreases in the money supply. Income again remains at Y_0. The economy behaves as if the *LM* schedule were flat at $i_0(LM_3)$. Under an interest rate target, income will not be affected by shifts in the demand for money.

Uncertainty in the Real Sector

Now let us reverse the conditions and assume certainty about the position of the *LM* function, but uncertainty about that of the *IS* function stemming from uncertainty about, say, investment or government spending. This function may shift between IS_1 and IS_2, as shown in Figure 33–8. Full-employment target income is again Y_0 at i_0. If the Fed sets money supply, the *LM* function will remain in place. A shift in the *IS* function down to IS_1 resulting from downward shifts in the underlying investment or government-expenditure functions causes equilibrium income to fall to Y_1 and interest rates to i_1. If the function shifts up to IS_2, income increases to Y_2 and interst rates to i_2. Income will fluctuate between Y_1 and Y_2. If, instead,

FIGURE

33–7

INTEREST RATE AND MONEY SUPPLY TARGETS WITH
UNCERTAINTY IN FINANCIAL SECTOR

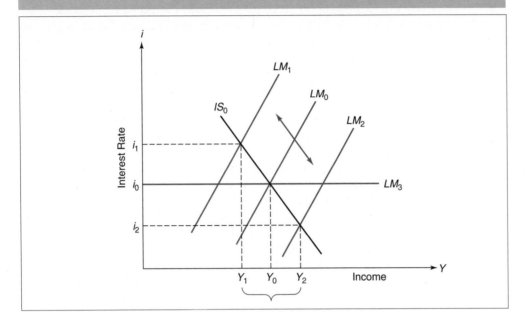

FIGURE

33–8

INTEREST RATE AND MONEY SUPPLY TARGETS WITH
UNCERTAINTY IN REAL SECTOR

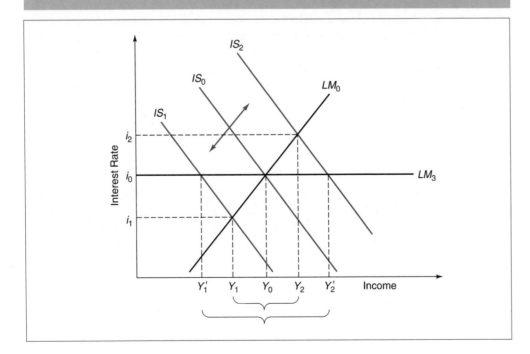

the Fed sets an interest rate target i_0, a shift to IS_1 will cause the Fed to decrease the money supply to offset the downward pressure in interest rates. At i_0, IS_1, income will decline to Y'_1. A shift to IS_2 will cause the Fed to increase the money supply to offset the upward pressure on interest rates. Income will increase to Y'_2. The LM function is effectively flat at i_0LM_3. The money supply changes procyclically in response to procyclical changes in interest rates, increasing when income increases and decreasing when income decreases. Although neither strategy restores income to Y_0 after a shift in the IS function, the money supply target constrains the change in income to a narrower band ($Y_1 - Y_2$) than the interest rate target ($Y'_1 - Y'_2$).

The moral of this analysis is clear. The choice of an intermediate target depends on the source of the uncertainty. If the disturbances originate in the financial sector, the Fed should use interest rates. If they originate in the real sector, the Fed should use money supply. But, although the analysis is clear, the solution is not unless you were certain about the source of the uncertainty. As we shall see in Chapter 35, a monetarist would argue that the uncertainty originates in the real sector and is attributable to previous erratic changes in the money supply, probably from the Fed's use of interest rates as a target. A Keynesian would argue with equal confidence that the disturbance originates in the financial sector from erratic shifts in the demand for money. But what if the disturbances originate in both? At a minimum, this analysis identifies the boundaries of the argument so that the costs and benefits of alternative strategies can be evaluated more accurately.

Federal Reserve Targets

What has the Federal Reserve used as intermediate targets?

1951–1965. Until the mid-1960s, the Fed relied primarily on short-term interest rate or closely related *money-market conditions* targets. Money-market conditions are defined to include a range of variables that reflect pressures in the short-term sector, such as the Fed-funds rate and borrowed reserves. A fairly typical policy paragraph in the directive issued by the Federal Open Market Committee to the manager of the Open Market Account in this period reads:

> To implement this policy, System open market operations until the next meeting of the Committee shall be conducted with a view to maintaining about the same conditions in the money market that have prevailed since the last meeting of the Committee.[1]

This directive was adopted November 23, 1965. It emphasized short-run interest rate stability, which, as noted earlier, has been a traditional concern of the Fed as a prerequisite for a broadly used financial market. To the extent that money-market conditions, like interest rates, are affected more by market forces than by immediate Federal Reserve actions, the operating

---

[1] Board of Governors of the Federal Reserve System, *Annual Report*, 1965, p. 148.

strategy called for by this directive was primarily *demand-driven*. This is the LM_3 scenario in Figure 33–8.

1966–1970. In the late 1960s, the acceleration in the rate of inflation, the increasing evidence that money supply was an important determinant of the rate of inflation, and the faster-than-desired rates of monetary growth that were obtained with interest rate targets caused the Fed to experiment with placing greater emphasis on monetary-aggregate targets. At first, monetary-aggregate targets, such as bank reserves, bank credit, or money supply, were included in the directive in the form of a *proviso clause* that instructed the manager to achieve a specified interest-rate target *provided* that some specified monetary aggregates did not change more than indicated. For example, the policy paragraph of the directive adopted June 7, 1966, the first to specify a proviso clause, reads:

> To implement this policy, System open market operations until the next meeting of the Committee shall be conducted with a view to maintaining net reserve availability and related money market conditions in about their recent ranges; provided, however, that if required reserves expand considerably more than seasonally expected, operations shall be conducted with a view to attaining some further gradual reduction in net reserve availability and firming of money market conditions.[2]

This change, however, did not appear to have resulted in better Fed control over the rapidly expanding money supply. Looking back, a Federal Reserve economist concluded:

> I do not believe that any member of the Federal Open Market Committee desired the progressive upward movements in the growth of money. From 1964 to 1973, the Federal Open Market Committee (FOMC) met 141 times and voted for a policy of restraint at seventy percent of these meetings. Only in 1967 and 1970 did the FOMC adopt a policy of ease at virtually every meeting.[3]

1971–1978. In 1971, shortly after the appointment of Arthur Burns as chairman of the Board of Governors, the committee elevated monetary aggregates to the primary intermediate target. This is seen in the first such directive, adopted on June 8:

> To implement this policy, the Committee seeks to moderate growth in monetary aggregates over the months ahead, taking account of developments in capital markets. System open market operations until the next meeting of the Committee shall be conducted with a view to achieving bank reserve and money market conditions consistent with those objectives.[4]

[2] Board of Governors of the Federal Reserve System, *Annual Report*, 1966, p. 151.

[3] Albert Burger, "The Current Inflation: The United States Experience," *Review*, Federal Reserve Bank of St. Louis, September 1974, p. 15.

[4] Board of Governors of the Federal Reserve System, *Annual Report*, 1971, p. 154.

But the Fed was reluctant to operate on money supply directly and chose instead to achieve its money targets indirectly by first achieving an assumed consistent interest rate operating target. This may be seen from the directive adopted April 18, 1978:

> The committee seeks to encourage near-term rates of growth in M-1 and M-2 on a path believed to be reasonably consistent with the longer-run ranges for monetary aggregates. . . . In the judgment of the Committee such growth rates are likely to be associated with a week-ly-average Federal funds rate slightly above the current level.[5]

Thus, interest rate stability remained an important concern.

1979–1982. In 1979, the FOMC acted to further increase its control over the money supply by operating directly to supply "the volume of bank reserves estimated to be consistent with the desired rates of growth in monetary aggregates, while permitting much greater fluctuations in the Federal funds rate than heretofore."[6] The directive adopted March 31, 1981, reflected this change in operating strategy:

> In the short run the Committee seeks behavior of reserve aggregates consistent with growth in M-1B from March to June at an annual rate of $5\frac{1}{2}$ percent or somewhat less . . . and growth in M-2 at an annual rate of about $10\frac{1}{2}$ percent. . . . If it appears during the period before the next meeting that fluctuations in the federal funds rate, taken over a period of time, within a range of 13 to 18 percent, are likely to be inconsistent with the monetary and related reserve paths, the Manager for Domestic Operations is promptly to notify the Chairman, who will then decide whether the situation calls for supplementary instructions from the Committee.[7]

The operating strategy required to achieve this directive could be termed *supply-driven*. As was widely expected, this change in procedures resulted in a sharp increase in the short-run volatility of interest rates, but also, as a surprise to almost all market participants, in an equally sharp increase in the short-run volatility of money supply. Monetarists argued that the sharp increase in interest rate and money volatility during the 1979–1982 regime reflected the Fed's use of inappropriate operating procedures and could have been avoided had the Fed really wanted to. Thus, they claim that this period did not represent a true "monetarist experiment." To them, it was a question of will, not of means.

1982–1985. In 1982, after only three years, in part as a result of the higher volatility of both interest rates and money supply, the Fed decreased its emphasis on monetary targeting and increased its emphasis on short-run money-market stability again. The directive adopted March 27, 1984, read:

[5] Board of Governors of the Federal Reserve System, *Annual Report*, 1978, p. 168.

[6] Board of Governors of the Federal Reserve System, *Annual Report*, 1979, p. 202.

[7] Board of Governors of the Federal Reserve System, *Annual Report*, 1981, p. 104. (M-1B was equivalent to the current M1.)

In the short run the Committee seeks to maintain pressures on bank reserve positions judged to be consistent with growth in M1, M2, and M3 at annual rates of around $6\frac{1}{2}$, 8, and $8\frac{1}{2}$ percent, respectively, during the period from March to June. Greater reserve restraint would be acceptable in the event of more substantial growth of the monetary aggregates, while somewhat lesser restraint might be acceptable if growth of the monetary aggregates slowed significantly.[8]

Reserve pressure was imposed through borrowed reserves. The greater the level of borrowed reserves relative to a target level, the more are banks believed to be under pressure to repay and the more temporary will be the reserve and monetary aggregate expansion. (This *bankers* theory is discussed more fully in Chapter 35.) To the extent that the amount of borrowed reserves outstanding reflects demand pressures, critics accused the Fed of returning to a demand-driven operating procedure. The Fed, however, argued that, unlike its pre-1979 procedures, it changes the target level of borrowed reserves frequently enough to minimize accommodating demand pressures. This procedure may be classified as *market-modified, supply-driven*.

1986—. In 1986, as M1 expanded sharply and M1 velocity declined sharply, the Fed found it a less useful target and reduced its emphasis on M1 by first downgrading the importance of the annual target range relative to those for M2 and M3, and then in 1987 by not specifying a range at all. This policy was evident in the directive adopted May 18, 1993, and shown on page 544. According to the Fed, this change did not alter its operating strategy, nor did it represent a further retreat from monetary targeting. In mid-1993, Chairman Greenspan announced that the Fed was temporarily downgrading M2 as well as M1 as an intermediate target because of its

> recognition that the relationship between spending and money holdings was departing markedly from historical norms. . . . The FOMC will continue to monitor the behavior of money supply measures for evidence about underlying economic and financial developments more generally, but it will still have to base its assessments regarding appropriate policy actions on a wide variety of economic indicators.[9]

The Chairman also announced that the Fed was broadening its range of potential intermediate targets and was considering real interest rates for the first time. However, as of the date this book went to press, the Fed had not announced any new targets.

In sum, it appears that the Fed relies primarily on interest rates and money-market condition targets when inflation is not a serious policy concern and shifts progressively more to money supply targets as inflation progressively becomes of greater concern.

---

[8] *Federal Reserve Bulletin*, June 1984, pp. 513–14.

[9] Board of Governors of the Federal Reserve System, 1994 *Monetary Policy Objectives*, Washington, D.C., February 22, 1994, p. 18.

How Good Has Federal Reserve Control Been?

The Fed had traditionally been able to hit its interest rate targets very closely. However, it has had less success in hitting its money supply targets. This may be seen from Table 28–3 and Figure 33–9. The solid blue line in the figure shows the actual rate of growth of M1 between 1975 and 1984. The continuous dotted line shows the average of the annual target growth rates specified in the directive for each period. This average differs from the rate of growth that would be required to achieve the target money supply at the end of 1984, because each growth-rate target for a year is based on the actual money stock outstanding at the beginning of the year, regardless of whether or not it was within the target range. The practice of basing each new growth target on the actual money stock outstanding at the beginning of the period rather than on the previously targeted amount for that date is referred to as **base drift.** As can be seen from the figure, actual money growth was considerably above the average target growth, and frequently even above the upper annual target range, shown by the discontinuous solid lines, which had drifted upward. Thus, most new targets were based on higher-than-targeted beginning money supplies. This helps to explain the faster-than-average target rate of M1 growth. This problem was a prime reason for the Fed's 1979 decision to operate more directly on the money supply. But the change in procedures did not appear to improve the Fed's abilities to hit its M1 targets. On the whole, the Fed overshot its target

FIGURE

33–9   ACTUAL AND TARGET RANGES FOR M1

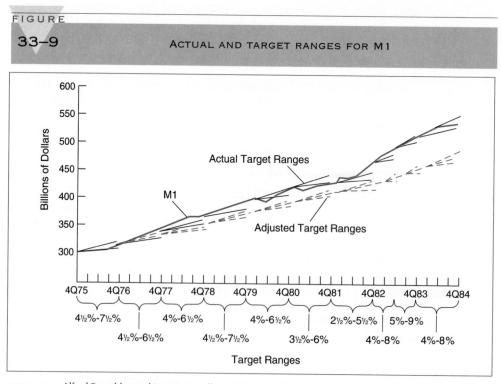

SOURCE: Alfred Broaddus and Marvin Goodfriend, "Base Drift and the Longer Run Growth of M1: Experience from a Decade of Monetary Targeting," *Economic Review*, Federal Reserve Bank of Richmond, November/December 1984, p. 9.

NOTE: M1 levels are quarterly averages and are adjusted for distortions from the deregulation of deposit accounts.

EXHIBIT

33–1

Beat Inflation or Lose Your Job

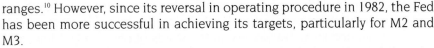

If New Zealand's new central bank governor doesn't wring inflation out of the economy, he might find himself out of a job.

Don Brash, who took over the Reserve Bank of New Zealand last month, said legislation expected to be enacted this year or early next year will make him accountable for the country's inflation performance. Wellington has set a goal of getting the rate below 2% by the early 1990s.

"It is my understanding that my contract will include a pretty specific target," Mr. Brash said in an interview. "And I suppose if I consistently fail to perform, just like any other chief executive, I can't continue to retain my job."

He said he didn't know whether he'd get a bonus if he did meet the target. But he did say he would be exempt from responsibility for the inflationary impact of developments outside his control, like tax increases.

Higher taxes don't seem likely anytime soon, however. The man with whom Mr. Brash will be negotiating his contract, Finance Minister Roger Douglas, has been pushing a tough brand of free-market economics that has come to be known as Rogernomics. Mr. Douglas has slashed the top tax rate to 33%, half what it was when he took office in 1984.

Mr. Brash's inflation-slaying assignment stems from a government decision in July to redefine the central bank's role. The bank was granted greater autonomy and told that its chief task is to keep prices down—an objective that had never been stated in so many words.

SOURCE: Martin Howell, "Win Inflation Fight or Lose Your Job, Monetary Boss Told," *The Wall Street Journal*, October 17, 1988, p. A11. Reprinted by permission of *The Wall Street Journal*, Dow Jones & Company, Inc. All Rights Reserved Worldwide.

ranges.[10] However, since its reversal in operating procedure in 1982, the Fed has been more successful in achieving its targets, particularly for M2 and M3.

Some critics of the Fed's operating procedures have argued that the Fed can freely miss its announced monetary aggregate and even ultimate objective targets because there is no penalty for doing so; these critics have urged the imposition of some form of penalty. An example, although probably somewhat extreme, of such a penalty was New Zealand and is described in Exhibit 33–1.

Fed Watching

Because of the historical reluctance of the Fed to announce its policy actions in plain English, its periodic changes in the variables it uses as intermediate targets, the large and volatile volume of defensive open-market operations, and disagreement about the best policy indicator, the direction and implications of Federal Reserve monetary policy are uncertain to

[10] The United States is not the only country in which actual money growth was outside target rates. Similar misses occurred in other countries. A review of target and actual rates of monetary growth in major countries is published annually in the *Annual Reports* of the Bank for International Settlements (BIS).

SOURCE: *American Banker*, July 16, 1981, p. 1. Reprinted by permission

large segments of the public, and even to many members of the financial
community. This is particularly true for investors in short-term and Treasury
securities, which are most directly affected by Fed operations. As a result,
some analysts specialize in following, deciphering, and even trying to predict Fed actions and their effects on the money market. Such people are
referred to as *Fed watchers*. In the words of one Fed watcher: "we . . . had to
sift through the tea leaves and figure out by looking at the daily open-market operations and [bank] reserve flows . . . if they changed policy."[11] Fed
watchers are employed by financial institutions to assist in their own
investment decisions and as a service for their clients. Fed watching provides lucrative employment opportunities both for former Fed employees,
who are most familiar with the technology, language, mystique, and
nuances of Fed operating procedures, and for former "China watchers," who
were thrown out of work when the United States recognized the previously
closed Communist regime and was able to collect information directly
through official channels. This importance of Fed watching is indicated by
the advertisement for this service placed by a large Treasury securities dealer in a major trade newspaper and shown in Figure 33–10. In 1994, partially in response to pressure from Congress, the Fed began to announce more
of its actions at the time they were taken. In part, this openness appears to
reflect its reduced emphasis on the use of intermediate targets. One newspaper heralded this change by noting that "the Temple doesn't have quite
so many secrets anymore."[12]

[11] David Wessel and Anita Raghavan, "A Growing Glasnost At The Fed Is Dispelling A Lot of
Its Mystique," *Wall Street Journal*, March 24, 1994, p. A9.

[12] Ibid, p. 1.

SUMMARY

The analysis developed in earlier chapters demonstrated that changes in money supply, represented by shifts in the *LM* function, have an immediate effect on interest rates in the opposite direction (from the old equilibrium to the new *LM* schedule at the same income level) and a delayed effect in the same direction (along the *LM* schedule to the new equilibrium). The first effect is termed the *liquidity effect*; the second, the *income effect*. In most instances, the liquidity effect is stronger than the income effect, and increases in money supply lead to lower equilibrium interest rates, and decreases to higher equilibrium rates. But changes in money supply also affect prices and price expectations. Changes in price expectations cause shifts in both the *LM* and *IS* schedules. The *price-expectations effect* on interest rates works to reinforce the income effect to offset the liquidity effect. The net effect of money supply on interest rates is the sum of the liquidity, income, and price-expectations effects. The strength of the price-expectations effect depends on the state of the economy. Generally, the closer the economy is to full employment, the stronger the effect. Thus, changes in money supply can lead to final changes in interest rates in either the opposite or the same direction and are difficult to predict.

Empirical evidence suggests that, on average, the sum of the income and price-expectations effects on interest rates outweighs the liquidity effects. Thus, interest rates are generally a poor indicator of the posture of monetary policy as reflected in the money supply.

Intermediate targets of monetary policy are financial variables at which the Fed directs monetary policy actions in order to gauge their success before they affect the ultimate goals of policy. Interest rates and money supply are both popular intermediary targets. But in a world of uncertainty, they can produce different results. If the source of the uncertainty originates in the real sector, use of money supply as an intermediate target would stabilize income more than would the use of interest rates. If the source of the uncertainty originates in the monetary sector through the demand for money, interest rates would be the better target of income stabilization. When inflation worsens, the Fed and other central banks place greater emphasis on monetary aggregates as their intermediate policy targets and change their operating procedures accordingly. In the last 30 years, the Fed has changed its operating targets and strategies a number of times as it has alternated between monetary and interest rate targeting. Under all targeting regimes, however, the Fed has missed its money supply target as often as it has hit it.

QUESTIONS

1. Identify and describe the three components of the complete effect of money on market rates of interest. Which effect do you think has the greatest popular appeal? Why?

2. Discuss the empirical evidence relating money supply and market interest rates. How does the U.S. experience compare with that of other countries?

3. If you were asked by Congress how to reduce interest rates, what would you reply? Defend your answer.

4. Why does the ultimate change in market interest rates after a Federal Reserve monetary action depend on the relative responses of investors (SSUs) and borrowers (DSUs)? Will the change be greater or less if all par-

ticipants anticipate the same price change? Why? What happens to both interest rates and income if they do not?

5. Define the liquidity effect part of the money–interest rate relationship. Why do most people tend to focus only on this effect? At what times is the liquidity effect observed most easily in practice and when is it most difficult to observe? Give examples from U.S. history since World War II. Do you think that liquidity effects are readily observable today? Why or why not?

6. Why and for whom are *indicators* of money policy necessary? Discuss the pros and cons of using interest rates and money supply as indicators.

7. Why does the Federal Reserve use intermediate targets? Discuss the pros and cons of market interest rates and money supply as intermediate targets. Under conditions of greater uncertainty in the real than in the financial sector, which intermediate target would produce less variability in income?

8. Why might the Fed have consistently missed its money supply target in the 1970s and in the early 1980s? In what directions did it miss? Why? Why has the Fed had a better record in more recent years?

9. Look up changes in the money supply, say, M1 or M2, for the first half of last year. What would these changes have told you about the posture of monetary policy? Why? What has happened in the economy since? Is this consistent with how you interpreted the earlier indicators? Discuss.

REFERENCES

Belognia, Michael T., and James A. Chalfant, "Alternative Measures of Money as Indicators of Inflation: A Survey and Some New Results," *Review*, Federal Reserve Bank of St. Louis, November/December 1990, pp. 20–33.

Black, Robert P., "Reflections on the Strategy of Monetary Policy," *Economic Review*, Federal Reserve Bank of Richmond, July/August 1990, pp. 3–7.

Broaddus, Alfred, and Marvin Goodfriend, "Base Drift and the Longer Run Growth of M1," *Economic Review*, Federal Reserve Bank of Richmond, November/December 1984, pp. 3–14.

Carlson, Keith M., and Scott E. Hein, "Monetary Aggregates as Monetary Indicators," *Review*, Federal Reserve Bank of St. Louis, November 1980, pp. 12–21.

Davis, Richard G., et al., *Intermediate Targets and Indicators for Monetary Policy.* New York: Federal Reserve Bank of New York, 1990.

Friedman, Milton, "Monetary Policy: Theory and Practice," *Journal of Money,* *Credit and Banking*, February 1982, pp. 98–118.

Garcia, Gillian, "The Right Rabbit: Which Intermediate Target Should the Fed Pursue?" *Economic Perspectives*, Federal Reserve Bank of Chicago, May/June 1984, pp. 15–31.

Heller, H. Robert, "Implementing Monetary Policy," *Federal Reserve Bulletin*, July 1988, pp. 419–29.

Hetzel, Robert L., "A Primer on the Importance of the Money Supply," *Economic Review*, Federal Reserve Bank of Richmond, September/October 1977, pp. 3–12.

Hetzel, Robert L., "The Rules versus Discretion Debate over Monetary Policy in the 1920s," *Economic Review*, Federal Reserve Bank of Richmond, November/December 1985, pp. 3–14.

Humphrey, Thomas M., "Can the Central Bank Peg Real Interest Rates? A Survey of Classical and Neoclassical Opinion," *Economic Review*, Federal Reserve Bank of Richmond, September/October 1984, pp. 12–21.

Kane, Edward J., "Selecting Monetary Targets in a Changing Financial Environment," *Monetary Policy Issues in the 1980s*, Federal Reserve Bank of Kansas City, 1982, pp. 181–206.

Kasman, Bruce, "A Comparison of Monetary Policy Operating Procedures in Six Industrial Countries," *Quarterly Review*, Federal Reserve Bank of New York, Summer 1992, pp. 5–24.

Kaufman, George G., "The Fed's Post-October Technical Operating Procedures under Lagged Reserve Requirements: Reduced Ability to Control Money," *Financial Review*, November 1982, pp. 279–94.

Kaufman, George G., "Monetarism at the Fed," *Journal of Contemporary Studies*, Winter 1983, pp. 27–36.

Leeper, Eric M., "Facing Up to Our Ignorance about Measuring Monetary Policy Effects," *Economic Review*, Federal Reserve Bank of Atlanta, May/June 1992, pp. 1–16.

Lombra, Raymond E., and Raymond G. Torto, "The Strategy of Monetary Policy," *Economic Review*, Federal Reserve Bank of Richmond, September/October 1975, pp. 3–14.

Mehre, Yash, "Inflationary Expectations, Money Growth, and the Vanishing Liquidity Effect of Money and Interest," *Economic Review*, Federal Reserve Bank of Richmond, March/April 1985, pp. 23–35.

Meltzer, Allan, et al., "Is the Federal Reserve's Monetary Control Policy Misdirected? A Debate," *Journal of Money, Credit and Banking*, February 1982, pp. 119–47.

Melvin, Michael, "The Vanishing Liquidity Effect of Money on Interest: Analysis and Implications for Policy," *Economic Inquiry*, April 1983, pp. 188–202.

Meulendyke, Ann-Marie, "Reserve Requirements and the Discount Window in Recent Decades," *Quarterly Review*, Federal Reserve Bank of New York, Autumn 1992, pp. 25–43.

Meulendyke, Ann-Marie, U.S. *Monetary Policy and Financial Markets*. New York: Federal Reserve Bank of New York, 1989.

Mote, Larry R., "Looking Back: The Use of Interest Rates in Monetary Policy," *Economic Perspectives*, Federal Reserve Bank of Chicago, January/February 1988, pp. 15–29.

Poole, William, "Interest Rate Stability as a Monetary Goal," *New England Economic Review*, Federal Reserve Bank of Boston, May/June 1976, pp. 30–37.

Poole, William, *Money and the Economy: A Monetarist View*. Reading, Mass.: Addison-Wesley, 1978.

Poole, William, et al., "Reforming the Monetary Regime," *The CATO Journal*, Winter 1986.

"Rational Expectations—Fresh Ideas That Challenge Some Established Views of Policy Making," *Annual Report 1977*, Federal Reserve Bank of Minneapolis, 1978.

Wallich, Henry C., et al., "Recent Techniques of Monetary Policy," *Journal of the Midwest Finance Association*, 1984, pp. 1–21.

Wessel, David and Anita Reghavan, "A Growing Glasnost At The Fed Is Dispelling A Lot Of Mistique," *Wall Street Journal*, March 24, 1994, pp. A1,9.

Wheelock, David C., "Monetary Policy in the Great Depression: What the Fed Did and Why," *Review*, Federal Reserve Bank of St. Louis, March/April 1992, pp. 3–28.

Inflation, The Phillips Curve, and Central Bank Independence

Inflation is defined as a prolonged increase in the overall price level and a concomitant deterioration in the purchasing power of money. Not all prices need rise equally. Some may rise faster than average, some slower, and some may even decline. An abrupt slowdown in the rate of inflation is often referred to as **disinflation** and a decline in the overall price level as **deflation.** Because prices have been increasing almost continuously since World War II in all developed countries, not only in the United States, we shall limit our analysis to inflation. But it should be kept in mind that the undesirable aspects of inflation apply equally to deflation or more generally to any volatility in the price level.

Although rising prices have been the rule rather than the exception throughout U.S. history, the public has become more concerned about inflation as its rate has remained high relative to other peacetime periods and briefly even accelerated to double digits in the early 1980s. Concern with inflation has not been confined to the United States; inflation has plagued almost all countries. Rates of inflation between 1973 and 1992 are shown in Table 34–1 for a sample of industrial countries. For the period as a whole, the inflation rate in the United States was about average, not nearly as high as in Italy and the United Kingdom but not nearly as low as in Japan.

As discussed earlier, inflation occurs when "too many dollars chase too few goods"; that is, when demand exceeds supply at or near full employment. Why this happens is more complex. At times, it may be the result of overexpansive monetary or fiscal policies. At other times, it may

TABLE 34–1	INFLATION RATE IN SELECTED INDUSTRIAL COUNTRIES, 1973–1992 (ANNUAL RATE)
	Percent
Canada	6.8
France	8.1
West Germany	3.7
Italy	12.5
Japan	−2.7
Netherlands	4.0
Switzerland	3.9
United Kingdom	9.8
United States	5.8

SOURCE: Federal Reserve Bank of St. Louis, *International Economic Conditions, Annual Edition,* July 1993.

FIGURE

34–1

UNTIL THE 1980S, PERCENT CHANGES IN MONEY SUPPLY HAVE BEEN
CLOSELY RELATED TO PERCENT CHANGES IN PRICES TWO YEARS LATER.

641

▼

INFLATION, THE
PHILLIPS CURVE,
AND CENTRAL BANK
INDEPENDENCE

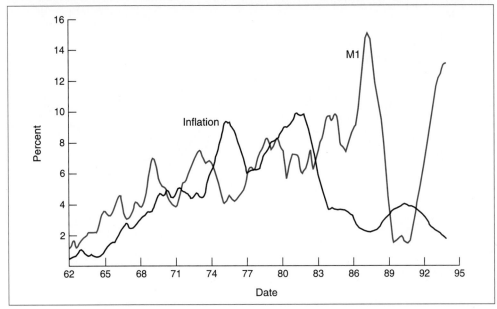

SOURCE: Federal Reserve Bank of Chicago

NOTE: Inflation = GDP price deflator, money = M1. Observations of M1 are plotted two years after they occurred.

result from cutbacks in supply—say, because of bad weather's reducing crops, monopolistic curtailment of petroleum production or labor supply, or wartime shifts in production from consumer to military goods. History suggests that every major inflation has been preceded or accompanied by increases in the money supply. Thus, to many analysts, inflation is basically a monetary phenomenon.

Monetarists point to a close relationship between changes in money supply and changes in inflation some two years later. For example, Figure 34–1 plots changes in M1 from 1961 to 1993 and the changes in the GDP deflator two years later. The close correlation in the early years is evident. Changes in money supply explain most of the changes in the rates of inflation even in 1973–1975 and 1979–1980, when the primary effects of the OPEC I and II increases in oil prices were being felt, and the sharp slowing of inflation in both 1976 and 1981. This close relationship underlies the conclusion of many analysts that inflation is a *monetary phenomenon.* However, changes in money explain less of the sharp decline in the rate of inflation after 1982, and the two have not been very closely correlated since.

The close money–inflation relationship through the early 1980s and the breakdown since is not unique to the United States. As can be seen from Figure 34–2, a similar relationship is evident for 24 major Western industrial countries. The reasons for the breakdown in the money–inflation relationship are not yet fully understood, nor is it clear whether the breakdown is permanent or represents a one-time shift in the structure of industrial countries as a result of the abrupt slowing in inflation. M1 velocity

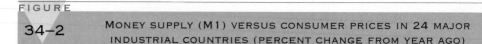

FIGURE

34–2

MONEY SUPPLY (M1) VERSUS CONSUMER PRICES IN 24 MAJOR
INDUSTRIAL COUNTRIES (PERCENT CHANGE FROM YEAR AGO)

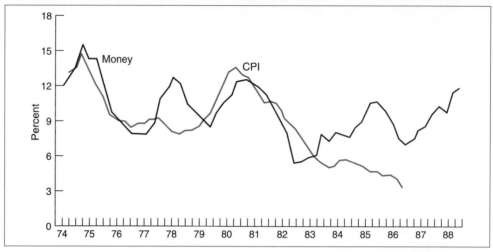

SOURCE: *Business News & Trends* (PNC Financial Corp., Pittsburgh, Pa.), Fourth Quarter 1986, p. 3.
NOTE: Money is pushed forward by eight quarters.

declined sharply in almost all countries in this period, at least temporarily reversing a long-time upward trend (Figure 29–1). Monetarists consider the breakdown only temporary and expect the close relationship to be reestablished again in future years. Others say money by itself is too simple an explanation of inflation, and they search for causes underlying the monetary expansion. Regardless of the reason for the monetary expansion, however, money—or, more precisely, an overabundance of money—is a prime contributor to price inflation.

Costs of Inflation

As discussed in Chapter 26, avoiding inflation or more generally rapid price level changes in either direction is an important goal of all economies. However, public concern over inflation is generally not as strong as it is over the failure to achieve some other goals. This is because the costs of not achieving price stability often are not immediately visible to the public at large, and only some households are affected adversely; others benefit. Moreover, unlike unemployment, the harm tends to be spread over many households so that any one unit suffers relatively little.

If all prices increased at the same rate, if all households and business firms knew this in advance, and if the costs of adjustment were zero, inflation would do little else than put additional zeros after prices. There would be no effects on the distribution of income and only small effects on aggregate income measured in real or constant-purchasing-power dollars. All people would anticipate the price increases equally and adjust their economic behavior accordingly. All prices and costs would be marked up by the anticipated rate of inflation, so that real prices and costs would remain unchanged. If prices were expected to rise by 10 percent across the board, workers might be expected to demand 10 percent higher wages than otherwise, and employers might be expected to be willing to grant this increase because it would not disturb their costs or profits. Other than suffering minor costs from changing prices frequently, no one would expect to be any better or worse off.

Unfortunately, however, in real life not everyone anticipates the same rate of inflation, all prices do not increase uniformly, information on price changes is not free, contracts cannot be changed in midstream (unless you are a star athlete), and anticipated price increases are not always realized. Unanticipated inflation—either accelerations or decelerations—creates two important problems. First, resources are shifted from productive to less productive uses, reducing aggregate income and welfare in the economy. Second, to the extent that different households and business firms are not all equally good in predicting the actual rate of inflation or in putting their predictions into practice, income is redistributed among them. We shall examine each effect in greater detail.

Aggregate Income Loss

If not all prices change uniformly and price information is not free, resources must be devoted to gathering, compiling, and interpreting price data for use in decision making. Because different sellers are likely to

"On the bright side, it's taking more people to keep track of inflation . . . that means more jobs!"

SOURCE: DUNAGIN'S PEOPLE by Ralph Dunagin. Copyright © 1978 King Features Syndicate. Reprinted with special permission of North American Syndicate.

charge different prices for the same items, at least temporarily, additional time is required to search out the lowest price. Long-established seller-buyer relationships based on faith break down. Price lists must be updated by the seller and scrutinized by the buyer more frequently. Price forecasts must be made and revised by more people more frequently. The additional resources needed to accomplish these tasks are transferred from more productive uses, or from potentially more productive uses if the economy is operating at less than full capacity. (This waste of resources to carry out the ordinary, everyday business of shopping is nicely described by Hans Bethe in his recollections of the German hyperinflation quoted in Chapter 2.) In addition, to the extent that prices do not contain fully accurate information, they are apt to transmit incorrect signals and not allocate resources most efficiently.

If expectations become either more difficult to form or increasingly unreliable, uncertainty increases. Increased uncertainty increases both transactions costs and risk, making decision units more reluctant to enter into riskier ventures. Unless the return for risk increases commensurately, activities undertaken in more certain times, particularly long-term capital investment, would not be undertaken, thus changing the output mix. Attempts to reduce risk include the increased use of financial futures and options markets (described in Chapter 22), which absorb both time and expense. Long-term contractors—labor, buyers, sellers, or financial—who find themselves unexpectedly seriously disadvantaged become more willing to breach or default on the contract. As a result, aggregate welfare for a given level of input will be lower than what it would have been had prices been more stable. The faster the rate of inflation, the more volatile it is likely to be, the greater would be costs of collecting information, the less reliable would prices be, the greater the uncertainty, the lower both saving and investment, and the greater the welfare loss.

Bank Failures

Some other costs of inflation have become evident only more recently in the United States. The financial system becomes more fragile and vulnerable to both credit and interest rate risk. The inflation of the 1980s hit depository institutions with a double whammy. First, the unexpected jump in interest rates produced by the unexpected acceleration in inflation in the late 1970s sharply reduced the market value of long-term fixed-coupon-rate debt. This particularly affected traditional mortgage-lending institutions, such as savings and loan associations and savings banks, whose interest earnings on their portfolios of old mortgage loans remained constant while their interest costs on shorter-term deposits increased sharply with the rise in market rates. By 1981, the majority of thrift institutions were experiencing severe financial strains from interest rate risk and were threatened with failure.

As discussed in Chapter 12, two-thirds of all SLAs lost money in 1982, and the economic net worth of the industry was negative by nearly $100 billion. In addition, because market interest rates had increased above the ceilings on deposit rates then in effect (Regulation Q), disintermediation threatened to shrink the industry substantially. Most institutions kept from closing only by merger with other institutions and/or government financial assistance. To protect themselves against future unexpected inflation and interest rate shocks, many mortgage lenders changed from making mostly fixed-rate loans to making mostly variable-rate loans, thereby shifting much of the inflation and interest rate risk onto the borrower (Chapter 21).

Moreover, many of the surviving institutions had greatly weakened capital bases. This encouraged a number of them to take bigger-than-normal interest and credit gambles, as they had little more of their own shareholders' funds to lose and much to gain. Because most of these gambles failed, the losses from interest rate risk in the early 1980s led to further losses in the later 1980s and contributed significantly to the near $200 billion cumulative deficit in the net worth of SLAs by 1991 and the near destruction of the industry.

Second, inflation tends to become incorporated in future income projections and asset values, which are used to justify and collateralize loans from banks and thrift institutions. If inflation slows unexpectedly, the market values of these incomes and assets will be lower than expected and the loans made on the basis of the projected values will be more likely to go into default. Losses from default risk were the cause of many bank and thrift failures in the mid- and late 1980s, particularly in the agricultural and energy belts of the country where the rapid runup in prices was followed by almost equally rapid price rundowns. Indeed, Anna Schwartz, a student of banking, concludes that price level instability is the major single threat to the stability of the banking system.

The high interest rates also encouraged savers to reduce their balances to the minimum at depository institutions that were restricted at the time by deposit rate ceilings to pay no interest or below-market rates of interest. This resulted in the development of new techniques, financial instruments, and even institutions, that could offer the same services but at a higher interest return. Institutions that did not react fast enough experienced deposit losses. Ironically, a considerable amount of the financial innovation since the 1970s can be traced to the needs of households and business firms to protect themselves from inflation and thus did not add to the country's economic welfare, although it did serve to minimize losses. The increase in the variety and complexity of new financial instruments makes it more difficult for households to feel confident that they have invested their funds at the highest interest rates and have borrowed at the lowest.

Income and Wealth Redistribution

If not all people hold the same expectations of the rate of price increase over a specified future time period, or if they do but are unable to adjust their economic behavior at the same rate or at the same cost, or if the expected rates of price increases do not materialize, inflation will affect different spending units differently. Income and wealth will be redistributed. There will be winners and losers. Those who had correctly estimated the rate of inflation and were able to put their expectations into action at little cost will gain relative to those who guessed wrong or were slow to act. Spending units that fail to adjust to expected inflation because they see only the increases in their money incomes but not in the prices they pay are said to operate under **money illusion.** The more volatile the rate of inflation, the more difficult and costly these adjustments are apt to be, and the wider the variance in individual price expectations is apt to be. Redistribution results from unanticipated inflation; the greater the unanticipated inflation, the greater the redistribution. It is unlikely that the redistribution of income caused by unanticipated inflation is consistent with that considered equitable by members of the economy and chosen as a goal. Thus, inflation produces inequities in income and wealth.

Income Effect.   To evaluate the implications of unanticipated inflation, it is necessary to identify the winners and the losers. With respect to income, the winners may be expected to be those spending units that are most knowledgeable about the workings of the economic system, can gather and evaluate price data most cheaply and most quickly, and have the ability to adjust the prices of their services, the products they produce, and the items they purchase. That is, the winners are those groups that operate under money illusion the least. These adjustments are particularly important in contracts that extend for a period of time. If, for example, after a period of price stability, prices are expected to increase by 10 percent in the next year, a previously negotiated 15 percent salary increase on a $40,000 salary base would still represent a nominal pay increase of $6,000 but a real increase of less than $2,000 [($46,000/1.10) − $40,000 = $1,818]. The employee loses, to the gain of the employer. It appears reasonable that better-educated people would be able to undertake these tasks better than the less educated. To the extent that education is correlated with personal income, in the absence of differential employment effects, higher-income households may be expected to protect their income better during inflationary periods than lower-income households.

Wealth Effect.   Unanticipated inflation also affects the market value of a spending unit's wealth. Wealth is the net difference between the assets and liabilities on a person's balance sheet. If the value of the assets exceeds that of the liabilities, wealth is positive. If the value of the liabilities exceeds that of the assets, wealth is negative. Increases in the value of assets increase wealth, and increases in the value of liabilities decrease it. As the price level changes, the values of some of the assets and liabilities, and therefore also wealth, may change.

Assets and liabilities may be divided into two types, according to how they respond to price changes. The value of **fixed-value assets** and **liabilities** are fixed in nominal dollars and do not change as prices change. Examples of such assets are currency, demand deposits, and savings deposits; of such liabilities, consumer and mortgage debt contracts. As the price level rises, the real or purchasing-power values of these assets and liabilities decline. The decline in the real value of the assets decreases real wealth; the decline in the real value of the liabilities increases real wealth.

Variable-value assets and **liabilities** are those whose nominal values change more or less in line with changes in the price level. Variable-value assets include real assets, such as houses, equipment, and automobiles; and financial claims on the earnings of these assets, such as stocks. Variable-value liabilities are much rarer. They would be commitments to sell particular assets at a future time at the market price at that time. Because their nominal values change with changes in the price level, the real values of variable-value assets and liabilities remain relatively constant on average. Thus, price-level changes should cause little change in real wealth through these assets and liabilities; the owners are "hedged" against inflation. Variable-value assets are sometimes referred to as **inflation hedges.**

It follows that the effect of unanticipated inflation on real wealth depends on the composition of the balance sheet. The larger the proportion of fixed-value assets and the smaller the ratio of fixed-value liabilities to total assets, the more will unanticipated accelerations in inflation reduce real wealth. Conversely, the larger the proportion of variable-value assets and the larger the ratio of fixed-value liabilities to total assets, the more will unexpected accelerations in inflation have little effect or a possibly beneficial effect on wealth. Unanticipated decelerations in the rate of inflation or disinflation as in the early 1980s, have the opposite effects for a given balance sheet.

The Evidence. Evidence suggests that the proportion of a household's assets in fixed-value form is inversely related to its income. The higher its income, the less will the average household hold its assets in fixed-value form. The evidence for fixed-value liabilities is less clear. This is because the largest groups of liabilities are owed by governments and corporations rather than by households. Because these groups are not real people, the liabilities have to be allocated to households that will ultimately service and repay the debt.

This is not easily done. To the extent that taxpayers actually service government debt, and that the federal tax structure is slightly progressive on average and that of state and local governments is slightly regressive, the government debt may be allocated proportionately to a household's income. Corporate debt payments are ultimately made by customers, labor, suppliers, stockholders, or, most likely, some combination of these four groups. For lack of better evidence, corporate debt may also be allocated proportionately to income. The debt that is owed directly by households, such as mortgage and consumer debt, varies directly with income. Although the debt of lower-income groups is widely discussed, these groups frequently have difficulty obtaining credit of any type. This analysis suggests that increases in the rate of inflation will decrease the real wealth of lower-income groups, who hold proportionately more fixed-value assets, more than of higher-income groups, who may actually experience increases in real wealth if they have large amounts of fixed-value liabilities.

In actuality, however, not all variable-value assets always change proportionately with the commodity price level or with each other. The annual rates of return for 14 investment assets over the period 1970–1990 are shown in Table 34–2. These varied from a high of 17 percent over the entire 20-year period for U.S. coins to a low of 4 percent for foreign exchange. Consumer prices increased at an annual rate of 6 percent in this period. But these rankings differ greatly in periods of different rates of inflation. As can be seen in panel b of Figure 34–3, in the 1970s, when inflation was rapid and accelerating, nonfinancial assets such as gold, silver, and oil did well and outpaced inflation. Financial assets, such as stocks and bonds, did poorly and increased more slowly than inflation. The situation reversed dramatically in the 1980s when inflation decelerated. Financial assets did

TABLE

34–2

RETURN ON SELECTED FINANCIAL AND
TANGIBLE ASSETS, 1970–1990

	Annual Rate (percent)	Rank
U.S. coins	17.3	1
Chinese ceramics	14.4	2
Stocks	12.7	3
Old masters	12.7	4
Gold	12.3	5
Diamonds	10.7	6
Bonds	9.6	7
Oil	9.0	8
Treasury bills	8.6	9
Housing	7.4	10
Farm land	6.5	11
CPI	6.2	12
Silver	5.4	13
Foreign exchange	4.4	14

SOURCE: R.S. Salomon, Jr., et al., "Annual Survey of Financial and Tangible Assets," New York, Salomon Brothers, June 4, 1990. By permission.

best and nonfinancial assets did worst, with some actually having negative rates of return. See Figure 34–3a.

Real estate buyers were big winners in the inflation of the 1970s on two counts: (1) as is evident from Figure 34–3, the value of real estate increased on average faster than both financial assets and prices, and (2) mortgage rates throughout most of the period underestimated the acceleration in the inflation rate and were lower, in retrospect, than required to maintain the purchasing power of the loan. The gain accrued to the borrower. The importance of these two effects can be gauged by noting that if a family with an average income of $10,285 had purchased an average-priced home of $24,800 in 1971 and borrowed 90 percent of its value on a 30-year, $7\frac{1}{2}$ percent mortgage, the monthly payments would have been $160, equal to 19 percent of monthly income. By 1980, the value of the average home had increased by 150 percent to $62,200, faster than the 110 percent increase in average family income to $21,652. A new 30-year mortgage loan would have carried an interest rate of $12\frac{1}{2}$ percent, and the monthly payments of $600 would have been equal to 34 percent of monthly income. In contrast, if the income of the family that purchased their home in 1971 had increased at the average rate, the constant monthly payments would be equal to less than 10 percent of its income in 1980. However, real estate buyers fared more poorly in the 1980s. In most areas of the country real estate prices increased no faster than overall prices and interest rates declined so that the burden of old, high fixed-rate mortgages that were not refinanced increased as a percent of family income.

The overall redistribution effects of inflation in the United States in the postwar period have been difficult to measure empirically. The winners

FIGURE

34-3

649

▼

INFLATION, THE
PHILLIPS CURVE,
AND CENTRAL BANK
INDEPENDENCE

INFLATION AND RATES OF RETURN ON SELECTED ASSETS, 1970–1989
(A) THE 1980S—A DECADE FOR FINANCIAL ASSETS (COMPOUND ANNUAL
RATES OF RETURN) (B) THE 1970S—A DECADE FOR TANGIBLE ASSETS
(COMPOUND ANNUAL RATES OF RETURN)

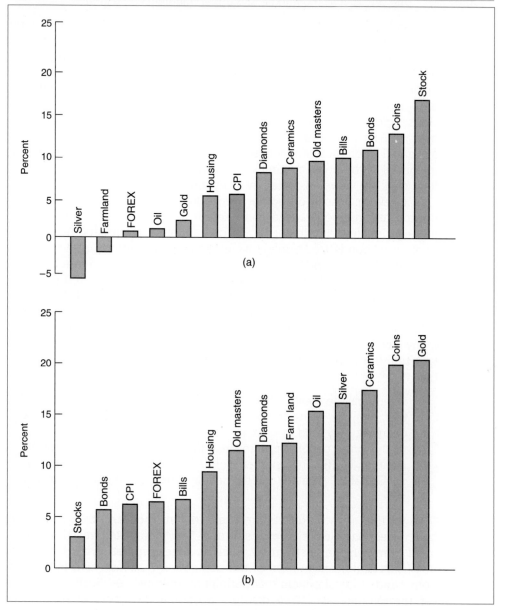

SOURCE: R.S. Salomon, Jr., et al., "Outlook Still Favors Financial Assets," *Investment Policy*, Research
Department, Salomon Brothers, June 5, 1989. Reprinted by permission.

and losers have been difficult to pinpoint. One representative study concluded:

> Overall, the redistributional effects of inflation are more complex than
> is often suggested, requiring analysis cutting across the broad func-
> tional income groups to individuals and smaller groups with lagging

incomes and substantial net creditor positions not offset by debts or large holdings of variable price assets. . . . Among households, inflation transfers purchasing power from older to younger people and, contrary to conventional wisdom, apparently from the very poor and the very rich to the middle and upper middle income groups.[1]

Inflation has important social and political as well as economic implications. In general, all prices and all incomes neither rise uniformly nor are perceived to rise uniformly. As a result, leads and lags arise. Many households whose incomes lag, or are perceived to lag, behind costs or the incomes of others consider themselves cheated. Accelerations in inflation also encourage an environment of accelerating further increases. Households may build up unrealistic expectations of future incomes on the basis of past increases or of a few well-publicized increases and become frustrated when these are not realized. They believe that they are no longer in control of their own destinies. The gains they achieve through their own hard work are viewed as eaten away by forces outside their control.

Likewise, losses on some fixed-value assets, such as bonds, from unexpected inflation-caused increases in interest rates are often viewed more seriously than similar losses on variable-value assets. As noted in Chapter 6, bonds traditionally were considered relatively riskless "fixed-income" securities and appealed to investors who wished to take little risk. If they had wanted to take more risk, they would have invested in stocks, commodities, and such! When the bonds purchased in the 1970s not only failed to deliver the fixed income promised but also declined sharply in value by 1980 to near 70 cents on the dollar for the longer-term issues, many owners felt that their "contract" had been broken and reacted bitterly. Arthur Burns, a former chairman of the Federal Reserve System, said that this

> is perhaps the greatest harm that inflation can do. When people feel that they are being treated unfairly, when they feel damaged and deprived, they tend to react in unpleasant ways. Here and there, formerly honest people begin to cheat in their dealings with the government and with one another. Formerly compassionate people turn uncharitable. Formerly gentle people strike out in frustration and rage.[2]

Victims of these effects are likely to vent their anger on those they believe responsible for their misfortune. The "villain" is often the government or impersonal institutions, such as large corporations or large labor unions. A significant portion of the population may lose faith in the economic and political system that permits these injustices. Social and political turmoil increase. This disrupts economic activity and encourages governments to take policy actions that appear to provide immediate relief but are likely to have less-favorable longer-term economic implications. Unexpected slowdowns in inflation cause similar problems.

---

[1] G.I. Bach and James B. Stephenson, "Inflation and the Redistribution of Wealth," *Review of Economics and Statistics*, 56 (February 1974), 13.

[2] Arthur F. Burns, *How Inflation Influences Our Lives*, Reprint No. 113 (Washington, D.C.: American Enterprise Institute, June 1980).

Similar to the severity of the economic implications, the severity of social and political effects varies directly with the rate and volatility of the inflation. Because faster rates of inflation are often associated with greater volatility, faster rates tend to produce the more marked effects. Most countries that have experienced very fast rates of inflation—say, 50 percent or higher annually—have also experienced nondemocratic changes in their government.

In sum, inflation and the subsequent disinflation are harmful on four accounts. They reduce aggregate economic welfare, increase financial instability, arbitrarily redistribute income and wealth, and may lead to undesirable social and political upheavals that undermine individual freedoms and democratic institutions.

The Phillips Curve

Although undesirable by itself, does inflation have any redeeming economic or social value? A widely held belief is that inflation is related inversely to unemployment. The higher the rate of inflation, the lower is unemployment. From this premise it is sometimes argued that economic policy can reduce unemployment by stimulating inflation. Others state that no relation exists between inflation and unemployment and that policies aimed at reducing unemployment by generating faster rates of inflation produce only faster inflation at the same or a higher rate of unemployment. This section examines the basis for any relation between the two variables. Knowledge of this relationship makes it easier to break changes in nominal income produced by policy actions into real-income and price components.

The relation between inflation and unemployment is generally described in terms of the **Phillips Curve.** The curve is named after A. W. Phillips, a British economist, who noted that the rate of change in wages in England between the mid-1800s and the mid-1900s was inversely related to the unemployment rate.[3] (Note that the relationship considers the *rate of change* in wages, not the *level* of wages.) Wages tended to increase faster when unemployment was low than when it was high. Moreover, the rate of wage increase accelerated as unemployment declined. If we replace the rate of change in wages with the rate of change in prices, the Phillips Curve can be depicted by the line in Figure 34–4. The rate of change in prices or the rate of inflation (P) is measured on the vertical axis and the percent of the labor force unemployed (U) on the horizontal axis. In equation form, the Phillips Curve may be written:

$$\dot{P} = f(\overline{U}) \tag{34–1}$$

---

[3] The relationship between inflation and unemployment was developed earlier by David Hume and Henry Thornton in the 1700s, John Stuart Mill in the 1800s, and Irving Fisher in the early 1900s, among others. Phillips's version was not published until 1948, when it caught the imagination of policy-oriented economists. Thomas Humphrey argues that the Phillips Curve illustrates the workings of two well-known "laws": (1) Stephen Stigler's Law of Eponymy, which states that no scientific discovery is named after its original discoverer; and (2) C. A. E. Goodheart's law that any observed statistical regularity will collapse once policymakers attempt to use it for policy purposes. Thomas M. Humphrey, A *History of the Phillips Curve.* Richmond, Va.: Federal Reserve Bank of Richmond, 1986.

FIGURE

▼

34–4

PHILLIPS CURVE

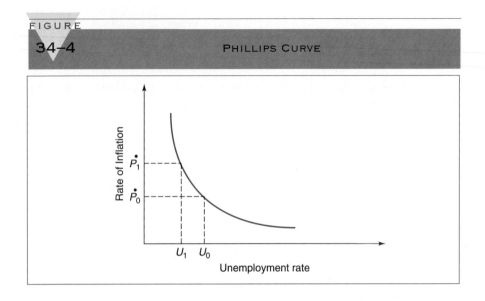

Because increases in price (a bad) are associated in this analysis with decreases in unemployment (a good), inflation is frequently tolerated more by the public and policymakers than are decreases in prices (a bad) and the associated increases in unemployment (also a bad).

The Phillips Curve has a great deal of intuitive appeal. For example, casual observation suggests that as production is increased and unemployment is reduced, less and less efficient labor and capital are brought on line. This should exert upward price pressures at an accelerating rate. In contrast, when employment is reduced, the less efficient units of production are the first to be laid off, and price pressures ease sharply.

From a policy point of view, the Phillips Curve suggests the possibility of trade-offs between inflation and unemployment. If the policymakers wished to reduce unemployment, they could do so only at the cost of a higher rate of inflation. Likewise, if they wished to slow inflation, they could do so only at the cost of higher unemployment. However, the Phillips Curve also suggests that policymakers can aim at a combined unemployment-inflation target. The extent of the potential trade-offs depends on the slope of the curve. The steeper the Phillips Curve, the more inflation is traded off for a given change in unemployment.

The Phillips Curve makes it possible to divide a change in nominal income, say as a result of the monetary or fiscal policy actions described in earlier chapters, between a change in real income and employment and a change in prices or inflation. The rate of unemployment at any time may be related to the gap between the level of aggregate real income in the economy at that time and the real income potential at full employment. The lower the current level of real income relative to full-employment real income, the higher will unemployment be. At first approximation, it is possible to relate the rate of unemployment to the gap between aggregate nominal income and full-employment nominal income or the deflationary or inflationary income gaps developed in Chapter 30. Thus, each level of nominal income, say Y_0, is associated with a rate of unemployment, say U_0, which (as shown in Figure 34–4) can be associated with a rate of inflation, say P_0, by the Phillips Curve. The higher the nominal income, the lower is unemployment, and the higher is inflation. Thus, a stimulative monetary policy that increases nominal income will reduce unemployment, say from U_0 to U_1, and accelerate the rate of inflation, say from $\dot{P}_0$ to $\dot{P}_1$. Note, however, that the degree of acceleration in the inflation rate depends on the initial unemployment rate. The higher the unemployment rate at the time the stimulative monetary policy action is taken, the more will the increase in nominal income result in a decrease in unemployment (increase in real income) and the less in an increase in inflation. Conversely, the lower the initial unemployment rate, the smaller will be the decrease in unemployment and the more will the increase in nominal income be absorbed in an increase in inflation.

Stability of the Phillips Curve

The stability and even the existence of the Phillips Curve is a subject of heated debate. Critics ask why such a relationship should exist between the rate of inflation and the rate of unemployment. If employers and employees are initially in equilibrium at a given real wage (nominal wages adjusted for changes in purchasing power) and both have the same price expectations, why would they change their behavior as prices change? A change in employment would occur only if the two sides had different price expectations. If, say, employees operated under money illusion longer than employers and were not fully aware of an acceleration in prices, they would be willing to offer additional labor services for increases in wage rates smaller than the expected price increases. They would fail to realize that their real wage was declining.

Employers, on the other hand, would recognize the fall in the real wage and increase their use of labor in place of capital up to the point where employees stopped operating under money illusion and demanded wage increases equal to price increases. At this point, the Phillips Curve would become a vertical line. However, it is likely that employees no longer under money illusion would also recognize that they were earning a lower real wage than before and would demand compensation for this loss. This would increase the real wage back to its initial level. In the light of the higher real cost of labor, employers would reduce employment to its initial level. If so, the economy would have the initial rate of unemployment at higher prices. Everyone would return to "go," but would be faced with higher prices the next time around!

Thus, the existence of the Phillips Curve and policy trade-offs depends on some groups' being fooled by inflation—that is, on unexpected inflation. Although this may happen at the onset of an inflation, it is less likely to happen after an inflation has set in. Even faculty members are unlikely to be fooled forever! Thus, critics argue, the Phillips Curve is for most practical policy purposes vertical at some equilibrium or "natural" rate of unemployment, and there is no relation between the rate of inflation and the rate of unemployment. Unemployment cannot be reduced by stimulating inflation. If it could, unemployment should have been near zero from 1979 to 1981, when the inflation rate exceeded 10 percent, rather than being nearly twice as high as in the 1960s, when the inflation rate was less than half as fast.

FIGURE

34–5

PERCENT CHANGE IN PRICES AND PERCENT
UNEMPLOYMENT 1948–1993

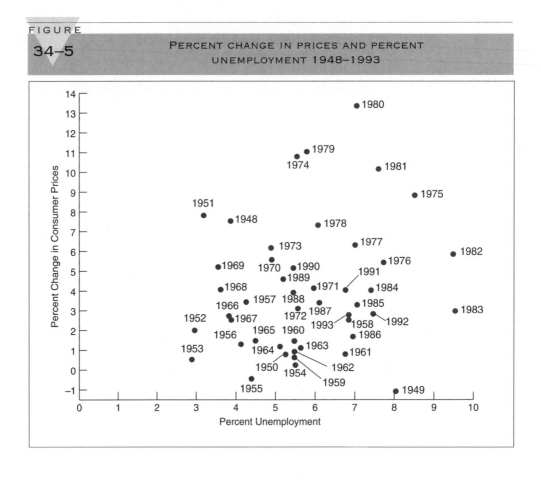

Which view of the Phillips Curve is correct can be determined only empirically. To which theory do the data conform better? The annual rate of change in consumer prices and the annual unemployment rate in the United States from 1948 through 1993 are plotted in Figure 34–5. It is evident from the scattering of the points that a clearly defined negative relationship does not exist for the period as a whole. The correlation between the two variables is close to zero, and a straight line fitted to the observations slopes upward rather than downward as suggested by the theory.

However, Phillips-type curves become visible to the naked eye if we divide the observations into groupings chronologically. As you may see by drawing in the lines, separate (and, until the mid-1980s, progressively farther out) negatively sloping convex hyperbolas (curves shaped as a Phillips Curve should) fit the observation in 1954–1969, 1970–1973, 1974–1979, 1986–1989 and 1990–1993 reasonably well, although some years tend to be outliers for reasons discussed below. This suggests, as is often the case, that both sides of the argument are partially correct. It appears that a conventional Phillips Curve relationship exists for periods in which price expectations are relatively constant or a significant portion of the work force is on long-term fixed contracts. In the former periods, the costs of operating under money illusion may be less for some groups than the costs of correcting for price changes. Thus, expansionary economic policies may temporarily reduce unemployment by permitting somewhat faster inflation.

FIGURE

34–6　　　　LOOPS AND SHIFTS IN PHILLIPS CURVE

655

▼

INFLATION, THE
PHILLIPS CURVE,
AND CENTRAL BANK
INDEPENDENCE

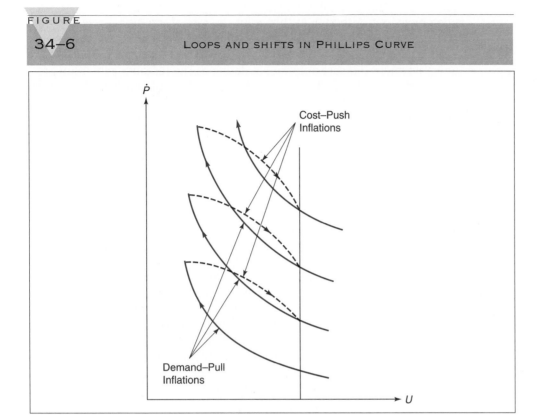

Because the acceleration in the rate of inflation is kicked off by an increase in demand, the stage of an inflation that is accompanied by a decline in unemployment and depicted by the negatively sloped convex Phillips Curve is referred to as ***demand-pull inflation.*** (See Figure 34–6.)

Similarly, restrictive policies may reduce inflation and temporarily increase unemployment, although the dynamic path along which this process occurs appears to differ from the convex Phillips Curve and to lie, say, along the concave dashed line in Figure 34–6. Assume that the Fed imposes a restrictive monetary policy after a period of accelerating inflation. Employers might be the first to recognize the change in policy and expect price increases to slow. They would be expected to slow money wage increases. However, employees operating under money illusion and expecting a continuation of the past rate of inflation would see only the slowing in money wage increases. They would interpret it as a cut in their real wages and would prefer to withhold their labor services. At the same time, employers would reduce employment if real wages rose as a result of employee reluctance to accept slower growth in money wages. Unemployment would increase sharply with only a small slowing in the inflation rate.

In time, as money illusion wears off, employees are willing to accept slower nominal wage increases in line with slower price increases and offer their labor services again. The real wage stops rising and the rate of unemployment stops increasing. Further slowing in inflation had little effect on unemployment. Although at this point the rate of inflation slows, inflation still exists as prices continue to rise. The cause of the inflation, however, is not excessive increases in demand as before. Indeed, the increases in unemployment indicate a decline in demand. The remaining inflation pressures are cost-related. This stage of an inflation, in which it slows more slowly than unemployment rises, is depicted by the concave part of the Phillips Curve loop (the dashed line in Figure 34–6) and is referred to as *cost-push inflation.* It is a lagged response to the earlier demand-pull inflation. The observations for 1958, 1975, and 1980–1981 in Figure 34–5, for example, appear to lie on the cost-push part of the Phillips Curve.

If, at the point where unemployment stops rising, economic policy becomes expansionary to offset the higher rate of unemployment, the rate of inflation may not return to its initial level. Expectations of faster inflation in the future are likely to shift the Phillips Curve outward toward the right, and the differences in expectations between employees and employers are likely to start the economy along the upward part of the Phillips Curve again. If such policies are continued, the Phillips Curve loop will shift along the lines shown in the figure. You can see that the shorter the length of the loops, the more will the long-run Phillips Curve resemble a vertical line. Figure 34–5 suggests that the time length of the loops may have become shorter in the 1970s. Likewise, when inflationary expectations are downgraded, the Phillips Curve shifts inward to the left. This can be seen in Figure 34–5 to have occurred in the mid-1980s, starting in 1983.

A direct relationship between the average rate of inflation and the steepness of the Phillips Curve was found in a cross-sectional study of major industrial countries. The authors concluded that "in countries with low inflation, the short-run Phillips curve is relatively flat. . . . In countries with high inflation, the Phillips curve is steep. . . . Countries that experience an increase in average inflation also typically experience an increased responsiveness of prices to aggregate demand [unemployment].[4]

In addition, abrupt changes or shocks in external nonpolicy forces, such as crop shortfalls or surpluses and major cutbacks or increases in petroleum production, are also likely to jolt price expectations and to shift the short-run Phillips Curve up or down. The resulting change in the rate of inflation is unlikely to affect unemployment greatly. Thus, the dramatic OPEC-induced increases in the rate of inflation in 1974 and again in 1979, which shifted the Phillips Curve up, were not accompanied by reduced unemployment.

Likewise, the sharp slowdown in inflation in the mid-1980s sparked by the even sharper decline in oil prices was not accompanied by an increase in unemployment. Indeed, some recent evidence suggests that while aggregate demand shocks, such as monetary and fiscal policies, may change inflation and unemployment in opposite directions, aggregate supply shocks, such as abrupt changes in the availability of important raw materials or disasters that destroy output capacity, are likely to change inflation and unemployment in the same direction.

This analysis suggests that price expectations are the key to the ability of policy to affect both real income and inflation. The Phillips Curve

---

[4] Lawrence Ball, N. Gregory Mankiw, and David Romer, "The New Keynesian Economics and the Output-Inflation Trade Off," *Brookings Papers on Economic Activity* (1988), p. 59.

equation may now be augmented to include expectations of future rates of inflation (P_E) as follows:

$$\overset{-\,+}{\dot{P} = f(U, \dot{P_E})} \tag{34-2}$$

It can be seen that the faster people expect the rate of inflation to be in the future, the greater will be the current rate of inflation and the greater will be the unemployment rate that is associated with any given rate of inflation. Conversely, the slower people expect the rate of inflation in the future, the lower will be the current rate of inflation and the lower will be the unemployment rate consistent with a given rate of inflation. Because of the important role of price expectations, inflation is, in part, a self-fulfilling prophecy.

It is possible to rewrite equation 34–2 to solve for unemployment as a function of actual and expected inflation as follows:

$$\overset{-\,+}{U = f(\dot{P}, \dot{P_E})} = f'(\overset{-}{\dot{P} - \dot{P_E}}) \tag{34-3}$$

The differences between actual and expected inflation represent unexpected inflation. Thus, the expected Phillips Curve analysis suggests that, *ceteris paribus*, changes in the rate of unemployment are caused by unexpected changes in the rate of inflation, or when people are fooled and operate under money illusion. To be effective in changing unemployment and real-sector activity then, monetary and fiscal policies must come as partial or total surprises. Expected changes in policy affect primarily prices.

The Phillips Curve permits us to complete the analysis of the impact of Federal Reserve monetary policy on the economy started in Chapter 31 by breaking down the change in nominal income between a change in real income and a change in prices (inflation). Price expectations may be expected to be based on past price changes, the current stage of the business cycle, the type and magnitude of current policy actions, and exogenous shocks to the system from political events and weather. Moderately expansive monetary actions taken near the bottom of an economic recession may reasonably be expected to generate an increase in nominal income, the major part of which may be expected to be in the form of an increase in real income (decrease in unemployment). The same Fed action taken in the later stages of a vigorous economic recovery may be expected to generate a similar increase in nominal income, the major part of which, however, will probably be in the form of price increases. Likewise, a moderate restrictive action will generate a decrease in nominal income accompanied by greater slowing in inflation the further the economy is from full employment and the lower are price expectations. Moderate restrictive actions imposed after a prolonged period of rapid inflation are likely to increase unemployment significantly before price expectations are revised downward.

Strong policy actions are apt to shift the public's price expectations quickly and to cause changes primarily in the rate of inflation, with only small changes in real incomes. Strong expansive actions are apt to accelerate the rate of inflation with little reduction in unemployment, and strong restrictive actions to slow the rate of inflation with little increase in unemployment. It follows that, strange as it may at first appear, the more credible policy actions are to the public, the more will the actions affect only prices. That is, the more the public believes that the policymakers will actually pursue a restrictive policy when they say so, the more successful in slowing inflation and the less painful in increasing unemployment the policy will be.

For example, after reviewing the process by which the German hyperinflation was slowed from an annual rate of 300,000 percent to virtually zero in 1923 with a loss of potential output of only 10 percent, Thomas Humphrey concluded that

> subduing inflation is easier
> —if the policymakers have established a record of credibility,
> —if they accurately convey their intentions to the public, and
> —if they convince the public of their resolve to stop inflation.[5]

He also concluded that to be successful, the "policy must focus on a single objective, namely, the elimination of inflation," and that "we should be wary of pessimistic conclusions that inflation can only be removed at the cost of a protracted and painful recession."[6] Similar conclusions were drawn by the IMF from an analysis of abrupt slowings in the rate of inflation in Argentina, Brazil, and Israel in 1985 to 1986 and by a study reviewing the slowing from more moderate rates of inflation in industrial countries during 1960 and 1991.[7]

Rational Expectations

The analysis above suggests that the Phillips Curve exists, even if only in the short run (however long that really is), and that policy trade-offs between unemployment and inflation are possible as long as some people operate under money illusion longer than others. If there were no differentials in money illusion, monetary or any other economic policies would affect only the rate of inflation, not real income. Whether and for how long people operate under money illusion depends on how they form their expectations. One recent school of thought believes that laymen are as knowledgeable about the workings of the economy as are the policymakers and process available economic and financial information efficiently. Thus, they are able to form accurate expectations about the effects of economic policy and are not likely to be fooled. If this is so, expected monetary policy actions will not affect real income and unemployment. The Phillips Curve will be vertical. Changes in nominal income will all be in the form of price changes. Policymakers can affect these variables only if they take unexpected actions that catch the public by surprise. Because this view attrib-

---

[5] Thomas Humphrey, "Eliminating Runaway Inflation: Lessons from the German Hyperinflation," *Economic Review*, Federal Reserve Bank of Richmond, July/August 1980, p. 6.

[6] Ibid., pp. 6–7.

[7] Peter Knight et al., "Escaping Hyperinflation: Argentina, Brazil, and Israel," *Finance and Development*, December 1986; and Laurance Ball, "What Determines the Sacrifice Ratio?", Working Paper 4306, Cambridge, Mass.: National Bureau of Economic Research, March 1993.

utes to all decision-making units substantial knowledge about the economy that they use fully to form their expectations as far as the availability of data permits, it is termed **rational expectations.**

Central Bank Independence

The analyses in this and the previous chapters clearly demonstrate why economic policymakers operating in the real world of political pressures may be biased toward expansive rather than restrictive stabilization policies. Policy actions affect different variables along the transmission chain with different time lags. Because, as discussed in Chapter 31, in the absence of sharp policy shocks, the rate of inflation is heavily dependent on past rates of inflation, policy actions affect real levels of output before they affect price levels. Thus, expansive actions tend to decrease unemployment before they increase inflation, and restrictive actions tend to increase unemployment before they slow inflation.

Moreover, because their intent is to increase incomes and decreases unemployment, expansive policies are popular, while restrictive policies, whose intent is to decrease incomes and increase unemployment, are not. Expansive policies are thus likely to achieve popular results first and unpopular results only later. Policymakers will receive immediate praise for their actions and, when inflation does accelerate later, few laypersons are likely to associate it with policy actions taken many months earlier and therefore will not fault the policymakers. Rather, they are likely to associate it with some concurrent events, such as poor crop harvest, greedy business firms, or greedy labor unions. Conversely, restrictive policies are likely to achieve unpopular increases in unemployment first and popular slowing in inflation only later. Policymakers will receive immediate blame and, when inflation does slow, few will associate it with the earlier policy actions and therefore will not credit the policymakers. Rather, they will associate it with and praise some concurrent happenings, such as good weather for crops, increased productivity, or more intelligent business managers.

As was discussed in Chapter 27, while the Federal Reserve is more independent of politics in the short term than in the long term, it nevertheless is subject to political influences. Central banks in other countries are each organized differently and thus are subject to different degrees of political influence. The argument above suggests that the more politically independent a country's central bank is, the more likely it is to pursue price stability. Conversely, the less independent the central bank is, the more likely it is to accept inflation in order to achieve lower unemployment, even only temporarily.

A recent study tested this hypothesis. It ranked the political independence of central banks in 16 major countries.[8] On a scale of $+2$ (most independence) to -2 (least independence), it found the central banks in Germany (1.8) and Switzerland (1.6) to have the most independence and the central banks in New Zealand (-1.5) and Spain (-1.2) to have the least.

---

[8] J. Bradford DeLong and Lawrence H. Summers, "Macroeconomic Policy and Long-Run Growth," *Economic Review*, Federal Reserve Bank of Kansas City, Fourth Quarter 1992, pp. 5–30.

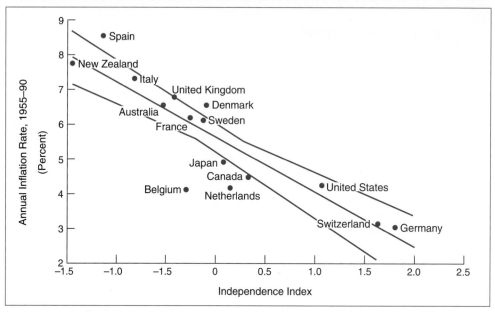

SOURCE: J. Bradford DeLong and Lawrence H. Summers, "Macroeconomic Policy and Long-Run Growth," *Economic Review*, Federal Reserve Bank of Kansas City, Fourth Quarter 1992, p. 14.

The U.S. Federal Reserve System had the third highest independence rating of 1.1. Figure 34–7 shows the relationship between the independence rating (plotted on the horizontal axis) and the average annual rate of inflation (plotted on the vertical axis) in each country from 1955 to 1990. The relationship is clearly inverse, as hypothesized. The less independent is the central bank, the higher, on average, is that country's rate of inflation. Germany, with the most politically independent central bank, had the lowest inflation rate and New Zealand, with the least independent central bank, experienced the second highest inflation rate. (Perhaps this is the reason that New Zealand moved to increase the independence of its central bank and impose penalties on it if it did not succeed in slowing the rate of inflation as was described in Exhibit 33–1.) Did the greater allegiance to price stability slow economic growth in countries with more politically independent central banks? It appears not. Figure 34–8 shows the relationship between central bank independence and real economic growth, after adjustment for differences in the initial productivity of labor in each country. The relationship is clearly positive. Economic growth was faster, on average, in more independent than in less independent central bank countries. This suggests that good politics is consistent, on average, with good economics. Unfortunately, politicians are not always elected on average!

FIGURE

34–8   CENTRAL BANK INDEPENDENCE AND ECONOMIC GROWTH, CONTROLLING
FOR INITIAL GDP PER WORKER LEVELS

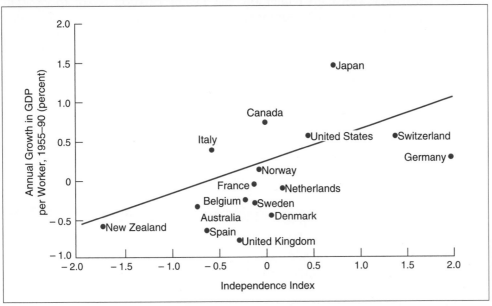

SOURCE: J. Bradford DeLong and Lawrence H. Summers, "Macroeconomic Policy and Long-Run Growth,"
Economic Review, Federal Reserve Bank of Kansas City, Fourth Quarter 1992, p. 16.

SUMMARY

Inflation has been the major economic problem in almost all industrial
countries since the 1960s. If inflation, or more generally the rate of change
in the price level either up or down, were uniformly and correctly expected
by all spending units at no cost for the information needed to make correct
deductions, it would have little effect on economic performance. But this is
unrealistic. All spending units do not adjust equally, and the cost of information is not free. Unexpected inflation has two costs to the economy. It
shifts resources from productive uses to less productive uses of gathering
data on price changes and making appropriate adjustments; and it redistributes income arbitrarily among income, wealth, and other socioeconom-
ic groups according to their abilities to adjust. Unanticipated accelerations
in the rate of inflation shift income to those groups that can adjust their
income and expense contracts quickest and that have the largest relative
holdings of variable-value assets and fixed-value liabilities. In the 1970s,
middle-income people who purchased their homes before the late 1970s
with large mortgages did best on average. But the costs of inflation are
more than economic; they are also social, political, and psychological, arising from a widespread feeling of "being cheated." Unanticipated slowing in
inflation (disinflation) causes similar problems.

Inflation is often said to be acceptable as long as it reduces unemployment. The relation between inflation and unemployment is described by the Phillips Curve. For given price expectations, lower unemployment is consistent with higher inflation. But higher inflation is apt to generate expectations of still higher inflation, and the unemployment–price-change curve will shift out. Thus, any unemployment-inflation trade-off may be only temporary. Whether the shifts in the curve are sufficiently infrequent to permit policymakers to use the unemployment-inflation trade-off or sufficiently fast so that the curve is effectively vertical and no trade-offs are possible, is subject to considerable public and technical debate.

Because controlling inflation is frequently seen as increasing unemployment, at least in the short run, political pressures may be exerted on a country's central bank to be less restrictive than otherwise. The evidence suggests that inflation is slower in countries whose central banks are relatively more insulated from political pressure.

QUESTIONS

1. Differentiate between expected (anticipated) and unexpected (unanticipated) inflation. Why would the economic implications of these two types of inflation differ? Which type would you expect to produce the greater costs?

2. Discuss the income and wealth effects of unexpected inflation. What can you conclude about the direction of the forecasting errors? Why? Define *inflation hedge*.

3. Why did financial assets perform poorly relative to real assets in the 1970s and relatively well in the 1980s? Was this only a one-time happening or would you expect to have this happen again? If the last, when?

4. Describe the Phillips Curve. What are its important policy implications? What condition is necessary for these implications to be useful?

5. Use Phillips-type curve lines to fit the points in Figure 34–5. Why does it take more than one curve? Identify the outliers. What explanation can you

think of for their behavior?

6. What might account for the apparent instability in the Phillips Curve in the 1970s and 1980s? What are the policy implications of this instability? How may this explain the frequent "stubbornness" of inflation?

7. Why does the Phillips Curve appear to be more stable again in recent years than in the 1970s and 1980s? How long do you think this may continue? Why?

8. Differentiate between demand-pull and cost-push inflation. How are the two depicted on the Phillips Curve diagram?

9. Why do many analysts believe that it is important to have an independent central bank? Independence from whom? What has been the evidence on the relationship of the performance of central banks and their political independence in different countries? Where does the Fed rank?

REFERENCES

Ball, Laurence, "How Costly Is Disinflation? The Historical Evidence," *Business Review*, Federal Reserve Bank of Philadelphia, November/December 1993, pp. 17–28.

Ball, Laurence, N. Gregory Mankiw, and David Romer, "The New Keynesian Economics and the Output-Inflation Trade Off," *Brookings Papers on Economic Activity*, 1, (1988), pp. 1–82.

Brookings Institution, "Innovative Policies to Slow Inflation," *Brookings Papers on Economic Activity*, 2 (1978).

Council on Wage and Price Stability, *Special Report on Inflation*. Washington, D.C.: U.S. Government Printing Office, April 1978.

Croushore, Dean, "What Are the Costs of Disinflation?" *Business Review*, Federal Reserve Bank of Philadelphia, May/June 1992, pp. 3–16.

DeLong, J. Bradford, and Lawrence H. Summers, "Macroeconomic Policy and Long-Run Growth," *Economic Review*, Federal Reserve Bank of Kansas City, Fourth Quarter, 1992, pp. 5–30.

Federal Reserve Bank of Kansas City, *Price Stability and Public Policy*. Kansas City, Mo., 1984.

Federal Reserve Bank of Minneapolis, "Rational Expectations—Fresh Ideas That Challenge Some Established Views of Policy Making," *Annual Report*, 1977. Minneapolis, 1978, pp. 1–13.

Feldstein, Martin, "Inflation and the American Economy," *The Public Interest*, Spring 1982, pp. 63–76.

Fellner, William, ed., *Essays on Contemporary Economic Problems: Disinflation*. Washington, D.C.: American Enterprise Institute, 1984.

Fischer, Stanley, and John Huizinga, "Inflation, Unemployment and Public Opinion Polls," *Journal of Money, Credit and Banking*, February 1982, pp. 1–19.

Humphrey, Thomas M., *Essays on Inflation*, 4th ed. Richmond, Va.: Federal Reserve Bank of Richmond, 1983.

Humphrey, Thomas M., *A History of the Phillips Curve*. Richmond, Va.: Federal Reserve Bank of Richmond, 1986.

Kareken, John H., "Inflation: An Extreme View," *Quarterly Review*, Federal Reserve Bank of Minneapolis, Winter 1978, pp. 7–13.

Knight, Peter T., F. Desmond McCarthy, and Sweder van Wijnbergen, "Escaping Hyperinflation: Argentina, Brazil, and Israel," *Finance and Development*, December 1986, pp. 14–17.

McCulloch, J. Huston, *Money and Inflation*, 2nd ed. New York: Academic Press, 1982.

Meyer, Laurence H., and Robert H. Rashe, "On the Costs and Benefits of Anti-Inflation Policies," *Review*, Federal Reserve Bank of St. Louis, February 1980, pp. 3–14.

Minark, Joseph I., "Who Wins, Who Loses from Inflation?" *Challenge*, January/February 1979, pp. 26–31.

Mullineaux, Donald J., "Inflation Expectations in the U.S.: A Brief Anatomy," *Business Review*, Federal Reserve Bank of Philadelphia, July/August 1977, pp. 3–12.

Pollard, Patricia S., "Central Bank Independence and Economic Performance," *Review*, Federal Reserve Bank of St. Louis, July/August 1993, pp. 21–36.

Roll, Eric et al., *Independent and Accountable: A New Mandate for the Bank of England*, London, Center for Economic Policy Research, October 1993.

Santomero, Anthony M., and John J. Seater, "The Inflation-Unemployment Tradeoff: A Critique of the Literature," *Journal of Economic Literature*, June 1978, pp. 499–544.

Wicker, Elmus, "Terminating Hyperinflation in the Dismembered Hapsburg Monarchy," *American Economic Review*, June 1986, pp. 350–64.

Yeager, Leland B., et al., *Experiences with Stopping Inflation*. Washington, D.C.: American Enterprise Institute, 1981.

Keynesianism, Monetarism, and Other Isms

35

Because of the inability of economists and financial analysts to identify with certainty all the relationships in the economy, many important issues in monetary theory, and thereby also in monetary policy, remain unresolved. More than one theory about a particular phenomenon leads to more than one recommendation about the correct policy prescription. Although, as discussed in Chapter 29, there are many theories describing the relationship between the financial and real sectors of the economy, at the present time two theories have particularly widespread support among both economists and policymakers. One is the Keynesian theory, and the other is the monetarist theory. In this chapter we shall first examine and compare the major features of these two theories. Then we shall turn our attention to two other theories that are currently out of fashion, particularly among professional economists, but have had support in the past and may again in the future. Paraphrasing Milton Friedman, "A theory may be down, but it is not necessarily out for good."

Keynesians versus Monetarists

The Keynesian theory was developed in the 1930s, in large measure as an attempt to explain the Great Depression of that period. Its bible is *The General Theory of Employment, Interest and Money*, which was written by John Maynard Keynes, after whom the theory is named, in 1936. The theory gained support rapidly and became the dominant doctrine in most Western, developed nations in the three decades from the mid-1930s to the mid-1960s.

The monetarist theory has its roots in the old quantity theory, described in Chapter 29. As the Keynesian theory gathered support in the years following the depression, the quantity theory lost support and became a museum relic to be stared at but not used. Revised or modern versions of the basic Keynesian model are referred to as **neo-Keynesian.** The redirection of economic concern from unemployment to inflation beginning in the late 1960s, the apparent inability of the Keynesian theory to provide as appealing solutions for inflation as it had for unemployment, and the increasing empirical evidence linking money and prices give impetus to the resurrection of the quantity theory in modern dress. Monetarism is a sophisticated refinement of the quantity theory. Today, the two theories compete on more or less equal terms, although the period since 1982 has not been kind to either theory.

The Keynesians obviously accept the teaching and leadership of Lord Keynes, although they have incorporated numerous modifications in their guru's sermon and have in places even altered its contents. The monetarists have no lord on their side, but they do have a Nobel Prize winner, Milton

SOURCE: Dwane Powell, Copyright © 1980, Raleigh News & Observer. Reprinted with permission. Los Angeles Times Syndicate.

Friedman, and one of the few genuine Zurich gnomes who lived most of his life outside of Switzerland, the late Karl Brunner. (Just to even up the numbers, the Keynesian leadership also has a Nobel Laureate in Paul Samuelson, of economics textbook fame.) The monetarist school is sometimes referred to as the Chicago School, after the University of Chicago, at which Friedman and others of this persuasion toiled, at first unappreciated by those employed at more Keynesian institutions. But loneliness built perseverance!

Although the two theories have much in common, they also have much in conflict. We will focus only on the disagreements. We shall also make the simplifying assumption that all members of the same school hold identically the same views, even though this is far from the truth. Both schools have their extreme and moderate factions, and even much variety within them. But for ease of exposition, it will be assumed that only one view prevails for each school. The Keynesians and monetarists differ in the assumptions underlying their theories, in their descriptions of the transmission mechanism for monetary policy, and in their policy recommendations. These differences are summarized in Table 35–1. We shall start by examining their transmission mechanisms in greater detail.

Differences in Transmission

Keynesian models of the transmission process tend to be larger and more complex than monetarist models. This reflects the Keynesian belief that monetary policy affects spending in each of the various sectors of the economy directly (although not equally) and that the ultimate change in aggregate income is the sum of the changes in spending in each of these sectors. (The model developed earlier in Chapters 30 and 31 is basically a neo-Keynesian framework.) In terms of output and prices, says the Keynesian, the economy will go the way its important sectors go—automobiles, hous-

TABLE
35–1   MAJOR DIFFERENCES BETWEEN MONETARISTS AND KEYNESIANS

Monetarists	Keynesians
Assumptions	
Private economy is stable.	Private economy is unstable.
Major source of instability if manmade abrupt changes in money supply for stabilization purposes.	Major sources of instability are exogenous, beyond human control, and primarily in investment.
Government produces instability.	Government produces stability.
Transmission Mechanism	
Money supply can be controlled by Fed.	Money supply cannot be controlled adequately by Fed.
Demand for money is stable and predictable.	Demand for money is unstable and unpredictable.
No liquidity trap.	Possibility of liquidity trap.
Money supply affects aggregate nominal income directly. (Effect works from top down.)	Money supply affects real sectoral spending directly. (Effects works from bottom up.)
"The" interest rate is not a key linkage variable.	"The" interest rate is a key linkage variable.
Market interest rates are determined primarily by price expectations. (Interest rates and money are directly related.) Liquidity effect is fleeting.	Market interest rates are determined primarily by money supply. (Interest rates and money are inversely related.) Liquidity effect is long-lasting.
No one key spending sector.	Investment is the key spending sector.
Price level is determined primarily by money supply.	Price level is determined by cost markups in each sector and is sticky.
Phillips Curve is vertical, and there are no meaningful trade-offs between inflation and unemployment. Unemployment is sticky.	Phillips Curve is alive, well, and nonvertical. Inflation is sticky, and short-run trade-offs exist between inflation and unemployment.
Policy	
Policy lags are difficult to predict.	Policy lags are predictable.
Passive, directed at secular objectives.	Activist, directed at contracyclical stabilization.
Steady or almost steady growth in money supply. No fine tuning.	Varying of growth in money according to the needs of the economy and to affect interest rates. Fine tuning.
Fiscal policy has no lasting effect on aggregate income. Complete crowding out.	Fiscal policy has a strong, long-lasting, predictable effect on income. Little crowding out.
Interest rates have no special significance.	Interest rates are a key policy target.
Don't know enough to try more.	Know enough to try more.
Politics and Philosophy	
Conservative.	Liberal.
Concerned more with price stability than with unemployment.	Concerned more with unemployment than with price stability.
Favor smaller government.	Favor larger government.
Have faith in free market.	Doubt efficiency and fairness of the free market.
Short run is only transient and will quickly pass. Focus on long run.	In the long run we are all dead; we live in the short run. Focus on short run.

ing, steel, and so on. In contrast, the monetarists believe that monetary policy affects total spending and thereby aggregate nominal income directly, and that the ultimate distribution of spending among sectors is determined by market forces afterward. (Of course, for total spending to change, spending in individual sectors must change. But the monetarists do not view this initial spending as indicative of final spending by sector.) That is, the Keynesian model builds from the bottom up (from individual sectors to aggregate income), whereas the monetarist model works from the top down. Thus, if GDP is the variable to be predicted, a monetarist model can do so more simply than a Keynesian model can. However, because a separate equation is required for every variable to be predicted, if the prediction of spending in a number of different sectors is the objective, both models would have to be of approximately equal size. If we assume a small and equal number of sectors, we can summarize the key elements in each of the two transmission linkages for monetary policy schematically, as follows:

Monetarist Theory

$$\left. \begin{array}{l} OMO \\ \Delta rr \\ \Delta DR \end{array} \right\} R^E \rightarrow M \rightarrow Y \rightarrow \left\{ \begin{array}{l} y \\ \updownarrow \\ \dot{P} \end{array} \right\} \rightarrow i \rightarrow I, C$$

Keynesian Theory

$$\left. \begin{array}{l} OMO \\ \Delta rr \\ \Delta DR \end{array} \right\} R^E \rightarrow \left\{ \begin{array}{l} i \\ \updownarrow \\ M \end{array} \right\} \rightarrow I^* \rightarrow \left\{ \begin{array}{l} y \\ \updownarrow \\ \dot{P} \end{array} \right\} \rightarrow Y$$

where: OMO = open-market operations
DR = discount rate
rr = reserve requirements
R^E = effective reserves
M = money supply
i = market rate of interest
Y = nominal GDP
y = real GDP
$\dot{P}$ = rate of change in price level
C = nominal consumption
I = nominal investment
I^* = real investment

Note that the determination of Y comes considerably earlier chronologically in the monetarist scheme than in the Keynesian scheme.

In both schemes, the three Fed tools affect effective reserves. In the monetarist model, this produces a predictable change in money supply. In the Keynesian model, the change in reserves changes interest rates, which affects the banking system's desire to offer money balances and the public's demand to hold them. However, these relationships are uncertain and difficult to predict. Moreover, if the economy is in a liquidity trap (the demand for money and the LM functions are perfectly flat), the change in reserves will not change interest rates and the effect of the action will not be transmitted further. (However, the liquidity trap is not an integral part of the Keynesian theory.) The flatter the demand for money function, the less will a change in reserves affect income. Major differences in the Keynesian and

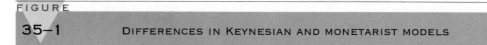

FIGURE

35–1   DIFFERENCES IN KEYNESIAN AND MONETARIST MODELS

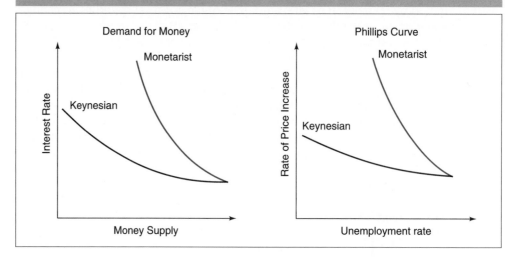

monetarist versions of the demand for money functions are shown in Figure 35–1. The Keynesian function is flatter than the monetarist function and is also less stable, that is, moves around more in an unpredictable way.

In the monetarist scheme, the change in money supply changes aggregate nominal income in a stable and predictable way. Spending units have more or less money than they wish to hold, and in the adjustment to the level of money balances they desire, they change their spending and thereby nominal income. The rate of inflation is determined both by current monetary policy and by expectations of future price changes, which is based to a large degree on past price changes. The Phillips Curve is relatively steep, so that most of the effect of the change in money is reflected in changes in prices (Figure 35–1). The close relationship between money and prices until recently is shown in Figure 34–1. The change in nominal income that is not absorbed by price changes becomes the change in real income. Both real income and price expectations affect interest rates, which, together with individual prices, determine nominal spending by sector.

In the Keynesian model, in contrast, interest rates are the major link between the financial and real sectors. All interest rates are summarized by changes in a single, "the" rate of interest. Changes in the rate of interest induced by monetary policy actions affect primarily real investment spending. Prices in each sector are determined by a markup over wages and other costs of production, which change only slowly. The Phillips Curve is relatively flat, so that most of the effect of the change in interest rates is reflected in changes in real output. Thus, price changes occur later in the Keynesian transmission process than in the monetarist process, and monetary policy has a longer-lasting effect on real income. Aggregate income is obtained by summing spending in the individual sectors.

More complete representations of these transmission processes are

FIGURE

35–2   FLOWCHART FOR MONETARIST FRB ST. LOUIS MODEL

669

▼

KEYNESIANISM,
MONETARISM, AND
OTHER ISMS

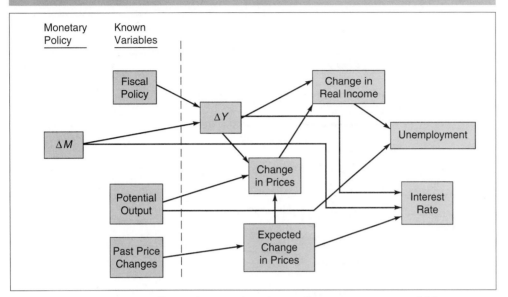

Monetary Policy   Known Variables

SOURCE: Adapted from Leonall C. Anderson and Keith M. Carlson, "A Monetarist Model for Economic Stabilization," *Review*, Federal Reserve Bank of St. Louis, April 1970, pp. 7–25.

shown in the form of flowcharts—in Figure 35–2 for a monetarist model and in Figure 35–3 for a Keynesian model. The monetarist model in the figure was developed by researchers at the Federal Reserve Bank of St. Louis, and the Keynesian model was developed jointly by researchers at the Board of Governors of the Federal Reserve System and at several academic institutions under the auspices of the Massachusetts Institute of Technology.[1] This model is referred to as the FRB-MIT model. Both models were developed in the late 1960s and are representative of other models of the same school of thought, although the FRB-MIT model incorporates refinements of the more traditional Keynesian theory and may be referred to more accurately as "neo-Keynesian." In addition, both models have undergone considerable modification since their initial construction and continue to be revised as new information and evidence become available. Nevertheless, we shall focus on these models because their economic underpinnings are more clearly defined than for most later, more complex models.

The FRB St. Louis model follows closely the monetarist linkage scheme just outlined and requires little additional explanation. Besides monetary policy (*MP*), users need to stipulate values only for fiscal policy (*FP*), the potential output of the economy (generally a given), and past price

[1] It is to the credit of the Federal Reserve that it permitted its researchers sufficient academic freedom to assist in the construction and funding of the two conflicting models.

FIGURE

35–3   FLOWCHART FOR KEYNESIAN FRB-MIT MODEL

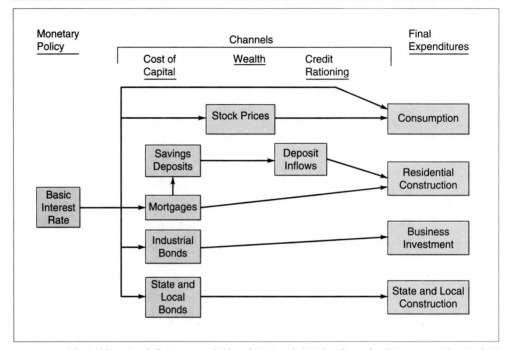

SOURCE: Adapted from Frank de Leeuw and Edward M. Gramlich, "The Channels of Monetary Policy," *Federal Reserve Bulletin*, June 1969, pp. 472–91.

changes (known). Monetary policy is measured by the money supply and fiscal policy by federal government spending and taxing, independent of any changes in these variables caused by feedback on them from changes in national income. The basic equation relates the change in nominal income to current and past changes in monetary and fiscal policies and to other, exogenous forces (Z):

$$\Delta Y_t = f(\Delta MP_t, \dots, \Delta MP_{t-n}; \Delta FP_t, \dots, \Delta FP_{t-n}; Z_t, \dots, Z_{t-n}) \qquad (35\text{–}1)$$

where t is the current observation period and n is any number so that $t - n$ represents a time period n periods earlier. The complete model solves sequentially for nominal income, prices, real income (output), unemployment, and interest rates. Note from the flowchart that the interest rate is determined by all three effects discussed in Chapter 33—the liquidity effect, the income effect, and the price-expectations effect.

The FRB-MIT model is more complex and requires some additional explanation. "The" rate of interest is determined by the response of the commercial banking system to changes in monetary policy. The effect of a change in the interest rate is transmitted to aggregate income through two channels.[2] One, it impinges directly on household spending on consumption goods, business investment spending for plant and equipment, and business and household spending for residential construction. This is termed the *cost-of-capital channel.* The change in the interest rate also has an indirect effect. The interest rate is an important determinant of the market value of household wealth, primarily of equities, which, in turn, is an important determinant of consumption spending. (Recall that interest rates and asset prices vary inversely. The higher interest rates are, the lower the market price of an asset.) This is the *wealth channel.*

Empirically, the direct cost-of-capital channel is most important in affecting spending on business investment and residential housing. The wealth effect impinges most strongly on consumption spending. Changes in spending on consumption and investment lead to changes in income.

Experiments on both models indicate that monetary policy first affects aggregate real income, but with different time lags. In the monetarist model, the effect is almost immediate and is gone within one year, as more of the policy effect is absorbed or crowded out by price changes, which occur more slowly. In the FRB-MIT model, the effect on real income lasts longer, as inflation adjusts even more slowly than in the monetarist model. The results for fiscal policy differ dramatically. In the FRB-MIT model, fiscal policy has a strong and quick effect on real income, particularly if the action involves changes in government spending. In the FRB St. Louis model, fiscal policy has no lasting effect whatsoever on real income. Changes in government spending produce small changes in real income in the expected direction immediately after the action, but these effects are only temporary. They are soon crowded out by induced changes in the opposite direction in private spending. Changes in tax rates have no effect either immediately or later. In both models, monetary and fiscal policy actions have delayed but long-run lasting effects only on prices. Thus, policymakers cannot play "alchemist" for long, turning paper money into real output and employment.

However, inflation is a much more direct process in the monetarist model. It is primarily a monetary phenomenon and bears a close relation to changes in money supply in earlier periods, as depicted in Figure 34–1. Overexpansion of the money supply is the primary continuing cause of inflation. In the FRB-MIT Keynesian model, inflation is affected more indirectly and less importantly by money supply. The effects of changes in the money supply work their way slowly through the more interest-sensitive

---

[2] The original FRB-MIT model also specified a third *credit-rationing channel.* This channel focused on the effects of a change in interest rates on the availability of mortgage funds from mortgage-lending institutions to finance home buying. These institutions give great importance to continuing long-term relationships with their borrower customers and are reluctant to change market mortgage rates abruptly as saving inflows change. Abrupt changes in rates may scare customers away. Rather, the institutions often introduce nominal rate changes slowly through time and, in the meantime, ration credit by such nonprice means as changing the amount of the down payment, the length to maturity, and the credit quality of their mortgages. These change the effective mortgage rate without immediately changing the nominal rate. The importance of credit rationing has declined in recent years with the removal of Regulation Q ceilings on deposit rates and the integration of the mortgage and capital markets. Explicit changes in deposit rates are more likely to encourage institutions to make explicit changes in mortgage rates.

"How can it fail? He's a staunch Keynesian and she just loves to shop."

SOURCE: Brian Savage, *Chicago Tribune*, January 29, 1984. Copyright © Brian Savage. Used with permission.

sectors, changing their output relative to full capacity and thereby the ability of producers to mark up prices above costs. The close correlation in many periods between changes in money and in aggregate prices shown in Figure 34–1 is believed to be only spurious. To Keynesians, inflation does not have a single unchanging primary cause. Rather, it is set off by different forces at different times, for instance, OPEC oil price increases, poor harvests, wars, and so on.

The finding of the FRB St. Louis model that, other than having a weak immediate effect, fiscal policy is completely impotent in affecting levels of aggregate income startled the economics profession and the public alike. It has not been replicated on most other models. Nevertheless, it directed attention to the possibility that public spending could crowd out private spending, and it contributed to a more skeptical attitude toward fiscal policy, similar to the one the Keynesians had developed toward monetary policy in the 1930s.

Differences in Assumptions

The monetarist believes that the economy is basically stable. When some disturbance shocks income and employment away from their equilibrium values, forces are automatically set in motion that will return the economy in time to equilibrium at full employment. The free market, monetarists

argue, will, on its own and if left alone, clear all markets and allocate goods and services efficiently. Many of the disturbances are viewed to be "manmade," originating in attempts by the government either to change the equilibrium levels of income and employment because they are not at their target levels or to accelerate the return to equilibrium after a shock.

Keynesians, on the other hand, view the economy as basically unstable. It is subject to numerous and frequent shocks from wars, natural catastrophes, and changes in expectations, technology, and weather. These will push the economy away from equilibrium. Moreover, the economy can be at equilibrium at subpar levels of economic performance. Natural forces are unlikely to restore the economy to full employment speedily. The free market does not clear all markets equally fast or efficiently. It is the function of the government to devise economic strategies that will offset the effects of the disturbances and guide the economy to a speedy return to target levels. Attainment of satisfactory economic performance is manmade, and the result of carefully planned "economic engineering."

Differences in Policy Recommendations

Because of the differences in their assumptions and in their analyses of the transmission mechanisms, the monetarists and Keynesians derive different policy recommendations for economic stabilization. The monetarists prefer a "hands-off" policy. Government, they say, is the source of most instabilities, and its actions, although well intentioned, can only make matters worse. Policy tries to do too much! Monetary policy is potent, but principally in affecting price levels. Real income is changed only temporarily. If it exists at all, the Phillips Curve is relatively steep. A given equilibrium rate of unemployment is pretty much built into the economy and is immune to short-run economic policy. Abrupt changes in money supply cause abrupt and short-lived near-term changes in real income, longer-term instability in prices, and confusion in people's expectations about future levels of economic activity. It is not that monetarists are callous about high unemployment; they believe that monetary policy can do little to improve it. It can, however, slow inflation significantly.

Moreover, active policymakers have a tendency to forget about lags and overreact on the basis of only current observations. Such behavior produces undesirable longer-term effects. Therefore, monetarists recommend, the money supply should be changed only moderately from a constant growth rate consistent with minimum inflationary pressure. Monetary policy should be directed primarily at secular goals, not at cyclical stabilization. We just do not know enough to try more. (Some stricter monetarists, such as Friedman, go even further and recommend a steady, unchanged rate of growth in money. They believe that any fluctuations in money supply would do more harm than good.)

Monetarists also believe that cyclical problems of allocation among sectors should be solved by the marketplace. Qualitative tools of monetary policy produce distortions in the short term and are ineffective in the long term. To monetarists, fiscal policy has little lasting effect on aggregate income. It primarily redistributes income between the private and public (government) sectors.

Keynesians prefer an "activist" policy. Because the economy is unstable and is continuously being bombarded by disturbances, the government must be continuously in action. Moreover, as the nature of each disturbance is likely to differ, no single policy strategy is effective at all times. Keynesians believe that we know enough about the economy to direct economic policy at both short-term stabilization and long-term secular goals.

Fiscal policy is the major Keynesian tool. Government spending can be used effectively to offset instability in private investment spending and produce equilibrium at full employment and stable prices. Changes in tax rates are somewhat less effective, because the effects on private spending are less reliable. Monetary policy is even less reliable, because of weak and unpredictable responses, first in money and interest rates to changes in bank reserves (a liquidity trap or variability in the deposit multiplier), and then in private spending to interest rate changes. However, because prices are sticky, so that the rate of inflation is effectively built in, when monetary policy is operative, it affects real income for significant periods of time. In this sense, it could be argued that it is the Keynesians who argue that "money matters" and the monetarists who argue that it does not, rather than the other way around, as is the usual case. The Phillips Curve exists and is relatively flat. Changes in unemployment have little effect on inflation in one direction or the other. Thus, one might just as well attempt to reduce it.

To Keynesians, monetary policy incorporates more than only changes in the money supply. They devote equal emphasis to credit, interest rates, and nonprice financial factors, such as credit rationing and allocation. Qualitative tools may be used to redirect credit and thereby spending among sectors. Since Keynesians do not view all sectors as equally economically important or socially desirable, this is an important aspect of policy.

The major differences between the monetarists and the Keynesians, summarized in Table 35–1, are polar views and are used for illustrative purposes. On many of the issues, most monetarists and Keynesians adopt more similar views. On the other hand, their economic differences are often sharpened by their political differences. On the average, monetarists tend to be political conservatives and Keynesians to be political liberals. But this division is not airtight. Some political liberals are monetarists and some political conservatives are neo-Keynesians in some or all of their beliefs. Because the public tends to accept theories that are most directly addressed to the pressing problem of the day, Keynesian theories tend to be accepted most widely when unemployment is high and monetarist theories when inflation is high.

In short, the monetarist credo for government economic policy, be it monetary or fiscal policy, is "Do no harm," generally by "Don't just do something, stand there," while that of the Keynesians is "Do good" by "Don't just stand there, do something."

Nevertheless, both models agree that in the long run, however long that may be defined in either model, neither monetary nor fiscal policy has a lasting effect on real income, only on prices and nominal measures. That is, changes in "paper" money or whether government spending is financed by taxes or borrowing cannot continually increase real resources. That can be done only by improvements in human capital or greater availability and more efficient use of available natural resources. If this were not so, there would be no poverty nor poor countries on earth, as nearly the first thing that every government learns is how to run the printing presses and print money. But alchemy is no more successful in economics than it is in chemistry!

Other Monetary Theories

Although the Keynesian and monetarist theories share most of the current spotlight, they are not the only theories of how monetary policy works. Other theories enjoyed equally wide appeal in earlier years and may be expected to attract interest again if the policy recommendations prescribed by the Keynesian and monetarist theories fail to provide satisfactory remedies to our economic problems. Like many veteran sports stars, they are sitting on the bench, waiting for the popular rookies of today to falter and for the populace to call for their return. At least two of these theories have been sufficiently important in the past to warrant their description here, both because they still surface periodically in the speeches and actions of policymakers and others and so that you can be prepared in case they are called back.[3] They are the **availability theory** and the **bankers theory.**

Availability Theory

The **credit availability theory** was developed shortly after World War II. In that period, liquidity was unusually high as a result of high savings during the war years, when many consumer goods and services were in limited supply. Deposits at nonbank financial intermediaries expanded rapidly. As a result, doubts arose about the usefulness of the traditional measures of money supply as a policy tool. Attempts by the Fed to change the money supply were postulated to be frustrated by changes in the opposite direction in the supply of other liquid assets (near-monies). That is, attempts to decrease the money supply by cutting back on bank reserves would lead to a transfer of funds by the public from banks to nonbanks that offered similar types of deposits but are not under Fed control.

The availability theory switched emphasis from measures of money to measures of credit. Unlike money balances, which were demanded for purposes other than transactions and thus could be held "idle," credit, in particular loans, was demanded to finance purchases. The theory postulated that this linked credit more closely than the money supply to aggregate income. Control of economic activity thus required control of credit.

---

[3] Two other theories—the supply-side theory and the rational expectations theory—have become popular in recent years, but they will not be discussed here; both have been noted earlier in the book. The supply-side theory focuses on reductions in federal government marginal tax rates and regulation to stimulate productivity and economic growth. Money, per se, plays a minor role. The rational expectations theory stresses the importance of expectations and the rapid processing of new information. It believes that market participants generally understand the basic functioning of the economy and that they base their expectations of future economic activity on this knowledge. They cannot be fooled easily. Monetary policy affects real economic activity only if it is unexpected and thus is not discounted at the time it occurs. Expected monetary policy actions affect only the rate of inflation.

The granting or "availability" of loans was hypothesized to be determined primarily by the state of liquidity of the lending institutions. The more liquid the lender, the more loans would be extended. The less liquid, the more reluctant was the institution to extend additional loans. The state of liquidity was determined by the market value of the lender's assets relative to their purchase prices. The higher the market value, the more liquid the lender. Conversely, the lower the market value, the larger the book losses, the less liquid the lender, and the more reluctant would the lender be to sell securities to finance additional loans. The lender was effectively "locked into" the portfolio. The market value of the lending institution's assets could be affected by the Fed's ability to change interest rates through changing reserves. The higher the interest rates, the lower the value of bank assets, and the smaller new loan extensions. Moreover, because banks and other lending institutions held large amounts of highly marketable long-term Treasury securities purchased during World War II, only small changes in interest rates would be required to produce large changes in their market values and thereby in liquidity. The key variables in the availability theory may be summarized schematically:

$$\left.\begin{array}{l} OMO \\ \Delta DR \\ \Delta rr \end{array}\right\} R^E \rightarrow i \rightarrow L \rightarrow K \rightarrow Y$$

where: L = liquidity
         K = credit

and the other variables are as defined on page 667.

The availability theory had considerable support in the United States through the mid-1960s and in some other countries, particularly the United Kingdom and Canada, until the early 1970s. Support for the theory declined because empirical investigations failed to find support for its major implications. Changes in near-monies did not vary inversely with changes in money. As we noted in Chapter 2, most definitions of money supply, including the broader definitions that encompass some liquid assets, mostly change in the same directions. The major exceptions stem from distortions caused by Regulation Q ceilings. Changes in interest rates had little noticeable effect on loan expansion by financial intermediaries in the hypothesized inverse direction, *ceteris paribus*. Last, in concept, credit proved more nebulous than money and, in practice, aggregate credit proved no better link to income.

Credit Channel Theory.   A modern version of the availability theory was developed in the late 1980s as the ***bank credit channel hypothesis.*** Basically, this theory looks at the impact of Federal Reserve actions on the asset or loan side of the banking system's balance sheet as well as on the liability or deposit side. It argues that for many borrowers, loans from other financial institutions are generally not very good substitutes for bank loans. That is, loans from different lending institutions are not all equal. Thus, as restrictive monetary policy actions shrink bank balance sheets, banks reduce their lending by more than their security investments, and some bank-dependent customers, particularly smaller business firms, are forced to search out higher-priced and less readily available credit sources. Some of these borrowers will be priced or rationed out of the loan market altogether and will cut back on their spending. A **credit crunch** will develop that does not affect all borrowers equally. The crunch also reduces aggregate income. In most versions of this theory, the bank credit channel is seen as a supplement to, not a replacement of, the money channel in the transmission mechanism modeled by both the Keynesians and the monetarists. Bank loans, as well as bank deposits, are "special."

The evidence of the existence of a bank credit channel is still preliminary. When the Fed takes restrictive actions, bank loans do decline and aggregate income slows. Some studies find that the decline in bank loans is greater than the decline in nonbank financing, such as commercial paper. This suggests that the Fed action has traveled to income through bank credit. Other studies, however, report that, once adjustment is made for different kinds of borrowers, for example, large versus small, bank loans decline no more than other credit and that bank credit plays no special or unique role in affecting aggregate income. Rather, the Fed action is transmitted to the economy through both total credit and money.

Bankers Theory

The **bankers theory** was developed in the United States in the early 1920s. Traces of this theory can be found earlier in some other countries. The bankers theory resembles the availability theory in that major emphasis is placed on credit rather than on money and on the willingness of lending institutions to extend credit. The bankers theory differs from the availability theory in the process by which the lender's willingness to extend credit is assumed to be affected by the central bank. The mix of bank reserves between borrowed and excess reserves replaces interest rates and liquidity as the key variable. (Recall that excess reserves are total reserves minus required reserves. The net difference between excess and borrowed reserves is termed **free reserves** or **net borrowed reserves** and sometimes is used in place of the two components.)

Reserves that member banks borrow at the Fed discount window (**borrowed reserves**) are postulated to be more restrictive than an equal dollar amount of reserves obtained elsewhere (**nonborrowed reserves**). Banks realize that they must repay the Fed shortly and the Fed encourages them to do so. In addition, some customers may view the bank's indebtedness to the Fed as a sign that the bank is experiencing financial difficulties. As a result, banks do not like to show borrowings from the Fed on their balance sheets. It follows that credit extended by banks that is supported by borrowed reserves is only temporary and will be reduced shortly.

Excess reserves are considered a smoldering log that could burst out into roaring credit expansion at any time. Thus, excess reserves are related to potential credit. The greater excess reserves are or the smaller borrowed reserves are, the greater is the potential for bank credit expansion. The smaller excess reserves are or the greater borrowed reserves are, the less is the potential for credit expansion. The Fed can affect the mix of bank reserves through the use of its policy tools. Cutbacks in reserves through open-market operations force banks to the discount window, and more liberal provision of nonborrowed reserves causes banks to build up excess reserves. The key variables in the linkage scheme implicit in the bankers theory are:

$$\left.\begin{array}{l} OMO \\ \Delta DR \\ \Delta rr \end{array}\right\} \quad R^E \begin{array}{c} \nearrow ER \searrow \\ \searrow BR \nearrow \end{array} K \rightarrow Y$$

where: ER = excess reserves
           BR = borrowed reserves

From the 1920s through the early post–World War II period, the bankers theory dominated Federal Reserve policy strategy in the United States, and, in somewhat different form, central bank strategy in other countries. In the first part of that era, the discount rate was a major tool of monetary policy and the discount window was a major source of changes in bank reserves. In the short run, changes in borrowed reserves determined changes in total reserves. Open-market operations had not yet been developed. In the second part, during the Great Depression of the 1930s, excess reserves were very large.

Empirical evidence failed to support the theory's interpretation of borrowed and excess reserves. *Ceteris paribus*, banks in the aggregate did not pursue more restrictive lending policies when their borrowings from the Fed were high or more liberal lending policies when their excess reserves were high. Changes in the financial environment after World War II further reduced any usefulness the theory may have had. The rapid growth of the Fed-funds and CD markets, and the greater emphasis on liability management reduced bank reluctance either to rely on purchased funds or to be in debt to the Fed.

At the same time, excess reserves were found to be excess only in the legal sense of the word, not in the economic. Banks have a demand for total reserves based, among other things, on their expectations of deposit losses. In the 1930s, the large number of bank failures motivated many banks to hold more reserves than their legal minimum in order to successfully meet potential deposit drains. These excess reserves were not held in readiness for future credit expansion. The fallacy of the argument became painfully evident in 1937. The Fed attempted to absorb excess reserves in that year through increases in reserve requirements to reduce the potential for future credit expansion. Rather than reduce their excess reserves to satisfy the higher reserve requirements, the banks cut back on their deposits to maintain almost the same ratio of excess reserves to deposits, and the money supply declined sharply. This policy action is generally believed to be a major contributor to the sharp economic downturn of 1937–1938 that delayed the recovery from the depression. Today, both because required reserves are generally greater than the amount banks would hold voluntarily and because of careful minute-to-minute liquidity management, excess reserves are almost nonexistent at larger banks and are only somewhat larger at smaller banks. Nevertheless, the Fed still uses part of the bankers theory to underpin its open-market operating procedures. As was noted in Chapter 33, since 1983, the Fed has at times relied on changes in borrowed reserves from a target level to produce the desired change in reserve and monetary aggregate expansion between meetings of the Federal Open Market Committee.

The two currently popular major competing monetary theories are the Keynesian theory and the monetarist theory. Keynesians believe that the economy is unstable, that monetary policy is transmitted through interest rates, that money supply is difficult to control and has an unpredictable effect on income, that prices reflect cost markups and change only slowly, that investment is the key private sector, and that fiscal policy is potent and necessary for stability. Monetarists believe that money supply can be controlled by the Fed and affects nominal income predictably; that the economy is stable, with instability the result of human error; that there is no single key sector; that fiscal policy has little lasting effect on aggregate income; and that prices go as money goes. As a result, their policy prescriptions differ.

Keynesians prefer active contracyclical monetary and fiscal policies and have concern for interest rates. They believe that unemployment is easier to affect with economic policy than is inflation. Monetarists prefer steady monetary growth and fiscal policy focusing on secular rather than cyclical stabilization, with little concern for interest rates. They believe that inflation is easier to control with economic policy than is unemployment. The basic underpinnings of these schools are incorporated in the neo-Keynesian FRB-MIT model and the monetarist FRB St. Louis model.

The two theories that are currently not as popular are the availability theory and the bankers theory. Both emphasize credit rather than money. The availability theory focuses on the state of liquidity of lenders. The more liquid, the more they are willing to extend credit that is used to finance aggregate spending. The Fed can affect liquidity through small adjustments in interest rates. The credit channel theory, which is a more modern subset of the availability theory that focuses on the response of bank lending to Fed actions, has gained popularity in recent years. The bankers theory focuses on excess and borrowed bank reserves. Excess reserves are waiting to be lent. Borrowed reserves must be repaid to the Fed and cause the banks to be more restrictive in their lending than otherwise. The Fed can influence bank lending and thereby economic activity by changing the mix of excess and borrowed reserves.

The support for each of the above theories has fluctuated through time as the empirical evidence for each has increased and decreased. In the 1950s and 1960s, the neo-Keynesian theory held sway, while the 1970s were the heydays for the monetarists. However, neither scored very well in predicting income and inflation in the 1980s and both lost some support. Note, for example, the poorer relationship between money and inflation in Figure 34–1 after 1982. But neither the availability theory nor the bankers theory did much better and neither gained greatly in favor. Rather, many analysts became more agnostic, picking and choosing different parts from different theories. As one observer summarized:

> We are all Keynesians now, thanks to Keynes. We are all monetarists now, thanks to Friedman. And we are all eclectics now, thanks to a turbulent world.[4]

This may be a fitting, although not very optimistic, note on which to end the book.

[4] Todd G. Buchhold, *New Ideas from Dead Economists* (New York: Plume, 1990), p. 24.

1. Why is more than one theory of how monetary policy affects the economy popular? What helps change people's minds about the usefulness of a particular theory at a particular time? "The simpler the theory, the more general it is and the more lasting it may be." Discuss.

2. Identify and discuss the basic differences in the Keynesian and monetarist views of the transmission mechanism. Which is the single most important or key transmission variable in each theory?

3. Discuss the basic differences between the monetarists and Keynesians in their assumptions about the behavior of the economy. How might these differences affect their policy recommendations?

4. To what primary factor would the monetarists and Keynesians attribute first the acceleration and then the slowing in inflation over the past 20 years? How might their policy prescriptions differ?

5. Why is the Federal Reserve Bank of St. Louis economic model considered monetarist and the FRB-MIT model Keynesian? How does each differ from stricter interpretations of their respective schools of thought?

6. Why are monetarists frequently viewed as "cold, uncaring" people and Keynesians as "warm, caring" people? Why do Keynesians, on the whole, believe in bigger government than monetarists? In the United States, are Keynesians more likely to be Democrats or Republicans, on average? Why?

7. Discuss how the role of money in the availability theory and bankers theory differs from that in the monetarist and Keynesian theories. How do the availability theory and bankers theory differ from each other?

8. How does the credit channel theory differ from the monetarist theory? How is it similar? What are the different implications for different types of business borrowers and the economy?

9. Why is the public frequently fickle with respect to the economic theory that they believe?

REFERENCES

Anderson, Leonall C., and Keith M. Carlson, "A Monetarist Model for Economic Stabilization," *Review*, Federal Reserve Bank of St. Louis, April 1970, pp. 7–25.

Barth, James R., "The Cost of Slowing Inflation: Four Views," *Economic Review*, Federal Reserve Bank of Atlanta, January 1982, pp. 39–49.

Batten, Dallas S., and Courtenay C. Stone, "Are Monetarists an Endangered Species?" *Review*, Federal Reserve Bank of St. Louis, May 1983, pp. 5–16.

Bernanke, Ben S., "Credit in the Macroeconomy," *Quarterly Review*, Federal Reserve Bank of New York, Spring 1993, pp. 50–70.

Bernanke, Ben S., "Monetary Policy Transmission through Money or Credit?" *Business Review*, Federal Reserve Bank of Philadelphia, November/December 1988, pp. 3–11.

Bernanke, Ben S., and Alan S. Blinder, "The Federal Funds Rate and Channels of Monetary Policy," *American Economic Review*, September 1992, pp. 901–21.

Brayton, Flint, and Eileen Mauskopf, "Structure and Uses of the MPS Quarterly Econometric Model of the

United States," *Federal Reserve Bulletin*, February 1987, pp. 93–109.

Brunner, Karl, "Has Monetarism Failed?" *CATO Journal*, Spring 1983, pp. 23–62.

Friedman, Milton, "Monetary Policy for the 1980s," in John H. Moore, ed., *To Promote Prosperity: U.S. Domestic Policy in the Mid-1980s*. Stanford, Calif.: Hoover Institute, 1984, pp. 23–60.

Friedman, Milton, "Nobel Lecture: Inflation and Unemployment," *Journal of Political Economy*, June 1977, pp. 451–72.

Friedman, Milton, and Walter W. Heller, *Monetary vs. Fiscal Policy*. New York: Norton, 1969.

Friedman, Milton, and Anna J. Schwartz, *Monetary Trends in the United States and the United Kingdom*. Chicago: University of Chicago Press, 1982.

Gibson, William E., and George G. Kaufman, *Monetary Economics: Readings on Current Issues*. New York: McGraw-Hill, 1971.

Goodfriend, Marvin, and Robert G. King, "Financial Deregulation, Monetary Policy and Central Banking," *Economic Review*, Federal Reserve Bank of Richmond, May/June 1988, pp. 3–22.

Hetzel, Robert L., "The Quantity Theory Tradition and the Role of Monetary Policy," *Economic Review*, Federal Reserve Bank of Richmond, May/June 1981, pp. 19–26.

Hetzel, Robert L., "The Rules versus Discretion Debate over Monetary Policy in the 1920s," *Economic Review*, Federal Reserve Bank of Richmond, November/December 1985, pp. 3–14.

Humphrey, Thomas M., "Keynes on Inflation," *1980 Annual Report*, Federal Reserve Bank of Richmond, 1981.

Humphrey, Thomas M., "Rival Notions of Money," *Economic Review*, Federal Reserve Bank of Richmond, September/October 1988, pp. 3–9.

Jordan, Jerry L., et al., "The Andersen-Jordan Approach after Nearly 20 Years," *Review*, Federal Reserve Bank of St. Louis, October 1986, entire issue.

Kaufman, George G., *Current Issues in Monetary Economics and Policy: A Review*. New York: Institute for Finance, New York University, May 1969.

Kretzmer, Peter E., "Monetary vs. Fiscal Policy: New Evidence on an Old Debate," *Economic Review*, Federal Reserve Bank of Kansas City, Second Quarter 1992, pp. 21–30.

Laidler, David, "The Legacy of the Monetarist Controversy," *Review*, Federal Reserve Bank of St. Louis, March/April 1990, pp. 49–64.

Machlup, Fritz, et al., "The Search for Stable Money," *CATO Journal*, Spring 1983.

Mauskopf, Eileen, "The Transmission Channels of Monetary Policy: How Have They Changed?" *Federal Reserve Bulletin*, December 1990, pp. 985–1008.

Mayer, Thomas, et al., *The Structure of Monetarism*. New York: Norton, 1978.

Meigs, A. James, *Money Matters*. New York: Harper, 1972.

Morgan, Donald P., "Are Bank Loans a Force in Monetary Policy?" *Economic Review*, Federal Reserve Bank of Kansas City, Second Quarter, 1992, pp. 31–41.

Mosser, Patracia C., "Changes in Monetary Policy Effectiveness: Evidence from Large Econometric Models," *Quarterly Review*, Federal Reserve Bank of New York, Spring 1992, pp. 36–51.

Oliner, Stephen D., and Glenn D. Rudebusch, "Is There a Bank Credit Channel for Monetary Policy?" *Finance and Economics Discussion Series* (93–8), Washington, D.C., Board of Governors of the Federal Reserve System, March 1993.

Stark, Tom, and Herb Taylor, "Activist Monetary Policy for Good or Evil?" *Business Review*, Federal Reserve Bank of Philadelphia, March/April 1991, pp. 17–25.

Tobin, James, "The Monetarist Counter-Revolution Today: An Appraisal," *Economic Journal*, March 1981, pp. 29–42.

Index

A

Accrual bonds, 457
Action lag, 594, 596
Active management, of interest rate risk, 328–30
Active strategy, for choosing bonds, 147–48
Adjustable-rate mortgages, 75, 419
Adjustment credit, 540
Aftermarket, 50
Aggregate income loss, 643–44
Allocative efficiency, 12, 38
Allstate Insurance Company, 251
Amercurrencies, 45, 466–67, 496
American Express, 157, 243, 251, 265, 454
American Telephone and Telegraph, 72, 454
Amortization, 85, 411
    of bonds, 139
    negative, 418
Amortized loans, 90
Amortized value, 60, 85
Annuities, 90
Appreciating exchange rate, 475
Artisans, and currency, 277
Asked yields, 62
Asset and liability management, 185, 325
Asset-backed commercial paper, 64
Asset-backed securities, 463
Asset liquidity management, 179
Assets
    of Federal Reserve, 530–31
    held by foreign banks in major countries, 213
Assistance services, of financial institutions, 46
At-the-money, 440
Auction market, 50–51
Automated clearinghouses (ACHs), 267–68
Automated teller machines (ATMs), 5, 268–69
Automatic Investment Services, 398

B

Availability theory, 675–77, 679

Bagehot, Walter, 34
Balance of payments, 483–86, 487, 603
    history of, 486
    stability in international, 511–12
Balance of trade, 483
Balance on current account, 484
Balance on goods and services, 484
Balance sheet
    bank, 180–85
    Federal Reserve, 533–34
BankAmerica, 376, 396
BankAmericard, 454
Bank balance sheet, 318–21
Bank capital, regulation of, 296–99
Bank credit channel hypothesis, 676
Bank discount basis, 88
Bankers' acceptances, 65–66
Bankers theory, 633, 675, 677–78, 679
Bank examination, 311–14
Bank failure, 173–74, 190–200, 350,644–45
    chronology of, 192–93
    history of, 195–96
    reasons for increase in, 196–99
Bank float, 259
Bank for Cooperatives, 71
Bank Holding Company Act, 203, 206, 302, 303
    Douglas Amendment to, 375
Banking
    deposit, 178–80
    fear of power concentrated in, 373
    fractional reserve, 171–73
    golden era of private, 390
    history of, 170–80
    international, 210–13
    interstate, 375–77
    merchant, 154
    mixing with commerce, 371–72
    nonpar, 261
    public policies toward, 292

    separation of commercial and investment, 390–404
    wildcat, 257
Banking Act of 1933. See Glass-Steagall Act.
Banking Acts of 1933 and 1935, 528
Bank Insurance Fund, 227, 308
Bank management, 185–87
Bank Merger Acts of 1960 and 1966, 302
Bank of America, 466
    and privately-issued pass-through mortgage securities, 424
Bank of International Settlements (BIS), 502
Bank of New England, 346
Bank performance, 186–87
Banks
    advantage of in obtaining financial information, 41
    balance sheet of, 180–85
    central, independence of, 659–60
    commercial, 159, 255, 409
    correspondent, 259
    creation of national-chartered, 391
    definition of, 42
    deposits of at Federal Reserve, 531
    equalizing conditions between national and state, 391
    establishment of central, 179
    Federal Reserve loans to, 530–31
    foreign with offices in U.S., 211–213
    industrial, 247
    insolvent, 360
    investment, 153–57
    loan commitments of, 183
    mortgage, 157–58
    overseas offices of, 210–11
    profitability of commercial, 199
    prohibited activities of, 370
    regional, 526–27
    reluctance of Congress to expand powers of commercial, 370
    restoring confidence in commercial, 392
    runs on, 174, 191–95

Banks (*cont.*)
  savings, 88, 164 fig., 226–27
  and secondary securities, 41
  size of, 206–08
  state-chartered insured, 309
  structure and organization of,
      200–209
  structure and performance of,
      208–09
  subsidiary, 212
  ten oldest in U.S., 181 fig.
  universal, 371–72
Barter, 17
Base drift, 634
Basis, 434
Basle standards, 297
Bear MIDs, 463
Best-effort basis, 154
Bethe, Professor Hans, 31, 644
Bid yields, 62
BIS standards, 297
Black, Fischer, 441 f
Black Monday, 9
Black-Scholes Model, 441 f
Bloom, Allan, 10
Board of Governors, 524–25
Bond financing, international, 500–503
Bond market, 50
Bond prices
  inverse relationship with market
      interest rates, 84
  mathematics of, 79–92
Bonds, 11, 58, 79
  accrual, 457
  active strategy for choosing, 147–48
  amortization of, 139
  consol, 89, 96
  corporate, 71, 73
  coupon discount, 96
  covenants of, 141–44
  credit quality of and interest rate,
      132
  defaulting, 135
  effect of changes in interest rates
      on, 86
  firm evaluating credit quality of,
      131–34
  fixed-coupon, 59
  fixed-rate, 81–88
  foreign, 73, 500–501
  forward, 121
  general obligation, 74
  high-yield, 5, 73, 132, 464–66
  junior, 131
  junk, 5, 73, 132, 464–66

losses on, 650
major sources of rate differences in,
    118
marketability of, 140–41
municipal, 60, 73–74
options and covenants of, 141–44
par value of, 83
premium, 96
realized returns in, 149–50
regular coupon, 96
relationship among, 90
relationship of duration and term to
    maturity, 95
relationship of prices to interest
    rates, 95
repriced, 89
revenue, 74
senior, 131
taxable municipal, 140
tax-exempt, 60
tax treatment of, 139–40
Treasury, 141, 431
variable-coupon, 59
variable-rate, 89–90
winning with, 145–49
Yankee, 73, 501
zero-coupon, 88–89, 457–58
Book-entry form, for sale of T-bills, 62
Borrowed reserves, 677
Borrowing, stimulation of by financial
    institutions, 45–46
Borrowing facilities, of IMF, 191–92
Boutiques, 156
Branches, 210
  interstate, 375–77
  regulations regarding, 374–75
Branching, 202–03
Brash, Don, 635
Brazil, hyperinflation in, 32
Bridge bank, 353
Bridge loans, 154
Broad markets, 49
Brokerage activities, of commercial
    banks, 396
Broker/dealers, 153
Brokers, 38
Brookings Study, 381
Brown Brothers Harriman, 202, 392
Brunner, Karl, 665
Buffer stock financing facility, for bor-
    rowing from IMF, 492
Building and loan associations, 217
Bull MIDs, 463
Burns, Arthur, 378, 381, 528, 631, 650
Bush, George, 358, 380

and S&L bailout, 223
Business cycle, expansions and con-
    tractions in, 601 fig.
Business finance companies, 250

C

Call options, 52, 60, 141, 150, 440
  of mortgages, 414
Call price, 141
Call yield premium, 142
CAMEL, 312, 345
Capital, of banks, 174–78
Capital account, 484
Capital forbearance, 220
Capital management, 175, 185
Capital market, 50
Capital-market instruments, 68–76
Capital requirements, risk-based,
    299 fig.
Capital-to-asset ratio, 339, 340 fig.
Carte Blanche, 265, 454
Carter, President Jimmy, 549
Cash coupon payments, 139
Cash item in the process of collection
    (CIPC), 259
Cash market, 52
Cash reserves, and transaction
    deposits, 280–81
Casualty insurance companies,
    233–35, 236, 449
Catastrophes, two costliest, 234 fig.
Cease and desist orders, 311
Ceilings, on deposit rates, 422
Centralization, 524
Central Liquidity Facility, 310
CDs. See Certificates of Deposit.
Certificates of Accrual on Treasury
    Securities (CATS), 458
Certificates of amortizing revolving
    debts (CARDs), 464
Certificates of automobile receivables
    (CARs), 464
Certificates of deposit (CDs), 5, 66–67,
    181
  negotiable, 181, 453
Charter, 201–02
  and Comptroller of the Currency,
      306
  as entry regulation, 296
  federal of savings and loan associa-
      tions, 218
  restrictions on, 301
Chase Manhattan Bank, 462

Check clearing, 258
Checking accounts, 178
    no-minimum-balance, 5
    special, 452–53
Checks, 20, 178, 258–65
Check volume, 264–65
Chicago Board of Options Exchange, 443
Chicago Board of Trade, 430
Chicago Mercantile Exchange, 430
Chicago school. *See* Monetarists.
Chinese Wall, 184
CHIPS, 176, 267
Citibank, 453
Citicorp, 204–05 fig., 206, 376, 396
Claim against issuer, securities and, 58
Clayton Antitrust Act, 302
Clearinghouse
    automated, 267–68
    local, example of, 259–61
    national, 262
Clinton, President Bill, 380, 385, 613
Closed-end funds, 238–42
Closed-end investment funds, of commercial banks, 398
Closure
    early, 354–55
    timing of bank, and losses, 354
Closure rule, 297, 342
Coins, 19, 255–56
Coinsurance, 351
Coldwell Banker, 251
Collateral, of security, 59
Collateralized mortgage obligations (CMOs), 5, 75, 424
Commercial banks, 159
    brokerage activities of, 396
    closed-end investment funds of, 398
    and mortgages, 409
    in payments system, 255
    securities trading by, 394–96
    trust departments of, 163 fig., 398
    underwriting by, 394–96
Commercial letters of credit, 183
Commercial paper, 63–64
Commission on Money and Credit, 375, 379
Commodity Futures Trading Commission, 433
Common stock, 58
Commonwealth Edison in Chicago, 72
Community Reinvestment Act, 294
Compensatory and contingency financing facility (CCFF), for

borrowing from IMF, 492
Competition, and commercial bank securities activities, 400–402
Competitive Equality Banking Act of 1987, 223, 357, 384
Compound interest, 83
Comptroller of the Currency, 306, 307 fig.
Concentration, and commercial bank securities activities, 400–402
Conditional debt, 158
Conflict of interest, and commercial bank securities activities, 403–04
Consol bonds, 89
    duration of, 96
Constant-dollar amounts, 26
Constant market basket price index, 24
Consumer finance companies, 247–49
Consumer Price Index (CPI), 24
    and purchasing power of dollar, 26
    Consumer protection, government regulation for, 294–95
Consumption goods, 573–76
Continental Illinois National Bank, 346, 353, 357
Contractions, business cycle, 601 fig.
Contract rate, 79
Contra-cyclical policy, 579
Convertibility options, 60
Convertible option, 143, 150
Convertible yield premium, 144
Convexity, 98
Corporate bonds, 71–73
Corrective actions, delays in and the S&L mess, 222
Correspondent banks, 259
Cost of borrowing, and tax rates, 109
Cost-of-capital channel, 671
Cost-of-living index, 24, 26
Cost-push inflation, 656
Costs, regulatory, to banking industry, 305
Counterparties, 461
Coupon change intervals (CCIs), 44, 59
Coupon discount bonds, duration of, 96
Coupon rate, 79, 83
Covenants, of bonds, 141–44
Covered call, 440
Credit, 79

Credit cards, 5, 265–66, 454—55
Credit Control Act of 1969, 549
Credit Control Program of 1980, 549–50
Credit crunch, 677
Credit quality swaps, 461
Credit-rationing channel, 671 f
Credit risk, 46
    and the S&L mess, 222
Credit-risk intermediation, 43
Credit tranche, 492
Credit unions, 227–28
    largest, 164 fig.
Crime, and currency, 277
Crisis failures, 350
Critically undercapitalized, 297
Cross-guarantees, 351
Cross-hedge, 436
Crowding in, 509–91
Crowding out, 590–91
Currency, 20, 179, 256–58, 275–78
    and deposit multiplier, 283–84
    excess, 276–78
    foreign, 44–46, 473
    held overseas, 277
    of securities, 60
    undervalued, 486
Current market basket price index, 26
Current yield, 90–91

D

Dealers, 39
Dean Witter, 251
Debentures, 59
Debit cards, 5, 266
Debt claims, 58
Debt securities, 158
Decentralization, 524
Deductible provision, 351
Deep markets, 49
Default risk, 80, 185
Default-risk premium (DRP), 130
Deferment periods, 142
Deferred availability cash item (DACI), 262
Deficits, 590–91
Deficit spending units (DSUs), 11
    borrowing in international markets, 499
    channeling funds to from SSUs, 37
    and collateral of securities, 59
    and demand for loanable funds, 111–12

Deficit spending units (DSUs), (*cont.*)
  options to satisfy need for funds, 12
  pattern as throughout lifetimes,
    37–38
Defined benefit, 243
Defined contribution, 243
Deflation, 28, 640
Deflationary gap, 581
Demand and supply relationships, 570
Demand deposits, 20, 178
Demand-pull inflation, 655
Denomination intermediation, 43, 45
Deposit banking, 178–80
Deposit expansion process, 288–91
Deposit insurance, reform of, 199–200
Deposit multiplier, 282–84
Depositor preference provision, 359
Depository Institutions Deregulation
    and Monetary Control Act of
    1980 (DIDMCA), 181, 188,
    220, 235, 262, 300, 305, 364,
    386, 548
  and Fed discount window, 541
  and Federal Reserve reserve require-
    ments powers, 539
  and Fed's power, 528
  major deregulation provisions of,
    369 fig.
  and mortgages, 411
  and NOW accounts, 456
  and reserve requirements, 308
Deposit payoff, 352
Deposit rate ceilings, 299–300
Deposits, 42
  at Federal Reserve, 531–32
  percent insured, 346–48
  total versus insured, 341–42
Deposit transfer, 353
Depreciating exchange rate, 475
Depreciation, 78, 576
Deregulation, 6
  and bank failures, 365
  banking, 365
  and bank safety, 377–78
Derivative markets, 428
Derivative securities, 428
DIDMCA. *See* Depository Institutions
    Deregulation and Monetary
    Control Act of 1980.
Diners Club, 265
Direct channeling, 55
Direct financial market. *See* Private
    financial market.
Direct redeposit, 191
Direct security, 40, 41

Dirty float, 480
Discomfort index, 516
Discount, in bond sales, 85
Discount basis, 60
Discount brokers, 155
Discount rate, 531, 540
Discount window, 541
Discover Card, 251, 454
Disinflation, 640
Disintermediation, 47–48
Distributed lag, 596
Dividend reinvestment plans, of com-
    mercial banks, 398
Dividends, 58
Dollar exchange rate, 474
Domestic currencies, 473
Domestic exchange rate, 474
Douglas Amendment, of Bank Holding
    Company Act, 375
Drexel Burnham, 465, 466
Dual banking system, 201
Due-on-sale clauses, 414
Durable goods, how financial markets
    impact spending on, 37
Duration, 95–100
Duration analysis, 321–25
Duration drift, 328
Duration gap, 323–24
Duration gap analysis, 317
  problems with applying, 331–36
Duration matching, 326
Dutch auction technique, 69

E

Earning assets, regulation of, 296
Eccles, Mariner, 528
Econometric models, 554
Economic growth, 509–10
Economic policy, 516–17
Economic recessions, and the S&L
    mess, 222
Economics, and politics, 517–20
Economic theory, 13–14
Economies of scale, and commercial
    bank securities activities, 402
Economy
  goals of, 506–15
  overview of U.S., 600–604
  responsibility for goals of, 515–16
Edge Act offices, 210
Effective reserves, 564
Efficiency, of economy, 514–15
Elastic currency, 524

Electronic funds transfer system
    (EFTS), 7, 266–71
Electronic payments, 176
Electronic transfer of funds, and blur-
    ring of distinctions between
    kinds of deposits, 368
Embedded options, 60
Employee Retirement Income Security
    Act (ERISA), 245
Employment Act of 1946, 515, 528
Endusers, 461
Enhanced structural adjustment facili-
    ty, for borrowing from IMF,
    492
Enlarged access facility, for borrowing
    from IMF, 492
Equation of exchange, 556
Equities, 11, 58
Escape clauses, 351
Eurobonds, 60, 500, 501
Eurocurrencies, 44, 68, 496
Eurodollar bonds, 73
Eurodollar CDs, 67
Eurodollars, 5, 44, 68, 495–98
  futures contracts on, 431
Euronotes, 500
European currency unit (ECU), 501,
    502–03
European Monetary System (EMS),
    502
Excess reserves, 282–83
Exchange rate, 487, 473–83
  as concern of IMF, 490
  relation of balance of payments to,
    485–86
  stability in, 511–12
Exchanges, 430
Exchange value, 19
Exercise price, 440
Exotic securities, 425, 448
Expansions, business cycle, 601 fig.
Expectations theory, and yield curve,
    120–26
Expedited Funds Availability Act, 294
Expiration, time to of option, 441
Export-Import Bank (X-M Bank), 71
Exports, 473
Extended credit, 541
Extended facility, for borrowing from
    IMF, 492

F

Failed banks, treatment of, 352–55

Fallen angels, 464
Family of funds, 241
Farm credit system, 71
Farm Credit System Financial
        Assistance Corporation, 71
Federal Agricultural Mortgage
        Corporation (Fannie Mac), 71
Federal Banking Commission, 380
    Federal Reserve opposition to, 385
Federal deposit insurance, 195, 198
Federal Deposit Insurance
        Corporation (FDIC), 195, 307
        fig., 308–10
    as insurer and regulator, 355–56
Federal Deposit Insurance
        Corporation Improvement
        Act (FDICIA), 199, 297, 298
        fig., 341, 358, 359, 385
    strengthening of capital base, 365
Federal Deposit Insurance
        Corporation insurance, 360
Federal Financial Institutions
        Examination Council, 312,
        384
Federal funds, 63
Federal Home Loan Bank Board
        (FHLBB), 218, 310, 385
    abolishment of, 223, 381
    and delayed recognition of failed
        savings and loans, 220
Federal Home Loan Banks, 69
Federal Home Loan Mortgage
        Corporation (Freddie Mac),
        69, 424
Federal Housing Authority (FHA), 71
Federal Housing Finance Board, cre-
        ation of, 224
Federal Intermediate Credit Banks, 71
Federal Land Banks, 71
Federal National Mortgage
        Association (Fannie Mae), 69
Federal Open Market Committee, 525
Federal Reserve Act of 1913, 308, 524
Federal Reserve Balance Sheet,
        529–34
Federal Reserve Bulletin, 525
Federal Reserve notes, 258, 531
Federal Reserve Regulations U, T, and
        G, 548
Federal Reserve System, 20, 262, 307
        fig., 308
    and amount of reserves, 281
    assets of, 530–31
    balance sheet of, 533–34
    and currency, 275

deposits at, 531–32
and DIDMCA, 528, 539, 541
establishment of, 194
and Federal Banking Commission,
        385
how good has control been, 634–35
independence of, 527–29, 659–60
instruments of, 538–51
intermediate targets of, 630–33
lending to undercapitalized institu-
        tions, 359
liabilities of, 531–32
loans to banks by, 530–31
and lower interest rates, 112
manipulation of financial variables
        by, 584
monetary control by, 303–04, 308
and Phillips curve, 657
qualitative tools of, 547–51
quantitative tools of, 538–47
stabilization activities of, 523
structure of the, 524–27
and supply of money, 112–13, 285
Federal Savings and Loan Association,
        (FSLIC), 195, 308
    abolishment of, 223
Federal Savings Bank, 218
Fed float, 263, 531
Fed-funds loans, 63
Fed watching, 635–36
Fedwire, 176, 267
Fee income, 184, 187
Fidelity Investments, 241, 242
Finance
    definition of, 1
    international, 472
Finance companies, 247–50
    largest, 167 fig.
Financial assets, 10
    savings in form of, 11
Financial centers, 53–55
Financial engineering, 443, 448
Financial failure, penalty for, 7
Financial futures, 428–39
Financial information, advantage of
        banks in obtaining, 41
Financial institutions
    assistance services of, 46
    despecialization of, 6
    different treatment of by different
        agencies, 381
    earning assets of major, 161 fig.
    geographic powers of, 373–77
    liquidity problem of, 420
    new, 448–52

private, 159
product powers of, 366–72
specialization of, 366
stimulation of borrowing by, 45–46
stimulation of saving by, 43–45
Financial Institutions and the Nation's
        Economy Study, 381
Financial Institutions Reform,
        Recovery and Enforcement
        Act (FIRREA), 195, 218, 308,
        358, 381, 385
    and Enforcement Act, passage of,
        223
    major provisions of, 224 fig.
    and Office of Thrift Supervision, 310
    and S&L bailout, 235
    separation of chartering and insur-
        ance powers, 383
    strengthening capital base, 365
Financial instruments, new, 452–67
Financial intermediaries, 217–35, 447
    characteristics of major private,
        160 fig.
    nonbank, 217, 243–50
Financial intermediation, 10–12
    interest rate risk and, 420–22
Financial management, object of, 2
Financial markets
    classification of, 49–53
    definition of, 37
    in different countries, 54–55
    efficiency in, 38
    evolution of, 6
    intermediation, 40–43
    international, 499–503
    private, 38–40
Financial options, 439–44
Financial production process, lack of
        understanding of, 7–8
Financial sector, 4, 571–72
    breakdowns in, 9
    importance of, 5–10
    relationship to rest of economy, 8
Financial securities, 11
Financial services industry, 6
Financial system, 4
Financial theory, 13–14
Fire-sale losses, 174
FIRREA. *See* Financial Institutions
        Reform, Recovery, and
        Enforcement Act.
First Bank of the United States, 257,
        523
First Boston Corporation, 453
First Capital, 232

First Executive Corporation, 232
Fiscal policy, 517, 577, 590–91, 607
Fisher, Irving, 102, 107
Fisher effect, 102–109, 116
Fixed-coupon (rate) bonds, 59
Fixed-coupon (rate) securities, 44
Fixed exchange rate, 477–83
Fixed-income securities, 145
Fixed-rate bonds, 81–88
Fixed-rate loans, hedging, 436–38
Fixed-rate mortgages, 411–16
   and inflation, 417
Fixed-value assets, 646
   losses on, 650
Fixed-value liabilities, 646
Flat money, 20
Flexible exchange rate, 477–83
Flight to currency, 191
Flight to quality, 191
Floating-coupon (rate) bonds, 59
Floating-coupon (rate) securities, 44
Flow of funds table, 112
Foreign bonds, 73, 500–501
Foreign currencies, 473
Foreign currency intermediation,
   44–46
Foreign currency risk, 44
Foreign currency swaps, 461
Foreign Exchange Market, 52–53, 499
Foreign exchange rates, 474
Foreign exchange value of the dollar,
   603
Foreign reserves, 485–86
Foreign securities market, 499
Forward bond, 121
Forward contract, 52, 183, 429
Forward market, 52
Forward price, 429
Forward rate, 121, 439
Fractional reserve banking, 171–73
Franklin National Bank, 346, 353
Fraud, and the S&L mess, 222
Free reserves, 677
Friedman, Milton, 10, 564, 556 f, 664,
   665
Full employment, 506–08
Full Employment and Balanced
   Growth Act of 1978, 528
Full-employment income, 579–81
Fully funded plan, 243
Fungible funds, 550
Futures, 5, 183
   differences from swaps, 462 fig.
Futures and options contracts, 428

Futures contract, 52, 429, 459
Futures interest rates, 439
Futures market, 52, 429
   default in, 430
   for financial instruments, 430–31
Future prices, 429
Future value, 81

G

Gap management, 186
Gapping period, 335
Garn-St. Germain Act of 1982, 206,
   220, 235, 300, 305, 364, 386,
   548
   major deregulation provisions of,
   369 fig.
   and MMDAs, 456
   and mortgages, 411
GDP deflator, 26
GE Capital, 251
General Electric, 157, 251
Generally accepted accounting princi-
   ples, and saving and loan
   losses, 220
General Motors Acceptance
   Corporation, 71, 249
General obligation bonds, 74
Geographic powers
   of financial institutions, 373–77
   regulation of, 301–02
Gerschenkron, Alexander, 371
Gibson, William, 350
Giro payments systems, 264
Glass, Senator Carter, 391
Glass-Steagall Act, 157, 296, 303, 364,
   374, 391–93, 528
   and mutual funds, 462
GLOBEX, 54 fig.
Gold, phasing out of, 493
Gold certificates, 530
Goldman Sachs, 157, 390
Goldsmiths, 170–71, 448
Gold standard, 480
Goodheart, C. A. E., 651 f
Government, 577–78
   in financial sector, 9
Government agency securities, 69
Government intervention, reduced, 6
Government National Mortgage
   Association (Ginnie Mae), 71,
   424, 430

Government policies, 9
Government regulation, reasons for,
   293–95
Government-sponsored enterprises,
   69
Graduated payment mortgages, 75,
   417–18
Greenspan, Alan, 525, 528, 633
Gross disintermediation, 47, 56
Guaranteed interest contracts, 232

H

Hedges, inflation, 647
Hedging, 429, 433–36
   of fixed-rate loans, 436–38
High-yield bonds, 5, 73, 132, 464–66
Hitler, Adolf, 9
Holding companies, 203–06
   largest commercial bank, 163 fig.
Holding-period yield, 91–92
Home Mortgage Disclosure Act, 295
Home Savings of America, 218
Hoover Commission, 381
Horizontal consolidation, regulation
   of, 302
Household Finance, 247
Human capital, source of productivity
   of, 7
Hume, David, 651 f
Humphrey, Thomas, 651 f, 658
Hurricane Andrew, 234
Hyperinflation, 30–34, 511

I

Immunization, 186, 326–28, 422
   bank, 324
   through duration matching, 98
Impact lag, 594–95, 596
Imported inflation, 481
Imports, 473
Income
   change in, 585
   definition of, 16
   equitable distribution of, 512–14
   and wealth redistribution, 645–51
Income effect, 619, 637, 646
Incomes policy, 517
Income velocity, 557, 559
Index funds, 241

Index interest rate, 418
Index number, 24
Index security, 458
Indicators of monetary policy, 623–25
Indirect channeling, 55
Indirect financial market. *See*
    Intermediation financial
    market.
Indirect redeposit, 191
Indirect securities. *See* Secondary
    securities.
Individual Retirement Account (IRA),
    245
Industrial banks, 247
Inflation, 27, 640–42
    and aggregate income, 511
    annual rate of, 603
    changes in money supply and, 641
    cost-push, 656
    costs of, 642–51
    demand-pull, 655
    and fixed-rate residential mort-
        gages, 369
    imported, 481
    inverse relation to unemployment,
        651–57
    market interest rates and, 107–09
    in monetarist model, 671
    solution to underestimation of rate
        of, 421–22
Inflationary gap, 581
Inflation hedges, 647
Inflation premium, 102–09, 116
Insolvent banks, handling, 360
Insolvent institutions, how regulations
    keep open, 340
Instrumental targets, 626
Insurance
    case for government, 350–51
    recent development in deposit,
        356–60
    reform of deposit, 199–200
    who provides, 349–52
Insurance companies, largest life and
    health, 165 fig.
Insurance groups, largest property and
    casualty, 165 fig.
Insurance intermediaries, 228–35
Insurance policies, 158
Insurance reform, basic deposit, 358
Insured pension funds, 231
Insured plans, 245
Intercity clearing, of checks, 261–63
Interest, 79

compound, 83
computation of on securities, 60
factors that determine, 102
simple, 83
Interest onlys (IOs), 5, 75
Interest-only strip, 425
Interest payment
    form of, 59–60
    of mortgage, 412–13
Interest rate caps, 458
Interest rate collars, 459
Interest rate futures, 431
Interest rate illusion, 105
Interest rate-income relationship, 571
Interest rate instruments, 428
Interest rate intermediation, income
    from, 317
Interest rate risk, 44, 46, 92, 186
    active management of, 328–30
    assessing exposure to, 317
    and financial intermediation,
        420–22
    managing, 325–30
Interest rates, 566–67, 609, 612
    and bond prices, 84
    and bond rate differences, 118
    changes in expectations for, and
        yield curve, 122–23
    and credit quality of bonds, 132
    decline in, 613
    definition of, 78–79
    and demand for loanable funds, 111
    determinants of, 110–114
    determination of equilibrium, 114
    effect of changes in on bonds, 86
    effect of on consumer expenditures,
        574–76
    effects of fiscal policy on, 590
    expectations of and yield curve, 120
    Fed target success, 634
    high, 197
    higher, and mortgages, 416
    increases in volatility of, 6
    as indicator of monetary policy,
        624–25
    interrelationships among, 144–45
    market, 106–09, 113
    mathematics of, 79–92
    or money supply as intermediate
        target, 626–28
    and mortgage debt, 409–11
    over business cycle, 114–16
    problems with dividing into its com-
        ponents, 105–08

    and quantity of money demanded,
        112
    Regulation Q restrictions on, 548
    relationship of bond prices to, 95
    relationship to money supplied by
        banks, 565
    relationship with money, 617–23
    and savings and loan associations,
        219–20
    short-term, 630
    and supply of loanable funds, 111
    taxes and changes in, 105–06
    and tax treatment of bonds, 139–40
    unexpected volatility in, 9
Interest rate sensitivity intermedia-
    tion, 45
Interest rate spread, 185
Interest rate swaps, 459–61
Intermediate targets
    of Federal Reserve, 630–33
    for monetary policy, 625–35
Intermediate-term financing, 500
Intermediation financial market,
    40–43, 43–49, 153, 158–67
    shift of funds to private financial
        market by, 47
Internal rate of return, 81–90
International Bank for Reconstruction
    and Development. *See* World
    Bank.
International banking, 210–13
International Banking Act of 1978, 211
International banking facilities, 211
International bond financing, 500–503
International Development
    Association, 495
International financial markets,
    499–503
International finance, 472
International Monetary Fund, 191–92,
    477, 490–493, 503
International money, issued by IMF,
    493
International Money Market, 459
International trade
    financing, 65
    link with international finance, 472
Interstate banking, 375–77
In-the-money, 440
Intrinsic value, 19
Inverse yield curve, 120
Investment, 576–77
Investment bankers, 39
Investment banks, 153–57

Investment banks, (*cont.*)
  merger of, 157
Investment companies, 238–42
Investment funds, 238
Investments, 180
  risky, and the S&L mess, 222
IS function, 578, 586–88, 628

J

Jones, E. D., 157
Junior bonds, 131
Junk bonds, 5, 73, 132, 464–66

K

Kane, Edward, 455
Keating, Charles, 357
Keating Five, 357
Keogh, Eugene, 245
Keogh plans, 245
Keynes, John Maynard, 13, 79, 515,
  560, 563 f, 664
Keynesians, versus monetarists,
  664–75
Keynesian theory, 560–64, 679
Kidder Peabody, 251
Kiting, 260
Kristol, Irving, 519
Kuhn Loeb, 390, 392

L

Lag
  between Fed actions and effects,
   593–97
  in fiscal policy, 596
Leakage, 283
Least cost resolution, 297
Lehman Brothers, 390, 392
Lender of last resort, 195
Leverage, 159
Leveraged buyout, 465
Leverage ratios, 297
Liabilities, of Federal Reserve, 531–32
Liability liquidity management, 179
Life insurance companies, 160–61,
  230–33, 236, 449
  and mortgages, 409
Limited branch states, 202
Liquidations, 354

Liquidity, 49
  of banks, 174–78
Liquidity effect, 567, 618, 637
Liquidity losses, 174
Liquidity management, 175, 185
Liquidity-preference theory, 112–14,
  116, 560
Liquidity premium theory, 124–26, 439
Liquidity problem, of financial institu-
  tion, 420
Liquidity trap, 562, 587
Lloyds of London, 233
LM function, 571, 585–86, 628
Load funds, 239
Loanable-funds theory, 110–12, 116
Loan commitments, bank, 183
Loans
  by Federal Reserve to banks, 530–31
  fixed-rate, 436–38
  losses on, 197
Long position, 434

M

Macaulay, Frederick, 95, 322
Macaulay measure, 95
Macaulay's duration, 322
McCabe, Thomas, 528
McFadden Act, 374, 375, 391
MACRO, 312
Macroliquidity, 49
Magnetic-link character recognition,
  264
Maine, and reciprocal interstate bank-
  ing, 376
Managed float, 480
Managed funds, 179
Marginal efficiency of investment, 577
Marginal propensity to consume, 574
Marginal propensity to save, 574
Margin requirements, 548–49
  in futures market, 430
Marketability
  of bonds, 140–41
  of securities, 59
Marketability yield premium, 141
Market basket, 23
Market discount, 85, 139
Market economy, 23
Market index deposits, 399, 461–63
Market interest rate
  determining, 113
  and inflation, 106–09

  inverse relationship with bond
   prices, 84
Market liquidity, 49
Market-modified supply-driven proce-
  dure, 633
Marketplace, as distributor of goods
  and services, 514–15
Market rate, 81
Market rate of interest, and price of an
  option, 441
Market-segmentation theory, 126–27,
  439
Mark to market, 429
Martin, William McChesney, 528, 529
Marx, Karl, 13
MasterCard, 265, 454
Matched-book strategy, 186
Matched sale-purchase agreement, 67
Matched sales-purchase transactions,
  544
Material well-being, and happiness,
  510
Maturity dates, deposit accounts with-
  out, 331
Maturity gaps, 333–36
Maturity intermediation, 43, 45
Maturity strategy, 148
Mellon Bank, and Dreyfus Funds, 399
Memorandum of understanding, 311
Merchant banking, 154
Mergers, of investment banking firms,
  157
Meritor Savings Bank, 226
Merrill, Lynch, Pierce, Fenner & Smith,
  39, 157, 457, 458
Metallic money standard, 19
Microliquidity, 49
Milken, Michael, 465, 466
Mill, John Stuart, 1, 651 f
Miller, G. William, 528
Minimum down payment, 549
Model, 554, 570
Modified purchase and assumption,
  353
Monarch, 232
Monetarists, versus Keynesians,
  664–75
Monetarist theory, 679
Monetary aggregates, 21, 631
Monetary control, by Federal Reserve
  System, 303–04
Monetary expansion, target rates of,
  546–47
Monetary phenomenon, inflation as,
  641

Monetary policy, 9, 516
   by Federal Reserve System, 303–04,
      308
   government regulation of, 295
   indicators of, 623–25
   intermediate targets for, 625–35
   1947-1960, 604–06
   1960-1970, 606–08
   1970-1980, 608–10
   1980-1990, 610–12
   1990- , 612–14
   path along which effects of travel,
      588–97
   strength of, 585–88
Monetary system, 4
Monetary value, 19
Money, 1, 10
   definition of, 16–18, 20–21, 275
   functions of, 18
   history of, 18–20
   international, 493
   measures of, 20–21
   precautionary demand for, 563 f
   present value of, 80–81
   quantity theory of, 556–59
   relationship with interest rate of,
      617–23
   renting, 79
   speculative demand for, 560–62
   as store of value, 18
   supply of, 34, 564–65
   supply of, and Federal Reserve
      System, 112–13, 285
   total demand for, 562–64
   value of, 21–27
Money illusion, 27, 645
Money management, 34
Money management services, of com-
      mercial banks, 398
Money market, 50
   conditions of as intermediate tar-
      get, 630
   short-run stability of as intermedi-
      ate target, 632–33
Money-market deposit accounts, 5,
      456–57
Money-market funds, 5, 160, 241–42,
      449
Money-market instruments, 61–68
Money-market mutual fund manage-
      ment companies, largest, 167
      fig.
Money-market mutual funds, 5–6
Money supply, 284–85, 625
   change in, 586–87

changes in and inflation, 641
Fed target success, 634
growth in, 603
or interest rates as intermediate tar-
   get, 626–28
Monte dei Paschi di Siena Bank, 180
Moody's, 132
Moral hazard, 339, 342
Moral suasion, 549, 610
Morgan, J. P., 390, 392, 396
Morgan Guaranty Trust Company, 392
Morris Plan banks, 247
Mortgage-backed securities, 5, 75, 409,
   423–24
Mortgage banks, 157–58
Mortgage debt, 408
   and interest rates, 409–11
Mortgage lending, three parts of, 408
Mortgage-lending institutions, 217
Mortgage loans, securitized, 463
Mortgages, 74–75
   adjustable-rate, 75, 419
   alternatives, 416–19
   breakdown by lender, 408, 409 fig.
   call options of, 414
   commercial banks and, 409
   DIDMCA and, 411
   fixed-rate, 411–16
   graduated-payment, 417–18
   inflation and attractiveness of fixed-
      rate, 369
   interest payment of, 412–13
   higher interest rates and, 416
   life insurance companies and, 409
   mathematics of, 411–16
   nonassumable, 414
   option features of, 414
   pooling of, 423
   prepayment provisions of, 414
   price-level-adjusted, 419
   principal repayment of, 412–13
   Regulation Q and, 410–11
   on secondary market, 414
   secondary market for, 423–25
   separation of financing and servic-
      ing aspects of, 423
   variable-rate, 75, 370, 418–19, 422
Mortgage tables, 413
Multibank holding companies, 203
Multiplier, changing, 539–40
Municipal bond mutual funds, 449
Municipal bonds, 60, 73–74
Mutual Benefit Life, 232
Mutual fund investment management
      companies, largest, 166 fig.

Mutual funds, 159, 238–42, 449
   brokerage of by commercial banks,
      399–400
   Glass-Steagall Act and, 462

N

Naked call, 440
Narrow bank proposal, 343, 352
National Association of Securities
      Dealers, 156
National Bank Act of 1863, 257, 306,
      374, 391
National Bank Acts of 1864 and 1865,
      194
National Credit Union Administration,
      307 fig., 310–11
National Credit Union Share Insurance
      Fund, 228, 310
Natural monopoly, 292
Negative amortization, 418
Negotiable certificates of deposit, 181,
      453
Negotiation market, 51
Neo-Keynesian, 664, 669
Net borrowed reserves, 677
Net disintermediation, 47, 56
Net income margin, 187
Net worth certificates, 220
New York City
   as major financial center, 53
   and reciprocal interstate banking,
      376
New York Federal Reserve Bank, 525
New York Mercantile Exchange, 430
New Zealand, 635
NINOW accounts, 456
Nixon, President Richard, 609
No-load funds, 239
Nonassumable mortgages, 414
Nonbank financial intermediaries, 217,
      243–50
Nonborrowed reserves, 677
Nonfinancial firms, 251
Noninsured plans, 245
Noninterest income, 187
Nonpar banking, 261
Nonprice rationing, 548
Nonproprietary funds, 399
Notes, 171
Not sufficient funds checks, 263 f
NOW accounts, 5, 455–56
Number of offices, regulation of, 301
Numeraire, 17

O

Off-balance sheet accounts, 183–85
Office of Thrift Supervision, 218, 307
    fig., 310
    creation of, 223, 381
Offsetting, of financial futures, 430
Old Age and Survivors Insurance
    Fund, 246
On-balance-sheet, 184
One-bank holding companies, 203,
    206
100 percent deposit insurance, 346
100 percent reserve banking, 172
Open bank assistance, 353
Open-end companies, 239
Open Market Account for Domestic
    Operations, 544
Open-market operations, 543–46
Operating risk, 46
Operating targets, 626
Operational efficiency, 12, 38
Option-adjusted yield, 142
Option and swap contracts, 5
Option features, of mortgages, 414
Option provisions, contracts with, 331
Options
    of bonds, 141–44
    factors in price of, 440–41
    in securities contracts, 60
Options contract, 52, 459
Options market, 52
Organized market, 51
Original issue discount bonds, 88,
    457–58
Original issue discounts, 85, 139
Original issue junk, 465
Out-of-money, 440
Outright purchases, 544
Overseas branches, deposits at, 343
Over-the-counter market, 52
Overvalued currency, 486
Ownership claims, 58
Ownership price, 78
Oxford-Provident Building
    Association, 217

P

Paper money standard, 20
Paper notes, 19
Paper transfer systems, 255–66
Par bonds, duration of, 96

Par value, of bonds, 83
Passive strategy, for choosing bonds,
    146–48
Pass-through certificates, 75
Pass-through security, 158
Pawnshops, 248–49
Payments, 483
Payments system
    commercial banks in, 255
    government regulations of, 293
Penney, J. C., 457
Pension Benefit Guaranty Corporation,
    245
Pension funds, 159, 243–47, 449
    largest public, 166 fig.
    private, 5, 165 fig., 245
    public, 246–47
PepsiCo, 457
Perfect hedge, 434, 435 fig., 436 fig.
Permanent income, 564
Permissible products, regulation of,
    302–03
Perpetuals, 43
Phibro, 157
Phillips, A. W., 651
Phillips Curve, 651–59, 668
Point-of-sale transfer system,
    269–71
Policies, 42
Politics, economics and, 517–20
Pollution, 509
Ponzi, Charles, 221 f
Ponzi scheme, 221
Poole, William, 628
Pooling, of mortgages, 423
Portability, 244
Portfolio risk, 340
Posner, Judge Richard, 386
Powell, Paul, 277
Precautionary demand for money,
    563 f
Preferred stock, 58
Premium bonds, duration of, 96
Premiums, 440
    in bond sales, 85
    determination of insurance, 342–45
    determining, 360
    flat versus risk-related, 343–45
    who pays, 348–49
Prepayment provisions, of mortgages,
    414
Presbyterian Minister's Fund, 230
Present value, 78, 80–81
President's Commission on Financial

Structure and Regulation,
    375, 380
President's Council on Wage and Price
    Stability, 305
Price and wage controls, 609
Price-expectations effect, 617, 619–21,
    637
Price-level-adjusted mortgages, 419
Price risk, 92, 98
Prices, 27–34
    in barter economy, 17
    future, 30
    past, 27–30
Price stability, 510–11
Primary market, 50
Primary offering, 154
Primary securities, 40, 41
Primerica, 157
Principal, unpaid, of mortgage, 412–13
Principal-agent problem, 339
Principal onlys, 5, 75
Principal-only strip, 425
Principal repayment, of mortgage,
    412–13
Private financial market, 38–40, 153–58
Private-label funds, 399
Private placement, 154
    by commercial banks, 397
    of corporate bonds, 73
Process innovations, 448
Producer Price Index, 25
Product innovations, 448
Productivity, and economic growth,
    509
Product powers, of financial institu-
    tions, 366–72
Program trading, 432
Prompt corrective action measures,
    297
Proprietary funds, 399
Prudential, 157
Prudential regulations, 295
Public issue, of corporate bonds, 73
Public offering, 154
Public policies, 9
    toward banking, 292
Purchase and assumption, 352
Purchased funds, 179
Purchasing power of the dollar, 26
Pure rental price, 78
Put options, 52, 60, 142, 150, 440
    of mortgages, 414
Put price, 142
Put yield premium, 143

692

Q

Qualitative tools, of Federal Reserve, 547–51
Quantitative tools, of Federal Reserve, 538–47, 584
Quantity theory of money, 556–59, 664

R

Rate risk, 80
Rating system, uniform supervisory, 311, 313 fig.
Rational expectations, 658, 675 f
Reagan, President Ronald, 380, 611
Real assets, 10
  savings in form of, 11
Real estate
  in inflation of 1970s, 648
  residential, return on, 3
Real estate investment trusts, 450
Real estate loans, 180
Real estate mortgage investment conduits, 75, 424, 449
Real interest rate, 102, 105, 116
  mortgages offered at, 419
Realized returns, in bonds, 149–50
Realized yield, 91–92
Real sector, 573–79
Receipts, 483
Reciprocal banking arrangements, 376
Reciprocal interstate banking, 376
Recognition lag, 594, 596
Refinancing, 415–16
Reform, prospects for, 384–86
Regional banks, 526–27
Regular coupon bonds, duration of, 96
Regulation Q, 47, 220, 241, 300, 538
  effects of on mortgages, 410–11
  removed from CDs, 610
Regulations
  evaluation of, 304–06
  first steps in redesigning, 364
  prudential, 295
  reform of, 365–78
  types of, 295–304
Regulators, and minimizing costs of regulation, 367–68
Regulatory accounting principles, 221
Regulatory agencies, 306–11
  case against multiple, 381–83
  case for multiple, 383–84
  reducing number of, 387

reform of, 378–86
Regulatory capture, 304
Regulatory policy, 9
Reinvestment risk, 92
Renegotiable-rate mortgages, 419
Rental price, 78
Reorganization, speed of and insurance losses, 344
Replenishments, 495
Repriced bond, 89
Repricing, of securities, 44
Repurchase agreements, 67–68, 543
Required-reserve ratios, changing, 539
Required reserves, 281, 308
Reserve position in the IMF, 485
Reserves
  changing amount of, 540–46
  control of Federal Reserve, 532–33
  effect of change in on transaction deposits, 288–90
  excess, 282–83
  meeting requirements for, 176–77
Reserve tranche, 491
Resetting, of coupons, 44
Resolution Funding Corporation, 71
Resolution Trust Corporation
  accumulation of losses by, 225 fig.
  creation of, 224
Return, 2
Return risk, 98–100
Revenue bonds, 74
Revenue sources, relative importance of, 154
Reverse repurchase agreement, 67
Reward for lending, and tax rates, 109
Risk, and commercial bank securities activities, 402–03
Risk-controlled arbitrage, 186
Riskiness
  evaluating bank, 343
  and premiums, 342
Risk management, 185
  forward contracts as, 429
Risk of default, 129–36
Risk of loss, 2
Risk weights, 297
Roll-over mortgages, 419
Run, on a bank, 174, 191–95

S

Safety
  deregulation and bank, 377–78

government regulation for, 293
  regulations for, 295–300
Sales finance companies, 249
Salomon Brothers, 458
Samuelson, Paul, 605
Save, financial markets as incentive to, 37
Saving, stimulation of by financial institutions, 43–45
Saving and loan associations, 160, 217–26, 449, 644
  failure and bailout of, 219–26
  failures of, 378
  federal charter of, 218
  and FIRREA, 235
  interest rates and, 219–20
  largest, 164 fig.
  and mortgages, 408
  problems in, 8
Savings Association Insurance Fund, 195, 218, 308
  creation of, 224, 381
Savings banks, 226–27, 644
  largest, 164 fig.
  U.S., 88
Saxon, James, 383
Scholes, Myron, 441 f
Schwartz, Anna, 645
Scott, Kenneth, 386
Search costs
  reduction of by financial institutions, 46
  reduction of through intermediation, 45
Sears Roebuck, 157, 251, 454
Sears Roebuck Acceptance Corporation, 249
Seasonal credit, 540
Secondary market, 50, 423–25
Secondary offering, 154
Secondary reserves, 175
Secondary securities, 41, 45
Second Bank of the United States, 257, 523
Second-generation mortgage-backed securities, 75
Section 20 subsidiaries, 396
Securities
  asset-backed, 463
  collateral of, 59
  definition of, 58
  derivative, 428
  exotic, 425, 448
  of Federal Reserve, 531

Securities (*cont.*)
  fixed-coupon, 44
  fixed-income, 145
  government agency, 69
  government-owned agencies that
      issue, 71
  index, 458
  marketability of, 59
  mortgage-backed, 5, 75, 409, 423–24
  pass-through, 158
  primary, 40, 41
  repricing of, 44
  secondary, 41, 45
  tax treatment of income from, 60
  types of, 61 fig.
  variable-coupon, 44
  variable-rate, 458–59
  volatility of and price of option, 441
  zero-coupon, 5, 62
Securities activities
  arguments for and against commer-
      cial bank involvement in,
      400–404
  nonpermissible bank, 399–400
  permissible bank, 394–99
Securities and Exchange commission,
    73
Securities dealers, 153
Securities trading, by commercial
    banks, 394–96
Securitization, 48–49, 423, 463–64
Security dealers, 39
Security Pacific National Bank, coop-
    erative venture with Fidelity
    Group, 397
Self-insurance, 348
Senior bonds, 131
Shakespeare, William, 16
Share draft accounts, 456
Share drafts, 228
Shares, 42, 238
  in credit unions, 228
Sherman Antitrust Act, 302
Short position, 434
Short-term financing, 500
Silverberg, Stanley, 383
Simple interest, 83
Small-loan companies, 247
Smith, Adam, 13
SNOW accounts, 456–57
Social Security, 246
Solvency problem, of financial institu-
    tion, 421
Sources and uses of funds tables, 112
Special drawing rights, 485, 530

and IMF, 493
Special purpose vehicles, 64
Specie, 19
Speculating, 438–39
Speculative demand for money,
    560–62
Spot market, 52
Spot price, 429
Spread, 62
Stabilization policy, 579
Stagflation, 608
Standard & Poor's, 132, 133–34 fig.
Standard mortgage contract, 423
Standby letters of credit, 183
State-chartered insured banks, 309
Statewide-branch states, 202
Stigler, Stephen, 651 f
Stochastic process, 332
Stock market, 50
Stocks, 11, 75–76
  options contracts on, 443
  return on, 2–3
Stopout rate, 63
Strike price, 440
STRIPS, 69, 458
Structural adjustment facility, for bor-
    rowing from IMF, 492
Structure
  government regulation of, 294
  regulations affecting, 301–03
Structured early intervention and reso-
    lution, 355
Student Loan Marketing Association
    (Sallie Mae), 71
Subbalances, 483
Subsidiaries, 210
Subsidiary banks, 212
Suffolk System, 257
Supervision, 293
Supply of money, 34, 564–65
  and Federal Reserve System,
      112–13, 285
Supply-side economics, 590, 675 f
Surplus spending units, 12
  channeling funds from to DSUs, 37
  investment of in securities, 238
  lending in international mar-
      ket, 499
  pattern as throughout lifetimes,
      37–38
  and supply of loanable funds,
      110–11
Swaps, 459–61
  differences from futures, 462 fig.
Swaptions, 443

Sweep systems, 468
Syndicate, 154
Syndicated loans, 500
Systemic transformation facility, for
    borrowing from IMF, 492

T

T accounts, 40
T&E charge cards, 454
Tangible accounting principles, 221
Task Group on Regulation of Financial
    Services, 380
Taxable municipal bonds, 140
Tax Act of 1986, 74 f
Taxes, and changes in interest rates,
    105–06
Tax-exempt bonds, 60
Tax laws, changes in federal, and the
    S&L mess, 222
Tax rates
  and cost of borrowing, 109
  and currency, 276
Tax treatment
  of bonds, 139–40
  of securities income, 60
T-bills, 61–63
Teachers Insurance and Annuity
    Association/College
    Retirement Equities Fund,
    245
Technology
  effects of advances in, 6
  new and new markets, 467–68
Term CDs, 67
Term loans, 180
Term premium, 124–26, 439
Term structure, 120
Term to maturity, 95, 118–29
Term to repricing, 59
Theory, role of monetary, 554–56
Third-generation transformation, 425
Thornton, Henry, 651 f
Thrift institutions, 217–28
Time-deposit accounts, 179
Time inconsistency problem, 518
T-notes, 68
Too-large-to-fail, 342, 357
  and FDIC protection, 358
Total demand for money, 562–64
Total spending, 578–79
Trade credit, 38
Trade-weighted dollar, 480
Transaction deposits, 278–84

effect of change in total reserves on, 288–91
Transactions demand for money, 560
Transactions velocity, 556
Transfer of funds, channels for, 40 fig.
Travel and entertainment cards, 265
Treasury Department, 531
  recommendations for modernizing the financial system, 372, 373 fig.
  recommendations for regulatory reform, 380
Treasury bills, 61–63, 88
  return on, 2–3
Treasury bonds, 141
  futures contracts on, 431
Treasury investment growth receipts, 457–58
Treasury notes and bonds, 68–69
Trust departments
  of commercial banks, 398
  largest commercial bank, 163 fig.
Trust funds, 184
Truth in Lending Act of 1968, 294

U

Unbiased-expectations theory, 122–23, 439
Uncertainty
  in financial sector, 628, 629 fig.
  in real sector, 628–30
Unconditional debt, 158
Uncovered call, 440
Underfunded plan, 244
Underground economy, 277
Undervalued currency, 486
Underwriting, 154

by commercial banks, 394–96
Unemployment
  changes in labor force and, 507
  inverse relation to inflation, 651–57
Unemployment rate, 602–03
Uniform Bank Performance Report, 312
Uninsurable risks, 230
Uninsured bank depositors, 354
Unit-banking states, 202
U.S. dollar, in international trade, 496
Unit of account, 501
Universal bank credit-card plan, 454
Universal banks, 371–72

V

Value of ownership, 78
Variability, of return on an investment, 2
Variable-coupon bonds, 59
Variable-coupon securities, 44
Variable-rate annuities, 231
Variable-rate bonds, 89–90
Variable-rate contracts, 331
Variable-rate loans, to reduce interest rate risk, 422
Variable-rate mortgages, 75, 370, 418–19
  and interest rate risk sharing, 422
Variable-rate securities, 458–59
Variable-value assets, 646–47
Variable-value liabilities, 646–47
Velocity of money, 556
Vending machines, and currency, 277
Vesting, 244
Visa, 265, 454
Volcker, Paul, 525, 528

W

Wealth
  definition of, 16
  equitable distribution of, 512–14
Wealth channel, 671
Wealth effect, 575, 646
Wealth redistribution, income and, 645–51
West, Morris, 8
Wholesale Price Index, 25
Wildcat banking, 257
Willie, Frank, 382
Wire transfers, 266–67
World Bank, 490, 494–95, 503

Y

Yankee bonds, 73, 501
Yield curve, 120
  bonds priced off, 131
  and changes in rate expectations, 122–23
  differences in unbiased- and biased-expectation theory predictions of, 120–26
  and market-segmentation theory, 126–27
  over business cycle, 127–29
  trap of the upward-sloping, 421
Yield to maturity, 81–90

Z

Zero-coupon bonds, 88–89, 457–58
Zero-coupon securities, 5, 62
Zombie institutions, 356, 360